Modern Systems Analysis and Design

Second Edition

JEFFREY A. HOFFER
University of Dayton

JOEY F. GEORGE
Louisiana State University

JOSEPH S. VALACICH
Washington State Universtiy

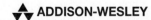 **ADDISON-WESLEY**

An imprint of Addison Wesley Longman, Inc.

Reading, Massachusetts • Menlo Park, California • New York • Harlow, England
Don Mills, Ontario • Sydney • Mexico City • Madrid • Amsterdam

Executive Editor: Mike Roche
Senior Project Manager: Mary Clare McEwing
Assistant Editor: Ruth Berry
Editorial Assistant: Adam Hamel
Senior Administrative Assistant: Dottie Dennis
Senior Production Supervisor: Juliet Silveri
Text Designer and Illustrations: Electronic Publishing Services Inc., NYC
Cover Design Manager: Regina Hagen
Cover Designers: Linda Manly Wade and Regina Hagen
Supplements Editor: Deborah Kiernan
Senior Marketing Manager: Tom Ziolkowski
Senior Marketing Coordinator: Deanna Storey
Technical Art Supervisor: Joseph K. Vetere
Print Buyer: Sheila Spinney
Project Coordination and Composition: Electronic Publishing Services Inc., NYC
Film House: PrePress Co., Inc.
Printer: World Color, Taunton
Cover Image: ©Mick Tarel for Artville

Library of Congress Cataloging-in-Publication Data

Hoffer, Jeffrey A.
    Modern systems analysis and design/Jeffrey A. Hoffer, Joey
George, Joe Valacich.–2nd ed.
        p. cm.
    Includes index
    ISBN 0-201-33841-6
    1. System design. 2. System analysis. I. George, Joey F.
II. Valacich, Joseph S. III. Title
QA76.9.S88H6197   1998
005. 1'2--dc21   98–25100
                                                  CIP

ISBN 0-201-33841-6

3456789—RNT—02010099

To Patty, for her sacrifices, encouragement
and support.
To my students, for being receptive and critical,
and challenging me to be a better teacher.
—Jeff

To Karen, Evan, and Caitlin, for your love,
support, and patience.
—Joey

To Jackie, Jordan, James and the rest of my family,
your love and support are my greatest
inspiration.
—Joe

Brief Table of Contents

Detailed Table of Contents

Preface

DESCRIPTION

Modern Systems Analysis and Design covers the concepts, skills, methodologies, techniques, tools, and perspectives essential for systems analysts to successfully develop information systems. The primary target audience is upper division undergraduates in a management information systems or computer information systems curriculum; a secondary target audience is MIS majors in MBA and M.S. programs. Although not explicitly written for the junior college and professional development markets, this book can also be used for these programs.

The book is written assuming that students have taken an introductory course on computer systems and have experience designing programs in several programming languages. We review basic system principles for those students who have not been exposed to the material on which systems development methods are based. We also assume that students have a solid background in computing literacy and a general understanding of the core elements of a business, including basic terms associated with the production, marketing, finance, and accounting functions.

Modern Systems Analysis and Design is characterized by the following themes:

1. *Systems development is firmly rooted in an organizational context.* The successful systems analyst requires a broad understanding of organizations, organizational culture, and operation.

2. *Systems development is a practical field.* A coverage of current practices as well as accepted concepts and principles are essential in a textbook.

3. *Systems analysis is a profession.* Standards of practice, a sense of continuing personal development, ethics, and a respect for and collaboration with the work of others are general themes in the textbook.

4. *Systems development has significantly changed with the explosive growth in databases and data-driven architectures for systems.* Systems development and database management can be and possibly should be taught in a highly coordinated fashion; this means that this textbook and the McFadden, Hoffer, and Prescott database text, *Modern Database Management*, fifth edition, also published by Addison Wesley Longman, should be compatible. In fact, the proper linking of these two textbooks is a strategic opportunity to meet the needs of the IS academic field.

5. *Success in systems analysis and design requires not only skills in methodologies and techniques but also in the management of projects: time, resources, and risks.* Thus, learning systems analysis and design requires a thorough understanding of the process as well as the techniques and deliverables of the profession.

6. *Systems development is increasingly becoming both automated and more strategic.* Students must understand the capabilities and limitations of such technologies as visual development tools and computer-aided software engineering (CASE) as well as know how systems relate to IS planning, business process reengineering, and systems integration initiatives.

Given these themes, this textbook emphasizes the following:

- A business rather than a technology perspective.

- The role, responsibilities, and mindset of the systems analyst as well as the systems project manager rather than those of the programmer or business manager.

- The methods and principles of systems development rather than the specific tools or tool-related skills of the field.

OUTSTANDING FEATURES

The following are some of the distinctive features of *Modern Systems Analysis and Design*:

1. This book is organized in parallel to the McFadden, Hoffer, and Prescott database text, *Modern Database Management*, Fifth Edition, which will facilitate consistency of frameworks, definitions, methods, examples, and notations to better support SA&D and database courses adopting both texts. Even with the strategic compatibilities between this text and *Modern Database Management*, each of these books is designed to stand alone as a market leader using the standard chapters found in each book.

2. Extensive coverage of oral and written communication skills including systems documentation, project management, team management, and a variety of systems development and acquisition strategies (e.g., life cycle, prototyping, rapid application development, object orientation, joint application development, participatory design, and systems reengineering).

3. A clear linkage of all dimensions of systems description and modeling—process, decision and temporal logic, and data modeling—into a comprehensive and compatible set of systems analysis and design approaches. Such a broad coverage is necessary for students in order to understand the advanced capabilities of many systems development methodologies and tools that are automatically generating a large percentage of code from design specifications.

4. The grounding of systems development in the typical architecture for systems in modern organizations, including database management and distributed and client/server systems.

5. Coverage of rules and principles of systems design, including decoupling, cohesion, modularity, and audits and controls.

6. Consideration of standards for the methodologies of systems analysis and the platforms on which systems are designed.

7. Discussion of systems development and implementation within the context of management of change, conversion strategies, and organizational factors in systems acceptance.

8. Careful attention to human factors in systems design that emphasize usability in both character-based and graphical user interface situations.

9. CASE technology is used throughout the text to illustrate typical systems analysis and design documents and CASE-based systems development is discussed; however, no specific CASE tool is assumed. A variety of CASE and visual development products are illustrated and the current limitations of CASE technologies are highlighted.

10. Chapter 2 highlights the talents that good systems analysts have (and previews the main themes of the text) and helps students identify important material throughout the text.

11. The text includes a separate chapter on systems maintenance. Given the type of job many graduates first accept and the large installed base of systems, this chapter covers an important and often neglected topic in SA&D texts.

NEW TO THE SECOND EDITION

The second edition of *Modern Systems Analysis and Design* follows the same overall outline as that of the first edition. Within this successful organization, several important changes have been made:

- *The text has been streamlined* Systems analysis and design is a comprehensive field, so long texts are common. This second edition, in comparison to the first edition, has moved one chapter (on a sample systems development project case study) to the text's Web site, combined two chapters (on systems implementation) into one Chapter (Chapter 20), and eliminated all appendices (two have been moved to the text's Web site and two are now full chapters — Chapters 12 and 13).

- *Expanded coverage of automated tools for systems development* The coverage of CASE has been slightly reduced, and the role of visual and emerging development environments, which are playing an increasingly important role in systems development, has been included in the new Chapter 4.

- *Integration of business process reengineering into relevant chapters* The role of BPR in systems development is treated within the context of systems analysis, as part of Chapter 7 on requirements determination and Chapter 8 on process modeling.

- *Thorough coverage of object-orientation* Chapter 12 is devoted to object-oriented systems analysis and design. This chapter explains the most significant and commonly used OO modeling and design techniques based on the UML standards. The chapter is positioned between the analysis and design sections of the text, consistent with the way in which object-orientation integrates these systems development steps.

- *Expanded coverage of Rapid Application Development (RAD)* Chapter 13 is devoted to this family of methodologies for iterative systems development. This chapter presents the frameworks on which RAD is based and shows how techniques and tools described in detail in the rest of the text are used in combination for effective rapid development of systems. The topic of RAD is also positioned between the analysis and design sections of the text to emphasize how these two systems development phases are blended together in RAD.

- *New coverage of enterprise resource planning packages as a system design strategy* Organizations of all sizes are adopting ERP packages such as R/3 from SAP America and Oracle Financials from Oracle Corporation. Chapter 11, which discusses selecting a systems design strategy at the end of the analysis phase of development, outlines the reasons for and hazards of the ERP approach to deploying systems.

- *New end-of-chapter review questions and new problems and exercises* All chapters have new questions and exercises, and many chapters have many new ones. Special attention has been given, where appropriate, to reordering problems and exercises in increasing order of difficulty.

- *CASE tool support for text significantly enhanced* All screen captures in the text have been updated to show the latest features of CASE and other automated tools. Many CASE tool screens are from Designer/2000, a leading CASE tool from Oracle Corporation.

THE ORACLE® CASE TOOLS EDITION

Modern Systems Analysis and Design, Second Edition, is the first systems analysis textbook on the market to offer students an outstanding CASE tools software package from Oracle Corporation. For a few dollars more than the price of the text alone, students will receive full editions of Designer/2000, release 2.1 for Microsoft® Windows 95; Developer 2000, release 2.1 for Microsoft Windows 95; and Personal Oracle7, release 7.3.4 for Microsoft Windows 95. We are proud to offer such a highly valued, powerful software package to students at such a low cost.

PEDAGOGY

Several elements in the design and implementation of the text and its supplements make it readable and practical, holding the reader's attention, and assisting the instructor in delivering a better course.

1. Fifteen of the twenty-one chapters include a running case study, Broadway Entertainment Company. This hypothetical, high-technology company provides a rich arena for bringing the concepts, skills, techniques, and tools explained in the chapter to life. Discussion questions for the case are provided in the *Instructor's Manual*.

2. Videotapes are available that will show practicing systems professionals engaged in meetings, interviews, and other tasks during the development of information systems. This series of videotapes also includes discussions by systems professionals on the critical success factors for systems developers and for the management of systems projects.

3. There are three case situations used throughout the book (several of these match cases used in the McFadden, Hoffer, and Prescott *Modern Database Management* text) to illustrate methods, notations, and design techniques.

4. End-of-chapter review questions and problems and exercises test students' knowledge of the material. An innovative addition is a set of field exercises

that give students an opportunity to explore the practice of SA&D in organizations.

5. Chapter objectives introduce each chapter to help the student identify the main topics within each chapter.

6. A comprehensive *Instructor's Manual* provides answers to all the review questions and problems and exercises from the text, plus teaching suggestions and selected questions and problems which may be used in tests or as supplemental exercises.

7. A comprehensive test bank of over 1,600 objective and short answer questions.

8. A Web site that provides extensive resources and links for both students and instructors. See the description of this site in the section on Supplements.

USING THIS TEXT

As stated earlier, the book is intended for mainstream SA&D courses. It may be used in a one-semester course on SA&D or over two quarters (first in a systems analysis and then in a systems design course). Because of the consistency with *Modern Database Management*, chapters from this book and from *Modern Database Management* can be used in various sequences suitable for your curriculum. The book will be adopted typically in business schools or departments, not in computer science programs. Applied computer science or computer technology programs may adopt the book.

The typical faculty member who will find this book most interesting is someone

- with a practical, rather than technical or theoretical, orientation

- with an understanding of databases and systems that use databases

- who uses practical projects and exercises in the course.

More specifically, academic programs that are trying to better relate their SA&D and database courses as part of a comprehensive understanding of systems development will be most attracted to this book.

The outline of the book generally follows the systems development life cycle, which allows for a logical progression of topics. However, the book emphasizes that various approaches (e.g., prototyping and iterative development) are also used, so what appears to be a logical progression often is a more cyclic process. Part I of the book provides an overview of systems development and previews the remainder of the book. Part I also covers those skills and concepts that are applied throughout systems development, including systems concepts, project management, and CASE and other automated development technologies. The remaining five sections provide thorough coverage of the seven phases of a generic systems development life cycle, interspersing coverage of alternatives to the SDLC as appropriate.

Some chapters may be skipped depending on the orientation of the instructor or the students' background. For example, Chapters 1 (environment of SA&D) and 2 (critical success factors for SA&D) cover topics that are emphasized in some introductory MIS courses. Chapter 5 (project identification and selection) can be skipped if the instructor wants to emphasize systems development once projects are identified or if there are fewer than 15 weeks available for the course. Chapters 10 (conceptual data modeling), 16 (logical data modeling), and 17 (physical database design) can be skipped or quickly scanned (as a refresher) if students have already had a thorough coverage of these topics in a previous database or data structures course. Chapter 12 (object-oriented analysis and design) and Chapter 13 (RAD) can be skipped or treated as advanced topics at the end of the course. Finally, Chapter 21 (maintenance and reengineering) can be skipped if these topics are beyond the scope of your course.

Because the material is presented within the flow of a systems development project, it is not recommended that you attempt to use the chapters out of sequence, with a few exceptions: Chapters 8 (process modeling), 9 (logic modeling), and 10 (conceptual data modeling) can be taught in any sequence; and Chapter 16 (logical data modeling) can be taught before Chapters 14 (output design) and 15 (interface design), but Chapters 14 and 15 should be taught in sequence.

SUPPLEMENTS

Instructor's Manual
by Jeffrey A. Hoffer, Joey F. George, Joseph S. Valacich, and Lisa Miller
The Instructor's Manual accompanying *Modern Systems Analysis and Design* provides teaching suggestions as well as answers to all text review questions, problems, and exercises. It is available electronically on the Instructor's Resource Disk (described below).

Test Bank
by Lisa Miller, University of Central Oklahoma
The Test Bank includes 40-60 multiple choice, 15 matching, and 5 essay questions per chapter. It is available in a computerized version on the Instructor's Resource Disk (described below). As an additional service to professors using the Hoffer/George/Valacich text, FastFax Testing is available through the Glenview Software Products Services Group. This group will create tests based on instructions from the professor via fax or mail. To receive more information or forms for requesting tests, please contact your local Addison Wesley Longman sales representative.

Instructor's Resource Disk
The Instructor's Resource Disk contains an electronic version of the Instructor's Manual, a computerized version of the Test Bank, and a PowerPoint Presentation. The Instructor's Manual is available in Word 97 for Windows. The computerized version of the Test Bank uses test generator software (TestGen-EQ with QuizMaster-EQ for Windows 95) which is fully networkable. TestGen-EQ's friendly graphical interface enables instructors to easily view, edit, and add questions; transfer questions to tests; and print tests in a variety of fonts and forms. Search-and-sort features let the instructor quickly locate questions and arrange them in a preferred order. QuizMaster-EQ automatically grades the exams, stores results on disk, and allows the instructor to view or print a variety of reports. The PowerPoint Presentation, consisting of key illustrations from the text, is available in PowerPoint 8 for Windows. Professors can customize the presentation by adding their own slides, or editing the existing ones. They can also print the slides out for distribution to the students.

Web Site
The web site accompanying *Modern Systems Analysis and Design*, Second Edition includes material on a sample systems development project case study (Pine Valley Furniture), appendixes on types of information systems and advanced topics in conceptual data modeling, and other useful resources and links for students and instructors. Visit the site at http://hepg.awl.com and use the keyword Hoffer.

EDS Video Series
by Electronic Data Systems Corporation (EDS)
This video series, prepared by EDS specifically to accompany *Modern Systems Analysis and Design*, consists of four video segments each approximately 15 minutes in length, that focus on systems analysis and design. Each includes an introduction and prologue from Professors Hoffer, George, and Valacich. A new video, in addition to this EDS Series, will be available with the second edition.*

ACKNOWLEDGMENTS

The authors have been blessed by considerable assistance from many people on all aspects of preparation of this text and its supplements. We are, of course, responsible for what eventually appears between the covers, but the insights, corrections, contributions, and proddings of others have greatly improved our manuscript. The people we recognize here all have a strong commitment to students, to the IS field, and to excellence. Their contributions have stimulated us, and frequently rejuvenated us during periods of waning energy for this project.

We would like to recognize the efforts of the many faculty and practicing systems analysts who have been reviewers of the several drafts of our manuscript. We have tried to deal with each reviewer comment, and although we did not always agree with specific points (within the approach we wanted to take in this book), all reviewers made us stop and think carefully about what and how we were writing. The reviewers were: Barbara Allen (Douglas College), Jay E. Aronson (University of Georgia), Susan Athey (Colorado State University), Penny Brunner (University of North Carolina, Asheville), Pedro Cabrejos (Champlain College), Donald Chand (Bentley College), Amir Dabirian (California State University, Fullerton), Mark Dishaw (University of Wisconsin at Oshkosh), Jerry Dubyk (Northern Alberta Institute of Technology), Barry Frew (Naval Post-Graduate School), Jim Gifford (University of Wisconsin), Mike Godfrey (California State University, Long Beach), Dale Gust (Central Michigan University), Alexander Hars (University of Southern California), Ellen Hoadley (Loyola College-Baltimore), Monica Holmes (Central Michigan University), Robert Jackson (Brigham Young University), Murray Jennex (University of Phoenix), Len Jessup (Indiana University), Robert Keim (Arizona State University), Mat Klempa (California State University at Los Angeles), Ned Kock (Temple University), Rebecca Koop (Wright State University), Sophie Lee (University of Massachusetts at Boston), Chang-Yang Lin (Eastern Kentucky University), Nancy Martin (USA Group, Indianapolis, Indiana), Roger McHaney (Kansas State University), Nancy Melone (University of Oregon), G. Premkumar (Iowa State University), Mary Prescott (University of South Florida), Terence Ryan (Southern Illinois University), Eugene Stafford (Iona College), Bob Tucker (Antares Alliance, Plano, Texas), Cheryl Welch (Ashland University), Connie Wells (Nicholls State University), Chris Westland (University of Southern California), Charles Winton (University of North Florida), and Terry Zuechow (EDS Corporation, Plano, Texas). All of the reviewers provided honest and helpful comments.

We wish to thank Atish Sinha of the University of Dayton for writing Chapter 12 on object-oriented analysis and design. Dr. Sinha, who has been teaching this topic for several years to both undergraduate and MBA students, executed a challenging assignment with creativity and cooperation. His chapter presents material that was released as our text was written. Atish — a remarkable job!

---

* The ancillary package is available to qualified domestic adopters and in some cases may not be available to international adopters because of legal and other restrictions.

We are also indebted to our undergraduate and MBA students at the University of Dayton, Florida State University, and Washington State University who have given us many helpful comments as they worked with drafts of this text.

We are most grateful to Oracle Corporation for making available their powerful modeling and development tools, Designer/2000, release 2.1 for Microsoft® Windows 95; Developer 2000, release 2.1 for Microsoft Windows 95; and Personal Oracle7, release 7.3.4 for Microsoft Windows 95, for students' use with this new edition of *Modern Systems Analysis and Design*. We believe that students will greatly benefit from having such easy access to these important CASE tools. We particularly thank Rene Bonvanie and Randy Baker of Oracle Corporation, as well as Maureen Dorhety, Diane Shorts, Marie Schmitt, Susan Andolsek, and other Oracle employees who worked behind the scenes to make this happen.

We also give special recognition to Pam Carter at Florida State University, who prepared all the Oracle Designer/2000 and Developer/2000 screens. Her work was timely and careful.

One unique supplement to this text is a series of four videotapes which illustrate common activities and situations encountered by systems analysts. We are very excited about the pedagogical value of these tapes, and compliment EDS Corporation for the sizable commitment of human and financial resources to develop and produce these tapes for exclusive use with our book. Specifically, we thank Stu Bailey, Michael Cummings, Vern Olsen, Chris Ryan, and Terry Zuechow of EDS, Bob Tucker of Antares Alliance, and Bill Satterwhite of Whitecap Productions for all of their work on this project.

We want to thank Lisa Miller from the University of Central Oklahoma who has prepared an extensive test bank and revised the Instructor's Manual for this text. We are also grateful to USA Group, Inc., Allison Engine Company, Cambridge Technology Partners (particularly Harold Gubnitsky, Elizabeth Brewer, and Kelly Wright), IVI Publishing, and Albertson's, Inc. for their valuable contributions in the construction of the case studies that open each part of this book.

Thanks also go to Fred McFadden (University of Colorado, Colorado Springs) and Mary Prescott (University of South Florida) for their assistance in coordinating this text with its companion book—*Modern Database Management*.

Finally, we have been fortunate to work with a large number of creative and insightful people at Addison Wesley Longman, who have added much to the development, format, and production of this text. We have been thoroughly impressed with their commitment to this text and to the IS education market. These people include: Mike Roche (Executive Editor); Mary Clare McEwing (Editor), who has supervised all stages of development and the best project manager with whom we have ever worked; Patty O'Connell and the staff of Electronic Publishing Services; Juliet Silveri (Senior Production Supervisor); Joe Vetere (Technical Art Supervisor); Ruth Berry (Assistant Editor); Deborah Kiernan (Supplements Editor); Dottie Dennis (Administrative Assistant); Anita Devine (Acquisitions Editor); Adam Hamel and Holly Rioux (Editorial Assistants); Deanna Storey (Senior Marketing Coordinator); and Gina Hagen (Designer).

The writing of this text has involved thousands of hours of time from the authors and from all of the people listed above. Although our names will be visibly associated with this book, we know that much credit goes to the individuals and organizations listed here for any success this book might achieve. It is important for the reader to recognize all the individuals and organizations who have been committed to the preparation and production of this book.

Jeffrey A. Hoffer (Dayton, Ohio)
Joey F. George (Baton Rouge, Louisiana)
Joseph S. Valacich (Pullman, Washington)
June, 1998

P A R T

I

Foundations for Systems Development

USA Group, Inc.

Application and Promissory Note for Federal Stafford Loans *(subsidized and unsubsidized)*

Guarantor or Program Identification

WARNING: Any person who knowingly makes a false statement or misrepresentation on this form is subject to penalties which may include fines or imprisonment under the United States Criminal Code and 20 U.S.C. 1097.

Borrower Section
Please print neatly or type. Read the instructions carefully.

1. Last Name	First Name	MI	2. Social Security Number

3. Permanent Street Address (If P.O. Box, see instructions.)	4. Telephone Number ( )	5. Loan Period (Month/Year) From: To:

City	State	Zip Code	6. Driver's License Number (List state abbreviation first.)

7. Lender Name	City	State	Zip Code	8. Lender Code, if known	9. Date of Birth (Month/Day/Year)

10. References: You must provide two separate references with different U.S. addresses. The first reference should be a parent or legal guardian (if living). Both references must be completed fully.

Name 1. _____ 2. _____
Permanent Address
City, State, Zip Code
Area Code/Telephone ( ) _____ ( ) _____
Relationship to Borrower

Loan Assistance Requested

11. I request the following loan type(s), to the extent I am eligible (see instructions):
☐ a. Subsidized Federal Stafford   ☐ b. Unsubsidized Federal Stafford

12. I request a total amount under these loan types not to exceed (see instructions for loan maximums): My school will certify my eligibility for each loan type for which I am applying. The amount and other details of my loan(s) will be described to me in a disclosure statement.
$ _____ .00

13. If I check yes, I am requesting postponement (deferment) of repayment for my Stafford and prior SLS loan(s) during the in-school and grace periods. If I check no, I do not want to defer repayment.
☐ a. Yes, I want a deferment   ☐ b. No, I do not want a deferment

14. If I check yes, I am requesting that the lender add the interest on my unsubsidized Stafford and prior SLS loan(s) which accrues during the in-school and deferment periods, to my loan principal (capitalization). If I check no, I prefer to pay the interest.
☐ a. Yes, I want my interest capitalized   ☐ b. No, I prefer to pay the interest

15. If my school participates in electronic funds transfer (EFT), I authorize the school to transfer the loan proceeds received by EFT to my student account.
☐ a. Yes, transfer funds   ☐ b. No, do not transfer funds

Promissory Note
Continued on the reverse side.

Promise to Pay: I promise to pay to the lender, or a subsequent holder of this Promissory Note, all sums disbursed (hereafter "loan" or "loans") under the terms of this Note, plus interest and other fees which may become due as provided in this Note. If I fail to make payments on this Note when due, I will also pay reasonable collection costs, including attorney's fees, court costs, and collection fees. I understand I may cancel or reduce the size of any loan by refusing to accept any disbursement that is issued. I understand that this is a Promissory Note. I will not sign this Note before reading it, including the writing on the reverse side, even if otherwise advised. I am entitled to an exact copy of this Promissory Note and the Borrower's Rights and Responsibilities. My signature certifies I have read, understand, and agree to the terms and conditions of this Application and Promissory Note, including the Borrower Certification and Authorization printed on the reverse side and the accompanying Borrower's Rights and Responsibilities statement.

THIS IS A LOAN(S) THAT MUST BE REPAID.

16. Borrower's Signature _____   Today's Date (Month/Day/Year) _____

School Section
To be completed by an authorized school official.

17. School Name	23. School Code/Branch	28. Telephone Number ( )

18. Street Address	24. Cost of Attendance $ .00	29. Recommended Disbursement Date(s) (Month/Day/Year) 1st _____ 2nd _____

City State Zip Code	25. Federal Expected Family Contribution $ .00	3rd _____ 4th _____

19. Loan Period (Month/Year) From: To:	26. Estimated Financial Aid $ .00	30. School Certification (See box on the reverse side.)

20. Grade Level	27. Certified Loan Amounts a. Subsidized $ .00	Signature of Authorized School Official

21. Enrollment Status (Check one.) ☐ Full Time ☐ At Least Half Time	b. Unsubsidized $ .00	Print or Type Name and Title

22. Anticipated Completion (Graduation) Date (Month/Day/Year)		Date Check box if electronically transmitted to guarantor: ☐

Lender Section
To be completed by an authorized lending official.

31. Lender Name	32. Lender Code/Branch	33. Telephone Number ( )	34. Lender Use Only

Street Address	35. Amount(s) Approved a. Subsidized $ .00 b. Unsubsidized $ .00	

City State Zip Code	36. Signature of Authorized Lending Official Print or Type Name, Title, and Date	

1/31/94

LENDER COPY

Role of Systems Analysts

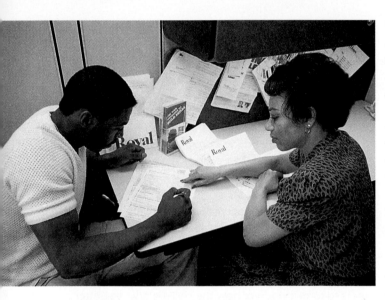

USA Group, Inc., in Indianapolis, Indiana, is one of the world's largest student loan management organizations. There are over 300 information systems people at USA Group, including general managers, project managers, systems analysts, programmers, programmer/analysts, technical analysts, and others. Systems analysts at USA Group hold salaried, professional positions, and project team leaders are considered the first line of management.

Analysts at lower grade levels do mostly analysis tasks, such as interviewing, while analysts at higher grade levels often coach junior analysts and serve as the team lead for projects. The team lead is responsible for coordinating the efforts of the team members, ensuring that the team's part of the system is well integrated with other parts of the system, and attending coordination meetings with other team leads, project managers, and

IS managers. Analysts fresh out of school are generally assigned simpler tasks, such as code maintenance on smaller projects, and are supervised by a more senior analyst. Many junior analysts begin as programmer/analysts and are later reclassified as analysts.

The role of the analyst at USA Group changes frequently depending on the project type and the phase of the project in the systems development life cycle. USA Group's largest system project, replacing their Guaranteed Student Loan (GSL) processing system, nicely illustrates the changing role of the analyst. The current system, Eagle 1, is used to process all GSL applications and to manage the loans throughout their lives. USA Group originally implemented Eagle 1 in order to use less paper, reduce errors, and perform loan processing faster. Approximately 150 systems personnel are now working on the new system, Eagle 2. Development cost for Eagle 2 will end up between $30 and $35 million. With Eagle 2, USA Group plans to further improve the loan processing system.

The Eagle 2 project is conducted by small, manageable teams working on subsystems such as (1) Options, Products, and Services, (2) Electronic Funds Transfers, and (3) Loan Approval. Team size changes throughout the life cycle as the need for more or fewer team members dictates. For example, one of the teams currently in the analysis phase includes about a dozen people but will double in size during the construction phase.

Because the project is in the analysis phase, analysts are primarily performing high-level activities, such as business area requirements analysis. Analysts work directly with executives, helping elicit their strategies, goals and objectives, and critical success factors. The analysts will then flesh out more detailed requirements in order to design the conceptual system. During this phase, they will work directly with users and modelers. Together the modelers and analysts draw the conceptual diagrams of how the system will look and function.

The project will then move into the technical design phase, when the systems analysts will work with technical analysts and designers. Next, the project will move into the final specs and code generation phases, when the analysts will work with programmer/analysts and programmers in order to make the system a tangible reality.

Throughout each of the phases of the systems development life cycle, the analysts work closely with project coordinators responsible for managing the CASE tools and related information. The analysts will also work with technical analysts who will be responsible for ensuring that the system and all subsystems have a consistent look and feel.

The systems analysts must know systems development methodologies and have some programming competency. In addition, they must have project management and CASE tool skills and, when acting as the lead on a project, they must have managerial skills, such as supervising team members and organizing work. However, interpersonal skills are perhaps most important. At USA Group, analysts spend a large portion of their time interacting with various people. Although there is some flexibility in assignments to projects and in assignments to tasks within projects, the analysts cannot escape having to interact with people. Systems personnel who prefer working alone are better suited to be programmers or technical analysts.

Analyst Nancy Martin estimates that she spends approximately 20 percent of her time in one-on-one interviews with various business and technical people. Perhaps more importantly, she estimates that she spends an additional, even larger, chunk of time in group meetings with managers, users, and her team members. In these meetings she and the other analysts ask key questions of users to elicit information about their business processes and needs. While the analysts are trying to learn how best to build the system, they are also helping users to better understand their own business processes. These types of meetings are especially prevalent at the front end of the systems projects.

The analysts work together as a team transcribing and translating users' business needs and trying to ask questions without making people feel defensive. The analysts also help the users stop fixating on the current system and the current way of doing things. They help users to form a vision of how they will be able to better accomplish their work.

Martin says that it is amusing to go out for lunch with other analysts from work. She admits that when together off-site they continue to analyze everything. On one lunch outing, they critically analyzed the restaurant layout including the design of the salad bar. They couldn't believe that someone had put the salad dressings, which drip a lot, at the back of the salad bar. Because of this design flaw the "user" was forced to drip salad dressing over everything in the salad bar placed in front of the dressing containers. She laughed and added that "a good system analyst wouldn't have designed it that way."

USA Group likes their systems analysts' penchant for analyzing things, particularly when the analysts are designing and building Eagle 2, the firm's costly, mission-critical loan processing application.

An Overview of Part I

Foundations for Systems Development

You are beginning a journey that will allow you to build on every aspect of your education and experience. Becoming a systems analyst is not a goal, it is a path to a rich and diverse career that will allow you to exercise and continue to develop a wide range of talents. We hope that this introductory part of the text helps open your mind to the opportunities of the systems analysis and design field and to the engaging nature of systems work.

Because what you do as a systems analyst occurs within a multifaceted organizational process involving other organizational members and external parties, in Chapter 1 we begin with a view of the "big picture" within which systems are developed. Systems analysis and design does not follow a cookbook-style, definitive process, and you, as a systems analyst, certainly do not work alone in the analysis and design process. Rather, because of the variety of

- Systems being developed
- People who develop those systems
- Systems analysis and design methods and procedures used by an organization
- Organizational philosophies about systems development
- Skills involved in systems development

you will learn many approaches to systems analysis and design and improve your communication and interpersonal skills as well. Understanding systems development requires an understanding of not only each technique, tool, and method but also how these elements cooperate, complement, and support each other within an organizational setting for systems development.

We presume that you have a general understanding of computer-based information systems as typically covered in introductory business information systems texts and courses. (If you do not have this background, you may want to go to a library and look through one or more books on management or business information systems.) Chapter 1 previews systems analysis and design by describing the environment and development of information systems. In this chapter, you will discover how the general approach to systems development has changed and continues to change as technology changes and users' expectations grow. Today, the modern approach to systems analysis and design integrates several views of systems with special emphasis on data as the core material.

Systems development is fascinating both to study and to participate in. Variety and change contribute to the fascination. First, contrary to popular belief and possibly inconsistent with your own experience with computer programming, systems analysis and design is a job with intense and frequent interpersonal contact. You will lead the development of systems by working with a diverse team of interested parties: other analysts, IS and business managers, programmers and other IS technical specialists, as well as the end users. Understanding how all these people fit into the systems development process will help you understand how to apply the skills, techniques, tools, and methods discussed later in the text.

Second, each system you develop will be different from every other system you have developed before. Systems of different types require emphasizing different aspects of systems analysis and design. Thus, understanding the differences among systems helps you choose the appropriate techniques, tools, and methods to apply in your work.

Finally, the systems analysis and design field is constantly changing and adapting to new situations (a source of job enrichment and a positive challenge for most people in this field). In part, such changes occur because of the strong commitment of the field to constantly improve—an inherent Total Quality Management (TQM) perspective is a tradition in systems analysis and design. Such changes also occur because the cultures of different organizations—with varying degrees of interest in consensus participatory management and leading-edge practices and technologies—favor different approaches to systems development. Thus, we complete our discussion of the environment for systems development with an overview of the various approaches taken in modern organizations. In this chapter and elsewhere, however, it is not our purpose to encourage any one approach over another. Our goal is to provide you with a mosaic of the skills needed to effectively work in whichever environment you find yourself, armed with the knowledge to determine the best practices for that situation and argue for them effectively.

Every field has some underlying principles that permeate it. In sports, conditioning, flexibility, health, coordination, and dedication are necessary traits. In the law, principles of precision, justice, and protection of rights span all aspects of practice. In systems development, there are certain fundamental principles and concepts that play a role in every phase of the systems development life cycle and that, in a sense, hold the systems development process together. The purpose of the remainder of Part I—Chapters 2, 3, and 4—is to outline those aspects of systems development that are independent of but applicable to each life cycle step. We cover these principles now since they will be used repeatedly in subsequent chapters, and it can be confusing to introduce them in a piecemeal fashion. A systems analyst and a systems development group must master at least a basic understanding of these principles before useful systems work can occur. We group these fundamental principles, necessary for preparing and organizing for systems development, into three chapters—critical success factors, project management, and automation of systems development.

There are individual factors for a systems analyst that contribute to successful systems development, and these critical success factors are the topic of Chapter 2. Various studies of successful systems analysis and design indicate that the systems analyst must possess analytical, technical, management, and interpersonal skills. Although these critical skills are held in common by most successful people in organizations, they take on special forms for systems analysts. Certainly the skill set changes—especially those skills related to technologies—but the changes tend to be more evolutionary than revolutionary. Because many systems analysis and design courses require significant project work, either in groups or in a real organizational setting, you will soon have an opportunity to practice the critical success factors. To help in these endeavors, this chapter sensitizes you to the skills you will soon need to practice. Later in the text, we will elaborate on the general skills outlined in this chapter by presenting specific versions of these general skills as they apply to systems development phases. As Chapter 2 ends, we develop an appreciation for systems analysis as a profession and show how these critical skills lead to standards, ethics, and career paths for the field.

Chapter 3 addresses a fundamental characteristic of life as a systems analyst working within the framework of projects with constrained resources. Although systems development efforts vary considerably in size and complexity, all systems work demands attention to deadlines, working within budgets, and coordinating the work of various people. The very nature of the systems development life cycle (SDLC) implies a systematic approach to managing systems development. This outlook is based on the notion that a project—a group of related activities—leads to a final deliverable. Projects must be planned, started, executed, and completed. The planned work of the project must be represented in such a way that all interested parties can review and understand it. Computer software can help systems analysts and project managers organize and track system project activities. In your first job as a systems analyst, you may not lead projects and hence you will not actually perform many of the project management steps outlined in Chapter 3. You will, however, have to work within the schedule and other project plans and thus it is important to understand the management process controlling your work. Even though you may have studied project management as part of other courses, this topic is so fundamental to systems development (and so often misunderstood), that we devote Chapter 3 to project management within the systems development setting.

Quality and productivity are essential to any job. For many years, the systems development field has been plagued by meager improvements due to small, incremental changes in our tools and techniques. Some believe that the only way to achieve quantum improvements is to provide automated support for systems development, just as we do for the rest of a business. Today, the focus for automated support for systems analysis and design (and for the total process of building systems) is on computer-aided software engineering, or CASE, and emerging development tools such as object-oriented development and visual programming. The purpose of CASE is to provide an engineering-style discipline with associated tools to enforce standards of practice and to greatly increase the speed by which systems are developed and maintained. Likewise, object-oriented development tools are helping to alleviate maintenance problems plaguing organizations that have multiple systems with redundant functions through the use of software objects that can be infinitely reused and literally become the building blocks for all systems. Visual development tools allow systems developers to quickly build new user interfaces, reports, and other features into new and existing systems in a fraction of the time previously required by allowing systems designers the ability to "draw" the design using predefined objects. Chapter 4 provides an overview of this rapidly changing and much discussed area. The goal of Chapter 4 is not to give you the skills for using these automated tools; rather, the intent is to make you a knowledgeable consumer of CASE and other development tools, able to know how and when to apply them.

Finally, Part I introduces Broadway Entertainment Company, Inc. (BEC). The BEC case, presented in separate sections after selected chapters, serves several purposes. First, whereas the book chapters emphasize the concepts, principles, and methods as being fundamental elements of the field, the BEC case helps demonstrate how these elements might fit into a practical situation. Second, besides illustrating the application of topics, BEC also provides a rich organizational setting for discussing issues about systems analysis and design.

Two BEC case sections are included after Chapter 4; the remaining book chapters through Chapter 20, with the exceptions of Chapters 12 and 13, each have an associated BEC case. The first BEC section introduces the company, summarizes its history, emphasizes its strategic and competitive business setting (which greatly influences the development of systems), and outlines the information systems applications in use. The second BEC section provides more detail on existing systems to aid in understanding BEC operations when we look at the requirements and design for new systems in later BEC case sections.

It is time to begin your journey.

1

The Systems Development Environment

LEARNING OBJECTIVES

After studying this chapter, you should be able to:

■ Define information systems analysis and design.

■ Discuss the modern approach to systems analysis and design that combines both process and data views of systems.

■ Describe the organizational roles, including systems analyst, involved in information systems development.

■ Describe the different types of information systems.

■ Describe the information systems development life cycle (SDLC).

■ List alternatives to the systems development life cycle and compare the advantages and deficiencies of the SDLC and its alternatives.

■ Explain briefly the role of computer-aided software engineering (CASE) tools in systems development.

INTRODUCTION

Information systems analysis and design is a complex, challenging, and stimulating organizational process that a team of business and systems professionals uses to develop and maintain computer-based information systems. Although advances in information technology continually give us new capabilities, the analysis and design of information systems is driven from an organizational perspective. An organization might consist of a whole enterprise, specific departments, or individual work groups. Organizations can respond to and anticipate problems and opportunities through innovative uses of information technology. Information systems analysis and design is, therefore, an organizational improvement process. Systems are built and rebuilt for organizational benefits. Benefits result from adding value during the process of creating, producing, and supporting the organization's products and services. Thus, the analysis and design of information systems is based on your understanding of the organization's objectives, structure, and processes as well as your knowledge of how to exploit information technology for advantage.

Few business careers present a greater opportunity for significant and visible impact on business as do careers in systems development. Furthermore, analyzing

Information systems analysis and design: The complex organizational process whereby computer-based information systems are developed and maintained.

and designing information systems will give you the chance to understand organizations at a depth and breadth that might take many more years to accomplish in other careers. According to *Money* magazine, the position of systems analyst will be the best job in America (Gilbert, 1994). *Money* predicted that over half a million new systems analyst jobs would be created between 1994 and 2005, more than doubling the total number of positions available in 1994. With such promising career prospects, combined with the challenges and opportunities of dealing with the rapid advances in information technologies, it is difficult to imagine a more exciting career choice than systems analysis and design.

Application software:
Computer software designed to support organizational functions or processes.

An important (but not the only) result of systems analysis and design is **application software;** that is, software designed to support a specific organizational function or process, such as inventory management, payroll, or market analysis. In addition to application software, the total information system includes the hardware and systems software on which the application software runs, documentation and training materials, the specific job roles associated with the overall system, controls, and the people who use the software along with their work methods. Although we will address all these various dimensions of the overall system, we will emphasize application software development—your primary responsibility as a systems analyst.

In the early years of computing, analysis and design was considered to be an art. Now that the need for systems and software has become so great, people in industry and academia have developed work methods that make analysis and design a disciplined process (similar to processes followed in engineering fields). Our goal is to help you develop the knowledge and skills needed to understand and follow such software engineering processes. Central to software engineering processes (and to this book) are various *methodologies, techniques,* and *tools* that have been developed, tested, and widely used over the years to assist people like you during systems analysis and design.

Methodologies are comprehensive, multiple-step approaches to systems development that will guide your work and influence the quality of your final product: the information system. A methodology adopted by an organization will be consistent with its general management style (for example, an organization's orientation toward consensus management will influence its choice of systems development methodology). Most methodologies incorporate several development techniques.

Techniques are particular processes that you, as an analyst, will follow to help ensure that your work is well thought-out, complete, and comprehensible to others on your project team. Techniques provide support for a wide range of tasks including conducting thorough interviews to determine what your system should do, planning and managing the activities in a systems development project, diagramming the system's logic, and designing the reports your system will generate.

Tools are typically computer programs that make it easy to use and benefit from the techniques and to faithfully follow the guidelines of the overall development methodology. To be effective, both techniques and tools must be consistent with an organization's systems development methodology. Techniques and tools must make it easy for systems developers to conduct the steps called for in the methodology. These three elements—methodologies, techniques, and tools—work together to form an organizational approach to systems analysis and design.

Systems analyst: The organizational role most responsible for the analysis and design of information systems.

Although many people in organizations are responsible for systems analysis and design, in most organizations the **systems analyst** has the primary responsibility. When you begin your career in systems development, you will most likely begin as a systems analyst or as a programmer with some systems analyst responsibilities. The primary role of a systems analyst is to study the problems and needs of an organization in order to determine how people, methods, and information technology can best be combined to bring about improvements in the organization.

A systems analyst helps system users and other business managers define their requirements for new or enhanced information services. As such, a systems analyst is an agent of change and innovation.

In the rest of this chapter, we will examine the systems approach to studying organizations and the systems approach to studying analysis and design. You will learn about the dominant complementary approaches to systems development—the data- and process-oriented approaches. You will also identify the various people who develop systems and the different types of systems they develop. The chapter ends with a discussion of some of the methodologies, techniques, and tools created to support the systems development process.

A MODERN APPROACH TO SYSTEMS ANALYSIS AND DESIGN

The analysis and design of computer-based information systems began in the 1950s. Since then, the development environment has changed dramatically, driven by organizational needs as well as by rapid changes in the technological capabilities of computers. In the 50s, the focus of the development effort was on the processes the software performed. Since computer power was a critical resource, efficiency of processing became the main goal. Computers were large, expensive, and not very reliable. Emphasis was placed on automating existing processes, such as purchasing or paying, often within single departments. All applications had to be developed in machine language or assembly language, and they had to be developed from scratch, as there was no software industry. Because computers were so expensive, computer memory was also at a premium, so system developers conserved as much memory for data storage as they could. Conserving memory helped lead to what is called the Year 2000 Problem (or Y2K), because the years in dates were stored as two digits instead of four. That worked fine as long as we were in the twentieth century, but doing all of the calculations that involved dates would cause problems as soon as we crossed into the twenty-first century. The Year 2000 Problem has become a major source of work in information systems departments in the late 1990s.

The first procedural or third-generation computer programming languages did not become available until the beginning of the 1960s. Computers were still large and expensive. But the 60s saw important breakthroughs in technology that enabled the development of smaller, faster, less expensive computers — mini-computers — and the beginnings of the software industry. Most organizations still developed their applications from scratch, using their in-house development staffs. System development was more of an art than a science. This view of systems development began to change in the 1970s, however, as organizations began to realize how expensive it was to develop customized information systems for every application. Systems development came to be more disciplined as many people worked to make it more like engineering. Early database management systems, using hierarchical and network models, helped bring discipline to the storage and retrieval of data. The development of database management systems helped shift the focus of systems development from processes first to data first.

The 1980s were also marked by major breakthroughs in computing in organizations, as microcomputers became key organizational tools. The software industry expanded greatly as more and more poeple began to write off-the-shelf software for microcomputers. Developers began to write more and more applications in fourth generation languages, which unlike procedural languages, instructed a computer on what to do instead of how to do it. Computer-aided software engineering (CASE) tools were developed to make systems developers' work easier and more consistent. As computers continued to get smaller, faster, and cheaper, and as the operating systems for computers moved away from line prompt interfaces to windows- and icon-based interfaces, organizations moved to applications with more graphics. Organizations developed less software in-house and bought relatively more from software vendors. The systems developer's job went through a transition from builder to integrator.

The current systems development environment in the late-1990s continues to be focused on systems integration. Developers use visual programming environments, like PowerBuilder or VisualBasic, to design the user interfaces for systems that run on client/server platforms. The database, which may be relational or object-oriented, and which may have been developed using software from firms such as Oracle, Microsoft, or Ingres, resides on the server. Alternatively, an organization may have decided to purchase their entire enterprise-wide system from companies such as SAP AG or PowerSoft Inc. Enterprise-wide systems are large, complex systems that consist of a series of independent system modules. Developers assemble systems by choosing and implementing specific modules. Today, many aspects of the organization's systems have been developed to interact with the Internet or with the firm's intranet.

Although the systems development environment has changed dramatically since its beginnings in the 1950s, some basic principles that govern the approach to systems development have been applicable through all the different eras of computing in organizations. One principle is the distinction between data, data flows, and processing logic, a distinction that will be considered in the next sections.

Separating Data and Processes That Handle Data

Every information system consists of three key components that must be clearly understood by anyone who analyzes and designs systems: data, data flows, and processing logic (see Figure 1-1). **Data** are raw facts that describe people, objects, and events in an organization, such as a customer's account number, the number of boxes of cereal bought, and whether someone is a Democrat or a Republican. Every information system depends on data in order to produce **information,** which is processed data presented in a form suitable for human interpretation. Systems developers must understand what kind of data a system uses and where the data originate. Data and the relationships among data may be described using various techniques, as we will see later. Figure 1-1 shows the structure of employee data as a simple table of rows (records about different employees) and columns (attributes describing each employee).

Data flows are groups of data that move and flow through a system and include a description of the sources and destinations for each data flow. For example, a customer's account number may be captured when he or she uses a credit card to pay for a purchased item. The account number may then be stored in a file within the system until needed to compile a billing statement or prepare a mailing address for a sales circular. When needed, the account number can be extracted from storage and used to complete a system function. Figure 1-1 illustrates data flows with directional lines that connect rounded rectangles which represent the processing steps that accept input data flows and produce output data flows.

Processing logic, the third component, describes the steps in the transformation of the data and the events that trigger these steps. For example, processing logic in a credit card application will explain how to compute available credit given the current credit balance and the amount of the current transaction. Processing logic will also indicate that the computation of the new credit balance will occur when a clerk presses a key on a credit card scanner to confirm the sales transaction. Figure 1-1, using an English-like language, illustrates the rules for calculating an

Data: Raw facts about people, objects, and events in an organization.

Information: Data that have been processed and presented in a form suitable for human interpretation, often with the purpose of revealing trends or patterns.

Data flow: Data in motion, moving from one place in a system to another.

Processing logic: The steps by which data are transformed or moved and a description of the events that trigger these steps.

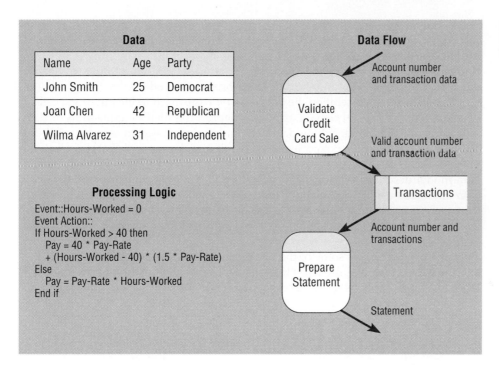

Figure 1-1
Differences among data, data flow, and processing logic

employee's pay and the event (receipt of a new hours-worked value) that causes this calculation to be made.

Traditionally, an information system's design was based upon what the system was supposed to do, such as billing and inventory control: the focus was on output and processing logic. Although the data the system used as input were important, data were subordinate to the application. The assumption was that we could anticipate all outputs and the proper processing steps with their need for data. Therefore, we could easily derive all data requirements from all known system deliverables. Furthermore, each application contained its own files and data storage capacity. The data had to match the specifications established in each application, and each application was considered separately.

This concentration on the flow, use, and transformation of data in an information system typified the **process-oriented approach** to systems development. The techniques and notations developed from this approach track the movement of data from their sources, through intermediate processing steps, and on to final destinations. Since various parts of an information system work on different schedules and at different speeds, the process-oriented approach also shows where data are temporarily stored until needed for processing. The natural structure of the data is, however, not specified within the traditional process-oriented approach. Until recently, techniques for the process-oriented approach did not address the timing or triggering of processing steps, only their sequence.

Data processing managers soon realized that there were problems with analyzing and designing systems using only a process-oriented approach. One result was the existence of several specialized files of data, each locked within different applications and programs. Many of the files in these different applications contained the same data elements (see Figure 1-2a). When a single data element changed, it had to be changed in each of these files. If, for example, such a system were in effect at your university and your address changed, it would have to be changed in the files of the library, the registrar's office, the financial aid office, and every other

Process-oriented approach:
An overall strategy to information systems development that focuses on how and when data are moved through and changed by an information system.

place your address was stored. It also became difficult to combine specialized data files. Even if the files contained the same data elements, each file might use a different name and format for the data. Since it was important to standardize how data elements were represented, data processing managers gradually came to separate the application programs and the data these programs used.

This focus on data typified the **data-oriented approach** to information systems development. The data-oriented approach depicts the ideal organization of data, independent of where and how data are used within a system (see Figure 1-2b). The techniques used for data orientation result in a data model that describes the kinds of data needed in systems and the business relationships among the data. A data model describes the rules and policies of a business. Some people believe a data model to be more permanent than a process model since a data model reflects the inherent nature of a business instead of the way a business operates, which is constantly changing. Some people refer to data-oriented approaches as *information engineering.*

Table 1-1 highlights some of the key distinctions between the process-oriented and the data-oriented approaches to systems development. Although we highlight these two approaches as separate competing orientations, we do so only to empha-

Data-oriented approach:
An overall strategy of information systems development that focuses on the ideal organization of data rather than where and how data are used.

Figure 1-2
Traditional relationship between data and applications, with redundant data, versus the database approach

(a) Traditional approach

(b) Database approach

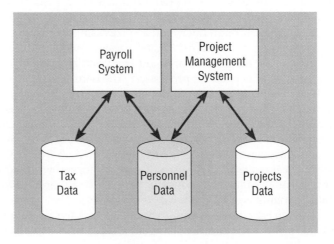

TABLE 1-1   Key Differences Between the Process-Oriented and Data-Oriented Approaches to Systems Development

Characteristic	Process-Orientation	Data-Orientation
System focus	What the system is supposed to do and when	Data the system needs to operate
Design stability	Limited, as business processes and the applications that support them change constantly	More enduring, as the data needs of an organization do not change rapidly
Data organization	Data files designed for each individual application	Data files designed for the enterprise
State of the data	Much uncontrolled duplication	Limited, controlled duplication

size their differences and unique contributions to systems analysis and design and to give you a sense of the historical evolution of systems analysis and design methodologies. As either approach is, by itself, inadequate, this book will cover the techniques and tools you will need to analyze and design both process and data aspects of systems.

Separating Databases and Applications

As data storage management technology advanced, it became possible to represent data not in separate files for each application but in coherent and shared databases. A **database** is a shared collection of logically related data organized in ways that facilitate capture, storage, and retrieval for multiple users in an organization. Databases involve methods of data organization that allow data to be centrally managed, standardized, and consistent. Instead of a proliferation of separate and distinct data files, the database approach allows central databases to be the sole source of data for many varied applications.

Database: A shared collection of logically related data designed to meet the information needs of multiple users in an organization.

Under the data-oriented approach to systems development, databases are designed around *subjects*, such as customers, suppliers, and parts. Designing databases around subjects enables you to use and revise databases for many different independent applications. This focus results in **application independence,** the separation of data and the definition of data from applications.

Application independence: The separation of data and the definition of data from the applications that use these data.

The central point of application independence is that data and applications are separate. For the data-oriented approach to be effective, however, another change in the system design is needed: Organizations that have centrally managed repositories of organizational data must design new applications to work with existing databases. Organizations that do not have centrally managed repositories of organizational data must design databases that will support both current and future applications.

YOUR ROLE AND OTHER ORGANIZATIONAL RESPONSIBILITIES IN SYSTEMS DEVELOPMENT

In an organization that develops its own information systems internally, there are several types of jobs involved. In medium to large organizations, there is usually a separate Information Systems (IS) department. Depending on how the organization is set up, the IS department may be a relatively independent unit, reporting to the organization's top manager. Alternatively, the IS department may be part of another functional department, such as Finance, or there may even be an IS department in several major business units. In any of these cases, the manager of an IS department will be involved in systems development. If the department is large enough, there will be a separate division for systems development, which would be homebase for systems analysts, and another division for programming, where programmers would be based (see Figure 1-3). The people for whom the systems are designed are located in the functional departments and are referred to as users or *end users.*

Some organizations use a different structure for their IS departments. Following this model, analysts are assigned and may report to functional departments. In this way, analysts learn more about the business they support. This approach is supposed to result in better systems, since the analyst becomes an expert in both systems development and the business area.

Regardless of how an organization structures its information systems department, systems development is a *team effort.* Systems analysts work together in a team, usually organized on a project basis. Team membership can be expanded to include IS managers, programmers, users, and other specialists who may be involved (throughout or at specific points) in the systems development project. It is rare to find an organizational information system project that involves only one person. Thus, learning how to work with others in teams is an important skill for any IS professional, and we will stress team skills throughout this book.

A good team has certain characteristics, some that are a result of how the group is assembled and others that must be acquired through effort on the part of team members (see Table 1-2). A good team is diverse and tolerant of diversity:

Figure 1-3
Organization chart for typical IS department

TABLE 1-2   Characteristics of Successful Teams

- Diversity in backgrounds, skills, and goals
- Tolerance of diversity, uncertainty, ambiguity
- Clear and complete communication
- Trust
- Mutual respect and putting one's own views second to the team
- Reward structure that promotes shared responsibility and accountability

- A diverse team has representation from all the different groups interested in a system, and the representation of these groups on the team increases the likelihood of acceptance of the changes a new system will cause.

- Diversity exposes team members to new and different ideas, ideas they might never think of were all team members from the same background, with the same skills and goals.

- New and different ideas can help a team generate better solutions to its problems and defend the course of action it chooses.

- Team members must be able to entertain new ideas without being overly critical, without dismissing new ideas out of hand simply because they are new.

- Team members must be able to deal with ambiguous information as well as with complexity and must learn to play a role on a team (and different roles on different teams) so that the talents of all team members can best be utilized.

In order to work well together, a good team must strive to communicate clearly and completely with its members. Team members will communicate more effectively if they trust each other. Trust, in turn, is built on mutual respect and an ability to place one's own goals and views secondary to the goals and views of the group. To help ensure that a team will work well together, management needs to develop a reward structure that promotes shared responsibility and accountability within the team. In addition to rewards for individual efforts, team members must be rewarded by IS managers for their work as members of an effective work unit.

Team success depends not only on how a team is assembled or the efforts of the group but also on the management of the team. Reward systems are one part of good team management. Effective project management is another key element of successful teams. Project management includes devising a feasible and realistic work plan and schedule, monitoring progress against this schedule, coordinating the project with its sponsors, allocating resources to the project, and sometimes even deciding whether and when a project should be terminated before completing the system.

The characteristics of each systems analysis and design project will dictate which types of individuals should be on the project team. In general, those involved in systems development include IS managers, systems analysts, programmers, end users, and business managers as well as additional IS managers, technicians, and specialists. We will now preview the role of each of these players and other **stakeholders** in systems development.

Stakeholder: A person who has an interest in an existing or new information system.

IS Managers in Systems Development

The manager of an IS department may have a direct role in the systems development process if the organization is small or if that is the manager's style. Typically, IS managers are more involved in allocating resources to and overseeing approved system development projects rather than in the actual development process. Thus, IS managers may attend some project review meetings and certainly will expect written status reports on project progress covering their areas of concern. IS managers may prescribe what methodologies, techniques, and tools are to be used and the procedure for reporting the status of projects. As department leaders, IS managers are also responsible for career planning and development for systems analysts and other employees and for solving problems that arise in the course of development projects.

There are, of course, several IS managers in any medium to large IS department (see Figure 1-3). The manager of an entire IS department may have the title Chief Information Officer and may report to the president or chairman of the firm. Each division of the IS department will also have a manager. Typical titles for these managers are Director of IS Development, IS Operations Manager, and IS Programming Director. The Director of IS Development may be responsible for several development projects at any given time, each of which has a project manager. The responsibilities and focus of any particular IS manager depend on his or her level in the department and on how the organization manages and supports the systems development process.

Systems Analysts in Systems Development

Systems analysts are the key individuals in the systems development process. To succeed as a systems analyst, you will need to develop four skills: analytical, technical, managerial, and interpersonal. *Analytical skills* enable you to understand the organization and its functions, to identify opportunities and problems, and to analyze and solve problems. One of the most important analytical skills you can develop is systems thinking, or the ability to see organizations and information systems as systems. Systems thinking provides a framework from which to see the important relationships among information systems, the organizations they exist in, and the environment in which the organizations themselves exist. *Technical skills* help you understand the potential and the limitations of information technology. As an analyst, you must be able to envision an information system that will help users solve problems and that will guide the system's design and development. You must also be able to work with programming languages, various operating systems, and computer hardware platforms. *Management skills* help you manage projects, resources, risk, and change. *Interpersonal skills* help you work with end users as well as with other analysts and programmers. As a systems analyst, you will play a major role as a liaison among users, programmers, and other systems professionals. Effective written and oral communication, including competence in leading meetings, interviewing, and listening, is a key skill analysts must master. Effective analysts successfully combine these four skills, as Figure 1-4, a typical advertisement for a systems analyst position, illustrates.

As with any profession, becoming a good systems analyst takes years of study and experience. Once hired by an organization, you will generally be trained in the development methodology used by the organization. There is usually a career path for systems analysts that allows them to gain experience and advance into project management and further IS or business management. Many academic IS departments train their undergraduate students to be systems analysts. As your career

Figure 1-4
Typical job ad for a systems analyst

SYSTEMS ANALYST
Distribution Center

We are the world's leading manufacturer of women's intimate apparel products. Our organization in the Far East has an opening for a Systems Analyst.

Requirements:

- Bachelor's degree (or comparable) in Computer Science and/or Business Administrations with 5 (+) years of working experience.

- In-depth understanding of Distribution and Manufacturing concepts (Allocation, Replenishment, Ship Floor Control, Production Scheduling, MRP)

- Working knowledge of project management and all phases of software development life cycle.

- Experience with CASE tools, PC and Bar Code equipment is essential.

- Working knowledge of an AS/400 and/or UNIX environment with the languages C, RPG400 and/or COBOL are desirable

The successful candidate will provide primary interface for all user problems, answer technical questions and requests within the applications development group; work with user areas to establish priorities; and provide recommendations and directions for process improvement through automation; skills in an Asian language is a plus.

We offer an attractive compensation package, relocation assistance and the technical and analytical challenges you would expect in a state-of-the-art environment. The position will report to Senior Management.

Please forward your resume, along with salary requirements to:

---

progresses, you may get the chance to become a manager inside or outside the IS area. In some organizations, you can opt to follow a technical career advancement ladder. As an analyst, you will become aware of a consistent set of professional practices, many of which are governed by a professional code of ethics, similar to other professions.

Programmers in Systems Development

Programmers convert the system specifications given to them by the analysts into instructions the computer can understand. Writing a computer program is sometimes called writing code, or *coding*. Programmers also write program documentation and programs for testing systems. For many years, programming was considered an art. However, computer scientists found that code could be improved if it were structured, so they introduced what is now called *structured programming* (Bohm and Jacopini, 1966). In structured programming, all computing instructions can be represented through the use of three simple structures: sequence, repetition, and selection. Becoming a skilled programmer takes years of training and experience. Many computer information systems undergraduates begin work as programmers or programmer/analysts.

Programming is very labor-intensive, therefore, special-purpose computing tools called *code generators* have been developed to generate reasonably good code from specifications, saving an organization time and money. Code generators do not put programmers out of work; rather, these tools change the nature of programming. Where code generators are in use, programmers take the generated code and fix problems with it, optimize it, and integrate it with other parts of the system. The goal of some computer-aided software engineering (CASE) tools is to provide a variety of code generators that can automatically produce 90 percent or more of code directly from the system specifications normally given a programmer. When this goal is achieved, the role of programmers on systems development teams will be changed further.

End Users in Systems Development

In the typical traditional systems development process, systems analysts interview, survey, and observe end users to determine what they need from an information system. **End users** are business professionals who are experts in their fields but who usually do not have the skills, time, desire, or responsibility required to develop information systems. Therefore, as an analyst, you will work with users to convert their knowledge of the business into supportive information systems. End users often are your clients or customers, the people for whom you are building a system. In many cases, end users will also serve on the systems development team, providing their expertise in very active ways. You and other IS professionals will also provide support and assistance for those more sophisticated end users who write, test, and implement their own information or data distribution systems.

End users: Non-information system professionals in an organization who specify the business requirements for and use software applications. End users often request new or modified applications, test and approve applications, and may serve on project teams as business experts.

Supporting End-User Development   As the number of user requests for new or improved information systems increases, an IS department will have to assign priorities to development projects. Prioritization means that some users will get their systems right away while others must wait. In the 1970s, with the spread of time-sharing systems that enabled several people to use the same computer at the same time, it became technically possible for end users to develop their own systems. As education and experience made end users aware of these technologies and they became skillful in using them, many users, impatient for their requested projects to be scheduled, developed their own applications. Consequently, a significant role for systems analysts and other IS professionals is to help end users develop their own systems, which are often stand-alone systems or data distribution systems designed to enhance an existing system developed by IS professionals.

End-user development: An approach to systems development in which users who are not computer experts satisfy their own computing needs through the use of high-level software and languages such as electronic spreadsheets and relational database management systems.

Support of **end-user development** has several dimensions. First, IS professionals must evaluate and make available suitable tools for end users. Second, IS professionals must train end users in the use of these tools and their proper application. Third, IS professionals must be available to assist end users and to answer questions or perform more complicated systems development work whenever end users have difficulties. Finally, IS professionals must continue to maintain the data capture and transfer applications that manage the databases from which end users extract the data needed in the systems they build.

End-user design and development of information systems has been somewhat controversial in the past (Alavi and Weiss, 1985; Davis, 1982). Some IS managers have worried about the quality of the systems end users produce. However, some end users believe there is no choice, especially if users must wait for the IS department to provide the desired and needed systems. Of course, if an organization is too small to have an IS department and outside consultants are too expensive, end users have little choice but to develop their own systems or settle for off-the-shelf software.

Business Managers in Systems Development

Another group important to systems development efforts is business managers, such as functional department heads and corporate executives. These managers are important to systems development because they have the power to fund development projects and to allocate the resources necessary for the projects' success. Because of their decision-making authority and knowledge of the firm's lines of business, department heads and executives are also able to set general requirements and constraints for development projects. In larger companies where the relative importance of systems projects is determined by a steering committee, these executives have additional power as they are usually members of the steering committees or systems planning groups. Business managers, therefore, have the power to set the direction for systems development, to propose and approve projects, and to determine the relative importance of projects that have already been approved and assigned to other people in the organization.

Other IS Managers/Technicians in Systems Development

In larger organizations where IS roles are more differentiated, there may be several additional IS professionals involved in the systems development effort. A firm with an existing set of databases will most likely have a *database administrator* who is usually involved in any systems project affecting the firm's databases. Network and *telecommunications experts* help develop systems involving data and/or voice communication, either internal or external to the organization. Some organizations have *human factors* departments which are concerned with system interfaces and ease-of-use issues, training users, and writing user documentation and manuals. Overseeing much of the development effort, especially for large or sensitive systems, are an organization's *internal auditors* who ensure that required controls are built into the system. In many organizations, auditors also have responsibility for keeping track of changes in the system's design. The necessary interaction of all these individuals makes systems development very much a team effort.

TYPES OF INFORMATION SYSTEMS
AND SYSTEMS DEVELOPMENT

As you can see, several different people in an organization can be involved in developing information systems. Given the broad range of people and interests represented in systems development, you might assume that it could take several different types of information systems to satisfy all an organization's information system needs. Your assumption would be correct.

Up until now we have been talking about information systems in generic terms, but there are actually several different types or classes of information systems. In general, these types are distinguished from each other on the basis of what the system does or by the technology used to construct the system. As a systems analyst, part of your job will be to determine which kind of system will best address the organizational problem or opportunity on which you are focusing. In addition, different classes of systems may require different methodologies, techniques, and tools for development.

From your prior studies and experiences with information systems, you are probably aware of at least four classes of information systems:

- Transaction processing systems

- Management information systems

- Decision support systems (for individuals, groups, and executives)

- Expert systems

In addition, many organizations recognize scientific (or technical) computing and office automation systems. To preview the diversity of systems development approaches, the following sections briefly highlight how systems analysis and design methods differ across the four major types of systems.

Transaction Processing Systems

Transaction processing systems (TPS) automate the handling of data about business activities or transactions, which can be thought of as simple, discrete events in the life of an organization. Data about each transaction are captured, transactions are verified and accepted or rejected, and validated transactions are stored for later aggregation. Reports may be produced immediately to provide standard summarizations of transactions, and transactions may be moved from process to process in order to handle all aspects of the business activity.

The analysis and design of a TPS means focusing on the firm's current procedures for processing transactions, whether those procedures are manual or automated. The focus on current procedures implies a careful tracking of data capture, flow, processing, and output. The goal of TPS development is to improve transaction processing by speeding it up, using fewer people, improving efficiency and accuracy, integrating it with other organizational information systems, or providing information not previously available.

Management Information Systems

A management information system (MIS) takes the relatively raw data available through a TPS and converts them into a meaningful aggregated form that managers need to conduct their responsibilities. Developing an MIS calls for a good understanding of what kind of information managers require and how managers use information in their jobs. Sometimes managers themselves may not know precisely what they need or how they will use information. Thus, the analyst must also develop a good understanding of the business and the transaction processing systems that provide data for an MIS.

Management information systems often require data from several transaction processing systems (for example, customer order processing, raw material purchasing, and employee timekeeping). Development of an MIS can, therefore, benefit from a data-orientation, in which data are considered an organization resource separate from the TPS in which they are captured. Because it is important to be able to draw on data from various subject areas, developing a comprehensive and accurate model of data is essential in building an MIS.

Decision Support Systems

Decision support systems (DSS) are designed to help organizational decision makers make decisions. Instead of providing summaries of data, as with an MIS, a DSS provides an interactive environment in which decision makers can quickly manipulate data and models of business operations. A DSS is composed of a database (which may be extracted from a TPS or MIS), mathematical or graphical models of business processes, and a user interface (or dialogue module) that provides a way for the decision maker, usually a non-technical manager, to communicate with the DSS. A DSS may use both hard historical data as well as judgments (or "what if" scenarios) about alternative histories or possible futures. One form of a DSS, an executive information system (EIS), emphasizes the unstructured capability for senior management to explore data starting at a high level of aggregation and selectively drilling down into specific areas where more detailed understandings of the business are required. In either case, a DSS is characterized by less structured and predictable use; rather, a DSS is a software resource intended to support a certain scope of decision-making activities (from problem finding to choosing a course of action).

The systems analysis and design for a DSS often concentrates on the three main DSS components: database, model base, and user dialogue. As with an MIS, a data-orientation is most often used for understanding user requirements. In addition, the systems analysis and design project will carefully document the mathematical rules that define inter-relationships among different data. These relationships are used to predict future data or to find the best solutions to decision problems. Thus, decision logic must be carefully understood and documented. Also, since a decision maker typically interacts with a DSS, the design of easy-to-use yet thorough user dialogues and screens is important. Because a DSS often deals with situations not encountered every day or situations that can be handled in many different ways, there can be considerable uncertainty on what a DSS should actually do. Thus, systems developers often use methods that prototype the system and iteratively and rapidly redevelop the system based on trial use. The development of a DSS, hence, often does not follow as formal a project plan as is done for a TPS or MIS, since the software deliverable is more uncertain at the beginning of the project.

Expert Systems

Different from any of the other classes of systems we have discussed so far, an expert system (ES) attempts to codify and manipulate knowledge rather than information. If-then-else rules or other knowledge representation forms describe the way an expert would approach situations in a specific domain of problems. Typically, users communicate with an ES through an interactive dialogue. The ES asks questions (that an expert would ask) and the end user supplies the answers. The answers are then used to determine which rules apply and the ES provides a recommendation based on the rules.

The focus on developing an ES is acquiring the knowledge of the expert in the particular problem domain. Knowledge engineers perform knowledge acquisition; they are similar to systems analysts but are trained to use different techniques, as determining knowledge is considered more difficult than determining data.

Summary of Information Systems Types

Many information systems you build or maintain will contain aspects of each of the four major types of information systems. Thus, as a systems analyst, you will likely employ specific methodologies, techniques, and tools associated with each of the four information system types. Table 1-3 summarizes the general characteristics and development methods for each type.

So far, we have concentrated on the context of information systems development, looking at the different organizations where software is developed, the people involved in development efforts, and the different types of information systems that exist in organizations. Now that we have a good idea of context, we can turn to the actual process by which many information systems are developed in organizations, the *systems development life cycle.*

DEVELOPING INFORMATION SYSTEMS AND THE SYSTEMS DEVELOPMENT LIFE CYCLE

Systems development methodology: A standard process followed in an organization to conduct all the steps necessary to analyze, design, implement, and maintain information systems.

Systems development life cycle (SDLC): The traditional methodology used to develop, maintain, and replace information systems.

Most organizations find it beneficial to use a standard set of steps, called a **systems development methodology,** to develop and support their information systems. Like many processes, the development of information systems often follows a life cycle. For example, a commercial product follows a life cycle in that it is created, tested, and introduced to the market. Its sales increase, peak, and decline. Finally, the product is removed from the market and replaced by something else. The **systems development life cycle (SDLC)** is a common methodology for systems development in many organizations, featuring several phases that mark the progress of the systems analysis and design effort. Every textbook author and information system development organization uses a slightly different life cycle model, with anywhere from three to almost twenty identifiable phases.

Although any life cycle appears at first glance to be a sequentially ordered set of phases, it actually is not (see Figure 1-5). The specific steps and their sequence are meant to be adapted as required for a project, consistent with management approaches. For example, in any given SDLC phase, the project can return to an earlier phase if necessary. Similarly, if a commercial product does not perform well just after its introduction, it may be temporarily removed from the market and im-

TABLE 1-3   Systems Development for Different IS Types

IS Type	IS Characteristics	Systems Development Methods
Transaction processing system	High-volume, data capture focus; goal is efficiency of data movement and processing and interfacing different TPSs	Process-orientation; concern with capturing, validating, and storing data and with moving data between each required step
Management information system	Draws on diverse yet predictable data resources to aggregate and summarize data; may involve forecasting future data from historical trends and business knowledge	Data-orientation; concern with understanding relationships between data so data can be accessed and summarized in a variety of ways; builds a model of data that supports a variety of uses
Decision support system	Provides guidance in identifying problems, finding and evaluating alternative solutions, and selecting or comparing alternatives; potentially involves groups of decision makers; often involves semi-structured problems and the need to access data at different levels of detail	Data- and decision logic-orientations; design of user dialogue; group communication may also be key and access to unpredictable data may be necessary; nature of systems require iterative development and almost constant updating
Expert system	Provides expert advice by asking users a sequence of questions dependent on prior answers that lead to a conclusion or recommendation	A specialized decision logic-orientation in which knowledge is elicited from experts and described by rules or other forms

Figure 1-5
The systems development life cycle

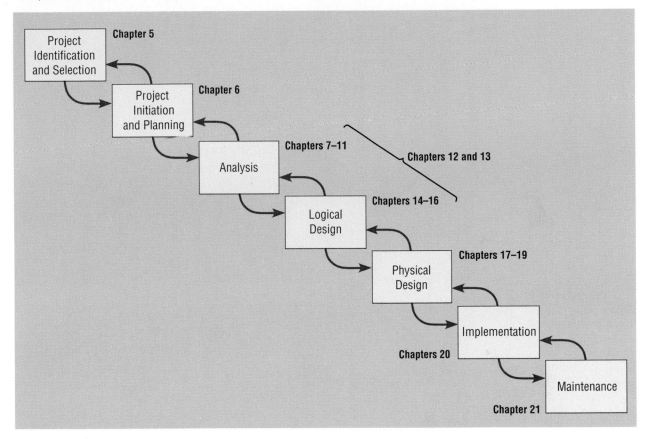

proved before being re-introduced. In the systems development life cycle, it is also possible to complete some activities in one phase in parallel with some activities of another phase. Sometimes the life cycle is iterative; that is, phases are repeated as required until an acceptable system is found. Such an iterative approach is especially characteristic of rapid application development methods, such as proto- typing, which we introduce later in the chapter (see Figure 1-6). Some people consider the life cycle to be a spiral, in which we constantly cycle through the phases at different levels of detail (see Figure 1-7). The life cycle can also be thought of as a circular process in which the end of the useful life of one system leads to the beginning of another project that will develop a new version or replace an existing system altogether. However conceived, the systems development life cycle used in an organization is an orderly set of activities conducted and planned for each de- velopment project. The skills required of a systems analyst apply to all life cycle models. Software is the most obvious end product of the life cycle; other essential outputs include documentation about the system and how it was developed as well as training for users.

Every medium to large corporation and every custom software producer will have its own specific, detailed life cycle or systems development methodology in place (see Figure 1-8). Even if a particular methodology does not look like a cycle, you will probably discover that many of the SDLC steps are performed and SDLC techniques and tools are used. Learning about systems analysis and design from

Figure 1-6
Rapid application development SDLC

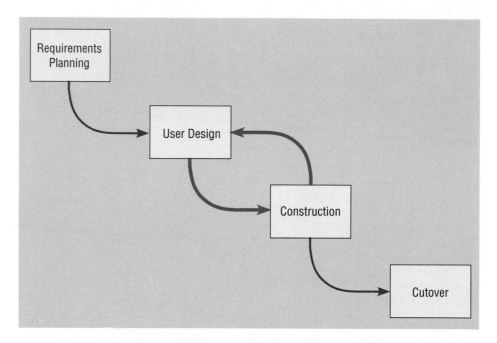

Figure 1-7
Evolutionary model SDLC

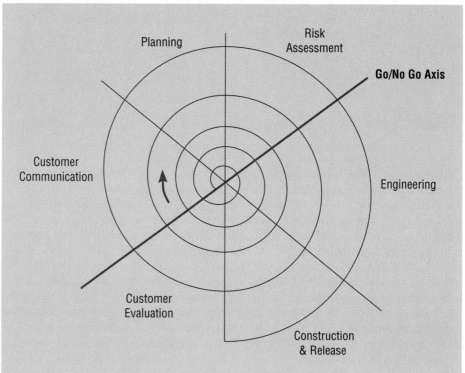

the life cycle approach will serve you well no matter which systems development methodology you use.

When you begin your first job, you are likely to spend several weeks or months learning your organization's SDLC and its associated methodologies, techniques, and tools. In order to make this book as general as possible, we follow a rather generic life cycle model, as described in more detail in Figure 1-5. Notice how our

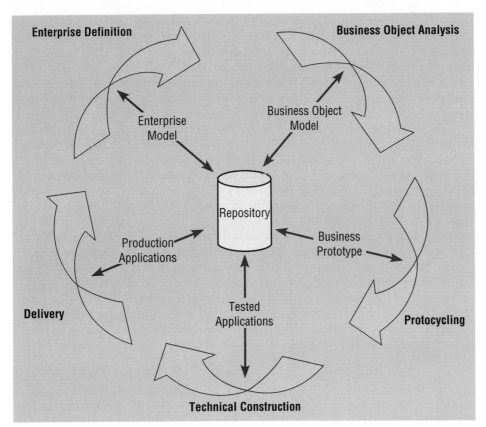

Figure 1-8
Seer Technologies, Inc., SDLC (The Seer Method™ is a trademark of Seer Technologies, Inc., all rights reserved.)

model resembles a staircase with arrows connecting each step to the step before it and to the step after it. This representation of the SDLC is sometimes referred to as the waterfall model. We use this SDLC as one example of a methodology but, more importantly, as a way to arrange the topics of systems analysis and design. Thus, what you learn in this book you can apply to almost any life cycle you might follow. As we describe this SDLC throughout the book, you will see that each phase has specific outcomes and deliverables that feed important information to other phases. At the end of each phase (and sometimes within phases for intermediate steps), a systems development project reaches a *milestone* and, as deliverables are produced, they are often reviewed by parties outside the project team. In the rest of this section we provide a brief overview of each SDLC phase. At the end of the section we summarize this discussion in a table listing the main deliverables or outputs from each SDLC phase.

The first phase in the SDLC is called **project identification and selection.** In this phase, someone identifies the need for a new or enhanced system. In larger organizations, this recognition may be part of a corporate and systems planning process. Information needs of the organization as a whole are examined, and projects to meet these needs are proactively identified. The organization's information system needs may result from requests to deal with problems in current procedures, from the desire to perform additional tasks, or from the realization that information technology could be used to capitalize on an existing opportunity. These needs can then be prioritized and translated into a plan for the IS department, including a schedule for developing new major systems. In smaller organizations (as well as in large ones), determination of which systems to develop may be affected by ad hoc user requests submitted as the need for new or enhanced

Project identification and selection: The first phase of the SDLC in which an organization's total information system needs are identified, analyzed, prioritized, and arranged.

Project initiation and planning: The second phase of the SDLC in which a potential information systems project is explained and an argument for continuing or not continuing with the project is presented; a detailed plan is also developed for conducting the remaining phases of the SDLC for the proposed system.

systems arises as well as from a formalized information planning process. In either case, during project identification and selection, an organization determines whether or not resources should be devoted to the development or enhancement of each information system under consideration. The outcome of the project identification and selection process is a determination of which systems development projects should be undertaken by the organization, at least in terms of an initial study.

The second phase is **project initiation and planning.** The two major activities in this phase are the formal, yet still preliminary, investigation of the system problem or opportunity at hand and the presentation of reasons why the system should or should not be developed by the organization. A critical step at this point is determining the scope of the proposed system. The project leader and initial team of systems analysts also produce a specific plan for the proposed project which the team will follow using the remaining SDLC steps. This baseline project plan customizes the standardized SDLC and specifies the time and resources needed for its execution. The formal definition of a project is based on the likelihood that the organization's IS department is able to develop a system that will solve the problem or exploit the opportunity and determine whether the costs of developing the system outweigh the benefits it could provide. The final presentation of the business case for proceeding with the subsequent project phases is usually made by the project leader and other team members to someone in management or to a special management committee with the job of deciding which projects the organization will undertake.

Analysis: The third phase of the SDLC in which the current system is studied and alternative replacement systems are proposed.

The next phase is **analysis.** During this phase, the analyst thoroughly studies the organization's current procedures and the information systems used to perform organizational tasks. Analysis has several sub-phases. The first is requirements determination. In this sub-phase, you and other analysts work with users to determine what the users want from a proposed system. This sub-phase usually involves a careful study of any current systems, manual and computerized, that might be replaced or enhanced as part of this project. Next, you study the requirements and structure them according to their inter-relationships and eliminate any redundancies. Third, you generate alternative initial designs to match the requirements. Then you compare these alternatives to determine which best meets the requirements within the cost, labor, and technical levels the organization is willing to commit to the development process. The output of the analysis phase is a description of (but not a detailed design for) the alternative solution recommended by the analysis team. Once the recommendation is accepted by those with funding authority, you can begin to make plans to acquire any hardware and system software necessary to build or operate the system as proposed.

Logical design: The fourth phase of the SDLC in which all functional features of the system chosen for development in analysis are described independently of any computer platform.

The fourth and fifth phases are devoted to designing the new or enhanced system. During design, you and the other analysts convert the description of the recommended alternative solution into logical and then physical system specifications. You must design all aspects of the system from input and output screens to reports, databases, and computer processes. Design occurs in two SDLC phases: logical design and physical design.

Logical design is not tied to any specific hardware and systems software platform. Theoretically, the system could be implemented on any hardware and systems software. The idea is to make sure that the system functions as intended. Logical design concentrates on the business aspects of the system (which is why some life cycles call this phase business design).

Physical design: The fifth phase of the SDLC in which the logical specifications of the system from logical design are transformed into technology-specific details from which all programming and system construction can be accomplished.

In **physical design,** you turn the logical design into physical, or technical, specifications. For example, you must convert diagrams that map the origin, flow, and processing of data in a system into a structured systems design that can then be broken down into smaller and smaller units for conversion to instructions written in a programming language. You design the various parts of the system to perform the physical operations necessary to facilitate data capture, processing, and information output. During physical design, the analyst team decides which programming languages the computer instructions will be written in, which database systems and file structures will be used for the data, and which hardware platform, operating system, and network environment the system will run under. These decisions finalize the hardware and software plans initiated at the end of the analysis phase. Now you can proceed with acquiring any new technology not already present in the organization. The final product of the design phase is the physical system specifications in a form ready to be turned over to programmers and other system builders for construction.

The physical system specifications are turned over to programmers as the first part of the **implementation** phase. During implementation, you turn system specifications into a working system that is tested and then put into use. Implementation includes coding, testing, and installation. During *coding,* programmers write the programs that make up the system. During *testing,* programmers and analysts test individual programs and the entire system in order to find and correct errors. During *installation,* the new system becomes a part of the daily activities of the organization. Application software is installed, or loaded, on existing or new hardware and users are introduced to the new system and trained. Begin planning for both testing and installation early as the project initiation and planning phase, since both testing and installation require extensive analysis in order to develop exactly the right approach.

Implementation: The sixth phase of the SDLC in which the information system is coded, tested, installed, and supported in the organization.

Implementation activities also include initial user support such as the finalization of documentation, training programs, and ongoing user assistance. Note that documentation and training programs are finalized during implementation; documentation is produced throughout the life cycle, and training (and education) occur from the inception of a project. Implementation can continue for as long as the system exists since ongoing user support is also part of implementation. Despite the best efforts of analysts, managers, and programmers, however, installation is not always a simple process. Many well-designed systems have failed because the installation process was faulty. Our point is that even a well-designed system can fail if implementation is not well managed. Since the management of implementation is usually done by the project team, we stress implementation issues throughout this book.

The final phase is **maintenance.** When a system (including its training, documentation, and support) is operating in an organization, users sometimes find problems with how it works and often think of better ways to perform its functions. Also, the organization's needs with respect to the system change over time. In maintenance, programmers make the changes that users ask for and modify the system to reflect changing business conditions. These changes are necessary to keep the system running and useful. In a sense, maintenance is not a separate phase but a repetition of the other life cycle phases required to study and implement the needed changes. Thus, you might think of maintenance as an overlay to the life cycle rather than a separate phase. The amount of time and effort devoted to maintenance depends a great deal on the performance of the previous phases of the life cycle. There inevitably comes a time, however, when an information system is no longer performing as desired, when maintenance costs become prohibitive, or when an organization's needs have changed substantially. Such problems indicate that it is time to begin designing the system's replacement, thereby completing the loop and starting the life cycle over again. Often the distinction between major maintenance and new development is not clear, which is another reason maintenance often resembles the life cycle itself.

Maintenance: The final phase of the SDLC in which an information system is systematically repaired and improved.

The SDLC is a highly linked set of phases whose products feed the activities in subsequent phases. Table 1-4 summarizes the outputs or products of each phase based on the above descriptions. The chapters on the SDLC phases will elaborate on the products of each phase as well as on how the products are developed.

Throughout the systems development life cycle, the systems development project itself needs to be carefully planned and managed. The larger the systems project, the greater the need for project management. Several project management techniques have been developed in this century and many have been made more useful through automation. Chapter 3 contains a more detailed treatment of project planning and management techniques. Next, we will discuss some of the criticisms of the systems development life cycle and alternatives developed to address those criticisms.

The Traditional SDLC

There are several criticisms of the traditional life cycle approach to systems development as followed exactly as outlined in Figure 1-5. One criticism relates to the way the life cycle is organized. Although we know that phases of the life cycle can sometimes overlap, traditionally one phase ended and another began once a *milestone* had been reached. The milestone usually took the form of some deliverable or pre-specified output from the phase. For example, the design deliverable is the set of detailed physical design specifications. Once the milestone had been reached and the new phase initiated, it became difficult to go back. Even though business conditions continued to change during the development process and analysts were pressured by users and others to alter the design to match changing conditions, it was necessary for the analysts to freeze the design at a particular point and go forward. The enormous amount of effort and time necessary to implement a specific design meant that it would be very expensive to make changes in a system once it was developed. There were no CASE tools, no code generators, and no fourth-generation languages when the SDLC was popularized in the 1960s. If the design

TABLE 1-4	Products of SDLC Phases
Phase	**Products, Outputs, or Deliverables**
Project identification and selection	Priorities for systems and projects; an architecture for data, networks, hardware, and IS management is the result of associated systems planning activities
Project initiation and planning	Detailed steps, or work plan, for project; specification of system scope and high-level system requirements or features; assignment of team members and other resources; system justification or business case
Analysis	Description of current system and where problems or opportunities are with a general recommendation on how to fix, enhance, or replace current system; explanation of alternative systems and justification for chosen alternative
Logical design	Functional, detailed specifications of all system elements (data, processes, inputs, and outputs)
Physical design	Technical, detailed specifications of all system elements (programs, files, network, system software, etc.); acquisition plan for new technology
Implementation	Code, documentation, training procedures, and support capabilities
Maintenance	New versions or releases of software with associated updates to documentation, training, and support

was not frozen, the system would never be completed, as programmers would no sooner be done with coding one design than they would receive requests for major changes. The traditional life cycle, then, had the property of locking in users to requirements that had been previously determined, even though those requirements might have changed.

Another criticism of the way the traditional life cycle is often used is that it tends to focus too little time on good analysis and design. The result is a system that does not match users' needs and one that requires extensive maintenance, unnecessarily increasing development costs. According to some estimates, maintenance costs account for as much as 70 percent of the system development costs (Aktas, 1987). Given these problems, people working in systems development began to look for better ways to conduct systems analysis and design.

Structured Analysis and Structured Design

Ed Yourdon and his colleagues developed *structured analysis* and *structured design* in the early 1970s as a way to address some of the problems with the traditional SDLC (Yourdon & Constantine, 1979). By making analysis and design more disciplined, similar to engineering fields, through the use of tools such as data flow diagrams and transform analysis, Yourdon and colleagues sought to emphasize and improve the analysis and design phases of the life cycle. The goal was to reduce maintenance time and effort. Structured analysis and design makes it easier to go back to earlier phases in the life cycle when necessary—for example, when requirements change. Finally, there is also an emphasis on partitioning or dividing a problem into smaller, more manageable units and on making a clear distinction between physical and logical design (DeMarco, 1979; Yourdon & Constantine, 1979). The life cycle used in this book is faithful to these structured principles.

Object-Oriented Analysis and Design

A more recent approach to systems development that is becoming more and more popular is **object-oriented analysis and design** (OOAD) (we elaborate on this approach in Chapter 12). OOAD is often called the third approach to systems development, after the process-oriented and data-oriented approaches. The object-oriented approach combines data and processes (call *methods*) into single entities called **objects.** Objects usually correspond to the real things an information system deals with, such as customers, suppliers, contracts, and rental agreements. Putting data and processes together in one place recognizes the fact that there are a limited number of operations for any given data structure. Putting data and processes together makes sense even though typical systems development keeps data and processes independent of each other. The goal of OOAD is to make system elements more reusable, thus improving system quality and the productivity of systems analysis and design.

Another key idea behind object-orientation is that of **inheritance.** Objects are organized into **object classes,** which are groups of objects sharing structural and behavioral characteristics. Inheritance allows the creation of new classes that share some of the characteristics of existing classes. For example, from a class of objects called "person," you can use inheritance to define another class of objects called "customer." Objects of the class "customer" would share certain characteristics with objects of the class "person": they would both have names, addresses, phone numbers, and so on. Since "person" is the more general class and "customer" is more specific, every customer is a person but not every person is a customer.

Object-oriented analysis and design (OOAD): Systems development methodologies and techniques based on objects rather than data or processes.

Object: A structure that encapsulates (or packages) attributes and methods that operate on those attributes. An object is an abstraction of a real-world thing in which data and processes are placed together to model the structure and behavior of the real-world object.

Inheritance: The property that occurs when entity types or object classes are arranged in a hierarchy and each entity type or object class assumes the attributes and methods of its ancestors; that is, those higher up in the hierarchy. Inheritance allows new but related classes to be derived from existing classes.

Object class: A logical grouping of objects that have the same (or similar) attributes and behaviors (methods).

As you might expect, you need a computer programming language that can create and manipulate objects and classes of objects in order to create object-oriented information systems. Several object-oriented programming languages have been created (e.g., C++, Eiffel, and ObjectPAL—for Paradox for Windows). In fact, object-oriented languages were developed first and object-oriented analysis and design techniques followed. Because OOAD is still relatively new, there is little consensus or standardization among the many OOAD techniques available. In general, the primary task of object-oriented analysis is identifying objects, defining their structure and behavior, and defining their relationships. The primary tasks of object-oriented design are modeling the details of the objects' behavior and communication with other objects so that system requirements are met and re-examining and redefining objects to better take advantage of inheritance and other benefits of object-orientation.

CONSIDERING DIFFERENT APPROACHES TO DEVELOPMENT

In the continuing effort to improve the systems analysis and design process, several different approaches have been developed. We will describe the more important alternatives in more detail in later chapters. Attempts to make system development less of an art and more of a science are usually referred to as *systems engineering* or *software engineering.* As the names indicate, rigorous engineering techniques are applied to systems development. A very influential practice borrowed from engineering is called prototyping. We will discuss prototyping next, followed by introductions to *Joint Application Design* and *Participatory Design.*

Prototyping

Prototyping: An iterative process of systems development in which requirements are converted to a working system that is continually revised through close work between an analyst and users.

Designing and building a scaled-down but functional version of a desired system is the process known as **prototyping.** You can build a prototype with any computer language or development tool, but special prototyping tools have been developed to simplify the process. A prototype can be developed with some fourth-generation languages (4GLs), with the query and screen and report design tools of a database management system, and with tools called *computer-aided software engineering (CASE)* tools.

Using prototyping as a development technique (see Figure 1-9), the analyst works with users to determine the initial or basic requirements for the system. The analyst then quickly builds a prototype. When the prototype is completed, the users work with it and tell the analyst what they like and do not like about it. The analyst uses this feedback to improve the prototype and takes the new version back to the users. This iterative process continues until the users are relatively satisfied with what they have seen. Two key advantages of the prototyping technique are the large extent to which prototyping involves the user in analysis and design and its ability to capture requirements in concrete, rather than verbal or abstract, form. In addition to being used stand-alone, prototyping may also be used to augment the SDLC. For example, a prototype of the final system may be developed early in analysis to help the analysts identify what users want. Then the final system is developed based on the specifications of the prototype. We discuss prototyping in greater detail in Chapter 7 and use various prototyping tools in Chapters 14 and 15 to illustrate the design of system outputs.

Prototyping is a form of rapid application development, or RAD. The fundamental principle of any RAD methodology is to delay producing detailed system

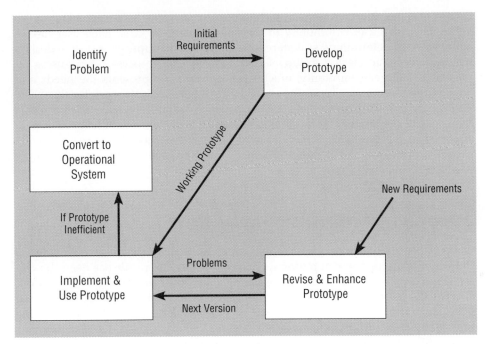

Figure 1-9
The prototyping methodology (Adapted from "Prototyping: The New Paradigm for Systems Development," by J. D. Naumann and A. M. Jenkins, *MIS Quarterly* 6 (3), pp. 29–44.)

design documents until after user requirements are clear. The prototype serves as the working description of needs. RAD methodologies emphasize gaining user acceptance of the human-system interface and developing core capabilities as quickly as possible, sacrificing computer efficiency for gains in human efficiency in rapidly building and rebuilding working systems. On the other hand, RAD methodologies can overlook important software engineering principles, the result of which are inconsistencies between system modules, noncompliance with standards, and lack of reusability of system components (Bourne, 1994). Chapter 13 addresses RAD in detail.

Joint Application Design

In the late 1970s, systems development personnel at IBM developed a new process for collecting information system requirements and reviewing system designs. The process is called **Joint Application Design (JAD).** The basic idea behind JAD is to bring structure to the requirements determination phase of analysis and to the reviews that occur as part of design. Users, managers, and systems developers are brought together for a series of intensive structured meetings run by a JAD session leader who maintains the structure and adheres to the agenda. By gathering the people directly affected by an IS in one room at the same time to work together to agree on system requirements and design details, time and organizational resources are better managed. As an added plus, group members are more likely to develop a shared understanding of what the IS is supposed to do. We will discuss JAD in more detail in Chapter 7.

Participatory Design

Developed in Northern Europe, **Participatory Design (PD)** represents a viable alternative approach to the SDLC. PD emphasizes the role of the user much more

Joint Application Design (JAD): A structured process in which users, managers, and analysts work together for several days in a series of intensive meetings to specify or review system requirements.

Participatory Design (PD): A systems development approach that originated in Northern Europe in which users and the improvement in their work lives is the central focus.

than traditional North American techniques do. In some instances, PD may involve the entire user community in the development process. Each user has an equal voice in determining system requirements and in approving system design. In other cases, an elected group of users controls the process. These users represent the larger community, much as a legislature represents the needs and wants of the electorate. Typically, under PD, systems analysts work for the users. The organization's management and outside consultants provide advice rather than control (Mumford, 1981). PD is partly a result of the roles of labor and management in the Northern European workplace where labor is more organized, carries more clout, and is more intimately involved with technological changes than is true in North America.

IMPROVING IS DEVELOPMENT PRODUCTIVITY

Other efforts to improve the system development process have taken advantage of the benefits offered by computing technology itself. The result has been the creation and fairly widespread use of *computer-aided software engineering* or *CASE* tools. CASE tools have been developed for internal use and for sale by several leading firms, including Intersolv (Excelerator™), Oracle (Designer/2000), and Sterling Software (COOL: Stuff), to name only a few.

CASE tools are built around a central repository for system descriptions and specifications, including information about data names, format, uses, and locations. The idea of a central repository of information about the project is not new—the manual form of such a repository is called a project dictionary or workbook. The difference is that CASE tools automate the repository for easier updating and for consistency. CASE tools also include diagramming tools for data flow diagrams and other graphical aids, screen and report design tools, and other special-purpose tools. CASE helps programmers and analysts do their jobs more efficiently and more effectively by automating routine tasks. There is more information on CASE in Chapter 4, and we relate many examples of the use of CASE throughout this book.

SUMMARY

This chapter introduced you to information systems analysis and design, the complex organizational process whereby computer-based information systems are developed and maintained. You read about the differences between the process-oriented and data-oriented approaches to systems analysis and design: Process-orientation focuses on what the system is supposed to do while data-orientation focuses on the data the system needs to operate. Process-orientation provides a less stable design than does data-orientation, as business processes change faster than do the data an organization uses. With process-orientation, data files are designed for specific applications whereas data files are designed for the whole enterprise with data-orientation; process-orientation leads to much uncontrolled data redundancy whereas data redundancy is controlled under data-orientation. You also learned about application independence, the separation of data from the computer applications that use the data. Data-orientation and application independence frame the way you learn about systems analysis and design in this book.

A major part of this chapter was devoted to examining the context of systems analysis and design. You read about the various people in organizations who develop systems, including systems analysts, programmers, IS managers, business managers, end users, database administrators, human factors experts, telecommunications experts, and auditors. You also learned that there are many different kinds of information systems used in organizations, from transaction processing systems to expert systems to office systems. Development techniques vary with system type.

Finally, you learned about the basic framework that guides systems analysis and design, the systems development life cycle, with its seven major phases: project identification and selection, project initiation and planning, analysis, logical design, physical design, implementation, and maintenance. The life cycle has had its share of criticism, which you read about, and other frameworks have been developed to address the life cycle's problems. These alternative frameworks include prototyping (a Rapid Application Development approach), Joint Application Design, and Participatory Design.

KEY TERMS

Analysis
Application independence
Application software
Data
Database
Data flow
Data-oriented approach
End users
End-user development
Implementation
Information
Information systems analysis and design

Inheritance
Joint Application Design (JAD)
Logical design
Maintenance
Object
Object class
Object-oriented analysis and design (OOAD)
Participatory Design (PD)
Physical design
Process-oriented approach
Processing logic

Project identification and selection
Project initiation and planning
Prototyping
Stakeholder
Systems analyst
Systems development life cycle (SDLC)
Systems development methodology

REVIEW QUESTIONS

1. Define each of the following terms:
   a. systems development life cycle
   b. data
   c. data flows
   d. processing logic
   e. object
   f. object class
   g. inheritance
   h. application software
   i. methodology
   j. technique
   k. tool

2. What is information systems analysis and design?

3. Explain the traditional application-based approach to systems development. How is this different from the data-based approach?

4. What are the organizational roles associated with systems development? Describe the responsibilities of each role.

5. List the different classes of information systems described in this chapter. How do they differ from each other?

6. List and explain the different phases in the systems development life cycle.

7. What are structured analysis and structured design?

8. What is prototyping?

9. What is JAD? What is Participatory Design?

10. What is object-oriented analysis and design?

11. Explain how systems analysis and design has changed from 1950–2000.

12. What are the characteristics of successful systems development teams?

PROBLEMS AND EXERCISES

1. Match the following terms to the appropriate definitions.

_____ maintenance	a. phase of the SDLC in which the information system is coded, tested, and installed
_____ analysis	b. phase of the SDLC in which an organization's total information system needs are analyzed and arranged
_____ design	c. phase of the SDLC in which the current system is studied and alternative other systems are proposed
_____ project initiation and planning	d. process of the SDLC in which the system chosen for development is described in detail with a particular physical form in mind
_____ project identification and selection	e. phase of the SDLC in which an information system is systematically improved
_____ implementation	f. phase of the SDLC in which a potential project is identified and an argument for the project is presented

2. Why is it important to use systems analysis and design methodologies when building a system? Why not just build the system in whatever way seems to be "quick and easy"? What value is provided by using an "engineering" approach?

3. Choose a business transaction you undertake regularly, such as using an ATM machine, buying groceries at the supermarket, or buying a ticket for a university's basketball game. For this transaction, define the data, draw the data flow diagram, and describe processing logic.

4. How is IBM's Joint Application Design (JAD) approach different from the Participatory Design (PD) approach developed in Northern Europe? You may have to do some digging at the library to answer this question adequately. What are the benefits in using approaches like this in building information systems? What are the barriers to using approaches like this?

5. How would you organize a project team of students to work with a small business client? How would you organize a project team if you were working for a professional consulting organization? How might these two methods of organization differ? Why?

6. How might prototyping be used as part of the SDLC?

7. Describe the difference in the role of a systems analyst in the SDLC versus prototyping.

8. Contrast process-oriented and data-oriented approaches to systems analysis and design. Why does this book make the point that these are complementary, not competing, approaches to systems development?

9. Compare Figures 1-7 and 1-9. What similarities and differences do you see?

10. Compare Figures 1-5 and 1-8. Can you match steps in Figure 1-8 with phases in Figure 1-5? How might you explain the differences?

11. Construct a table with the seven phases of the SDLC as columns and the various people/roles involved in a systems development project as the rows. Place a P in a cell if that person participates in that phase, and place an L in a cell if that person plays a leadership role in that phase. Explain your responses.

FIELD EXERCISES

1. Choose an organization with a fairly extensive information systems department. Get a copy of its organization chart (or draw one). At what level in the organization is the highest ranking information systems employee? What is his or her title? To whom does he or she report? What are his or her primary duties? Does the nature of this person's job description, responsibilities, and authority help or hinder this person in doing a good job?

2. Choose an organization and identify personnel who fulfill each of the following roles: IS manager, systems analyst, programmer, end user, business manager, database administrator, network and/or telecommunications manager, information system security manager. Are these roles filled formally or informally? Draw an organization chart linking these people. When these people build, use, and maintain the information systems, do they work together as a team or is their work fairly independent of each other? Why? Are they effective? Why or why not?

3. Choose an organization that you interact with regularly and list as many different "systems" (whether computer-based or not) as you can that are used to process transactions, provide information to managers and executives, help managers and executives make decisions, aid groups to make decisions together, capture knowledge and provide expertise, help design products and/or facilities, and assist people in communicating with each other. Draw a diagram that shows how each of these systems interacts (or should interact) with each other. Are these systems well integrated?

4. Imagine an information system built without using a systems analysis and design methodology and without any thinking about the SDLC. Use your imagination and describe any and all problems that might occur, even if they seem a bit extreme and absurd. Surprisingly, the problems you will describe have probably already happened in one setting or another.

5. Choose a relatively small organization that is just beginning to use information systems. What types of systems are being used? for what purposes? To what extent are these systems integrated with each other? with systems outside the organization? How are these systems developed and controlled? Who is involved in systems development, use, and control?

6. You may want to keep a personal journal of ideas and observations about systems analysis and design while you are studying this book. Use this journal to record comments you hear, summaries of news stories or professional articles you read, original ideas or hypotheses you create, and questions that require further analysis. Keep your eyes and ears open for anything related to systems analysis and design. Your instructor may ask you to turn in a copy of your journal from time to time in order to provide feedback and reactions. The journal is an unstructured set of personal notes that will supplement your class notes and can stimulate you to think beyond the topics covered within the time limitations of most courses.

REFERENCES

Aktas, A. Z. 1987. *Structured Analysis and Design of Information Systems.* Englewood Cliffs, NJ: Prentice-Hall.

Alavi, M., and I. R. Weiss. 1985. "Managing the Risks Associated with End-User Computing." *Journal of MIS* 2 (Winter): 5–20.

Bohm, C., and I. Jacopini. 1966. "Flow Diagrams, Turing Machines, and Languages with Only Two Formation Rules." *Communications of the ACM* 9 (May): 366–71.

Bourne, K. C. 1994. "Putting Rigor Back in RAD." *Database Programming & Design* 7(8) (Aug.): 25–30.

Davis, G. B. 1982. "CAUTION: User-Developed Systems Can Be Dangerous To Your Organization." *End-User Computing: Concepts, Issues and Applications.* 1989. R. R. Nelson (ed.). New York: Wiley: 209–228.

DeMarco, T. 1979. *Structured Analysis and System Specification.* Englewood Cliffs, NJ: Prentice-Hall.

Gilbert. J. 1994. "The Best Jobs in America." *Money* 23 (March): 70–73.

Mumford, E. 1981. "Participative Systems Design: A Structure and Method." *Systems, Objectives, Solutions* 1 (1): 5–19.

Naumann, J. D., and A. M. Jenkins. 1982. "Prototyping: The New Paradigm for Systems Development." *MIS Quarterly* 6 (3): 29–44.

Yourdon, E., and L. L. Constantine. 1979. *Structured Design.* Englewood Cliffs, NJ: Prentice-Hall.

2

Succeeding as a
Systems Analyst

After studying this chapter, you should be able to:

■ Discuss the analytical skills, including systems thinking, needed for a systems analyst to be successful.

■ Describe the technical skills required of a systems analyst.

■ Discuss the management skills required of a systems analyst.

■ Identify the interpersonal skills required of a systems analyst.

■ Describe the systems analysis profession.

INTRODUCTION

In the first chapter, you learned about the different types of information systems developed in organizations, the people who develop them, and the project environment in which systems are developed. Before we explore the systems development life cycle in more detail, however, we need to examine the skills needed to succeed as a systems analyst. You will first examine the analytical skills a systems analyst needs, then discuss the technical, management, and interpersonal skills required of a good analyst. One of the key analytical skills you will study is systems thinking, or the ability to see things as *systems*. You probably learned about systems and systems thinking in your introductory information systems class, so we will review here the highlights of systems and systems thinking that directly affect the design of information systems and how a systems analyst develops systems.

As illustrated in Figure 2-1, an analyst works throughout all phases of the systems development life cycle. The life cycle model represents the process of developing information systems, the same process you read about in Chapter 1. The skills the analyst needs to be successful are represented by the objects placed in the diagram. The laptop computer represents technical skills; the briefcase represents management skills; the magnifying glass represents analytical skills; and the telephone represents interpersonal skills. As you can see, to follow the guidelines established by any development methodology, an analyst needs to rely on many skills. Although we cannot possibly provide thorough coverage of these skills in this chapter, some will be covered in considerable depth in later chapters while others are discussed more generally. Our goal for these general skills is to sensitize you to abilities that you need to develop from other courses and materials in order to become a successful systems analyst. The chapter ends by stepping back from these specific skills to examine systems analysis as a profession, with its own standards of practice, ethics, and career paths.

ANALYTICAL SKILLS FOR SYSTEMS ANALYSTS

Given the title systems analyst, you might think that analytical skills are the most important. While there is no question that analytical skills are essential, other skills are equally required. First, however, we will focus on the four sets of analytical skills: systems thinking, organizational knowledge, problem identification, and problem analyzing and solving.

Systems Thinking: A Review

If you counted the number of times each key term is used in this book, the key term used most frequently would undoubtedly be *system.* Let's take the time now to examine systems in general and information systems in particular. (For a more thorough

Figure 2-1
The relationship between a systems analyst's skills and the systems development life cycle

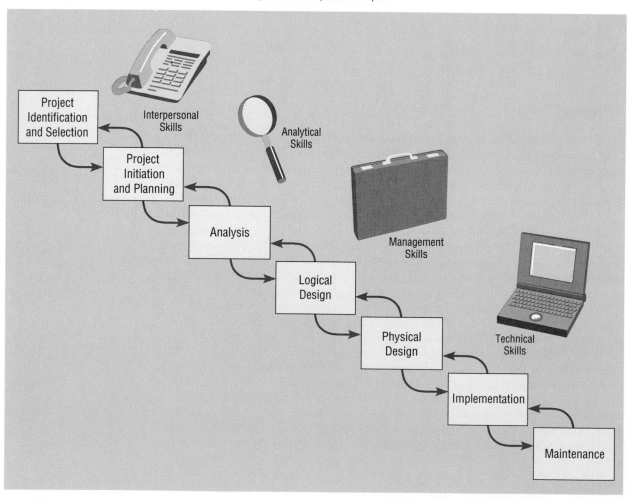

treatment of system concepts, see Martin, et al., 1994). Let's start by examining what we mean by a system and identify the characteristics that define a system.

Definitions of a System and Its Parts   A **system** is an inter-related set of components with an identifiable boundary, working together for some purpose. A system has nine characteristics (see Figure 2-2):

1. Components
2. Inter-related components
3. A boundary
4. A purpose
5. An environment
6. Interfaces
7. Input
8. Output
9. Constraints

A system is made up of components. A **component** is either an irreducible part or an aggregate of parts, also called a *subsystem*. The simple concept of a component is very powerful. For example, just as with an automobile or a stereo system

> **System:** An inter-related set of components, with an identifiable boundary, working together for some purpose.

> **Component:** An irreducible part or aggregation of parts that make up a system, also called a subsystem.

Figure 2-2
A general depiction of a system

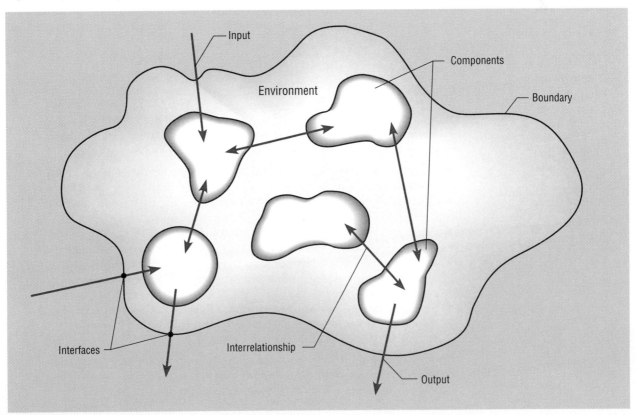

Inter-related components: Dependence of one subsystem on one or more subsystems.

Boundary: The line that marks the inside and outside of a system and which sets off the system from its environment.

Purpose: The overall goal or function of a system.

Environment: Everything external to a system that interacts with the system.

Interface: Point of contact where a system meets its environment or where subsystems meet each other.

Constraint: A limit to what a system can accomplish.

with proper design, we can repair or upgrade the system by changing individual components without having to make changes throughout the entire system. The components are **inter-related;** that is, the function of one is somehow tied to the functions of the others. For example, the work of one component, such as producing a daily report of customer orders received, may not progress successfully until the work of another component is finished, such as sorting customer orders by date of receipt. A system has a **boundary,** within which all of its components are contained and which establishes the limits of a system, separating the system from other systems. Components within the boundary can be changed whereas things outside the boundary cannot be changed. All of the components work together to achieve some overall **purpose** for the larger system: the system's reason for existing.

A system exists within an **environment**—everything outside the system's boundary. For example, we might consider the environment of a state university to include the legislature, prospective students, foundations and funding agencies, and the news media. Usually the system interacts with its environment, exchanging, in the case of an information system, data and information. The points at which the system meets its environment are called **interfaces,** and there are also interfaces between subsystems (Figure 2-3 provides a list of functions performed by interfaces). An example of a subsystem interface is the clutch subsystem which acts as the point of interaction between the engine and transmission subsystems of a car. As can be seen from Figure 2-3, interfaces may include much functionality. You will spend a considerable portion of time in systems development dealing with interfaces, especially interfaces between an automated system and its users (manual systems) and interfaces between different information systems. It is the design of good interfaces that permits different systems to work together without being too dependent on each other.

A system must face **constraints** in its functioning because there are limits (in terms of capacity, speed, or capabilities) to what it can do and how it can achieve its purpose within its environment. Some of these constraints are imposed inside the

Figure 2-3
Special characteristics
of interfaces

INTERFACE FUNCTIONS

Because an interface exists at the point where a system meets its environment, the interface has several special, important functions. An interface provides

- *Security,* protecting the system from undesirable elements that may want to infiltrate it
- *Filtering* unwanted data, both for elements leaving the system and entering it
- *Coding and decoding* incoming and outgoing messages
- *Detecting and correcting errors* in its interaction with the environment
- *Buffering,* providing a layer of slack between the system and its environment, so that the system and its environment can work on different cycles and at different speeds
- *Summarizing* raw data and transforming them into the level of detail and format needed throughout the system (for an input interface) or in the environment (for an output interface)

Because interface functions are critical in communication between system components or a system and its environment, interfaces receive much attention in the design of information systems (see Chapters 14 and 15).

system (for example, a limited number of staff available) and others are imposed by the environment (for example, due dates or regulations). A system takes **input** from its environment in order to function. Mammals, for example, take in food, oxygen, and water from the environment as input. Finally, a system returns **output** to its environment as a result of its functioning and thus achieves its purpose.

Now that you know the definition of a system and its nine important characteristics, let's take an example of a system and use it to illustrate the definition and each system characteristic. Consider a system that is familiar to you: a fast food restaurant (see Figure 2-4).

How is a fast food restaurant a system? Let's take a look at the fictional Hoosier Burger Restaurant in Bloomington, Indiana. First, Hoosier Burger has components or subsystems. We can figure out what the subsystems are in many ways but, for the sake of illustration, let's focus on Hoosier Burger's physical subsystems as follows: kitchen, dining room, counter, storage, and office. As you might expect, the subsystems are inter-related and work together to prepare food and deliver it to customers, one purpose for the restaurant's existence. Food is delivered to Hoosier Burger early in the morning, kept in storage, prepared in the kitchen, sold at the counter, and often eaten in the dining room. The boundary of Hoosier Burger is represented by its physical walls and the primary purpose for the restaurant's existence is to make a profit for its owners, Bob and Thelma Mellankamp.

Hoosier Burger's environment consists of those external elements that interact with the restaurant, such as customers (many of whom come from nearby Indiana University), the local labor supply, food distributors (much of the produce is grown locally), banks, and neighborhood fast food competitors. Hoosier Burger has one interface at the counter where customers place orders and another at the back door where food and supplies are delivered. Still another interface is the telephone which managers use regularly to talk with bankers and food distributors. The restaurant faces several constraints. It is designed for the easy and cost-effective preparation

Input: Whatever a system takes from its environment in order to fulfill its purpose.

Output: Whatever a system returns to its environment in order to fulfill its purpose.

Figure 2-4
A fast food restaurant as a system

of certain popular foods, such as hamburgers and milk shakes, which constrains the restaurant in the foods it may offer for sale. Hoosier Burger's size and its location in the university neighborhood constrain how much money it can make on any given day. The Monroe County Health Department also imposes constraints, such as rules governing food storage. Inputs include, but are not limited to, ingredients for the burgers and other food as well as cash and labor. Outputs include, but are not limited to, prepared food, bank deposits, and trash.

Important System Concepts   Once we have recognized something as a system and identified the system's characteristics, how do we understand the system? Further, what principles or concepts about systems guide the design of information systems? A key aspect of a system for building systems is the system's relationship with its environment. Some systems, called **open systems,** interact freely with their environments, taking in input and returning output. As the environment changes, an open system must adapt to the changes or suffer the consequences. A **closed system** does not interact with the environment; changes in the environment and adaptability are not issues for a closed system. However, all business information systems are open, and in order to understand a system and its relationships to other information systems, to the organization, and to the larger environment, you must always think of information systems as open and constantly interacting with the environment.

There are several other important systems concepts with which systems analysts need to become familiar:

- Decomposition

- Modularity

- Coupling

- Cohesion

In addition, you need to understand the differences between viewing a system at a logical and at a physical level, each with associated descriptions concentrating on different aspects of a system.

Decomposition deals with being able to break down a system into its components. These components may themselves be systems (subsystems) and can be broken down into their components as well. How does decomposition aid understanding of a system? Decomposition results in smaller and less complex pieces that are easier to understand than larger, complex pieces. Decomposing a system also allows us to focus on one particular part of a system, making it easier to think of how to modify that one part independently of the entire system (Figure 2-5). Figure 2-6 shows the decomposition of a portable compact disc (CD) player. At the highest level of abstraction, this system simply accepts CDs and settings of the volume and tone controls as input and produces music as output. Decomposing the system into subsystems reveals the system's inner workings: there are separate systems for reading the digital signals from the CDs, for amplifying the signals, for turning the signals into sound waves, and for controlling the volume and tone of the sound. Breaking the subsystems down into their components would reveal even more about the inner workings of the system and greatly enhance our understanding of how the overall system works.

Modularity, a direct result of decomposition, refers to dividing a system up into chunks or modules of a relatively *uniform* size. Modules can represent a system simply, making it not only easier to understand but also easier to redesign and rebuild.

Coupling is the extent to which subsystems are dependent on each other. Subsystems should be as independent as possible. If one subsystem fails and other

Open system: A system that interacts freely with its environment, taking input and returning output.

Closed system: A system that is cut off from its environment and does not interact with it.

Modularity: Dividing a system up into chunks or modules of a relatively uniform size.

Coupling: The extent to which subsystems depend on each other.

Figure 2-5
Purposes of decomposition

DECOMPOSITION FUNCTIONS
Decomposition aids a systems analyst and other systems development
project team members by

• Breaking a system into smaller, more manageable and understandable
  subsystems
• Facilitating the focusing of attention on one area (subsystem) at a time
  without interference from other parts
• Allowing attention to concentrate on the part of the system pertinent to a
  particular audience, without confusing people with details irrelevant to
  their interests
• Permitting different parts of the system to be built at independent times
  and/or by different people

Figure 2-6
An example of system decomposition

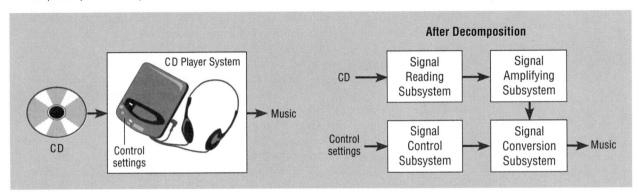

subsystems are highly dependent on it, the others will either fail themselves or have
problems functioning. Looking at Figure 2-6, we would say the components of a portable CD player are tightly coupled. The amplifier and the unit that reads the CD
signals are wired together in the same container, and the boundaries between these
two subsystems may be difficult to draw clearly. If one subsystem fails, the entire CD
player must be sent off for repair. In a home stereo system, the components are loosely
coupled since the subsystems, such as the speakers, the amplifier, the receiver, and
the CD player, are all physically separate and function independently. For example, if
the amplifier in a home stereo system fails, only the amplifier needs to be repaired.

Finally, **cohesion** is the extent to which a subsystem performs a single function.
In biological systems, subsystems tend to be well differentiated and thus very cohesive. In man-made systems, subsystems are not always as cohesive as they should
be. We will discuss the concepts of coupling and cohesion and how they apply to
information systems in detail in Chapter 18.

One final key systems concept with which you should be familiar is the difference between logical and physical systems. Any description of a system is abstract
since the definition is not the system itself. When we talk about logical and physical
systems, we are actually talking about logical and physical system descriptions.

A **logical system description** portrays the purpose and function of the system
without tying the description to any specific physical implementation. For example,
in developing a logical description of the portable CD player, we describe the basic
components of the player (signal reader, amplifier, speakers, controls) and their relations to each other, focusing on the function of playing CDs using a self-contained,

Cohesion: The extent
to which a system or a
subsystem performs a
single function.

Logical system description:
Description of a system that
focuses on the system's function and purpose without
regard to how the system will
be physically implemented.

portable unit. We do not specify whether the earphone jack contains aluminum or gold, where we could buy the laser that reads the CDs, or how much the jack or the laser cost to produce.

Physical system description: Description of a system that focuses on how the system will be materially constructed.

The **physical system description,** on the other hand, is a material depiction of the system, a central concern of which is building the system. A physical description of the portable CD player would provide details on the construction of each sub-unit, such as the design of the laser, the composition of the earphones, and whether the controls feature digital readouts. A systems analyst should deal with function (logical system description) before form (physical system description), just as an architect does for the analysis and design of buildings.

Benefiting from Systems Thinking   The first step in systems thinking is to be able to identify something as a system. This identification also involves recognizing each of the system's characteristics, for example, identifying where the boundary lies and all of the relevant inputs. But once you have identified a system, what is the value of thinking of something as a system? Visualizing a set of things and their inter-relationships as a system allows you to translate a specific physical situation into more general, abstract terms. From this abstraction, you can think about the essential characteristics of a specific situation. This in turn allows you to gain insights you might never get from focusing too much on the details of the specific situation. Also, you can question assumptions, provide documentation, and manipulate the abstract system without disrupting the real situation.

Let's look again at Hoosier Burger. How can visualizing a fast food restaurant as a system help us gain insights about the restaurant that we might not get otherwise? Let's imagine that Hoosier Burger is facing more demand for its food than it can handle. Some people are convinced that its hamburgers are the best in Bloomington, maybe even in Southern Indiana. Many people, especially IU students and faculty, frequently eat at Hoosier Burger, and the staff is having a difficult time keeping up with the demand. For the owner-managers, Bob and Thelma Mellankamp, the high level of demand is both a problem and an opportunity. The problem is that if the restaurant can't keep up with demand, people will stop coming to eat here, and the owners will lose money. The opportunity is to capitalize on Hoosier Burger's popularity and serve even more customers every day, making larger profits for the owners (which is the purpose of their system).

How does looking at Hoosier Burger as a system help? By decomposing the restaurant into subsystems, we can analyze each subsystem separately and discover if one or more subsystems is at capacity. Capacity is a general problem common to many systems. Let's say, after careful study, we discover that the kitchen, storage, and dining room subsystems have plenty of available capacity. However, the counter is unable to handle the rush of people. Customers have to wait in line for several minutes to place and receive their orders. The counter is the restaurant's bottleneck; thus the capacity of the counter needs to be increased. If we redesign the counter area or the procedures for taking customer orders, then we can increase the counter's capacity and better match it to the kitchen's capacity. Customers will have to wait in line less time to place their orders and they will get their food faster. Fewer customers will turn away because of long lines, which should translate into more food sold and higher profits.

There are other aspects of the system we could have examined, such as outputs, inputs, or environmental conditions, but to make the example more clear and concise, we looked only at subsystems. For this particular problem, decomposing Hoosier Burger into its subsystems enabled us to determine its problem with demand. Other problems may have required an examination of all aspects of the restaurant system.

Applying Systems Thinking to Information Systems   None of the examples of systems we have examined so far in this chapter have been information systems, even though information systems are the focus of this book. There are two reasons why we have looked at other types of systems first. One is so that you will become accustomed to thinking of some of the many different things you encounter daily as systems and realize how useful systems thinking can be. The second is that thinking of organizations as systems is a useful perspective from which to begin developing information systems. *Information systems can be seen as subsystems in larger organizational systems, taking input from, and returning output to, their organizational environments.*

Let's examine a simplified version of an information system as a special kind of system. In our fast food restaurant example, Hoosier Burger uses an information system to take customer orders, send the orders to the kitchen, monitor goods sold and inventory, and generate reports for management. The information system is depicted as a data flow diagram in Figure 2-7 (you will learn how to draw data flow diagrams in Chapter 8).

As the diagram illustrates, Hoosier Burger's customer order system contains four components or subsystems: Process Customer Food Order, Update Goods Sold File, Update Inventory File, and Produce Management Reports. The arrows in the diagram show how these subsystems are inter-related. For example, the first process produces four outputs: a Kitchen Order, a Receipt, Goods Sold data, and Inventory Data. The latter two outputs serve as input for other subsystems. The dotted line illustrates the boundary of the system. Notice that the Customer, the Kitchen, and the Restaurant Manager (Bob Mellankamp) are all considered to be outside the customer order system. The specific purpose of the system is to

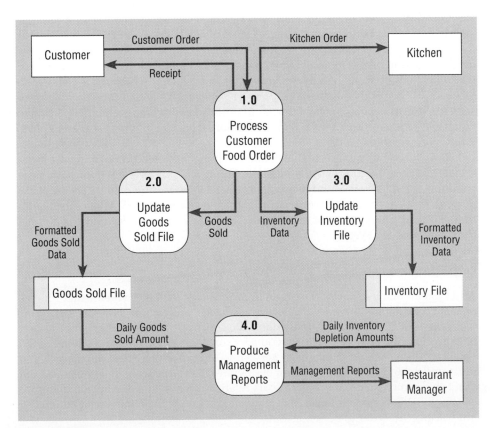

Figure 2-7

A fast food restaurant's customer order information system depicted in a data flow diagram facilitate customer orders, monitor inventory, and generate reports; the system's general purpose is to improve the efficiency of the restaurant's operations.

Since this information system is smaller in scope and purpose than the Hoosier Burger system itself, its environment is also smaller. For our purposes, we can limit the environment to those entities that interact with the system: Customers, the Kitchen, and the Restaurant Manager. Constraints on the system may or may not be apparent from the diagram. For example, the diagram implicitly shows (by omission) that there is no direct data exchange between the customer order system and information systems used by the restaurant's suppliers; this prevents the system from automatically issuing an order for supplies directly to the suppliers when inventory falls below a certain level. We do not know, however, if any other Hoosier Burger system supports such direct data exchange. Another constraint may be the system's inability to provide on-line, real-time information on inventory levels, limiting Bob Mellankamp to receiving nightly batched reports. This is not at all clear from Figure 2-7. In contrast, system input and output are very clear. The only system input is the Customer Order and there are three overall system outputs: a Receipt for the customer, a Kitchen Order, and Management Reports.

On one level of analysis and description, Hoosier Burger's customer order system is a physical system that takes input, processes data, and returns output. The physical system consists of a computerized cash register that a clerk uses to enter a customer order and return a paper receipt to the customer. Another piece of paper, the kitchen order, is generated from a printer in the restaurant's kitchen. The cash register sends data on the order about goods sold and inventory to a computer in Hoosier Burger's office, where computer files on goods sold and inventory are updated by applications software. Other application software uses data in the Goods Sold and Inventory files to generate and print reports on a laser printer in the office.

On another level of analysis and description, Hoosier Burger's customer order system can be explained using a logical description of an information system that focuses on the flow and transformation of data. The physical system is one possible implementation of the more abstract, logical information system description. For the logical information system description, it is irrelevant whether the customer's order shows up in the kitchen as a piece of paper or as lines of text on a monitor screen. What's important is the information that is sent to Hoosier Burger's kitchen. For every logical information system description, there can be several different physical implementations of it.

The way we draw information systems shows how we think of them as systems. Data flow diagrams clearly illustrate inputs, outputs, system boundaries, the environment, subsystems, and inter-relationships. Purpose and constraints are much more difficult to illustrate and must therefore be documented using other notations. In total, all elements of the logical system description must address all nine characteristics of a system.

Organizational Knowledge

As a systems analyst, you will work in organizations. Whether you are an in-house or contract custom software developer, you must understand how organizations work. In addition, you must understand the functions and procedures of the particular organization (or enterprise) you are working for. Furthermore, many of the systems you will build or maintain serve one organizational department and you must understand how that department operates, its purpose, its relationships with other departments and, if applicable, its relationships with customers and suppliers. Table 2-1 lists various kinds of organizational knowledge that a systems analyst must acquire in order to be successful.

Problem Identification

What is a problem? Pounds (1969) defines a problem as the difference between an existing situation and a desired situation. For him, the process of identifying problems is the process of defining differences, so problem solving is the process of finding a way to reduce differences. According to Pounds, a manager defines differences by comparing the current situation to the output of a model that predicts what the output should be. For example, at Hoosier Burger, a certain portion of the food ordered from local produce distributors is expected to go bad before it can be used. Comparing a current food spoilage rate of 10 percent to a desired spoilage rate of 5 percent defines a difference and therefore identifies a problem. In this case, Bob Mellankamp has used a model to determine the desired spoilage rate of 5 percent. The particular model used, showing how fast produce ripens after harvesting, typical delivery times, and how long produce will stay fresh in a refrigerator, has come from research carried out at Purdue University's College of Agriculture. Based on the research, the Mellankamps have set a standard of a 5 percent spoilage rate, with an acceptable variance of 2 percent in either direction. According to this standard, a 5 percent variance between desired and actual is clearly out of line and merits attention. Another model might have indicated that a

TABLE 2-1   Selected Areas of Organizational Knowledge for a Systems Analyst
How Work Officially Gets Done in a Particular Organization
Terminology, abbreviations, and acronyms
Policies
Standards and procedures
Standards of practice
Formal organization structure
Job descriptions
Understanding the Organization's Internal Politics
Influence and inclinations of key personnel
Who the experts are in different subject areas
Critical incidents in the organization's history
Informal organization structure
Coalition membership and power structures
Understanding the Organization's Competitive and Regulatory Environment
Government regulations
Competitors, domestic and international
Products, services, and markets
Role of technology
Understanding the Organization's Strategies and Tactics
Short- and long-term strategy and plans
Values and mission

10 percent spoilage rate was acceptable. You can see that understanding how managers identify problems is understanding the models they use to define differences.

In order to identify problems that need solving, you must be able to compare the current situation in an organization to the desired situation. You must develop a repertoire of models to define the differences between what is and what ought to be. It is also important that you appreciate the models that information systems users rely on to identify problems. Every functional area of the organization will use different models to find problems; what is helpful in accounting will not necessarily work well in manufacturing. Often you must be able to see problems from a broader perspective. By relying on models from their own particular functional areas, users may not see the real problem from an organizational view.

Problem Analyzing and Solving

Once a problem has been identified, you must analyze the problem and determine how to solve it. Analysis entails finding out more about the problem. Systems analysts learn through experience, with guidance from proven methods, how to get the needed information from people as well as from organizational files and documents. As you seek out additional information, you also begin to formulate alternative solutions to the problem. Devising solutions leads to a search for more information, which in turn leads to improvements in the alternatives. Obviously, such a process could continue indefinitely, but at some point, the alternatives are compared and typically one is chosen as the best solution. Once the analyst, users, and management agree on the general suitability of the solution, they devise a plan for implementing it.

The approach for analyzing and solving problems we describe was formally described by Herbert Simon and colleagues (Simon, 1960). The approach has four phases: intelligence, design, choice, and implementation. During the intelligence phase, all information relevant to the problem is collected. During the design phase, alternatives are formulated and, during choice the best alternative solution is chosen. The solution is put into practice during the implementation phase.

This problem-analysis and -solving approach should be familiar to you: it is essentially the same general process as that described earlier in the systems development life cycle (see Figure 2-8). Simon's intelligence phase corresponds roughly to the first three phases in the life cycle: project identification and selection, project initiation and planning, and analysis. Simon's design phase corresponds to that part of analysis where alternative solutions are formulated. The detailed solution formulation (once the solution is chosen), however, would be performed in the life cycle's logical and physical design phases. Choice of the best solution is made in stages, first at the end of the analysis phase and then during physical design. In our life cycle model, activities that occur in logical design, physical design, implementation, and maintenance correspond to Simon's implementation phase.

Simon's problem-solving model is a useful one which lends insight into how people solve certain kinds of problems, but there are other factors in organizations that influence how problems are solved. Among these are personal interests, political considerations, and limits in time and cognitive ability that affect how much information people can gather and process. We will say more about these factors in later chapters; now we will turn to an examination of the technical skills required of systems analysts.

TECHNICAL SKILLS

Many aspects of your job as a systems analyst are technically oriented. In order to develop computer-based information systems, you must understand how comput-

Figure 2-8
The systems development life cycle and Simon's problem-solving model

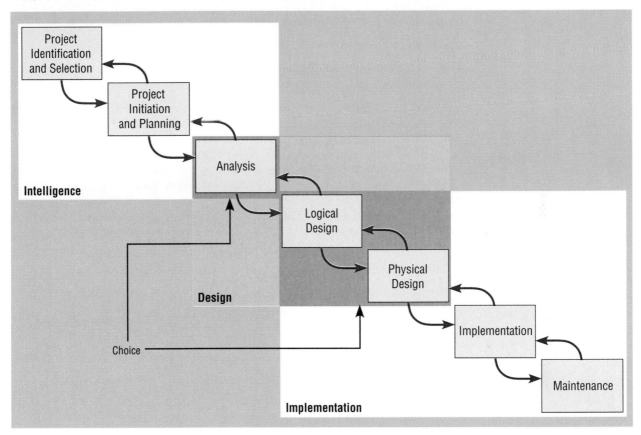

ers, data networks, database management and operating systems, and a host of other technologies work as well as their potential and limitations. Further, you must be technically adept with different notations for representing, or modeling, various aspects of information systems. You need these technical skills not only to perform tasks assigned to you but also to communicate with the other people with whom you work in systems development (see Chapter 1 for a discussion of the roles of various people in systems analysis and design). Rather than develop a single set of technical skills to use throughout your career, you must constantly re-educate yourself about information technology, techniques, and methodologies. These information technology, techniques, and methodologies change quickly, and you must keep up with the changes. You need to understand alternative technologies (like Microsoft Windows and UNIX operating environments) as organizational preferences, since choices vary across companies and over time. Versatility, based on a sound understanding of technical concepts rather than specific tools, gives you the flexibility needed for such a changing skill set.

The following activities will help you stay versatile and up-to-date:

- Read trade publications (for example, *Computerworld, Datamation,* or *PCWeek*) and books.

- Join professional societies (for example, the *Association of Information Technology Professionals* or the *Association for Computing Machinery*) or other clubs and their meetings.

- Attend classes or teach at a local college. Teaching is a wonderful way to force yourself to stay current and to learn from others.

- Attend any courses or training sessions offered by your organization.

- Attend professional conferences, seminars, or trade shows.

- Participate in electronic bulletin boards, news groups, or conferences on local, national, or international networks.

Maybe you have seen the cartoon of the person wearing tattered clothes, looking thin, sitting on a park bench feeding the birds. The caption reads, "He was an outstanding systems analyst, but he took a six-month vacation and fell too far behind in his field." Being a systems analyst working in the systems field requires continuous learning.

Because of the rapid changes that occur in technology, we do not dwell on specifics in this section. For example, when this book was being written, object-oriented database technology was considered new and experimental. It is quite possible, however, that this technology may be popular and widespread when you read this book. In general, you should be as familiar as possible with such families of technologies as

- Microcomputers, workstations, minicomputers, and mainframe computers

- Programming languages

- Operating systems, both for single machines and networks

- Database and file management systems

- Data communication standards and software for local and wide area networks

- Systems development tools and environments (such as form and report generators and graphical interface design tools)

- Decision support system generators and data analysis tools

as well as modern methods and techniques for describing, modeling, and building systems. How technical you must be will vary by job assignment and where you are in your career. Often, you will be asked to be more technical in the early stages of your career, and then you will assume more managerial responsibilities as you gain experience. We discuss career progression later in this chapter.

MANAGEMENT SKILLS

Systems analysts are almost always members of project teams and are frequently asked to lead teams. Management skills are very useful for anyone in a leadership role. As an analyst, you also need to know how to manage your own work and how to use organizational resources in the most productive ways possible. Self-management, then, is an important skill for an analyst. In this section, we describe four categories of management skills: resource, project, risk, and change management.

Resource Management

Any organizational worker must know how to obtain and work effectively with organizational resources. A systems analyst must know how to get the most out of a wide range of resources: system documentation, information technology, and money. For an analyst leading a team, the most important resource is people. A team leader must learn how to best utilize the particular talents of other team members. He or she must also be able to delegate responsibility, empowering people to do the tasks they have been assigned.

Resource management includes the following capabilities:

- Predicting resource usage (budgeting)

- Tracking and accounting for resource consumption

- Learning how to use resources effectively

- Evaluating the quality of resources used

- Securing resources from abusive use

- Relinquishing resources when no longer needed and obsoleting resources when they can no longer be useful

Project Management

Effectively managing projects is crucial to a systems analyst's job. Information systems development projects range from one-person projects that take very little time and effort to multi-person, multi-year efforts costing millions of dollars. The goal of project management is to prevent projects from coming in late and going over budget. In addition, project management is designed to help managers keep track of the project's progress.

Even if you are not a project leader, you will be given responsibilities for parts of a project, or subprojects. In the role of project or subproject manager, you first need to decompose a (sub)project into several independent tasks. The next step is to determine how the tasks are related to each other and who will be responsible for each task. As we will see in Chapter 3, analysts use established tools and techniques to help manage projects. The most important element, however, is managing the people working on the project. Successful analysts motivate people to work together and instill a sense of trust and interdependence among them. Project management extends beyond the organization to any vendors or contractors working on the project.

Often, in today's development environment, many aspects of a project may be farmed out to various contractors outside the organization. Using independent contractors has many advantages. A particular contractor may be more skilled than internal personnel in a technology or may be less expensive. If a project is short on time, it may also make sense to contract out some parts of a development project to help speed up the overall process. Many times, however, contractors deliver work that is late or of low quality, or that does not meet requirements. If the system requirements are unstable or not well defined, the potential problems with contractors can be exaggerated. For these reasons, it is just as important to manage outside contractors as it is to manage everyone else involved in a project. Two mechanisms that help manage contractors are contracts and relationship managers. Very well-specified contracts that spell out just exactly what is expected and when, and that lay out explicit sanctions for nonperformance, may motivate contractors to perform up to expectations. On the other hand, very explicit contracts many scare off contractors who know that they cannot live up to such a contract's terms. Relationship managers act as liaisons between your firm and the contractors. By establishing personal relationships with the parties involved, relationship managers may be in a position to sense trouble before it happens and work with both parties toward reasonable settlements.

Risk Management

Risk management is the ability to anticipate what might go wrong in a project. Once risks to the project have been identified, you must be able to minimize the likelihood that those risks will actually occur. If minimizing risk is not possible, then you try to minimize the damage that might result. Risk management also includes knowing where to place resources (such as people) where they can do the most good and prioritizing activities to achieve the greatest gain. We discuss a key part of risk management that is carried out during project justification—risk assessment—in Chapter 6.

Change Management

Introducing a new or improved information system into an organization is a change process. In general, people do not like change and tend to resist it; therefore, any change in how people perform their work in an organization must be carefully managed. Change management, then, is a very important skill for systems analysts, who are organizational *change agents.* You must know how to get people to make a smooth transition from one information system to another, giving up their old ways of doing things and accepting new ways. Change management also includes the ability to deal with technical issues related to change, such as obsolescence and reusability. You will learn more about managing the change that accompanies a new information system in Chapter 20.

INTERPERSONAL SKILLS

Although, as a systems analyst, you will be working in the technical area of designing and building computer-based information systems, you will also work extensively with all types of people. Perhaps the most important skills you will need to master are interpersonal. In this part of the chapter, we will discuss the various interpersonal skills necessary for successful systems analysis work: communication skills; working alone and with a team; facilitating groups; and managing expectations of users and managers.

Communication Skills

The single most important interpersonal skill for an analyst, as well as for any professional, is the ability to communicate clearly and effectively with others. Analysts should be able to successfully communicate with users, other information systems professionals, and management. Analysts must establish a good, open working relationship with clients early in the project and maintain it throughout by communicating effectively.

Communication takes many forms, from written (memos, reports) to verbal (phone calls, face-to-face conversations) to visual (presentation slides, diagrams). The analyst must be able to master as many forms of communication as possible. Oral communication and listening skills are considered by many information system professionals as the most important communication skills analysts need to succeed. Interviewing skills are not far behind. All types of communication, however, have one thing in common: They improve with experience. The more you practice, the better you get. Some of the specific types of communication we will mention are interviewing and listening, the use of questionnaires, and written and oral presentations.

Interviewing, Listening, and Questionnaires   Interviewing is one of the primary ways analysts gather information about an information systems project. Early in a project, you may spend a large amount of time interviewing users about their work and the information they use. There are many ways to effectively interview someone, and becoming a good interviewer takes practice. We will discuss interviewing in more detail in Chapter 7, but it is important to point out now that asking questions is only one part of interviewing. Listening to the answers is just as important, if not more so. Careful listening helps you understand the problem you're investigating and, many times, the answers to your questions lead to additional questions that may be even more revealing and probing than the questions you prepared before your interview.

Although interviews are very effective ways of communicating with people and obtaining important information from them, interviews can also be very expensive and time-consuming. Because questionnaires provide no direct means by which to ask follow-up questions, they are generally less effective than interviews. It is possible, however, though time-consuming, to call respondents and ask them follow-up questions. Questionnaires are less expensive to conduct because the questioner does not have to invest the same amount of time and effort to collect the same information using a questionnaire as he or she does in conducting an interview. For example, using a written questionnaire that respondents complete themselves, you could gather the same information from 100 people in one hour that you could collect from only one person in a one-hour interview. In addition, questionnaires have the advantage of being less biased in how the results are interpreted because the questions and answers are standardized. Creating good questionnaires is a skill that comes only with practice and experience. You will learn more about questionnaire design in Chapter 7.

Written and Oral Presentations   At many points during the systems development process, you must document the progress of the project and communicate that progress to others. This communication takes the following forms:

- Meeting agenda

- Meeting minutes

- Interview summaries

- Project schedules and descriptions

- Memoranda requesting information, an interview, participation in a project activity, or the status of a project

- Requests for proposal from contractors and vendors

and a host of other documents. This documentation is essential to provide a written, not just oral, history for the project, to convey information clearly, to provide details needed by those who will maintain the system after you are off the project team, and to obtain commitments and approvals at key project milestones.

The larger the organization and the more complicated the systems development project, the more writing you will have to do. You and your team members will have to complete and file a report at the end of each stage of the systems development life cycle. The first report will be the business case for getting approval to start the project. The last report may be an audit of the entire development process. And at each phase, the analysis team will have to document the system as it evolves. To be effective, you need to write both clearly and persuasively.

As there are often many different parties involved in the development of a system, there are many opportunities to inform people of the project's status. Periodic written status reports are one way to keep people informed, but there will also be unscheduled calls for ad hoc reports. Many projects will also involve scheduled and unscheduled oral presentations. Part of oral presentations involves preparing slides, overhead transparencies, or multimedia presentations, including system demonstrations. Another part involves being able to field and answer questions from the audience.

How can you improve your communication skills? We have four simple yet powerful suggestions:

1. Take every opportunity to practice. Speak to a civic organization about trends in computing. Such groups often look for local speakers to present talks on topics of general interest. Conduct a training class on some topic on which you have special expertise. Some people have found participation in Toastmasters, an international organization with local chapters, a very helpful way to improve oral communication skills.

2. Videotape your presentations and do a critical self-appraisal of your skills. You can view videotapes of other speakers and share your assessments with each other.

3. Make use of writing centers located at many colleges as a way to critique your writing.

4. Take classes on business and technical writing from colleges and professional organizations.

Working Alone and with a Team

As a systems analyst, you must often work alone on certain aspects of any systems development project. To this end, you must be able to organize and manage your own schedule, commitments, and deadlines. Many people in the organization will depend on your individual performance, yet you are almost always a member of a team and must work with the team toward achieving project goals. As we saw in Chapter 1, working with a team entails a certain amount of give and take. You need to know when to trust the judgment of other team members as well as when to question it. For example, when team members are speaking or acting from their base of experience and expertise, you are more likely to trust their judgment than when they are talking about something beyond their knowledge. For this reason, the analyst leading the team must understand the strengths and weaknesses of the other team members. To work together effectively and to ensure the quality of the group product, the team must establish standards of cooperation and coordination that guide their work (review Table 1-2 for the characteristics of a successful team).

There are several dimensions to the cooperation and coordination that influence team work. Table 2-2 lists the twelve characteristics of a high performance team (McConnell, 1996). The first characteristic is a shared vision, which allows each team member to have a clear understanding of the project's objectives. A shared vision helps team members keep their priorities straight and not allow small items of little significance to become overwhelming and distracting. To provide motivation for team members, the vision also needs to present a challenge to team members. The second characteristic, team identity, emerges as team members work together closely and begin to share a common language and sense of humor. Team identity can lead to the synergy of effort only possible when groups work together well.

Shared vision and team identity are important but they alone may not be enough for a team to actually accomplish something. The third characteristic of high performance teams is how the teams are organized. A result-driven structure is one that depends on clear roles, effective communication systems, means of monitoring individual performance, and decision making based on facts rather than emotions. Choosing the right people for the team is the fourth characteristic. McConnell (1996) reports that team performance may differ by as much as a factor of 5, depending only on the skills and attitudes of a team's members. Although the skills of each team member are important determinants of how well the team will perform, all members must be committed to the team, the fifth characteristic of high performance teams. A group of the best and brightest individuals, committed only to their own self-interests, cannot outperform a true team of lesser talents who are genuinely committed to each other and to their joint effort.

The next five characteristics of high performance teams all have to do with how the team members interact with each other. It is very important that team members develop genuine trust for each other. The need for trust is why you see so many team-building exercises; for example, an individual falls backwards into the arms of a fellow team member, not knowing if the other person is really there but trusting that he or she will be. Similarly, members of high-performance teams work interdependently, relying on each others' strengths; develop effective means of communication; give each team member the autonomy to do whatever he or she believes is best for the team and for the project; and empower each team member.

All of these high performance characteristics seem to work best, according to McConnell (1996), in small teams no larger than eight to ten people. Finally, it is important that teams have fun. Enjoying working together leads to increased team cohesiveness, which has been shown to be a key ingredient of team productivity (Lakhanpal, 1993).

TABLE 2-2   Characteristics of a High Performance Team (McConnell, 1996)

1. Shared, elevated vision or goal
2. Sense of team identity
3. Result-driven structure
4. Competent team members
5. Commitment to the team
6. Mutual trust
7. Interdependence among team members
8. Effective communication
9. Sense of autonomy
10. Sense of empowerment
11. Small team size
12. High level of enjoyment

Facilitating Groups

Sometimes you need to interact with a group in order to communicate and receive information. In Chapter 1, we introduced you to the Joint Application Design (JAD) process in which analysts actively work with groups during systems development. Analysts use JAD sessions to gather systems requirements and to conduct design reviews. The assembled group is the most important resource the analyst has access to during a JAD and you must get the most out of that resource; successful group facilitation is one way to do that. In a typical JAD, there is a trained session leader running the show. He or she has been specially trained to facilitate groups, to help them work together, and to help them achieve their common goals. Facilitation necessarily involves a certain amount of neutrality on the part of the facilitator. The facilitator must guide the group without being part of the group and must work to keep the effort on track by ferreting out disagreements and helping the group resolve differences. Obviously, group facilitation requires training. Many organizations that rely on group facilitation train their own facilitators. Figure 2-9 lists some guidelines for running an effective meeting, a task that is fundamental to facilitating groups.

Managing Expectations

Systems development is a change process, and any organizational change is greeted with anticipation and uncertainty by organization members. Organization members will have certain ideas, perhaps based on their hopes and wishes, about what a new information system will be able to do for them; these expectations about the new system can easily run out of control. Ginzberg (1981) found that successfully managing user expectations is related to successful systems implementation. For you to successfully manage expectations, you need to understand the technology and what it can do. You must understand the work flows that the technology will support and how the new system will affect them. More important than understanding, however, is your ability to communicate a realistic picture of the new system and what it will do for users and managers. Managing expectations begins with the development of the business case for the system and extends all the way through training people to use the finished system. You need to educate those who

Figure 2-9

Some guidelines for running effective meetings (Adapted from Option Technologies, Inc. [1992])

- Become comfortable with your role as facilitator by gaining confidence in your ability, being clear about your purpose, and finding a style that is right for you.
- At the beginning of the meeting, make sure the group understands what is expected of them and of you.
- Use physical movement to focus on yourself or on the group, depending on which is called for at the time.
- Reward group member participation with thanks and respect.
- Ask questions instead of making statements.
- Be willing to wait patiently for group members to answer the questions you ask them.
- Be a good listener.
- Keep the group focused.
- Encourage group members to feel ownership of the group's goals and of their attempts to reach those goals.

have few expectations as well as temper the optimism of those who expect the new system to perform miracles.

SYSTEMS ANALYSIS AS A PROFESSION

Even though systems analysis is a relatively new field, those in the field have established standards for education, training, certification, and practice. Such standards are required for any profession.

Whether or not systems analysis is a profession is open to debate. Some feel systems analysis is not a profession because it simply has not been around long enough to have established the rigorous standards that define a profession. Others feel that at least some standards are already in place. There are guidelines for college curricula and there are standard ways of analyzing, designing, and implementing systems. Professional societies that systems analysts may join include the Society for Information Management, the Association of Information Technology Professionals, and the Association for Computing Machinery (ACM). There is a Certified Data Processing Certificate (CDP) exam, much like the Certified Public Accountant (CPA) exam, that you can take to prove your competency in the field, although, unlike the CPA certificate, very few jobs and employers in the IS field require you to have the CDP certificate. Codes of ethics to govern behavior also exist. In this section, we will discuss several aspects of a systems analyst's job: standards of practice, the ACM code of ethics, and career paths for those choosing to become systems analysts.

Standards of Practice

Standard methods or practices of performing systems development are emerging that make systems development less of an art and more of a science. Standards are developed through education and practice and spread as systems analysts move from one organization to another. We will focus here on four standards of practice: an endorsed development methodology, approved development platforms, well-defined roles for people in the development process, and a common language.

There are several different development methodologies now being used in organizations. Although there is no standardization of a single methodology across all organizations, a few prominent methodologies are in common use. An *endorsed development methodology* lays out specific procedures and techniques to be used during the development process. These standards are central to promoting consistency and reliability in methods across all of an organization's development projects. Some methodologies are spread through the work of well-known consultants, such as James Martin's Information Engineering™. Others are spread through major consulting firms, such as Andersen Consulting's Foundation/1™.

Closely associated with endorsed methodologies are approved development platforms. Some methodologies are closely tied to platforms, as is Andersen's methodology and their Foundation® CASE tool. Other methodologies are more adaptable and can work in close accordance with development platforms that exist in the organization, such as database management systems and 4GLs. The point is that organizations, and hence the analysts who work for them, are standardizing around specific platforms, and standards for development emerge from this standardization.

Roles for the various people involved in the development process are also becoming standardized. End users, managers, and analysts are each assigned certain responsibilities for development projects. The training that analysts receive in college, on their first jobs, and during their interactions with other analysts, combine to create a gestalt of the analyst's job. For example, as you study this book and talk about systems development in your class, you are forming certain ideas about what systems analysts do and how systems are developed in organizations. Your ideas are also shaped and reinforced by the other IS courses you take in college. Once you get your first job, you will receive additional training and you will adjust your understanding of systems analysis accordingly. As you gain experience working on projects and interacting with other analysts, who may have been trained at other universities and in other organizations, your ideas will continue to change and grow, but the basic core of what systems analysis means to you will have been established. Many of the experiences you have on the job will reinforce much of what you have already learned about systems analysis. When you leave an organization and go to work elsewhere, you will carry your understanding of systems analysis with you. Over time, as you and other analysts change jobs and move from one organization to another, what it means to be an analyst becomes standardized across organizations, and the standards of practice in the field help define what it means to be an analyst.

Another factor moving the job of the systems analyst toward professionalism is the development of a common language analysts use to talk to each other. Analysts communicate on the job, at meetings of professional societies, and through publications. As analysts develop a special language for communication among themselves, their language becomes standardized. For example, since the late 1970s, systems analysts have begun to rely on data flow diagramming as a means of communication. There are now two primary standards for data flow diagramming: Yourdon, and Gane and Sarson (see Chapter 8). In time, only one may be used. Other examples of communication becoming standardized include the widespread use of common programming languages such as COBOL and C and the spread of SQL as the language of choice for data definition and manipulation for relational databases. As their common language develops, analysts become more cohesive as a group—a characteristic of professions.

Ethics

The ACM is a large professional society made up of information system professionals and academics. It has over 85,000 members. Founded in 1947, the ACM is dedicated to promoting information processing as an academic discipline and to encouraging the responsible use of computers in a wide range of applications. Because of its size and membership, it has much influence in the information systems community. The ACM has developed a code of ethics for its members called the "ACM Code of Ethics and Professional Conduct." The full statement is reproduced in Figure 2-10. The code applies to all ACM members and directly applies to systems analysts.

Note the emphasis in the Code on personal responsibility, on honesty, and on respect for relevant laws. Notice also that compliance with a code of ethics such as this one is voluntary, although article 4.2 calls for, at a minimum, peer pressure for compliance. No one can force an information systems professional to follow these guidelines. However, it is voluntary compliance with the guidelines that makes someone a professional in the first place. Notice that for leaders there is the burden of educating non-IS professionals about computing—about what computing can and cannot do. The Code also expresses concern for the quality of work life and for protecting the dignity and privacy of others when performing professional work, such as developing information systems.

Association for Computing Machinery Professional Code of Ethics

Preamble

These statements of intended conduct are expected of every member (voting members, associate members, and student members) of the Association for Computing Machinery (ACM). Section 1.0 consists of fundamental ethical considerations; section 2.0 includes additional considerations of professional conduct; statements in 3.0 pertain to individuals who have a leadership role; and section 4.0 deals with compliance. ACM shall prepare and maintain an additional document for interpreting and following this Code.

(1.0) General Moral Imperatives

(As an ACM member I will . . .)
(1.1) Contribute to society and human well-being.
(1.2) Avoid harm to others.
(1.3) Be honest and trustworthy.
(1.4) Be fair and take action not to discriminate.
(1.5) Respect property rights (Honor copyrights and patents; give proper credit; not steal, damage, or copy without permission).
(1.6) Respect the privacy of others.
(1.7) Honor confidentiality.

(2.0) Additional Professional Obligations

(As an ACM computing professional I will ...)
(2.1) Strive to achieve the highest quality in the processes and products of my work.
(2.2) Acquire and maintain professional competence.
(2.3) Know and respect existing law pertaining to my professional work.
(2.4) Encourage review by peers and all affected parties.
(2.5) Give well-grounded evaluations of computer systems, their impacts, and possible risks.
(2.6) Honor contracts, agreements, and acknowledged responsibilities.
(2.7) Improve public understanding of computing and its consequences.

(3.0) Organizational Leadership Imperatives

(As an organizational leader I will . . .)
(3.1) Articulate social responsibilities of members of the organizational unit and encourage full participation in these responsibilities.
(3.2) Shape information systems to enhance the quality of working life.
(3.3) Articulate proper and authorized uses of organizational computer technology and enforce those policies.
(3.4) Ensure participation of users and other affected parties in system design, development and implementation.
(3.5) Support policies that protect the dignity of users and others affected by a computerized system.
(3.6) Support opportunities for learning the principles and limitations of computer systems.

(continued)

Figure 2-10
ACM Code of Ethics and Professional Conduct, Revision Draft No. 19 (9/19/91). (Copyright © Association for Computing Machinery, reprinted with permission.)

Figure 2-10 *(continued)*

> **(4.0) Compliance with Code**
>
> (4.1) I will uphold and promote the principles of this Code.
> (4.2) If I observe an apparent violation of this Code, I will take appropriate action leading to a remedy.
> (4.3) I understand that violation of this Code is inconsistent with continued membership in the ACM.

Though not written specifically for systems analysts, the ACM Code of Ethics can easily be adapted to the systems analysis job. Many systems development projects deal directly with many of the issues addressed in the Code: privacy, quality of work life, user participation, and managing expectations. When an analyst must confront one or more of these issues, the Code can be used as a guide for professional conduct.

Career Paths

A typical first job for a recent college graduate who wants to become a systems analyst is as an analyst or programmer/analyst trainee for a corporation or large consulting firm. Other typical entry-level opportunities are as

- End-user support specialist, assisting non-IS professional and clerical staff to better use computer resources

- Decision support analyst, in which you design database queries and data analysis routines to support business analysis and decision making, often for one department, such as market research or investments

- Trainer, in which you prepare and conduct various classes on information systems and technologies

- Computer technology sales and customer support, in which you either sell hardware, software, or services or support the sales staff by installing technology and responding to customer questions

Larger firms usually have their own intensive training programs to instruct trainees in the way the firm develops and maintains systems. Every firm handles systems development a little bit differently. Once trained, the entry-level systems analyst begins a career path, which differs from one firm to another.

For example, in one particular firm where the authors have done research—which we'll call the JKL Corporation—an analyst typically begins as an assistant analyst. The qualifications for this position are a bachelor's degree with little or no experience. Typically after two years of work, the assistant analyst is promoted to an associate analyst. Another two to three years of work experience qualify the associate analyst to become an analyst. The next two steps up the ladder are senior analyst and staff analyst. Of course, not everyone makes it to staff analyst. Many analysts leave after one or two promotions to work for other firms or settle into a position along the way.

At this point in his or her career at JKL Corp., the staff analyst must decide whether he or she wants to pursue a management ladder or a technical ladder. Analysts who are more technically oriented might prefer not to follow a management career path (see Figure 2-11). The management ladder continues upward with the

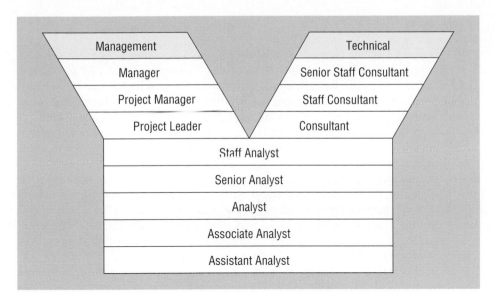

Figure 2-11
Information systems career
ladder for the JKL Corp.

positions of project leader, project manager, and manager. A manager is responsible for planning, developing, and implementing information technology at JKL Corp., for training and staff development, and for establishing and managing budgets. The technical ladder continues upward with the positions of consultant, staff consultant, and senior staff consultant. A senior staff consultant is responsible for major research and development projects. Creativity and vision are necessary for successful performance as a senior staff consultant.

It should be pointed out that not everyone hired by JKL Corp. starts out as an assistant analyst and works his or her way up in the corporation. Some employees are hired directly into higher-level jobs, based on their work experience and education. For example, someone with a master's degree and little or no experience can be hired directly into the associate analyst position. On the other hand, a person with a bachelor's degree and 14 or more years of proven experience can be hired directly into the manager's position.

Besides progression within the IS organization, some IS professionals choose to make a lateral move into general management positions and then return to senior IS management positions later in their careers. IS is an excellent entry point into any general business career since the process of systems analysis and design gives you a thorough understanding of the business, and your acquired general business knowledge is extremely valuable in general management positions.

For those who enter the consulting world, career progression is typically geared toward becoming a partner or principle of the business. These positions often focus on generating business and maintaining customer relationships. Another interesting option for people with more of an entrepreneurial spirit is to start your own business. You may develop expertise in a certain area or have a unique idea for some software tool that can flourish only in your own company. Many niche products, such as specialized data analysis tools or systems for particular types of functions or businesses, exist in the information systems field. Many of these were created by systems analysts who, after years of experience and continuing development, got a bright idea, networked with contacts, acquired funding, and started their own business. This is one way to become president of the company!

SUMMARY

In this chapter, we have surveyed the skills necessary for success as a systems analyst. The requisite skills are analytical, technical, management, and interpersonal. Analytical skills include the concept of systems thinking, which is one of the most important skills an analyst can learn. Systems thinking provides a disciplined foundation on which all other analyst skills can build. In addition, an analyst needs to understand the nature of business and of the particular enterprise he or she serves and to be able to identify, analyze, and solve problems.

Technical skills change over time as technology changes and analysts need to keep current with changing information technology. This can be accomplished through reading trade journals, joining professional societies, attending or teaching classes, attending conferences, and participating in electronic bulletin boards and news groups. Some technology areas that play a continuing important role are programming languages, operating systems, database management systems, data communications, and systems development techniques and tools.

A useful skill is the ability to manage resources, projects, risk, and change. Interpersonal skills, especially clear communication, are also important. Analysts communicate with team members in interviews, with questionnaires, through written and oral presentations, and through facilitating groups. A key component of communicating about information systems is managing the expectations of both users and managers.

The chapter concluded with an examination of the system analyst's position, the standards of practice, the ACM Code of Ethics, and possible career paths. Systems analysis is becoming more of a science and less of an art as the systems analysis field becomes a profession.

KEY TERMS

Boundary	Environment	Open system
Closed system	Input	Output
Cohesion	Interface	Physical system
Components	Inter-related components	description
Constraints	Logical system description	Purpose
Coupling	Modularity	System

REVIEW QUESTIONS

1. Define each of the following terms:
   a. system
   b. interface
   c. boundary
   d. purpose
   e. modularity

2. What is systems thinking? How is it useful for thinking about computer-based information systems?

3. What is decomposition? coupling? cohesion?

4. In what way are organizations systems?

5. What are the differences between problem identification and problem solving?

6. How can a systems analyst determine if his or her technical skills are up-to-date?

7. Explain the management skills needed by systems analysts.

8. Which communication skills are important for analysts? Why?

9. Is systems analysis a profession? Why or why not?

10. What is a code of ethics?

11. What's the difference between a logical system description and a physical system description?

12. Which areas of organizational knowledge are important for a systems analyst to know?

13. What's the difference between an open and a closed system?

14. What kinds of tasks are included in resource management?

15. Why is the development of an information sometimes done by independent contractors?

16. What are the twelve characteristics of high performance teams? Compare Table 2-2 with Table 1-2. What differences do you see between these two tables?

P R O B L E M S   A N D   E X E R C I S E S

1. Match the following terms to the appropriate definitions.

_____ closed system	a. systems that interact freely with their environments, taking input and returning output
_____ open system	b. systems that are cut off from their environments and do not interact with them
_____ components	c. everything external to a system
_____ constraint	d. limits to what a system can accomplish
_____ environment	e. the parts or subsystems that make up a system

2. Describe your university or college as a system. What is the input? the output? the boundary? the components? their inter-relationships? the constraints? the pupose? the interfaces? the environment? Draw a diagram of this system.

3. a. A car is a system with several subsystems, including the braking subsystem, the electrical subsystem, the engine, the fuel subsystem, the climate control subsystem, and the passenger subsystem. Draw a diagram of a car as a system and label all of its system characteristics.

   b. Your personal computer is a system. Draw and label a personal computer as a system as you did for a car in part (a).

4. Describe yourself in terms of your abilities at resource, project, risk, and change management. Among these categories, what are your strengths and weaknesses? Why? How can you best capitalize on your strengths and strengthen areas where

you are weak? If you do not have managerial or supervisory experience, answer these questions as if you were generalizing from your experiences thus far to your performance later as a manager.

5. Describe yourself in terms of your abilities at each of the following interpersonal skills: working alone versus working with a team, interviewing, listening, writing, presenting, facilitating a group, and managing expectations. Where are your strengths and weaknesses? Why? What can you do to capitalize on your strengths and strengthen areas where you are weak?

6. Use your imagination and hypothesize what a systems analyst would be like if he or she were a person with no personal or professional ethics. What types of systems would that person help to create, and how might they go about building such systems? What would the consequences of these actions be, with what implications for the analyst, for his or her information systems department, for his or her users, for the organization? Specifically, how would a code of ethics and professional conduct help curb the behavior of this person? This may seem like a silly exercise, but even your wildest guesses about the things an unethical analyst might do have probably happened in some setting.

7. You likely receive (and pay) one or more bills each month or semester (for example, tuition, rent, utilities, or telephone). Describe one of these billing systems as an information system. Be sure to list at least one example of each of the nine characteristics of a system for your example billing system.

8. The chapter mentioned that choosing the boundary for a system is a crucial step in analyzing and studying a system. What criteria would you use to determine where to draw a system boundary? What are the ramifications of setting too broad a boundary? Too narrow a boundary?

9. Make a list of the technical skills you have developed at school, as part of any job you've held, and on your own. Using newspaper want ads, trade journals, and other sources, determine if your technical skills are up-to-date. If not, devise a plan to update your technical skills.

10. Recall a team on which you have worked in a job or course project. How well did this team follow the twelve characteristics of high-performance teams? How could you have improved the performance of this team?

11. Chapter 1 outlined the role of systems analyst and others in systems development. How might these roles change if contractors are used on a project? Which of these roles might a contractor provide?

FIELD EXERCISES

1. Describe an organization of your choice as an open system. What factors lead you to believe that this system is open? Describe the organization in terms of decomposition, coupling, cohesion, and modularity. What is beneficial about thinking of the organization in this way?

2. Think about a problem you have, perhaps with a grade in a class, with a job you're not satisfied with, or with a co-worker on the job. Describe the problem as a difference between "what is" and "what should be." What must happen to shift your situation from "what is" to "what should be" to bring about a situation that you are satisfied with? What specific actionable steps must you take to make this change happen? What information, if any, will you need to gather about this situation? From where, and/or from whom, must the information come? How can you get this information?

3. Choose a manager you know in any area and describe this person in terms of his or her abilities at resource, project, risk, and change management. Overall, is he or she successful or not? Why or why not?

4. Investigate where on your campus and community you could go to get help and practice with public speaking. Talk with other students, contact your instructors, look in the telephone book and directory of services at your college, and explore avenues to uncover as many sources of public speaking help you can find.

5. Many organizations have an approved technology list from which units are free to purchase hardware and software for application development. Contact the computing services unit at your college (or other organization) and find out what hardware and software are supported on your campus for administrative computing. Given this list of supported technologies, what would you infer are the technical skills required for a systems analyst at your college (or other organization)?

REFERENCES

Ginzberg, M. J. 1981. "Early Diagnosis of MIS Implementation Failure: Promising Results and Unanswered Questions." *Management Science* 27 (April): 459–78.

Lakhanpal, B. 1993. "Understanding the Factors Influencing the Performance of Software Development Groups: An Exploratory Group-level Analysis." *Information & Software Technology* 35(8):468–73.

Martin. E. W., D. W. DeHayes, J. A. Hoffer, and W. C. Perkins. 1994. *Managing Information Technology: What Managers Need to Know.* 2nd ed. New York: Macmillan Publishing Company.

McConnell, S. 1996. *Rapid Development.* Redmond, WA: Microsoft Press.

Option Technologies, Inc. 1992. *Just-In-Time Knowledge for Teams.* Mendotta Heights, MN.

Pounds, W. F. 1969. "The Process of Problem Finding." *Industrial Management Review* (Fall): 1–19.

Simon, H. A. 1960. *The New Science of Management Decision.* New York: Harper & Row.

3

Managing the Information Systems Project

L E A R N I N G   O B J E C T I V E S

After studying this chapter, you should be able to:

■ Explain the process of managing an information systems project.

■ Describe the skills required to be an effective project manager.

■ List and describe the skills and activities of a project manager during project initiation, project planning, project execution, and project close-down.

■ Explain what is meant by critical path scheduling and describe the process of creating Gantt and PERT charts.

■ Explain how commercial project management software packages can be used to assist in representing and managing project schedules.

INTRODUCTION

Many aspects of information technology in general and the development of information systems in particular are more glamorous than the management of development projects. This view is underscored by a quote from a book that focuses on the management of information systems projects:

> Project management has rarely received the attention it deserves, and particularly within the computing profession, it has been overshadowed by the battles within the technological arena: Manufacturer versus manufacturer, development language versus development language, mainframe versus micro, operating system versus operating system are the stuff from which great legends are born and great leaders emerge as role models . . . Pity the humble project manager who manages to bring the general ledger system in on time, within budget, and working to the users' satisfaction (Thomsett, 1985).

As the above quotation typifies, some may not view project management to be a glamorous occupation. Yet, project management is an important aspect of the development of information systems and a critical skill for a systems analyst. The focus of project management is to assure that system development projects meet customer expectations and are delivered within budget and time constraints. This chapter describes how you can wear many different hats while managing all or part of a project.

The project manager is responsible for virtually all aspects of a systems development project: what you experience as a project manager is an environment of continual change and problem solving. In some organizations the project manager is a senior systems analyst who "has been around the block" a time or two. In others, both junior and senior analysts are expected to take on this role, managing parts of a project or actively supporting a more senior colleague who is assuming this role. Consequently, it is important that you gain an understanding of the project management process; this will become a critical skill for your future success.

In this chapter we focus on the systems analyst's role in managing information systems projects and will refer to this role as the project manager. The next section will provide the background for Pine Valley Furniture, a manufacturing company that we will visit throughout the remainder of the book. The following section will provide you with an understanding of the project manager's role and the project management process. The subsequent section examines techniques for reporting project plans using Gantt and PERT charts. The chapter will conclude by discussing the use of commercially available project management software that can be used to assist with a wide variety of project management activities.

PINE VALLEY FURNITURE COMPANY BACKGROUND

Pine Valley Furniture Company (PVF) manufactures high-quality, all-wood furniture and distributes it to retail stores within the United States. Their product lines include dinette sets, stereo cabinets, wall units, living room furniture, and bedroom furniture. PVF currently employs about 50 people and is growing rapidly.

When PVF was founded 15 years ago by Donald Knotts, managing data and information systems was relatively simple. Don founded PVF out of his garage where he made custom furniture as a hobby. When business expanded into a rented warehouse, Don hired a part-time bookkeeper. When the company moved into its present location ten years ago, the product line had multiplied, sales volume had doubled, and the size of the staff had increased. Due to the added complexity of the company's operations, Don reorganized the company into functional areas: Manufacturing, which was further subdivided into three separate functions—Fabrication, Assembling, and Finishing; Sales; Orders; Accounting; and Purchasing. Don and the heads of the functional areas established manual information systems that worked well for a time but, eventually, PVF selected and installed a minicomputer to automate applications.

When the applications were first computerized, each separate application had its own individual data files tailored to the needs of each functional area. As is typical in such situations, the applications closely resembled the manual systems on which they were based. (Three of the computer applications at Pine Valley Furniture are depicted in Figure 3-1.) In the late 1980s, PVF formed a task force to study the possibility of moving to a database approach. After the preliminary study was completed, management decided to convert their information systems to the database approach. They upgraded their minicomputer and implemented a database management system. By the time we catch up with Pine Valley Furniture, it has successfully designed and populated a company-wide database and has converted its applications to work with the database. However, PVF is continuing to grow at a rapid rate, putting pressure on its current application systems.

The computer-based applications at PVF parallel the processes that are part of doing business in the company. When customers order furniture, their orders must be processed appropriately so that customers receive what they order and are billed correctly. To fill the orders, furniture has to be built and shipped to customers. Employees have to be paid for their work. Accordingly, most computer-based applications at PVF are in the accounting and financial areas. The applications include order filling, invoicing, accounts receivable, inventory control, accounts payable, payroll, and general ledger. As we stated earlier, each application once had its own data files. For example, there was a customer master file, an inventory master file, a back order file, an inventory pricing file, and an employee

Figure 3-1

Three application systems at Pine Valley Furniture (Source: McFadden, Hoffer, and Prescott, 1999)

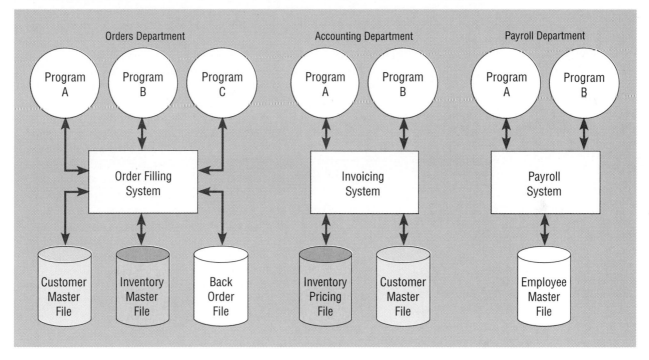

master file. The order-filling system used data from three files: customer master, inventory master, and back order. With PVF's new centralized database, data are organized around *entities,* or subjects, such as customers, invoices, and orders.

Pine Valley Furniture, like many firms, decided to develop its application software in-house; that is, it hired staff and bought equipment necessary to build application software suited to its own needs. There are, of course, other ways for firms to obtain application software, as explained more fully in Chapter 11.

MANAGING THE INFORMATION SYSTEMS PROJECT

Successful projects require managing resources, activities, and tasks needed to complete the project. A **project** is a planned undertaking of a series of related activities to reach an objective that has a beginning and an end. The first question you might ask yourself is "Where do projects come from?" and, after considering all the different things that you could be asked to work on within an organization, "How do I know which projects to work on?" The ways in which each organization answers these questions can vary. Throughout the remainder of this section, we will describe the process followed by Juanita Lopez and Chris Martin during the development of Pine Valley Furniture's (PVF) Purchasing Fulfillment System. (A detailed description of this project is available on the World Wide Web site for *Modern Systems Analysis and Design* at http://hepg.awl.com/.) Juanita, having observed problems with the way orders were processed and reported, contacted Chris, a systems analyst within PVF's systems development group. Together they worked on this project.

The first deliverable that Chris and Juanita produced was a System Service Request (SSR), a standard form PVF uses for requesting systems development work (see Figure 3-2). This request was then evaluated by the Systems Priority Board. The

Project: A planned undertaking of related activities to reach an objective that have a beginning and an end.

Figure 3-2
System Service Request for Purchasing Fulfillment System

Pine Valley Furniture
System Service Request

REQUESTED BY ___Juanita Lopez___ DATE ___November 1, 1998___

DEPARTMENT ___Purchasing, Manufacturing Support___

LOCATION ___Headquarters, 1-322___

CONTACT ___Tel: 4-3267   FAX: 4-3270   e-mail: jlopez___

TYPE OF REQUEST   URGENCY

[X]   New System   [   ]   Immediate – Operations are impaired or
                                               opportunity lost

[   ]   System Enhancement   [   ]   Problems exist, but can be worked around
[   ]   System Error Correction   [X]   Business losses can be tolerated until new
                                               system installed

PROBLEM STATEMENT

Sales growth at PVF has caused greater volume of work for the manufacturing support unit within
Purchasing. Further, more concentration on customer service has reduced manufacturing lead times,
which puts more pressure on purchasing activities. In addition, cost-cutting measures force Purchasing
to be more agressive in negotiating terms with vendors, improving delivery times, and lowering our
investments in inventory. The current modest systems support for manufacturing purchasing is not
responsive to these new business conditions. Data are not available, information cannot be summarized,
supplier orders cannot be adequately tracked, and commodity buying is not well supported. PVF is
spending too much on raw materials and not being responsive to manufacturing needs.

SERVICE REQUEST

I request a thorough analysis of our current operations with the intent to design and build a completely
new information system. This system should handle all purchasing transactions, support display and
reporting of critical purchasing data, and assist purchasing agents in commodity buying.

IS LIAISON   Chris Martin (Tel: 4-6204   FAX: 4-6200   e-mail: cmartin)

SPONSOR   Sal Divario, Director, Purchasing

------------------------- TO BE COMPLETED BY SYSTEMS PRIORITY BOARD -------------------------

[   ]   Request approved   Assigned to _____
                           Start date _____
[   ]   Recommend revision
[   ]   Suggest user development
[   ]   Reject for reason _____
                         _____
                         _____

Board evaluates development requests in relation to the business problems or opportunities the system will solve or create and also considers how the proposed project fits within the broader scope of the organization's Information Systems architecture and long-range development plans. Both the IS architecture and long-range systems plans are additional sources for projects. Thus, the Board considers all requests with respect to the overall plans and architecture of the organization when choosing projects to approve or reject. Since all organizations have limited time and resources, not all requests can be approved. The review board selects those projects that best meet overall organizational goals. (Chapter 5 provides you with a detailed description of the IS planning process and how projects are identified and selected.) In the case of the Purchasing Fulfillment System request, the Board found merit in the request and approved a more detailed feasibility study and, eventually, the construction of the system. Figure 3-3 provides a graphical view of the steps followed during the project initiation of the Purchasing Fulfillment System.

In summary, systems development projects are undertaken for two *primary* reasons: to take advantage of business *opportunities* or to solve business *problems*. Taking advantage of an opportunity might occur by providing an innovative service to customers through the creation of a new system. Solving a business problem could occur by modifying the way in which an existing system processes data so that more accurate or timely information is provided to users.

Projects are not always initiated for the rational reasons (solving business problems or taking advantage of business opportunities) stated above. For example, we have all read or heard of instances in organizations and in government where projects were undertaken to spend resources, to attain or pad budgets, to keep people busy, or to help train people and develop their skills. The goal of this chapter is not

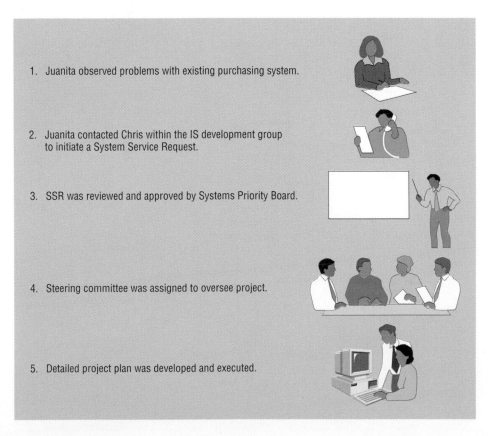

1. Juanita observed problems with existing purchasing system.

2. Juanita contacted Chris within the IS development group to initiate a System Service Request.

3. SSR was reviewed and approved by Systems Priority Board.

4. Steering committee was assigned to oversee project.

5. Detailed project plan was developed and executed.

Figure 3-3
Overview of the steps followed during the Purchasing Fulfillment System project

to examine issues related to how and why organizations undertake the projects they do but to focus on the project management process in the context of developing information systems. In other words, our focus is not necessarily on *how* and *why* organizations identify projects but on the management of projects *once they have been identified.*

Once a potential project has been identified, an organization must determine the resources required for a project's completion. This understanding is gained by analyzing the scope of the project and determining the probability of successful completion. After gaining this understanding, the organization can then determine whether solving a particular problem or taking advantage of an opportunity is feasible within time and resource constraints. If deemed feasible, a more detailed project analysis is then conducted.

Project manager: An individual with a diverse set of skills—management, leadership, technical, conflict management, and customer relationship—who is responsible for initiating, planning, executing, and closing down a project.

The **project manager** is responsible for creating high-level feasibility plans and detailed project plans as well as staffing the project team. As you will see, determining the size, scope, and resource requirements for a project are just a few of the many skills that a project manager must possess. The skills required to be an effective project manager are varied. A project manager is often referred to as a juggler keeping aloft many balls that reflect the various aspects of a project's development (see Figure 3-4).

In order to be successful in orchestrating the construction of a complex information system, a project manager must have interpersonal skills, leadership skills, and technical skills. Table 3-1 lists many of the project manager's common skills and activities. Note that many of the skills are personnel- or general management-related, not simply technical skills. The capabilities of an effective project manager

Figure 3-4
A project manager juggles numerous items during a project

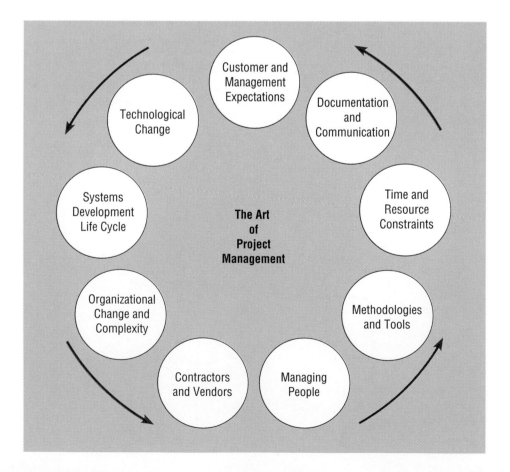

TABLE 3-1 Common Activities and Skills of a Project Manager

Activity	Description	Skill
Leadership	Influencing the activities of others toward the attainment of a common goal through the use of intelligence, personality, and abilities	Communication; liaison between management, users, and developers; assigning activities; monitoring progress
Management	Getting projects completed through the effective utilization of resources	Defining and sequencing activities; communicating expectations; assigning resources to activities; monitoring outcomes
Customer Relations	Working closely with customers to assure project deliverables meet expectations	Interpreting system requests and specifications; site preparation and user training; contact point for customers
Technical Problem Solving	Designing and sequencing activities to attain project goals	Interpreting system requests and specifications; defining activities and their sequence; making tradeoffs between alternative solutions; designing solutions to problems
Conflict Management	Managing conflict within a project team to assure that conflict is not too high or too low (see Figure 3-5)	Problem solving; smoothing out personality differences; compromising; goal setting
Team Management	Managing the project team for effective team performance	Communication within and between teams; peer evaluations; conflict resolution; team building; self management
Risk and Change Management	Identifying, assessing, and managing the risks and day-to-day changes that occur during a project	Environmental scanning; risk and opportunity identification and assessment; forecasting; resource re-deployment

augment those of the systems analyst outlined in Chapter 2. Table 3-1 shows that not only must a project manager have varied skills, but is also arguably the most instrumental person to the successful completion of any project (Boehm, 1981). Table 3-1 also shows that a project manager has to deal with a wide variety of issues and tasks that go far beyond simply *constructing* an information system.

Because there are many people with diverse interests involved in a project (as team members, clients, stakeholders), conflict can arise. Although mitigating conflict is typically desirable, conflict can also be used to advantage. For example, Figure 3-5 describes how conflict can be used as a stimulant for creativity. Yet, too much conflict within a team has been found to make people apprehensive of making contributions due to fear of being ridiculed for having a "dumb idea." This

Figure 3-5
Role of conflict in software teams (Adapted from Zachary [1993])

Researchers and experts in the field of organizational behavior and group dynamics have repeatedly found that some conflict in project teams is not always a bad thing. Conflict can be viewed as a stimulus. For example, many effective teams like to use conflict inducing techniques such as devil's advocacy, a technique where a member of the group tries to improve team performance by surfacing all things that may be wrong with a suggested idea. Thus, at the right levels, conflict has been found to improve overall team performance. An example of conflict having a positive influence on the Microsoft Windows NT software development project team was reported in the Wall Street Journal: Innovation requires "dogged system-building and the ability to hold large teams together while allowing—even cultivating—conflict. Conflict lies at the core of innovation . . . When there's no conflict, a lab is no good."

Project management:
A controlled process of initiating, planning, executing, and closing down a project.

means that the project manager must balance the negative and positive influences of conflict.

The focus of the following section is on the **project management** process. The activities involved in managing a project occur in four phases:

1. Initiating the project

2. Planning the project

3. Executing the project

4. Closing down the project

Each phase of the project management process requires that several activities be performed. Research has found that project success is strongly related to the characteristics of the process used to manage the project. In essence, following a formal project management process greatly increases the likelihood of project success. Descriptions of the activities performed during each of the project management processes are presented in the following sections.

Initiating a Project

Project initiation: The first phase of the project management process in which activities are performed to assess the size, scope, and complexity of the project and to establish procedures to support later project activities.

During **project initiation** the project manager performs several activities that lay the foundation for the rest of the project. Depending upon the size, scope, and complexity of the project, some project initiation activities may be unnecessary and some may be very involved. Your goal should be to initiate the project so that you will be able to effectively perform subsequent project activities. The types of activities you will perform when initiating a project include the following:

1. *Establishing the Project Initiation Team.* This activity focuses on organizing an initial core of project team members who assist in accomplishing the project initiation activities. For example, during the Purchasing Fulfillment System project at PVF, Chris Martin was assigned to support the Purchasing department. It is a PVF policy that all initiation teams consist of at least one user representative, in this case Juanita Lopez, and one member of the IS development group. Therefore, the project initiation team consisted of Chris and Juanita; Chris was the project manager.

2. *Establishing a Relationship with the Customer.* A thorough understanding of your customer builds stronger partnerships and higher levels of trust. At PVF, management has tried to foster strong working relationships between business units (like Purchasing) and the IS development group by assigning a specific individual to work as a liaison between both groups. Since Chris had been assigned to the Purchasing unit for some time, he was already aware of some of the problems with the existing Purchasing systems. PVF's policy of assigning specific individuals to each business unit helped to assure that both Chris and Juanita were comfortable working together prior to the initiation of the project. Many organizations use a similar mechanism for establishing relationships with customers.

3. *Establishing the Project Initiation Plan.* This activity focuses on defining the activities required to organize the initiation team while they are working to define the scope of the project. Chris's role was to help Juanita translate her business requirements into a specification for an improved information system. This required the collection, analysis, organization, and transformation of a lot of information. Since Chris and Juanita were already familiar with

each other and their roles within a development project, they next needed to define when and how they would communicate, define deliverables and project steps, and set deadlines. Their initiation plan included agendas for several meetings. These steps eventually led to the creation of their SSR.

4. *Establishing Management Procedures.* Successful projects require the development of effective management procedures. Within PVF, many of these management procedures had been established as standard operating procedures by the Systems Priority Board and the IS development group. For example, all project development work is charged back to the functional unit requesting the work. In other organizations, each project may have unique procedures tailored to its needs. Yet, in general when establishing procedures, you are concerned with developing team communication and reporting procedures, job assignments and roles, project change procedures, and determining how project funding and billing will be handled. It was fortunate for Chris and Juanita that most of these procedures were already established at PVF, allowing them to quickly move on to other project activities.

5. *Establishing the Project Management Environment and Project Workbook.* The focus of this activity is to collect and organize the tools that you will use while managing the project and to construct the **project workbook.** If the system is being developed with the assistance of CASE, as in the Purchasing Fulfillment System, most diagrams, charts, descriptions, and other repository contents can be printed to produce much of the project workbook contents. Thus, the project workbook serves as a repository for all project correspondence, inputs, outputs, deliverables, procedures, and standards established by the project team (Rettig, 1990). The project workbook can be stored as an online electronic document or large three-ring binder. The project workbook is used by all team members and is useful for project audits, orientation of new team members, communication with management and customers, scoping future projects, and performing post-project reviews. The establishment and diligent recording of all project information in the workbook is one of the most important activities you will perform as project manager.

Project workbook: An online or hardcopy repository for all project correspondence, inputs, outputs, deliverables, procedures, and standards that is used for performing project audits, orientation of new team members, communication with management and customers, scoping future projects, and performing post-project reviews.

Figure 3-6 shows the project workbook for the Purchasing Fulfillment System. It consists of both a large hardcopy binder and electronic diskettes where the system data dictionary and diagrams are stored. For this system, a single binder is currently able to contain all project documents. It is not unusual, however, for project documentation to be spread over several binders. As more information is captured and recorded electronically, however, fewer hardcopy binders may be needed.

Once all these activities have been performed, project initiation is complete (see Table 3-2). Before moving on to the next phase of the project, a review of the work performed during project initiation usually occurs. This review meeting is a formal process that is attended by management, customers, and project team members. An outcome of this meeting is a decision to continue the project, modify it in some way, or to abandon it. In the case of the Purchasing Fulfillment System project, the SSR was accepted by the Board, the Board then selected a project steering committee to monitor project progress and to provide guidance to the team members during subsequent activities. If the scope of the project is modified, it may be necessary to return to project initiation activities and collect additional information. Once a decision is made to continue the project, a much more detailed project plan is developed during the project planning phase.

Figure 3-6
The project workbook for the Purchasing Fulfillment System project contains both hardcopy and electronic documents

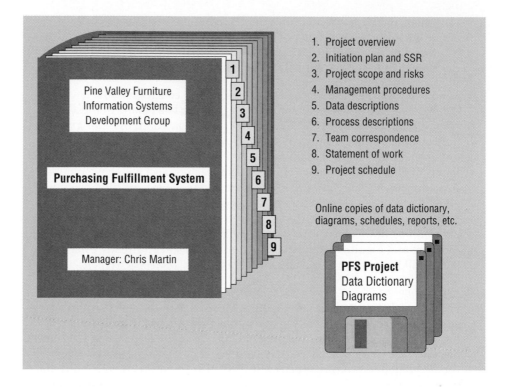

1. Project overview
2. Initiation plan and SSR
3. Project scope and risks
4. Management procedures
5. Data descriptions
6. Process descriptions
7. Team correspondence
8. Statement of work
9. Project schedule

Online copies of data dictionary, diagrams, schedules, reports, etc.

PFS Project
Data Dictionary
Diagrams

Planning the Project

Project planning: The second phase of the project management process which focuses on defining clear, discrete activities and the work needed to complete each activity within a single project.

The next step in the project management process is **project planning.** Distinct from general information systems planning, which focuses on assessing the information systems needs of the *entire* organization (Chapter 5), project planning is the process of defining clear, discrete activities and the work needed to complete each activity within a *single* project. Project planning often requires you to make numerous assumptions about resource availability and potential problems. It is much easier to plan nearer-term activities than those occurring in the future. In actual fact, you often have to construct longer-term plans that are more general in scope and nearer-term plans that are more detailed. The repetitive nature of the project management process requires that plans be constantly monitored throughout the project and periodically updated (usually after each phase) based upon the most recent information.

Figure 3-7 illustrates the principle that nearer-term plans are typically more specific and firm than longer-term plans. For example, it is virtually impossible to rigorously plan activities late in the systems development life cycle (SDLC) without first completing the analysis phase. Also, the outcome of activities performed earlier in the project are likely to have impact on later activities. This means that it is very difficult, and very likely inefficient, to try to plan detailed solutions for activities that will occur far into the future.

TABLE 3-2   Elements of Project Initiation

- Establishing the Project Initiation Team
- Establishing a Relationship with the Customer
- Establishing the Project Initiation Plan
- Establishing Management Procedures
- Establishing the Project Management Environment and Project Workbook

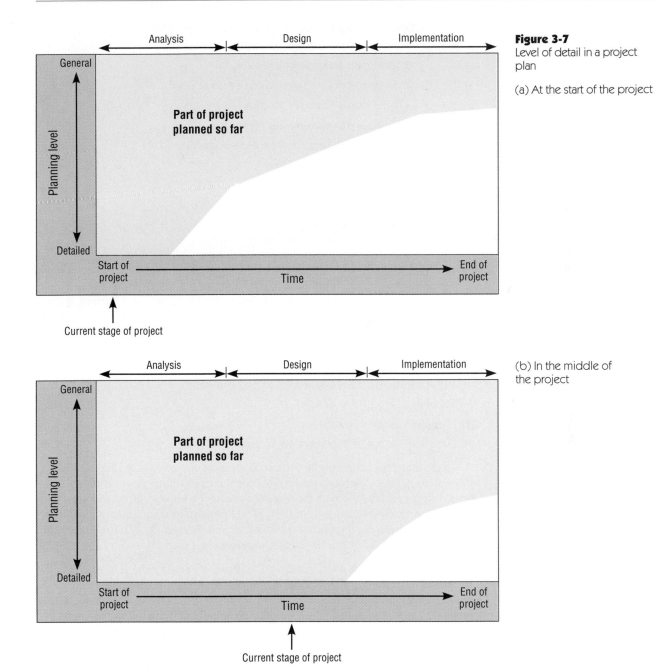

Figure 3-7
Level of detail in a project
plan

(a) At the start of the project

(b) In the middle of
the project

The types of activities that must be performed during project planning are varied and numerous (see Table 3-3). As with the project initiation process, the size,
scope, and complexity of a project will dictate the comprehensiveness of the project
planning process. For example, during the Purchasing Fulfillment System project,
Chris and Juanita developed a plan that was approximately ten pages in length, not
including figures. However, project plans for very large systems may be several
hundred pages in length. The types of activities that you can perform during project planning include the following elements:

1. *Describing Project Scope, Alternatives, and Feasibility.* The purpose of this activity
   is to develop an understanding of the content and complexity of the project.

TABLE 3-3   Elements of Project Planning

1. Describing Project Scope, Alternatives, and Feasibility

2. Dividing the Project into Manageable Tasks

3. Estimating Resources and Creating a Resource Plan

4. Developing a Preliminary Schedule

5. Developing a Communication Plan

6. Determining Project Standards and Procedures

7. Identifying and Assessing Risk

8. Creating a Preliminary Budget

9. Developing a Statement of Work

10. Setting a Baseline Project Plan

Within PVF's system development methodology, it is required that one of the first meetings focus on defining a project's scope. Although project scope information was not included in the SSR developed by Chris and Juanita, it was important that both shared the same vision for the project before moving too far along. During this activity, you should try to gain answers to and agreement on the following types of questions:

- What problem or opportunity does the project address?

- What are the quantifiable results to be achieved?

- What needs to be done?

- How will success be measured?

- How will we know when we are finished?

After defining the scope of the project, your next objective is to identify and document general alternative solutions for the current business problem or opportunity and assess each for feasibility so that a choice can be made as to which to consider during subsequent SDLC phases. In some instances, an off-the-shelf solution can be found. It is also important that any unique problems, constraints, and assumptions about the project be clearly stated.

2. *Dividing the Project into Manageable Tasks.* This is a very critical activity during the project planning process. Here, you must divide the entire project into manageable tasks, and then logically order them to ensure a smooth evolution between tasks. The definition of tasks and their sequence is often referred to as the **work breakdown structure.** Some tasks may be performed in parallel while others must follow one another sequentially. Task sequence will depend on which tasks produce deliverables needed in other tasks, when critical resources are available, constraints placed on the project by the client, and the process outlined in the SDLC.

As you will learn in later chapters, the SDLC consists of several phases. And within each phase, several activities need to be carried out. For example, during the analysis phase, activities must be performed to develop data and process flows. Within each activity, numerous tasks must be completed. For example, when developing a data flow diagram, tasks might include interviewing managers; identifying processes and data inflows, outflows, and transformations; and refining the data flow diagrams. The identification of processes and data flows and their combination into a data flow diagram represent separate tasks. Creating a work breakdown structure requires that you decompose phases into activities and activities into tasks.

Work breakdown structure: The process of dividing the project into manageable tasks and logically ordering them to ensure a smooth evolution between tasks.

It is important that each task be defined at an appropriate level of detail. Defining tasks in too much detail will make the management of the project unnecessarily complex. Discovering the optimal level of detail for representing tasks is a skill that you will develop through experience. For example, it may be very difficult to list tasks that require less than one hour of time to complete in a final work breakdown structure. Alternatively, choosing tasks that are too large in scope (for example, several weeks long) will not provide you with a clear sense of the status of the project or of the interdependencies between tasks. Some guidelines for defining a task are that a task should

- Be done by one person or a well-defined group
- Have a single and identifiable deliverable (The task is, however, the process of creating the deliverable.)
- Have a known method or technique
- Have well accepted predecessor and successor steps
- Be measurable so that percent completed can be determined

3. *Estimating Resources and Creating a Resource Plan.* The focus of this activity is on estimating resource requirements for each project activity and using this information to create a project resource plan. The resource plan is used to help assemble and deploy resources in the most effective manner (for example, you would not want to bring additional programmers onto the project at a rate faster than you could prepare them for useful work). Project estimating and deploying human resources is typically the most important resource planning activity as people are the most expensive element. Commonly used methods for estimating project size and thus the resource requirements for a project are briefly described in Figure 3-8. A detailed review of this topic is beyond the scope of our discussion; the interested reader is encouraged to see Pressman (1992).

Figure 3-8
Methods for estimating project size

Three commonly used techniques for estimating project size are decomposition, modeling, and function point estimating.

1. *Decomposition* is the process of breaking a project down into small manageable pieces that can be estimated (see Pressman, 1992). Estimates are obtained by "best guesses" and by reviewing historic productivity matrices for similar projects. When assigning human resources, average productivity should reflect the complexity of the project, experience of the person being assigned, or effects of project member turnover (see Abdel-Hamid, 1992). Due to its simplicity, decomposition is the most widely used estimation technique.
2. An example of a *modeling* technique is Boehm's (1981) *COnstructive COst MOdel* (COCOMO), an estimation model for determining the number of person months required for completing a project. The model uses parameters that were derived from prior projects of differing complexity (that is, the model was empirically developed). COCOMO uses these different parameters to predict human resource requirements for basic, intermediate, and very complex systems.
3. *Function point estimating* obtains a score for a particular project based upon the number and complexity of external inputs, external outputs, internal and external files, and system inquiries (e.g., a help screen) (see Grupe and Clevenger, 1991). Once a function point score is calculated for a given project, it can be compared to the number of function points of prior projects so that a project time estimate can be made.

Project time estimates for task completion and overall system quality are significantly influenced by the assignment of people to tasks. Although it is important to develop staff by assigning them new tasks in which they can learn new skills, it is equally important to make sure that project members are not in "over their heads" or working on a task that is not well suited to their skills. In essence, the assignment of one person to a task rather than some other person may have significant effects on the completion of an activity. This means that resource estimates may need to be revised based upon the skills of the actual person (or people) assigned to a particular activity. Figure 3-9 shows this relationship by indicating the relative programming speed versus the relative programming quality for three programmers. The figure suggests that Carl should not be assigned tasks in which completion time is critical and that Brenda should be assigned to tasks in which high quality is most vital.

One task assignment approach is to assign a single task type (or only a few task types) to each worker for the duration of the project. For example, you could assign one worker to create all computer displays and another to create all system reports. Such specialization ensures that both workers become efficient at their own particular tasks. Unfortunately, such an assignment may become boring if the task is too specialized or is long in duration. Alternatively, you could assign workers to a wider variety of tasks. This approach may lead, however, to lowered task efficiency. A middle ground would be to make assignments with a balance of both specialization and task variety. Of course, possible assignments depend upon the size of the development project and the skills of the project team. Regardless of the manner in which you assign tasks, make sure that each team member only works on one task at a time. Exceptions to this rule can occur when a task occupies only a small portion of a team member's time (for example, testing the programs developed by another team member) or during an emergency.

4. *Developing a Preliminary Schedule.* During this activity, you use the information regarding tasks and resource availability to assign time estimates to each activity in the work breakdown structure. This assignment will allow for the creation of target starting and ending dates for the project. Often the develop-

Figure 3-9
Tradeoffs between the quality of the program code versus the speed of programming (Adapted from Page-Jones, 1985)

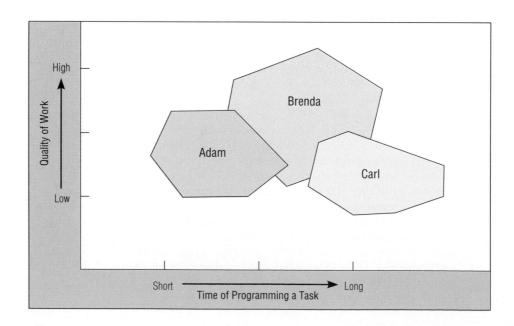

ment of target dates is an iterative process until a schedule is produced that is acceptable to the customer. Determining an acceptable schedule may require that you find additional or different resources or that the scope of the project be changed. The schedule may be represented as a Gantt or PERT chart, as discussed later in this chapter.

5. *Developing a Communication Plan.* The focus of this activity is to outline the communication procedures among management, project team members, and the customer. The communication plan includes when and how written and oral reports will be provided by the team, how team members will coordinate work, what messages will be sent to announce the project to interested parties, and what kinds of information will be shared with vendors and external contractors involved with the project. It is important that free and open communication occur among all parties, with respect for proprietary information and confidentiality with the customer (see Kettelhut, 1991).

6. *Determining Project Standards and Procedures.* During this activity, you will specify how various deliverables are produced and tested by you and your project team. For example, the team must decide on which CASE tools to use, how the standard SDLC might be modified, which SDLC methods will be used, documentation styles (for example, type fonts and margins for user manuals), how team members will report the status of their assigned activities, and terminology. In essence, setting project standards and procedures for work acceptance is a way to assure the development of a high-quality system. Also, you will find it much easier to train new team members when clear standards are in place. Organizational standards for project management and conduct make the determination of individual project standards easier and the interchange or sharing of personnel among different projects feasible.

7. *Identifying and Assessing Risk.* The focus of this activity is to identify sources of project risk and to estimate the consequences of those risks. Risks might arise from the use of new technology, resistance to change, availability of critical resources, competitive or regulatory actions, or team member inexperience with technology or the business area. Thus, you should continually try to identify and assess project risk. We discuss this important topic in greater detail in Chapter 6.

   The identification and assessment of risks are needed when making subsequent planning decisions. Since the identification of project risks is also a requirement of PVF's system development methodology, another early meeting between Chris and Juanita focused on risk assessment. At this meeting, they focused on identifying and describing possible negative outcomes of the project and their corresponding probabilities of occurrence. Although we have listed the identification of risks and the outline of project scope as discrete activities, both are highly related and often concurrently discussed.

8. *Creating a Preliminary Budget.* During this phase, you need to create a preliminary budget that outlines the planned expenses and revenues associated with your project. The project justification, or business case, will demonstrate that the benefits are worth these costs. The project budget is one part of the overall business case for the application and we will fully discuss the development of project budgets in Chapter 6.

9. *Developing a Statement of Work.* A major activity that occurs near the end of the project planning phase is the development of the statement of work. Developed primarily for the customer, this document outlines a description of all work that will be done and makes clear what the project will deliver. The

statement of work is useful to make sure that you, the customer, and other project team members have a clear understanding of the intended project size, duration, and outcomes.

10. *Setting a Baseline Project Plan.* Once all of the prior project planning activities have been completed, you will be able to develop a baseline project plan. This baseline plan reflects the best estimate of the project's tasks and resource requirements and is used to guide the next project phase—execution. It is worth noting that the baseline project plan is often changed after the project execution begins. As new information is acquired during project execution, the baseline plan will be updated.

At the end of the project planning phase, a review of the baseline project plan is conducted. The focus of this activity is to double-check all information in the baseline plan. As with the project initiation phase, it may be necessary to modify the plan; this means returning to prior project planning activities before proceeding. As with the Purchasing Fulfillment System project, you may submit the plan and make a brief presentation to the project steering committee at this time. At this meeting, the committee can endorse the plan, ask for modifications, or determine that it is not wise to continue the project (at least as currently outlined).

Executing the Project

Project execution: The third phase of the project management process in which the plans created in the prior phases (project initiation and planning) are put into action.

Project execution puts the baseline project plan into action. Within the context of the SDLC, project execution occurs primarily during the *analysis, design,* and *implementation* phases. During the development of the Purchasing Fulfillment System, Chris Martin was responsible for several activities during project execution, activities that could be generally described as follows:

1. *Executing the Baseline Project Plan.* Your primary focus is to oversee the execution of the baseline plan. This means that you initiate the execution of project activities, acquire and assign resources, orient and train new team members, keep the project on schedule, and assure the quality of project deliverables. As you might expect, this is a formidable task, but a task made much easier through the use of sound project management techniques. During the project, members will come and go from the project team at different times. You are responsible for initiating each team member into the team, including not only providing them with the resources they need but also building and rebuilding the team as a unit. You may want to plan social events, regular team project status meetings, team-level reviews of project deliverables, and other group events to mold the group into an effective team (see the box on "The Project Juke Box").

2. *Monitoring Project Progress Against the Baseline Plan.* One aspect of executing the baseline project plan relates to monitoring your actual progress against the baseline plan. If the project gets ahead of (or behind) schedule, you may have to make adjustments to resources, activities, and budgets. Monitoring project activities not only enables modifications to be made to the current plan but also provides insights for estimating future activities and projects. Additionally, measuring the time and effort expended on each activity will help you improve the accuracy of future estimations. It is possible with project schedule charts, like Gantt charts (see Figure 3-10a later in this chapter), to show progress against a plan; and it is easy with PERT charts (see Figure 3-10b later in this chapter) to understand the ramifications of delays in an

activity. Monitoring progress also means that the team leader must evaluate and appraise each team member, occasionally change work assignments or request changes in personnel, and provide feedback to the employee's supervisor.

3. *Managing Changes to the Baseline Project Plan.* You will also encounter pressure to make changes to the baseline plan. At PVF, policies dictate that only approved changes to the project specification can be made and all changes must be reflected in the baseline plan and project workbook, including all charts. For example, if Juanita suggests a significant change to the existing design of the Purchasing Fulfillment System, a formal change request must be approved by the steering committee. In this request, it should be made clear why changes are desired and include a description of all possible impacts on prior and subsequent activities, project resources, and the overall project schedule. Of course, Chris would have to help Juanita develop such a request. This information will allow the project steering committee to more easily evaluate the costs and benefits of a significant midcourse change.

> **The Project Juke Box**
>
> Project leaders have been known to use various means to motivate team members and to create a collective sense of responsibility. One project leader discovered that many of his team members had a common interest in bebop and doowap music and arranged for a juke box filled with such music to be installed in the lunch room of the temporary offices of his team. The juke box became the team's symbol and the envy of other company employees. The leader also planned a racquetball tournament, a trip to a play, and a group reservation at a outdoor challenge camp and at a professional conference. Although the team members came from eight different departments and only two knew each other before the project, team morale remained high, the team was given a productivity award by upper management, and team members formed lasting friendships that had many benefits after the project was over. As a final gift, the leader gave each team member a custom-made pin of a juke box at the project close-down party.

In addition to changes occurring through formal request, changes may also occur from events far outside your control. In fact, there are numerous events that may motivate making a change to the baseline project plan, including the following possibilities:

- A slipped completion date for an activity

- A bungled activity that must be re-done

- The identification of a new activity that becomes evident later in the project

- An unforeseen change in personnel due to sickness, resignation, or termination

When an event occurs that delays the completion of an activity, you typically have two choices: devise a way to get back on schedule or revise the plan. Devising a way to get back on schedule is the preferred approach because no changes to the plan will have to be made. The ability to head off and smoothly work around problems is a critical skill that you need to master.

As you will see later in the chapter, project schedule charts are very helpful in assessing the impact of change. Using such charts, you can quickly see if the completion time of other activities will be affected by changes in the duration of a given activity or if the whole project completion date will change. Often you will have to find a way to rearrange the activities since the ultimate project completion data may be rather fixed. There may be a penalty to the organization (even legal action) if the expected completion date is not met.

4. *Maintaining the Project Workbook.* As in all project phases, maintaining complete records of all project events is necessary. The workbook provides the documentation new team members require to quickly assimilate project tasks; it provides a history to explain why certain design decisions were made; and it is a primary source of information for producing all project reports.

5. *Communicating the Project Status.* The project manager is responsible for keeping all team members—system developers, managers, and customers—abreast of the project status. Clear communication is a requirement for creating a shared understanding of the activities and goals of the project; such an understanding assures better coordination of activities. This means that the entire project plan should be shared with the entire project team and any revisions to the plan should be communicated to all interested parties so that everyone understands how the plan is evolving. Procedures for communicating project activities can range from formal activities to more informal ones. Keep in mind that different types of procedures are appropriate for different types of communication. Some are useful for *informing* others of project status, others for *resolving* issues, and others for keeping *permanent records* of information and events. Table 3-4 lists numerous communication procedures, their level of formality, and most likely use. Whichever procedure you use, frequent communication helps to assure project success (Kettelhut, 1991).

This section outlined your role as the project manager during the execution of the baseline project plan (see Table 3-5). The ease with which the project can be managed is significantly influenced by the quality of prior project phases. If you develop a high-quality project plan, it is much more likely that the project will be successfully executed. The next section describes your role during project close-down, the final phase of the project management process.

TABLE 3-4   Project Team Communication Methods

Procedure	Formality	Use
Project Workbook	High	Inform Permanent Record
Meetings	Medium to High	Resolve Issues
Seminars and Workshops	Low to Medium	Inform
Project Newsletters	Medium to High	Inform
Status Reports	High	Inform
Specification Documents	High	Inform Permanent Record
Minutes of Meetings	High	Inform Permanent Record
Bulletin Boards	Low	Inform
Memos	Medium to High	Inform
Brown Bag Lunches	Low	Inform
Hallway Discussions	Low	Inform Resolve Issues

TABLE 3-5   Elements of Project Execution

1. Executing the Baseline Project Plan
2. Monitoring Project Progress Against the Baseline Plan
3. Managing Changes to the Baseline Project Plan
4. Maintaining the Project Workbook
5. Communicating the Project Status

Closing Down the Project

The focus of **project close-down** is to bring the project to an end. Projects can conclude with a *natural* or an *unnatural* termination. A natural termination occurs when the requirements of the project have been met—the project has been completed and is a success. An unnatural termination occurs when the project is stopped before completion. Several events can cause an unnatural termination to a project. For example, it may be learned that the assumption used to guide the project proved to be false, or that the performance of the system or development group was somehow inadequate, or that the requirements are no longer relevant or valid in the customer's business environment. The most likely reasons for the unnatural termination of a project relates to running out of time or money, or both (for a humorous "Top 10" list related to signs of project failure, see Table 3-6). Regardless of the project termination outcome, there are several activities that must be performed: closing down the project, conducting post-project reviews, and closing the customer contract. Within the context of the SDLC, project close-down occurs after the *implementation* phase; the system *maintenance* phase typically represents an ongoing series of projects, each needing to be individually managed.

Project close-down: The final phase of the project management process that focuses on bringing a project to an end.

1. *Closing Down the Project.* During close-down, you will perform several diverse activities. If, for example, you have several team members working with you, project completion may signify job and assignment changes for some members. You will likely be required to assess each team member and provide an appraisal for personnel files and for salary determination. You may also want to provide career advice to team members, write letters to superiors praising special accomplishments of team members, and send thank you letters to those who helped but were not team members. As project manager, you must be prepared to handle possible negative personnel issues such as job termination, especially if the project was not successful. When closing down the project, it is also important to notify all interested parties that the project has been completed and to finalize all project documentation and financial records so that a final review of the project can be conducted. You should also celebrate the accomplishments of the team. Some teams will hold a party, and

TABLE 3-6 Top 10 Signs of IS Project Failure—With Apologies to David Letterman

10. All software purchased is Version 1.0.

9. All hardware purchased comes from a discount company called Kludges "R" Us.

8. Project manager is spotted reading *PCs for Dummies.*

7. Application developers think Java OLE is something to be ordered at a coffee shop.

6. Network administrators question the usefulness of an ATM system that doesn't accept bank cards.

5. Hardware technicians try to use RAID to cure software bugs.

4. Size of database balloons reaches IWSTBTB (It Wasn't Supposed To Be That Big) proportions.

3. Consultants revamp system architecture, which had been totally revamped only a month ago by a different group of consultants.

2. After system is finally deployed, end users mistake their computer mouses for foot pedals.

1. CIO is seen faxing his resume.

Reprinted with permission of Cahners Publishing Company, a division of Reed Elsevier Business Information, Inc.

each team member may receive memorabilia (for example, a tee shirt with "I survived the X project"). The goal is to celebrate the team's effort to bring a difficult task to a successful conclusion.

2. *Conducting Post-Project Reviews.* Once you have closed down the project, final reviews of the project should be conducted with management and customers. The objective of these reviews is to determine the strengths and weaknesses of project deliverables, the processes used to create them, and the project management process. It is important that everyone understands what went right and what went wrong in order to improve the process for the next project. Remember, the systems development methodology adopted by an organization is a living guideline that must undergo continual improvement.

3. *Closing the Customer Contract.* The focus of this final activity is to ensure that all contractual terms of the project have been met. A project governed by a contractual agreement is typically not completed until agreed to by both parties, often in writing. Thus, it is paramount that you gain agreement from your customer that all contractual obligations have been met and that further work is either their responsibility or covered under another system service request or contract.

Close-down is a very important activity since a project is not complete until it is closed and it is at close-down that projects are deemed a success or failure. Completion also signifies the chance to begin a new project and apply what you have learned. Now that you have an understanding of the project management process, the next section will describe specific techniques used in systems development for representing and scheduling activities and resources.

REPRESENTING AND SCHEDULING PROJECT PLANS

Gantt chart: A graphical representation of a project that shows each task activity as a horizontal bar whose length is proportional to its time for completion.

A project manager has a wide variety of techniques available for depicting and documenting project plans. These planning documents can take the form of graphical or textual reports although graphical reports have become most popular for depicting project plans (see Figure 3-10). A **Gantt chart** is a graphical representation of a project that shows each task activity as a horizontal bar whose length is proportional to its time for completion (Figure 3-10a). Different colors, shades, or shapes can be used to highlight different kinds of tasks. For example, those activities on the critical path (defined below) may be in red and a summary task (a subproject) could have a special bar. Planned versus actual times or progress for an activity can be compared by parallel bars of different colors, shades, or shapes. Gantt charts do not show how tasks must be ordered (precedence), but simply show when an activity should begin and when it should end. Consequently, Gantt charts are often more useful for depicting relatively simple projects or subparts of a larger project, the activities of a single worker, and for monitoring the progress of activities compared to scheduled completion dates.

PERT chart: A diagram that depicts project activities and their inter-relationships. PERT stands for Program Evaluation Review Technique.

A **PERT** (Program Evaluation Review Technique) **chart** is a graphical depiction of project task activities and their inter-relationships (Figure 3-10b). As with a Gantt chart, different types of tasks can be highlighted by different features on the PERT chart. The distinguishing feature of a PERT is that the ordering of activities is shown by connecting an activity with its predecessor and successor activities. However, the relative size of a node, which represents an activity, or arcs does not imply the activity's duration.

Figure 3-10

Graphical diagrams for depicting project plans

(a) Gantt chart

(b) PERT chart

Sometimes a PERT chart is preferable; other times a Gantt chart more easily shows certain aspects of a project:

- Gantt visually shows the duration of activities whereas PERT visually shows the sequence dependencies between activities

- Gantt visually shows the time overlap of activities whereas PERT does not show time overlap but which activities could be done in parallel

- Some forms of Gantt charts can visually show slack time available within an earliest start and latest finish duration whereas PERT shows this by data within activity rectangles

Project managers also use textual reports depicting resource utilization by tasks, project variances, and cost distributions to control activities. For example, Figure 3-11 shows a screen from Microsoft Project for Windows® that summarizes all project activities, their durations in weeks, and their scheduled starting and ending dates. Regardless of the project reporting or representation technique, most project managers use computer-based systems to help develop their graphical and textual reports. Later in this chapter, we will discuss these automated systems in more detail.

When managing a project, a manager will periodically review the status of all ongoing project activities. During this review, the manager will assess whether the activities will be completed early, on time, or late. If early or late, the duration of the activity (see column 2 of Figure 3-11) can be updated. Once changed, the scheduled start and finish times of all subsequent activities will also change. Making such a change will also alter a Gantt or PERT chart used to represent the project activities. The ability to easily make changes to a project is a very powerful feature of most project management environments. It allows the project manager to easily gain a clear idea of how activity duration changes impact the overall project completion date. It is also useful for examining "what if" scenarios of adding or reducing resources for an activity and assessing the overall impact on the project.

Resource: Any person, group of people, piece of equipment, or material used in accomplishing an activity.

Critical path scheduling: A scheduling technique where the order and duration of the sequence of activities directly affect the completion date of a project.

Representing Project Plans

Project scheduling and management require that time, costs, and resources be controlled. **Resources** are any person, group of people, piece of equipment, or material used in accomplishing an activity and PERT is a **critical path scheduling** technique

Figure 3-11
Textual report showing project activities, their duration, and scheduled starting and ending dates

used for controlling resources. A critical path refers to a sequence of activities whose order and durations directly affect the completion date of a project. Of the many project scheduling methods, PERT is one of the most widely used and best-known and requires that a project have

- Well-defined activities that have a clear beginning and end point

- Activities that can be worked on independently of other activities

- Activities that are ordered

- Activities that when completed serve the purpose of the project

A major strength of the PERT technique is its ability to represent completion time variability. Because of this, it is more often used than Gantt charts to manage projects such as information systems development where variability in the duration of activities is the norm. PERT charts use a graphical network diagram composed of circles or boxes representing activities and connecting arrows showing required work flows (see Figure 3-12).[1]

Constructing a Gantt and PERT Chart at Pine Valley Furniture

Although Pine Valley Furniture has historically been strictly a manufacturing company, they have recently entered the direct sales market for selected target markets. One of the fastest growing of these is economically priced furniture suitable for college students. Management has requested that a new Sales Promotion Tracking System (SPTS) be developed. This project has already successfully moved through project initiation and is currently in the detailed project planning stage, which corresponds to the SDLC phase of *project initiation and planning.* The SPTS will be used to track the sales purchases by college students for the next fall semester. Students typically purchase low-priced beds, bookcases, desks, tables, chairs, and dressers. Since PVF does not normally stock a large quantity of lower-priced items, management feels that a tracking system will help provide information about the college student market that can be used for follow-up sales promotions (for example, a midterm futon sale).

---

[1]There are several variations as to how PERT diagrams can be drawn. For example, it is common to use arrows to represent activities and circles or boxes to represent the event of starting or ending an activity. The discussion of these subtle differences is not important for our presentation. We have chosen to use the PERT diagram style most commonly used in project management software.

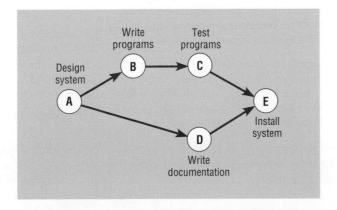

Figure 3-12
PERT chart showing activities and sequence

The project, then, is to design, develop, and implement this information system before the start of the fall term in order to collect sales data at the next major buying period. This deadline gives the project team 24 weeks to develop and implement the system. The Systems Priority Board at PVF wants to make a decision this week based on the feasibility of completing the project within the 24-week deadline. Using PVF's project planning methodology, the project manager, Jim Woo, knows that the next step is to construct Gantt and PERT charts of the project to represent the baseline project plan so that he can use these charts to estimate the likelihood of completing the project within 24 weeks. A major activity of project planning focuses on dividing the project into manageable activities, estimating times for each, and sequencing their order. The steps Jim followed to do this are outlined below.

1. *Identify each activity to be completed in the project.* After discussing the project with PVF's management, sales, and development staff, Jim identified the following major activities for the project:

   - Requirements collection
   - Screen design
   - Report design
   - Database construction
   - Software programming
   - System testing
   - User documentation creation
   - System installation

2. *Determine time estimates and calculate the expected completion time for each activity.* A standard method for determining the expected completion time for an activity is based on a calculation using three time estimates: the *optimistic time, realistic time,* and *pessimistic time.* The optimistic (o) and pessimistic (p) times reflect the minimum and maximum possible periods of time for an activity to be completed. The realistic time (r) reflects the planner's "best guess" of the amount of time the activity actually will require for completion. Once each of these estimates is made for an activity, an estimated time (ET) can be calculated. Since the estimated completion time should be closest to the realistic time (r), it is weighted four times more than the optimistic (o) and pessimistic (p) times using the following formula:

$$ET = \frac{o + 4r + p}{6} \qquad 1$$

   where
   ET = estimated time for the completion for an activity
   o = optimistic completion time for an activity
   r = realistic completion time for an activity
   p = pessimistic completion time for an activity

   In conclusion, after identifying the major project activities, Jim established optimistic, realistic, and pessimistic time estimates for each activity. These numbers were then used to calculate the expected completion times for all project activities. Figure 3-13 shows the estimated time calculations for each activity of the SPTS project.

3. *Determine the sequence of the activities and precedence relationships among all activities by constructing a Gantt and PERT chart.* This step makes it possible to understand the interrelationships among all activities within the overall proj-

| | TIME ESTIMATE | | | EXPECTED TIME (ET) |
| | (in weeks) | | | $\dfrac{o + 4r + p}{6}$ |
ACTIVITY	o	r	p	6
1. Requirements Collection	1	5	9	5
2. Screen Design	5	6	7	6
3. Report Design	3	6	9	6
4. Database Construction	1	2	3	2
5. User Documentation	3	6	7	5.5
6. Programming	4	5	6	5
7. Testing	1	3	5	3
8. Installation	1	1	1	1

Figure 3-13
Estimated time calculations
for the SPTS project

ect. Jim starts by determining the precedence relationships between activities. Depending upon the complexity and size of the project, several project members may be asked to assist in making activity time and sequencing estimates. The results of this analysis for the SPTS project are shown in Figure 3-14. The first row of this figure shows that no activities precede requirements collection. Row 2 shows that screen design must be preceded by requirements collection and row 4 shows that both screen and report design must precede database construction. Thus, activities may be preceded by zero, one, or more activities.

Using the estimated time and activity sequencing information (Figures 3-13 and 3-14), Jim can now construct Gantt and PERT charts of the project's activities. To construct the Gantt chart, a horizontal bar is drawn for each activity that reflects its sequence and duration (Figure 3-15). The Gantt chart may not, however, show direct interrelationships between activities. For example, just because the database design activity begins right after the screen design and report design bars finish does not imply that these two activities must finish before database design can begin. To show such precedence relationships, a PERT chart must be used. The Gantt chart in Figure 3-15 does, however, show precedence relationships.

PERT charts have two major components: arrows and nodes. Arrows reflect the sequence of activities while nodes reflect activities that consume time and resources. A PERT chart for the SPTS project is shown in Figure 3-16. This diagram has eight nodes labeled 1 through 8.

4. *Determine the critical path.* The critical path of a PERT network is represented by the sequence of connected activities that produce the longest overall time period. All nodes and activities within this sequence are referred to as being "on"

ACTIVITY	PRECEDING ACTIVITY
1. Requirements Collection	—
2. Screen Design	1
3. Report Design	1
4. Database Construction	2,3
5. User Documentation	4
6. Programming	4
7. Testing	6
8. Installation	5,7

Figure 3-14
Sequencing of activities
within the SPTS project

the critical path. The critical path represents the shortest time in which a project can be completed. In other words, any activity on the critical path that is delayed in completion will result in delaying the entire project. Nodes not on the critical path, however, can be delayed (for some amount of time) without delaying the final completion of the project. These nodes are said to contain **slack time** and allow the project manager some flexibility in scheduling.

Slack time: The amount of time that an activity can be delayed without delaying the project.

Figure 3-17 shows the PERT diagram for the SPTS project in the form Jim used to determine the critical path and expected completion time for the project. To determine the critical path, Jim calculated the earliest and latest expected completion time for each activity. He found each activity's *earliest* expected completion time (T_E) by summing the estimated time (ET) for each activity from left to right (that is, in precedence order), starting at activity 1 and working toward activity 8. In this case T_E for activity 8 is equal to 22 weeks. If two or more activities precede an activity, the largest expected completion time of these activities is used in calculating the new activity's

Figure 3-16
PERT chart for the SPTS
project

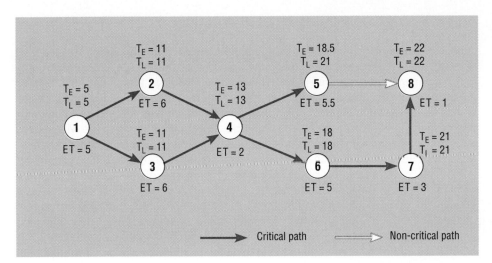

expected completion time. For example, since activity 8 is preceded by both activities 5 and 7, the largest expected completion time between 5 and 7 is 21, so T_E for activity 8 is 21 + 1, or 22. The earliest expected completion time for the last activity of the project represents the amount of time the project *should* take to complete. Because the time of each activity can vary, however, the projected completion time only represents an estimate. The project may in fact require more or less time for completion.

The *latest* expected completion time (T_L) refers to the time in which an activity can be completed without delaying the project. To find the values for each activity's latest expected completion time (T_L), Jim started at activity 8 and set T_L equal to the final T_E (22 weeks). Next, he worked right to left toward activity 1 and subtracted the expected time for each activity. The slack time for each activity is equal to the difference between its latest and earliest expected completion time ($T_L - T_E$). Figure 3-18 shows the slack time calculations for all activities of the SPTS project. *All activities with a slack time equal to zero are on the critical path.* Thus, all activities except 5 are on the critical path. Part of the diagram shows two critical paths (see Figure 3-17), between activities 1-2-4 and 1-3-4, since both of these *parallel* activities have zero slack.

It is also possible to determine the probability of completing a project by a given date when using PERT. Using the activity completion time estimates, that is, the optimistic, pessimistic, and realistic time estimates for each activity, it is possible to calculate the probability of completing the entire project by a given date. The steps used to conduct this analysis are beyond the scope of this chapter. The interested reader is encouraged to see Miller (1989).

ACTIVITY	T_E	T_L	SLACK $T_L - T_E$	ON CRITICAL PATH
1	5	5	0	✓
2	11	11	0	✓
3	11	11	0	✓
4	13	13	0	✓
5	18.5	21	2.5	
6	18	18	0	✓
7	21	21	0	✓
8	22	22	0	✓

Figure 3-18
Activity slack time calculations for the SPTS project

USING PROJECT MANAGEMENT SOFTWARE

A wide variety of automated project management tools are available to help you manage a development project and new versions of these tools are continuously being developed and released by software vendors. Most of the available tools have a common set of features that include the ability to define and order tasks, assign resources to tasks, and easily modify tasks and resources. Project management tools are available to run on IBM-compatible personal computers, the Macintosh, and larger mainframe and workstation-based systems. Key dimensions on which these systems vary include the number of task activities supported, the complexity of relationships, system processing and storage requirements, and, of course, cost. Prices for these systems can range from a few hundred dollars for personal computer-based systems to more than $100,000 for large-scale multi-project systems. According to Julia M. Wilson of the *Project Management Institute,* project managers need high-end project management systems when projects exceed 500 independent tasks on the work breakdown structure (Thé, 1996). Yet a lot can be done with systems like Microsoft Project as well as public domain and shareware systems. For example, there are numerous shareware project management programs (e.g., Calendar Quick, Delegator, and SureTrak) that can be downloaded from the World Wide Web (e.g., www. download.com) and online bulletin boards. Since these systems are continuously changing, you should comparison shop before choosing a particular package. Many computer publications such as *PC Magazine, PC Week, MacUser,* and *Datamation* regularly review and contrast available systems (see box "Automating Process Management" for the possible results from using project management software).

> **Automating Process Management**
>
> The most sophisticated project management software do not provide automated support for just project planning but rather for all activities needed to control a project's outcome. These include not only planning (such as with Gantt and PERT charts) but also project tracking, cost estimating, estimating size of software and other project deliverables (which aids in planning), measuring quality and defects, assessing alternative plans, and measuring project productivity. Through a combination of a well-proven systems development methodology (supported by a CASE tool called Process Engineer from LBMS, Inc.) and process management automation (including Microsoft Project) involving support in all of these areas, Holiday Inns Worldwide achieved roughly a 33 percent reduction in the number of tasks needed in systems development projects.
>
> *(Adapted from Butler, 1994)*

To help you get a feel for using project management software, examples of the types of activities you would perform when using a system are illustrated in this section. One particular project management system that has had consistent high marks in computer publication reviews is Microsoft Project for Windows. When using this system to manage a project, you need to perform at least the following activities:

- Establish a project starting or ending date

- Enter activities and assign activity relationships

- Select a scheduling method to review project information

Establishing a Project Starting Date

When using a project management system, the first step is to define the general project information. This information typically includes the name of the project and project manager and the starting or ending date of the project. Starting and ending dates are used to schedule future activities or backdate others (see below) based upon their duration and relationships to other activities. An example from Microsoft Project for Windows of the data entry screen for establishing a project starting or ending date is shown in Figure 3-19. This shows PVF's Purchasing Fulfillment System project. Here, the starting date for the project is Monday, November 23, 1998.

Figure 3-19
Establishing a project starting date in Microsoft Project for Windows

Entering Tasks and Assigning Task Relationships

The next step in defining a project is to define project tasks and their relationships. For the Purchasing Fulfillment System project, Chris defined twelve tasks to be completed when performing the initial system analysis activities of the project. The task entry screen is shown in Figure 3-20 and is much like a financial spreadsheet program in the way in which information is entered. Specifically, the user moves the cursor to a cell with arrow keys or the mouse and then simply enters a textual *Name* and a numeric *Duration* for each activity. *Scheduled Start* and *Scheduled Finish* are automatically entered based upon the project start date and duration. To set an activity relationship, the *ID* number (or numbers) of the activity that must be completed before the start of the current activity is entered in the *Predecessors* column. Additional codes under this column make the precedence relationships more precise. For example, consider the Predecessor column for ID 6. The entry in this cell says that activity 6 cannot start until one day before the finish of activity 5. Microsoft Project provides many different options for precedence and delays such as in this example, but discussion of these is beyond the scope of our coverage. The project management software uses this information to construct Gantt, PERT, and other project-related reports.

Selecting a Scheduling Method and Reviewing Project Reports

Once information about all the activities for a project has been entered, it is very easy to review the information in a variety of graphical and textual formats using displays or printed reports. For example, Figure 3-20 shows the project information in a Gantt chart screen while Figure 3-21 shows the project information in a condensed PERT chart display. You can easily change how you view the information by making a selection from the *View* menu shown in Figure 3-21.

Figure 3-20
Entering tasks and assigning task relationships in Microsoft Project for Windows

Figure 3-21
Viewing project information as a PERT chart in Microsoft Project for Windows

As mentioned in the chapter, interim project reports to management will often compare actual progress to plans. Figure 3-22 illustrates how Microsoft Project shows progress, by a solid line within the activity bar. In this figure, activities 2 and 3 are almost done, but there remains a small percentage of work on each activity, as shown by the incomplete solid lines within the bars for these activities. Assuming that this screen represents the status of the project on December 10, 1998, the third

Figure 3-22
Gantt chart showing progress
on activities versus planned
durations

activity is approximately on schedule, but the second activity is behind its expected completion date. Tabular reports can summarize the same information.

This brief introduction to project management software has only scratched the surface to show you the power and the features of these systems. Other features that are widely available and especially useful for multi-person projects relate to resource usage and utilization. Resource-related features typically allow you to define resource characteristics such as standard costing rates and daily availability via a calendar that records holidays, working hours, and vacations—particularly useful for billing and scoping project costs. Often, resources are shared across multiple projects which could significantly affect a project's schedule. Depending upon how projects are billed within an organization, assigning and billing resources to tasks is a very time-consuming activity for most project managers. The features provided in these powerful tools can greatly ease both the planning and managing of projects so that both project and management resources are effectively utilized.

SUMMARY

The focus of this chapter was on managing information system projects and the role of the project manager in this process. A project manager has both technical and managerial skills and is ultimately responsible for determining the size, scope, and resource requirements for a project. Once a project is deemed feasible by an organization, the project manager ensures that the project meets the customer's needs and is delivered within budget and time constraints. To manage the project, the project manager must execute four primary activities: project initiation, project planning, project execution, and project close-down. The focus of project initiation is on assessing the size, scope, and complexity of a project and establishing procedures to support later project activities. The focus of project planning is on defining clear, discrete activities and the work needed to complete each activity. The focus of project execution is on putting the plans developed in project initiation and planning into action. Project close-down focuses on bringing the project to an end.

Gantt and PERT charts are powerful graphical techniques used in planning and controlling projects. Both Gantt and PERT scheduling techniques require that a project have activities that can be defined as having a clear beginning and end, can be worked on independently of other activities, are ordered, and are such that their completion signifies the end of the project. Gantt charts use horizontal bars to represent the beginning, duration, and ending of an activity. PERT is a critical path scheduling method that shows the inter-relationships between activities. Critical path scheduling refers to planning methods whereby the order and duration of the project's activities directly affect the completion date of the project. These charts show when activities can begin and end, which activities cannot be delayed without delaying the whole project, how much slack time each activity has, and progress against planned activities. PERT's ability to use probability estimates in determining critical paths and deadlines makes it a widely used technique for very complex projects.

A wide variety of automated tools for assisting the project manager are available. Most tools have common features including the ability to define and order tasks, assign resources to tasks, and modify tasks and resources. Systems vary regarding the number of activities supported, the complexity of relationships, processing and storage requirements, and cost.

K E Y   T E R M S

Critical path scheduling	Project execution	Project workbook
Gantt chart	Project initiation	Resource
PERT chart	Project management	Slack time
Project	Project manager	Work breakdown
Project close-down	Project planning	structure

R E V I E W   Q U E S T I O N S

1. Define each of the following terms:
   a. critical path scheduling
   b. Gantt chart
   c. PERT
   d. project close-down
   e. project execution
   f. project initiation
   g. project planning
   h. project workbook
   i. resource
   j. slack time
   k. baseline project plan
   l. earliest expected completion time
   m. latest expected completion time

2. Contrast the following terms:
   a. critical path scheduling, Gantt, PERT, slack time
   b. project, project management, project manager
   c. project initiation, project planning, project execution, project close-down
   d. project workbook, resources, work breakdown structure

3. Discuss the reasons why organizations undertake information system projects.

4. List and describe the common skills and activities of a project manager. Which skill do you think is most important? Why?

5. Describe the activities performed by the project manager during project initiation.

6. Describe the activities performed by the project manager during project planning.

7. Describe the activities performed by the project manager during project execution.

8. List various project team communication methods and describe an example of the type of information that might be shared among team members using each method.

9. Describe the activities performed by the project manager during project close-down.

10. What characteristics must a project have in order for critical path scheduling to be applicable?

11. Describe the steps involved in making a Gantt chart.

12. Describe the steps involved in making a PERT chart.

13. In which phase of the systems development life cycle does project planning typically occur? In which phase does project management occur?

14. What are some reasons why one activity may have to precede another activity before the second activity can begin? In other words, what causes precedence relationships between project activities?

PROBLEMS AND EXERCISES

1. Match the following terms to the appropriate definitions.

    _____ project

    _____ project workbook

    _____ Gantt chart
    _____ PERT chart

    _____ baseline project plan

    _____ critical path

   a. those activities whose order and durations directly affect the project completion date
   b. the best estimate of a project's tasks and resource requirements
   c. a repository of all project documentation
   d. a planned undertaking of related activities to reach an objective that has a beginning and an end
   e. a graphical representation of project activities using horizontal bars
   f. program evaluation review technique

2. Which of the four phases of the project management process do you feel is most challenging? Why?

3. What are some sources of risk in a systems analysis and design project and how does a project manager cope with risk during the stages of project management?

4. Search computer magazines for recent reviews of project management software. Which packages seem to be most popular? What are the relative strengths and weaknesses of each package software? What advice would you give to someone intending to buy project management software for their PC? Why?

5. How are information system projects similar to other types of projects? How are they different? Are the project management packages you evaluated in Problem and Exercise 4 suited for all types of projects or for particular types of projects? Which package is best suited for information systems projects? Why?

6. If given the chance, would you become the manager of an information systems project? If so, why? Prepare a list of the strengths that you would bring to the project as its manager. If not, why not? What would it take for you to feel more comfortable managing an information systems project? Prepare a list and timetable

for the necessary training you would need to feel more comfortable about managing an information systems project.

7. Calculate the expected time for the following tasks.

Task	Optimistic Time	Most Likely Time	Pessimistic Time	Expected Time
A	3	7	11	
B	5	9	13	
C	1	2	9	
D	2	3	16	
E	2	4	18	
F	3	4	11	
G	1	4	7	
H	3	4	5	
I	2	4	12	
J	4	7	9	

8. A project has been defined to contain the following list of activities along with their required times for completion.

Activity	Time (weeks)	Immediate Predecessors
1 - collect requirements	2	—
2 - analyze processes	3	1
3 - analyze data	3	2
4 - design processes	7	2
5 - design data	6	2
6 - design screens	1	3, 4
7 - design reports	5	4, 5
8 - program	4	6, 7
9 - test and document	8	7
10 - install	2	8, 9

a. Draw a PERT chart for the activities.
b. Calculate the earliest expected completion time.
c. Show the critical path.
d. What would happen if Activity 6 was revised to take six weeks instead of one week?

9. Construct a Gantt chart for the project defined in Problem and Exercise 8 above.

10. Look again at the activities outlined in Problem and Exercise 8. Assume that your team is in its first week of the project and has discovered that each of the activity duration estimates is wrong. Activity 2 will take only two weeks to complete. Activities 4 and 7 will each take three times longer than anticipated. All other activities will take twice as long to complete as previously estimated. In addition, a new activity, number 11, has been added. It will take one week to complete and its immediate predecessors are activities 10 and 9. Adjust the PERT chart and recalculate the earliest expected completion times.

11. Construct Gantt and PERT charts for a project you are or will be involved in. Choose a project of sufficient depth at either work, home, or school. Identify the activities to be completed, determine the sequence of the activities, and construct a diagram reflecting the starting, ending, duration, and precedence (PERT only) relationships among all activities. For your PERT chart, use the procedure in this chapter to determine time estimates for each activity and calculate the expected time for each activity. Now determine the critical path and the early and late starting and finishing times for each activity. Which activities have slack time?

12. For the project you described in Problem and Exercise 11, assume that the worst has happened. A key team member has dropped out of the project and has been assigned to another project in another part of the country. The remaining team members are having personality clashes. Key deliverables for the project are now due much earlier than expected. In addition, you have just determined that a key phase in the early life of the project will now take much longer than you had originally expected. To make matters worse, your boss absolutely will not accept that this project cannot be completed by this new deadline. What will you do to account for these project changes and problems? Begin by reconstructing your Gantt and PERT charts and determine a strategy for dealing with the specific changes and problems described above. If new resources are needed to meet the new deadline, outline the rationale that you will use to convince your boss that these additional resources are critical to the success of the project.

13. Assume you have a project with seven activities labeled A–G (below). Derive the earliest completion time (or early finish—EF), latest completion time (or late finish—LF), and slack for each of the following tasks (begin at time = 0). Which tasks are on the critical path? Draw a Gantt chart for these tasks.

Task	Preceding Event	Expected Duration	EF	LF	Slack	Critical Path?
A	—	5				
B	A	3				
C	A	4				
D	C	6				
E	B, C	4				
F	D	1				
G	D, E, F	5				

14. Draw a PERT chart for the tasks shown in Problem 13. Highlight the critical path.

15. Assume you have a project with 10 activities labeled A–J (below). Derive the earliest completion time (or early finish—EF), latest completion time (or late finish—LF), and slack for each of the following tasks (begin at time = 0). Which tasks are on the critical path? Highlight the critical path on your PERT chart.

Activity	Preceding Event	Expected Duration	EF	LF	Slack	Critical Path?
A	—	4				
B	A	5				
C	A	6				
D	A	7				
E	A, D	6				
F	C, E	5				
G	D, E	4				
H	E	3				
I	F, G	4				
J	H, I	5				

16. Draw a Gantt chart for the tasks shown in Problem 15.

17. Assume you have a project with 11 activities labeled A–K (below). Derive the earliest completion time (or early finish—EF), latest completion time (or late finish—LF), and slack for each of the following tasks (begin at time = 0). Which tasks are on the critical path? Draw both Gantt and PERT charts for these tasks and make sure you highlight the critical path on your PERT chart.

Activity	Preceding Event	Expected Duration	EF	LF	Slack	Critical Path?
A	—	2				
B	A	3				
C	B	4				
D	C	5				
E	C	4				
F	D, E	3				
G	F	4				
H	F	6				
I	G, H	5				
J	G	2				
K	I, J	4				

18. Make a list of the tasks that you performed when designing your schedule of classes for this term. Develop a table showing each task, its duration, preceding event(s), and expected duration. Develop a PERT chart for these tasks. Highlight the critical path on your PERT chart.

FIELD EXERCISES

1. Identify someone who manages an information systems project in an organization. Describe to him or her each of the skills and activities listed in Table 3-1. Determine which items they are responsible for on the project. Of those they are responsible for, determine which are the more challenging and why. Of those they are not responsible for, determine why not and who is responsible for these activities. What other skills and activities, not listed in Table 3-1, is this person responsible for in managing this project?

2. Identify someone who manages an information systems project in an organization. Describe to him or her each of the project planning elements in Table 3-3. Determine the extent to which each of these elements is part of that person's project planning process. If that person is not able to perform some of these planning activities, or if he or she cannot spend as much time on any of these activities as he or she would like, determine what barriers are prohibitive for proper project planning.

3. Identify someone who manages an information systems project (or other team-based project) in an organization. Describe to him or her each of the project team communication methods listed in Table 3-4. Determine which types of communication methods are used for team communication and describe which he or she feels are best for communicating various types of information.

4. Identify someone who manages an information systems project in an organization. Describe to them each of the project execution elements in Table 3-5. Determine the extent to which each of these elements is part of that person's project execution process. If that person does not perform some of these activities, or if he or she cannot spend much time on any of these activities, determine what barriers or reasons prevent performing all project execution activities.

5. Interview a sample of project managers. Divide your sample into two small sub-samples, one for managers of information systems projects and one for managers of other types of projects. Ask each respondent to identify personal leadership attri-

butes that contribute to successful project management and explain why these are important. Summarize your results. What seem to be the attributes most often cited as leading to successful project management, regardless of the type of project? Are there any consistent differences between the responses in the two subsamples? If so, what are these differences? Do they make sense to you? If there are no apparent differences between the responses of the two subsamples, why not? Are there no differences in the skill sets necessary for managing information system projects versus managing other types of projects?

6. Observe a real information systems project team in action for an extended period of time. Keep a notebook as you watch individual members performing their individual tasks, as you review the project management techniques used by the team's leader, and as you sit in on some of their meetings. What seem to be the team's strengths and weaknesses? What are some areas in which the team can improve?

REFERENCES

Abdel-Hamid, T. K. 1992. "Investigating the Impacts of Managerial Turnover/Succession on Software Project Performance." *Journal of Management Information Systems* 9 (2): 127–144.

Boehm, B. W. 1981. *Software Engineering Economics.* Englewood Cliffs, NJ: Prentice-Hall.

Butler, J. 1994. "Automating Process Trims Software Development Fat." *Software Magazine* 14(8) (Aug): 37–46.

Datamation. 1996. "Top 10 Signs of IS Project Failure." June 1: 19.

Grupe, F. H., and D. F. Clevenger. 1991. "Using function point analysis as a software development tool." *Journal of Systems Management* 42 (December): 23–26.

Kettelhut, M. C. 1991. "Avoiding group-induced errors in systems development." *Journal of Systems Management* 42 (December): 13–17.

McFadden, F. R., J. A. Hoffer, and M. B. Prescott. 1999. *Modern Database Management.* Reading, MA: Addison Wesley Longman.

Miller, R. W. 1989. "How to plan and control with PERT." *Managing Projects and Programs,* Harvard Business School Press. Boston, MA: Harvard.

Page-Jones, M. 1985. *Practical Project Management.* New York: Dorset House.

Pressman, R. S. 1992. *Software Engineering.* 3d ed. New York: McGraw-Hill.

Rettig, M. 1990. "Software Teams." *Communications of the ACM* 33 (10): 23–27.

Thé, L. 1996. IS-Friendly Project Management, *Datamation,* April 1: 79–82.

Thomsett, R. 1985. Foreword to *Practical Project Management,* by M. Page-Jones. New York: Dorset House.

Zachary, G. P. 1993. "Agony and Ecstasy Of 200 code writers beget Windows NT." *The Wall Street Journal* (May 26): A1–A6.

4

Automated Tools
for Systems Development

After studying this chapter, you should be able to:

■ Identify the trade-offs when using CASE to support systems development activities.

■ Describe organizational forces for and against the adoption of CASE tools.

■ Describe the role of CASE tools and how they are used to support activities within the SDLC.

■ List and describe the typical components of a comprehensive CASE environment.

■ Describe the general functions of upper CASE tools, lower CASE tools, cross life cycle CASE tools, and the CASE repository.

■ Describe visual and emerging development tools and how they are being used.

INTRODUCTION

In the past, system development was viewed by many as an art that only a few skilled individuals could master. Within many organizations, the techniques employed by each developer could also vary substantially. This lack of consistency in technique and methodology often made it difficult to integrate systems and data or to quickly construct new systems. As a result, many organizations faced a growing backlog of applications to be developed; once developed, many of these systems were error-ridden, over budget, and late. Lack of standards also made maintenance difficult.

To address these problems, information systems professionals concluded that software development needed an engineering-type discipline (Nunamaker, 1992). The goal was to concentrate on developing common techniques, standard methodologies, and automated tools in a manner similar to the traditional engineering field. This chapter covers the evolution and use of automated tools to support the information systems development process. **Computer-aided software engineering (CASE)** refers to automated software tools used by systems analysts to develop information systems. These tools can be used to automate or support activities throughout the systems development process with the objective of increasing productivity and improving the overall quality of systems. Additionally, systems development and programming environments are continuously evolving to include *visual* and CASE-like features. This evolution is occurring rapidly and people with skill in using these tools are in hot demand.

Computer-aided software engineering (CASE): Software tools that provide automated support for some portion of the systems development process.

In the next section, we will describe how CASE is being used within organizations and examine the typical components of a comprehensive CASE environment. Next, visual and emerging development tools will be described with a focus on object-oriented tools, visual programming, and systems development tools of the future.

THE USE OF CASE IN ORGANIZATIONS

The purpose of CASE is to make it much easier to enact a single design philosophy within an organization with many projects, systems, and people. CASE can support most of the system development activities; Figure 4-1 highlights selected CASE facilities for each life cycle phase. Although CASE tools run on a variety of mini and mainframe systems, recent advances in microcomputers have made the PC the predominant CASE workstation. CASE helps provide an engineering-type discipline to software development and to the automation of the entire software life cycle process, sometimes with a single family of integrated software tools. In general,

Figure 4-1
CASE can provide effective support for most system development activities

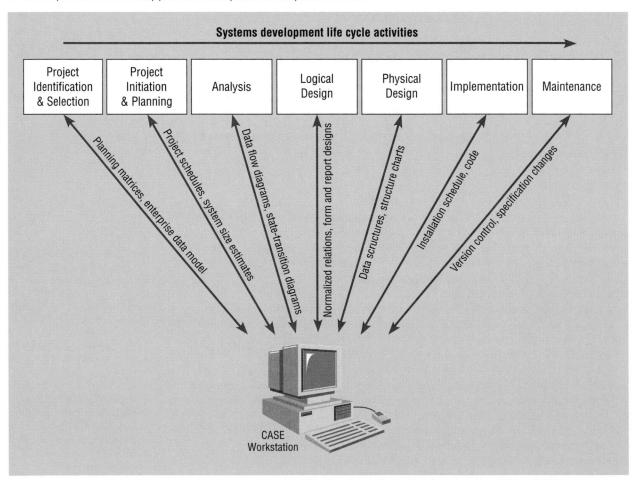

CASE assists systems builders in managing the complexities of information system projects and helps assure that high-quality systems are constructed on time and within budget.

From a systems analyst's perspective, the reason for using CASE may stem from a very straightforward and practical decision such as, "It makes my life easier." However, from an organizational perspective, the reasons for using CASE are much broader (see Table 4-1). Organizations primarily adopt CASE to improve the quality and speed of the systems development process. It is easy to argue that all organizations should openly embrace the adoption and deployment of CASE, since the objectives of CASE are consistent with the objectives of most organizations.

For example, Collect America, Ltd. (CA), a company that collects long overdue customer and commercial debts, uses Oracle Designer/2000 and Developer/2000 CASE tools for developing their information systems (Oracle, 1998). Based in Denver, Colorado, CA tracks and monitors debtors using an Oracle database environment. To make collections, CA has franchise agreements with regional law firms in the United States, Canada, and Mexico. As their business has grown, so too have their information management needs. CA's use of Oracle's CASE tools to design, construct, and maintain their applications has improved system quality and speed ove their previously non-CASE developed systems. The main reason is that systems developed using CASE allow applications to be easily moved from one hardware platform to another. Consequently, as the hardware infrastructure in CA has evolved, their applications have also evolved without major changes. For example, with the rapid growth and easy accessibility of the World Wide Web, CA could save a lot of money if franchise offices around North America used the Web to access CA's database. Using Oracle's CASE tools, system developers reconstructed applications so that they would operate via Java Applets inside a standard Web browser. Today, because access to this information is through the Web, huge cost savings are being realized by CA; the company no longer has to invest in routers, dedicated lines, and all the other technology needed to manage a dedicated network. For CA, CASE has really paid off.

Yet, adopting CASE can have numerous and widespread effects on an organization and its information systems development process beyond quality and speed

TABLE 4-1   Objectives of CASE

Most organizations use CASE to

- Improve the quality of the systems developed
- Increase the speed with which systems are designed and developed
- Ease and improve the testing process through the use of automated checking
- Improve the integration of development activities via common methodologies
- Improve the quality and completeness of documentation
- Help standardize the development process
- Improve the management of the project
- Simplify program maintenance
- Promote reusability of modules and documentation
- Improve software portability across environments

improvements. As a result, the deployment of CASE within organizations has been slower than expected, with several factors inhibiting widespread deployment.

Most agree that the start-up cost of using CASE is the greatest single factor. Integrated CASE environments range in price from less than $5,000 per analyst to more than $50,000! Lower-end systems are often low in functionality and fail to provide substantial productivity benefits. Furthermore, without adequate CASE training, most people are not able to gain the expertise needed to fully use CASE. For every dollar a company spends on tools, it is projected that from 50 cents to $1 must also be spent on training (Jones, 1993). CASE, an expensive technology, often leaves only large-scale system builders capable of making the investment required for organization-wide adoption. For example, it has been estimated that equipping a 150-person IS organization with CASE technology, including software, hardware, training, and maintenance, could exceed $3,000,000 over a five-year period (*I/S Analyzer,* 1993). A practical guideline is that it costs between $5,000 and $15,000 per year to provide CASE to one systems analyst. In spite of this, smaller organizations have effectively deployed CASE by using fewer and less sophisticated tools to automate only a subset of all development activities, thus substantially reducing deployment costs. Nonetheless, adopting CASE is an important decision that must be made at the highest levels of the organization.

Another factor influencing CASE adoption relates to how organizations evaluate their return on investments. The big benefits to using CASE come in the late stages of the SDLC: system construction, testing, implementation, and especially maintenance. Additionally, CASE often lengthens the duration of early stages of the project, sometimes by more than 40 percent (Stone, 1993). This increase in front-end effort is necessitated by the need to completely finish the system design before using automated code generators during system construction. In essence, although CASE provides the potential to significantly shorten the *overall* process, many users and managers are often frustrated by the seemingly long duration of planning, analysis, and design when using CASE. As a result, enthusiasm for CASE can dwindle. Organizations must be patient when making CASE investments—it is likely that the long-term payback from CASE takes more time than some organizations are willing to accept.

Other factors can also influence CASE adoption. One factor, cited as a significant productivity bottleneck, is that some CASE tools cannot easily share information between tools. A related issue is the extent to which CASE can support all SDLC activities. Providing a complete set of tools for all aspects of the SDLC turns out to be more difficult than first imagined. This has left many organizations with distinct tools that "refuse to talk to each other."

The adoption of CASE is highly related to use of a formal systems development process. Many CASE products force or encourage analysts to follow a specific methodology or philosophy for systems development. Thus, an organization without a widely used methodology or one that is not compatible with CASE tools will find it difficult to use CASE. Without a match between a methodology and CASE, CASE is simply another graphical drawing, word processing, and reporting package.

Despite these issues, the long-term prognosis for CASE is very good. The functionality of CASE tools is increasing and the costs are coming down (*PC Magazine,* 1997). During the next several years, CASE technologies and the market for CASE will begin to mature. This should help improve product offerings and reduce system costs. Additionally, by exposing more systems analysts to CASE technology earlier in their education and career, adoption with less training and better results should result.

Another factor that should stimulate the market for CASE products is the desire of organizations to extend the life of existing systems. Categories of CASE products referred to as *reverse engineering* and *reengineering* tools are "breathing new life" into existing systems by allowing old programs to be more easily modified to run on new hardware configurations (Pfrenzinger, 1992).

Reverse engineering refers to the process of creating design specifications for a system or program module from program code and data definitions. For example, CASE tools that support reverse engineering read program source code as input, perform an analysis, and extract information such as program control structures, data structures, logic, and data flow. Once a program is represented at a design level using both graphical and textual representations, the systems analyst can more effectively restructure the code to current business needs or programming practices. Figure 4-2 shows a screen from Imagix 4D that graphically displays how symbols within an information system are related to one another. This tool provides analysts with a powerful method to quickly explore and understand a system. For example, Figure 4-2 shows a mapping between variables and program procedures. This high-level view of a program allows programmers to see more quickly the interrelationships and structure of a program, making it easier to understand and maintain. As with many legacy systems, only the source code may exist, yet additional documentation is necessary to make program maintenance productive.

Reengineering tools are similar to reverse engineering tools but include analysis features that can automatically, or interactively with a systems analyst, alter an existing system in an effort to improve its quality or performance. Although most organizations may have numerous systems that are candidates for reverse engineering or reengineering, the complexity and effort in using these tools have limited their widespread use. Additionally, most CASE environments do not yet have reverse or reengineering capabilities. However, as automated development environments evolve to support these features, CASE should evolve to have greater impact beyond what the technology has so far experienced.

Besides financial and productivity issues, the culture of an organization can significantly influence the success of CASE adoption. IS personnel with different career orientations have different attitudes toward CASE (Orlikowski, 1989). IS personnel

Reverse engineering: Automated tools that read program source code as input and create graphical and textual representations of program design-level information such as program control structures, data structures, logical flow, and data flow.

Reengineering: Automated tools that read program source code as input, perform an analysis of the program's data and logic, and then automatically, or interactively with a systems analyst, alter an existing system in an effort to improve its quality or performance.

Figure 4-2
Sample screen of reverse engineering tool from Imagix (Source: Imagix, 1998)

with a managerial orientation welcome CASE because they believe it helps reduce the risk and uncertainty in managing the SDLC. IS personnel with a more technical orientation tend to resist CASE because they feel threatened by the technology's ability to replace some skills they have taken years to master. Table 4-2 lists several possible impacts of CASE on the roles of individuals within organizations. It should be clear after reviewing this table that the adoption of CASE should be a well thought-out and highly orchestrated activity.

A report prepared by a large accounting firm identified several driving and resisting forces that influence CASE adoption (Chen and Norman, 1992). Forces were identified from both an organization-wide and an individual perspective (see Tables 4-3 and 4-4). Organizational forces came from the pressures to develop and market information-intensive products and services, the increasingly shorter time-to-market, the transition to information-based organizations, and the potential for using information systems to support the organization's competitive strategy. Other factors included the increasing pressure to improve developer productivity and system quality. CASE was also viewed as an attractive vehicle for training, for building systems independent of specific implementation platforms, and for more easily managing projects. From the individual perspective, IS professionals who viewed CASE favorably felt that understanding how to use CASE was a valuable and marketable skill, that CASE automated many routine and boring

TABLE 4-2   Common Impacts of CASE on Individuals within Organizations

Individuals	Common Impact
Systems Analysts	CASE automates many routine tasks of the analyst, making the communication skills (rather than analytical skills) of the analyst most critical.
Programmers	Programmers will piece together objects created by code generators and 4th-generation languages. Their role will include more of maintaining designs using diagramming tools rather than source code.
Users	Users will be much more active in the systems development process through the use of upper CASE tools.
Top Managers	Top managers will play a more active role in setting priorities and strategic directions for IS by using CASE-based planning and through user-oriented system development methods.
Functional Managers	Functional managers will play a greater role in leading development projects by using CASE to reengineer their business processes.
IS Project Managers	IS project managers will have greater control over development projects and resources.

Adapted from Chen and Norman, 1992

TABLE 4-3   Driving Organizational Forces for the Adoption of CASE

Organizations adopt CASE to

- Provide new systems with shorter development time
- Improve the productivity of the systems development process
- Improve the quality of the systems development process
- Improve worker skills
- Improve the portability of new systems
- Improve the management of the systems development process

TABLE 4-4   Resisting Organizational Forces for the Adoption of CASE

Organizations reject CASE because of

- The high cost of purchasing CASE
- The high cost of training personnel
- Low organizational confidence in the IS department to deliver high-quality systems on time and within budget
- Lack of methodology standards within the organization
- Viewing CASE as a threat to job security
- Lack of confidence in CASE products

TABLE 4-5 CASE Implementation Issues and Strategies

Top Management Support	CASE requires a substantial long-term investment. Top management support is essential for success.
Contribution	CASE adoption is a business decision that must be justified as bringing business value to the organization by addressing or overcoming some identifiable problem in the development of information systems.
Manage Expectation	History has shown that the benefits of CASE are often long-term (for example, easier maintenance). IS managers must be careful not to oversell CASE as a cure-all for the development of information systems.
Prevent Resistance	The resistance to CASE can come from both inside and outside the IS department. Effectively managing expectations, providing extensive training, and selecting the right pilot projects and personnel will ease adoption and diffusion.
Deploy Carefully	CASE deployment should be done with care. Initial projects and personnel should be selected carefully. Personnel should be respected individuals with high credibility, training, and expertise.
Evaluate Continuously	The effects of CASE (and all other substantial investments) on the organization should be continuously monitored so that timely adjustments in strategy can be made.

Adapted from Chen and Norman, 1992

tasks, and that it was an effective method for enforcing a common development methodology.

There were several resisting forces that had acted to preclude many organizations from making the investment in CASE. From an organizational perspective, it was reported that many business managers were losing confidence in the IS department's ability to deliver quality systems on time. Thus, organizations were investing in other options such as end-user computing and outsourcing.

Effective CASE adoption requires using a common design methodology. Thus, if an organization does not *first* have a standard methodology for developing systems, it is unlikely that CASE will be successfully adopted. Additionally, individuals within the IS organization may view CASE as a career threat if no coherent strategy for adoption and deployment is instituted.

This section has described the use of CASE within organizations and discussed several issues surrounding the adoption of CASE. It should now be clear to you that adopting and using CASE is a significant event in any organization. In view of this, the adoption of CASE, or any other technology with so many potential impacts, should be guided with a clear strategy. Table 4-5 outlines many critical issues and implementation strategies. Although all items listed in this table are important, our personal experience is that without top management support, any significant systems project is destined for failure.

COMPONENTS OF CASE

CASE tools are used to support a wide variety of SDLC activities. CASE tools can be used to help in the project identification and selection, project initiation and planning, analysis, and design phases (**upper CASE**) and/or in the implementation and maintenance phases (**lower CASE**) of the SDLC (see Figure 4-3). A third category of CASE, **cross life cycle CASE,** is tools used to support activities that occur

Upper CASE: CASE tools designed to support the information planning and the project identification and selection, project initiation and planning, analysis, and design phases of the systems development life cycle.

Lower CASE: CASE tools designed to support the implementation and maintenance phases of the systems development life cycle.

Cross life cycle CASE: CASE tools designed to support activities that occur *across* multiple phases of the systems development life cycle.

Figure 4-3
The relationship between CASE tools and the systems development life cycle

across multiple phases of the SDLC. For example, tools used to assist in ongoing activities such as managing the project, developing time estimates for activities, and creating documentation are often considered cross life cycle tools. Over the past several years, vendors of upper, lower, and cross life cycle CASE products have "opened up" their systems through the use of standard databases and data conversion utilities to more easily share information across products and tools. An integrated and standard database called a *repository* is the common method for providing product and tool integration and has been a key factor in enabling CASE to more easily manage larger, more complex projects and to seamlessly *integrate* data across various tools and products. Integrated CASE or *I-CASE* will be described in more detail later in the chapter. User interface standards such as Microsoft's Windows™ have also greatly eased the integration and deployment of these systems. The general types of CASE tools are listed below:

- *Diagramming tools* that enable system process, data, and control structures to be represented graphically.

- *Computer display and report generators* that help prototype how systems "look and feel" to users. Display (or form) and report generators also make it easier for the systems analyst to identify data requirements and relationships.

- *Analysis tools* that automatically check for incomplete, inconsistent, or incorrect specifications in diagrams, forms, and reports.

- A central *repository* that enables the integrated storage of specification, diagrams, reports, and project management information.

- *Documentation generators* that help produce both technical and user documentation in standard formats.

- *Code generators* that enable the automatic generation of program and database definition code directly from the design documents, diagrams, forms, and reports.

Besides providing an array of tools, most CASE products also support ad hoc inquiry into and extraction from the repository. Security features, which may be important in some development environments, are also widely available. For example, if you contract with a custom software developer, you may expect them to secure your system specifications so that other project teams may not access your system requirements, design, and code. Some more advanced CASE products also support version control, which allows one repository to contain the description of several versions or releases of the same application system. Also, some CASE products provide import and export facilities to automatically move data between the CASE repository and other software development tools such as word processors, software libraries, and testing environments. Finally, as a shared development database, CASE environments should provide facilities for backup and recovery, user account management, and usage accounting. In other words, to provide the greatest benefits, CASE should be used to support all activities within the SDLC.

Nonetheless, many organizations that use CASE tools do not use them to support all phases of the SDLC. Some organizations may extensively use the diagramming features but not use code generators. Table 4-6 summarizes how CASE is commonly used within each SDLC phase. There are a variety of reasons why organizations choose to adopt CASE partially or to not use it at all. These reasons range from a lack of vision for applying CASE to all aspects of the SDLC to the belief that CASE technology will fail to meet an organization's unique system development needs. Several key differences between using traditional non-integrated system development processes versus CASE-based development are summarized in Table 4-7.

In traditional systems development, much of the time is spent on coding and testing. When software changes are approved, often the code is first changed and then tested. Once the functionality of the code is assured, the documentation and specification documents are updated to reflect system changes. In effect, this means the systems analyst's job is that of *maintaining code and documentation*. Changes to the system "ripple" through all aspects of the system and supporting documentation and maintaining systems requires that all discrete system documents be updated. For example, if you use a word processing system for logging documentation changes, these files need to be updated. If you use a separate program to graphically reflect

TABLE 4-6 Examples of CASE Usage Within the SDLC

SDLC Phase	Key Activities	CASE Tool Usage
Project identification and selection	Display and structure high-level organizational information	Diagramming and matrix tools to create and structure information
Project initiation and planning	Develop project scope and feasibility	Repository and documentation generators to develop project plans
Analysis	Determine and structure system requirements	Diagramming to create process, logic, and data models
Logical and physical design	Create new system designs	Form and report generators to prototype designs; analysis and documentation generators to define specifications
Implementation	Translate designs into an information system	Code generators and analysis, form, and report generators to develop system; documentation generators to develop system and user documentation
Maintenance	Evolve information system	All tools are used (repeat life cycle)

TABLE 4-7 Traditional Systems Development versus CASE-Based Development

Traditional Systems Development	CASE-Based Systems Development
Emphasis on coding and testing	Emphasis on analysis and design
Paper-based specification	Rapid interactive prototyping
Manual coding of programs	Automated code generation
Manual documenting	Automated documentation generation
Intensive software testing	Automated design checking
Maintain code and documentation	Maintain design specifications

Adapted from McClure, 1989

process flow and data, changes to these diagrams must occur. Additionally, all other documents must be updated to reflect even the most minuscule changes to the system. The process of keeping all system documentation current can be a very boring and time-consuming activity that is often neglected. This neglect makes future maintenance by the same or (more likely) different programmers difficult at best. Experienced analysts know that complete and consistent documentation is the most important determinant to maintaining large computer systems. Thus, a primary drawback to the traditional development approach is the lack of integration among specification documents, program code, and supporting documentation.

A primary objective of the CASE-based approach to systems development is to overcome the drawbacks of the traditional approach. When using an integrated CASE environment, your primary role is to maintain the design documents, as most other aspects of the system can "flow" directly from these diagrams, forms, and report templates. In the remainder of this section, we discuss the components of CASE.

CASE Diagramming Tools

Diagramming tools: CASE tools that support the creation of graphical representations of various system elements such as process flow, data relationships, and program structures.

CASE **diagramming tools** allow you to represent a system and its various components visually. Diagrams are very effective for representing process flows, data structures, and program structures. For example, a diagramming technique called data flow diagramming is often used to represent the movement of data between business processes.

An example of a business process is customer billing within a company when invoices are received from a customer, a bill is produced, and this bill is sent to the the customer; each of these activities is a business process. A data flow diagram (DFD) is used to model business processes as information flows through an organization. For example, Figure 4-4 shows a DFD from Designer/2000 CASE system from Oracle Corporation. This view shows some of the business processes within a department of motor vehicles, specifically the processes related to that of issuing a driver's license to an applicant. The diagram shows process 1.2, Issue License, as consisting of three subprocesses, (1.2.3) Update DMV database, (1.2.1) Get photograph of applicant, and (1.2.2) Create drivers license. Arrows, called data flows, move information between processes, data stores (e.g., DMV database), and between sources and sinks of information. In this figure, the DMV Evaluator is a source that provides the data flow, Successful Test Results. Likewise, the Applicant is a sink that receives information from the data flow, Drivers License. Note that processes could be automated or nonautomated. Additionally, the CASE tool allows the system designer to easily decompose higher-level processes into more specific subprocesses. CASE allows the designer to examine the system processes at a

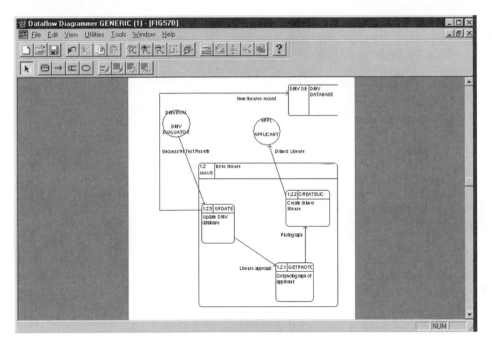

Figure 4-4
A data flow diagram (DFD)
from Oracle's Designer/2000
CASE environment

high aggregate level or at a highly detailed level. For example, Figure 4-5 provides a high-level view of the motor vehicle system in a functional hierarchy diagram.

In addition to providing methods for modeling business processes, most CASE systems provide numerous options for representing other types of system-related information. A common method for representing data is the entity-relationship diagram (ERD). An example of a CASE-drawn ERD is shown in Figure 4-6 and is again from Oracle's Designer/2000. In this diagram, there are four separate *entities*—supplier, shipment, product, and task. The lines connecting these entities

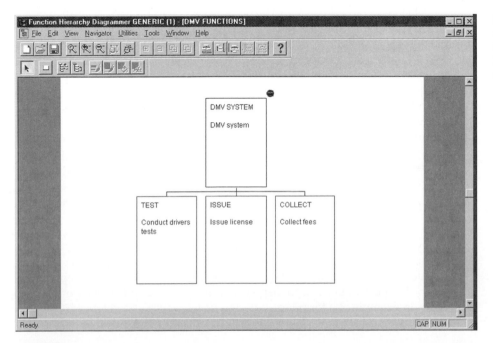

Figure 4-5
A functional hierarchy
diagram from Oracle's
Designer/2000 CASE
environment

Figure 4-6

An entity-relationship diagram (ERD) from Oracle's Designer/2000 CASE environment

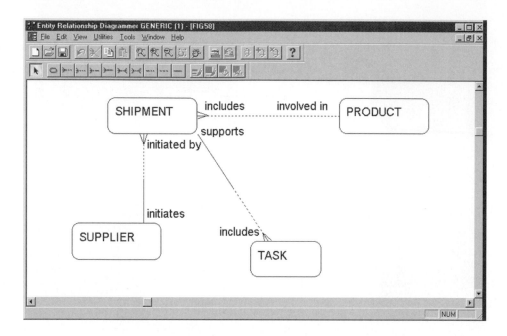

represent relationships between entities, which means these entities can be joined together to provide information. For example, the product entity lists all of a company's products. When joined with the shipment entity, and when the supplier entity is joined with the shipment entity, it is easy to identify the products contained in a given shipment from a given supplier. Systems designers use these high-level models to gain a clear understanding of the interrelationships among different entities. Most CASE tools can generate the database schema—the separate tables needed to physically store the data in the database—directly from the ERD.

As with DFDs, most CASE environments allow you to display data models at higher or lower levels of detail. In addition, not only can you "link" higher and lower level views, you can also associate items in one diagram with items in another. For example, an entity of an ERD can be linked to a data store on a DFD, and the data elements in a data flow on a DFD can be linked to data elements of an entity and defined in the repository. The types of diagrams you will use depend upon the methodology standards within your organization and the type of information you are trying to represent. Most IS professionals believe the old proverb that "a picture is worth a thousand words" and have found this to be especially true when representing business processes and complex data relationships. Diagrams are an effective method for developing a common language that users and analysts can use to discuss system requirements. This has resulted in making the diagramming capabilities of most CASE environments a fundamental and indispensable component.

CASE Form and Report Generator Tools

Form and report generators: CASE tools that support the creation of system forms and reports in order to prototype how systems will "look and feel" to users.

Automated tools for developing computer displays (forms) and reports help the systems analyst design how the user will interact with the new system. These tools, referred to as **form and report generators,** are most commonly used for two purposes: (1) to create, modify, and test prototypes of computer display forms and reports and (2) to identify which data items to display or collect for each form or report. Figure 4-7 shows an example of a form layout design using Oracle's Developer/2000 form design facility. This facility has numerous features to help you quickly design forms

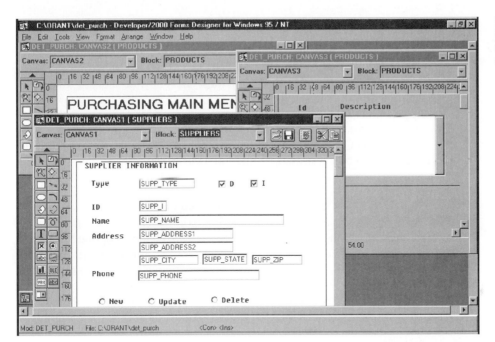

Figure 4-7
Form design tool from
Oracle's Developer/2000
CASE environment

and windows that look and feel consistent to your users. For example, Developer/2000 has a template feature that allows you to define common headings, footers, and function key assignments. Once defined, all forms in the system inherit these template definitions. Also, if a common change is desired for all forms, you can simply change the template definition and all system forms will automatically inherit this change. Once you are happy with the design, you can quickly test its usability by converting the design template (Figure 4-7) into a working prototype.

You will find that using automated tools for developing forms and reports is useful for both you and the eventual users of your system. For users, interacting with you during the early stages of the SDLC as forms and reports are outlined may help to ease system implementation. Involved users will be more familiar with the system when it is completed. As a result, these users may require less training than uninvolved users. Additionally, they may feel more positive that the system will meet their needs. From your perspective as the analyst, close interaction with users will help you develop a common frame of reference and enable you to better understand their data and processing requirements.

CASE Analysis Tools

One important objective of CASE is to help you handle the complexities of building large systems. We have described how CASE environments automate the creation of diagrams to represent system process flows, data, and structures in addition to constructing forms and reports. **Analysis tools** generate reports that help you identify possible inconsistencies, redundancies, and omissions in these diagrams, forms, and reports. For example, many analysis activities can be performed on the graphical diagrams created by the analyst. Each general diagramming technique has numerous rules that govern how a diagram can be drawn; for example, the "balancing" rule must be followed when creating a lower-level DFD from a higher-level DFD. This rule requires that the number of data flows or arrows flowing into and out of a high-level process must equal those flowing into and out of all this

Analysis tools: CASE tools that enable automatic checking for incomplete, inconsistent, or incorrect specifications in diagrams, forms, and reports.

process' lower-level sub-processes. Figure 4-8 shows a violation of the balancing rule: Data flow "C" flows out of process 1.2 on the Level-1 diagram, but it does not flow out of process 1 on the Level-0 diagram—dataflow X is a product produced within process 1 and would not be identified as an error. Thus, these diagrams are out of balance. An analysis performed on these Level-0 and Level-1 diagrams would alert you to this rule violation.

It is important to note that the types of analyses vary depending upon the organization's development methodology and the features of the CASE environment in use. In addition, many CASE systems support the creation of customized analysis reports. Typically, however, CASE analysis functions focus primarily on data structures and usage and on diagram completeness and consistency. For example, an analysis of all data input forms for a system could be performed. One report generated from this analysis could identify all input forms where the data elements contained on one form were identical to those contained on another (completely redundant forms). A second report could identify those forms where the data elements of one form were completely contained as a subset of the elements on another form (a partially redundant form). Such an analysis may identify that data are being entered into the system from more than one source—a possible data control violation. Such analysis capabilities are especially useful after the work of several systems analysts is combined.

CASE Repository

Substantial benefits when using CASE can only be achieved through the *integration* of various CASE tools and their data. Integrated CASE, or **I-CASE**, tools rely on common terminology, notations, and methods for systems development across all tools. Furthermore, all integrated CASE tools have a common user interface and can share system representations without systems analysts having to convert between different formats used by different tools. Hence, central to I-CASE is the idea of using a common repository for all tools so that this information can be easily shared between tools and SDLC activities. The **repository,** a centralized database, is the nucleus of a comprehensive I-CASE environment and is paramount to the smooth integration of the tools used during the various SDLC phases (Hanna, 1996). This means that the repository holds the complete information needed to cre-

I-CASE: An automated systems development environment that provides numerous tools to create diagrams, forms, and reports; provides analysis, reporting, and code generation facilities; and seamlessly shares and integrates data across and between tools.

Repository: A centralized database that contains all diagrams, forms and report definitions, data structure, data definitions, process flows and logic, and definitions of other organizational and system components; it provides a set of mechanisms and structures to achieve seamless data-to-tool and data-to-data integration.

Figure 4-8
Out of balance data flow diagrams

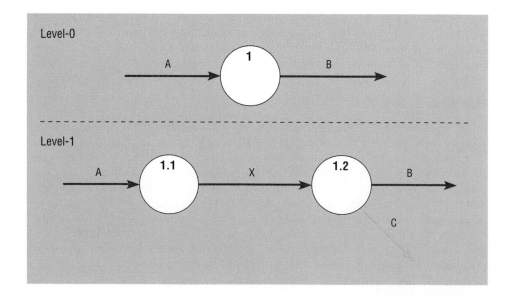

ate, modify, and evolve a software system from project initiation and planning to code generation and maintenance (see Figure 4-9). With a true I-CASE product, all tools throughout the entire life cycle will use a common repository. In this book, we will interchangeably use both CASE and I-CASE to refer to automated environments used to support the creation of information systems.

For years common development repositories have been used to create information systems independent of CASE. Figure 4-10 reflects the common components of

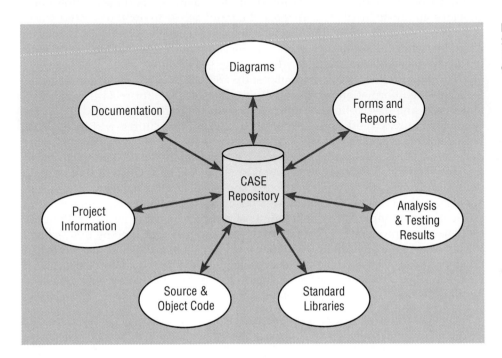

Figure 4-9
System development items stored in the CASE repository

Figure 4-10
Common components of a comprehensive CASE repository

a comprehensive CASE repository. The application development environment is one in which either information specialists or end users use CASE tools, high-level languages, and other tools to develop new applications. The production environment is one in which these same people use applications to build databases, keep the data current, and extract data from databases.

Within a repository there are two primary segments: the information repository and the data dictionary. The **information repository** combines information about an organization's business information and its application portfolio and provides automated tools to manage and control access to the repository (Bruce, Fuller, and Moriarty, 1989). Business information is the data stored in the corporate databases while the application portfolio consists of the application programs used to manage business information.

The **data dictionary** is a computer software tool used to manage and control access to the information repository. It provides facilities for recording, storing, and processing descriptions of an organization's significant data and data processing resources (Lefkovitz, 1985). Data dictionary features within a CASE repository are especially valuable for the systems analyst when cross referencing data items. **Cross referencing** enables one description of a data item to be stored and accessed by all individuals (systems analysts and end users) so that a single definition for a data item is established and used. Such a description helps to avoid data duplication and makes systems development and maintenance more efficient. For example, if the field length of a data element is changed, the data dictionary can produce a report identifying all programs affected by this change. Within an I-CASE environment, all diagrams, forms, reports, and programs can be automatically updated by the single change to the data dictionary definition. Each entry in a data dictionary has a standard "definition" that can include information such as the following attributes:

1. Element name and any aliases (can include both data items and programs)

2. Textual description of the element

3. List of related elements

4. Element type and format (for example, a calendar date might be of data type "date" and be of the format 12-Jan-99)

5. Range of acceptable values

6. Other information unique to the proper processing of this element

Figure 4-11 shows two computer screens that display information from Oracle's repository tool within the Designer/2000 and Developer/2000 CASE environment. Figure 4-11a shows a screen from the standard reporting system. Using this tool, one can view exhaustive information on all repository contents. In this figure, a report on the SHIP_AND_RECEIVE ERD is being viewed. The details on any individual item in the repository can be viewed by moving sequentially through each item or by locating an item through an interactive query. For example, Figure 4-11b shows a screen examining the data dictionary details of the NAME attribute of the SUPPLIER entity. In these details, we see that supplier names are a required field within a maximum length of 25 characters.

CASE Repository and the SDLC   During the project initiation and planning phase, the repository is used to store all information, both textual and graphical, related to the problem being solved. Details such as the problem domain, project resources and history, and organizational context are stored in the repository. As the project

Information repository: Automated tools used to manage and control access to organizational business information and application portfolio as components within a comprehensive repository.

Data dictionary: The repository of all data definitions for all organizational applications.

Cross referencing: A feature performed by a data dictionary that enables one description of a data item to be stored and accessed by all individuals so that a single definition for a data item is established and used.

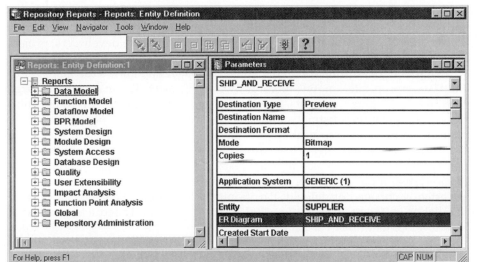

Figure 4-11
Sample CASE repository
contents

(a) Screen from Oracle's
information repository
showing standard reports

(b) Screen from Oracle's
repository showing data
dictionary details

evolves, the repository becomes the basis for the integration of the various SDLC
activities and phases.

During the analysis and design phases of the SDLC, the CASE repository is
used to store graphical diagrams and prototype forms and reports. When completeness and consistency analyses are done, the repository allows the data from
all diagrams, forms, and reports to be accessed simultaneously for comprehensive
analysis. The data stored in the repository are also used as the foundation for the
generation of code and documentation. Thus, the CASE repository is the integrating mechanism on all cross life cycle tools and activities.

Additional Advantages of a CASE Repository   Besides specific tool integration,
there are two additional advantages of using a comprehensive CASE repository

that relate to project management and reusability. The development of most software systems requires that more than one person work on the project; therefore, to coordinate most effectively the activities of multiple developers, project management techniques should be used (Chapter 3). The CASE repository provides a wealth of information to the project manager and allows the manager to exert an appropriate amount of control on the project. For example, on large software development projects, it is customary (and more efficient) to partition the development into distinct subprojects where one or a few people (that is, a team) have primary responsibility for their development. Through the CASE repository, the project manager can restrict members' access to only those aspects of the system for which they are responsible. This reduces the complexity of the system for a given team and provides security such that data are not inadvertently changed or deleted. Partitioning allows multiple teams to work in parallel on different aspects of a single system, potentially reducing total system development time.

Reusability: The ability to design software modules in a manner so that they can be used again and again in different systems without significant modification.

Another important use of the CASE repository relates to software **reusability.** In a large organization with many software systems, up to 75 percent of the application programs contain a significant amount of identical functions (Jones, 1986). In addition, as much as 50 percent of systems-level programs and upwards of 70 percent of telecommunications programs contain a significant amount of identical functions. Thus, one easy way for systems developers to enhance their productivity is to stop "reinventing the wheel" (or here, reinventing the function). If all organizational systems were created using CASE technology with a common repository, it would be possible to reuse significant portions of prior systems (or the design of prior systems) in the development of new ones. There are many items that can be reused besides programming code such as design documents (diagrams, specification documents, form and report layouts) and project management modules (schedules, assignments, report formats, project plans). The benefits of reusability are reduced development time and cost and improved software quality by using time-tested modules.

CASE without a Common Repository   Organizations that do not adopt a single integrated CASE environment must share design and development information among tools. Sharing may be necessary since different, nonintegrated tools may be used on the same project or on different projects for coupled systems. Besides using a single CASE repository, you can share data between CASE tools by the following methods:

- Manually entering specifications contained in one repository into another repository (obviously, not a very desirable approach).

- Converting repository contents into some neutral format, like an ASCII file, and then importing these into another repository. This is a better solution in terms of human effort but there still may be considerable loss of information or extra manual effort since the structure of the specifications may be lost in such a conversion.

- Converting the specifications in different repositories by using vendor or third-party utilities that translate either directly or through an industry standard exchange format among the repository formats of different CASE tools (IBM External Source Format and the CASE Data Interchange Format provide this type of passive repository sharing, if supported by the CASE tool).

- Allowing one CASE tool to directly read the repository of another CASE tool. This more active type of sharing across CASE tools is possible only if a CASE vendor opens up its database format, as many DBMS vendors have done.

CASE Documentation Generator Tools

Each phase of the SDLC produces documentation. The types of documentation that flow from one phase to the next vary depending upon the organization, methodologies employed, and type of system being built. **Documentation generators** are modules that can create standard reports based upon the contents of the repository. Typically, SDLC documentation includes textual descriptions of needs, solution trade-offs, diagrams of data and processes, prototype forms and reports, program specifications, and user documentation including application and reference materials. A system that does not have adequate documentation is virtually impossible to use and maintain (Brooks, 1995).

A common problem when developing systems is that ". . . programmers concentrate on getting the application software up and running, rather than producing a document at the end of each development phase" (Hanna, 1992). Thus, documentation is a task that is often left to be dealt with *after* the programs have been completed. This time lag between when development activities occur and when documentation of these activities is produced often results in lower-quality documentation. The value of good documentation in relation to system maintenance is shown in Figure 4-12. This figure shows that the system maintenance effort takes 400 percent longer with poor-quality documentation. High-quality documentation leads to an 80 percent reduction in the system maintenance effort when compared to average-quality documentation. The practical implication of this is that there are some benefits for taking steps to improve the quality of system documentation and severe disadvantages for producing less-than-average-quality documentation.

Documentation generators within a CASE environment provide a method for managing the vast amounts of documentation created during the SDLC. Documentation generators allow the creation of master templates that can be used to verify that the documentation created for each SDLC phase conforms to a standard and that all required documents have been produced. Documentation is an often overlooked aspect of systems development yet, as pointed out in Figure 4-12, is decidedly the most important aspect to building *maintainable* systems. (The interested reader

Documentation generators: CASE tools that enable the easy production of both technical and user documentation in standard formats.

Figure 4-12
Impact of documentation quality on system maintenance (Source: Hanna, 1992)

is encouraged to read the classic discussion of systems development and documentation by Brooks [1995] in *The Mythical Man-Month.*)

CASE Code Generation Tools

Code generators: CASE tools that enable the automatic generation of program and database definition code directly from the design documents, diagrams, forms, and reports stored in the repository.

Code generators are automated systems that produce high-level program source code from diagrams and forms used to represent the system. As target environments vary on several dimensions, such as hardware and operating system platforms, many code generators are designed to be special-purpose systems that produce source code for a particular environment in a particular programming language. Most CASE tools that generate source code take a more flexible approach by producing standard source code and database definitions. Using standard language conventions, CASE-generated code can typically be compiled and executed on numerous hardware and operating system platforms with no, or very minor, changes. Yet standard code and definitions may not take advantage of special hardware or operating system features of specific environments.

VISUAL AND EMERGING DEVELOPMENT TOOLS

Systems development tools are rapidly evolving. In particular, programming tools are undergoing radical changes to make programming much faster and easier. Without these powerful tools, programming would remain a slow and tedious process. The following three subsections describe some of these tools: The first describes object-oriented development, the second describes visual development, and the third examines the evolution and future of systems development tools.

Object-Oriented Development Tools

Development tools with object-oriented capabilities are among the newest type of programming languages. Object-oriented development tools are helping to alleviate maintenance problems plaguing organizations that have multiple systems with redundant functions. To understand how object-oriented tools work, let's start by describing an *object*. In simple terms, an object is a chunk of program and data that is built to perform common functions within a system. The idea is to make objects that can be *easily* reused and literally become the building blocks for all systems. This is very different from traditional programming languages where variables, procedures, and data are managed separately. This process of grouping the data and instructions together into a single object is called *encapsulation* (see Chapter 12). By encapsulating the instructions and data together, programs are easier to maintain because the objects that are grouped together are protected or isolated from other parts of the program. An example of an object might include employee identification and payroll information with a set of corresponding rules for calculating monthly payroll for a variety of job classifications and tax rules. Another example might be a printing object that can be used in multiple applications. Then, when a modification to the print object needs to be made—for example, let's suppose we want to modify the print object to support color printing—*one* module can be changed and *all* systems that use this common object can include the enhanced color printing functionality.

Consequently, one of the major advantages of object-oriented development is that each object contains easily reusable code. This means that objects used in one program can simply be inserted into a different program without having to be recreated or reprogrammed. In other words, once an object is created, it can be plugged into a number of different applications, avoiding the time (and expense!) of having to reprogram that particular set of instructions. Just as a radio made by Pioneer can be plugged into several different cars, an object can be plugged into several different applications. For example, when using an object-oriented development environment like Visual C++, a developer has numerous controls (that is, objects) that are built directly into the development tool. This means that when developing a user interface or input form, the programmer can use predefined objects—each object has a predefined look and numerous predefined properties that are associated with the object. Figure 4-13 shows a form from Pine Valley Furniture with three command buttons at the bottom of the form—Help, Prior Screen, and Exit. Figure 4-14 shows the button property customization form for the Exit button of Figure 4-13 where the programmer can set specific properties for that object. Using this method of development, the object can be customized and be easily reused in other systems. Thus, the goal of object-oriented development is to make software easier to create, simpler and more consistent to use, and far more reliable (Verity and Schwartz, 1994). An easy way to think about object-oriented development for building information systems is to think about using Lego™ Bricks for building model bridges, planes, and buildings. The Lego Bricks are reusable in an infinite number of structures. Likewise, the well-designed software object is also infinitely reusable.

Object-oriented languages are currently among the most popular and their use continues to grow. For example, C++ is an object-oriented enhancement of the original C programming language. Java has become a very popular object-oriented

Pine Valley Furniture				

Pine Valley Furniture
Detail Customer Account Information

Page: 2 of 2
Today: 11-OCT-98

Customer Number: 1273
Name: Contemporary Designs

DATE	PURCHASE	PAYMENT		CURRENT BALANCE
01-Jan-98				0.00
21-Jan-98	(22,000.00)			(22,000.00)
21-Jan-98		13,000.00		(9,000.00)
02-Mar-98	(16,000.00)			(25,000.00)
02-Mar-98		15,500.00		(9,500.00)
23-May-98		5,000.00		(4,500.00)
12-Jul-98	(9,285.00)			(13,785.00)
12-Jul-98		3,785.00		(10,000.00)
21-Jul-98		5,371.65		(4,628.35)
YTD-SUMMARY	(47,285.00)	42,656.65		(4,628.35)

Help	Prior Screen	Exit

Figure 4-13
A form designed in Visual C++

Figure 4-14
Button property
customization in Visual C++

development language for building Internet Web applications. As you might expect, there are object-oriented extensions to many other traditional programming languages including COBOL, FORTRAN, and BASIC. The biggest growth area in object-oriented development is the area of visual development tools. This will be described next.

Visual Development Tools

Visual development tools are a relatively new and extremely powerful way to rapidly develop systems. Visual Basic by Microsoft, PowerBuilder by Powersoft, Delphi by Borland International, and other visual development tools are some of the most widely used development environments today. These visual tools allow systems developers to quickly build new user interfaces, reports, and other features into new and existing systems in a fraction of the time previously required. Instead of building a screen, report, or menu by typing crude commands, designers use visual tools to "draw" the design using predefined objects. For example, to build a menu system in a visual programming environment is simple. Analysts can quickly list the order of menu commands in a development module called the Menu Editor (see Figure 4-15a) and instantly test the look of their design (see Figure 4-15b). In fact, once designed, these systems convert the design into the appropriate computer instructions, but all these details are hidden from the developer.

Although the popularity and the capabilities of most visual programming environments continue to expand, each environment has its own way of doing things. Yet, all have similar functions and capabilities. The market for these tools is very competitive, therefore, if one tool adds a new feature, most others quickly follow. Consequently, each tool has its strengths and weaknesses; it would be impossible to generalize that one system or approach to visual development is best. Visual Basic is arguably the most popular visual development tool and is very powerful and easy to use (see Figure 4-16 for an example of this development environment). In fact, Visual Basic is the macro programming language in the Microsoft software suite of tools such as Word and Excel. This means that Visual Basic has a wide range of users, from individuals streamlining their home expense budget in Excel to professional systems developers in organizations such as Xerox and the Vancouver Port Authority (see Microsoft, 1998).

PowerBuilder is another visual development environment that is extremely powerful and somewhat more expensive than Visual Basic (see Figure 4-17 for an example of this development environment). PowerBuilder's greatest strength is that it runs and develops applications for a broad range of hardware, computing platforms, and databases. PowerBuilder is primarily used by professional systems developers in larger organizations such as American Express, Fox Broadcasting, Nissan Motors, and Sega Video Games (see Powersoft, 1998). Delphi is another powerful visual programming tool that has a large and loyal following among professional developers (see Figure 4-18). Delphi, like Visual Basic and PowerBuilder, has extensive object-oriented capabilities that developers can quickly and easily include in their systems. Organizations such as American Airlines, BMW, Coors, NASA, and countless others have reported great success when using Delphi (see Borland, 1998). Given the popularity of visual development, if you haven't yet used these tools, you soon will!

Evolution and Future of Development Tools

We have already described two other approaches—object-oriented and visual development tools—which are rapidly being deployed to ease and empower the development process. A third way that is also emerging is to embed artificial intelligence into development environments. For example, in the near future, developers will be able to go well beyond 4GLs and develop large-scale information systems by simply telling the computer what they want it to do by using intelligent

Figure 4-16
Visual Basic development environment

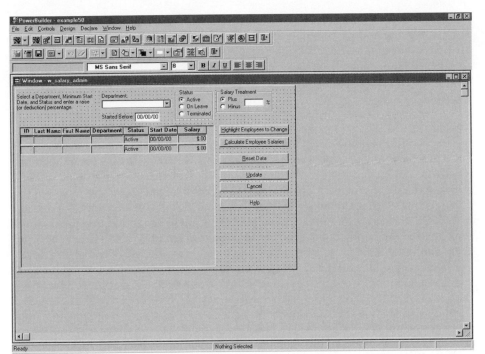

Figure 4-17
PowerBuilder development environment (Source: Borland, 1998)

Figure 4-18
Delphi development environment (Source: Inprise Corporation, 1998)

agents, created by other programmers, that will reside in the computer. A user or programmer would make a request to the agent through a conversational dialogue. The agents would use preestablished objects and visually display the results of the evolving system. In sum, the evolution and future of development tools will include extensive use of object-oriented modules and the visual display of results. As you will experience in your career, the evolution of development tools and techniques will be ongoing and continuous. This will result in more capable and complex systems for users and more capable and complex development environments. Hang on!

SUMMARY

The purpose of this chapter has been to introduce you to the use of automated tools to support the systems development process. First, we examined how CASE is being used within organizations. The objectives of CASE are to aid the systems analyst with automated tools so that higher-quality systems are constructed on time and within budget, maintained economically, and changed rapidly.

Yet, with all the potential benefits of adoption, CASE can affect many individuals within the organization in a variety of ways. Systems development personnel will focus more on their interpersonal and communication skills than solely on their analytical skills. Likewise, users will be much more involved in the development process by actively working with development personnel when defining requirements, finalizing designs, and testing features and capabilities. Additionally, managers will play a more active role in setting project and design priorities. Overall, CASE acts to make the development process more collaborative. It should be clear that implementing CASE is not a small undertaking for most organizations. A long-term perspective must be taken or the potential benefits of CASE may not be realized.

Different categories of CASE tools were introduced, such as reverse and re-engineering tools for rebuilding legacy systems. The components of a comprehensive CASE system are divided into upper, lower, and cross life cycle CASE tools, covering different segments of the SDLC. Upper CASE tools—diagramming tools, form and report generators, and analysis tools—are used primarily to support project identification and selection, project initiation and planning, analysis, and design. Lower CASE tools—code generators—are used primarily to support system implementation and maintenance. Cross life cycle tools—project management tools—coordinate project activities. The repository and documentation generators are used across multiple life cycle phases to support project management, activity estimation, and documentation creation.

The final major section of the chapter examined visual and emerging development tools, focusing primarily on object-oriented and visual development. These modern tools are being rapidly deployed because they are enabling organizations to more quickly and easily develop and maintain systems. In short, object-oriented tools allow the use of software objects that encapsulate the programming instructions and data together, making programs easier to develop and maintain. A big benefit of object-oriented development is the ease with which software objects can be reused in other systems. Many development environments and programming languages use object-orientated capabilities, including C++, COBOL, FORTRAN, and BASIC. Visual development tools allow systems developers to quickly build new user interfaces, reports, and other features into new and existing systems in a fraction of the time previously required. Through the use of development tools like Visual Basic by Microsoft, PowerBuilder by Powersoft, or Delphi by Borland International, new systems are constructed by piecing together predefined "visual" objects rather than typing crude programming commands as was done in the past. This evolution in development is radically changing how systems are designed, developed, and maintained. As a result, more powerful systems can be constructed in a fraction of the time previously required. In the next chapter, we look in detail at the SDLC by focusing on project identification and selection.

KEY TERMS

Analysis tools
Code generators
Computer-aided software
   engineering (CASE)
Cross life cycle CASE
Cross referencing

Data dictionary
Diagramming tools
Documentation generators
Form and report generators
I-CASE
Information Repository

Lower CASE
Reengineering
Repository
Reusability
Reverse engineering
Upper CASE

REVIEW QUESTIONS

1. Define each of the following terms:

   a. CASE
   b. code generators
   c. cross referencing
   d. data dictionary
   e. I-CASE
   f. information repository
   g. lower CASE
   h. reengineering
   i. reverse engineering

   j. repository
   k. reusability
   l. upper CASE
   m. version control (within CASE repository)
   n. active in development
   o. active in production
   p. cross life cycle CASE

2. Describe the evolution of CASE and its outlook for the future.

3. List five objectives for CASE within organizations.

4. How does or can the role of CASE change in relation to the size of the organization?

5. How does or can the role of CASE change in relation to the type of information systems developed by an organization?

6. Who are the individuals impacted by the adoption of CASE within an organization, and how are they impacted?

7. What are the driving forces behind the adoption of CASE? What are the resisting forces?

8. Describe each major component of a comprehensive CASE system. Is any component more important than any other?

9. Contrast the differences between a data dictionary and repository.

10. Contrast the difference between traditional nonautomated systems development and CASE-based systems development.

11. Describe how CASE is used to support each phase of the SDLC.

12. Describe the concept of software reusability. Is reusability possible without CASE?

PROBLEMS AND EXERCISES

1. Match the following terms to the appropriate definitions.

   _____ lower CASE

   a. tools used to manage and control access to a CASE repository

_____ upper CASE	b. CASE tools designed to support early phases of the SDLC
_____ I-CASE	c. CASE tools designed to support late phases of the SDLC
_____ reverse engineering	d. maintaining consistency between a more general and a more detailed data flow diagram
_____ reengineering	e. the repository of all data definitions
_____ balancing	f. tools which study programs and restructure them to improve quality or performance
_____ data dictionary	g. tools which study programs and produce documentation which models the programs and data used in the programs
_____ information repository	h. a CASE environment that allows the seamless sharing of data across CASE tools

2. Review the driving and resisting forces for CASE described in Tables 4-3 and 4-4 and the CASE implementation issues listed in Table 4-5. What do you forecast for CASE evolution and adoption in the future? Why? Would you recommend to colleagues that they adopt CASE tools? If so, under what circumstances? Why? If you wouldn't recommend using CASE tools now, why not, and what must change to cause you to recommend CASE tool adoption?

3. Review the sample computer forms in Figure 4-7. How is a form generator different from a standard graphics package like, say, Microsoft Windows Paintbrush® or PowerPoint? Why not simply use one of these graphics packages instead of using a CASE tool? What is gained by using a CASE tool rather than a graphics package? To answer these questions adequately, you may need to call a CASE tool vendor directly or find CASE tool product evaluations in the popular press.

4. Using a university or your workplace as the setting, list as many data elements (e.g., student identification number or customer identification number) as you can. Imagine how much information would be gathered and organized in this organization's database files and data dictionary. Estimate how much computer-based storage space would be needed to store, process, and back up this information. In an environment with computers, but without CASE tools, how would this organization store, organize, and retrieve this information? What are the limitations, weaknesses, and potential problems in trying to do this without the data dictionary component of a CASE tool?

5. What forms of user documentation, either hard copy or on-line, came with your PC, operating system, network operating system, and applications software at work, home, or school? Is this documentation accessible and helpful? At what level would you rate the quality of the documentation—high, average or low? Why? What could be done to improve the documentation? How could CASE help to improve documentation?

6. A goal stated by many vendors of CASE products is to have CASE ultimately be able to automatically generate (and regenerate to any platform and with any changes) 100 percent of the code, error-free, for a new or modified information system. This goal is considered important in order to achieve systems development productivity gains necessary to deal with systems backlog, to improve system quality, and to enhance our ability to maintain systems. Do you think this goal is possible? Why or why not?

7. What problems might occur during systems development if an organization used different CASE tools that did not share a common repository? What parallels can you make between the purpose of shared databases and the purpose of I-CASE?

8. Review the data dictionary entries on the SUPPLIER data entity in Figure 4-11b. What other data about an entity would you suggest be included in such a data dictionary entry? Why?

9. Contrast the differences between CASE, object-oriented, and visual development tools. How are these tools similar? How are they different?

FIELD EXERCISES

1. Interview a systems analyst, programmer, or an IS project manager to elicit their views of CASE, object-oriented, or visual development tools. Are they or their organization using any of these tools? If so, what are their evaluations thus far? What effects have these tools had on their jobs? If they use CASE, do their perceptions fit with those summarized in Table 4-2? If they are not using these development tools, why not? What must happen before they adopt one of these tools?

2. Find a detailed description of a CASE, object-oriented, or visual development tool and determine which of the functions and/or capabilities discussed in the chapter this tool supports. To do this, you may need to call a tool vendor directly, find a product evaluation in the popular press, or search a company's Web site.

3. Interview information systems professionals who use CASE, object-oriented, or visual development tools and find out how they use the tools throughout the SDLC process. Ask them what advantages and disadvantages they see in using the tools that they do.

4. The systems development tool market is rapidly changing. Search through recent trade publications, like *Computerworld, PCWeek, Database Programming & Design*, and *Software Magazine* (many of these publications can now be found on the Web). Find ads or articles that list and/or evaluate tools. Develop a list of these products. What are the benefits claimed for each in these ads and articles? What features do the vendors promote?

5. Choose an organization that is developing information systems without CASE tools. Talk to the people involved in building the systems and find out more about how they build them. Determine the parts of the systems development process that could be better done using CASE tools. Estimate the time and expense involved in those parts of the process that could be better done using CASE tools. Does it make sense for this organization to adopt CASE tools? Why or why not?

6. Go to a CASE tool vendor's Web site and determine the product's price, functionality, and advantages. Try to find information related to any future plans for the product. If changes are planned, what changes and/or enhancements are planned for future versions? Why are these changes being made?

REFERENCES

Borland, 1998. Information from: *www.borland.com*. Information verified: February 14, 1998.

Brooks, F. P., Jr. 1995. *The Mythical Man-Month: Essays on Software Engineering*. Reading, MA: Addison-Wesley.

Bruce, T., J. Fuller, and T. Moriarty. 1989. "So You Want a Repository." *Database Programming & Design* 2(May): 60–69.

Chen M., and R. J. Norman. 1992. "Integrated Computer-aided Software Engineering (CASE): Adoption, Implementation, and Impacts." *Proceedings of the Hawaii International Conference on System Sciences,* edited by J. F. Nunamaker, Jr. Los Alamitos, CA: IEEE Computer Society Press, Vol. 3: 362–73.

Hanna, M. 1992. "Using Documentation as a Life-cycle Tool." *Software Magazine* 12(12) (Dec.): 41–51.

Hanna, M. 1996. "Can Tool Vendors Get It Together?" *Software Magazine* (Jan.): 59–62.

Imagix, 1998. Information from: *www.imagix.com.* Information verified: February 14, 1998.

I/S Analyzer. 1993. "The Cost and Benefits of CASE." Rockville, MD: United Communications Group. 31(6) (June).

Jones, C. 1986. *Programming Productivity.* New York, NY: McGraw-Hill.

Jones, T. C. 1993. "Equipping the Software Engineer." *Software Magazine* 13(1) (January): 100–109.

Lefkovitz, H. C. 1985. *Proposed American National Standards Information Resource Dictionary System.* Wellesley, MA: QED Information Sciences.

McClure, C. L. 1989. *CASE is Software Automation.* Englewood Cliffs, NJ: Prentice-Hall.

Microsoft, 1998. Information from: *www.microsoft.com.* Information verified: February 14, 1998.

Nunamaker, J. F. 1992. "Build and Learn, Evaluate and Learn." *Informatica* 1(1): 1–6.

Oracle, 1998. Information from: *www.oracle.com.* Information verified: February 14, 1998.

Orlikowski, W. J. 1989. "Division Among the Ranks: The Social Implications of CASE Tools for System Developers." *Proceedings of the Tenth International Conference on Information Systems.* 199–210.

Pfrenzinger, S. 1992. "Reengineering Goals Shift Toward Analysis, Transition." *Software Magazine* 12(10) (Oct.): 44–57.

Powersoft, 1998. Information from: *www.powersoft.com.* Information verified: February 14, 1998.

Stickel, E. U. 1993. "An Experience with CASE Tool Support for Financial Product Design." *Data Base* 24(4) (Nov.): 31–35.

Stone, J. 1993. *Inside ADW and IEF: The Promise and Reality of CASE.* New York, NY: McGraw-Hill.

Verity, J.W., and E.I. Schwartz. 1994. Software Made Simple. In P. Gray, W.R. King, E.R. McLean, and H.J. Watson (eds.), *Management of Information Systems*, 2nd ed., pp. 293-299. Fort Worth, TX: The Dryden Press.

BROADWAY ENTERTAINMENT COMPANY, INC.

Case Introduction

OUR RUNNING CASE: BROADWAY ENTERTAINMENT COMPANY

Starting with Chapter 4, we will follow all chapters through Chapter 19 (except Chapters 12 and 13) with a case example featuring the Broadway Entertainment Company, Inc. Broadway Entertainment is a fictional company in the video rental and recorded music retail industry, but its size, strategies, and business problems (and opportunities) are comparable to those of real businesses in this fast-growing industry.

The first case is designed to introduce you to the company and the people who work for it. The second case follows this one and will present the company's information systems portfolio. The third case will follow Chapter 5 where we discuss the idea for a new information system, which begins the systems development life cycle. A new case will be presented at the end of most subsequent chapters. Each case will deal with that phase of the life cycle discussed in the adjoining chapter. The last Broadway case will follow Chapter 19 and covers data privacy issues for the new system.

Our aim is to provide you with a realistic case example of how the systems development life cycle proceeds through its phases and how analysts, managers, and users work together to develop an information system. Reading about a phase of the life cycle and the techniques and tools that can support that phase is one thing; seeing the techniques and tools in action is another. Our hope is that the book chapters and Broadway Entertainment sections will complement each other as you learn about information systems development following the systems development life cycle.

THE COMPANY

The Broadway Entertainment Company, Inc., owns and operates Broadway Entertainment Company, or BEC, retail outlets. As of January 1998, Broadway owned 2,125 outlets across the United States, Canada, Mexico, and Costa Rica. There is at least one BEC outlet in every state (except Montana) and in each Canadian province. There are 32 Canadian stores, two in Mexico, and one in Costa Rica. The company is currently struggling to open a retail outlet in Japan and plans to expand into the European Union (EU) within five years. Broadway is headquartered in Spartanburg, S.C. Canadian operations are headquartered in Vancouver, B.C., and Latin American operations are based in Mexico City.

Each BEC outlet offers for sale two product lines, recorded music and video games, and rents to customers two product lines, recorded videos and video games. Recorded music is sold in two formats: cassette tapes and compact discs (CDs); videos are also rented in two formats: video tapes and laser discs. In calendar year 1997, music sales and video rentals together accounted for over 85 percent of Broadway's U.S. revenues. (See Table 1 for a breakdown of Broadway's domestic revenues for 1997.) Foreign operations added another $17,500,000 to company revenues.

TABLE 1 Calendar 1997 Domestic Revenue by Category		
Category	Revenues (in $000s)	Percent
Music Sales	500,000	37.0
Compact Discs	300,000	22.2
Cassettes	200,000	14.8
Video Game Sales	80,000	5.9
Video Game Rentals	120,000	8.9
Video Rentals	650,000	48.2
Video Tapes	585,000	43.4
Laser Discs	65,000	4.8
Total	1,350,000	100.0

The home video and music retail industries are strong and growing, both domestically and internationally. Worldwide retail home video revenue for 1993 exceeded $25 billion. U.S. video rentals exceeded $10.6 billion in 1996, while U.S. video sales exceeded $6 billion for the same year.

For several years, home video has generated more revenue than either theatrical box office or movie pay-per-view. U.S. revenues for the home video industry (rental and sales) are expected to exceed $21 billion by 2000, yet the total domestic revenue for the industry was only $700 million in 1982. The music retail industry, on the other hand, had worldwide revenues of $29 billion in 1992.

Revenues in the United States alone exceeded $13 billion in 1997. In 1995, Broadway controlled 5 percent of the domestic market for both home video and music.

To get a good idea of the industry in which Broadway competes, we can use Porter's Five Forces Model of Industry Structure (1980). According to Porter, any industry can be analyzed by focusing on five aspects of its structure: (1) suppliers, (2) buyers, (3) substitutes, (4) barriers to entry, and (5) rivalries among firms competing in the industry (see Figure 1). For suppliers, Broadway deals with all of the major distributors of recorded music (Sony, Matsushita, Time Warner), video games (Nintendo, Sega), and recorded videos (CBS Fox, Viacom). Customers (buyers) consist entirely of individual consumers—Broadway does not provide product for rebroadcast or public showings and does not deal with groups or associations. Substitutes for Broadway's entertainment offerings include television (broadcast, cable, satellite), first-run movies, theater, radio, concerts, and sporting events.

On one level, the barriers to entry into Broadway's business are relatively low. To open a single retail outlet that sells music and video games and rents videos does not take a large amount of capital or experience. On the other hand, to create a company that could compete with Broadway on the same national and international scale would take quite a bit of capital and experience. Broadway's management is not worried about the so-called "Mom and Pop" record and video stores. They are worried about such things as alliances between telecommunications and entertainment companies to create cable television that lets consumers choose from a large number and variety of videos from a computerized menu system in their homes. Such a system, which can be thought of as a much larger pay-per-view setup, would obviate the need for consumers to ever set foot in a video store. They could see whichever movie or entertainment event they wanted without leaving home and without having to worry about returning any product to the store.

As for rivalries in the industry, Broadway is most concerned about two types of rivals: the large music chains and the large video chains. In the video area, the biggest competitor by far is Blockbuster Entertainment. At the end of 1997, Blockbuster had 6,000 video stores in 50 states and 25 foreign countries. In 1992, Blockbuster entered the music business by acquiring 238 music stores and by entering into a joint agreement with Virgin Retail Group to open 20 "megastores," primarily in Europe. By the end of June 1994, Blockbuster owned 521 music stores in addition to the "megastores," making Blockbuster one of the largest music retailers as well as the largest video rental operator. Other retail music competitors include Musicland, Tower Records, and the Wherehouse. (See Table 2 for the recent revenues of Broadway's chief competitors.)

Figure 1
Porter's Five Forces Model of Industry Structure

COMPANY HISTORY

Broadway Entertainment Company, Inc., started as one of the "Mom and Pop" stores that Broadway's management no longer fears. The first BEC outlet opened in the Westgate Mall in Spartanburg, S.C., in 1977 as a music sales store or, as it was popularly known at that time, a record store. The first store exclusively sold recorded music, primarily in vinyl format, but also stocked cassette tapes. Broadway's founder and current chairman of the board, Nigel Broad, had immigrated to South Carolina from his native Great Britain in 1968. In Britain, Nigel had worked in several record stores and as a disc jockey for two different rock radio stations. He moved to South Carolina to be near his last remaining uncle, Albert. After nine years of numerous music-related jobs, Nigel took the money he had been left by his mother, formed Broadway Entertainment Company, Inc., and opened the first BEC outlet in the newly opened Westgate Mall on Spartanburg's west side.

Sales were steady and profits increased. Soon Nigel was able to open a second outlet and then a third. Predicting that his BEC stores had already met Spartanburg's demand for recorded music, Nigel decided to open his fourth store in nearby Greenville in 1981. At about the same time, he added a new line—Atari video game cartridges. Atari's release of its Space Invaders game cartridge resulted in huge profits for Nigel. The company continued to grow and Broadway expanded beyond South Carolina into neighboring states.

When Nigel first started his business, he had the insight to not stock eight-track tapes. His insight paid off as eight-tracks soon died as a recorded music format. In the early 1980s, Nigel saw the potential in video cassette recorders and video tapes. A few video rental outlets had opened in some of Broadway's markets, but they were all small independent operations. Most video stores had similar business practices: customers had to join a video club and pay some type of membership fee, usually $30 to $40 per family; customers had to return the video within 24 hours of the time they rented it; most stores had limited selections. Nigel saw the opportunity to combine video rentals with music sales in one place. He also decided that he could rent more videos to customers if he changed some of the video store rules such as eliminating the heavy membership fee and allowing customers to keep videos more than one night. Nigel also wanted to offer the best selection of videos anywhere.

Nigel opened his first joint music and video store at the original BEC outlet in Spartanburg in 1985. Customer response was overwhelming. In 1986, Nigel decided to turn all 17 BEC outlets into joint music and video stores. Nigel realized that the expansion would require a large amount of capital to finance the purchase of a large video tape library. Up until this time, Broadway Entertainment had been a closely held company. To move into the video rental business in a big way, Nigel decided to have a public offering later that year. Nigel and his chief financial officer, Bill Patton, put together the basic terms of the offer: 1,000,000 shares of stock to sell for $7 each. They were happily surprised when all one million shares sold. The proceeds allowed Broadway to offer video rentals in all 17 BEC outlets and to revive the dying video games line by dropping Atari and adding the newly released Nintendo game cartridges.

Profits from BEC outlets continued to grow throughout the 1980s, and Broadway continued to expand. Important events in the expansion are listed in Table 3. One of the most important decisions Nigel made was to acquire existing music and video store chains and convert them to BEC stores. From 1987 through 1993, the number of BEC outlets roughly doubled each year. The decision to go international, made in 1991, was also important, resulting in 12 Canadian

TABLE 2 Comparison Data on Some of Broadway's Closest Competitors

Competitor	Number of stores	1996 Revenues (in $ millions)	1997 Revenues (in $millions)
Blockbuster Entertainment	6000	3,500	3,900 (estimate)
Hollywood Entertainment	900	302	495 (estimate)
MST (Tower Records)	180	1,000	1,000
Musicland	1400	1,820	1,768
Wherehouse	297	433	365

stores that year, with 10 more added in 1992 and 1993. All three Latin American stores were opened in mid-1994. From its beginnings in 1977, with 10 employees and $398,000 in revenues, Broadway Entertainment Company, Inc., grew to 24,225 employees and worldwide revenues of $1,367,500,000 by January 1, 1998.

COMPANY ORGANIZATION

Since 1977 when he founded the company, Nigel Broad has been intimately involved in the growth and development of Broadway Entertainment Company, Inc. In 1992, when the company was about to open its one-thousandth store, Nigel decided that he no longer

TABLE 3   Important Events in Broadway's History

Year	Event
1988	Decision to acquire 30-store MAP Video Store chain
1989	Acquisition of 52-store Buddy's Records chain
1989	Second public offering, 30,000,000 shares offered
1990	Acquisition of 98-store Chang Video Market chain
1991	Decision to expand to Canada, 12 stores opened
1991	Acquisition of 208-store Music World chain
1991	Decision to rent video games
1992	Third public offering, 100,000,000 shares offered
1993	Decision to expand to Latin America

wanted to be the chief executive officer of the company. Nigel decided to fill only the position of chairman and he promoted his close friend Ira Abramowitz to the offices of president and CEO (see Figure 2).

Most of Broadway's other senior officers have also been promoted from within. Bill Patton, the chief financial officer, had been with Broadway from the beginning, starting out as the fledgling company's bookkeeper and accountant. Karen Gardner had been part of the outside consulting team that had built Broadway's first information system in 1986 and 1987. She became the vice-president in charge of IS for BEC in 1990. Bob Panofsky, the vice-president for human resources, had been with the company since 1981 and had worked his way up to the vice-president level. An exception to the promote-from-within tendency, W. D. Nancy Chen, the vice-president for domestic operations, had been recruited from Music World in 1991, shortly before the chain was purchased by Broadway. Oscar Morales had been hired in 1992 from Blockbuster Entertainment, where he had been in charge of Latin American expansion.

INFORMATION SYSTEMS

Broadway Entertainment Company operated from 1977 until 1984 without any information systems support. During its first five years of business, Broadway operated five or fewer music outlets. Like many businesses this size, the owner did not have the expertise or the capital for developing the company's own information systems. Bill Patton, the company's accountant,

Figure 2
Broadway Entertainment Company, Inc. organization chart

did all of the company business, including the management of inventory, by hand until he bought an IBM AT in 1984. After he had successfully converted Broadway's accounting and other business functions to work on the AT using prepackaged software purchased from a local computer store, Bill wondered how he had ever worked without it. Bill told anyone who would listen that computerizing the company had made the expansion to 10 stores in 1984 much easier. In 1985, Nigel expanded the original Spartanburg BEC store to handle video rentals, and by 1986, Broadway had expanded to 17 outlets and was considering its first public offering. The change in the business scope would clearly swamp Bill Patton and his IBM AT. The dramatically increased demands on inventory alone seemed to warrant increased computerization.

BEC had nobody trained in information systems on staff and all the BEC managers were quite busy coping with the business expansion. Nigel and Bill considered hiring a small IS department from outside, but they were reluctant to do so since they did not know how a new group should be managed, how to select quality staff, or what to expect from such employees. From their limited experience with computers, Nigel and Bill realized that computer software could be quite complicated, and building systems for a rapidly changing organization could be quite a challenge. Nigel and Bill also knew that building information systems required discipline and this discipline needed to be a part of systems development from the beginning. Thus, they wanted experienced people, but had no idea how much effort was involved or what expertise would be required. So Nigel, after contacting several other South Carolina businesses, contacted the information consulting firm of Fitzgerald McNally, Inc., about designing and building a custom computer-based information system for Broadway.

Nigel and Bill wanted the new system to perform all of the functions Bill's current system could handle, i.e., accounting, payroll, and inventory. Nigel wanted the system to be readily expandable as he was planning for Broadway's rapid growth. At the operational level, Nigel realized that the video rental business would require new features in their information system, features not needed for prerecorded music. For one thing, rental customers would not only be taking product from the store, they would also be returning it at the end of the rental period. Further, customers would be required to register with Broadway and attach some kind of deposit to their account in order to help ensure that videos would be returned.

At a managerial level, Nigel wanted the movement of videos in and out of the stores and all customer accounts computerized and easy to track. Being new to the video rental business, Nigel also wanted to be able to search through the data on Broadway's customers describing their rental habits. He wanted to know which videos were the most popular, and he wanted to know who Broadway's most frequent customers were, not only in South Carolina but in every location where Broadway did business.

Fitzgerald McNally, Inc., was happy to get Broadway's account. They assigned Karen Gardner to head up the development team. Karen led a team of her own staff of analysts and programmers, along with participation by several BEC managers, in a thorough analysis and design study. Fitzgerald McNally had recently adopted a CASE tool and associated methodology. This methodology provided the discipline needed for such a major systems development effort. The methodology began with information planning and continued through all phases of the systems development life cycle. Fortunately for the development team, BEC had been doing annual and long-term business planning and was very cooperative at every step of the total process.

After working for almost two years on the project, Karen and her team delivered and installed the system Broadway had requested. The system was centralized, with an IBM 4381 mainframe installed at headquarters in Spartanburg, and three terminals, three light pens, and three dot matrix printers installed in each BEC outlet. The light pens were used to track videotapes, recording when the tapes were rented and when they were returned by reading the bar code on the cassette. The light pens were also used to read the customer's account number, which was recorded in a bar code on the customer's BEC account card. The printers generated receipts. The same equipment was used for video game rentals and for video game and music sales. In addition, the system included a small personal computer and printer to handle a few office functions such as the ordering and receiving of goods. The primary software product Fitzgerald McNally built for Broadway, then, monitored and updated inventory levels. Another software product generated and updated the customer database while other parts of the final software package were designed for accounting and payroll. By the time the system was installed and running at the end of 1987, Broadway had expanded to 33 stores, and the system was able to handle Broadway's business demands with few problems.

In 1988, Karen Gardner left Fitzgerald McNally to start her own consulting firm. In 1990, she joined Broadway as the head of its information systems group. Karen led the effort to expand and enhance Broadway's information systems as the company grew to over 2,000 company-owned stores in 1995. Broadway now relies on several IBM 3090 mainframes and in-store point-of-sale computer systems to handle the transaction volume generated by millions of customers at all BEC outlets. Karen and her team have been thinking seriously about decentralizing Broadway's information systems and changing to a client/server network. None of these issues, however, has been resolved.

SUMMARY

Broadway Entertainment Company (BEC) is a $1.37-billion international chain of music, video, and game rental and sales outlets. BEC operates in a highly competitive and rapidly changing industry not only involving some of the largest electronics and entertainment companies but also providing the opportunity for new entrants with innovative delivery systems and service.

BEC started with one store in Spartanburg, S.C., in 1977 and has grown through astute management and capitalization into over 2,000 stores in four countries today. BEC is headed by Chairman of the Board of Directors Nigel Broad, who has relinquished all operating duties to a team of executives including Ira Abramowitz (CEO), Bill Patton (CFO), and Karen Gardner (VP for information systems). Computer systems began with one PC. Through the guidance of an outside consultant, quality systems were developed and eventually an internal IS function was created, headed by Karen Gardner, formerly with the consulting firm. Today, BEC systems run on an IBM mainframe at corporate headquarters and distributed point-of-sale equipment in retail stores. You will learn more about these systems in the next case study.

BROADWAY ENTERTAINMENT COMPANY, INC.

The Existing Application Portfolio

INTRODUCTION

Broadway Entertainment Company (BEC) has developed computer applications for both local stores as well as corporate functions. BEC has two systems development and support groups, one responsible for in-store applications and the other responsible for corporate applications. The corporate group is further divided by functional area, such as accounting, marketing, and human resources. Each corporate development group also has liaison staff with the in-store group, since data in many corporate systems feed or are fed by in-store applications (for example, market analysis systems depend on transaction data collected by the in-store systems). BEC creates both one-year and three-year IS plans that encompass both store and corporate functions. Regional and country management operations are supported within the corporate IS plan and development group.

The functions of the original in-store systems at BEC have changed very little since they were installed in 1987—customer and inventory tracking is still done by pen-based, bar code scanning of product labels and membership cards, and basic accounting and payroll functions are automated. Daily transactional data (rentals and returns, sales, and other changes in inventory as well as employee time in and out) are all captured at the store in electronic form via a local point-of-sale (POS) computer system and transmitted in batch at night using modems and regular telephone connections to corporate headquarters where all records are centralized on an IBM 3090 mainframe for all stores (Figure 1 depicts BEC's hardware and network architecture). Software updates for the store systems are also distributed electronically via the public data network.

As shown in Figure 1, each BEC store has an NCR computer that serves as a host for a number of POS terminals at check-out counters. The computer also serves as the store manager's workstation for generating reports and performing other administrative in-store applications. Some managers have also learned how to use spreadsheet, word processing, and other packages to handle functions not supported by systems provided by BEC for in-store use. Each store computer includes a modem to allow communication with the corporate host computer via a communications front-end processor. The front-end processor at corporate headquarters offloads communications traffic from the IBM mainframe so that it can concentrate on data processing applications. BEC's communication protocol is SNA, an IBM standard. Corporate databases are managed by IBM's relational DBMS DB2. BEC uses a variety of programming environments, including C, COBOL, SQL (as part of DB2), and code generators.

All inventory control (e.g., purchasing of new items, retirement of items) is done centrally and, since local stores are corporate owned, employees are paid by the corporation. Today, each store is an isolated outlet; that is, each store has electronic records of only its own activity, including inventory. Profit and loss, balance sheets, and other financial statements are produced for each store by centralized systems. Each store manager is responsible for all local personnel matters (hiring, evaluating, scheduling, and firing employees), local property management (cleaning, day-to-day dealings with property owner if the property is leased, store layout within company guidelines, and so forth), managing local promotions within a budget set by BEC for each store, and customer relations. The local manager also influences stocking decisions, but final decisions are made at headquarters based on store transaction history and market trends. Practically all other functions are managed centrally. The following sections review many of the applications that exist in the stores and at the corporate level.

Figure 1
BEC hardware and network architecture

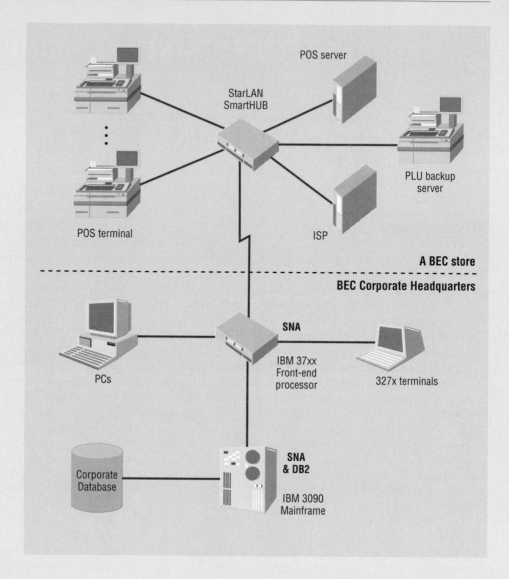

IN-STORE SYSTEMS

Table 1 lists the application systems installed in each store. BEC has developed a turnkey package of hardware and software (called Entertainment Tracker—ET) that is installed in each store worldwide. Besides English, the system also works in Spanish and French; BEC has developed one store system in which the language is set as a parameter when the system is installed in a store. The store system uses NCR point-of-sale (POS) technology, which is Intel microprocessor-based. BEC chose NCR equipment because NCR is a worldwide leader in point-of-sale equipment with sales and support offices in all international locations where BEC plans to operate. NCR equipment and system software is also compatible with the IBM mainframes

used at corporate headquarters, so data transmission between headquarters and stores is not complicated.

As you can see from Table 1, all of these applications are transaction processing systems. In fact, there is a master screen on the POS terminals that leads to all systems, and the type of transaction selected on this master screen determines which ET application is activated. These systems work off a local decentralized database, and there is a similarly structured database for each store. Databases are not distributed. For example, the database of a store in San Diego, California, is not accessible from a store in Ft. Collins, Colorado. Furthermore, store databases are not accessible interactively from corporate headquarters, although various batched data transfers occur between corporate and store systems at night (store trans-

TABLE 1　List of BEC In-Store (Entertainment Tracker) Applications

System Name	Description
Membership	Supports enrollment of new members, issuing membership cards, reinstatement of inactive members, and local data management for transient members
Rental	Supports rentals and returns of all products and outstanding rental reports
Sales	Supports sales and returns of all products (including videos, music, snack food, BEC apparel, and gift certificates)
Inventory Control	Supports all changes in rental and sales inventory that are not sales-based (e.g., receipt of a new tape for rental, rejection of goods damaged in shipment, and transfer of an item from rental to sales categories)
Employee	Supports hiring and terminating hourly employees, as well as all time-reporting activities

actions, price and membership data updates, etc.). Figure 2 depicts a conceptual view of the database structure in each store. The database contains only current data—the history of customer sales and rentals is retained in a corporate database. Daily sales transactions are transmitted nightly to corporate databases and purged from the local database each night; daily rental data are also transmitted overnight, but a rental transaction is not purged until the items are returned and the completed rental transaction data are transmitted that night. Thus, local stores do not retain any customer sales and rental activity (except for open rentals).

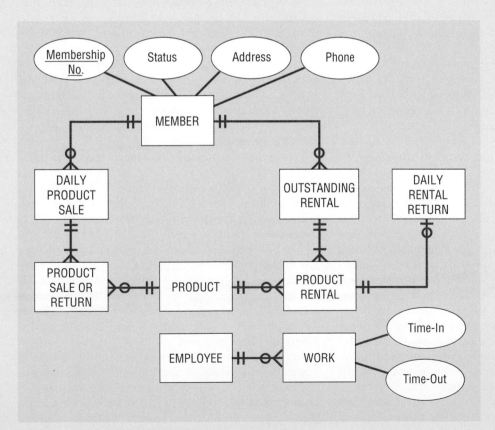

Figure 2
Store database

Data for those members who have had no activity at a local store for more than one year are purged from the local database. Approximately 3 percent of a store's transactions are made by infrequent or transient BEC members. Transient members are those who might use several stores in the same metropolitan area or who rent or purchase items while travelling away from their home. In certain locations, like resorts and college towns, transient customer transactions occur at a much higher percentage. When members use a BEC membership card and no member record exists in the local database, members are asked to provide a local address and phone number where they can be contacted.

All store employees, except the store manager who is on salary, are paid on an hourly basis, so clock-in and clock-out times are entered as a transaction, using employee badges with a bar code strip, on the same point-of-sale terminal used for member transactions. Paychecks are delivered by express mail twice a month. Employee reports (for example, attendance, payroll, and productivity) are produced by corporate systems and sent to store managers. Store managers have been asking for more time and attendance management support functions in the local computer system, but the functionality is currently minimal. Some store managers use stand-alone personal computers to manage personnel scheduling using packaged calendaring and project management software.

All other store record-keeping is manual and local stores do not pay any bills. Most bills, such as rent, utilities, and local advertisements, are sent directly to BEC headquarters; those which do come to a local store are simply forwarded to corporate offices by the store manager. Thus, the local store is not concerned with check writing, accounts payable, banking, or any other financial functions. Accounts receivable is a corporate function. Although the local store manager is responsible for contacting via phone or mail members who are late in returning rented items, the corporate accounts receivable department has final collection responsibilities including cancelling a member's membership. Each night a file of delinquent members is transmitted to each store and, if a member tries to use a delinquent membership, the member is asked to return all outstanding rentals before renting any more items and the current transaction is invalidated. Accounts receivable can also terminate a member for frequent delinquency or for other reasons. When terminated members try to use their cards, a BEC store clerk keeps the membership card and members are given a printed form which explains their rights at that point. Stolen membership cards are handled similarly, except that the store manager deals personally with people using cards that have been reported stolen.

CORPORATE SYSTEMS

Corporate systems run on IBM mainframes using IBM's DB2 relational database management system, although some run on PCs. Application software is written in COBOL, C, SQL (a database processing language), and several 4GLs, and all systems are developed by BEC. Clerks and managers use IBM 327x terminals and PCs for interactive access into corporate systems. There are also many PCs used by managers for stand-alone, end-user applications such as word processing, spreadsheets, specialized databases, and business graphics.

There are more than 20 major corporate systems with over 350 programs and approximately 500,000 lines of code. There are many more specialized systems, often developed for individual managers, projects, or special events. Table 2 lists some of the most active and largest of the major corporate systems. Most of these systems are a combination of transaction processing and MIS or MIS and DSS types. For example, the General Ledger and Financial Accounting application handles both transaction entries as well as management reports which summarize costs and revenues in a variety of ways. Since BEC does not hold any product inventory at the corporate level (all items are shipped directly from suppliers or distributors to the stores), there is no warehousing application.

One interesting aspect of the Banking application is that since stores have no financial responsibilities, BEC uses a local bank only for daily deposits and getting change. BEC's corporate bank, NCNB, arranges correspondent banking relationships for BEC so that local deposits are electronically transferred to BEC's corporate accounts with NCNB.

BEC's applications are still expanding, and they are under constant revision. For example, a current enhancement to the Sales Tracking and Analysis application deals with transient members. In cooperation with several hotel and motel chains that provide VCRs for rental, BEC is undertaking a new marketing campaign aimed at frequent travellers. Another study is underway to assess the costs of redesigning the Sales Tracking and Analysis application to support sales and rentals of business and training products to corporate members; this study will be used to help build the business case for this new market BEC is consider-

TABLE 2   List of BEC Corporate Applications

System Name	Description
Human Resources	Supports all employee functions, including payroll, benefits, employment and evaluation history, training, and career development (including a college scholarship for employees and dependents)
Accounts Receivable	Supports notification of overdue fees and collection of payment from delinquent customers
Banking	Supports interactions with banking institutions, including account management, electronic funds transfers
Accounts Payable, Purchasing, and Shipping	Supports ordering products and all other purchased items used internally and resold/rented, distribution of products to stores, and payment of vendors
General Ledger and Financial Accounting	Supports all financial statement and reporting functions
Property Management	Supports the purchasing, rental, and management of all properties and real estate used by BEC
Member Tracking	Supports record-keeping on all BEC members and transmits and receives member data between corporate and in-store systems
Inventory Management	Supports tracking inventory of items in stores and elsewhere and reordering those items that must be replenished
Sales Tracking and Analysis	Supports a variety of sales analysis activities in support of marketing and product purchasing functions based on sales and rental transaction data transmitted nightly from stores
Store Contact	Supports transmittal of data between corporate headquarters and stores nightly, and the transfer of data to and from corporate and store systems
Fraud	Supports monitoring abuse of membership privileges
Shareholder Services	Supports all shareholder activities, including recording stock purchases and transfers, disbursement of dividends, and reporting
Store and Site Analysis	Supports the activity and profit analysis of stores and the analysis of potential sites for stores

ing entering. At any one time, there are approximately 10 major system changes or new systems under development for corporate applications with over 250 change requests received annually covering requirements from minor bug fixes to reformatting or creating new reports to whole new systems.

STATUS OF SYSTEMS

A rapidly expanding business, BEC has created significant growth for the information systems group Karen Gardner manages. To date, BEC's international operations, headed by Oscar Morales, has not had its own development and support staff, but Karen is considering reorganizing her staff to provide focused attention to this important area. Since BEC wants to invest as much as possible in expansion—especially international—managers have been charged with increasing productivity without adding full-time staff. BEC still uses the services of Fitzgerald McNally, but on a very selective basis, such as when Karen's resources are fully committed. Karen's department includes 33 developers (programmers, analysts, and other specialists in database, networking, etc.) plus data center staff and is now large and technically skilled enough to handle almost all requests. Karen has created as professional an environment in BEC's IS group as exists at Fitzgerald McNally. For example, BEC recently acquired a CASE tool and adopted a standardized systems development methodology consistent with this tool.

Karen's current challenge in managing the IS group is keeping her staff current in the skills they need to successfully support the systems in a rapidly changing and competitive business environment. Besides adapting to new technical skills, Karen's staff needs to be excellent project managers, to completely understand the business, and to exhibit excellent communication with clients and each other. Karen is also concerned about information systems literacy among BEC management and that technology is not being as thoroughly exploited as it could be.

To deal with this situation, Karen is considering several initiatives. First, she has requested a sizeable increase in her training budget and has asked BEC to consider expanding the benefits of its college tuition reimbursement program. Second, Karen is considering instituting a management development program that will better develop junior staff members and will involve various user departments. As part of this program, BEC personnel will rotate in and out of the IS group as part of normal career progression. This program should greatly improve relationships with user departments and increase end-user understanding of technology. The development of this set of technical, managerial, business, and interpersonal skills in and outside IS is a critical success factor for Karen's group in responding to the significant demands and opportunities of the IS area.

SUMMARY

BEC has a hardware and software environment that is similar to that used by many national retail chains. Each store has a computer system with point-of-sale terminals which run mainly sales and rental transaction processing applications, such as product sales and rental, membership, store-level inventory, and employee pay activities. Corporate systems are executed on a mainframe computer at a corporate data center. Corporate systems handle all accounting, banking, property, sales and member tracking, and other applications that involve data from all stores.

BEC is a rapidly growing business with significant demand for information services. To build and maintain systems, BEC has divided its staff into functional area groups for both domestic and international needs. BEC uses modern database management and programming language technologies, including a CASE tool. The BEC IS organization is challenged by keeping current in both business and technology areas. We will see in subsequent case studies after subsequent chapters how BEC responds to a request for a new system within the business and technology environment described in the first two BEC case segments.

PART

II

Making the Business Case

Allison Engine Company

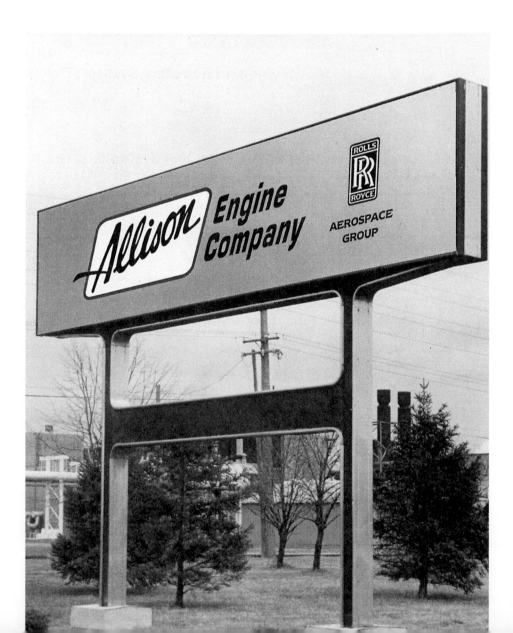

How Organizational and IS Strategies Are Related

Allison Engine Co., now owned by Rolls Royce, Inc., was formerly Allison Gas Turbine, a division of General Motors (GM), Inc. Allison manufactures gas turbine engines used in helicopters and various aircraft and does work relating to national defense.

While a division of GM, much of Allison's information systems needs were handled "back at corporate." Thus, while Allison employees did some processing locally on personal computers, the bulk of their business information systems was handled by GM. In the mid-80s GM bought Electronic Data Systems, Inc. (EDS), which eventually took over much of GM's information systems.

To process applications from its various divisions,

GM uses many mainframe class computers spread throughout the country. For example, some of the processing for Allison is done on a GM corporate-wide computer host in Plano, Texas, while other processing is done at various Information Processing Centers (IPCs) in Indianapolis, Michigan, and other locations. These various hosts are linked through EDSNET, a worldwide network enabling users to access information around the globe.

As with other firms, systems applications involving personnel processes are central to Allison's business processes. Yet nearly all of their personnel applications were handled off site by GM. To the employees at Allison, these personnel applications being run by GM at a distant IPC were to a great extent a "black box." Allison employees sent personnel information (for example, hours worked for each employee) to the GM IPC and GM would later send back output (for example, paychecks) to Allison. The IPC would charge Allison for each use depending on things such as connect time, cycle time, and number of pages in reports. This off-site processing was becoming very expensive to Allison.

Due to increased competitiveness in their industry, Allison management realized that they could not continue to pay for this expensive processing and remain competitive. Their organizational strategy was to become more and more cost-conscious and efficient, as were all other manufacturers in the aircraft and defense areas. In addition, the increased competitiveness necessitated changes in the way Allison reacted to their environment and ran their business. They needed to be more flexible and adaptable, better able to manage change. Allison needed to have more control over their own business processes and to quickly and easily access their internal business data for decision-making purposes.

Motivated by the changes in their environment and the pressures internally to cut costs, operate more efficiently, and take control of their own processes and data, Allison management decided to evaluate other information systems alternatives for their personnel applications. What they needed was a system that would fit better with their current environment and changing organizational strategy.

To address the concerns for control over processes and data, Allison management decided they needed a system developed and/or managed in-house. Further, there was a great deal of support internally for a client/server approach versus buying their own mainframe with terminals distributed throughout the site. It was thought that a client/server environment would provide more control over processes and better data access than would a mainframe. Given the concerns for costs, the in-house, client/server approach was additionally attractive from a financial perspective.

Allison and EDS ultimately implemented a UNIX-based Sun SparcStation, running People Soft personnel applications, less expensive even than a smaller main-

frame running similar software. These applications are accessible from any PC on the site if it is on the network and if the user has been granted access to the system. This alternative satisfied the criteria of decreased costs, increased control, and increased flexibility better than did other alternatives. Perhaps more importantly, this alternative satisfied the desire to move to a client/server environment.

Access to data is now much faster than before and, in many cases, access is instant. Users can query the system spontaneously and perform ad hoc reporting. Many users have a high-end PC on their desk connected to the new personnel application through the network. They can retrieve data from the personnel application and paste into their Microsoft Windows applications (for example, into Microsoft Excel) so that they can manipulate and graph the data. As a result, they are more in touch with their own data and in better control over their own business processes.

Allison employees feel that they now have an information system that better fits their organizational strategy for dealing with industry changes. Their new system satisfied objective criteria involving costs, control, and flexibility, and it satisfied the desire to move into new technologies.

An Overview of Part II

Making the Business Case

The demand for new or replacement systems exceeds the ability and resources of most organizations to conduct systems development projects by either themselves or consultants. (An advantage of this is, of course, that there is plenty of work for systems professionals, which is why most surveys of "hot careers" by *Money Magazine* and other sources consistently point to systems analysis as one of the leading current and future job areas.) Thus, organizations must set priorities and a direction for systems development that will yield development projects with the greatest net benefits. As a systems analyst, you must not only analyze user information requirements but also help make the business case, or justify why the system should be built and the development project conducted.

The reason for any new or improved information system is to add value to the organization. As systems analysts, we must choose to use systems development resources to build the mix of systems that adds the greatest value to the organization. How can we determine the business value of systems and identify those applications that provide the most critical gains? Part II addresses this topic, which we call making the business case. Business value comes from supporting the most critical business goals and helping the organization deliver on its business strategy. All systems, whether supporting operational or strategic functions, must be linked to business goals. The chapters in this part of the book show how to make this linkage.

The source of systems projects is either initiatives from information systems planning (proactive identification of systems) or requests from users or IS professionals (reactions to problems or opportunities) for new or enhanced systems. In Chapter 5 we outline the linkage among corporate planning, information systems planning, and the identification and selection of projects. We do not include IS planning as part of the SDLC, but the results of IS planning greatly influence the birth and conduct of systems projects. Chapter 5 makes a strong argument that IS planning provides not only insights into choosing which systems an organization needs, but also describes the strategies necessary for evaluating the viability of any potential systems project.

IS planning produces three key deliverables included in CASE repositories and project dictionaries—the information bases referenced throughout the systems development process. These deliverables are listed as follows:

1. IS plans for specific business areas, including general information requirements of projects for new or improved systems

2. Business area analyses that outline business strategy, objectives, critical success factors, and major business processes and data subjects for different business areas and the organization as a whole

3. A framework or architecture for systems that allows systems development teams and management to work together to build compatible and comprehensive systems.

Chapter 5 briefly outlines the process of IS planning and emphasizes these deliverables. Because of its periodic (usually annual) timing and macro orientation, IS planning is not a frequent activity conducted by systems analysts. The results of IS planning, however, directly affect and are used within systems development work, which is why Chapter 5 concentrates on the linkage between IS planning and projects. The organizations that are most successful in deploying systems are those that link their IS application portfolio to business and IS plans—thus the importance of this topic in our discussion of systems analysis and design.

We continue with the Broadway Entertainment Company (BEC) case following Chapter 5. In this case, we show how an idea for a new information system was stimulated from a synergy of corporate strategic planning and the creativity of an individual business manager. We also show how this idea is initially evaluated and how it leads to the initiation of a systems development project.

The actual SDLC itself starts when a potential development project is identified. As stated previously, IS planning can result in an outline for a systems project to build some needed system or to replace a system that is identified as inconsistent with or seriously harming business directions. Another, more frequent source of project identification originates from system service requests (SSRs) from business managers and IS professionals, usually for very focused systems or incremental improvements in existing systems. User managers request a new or replacement system when they believe that improved information services will help them do their jobs. IS professionals may request system updates when technological changes make current system implementations obsolete or when the performance of an existing system needs improvement. In either case, the request for service must be understood by management and a justification for the system and associated project must be developed. The SDLC initial phase, consisting of project initiation and planning, is the subject of Chapter 6. (Project initiation and planning are also the first two steps of project management, as described in Chapter 3 in Part I.)

During project initiation and planning, a brief study is conducted to investigate the proposed system request. This study develops a better understanding of the scope of the potential system change and the nature of the needed system features. From this preliminary understanding of system requirements, a project plan is developed which shows both the detailed steps and resources needed in order to conduct the analysis phase of the life cycle and the more general steps for subsequent phases. The feasibility and potential risks of the requested system are also outlined and an economic cost-benefit analysis is conducted to show the potential impact of the system change. In addition to the economic feasibility or justification of the system, technical, organizational, political, legal, schedule, and other feasibilities are assessed. Potential risks—unwanted outcomes—are identified and plans for dealing with these possibilities are identified. Project initiation and planning ends when a formal proposal for the systems development project is completed and submitted for approval to whomever must commit the resources to systems development. If approved, the project moves into the analysis phase.

The reason for the project initiation and planning phase is found, in part, in the notion of incremental commitment. The main purpose of project initiation and planning is to assess the worthiness of the identified system and to decide if there is enough potential benefit for the organization to invest in the project further. Thus, project initiation and planning, although critical in the SDLC, must be conducted with minimal time and resources in order to minimize sunk costs. Consequently, the ability to conduct this phase, often done by only one analyst in conjunction with the project requester, is of the utmost importance to successful systems analysis and design.

We illustrate a typical project initiation and planning phase in a BEC case following Chapter 6. In this case, we show how BEC identified one critically important business goal, which provided the motivation for a requested system. The case further shows how an analysis of this business goal leads to the justification for a system with a competitive advantage for BEC and then to the associated development project plan.

CHAPTER

5

Identifying and Selecting Systems Development Projects

INTRODUCTION

The scope of information systems today is the whole enterprise. Managers, knowledge workers, and all other organizational members expect to easily access and retrieve information, regardless of its location. Non-integrated systems used in the past—often referred to as "islands of information"—are being replaced with cooperative, integrated enterprise systems that can easily support information sharing (Morton, 1992). While the goal of building bridges between these "islands" will take some time to achieve, it represents a clear direction for information systems development.

Obtaining integrated enterprise-wide computing presents significant challenges for both corporate and information systems management. For example, given the proliferation of personal and departmental computing wherein disparate systems and databases have been created, how can the organization possibly control and maintain all of these systems and data? In many cases they simply cannot because it is nearly impossible to track who has which systems and what data, where there are overlaps or inconsistencies, and how accurate the information is. The reason that personal and departmental systems and databases abound is that users are either unaware of the information that exists in corporate databases or they cannot easily get at it, so they create and maintain their own information and systems (Reingruber and Spahr, 1992). Intelligent identification and selection of systems development projects, for both new and replacement systems, are critical steps in gaining control of systems and data.

The acquisition, development, and maintenance of information systems consume substantial resources for most organizations. This suggests that organizations can benefit from following a formal process for identifying and selecting projects. The first phase of the systems development life cycle—project identification and selection—deals with this issue. In the next section, you will learn about a general method for identifying and selecting projects and the deliverables and outcomes from this process. This is followed by brief descriptions of corporate strategic planning and information systems planning, two activities that can greatly improve the project identification and selection process.

IDENTIFYING AND SELECTING SYSTEMS DEVELOPMENT PROJECTS

The first phase of the SDLC is project identification and selection. During this activity, a senior manager, a business group, an IS manager, or a steering committee identify and assess all possible systems development projects that an organization unit could undertake. Next, those projects deemed most likely to yield significant organizational benefits, given available resources, are selected for subsequent development activities. Organizations vary in their approach to identifying and selecting projects. In some organizations, project identification and selection is a very formal process in which projects are outcomes of a larger overall planning process. For example, a large organization may follow a formal project identification process whereby a proposed project is rigorously compared to all competing projects. Alternatively, a small organization may use informal project selection processes that allow the highest-ranking IS manager to independently select projects or allow individual business units to decide on projects after agreeing to provide project funding.

There is a variety of sources for information systems development requests. One source is requests by managers and business units for replacing or extending an existing system to gain needed information or to provide a new service to customers. Another source for requests is IS managers who want to make a system more efficient, less costly to operate, or want to move it to a new operating environment. A final source of projects is a formal planning group which identifies projects for improvement that would help the organization meet its corporate objectives (for example, a new system to provide better customer service). Regardless of how a given organization actually executes the project identification and selection process, there is a common sequence of activities that occurs. In the following sections, we describe a general process for identifying and selecting projects and producing the deliverables and outcomes of this process.

The Process of Identifying and Selecting IS Development Projects

As shown in Figure 5-1, project identification and selection consists of three primary activities:

1. Identifying potential development projects

2. Classifying and ranking projects

3. Selecting projects for development

Figure 5-1
Systems development life cycle with project identification and selection highlighted

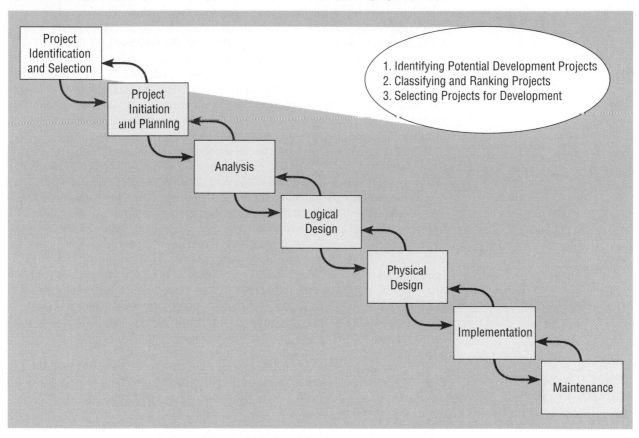

Each of these steps is described below:

1. *Identifying Potential Development Projects.* Organizations vary as to how they identify projects. This process can be performed by

   - A key member of top management, either the CEO of a small- or medium-sized organization or a senior executive in a larger organization

   - A steering committee, composed of a cross section of managers with an interest in systems

   - User departments, in which either the head of the requesting unit or a committee from the requesting department decides which projects to submit (often you, as a systems analyst, will help users prepare such requests)

   - The development group or a senior IS manager

   All methods of identification have been found to have strengths and weaknesses. Research has found, for example, that projects identified by top management more often have a strategic organizational focus. Alternatively, projects identified by steering committees more often reflect the diversity of the committee and therefore have a cross-functional focus. Projects identified by individual departments or business units most often have a narrow, tactical focus. Finally, a dominant characteristic of projects identified by the development group is the ease with which existing hardware and systems will integrate with the proposed project. Other factors, such as project cost, duration, complexity, and risk, are also influenced by the source of a given project. Characteristics of each selection method are briefly summarized in Table 5-1.

Of all the possible project sources, those identified by top management and steering committees most often reflect the broader needs of the organization. This occurs because top management and steering committees are likely to have a broader understanding of overall business objectives and constraints. Projects identified by top management or by a diverse steering committee are therefore referred to as coming from a top-down source.

Projects identified by a functional manager, business unit, or by the information systems development group are often designed for a particular business need within a given business unit. In other words, these projects may not reflect the overall objectives of the organization. This does not mean that projects identified by individual managers, business units, or the IS development group are deficient, only that they may not consider broader organizational issues. Project initiatives stemming from managers, business units, or the development group are generally referred to as coming from a bottom-up source. These are the types of projects in which you, as a systems analyst, will have the earliest role in the life cycle as part of your ongoing support of users. You will help user managers provide the description of information needs and the reasons for doing the project that will be evaluated in selecting, among all submitted projects, which ones will be approved to move into the project initiation and planning phase of the SDLC.

In sum, projects are identified by both top-down and bottom-up initiatives. The formality of the process of identifying and selecting projects can

TABLE 5-1 Characteristics of Alternative Methods for Making Information Systems Identification and Selection Decisions

Selection Method	Characteristics
Top Management	Greater strategic focus
	Largest project size
	Longest project duration
Steering Committee	Cross-Functional focus
	Greater organizational change
	Formal cost-benefit analysis
	Larger and riskier projects
User Department	Narrow, non-strategic focus
	Faster development
	Fewer users, management layers, and business functions
Development Group	Integration with existing systems focus
	Fewer development delays
	Less concern on cost-benefit analysis

Adapted from McKeen, Guimaraes, and Wetherbe, 1994

vary substantially across organizations. Also, since limited resources preclude the development of all proposed systems, most organizations have some process of classifying and ranking the merit of each project. Those projects deemed to be inconsistent with overall organizational objectives, redundant in functionality to some existing system, or unnecessary will thus be removed from consideration. This topic is discussed next.

2. *Classifying and Ranking IS Development Projects.* The second major activity in the project identification and selection process focuses on assessing the relative merit of potential projects. As with the project identification process, classifying and ranking projects can be performed by top managers, a steering committee, business units, or the IS development group. Additionally, the criteria used when assigning the relative merit of a given project can vary. Commonly used criteria for assessing projects are summarized in Table 5-2. In any given organization, one or several criteria might be used during the classifying and ranking process.

As with the project identification and selection process, the actual criteria used to assess projects will vary by organization. If, for example, an organization uses a steering committee, it may choose to meet monthly or quarterly to review projects and use a wide variety of evaluation criteria. At these meetings, new project requests will be reviewed relative to projects already identified, and ongoing projects are monitored. The relative ratings of projects are used to guide the final activity of this identification process—project selection.

An important project evaluation method that is widely used for assessing information systems development projects is called **value chain analysis** (Porter, 1985; Shank and Govindarajan, 1993). Value chain analysis is the process of analyzing an organization's activities for making products and/or services to determine where value is added and costs are incurred. Once an organization gains a clear understanding of its value chain, improvements in the organization's operations and performance can be achieved. Information systems projects providing the greatest benefit to the value chain will be given priority over those with fewer benefits.

As you might have guessed, information systems have become one of the primary ways for organizations to make changes and improvements in their

Value chain analysis:
Analyzing an organization's activities to determine where value is added to products and/or services and the costs incurred for doing so; usually also includes a comparison with the activities, added value, and costs of other organizations for the purpose of making improvements in the organization's operations and performance.

TABLE 5-2 Possible Evaluation Criteria When Classifying and Ranking Projects

Evaluation Criteria	Description
Value Chain Analysis	Extent to which activities add value and costs when developing products and/or services
Strategic Alignment	Extent to which the project is viewed as helping the organization achieve its strategic objectives and long-term goals
Potential Benefits	Extent to which the project is viewed as improving profits, customer service, etc. and the duration of these benefits
Resource Availability	Amount and type of resources the project requires and their availability
Project Size/Duration	Number of individuals and the length of time needed to complete the project
Technical Difficulty/Risks	Level of technical difficulty to successfully complete the project within given time and resource constraints

value chains. Many organizations, for example, are using the Internet to exchange important business information with suppliers and customers such as orders, invoices, and receipts. To conduct a value chain analysis for an organization, think about an organization as a big input/output process (see Figure 5-2). At one end are the inputs to the organization, for example, supplies that are purchased. Within the organizations, those supplies and resources are integrated in some way to produce products and services. At the other end are the outputs, which represent the products and services that are marketed, sold, and then distributed to customers. In value chain analysis, you must first understand each activity, function, and process where value is or should be added. Next, determine the costs (and the factors that drive costs or cause them to fluctuate) within each of the areas. After understanding your value chain and costs, you can benchmark (compare) your value chain and associated costs with those of other organizations, preferably your competitors. By making these comparisons, you can identify priorities for applying information systems projects.

3. *Selecting IS Development Projects.* The final activity in the project identification and selection process is the actual selection of projects for further development. Project selection is a process of considering both short- and long-term projects and selecting those most likely to achieve business objectives. Additionally, as business conditions change over time, the relative importance of any single project may substantially change. Thus, the identification and selection of projects is a very important and ongoing activity.

Figure 5-2
Organizational value chain
(Source: reprinted with the permission of The Free Press, a Division of Simon & Schuster, Inc. from *Competitive Advantage: Creating and Sustaining Superior Performance* by Michael E. Porter. Copyright © 1985 by Michael Porter.)

Numerous factors must be considered when making project selection decisions. Figure 5-3 shows that a selection decision requires that the perceived needs of the organization, existing systems and ongoing projects, resource availability, evaluation criteria, current business conditions, and the perspectives of the decision makers will all play a role in project selection decisions. Numerous outcomes can occur from this decision process. Of course, projects can be accepted or rejected. Acceptance of a project usually means that funding to conduct the next phase of the SDLC has been approved. Rejection means that the project will no longer be considered for development. However, projects may also be conditionally accepted; projects may be accepted pending the approval or availability of needed resources or the demonstration that a particularly difficult aspect of the system *can* be developed. Projects may also be returned to the original requesters who are told to develop or purchase the requested system themselves. Finally, the requesters of a project may be asked to modify and resubmit their request after making suggested changes or clarifications.

Deliverables and Outcomes

The primary deliverable from the first SDLC phase is a schedule of specific IS development projects, coming from both top-down and bottom-up sources, to move into the next SDLC phase—project initiation and planning (see Figure 5-4). An outcome of this phase is the assurance that careful consideration was given to project selection, with a clear understanding of how each project can help the organization reach its objectives. Due to the principle of **incremental commitment,** a selected project does not necessarily result in a working system. After each subsequent SDLC phase, you, other members of the project team, and organizational officials will reassess your project to determine whether the business conditions have changed or whether a more detailed understanding of a system's costs, benefits, and risks would suggest that the project is not as worthy as previously thought.

Many organizations have found that in order to make good project selection decisions and to provide sound guidance as issues arise in your work as a systems

Incremental Commitment:
A strategy in systems analysis and design in which the project is reviewed after each phase and continuation of the project is rejustified in each of these reviews.

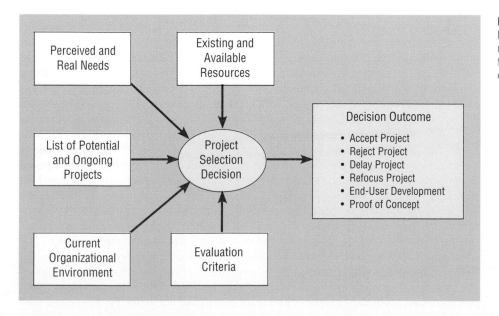

Figure 5-3
Project selection decisions must consider numerous factors and can have numerous outcomes

Figure 5-4

Information systems development projects come from both top-down and bottom-up initiatives

analyst on a project, a clear understanding of overall organizational business strategy and objectives is required. This means that a clear understanding of the business and the desired role of information systems in achieving organizational goals is a precondition to improving the identification and selection process. In the next section we provide a brief overview of the process many organizations follow, involving corporate strategic planning and information systems planning, when setting their business strategy and objectives and when defining the role of information systems in their plans.

CORPORATE AND INFORMATION SYSTEMS PLANNING

Although there are numerous motivations for carefully planning the identification and selection of projects (see Atkinson, 1990; Atkinson and Montgomery, 1990), organizations have not traditionally used a systematic planning process when determining how to allocate IS resources. Instead, projects have often resulted from attempts to solve isolated organizational problems. In effect, organizations have asked the question: "What procedure (application program) is required to solve *this particular problem* as it exists today?" The difficulty with this approach is that the required organizational procedures are likely to change over time as the environment changes. For example, a company may decide to change its method of billing customers or a university may change its procedures for registering students. When such changes occur, it is usually necessary to again modify existing information systems.

In contrast, planning-based approaches essentially ask the question: "What information (or data) requirements will satisfy the decision-making needs or business processes of the enterprise today and well into the future?" A major advantage of this approach is that an organization's informational needs are less likely to change (or will change more slowly) than its business processes. For example, unless an organization fundamentally changes its business, its underlying data structures may remain reasonably stable for more than ten years. However, the procedures used to access and process the data may change many times during that period. Thus, the challenge of most organizations is to design comprehensive information models containing data that are relatively independent from the languages and programs used to access, create, and update them.

To benefit from a planning-based approach for identifying and selecting projects, an organization must analyze its information needs and plan its projects carefully. Without careful planning, organizations may construct databases and systems that support individual processes but do not provide a resource that can be easily shared throughout the organization. Further, as business processes change, lack of data and system integration will hamper the speed at which the organization can effectively make business strategy or process changes.

The need for improved information systems project identification and selection is readily apparent when we consider factors such as the following:

1. The cost of information systems has risen steadily and approaches 40 percent of total expenses in some organizations.

2. Many systems cannot handle applications that cross organizational boundaries.

3. Many systems often do not address the critical problems of the business as a whole nor support strategic applications.

4. Data redundancy is often out of control and users may have little confidence in the quality of data.

5. Systems maintenance costs are out of control as old, poorly planned systems must constantly be revised.

6. Application backlogs often extend three years or more and frustrated end users are forced to create (or purchase) their own systems, often creating redundant databases and incompatible systems in the process.

Careful planning and selection of projects alone will certainly not solve all of these problems. We believe, however, that a disciplined approach, driven by top management commitment, is a prerequisite to most effectively apply information systems in order to reach organizational objectives. The focus of this section is to provide you with a clear understanding of how specific development projects with a broader organizational focus can be identified and selected. Specifically, we describe corporate strategic planning and information systems planning, two processes that can significantly improve the quality of project identification and selection decisions. This section also outlines the types of information about business direction and general systems requirements that can influence the selection decisions and guide the direction of approved projects.

Corporate Strategic Planning

A prerequisite to making effective project selection decisions is to gain a clear idea of where an organization is, its vision of where it wants to be in the future, and how to make the transition to its desired future state. Figure 5-5 represents this as a three-step process. The first step focuses on gaining an understanding of the current enterprise. In other words, if you don't know where you are, it is impossible to tell where you are going. Next, top management must determine where it wants the enterprise to be in the future. Finally, after gaining an understanding of the current and future enterprise, a strategic plan can be developed to guide this transition. The process of developing and refining models of the current and future enterprise as well as a transition strategy is often referred to as **corporate strategic planning.**

Corporate strategic planning: An ongoing process that defines the mission, objectives, and strategies of an organization.

Figure 5-5
Corporate strategic planning
is a three-step process

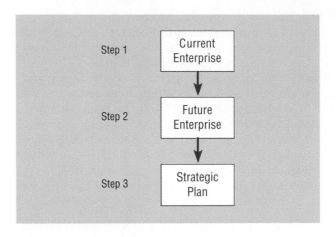

During corporate strategic planning, executives typically develop a mission statement, statements of future corporate objectives, and strategies designed to help the organization reach its objectives.

Mission statement: A statement that makes it clear what business a company is in.

All successful organizations have a mission. The **mission statement** of a company typically states in very simple terms what business the company is in. For example, the mission statement for Pine Valley Furniture (PVF) is shown in Figure 5-6. After reviewing the mission statement from PVF, it becomes clear that they are in the business of constructing and selling high-quality wood furniture to the general public, businesses, and institutions such as universities and hospitals. It is also clear that PVF is not in the business of fabricating steel file cabinets or selling their products through wholesale distributors. Based on this mission statement, you could conclude that PVF does not need a retail sales information system; instead, a high-quality human resource information system would be consistent with their goal.

Objective statements: A series of statements that express an organization's qualitative and quantitative goals for reaching a desired future position.

After defining its mission, an organization can then define its objectives. The **objective statements** refer to "broad and timeless" goals for the organization. These goals can be expressed as a series of statements that are either qualitative or quantitative but that typically do not contain details likely to change substantially over time. Objectives are often referred to as "critical success factors." Here, we will simply use the term "objectives." The objectives for PVF are shown in Figure 5-7,

Figure 5-6
Mission statement (Pine
Valley Furniture)

Pine Valley Furniture
Corporate Mission Statement

We are in the business of designing,
fabricating, and selling to retail stores
high-quality wood furniture for
household, office, and institutional use.
We value quality in our products and
in our relationships with customers and
suppliers. We consider our employees
our most critical resource.

Figure 5-7
Statement of corporate
objectives (Pine Valley
Furniture)

Pine Valley Furniture
Statement of Objectives

1. PVF will strive to increase market share and profitability (prime objective).

2. PVF will be considered a market leader in customer service.

3. PVF will be innovative in the use of technology to help bring new products to market faster than our competition.

4. PVF will employ the fewest number of the highest-quality people necessary to accomplish our prime objective.

5. PVF will create an environment that values diversity in gender, race, values, and culture among employees, suppliers, and customers.

with most relating to some aspect of the organizational mission. For example, objective number two relates to how PVF views its relationships with customers. This goal would suggest that PVF might want to invest in electronic data interchange or on-line order status systems that would contribute to high-quality customer service. Once a company has defined its mission and objectives, a competitive strategy can be formulated.

A **competitive strategy** is the method by which an organization attempts to achieve its mission and objectives. In essence, the strategy is an organization's game plan for playing in the competitive business world. In his classic book on competitive strategy, Michael Porter (1980) defined three generic strategies—low-cost producer, product differentiation, and product focus or niche—for reaching corporate objectives (see Table 5-3). These generic strategies allow you to more

Competitive strategy: The method by which an organization attempts to achieve its mission and objectives.

TABLE 5-3   Generic Competitive Strategies

Strategy	Description
Low-Cost Producer	This strategy reflects competing in an industry on the basis of product or service cost to the consumer. For example, in the automobile industry, the South Korean-produced Hyundai is a product line that competes on the basis of low cost.
Product Differentiation	This competitive strategy reflects capitalizing on a key product criterion requested by the market (for example, high quality, style, performance, roominess). In the automobile industry, many manufacturers are trying to differentiate their products on the basis of quality (for example, "At Ford, quality is job one.").
Product Focus or Niche	This strategy is similar to both the low-cost and differentiation strategies but with a much narrower market focus. For example, a niche market in the automobile industry is the convertible sports car market. Within this market, some manufacturers may employ a low-cost strategy while others may employ a differentiation strategy on performance or style.

Adapted from Porter, 1980

easily compare two companies in the same industry that may not employ the same competitive strategy. In addition, organizations employing different competitive strategies often have different informational needs to aid decision making. For example, Rolls Royce and GEO are two car lines with different strategies: one is a high-prestige line in the ultra-luxury *niche* while the other is a relatively *low-priced* line for the general automobile market. Rolls Royce may build information systems to collect and analyze information on customer satisfaction to help manage a key company objective. Alternatively, GEO may build systems to track plant and material utilization in order to manage activities related to their low-cost strategy.

To effectively deploy resources such as the creation of a marketing and sales organization, *or to build the most effective information systems,* an organization must clearly understand its mission, objectives, and strategy. A lack of understanding will make it impossible to know which activities are essential to achieving business objectives. From an information systems development perspective, by understanding which activities are most critical for achieving business objectives, an organization has a much greater chance to identify those activities that need to be supported by information systems. In other words, **it is only through the clear understanding of the organizational mission, objectives, and strategies that IS development projects should be identified and selected.** The process of planning how information systems can be employed to assist organizations to reach their objectives is the focus of the next section.

Information Systems Planning

Information systems planning (ISP): An orderly means of assessing the information needs of an organization and defining the systems, databases, and technologies that will best satisfy those needs.

The second planning process that can play a significant role in the quality of project identification and selection decisions is called **information systems planning (ISP).** Information systems planning is an orderly means of assessing the information needs of an organization and defining the information systems, databases, and technologies that will best satisfy those needs (Carlson, Gardner, and Ruth, 1989; Parker and Benson, 1989). This means that during ISP you (or, more likely, senior IS managers responsible for the IS plan) must model current and future organization informational needs, and develop strategies and *project plans* to migrate the current information systems and technologies to their desired future state. ISP is a top-down process that takes into account the outside forces—industry, economic, relative size, geographic region, and so on—critical to the success of the firm. This means that ISP must look at information systems and technologies in terms of how they help the business achieve its objectives defined during corporate strategic planning.

The three key activities of this modeling process are represented in Figure 5-8. Like corporate strategic planning, ISP is a three-step process in which the first step is to assess current IS-related assets—human resources, data, processes, and technologies. Next, target blueprints of these resources are developed. These blueprints reflect the desired future state of resources needed by the organization to reach its objectives as defined during strategic planning. Figures 5-9, 5-10, and Table 5-4 describe one popular framework for representing these blueprints—an information systems architecture. Finally, a series of scheduled projects is defined to help move the organization from its current to its future desired state. (Of course, scheduled projects from the ISP process are just one source for projects. Others include bottom-up requests from managers and business units like the System Service Request in Figure 3-2.)

In terms of an information systems architecture as described in Figure 5-10, the purpose of a project is to improve the functionality or operation of information systems in one or more cells of this matrix. For example, a project may focus on

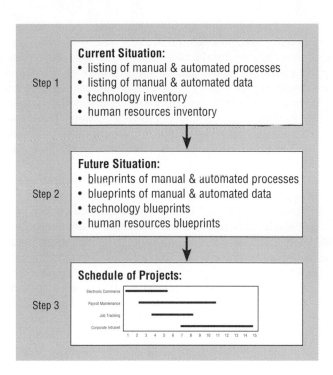

Figure 5-8
Information systems planning
is a three-step process

reconfiguration of a telecommunications network to speed data communications (row 5 of the Network column), or may restructure work and data flows between business areas (possibly row 3 and below of the process column). Projects can include not only the development of new information systems or the modification of existing ones but also the acquisition and management of new systems, technologies, and platforms. These three activities parallel those of corporate strategic planning and this relationship is shown in Figure 5-11. Numerous methodologies such as Business Systems Planning (BSP) and Information Engineering (IE) have been developed to support the ISP process[1]; most contain the three key activities described below:

1. *Describing the Current Situation.* The most widely used approach for describing the current organizational situation is generically referred to as top-down planning. **Top-down planning** attempts to gain a broad understanding of the informational needs of the entire organization. The approach begins by conducting an extensive analysis of the organization's mission, objectives, and strategy and determining the information requirements needed to meet each objective. This approach to ISP implies by its name a high-level organizational perspective with active involvement of top-level management. The top-down approach to ISP has several advantages over other planning approaches, and these are summarized in Table 5-5.

   In contrast to the top-down planning approach, a **bottom-up planning** approach requires the identification of business problems and opportunities which are used to define projects. Using the bottom-up approach for creating

Top-down planning: A generic information systems planning methodology that attempts to gain a broad understanding of the information system needs of the entire organization.

Bottom-up planning: A generic information systems planning methodology that identifies and defines IS development projects based upon solving operational business problems or taking advantage of some business opportunities.

---

[1]For an overview of several information systems planning methodologies, see Koory and Medley (1987) or Martin (1990).

Figure 5-9
Representing information
systems plans using an
information systems
architecture

If you were planning to build a new home, you would certainly want to have a blueprint or set of architectural plans before starting construction. In fact, almost any large-scale creative endeavor requires the early development of a vision or architectural plan if that endeavor is to be successfully completed. Designing the blueprints for the future vision of information systems is one of the greatest challenges facing most organizations today. You may be surprised to learn that (unfortunately) many organizations do not have a comprehensive architectural plan for their information systems, although this is changing.

In 1987, John Zachman (then of IBM) developed a comprehensive framework for portraying an information systems architecture (ISA) which is shown in Figure 5-10 (Zachman, 1987). In this framework every information system can be visualized as a combination of three major components: Data, Process, and Network. The Data column represents the "what" in an information system. For example, in a manufacturing system, the "what" might correspond to a bill of materials listing the components required to assemble a finished product. The Process column represents "how." For example, the list of instructions that specify "how" a finished product is assembled from its components. The Network column represents "where," such as the locations of data, processing, and other resources.

The ISA has six rows that represent different views of the data, processes, and network components. Zachman used a construction industry analogy to describe the roles individuals within an organization play when sponsoring, designing, building, and using an information system. Each role corresponds to a row within the framework (see Table 5-4). During its evolution, an information system should move through the cells of the framework from the top of the framework to the bottom. As this occurs, top-level information is transformed into more concrete representations of the system. The lowest level represents an actual information system.

In more recent work, Sowa and Zachman (1992) extend the concepts of the information systems architecture to also include "who, when, and why" components. These three components extend the "what, how, and where" components so that all English language question words are included in the model. Who refers to the concept of determining *who* works with the system. When reflects information related to understanding *when* events occur. Information related to why helps to uncover *why* events occur. The objective of the extended ISA model is to create a systematic taxonomy for relating things in the world to representations in the computer. In other words, the extended ISA framework provides a structured way for viewing information systems from many different perspectives and showing how each is related. Using formal methods such as the ISA framework to represent information systems and plans is becoming more common. If you have not already, it is likely that you will have the opportunity to learn more about this or some similar technique as your career evolves.

IS plans can be faster and less costly to develop than using the top-down approach and also has the advantage of identifying pressing organizational problems. Yet, the bottom-up approach often fails to view the informational needs of the *entire* organization. This can result in the creation of disparate information systems and databases that are redundant or not easily integrated without substantial rework.

Figure 5-10
Information systems architecture framework (Adapted from Zachman, 1987)

		Data	Process	Network
1	Business Scope	List of Entities Important to the Business	List of Functions the Business Performs	List of Locations in which the Business Operates
2	Business Model	Business Entities and their Inter-relationships	Function and Process Decomposition	Communications Links between Business Locations
3	Information Systems Model	Model of the Business Data and their Inter-relationships	Flows between Application Processes	Distribution Network
4	Technology Model	Database Design	Process Specifications	Configuration Design
5	Technology Definition	Database Schema and Subschema Definition	Program Code and Control Blocks	Configuration Definition
6	Information System	Data and Information	Application Programs	System Configuration

The process of describing the current situation begins by selecting a planning team that includes executives chartered to model the existing situation. To gain this understanding, the team will need to review corporate documents; interview managers, executives, and customers; and conduct detailed reviews of competitors, markets, products, and finances. The type of information that must be collected to represent the current situation includes the identification of all organizational locations, units, functions, processes, data (or data entities), and information systems.

TABLE 5-4 Models and Roles in the Information Systems Framework		
Model Name	**Role or Perspective**	**Role Description**
Business Scope	Owner	Provides a strategic overview including business scope, mission, and direction
Business Model	Architect	Develops business models that describe the business scope, mission, and direction
Information Systems Model	Designer	Develops information systems models that support the business
Technology Model	Builder	Converts information systems models into a design that conforms to the features and constraints of the technology
Technology Definition	Contractor	Converts technology models into statements to generate the actual information system
Information System	User	Manages, uses, and operates the completed information system

Adapted from Moriarty, 1991

Figure 5-11
Parallel activities of corporate strategic planning and information systems planning

Within Pine Valley Furniture, for example, organizational locations would consist of a list of all geographic areas in which the organization operates (for example, the locations of the home and branch offices). Organizational units represent a list of people or business units that operate within the organization. Thus, organizational units would include vice president manufacturing, sales manager, sales person, and clerk. Functions are cross-organizational col-

TABLE 5-5 Advantages to the Top-Down Planning Approach over Other Planning Approaches

Advantage	Description
Broader Perspective	If not viewed from the top, information systems may be implemented without first understanding the business from general management's viewpoint.
Improved Integration	If not viewed from the top, totally new management information systems may be implemented rather than planning how to evolve existing systems.
Improved Management Support	If not viewed from the top, planners may lack sufficient management acceptance of the role of information systems in helping them achieve business objectives.
Better Understanding	If not viewed from the top, planners may lack the understanding necessary to implement information systems across the entire business rather than simply to individual operating units.

IBM, 1982; pp. 236–37

lections of activities used to perform day-to-day business operations. Examples of business functions might include research and development, employee development, purchasing, and sales. Processes represent a list of manual or automated procedures designed to support business functions. Examples of business processes might include payroll processing, customer billing, and product shipping. Data entities represent a list of the information items generated, updated, deleted, or used within business processes. Information systems represent automated and non-automated systems used to transform data into information to support business processes. For example, Figure 5-12 shows portions of the business functions, data entities, and information systems of PVF. Once high-level information is collected, each item can typically be decomposed into smaller units as more detailed planning is performed. Figure 5-13 shows the decomposition of several of PVF's high-level business functions into more detailed supporting functions.

After creating these lists, a series of matrices can be developed to cross reference various elements of the organization. The types of matrices typically developed include the following:

- *Location-to-Function:* This matrix identifies which business functions are being performed at various organizational locations.

- *Location-to-Unit:* This matrix identifies which organizational units are located in or interact with a specific business location.

FUNCTIONS:
- business planning
- product development
- marketing and sales
- production operations
- finance and accounting
- human resources
…

DATA ENTITIES:
- customer
- product
- vendor
- raw material
- order
- invoice
- equipment
…

INFORMATION SYSTEMS:
- payroll processing
- accounts payable
- accounts receivable
- time card processing
- inventory management
…

Figure 5-12
Information systems planning information (Pine Valley Furniture)

Figure 5-13
Functional decomposition of information systems planning information (Pine Valley Furniture)

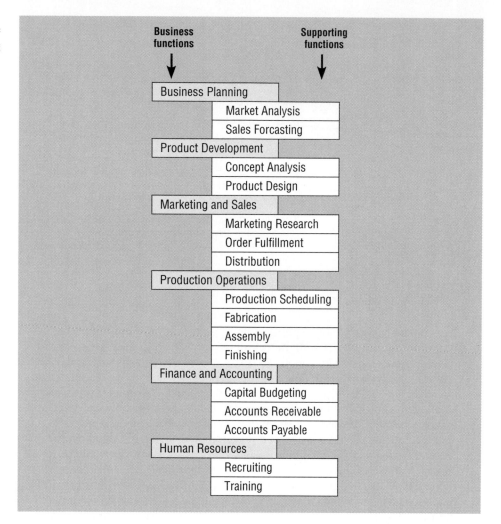

- *Unit-to-Function:* This matrix identifies the relationships between organizational entities and each business function.
- *Function-to-Objective:* This matrix identifies which functions are essential or desirable in achieving each organizational objective.
- *Function-to-Process:* This matrix identifies which processes are used to support each business function.
- *Function-to-Data Entity:* This matrix identifies which business functions utilize which data entities.
- *Process-to-Data Entity:* This matrix identifies which data are captured, used, updated, or deleted within each process.
- *Process-to-Information System:* This matrix identifies which information systems are used to support each process.
- *Data Entity-to-Information System:* This matrix identifies which data are created, updated, accessed, or deleted in each system.
- *Information System-to-Objective:* This matrix identifies which information systems support each business objective as identified during organizational planning.

For example, Figure 5-14 shows a portion of the Data Entity-to-Function matrix for Pine Valley Furniture. The "X" in various cells of the matrix represents which business functions utilize which data entities. A more detailed picture of data utilization would be shown in the Process-to-Data Entity matrix (not shown here), where the cells would be coded as "C" for the associated process that creates or captures data for the associated data entity, "R" for retrieve (or used), "U" for update, and "D" for delete.

Different matrices will have different relationships depending upon what is being represented. For example, Figure 5-15 shows a portion of the Information System-to-Objective matrix. In this matrix, those objectives that are *currently* supported by existing information systems are labeled "C," and objectives intended to be supported by *future* development are represented by "F." One way this matrix would be useful in project selection of a bottom-up project would be as follows. Suppose a request came in to make changes to the Payroll system. You can see from the C in the Payroll row and Profit column that this system currently supports the profit objective well; the requested change should be based on making a contribution to other objectives (for example, personnel) in order to be considered worthwhile. Various impact analyses like this are possible via one matrix or combination of matrices. Through the creation and analysis of these matrices, planners can gain a clear understanding of the organization's current situation (Kerr, 1990). A primer on using matrices for information systems planning is provided in Figure 5-16.

2. *Describing the Target Situation, Trends, and Constraints.* After describing the current situation, the next step in the ISP process is to define the target situation

Figure 5-14
Data Entity-to-Function matrix (Pine Valley Furniture)

Business Functions \ Data Entity Types	Customer	Product	Vendor	Raw Material	Order	Work Center	Equipment	Employees	Invoice	Work Order	...
Marketing and Sales											
Marketing Research	X	X									
Order Fulfillment	X	X			X				X		
Distribution	X	X									
Production Operations											
Production Scheduling						X	X	X		X	
Fabrication						X	X	X		X	
Assembly						X	X	X		X	
Finishing						X	X	X		X	
Finance and Accounting											
Capital Budgeting						X	X				
Accounts Receivable	X	X			X						
Accounts Payable			X	X	X				X		
Human Resources											
Recruiting								X			
Training								X			
...											

X = data entity is used within business function

Figure 5-15
Information System-to-Objective matrix (Pine Valley Furniture)

Information System	Profit	Service	Innovation	Personnel	Diversity
Transaction Processing					
Order Tracking	F	F		F	
Order Processing	C	C		C	
Plant Scheduling	F	F		F	
Payroll	C				
Accounts Payable	C			C	
Accounts Receivable	C	C		C	
Cash Management	F		F		
. . .					
Management Information Systems					
Sales Management	C	F	F	C	F
Sales Region Analysis	F	F	F	F	F
Inventory Control	C	C	C		
Production Scheduling	F	F	F	F	
. . .					

C = objective currently supported by existing systems
F = objective is planned to be supported by future system

which reflects the desired future state of the organization. This means that the target situation consists of the desired state of the locations, units, functions, processes, data, and information systems (see Figure 5-8). For example, if a desired future state of the organization is to have several new branch offices or a new product line which require several new employee positions, functions, processes, and data, then most lists and matrices will need to be updated to reflect this vision. The target situation must be developed in light of technology and business trends, in addition to organizational constraints. This means that lists of business trends and constraints should also be constructed in order to help assure that the target situation reflects these issues.

In summary, to create the target situation, planners must first edit their initial lists and record the *desired* locations, units, functions, processes, data, and information systems within the constraints and trends of the organization environment (for example, time, resources, technological evolution, competition, and so on). Next, matrices are updated to relate information in a manner consistent with the desired future state. Planners then focus on the *differences* between the current and future lists and matrices to identify projects and transition strategies.

3. *Developing a Transition Strategy and Plans.* Once the creation of the current and target situations is complete, a detailed transition strategy and plan are developed by the IS planning team. This plan should be very comprehensive, reflecting both broad, long-range issues in addition to providing sufficient detail to guide all levels of management concerning what needs doing, how, when, and by whom in the organization. The components of a typical information systems plan are outlined in Figure 5-17.

Figure 5-16
Making sense out of planning matrices

During the information systems planning process, before individual projects are identified and selected, a great deal of "behind the scenes" analysis takes place. During this planning period, which can span from six months to a year, IS planning team members develop and analyze numerous matrices like those described in the associated text. Matrices are developed to represent the current and the future views of the organization. Matrices of the "current" situation are called "as is" matrices. In other words, they describe the world "as" it currently "is." Matrices of the target or "future" situation are called "to be" matrices. Contrasting the current and future views provides insights into the relationships existing in important business information, and most importantly, forms the basis for the identification and selection of specific development projects. Many CASE tools provide features that will help you make sense out of these matrices in at least three ways:

1. *Management of Information.* A big part of working with complex matrices is managing the information. Using the dictionary features of the CASE tool repository, terms (such as business functions and process and data entities) can be defined or modified in a single location. All planners will therefore have the most recent information.
2. *Matrix Construction.* The reporting system within the CASE repository allows matrix reports to be easily produced. Since planning information can be changed at any time by many team members, an easy method to record changes and produce the most up-to-date reports is invaluable to the planning process.
3. *Matrix Analysis.* Possibly the most important feature CASE tools provide to planners is the ability to perform complex analyses within and across matrices. This analysis is often referred to as **affinity clustering.** Affinity refers to the extent to which information holds things in common. Thus, affinity clustering is the process of arranging matrix information so that clusters of information with some predetermined level or type of affinity are placed next to each other on a matrix report. For example, an affinity clustering of a Process-to-Data Entry matrix would create roughly a block diagonal matrix with processes that use similar data entities appearing in adjacent rows and data entities used in common by the same processes grouped into adjacent columns. This general form of analysis can be used by planners to identify items that often appear together (or should!). Such information can be used by planners to most effectively group and relate information (e.g., data to processes, functions to locations, and so on). For example, those data entities used by a common set of processes are candidates for a specific database. And those business processes that relate to a strategically important objective will likely receive more attention when managers from those areas request system changes.

Affinity clustering: The process of arranging planning matrix information so the clusters of information with some predetermined level or type of affinity are placed next to each other on a matrix report.

The IS plan is typically a very comprehensive document that looks at both short- and long-term organizational development needs. The short- and long-term developmental needs identified in the plan are typically expressed as a series of projects (see Figure 5-18). Projects from the long-term plan tend to build a foundation for later projects (such as transforming databases from old technology into newer technology). Projects from the short-term plan consist of specific steps to fill the gap between current and desired systems or respond to dynamic business conditions. The top-down (or plan-driven) projects join a set of bottom-up or needs-driven projects submitted as system

Figure 5-17
Outline of an information systems plan

I. **Organizational Mission, Objectives, and Strategy**
Briefly describes the mission, objectives, and strategy of the organization. The current and future views of the company are also briefly presented (i.e., where are we, where do we want to be).

II. **Informational Inventory**
This section provides a summary of the various business processes, functions, data entities, and information needs of the enterprise. This inventory will view both current and future needs.

III. **Mission and Objectives of Information Systems**
Description of the primary role IS will play in the organization to transform the enterprise from its current to future state. While it may later be revised, it represents the current best estimate of the overall role for IS within the organization. This role may be as a necessary cost, an investment, or a strategic advantage, for example.

IV. **Constraints on IS Development**
Briefly describes limitations imposed by technology and current level of resources within the company—financial, technological, and personnel.

V. **Overall Systems Needs and Long-Range IS Strategies**
Presents a summary of the overall systems needed within the company and the set of long-range (2–5 years) strategies chosen by the IS department to fill the needs.

VI. **The Short-Term Plan**
Shows a detailed inventory of present projects and systems and a detailed plan of projects to be developed or advanced during the current year. These projects may be the result of the long-range IS strategies or of requests from managers which have already been approved and are in some stage of the life cycle.

VII. **Conclusions**
Contains likely but not-yet-certain events that may affect the plan, an inventroy of business change elements as presently known, and a description of their estimated impact on the plan.

Figure 5-18
Systems development projects flow from the information systems plan

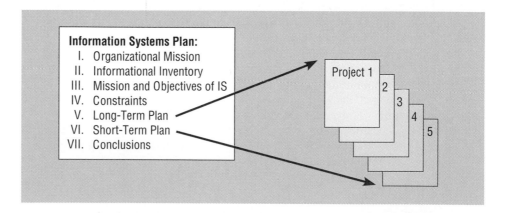

service requests from managers to form the short-term systems development plan. Collectively, the short- and long-term projects set clear directions for the project selection process. The short-term plan includes not only those projects identified from the planning process but also those selected from among bottom-up requests. The overall IS plan may also influence all development projects. For example, the IS mission and IS constraints may cause projects to choose certain technologies or emphasize certain application features as systems are designed.

In this section, we outlined a general process for developing an IS plan. ISP is a detailed process and an integral part of deciding how to best deploy information systems and technologies to help reach organizational goals. It is beyond the scope of this chapter, however, to extensively discuss ISP, yet it should be clear from our discussion that planning-based project identification and selection will yield substantial benefits to an organization. It is probably also clear to you that, as a systems analyst, you are not usually involved in IS planning, since this process requires senior IS and corporate management participation. On the other hand, the results of IS planning, such as planning matrices like those in Figures 5-14 and 5-15 can be a source of very valuable information as you identify and justify projects.

The planning process that we have described requires collecting, organizing, and analyzing vast amounts of data. This process can be eased by using upper CASE tools to more effectively deal with the vast amounts of information and to assist in providing (and enforcing) a common methodology throughout the process. In short, as information is collected during information systems planning, for example, it can be stored in the CASE repository. This information can then be summarized as needed to help identify and select specific development projects. For example, a particular matrix, like Information System-to-Objective, could be generated from the repository to help identify projects that address upgrading or replacing a specific system in order to better achieve prime objectives. In this simple way CASE can be used to improve the project identification and selection process. For more information on the role of CASE during the project identification and selection process, see Chapter 4.

SUMMARY

In this chapter, we described the first phase of the SDLC—project identification and selection. Project identification and selection consists of three primary activities: identifying potential development projects, classifying and ranking projects, and selecting projects for development. A variety of organizational members or units can be assigned to perform this process including top management, a diverse steering committee, business units and functional managers, the development group, or the most senior IS executive. Potential projects can be evaluated and selected using a broad range of criteria such as value chain analysis, alignment with business strategy, potential benefits, resource availability and requirements, and risks.

The quality of the project identification and selection process can be improved if decisions are guided by corporate strategic planning and information systems planning. Corporate strategic planning is the process of identifying the mission, objectives, and strategies of an organization. Crucial in this process is selecting a competitive strategy which states how the organization plans to achieve its objectives.

Information systems planning is an orderly means for assessing the information needs of an organization and defining the systems and databases that will best satisfy those needs. ISP is a top-down process that takes into account outside forces that drive the business and the factors critical to the success of the firm. ISP evaluates the current inventory of systems, the desired future state of the organization and its system, and determines which projects are needed to transform systems to meet the future needs of the organization.

Corporate and IS planning are highly inter-related. Conceptually, these relationships can be viewed via various matrices that show how organizational objectives, locations, units, functions, processes, data entities, and systems relate to one another. Selected projects will be those viewed to be most important in supporting the organizational strategy.

The focus of this chapter was to provide you with a clearer understanding of how organizations identify and select projects. The need for improved project identification and selection is apparent for reasons such as the following: the cost of information systems is rising rapidly, systems cannot handle applications that cross organizational boundaries, systems often do not address critical organizational objectives, data redundancy is often out of control, and system maintenance costs continue to rise. Thus, effective project identification and selection is essential if organizations are to realize the greatest benefits from information systems.

KEY TERMS

Affinity clustering
Bottom-up planning
Competitive strategy
Corporate strategic
    planning

Incremental commitment
Information systems
    planning (ISP)
Mission statement
Objective statements

Top-down planning
Value chain analysis

REVIEW QUESTIONS

1. Define each of the following terms:
   a. bottom-up planning
   b. competitive strategy
   c. corporate strategic planning
   d. information systems planning
   e. mission statement
   f. objective statements
   g. top-down planning
   h. affinity clustering
   i. value chain analysis

2. Contrast the following terms:
   a. mission; objective statements; competitive strategy
   b. corporate strategic planning; information systems planning
   c. top-down planning; bottom-up planning
   d. low-cost producer; product differentiation; product focus or niche
   e. data entity; information system

3. Describe the project identification and selection process.

4. Describe several project evaluation criteria.

5. Describe value chain analysis and how organizations use this technique to evaluate and compare projects.

6. Discuss several factors that provide evidence for the need for improved information systems planning today.

7. Describe the steps involved in corporate strategic planning.

8. What are three generic competitive strategies?

9. Describe what is meant by information systems planning and the steps involved in the process.

10. List and describe the advantages of top-down planning over other planning approaches.

11. Briefly describe nine planning matrices that are used in information systems planning and project identification and selection.

PROBLEMS AND EXERCISES

1. Match the following terms to the appropriate definitions.

_____ corporate strategic planning	a. statement that expresses an organization's qualitative and quantitative goals for reaching a desired future position
_____ mission statement	b. method by which an organization attempts to achieve its mission and objectives
_____ objective statement	c. statement that makes it clear what business a company is in
_____ competitive strategy	d. ongoing process that defines the mission, objectives, and strategies of an organization
_____ information systems planning	e. orderly means of assessing the information needs of an organization and defines the systems, databases, and technologies that will best satisfy those needs
_____ value chain analysis	f. process of arranging planning matrix information so that clusters of information with some pre-determined level or type of affinity are placed next to each other on a matrix report
_____ top-down planning	g. generic information systems planning methodology that attempts to gain a broad understanding of the information system needs of the entire organization
_____ bottom-up planning	h. generic information systems planning methodology that identifies and defines the IS development projects based upon solving operational business problems or taking advantage of some business opportunities
_____ affinity clustering	i. process of analyzing an organization's activities to determine where value is added to products and/or services and the costs incurred for doing so

2. Write a mission statement for a business that you would like to start. The mission statement should state the area of business you will be in and what aspect of the business you value highly.

3. When you are happy with the mission statement you have developed in response to the prior question, describe the objectives and competitive strategy for achieving that mission.

4. Consider an organization that you believe does not conduct adequate strategic IS planning. List at least six reasons why this type of planning is not done appropriately (or is not done at all). Are these reasons justifiable? What are the implications

of this inadequate strategic IS planning? What limits, problems, weaknesses, and barriers might this present?

5. IS planning, as depicted in this chapter, is highly related to corporate strategic planning. What might those responsible for IS planning have to do if they operate in an organization without a formal corporate planning process?

6. The economic analysis carried out during the project identification and selection phase of the systems development life cycle is rather cursory. Why is this? Consequently, what factors do you think tend to be most important for a potential project to survive this first phase of the life cycle?

7. In those organizations that do an excellent job of IS planning, why might projects identified from a bottom-up process still find their way into the project initiation and planning phase of the life cycle?

8. Figure 5-16 introduces the concept of affinity clustering. Suppose that through affinity clustering it was found that three business functions provided the bulk of the use of five data entities. What implications might this have for project identification and subsequent steps in the systems development life cycle?

9. Timberline Technology manufactures membrane circuits in its northern California plant. In addition, all circuit design and R&D work occur at this site. All finance, accounting, and human resource functions are headquartered at the parent company in the upper-Midwest. Sales take place through six sales representatives located in various cities across the country. Information systems for payroll processing, accounts payable, and accounts receivable are located at the parent office while systems for inventory management and computer-integrated manufacturing are at the California plant. As best you can, list the locations, units, functions, processes, data entities, and information systems for this company.

10. For each of the following categories, create the most plausible planning matrices for Timberline Technology, described in Problem and Exercise 9: function-to-data entity, process-to-data entity, process-to-information system, data entity-to-information system. What other information systems not listed is Timberline likely to need?

11. The owners of Timberline Technology (described in Problem and Exercise 9) are considering adding a plant in Idaho and one in Arizona and six more sales representatives at various sites across the country. Update the matrices from Problem and Exercise 10 so that the matrices account for these changes.

FIELD EXERCISES

1. Obtain a copy of an organization's mission statement. (One can typically be found in the organization's Annual Report which are often available in university libraries or in corporate marketing brochures. If you are finding it difficult to locate this material, write or call the organization directly and ask for a copy of the mission statement.) What is this organization's area of business? What does the organization value highly (e.g., high-quality products and services, low cost to consumers, employee growth and development, etc.)? If the mission statement is well written, these concepts should be clear. Do you know anything about the information systems in this company that would demonstrate that the types of systems in place reflect the organization's mission? Explain.

2. Interview the managers of the information systems department of an organization to determine the level and nature of their strategic information systems planning. Does it appear to be adequate? Why or why not? Obtain a copy of that organization's mission statement. To what degree do the strategic IS plan and the organizational strategic plan fit together? What are the areas where the two plans fit

and do not fit? If there is not a good fit, what are the implications for the success of the organization? For the usefulness of their information systems?

3. Choose an organization that you have contact with, perhaps your employer or university. Follow the "Outline of an information systems plan" shown in Figure 5-17 and complete a short information systems plan for the organization you chose. Write at least a brief paragraph for each of the seven categories in the outline. If IS personnel and managers are available, interview them to obtain information you need. Present your mock plan to the organization's IS manager and ask for feedback on whether or not your plan fits the IS reality for that organization.

4. Choose an organization that you have contact with, perhaps your employer or university. List significant examples for each of the items used to create planning matrices. Next, list possible relationships among various items and display these relationships in a series of planning matrices.

5. Write separate mission statements that you believe fit well for Microsoft, IBM, and AT&T. Compare your mission statements with the real mission statements of these companies. Their mission statements can typically be found in their Annual Reports. Were your mission statements comparable to the real mission statements? Why or why not? What differences and similarities are there among these three mission statements? What information systems are necessary to help these companies deliver on their mission statements?

6. Choose an organization that you have contact with, perhaps your employer or university. Determine how information systems projects are identified. Are projects identified adequately? Are they identified as part of the information systems planning or the corporate strategic planning process? Why or Why not?

REFERENCES

Atkinson, R. A. 1990. "The Motivations for Strategic Planning." *Journal of Information Systems Management* 7 (4): 53–56.

Atkinson, R. A., and J. Montgomery. 1990. "Reshaping IS Strategic Planning." *Journal of Information Systems Management* 7 (4): 9–15.

Carlson, C. K., E. P. Gardner, and S. R. Ruth. 1989. "Technology-Driven Long-Range Planning." *Journal of Information Systems Management* 6 (3): 24–29.

IBM. 1982. "Business Systems Planning." In *Advanced System Development/Feasibility Techniques,* edited by J. D. Couger, M. A. Colter, and R. W. Knapp. New York, NY: Wiley: 236–314.

Kerr, J. 1990. "The Power of Information Systems Planning." *Database Programming & Design* 3 (December): 60–66.

Koory, J. L. and D. B. Medley. 1987. *Management Information Systems: Planning and Decision Making,* Cincinnati, OH: South-Western.

Martin, J. (1990). *Information Engineering.* Englewood Cliffs, NJ: Prentice-Hall, Inc.

McKeen, J. D., T. Guimaraes, and J. C. Wetherbe. 1994. "A Comparative Analysis of MIS Project Selection Mechanisms." *Data Base* 25 (February): 43–59.

Moriarty, T. 1991. "Framing Your System." *Database Programming & Design* 4 (June): 57–59.

Morton, C. 1992. "Information Competition: Can OLTP and DSS Peacefully Coexist?" *Data Base Management* 2 (June): 24–28.

Parker, M. M., and R. J. Benson. 1989. "Enterprisewide Information Management: State-of-the-Art Strategic Planning." *Journal of Information Systems Management* 6 (Summer): 14–23.

Porter, M. 1980. *Competitive Strategy: Techniques for Analyzing Industries and Competitors.* New York, NY: Free Press.

Porter, M. 1985. *Competitive Advantage.* New York, NY: Free Press.

Reingruber, M. J. and D. L. Spahr. 1992. "Putting Data Back in Database Design." *Data Base Management* 2 (March): 19–21.

Shank, J. K., and V. Govindarajan. 1993. *Strategic Cost Management.* New York, NY: Free Press.

Sowa, J. F. and J. A. Zachman. 1992. "Extending and Formalizing the Framework for Information Systems Architecture." *IBM Systems Journal* 31 (3): 590–616.

Zachman, J. A. 1987. "A Framework for Information Systems Architecture." *IBM Systems Journal* 26 (March): 276–92.

Identifying and Selecting the Customer Activity Tracking System

INTRODUCTION

Over the last two days, all BEC top executives participated in the annual off-site strategic planning session. During the first day, BEC executives reviewed major events and accomplishments of the prior year. They also reviewed and updated BEC corporate objectives and generated ideas on how to continuously improve BEC business practices. On the second day, Nigel Broad, the chair of BEC, worked with the group to develop a forward-looking document that they called BEC's Blueprint for the Decade (Figure 1). In this document, BEC's mission, objectives, and strategy were reviewed, updated, and clearly laid out so that they could be easily expressed to all BEC employees. Nigel believes that all employees need to clearly understand BEC's mission, objectives, and strategy if profit and growth targets are to be realized.

AN IDEA FOR A NEW SYSTEM IS BORN

After completing this intensive two-day session, Nancy Chen, director of U.S. operations, returned home to relax and reflect on the intensive planning session. Upon arrival, she found her mailbox full of new catalogs from companies she had never heard of, and thought to herself, "Where do these catalogs come from? Where do these companies get my name and address? How do these companies know that I like to fly fish in the Rockies? They seem to know exactly what I like to do; I wonder how?" With this, she fixed her dinner and looked forward to browsing through her new catalogs. Later that night while watching a "Next Generation" rerun, she flipped though the catalog titled *Remote B&Bs*. While reading, she remembered that she had recently stayed in a beautiful bed and breakfast while on a fishing expedition outside Missoula, Montana. "Ah, maybe that's where they got my name." This also gave her an idea: Could BEC use customer data in a similar way?

While thinking her idea through, she remembered Nigel stressing the importance of "leveraging our existing customer base to get more frequent purchase and rental activity" and the Blueprint's objective of applying technology in innovative ways to provide better customer service. Maybe her idea could serve as a model for the point Nigel was making.

After arriving at work the following day, Nancy searched the Internet for information related to direct marketing and customer profiling. This search yielded several articles and references. In one particular article from the *Wall Street Journal* she read how numerous mail order companies have enhanced promotional efforts and profitability by profiling customer buying habits and then sending their customers specific types of catalogs based upon their profiles. For example, households profiled to have young children are mailed catalogs that include children-related items in addition to adult clothing whereas households profiled as not having children are sent catalogs with no children-related sections. It was reported that companies using these and similar profiling techniques are experiencing substantially improved "hit rates" for promotions. Nancy felt that similar profiling of BEC customers could be performed using customer transaction data. She felt that an analysis of the customer rental and buying patterns could lead to the creation of profiles that might be useful for targeting new product releases and promotions. This would help BEC better utilize its marketing expenditures and provide an innovative customer service through the use of information technology.

To see if her idea were possible, Nancy first contacted Karen Gardner, VP of Information Systems, to get Karen's views on the project idea. Nancy had been very impressed with Karen at the strategic planning session when Karen had reviewed the strengths and weaknesses of BEC's IS organization. After Nancy gave a brief explanation of her ideas on customer rental and buying patterns, Karen felt that the ideas had merit. She reminded Nancy that, since it appeared that Nancy's ideas would require a costly systems development

Figure 1
Broadway Entertainment Company's mission, objectives, and strategy

---

BLUEPRINT FOR THE DECADE

FORWARD

This blueprint provides guidance to Broadway Entertainment Corporation (BEC), Incorporated for the coming decade. It shows how our mission, objectives, and strategy fit together and provides direction for all individuals and decisions of the Corporation.

OUR MISSION

BEC is a publicly held, for-profit organization focusing on the home entertainment industry that has a global focus for operations. BEC exists to serve customers with a primary goal of enhancing shareholders' investment through the pursuit of excellence in everything we do. BEC will operate under the highest ethical standards, will respect the dignity, rights, and contributions of all employees, and strive to better society.

OUR OBJECTIVES

1. BEC will strive to increase market share and profitability (prime objective).
2. BEC will be a leader in all areas of our business—human resources, technology, operations, and marketing.
3. BEC will be cost-effective in the use of all resources.
4. BEC will rank among industry leaders in both profitability and growth.
5. BEC will be innovative in the use of technology to help bring new products and services to market faster than our competition and to provide better service to our customers.
6. BEC will create an environment that values diversity in gender, race, values, and culture among employees, suppliers, and customers.

OUR STRATEGY

BEC will be a *global* provider of home entertainment products and services by providing the highest quality *customer service*, the *broadest range of products and services*, at the *lowest possible price*.

---

effort and that the new system would need to access corporate databases, a formal request must be developed and approved by the Systems Priority Board (SPB) before proceeding. Nancy remembered Karen's remarks at the strategic planning session about how IS needed to drive its systems development more from corporate strategy and objectives in order to better manage the deluge of requests for new and improved systems. Nancy asked Karen some questions about how to show the linkage between an IS request, corporate strategy and objectives, and the annual IS plan. Karen suggested that Nancy's request could be a good test case for trying out some ways to show this linkage.

Karen assigned Jordan Pippen, a senior systems analyst at BEC, to assist Nancy with the development of a formal Systems Service Request (SSR). As Jordan had led an internal IS study on aligning systems development with corporate plans, she would be especially helpful to Nancy. Over the next two weeks Jordan and Nancy met three times. At the first meeting, Nancy explained her vision of the project to Jordan. This information provided Jordan with adequate information to develop a high-level project statement that she shared with Nancy prior to their second meeting. During their second meeting, they jointly edited this statement as it developed into the Problem Statement within the SSR. At the third meeting, they finalized the wording of the entire SSR before forwarding it to the SPB (see Figure 2).

Figure 2
System service request for the CATS project

**Broadway Entertainment
System Service Request**

REQUESTED BY   Nancy Chen   DATE: April 23, 1998

DEPARTMENT   Operations

LOCATION   Headquarters, 4409

CONTACT   Tel: 6-7755   FAX: 6-7750   e-mail: chen

TYPE OF REQUEST   URGENCY
  [X] New System   [ ] Immediate – Operations are impaired or opportunity lost
  [ ] System Enhancement   [ ] Problems exist, but can be worked around
  [ ] System Error Correction   [X] Business losses can be tolerated until new system installed

PROBLEM STATEMENT

Market, sales, and profit growth at BEC is limited by the extent to which we can leverage each customer to increase the frequency and/or amount of rental or purchase activity. A possible method for BEC to achieve its growth targets has been stated as a desire to "leverage our existing customer base to get more frequent purchase and rental activity." One method to achieve this goal would be to use existing customer information and behavior to develop a purchase and rental profile for each customer. This profile could then be used to target customers who would be more likely to rent a particular movie or purchase a particular music title. Customer profiles would be matched against new product releases. Once a match has been made, customers would then be notified of the pending product release (for example, using a post card) and be informed that the product will be held for the customer at a local store if the customer so desires. To reserve a product, the customer would simply have to call an 800 number, give a code number that is printed on the card to identify the product, store, and customer, and a product would be earmarked for the customer. Inventory management systems would be modified to use this information to assure that specific product is at the right store at the right time. Stores would be given a listing of customers and reserved products so that appropriate measures would be taken to hold back adequate inventory supplies for profiled customers.

SERVICE REQUEST

I request a thorough analysis of this idea be conducted. We currently are underutilizing our information on customer transaction data. This application would provide us with a system that could differentiate BEC from our competitors and help achieve one of our strategic objectives.

IS LIAISON   Jordan Pippen 6-5519 FAX: 6-5550 e-mail: pippen

SPONSOR   Nancy Chen, VP of U.S. Operations

---------------------- TO BE COMPLETED BY SYSTEMS PRIORITY BOARD ------------------------
  [ ] Request approved   Assigned to _____
                        Start date _____
  [ ] Recommend revision
  [ ] Suggest user development
  [ ] Reject for reason _____
             _____

At the last meeting, Jordan and Nancy gave their project a name—the Customer Activity Tracking System (CATS).

About one year ago Karen had received corporate board approval to form the Systems Priority Board. Overall growth at BEC had created extensive demand on the IS organization and Karen wanted general management validation that IS was working on the most important projects. At this time, Karen convenes the SPB, but she is the only IS department representative of the six SPB members. Not all requests must pass before the SPB: requests to fix system errors or to comply with legal/regulatory edicts are simply summarized for SPB awareness. Also, enhancement and new system requests that require less than $2,000 of IS development cost and which do not change existing corporate systems and databases are only summarized for review. The SPB discusses such requests only if an abnormal pattern of these requests arises (for example, more than $20,000 of requests from the same department over 6–12 months).

A primary function of the SPB is to assess an SSR in terms of its alignment with systems development objectives defined in BEC's information systems plan (ISP), updated annually after the corporate strategic planning session. The CATS request was a bottom-up request that was developed outside the normal information systems planning process. The request must now be assessed in light of all projects currently selected for project initiation and planning, the second phase of BEC's systems development life cycle. The SPB must assess how well this request fits in with corporate and IS strategy and existing IS architecture compared to other requests with which it must compete for resources.

If the SPB feels that the request is adequately aligned with their ISP, they will likely approve a more detailed study to outline the development project in detail. If the SPB feels that the request is not adequately aligned with the ISP, they will most likely reject the proposal and provide feedback to Nancy as to why it was rejected. In project initiation and planning, only projects deemed to be adequately aligned with the objectives of BEC's information system plan are given approval for more detailed study.

For this reason, Jordan and Nancy decided to supplement the standard BEC SSR form with information showing the relationship of CATS to the Blueprint for the Decade and to the IS plan (see Figure 3). Although at a very high level, this information nonetheless helped

Figure 3
CATS alignment with ISP

	CATS	Legend
Blueprint Objectives		
1. Increase market share and profitability	C,E	
2. Leader in all areas of business	C,E	C = major contribution
3. Cost-effective use of resources	E	by CATS
4. Industry leader in profitability and growth	C,E	E = major contribution
5. Innovative use of technology	C	by existing systems
6. Value diversity	C	
ISP Objectives		
1. Better align IS development with corporate objectives	P	
2. Deliver global system solutions	S	P = primary goal of CATS
3. Reduce systems development backlog	S	S = secondary goal of CATS
4. Increase skill level of IS staff		
Relationship with Current Systems		
Rental	F,S	
Sales	F,S	F = CATS to be fed data
Inventory Control	S	from this system
Member Tracking	F	S = CATS can provide
Inventory Management	F,S	information to this system
Sales Tracking and Analysis	F,S	

the SPB to see the potential scope of CATS and the potential areas where CATS might have impact. Based on the SSR and this supplemental information, the SPB approved the selection of the CATS project, thereby initiating the development of a Baseline Project Plan to be created during the second phase of the SDLC—project initiation and planning.

The SPB did raise two issues needing to be addressed during the next and subsequent phases. First, Karen noted that many existing systems (see Figure 3) could have some form of interface to CATS, primarily in providing data used by profiling routines in CATS; her concern was that duplication and lack of synchronization of data across these systems might cause problems for CATS. Second, Dwight Ford, BEC legal counsel and member of the SPB, asked that an investigation about the legality and ethics of buying and

selling sales activity data be carried out during the project. Dwight had been a strong proponent of the statements on "highest ethical standards" and supporting diversity in the Blueprint for the Decade.

SUMMARY

The objective of this section was to describe how the Customer Activity Tracking System was identified and selected at BEC. CATS, like many systems, was the brainchild of one manager, creatively connecting information she had received from apparently unrelated activities. This idea led to a request to fund further study of a potential new system—CATS. At the end of each subsequent chapter dealing with a phase of the SDLC, the story of CATS will unfold.

6

Initiating and Planning Systems Development Projects

After studying this chapter, you should be able to:

■ Describe the steps involved in the project initiation and planning process.

■ Explain the need for and the contents of a Statement of Work and Baseline Project Plan.

■ List and describe various methods for assessing project feasibility.

■ Describe the differences between tangible and intangible benefits and costs and between one-time and recurring benefits and costs.

■ Perform cost-benefit analysis and describe what is meant by the time value of money, present value, discount rate, net present value, return on investment, and break-even analysis.

■ Describe the general rules for evaluating the technical risks associated with a systems development project.

■ Describe the activities and participant roles within a structured walkthrough.

INTRODUCTION

The first phase of the systems development life cycle is project identification and selection, during which the need for a new or enhanced system is recognized. This first life cycle phase does not deal with a specific project but rather identifies the portfolio of projects to be undertaken by the organization. Thus, project identification and selection is a pre-project step in the life cycle. This recognition of potential projects may come as part of a larger planning process, information systems planning, or from requests from managers and business units. Regardless of how a project is identified and selected, the next step is to conduct a more detailed assessment of one particular project selected during the first phase. This assessment does not focus on how the proposed system will operate but rather on understanding the scope of a proposed project and its feasibility of completion given the available resources. It is crucial that organizations understand whether resources should be devoted to a project, otherwise very expensive mistakes can be made. The focus of this chapter is on this process. In other words, project initiation and planning is where projects are either accepted for development, rejected, or redirected. This is also where you, as a systems analyst, begin to play a major role in the systems development process.

In the next section, the project initiation and planning process is briefly reviewed. Next, numerous techniques for assessing project feasibility are described. The information uncovered during feasibility analysis is organized into a document called a Baseline Project Plan. Once this plan is developed, a formal review of the project can be conducted. The process of building this plan is discussed next. Yet, before the project can evolve to the next phase of the systems development life cycle—analysis—the project plan must be reviewed and accepted. In the final major section of the chapter, we provide an overview of the project review process.

INITIATING AND PLANNING SYSTEMS DEVELOPMENT PROJECTS

A key consideration when conducting project initiation and planning (PIP) is deciding when PIP ends and when analysis, the next phase of the SDLC, begins. This is a concern since many activities performed during PIP could also be completed during analysis. Pressman (1992) speaks of three important questions that must be considered when making this decision on the division between PIP and analysis:

1. *How much effort should be expended on the project initiation and planning process?*

2. *Who is responsible for performing the project initiation and planning process?*

3. *Why is project initiation and planning such a challenging activity?*

Finding an answer to the first question, how much effort should be expended on the PIP process, is often difficult. Practical experience has found, however, that the time and effort spent on initiation and planning activities easily pay for themselves later in the project. Proper and insightful project planning, including determining project scope as well as identifying project activities, can easily reduce time in later project phases. For example, a careful feasibility analysis which leads to deciding that a project is not worth pursuing can save a considerable expenditure of resources. The actual amount of time expended will be affected by the size and complexity of the project as well as by the experience of your organization in building similar systems. A rule of thumb is that between 10 and 20 percent of the entire development effort should be expended on the PIP study. Thus, you should not be reluctant to spend considerable time in PIP in order to fully understand the motivation for the requested system.

For the second question, who is responsible for performing the PIP, most organizations assign an experienced systems analyst, or team of analysts for large projects, to perform PIP. The analyst will work with the proposed customers (managers and users) of the system and other technical development staff in preparing the final plan. Experienced analysts working with customers who well understand their information services needs should be able to perform PIP without the detailed analysis typical of the analysis phase of the life cycle. Less experienced analysts with customers who only vaguely understand their needs will likely expend more effort during PIP in order to be certain that the project scope and work plan are feasible.

Third, the project initiation and planning process is viewed as a challenging activity because the objective of the PIP study is to transform a vague system request document into a tangible project description. This is an open-ended process. The analyst must clearly understand the motivation for and objectives of the proposed system. Therefore, effective communication among the systems analyst, users, and management is crucial to the creation of a meaningful project plan. Getting all parties to agree on the direction of a project may be difficult for cross-department projects when different parties have different business objectives. Thus, more complex organizational settings for projects will result in more time required for analysis of the current and proposed systems during PIP.

In the remainder of this chapter, we will describe the necessary activities used to answer these questions. In the next section, we will revisit the project initiation and planning activities originally outlined in Chapter 3 in the section on Managing the Information Systems Project. This is followed by a brief description of the deliverables and outcomes from this process.

The Process of Initiating and Planning Systems Development Projects

As its name implies, two major activities occur during the second phase of the SDLC, project initiation and planning (Figure 6-1). As the steps in the project initiation and planning process were explained in Chapter 3, our primary focus in this chapter is to describe several techniques that are used when performing this process. Therefore, we will only briefly review the PIP process.

Project initiation focuses on activities designed to assist in *organizing* a team to conduct project planning. During initiation, one or more analysts are assigned to work with a customer—that is, a member of the business group that requested or will be impacted by the project—to establish work standards and communication procedures. Examples of the types of activities performed are shown in Table 6-1.

Figure 6-1
Systems development life cycle with project initiation and planning highlighted

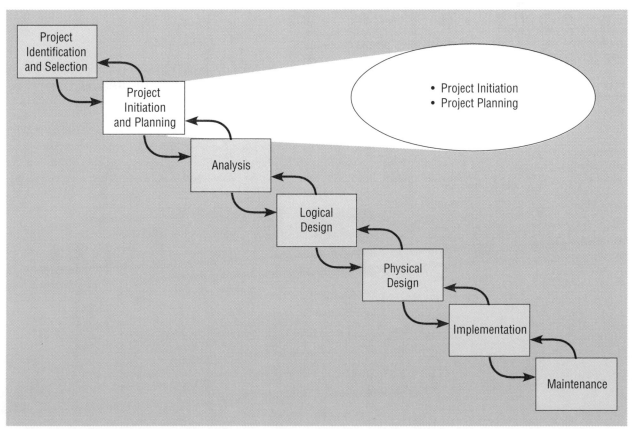

TABLE 6-1   Elements of Project Initiation

- Establishing the Project Initiation Team
- Establishing a Relationship with the Customer
- Establishing the Project Initiation Plan
- Establishing Management Procedures
- Establishing the Project Management Environment and Project Workbook

Depending upon the size, scope, and complexity of the project, some project initiation activities may be unnecessary or may be very involved. Also, many organizations have established procedures for assisting with common initiation activities.

Project planning, the second activity within PIP, is distinct from general information systems planning which focuses on assessing the information systems needs of the *entire* organization (discussed in Chapter 5). Project planning is the process of defining clear, discrete activities and the work needed to complete each activity within a *single* project. The objective of the project planning process is the development of a *Baseline Project Plan* (*BPP*) and the *Statement of Work* (*SOW*). The BPP becomes the foundation for the remainder of the development project. The SOW produced by the team clearly outlines the objectives and constraints of the project for the customer. As with the project initiation process, the size, scope, and complexity of a project will dictate the comprehensiveness of the project planning process and resulting documents. Further, numerous assumptions about resource availability and potential problems will have to be made. Analysis of these assumptions and system costs and benefits forms a **business case.** The range of activities performed during project planning are listed in Table 6-2.

Business case: The justification for an information system, presented in terms of the tangible and intangible economic benefits and costs, and the technical and organizational feasibility of the proposed system.

Baseline Project Plan (BPP): A major outcome and deliverable from the project initiation and planning phase which contains the best estimate of a project's scope, benefits, costs, risks, and resource requirements.

Deliverables and Outcomes

The major outcomes and deliverables from the project initiation and planning phase are the Baseline Project Plan and the Statement of Work. The **Baseline Project Plan (BPP)** contains all information collected and analyzed during project initiation and planning. The plan reflects the best estimate of the project's scope, benefits, costs, risks, and resource requirements given the current understanding of the project. The BPP specifies detailed project activities for the next life cycle phase—analysis—and less detail for subsequent project phases (since these depend on the results of the analysis phase). Similarly, benefits, costs, risks, and resource requirements will be-

TABLE 6-2   Elements of Project Planning

- Describing the Project Scope, Alternatives, and Feasibility
- Dividing the Project into Manageable Tasks
- Estimating Resources and Creating a Resource Plan
- Developing a Preliminary Schedule
- Developing a Communication Plan
- Determining Project Standards and Procedures
- Identifying and Assessing Risk
- Creating a Preliminary Budget
- Developing a Statement of Work
- Setting a Baseline Project Plan

come more specific and quantifiable as the project progresses. The BPP is used by the project selection committee to help decide whether the project should be accepted, redirected, or canceled. If selected, the BPP becomes the foundation document for all subsequent SDLC activities; however, it is also expected to evolve as the project evolves. That is, as new information is learned during subsequent SDLC phases, the baseline plan will be updated. Later in the chapter we describe how to construct the BPP.

The **Statement of Work (SOW)** is a short document prepared for the customer that describes what the project will deliver and outlines all work required to complete the project. The SOW assures that both you and your customer gain a common understanding of the project and is a very useful communication tool. The SOW is a very easy document to create because it typically consists of a high-level summary of the BPP information (described later). A sample SOW is shown in Figure 6-2. Depending upon your relationship with your customer, the role of the SOW may vary. At one extreme, the SOW can be used as the basis of a formal contractual agreement outlining firm deadlines, costs, and specifications. At the other extreme, the SOW can simply be used as a communication vehicle to outline the current best estimates of what the project will deliver, when it will be completed, and the resources it may consume. A contract programming or consulting firm, for example, may establish a very formal relationship with a customer and use a SOW that is extensive and formal. Alternatively, an internal development group may develop a SOW that is only one-to-two pages in length and is intended to inform customers rather than to set contractual obligations and deadlines.

Statement of Work (SOW):
Document prepared for the customer during project initiation and planning that describes what the project will deliver and outlines generally at a high level all work required to complete the project.

ASSESSING PROJECT FEASIBILITY

All projects are feasible given unlimited resources and infinite time (Pressman, 1992). Unfortunately, most projects must be developed within tight budgetary and time constraints. This means that assessing project feasibility is a required activity for all information systems projects and is potentially a large undertaking. It requires that you, as a systems analyst, evaluate a wide range of factors. Typically, some of these factors will be more important than others for some projects and relatively unimportant for other projects. Although the specifics of a given project will dictate which factors are most important, most feasibility factors are represented by the following categories:

- *Economic*
- *Technical*
- *Operational*
- *Schedule*
- *Legal and Contractual*
- *Political*

Together, the culmination of these feasibility analyses form the business case that justifies the expenditure of resources on the project. In the remainder of this section, we will examine various feasibility issues. We begin by examining issues related to economic feasibility and demonstrate techniques for conducting this analysis. This is followed by a discussion of techniques for assessing technical project risk. Finally, issues not directly associated with economic and technical feasibility, but no less important to assuring project success, are discussed.

To help you better understand the feasibility assessment process, we will examine a project at Pine Valley Furniture. For this project, a Systems Service Request

Figure 6-2
Statement of Work for the
Customer Tracking System
(Pine Valley Furniture)

Pine Valley Furniture   **Prepared: 9/20/98**
Statement of Work

Project Name: Customer Tracking Systems
PVF Project Manager: Jim Woo

Customer: Marketing
Project Sponsor: Jackie Judson

Project Start / End (projected):   10/1/98–2/1/99

PVF Development Staff Estimates (man-months):
    Programmers: 2.0
    Jr. Analysts: 1.5
    Sr. Analysts: 0.3
    Supervisors: 0.1
    Consultants: 0.0
    Librarian: 0.1

    TOTAL: **4.0**

Project Description

Goal
    This project will implement a customer tracking system for the
    marketing department. The purpose of this system is to
    automate the … to save employee time, reduce errors, have
    more timely information, …

Objective
    • minimize data entry errors
    • provide more timely information
    • …

Phases of Work
    The following tasks and deliverables reflect the current
    understanding of the project:
    In Analysis, …
    In Design, …
    In Implementation, …

(SSR) was submitted by Pine Valley Furniture's (PVF) vice-president of Marketing, Jackie Judson, to develop a Customer Tracking System (Figure 6-3). Jackie feels that this system would allow PVF's marketing group to better track customer purchase activity and sales trends. She also feels that, if constructed, the Customer Tracking System (CTS) would provide many tangible and intangible benefits to PVF. This project was selected by PVF's Systems Priority Board for a project initiation and planning study. During project initiation, senior systems analyst Jim Woo was assigned to work with Jackie to initiate and plan the project. At this point in the project, all project initiation activities have been completed. Jackie and Jim are now focusing on project planning activities in order to complete the BPP.

Figure 6-3
System service request for Customer Tracking System (Pine Valley Furniture)

Pine Valley Furniture
System Service Request

REQUESTED BY _____Jackie Judson_____ DATE: ___August 23, 1998___

DEPARTMENT ___Marketing_____

LOCATION _____Headquarters, 570c_____

CONTACT _____Tel: 4-3290   FAX: 4-3270   e-mail: jjudson_____

TYPE OF REQUEST   URGENCY
  [X] New System   [   ] Immediate – Operations are impaired or opportunity lost
  [   ] System Enhancement   [   ] Problems exist, but can be worked around
  [   ] System Error Correction   [X] Business losses can be tolerated until new system installed

PROBLEM STATEMENT

Sales growth at PVF has caused a greater volume of work for the marketing department. This volume of work has greatly increased the volume and complexity of the data we need to deal with and understand. We are currently using manual methods and a complex PC-based electronic spreadsheet to track and forecast customer buying patterns. This method of analysis has many problems: (1) we are slow to catch buying trends as there is often a week or more delay before data can be taken from point of sales system and manually enter it into our spreadsheet; (2) the process of manual data entry is prone to errors (which makes the results of our subsequent analysis suspect); and (3) the volume of data and the complexity of analyses conducted in the system seem to be overwhelming our current system—sometimes the program starts recalculating and never returns while for others it returns information that we know cannot be correct.

SERVICE REQUEST

I request a thorough analysis of our current method of tracking and analysis of customer purchasing activity with the intent to design and build a completely new information system. This system should handle all customer purchasing activity, support display and reporting of critical sales information, and assist marketing personnel in understanding the increasingly complex and competitive business environment. I feel that such a system will improve the competitiveness of PVF, particularly in our ability to better serve our customers.

IS LIAISON   Jim Woo, 4-6207 FAX: 4-6200 e-mail: jwoo_____

SPONSOR   Jackie Judson, Vice-President, Marketing_____

---------------------- TO BE COMPLETED BY SYSTEMS PRIORITY BOARD -----------------------
  [   ] Request approved   Assigned to _____
                                   Start date _____
  [   ] Recommend revision
  [   ] Suggest user development
  [   ] Reject for reason _____
                           _____

Assessing Economic Feasibility

Economic feasibility: A process of identifying the financial benefits and costs associated with a development project.

The purpose for assessing **economic feasibility** is to identify the financial benefits and costs associated with the development project; economic feasibility is often referred to as cost-benefit analysis. During project initiation and planning, it will be impossible for you to precisely define all benefits and costs related to a particular project. Yet, it is important that you spend adequate time identifying and quantifying these items or it will be impossible for you to conduct an adequate economic analysis and make meaningful comparisons between rival projects. Here we will describe typical benefits and costs resulting from the development of an information system and provide several useful worksheets for recording costs and benefits. Additionally, several common techniques for making cost-benefit calculations are presented. These worksheets and techniques are used after each SDLC phase as the project is reviewed in order to decide whether to continue, redirect, or kill a project.

Determining Project Benefits   An information system can provide many benefits to an organization. For example, a new or renovated IS can automate monotonous jobs, reduce errors, provide innovative services to customers and suppliers, and improve organizational efficiency, speed, flexibility, and morale. In general, the benefits can be viewed as being both tangible and intangible. **Tangible benefits** refer to items that can be measured in dollars and with certainty. Examples of tangible benefits might include reduced personnel expenses, lower transaction costs, or higher profit margins. It is important to note that not all tangible benefits can be easily quantified. For example, a tangible benefit that allows a company to perform a task in 50 percent of the time may be difficult to quantify in terms of hard dollar savings. Most tangible benefits will fit within the following categories:

Tangible benefit: A benefit derived from the creation of an information system that can be measured in dollars and with certainty.

- Cost reduction and avoidance
- Error reduction
- Increased flexibility
- Increased speed of activity
- Improvement of management planning and control
- Opening new markets and increasing sales opportunities

Within the Customer Tracking System at PVF, Jim and Jackie identified several tangible benefits, summarized on a tangible benefits worksheet shown in Figure 6-4. Jackie and Jim had to establish the values in Figure 6-4 after collecting information from users of the current customer tracking system. They first interviewed the person responsible for collecting, entering, and analyzing the correctness of the current customer tracking data. This person estimated that they spent 10 percent of their time correcting data entry error. Given that this person's salary is $25,000, Jackie and Jim estimated an *error reduction* benefit of $2,500. Jackie and Jim also interviewed managers who used the current customer tracking reports. Using this information they were able to estimate other tangible benefits. They learned that *cost reduction or avoidance* benefits could be gained due to better inventory management. Also, *increased flexibility* would likely occur from a reduction in the time normally taken to manually reorganize data for different purposes. Further, *improvements in management planning or control* should result from a broader range of analyses in the new system. Overall, this analysis forecasts that benefits from the system would be approximately $50,000 per year.

Intangible benefit: A benefit derived from the creation of an information system that cannot be easily measured in dollars or with certainty.

Jim and Jackie also identified several intangible benefits of the system. Although they could not quantify these benefits, they will still be described in the final BPP. **Intangible benefits** refer to items that *cannot* be easily measured in dol-

```
┌────────────────────────────────────────────────────────┐
│                                                          │
│              TANGIBLE BENEFITS WORKSHEET                 │
│               Customer Tracking System Project           │
│                                                          │
│                                         Year 1 through 5 │
│                                                          │
│   A.  Cost reduction or avoidance            $  4,500    │
│                                                          │
│   B.  Error reduction                            2,500   │
│                                                          │
│   C.  Increased flexibility                      7,500   │
│                                                          │
│   D.  Increased speed of activity               10,500   │
│                                                          │
│   E.  Improvement in management                          │
│       planning or control                      25,000   │
│                                                          │
│   F.  Other _____      0    │
│                                                          │
│   TOTAL tangible benefits                     $50,000    │
│                                                          │
└────────────────────────────────────────────────────────┘
```

Figure 6-4
Tangible benefits for
Customer Tracking System
(Pine Valley Furniture)

lars or with certainty. Intangible benefits may have direct organizational benefits such as the improvement of employee morale or they may have broader societal implications such as the reduction of waste creation or resource consumption. Potential tangible benefits may have to be considered intangible during project initiation and planning since you may not be able to quantify them in dollars or with certainty at this stage in the life cycle. During later stages, such intangibles can become tangible benefits as you better understand the ramifications of the system you are designing. In this case, the BPP is updated and the business case revised to justify continuation of the project to the next phase. Table 6-3 lists numerous intangible benefits often associated with the development of an information system. Actual benefits will vary from system to system. After determining project benefits, project costs must be identified.

Determining Project Costs   Similar to benefits, an information system can have both tangible and intangible costs. **Tangible costs** refer to items that you can easily measure in dollars and with certainty. From an IS development perspective, tangible costs include items such as hardware costs, labor costs, and operational costs such as employee training and building renovations. Alternatively, intangible costs are those items that you cannot easily measure in terms of dollars or with certainty.

Tangible cost: A cost associated with an information system that can be measured in dollars and with certainty.

TABLE 6-3   Intangible Benefits from the Development of an Information System

- Competitive necessity
- More timely information
- Improved organizational planning
- Increased organizational flexibility
- Promotion of organizational learning and understanding
- Availability of new, better, or more information
- Ability to investigate more alternatives

- Faster decision making
- Information processing efficiency
- Improved asset utilization
- Improved resource control
- Increased accuracy in clerical operations
- Improved work process that can improve employee morale
- Positive impacts on society

Adapted from Parker and Benson, 1988

Intangible cost: A cost associated with an information system that cannot be easily measured in terms of dollars or with certainty.

One-time cost: A cost associated with project start-up and development, or system start-up.

Recurring cost: A cost resulting from the ongoing evolution and use of a system.

Intangible costs can include loss of customer goodwill, employee morale, or operational inefficiency. Table 6-4 provides a summary of common costs associated with the development and operation of an information system. Predicting the costs associated with the development of an information system is an inexact science. IS researchers, however, have identified several guidelines for improving the cost-estimating process (see Table 6-5). Both underestimating and overestimating costs are problems you must avoid (Lederer and Prasad, 1992). Underestimation results in cost overruns while overestimation results in unnecessary allocation of resources that might be better utilized.

Besides tangible and intangible costs, you can distinguish IS-related development costs as either one-time or recurring (the same is true for benefits although we do not discuss this difference for benefits). **One-time costs** refer to those associated with project initiation and development and the start-up of the system. These costs typically encompass activities such as system development, new hardware and software purchases, user training, site preparation, and data or system conversion. When conducting an economic cost-benefit analysis, a worksheet should be created for capturing these expenses. For very large projects, one-time costs may be staged over one or more years. In these cases, a separate one-time cost worksheet should be created for each year. This separation will make it easier to perform present value calculations (see below). **Recurring costs** refer to those costs resulting from the ongoing evolution and use of the system. Examples of these costs typically include

- Application software maintenance
- Incremental data storage expense
- Incremental communications

TABLE 6-4   Possible Information Systems Costs

Types of Costs	Examples	Types of Costs	Examples
Procurement	Consulting costs	Project-Related	Application software
	Equipment purchase or lease		Software modifications to fit local systems
	Equipment installation costs		Personnel, overhead, et al., from in-house development
	Site preparation and modifications		Training users in application use
	Capital costs		Collecting and analyzing data
	Management and staff time		Preparing documentation
Start-Up	Operating system software		Managing development
	Communications equipment installation	Operating	System maintenance costs (hardware, software, and facilities)
	Start-up personnel		
	Personnel searches and hiring activities		Rental of space and equipment
	Disruption to the rest of the organization		Asset depreciation
	Management to direct start-up activity		Management, operation, and planning personnel

Adapted with the permission of the Association for Computing Machinery. Copyright ©1978 J.L. King and E. Schrems

TABLE 6-5 Guidelines for Better Cost Estimating

1. Assign the initial estimating task to the final developers.
2. Delay finalizing the initial estimate until the end of a thorough study.
3. Anticipate and control user changes.
4. Monitor the progress of the proposed project.
5. Evaluate proposed project progress by using independent auditors.
6. Use the estimate to evaluate project personnel.
7. Study the cost estimate carefully before approving it.
8. Rely on documented facts, standards, and simple arithmetic formulas rather than guessing, intuition, personal memory, and complex formulas.
9. Don't rely on cost-estimating software for an accurate estimate.

Adapted with the permission of the Association for Computing Machinery. Copyright ©1992 A.L. Lederer and J. Prasad.

- New software and hardware leases
- Supplies and other expenses (for example, paper, forms, data center personnel)

Both one-time and recurring costs can consist of items that are fixed or variable in nature. Fixed costs refer to costs that are billed or incurred at a regular interval and usually at a fixed rate (a facility lease payment). Variable costs refer to items that vary in relation to usage (long distance phone charges).

During the process of determining project costs, Jim and Jackie identified both one-time and recurring costs for the project. These costs are summarized in Figures 6-5 and 6-6. These figures show that this project will incur a one-time cost of $42,500 and a recurring cost of $28,500 per year. One-time costs were established by discussing the system with Jim's boss who felt that the system would require

Figure 6-5
One-time costs for Customer Tracking System (Pine Valley Furniture)

ONE-TIME COSTS WORKSHEET Customer Tracking System Project	Year 0
A. Development costs	$20,000
B. New hardware	15,000
C. New (purchased) software, if any 1. Packaged applications software	5,000
2. Other _____	0
D. User training	2,500
E. Site preparation	0
F. Other _____	0
TOTAL one-time cost	$42,500

Figure 6-6
Recurring costs for Customer Tracking System (Pine Valley Furniture)

RECURRING COSTS WORKSHEET *Customer Tracking System Project*	
	Year 1 through 5
A. Application software maintenance	$25,000
B. Incremental data storage required: 20 MB × $50. (estimated cost/MB = $50)	1,000
C. Incremental communications (lines, messages, . . .)	2,000
D. New software or hardware leases	0
E. Supplies	500
F. Other _____	0
TOTAL recurring costs	**$28,500**

approximately four months to develop (at $5,000 per month). To effectively run the new system, the Marketing department would need to upgrade at least five of their current workstations (at $3,000 each). Additionally, software licenses for each workstation (at $1,000 each) and modest user training fees (ten users at $250 each) would be necessary.

As you can see from Figure 6-6, Jim and Jackie believe the proposed system will be highly dynamic and will require, on average, five months of annual maintenance, primarily for enhancements as users expect more from the system. Other ongoing expenses such as increased data storage, communications equipment, and supplies should also be expected. You should now have an understanding of the types of benefit and cost categories associated with an information systems project. It should be clear that there are many potential benefits and costs associated with a given project. Additionally, since the development and useful life of a system may span several years, these benefits and costs must be normalized into present-day values in order to perform meaningful cost-benefit comparisons. In the next section, we address the relationship between time and money.

The Time Value of Money   Most techniques used to determine economic feasibility encompass the concept of the *time value of money* (TVM). TVM refers to the concept of comparing present cash outlays to future expected returns. As previously discussed, the development of an information system has both one-time and recurring costs. Furthermore, benefits from systems development will likely occur sometime in the future. Since many projects may be competing for the same investment dollars and may have different useful life expectancies, all costs and benefits must be viewed in relation to their *present value* when comparing investment options.

A simple example will help in understanding the TVM. Suppose you want to buy a used car from an acquaintance and she asks that you make three payments of $1,500 for three years, beginning next year, for a total of $4,500. If she would agree to a single lump sum payment at the time of sale (and if you had the money!), what amount do you think she would agree to? Should the single payment be $4,500? Should it be more or less? To answer this question, we must consider the time value of money. Most of us would gladly accept $4,500 today rather than three payments of $1,500, because a dollar today (or $4,500 for that matter) is worth more than a dollar tomorrow or next year, because money can be invested. The rate at which money can be borrowed or invested is called the *cost of capital,* and is called the **discount rate** for TVM calculations. Let's suppose that the seller could put the money received for the sale of the car in the bank and receive a 10% return on her investment. A simple formula can be used when figuring out the **present value** of the three $1,500 payments:

$$PV_n = Y \times \left[\frac{1}{(1 + i)^n} \right]$$

where PV_n is the present value of Y dollars n years from now when i is the discount rate.

From our example, the present value of the three payments of $1,500 can be calculated as

$$PV_1 = 1500 \times \left[\frac{1}{(1 + .10)^1} \right] = 1500 \times .9091 = 1363.65$$

$$PV_2 = 1500 \times \left[\frac{1}{(1 + .10)^2} \right] = 1500 \times .8264 = 1239.60$$

$$PV_3 = 1500 \times \left[\frac{1}{(1 + .10)^3} \right] = 1500 \times .7513 = 1126.95$$

where PV_1, PV_2, and PV_3 reflect the present value of each $1,500 payment in year one, two, and three, respectively.

To calculate the *net present value* (NPV) of the three $1,500 payments, simply add the present values calculated above (NPV = $PV_1 + PV_2 + PV_3$ = 1363.65 + 1239.60 + 1126.95 = $3730.20). In other words, the seller could accept a lump sum payment of $3,730.20 as equivalent to the three payments of $1,500, given a discount rate of 10 percent.

Given that we now know the relationship between time and money, the next step in performing the economic analysis is to create a summary worksheet reflecting the present values of all benefits and costs as well as all pertinent analyses. Due to the fast pace of the business world, PVF's System Priority Board feels that the useful life of many information systems may not exceed five years. Therefore, all cost-benefit analysis calculations will be made using a five-year time horizon as the upper boundary on all time-related analyses. In addition, the management of PVF has set their cost of capital to be 12% (that is, PVF's discount rate). The worksheet constructed by Jim is shown in Figure 6-7.

Cell H11 of the worksheet displayed in Figure 6-7 summarizes the NPV of the total tangible benefits from the project. Cell H19 summarizes the NPV of the total costs from the project. The NPV for the project ($35,003) shows that, overall, benefits from the project exceed costs (see cell H22).

The overall return on investment (ROI) for the project is also shown on the worksheet in cell H25. Since alternative projects will likely have different benefit and cost values and, possibly, different life expectancies, the overall ROI value is very useful for making project comparisons on an economic basis. Of course, this example shows ROI for the overall project. An ROI analysis could be calculated for each year of the project.

The last analysis shown in Figure 6-7 is a break-even analysis. The objective of the break-even analysis is to discover at what point (if ever) benefits equal costs (that is, when break-even occurs). To conduct this analysis, the NPV of the yearly cash flows are determined. Here, the yearly cash flows are calculated by subtracting both the one-time cost and the present values of the recurring costs from the present value of the yearly benefits. The overall NPV of the cash flow reflects the total cash flows for all preceding years. Examination of line 30 of the worksheet shows that break-even occurs between years 2 and 3. Since year three is the first in

Discount rate: The rate of return used to compute the present value of future cash flows.

Present value: The current value of a future cash flow.

Figure 6-7

Summary spreadsheet reflecting the present value calculations of all benefits and costs for the Customer Tracking System (Pine Valley Furniture)

	A	B	C	D	E	F	G	H
1	*Pine Valley Furniture*							
2	*Economic Feasibility Analysis*							
3	*Customer Tracking System Project*							
4								
5					Year of Project			
6		*Year 0*	*Year 1*	*Year 2*	*Year 3*	*Year 4*	*Year 5*	*TOTALS*
7	Net economic benefit	$0	$50,000	$50,000	$50,000	$50,000	$50,000	
8	Discount rate (12%)	*1.0000*	*0.8929*	*0.7972*	*0.7118*	*0.6355*	*0.5674*	
9	PV of benefits	$0	$44,643	$39,860	$35,589	$31,776	$28,371	
10								
11	*NPV of all BENEFITS*	$0	$44,643	$84,503	$120,092	$151,867	$180,239	$180,239
12								
13	*One-time COSTS*	($42,500)						
14								
15	Recurring Costs	$0	($28,500)	($28,500)	($28,500)	($28,500)	($28,500)	
16	Discount rate (12%)	*1.0000*	*0.8929*	*0.7972*	*0.7118*	*0.6355*	*0.5674*	
17	PV of Recurring Costs	$0	($25,446)	($22,720)	($20,286)	($18,112)	($16,172)	
18								
19	*NPV of all COSTS*	($42,500)	($67,946)	($90,666)	($110,952)	($129,064)	($145,236)	($145,236)
20								
21								
22	*Overall NPV*							$35,003
23								
24								
25	*Overall ROI - (Overall NPV / NPV of all COSTS)*							0.24
26								
27								
28	*Break-even Analysis*							
29	Yearly NPV Cash Flow	($42,500)	$19,196	$17,140	$15,303	$13,664	$12,200	
30	Overall NPV Cash Flow	($42,500)	($23,304)	($6,164)	$9,139	$22,803	$35,003	
31								
32	Project break-even occurs between years 2 and 3							
33	Use first year of positive cash flow to calculate break-even fraction - ((15303 - 9139) / 15303) = .403							
34	*Actual break-even occurred at 2.4 years*							
35								
36	Note: All dollar values have been rounded to the nearest dollar							

which the general NPV cash flows figure is non-negative, the identification of what point during the year break-even occurs can be derived as follows:

$$\text{Break-Even Ratio} = \frac{\text{Yearly NPV Cash Flow} - \text{general NPV Cash Flow}}{\text{Yearly NPV Cash Flow}}$$

Using data from Figure 6-7,

$$\text{Break-Even Ratio} = \frac{15{,}303 - 9{,}139}{15{,}303} = .404$$

Therefore, project break-even occurs at approximately 2.4 years. A graphical representation of this analysis is shown in Figure 6-8. Using the information from the

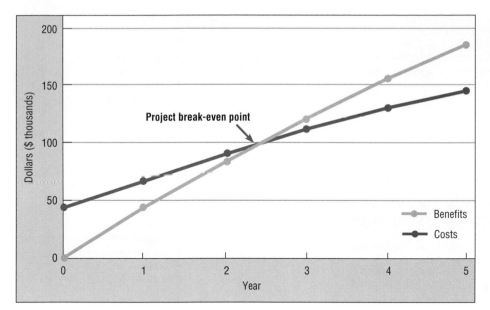

economic analysis, PVF's Systems Priority Board will be in a much better position to understand the potential economic impact of the Customer Tracking System. It should be clear from this analysis that, without such information, it would be virtually impossible to know the cost-benefits of a proposed system and impossible to make an informed decision regarding approval or rejection of the service request.

There are many techniques that you can use to compute a project's economic feasibility. Because most information systems have a useful life of more than one year and will provide benefits and incur expenses for more than one year, most techniques for analyzing economic feasibility employ the concept of the TVM. Some of these cost-benefit analysis techniques are quite simple while others are more sophisticated. Table 6-6 describes three commonly used techniques for conducting economic feasibility analysis. For a more detailed discussion of TVM or cost-benefit analysis techniques in general, the interested reader is encouraged to review an introductory finance or managerial accounting textbook.

A systems project, to be approved for continuation, may not have to achieve break-even or have an ROI above some organizational threshold as estimated during project initiation and planning. Since you may not be able to quantify many

TABLE 6-6 Commonly Used Economic Cost-Benefit Analysis Techniques	
Analysis Technique	**Description**
Net Present Value (NPV)	NPV uses a discount rate determined from the company's cost of capital to establish the present value of a project. The discount rate is used to determine the present value of both cash receipts and outlays.
Return on Investment (ROI)	ROI is the ratio of the net cash receipts of the project divided by the cash outlays of the project. Tradeoff analysis can be made among projects competing for investment by comparing their representative ROI ratios.
Break-Even Analysis (BEA)	BEA finds the amount of time required for the cumulative cash flow from a project to equal its initial and ongoing investment.

Measuring Web ROI

Over the past few years, the World Wide Web has been getting a lot of attention by all types of businesses. Yet, with all the hype and activity on the Web, many businesses struggle with economically justifying their Web-based systems. Forrester Research predicts that an average corporate Web site used only for product promotion cost $681,000 in 1997 (Radosevich, 1996). A full-blown electronic commerce site with on-line transaction processing was estimated to cost $4,224,000! When designing a Web site, organizations must consider a broad range of costs that you may not consider when building a more traditional information system (see Table 6-7). When building Web sites, a big variation in costs was found not only among the types of sites but also depending on whether the site was built and maintained by the company itself or outsourced to a company specializing in the design and management of Web-based systems—in some cases, costs were found to be more than 10 times lower when outsourced. In addition to having difficulty estimating costs, identifying tangible benefits is also often difficult. For example, Hershey Foods (www.hershey.com) has developed a promotional site to provide visitors with information on financial performance and chocolate recipes. Hershey made a decision early on to keep its site simple. According to Tom Loser, Webmaster and database administrator for Hershey, "We can't afford to sell a single candy bar over the net, so ours is just an information source" (Radosevich, 1996; p. 94). Consequently, many of the benefits derived from its site may show no measurable economic benefits. Nonetheless, Hershey feels that the site provides valuable benefits and has no plans to discontinue its Web presence.

TABLE 6-7 Web-based System Costs

Cost Category	Examples
Platform costs	• Web-hosting service • Web server • Server software • Software plug-ins • Firewall server • Router • Internet connection
Content and service	• Creative design and development • Ongoing design fees • Web project manager • Technical site manager • Content staff • Graphics staff • Support staff • Site enhancement funds • Fees to license outside content • Programming, consulting, and research • Training and travel
Marketing	• Direct mail • Launch and ongoing public relations • Print advertisement • Paid links to other Web sites • Promotions • Marketing staff • Advertising sales staff

benefits or costs at this point in a project, such financial hurdles for a project may be unattainable. In this case, simply doing as thorough an economic analysis as possible, including producing a long list of intangibles, may be sufficient for the project to progress. One other option is to run the type of economic analysis shown in Figure 6-7 using pessimistic, optimistic, and expected benefit and cost estimates during project initiation and planning. This range of possible outcomes, along with the list of intangible benefits and the support of the requesting business unit, will often be enough to allow the project to continue to the analysis phase. You must, however, be as precise as you can with the economic analysis, especially when investment capital is scarce. In this case, it may be necessary to conduct some typical analysis phase activities during project initiation and planning in order to clearly identify inefficiencies and shortcomings with the existing system and to explain how a new system will overcome these problems. Thus, building the economic case for a systems project is an open-ended activity; how much analysis is needed depends on the particular project, stakeholders, and business conditions. Also, conducting economic feasibility analyses for new types of information systems if often very difficult (see box titled "Measuring Web ROI").

Technical feasibility:
A process of assessing the development organization's ability to construct a proposed system.

Assessing Technical Feasibility

The purpose of assessing **technical feasibility** is to gain an understanding of the organization's ability to construct the proposed system. This analysis should include an assessment of the development group's understanding of the possible target hardware, software, and operating environments to be used as well as system size, complexity, and the group's experience with similar systems. In this section, we will discuss a framework you can use for assessing the technical feasibility of a project in which a level of project risk can be determined after answering a few fundamental questions.

It is important to note that all projects have risk and that risk is not necessarily something to avoid. Yet it is also true that, because organizations typically expect a greater return on their investment for riskier projects, understanding the sources and types of technical risks proves to be a valuable tool when you assess a project. Also, risks need to be managed in order to be minimized; you should, therefore, identify potential risks as early as possible in a project. The potential consequences of not assessing and managing risks can include the following outcomes:

1. Failure to attain expected benefits from the project

2. Inaccurate project cost estimates

3. Inaccurate project duration estimates

4. Failure to achieve adequate system performance levels

5. Failure to adequately integrate the new system with existing hardware, software, or organizational procedures

You can manage risk on a project by changing the project plan to avoid risky factors, assigning project team members to carefully manage the risky aspects, and setting up monitoring methods to determine whether or not potential risk is, in fact, materializing.

The amount of technical risk associated with a given project is contingent on four primary factors: project size, project structure, the development group's experience with the application and technology area, and the user group's experience with development projects and application area. Aspects of each of these risk areas are summarized in Table 6-8. Using these factors for conducting a technical risk assessment, four general rules emerge:

1. *Large projects are riskier than small projects.* Project size, of course, relates to the relative project size that the development group is familiar working with. A "small" project for one development group may be relatively "large" for another. The types of factors that influence project size are listed in Table 6-8.

2. *A system in which the requirements are easily obtained and highly structured will be less risky than one in which requirements are messy, ill-structured, ill-defined, or subject to the judgement of an individual.* For example, the development of a payroll system has requirements that may be easy to obtain due to legal reporting requirements and standard accounting procedures. On the other hand, the development of an executive support system would need to be customized to the particular executive decision style and critical success factors of the organization, thus making its development more risky (see Table 6-8).

3. *The development of a system employing commonly used or standard technology will be less risky than one employing novel or non-standard technology.* A project has a greater likelihood of experiencing unforeseen technical problems when the development group lacks knowledge related to some aspect of the technology environment. A less risky approach is to use standard development tools and hardware environments. It is not uncommon for experienced system developers to talk of the difficulty of using leading-edge (or in their words, *bleeding edge*) technology (see Table 6-8).

TABLE 6-8 Project Risk Assessment Factors

Risk Factor	Examples
Project Size	Number of members on the project team
	Project duration time
	Number of organizational departments involved in project
	Size of programming effort (e.g., hours, function points)
Project Structure	New system or renovation of existing system(s)
	Organizational, procedural, structural, or personnel changes resulting from system
	User perceptions and willingness to participate in effort
	Management commitment to system
	Amount of user information in system development effort
Development Group	Familiarity with target-hardware, software development environment, tools, and operating system
	Familiarity with proposed application area
	Familiarity with building similar systems of similar size
User Group	Familiarity with information systems development process
	Familiarity with proposed application area
	Familiarity with using similar systems

Adapted from Cash, McFarlan, McKenney, and Applegate, 1992

4. *A project is less risky when the user group is familiar with the systems development process and application area than if unfamiliar.* Successful IS projects require active involvement and cooperation between the user and development groups. Users familiar with the application area and the systems development process are more likely to understand the need for their involvement and how this involvement can influence the success of the project (see Table 6-8).

A project with high risk may still be conducted. Many organizations look at risk as a portfolio issue: considering all projects, it is okay to have a reasonable percentage of high-, medium-, and low-risk projects. Given that some high-risk projects will get into trouble, an organization cannot afford to have too many of these. Having too many low-risk projects may not be aggressive enough to make major breakthroughs in innovative uses of systems. Each organization must decide on its acceptable mix of projects of varying risk.

A matrix for assessing the relative risks related to the general rules described above is shown in Figure 6-9. Using the risk factor rules to assess the technical risk level of the Customer Tracking System, Jim and Jackie concluded the following about their project:

1. The project is a relatively *small project* for PVF's development organization. The basic data for the system is readily available so the creation of the system will not be a large undertaking.

2. The requirements for the project are *highly structured* and easily obtainable. In fact, an existing spreadsheet-based system is available for analysts to examine and study.

		Low Structure	High Structure
High Familiarity with Technology or Application Area	Large Project	(1) Low risk (very susceptible to mismanagement)	(2) Low risk
	Small Project	(3) Very low risk (very susceptible to mismanagement)	(4) Very low risk
Low Familiarity with Technology or Application Area	Large Project	(5) Very high risk	(6) Medium risk
	Small Project	(7) High risk	(8) Medium-low risk

Figure 6-9
Effects of degree of project structure, project size, and familiarity with application area on project implementation risk (Adapted from: Cash et al., 1999)

3. The *development group is familiar* with the technology that will likely be used to construct the system, as the system will simply extend current system capabilities.

4. The *user group is familiar* with the application area since they are already using the PC-based spreadsheet system described in Figure 6-3.

Given this risk assessment, Jim and Jackie mapped their information into the risk framework of Figure 6-9. They concluded that this project should be viewed as having "very low" technical risk (cell 4 of the figure). Although this method is useful for gaining an understanding of technical feasibility, numerous other issues can influence the success of the project. These non-financial and non-technical issues are described in the following section.

Assessing Other Feasibility Concerns

In this section, we will briefly conclude our discussion of project feasibility issues by reviewing other forms of feasibility that you may need to consider when formulating the business case for a system during project planning. The first relates to examining the likelihood that the project will attain its desired objectives, called **operational feasibility.** Its purpose is to gain an understanding of the degree to which the proposed system will likely solve the business problems or take advantage of the opportunities outlined in the systems service request or project identification study. For a project motivated from information system planning, operational feasibility includes justifying the project on the basis of being consistent with or necessary for accomplishing the IS plan. In fact, the business case for any project can be enhanced by showing a link to the business or information systems plan. Your assessment of operational feasibility should also include an analysis of how the proposed system will affect organizational structures and procedures. Systems that have substantial and widespread impact on an organization's structure or procedures are typically riskier projects to undertake. Thus, it is important for you to have a clear understanding of how an IS will fit into the current day-to-day operations of the organization.

Operational feasibility: The process of assessing the degree to which a proposed system solves business problems or takes advantage of business opportunities.

Schedule feasibility: The process of assessing the degree to which the potential time frame and completion dates for all major activities within a project meet organizational deadlines and constraints for affecting change.

Another feasibility concern relates to project duration and is referred to as assessing schedule feasibility. The purpose of assessing **schedule feasibility** is for you, as a systems analyst, to gain an understanding of the likelihood that all potential timeframes and completion date schedules can be met and that meeting these dates will be sufficient for dealing with the needs of the organization. For example, a system may have to be operational by a government-imposed deadline, by a particular point in the business cycle (such as the beginning of the season when new products are introduced), or at least by the time a competitor is expected to introduce a similar system. Further, detailed activities may only be feasible if resources are available when called for in the schedule. For example, the schedule should not call for system testing during rushed business periods or for key project meetings during annual vacation or holiday periods. The schedule of activities produced during project initiation and planing will be very precise and detailed for the analysis phase. The estimated activities and associated times for activities after the analysis phase are typically not as detailed (e.g., it will take two weeks to program the payroll report module) but are rather at the life-cycle phase level (e.g., it will take six weeks for physical design, four months for programming, and so on). This means that assessing schedule feasibility during project initiation and planning is more of a "rough-cut" analysis of whether the system can be completed within the constraints of the business opportunity or the desires of the users. While assessing schedule feasibility you should also evaluate scheduling tradeoffs. For example, factors such as project team size, availability of key personnel, subcontracting or outsourcing activities, and changes in development environments may all be considered as having possible impact on the eventual schedule. As with all forms of feasibility, schedule feasibility will be reassessed after each phase, when you can specify with greater certainty the detailed steps and their duration for the next phase.

Legal and contractual feasibility: The process of assessing potential legal and contractual ramifications due to the construction of a system.

A third concern relates to assessing **legal and contractual feasibility** issues. In this area, you need to gain an understanding of any potential legal ramifications due to the construction of the system. Possible considerations might include copyright or nondisclosure infringements, labor laws, antitrust legislation (which might limit the creation of systems to share data with other organizations), foreign trade regulations (for example, some countries limit access to employee data by foreign corporations), and financial reporting standards as well as current or pending contractual obligations. Contractual obligations may involve ownership of software used in joint ventures, license agreements for use of hardware or software, nondisclosure agreements with partners, or elements of a labor agreement (for example, a union agreement may preclude certain compensation or work-monitoring capabilities a user may want in a system). A common situation is that development of a new application system for use on new computers may require new or expanded, and more costly, system software licenses. Typically, legal and contractual feasibility is a greater consideration if your organization has historically used an outside organization for specific systems or services that you now are considering handling yourself. In this case, ownership of program source code by another party may make it difficult to extend an existing system or link a new system with an existing, purchased system.

Political feasibility: The process of evaluating how key stakeholders within the organization view the proposed system.

A final feasibility concern focuses on assessing **political feasibility** in which you attempt to gain an understanding of how key stakeholders within the organization view the proposed system. Since an information system may affect the distribution of information within the organization, and thus the distribution of power, the construction of an IS can have political ramifications. Those stakeholders not supporting the project may take steps to block, disrupt, or change the intended focus of the project.

In summary, depending upon the given situation, numerous feasibility issues must be considered when planning a project. This analysis should consider economic, technical, operational, schedule, legal, contractual, and political issues related to the project. In addition to these considerations, project selection by an organization may be influenced by issues beyond those discussed here. For example, projects may be selected for construction given high project costs and high technical risk if the system is viewed as a strategic necessity; that is, a project viewed by the organization as being critical to its survival. Alternatively, projects may be selected because they are deemed to require few resources and have little risk. Projects may also be selected due to the power or persuasiveness of the manager proposing the system. This means that project selection may be influenced by factors beyond those discussed here and beyond items that can be analyzed. Understanding the reality that projects may be selected based on factors beyond analysis, your role as a systems analyst is to provide a thorough examination of the items that can be assessed. Your analysis will ensure that a project review committee has as much information as possible when making project approval decisions. In the next section, we discuss how project plans are typically reviewed.

BUILDING THE BASELINE PROJECT PLAN

All the information collected during project initiation and planning is collected and organized into a document called the Baseline Project Plan. Once the BPP is completed, a formal review of the project can be conducted with project clients and other interested parties. This presentation is called a *walkthrough* and is discussed later in the chapter. The focus of this review is to verify all information and assumptions in the baseline plan before moving ahead with the project. As mentioned above, the project size and organizational standards will dictate the comprehensiveness of the project initiation and planning process as well as the BPP. Yet, most experienced systems builders have found project planning and a clear project plan to be invaluable to project success. An outline of a Baseline Project Plan is provided in Figure 6-10, which shows that it contains four major sections:

1. Introduction

2. System Description

3. Feasibility Assessment

4. Management Issues

The purpose of the *Introduction* is to provide a brief overview of the entire document and outline a recommended course of action for the project. The entire Introduction section is often limited to only a few pages. Although the Introduction section is sequenced as the first section of the BPP, it is often the final section to be written. It is only after performing most of the project planning activities that a clear overview and recommendation can be created. One activity that should be performed initially is the definition of project scope.

When defining scope for the Customer Tracking System within PVF, Jim Woo first needed to gain a clear understanding of the project's objectives. To do this, Jim briefly interviewed Jackie Judson and several of her colleagues to gain a clear idea of their needs. He also spent a few hours reviewing the existing system's functionality, processes, and data use requirements for performing customer tracking

Figure 6-10
Outline of a Baseline Project Plan

BASELINE PROJECT PLAN REPORT

1.0 *Introduction*
    A. Project Overview—Provides an executive summary that specifies the project's scope, feasibility, justification, resource requirements, and schedules. Additionally, a brief statement of the problem, the environment in which the system is to be implemented, and constraints that affect the project are provided.
    B. Recommendation—Provides a summary of important findings from the planning process and recommendations for subsequent activities.

2.0 *System Description*
    A. Alternatives—Provides a brief presentation of alternative system configurations.
    B. System Description—Provides a description of the selected configuration and a narrative of input information, tasks performed, and resultant information.

3.0 *Feasibility Assessment*
    A. Economic Analysis—Provides an economic justification for the system using cost-benefit analysis.
    B. Technical Analysis—Provides a discussion of relevant technical risk factors and an overall risk rating of the project.
    C. Operational Analysis—Provides an analysis of how the proposed system solves business problems or takes advantage of business opportunities in addition to an assessment of how current day-to-day activities will be changed by the system.
    D. Legal and Contractual Analysis—Provides a description of any legal or contractual risks related to the project (e.g., copyright or nondisclosure issues, data capture or transferring, and so on).
    E. Political Analysis—Provides a description of how key stakeholders within the organization view the proposed system.
    F. Schedules, Timeline, and Resource Analysis—Provides a description of potential timeframe and completion date scenarios using various resource allocation schemes.

4.0 *Management Issues*
    A. Team Configuration and Management—Provides a description of the team member roles and reporting relationships.
    B. Communication Plan—Provides a description of the communication procedures to be followed by management, team members, and the customer.
    C. Project Standards and Procedures—Provides a description of how deliverables will be evaluated and accepted by the customer.
    D. Other Project-Specific Topics—Provides a description of any other relevant issues related to the project uncovered during planning.

activities. These activities provided him with the information needed to define the project scope and to identify possible alternative solutions. Alternative system solutions can relate to different system scopes, platforms for deployment, or approaches to acquiring the system. We elaborate on the idea of alternative solutions, called design strategies, when we discuss the analysis phase of the life cycle. During project initiation and planning, the most crucial element of the design strategy is the system's scope. In sum, a determination of scope will depend on these factors:

- Which organizational units (business functions and divisions) might be affected by or use the proposed system or system change?

- With which current systems might the proposed system need to interact or be consistent, or which current systems might be changed due to a replacement system?

- Who inside and outside the requesting organization (or the organization as a whole) might care about the proposed system?

- What range of potential system capabilities are to be considered?

The statement of project scope for the Customer Tracking System project is shown in Figure 6-11.

For the Customer Tracking System (CTS), project scope was defined using only textual information. It is not uncommon, however, to define project scope using diagrams such as data flow diagrams and entity-relationship models. For example, Figure 6-12 shows a context-level data flow diagram used to define system scope for PVF's Purchasing Fulfillment System described on the *Modern Systems Analysis and Design*'s World Wide Web site (http://hepg.awl.com/). The other items in the Introduction section of the BPP are simply executive summaries of the other sections of the document.

The second section of the BPP is the *System Description* where you outline possible alternative solutions in addition to the one deemed most appropriate for the given situation. Note that this description is at a very high level, mostly narrative in form. For example, alternatives may be stated as simply as this:

1. Mainframe with central database

2. Distributed with decentralized databases

3. Batch data input with on-line retrieval

4. Purchasing of a pre-written package

If the project is approved for construction or purchase, you will need to collect and structure information in a more detailed and rigorous manner during the analysis phase and evaluate in greater depth these and other alternative directions for the system. At this point in the project, your objective is only to identify the most obvious alternative solutions.

When Jim and Jackie were considering system alternatives for the CTS, they focused on two primary issues. First, they discussed how the system would be acquired and considered three options: *purchase* the system if one could be found that met PVF's needs, *outsource* the development of the system to an outside organization, or *build* the system within PVF. The second issue focused on defining the comprehensiveness of the system's functionality. To complete this task, Jim asked Jackie to write a series of statements listing the types of tasks that she envisioned marketing personnel would be able to accomplish when using the CTS. This list of statements became the basis of the system description and was instrumental in helping them make their acquisition decision. After considering the unique needs of the marketing group, both decided that the best decision was to build the system within PVF.

Figure 6-11
Statement of project scope (Pine Valley Furniture)

Pine Valley Furniture *Statement of Project Scope*	Prepared by: Jim Woo Date: September 18, 1998

General Project Information
    Project Name: Customer Tracking System
    Sponsor: Jackie Judson, VP Marketing
    Project Manager: Jim Woo

Problem/Opportunity Statement:
    Sales growth has out-paced the marketing department's ability to accurately track and forecast customer buying trends. An improved method for performing this process must be found in order to reach company objectives.

Project Objectives:
    To enable the marketing department to accurately track and forecast customer buying patterns in order to better serve customers with the best mix of products. This will also enable PVF to identify the proper application of production and material resources.

Project Description:
    A new information system will be constructed that will collect all customer purchasing activity, support display and reporting of sales information, aggregate data and show trends in order to assist marketing personnel in understanding dynamic market conditions. The project will follow PVF's systems development life cycle.

Business Benefits:
    Improved understanding of customer buying patterns
    Improved utilizaton of marketing and sales personnel
    Improved utilization of production and materials

Project Deliverables:
    Customer tracking system analysis and design
    Customer tracking system programs
    Customer tracking documentation
    Training procedures

Estimated Project Duration:
    5 months

In the third section, *Feasibility Assessment,* issues related to project costs and benefits, technical difficulties, and other such concerns are outlined. This is also the section where high-level project schedules are specified using PERT and Gantt charts. Recall from Chapter 3 that this process is referred to as a work breakdown structure. During project initiation and planning, task and activity estimates are

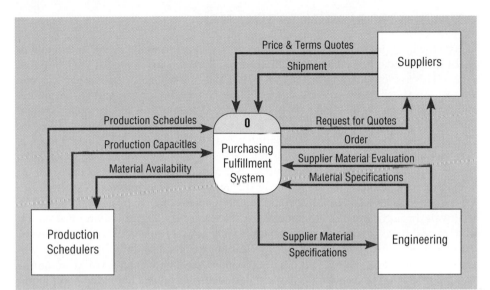

Figure 6-12
Context-level data flow diagram showing project scope for Purchasing Fulfillment System (Pine Valley Furniture)

not generally detailed. An accurate work breakdown can only be done for the next one or two life cycle activities. After defining the primary tasks for the project, an estimate of the resource requirements can be made. As with defining tasks and activities, this activity is primarily concerned with gaining rough estimates of the human resource requirements, since people are the most expensive resource element. Once you define the major tasks and resource requirements, a preliminary schedule can be developed. Defining an acceptable schedule may require that you find additional or different resources or that the scope of the project be changed. The greatest amount of project planning effort is typically expended on these Feasibility Assessment activities.

The final section, *Management Issues,* outlines a number of managerial concerns related to the project. This will be a very short section if the proposed project is going to be conducted exactly as prescribed by the organization's standard systems development methodology. Most projects, however, have some unique characteristics that require minor to major deviation from the standard methodology. In the Team Configuration and Management portion, you identify the types of people to work on the project, who will be responsible for which tasks, and how work will be supervised and reviewed. In the Communications Plan portion, you explain how the user will be kept informed about project progress (such as periodic review meetings or even a newsletter) and which mechanisms will be used to foster sharing of ideas among team members, such as some form of computer-based conference facility. An example of the type of information contained in the Project Standards and Procedures portion would be procedures for submitting and approving project change requests and any other issues deemed important for the project's success.

You should now have a feel for how a BPP is constructed and the types of information it contains. Its creation is not meant to be a project in and of itself but rather a step in the overall systems development process. Developing the BPP has two primary objectives. First, it helps to assure that the customer and development group share a common understanding of the project. Second, it helps to provide the sponsoring organization with a clear idea of the scope, benefits, and duration of the project.

REVIEWING THE BASELINE PROJECT PLAN

Before the next phase of the SDLC can begin, the users, management, and development group must review the Baseline Project Plan in order to verify that it makes sense. This review takes place before the BPP is submitted or presented to some project approval body, such as an IS steering committee or the person who must fund the project. The objective of this review is to assure that the proposed system conforms to organizational standards and to make sure that all relevant parties understand and agree with the information contained in the Baseline Project Plan. A common method for performing this review (as well as reviews during subsequent life cycle phases) is called a structured **walkthrough.** Walkthroughs are peer group reviews of any product created during the systems development process and are widely used by professional development organizations. Experience has shown that walkthroughs are a very effective way to ensure the quality of an information system and have become a common day-to-day activity for many system analysts.

Walkthrough: A peer group review of any product created during the systems development process. Also called structured walkthrough.

Most walkthroughs are not rigidly formal or exceeding long in duration. It is important, however, that a specific agenda be established for the walkthrough so that all attendees understand what is to be covered and the expected completion time. At walkthrough meetings, there is a need to have individuals play specific roles. These roles are as follows (Yourdon, 1989):

- *Coordinator.* This person plans the meeting and facilitates a smooth meeting process. This person may be the project leader or a lead analyst responsible for the current life cycle step.

- *Presenter.* This person describes the work product to the group. The presenter is usually an analyst who has done all or some of the work being presented.

- *User.* This person (or group) makes sure that the work product meets the needs of the project's customers. This user would usually be someone not on the project team.

- *Secretary.* This person takes notes and records decisions or recommendations made by the group. This may be a clerk assigned to the project team or it may be one of the analysts on the team.

- *Standards bearer.* The role of this person is to ensure that the work product adheres to organizational technical standards. Many larger organizations have staff groups within the unit responsible for establishing standard procedures, methods, and documentation formats. These standards bearers validate the work so that it can be used by others in the development organization.

- *Maintenance oracle.* This person reviews the work product in terms of future maintenance activities. The goal is to make the system and its documentation easy to maintain.

After Jim and Jackie completed their BPP for the Customer Tracking System, Jim approached his boss and requested that a walkthrough meeting be scheduled and that a walkthrough coordinator be assigned to the project. PVF assists the coordinator by providing a Walkthrough Review Form, shown in Figure 6-13. Using this form, the coordinator can more easily make sure that a qualified individual is assigned to each walkthrough role, that each member has been given a copy of the review materials, and that each member knows the agenda, date, time, and location of the meeting. At the meeting, Jim presented the BPP and Jackie added comments from a user perspective. Once the walkthrough presentation was completed, the coordinator polled each representative for his or her recommendation concerning the work product. The results of this voting may result in validation of the work

Figure 6-13
Walkthrough review form (Pine Valley Furniture)

Pine Valley Furniture
Walkthrough Review Form

Session Coordinator:

Project/Segment:

Coordinator's checklist:

1. Confirmation with producer(s) that material is ready and stable: _____
2. Issue invitations, assign responsibilities, distribute materials: [ ] Y   [ ] N
3. Set date, time, and location for meeting:

   Date: ___ / ___ / ___   Time: _____ a.m. / p.m. (circle one)

   Location: _____

Responsibilities	*Participants*	*Can Attend*	*Received Materials*
Coordinator	_____	[ ] Y [ ] N	[ ] Y [ ] N
Presenter	_____	[ ] Y [ ] N	[ ] Y [ ] N
User	_____	[ ] Y [ ] N	[ ] Y [ ] N
Secretary	_____	[ ] Y [ ] N	[ ] Y [ ] N
Standards	_____	[ ] Y [ ] N	[ ] Y [ ] N
Maintenance	_____	[ ] Y [ ] N	[ ] Y [ ] N

Agenda:
_____ 1. All participants agree to follow PVF's Rules of a Walkthrough
_____ 2. New material: walkthrough of all material
_____ 3. Old material: item-by-item checkoff of previous action list
_____ 4. Creation of new action list (contribution by each participant)
_____ 5. Group decision (see below)
_____ 6. Deliver copy of this form to the project control manager

Group Decision:
_____ Accept product as-is
_____ Revise (no further walkthrough)
_____ Review and schedule another walkthrough

Signatures		

product, validation pending changes suggested during the meeting, or a suggestion that the work product requires major revision before being presented for approval. In this latter case, substantial changes to the work product are usually requested after which another walkthrough must be scheduled before the project can be proposed to the Systems Priority Board (steering committee). In the case of the Customer Tracking System, the BPP was supported by the walkthrough panel pending some minor changes to the duration estimates of the schedule. These suggested changes were recorded by the secretary on a Walkthrough Action List (see Figure 6-14) and given to Jim to incorporate into a final version of the baseline plan presented to the steering committee.

As suggested above, walkthrough meetings are a common occurrence in most systems development groups and can be used for more activities than reviewing the BPP, including the following:

- System specifications

- Logical and physical designs

- Code or program segments

- Test procedures and results

- Manuals and documentation

One of the key advantages to using a structured review process is to ensure that formal review points occur during the project. At each subsequent phase of the project, a formal review should be conducted (and shown on the project schedule) to make sure that all aspects of the project are satisfactorily accomplished before assigning additional resources to the project. This conservative approach of reviewing each major project activity with continuation contingent on successful completion of the prior phase is called *incremental commitment*. It is much easier to stop or redirect a project at any point when using this approach.

SUMMARY

The project initiation and planning phase is a critical activity in the life of a project. It is at this point that projects are accepted for development, rejected as infeasible, or redirected. The objective of this process is to transform a vague system request into a tangible system description clearly outlining the objectives, feasibility issues, benefits, costs, and time schedules for the project.

Project initiation includes forming the project initiation team, establishing customer relationships, developing a plan to get the project started, setting project management procedures, and creating an overall project management environment. A key activity in project planning is the assessment of numerous feasibility issues associated with the project. Feasibilities include economic, technical, operational, schedule, legal and contractual, and political. These issues are influenced by the project size, the type of system proposed, and the collective experience of the development group and potential customers of the system. High project costs and risks are not necessarily bad; rather it is more important that the organization understands the costs and risks associated with a project and with the portfolio of active projects before proceeding.

After completing all analyses, a Baseline Project Plan can be created. A BPP includes a high-level description of the proposed system or system change, an outline of the various feasibilities, and an overview of management issues specific to the project. Before the development of an information system can begin, the users,

Figure 6-14
Walkthrough action list (Pine Valley Furniture)

Pine Valley Furniture	
Walkthrough Action List	
Session Coordinator:	
Project/Segment:	
Date and Time of Walkthrough:	
Date: ____ /____ /____ Time: _____ a.m. / p.m. (circle one)	

Fixed (✓)	*Issues raised in review:*

management, and development group must review and agree on this specification. The focus of this walkthrough review is to assess the merits of the project and to assure that the project, if accepted for development, conforms to organizational standards and goals. An objective of this process is to also make sure that all relevant parties understand and agree with the information contained in the plan before subsequent development activities begin.

Project initiation and planning is a challenging and time-consuming activity that requires active involvement from many organizational participants. The eventual success of development projects, and the MIS function in general, hinges on the effective use of disciplined, rational approaches such as the techniques outlined in this chapter. In subsequent chapters you will be exposed to numerous other tools that will equip you to become an effective designer and developer of information systems.

KEY TERMS

Baseline Project Plan (BPP)
Business case
Discount rate
Economic feasibility
Intangible benefit
Intangible cost
Legal and contractual
    feasibility

One-time cost
Operational feasibility
Present value
Political feasibility
Recurring cost
Schedule feasibility
Statement of Work (SOW)
Tangible benefit

Tangible cost
Technical feasibility
Walkthrough

REVIEW QUESTIONS

1. Define each of the following terms:
   a. Baseline Project Plan
   b. discount rate
   c. one-time cost
   d. recurring cost
   e. walkthrough
   f. Statement of Work

2. Contrast the following terms:
   a. break-even analysis, present value, net present value, return on investment
   b. economic feasibility, legal and contractual feasibility, operational feasibility, political feasibility, schedule feasibility
   c. intangible benefit, tangible benefit
   d. intangible cost, tangible cost

3. List and describe the steps in the project initiation and planning process.

4. What is contained in a Baseline Project Plan? Is the content and format of all baseline plans the same? Why or why not?

5. Describe three commonly used methods for performing economic cost-benefit analysis.

6. List and discuss the different types of project feasibility factors. Is any factor most important? Why or why not?

7. What are the potential consequences of not assessing the technical risks associated with an information systems development project?

8. In what ways could you identify an IS project that was riskier than another?

9. What are the types or categories of benefits from an IS project?

10. What intangible benefits might an organization obtain from the development of an IS?

11. Describe the concept of the time value of money. How does the discount rate affect the value of $1 today versus one year from today?

12. Describe the structured walkthrough process. What roles need to be performed during a walkthrough?

PROBLEMS AND EXERCISES

1. Match the following terms to the appropriate definitions.

_____ Baseline Project Plan	a. benefit derived from the creation of an information system that can generally be easily measured in dollars and with certainty
_____ economic feasibility	b. process of assessing the potential time-frame and completion dates for all major activities within a project
_____ tangible benefits	c. cost associated with project start-up and development, or system start-up
_____ intangible benefits	d. process of assessing the development organization's ability to construct a proposed system
_____ one-time cost	e. process of identifying the financial benefits and costs associated with a development project
_____ recurring cost	f. process of assessing the degree to which a proposed system solves business problems or takes advantage of business opportunities
_____ technical feasibility	g. cost resulting from the ongoing evolution and use of system
_____ operational feasibility	h. major outcome and deliverable from the project initiation and planning phase and contains the best estimate of a project's scope, benefits, costs, risks, and resource requirements
_____ schedule feasibility	i. process of assessing potential legal and contractual ramifications due to the construction of a system
_____ legal and contractual feasibility	j. benefit derived from the creation of an information system that cannot be easily measured in dollars or with certainty
_____ political feasibility	k. process of evaluating how key stakeholders within the organization view the proposed system

2. Consider the purchase of a PC and laser printer for use at your home and assess risk for this project using the project risk assessment factors in Table 6-8.

3. Consider your use of a PC at either home or work and list tangible benefits from an information system. Based on this list, does your use of a PC seem to be beneficial? Why or why not? Now do the same using Table 6-3, the intangible benefits from an information system. Does this analysis support or contradict your previous analysis? Based on both analyses, does your use of a PC seem to be beneficial?

4. Consider, as an example, buying a network of PCs for a department at your workplace or, alternatively, consider outfitting a laboratory of PCs for students at a university. For your example, estimate the costs outlined in Table 6-4, one-time and recurring costs.

5. Assuming monetary benefits of an information system at $85,000 per year, one-time costs of $75,000, recurring costs of $35,000 per year, a discount rate of 12%, and a five-year time horizon, calculate the Net Present Value of these costs and benefits of an information system. Also calculate the overall Return on Investment of the project and then present a Break-Even Analysis. At what point does break-even occur?

6. Choose as an example one of the information systems you described in Problem and Exercise 4 above, either buying a network of PCs for a department at your workplace or outfitting a laboratory of PCs for students at a university. Estimate the costs and benefits for your system and calculate the Net Present Value, Return on Investment and present a Break-Even Analysis. Assume a discount rate of 12% and a five-year time horizon.

7. Use the outline for the Baseline Project Plan provided in Figure 6-10 to present the system specifications for the information system you chose for Problems and Exercises 4 and 6 above.

8. Change the discount rate for Problem and Exercise 5 to 10% and redo the analysis.

9. Change the recurring costs in Problem and Exercise 5 to $40,000 and redo the analysis.

10. Change the time horizon in Problem and Exercise 5 to 3 years and redo the analysis.

11. Assume monetary benefits of an information system of $50,000 the first year and increasing benefits of $5,000 a year for the next four years (Year 1 = 50,000; Year 2 = 55,000; Year 3 = 60,000; Year 4 = 65,000; Year 5 = 70,000). One-time development costs were $90,000 and recurring costs beginning in Year 1 were $40,000 over the duration of the system's life. The discount rate for the company was 10%. Using a five-year horizon, calculate the Net Present Value of these costs and benefits. Also calculate the overall Return on Investment of the project and then present a Break-Even analysis. At what point does break-even occur?

12. Change the discount rate for Problem and Exercise 11 to 12% and redo the analysis.

13. Change the recurring costs in Problem and Exercise 11 to $60,000 and redo the analysis.

14. Change the time horizon in Problem and Exercise 5 to 3 years and redo the analysis.

15. For the system you chose for Problems and Exercises 4 and 6, complete section 1.0, A, Project Overview, of the Baseline Project Plan Report. How important is it that this initial section of the Baseline Project Plan Report be done well? What could go wrong if this section is incomplete or incorrect?

16. For the system you chose for Problems and Exercises 4 and 6, complete section 2.0, A, Alternatives, of the Baseline Project Plan Report. Without conducting a full-blown feasibility analysis, what is your gut feeling as to the feasibility of this system?

17. For the system you chose for Problems and Exercises 4 and 6, complete section 3.0, A–F, Feasibility Analysis, of the Baseline Project Plan Report. How does this feasibility analysis compare with your gut feeling from the previous question? What might go wrong if you rely on your gut feeling in determining system feasibility?

18. For the system you chose for Problems and Exercises 4 and 6, complete section 4.0, A–C, Management Issues, of the Baseline Project Plan Report. Why might people

sometimes feel that these additional steps in the project plan are a waste of time? What would you say to them to convince them that these steps are important?

FIELD EXERCISES

1. Describe several projects you are involved in or plan to undertake, whether they be related to your education or to your professional or personal life. Some examples are purchasing a new vehicle, learning a new language, renovating a home, and so on. For each, sketch out a Baseline Project Plan like that outlined in Figure 6-10. Focus your efforts on item number 1.0 (Introduction) and 2.0 (System Description).

2. For each project from the previous question, assess the feasibility in terms of economic, operational, technical, schedule, legal and contractual, as well as political aspects.

3. Network with a contact you have in some organization that conducts projects (these might be IS projects, but they could be construction, product development, research and development, or any type of project). Interview a project manager and find out what type of Baseline Project Plan is constructed. For a typical project, in what ways are baseline plans modified during the life of a project? Why are plans modified after the project begins? What does this tell you about project planning?

4. Through a contact you have in some organization that uses packaged software, interview an IS manager responsible for systems in an area that uses packaged application software. What contractual limitations, if any, has the organization encountered with using the package? If possible, review the license agreement for the software and make a list of all the restrictions placed on a user of this software.

5. Choose an organization that you are familiar with and determine what is done to initiate information systems projects. Who is responsible for performing this? Is this process formal or informal? Does this appear to be a top-down or bottom-up process? How could this process be improved?

6. Find an organization that does not use Baseline Project Plans for their IS projects. Why doesn't this organization use this method? What are the advantages and disadvantages of not using this method? What benefits could be gained from implementing the use of Baseline Project Plans? What barriers are there to implementing this method?

REFERENCES

Cash, J. I., F. W. McFarlan, J. L. McKenney, and L. M. Applegate. 1992. *Corporate Information Systems Management.* 3rd ed. Boston, MA: Irwin.

King, J. L. and E. Schrems. 1978. "Cost Benefit Analysis in Information Systems Development and Operation. *ACM Computing Surveys* 10 (1): 19–34.

Lederer, A. L., and J. Prasad. 1992. "Nine Management Guidelines for Better Cost Estimating." *Communications of the ACM* 35(2): 51–59.

Parker, M. M. and R. J. Benson. 1988. *Information Economics,* Englewood Cliffs, NJ: Prentice-Hall.

Pressman, R. S. 1992. *Software Engineering.* 3rd ed. New York, NY: McGraw-Hill.

Radosevich, L. 1996. "Can You Measure Web ROI?" *Datamation* July: 92–96.

Yourdon, E. 1989. *Structured Walkthroughs,* 4th ed. Englewood Cliffs, NJ: Prentice-Hall.

Initiating and Planning the Customer Activity Tracking System

INTRODUCTION

Having gained approval from the Systems Priority Board to start the Customer Activity Tracking System (CATS) project, Nancy Chen and Jordan Pippen begin the second phase of the systems development life cycle—project initiation and planning. Creation of a Baseline Project Plan (BPP) is the primary outcome and deliverable during this phase. Once the BPP is created, it is then reviewed by the Systems Priority Board in a formal approval session. If the project is approved, it can then move from the project initiation and planning phase to the third SDLC phase—analysis. The objective of this case is to describe the initiation and planning process that occurred at BEC with the Customer Activity Tracking System (CATS).

INITIATING AND PLANNING THE PROJECT

After gaining project selection approval, Jordan and Nancy met numerous times over several weeks to initiate and plan the CATS project. Since Jordan and Nancy had not asked the Systems Priority Board for any additional personnel for the project initiation team, Karen Gardner continued to ensure that Jordan's workload permitted working on initiating and planning CATS. Jordan and/or Nancy held meetings with several BEC managers and IS staff members in order to collect information about data availability and current BEC business processes. Nancy composed and distributed a brief memo to everyone in U.S. operations and to a few key people in other units (for example, international operations) announcing the project and requesting cooperation during the initiation phase.

During initiation and planning, Nancy took the lead in developing a more detailed requirements statement (see Figure 1) and business case that included potential costs and benefits as well as risks (see Figure 2). The system requirements are still described

in words, and details are purposefully vague. These details will be studied during the analysis phase, but Figure 1 will give the analysis team direction for their work. The potential costs and benefits are listed without being quantified, although costs and tangible benefits should be quantified during later systems development phases, probably during the analysis phase. Where possible, benefits are related to BEC's Blueprint for the Decade objectives, listed when the CATS project was requested. The only anticipated element of risk with CATS is that the system requirements are somewhat ill-defined, since customer profiling and target marketing are new concepts at BEC. Problem issues concerning technical, operational, schedule, legal/contractual, or political feasibility are not expected.

In addition to developing a possible schedule for the project (see Figures 3 and 4), Jordan and Nancy jointly worked out a request for resources and an initial project time line. Figure 3 shows an estimate of approximately six months' calendar time for subsequent SDLC phases. The installation is the longest phase for this project in order to handle the rollout of CATS to all stores, including those outside the U.S. operations area. Jordan was instrumental in developing this schedule, in part by studying prior similar project schedules. Figure 4 breaks out the analysis phase activities into more detail. Note that there are activities which respond to the concerns raised by the SPB during project identification and selection about data exchanges among CATS and about existing systems and data privacy. The exchange of data between CATS and existing systems will, however, be addressed in most subsequent phases.

Resource requirements for the 30-day analysis phase are as follows:

- Two full-time systems analysts and a full-time market researcher from Nancy Chen's staff

- Five days of assistance from a data analyst from the data administration staff

1. Profile Each Customer
A profile for each customer will be created based upon prior purchasing and rental activity of both music and videos. Profiles would be updated on a periodic basis, using both past and recent transaction data. Profiles will be ordered based upon rental and purchase volume.

2. Profile New Product Offerings
Each new product being released by music and video distributors will be profiled prior to its release. For example, a profile for a video release could include information such as rating, movie type (e.g., action, thriller, comedy), actors, and so on.

3. Profile Matching
An automated system would then match product profiles to customers most likely to rent or purchase a newly released item. Matched profiles are then sorted based on the strength of the association between the customer-product profile.

4. Profile Selection
Based upon the strength of the association of the profile matches, profiles could be selected that represent those most likely to lead to additional sales. BEC management could use interactive decision support tools to segment profiles by geographic location, customer or product characteristic, in addition to association strength.

5. Produce Product Announcement Card
An automated system will produce post cards addressed to selected customers announcing the new product releases and the information needed to make a reservation.

6. Track Customer Reservations
A customer service agent at BEC would be available for customers to contact using an 800 number to make product reservations. The agent would record reservation information into an automated system that would update BEC's inventory control system.

7. Delivery of Reserved Product to Customer
Products earmarked for profiled customers will be shipped to local BEC stores with a report showing how to notify customers of product arrival.

Figure 1
Statement of system requirement for the CATS project

POSSIBLE COSTS	
One-Time System design System development Changing existing systems	*Ongoing* Increased staff System maintenance Operating costs
POSSIBLE BENEFITS	
Tangible Increased sales and rentals (increased market share and profitability)	*Intangible* Improved planning New information Better asset utilization Better resource control Better customer service (appeal to diverse customers) Recognition as industry leader
POSSIBLE RISKS	
Lack of experience with target marketing and customer profiling	

Figure 2
Possible costs, benefits, and risks for the CATS project

Figure 3
Gantt chart excerpt
for the CATS project

Figure 4
Analysis phase schedule
for CATS project

(a) Analysis phase
Gantt chart

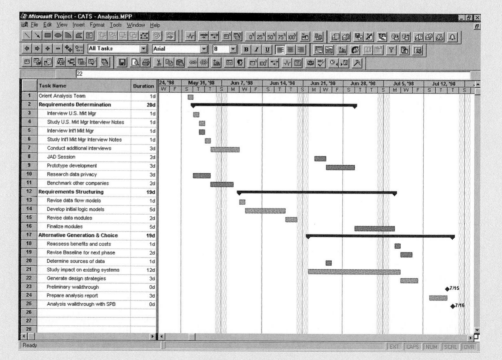

- Ten hours of research time from the office of the legal counsel

- An unspecified amount of time from a variety of managers for gathering system requirements in interviews, during a JAD session, and while reviewing system prototypes

- Unlimited access to documentation on existing systems

- $500 travel budget to visit a nearby mail-order catalog firm that has been experimenting with customer profiling and target marketing

Figure 4 *(continued)*

(b) Analysis phase PERT chart

In addition, Nancy will spend about 10 percent of her time on this project and asks that Jordan be assigned full-time as project manager for CATS. As a senior systems analyst, Jordan is quite familiar with standard systems development procedures at BEC, and she recommends that the CATS project follow these procedures closely. This includes using Oracle Designer/2000 and other CASE tools throughout the project. In total, the resource requirements for the analysis phase represent approximately a $15,000 investment, exclusive of managerial time for interviews, JADs, and other requirements determination activities.

Since the proposed system will tie into existing applications and access several databases, Jordan felt it was necessary, when putting together the project schedule, to develop high-level process and data models for the proposed system that begin to show possible interfaces between CATS and other systems. Figure 5 shows the scope of CATS via a level-0 data flow diagram (DFD) as drawn using Oracle's Designer/2000. The sources/sinks (or entities outside CATS) that will interface with the system are BEC customers and store managers. The diagram shows that a customer will receive a notice about a particular product and will then notify BEC if he or she wants to reserve the product for purchase or rental. Local store managers will receive lists of customers who have been profiled and contacted. If a customer contacts BEC to reserve a product, this reservation is logged into a reservation database and a report containing all customer reser-

vations is forwarded to each store. Whether or not a customer actually rents or purchases a reserved item is handled by feeds from other existing BEC systems and is not shown on this diagram, although the analysis phase project schedule (see Figure 4) includes activities to investigate this area.

Figure 5 also shows that six high-level processes are initially identified within the proposed system: Profiling Customers, Profiling Products, Profile Matching & Selection, Announcement Production & Mailing, Store Notification, and Reservation Processing. Data stores are encapsulated within processes for the data flow notation used by Designer/2000. Once it is known exactly what data are needed from these data stores, the data analyst will identify which databases from the existing systems will map to these data stores. The data analyst will also decide whether changes need to be made in other systems to capture new data that CATS will need; the data and systems analysts will also have to identify the changes that must be made in other systems to accommodate recording sales and rentals of reserved products.

Jordan also developed another view of the scope of CATS via a high-level (or enterprise) data model using entity-relationship (E-R) diagramming (Figure 6). The entities identified included Stores, Customers, Customer Profiles, Customer Transactions, Products, Product Profiles, and Product Reservations. Again, it is not known at this time what data will be kept about each of these entities or which of these data will come

Figure 5
Level-0 data flow diagram
for the CATS project

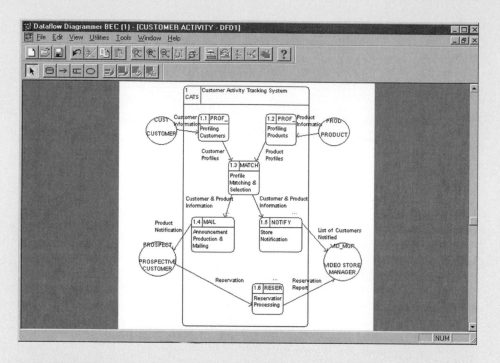

Figure 6
Entity-relationship diagram
for the CATS project

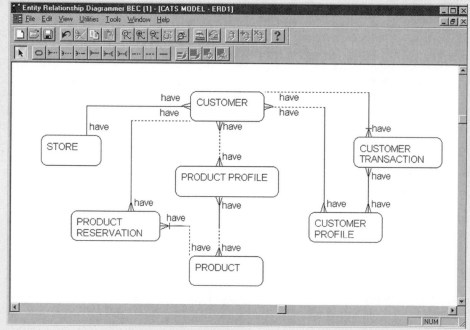

from existing databases. The relationship between Stores and Customers, for example, implies that "each Store has one-to-many Customers" and "each Customer is assigned to only one Store" (at least at a particular point in time). The diagram also reflects the fact that Customer(s) have transactions and that a Customer Profile, a combination of customer descriptors, applies to one or many Customers and a Customer may have several Customer Profiles. A Product Reservation contains information that is stored after a given Customer contacts BEC about reserving a particular Product.

After several weeks of hard work, Nancy and Jordan completed the Baseline Project Plan (BEC's format for a Baseline Project Plan is very similar to the template presented in Figure 6-10). This plan was submitted to

BEC's System Priority Board for review. A formal review of the plan was then scheduled for the following Friday morning.

REVIEWING THE BASELINE PROJECT PLAN

At the review meeting of the Baseline Project Plan, both Nancy and Jordan presented information to the SPB. Their presentation was an abridged version of their project plan. An agenda for their presentation is shown in Figure 7.

As with most walkthroughs, Nancy, Jordan, and the SPB had different roles to play in the meeting. Nancy focused on presenting an overview of issues surrounding what CATS was and how CATS would address a key BEC objective. In other words, as the system client and requester, Nancy focused primarily on the business reasons why CATS needed to be constructed. Jordan, on the other hand, focused on explaining the relationship between CATS and the existing information systems portfolio, with particular emphasis on feasibility issues such as system compatibility, complexity, costs, and schedules. The SPB's role was to assess the extent to which CATS was a unique and valuable system that would help BEC reach its strategic objective of providing superior customer service through the use of technology. In other words, the SPB's responsibility is to compare CATS to other projects and, since limited resources preclude all projects from being developed, to select or reject it for continued development.

Both Nancy and Jordan carefully prepared overhead transparencies to assist in making their presentation. They also practiced their presentation several times before the meeting. A common practice at BEC is for presenters to provide copies of their slides as hand-outs to all SPB members. During the question and answer session, Nancy was asked for a rough estimate of the possible benefits. She reported that the *Wall Street Journal* and other articles she had read (which had been the seed for the CATS request) had mentioned a range of 3 to 10 percent increase in sales, which would mean $400,000 to $1,000,000 to BEC at current annual sales and rental levels. Nancy felt that being the first home entertainment company to provide this service could yield returns at the high end of this range—at least until the competition could catch up. The halo effect from better customer service could be longer lasting. Further, the intangible benefit of "better resource control" might be significant, since the reservation system could lead to a significant reduction in inventory levels and would allow more central planning of inventory.

An SPB member then asked Jordan about the potential costs. Jordan responded that, other than the initial $15,000 investment for the analysis phase, she was rather uncertain about subsequent costs. CATS represented a new type of system for BEC (thus the risk statement in Figure 2). Depending on the determination of exactly what a customer profile is and the specifics of interfaces between CATS and existing systems, the cost to design and (re)program CATS and existing systems was uncertain. Jordan saw no need for new hardware or software to support CATS. Although a decision about the development platform for CATS would be made in analysis, Jordan thought that the programming languages, data analysis tools, and database management systems used at BEC would be sufficient to develop CATS. The analysis phase, however, would clarify all of these issues in the recommended design strategy.

After the presentation, Nancy took Jordan to lunch as a small gesture for all the hard work she had done. This lunch turned out to be a celebration, as the CATS project was approved by the SPB to move into the analysis phase. Both Jordan and Nancy knew that this could be the beginning of a long relationship and that much more work was ahead of them before BEC would realize any benefits from the development of this system.

TOPIC	PRESENTER
Introduction to the CATS Project	Nancy (5 minutes)
Functional Description and Scope	Nancy & Jordan (15 minutes)
Schedule	Jordan (5 minutes)
Feasibility Analysis and Risks	Jordan (10 minutes)
Resources Requirements and Costs	Jordan (10 minutes)
Question and Answer Period	Nancy & Jordan (15 minutes)

Figure 7
Agenda for the Baseline Project Plan walkthrough

SUMMARY

The project initiation and planning phase of the CATS project demonstrates the need to carefully develop a Baseline Project Plan. CATS has great potential benefit in increased sales and rentals and many potential intangible benefits. However both one-time and ongoing costs as well as the risks of implementing a new system make the success of such projects dubious. Since the motivation for the CATS project was linked to several important BEC objectives, the phased development cycle allows for frequent review of the project, and there is close cooperation between IS and the client organization, the Systems Priority Board approved funding for the analysis phase and is eager to see the results of the analysis phase.

PART

III

Analysis

Karl's Vineyard and Winery*

Karl's Winery

SAUVIGNON
BLANC
1996

Estate Bottled

---

* This case is developed from *Rapid Application Development with Oracle® Designer/2000* by Chris Billings, Maria Billings, and Julia Tower. 1997. Addison Wesley Longman, Inc.

Use of CASE to Support Rapid Systems Analysis

The development of an enterprise-wide information system requires considerable planning and coordination. The IS manager at Karl's Vineyard and Winery (KVW) believed that the best way to document and monitor the development of new systems across the enterprise was to build over time a business model using an integrated CASE package. KVW chose Oracle's Designer/2000 for this modeling effort.

Due to pressing business issues and in order to introduce CASE-based systems analysis and development to KVW, the IS manager decided to conduct a rapid analysis workshop on a limited-scope project, one for which the analysis and design phases could be completed in roughly ten days with the help of Designer/2000. Such a beginning seemed wise since it is necessary to evolve to an enterprise-wide system by modular development. Due to lagging sales, sales administration was chosen as the most critical area of the business in which new systems development could have the most impact.

Over the ten working days, the workshop included members of the sales administration staff, systems analysts, programmers, database specialists, and a workshop facilitator. During the first session all attendees introduced themselves, the facilitator reviewed the systems development life cycle as used in the workshop (a modified version of the structured systems development life cycle), and a short Q&A session helped everyone to clarify the goals and process for the workshop. The facilitator then presented an overview of KVW's mission statement, recent annual report, and organization chart, and indicated that other more detailed documents, such as procedure manuals, were available for reference. Then detailed work began.

The first major section of the workshop was interviewing. Each interview was conducted by two systems analysts, one who asked questions and the other who took notes. Senior sales administration staff were interviewed prior to the workshop since their answers guided the choice of who was invited to the workshop and the questions to explore during these subsequent interviews. These initial interviews helped to clarify the mission of the sales administration unit, its critical success factors, and special concerns of individual senior managers (for example, special issues for international sales).

During the workshop interviews and subsequent discussions, the systems analysts used various Designer/2000 tools to record the information they learned. These tools included:

- *Function hierarchy diagrammer*–each business function is recursively described in more detail by its subfunctions.
- *Process modeller*–each business process (such as sales administration or its subprocesses) is represented as a sequence of steps, what data and materials move between those steps and when, data and material stores where these items are retained, who is responsible for each step, and events that trigger a process or are the result of a process. One process model can be decomposed into models for subprocesses.
- *Entity-relationship diagrammer*–each object about which data must be kept is shown along with the data associated with it and the associations it has with other objects.

- *Matrix diagrammer*–a general purpose tool to build two dimensional matrices or tables to show how lists of items are connected with each other.

The interviews, some of which were as long as half a day but more typically about two hours, raised a wide variety of issues and needs, from limitations of working with a product that has annual production to problems of interactions between current sales administration and production systems. All comments were recorded via Designer/2000, many of which were associated with objects identified via one of the diagramming tools. These comments, along with other descriptive information on the objects, were stored in the Designer/2000 repository, so that they could be recalled at any time. Extra effort was taken so that thorough, clear, and unique descriptions were developed for all objects. Thorough definitions help to avoid confusion later, reconcile what different analysts hear from different interviews, and provide useful input to later systems development steps. For example, when a systems analyst identified a potential data entity, that entity is described by: short name, long name, nicknames, plural name, textual description, notes from the analysts concerning nuances about the entity, and volume information (for example, initial and maximum quantity, growth rate).

The matrix diagrammer is also helpful to clarify the meaning of objects identified during analysis and to provide a completeness and consistency check. For example, the matrix of each business function versus each data entity was used during one workshop session. The attendees discussed which function created, updated, deleted, or used each entity. The matrix was a convenient, compact, and visual way to check that each entity was at least created and used, and that each function used at least some entity.

Since Designer/2000 recorded and helped to structure all the information learned during the workshop, the repository was the source of the information needed to produce many of the diagrams and reports discussed in various sessions during the workshop. Most of the time a standard Designer/2000 report was sufficient, but occasionally an analyst would have to design a customized report.

The use of one business modeling tool for systems analysis made communication among the different analysts and users easy. Everyone was using the same terminology, and the results of one interview or a discussion session were immediately available in a common format to all workshop participants. Although not intrinsically important to analysis, having all analysis documentation in one source, the Designer/2000 repository for this project, made subsequent design steps more efficient. First, all the information for design was in one, consistent format. Second, the automatic design and generator tools (Wizards) within Designer/2000 allowed rapid development of screens, reports, database definitions, and even program code from the information produced during analysis.

An Overview of Part III

Analysis

nalysis is the first systems development life cycle (SDLC) phase where you begin to understand, in depth, the needs for system changes. Systems analysis involves a substantial amount of effort and cost and is therefore undertaken only after management has decided that the systems development project under consideration has merit and should be pursued through this phase. The project initiation and planning phase provides the basis for a go-ahead decision for analysis, and the Baseline Project Plan (BPP) provides the structure for conducting the analysis phase. The analysis team should not take the analysis process for granted or attempt to speed through it. Most observers today would agree that many of the errors in developed systems are directly traceable to inadequate efforts in the analysis and design phases of the life cycle. As analysis is a large and involved process, we divide it into three main activities to make the overall process easier to understand. As depicted in Figure 1, analysis includes the following steps:

- *Requirements determination.* This is primarily a fact-finding activity.

- *Requirements structuring.* This activity creates a thorough and clear description of current business operations and new information processing services. Requirements structuring has three subactivities that concentrate on structuring different views or dimensions of the information system.

- *Alternative generation and selection.* This process results in a choice among alternative strategies for subsequent systems design.

The purpose of analysis is to determine what information and information processing services are needed to support selected objectives and functions of the organization; consequently, analysis is fundamentally an intelligence activity in which analysts capture and structure information. Gathering this information about both the current and the replacement systems is called requirements determination, the subject of Chapter 7. The fact-finding techniques in Chapter 7 are used to learn about the current system (if one exists), the organization that the new or replacement system will support, and user requirements or expectations for the replacement system.

During the requirements determination process, the systems development team attempts to discover important information about how employees now perform and how they will need to perform their jobs in order to meet future

Figure 1

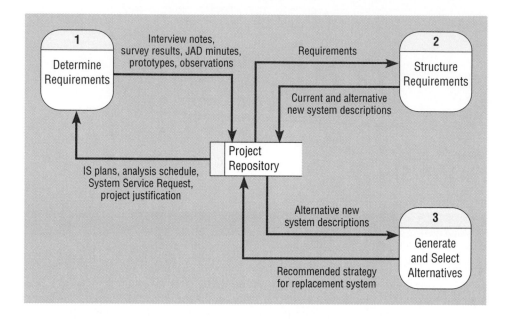

business conditions. Included in this information will be answers to the following questions:

- How does the current system function? Is the system manual or automated?
- What data are necessary for proper functioning of the supported business area?
- What kinds of reports are generated?
- How do people use the system to perform their work?

A study of current operations gives insights on system requirements, grounds analysis in actual information system activity, is the basis for discovering possible incremental improvements, and provides necessary information for subsequent steps involved in converting from the current to a replacement system. Moreover, analysts must focus on the following additional questions:

- How should a new or replacement system function?
- What data would be needed for it to operate smoothly?
- What kinds of reports would it need to generate?
- How would a new system alter employees' jobs?
- What new or improved information services are needed to support the future organizational goals, objectives, strategies, and functions?

In Chapter 7, we also discuss one of the major sources of new systems today, Business Process Reengineering (BPR). In contrast to the incremental improvements that might drive many systems development projects, BPR results in radical redesign of the processes that information systems are designed to support. New, or disruptive technologies, can make current business processes obsolete, requiring extensive system maintenance, or even new systems. We show how BPR relates to information systems analysis in Chapter 8, where we use data flow diagrams to support the reengineering process.

After Chapter 7, the Broadway Entertainment Company (BEC) running case shows how the results of an interview can be used to better understand the requirements for a new system and how different requirements determination techniques can be used in combination to gain a thorough understanding of requirements.

Information about current operations and requirements for a replacement system must somehow be organized in order to be useful during analysis and, subsequently, to a design team. Organizing, or structuring, system requirements is the second major activity of the analysis phase. The requirements structuring techniques described in Chapters 8-10 are used to unambiguously describe and structure the current system and the alternatives for the replacement system. These techniques produce diagrams and descriptions (models) that can be analyzed to show deficiencies, inefficiencies, missing elements, and illogical components of the current business operation and information systems. Along with user requirements, they are used to determine the strategy for the replacement system.

The results of the requirements determination can be structured according to three essential views of the current and replacement information systems:

- *Process*—the sequence of data movement and handling operations within the system

- *Logic and timing*—the rules by which data are transformed and manipulated and an indication of what triggers data transformation

- *Data*—the inherent structure of data independent of how or when it is processed

The goal is to capture as complete a specification of the required system as is possible. Ideally, the specification would be so complete that, along with the necessary steps in the design phase, the replacement or new system could be generated without human programming. Today, 100 percent generation from functional specifications is not possible, although reports of 70-90 percent code generation have appeared. Generating computer display and report programs is now fairly common once a data model, as well as display and report layouts, are specified. No matter what percentage of code is automatically generated, the structured specifications provide a clear picture for later design, implementation, and, most importantly, maintenance activities. Maintaining systems from functional specifications is more reliable and significantly more productive than manually modifying code as the inevitable system changes occur.

The *process* view of a system can be represented by data flow diagrams, the subject of Chapter 8. *System logic and timing,* or what goes on inside the black boxes that are identified as processes in data flow diagrams and when these processes occur, can be represented in many ways, including Structured English, decision tables, and decision trees. Modeling system logic is the subject of Chapter 9. Finally, the *data* view of a system shows the rules that govern the structure and integrity of data and concentrates on what data about business entities and relationships among these entities must be accessed within the system. Data modeling pertinent to analysis is the subject of Chapter 10.

Broadway Entertainment Company (BEC) cases appear following Chapters 8, 9, and 10. These cases describe the sample Customer Activity Tracking System to illustrate the process, logic, and data models that describe this new system. They also illustrate how diagrams and models for each of these three views of an information system are related to one another to form a consistent and thorough structured description of a proposed system.

Chapter 11 discusses the final step within analysis—how to choose among alternative competing sets of requirements. Chapter 11, in part, returns to tasks similar to those carried out in project initiation and planning activities. That is, once the requirements for the replacement system have been structured and documented, the systems development team realizes that there are many strategies to consider before actually designing and implementing the replacement system. For example, analysts must decide on the proper mix of on-line versus batch processing, what functionality to include when all user requirements cannot be justifiably met, and what scope is necessary for an effective system—the world of computing offers many choices. Before proceeding with the design step, systems analysts must choose the best design strategy to pursue by balancing a variety of economic, organizational, technical, legal, and other factors.

To find the best strategy, analysts will first generate several competing alternative strategies. One strategy may be high-end, involving state-of-the-art technology and implementing every conceivable function in the new system. Another strategy may be low-end, involving a minimal number of changes and improving functionality while keeping costs and risks low. Still another strategy may be somewhere between these two extremes, and there may be a host of other design strategies that are also contenders.

When alternatives have been identified and documented, the systems development team must present its best choice to management for the purpose of gaining approval for further development. Once the best system design strategy has been identified and recommended, the analysis phase ends. At this point, management has to decide whether to continue the project and proceed to design and, if so, how the design phase of the project should be structured. Management may also decide at this time that packaged software is a viable option, or that contracting one or more subsequent life cycle steps to a consulting firm might be an appropriate strategy. The work carried out in analysis is essential to identify and describe the proper system requirements in an unambiguous format for subsequent systems development work.

Chapter 11 shows how project management, incremental commitment, the iterative nature of project management, and the evolving nature of details in project plans apply as we move through the life cycle. Since Chapter 11 brings to a close the section on the analysis phase of the life cycle, a major project milestone is reached. So, Chapter 11 also discusses updating the Baseline Project Plan and the transition from analysis to design.

We conclude Part III with a Broadway Entertainment Company (BEC) case. This case shows how alternative design strategies for the Customer Activity Tracking System are generated and evaluated and the best strategy selected. The case also explains how the Baseline Project Plan is updated and presented to management to determine if and how the project should continue.

7

Determining System Requirements

After studying this chapter, you should be able to:

■ Describe options for designing and conducting interviews and develop a plan for conducting an interview to determine system requirements.

■ Design, distribute, and analyze questionnaires to determine system requirements.

■ Explain the advantages and pitfalls of observing workers and analyzing business documents to determine system requirements.

■ Explain how computing can provide support for requirements determination.

■ Participate in and help plan a Joint Application Design session.

■ Use prototyping during requirements determination.

■ Select the appropriate methods to elicit system requirements.

INTRODUCTION

Systems analysis is the part of the systems development life cycle in which you determine how the current information system functions and assess what users would like to see in a new system. As you learned in Chapter 1, there are three subphases in analysis: requirements determination, requirements structuring, and alternative generation and choice.

In this chapter, you will learn about the beginning subphase of analysis—determining system requirements. Techniques used in requirements determination have evolved over time to become more structured and, as we will see in this chapter, current methods increasingly rely on the computer for support. We will first study the more traditional requirements determination methods including interviewing, using questionnaires, observing users in their work environment, and collecting procedures and other written documents. We will then discuss modern methods for collecting system requirements. The first of these methods is Joint Application Design (JAD), which you first read about in Chapter 1. Next, you will read about how analysts rely more and more on information systems to help them perform analysis. As you will see, group support systems have been used to support systems analysis, especially as part of the JAD process. CASE tools, discussed in Chapter 4, are also very useful in requirements determination. Finally, you will learn how prototyping can be used as a key tool for some requirements determination efforts.

PERFORMING REQUIREMENTS DETERMINATION

As stated earlier and shown in Figure 7-1, there are three subphases to systems analysis: requirements determination, requirements structuring, and generating alternative system design strategies and selecting the best one. We will address these as three separate steps, but you should consider these steps as somewhat parallel and iterative. For example, as you determine some aspects of the current and desired system(s), you begin to structure these requirements or to build prototypes to show users how a system might behave. Inconsistencies and deficiencies discovered through structuring and prototyping lead you to explore further the operation of current system(s) and the future needs of the organization. Eventually your ideas and discoveries converge on a thorough and accurate depiction of current operations and what the requirements are for the new system. As you think about beginning the analysis phase, you probably wonder what exactly is involved in requirements determination. We discuss this process in the next section.

Figure 7-1
Systems development life cycle with analysis phase highlighted

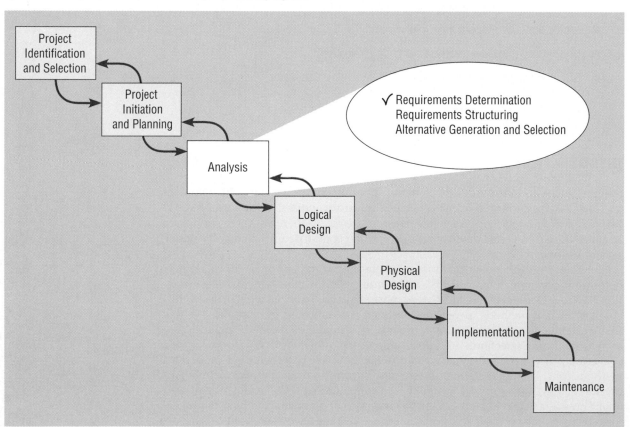

The Process of Determining Requirements

Once management has granted permission to pursue development of a new system (this was done at the end of the project identification and selection phase of the SDLC) and a project is initiated and planned (see Chapter 6), you begin determining what the new system should do. During requirements determination, you and other analysts gather information on what the system should do from as many sources as possible: from users of the current system, from observing users, and from reports, forms, and procedures. All of the system requirements are carefully documented and made ready for structuring, the subject of Chapters 8 through 10.

In many ways, gathering system requirements is like conducting any investigation. Have you read any of the Sherlock Holmes or similar mystery stories? Do you enjoy solving puzzles? From these experiences, we can detect some similar characteristics for a good systems analyst during the requirements determination subphase. These characteristics include

- *Impertinence.* You should question everything. You need to ask such questions as: Are all transactions processed the same way? Could anyone be charged something other than the standard price? Might we someday want to allow and encourage employees to work for more than one department?

- *Impartiality:* Your role is to find the best solution to a business problem or opportunity. It is not, for example, to find a way to justify the purchase of new hardware or to insist on incorporating what users think they want into the new system requirements. You must consider issues raised by all parties and try to find the best organizational solution.

- *Relax constraints:* Assume anything is possible and eliminate the infeasible. For example, do not accept this statement: "We've always done it that way, so we have to continue the practice." Traditions are different from rules and policies. Traditions probably started for a good reason but, as the organization and its environment change, traditions may turn into habits rather than sensible procedures.

- *Attention to details:* Every fact must fit with every other fact. One element out of place means that the ultimate system will fail at some time. For example, an imprecise definition of who a customer is may mean that you purge customer data when a customer has no active orders; yet these past customers may be vital contacts for future sales.

- *Reframing:* Analysis is, in part, a creative process. You must challenge yourself to look at the organization in new ways. You must consider how each user views his or her requirements. You must be careful not to jump to this conclusion: "I worked on a system like that once—this new system must work the same way as the one I built before."

Deliverables and Outcomes

The primary deliverables from requirements determination are the various forms of information gathered during the determination process: transcripts of interviews; notes from observation and analysis of documents; analyzed responses from questionnaires; sets of forms, reports, job descriptions, and other documents; and computer-generated output such as system prototypes. In short, anything that the analysis team collects as part of determining system requirements is included in the deliverables resulting from this subphase of the systems development life cycle.

Table 7-1 lists examples of some specific information that might be gathered during requirements determination.

These deliverables contain the information you need for systems analysis within the scope of the system you are developing. In addition, you need to understand the following components of an organization:

- The business objectives that drive what and how work is done

- The information people need to do their jobs

- The data (definition, volume, size, etc.) handled within the organization to support the jobs

- When, how, and by whom or what the data are moved, transformed, and stored

- The sequence and other dependencies among different data-handling activities

- The rules governing how data are handled and processed

- Policies and guidelines that describe the nature of the business and the market and environment in which it operates

- Key events affecting data values and when these events occur

As should be obvious, such a large amount of information must be organized in order to be useful. This is the purpose of the next subphase—requirements structuring.

From just this subphase of analysis, you probably already realize that the amount of information to be gathered could be huge, especially if the scope of the system under development is broad. The time required to collect and structure a great deal of information can be extensive and, because it involves so much human effort, quite expensive. Too much analysis is not productive and the term "analysis paralysis" has been coined to describe a systems development project that has bogged down in an abundance of analysis work. Because of the dangers of excessive analysis, today's systems analysts focus more on the system to be developed than on the current system. The techniques you will learn about later in the chapter, JAD and prototyping, were developed to keep the analysis effort at a minimum yet still effective. Other processes have been developed to limit the analysis commitment even more, providing an alternative to the SDLC. One of these processes is called *Rapid Application Development (RAD)* and is the subject of Chapter 13. As you will learn, RAD relies on JAD, prototyping, and integrated CASE tools to be effective. Even RAD, as well as the structured analysis methods discussed in subsequent chapters in the analysis section of this book, rely on a basic understanding of the business area served by an information system. Thus, before you can fully appreciate RAD, you need to learn about traditional fact-gathering techniques. These techniques are the subject of the next section.

TABLE 7-1 Deliverables for Requirements Determination

1. **Information collected from conversations with or observations of users:** interview transcripts, questionnaire responses, notes from observation, meeting minutes

2. **Existing written information:** business mission and strategy statements, sample business forms and reports and computer displays, procedure manuals, job descriptions, training manuals, flow charts and documentation of existing systems, consultant reports

3. **Computer-based information:** results from Joint Application Design sessions, transcripts or files from group support system sessions, CASE repository contents and reports of existing systems, and displays and reports from system prototypes.

TRADITIONAL METHODS FOR DETERMINING REQUIREMENTS

At the core of systems analysis is the collection of information. At the outset, you must collect information about the information systems that are currently being used and how users would like to improve the current systems and organizational operations with new or replacement information systems. One of the best ways to get this information is to talk to the people who are directly or indirectly involved in the different parts of the organizations affected by the possible system changes: users, managers, funders, etc. Another way to find out about the current system is to gather copies of documentation relevant to current systems and business processes. In this chapter, you will learn about various ways to get information directly from stakeholders: interviews, questionnaires, group interviews, and direct observation. You will learn about collecting documentation on the current system and organizational operation in the form of written procedures, forms, reports, and other hard copy. These traditional methods of collecting system requirements are listed in Table 7-2.

Interviewing and Listening

Interviewing is one of the primary ways analysts gather information about an information systems project. Early in a project, an analyst may spend a large amount of time interviewing people about their work, the information they use to do it, and the types of information processing that might supplement their work. Other stakeholders are interviewed to understand organizational direction, policies, expectations managers have on the units they supervise, and other nonroutine aspects of organizational operations. During interviewing you will gather facts, opinions, and speculation and observe body language, emotions, and other signs of what people want and how they assess current systems.

There are many ways to effectively interview someone and no one method is necessarily better than another. Some guidelines you should keep in mind when you interview, summarized in Table 7-3, are discussed next.

First, you should prepare thoroughly before the interview. Set up an appointment at a time and for a duration convenient for the interviewee. The general nature of the interview should be explained to the interviewee in advance. You may ask the interviewee to think about specific questions or issues or to review certain

TABLE 7-2 Traditional Methods of Collecting System Requirements

- Individually *interview* people informed about the operation and issues of the current system and needs for systems in future organizational activities
- Survey people via *questionnaires* to discover issues and requirements
- *Interview groups* of people with diverse needs to find synergies and contrasts among system requirements
- *Observe workers* at selected times to see how data are handled and what information people need to do their jobs
- *Study business documents* to discover reported issues, policies, rules, and directions as well as concrete examples of the use of data and information in the organization

TABLE 7-3   Guidelines for Effective Interviewing

Plan the Interview

- Prepare interviewee: appointment, priming questions
- Prepare checklist, agenda, and questions

Listen carefully and take notes (tape record if permitted)

Review notes within 48 hours of interview

Be neutral

Seek diverse views

documentation to prepare for the interview. You should spend some time thinking about what you need to find out and write down your questions. Do not assume that you can anticipate all possible questions. You want the interview to be natural and, to some degree, you want to spontaneously direct the interview as you discover what expertise the interviewee brings to the session.

You should prepare an interview guide or checklist so that you know in which sequence you intend to ask your questions and how much time you want to spend in each area of the interview. The checklist might include some probing questions to ask as follow-up if you receive certain anticipated responses. You can, to some degree, integrate your interview guide with the notes you take during the interview, as depicted in a sample guide in Figure 7-2. This same guide can serve as an outline for a summary of what you discover during an interview.

The first page of the sample interview guide contains a general outline of the interview. Besides basic information on who is being interviewed and when, you list major objectives for the interview. These objectives typically cover the most important data you need to collect, a list of issues on which you need to seek agreement (for example, content for certain system reports), and which areas you need to explore, not necessarily with specific questions. You also include reminder notes to yourself on key information about the interviewee (for example, job history, known positions taken on issues, and role with current system). This information helps you to be personal, shows that you consider the interviewee important, and may assist you in interpreting some answers. Also included is an agenda for the interview with approximate time limits for different sections of the interview. You may not follow the time limits precisely but the schedule helps you cover all areas during the time the interviewee is available. Space is also allotted for general observations that do not fit under specific questions and for notes taken during the interview about topics skipped or issues raised that could not be resolved.

On subsequent pages you list specific questions; the sample form in Figure 7-2 includes space for taking notes on these questions. Because unanticipated information arises, you will not strictly follow the guide in sequence. You can, however, check off the questions you have asked and write reminders to yourself to return to or skip certain questions as the dynamics of the interview unfold.

Choosing Interview Questions   You need to decide what mix and sequence of open-ended and closed-ended questions you will use. **Open-ended questions** are usually used to probe for information for which you cannot anticipate all possible responses or for which you do not know the precise question to ask. The person being interviewed is encouraged to talk about whatever interests him or her within the general bounds of the question. An example is, "What would you say is the best thing about the information system you currently use to do your job?" or "List the

Open-ended questions:
Questions in interviews and on questionnaires that have no pre-specified answers.

Figure 7-2
Typical interview guide

Interview Outline	
Interviewee: *Name of person being interviewed*	Interviewer: *Name of person leading interview*
Location/Medium: *Office, conference room, or phone number*	Appointment Date: Start Time: End Time:
Objectives: *What data to collect* *On what to gain agreement* *What areas to explore*	Reminders: *Background/experience of interviewee* *Known opinions of interviewee*

Agenda:
Introduction
Background on Project
Overview of Interview
   Topics To Be Covered
   Permission to Tape Record
Topic 1 Questions
Topic 2 Questions
…
Summary of Major Points
Questions from Interviewee
Closing
	Approximate Time:
	1 minute
	2 minutes
	
	1 minute
	
	5 minutes
	7 minutes
	…
	2 minutes
	5 minutes
	1 minute

General Observations:

   Interviewee seemed busy — probably need to call in a few days for follow-up questions since he gave only short answers. PC was turned off —probably not a regular PC user.

Unresolved Issues, Topics not Covered:

   He needs to look up sales figures from 1996. He raised the issue of how to handle returned goods, but we did not have time to discuss.

(continues)

three most frequently used menu options." You must react quickly to answers and determine whether or not any follow-up questions are needed for clarification or elaboration. Sometimes body language will suggest that a user has given an incomplete answer or is reluctant to divulge some information; a follow-up question might yield additional insight. One advantage of open-ended questions in an interview is that previously unknown information can surface. You can then continue exploring along unexpected lines of inquiry to reveal even more new information.

Figure 7-2 *(continued)*
Typical interview guide

Interviewee:	Date:
Questions:	Notes:
When to ask question, if conditional *Question number: 1* Have you used the current sales tracking system? If so, how often? *If yes, go to Question 2*	*Answer* Yes, I ask for a report on my product line weekly *Observations* Seemed anxious — may be over-estimating usage frequency
Question: 2 What do you like least about this system?	*Answer* Sales are shown in units, not dollars *Observations* System can show sales in dollars, but user does not know this.

Open-ended questions also often put the interviewees at ease since they are able to respond in their own words using their own structure; open-ended questions give interviewees more of a sense of involvement and control in the interview. A major disadvantage of open-ended questions is the length of time it can take for the questions to be answered. In addition, open-ended questions can be difficult to summarize.

Closed-ended questions:
Questions in interviews and on questionnaires that ask those responding to choose from among a set of specified responses.

Closed-ended questions provide a range of answers from which the interviewee may choose. Here is an example:

Which of the following would you say is the one best thing about the information system you currently use to do your job (pick only one):
a. Having easy access to all of the data you need
b. The system's response time
c. The ability to run the system concurrently with other applications

Closed-ended questions work well when the major answers to questions are well known. Another plus is that interviews based on closed-ended questions do not necessarily require a large time commitment—more topics can be covered. As opposed to collecting such information via questionnaires, you can see body language and hear voice tone which can aid in interpreting the interviewee's responses. Closed-ended questions can also be an easy way to begin an interview and to determine which line of open-ended questions to pursue. You can include an "other" option to encourage the interviewee to add unanticipated responses. A major disadvantage of closed-ended questions is that useful information that does not quite fit into the defined answers may be overlooked as the respondent tries to make a choice instead of providing his or her best answer.

Closed-ended questions, like objective questions on an examination, can follow several forms, including these choices:

- True or false.

- Multiple choice (with only one response or selecting all relevant choices).

- Rating a response or idea on some scale, say from bad to good or strongly agree to strongly disagree. Each point on the scale should have a clear and consistent meaning to each person and there is usually a neutral point in the middle of the scale.

- Ranking items in order of importance.

Interview Guidelines   First, with either open- or closed-ended questions, do not phrase a question in a way that implies a right or wrong answer. The respondent must feel that he or she can state his or her true opinion and perspective and that his or her idea will be considered equally with those of others. Questions such as, "Should the system continue to provide the ability to override the default value, even though most users now do not like the feature?" should be avoided as such wording predefines a socially acceptable answer.

The second guideline to remember about interviews is to listen very carefully to what is being said. Take careful notes or, if possible, record the interview on a tape recorder (be sure to ask permission first!). The answers may contain extremely important information for the project. Also, this may be the only chance you have to get information from this particular person. If you run out of time and still need to get information from the person you are talking to, ask to schedule a follow-up interview.

Third, once the interview is over, go back to your office and type up your notes within 48 hours. If you recorded the interview, use the recording to verify the material in your notes. After 48 hours, your memory of the interview will fade quickly. As you type and organize your notes, write down any additional questions that might arise from lapses in your notes or from ambiguous information. Separate facts from your opinions and interpretations. Make a list of unclear points that need clarification. Call the person you interviewed and get answers to these new questions. Use the phone call as an opportunity to verify the accuracy of your notes. You may also want to send a written copy of your notes to the person you interviewed so the person can check your notes for accuracy. Finally, make sure you thank the person for his or her time. You may need to talk to your respondent again. If the interviewee will be a user of your system or is involved in some other way in the system's success, you want to leave a good impression.

Fourth, be careful during the interview not to set expectations about the new or replacement system unless you are sure these features will be part of the delivered system. Let the interviewee know that there are many steps to the project and the perspectives of many people need to be considered, along with what is techni-cally possible. Let respondents know that their ideas will be carefully considered, but that due to the iterative nature of the systems development process, it is prema-ture to say now exactly what the ultimate system will or will not do.

Fifth, seek a variety of perspectives from the interviews. Find out what poten-tial users of the system, users of other systems that might be affected by changes, managers and superiors, information systems staff who have experience with the current system, and others think the current problems and opportunities are and what new information services might better serve the organization. You want to understand all possible perspectives so that in a later approval step you will have information on which to base a recommendation or design decision that all stake-holders can accept.

Administering Questionnaires

Interviews are very effective ways of communicating with people and obtaining im-portant information from them. However, interviews are also very expensive and time-consuming to conduct. Thus, a limited number of questions can be covered and people contacted. In contrast, questionnaires are passive and often yield less depth of understanding than interviews; however, questionnaires are not as expen-sive to administer per respondent. In addition, questionnaires have the advantage of gathering information from many people in a relatively short time and of being less biased in the interpretation of their results.

Choosing Questionnaire Respondents   Sometimes there are more people to survey than you can handle and you must decide which set of people to send the question-naire to or which questionnaire to send to which group of people. Whichever group of respondents you choose, it should be representative of all users. In general, you can achieve a representative sample by any one or any combination of these four methods:

1. Those *convenient to* sample: these may be people at a local site, those willing to be surveyed, or those most motivated to respond

2. A *random* group: if you get a list of all users of the current system, simply choose every nth person on the list; or, you could select people by skipping names on the list based on numbers from a random number table

3. A *purposeful* sample: here you may specify only people who satisfy certain cri-teria, such as users of the system for more than two years or users who use the system most often

4. A *stratified* sample: in this case, you have several categories of people whom you definitely want to include—choose a random set from each category (e.g., users, managers, foreign business unit users)

Samples which combine characteristics of several approaches are also common. In any case, once the questionnaires are returned, you should check for non-response bias; that is, a systematic bias in the results since those who responded are different from those who did not respond. You can refer to books on survey research to find out how to determine if your results are confounded by non-response bias.

Designing Questionnaires   Questionnaires are usually administered on paper al-though they can be administered in person (resembling a structured interview), over the phone (computer-assisted telephone interviewing), or even on diskette.

Questionnaires are less expensive, however, if they do not require a person to administer them directly; that is, if the people answering the questions can complete the questionnaire without help. Also, answers can be provided at the convenience of the respondent, as long as the answers are returned by a specific date.

Questionnaires typically include closed-ended questions, more than can be effectively asked in an interview, and sometimes contain open-ended questions as well. Closed-ended questions are preferable because they are easier to complete and they define the exact coverage required. A few open-ended questions give the person being surveyed an opportunity to add insights not anticipated by the designer of the questionnaire. In general, questionnaires take less time to complete than interviews structured to obtain the same information. In addition, questionnaires are given to many people simultaneously whereas interviews are usually limited to one person at a time.

Questionnaires are generally less rich in information content than interviews, however, because they provide no direct means by which to ask follow-up questions (although it is possible, though time-consuming, to contact respondents after they have returned their completed questionnaires to ask for further information). Also, since questionnaires are written, they do not provide the opportunity to judge the accuracy of the responses. In an interview, you can sometimes determine if people are answering truthfully or fully by the words they use, whether they make direct eye contact, the tone of voice they use, or their body language.

The ability to create good questionnaires is a skill that improves with practice and experience. Because the questions are written, they must be extremely clear in meaning and logical in sequence. When a person is completing a questionnaire, he or she only has the written questions to interpret and answer. You are not there to clarify each question's meaning. For example, what if a closed-ended question were phrased in this way:

> How often do you back up your computer files?
> a. Frequently
> b. Sometimes
> c. Hardly at all
> d. Never

There are at least two sources of ambiguity in the wording of the question. The first source of ambiguity is the categories offered for the answer: the only non-ambiguous answer is "never." "Hardly at all" could mean anything from once per year to once per month, depending on who is answering the question. "Sometimes" could cover the same range of possibilities as "Hardly at all." "Frequently" could be anything from once per hour to once per week. The second source of ambiguity is in the question itself. Does the term "computer files" pertain only to those on my hard disk? Or does it also mean the files I have stored on floppy disk? What if I have more than one PC in my office? And what about the files I have stored on the mini-computer I use for certain applications? I don't back up those files; the system operator does it on a regular basis for all minicomputer files, not just mine. With no questioner present to explain the ambiguities, the respondent is at a loss and must try to answer the question in the best way he or she knows how. Whether the respondent's interpretation is the same as other respondents' is anyone's guess. The respondent cannot be there when the data are analyzed to tell exactly what was meant.

A less ambiguous way to phrase the question and its response categories would be something like this:

> How often do you back up the computer files stored on the hard disk on the PC you use for over 50% of your work time?

    a. *Frequently (at least once per week)*
    b. *Sometimes (from one to three times per month)*
    c. *Hardly at all (once per month or less)*
    d. *Never*

As you can see from the wording of the question, the phrasing is a bit awkward, but it avoids ambiguity. You may want to break up a single question into multiple questions, or a set of questions and statements, to avoid awkward phrasing. Notice also that the possible responses are much clearer now that they have been specifically defined, and they cover the full range of possibilities, from never to at least once per week with no overlapping time periods.

Obviously, care must be taken in the task of composing closed-ended and open-ended questions. Further, you should be as careful in composing questions for interviews as for questionnaires, since sloppily worded questions cannot be identified every time in an interview unless the interviewee asks for clarification. For both interviews and questionnaires, it is wise to pretest your questions. Pose the questions in a simulated interview and ask the interviewee to rephrase each question as he or she interprets the question. Check responses for reasonableness. You can even ask the same question in what you think are several different ways to see if you receive a materially different response. Use this feedback to adjust the questions to make them less ambiguous.

Questionnaires are most useful in the requirements determination process when used for very specific purposes rather than for more general information gathering. For example, one useful application of questionnaires is to measure levels of user satisfaction with a system or with particular aspects of it. Another useful application is to have several users choose from among a list of system features available in many off-the-shelf software packages. You could ask users to choose the features they most want and quickly tabulate the results to find out which features are most in demand. You could then recommend a system solution based on a particular software package to meet the demands of most of the users.

Choosing Between Interviews and Questionnaires

To summarize the previous sections, you can see that interviews are good tools for collecting rich, detailed information and that interviews allow exploration and follow-up (see Table 7-4). On the other hand, interviews are quite time-intensive and expensive. In comparison, questionnaires are inexpensive and take less time, as specific information can be gathered from many people at once without the personal intervention of an interviewer. The information collected from a questionnaire is less rich, however, and is potentially ambiguous if questions are not phrased precisely. In addition, follow-up to a questionnaire is more difficult as it often involves interviews or phone calls, adding to the expense of the process.

These differences and others are important for you to remember during the analysis phase. Deciding which method to use and what strategy to employ to gather information will vary with the system being studied and its organizational context. For example, if the organization is large and the system being studied is vast and complex, then there will probably be dozens of affected users and stakeholders. If you know little about the system or the organization, a good strategy is to identify key users and stakeholders and interview them. You would then use the information gathered in the interviews to create a questionnaire which would be distributed to a large number of users. You could then schedule follow-up interviews with a few users. At the other extreme, if the system and organization are small and you understand them well, the best strategy may be to interview only one or two key users or stakeholders.

TABLE 7-4 Comparison of Interviews and Questionnaires

Characteristic	Interviews	Questionnaires
Information Richness	High (many channels)	Medium to low (only responses)
Time Required	Can be extensive	Low to moderate
Expense	Can be high	Moderate
Chance for Follow-up and Probing	Good: probing and clarification questions can be asked by either interviewer or interviewee	Limited: probing and follow-up done after original data collection
Confidentiality	Interviewee is known to interviewer	Respondent can be unknown
Involvement of Subject	Interviewee is involved and committed	Respondent is passive, no clear commitment
Potential Audience	Limited numbers, but complete responses from those interviewed	Can be quite large, but lack of response from some can bias results

Interviewing Groups

One drawback to using interviews and questionnaires to collect systems requirements is the need for the analyst to reconcile apparent contradictions in the information collected. A series of interviews may turn up inconsistent information about the current system or its replacement. You must work through all of these inconsistencies to figure out what the most accurate representation of current and future systems might be. Such a process requires several follow-up phone calls and additional interviews. Catching important people in their offices is often difficult and frustrating, and scheduling new interviews may become very time-consuming. In addition, new interviews may reveal new questions that in turn require additional interviews with those interviewed earlier. Clearly, gathering information about an information system through a series of individual interviews and follow-up calls is not an efficient process.

Another option available to you is the group interview. In a group interview, you interview several key people at once. To make sure all of the important information is collected, you may conduct the interview with one or more analysts. In the case of multiple interviewers, one analyst may ask questions while another takes notes, or different analysts might concentrate on different kinds of information. For example, one analyst may listen for data requirements while another notes the timing and triggering of key events. The number of interviewees involved in the process may range from two to however many you believe can be comfortably accommodated.

A group interview has a few advantages. One, it is a much more effective use of your time than is a series of interviews with individuals (although the time commitment of the interviewees may be more of a concern). Two, interviewing several people together allows them to hear the opinions of other key people and gives them the opportunity to agree or disagree with their peers. Synergies also often occur. For example, the comments of one person might cause another person to say, "That reminds me of . . ." or "I didn't know that was a problem." You can benefit from such a discussion as it helps you identify issues on which there is general agreement and areas where views diverge widely.

The primary disadvantage of a group interview is the difficulty in scheduling it. The more people involved, the more difficult it will be finding a convenient time and place for everyone. Modern technology such as video conferences and video phones can minimize the geographical dispersion factors that make scheduling meetings so difficult. Group interviews are at the core of the Joint Application Design process, which we discuss in a later section in this chapter.

Directly Observing Users

All the methods of collecting information that we have been discussing up until now involve getting people to recall and convey information they have about an organizational area and the information systems which support these processes. People, however, are not always very reliable informants, even when they try to be reliable and tell what they think is the truth. As odd as it may sound, people often do not have a completely accurate appreciation of what they do or how they do it. This is especially true concerning infrequent events, issues from the past, or issues for which people have considerable passion. Since people cannot always be trusted to reliably interpret and report their own actions, you can supplement and corroborate what people tell you by watching what they do or by obtaining relatively objective measures of how people behave in work situations. (See the box "Lost Soft Drink Sales" for an example of the importance of systems analysts learning firsthand about the business for which they are designing systems.)

For example, one possible view of how a hypothetical manager does her job is that a manager carefully plans her activities, works long and consistently on solving problems, and controls the pace of her work. A manager might tell you that is how she spends her day. When Mintzberg (1973) observed how managers work, however, he found that a manager's day is actually punctuated by many, many interruptions. Managers work in a fragmented manner, focusing on a problem or on a communication for only a short time before they are interrupted by phone calls or visits from their subordinates and other managers. An information system designed to fit the work environment described by our hypothetical manager would not effectively support the actual work environment in which that manager finds herself.

As another example, consider the difference between what another employee might tell you about how much he uses electronic mail and how much electronic mail use you might discover through more objective means. An employee might tell you he is swamped with e-mail messages and that he spends a significant proportion of his time responding to e-mail messages. However, if you were able to check electronic mail records, you might find that this employee receives only three e-mail messages per day on average, and that the most messages he has ever received during one eight-hour period is ten. In this case, you were able to obtain an

---

Lost Soft Drink Sales

A systems analyst was quite surprised to read that sales of all soft drink products were lower, instead of higher, after a new delivery truck routing system was installed. The software was designed to reduce stock-outs at customer sites by allowing drivers to visit each customer more often using more efficient delivery routes.

Confused by the results, management asked the analyst to delay a scheduled vacation, but he insisted that he could look afresh at the system only after a few overdue days of rest and relaxation.

Instead of taking a vacation, however, the analyst called a delivery dispatcher he had interviewed during the design of the system and asked to be given a route for a few days. The analyst drove a route (for a regular driver actually on vacation), following the schedule developed from the new system. What the analyst discovered was that the route was very efficient, as expected; so at first the analyst could not see any reason for lost sales.

During the third and last day of his "vacation" the analyst stayed overtime at one store to ask the manager if she had any ideas why sales might have dropped off in recent weeks. The manager had no explanation, but did make a seemingly unrelated observation that the regular route driver appeared to have less time to spend in the store. He did not seem to take as much interest in where the products were displayed and did not ask for promotional signs to be displayed, as he had often done in the past.

From this conversation, the analyst concluded that the new delivery truck routing system was, in one sense, too good. It placed the driver on such a tight schedule that a driver had no time left for the "schmoozing" required to get special treatment, that gave the company's products an edge over the competition.

Without first-hand observation of the system in action participating as a system user, the analyst might never have discovered the true problem with the system design. Once time was allotted for not only stocking new products but also for necessary marketing work, product sales returned to and exceeded levels achieved before the new system had been introduced.

accurate behavioral measure of how much e-mail this employee copes with without having to watch him read his e-mail.

The intent behind obtaining system records and direct observation is the same, however, and that is to obtain more firsthand and objective measures of employee interaction with information systems. In some cases, behavioral measures will be a more accurate reflection of reality than what employees themselves believe. In other cases, the behavioral information will substantiate what employees have told you directly. Although observation and obtaining objective measures are desirable ways to collect pertinent information, such methods are not always possible in real organizational settings. Thus, these methods are not totally unbiased, just as no other one data-gathering method is unbiased.

For example, observation can cause people to change their normal operating behavior. Employees who know they are being observed may be nervous and make more mistakes than normal, may be careful to follow exact procedures which they do not typically follow, and may work faster or slower than normal. Moreover, since observation typically cannot be continuous, you receive only a snapshot image of the person or task you observe which may not include important events or activities. Since observation is very time-consuming, you will not only observe for a limited time but also a limited number of people and at a limited number of sites. Again, observation yields only a small segment of data from a possibly vast variety of data sources. Exactly which people or sites to observe is a difficult selection problem. You want to pick both typical and atypical people and sites and observe during normal and abnormal conditions and times to receive the richest possible data from observation.

Analyzing Procedures and Other Documents

As noted above, asking questions of the people who use a system every day or who have an interest in a system is an effective way to gather information about current and future systems. Observing current system users is a more direct way of seeing how an existing system operates, but even this method provides limited exposure to all aspects of current operations. These methods of determining system requirements can be enhanced by examining system and organizational documentation to discover more details about current systems and the organization these systems support.

Although we discuss here several important types of documents that are useful in understanding possible future system requirements, our discussion does not exhaust all possibilities. You should attempt to find all written documents about the organizational areas relevant to the systems under redesign. Besides the few specific documents we discuss, organizational mission statements, business plans, organization charts, business policy manuals, job descriptions, internal and external correspondence, and reports from prior organizational studies can all provide valuable insight.

What can the analysis of documents tell you about the requirements for a new system? In documents you can find information about

- Problems with existing systems (e.g., missing information or redundant steps)

- Opportunities to meet new needs if only certain information or information processing were available (e.g., analysis of sales based on customer type)

- Organizational direction that can influence information system requirements (e.g., trying to link customers and suppliers more closely to the organization)

- Titles and names of key individuals who have an interest in relevant existing systems (e.g., the name of a sales manager who led a study of buying behavior of key customers)

- Values of the organization or individuals who can help determine priorities for different capabilities desired by different users (e.g., maintaining market share even if it means lower short-term profits)

- Special information processing circumstances that occur irregularly that may not be identified by any other requirements determination technique (e.g., special handling needed for a few very large-volume customers and which requires use of customized customer ordering procedures)

- The reason why current systems are designed as they are, which can suggest features left out of current software which may now be feasible and more desirable (e.g., data about a customer's purchase of competitors' products were not available when the current system was designed; these data are now available from several sources)

- Data, rules for processing data, and principles by which the organization operates that must be enforced by the information system (e.g., each customer is assigned exactly one sales department staff member as a primary contact if the customer has any questions)

One type of useful document is a written work procedure for an individual or a work group. The procedure describes how a particular job or task is performed, including data and information that are used and created in the process of performing the job. For example, the procedure shown in Figure 7-3 includes data (list of features and advantages, drawings, inventor name, and witness names) required to prepare an invention disclosure. It also indicates that besides the inventor, the vice president for research and department head and dean must review the material, and that a witness is required for any filing of an invention disclosure. These insights clearly affect what data must be kept, to whom information must be sent, and the rules that govern valid forms.

Procedures are not trouble-free sources of information, however. Sometimes your analysis of several written procedures will reveal a duplication of effort in two or more jobs. You should call such duplication to the attention of management as an issue to be resolved before system design can proceed. That is, it may be necessary to redesign the organization before the redesign of an information system can achieve its full benefits. Another problem you may encounter with a procedure occurs when the procedure is missing. Again, it is not your job to create a document for a missing procedure—that is up to management. A third and common problem with a written procedure happens when the procedure is out of date. You may realize the procedure is out of date when you interview the person responsible for performing the task described in the procedure. Once again, the decision to rewrite the procedure so that it matches reality is made by management, but you may make suggestions based upon your understanding of the organization. A fourth problem often encountered with written procedures is that the formal procedures may contradict information you collected from interviews, questionnaires, and observation about how the organization operates and what information is required. As in the other cases, resolution rests with management.

All of these problems illustrate the difference between **formal systems** and **informal systems.** Formal systems are systems recognized by the official documentation of the organization; informal systems are the way in which the organization actually works. Informal systems develop because of inadequacies of formal procedures, individual work habits and preferences, resistance to control, and other

Formal system: The official way a system works as described in organizational documentation.

Informal system: The way a system actually works.

Figure 7-3
Example of a procedure

GUIDE FOR PREPARATION OF INVENTION DISCLOSURE
(See FACULTY and STAFF MANUALS for detailed Patent Policy and routing procedures.)

(1) DISCLOSE ONLY ONE INVENTION PER FORM.

(2) PREPARE COMPLETE DISCLOSURE.

The disclosure of your invention is adequate for patent purposes ONLY if it enables a person skilled in the art to understand the invention.

(3) CONSIDER THE FOLLOWING IN PREPARING A COMPLETE DISCLOSURE:

(a) All essential elements of the invention, their relationship to one another, and their mode of operation.

(b) Equivalents that can be substituted for any elements.

(c) List of features believed to be new.

(d) Advantages this invention has over the prior art.

(e) Whether the invention has been built and/or tested.

(4) PROVIDE APPROPRIATE ADDITIONAL MATERIAL.

Drawings and descriptive material should be provided as needed to clarify the disclosure. Each page of this material must be signed and dated by each inventor and properly witnessed. A copy of any current and/or planned publication relating to the invention should be included.

(5) INDICATE PRIOR KNOWLEDGE AND INFORMATION.

Pertinent publications, patents or previous devices, and related research or engineering activities should be identified.

(6) HAVE DISCLOSURE WITNESSED.

Persons other than co-inventors should serve as witnesses and should sign each sheet of the disclosure only after reading and understanding the disclosure.

(7) FORWARD ORIGINAL PLUS ONE COPY (two copies if supported by grant/contract) TO VICE PRESIDENT FOR RESEARCH VIA DEPARTMENT HEAD AND DEAN.

factors. It is important to understand both formal and informal systems since each provides insight into information requirements and what will be required to convert from present to future information services.

A second type of document useful to systems analysts is a business form (see a mock-up of a form in Figure 7-4). Forms are used for all types of business functions, from recording an order to acknowledging the payment of a bill to indicating what

Figure 7-4
Example of a business form (Generated from Microsoft Access™)

Company Name

INVOICE

Company Slogan
Enter Address Here
City, State, Zip/Postal Code
Phone: (000) 000-0000

INVOICE #	*1*
INVOICE DATE	*3/31/98*
YOUR ORDER #	*84456*
TERMS	*Net 10*
SALESMAN	*George*
F.O.B.	*Hartford, CT*

SOLD TO:
Sam Jones
25 Herky Ave.
Montreal, H9J1A2 Canada
(555) 555-7744

SHIPPED TO:
Sue Michaels
60 Krawski Dr.
Mainville, KY 64423 USA
(555) 644-5891

Shipped via
◉ UPS
◯ **US Mail**
◯ **Overnight**

Payment type
◉ Collect
◯ **Prepaid**

ITEM #	Quantity	Description	Price	Amount
12223	78	#2 Pine Boards	$12.23	$953.94
14206	5	Widgets	$5.01	$25.05
14456	7	Screws	$12.34	$86.38
17885	1	Nail Gun	$65.00	$65.00
24553	7	Hammers	$37.23	$260.61
26453	3	Gadgets	$10.00	$30.00
41165	5	Nails	$43.23	$216.15
63342	45	Roof Truss	$125.23	$5,635.35
		SUBTOTAL		$7,272.48
		TAX		$42.00
		FREIGHT		$5.50
		PAY THIS AMOUNT ☞		$7,319.98

If you have any questions concerning this invoice, call

Name   Phone Number

MAKE CHECKS PAYABLE TO
Enter Company Name Here

THANK YOU FOR YOUR BUSINESS

goods have been shipped. Forms are important for understanding a system because they explicitly indicate what data flow in or out of a system and which are necessary for the system to function. In the sample invoice form in Figure 7-4, we see data such as the name of the customer, the customer's sold to and ship to addresses, method of payment, data (item number, quantity, etc.) about each line item on the invoice, and calculated data such as tax and totals.

The form gives us crucial information about the nature of the organization. For example, the company can ship and bill to different addresses; item numbers appear to be all-numeric and five digits long; and the freight expense is charged to the customer. A printed form may correspond to a computer display that the system will generate for someone to enter and maintain data or to display data to on-line users. Forms are most useful to you when they contain actual organizational data (as in Figure 7-4), as this allows you to determine the characteristics of data which are actually used by the application. The ways in which people use forms change over time, and data that were needed when a form was designed may no longer be required. You can use the systems analysis techniques presented in Chapters 8 through 10 to help you determine which data are no longer required.

A third type of useful document is a report generated by current systems. As the primary output for some types of systems, a report enables you to work backwards from the information on the report to the data that must have been necessary to generate them. Figure 7-5 presents an example of a typical report prepared for management in a video rental business. This report shows that the system must be able to identify categories for each video and associate customers with the videos they rent. The date near the top of the report is probably the date on which the report was prepared and need not be kept by the system. You would analyze such reports to determine which data need to be captured over what time period and what manipulation of these raw data would be necessary to produce each field on the report.

If the current system is computer-based, a fourth set of useful documents are those that describe the current information systems—how they were designed and how they work. There are a lot of different types of documents that fit this description, everything from flow charts to data dictionaries and CASE tool reports to user manuals. An analyst who has access to such documents is lucky, as many in-house–developed information systems lack complete documentation (unless a CASE tool has been used).

Analysis of organizational documents and observation, along with interviewing and questionnaires, are the methods most used for gathering system requirements. In Table 7-4 we summarized the comparative features of interviews and questionnaires. Table 7-5 summarizes the comparative features of observation and analysis of organizational documents.

MODERN METHODS FOR DETERMINING SYSTEM REQUIREMENTS

Even though we called interviews, questionnaires, observation, and document analysis traditional methods for determining a system's requirements, all of these methods are still very much used by analysts to collect important information. Today, however, there are additional techniques to collect information about the current system, the organizational area requesting the new system, and what the new system should be like. In this section, you will learn about several modern information-gathering techniques for analysis (listed in Table 7-6): Joint Application Design (JAD), group support systems, CASE tools, and prototyping. As we said

Figure 7-5
Example of a report

```
========================================
Who rents what category of videos?

28-Feb-98                              1
========================================
Video Category      Customer Name
========================================

action
                    Eleanor Johnson
                    Miles Standish
foreign
                    Alan Alda
                    Bob Hope
                    Eleanor Johnson
                    Jane Smith
                    Juan Valdez
sf
                    Alan Alda
                    Alexi Kosygin
                    Bob Hope
                    Eleanor Johnson
                    Jane Smith
                    John Smith
                    Wanda Orlikowski
western
                    Alexi Kosygin
                    Bob Hope
                    Jane Smith
                    Juan Valdez
                    Miles Standish
                    Wilma Randolph
```

earlier, these techniques can support effective information collection and structuring while reducing the amount of time required for analysis. An alternative to the SDLC, RAD, which combines JAD, CASE tools, and prototyping, is described in more detail in Chapter 13.

Joint Application Design

You were introduced to Joint Application Design, or JAD, in Chapter 1. There you learned JAD started in the late 1970s at IBM and that since then the practice of JAD has spread throughout many companies and industries. For example, it is quite popular in the insurance industry in Connecticut where a JAD users group has been formed. In fact, several generic approaches to JAD have been documented and popularized (see Wood and Silver, 1989, for an example). You also learned in Chapter 1 that the main idea behind JAD is to bring together the key users, managers, and systems analysts involved in the analysis of a current system. In that respect, JAD is similar to a group interview; a JAD, however, follows a particular structure of roles and agenda that is quite different from a group interview during

TABLE 7-5 Comparison of Observation and Document Analysis

Characteristic	Observation	Document Analysis
Information Richness	High (many channels)	Low (passive) and old
Time Required	Can be extensive	Low to moderate
Expense	Can be high	Low to moderate
Chance for Follow-up and Probing	Good: probing and clarification questions can be asked during or after observation	Limited: probing possible only if original author is available
Confidentiality	Observee is known to interviewer; observee may change behavior when observed	Depends on nature of document; does not change simply by being read
Involvement of Subject	Interviewees may or may not be involved and committed depending on whether they know if they are being observed	None, no clear commitment
Potential Audience	Limited numbers and limited time (snapshot) of each	Potentially biased by which documents were kept or because document not created for this purpose

TABLE 7-6 Modern Methods for Collecting System Requirements

- Bringing together in a *Joint Application Design (JAD)* session users, sponsors, analysts and others to discuss and review system requirements

- Using *group support systems* to facilitate the sharing of ideas and voicing opinions about system requirements

- Using *CASE tools* to analyze current systems to discover requirements to meet changing business conditions

- Iteratively developing system *prototypes* that refine the understanding of system requirements in concrete by showing working versions of system features

which analysts control the sequence of questions answered by users. The primary purpose of using JAD in the analysis phase is to collect systems requirements simultaneously from the key people involved with the system. The result is an intense and structured, but highly effective, process. As with a group interview, having all the key people together in one place at one time allows analysts to see where there are areas of agreement and where there are conflicts. Meeting with all these important people for over a week of intense sessions allows you the opportunity to resolve conflicts, or at least to understand why a conflict may not be simple to resolve.

JAD sessions are usually conducted in a location other than the place where the people involved normally work. The idea behind such a practice is to keep participants away from as many distractions as possible so that they can concentrate on systems analysis. A JAD may last anywhere from four hours to an entire week and may consist of several sessions. A JAD employs thousands of dollars of corporate resources, the most expensive of which is the time of the people involved. Other expenses include the costs associated with flying people to a remote site and putting them up in hotels and feeding them for several days.

The typical participants in a JAD are listed below:

JAD session leader: The trained individual who plans and leads Joint Application Design sessions.

- **JAD session leader:** The JAD leader organizes and runs the JAD. This person has been trained in group management and facilitation as well as in systems analysis. The JAD leader sets the agenda and sees that it is met. The JAD leader remains neutral on issues and does not contribute ideas or opinions but rather concentrates on keeping the group on the agenda, resolving conflicts and disagreements, and soliciting all ideas.

- Users: The key users of the system under consideration are vital participants in a JAD. They are the only ones who have a clear understanding of what it means to use the system on a daily basis.

- Managers: Managers of the work groups who use the system in question provide insight into new organizational directions, motivations for and organizational impacts of systems, and support for requirements determined during the JAD.

- Sponsor: As a major undertaking due to its expense, a JAD must be sponsored by someone at a relatively high level in the company. If the sponsor attends any sessions, it is usually only at the very beginning or the end.

- Systems Analysts: Members of the systems analysis team attend the JAD although their actual participation may be limited. Analysts are there to learn from users and managers, not to run or dominate the process.

Scribe: The person who makes detailed notes of the happenings at a Joint Application Design session.

- **Scribe:** The scribe takes notes during the JAD sessions. This is usually done on a personal computer or laptop. Notes may be taken using a word processor, or notes and diagrams may be entered directly into a CASE tool.

- IS staff: Besides systems analysts, other IS staff, such as programmers, database analysts, IS planners, and data center personnel, may attend to learn from the discussion and possibly to contribute their ideas on the technical feasibility of proposed ideas or on technical limitations of current systems.

JAD sessions are usually held in special-purpose rooms where participants sit around horseshoe-shaped tables, as in Figure 7-6. These rooms are typically equipped with whiteboards (possibly electronic, with a printer to make copies of what is written on the board). Other audio-visual tools may be used, such as transparencies and overhead projectors, magnetic symbols that can be easily rearranged on a whiteboard, flip charts, and computer-generated displays. Flip chart paper is typically used for keeping track of issues that cannot be resolved during the JAD or for those issues requiring additional information that can be gathered during breaks in the proceedings. Computers may be used to create and display form or report designs or for diagramming existing or replacement systems. In general, however, most JADs do not benefit much from computer support (Carmel, 1991).

When a JAD is completed, the end result is a set of documents that detail the workings of the current system related to the study of a replacement system. Depending on the exact purpose of the JAD, analysts may also walk away from the JAD with some detailed information on what is desired of the replacement system.

Taking Part in a JAD   Imagine that you are a systems analyst taking part in your first JAD. What might participating in a JAD be like? Typically, JADs are held off site, in comfortable conference facilities. On the first morning of the JAD, you and your fellow analysts walk into a room that looks much like the one depicted in Figure 7-6.

Figure 7-6
Illustration of the typical room layout for a JAD
(Adapted from Wood and Silver, 1989)

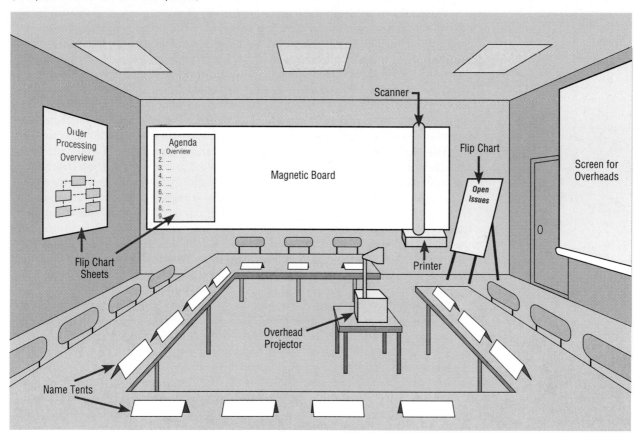

The JAD facilitator is already there; she is finishing writing the day's agenda on a flip chart. The scribe is seated in a corner at a microcomputer, preparing to take notes on the day's activities. Users and managers begin to enter in groups and seat themselves around the U-shaped table. You and the other analysts review your notes describing what you have learned so far about the information system you are all here to discuss. The session leader opens the meeting with a welcome and a brief run-down of the agenda. The first day will be devoted to a general overview of the current system and major problems associated with it. The next two days will be devoted to an analysis of current system screens. The last two days will be devoted to analysis of reports.

The session leader introduces the corporate sponsor who talks about the organizational unit and current system related to the systems analysis study and the importance of upgrading the current system to meet changing business conditions. He leaves, and the JAD session leader takes over. She yields the floor to the senior analyst who begins a presentation on key problems with the system that have already been identified. After the presentation, the session leader opens the discussion to the users and managers in the room.

After a few minutes of talk, a heated discussion begins between two users from different corporate locations. One user, who represents the office which served as the model for the original systems design, argues that the system's perceived lack of flexibility is really an asset, not a problem. The other user, who represents an office that was part of another company before a merger, argues that the current system is so inflexible as to be virtually unusable. The session leader intervenes and tries to help the users isolate particular aspects of the system that may contribute to the system's perceived lack of flexibility.

Questions arise about the intent of the original developers. The session leader asks the analysis team about their impressions of the original system design. Because these questions cannot be answered during this meeting, as none of the original designers are present and none of the original design documents are readily available, the session leader assigns the question about intent to the "to do" list. This question becomes the first one on a flip chart sheet of "to do" items and the session leader gives you the assignment of finding out about the intent of the original designers. She writes your name next to the "to do" item on the list and continues with the session. Before the end of the JAD, you must get an answer to this question.

The JAD will continue like this for its duration. Analysts will make presentations, help lead discussions of form and report design, answer questions from users and managers, and take notes on what is being said. After each meeting, the analysis team will meet, usually informally, to discuss what has occurred that day and to consolidate what they have learned. Users will continue to contribute during the meetings and the session leader will facilitate, intervening in conflicts, seeing that the group follows the agenda. When the JAD is over, the session leader and her assistants must prepare a report that documents the findings in the JAD and is circulated among users and analysts.

CASE Tools During JAD   The CASE tools most useful to analysis during a JAD are those referred to as upper CASE (see Chapter 4), as they apply most directly to activities occurring early in the systems development life cycle. Upper CASE tools usually include planning tools (see Chapter 5), diagramming tools (see Chapter 8 for examples of diagrams used during systems analysis), and prototyping tools, such as computer display and report generators. For requirements determination and structuring, the most useful CASE tools are for diagramming and for display and report generation. The more interaction analysts have with users during this phase, the more useful this set of tools. The analyst can use diagramming and prototyping tools to give graphic form to system requirements, show the tools to users, and make changes based on the users' reactions. The same tools are very valuable for requirements structuring as well. Using common CASE tools during requirements determination and structuring makes the transition between these two sub-phases easier and reduces the time spent. In structuring, CASE tools which analyze requirements information for correctness, completeness, and consistency are also useful. Finally, for alternative generation and selection, diagramming and prototyping tools are key to presenting users with graphic illustrations of what the alternative systems will look like. Such a practice provides users and analysts with better information to select the most desirable alternative system.

Some observers advocate using CASE tools during JADs (Lucas, 1993). Running a CASE tool during a JAD allows analysts to enter system models directly into a CASE tool, providing consistency and reliability in the joint model-building process. The CASE tool captures system requirements in a more flexible and useful way than can a scribe or an analysis team making notes. Further, the CASE tool can be used to project menu, display, and report designs, so users can directly observe old and new designs and evaluate their usefulness for the analysis team. Some CASE tools are too slow for the real-time pace of most JADs, however, so the session leader may want analysts to enter information into the CASE tool after the day's meeting is over. Users and managers can be shown the results of their work the next morning.

Supporting JAD with GSS   The JAD process is typically not well supported by computing, despite suggestions to augment JADs with CASE tools and other computer-based aids. Most traditional JADs rely on one computer for the scribe to use and maybe another for displaying screen and report designs. Since JAD is a structured group process, JAD can benefit from the same computer-based support that can be applied to any group process. Group support systems (GSS) can be used to support group meetings. Here we will discuss how JAD can benefit from GSS use.

One disadvantage to a JAD session is that it suffers from many of the same problems as any group meeting. For example, the more people in a group, the less time there is for all of them to speak and state their views. Even if you assumed that they all spoke for an equal amount of time, no one would have much time to talk in a one-hour meeting for 12 people (only five minutes each!). The assumption about speaking equally points out a second problem with meetings—one or a few people always dominate the discussion. On the other hand, some people will say absolutely nothing. Whatever outcome the meeting produces tends to be tilted toward those who spoke the most during the meeting and others may not be fully committed to the conclusions reached. A third problem with group meetings is that some people are afraid to speak out for fear they will be criticized. A fourth problem is that most people are not willing to criticize or challenge their bosses in a meeting, even if what the boss is saying is wrong.

JADs suffer from all of these problems with meetings. The result is that important views often are not aired. Such an outcome is unfortunate as the design of the new system could be adversely impacted and the system may have to be reworked at great expense when those important views finally become known.

GSSs have been designed specifically to help alleviate some of the problems with group meetings. In order to provide everyone in the meeting with the same chance to contribute, group members type their comments into computers rather than speak them. The GSS is set up so that all members of the group can see what every other member has been typing. In the one-hour meeting for 12 people mentioned earlier, all 12 can contribute for the full hour, instead of just for five minutes, using a GSS. If everyone in the meeting is typing, not talking, and everyone has the same chance to contribute, then the chances of domination of the meeting by any one individual are greatly reduced. Also, comments typed into a GSS are anonymous. Anonymity helps those who fear criticism because only the comment, and not the person, can be criticized, since no one knows who typed what. Anonymity also provides the ability to criticize your boss.

Supporting a JAD with a GSS has many potential benefits. Using a GSS, a JAD session leader is more likely to obtain contributions from everyone, rather than from just a few. Important ideas are less likely to be missed. Similarly, poor ideas are more likely to be criticized. A study comparing traditional JAD to JAD supported with GSS found that using a GSS did lead to certain enhancements in the JAD process (Carmel, George, and Nunamaker, 1992). Among the findings were that GSS-supported JADs tended to be more time-efficient than traditional JAD and participation was more equal because there was less domination by certain individuals than in traditional JAD. The study also found that introducing a GSS into a JAD session had other, less desirable, effects. GSS-supported JADs tended to be less structured and it was more difficult to identify and resolve conflicts when a GSS was used, due in part to the anonymity of interaction. Supporting a JAD with GSS, then, does seem to provide some benefits through altering how the group works together. Yet a reduction in the JAD leader's ability to resolve conflicts could be a problem, especially since JAD was designed to help uncover and resolve conflicts.

Using Prototyping During Requirements Determination

You were introduced to prototyping in Chapter 1 (see Figure 1-9 for an overview of prototyping). There you learned that prototyping is an iterative process involving analysts and users whereby a rudimentary version of an information system is built and rebuilt according to user feedback. You also learned that prototyping could replace the systems development life cycle or augment it. What we are interested in here is how prototyping can augment the requirements determination process.

In order to gather an initial basic set of requirements, you will still have to interview users and collect documentation. Prototyping, however, will allow you to quickly convert basic requirements into a working, though limited, version of the desired information system. The prototype will then be viewed and tested by the user. Typically, seeing verbal descriptions of requirements converted into a physical system will prompt the user to modify existing requirements and generate new ones. For example, in the initial interviews, a user might have said that he wanted all relevant utility billing information on a single computer display form, such as the client's name and address, the service record, and payment history. Once the same user sees how crowded and confusing such a design would be in the prototype, he might change his mind and instead ask for the information to be organized on several screens, but with easy transitions from one screen to another. He might also be reminded of some important requirements (data, calculations, etc.) that had not surfaced during the initial interviews.

You would then redesign the prototype to incorporate the suggested changes. Once modified, users would again view and test the prototype. And, once again, you would incorporate their suggestions for change. Through such an iterative process, the chances are good that you will be able to better capture a system's requirements. The goal with using prototyping to support requirements determination is to develop concrete specifications for the ultimate system, not to build the ultimate system from prototyping.

Prototyping is possible with several 4GLs and with CASE tools, as pointed out in Chapter 4 and the earlier section on CASE tools and analysis in this chapter. As we saw there, you can use CASE tools as part of a JAD to provide a type of limited prototyping with a group of users.

Prototyping is most useful for requirements determination when

- User requirements are not clear or well understood, which is often the case for totally new systems or systems that support decision making

- One or a few users and other stakeholders are involved with the system

- Possible designs are complex and require concrete form to fully evaluate

- Communication problems have existed in the past between users and analysts and both parties want to be sure that system requirements are as specific as possible

- Tools (such as form and report generators) and data are readily available to rapidly build working systems

Prototyping also has some drawbacks as a tool for requirements determination. These include

- A tendency to avoid creating formal documentation of system requirements which can then make the system more difficult to develop into a fully working system

- Prototypes can become very idiosyncratic to the initial user and difficult to diffuse or adapt to other potential users

- Prototypes are often built as stand-alone systems, thus ignoring issues of sharing data and interactions with other existing systems

- Checks in the SDLC are bypassed so that some more subtle, but still important, system requirements might be forgotten (e.g., security, some data entry controls, or standardization of data across systems)

RADICAL METHODS FOR DETERMINING SYSTEM REQUIREMENTS

Whether traditional or modern, the methods for determining system requirements that you have read about in this chapter apply to any requirements determination effort, regardless of its motivation. But most of what you have learned has traditionally been applied to systems development projects that involve automating existing processes. Analysts use system requirements determination to understand current problems and opportunities, as well as what is needed and desired in future systems. Typically, the current way of doing things has a large impact on the new system. In some organizations, though, management is looking for new ways to perform current tasks. These new ways may be radically different from how things are done now, but the payoffs may be enormous: fewer people may be needed to do the same work, relationships with customers may improve dramatically, and processes may become much more efficient and effective, all of which can result in increased profits. The overall process by which current methods are replaced with radically new methods is generally referred to as **business process reengineering** or **BPR**.

> **Business Process Reengineering (BPR):** The search for, and implementation of, radical change in business processes to achieve breakthrough improvements in products and services.

To better understand BPR, consider the following analogy. Suppose you are a successful European golfer who has tuned your game to fit the style of golf courses and weather in Europe. You have learned how to control the flight of the ball in heavy winds, roll the ball on wide open greens, putt on large and undulating greens, and aim at a target without the aid of the landscaping common on North American courses. When you come to the United States to make your fortune on the U.S. tour, you discover that incrementally improving your putting, driving accuracy, and sand shots will help, but the new competitive environment is simply not suited to your style of the game. You need to reengineer your whole approach, learning how to aim at targets, spin and stop a ball on the green, and manage the distractions of crowds and press. If you are good enough, you may survive, but without reengineering, you will never be a winner.

Just as the competitiveness of golf forces good players to adapt their games to changing conditions, the competitiveness of our global economy has driven most companies into a mode of continuously improving the quality of their products and services (Dobyns and Crawford-Mason, 1991). Organizations realize that creatively using information technologies can yield significant improvements in most business processes. The idea behind BPR is not just to improve each business process but, in a systems modeling sense, to reorganize the complete flow of data in major sections of an organization to eliminate unnecessary steps, achieve synergies among previously separate steps, and become more responsive to future changes. Companies such as IBM, Procter & Gamble, Wal-Mart, and Ford are actively pursuing BPR efforts and have had great success. Yet, many other companies have found difficulty in applying BPR principles (Moad, 1994). Nonetheless, BPR concepts are actively applied in both corporate strategic planning and information systems planning as a way to radically improve business processes (as described in Chapter 5).

BPR advocates suggest that radical increases in the quality of business processes can be achieved through creative application of information technologies. BPR advocates also suggest that radical improvement cannot be achieved by tweaking existing processes but rather by using a clean sheet of paper and asking "If we were a new organization, how would we accomplish this activity?" Changing the way work is performed also changes the way information is shared and stored, which means that the results of many BPR efforts are the development of information system maintenance requests or requests for system replacement. It is likely that you will encounter or have encountered BPR initiatives in your own organization. A recent survey of IS executives found that they view BPR to be a top IS priority for the coming years (Hayley, Plewa, and Watts, 1993).

Identifying Processes to Reengineer

Key business processes:
The structured, measured set of activities designed to produce a specific output for a particular customer or market.

A first step in any BPR effort relates to understanding what processes to change. To do this, you must first understand which processes represent the **key business processes** for the organization. Key business processes are the structured set of measurable activities designed to produce a specific output for a particular customer or market. The important aspect of this definition is that key processes are focused on some type of organizational outcome such as the creation of a product or the delivery of a service. Key business processes are also customer-focused. In other words, key business processes would include all activities used to design, build, deliver, support, and service a particular product for a particular customer. BPR efforts, therefore, first try to understand those activities that are part of the organization's key business processes and then alter the sequence and structure of activities to achieve radical improvements in speed, quality, and customer satisfaction. The same techniques you learned to use for systems requirement determination can be used to discover and understand key business processes. Interviewing key individuals, observing activities, reading and studying organizational documents, and conducting JADs can all be used to find and fathom key business processes.

After identifying key business processes, the next step is to identify specific activities that can be radically improved through reengineering. Hammer and Champy (1993), the two people most identified with the term BPR, suggest that three questions be asked to identify activities for radical change:

1. How important is the activity to delivering an outcome?

2. How feasible is changing the activity?

3. How dysfunctional is the activity?

The answers to these questions provide guidance for selecting which activities to change. Those activities deemed important, changeable, yet dysfunctional, are primary candidates. To identify dysfunctional activities, they suggest you look for activities where there are excessive information exchanges between individuals, where information is redundantly recorded or needs to be rekeyed, where there are excessive inventory buffers or inspections, and where there is a lot of rework or complexity. Many of the tools and techniques for modeling data, processes, events, and logic within the IS development process are also being applied to model business processes within BPR efforts (see Davenport, 1993). Thus, the skills of a systems analyst are often central to many BPR efforts.

Disruptive Technologies

Once key business processes and activities have been identified, information technologies must be applied to radically improve business processes. To do this,

TABLE 7-7 Long-Held Organizational Rules that are Being Eliminated through Disruptive Technologies

Rule	Disruptive Technology
Information can appear in only one place at a time.	Distributed databases allow the sharing of information.
Only experts can perform complex work.	Expert systems can aid nonexperts.
Businesses must choose between centralization and decentralization.	Advanced telecommunications networks can support dynamic organizational structures.
Managers must make all decisions.	Decision-support tools can aid nonmanagers.
Field personnel need offices where they can receive, store, retrieve, and transmit information.	Wireless data communication and portable computers provide a "virtual" office for workers.
The best contact with a potential buyer is personal contact.	Interactive communication technologies allow complex messaging capabilities.
You have to find out where things are.	Automatic identification and tracking technology know where things are.
Plans get revised periodically.	High-performance computing can provide real-time updating.

Hammer and Champy (1993) suggest that organizations think "inductively" about information technology. Induction is the process of reasoning from the specific to the general, which means that managers must *learn* the power of new technologies and *think* of innovative ways to alter the way work is done. This is contrary to deductive thinking where problems are first identified and solutions are then formulated.

Hammer and Champy suggest that managers especially consider **disruptive technologies** when applying deductive thinking. Disruptive technologies are those that enable the breaking of long-held business rules that inhibit organizations from making radical business changes. For example, Saturn is using production schedule databases and electronic data interchange (EDI) to work with its suppliers as if they and Saturn were one company. Suppliers do not wait until Saturn sends them a purchase order for more parts but simply monitor inventory levels and automatically send shipments as needed (Hammer and Champy, 1993: 90). Table 7-7 shows several long-held business rules and beliefs that constrain organizations from making radical process improvements. For example, the first rule suggests that information can only appear in one place at a time. However, the advent of distributed databases (see Chapter 19) has "disrupted" this long-held business belief.

In this section, we discussed how BPR is increasingly being used to identify ways to adapt existing information systems to changing organizational information needs and processes. It was our intent to provide a brief introduction to this topic, as the specific tools and techniques for performing BPR are still evolving. For more information on this exciting topic, the interested reader is encouraged to see the books by Davenport (1993) and Hammer and Champy (1993).

Disruptive technologies: Technologies that enable the breaking of long-held business rules that inhibit organizations from making radical business changes.

SUMMARY

As we saw in Chapter 1, there are three subphases in the systems analysis phase of the systems development life cycle: requirements determination, requirements structuring, and alternative generation and choice. Chapter 7 has focused on requirements determination, the gathering of information about current systems and the need for replacement systems. Chapters 8 through 10 will address techniques for structuring the requirements elicited during requirements determination. Chapter 11 closes Part III of the book by explaining how analysts generate alternative design strategies for replacement systems and choose the best one.

For requirements determination, the traditional sources of information about a system include interviews, questionnaires, observation, group interviews, and procedures, forms, and other useful documents. Often many or even all of these sources are used to gather perspectives on the adequacy of current systems and the requirements for replacement systems. Each form of information collection has its advantages and disadvantages, which were summarized in Tables 7-4 and 7-5. Selecting the methods to use depends on the need for rich or thorough information, the time and budget available, the need to probe deeper once initial information is collected, the need for confidentiality for those providing assessments of system requirements, the desire to get people involved and committed to a project, and the potential audience from which requirements should be collected.

Both open- and closed-ended questions can be posed during interviews or in questionnaires. In either case, you must be very precise in formulating a question in order to avoid ambiguity and to insure a proper response. During observation you must try not to intrude or interfere with normal business activities so that the people being observed do not modify their activities from normal processes. The results of all requirements gathering methods should be compared, since there may be differences between the formal or official system and the way people actually work, the informal system.

You also learned about alternative methods to collect requirements information, many of which themselves make use of information systems. Joint Application Design (JAD) begins with the idea of the group interview and adds structure and a JAD session leader to it. Typical JAD participants include the session leader, a scribe, key users, managers, a sponsor, and systems analysts. JAD sessions are usually held off site and may last as long as one week.

Although JAD sessions typically rely little on computer support, systems analysis is increasingly performed with computer assistance, such as group support systems. You also read how information systems can support requirements determination with CASE tools and for prototyping. As part of the prototyping process, users and analysts work closely together to determine requirements which the analyst then builds into a model. The analyst and user then work together on revising the model until it is close to what the user desires.

Business process reengineering (BPR) is an approach to radically changing business processes. BPR efforts are a source of new information requirements. Information systems and technologies often enable BPR by allowing an organization to eliminate or relax constraints on traditional business rules.

The result of requirements determination is a thorough set of information, including some charts, that describes the current systems being studied and the need for new and different capabilities to be included in the replacement systems. This information, however, is not in a form that makes analysis of true problems and clear statements of new features possible. Thus, you and other analysts will study this information and structure it into standard formats suitable for identifying problems and unambiguously describing the specifications for new systems. With modern information systems, structuring requires documenting the flow or movement of data throughout the organization and information systems, the logic of transforming data into information (including the timing of events that cause data to be transformed or processed), and the rules that govern the relationships between different data handled by the system. We discuss a variety of popular techniques for structuring requirements in the following three chapters.

K E Y   T E R M S

Business process re-
    engineering
Closed-ended questions
Disruptive technologies

Formal system
Informal system
JAD session leader
Key business processes

Open-ended questions
Scribe

R E V I E W   Q U E S T I O N S

1. Define each of the following terms:

    a. Joint Application Design
    b. prototyping
    c. Group Support System (GSS)
    d. requirements determination

    e. requirements structuring
    f. formal system
    g. informal system
    h. business process reengineering

2. Describe systems analysis and the major activities that occur during this phase of the systems development life cycle.

3. Describe four traditional techniques for collecting information during analysis. When might one be better than another?

4. Compare collecting information by interview and by questionnaire. Describe a hypothetical situation in which each of these methods would be an effective way to collect information system requirements.

5. What is JAD? How is it better than traditional information-gathering techniques? What are its weaknesses?

6. How has computing been used to support requirements determination?

7. How has computing been used to support JAD?

8. How can CASE tools be used to support requirements determination? Which type of CASE tools are appropriate for use during requirements determination?

9. Describe how prototyping can be used during requirements determination. How is it better or worse than traditional methods?

10. What unique benefits does a GSS provide for group methods of requirements determination, such as group interviews or JAD?

11. When conducting a business process reengineering study, what should you look for when trying to identify business processes to change? Why?

12. What are disruptive technologies and how do they enable organizations to radically change their business processes?

P R O B L E M S   A N D   E X E R C I S E S

1. Match the following terms to the appropriate definitions.

    _____ open-ended questions

    a. questions in interviews and on questionnaires that ask those answering the questions to choose from among a set of prespecified responses

_____ closed-ended questions

_____ JAD session leader

_____ scribe

_____ key business processes

b. trained individual who plans and leads Joint Application Design sessions
c. person who makes detailed notes of the happenings at a Joint Application Design session
d. responses to questions in interviews and on questionnaires that have no pre-specified answers
e. The structured, measured set of activities designed to produce a specific output for a particular customer or market.

2. Choose either CASE or GSS as a topic and review a related article from the popular press and from the academic research literature. Summarize the two articles and, based on your reading, prepare a list of arguments for why this type of system would be useful in a JAD session. Also address the limits for applying this type of system in a JAD setting.

3. One of the potential problems with gathering information requirements by observing potential system users mentioned in the chapter is that people may change their behavior when observed. What could you do to overcome this potential confounding factor in accurately determining information requirements?

4. Summarize the problems with the reliability and usefulness of analyzing business documents as a method for gathering information requirements. How could you cope with these problems to effectively use business documents as a source of insights on system requirements?

5. Suppose you were asked to lead a JAD session. List 10 guidelines you would follow to assist you in playing the proper role of a JAD session leader.

6. Prepare a plan, similar to Figure 7-2, for an interview with your academic advisor to determine which courses you should take to develop the skills you need to be hired as a programmer/analyst.

7. Write at least three closed-ended questions that you might use on a questionnaire that would be sent to users of a word processing package in order to develop ideas for the next version of the package. Test these questions by asking a friend to answer the questions; then interview your friend to determine why she responded as she did. From this interview, determine if she misunderstood any of your questions and, if so, rewrite the questions to be less ambiguous.

8. An interview lends itself easily to asking probing questions, or asking different questions depending on the answers provided by the interviewee. Although not impossible, probing and alternative questions can be handled in a questionnaire. Discuss how you could include probing or alternative sets of questions in a questionnaire.

9. Figure 7-2 shows part of a guide for an interview. How might an interview guide differ when a group interview is to be conducted?

10. Group interviews and JADs are very powerful ways to collect system requirements but special problems arise during group requirements collection sessions. Summarize the special interviewing and group problems that arise in such group sessions, and suggest ways that you, as a group interviewer or group facilitator, might deal with these problems.

11. Review the material in Chapter 5 on corporate and information systems strategic planning. How are these processes different from BPR? What new perspectives might BPR bring that classical strategic planning methods may not have?

FIELD EXERCISES

1. Effective interviewing is not something that you can learn from just reading about it. You must first do some interviewing, preferably a lot of it, as interviewing skills only improve with experience. To get an idea of what interviewing is like, try the following: Find three friends or classmates to help you complete this exercise. Organize yourselves into pairs. Write down a series of questions you can use to find out about a job your partner now has or once held. You decide what questions to use, but at a minimum, you must find out the following. (1) the job's title (2) the job's responsibilities (3) whom your partner reported to (4) who reported to your partner, if anyone did, and (5) what information your partner used to do his or her job. At the same time, your partner should be preparing questions to ask you about a job you have had. Now conduct the interview. Take careful notes. Organize what you find into a clear form that another person could understand (you might want to use a systems diagram like Figure 2-7, with boundaries, inputs, and outputs). Now repeat the process, but this time, your partner interviews you.

   While the two of you have been interviewing each other, your two other friends should have been doing the same thing. When all four of you are done, switch partners and repeat the entire process. When you are all done, each of you should have interviewed two people, and each of you should have been interviewed by two people. Now, you and the person who interviewed your original partner should compare your findings. Most likely, your findings will not be identical to what the other person found. If your findings differ, discover why. Did you use the same questions? Did the other person do a more thorough job of interviewing your first partner, since it was the second time he or she had conducted an interview? Did you both ask follow-up questions? Did you both spend about the same amount of time on the interview? Prepare a report with this person about why your findings differed. Now find both of the people who interviewed you. Does one set of findings differ from the other? Try and figure out why. Did one of them (or both of them) misrepresent or misunderstand what you told them? Each of you should now write a report on your experience, using it to explain why interviews are sometimes inconsistent and inaccurate and why having two people interview someone on a topic is better than having just one person do the interview. Explain the implications of what you have learned for the requirements determination subphase of the systems development life cycle.

2. Choose a work team at your work or university and interview them in a group setting. Ask them about their current system (whether computer-based or not) for performing their work. Ask each of them what information they use and/or need and from where/whom they get it. Was this a useful method for you to learn about their work? Why or why not? What comparative advantages does this method provide as compared to one-on-one interviews with each team member? What comparative disadvantages?

3. For the same work team you used in Field Exercise 2, examine copies of any relevant written documentation (e.g., written procedures, forms, reports, system documentation). Are any of these forms of written documentation missing? Why? With what consequences? To what extent does this written documentation fit with the information you received in the group interview?

4. Interview systems analysts, users, and managers who have been involved in JAD sessions. Determine the location, structure and outcomes of each of their JAD sessions. Elicit their evaluations of their sessions. Were they productive? Why or why not?

5. Survey the literature on JAD in the academic and popular press and determine the "state of the art." How is JAD being used to help determine system requirements? Is using JAD for this process beneficial? Why or why not? Present your analysis to the IS manager at your work or at your university. Does your analysis of JAD fit with his or her perception? Why or why not? Is he or she currently using JAD, or a JAD-like method, for determining system requirements? Why or why not?

6. With the help of other students or your instructor, contact someone in an organization that has carried out a BPR study. What effects did this study have on information systems? In what ways did IT (especially disruptive technologies) facilitate making the radical changes discovered in the BPR study?

REFERENCES

Carmel, E. 1991. *Supporting Joint Application Development with Electronic Meeting Systems: A Field Study.* Unpublished doctoral dissertation, University of Arizona.

Carmel, E., J. F. George, and J. F. Nunamaker, Jr. 1992. "Supporting Joint Application Development (JAD) with Electronic Meeting Systems: A Field Study." *Proceedings of the Thirteenth International Conference on Information Systems.* Dallas, TX, December: 223–32.

Carmel, E., R. Whitaker, and J. F. George. 1993 "Participatory Design and Joint Application Design: A Transatlantic Comparison." *Communications of the ACM* 36 (June): 40–48.

Davenport, T. H. 1993. *Process Innovation: Reengineering Work through Information Technology.* Boston, MA: Harvard Business School Press.

Dennis, A. R., J. F. George, L. Jessup, J. F. Nunamaker, Jr., and D. R. Vogel. 1988. "Information Technology to Support Electronic Meetings." *MIS Quarterly* 12 (December): 591–624.

Dobyns, L., and C. Crawford-Mason. 1991. *Quality or Else.* Boston, MA: Houghton-Mifflin.

Hammer, M., and J. Champy. 1993. *Reengineering the Corporation.* New York, NY: Harper Business.

Lucas, M.A. 1993. "The Way of JAD." *Database Programming & Design* 6 (July): 42–49.

Mintzberg, H. 1973. *The Nature of Managerial Work.* New York, NY: Harper & Row.

Moad, J. 1994. "After Reengineering: Taking Care of Business." *Datamation* 40 (20): 40–44.

Wood, J., and D. Silver. 1989. *Joint Application Design.* New York, NY: John Wiley & Sons.

Analysis: Requirements Determination for the Customer Activity Tracking System

INTRODUCTION

As seen from Figure 4 in the previous Broadway Entertainment Company case, the Baseline Project Plan for the requirements determination step included several interviews, analysis of relevant business documents, benchmarking customer profiling in other firms, and a (tentative) JAD session, among other steps. Space does not permit us to discuss all of these activities. To illustrate requirements determination, this section focuses on the results of the interview with the U.S. marketing manager conducted by one of the systems analysts assigned to the CATS project.

ANALYZING INTERVIEW RESULTS

Frank Napier walked into Jordan Pippen's office. In his hands, he carried several pages of printed notes. Frank had been with BEC for about nine months since his graduation from the computer information systems program at the University of Western Florida. Frank had worked on his first systems project at BEC with Jordan and Jordan had requested that Frank be assigned as one of the two analysts for the analysis phase of the CATS project. Frank was relatively inexperienced for such a highly placed project as CATS, but he was well trained and knew his limitations. Jordan and Nancy Chen, the CATS project client, had agreed that with Jordan's experience as project manager and Frank's excellent reputation in only nine months at BEC, Frank should work out well on the project.

"Hi Frank. What have you got there? Are those your notes on your interview with Wendy?"

"Yes," Frank said, handing the notes to Jordan. At the top of the first page was typed:

Interview with: Wendy Yoshimuro, Marketing Manager, U.S. Operations

Interviewer: Frank Napier, Junior Systems Analyst
Date: May 31, 1998
Tape: CATS1
Topic: BEC Customer Activity Tracking System (CATS)

Jordan picked up Frank's notes and began leafing through them. Wendy Yoshimuro worked for Nancy Chen in the U.S. Operations office. Wendy was the marketing manager whose job responsibilities were most closely aligned with what the CATS system was about, namely, helping to determine product mix based on customer profiles. Wendy's office was responsible for maintaining and interpreting the customer information that was derived from the raw data on customer purchases and rentals collected at the store level. Jordan began to read Frank's interview notes:

Frank: What do the current customer profiles look like?

Wendy: I can give you a copy of the form we use to collect information from new customers (Figure 1) and I can give you a list of all the attributes we store, but I can tell you, too. We have the basic customer information, name, address, credit card number, that kind of stuff. As for video rentals, you know the consumer privacy law prevents us from recording specific video titles a customer rents, but we can record the category of video that was rented. BEC now has 87 different categories, so we can narrow down preferences quite a bit. For example, we don't have a single science fiction category. Instead, we have one category for Star Trek™ for all of the movies and for tapes of both original and "Next Generation" shows. We have another category for George Lucas movies, another category for science fiction movies from the '50s and '60s, and so on. Instead of a single category for action movies, we have Schwartzenegger movies, Stallone

Figure 1
Customer information form
for joining BEC

> ## BEC MEMBERSHIP INFORMATION
>
> Mr. Mrs. Ms. : _____
>
> Street Address: _____
>
> City: _____ State: _____ Zip: _____
>
> Telephone: (____) _____
>
> Credit Card Type: AE   MC   Visa   Discover
>
> Credit Card Number: _____
>
> Expiration Date: _____
>
> Social Security Number (optional): _____

movies, James Bond movies, Van Damme movies, etc. We are also allowed to keep a record of how many videos of each type a customer has rented.

Frank: What's the time period? Do you store totals per category for the month? For the year?

Wendy: By the month. We keep data on-line for two years and then we archive them. For the membership data, if someone has not been an active customer over a one-year period, we purge their records from our files. If they want to be a customer again, they have to reapply at their local BEC store.

Frank: What about other rentals, like video games?

Wendy: There are no laws that govern what we keep about the video games people rent, so we keep actual titles instead of categories and counts.

Frank: What about purchases, especially music?

Wendy: We keep a record of the titles customers purchase, whether the media is tape or CD.

Frank: What other kinds of information would you need to implement a system like the Customer Activity Tracking System that is proposed?

Wendy: Correct me if I'm wrong, but from what was in Nancy's memo announcing the project, from what she has told us in staff meetings, and from what I've read, one of the purposes of this system is to match customers with newly released products?

Frank: Yes, that's right.

Wendy: I think it would be helpful to get more customer information, such as income, education, age, those kinds of demographics. You have to understand the difference between what we do with this information now and what we would be doing with it in CATS. Right now, all we do is look at sales and rental trends over time. We want to know what types of products we should stock and in what quantities, at each store. You have to remember tastes vary by region of the country. We will sell a lot of Snoop Doggy Dogg CDs in Los Angeles but very few in Salt Lake City. But I'm digressing. When we use our customer information to determine what products we should be selling, we don't care about individuals. We only look at aggregates. For CATS, we **have** to focus on individuals. We have to know what each person's tastes are, but we also need to know how much product they can afford to buy. One other thing you might consider as part of this system is the frequency with which you send reminders to customers. For some customers, you might not want to send more than one notice per month. Some people have limited incomes and limited tastes in music. I mean, how often does Jimmy Buffett come out with a new album anyway? For others, like teenagers with lots of disposable income and wide musical tastes, you might want to send several notices per week.

Frank: That's a good suggestion. If you have any other ideas about CATS after the interview is over, please let me know. Let's see, we're almost done here. I just have a few questions left.

"This is all very useful information," Jordan said to Frank. "It sounds as if Wendy has a lot of good ideas we can use for CATS."

"Yeah," Frank said, "I think she can help us a lot. I have a follow-up interview with Wendy scheduled for next week; I wanted to talk with her in person to verify what I learned in our first interview and to ask some follow-up questions. I think Wendy will be someone we have to really satisfy to win approval for building the system. I understand that some of Nancy's direct reports are beginning to question the potential benefits of CATS. I think they fear that funding of CATS may lessen the chances for funding other marketing projects they want done. If we can convince Wendy of the system's value, this will give Nancy a strong advocate in her group. On another subject, I still haven't been able to find anything in the trade press about information systems similar to what we have in mind for CATS, but I did find this article on custom tailoring of catalogs."

"Oh, I saw that," said Jordan. "Maybe Jorge will find out more from the calls he's making to Lands' End, L.L. Bean, PowerUp!, and the other firms against which we are benchmarking." (Jorge Lopez is the other analyst assigned to the CATS project. Jorge has been with BEC for five years and has been responsible for developing many of the systems that support international operations.)

"I have a call in to one of the people mentioned in the article," Frank replied. "I want to see if they will send us some information on their system design, at least some charts used in training users, maybe some data flow diagrams. I talked to Jorge about this and he said I could go ahead and make the contact since I was so interested. I'll be sure to share what I get with him."

"What have you found out about product announcements from the record and video companies and about how we do product profiles?"

"Those were both on my list of questions for Wendy, but we ran out of time in the last interview. That's another reason I have the second interview with her scheduled. Jordan, I'm still surprised how talkative most of the BEC managers are. It's so difficult to keep them on the topic. I'll try to be a little more assertive in my next interview so that I get all questions covered to some degree. From the first interview, I think I got a pretty good idea about how customer profiles work, so I'm confident I'll be able to find out a lot of what we need to know about product announcements and product profiles."

"I think we're making good progress," said Jordan. "We already have one interview with Wendy in the can. We have the notes from the formal interview that we decided in our orientation meeting I ought to do with Nancy Chen, plus all of my notes from my many talks with her. We have copies of the customer information form they fill out to get BEC membership cards and you're going to get documents on customer and product profiles. We and Jorge have additional interviews scheduled with people who Nancy, Wendy, and others have suggested we meet, and you may be able to get some information on that catalog system. Did I tell you? Next week, I'm meeting with the managers of the seven BEC stores with the highest sales figures. One of them called Nancy after she distributed the project announcement memo and asked to meet with me. It will be a chance for me to understand their reactions to a system like CATS. You know, if implemented, CATS will put an additional burden on the store manager, since the initial conception makes them responsible for reserving merchandise for targeted customers."

"What about feedback?" asked Frank. "Does the current system conception make provisions for feedback? Don't we want to know if CATS works? If the customers we target actually do come in and either buy the records we have reserved for them or rent the tapes we set aside? Isn't that another burden for the store managers? More record keeping."

"That's a good point," Jordan said. "Look at the initial DFD Nancy and I presented to the Systems Priority Board (Figure 2). There is a reservation report on here, but that goes from the system to the stores. Make a note to remember that we'll probably need to add some flow from the stores back to CATS, or maybe we'll need to modify the Rental and Sales systems to capture this and note reservation sales differently in the transaction files. But I'm not sure exactly what changes would have to be made to our existing systems to accommodate the feedback function. It probably wouldn't entail much, if any, extra record keeping at the store level, but it definitely would affect existing systems. I'll ask the store managers about this when I talk with them. That reminds me. We really need someone else on this team who knows the existing related systems. Jorge knows the international systems, so he can help, but you and Jorge are really busy with

Figure 2
Level-0 data flow diagram
for the CATS project

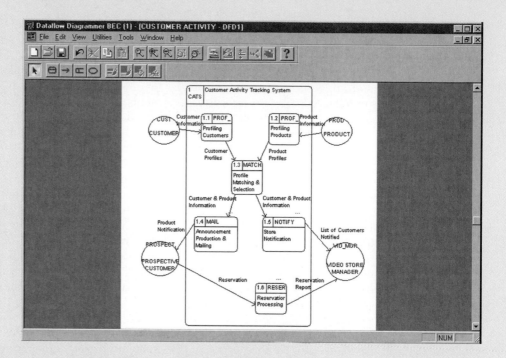

your other assignments. Nancy told me that she can allocate some extra money from her systems budget if the CATS analysis phase budget approved by the SPB comes up short. We can use that to 'borrow' somebody for a few weeks. Let me talk to Karen about it."

"Have you given any more thought to whether we need to have the tentatively scheduled JAD for requirements determination?" Frank asked. "Based on the initial information we have collected so far, I'm beginning to think a one- or two-day JAD really would be a good idea."

"You may be right," Jordan answered. "I'll talk to Karen about that, too. We'll make sure we get a professional JAD facilitator this time. After that rather hostile JAD you and I were part of about six months ago, didn't

you tell me there is a professor at Western Florida who might be able to train us on running JADs?"

SUMMARY

Requirements determination is progressing on the CATS project. Interviews, such as the one with Wendy Yoshimuro, yield much insight into possible system requirements and features. Soon Frank, Jorge, and Jordan will need to begin to structure what they have learned into a set of consistent and complete diagrams and descriptions of CATS. In the next BEC segment, we will see how the structuring of data movement and processing requirements can be presented.

Structuring System Requirements: Process Modeling

After studying this chapter, you should be able to:

- Understand the logical modeling of processes through studying examples of data flow diagrams.

- Draw data flow diagrams following specific rules and guidelines that lead to accurate and well-structured process models.

- Decompose data flow diagrams into lower-level diagrams.

- Balance higher-level and lower-level data flow diagrams.

- Explain the differences among four types of DFDs: current physical, current logical, new physical, and new logical.

- Use data flow diagrams as a tool to support the analysis of information systems.

INTRODUCTION

In the last chapter, you learned about various methods used by systems analysts to collect the information necessary to determine information systems requirements. In this chapter, our focus will be on one tool used to coherently represent the information gathered as part of requirements determination—data flow diagrams. Data flow diagrams allow you to model how data flow through an information system, the relationships among the data flows, and how data come to be stored at specific locations. Data flow diagrams also show the processes that change or transform data. Because data flow diagrams concentrate on the movement of data between processes, these diagrams are called process models.

As the name indicates, a data flow diagram is a graphical tool that allows analysts (and users, for that matter) to depict the flow of data in an information system. The system can be physical or logical, manual or computer-based. In this chapter, you will learn the basic mechanics of drawing and revising data flow diagrams and you will learn the basic symbols and a set of rules for drawing them. You will learn about what to do and what *not* to do when drawing data flow diagrams. You will learn two important concepts related to data flow diagrams: *balancing* and *decomposition*. You will also learn the differences between four different types of data flow diagrams: current physical, current logical, new logical, and new physical. Finally, at the end of the chapter, you will learn how to use data flow diagrams as part of the analysis of an information system and as a tool for supporting business process reengineering.

PROCESS MODELING

Data flow diagram:
A picture of the movement of data between external entities and the processes and data stores within a system.

Process modeling involves graphically representing the functions, or processes, which capture, manipulate, store, and distribute data between a system and its environment and between components within a system. A common form of a process model is a **data flow diagram.** Over the years, several different tools have been developed for process modeling. In this chapter, we focus solely on data flow diagrams, the traditional process modeling technique of structured analysis and design and the technique most often used today for process modeling.

Data flow diagramming is one of several notations that are called structured analysis techniques. Although not all organizations use each structured analysis technique, collectively techniques like data flow diagrams have had a significant impact on the quality of the systems development process. For example, Raytheon (Gibbs, 1994) has reported a savings from 1988 through 1994 of $17.2 million in software costs by applying structured analysis techniques, due mainly to avoiding rework to fix requirements flaws. This represents a doubling of systems developers' productivity and helped them avoid costly system mistakes.

Modeling a System's Process

As Figure 8-1 shows, there are three subphases of the analysis phase of the systems development life cycle: requirements determination, requirements structuring, and generating alternative systems and selecting the best one. The analysis team enters requirements structuring with an abundance of information gathered during requirements determination. During requirements structuring, you and the other team members must organize the information into a meaningful representation of the information system that exists and of the requirements desired in a replacement system. In addition to modeling the processing elements of an information system and how data are transformed in the system, you must also model the processing logic and the timing of events in the system (Chapter 9) and the structure of data within the system (Chapter 10). Thus, a process model is only one of three major complementary views of an information system. Together, process, logic and timing, and data models provide a thorough specification of an information system and, with the proper supporting tools, also provide the basis for the automatic generation of many working information system components.

Deliverables and Outcomes

In structured analysis, the primary deliverables from process modeling are a set of coherent, inter-related data flow diagrams. Table 8-1 provides a more detailed list of the deliverables that result from studying and documenting a system's process. First, a context diagram shows the scope of the system, indicating which elements are inside and which are outside the system. Second, data flow diagrams of the current physical system specify which people and technologies are used in which processes to move and transform data, accepting inputs and producing outputs. These diagrams are developed into sufficient detail to understand the current system and to eventually determine how to convert the current system into its replacement. Third, technology-independent, or logical, data flow diagrams of the

Figure 8-1
Systems development life cycle with the analysis phase highlighted

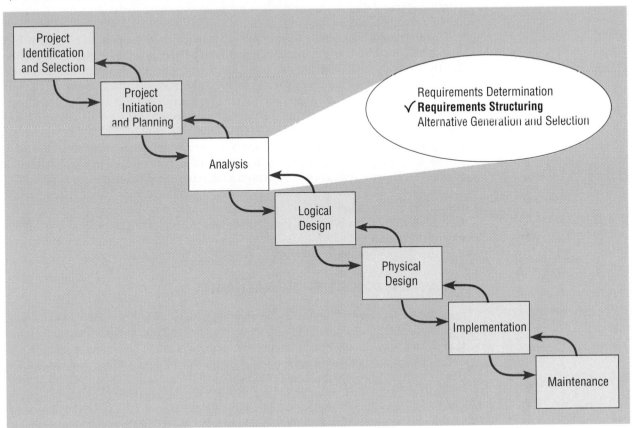

TABLE 8-1   Deliverables for Process Modeling
1. Context data flow diagram (DFD)
2. DFDs of current physical system (adequate detail only)
3. DFDs of current logical system
4. DFDs of new logical system
5. Thorough descriptions of each DFD component

current system show what data processing functions are performed by the current information system. Fourth, the data movement, or flow, structure, and functional requirements of the new system are represented in logical data flow diagrams. Finally, entries for all of the objects included in all diagrams are included in the project dictionary or CASE repository. This logical progression of deliverables allows you to understand the existing system. You can then abstract this system into its essential elements to show the way in which the new system should meet its information processing requirements identified during requirements determination. Remember, the deliverables of process modeling are simply stating *what* you learned during requirements determination; in later steps in the systems development life cycle, you and other project team members will make decisions on exactly *how* the new system will deliver these new requirements in specific manual and automated functions. Since requirements determination and structuring are often parallel steps, data flow diagrams evolve from the more general to the more detailed as current and replacement systems are better understood.

Even though data flow diagrams remain popular tools for process modeling and can significantly increase software development productivity, as reported above for Raytheon, data flow diagrams are not used in all systems development methodologies. Some organizations, like Electronic Data Systems, have developed their own type of diagrams to model processes. Some methodologies, such as Rapid Application Development (RAD), do not model process separately at all. Instead RAD builds process into the prototypes that are created as the core of its development life cycle (see Chapter 13). However, even if you never formally use data flow diagrams in your professional career, they remain a part of system development's history. DFDs give you a notation as well as illustrate important concepts about the movement of data between manual and automated steps and a way to depict work flow in an organization. DFDs continue to be beneficial to information systems professionals as tools for both analysis and communication. For that reason, we devote an entire chapter to DFDs.

DATA FLOW DIAGRAMMING MECHANICS

Data flow diagrams are versatile diagramming tools. With only four symbols, you can use data flow diagrams to represent both physical and logical information systems. Data flow diagrams (DFDs) are not as good as flow charts for depicting the details of physical systems; on the other hand, flow charts are not very useful for depicting purely logical information flows. In fact, flow charting has been criticized by proponents of structured analysis and structured design because it is too physically oriented. Flow charting symbols primarily represent physical computing equipment, such as punch cards, terminals, and tape reels. One continual criticism of system flow charts has been that reliance on them tends to result in premature physical system design. Consistent with the incremental commitment philosophy of the SDLC, you should wait to make technology choices and to decide on physical characteristics of an information system until you are sure all functional requirements are right and accepted by users and other stakeholders.

DFDs do not share this problem of premature physical design because they do not rely on any symbols to represent specific physical computing equipment. They are also easier to use than flow charts as they involve only four different symbols.

Definitions and Symbols

There are two different standard sets of data flow diagram symbols, but each set consists of four symbols that represent the same things: data flows, data stores, processes, and sources/sinks (or external entities). The set of symbols we will use in this book was devised by Gane and Sarson (1979). The other standard set was developed by DeMarco and Yourdon (DeMarco, 1979; Yourdon and Constantine, 1979).

A *data flow* can be best understood as data in motion, moving from one place in a system to another. A data flow could represent data on a customer order form or a payroll check. A data flow could also represent the results of a query to a database, the contents of a printed report, or data on a data entry computer display form. A data flow is data that move together. Thus, a data flow can be composed of many individual pieces of data that are generated at the same time and flow together to common destinations. A **data store** is data at rest. A data store may represent one of

Data store: Data at rest, which may take the form of many different physical representations.

many different physical locations for data, for example, a file folder, one or more computer-based file(s), or a notebook. To understand data movement and handling in a system, the physical configuration is not really important. A data store might contain data about customers, students, customer orders, or supplier invoices. A **process** is the work or actions performed on data so that they are transformed, stored, or distributed. When modeling the data processing of a system, it doesn't matter whether a process is performed manually or by a computer. Finally, a **source/sink** is the origin and/or destination of the data. Source/ sinks are sometimes referred to as external entities because they are outside the system. Once processed, data or information leave the system and go to some other place. Since sources and sinks are outside the system we are studying, there are many characteristics of sources and sinks that are of no interest to us. In particular, we do not consider the following:

- Interactions that occur between sources and sinks

- What a source or sink does with information or how it operates (that is, a source or sink is a "black box")

- How to control or redesign a source or sink since, from the perspective of the system we are studying, the data a sink receives and often what data a source provides are fixed

- How to provide sources and sinks direct access to stored data since, as external agents, they cannot directly access or manipulate data stored within the system; that is, processes within the system must receive or distribute data between the system and its environment

These principles are consistent with the concepts of system, boundaries, and environment presented in Chapter 2.

The symbols for each set of DFD conventions are presented in Figure 8-2. For both conventions, a data flow is depicted as an arrow. The arrow is labeled with a

Process: The work or actions performed on data so that they are transformed, stored, or distributed.

Source/sink: The origin and/or destination of data, sometimes referred to as external entities.

Figure 8-2
Comparison of DeMarco & Yourdan and Gane & Sarson DFD symbol sets

meaningful name for the data in motion; for example, customer order, sales receipt, or paycheck. The name represents the aggregation of all the individual elements of data moving as part of one packet, that is, all the data moving together at the same time. A square is used in both conventions for sources/sinks and has a name which states what the external agent is, such as customer, teller, EPA office, or inventory control system. The Gane & Sarson symbol for a process is a rectangle with rounded corners; it is a circle for DeMarco & Yourdon. The Gane & Sarson rounded rectangle has a line drawn through the top. The upper portion is used to indicate the number of the process. Inside the lower portion is a name for the process, such as generate paycheck, calculate overtime pay, or compute grade point average. The Gane & Sarson symbol for a data store is a rectangle that is missing its right vertical side. At the left end is a small box used to number the data store and inside the main part of the rectangle is a meaningful label for the data store, such as student file, transcripts, or roster of classes. The DeMarco data store symbol consists of two parallel lines, which may be depicted horizontally or vertically.

As stated earlier, sources/sinks are *always* outside the information system and define the boundaries of the system. Data must originate outside a system from one or more sources and the system must produce information to one or more sinks (these are principles of open systems, and almost every information system is an example of an open system). If any data processing takes place inside the source/ sink, we are not interested in it, as this processing takes place outside of the system we are diagramming. A source/sink might consist of the following:

- Another organization or organization unit which sends data to or receives information from the system you are analyzing (for example, a supplier or an academic department—in either case, this organization is external to the system you are studying)

- A person inside or outside the business unit supported by the system you are analyzing and who interacts with the system (for example, a customer or loan officer)

- Another information system with which the system you are analyzing exchanges information

Many times students who are just learning how to use DFDs will be confused about whether something is a source/sink or a process within a system. This dilemma occurs most often when the data flows in a system cross office or departmental boundaries so that some processing occurs in one office and the processed data is moved to another office where additional processing occurs. Students are tempted to identify the second office as a source/sink to emphasize the fact that the data have been moved from one physical location to another (Figure 8-3a). However, we are not concerned with where the data are physically located. We are more interested in how they are moving through the system and how they are being processed. If the processing of data in the other office may be automated by your system or the handling of data there may be subject for redesign, then you should represent the second office as one or more processes rather than as a source/sink (Figure 8-3b).

Developing DFDs: An Example

To illustrate how DFDs are used to model the logic of data flows in information systems, we will present and work through an example. Consider Hoosier Burger's

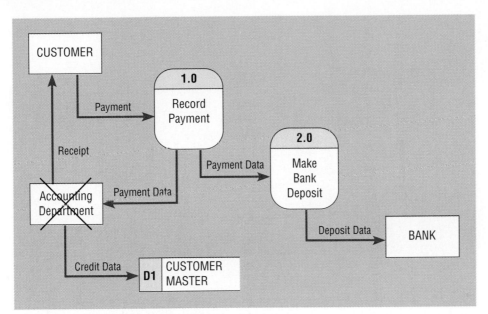

Figure 8-3
Differences between
sources/sinks and
processes

(a) An improperly drawn
DFD showing a process as
a source/sink

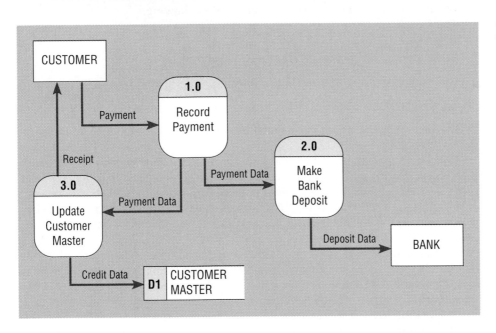

(b) A DFD showing proper
use of a process

food ordering system, which you first saw in Chapter 2. The highest-level view of
this system, a **context diagram,** is shown in Figure 8-4. You will notice that this context diagram contains only one process, no data stores, four data flows, and three
sources/sinks. The single process, labeled "0," represents the entire system; all context diagrams have only one process labeled "0." The sources/sinks represent its
environmental boundaries. Since the data stores of the system are conceptually inside the one process, no data stores appear on a context diagram.

The next step for the analyst is to think about which processes are represented
by the single process in the context diagram. As you can see in Figure 8-5, we

Context diagram: An overview of an organizational
system that shows the system
boundaries, external entities
that interact with the system,
and the major information
flows between the entities and
the system.

Figure 8-4
Context diagram of Hoosier
Burger's food ordering
system

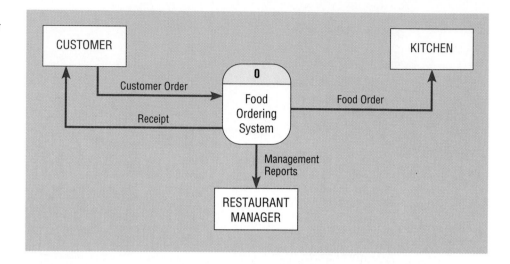

have identified four separate processes, providing more detail of the system we are studying. The main processes represent the major functions of the system and these major functions correspond to such actions as the following:

1. Capturing data from different sources (e.g., Process 1.0)

2. Maintaining data stores (e.g. Processes 2.0 and 3.0)

3. Producing and distributing data to different sinks (e.g., Process 4.0)

4. High-level descriptions of data transformation operations (e.g., Process 1.0).

Often, these major functions correspond to the selections of activities on the main system menu.

We see the system begins with an order from a customer, as was the case with the context diagram. In the first process, labeled "1.0," we see that the customer order is processed. The results are four streams or flows of data: (1) the food order is transmitted to the kitchen (2) the customer order is transformed into a list of goods sold (3) the customer order is transformed into inventory data and (4) the process generates a receipt for the customer.

Notice that the sources/sinks are the same in the context diagram and in this diagram: the customer, the kitchen, and the restaurant's manager. This diagram is called a **level-0 diagram** as it represents the primary individual processes in the system at the highest possible level. Each process has a number which ends in .0 (corresponding to the level number of the DFD).

Two of the data flows generated by the first process, "Receive and Transform Customer Food Order," go to external entities, so we no longer have to worry about them. We are not concerned about what happens outside of our system. Let's trace the flow of the data represented in the other two data flows. First, the data labeled Goods Sold goes to Process 2.0, Update Goods Sold File. The output for this process is labeled Formatted Goods Sold Data. This output updates a data store labeled Goods Sold File. If the customer order was for two cheeseburgers, one order of fries, and a large soft drink, each of these categories of goods sold in the data store would be incremented appropriately. The daily goods sold amounts are then used as input to Process 4.0, Produce Management Reports. Similarly, the remaining data flow generated by Process 1.0, called Inventory Data, serves as input for Process 3.0, Update Inventory File. This process updates the Inventory File data store, based

Level-0 diagram: A data
flow diagram that represents
a system's major processes,
data flows, and data stores at
a high level of detail.

on the inventory that would have been used to create the customer order. For example, an order of two cheeseburgers would mean that Hoosier Burger now has two fewer hamburger patties, two fewer burger buns, and four fewer slices of American cheese. The Daily Inventory Depletion Amounts are then used as input to Process 4. The data flow leaving Process 4.0, Management Reports, goes to the sink Restaurant Manager.

Figure 8-5 illustrates several important concepts about information movement. Consider the data flow Inventory Data moving from Process 1.0 to Process 3.0. We know from this diagram that Process 1.0 produces this data flow and that Process 3.0 receives it. However, we do not know the timing of when this data flow is produced, how frequently it is produced, or what volume of data is sent. Thus, this DFD hides many physical characteristics of the system it describes. We do know, however, that this data flow is needed by Process 3.0 and that Process 1.0 provides this needed data.

Also implied by the Inventory Data data flow is that whenever Process 1.0 produces this flow, Process 3.0 must be ready to accept it. Thus, Processes 1.0 and 3.0 are coupled to each other. In contrast, consider the link between Process 2.0 and Process 4.0. The output from Process 2.0, Formatted Goods Sold Data, is placed in a data store and, later, when Process 4.0 needs such data, it reads Daily Goods Sold Amounts from this data store. In this case, Processes 2.0 and 4.0 are decoupled by placing a buffer, a data store, between them. Now, each of these processes can work

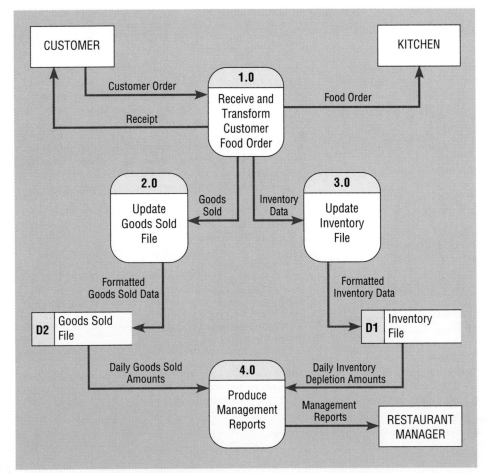

Figure 8-5
Level-0 DFD of Hoosier Burger's food ordering system

at their own pace and Process 4.0 does not have to be vigilant by being able to accept input at any time. Further, the Goods Sold File becomes a data resource that other processes could potentially draw upon for data.

Data Flow Diagramming Rules

There is a set of rules you must follow when drawing data flow diagrams. Unlike system flow charts, these rules allow you (or a CASE tool) to evaluate DFDs for correctness. The rules for DFDs are listed in Table 8-2. Figure 8-6 illustrates incorrect ways to draw DFDs and the corresponding correct application of the rules. The rules that prescribe naming conventions (rules C, G, I, and P) and those that explain how to interpret data flows in and out of data stores (rules N and O) are not illustrated in Figure 8-6.

Besides the rules of Table 8-2, there are two DFD guidelines that apply most of the time:

- *The inputs to a process are different from the outputs of that process:* The reason is that processes, to have a purpose, typically transform inputs into outputs, rather than simply pass the data through without some manipulation. What may happen is that the same input goes in and out of a process but the process also produces other new data flows that are the result of manipulating the inputs.

TABLE 8-2   Rules Governing Data Flow Diagramming

Process:

A. No process can have only outputs. It is making data from nothing (a miracle). If an object has only outputs, then it must be a source.

B. No process can have only inputs (a black hole). If an object has only inputs, then it must be a sink.

C. A process has a verb phrase label.

Data Store:

D. Data cannot move directly from one data store to another data store. Data must be moved by a process.

E. Data cannot move directly from an outside source to a data store. Data must be moved by a process which receives data from the source and places the data into the data store.

F. Data cannot move directly to an outside sink from a data store. Data must be moved by a process.

G. A data store has a noun phrase label.

Source/Sink:

H. Data cannot move directly from a source to a sink. It must be moved by a process if the data are of any concern to our system. Otherwise, the data flow is not shown on the DFD.

I. A source/sink has a noun phrase label.

Data Flow:

J. A data flow has only one direction of flow between symbols. It may flow in both directions between a process and a data store to show a read before an update. The latter is usually indicated, however, by two separate arrows since these happen at different times.

K. A fork in a data flow means that exactly the same data goes from a common location to two or more different processes, data stores, or sources/sinks (this usually indicates different copies of the same data going to different locations).

L. A join in a data flow means that exactly the same data comes from any of two or more different processes, data stores, or sources/sinks to a common location.

M. A data flow cannot go directly back to the same process it leaves. There must be at least one other process which handles the data flow, produces some other data flow, and returns the original data flow to the beginning process.

N. A data flow to a data store means update (delete or change).

O. A data flow from a data store means retrieve or use.

P. A data flow has a noun phrase label. More than one data flow noun phrase can appear on a single arrow as long as all of the flows on the same arrow move together as one package.

Adapted from Celko, 1987

Figure 8-6
Incorrect and correct ways
to draw data flow diagrams

- *Objects on a DFD have unique names:* Every process has a unique name. There is no reason to have two processes with the same name. To keep a DFD uncluttered, however, you may repeat data stores and sources/sinks. When two arrows have the same data flow name, you must be careful that these flows are exactly the same. It is easy to reuse the same data flow name when two packets of data are almost the same, but not identical. A data flow name represents a specific set of data, and another data flow that has even one more or one less piece of data must be given a different, unique name.

Decomposition of DFDs

Functional decomposition: An iterative process of breaking the description of a system down into finer and finer detail which creates a set of charts in which one process on a given chart is explained in greater detail on another chart.

In the earlier example of Hoosier Burger's food ordering system, we started with a high-level context diagram. Upon thinking more about the system, we saw that the larger system consisted of four processes. The act of going from a single system to four component processes is called *(functional) decomposition*. **Functional decomposition** is an iterative process of breaking the description or perspective of a system down into finer and finer detail. This process creates a set of hierarchically related charts in which one process on a given chart is explained in greater detail on another chart. For the Hoosier Burger system, we broke down or decomposed the larger system into four processes. Each of those processes (or subsystems) are also candidates for decomposition. Each process may consist of several sub-processes. Each sub-process may also be broken down into smaller units. Decomposition continues until you have reached the point where no sub-process can logically be broken down any further. The lowest level of DFDs is called a *primitive DFD,* which we define later in this chapter.

Let's continue with Hoosier Burger's food ordering system to see how a level-0 DFD can be further decomposed. The first process in Figure 8-5, called Receive and Transform Customer Food Order, transforms a customer's verbal food order (for example, "Give me two cheeseburgers, one small order of fries, and one regular orange soda.") into four different outputs. Process 1.0 is a good candidate process for decomposition. Think about all of the different tasks that Process 1.0 has to perform: (1) receive a customer order (2) transform the entered order into a form meaningful for the kitchen's system (3) transform the order into a printed receipt for the customer (4) transform the order into goods sold data (5) transform the order into inventory data. There are at least these five logically separate functions that occur in Process 1.0. We can represent the decomposition of Process 1.0 as another DFD, as shown in Figure 8-7.

Note that each of the five processes in Figure 8-7 are labeled as sub-processes of Process 1.0: Process 1.1, Process 1.2, and so on. Also note that, just as with the other data flow diagrams we have looked at, each of the processes and data flows are named. You will also notice that there are no sources or sinks represented. Although you may include sources and sinks, the context and level-0 diagrams show the sources and sinks. The data flow diagram in Figure 8-7 is called a level-1 diagram. If we should decide to decompose Processes 2.0, 3.0, or 4.0 in a similar manner, the DFDs we create would also be called level-1 diagrams. In general, a **level-*n* diagram** is a DFD that is generated from *n* nested decompositions from a level-0 diagram.

Level-*n* diagram: A DFD that is the result of *n* nested decompositions of a series of sub-processes from a process on a level-0 diagram.

Processes 2.0 and 3.0 perform similar functions in that they both use data input to update data stores. Since updating a data store is a singular logical function, neither of these processes need to be decomposed further. We can, on the other hand, decompose Process 4.0, Produce Management Reports, into at least three sub-processes: Access Goods Sold and Inventory Data, Aggregate Goods Sold and

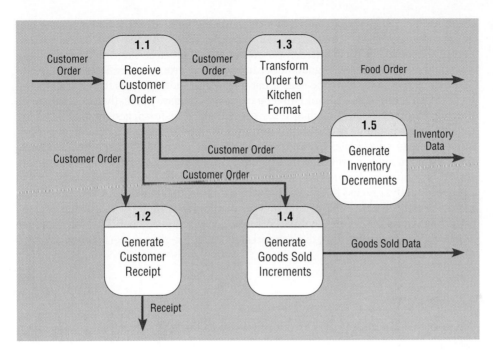

Figure 8-7
Level-1 diagram showing the decomposition of Process 1.0 from the level-0 diagram for Hoosier Burger's food ordering system

Inventory Data, and Prepare Management Reports. The decomposition of Process 4.0 is shown in the level-1 diagram of Figure 8-8.

Each level-1, -2, or -n DFD represents one process on a level-n-1 DFD; each DFD should be on a separate page. As a rule of thumb, no DFD should have more than about seven processes in it, as too many processes will make the diagram too crowded and more difficult to understand.

To continue with the decomposition of Hoosier Burger's food ordering system, we examine each of the sub-processes identified in the two level-1 diagrams we have produced, one for Process 1.0 and one for Process 4.0. Should we decide that any of

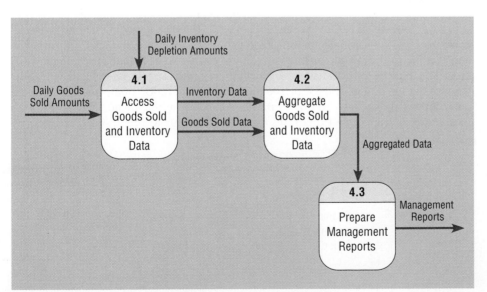

Figure 8-8
Level-1 diagram showing the decomposition of Process 4.0 from the level-0 diagram for Hoosier Burger's food ordering system

these sub-processes should be further decomposed, we would create a level-2 diagram showing that decomposition. For example, if we decided that Process 4.3 in Figure 8-8 should be further decomposed, we would create a diagram that looks like something like Figure 8-9. Again, notice how the sub-processes are labeled.

Just as the labels for processes must follow numbering rules for clear communication, process names should also be clear yet concise. Typically, process names begin with an action verb, such as receive, calculate, transform, generate, or produce. Often process names are the same as the verbs used in many computer programming languages. Examples include merge, sort, read, write, and print. Process names should capture the essential action of the process in just a few words, yet be descriptive enough of the process' action so that anyone reading the name gets a good idea of what the process does. Many times, students just learning DFDs will use the names of people who perform the process or the department in which the process is performed as the process name. This practice is not very useful, as we are more interested in the action the process represents than the person performing it or the place where it occurs.

Balancing DFDs

Balancing: The conservation of inputs and outputs to a data flow diagram process when that process is decomposed to a lower level.

When you decompose a DFD from one level to the next, there is a conservation principle at work. You must conserve inputs and outputs to a process at the next level of decomposition. In other words, Process 1.0, which appears in a level-0 diagram, must have the same inputs and outputs when decomposed into a level-1 diagram. This conservation of inputs and outputs is called **balancing.**

Let's look at an example of balancing a set of DFDs. Look back at Figure 8-4. This is the context diagram for Hoosier Burger's food ordering system. Notice that there is one input to the system, the customer order, which originates with the customer. Notice also that there are three outputs: the customer receipt, the food order intended for the kitchen, and management reports. Now look at Figure 8-5. This is the level-0 diagram for the food ordering system. Remember that all data stores and flows to or from them are internal to the system. Notice that the same single input to the system and the same three outputs represented in the context diagram also appear at level-0. Further, no new inputs to or outputs from the system have been introduced. Therefore, we can say that the context diagram and level-0 DFDs are balanced.

Now look at Figure 8-7, where Process 1.0 from the level-0 DFD has been decomposed. As we have seen before, Process 1.0 has one input and four outputs. The single input and multiple outputs all appear on the level-1 diagram in Figure 8-7. No new inputs or outputs have been added. Compare Process 4.0 in Figure 8-5 to its decomposition in Figure 8-8. You see the same conservation of inputs and outputs.

Figure 8-10 shows you one example of what an unbalanced DFD could look like. Here, in the context diagram, there is one input to the system, A, and one

Figure 8-9
Level-2 diagram showing the decomposition of Process 4.3 from the level-1 diagram for Process 4.0 for Hoosier Burger's food ordering system

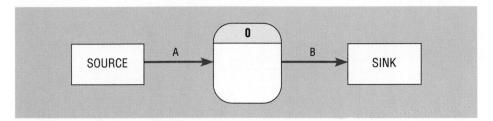

Figure 8-10
An unbalanced set of data
flow diagrams

(a) Context diagram

(b) Level-0 diagram

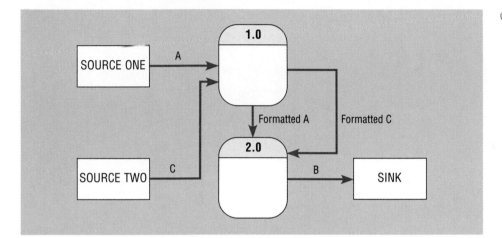

output, B. Yet, in the level-0 diagram, there is an additional input, C, and flows A and C come from different sources. These two DFDs are not balanced. If an input appears on a level-0 diagram, it must also appear on the context diagram. What happened in this example? Perhaps, when drawing the level-0 DFD, the analyst realized that the system also needed C in order to compute B. A and C were both drawn in the level-0 DFD, but the analyst forgot to update the context diagram. In making corrections, the analyst should also include "SOURCE ONE" and "SOURCE TWO" on the context diagram. It is very important to keep DFDs balanced, from the context diagram all the way through each level diagram you must create.

A data flow consisting of several sub-flows on a level-n diagram can be split apart on a level-$n+1$ diagram for a process which accepts this composite data flow as input. For example, consider the partial DFDs from Hoosier Burger illustrated in Figure 8-11. In Figure 8-11a we see that a composite, or package, data flow, Payment and Coupon, is input to the process. That is, the payment and coupon always flow together and are input to the process at the same time. In Figure 8-11b the process is decomposed (sometimes called exploded or nested) into two sub-processes, and each sub-process receives one of the components of the composite data flow from the higher-level DFD. These diagrams are still balanced since exactly the same data are included in each diagram.

The principle of balancing and the goal of keeping a DFD as simple as possible lead to four additional, advanced rules for drawing DFDs. These advanced rules are summarized in Table 8-3. Rule Q covers the situation illustrated in Figure 8-11. Rule R covers a conservation principle about process inputs and outputs. Rule S addresses one exception to balancing. Rule T tells you how you can minimize clutter on a DFD.

Figure 8-11
Example of data flow
splitting

(a) Composite data flow

(b) Disaggregated data flows

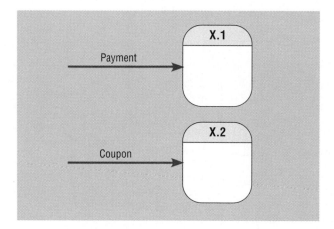

TABLE 8-3   Advanced Rules Governing Data Flow Diagramming
Q. A composite data flow on one level can be split into component data flows at the next level, but no new data can be added and all data in the composite must be accounted for in one or more sub-flows.
R. The inputs to a process must be sufficient to produce the outputs (including data placed in data stores) from the process. Thus, all outputs can be produced, and all data in inputs move somewhere, either to another process or to a data store outside the process or on a more detailed DFD showing a decomposition of that process.
S. At the lowest level of DFDs, new data flows may be added to represent data that are transmitted under exceptional conditions; these data flows typically represent error messages (e.g., "Customer not known; do you want to create a new customer") or confirmation notices (e.g., "Do you want to delete this record").
T. To avoid having data flow lines cross each other, you may repeat data stores or sources/sinks on a DFD. Use an additional symbol, like a double line on the middle vertical line of a data store symbol, or a diagonal line in a corner of a sink/source square, to indicate a repeated symbol.

Adapted from Celko, 1987

FOUR DIFFERENT TYPES OF DFDS

There are actually four different types of data flow diagrams used in the systems development process: (1) current physical (2) current logical (3) new logical (4) new physical. When structured analysis and design was first introduced in the late 1970s, it was argued that analysts should prepare all four types of DFDs, in this particular order.

In a current physical DFD, process labels include the names of people or their positions or the names of computer systems that might provide some of the overall system's processing. That is, the label includes an identification of the "technology" used to process the data. Similarly, data flows and data stores are often labeled with the names of the actual physical media on which data flow or in which data are stored, such as file folders, computer files, business forms, or computer tapes. For the current logical model, the physical aspects of the system are removed as much as possible so that the current system is reduced to its essence, to the data and the processes that transform them, regardless of actual physical form. The new logical model would be exactly like the current logical model if the user were completely happy with the functionality of the current system but had problems with how it was implemented. Typically, though, the new logical model will differ from the current logical model by having additional functions, obsolete functions removed, and inefficient flows reorganized. Finally, the DFDs for the new physical system represent the physical implementation of the new system. The DFDs for the new physical system will reflect the decision of the analysts about which system functions, including those added in the new logical model, will be automated and which will be manual.

To illustrate the differences among the different types of DFDs, we will look at another example from Hoosier Burger. We saw that the food ordering system generates two types of usage data, for goods sold and for inventory. At the end of each day, the manager, Bob Mellankamp, generates the inventory report which tells him how much inventory should have been used for each item associated with sales. The amounts shown on the inventory report are just one input to a largely manual inventory control system Bob uses every day. Figure 8-12 lists the steps involved in Bob's inventory control system.

The data flow diagrams that model the current physical system are shown in Figure 8-13. The context diagram (Figure 8-13a) shows three sources of data outside the system: suppliers, the food ordering system inventory report, and stock-on-hand. Suppliers provide invoices as input, and the system returns payments and orders as outputs to the suppliers. Both the inventory report and the stock-on-hand provide inventory counts as system inputs. The level-0 DFD for Hoosier Burger's inventory system (Figure 8-13b) shows six different processes, most of which also appear in the list of inventory activities in Figure 8-12. You can see from the diagram that when Bob receives invoices from suppliers, he records their receipt on an invoice log sheet and files the actual invoices in his accordion file. Using the invoices, Bob records the amount of stock delivered on the stock logs, which are

---

1. Meet delivery trucks before opening restaurant.

2. Unload and store deliveries.

3. Log invoices and file in accordion file.

4. Manually add amounts received to stock logs.

5. After closing, print inventory report.

6. Count physical inventory amounts.

7. Compare inventory report totals to physical count totals.

8. Compare physical count totals to minimum order quantities; if the amount is less, make order; if not, do nothing.

9. Pay bills that are due and record them as paid.

Figure 8-12
List of activities involved in Bob Mellankamp's inventory control system for Hoosier Burger

paper forms posted near the point of storage for each inventory item. Figure 8-13 also illustrates that a physical DFD shows only data movement, not the movement of materials or other physical items (e.g., energy). Data about physical items such as an Invoice which is data about a shipment to Hoosier Burger, are shown on a physical DFD; the data about a physical item may or may not move with the actual physical item.

Figure 8-13
Hoosier Burger's current physical inventory control system

(a) Context diagram

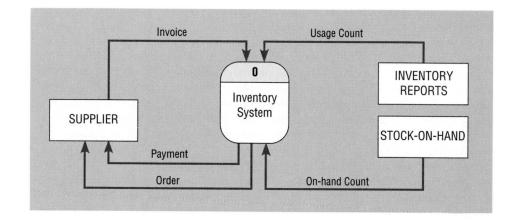

(b) Level-0 data flow diagram

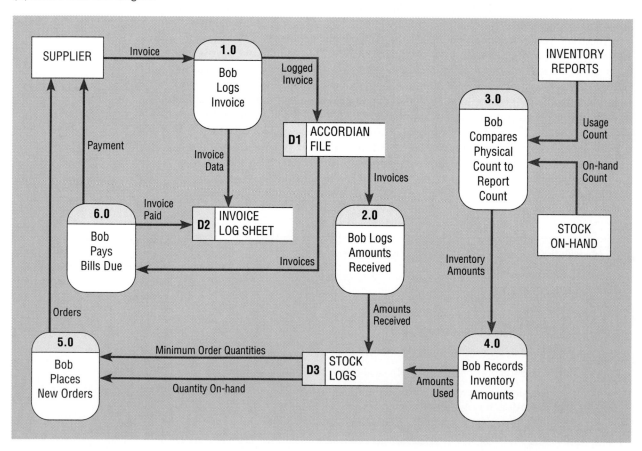

Figure 8-14 gives a partial example of Hoosier Burger's stock log. Notice that the minimum order quantities—the stock level at which orders must be placed in order to avoid running out of an item—appear on the log form. There are also spaces for entering the starting amount, amount delivered, and the amount used for each item. Amounts delivered are entered on the sheet when Bob logs stock deliveries; amounts used are entered after Bob has compared the amounts of stock used according to a physical count and according to the numbers on the inventory report generated by the food ordering system. We should note that Hoosier Burger has standing daily delivery orders for some perishable items that are used every day, like burger buns, meats, and vegetables.

As the DFD in Figure 8-13b shows, Bob uses the minimum order quantities and the amount of stock on hand to determine which orders need to be placed. He uses the invoices to determine which bills need to be paid, and he carefully records each payment.

To continue to the next step, creating the current logical model using DFDs, we need to identify the essence of the inventory system Bob has established. What are the key data necessary to keep track of inventory and to pay bills? What are the key processes involved? We also need to remove all elements of the physical system, such as Bob and the physical file folders he uses. There are at least four key processes that make up the Hoosier Burger's inventory system: (1) account for anything added to inventory (2) account for anything taken from inventory (3) place orders (4) pay bills. Key data used by the system include inventories and stock-on-hand counts, however determined. Major outputs from the system continue to be orders and payments. Focusing on the essential elements of the system results in the DFD for the current logical system shown in Figure 8-15.

The purpose of the new logical DFD is (1) to show any additional functionality necessary in the new system (2) to indicate which, if any, obsolete components have been eliminated, and (3) to describe any changes in the logical flow of data between system components, including different data stores. For Hoosier Burger's inventory system, Bob Mellankamp would like to add three additional functions. First, Bob would like data on new shipments to be entered into an automated system, thus doing away with paper stock log sheets. Bob would like shipment data to be as current as possible by being entered into the system as soon as the new stock arrives at the restaurant. Second, Bob would like the system to determine automatically

Figure 8-14

Hoosier Burger's stock log form

Stock Log					
Date:		**Jan 1**			**Jan 2**
	Reorder	Starting	Amount	Amount	Starting
Item	*Quantity*	Amount	Delivered	Used	Amount
Hamburger buns	50 dozen	5	50	43	12
Hot dog buns	25 dozen	0	25	22	3
English muffins	10 dozen	6	10	12	4
Napkins	2 cases	10	0	2	8
Straws	1 case	1	0	1	0

Figure 8-15
Level-0 data flow diagram for Hoosier Burger's current logical inventory control system

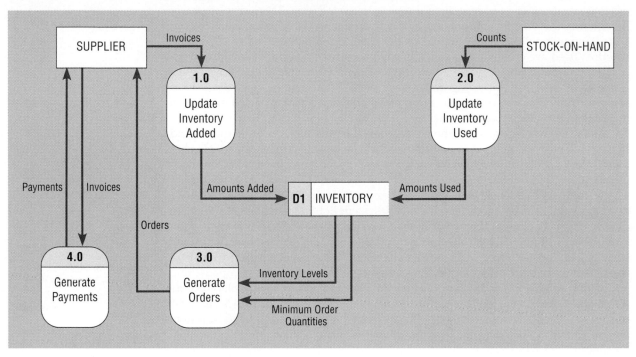

whether a new order should be placed. Automatic ordering would relieve Bob of worrying about whether Hoosier Burger has enough of everything in stock at all times. Finally, Bob would like to be able to know, at any time, the approximate inventory levels for all goods in stock. For some goods, such as hamburger buns, Bob can visually inspect the amount in stock and determine approximately how much is left and how much more is needed before closing time. For other items, however, Bob may need a quick, rough estimate of what is in stock more quickly than it would take him to do a visual inspection.

The new logical data flow diagram for Hoosier Burger's inventory system is shown in Figure 8-16. Notice how the DFD is almost identical to the DFD for current logical, in Figure 8-15. The only difference is a new Process 5.0, which allows for querying the inventory data to get an estimate of how much of an item is in stock. Bob's two other requests for change can both be handled within the existing logical view of the inventory system. Process 1.0, Update Inventory Added, does not indicate whether the updates are in real-time or batched or whether the updates occur on paper or as part of an automated system. Therefore, immediately entering shipment data into an automated system is encompassed by Process 1.0. Similarly, Process 2.0, Generate Orders, does not indicate whether Bob or a computer generates orders or whether the orders are generated on a real-time or batch basis, so Bob's request that orders be generated automatically by the system is already represented by Process 3.0. The next step would be to create a data flow diagram for the new physical system to represent the requests Bob has made. That step will be deferred, however, until several alternative solutions to Bob's inventory problems have been considered in Chapter 11.

You may be asking if it is really necessary for an analyst to construct not just one but four complete sets of data flow diagrams for each system on which he or

Figure 8-16
Level-0 data flow diagram for Hoosier Burger's new logical inventory control system

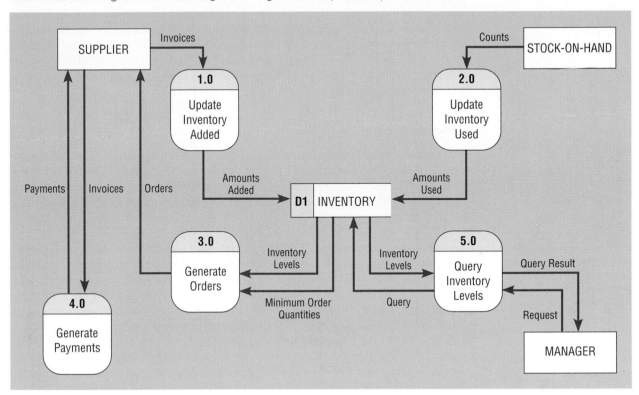

she works. Many experts today say no, it is not necessary, that analysts should begin as quickly as possible with the new logical DFD. Experts used to recommend that all four levels of DFDs be constructed because of three assumptions:

1. Analysts knew little about the user's business and needed to develop a detailed current physical DFD in order to understand the business.

2. Users were not able to work with a new logical DFD right away.

3. There is not much work in turning current logical DFDs into new logical DFDs.

These assumptions proved to be correct (Yourdon, 1989) but overlooked a greater danger: analysts tended to devote a great deal of time to creating and refining a detailed set of DFDs for the current physical system, most of which was thrown away in the transition to the current logical DFDs. We recommend that you create a set of DFDs for the current physical system but that those DFDs only be detailed enough so that you come away with a good overview of the current system. We agree with the experts that the focus should be on the new logical system.

USING DATA FLOW DIAGRAMMING IN THE ANALYSIS PROCESS

Learning the mechanics of drawing data flow diagrams is important to you, as data flow diagrams have proven to be essential tools for the structured analysis process.

Beyond the issues of drawing mechanically correct DFDs, there are other issues related to process modeling with which you as an analyst must be concerned. Such issues, including whether the DFDs are complete and consistent across levels, are dealt with in the next section on guidelines for drawing DFDs. Another issue to consider is how you can use data flow diagrams as a useful tool for analysis, discussed in the final section of the chapter. In these final sections, we also illustrate features of CASE tools that aid in compliance with rules and guidelines, as well as in good systems analysis.

Guidelines for Drawing DFDs

In this section, we will consider additional guidelines for drawing DFDs that extend beyond the simple mechanics of drawing diagrams and making sure that the rules listed in Tables 8-2 and 8-3 are followed. These guidelines include (1) completeness (2) consistency (3) timing considerations (4) the iterative nature of drawing DFDs, and (5) drawing primitive DFDs.

DFD completeness: The extent to which all necessary components of a data flow diagram have been included and fully described.

Completeness   The concept of **DFD completeness** refers to whether you have included in your DFDs all of the components necessary for the system you are modeling. If your DFD contains data flows that do not lead anywhere, or data stores, processes, or external entities that are not connected to anything else, your DFD is not complete. Most CASE tools have built-in facilities that you can run to help you find incompleteness in your DFDs. For example, Figure 8-17a shows a draft of a DFD from Oracle's Designer/2000 CASE tool for the process Bob Mellankamp follows to hire new employees for Hoosier Burger. Figure 8-17b shows an analysis report that a CASE tool would generate indicating the three errors of completeness found on this DFD. Did you identify all the same errors found by the CASE tool? To which of the rules in Tables 8-2 and 8-3 are these errors associated? When you draw many DFDs for a system, it is not uncommon to make errors like those in Figure 8-17; either CASE tool analysis functions or walkthroughs with other analysts can help you identify such problems.

Not only must all necessary elements of a DFD be present, each of the components must be fully described in the project dictionary. With most CASE tools, the project dictionary is linked to the diagram. That is, when you define a process, data flow, source/sink, or data store on a DFD, an entry is automatically created in the repository for that element. You must then enter the repository and complete the element's description. Different descriptive information can be kept about each of the four types of elements on a DFD, and each CASE tool or project dictionary standard an organization adopts has different entry information. Figure 8-18 shows a display of the contents of the Oracle Designer/2000 repository entry for the Request for Reference data flow on Figure 8-17. This data flow repository entry includes

- The label or name (e.g., Request for Reference) for the data flow as entered on DFDs (*Note:* Case and punctuation of the label matter, but if exactly the same label is used on multiple DFDs, whether nested or not, then the same repository entry applies to each reference.)

- A short description defining the data flow

- A list of other repository objects grouped into categories by type of object

- The composition or list of data elements contained in the data flow

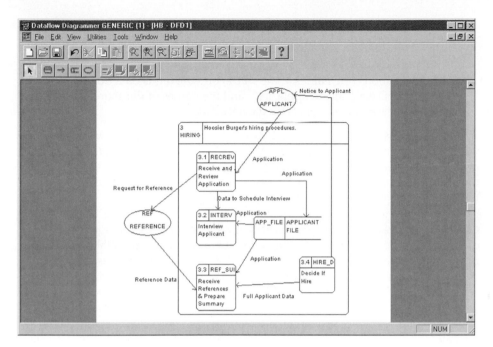

Figure 8-17
Hoosier Burger's hiring procedures

(a) Data flow diagram

DFD Analysis Errors [Project 'S330']
Error: Process labeled 'Interview Applicant' is an input only Process.
Error: Process labeled 'Receive References & Prepare Summary' is an input only Process.
Error: Process labeled 'Decide If Hire' is an output only Process.

(b) Analysis of completeness report from CASE tool

Figure 8-18
Repository entry for a data flow

- Notes supplementing the limited space for the description which go beyond defining the data flow to explaining the context and nature of this repository object

- A list of locations (the names of the DFDs) on which this data flow appears (e.g., the DFD was called "applicant") and the names of the sources and destinations on each of these DFDs for the data flow

By the way, it is this tight linkage between diagrams and the CASE repository which creates much of the value of a CASE tool. Although very sophisticated drawing tools as well as forms and word processing systems exist, these stand-alone tools do not integrate graphical objects with their textual descriptions as CASE tools do.

DFD consistency: The extent to which information contained on one level of a set of nested data flow diagrams is also included on other levels.

Consistency   The concept of **DFD consistency** refers to whether or not the depiction of the system shown at one level of a nested set of DFDs is compatible with the depictions of the system shown at other levels. A gross violation of consistency would be a level-1 diagram with no level-0 diagram. Another example of inconsistency would be a data flow that appears on a higher level DFD but not on lower levels (a violation of balancing). Yet another example of inconsistency is a data flow attached to one object on a lower level diagram but attached to another object at a higher level. For example, a data flow named "Payment," which serves as input to Process 1 on a level-0 DFD, appears as input to Process 2.1 on a level-1 diagram for Process 2.

CASE tools also have analysis facilities you can use to detect such inconsistencies across nested data flow diagrams. For example, to help you avoid making DFD consistency errors when you draw a DFD using a CASE tool, most tools will automatically place the inflows and outflows of a process on the DFD you create when you inform the tool to decompose that process. In manipulating the lower-level diagram, you could accidentally delete or change a data flow which would cause the diagrams to be out of balance; thus, a consistency check facility with a CASE tool is quite helpful.

Timing   You may have noticed in some of the DFD examples we have presented that DFDs do not do a very good job of representing time. On a given DFD, there is no indication of whether a data flow occurs constantly in real-time, once per week, or once per year. There is also no indication of when a system would run. For example, many large transaction-based systems may run several large, computing-intensive jobs in batch mode at night, when demands on the computer system are lighter. A DFD has no way of indicating such overnight batch processing. When you draw DFDs, then, draw them as if the system you are modeling has never started and will never stop. You will learn in Chapter 12 that another type of diagram, a state-transition diagram, is used to show the timing of processes associated with a system.

Iterative Development   The first DFD you draw will rarely capture perfectly the system you are modeling. You should count on drawing the same diagram over and over again, in an iterative fashion. With each attempt, you will come closer to a good approximation of the system or aspect of the system you are modeling. Iterative DFD development recognizes that requirements determination and requirements structuring are interacting, not sequential sub-phases of the analysis phase of the SDLC. One rule of thumb is that it should take you about three revisions for each DFD you draw. Fortunately, CASE tools make revising drawings a lot easier than it would be if you had to draw each revision with pencil and template.

Primitive DFDs One of the more difficult decisions you need to make when drawing DFDs is when to stop decomposing processes. One rule is to stop drawing when you have reached the lowest logical level; however, it is not always easy to know what the lowest logical level is. Other more concrete rules for when to stop decomposing are

- When you have reduced each process to a single decision or calculation or to a single database operation, such as retrieve, update, create, delete, or read

- When each data store represents data about a single entity, such as a customer, employee, product, or order

- When the system user does not care to see any more detail, or when you and other analysts have documented sufficient detail to do subsequent systems development tasks

- When every data flow does not need to be split further to show that different data are handled in different ways

- When you believe that you have shown each business form or transaction, computer on-line display, and report as a single data flow (This often means, for example, that each system display and report title corresponds to the name of an individual data flow)

- When you believe there is a separate process for each choice on all lowest-level menu options for the system

Obviously, the iteration guideline discussed earlier and the various feedback loops in the SDLC (see Figure 8-1) suggest that when you think you have met the above rules for stopping, you may later discover nuances to the system that require you to further decompose a set of DFDs.

By the time you stop decomposing DFDs, a DFD can become quite detailed. Seemingly simple actions, such as generating an invoice, may pull information from several entities and may also return different results depending on the specific situation. For example, the final form of an invoice may be based on the type of customer (which would determine such things as discount rate), where the customer lives (which would determine such things as sales tax), and how the goods are shipped (which would determine such things as the shipping and handling charges). At the lowest level DFD, called a **primitive DFD,** all of these conditions would have to be met. Given the amount of detail called for in a primitive DFD, perhaps you can see why many experts believe analysts should not spend their time completely diagramming the current physical information system as much of the detail will be discarded when the current logical DFD is created.

Primitive DFD: The lowest level of decomposition for a data flow diagram.

Using these guidelines will help you create DFDs that are more than just mechanically correct. Your data flow diagrams will also be robust and accurate representations of the information system you are modeling. Such primitive DFDs also facilitate consistency checks with the documentation produced from other requirements structuring techniques as well as make it easy for you to transition to system design steps. Having mastered the skills of drawing good DFDs, you can now use them to support the analysis process, the subject of the next section.

Using DFDs as Analysis Tools

We have seen that data flow diagrams are versatile tools for process modeling and that they can be used to model systems that are either physical or logical, current or new. Data flow diagrams can also be used in analysis for a process called *gap analysis.*

In gap analysis, the role of the analyst is to discover discrepancies between two or more sets of data flow diagrams, representing two or more states of an information system, or discrepancies within a single DFD.

Once the DFDs are complete, you can examine the details of individual DFDs for such problems as redundant data flows, data that are captured but are not used by the system, and data that are updated identically in more than one location. These problems may not have been evident to members of the analysis team or to other participants in the analysis process when the DFDs were created. For example, redundant data flows may have been labeled with different names when the DFDs were created. Now that the analysis team knows more about the system they are modeling, analysts can detect such redundancies. Such redundancies can be seen most easily from various CASE tool repository reports. For example, many CASE tools can generate a report listing all the processes that accept a given data element as input (remember, a list of data elements is likely part of the description of each data flow). From the label of these processes you can determine whether or not it appears as if the data are captured redundantly or if more than one process is maintaining the same data stores. In such cases, the DFDs may well accurately mirror the activities occurring in the organization. As the business processes being modeled took many years to develop, sometimes with participants in one part of the organization adapting procedures in isolation from other participants, redundancies and overlapping responsibilities may well have resulted. The careful study of the DFDs created as part of analysis can reveal these procedural redundancies and allow them to be corrected as part of system design.

Inefficiencies can also be identified by studying DFDs, and there are a wide variety of inefficiencies that might exist. Some inefficiencies relate to violations of DFD drawing rules. For example, a violation of rule R from Table 8-3 could occur because obsolete data are captured but never used within a system. Other inefficiencies are due to excessive processing steps. For example, consider the correct DFD in item M of Figure 8-6. Although this flow is mechanically correct, such a loop may indicate potential delays in processing data or unnecessary approval operations.

Similarly, a set of DFDs that models the current logical system can be compared to DFDs that model the new logical system to better determine which processes systems developers need to add or revise while building the new system. Processes for which inputs, outputs, and internal steps have not changed can possibly be reused in the construction of the new system. You can compare alternative logical DFDs to identify those few elements which must be discussed in evaluating competing opinions on system requirements. The logical DFDs for the new system can also serve as the basis for developing alternative design strategies for the new physical system. As we saw with the Hoosier Burger example, a process on a new logical DFD can be implemented in several different physical ways.

Using DFDs in Business Process Reengineering

Data flow diagrams also make a useful tool for modeling processes in business process reengineering (BPR), which you read about in Chapter 7. To illustrate their usefulness, let's look at an example from Hammer and Champy (1993). Hammer and Champy use IBM Credit Corporation as an example of a firm that successfully reengineered its primary business process. IBM Credit Corporation provides financing for customers making large purchases of IBM computer equipment. Its job is to analyze deals proposed by salespeople and write the final contracts governing those deals.

According to Hammer and Champy, IBM Credit Corporation typically took six business days to process each financing deal. The process worked like this: First, the salesperson called in with a proposed deal. The call was taken by one of a half-dozen people sitting around a conference table. Whoever received the call logged it and wrote the details on a piece of paper. A clerk then carried the paper to a second person who initiated the next step in the process by entering the data in a computer system and checking the client's creditworthiness. This person then wrote the details on a piece of paper and carried the paper, along with the original documentation, to a loan officer. Step three, the loan officer modified the standard IBM loan agreement for the customer. This step involved a separate computer system from the one used in step two. Details of the modified loan agreement, along with the other documentation, were then sent on to the next station in the process, where a different clerk determined the appropriate interest rate for the loan. Step four also involved its own information system. In step five, the resulting interest rate, and all of the paper generated up to this point, were then carried to the next stop, where the quote letter was created. Once complete, the quote letter was sent via overnight mail back to the salesperson.

Only reading about this process makes it seem complicated. We can use data flow diagrams to illustrate how the overall process worked (see Figure 8-19). DFDs help us see that the process is not as complicated as it is tedious and wasteful, especially when you consider that so many different people and computer systems were used to support the work at each step.

According to Hammer and Champy, two IBM managers decided one day to see if they could improve the overall process at IBM Credit Corporation. They took a call from a salesperson and walked it through the system. These managers found the actual work being done on a contract only took 90 minutes. For much of the rest of the six days it took to process the deal, the various bits of documentation were sitting in someone's in-basket waiting to be processed.

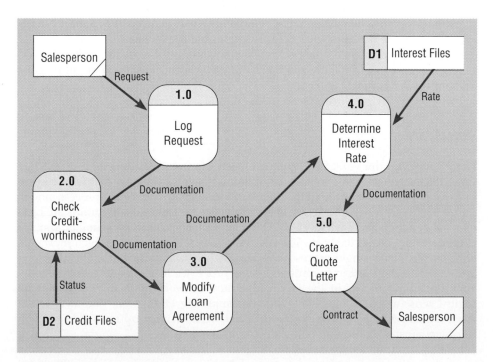

Figure 8-19
IBM Credit Corporation's primary work process before BPR (Copyright © 1993 Harper Business, an imprint of HarperCollins Publishers. Adapted with permission.)

Figure 8-20
IBM Credit Corporation's primary work process after BPR (Copyright © 1993 Harper Business, an imprint of HarperCollins Publishers. Adapted with permission.)

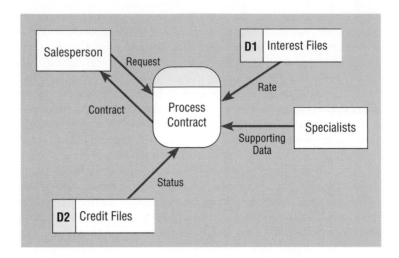

IBM Credit Corporation management decided to reengineer its entire process. The five sets of task specialists were replaced with generalists. Now each call from the field comes to a single clerk, who does all the work necessary to process the contract. Now instead of having different people check for creditworthiness, modify the basic loan agreement, and determine the appropriate interest rate, one person does it all. IBM Credit Corporation still has specialists for the few cases that are significantly different from what the firm routinely encounters. There is also a single supporting computer system. The new process is modeled by the DFD in Figure 8-20. The most striking difference between the DFD in Figure 8-19 and the DFD in Figure 8-20, other than the number of process boxes in each one, is the lack of documentation flow in Figure 8-20. The resulting process is much simpler and cuts down dramatically on any chance of documentation getting lost between steps. Redesigning the process from beginning to end allowed IBM Credit Corporation to increase the number of contracts it can handle by one-hundred-fold—not 100 percent, which would only be doubling the amount of work. BPR allowed IBM Credit Corporation to handle 100 times more work, in the same amount of time, and with fewer people!

SUMMARY

Data flow diagrams, or DFDs, are very useful for representing the overall data flows into, through, and out of an information system. Data flow diagrams rely on only four symbols to represent the four conceptual components of a process model: data flows, data stores, processes, and sources/sinks. Data flow diagrams are hierarchical in nature and each level of a DFD can be decomposed into smaller, simpler units on a lower-level diagram. You begin with a context diagram, which shows the entire system as a single process. The next step is to generate a level-0 diagram, which shows the most important high-level processes in the system. You then decompose each process in the level-0 diagram, as warranted, until it makes no logical sense to go any further. When decomposing DFDs from one level to the next, it is important that the diagrams be balanced; that is, inputs and outputs on one level must be conserved on the next level.

There are four sets of data flow diagrams. The first set you create models the current physical system. The next set models the current logical system. The third set models the new logical system, which may be different from the current logical system to the extent that it shows desired functionality, even though the new system may radically re-engineer the flow of data between system components. The fourth set models the new physical information system. Due to the time it takes to create a complete set of DFDs, many experts suggest that you begin work on the new logical DFDs as soon as possible.

Data flow diagrams should be mechanically correct, but they should also accurately reflect the information system being modeled. To that end, you need to check DFDs for completeness and consistency and draw them as if the system being modeled were timeless. You should be willing to revise DFDs several times. Complete sets of DFDs should extend to the primitive level where every component reflects certain irreducible properties; for example, a process represents a single database operation and every data store represents data about a single entity. Following these guidelines, you can produce DFDs to aid the analysis process by analyzing the gaps between existing procedures and desired procedures and between current and new systems.

KEY TERMS

Balancing	DFD consistency	Level-n diagram
Context diagram	Data store	Primitive DFD
Data flow diagram	Functional decomposition	Process
DFD completeness	Level-0 diagram	Source/sink

REVIEW QUESTIONS

1. Define each of the following terms:

   a. new logical data flow diagram
   b. current logical data flow diagram
   c. decomposition
   d. balancing
   e. level-0 data flow diagram
   f. context diagram
   g. process modeling
   h. primitive DFD

2. What is a data flow diagram? Why do systems analysts use data flow diagrams?

3. Explain the rules for drawing good data flow diagrams.

4. What is decomposition? What is balancing? How can you determine if DFDs are not balanced?

5. Explain the convention for naming different levels of data flow diagrams.

6. What are the primary differences between current physical and current logical data flow diagrams?

7. Why don't analysts usually draw four complete sets of DFDs?

8. How can data flow diagrams be used as analysis tools?

9. Explain the guidelines for deciding when to stop decomposing DFDs.

10. How do you decide if a system component should be represented as a source/sink or as a process?

11. What unique rules apply to drawing context diagrams?

PROBLEMS AND EXERCISES

1. Match the following terms to the appropriate definitions.

_____ source/sink		a. data in motion, moving from one place in a system to another
_____ data flow		b. data at rest, which may take the form of many different physical representations
_____ data store		c. work or actions performed on data so that they are transformed or stored or distributed
_____ process		d. the origin and/or destination of data, sometimes referred to as external entities
_____ DFD completeness		e. extent to which information contained on one level of a set of nested data flow diagrams is also included on other levels
_____ DFD consistency		f. extent to which all necessary components of a data flow diagram have been included

2. Using the example of a retail clothing store in a mall, list relevant data flows, data stores, processes, and sources/sinks. Observe several sales transactions. Draw a context diagram and a level-0 diagram that represent the selling system at the store. Explain why you chose certain elements as processes versus sources/sinks.

3. Choose a transaction that you are likely to encounter, perhaps ordering a cap and gown for graduation, and develop a high-level DFD, or context diagram. Decompose this to a level-0 diagram.

4. Evaluate your level-0 DFD from the previous question using the rules for drawing DFDs in this chapter. Edit your DFD so that it does not break any of these rules.

5. Choose an example like that in the second question and draw a context diagram. Decompose this diagram until it doesn't make sense to continue. Be sure that your diagrams are balanced as discussed in this chapter.

6. Refer to Figure 8-21 which contains drafts of a context and level-0 DFD for a university class registration system. Identify and explain potential violations of rules and guidelines on these diagrams.

7. Why should you develop both logical and physical DFDs for systems? What advantage is there for drawing a logical DFD before a physical DFD for a new information system?

8. What is the relationship between DFDs and entries in the project dictionary or CASE repository?

9. This chapter has shown you how to model, or structure, just one aspect, or view, of an information system, namely the process view. Why do you think analysts have different types of diagrams and other documentation to depict different views (for example, process, logic, and data) of an information system?

10. Consider the DFD in Figure 8-22. List three errors (rule violations) on this DFD.

11. Consider the three DFDs in Figure 8-23. List three errors (rule violations) on these DFDs.

12. Starting with a context diagram, draw as many nested DFDs as you consider necessary to represent all the details of the employee hiring system described in the following narrative. You must draw at least a context and a level-0 diagram. In drawing these diagrams, if you discover that the narrative is incomplete, make up

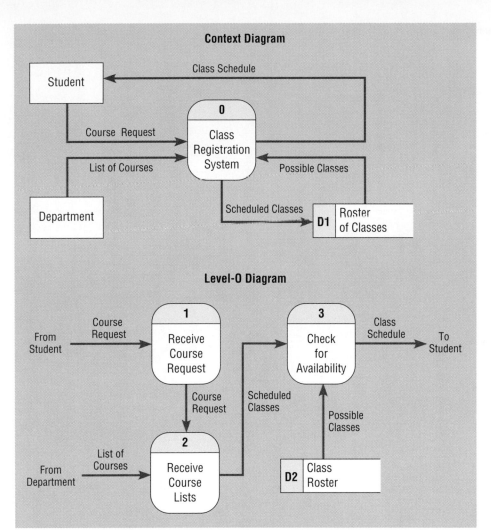

Figure 8-21
Class registration system
for Problem and Exercise 6

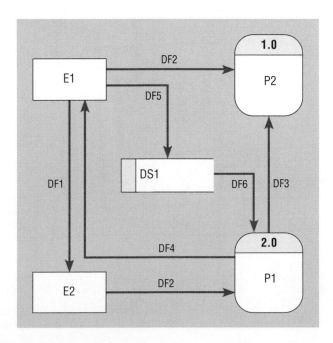

Figure 8-22
DFD for Problem and
Exercise 10

Figure 8-23
DFD for Problem and
Exercise 11

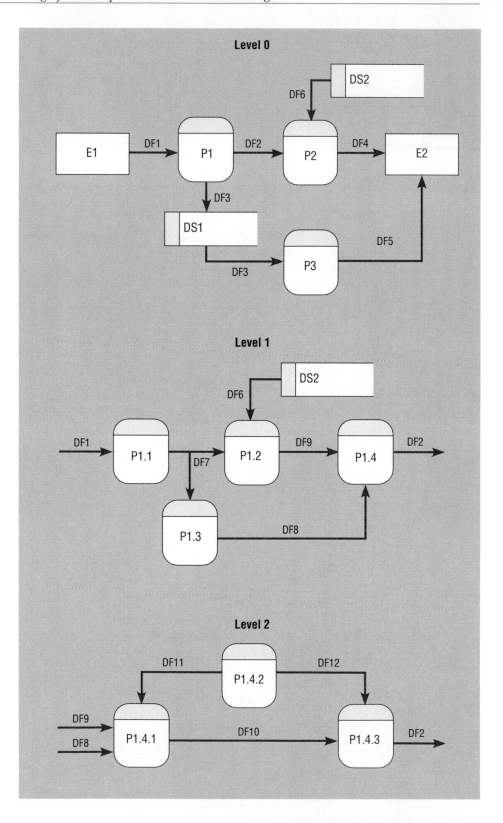

reasonable explanations to complete the story. Supply these extra explanations along with the diagrams. Here is the narrative. Projects, Inc. is an engineering firm with approximately 500 engineers of different types. The company keeps records on all employees, their skills, projects assigned, and departments worked in. New employees are hired by the personnel manager based on data in an application form and evaluations collected from other managers who interview the job candidates. Prospective employees may apply at any time. Engineering managers notify the personnel manager when a job opens and list the characteristics necessary to be eligible for the job. The personnel manager compares the qualifications of the available pool of applicants with the characteristics of an open job, then schedules interviews between the manager in charge of the open position and the three best candidates from the pool. After receiving evaluations on each interview from the manager, the personnel manager makes the hiring decision based upon the evaluations and applications of the candidates and the characteristics of the job, and then notifies the interviewees and the manager about the decision. Applications of rejected applicants are retained for one year, after which time the application is purged. When hired, a new engineer completes a nondisclosure agreement, which is filed with other information about the employee.

13. a. Starting with a context diagram, draw as many nested DFDs as you consider necessary to represent all the details of the system described in the following narrative. In drawing these diagrams, if you discover that the narrative is incomplete, make up reasonable explanations to make the story complete. Supply these extra explanations along with the diagrams. Here is the narrative. Maximum Software is a developer and supplier of software products to individuals and businesses. As part of their operations, Maximum provides an 800 telephone number help desk for clients who have questions about software purchased from Maximum. When a call comes in, an operator inquires about the nature of the call. For calls that are not truly help desk functions, the operator redirects the call to another unit of the company (such as Order Processing or Billing). Since many customer questions require in-depth knowledge of a product, help desk consultants are organized by product. The operator directs the call to a consultant skilled on the software that the caller needs help with. Since a consultant is not always immediately available, some calls must be put into a queue for the next available consultant. Once a consultant answers the call, he determines if this is the first call from this customer about this problem. If so, he creates a new call report to keep track of all information about the problem. If not, he asks the customer for a call report number, and retrieves the open call report to determine the status of the inquiry. If the caller does not know the call report number, the consultant collects other identifying information such as the caller's name, the software involved, or the name of the consultant who has handled the previous calls on the problem in order to conduct a search for the appropriate call report. If a resolution of the customer's problem has been found, the consultant informs the client what that resolution is, indicates on the report that the customer has been notified, and closes out the report. If resolution has not been discovered, the consultant finds out if the consultant handling this problem is on duty. If so, he transfers the call to the other consultant (or puts the call into the queue of calls waiting to be handled by that consultant). Once the proper consultant receives the call, he records any new details the customer may have. For continuing problems and for new call reports, the consultant tries to discover an answer to the problem by using the relevant software and looking up information in reference manuals. If he can now resolve the problem, he tells the customer how to deal with the problem,

and closes the call report. Otherwise, the consultant files the report for continued research and tells the customer that someone at Maximum will get back to him, or if the customer discovers new information about the problem, to call back identifying the problem with a specified call report number.

b. Analyze the DFDs you created in part (a) of this question. What recommendations for improvements in the help desk system at Maximum can you make based upon this analysis? Draw new logical DFDs that represent the requirements you would suggest for an improved help desk system. Remember, these are to be logical DFDs, so consider improvements independent of technology that can be used to support the help desk.

14. Develop a context diagram and level-0 diagram for the hospital pharmacy system described in the following narrative. If you discover that the narrative is incomplete, make up reasonable explanations to complete the story. Supply these extra explanations along with the diagrams. Here is the narrative. The pharmacy at Mercy Hospital fills medical prescriptions for all patients and distributes these medications to the nurse stations responsible for the patient's care. Medical prescriptions are written by doctors and sent to the pharmacy. A pharmacy technician reviews the prescriptions and send them to the appropriate pharmacy station. Prescriptions for drugs that must be formulated (made on-site) are sent to the lab station, prescriptions for off-the-shelf drugs are sent to the shelving station, and prescriptions for narcotics are sent to the secure station. At each station, a pharmacist reviews the order, check the patient's file to determine the appropriateness of the prescriptions, and fills the order if the dosage is at a safe level and it will not negatively interact with the other medications or allergies indicated in the patient's file. If the pharmacist does not fill the order, the prescribing doctor is contacted to discuss the situation. In this case, the order may ultimately be filled or the doctor may write another prescription depending on the outcome of the discussion. Once filled, a prescription label is generated listing the patient's name, the drug type and dosage, an expiration date, and any special instructions. The label is placed on the drug container and the orders are sent to the appropriate nurse stations. The patient's admission number, the drug type and amount dispensed, and the cost of the prescription are then sent to the billing department.

15. Develop a context diagram and a level-0 diagram for the contracting system described in the following narrative. If you discover that the narrative is incomplete, make up reasonable explanations to complete the story. Supply these extra explanations along with the diagrams. Here is the narrative. Government Solutions Company (GSC) sells computer equipment to federal government agencies. Whenever a federal agency needs to purchase equipment from GSC, it issues a purchase order against a standing contract previously negotiated with the company. GSC holds several standing contracts with various federal agencies. When a purchase order is received by GSC's contracting officer, the contract number referenced on the purchase order is entered into the contract database. Using information from the database, the contracting officer reviews the terms and conditions of the contract and determines whether the purchase order is valid. The purchase order is valid if the contract has not expired, the type of equipment ordered is listed on the original contract, and the total cost of the equipment does not exceed a predetermined limit. If the purchase order is not valid, the contracting officer sends the purchase order back to the requesting agency with a letter stating why the purchase order cannot be filled, and a copy of the letter is filed. If the purchase order is valid, the contracting officer enters the purchase order number into the contract database and flags the order as outstanding. The purchase

order is then sent to the order fulfillment department. Here the inventory is checked for each item ordered. If any items are not in stock, the order fulfillment department creates a report listing the items not in stock and attaches it to the purchase order. All purchase orders are forwarded to the warehouse where the items in stock are pulled from the shelves and shipped to the customer. The warehouse then attaches to the purchase order a copy of the shipping bill listing the items shipped and sends it to the contracting officer. If all items were shipped, the contracting officer closes the outstanding purchase order record in the database. The purchase order, shipping bill, and exception report (if attached) are then filed in the contracts office.

16. Develop a context diagram and as many nested DFDs as you consider necessary to represent all the details of the training logistics system described in the following narrative. If you discover that the narrative is incomplete, make up reasonable explanations to complete the story. Supply these extra explanations along with the diagrams. Here is the narrative. Training, Inc., conducts training seminars in major U.S. cities. For each seminar, the logistics department must make arrangements for the meeting facilities, the training consultant's travel, and the shipment of any seminar materials. For each scheduled seminar, the bookings department notifies the logistics coordinator of the type of seminar, the dates and city location, and the name of the consultant who will conduct the training. To arrange for meeting facilities, the logistics coordinator gathers information on possible meeting sites in the scheduled city. The meeting site location decision is made based on date availability, cost, type of meeting space available, and convenience of the location. Once the site decision is made, the coordinator speaks with the sales manager of the meeting facility to reserve the meeting room(s), plan the seating arrangement(s), and reserve any necessary audio-visual equipment. The coordinator estimates the number and size of meeting rooms, the type of seating arrangements, and the audio-visual equipment needed for each seminar from the information kept in a logistics database on each type of seminar offered and the number of anticipated registrants for a particular booking. After negotiations are conducted by the logistics coordinator and the sales manager of the meeting facility, the sales manager creates a contract agreement specifying the negotiated arrangements and sends two copies of it to the logistics coordinator. The coordinator reviews the agreement and approves it if no changes are needed. One copy of the agreement is filed and the other copy is sent back to the sales manager. If changes are needed, the agreement copies are changed and returned to the sales manager for approval. This approval process continues until both parties have approved the agreement. The coordinator must also contact the training consultant to make travel arrangements. First, the coordinator reviews the consultant's travel information in the logistics database and researches flight schedules. Then the consultant is contacted to discuss possible travel arrangements; subsequently, the coordinator books a flight for the consultant with a travel agency. Once the consultant's travel arrangements have been completed, a written confirmation and itinerary are sent to the consultant. Two weeks before the date of the seminar, the coordinator determines what, if any, seminar materials (e.g., transparencies, training guides, pamphlets, etc.) need to be sent to the meeting facility. Each type of seminar has a specific set of materials assigned to it. For some materials, the coordinator must know how many participants have registered for the seminar in order to determine how many to send. A request for materials is sent to the material-handling department where the materials are gathered, boxed, and sent to the meeting address listed on the request. Once the requested materials have been shipped, a notification is sent to the logistics coordinator.

FIELD EXERCISES

1. Talk to systems analysts who work at an organization. Ask the analyst to show you a complete set of DFDs from a current project. Interview the analyst about his or her views about DFDs and their usefulness for analysis.

2. Interview several people in an organization about a particular system. What is the system like now and what would they like to see changed? Create a complete set of DFDs for the current physical, current logical, and new logical system. Show some of the people you interviewed your DFDs and ask for their reactions. What kinds of comments do they make? What kinds of suggestions?

3. Talk to systems analysts who use a CASE tool. Investigate what capabilities that CASE tool has for automatically checking for rule violations in DFDs. What reports can the CASE tool produce with error and warning messages to help analysts correct and improve DFDs?

4. Find out which, if any, drawing packages, word processors, forms design, and database management systems your university or company supports. Research these packages to determine how they might be used in the production of a project dictionary. For example, do the drawing packages include either set of standard DFD symbols in their graphic symbol palette?

5. At an organization with which you have contact, ask one or more employees to draw a "picture" of the business process they interact with at that organization. Ask them to draw the process using whatever format suits them. Ask them to depict in their diagram each of the components of the process and the flow of information among these components at the highest level of detail possible. What type of diagram have they drawn? Why? In what ways does it resemble (and not resemble) a data flow diagram? Why? When they have finished, help them to convert their diagram to a standard data flow diagram as described in this chapter. In what ways is the data flow diagram stronger and/or weaker than the original diagram?

REFERENCES

Celko, J. 1987. "I. Data Flow Diagrams." *Computer Language* 4(January): 41–43.

DeMarco, T. 1979. *Structured Analysis and System Specification.* Englewood Cliffs, NJ: Prentice-Hall.

Gane, C. and T. Sarson. 1979. *Structured Systems Analysis.* Englewood Cliffs, NJ: Prentice-Hall.

Gibbs, W. W. 1994. "Software's Chronic Crisis." *Scientific American* 271(Sept.): 86–95.

Hammer, M., and J. Champy. 1993. *Reengineering the Corporation.* New York, NY: Harper Business.

Yourdon, E. 1989. *Managing the Structured Techniques,* 4th ed. Englewood Cliffs, NJ: Prentice-Hall.

Yourdon, E. and L. L. Constantine. 1979. *Structured Design.* Englewood Cliffs, NJ: Prentice-Hall.

Structuring System Requirements: Process Modeling for the Customer Activity Tracking System

INTRODUCTION

Requirements determination had generated a lot of ideas about possible ways to profile customers and products and about various functions to provide in CATS. So far, the only structured descriptions of CATS that the project team had to work with were the original data flow diagrams and entity-relationship diagram developed during the initiation and planning of the CATS project. Although more requirements determination activities would occur, such as a JAD session, it was time for Frank and the other team members to organize what had been discovered so far. Further, the JAD could be a useful opportunity to obtain reactions to the requirements, and the requirements had to be structured and diagrammed to facilitate feedback at the JAD.

DEVELOPING DETAILED DFDS FOR CATS

Frank Napier was studying the level-0 data flow diagram Jordan Pippen had prepared for BEC's Customer Activity Tracking System (CATS) (Figure 1). It was late at night, and Jordan was in Miami getting ready to meet with the managers of the seven stores with the highest sales figures. Frank's job, as part of the "Revise data flow models" activity in the Baseline Project Plan, was to decompose this DFD. Such DFDs were essential so that everyone on the project team could have a common understanding of CATS. Frank sat at his computer, using Oracle's Designer/2000 CASE tool, drawing level-1 DFDs for processes 4, 5, and 6. Frank had begun sketching some of these diagrams by hand while studying his notes from several interviews he, Jorge Lopez, and Jordan had conducted. As none of the interview notes very clearly described what CATS would have to do, drawing the DFDs would prove challenging and would call for much creativity on Frank's part.

Process 4, Announcement Production & Mailing, seemed straightforward enough, however. Frank understood that the purpose of process 4 was to take a match that had been made between a given new product and a given customer in process 3 and print an announcement addressed to that customer. The announcement would indicate that the product could be reserved for that person at his regular BEC store. Looking at the various materials he and the analysis team had gathered during requirements determination, Frank knew that the announcement would contain a product/customer/store (PCS) code, which the customer would call in to an 800 number to ask that the product be held for the customer at the BEC store. Each announcement would have only one PCS, so separate ones would be generated even if a customer was matched with several new products in the same CATS run. Frank decided process 4 had to contain the logic to generate that code, as he did not see a more appropriate place to create the code anywhere else in the system. Frank drew a subprocess that would create the PCS code and change the customer state from Selected to Notified. Produce Notifications became the subprocess where the announcement would be created. The only process left to do was print and mail the postcard. Frank's decomposition of process 4 is shown in Figure 2.

The CASE tool automatically created an entry in the repository for each DFD element. Before the analysis phase was complete, the CATS project team would need to enter full descriptions and other information about each process, data flow, and source/sink. For now, Frank entered a few notes, in outline form, under the description of each element so that other members of the team would have a basic idea of what Frank meant by each term.

Figure 1
Level-0 data flow diagram
for the CATS project

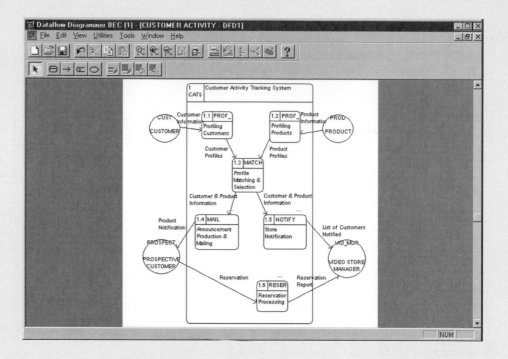

Figure 2
Level-1 diagram for
process 4, Announcement
Production and Mailing

Frank next turned to the decomposition of process 5, Store Notification. Frank reasoned that the customer-product match data would have to be sorted by customer and then by product. The result would be a list of customer-product match instances by customer first and, within customer, by product. As noted above, some customers might have been matched with more than one product each time CATS was run. Once sorted, the customers had to be matched with the store where they were registered. Once all of the customer-product match instances had been grouped by store, the customer profile report could be formatted, generated, and sent to the individual stores. One of the questions Jordan was going to ask the store managers she was meeting with in Miami concerned the utility of the customer profile report. Frank had pointed out to Jordan before she left that this report showed only potential reservations, but it was the reservation report that told store managers which customers had asked for reservations of which products. Figure 3 shows Frank's decomposition for process 5, which Frank left still fairly general until the issues mentioned above are resolved.

Process 6, Reservation Processing was more complicated. Within this process, customers had to be able to make reservations, the product reservations data store had to be updated, new product orders had to be initiated via a message sent to the central inventory control system, and the reservation report had to be generated and sent to individual stores. Frank's decomposition for process 6 appears as Figure 4. As with prior decompositions, as Frank structured the process at a finer detail, he identified flaws in the level-0 diagram which he would have to fix later in order to eliminate error messages from the CASE tool's DFD validity checker. An example was the need for Process 6 to retrieve data from the Inventory data store and for an interface with the central inventory control system.

Customer reservation confirmations phoned in to the 800 number would be used to update product reservation records. This information would be collected and batched by store; Frank thought this could be suit-

ably done as a batch process, but the decision about whether the Product Reservations data store would be updated on-line by the 800 number operators or entered on-line for later batch updating would be made during the design phase. Several times per day, the names and amounts of each CATS product each store needed would be generated and compared to current inventory levels for those products. If additional product was needed, that information would be used to order additional product through BEC's centralized inventory control system. Order information and product reservation information would be used to generate a reservation report for the stores.

The reservation report contained information about the products the store was supposed to reserve and the customers the products were to be reserved for, and information about how much product had been ordered from BEC's warehouses. Frank thought back to a conversation he had had earlier with Jordan Pippen, his boss on the CATS project.

Frank had asked Jordan about feedback and how much of a burden a feedback requirement would place on local stores. Jordan had replied she thought that maybe the reservation report served a feedback function. Now that he was decomposing the level-0 DFD, Frank realized that the reservation report served only to *tell* the stores which products they had to set aside and for whom and also about any new orders connected

Figure 3

Level-1 diagram for process 5, Store Notification

Figure 4
Level-1 diagram for process
6, Reservation Processing

with the reservations. Frank also realized that store managers needed to keep track of the reservations and whether customers who made reservations actually came in to the stores and bought the reserved product. Right now, since CATS was a totally new system for BEC, they had no way of really knowing how many of those reservations would turn into sales. Yet the success rate would determine how much product would be automatically ordered for each store, based on reservations. If only 40 percent of the reservations resulted in sales, then less product would be automatically ordered than if 60 or 70 percent of the reservations resulted in sales. Clearly this would be valuable information.

The rental and sales systems could be modified to capture purchases of reserved versus non-reserved items, but modifying these systems would delay the deployment of CATS. An alternative would be to try to capture this in a separate component of CATS at the store level. Store managers would have to assume an additional burden under this alternative design—that is, clerks would enter purchase data through the sale and rental systems and the manager or a clerk would also have to enter it in the CATS store system—using this approach CATS could be a reality a lot sooner. Frank did not think this would be too much of an extra burden for the manager or clerks in a store. Frank realized his conclusions would be important for Jordan to know before her meetings with the store managers were over since the managers could best judge if such double entry created any problems. Frank created a

level-0 DFD for a store-level CATS subsystem, as shown in Figure 5. Frank also made some notes in his personal journal that he kept for each project; he would refer to his notes at the next weekly CATS team meeting and raise the possibility of these alternative design strategies.

The inputs for the store level system would include new order data from BEC's central inventory system, the reservation report from central CATS, and the purchase of reserved products by customers. New order data would be used to update the store inventory records. The reservations report (which would now consist of a transaction file downloaded to the store as well as a printed report) would be used to update product reservations records. Customer purchase data would be used to update customer transaction records for reservation purchases. This current information would serve as input in updating product reservations and store inventory records. The updated product reservations records would then be used to generate a success rate report for the store manager and for the CATS manager. The data in that report would at the very least be used to adjust the ordering thresholds for CATS.

Frank made some notes about the need he had identified for a store-level CATS component and for the relative lightness of the feedback burden for store managers. He printed out his notes and DFDs and faxed them to Jordan at her hotel in Miami. Whether or not she agreed with his conclusions, Jordan at least needed to be made aware of them. After all, her meeting with the store managers was not just for gathering

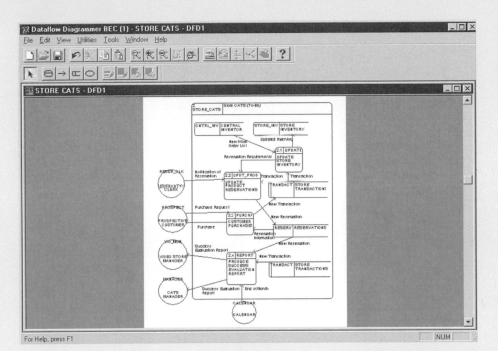

Figure 5
Level-0 data flow diagram
for a store-level CATS
component

additional information; it was also intended to sell the store managers on CATS and let them know how useful it would be to them and to BEC.

SUMMARY

The diagrams presented in this case are only a few of many DFDs that Frank, Jorge, and Jordan would need to develop to show all of the data movement between CATS components. With the large number of diagrams, the CASE tool and repository are invaluable in ensuring that the diagrams and associated repository entries are consistent and complete. The diagrams show valuable information useful in other analysis and subsequent design steps. Each data flow coming from a source means an automated or manual procedure has to be developed to capture these data, including the possible development of a business form on which to record the data. Each data flow going to a sink implies a file transfer, printed report, or data for computer

display. Data flows going into a data store represent database update operations, and data flows coming from a data store represent a query to the database. The number of processes indicates how much design and programming work must be done in subsequent project phases, which must be outlined in the updated Baseline Project Plan prepared at the end of the analysis phase. No matter how detailed the analysis team makes the DFDs, the actual logic of processing the data (for example, how the Produce Notifications process in Figure 2, works) still needs to be defined in a more algorithmic fashion. Also, since some processes involve multiple data stores, the analysis team will have to develop structures that show how to relate data in associated data stores. The development of the DFDs, however, clarifies many of the elements required in CATS and identifies what general kinds of information users would receive and need to provide. Whether these requirements make sense or not would be validated later in analysis during the JAD and several walkthrough sessions.

Structuring System Requirements: Logic Modeling

After studying this chapter, you should be able to:

■ Use Structured English as a tool for representing steps in logical processes in data flow diagrams.

■ Use decision tables and decision trees to represent the logic of choice in conditional statements.

■ Select among Structured English, decision tables, and decision trees for representing processing logic.

INTRODUCTION

In Chapter 8 you learned how the processes that convert data to information are key parts of information systems. As good as data flow diagrams are for identifying processes, they are not very good at showing the logic inside the processes. Even the processes on the primitive-level data flow diagrams do not show the most fundamental processing steps. Just what occurs within a process? How are the input data converted to the output information? Since data flow diagrams are not really designed to show the detailed logic of processes, you must model process logic using other techniques. This chapter is about the techniques you use for modeling process decision logic.

First you will be introduced to Structured English, a modified version of the English language that is useful for representing the logic in information system processes. You can use Structured English to represent all three of the fundamental statements necessary for structured programming: choice, repetition, and sequence.

Second, you will learn about decision tables. Decision tables allow you to represent a set of conditions and the actions that follow from them in a tabular format. When there are several conditions and several possible actions that can occur, decision tables can help you keep track of the possibilities in a clear and concise manner.

Third, you will also learn how to model the logic of choice statements using decision trees. Decision trees model the same elements as a decision table but in a more graphical manner.

Fourth, you will have to decide when to use Structured English, decision tables, and decision trees. In this chapter, you will learn about the criteria you can use to make a choice among these three logic modeling techniques.

LOGIC MODELING

In Chapter 7, you learned how the requirements for an information system are collected. Analysts structure the requirements information into data flow diagrams that model the flow of data into and through the information system. Data flow diagrams, though versatile and powerful techniques, are not adequate for modeling all of the complexity of an information system. Although decomposition allows you to represent a data flow diagram's processes at finer and finer levels of detail, the process names themselves cannot adequately represent what a process does and how it does it. For that reason, you must represent the logic contained in the process symbols on DFDs with other modeling techniques.

Logic modeling involves representing the internal structure and functionality of the processes represented on data flow diagrams. These processes appear on DFDs as little more than black boxes, in that we cannot tell from only their names or CASE repository descriptions precisely what they do and how they do it. Yet the structure and functionality of a system's processes are a key element of any information system. Processes must be clearly described before they can be translated into a programming language. In this chapter, we will focus on techniques you can use during the analysis phase to model the logic within processes; that is, data-to-information transformations and decisions. In the analysis phase, logic modeling will be complete and reasonably detailed, but it will also be generic in that it will not reflect the structure or syntax of a particular programming language. You will focus on more precise, language-based logic modeling in the design phase of the life cycle.

Modeling a System's Logic

The three subphases to systems analysis are requirements determination, requirements structuring, and generating alternative systems and selecting the best one (Figure 9-1). Modeling a system's logic is part of requirements structuring, just as was representing the system with data flow diagrams. Here our focus is on the processes pictured on the data flow diagrams and the logic contained within each. You can also use logic modeling to indicate when processes on a DFD occur (for example, when a process extracts a certain data flow from a given data store). Just as we use logic modeling to represent the logic contained in a data flow diagram's processes, we will use data modeling to represent the contents and structure of a data flow diagram's data flows and data stores.

Deliverables and Outcomes

In structured analysis, the primary deliverables from logic modeling are structured descriptions and diagrams that outline the logic contained within each DFD process as well as diagrams that show the temporal dimension of systems—when processes or events occur and how these events change the state of the system. Table 9-1 provides a list of deliverables that result from documenting the logic of a system's processes. Note that the analyst decides if a process requires more than one representation of its logic. Deliverables can also take the form of new entries into the project dictionary or CASE repository. These entries may update process descriptions or, if possible, store the new diagrams from logic and event-response modeling along with associated repository entries.

Creating diagrams and descriptions of process logic is not an end in itself. Rather, these diagrams and descriptions are created ultimately to serve as part of an unambiguous and thorough explanation of the system's specifications. These specifications are used to explain the system requirements to developers, whether

Figure 9-1
Systems development life cycle with the analysis phase highlighted

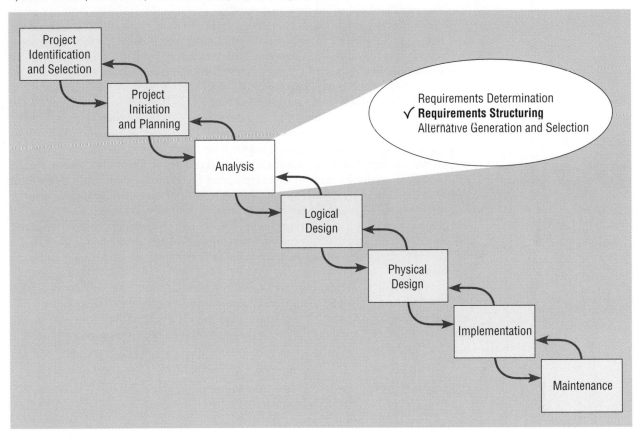

people or automated code generators. Users, analysts, and programmers use logic diagrams and descriptions throughout analysis to incrementally specify a shared understanding of requirements, without regard for programming languages or development environments. Such diagrams may be discussed during JAD sessions or project review meetings. Alternatively, system prototypes generated from such diagrams may be reviewed, and requested changes to a prototype will be implemented by changing logic diagrams and generating a new prototype from a CASE tool or other code generator.

TABLE 9-1   Deliverables for Logic Modeling

Where appropriate, each process on the lowest- (primitive-) level data flow diagrams will be represented with one or more of the following:

- Structured English representation of process logic
- Decision table representation
- Decision tree representation
- State-transition diagram or table (see Chapter 12)

MODELING LOGIC WITH STRUCTURED ENGLISH

You must understand more than just the flow of data into, through, and out of an information system. You must also understand what each identified process does and how it accomplishes its task. Starting with the processes depicted in the various sets of data flow diagrams you and others on the analysis team have produced, you must now begin to study and document the logic of each process. *Structured English* is one method used to illustrate process logic.

Structured English:
Modified form of the English language used to specify the logic of information system processes. Although there is no single standard, Structured English typically relies on action verbs and noun phrases and contains no adjectives or adverbs.

Structured English is a modified form of English that is used to specify the contents of process boxes in a DFD. It differs from regular English in that it uses a subset of English vocabulary to express information system process procedures. The same action verbs we listed in Chapter 8 for naming processes are also used in Structured English. These include such verbs as read, write, print, sort, move, merge, add, subtract, multiply, and divide. Structured English also uses noun phrases to describe data structures, such as patron-name and patron-address. Unlike regular English, Structured English does not use adjectives or adverbs. The whole point of using Structured English is to represent processes in a shorthand manner that is relatively easy for users and programmers to read and understand. As there is no standard version, each analyst will have his or her own particular dialect of Structured English.

It is possible to use Structured English to represent all three processes typical to structured programming: sequence, conditional statements, and repetition. Sequence requires no special structure but can be represented with one sequential statement following another. Conditional statements can be represented with a structure like the following:

```
BEGIN IF
    IF Quantity-in-stock is less than Minimum-order-quantity
    THEN GENERATE new order
    ELSE DO nothing
END IF
```

Another type of conditional statement is a case statement where there are many different actions a program can follow, but only one is chosen. A case statement might be represented as:

```
READ Quantity-in-stock
SELECT CASE
    CASE 1 (Quantity-in-stock greater than Minimum-order-quantity)
        DO nothing
    CASE 2 (Quantity-in-stock equals Minimum-order-quantity)
        DO nothing
    CASE 3 (Quantity-in-stock is less than Minimum-order-quantity)
        GENERATE new order
    CASE 4 (Stock out)
        INITIATE emergency reorder routine
END CASE
```

Repetition can take the form of Do-Until loops or Do-While loops. A Do-Until loop might be represented as follows:

```
DO
    READ Inventory records
    BEGIN IF
```

```
            IF Quantity-in-stock is less than Minimum-order-quantity
            THEN GENERATE new order
            ELSE DO nothing
        END IF
    UNTIL End-of-file
```

A Do-While loop might be represented as follows:

```
    READ Inventory records
    WHILE NOT End-of-File DO
        BEGIN IF
            IF Quantity-in-stock is less than Minimum-order-quantity
            THEN GENERATE new order
            ELSE DO nothing
        END IF
    END DO
```

Let's look at an example of how Structured English would represent the logic of some of the processes identified in Hoosier Burger's current logical inventory control system. Figure 8-15 is reproduced below as Figure 9-2.

There are four processes depicted in Figure 9-2: Update Inventory Added, Update Inventory Used, Generate Orders, and Generate Payments. Structured English representations of each process are shown in Figure 9-3. Notice that in this version of Structured English the file names are connected with hyphens and file names and variable names are capitalized. Terms that signify logical comparisons, such as greater than and less than, are spelled out rather than represented by their arithmetic symbols. Also notice how short the Structured English specifications are,

Figure 9-2

Current logical DFD for Hoosier Burger's inventory control system

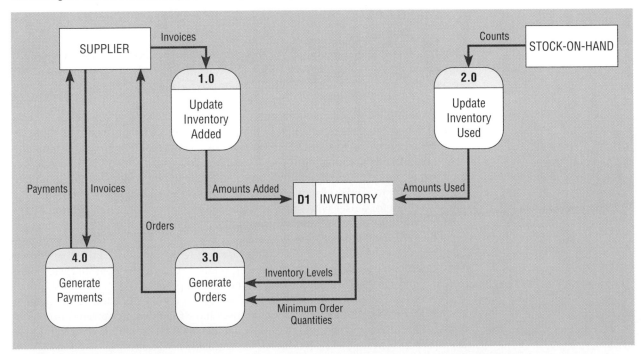

Figure 9-3

Structured English representations of the four processes depicted in Figure 9-2

```
Process 1.0: Update Inventory Added
DO
    READ next Invoice-item-record
    FIND matching Inventory-record
    ADD Quantity-added from Invoice-item-record to Quantity-in-stock on
        Inventory-record
UNTIL End-of-file
```

```
Process 2.0: Update Inventory Used

    READ next Stock-item-record
    FIND matching Inventory-record
    SUBTRACT Quantity-used on Stock-item-record from Quantity-in-stock
        on Inventory-record
UNTIL End-of-file
```

```
Process 3.0: Generate Orders
DO
    READ next Inventory-record
    BEGIN IF
        IF Quantity-in-stock is less than Minimum-order-quantity
        THEN GENERATE Order
    END IF
UNTIL End-of-file
```

```
Process 4.0: Generate Payments
READ Today's-date
DO
    SORT Invoice-records by Date
    READ next Invoice-record
    BEGIN IF
        IF Date is 30 days or greater than Today's-date
        THEN GENERATE Payments
    END IF
UNTIL End-of-file
```

considering that these specifications all describe level-0 processes. The final specifications would model the logic in the lowest-level DFDs only. From reading the process descriptions in Figure 9-3, it should be obvious to you that much more detail would be required to actually perform the processes described. In fact, creating Structured English representations of processes in higher-level DFDs is one method you can use to help you decide if a particular DFD needs further decomposition.

Notice how the format of the Structured English process description mimics the format usually used in programming languages, especially the practice of indentation. This is the "structured part" of Structured English. Notice also that the language used is similar to spoken English, using verbs and noun phrases. The language is simple enough for a user who knows nothing about computer programming to understand the steps involved in performing the various processes, yet the structure of the descriptions makes it easy to eventually convert to a programming language. Using Structured English also means not having to worry about initializing variables, opening and closing files, or finding related records in separate files. These more technical details are left for later in the design process.

Structured English is intended to be used as a communication technique for analysts and users. Analysts and programmers have their own communication technique, *pseudocode,* which we will study later in this book. Whereas Structured English resembles spoken English, pseudocode resembles a programming language.

MODELING LOGIC WITH DECISION TABLES

Structured English can be used to represent the logic contained in an information system process, but sometimes a process' logic can become quite complex. If several different conditions are involved, and combinations of these conditions dictate which of several actions should be taken, then Structured English may not be adequate for representing the logic behind such a complicated choice. Not that Structured English cannot represent complicated logic; rather, Structured English becomes more difficult to understand and verify as logic becomes more complicated. Research has shown, for example, that people become confused in trying to interpret more than three nested IF statements (Yourdon, 1989a). Where the logic is complicated, then, a diagram may be much clearer than a Structured English statement. A **decision table** is a diagram of process logic where the logic is reasonably complicated. All of the possible choices and the conditions the choices depend on are represented in tabular form, as illustrated in the decision table in Figure 9-4.

The decision table in Figure 9-4 models the logic of a generic payroll system. There are three parts to the table: the **condition stubs,** the **action stubs,** and the **rules.** The condition stubs contain the various conditions that apply in the situation the table is modeling. In Figure 9-4, there are two condition stubs for employee type and hours worked. Employee type has two values: "S," which stands for salaried, and "H," which stands for hourly. Hours worked has three values: less than 40, exactly 40, and more than 40. The action stubs contain all the possible courses of action that result from combining values of the condition stubs. There are four possible courses of action in this table: Pay base salary, Calculate hourly wage, Calculate overtime, and Produce Absence Report. You can see that not all actions are triggered by all combinations of conditions. Instead, specific combinations trigger specific actions. The part of the table that links conditions to actions is the section that contains the rules.

To read the rules, start by reading the values of the conditions as specified in the first column: Employee type is "S," or salaried, and hours worked are less than 40. When both of these conditions occur, the payroll system is to pay the base salary. In the next column, the values are "H" and "<40," meaning an hourly worker who worked less than 40 hours. In such a situation, the payroll system calculates the hourly wage and makes an entry in the Absence Report. Rule 3 addresses the situation when a salaried employee works exactly 40 hours. The system pays the base salary, as was the case for Rule 1. For an hourly worker who has worked exactly 40 hours, Rule 4 calculates the hourly wage. Rule 5 pays the base salary for salaried employees who work more than 40 hours. Rule 5 has the same

Decision table: A matrix representation of the logic of a decision, which specifies the possible conditions for the decision and the resulting actions.

Condition stubs: That part of a decision table that lists the conditions relevant to the decision.

Action stubs: That part of a decision table that lists the actions that result for a given set of conditions.

Rules: That part of a decision table that specifies which actions are to be followed for a given set of conditions.

	Conditions/ Courses of Action	Rules					
		1	2	3	4	5	6
Condition Stubs	Employee type	S	H	S	H	S	H
	Hours worked	<40	<40	40	40	>40	>40
Action Stubs	Pay base salary	X		X		X	
	Calculate hourly wage		X		X		X
	Calculate overtime						X
	Produce Absence Report		X				

Figure 9-4
Complete decision table for payroll system example

Indifferent condition: In a decision table, a condition whose value does not affect which actions are taken for two or more rules.

action as Rules 1 and 3, and governs behavior with regard to salaried employees. The number of hours worked does not affect the outcome for Rules 1, 3, or 5. For these rules, hours worked is an **indifferent condition** in that its value does not affect the action taken. Rule 6 calculates hourly pay and overtime for an hourly worker who has worked more than 40 hours.

Because of the indifferent condition for Rules 1, 3, and 5, we can reduce the number of rules by condensing Rules 1, 3, and 5 into one rule, as shown in Figure 9-5. The indifferent condition is represented with a dash. Whereas we started with a decision table with six rules, we now have a simpler table that conveys the same information with only four rules.

In constructing these decision tables, we have actually followed a set of basic procedures, as follows:

1. *Name the conditions and the values each condition can assume.* Determine all of the conditions that are relevant to your problem, and then determine all of the values each condition can take. For some conditions, the values will be simply "yes" or "no" (called a limited entry). For others, such as the conditions in Figures 9-4 and 9-5, the conditions may have more values (called an extended entry).

2. *Name all possible actions that can occur.* The purpose of creating decision tables is to determine the proper course of action given a particular set of conditions.

3. *List all possible rules.* When you first create a decision table, you have to create an exhaustive set of rules. Every possible combination of conditions must be represented. It may turn out that some of the resulting rules are redundant or make no sense, but these determinations should be made only *after* you have listed every rule so that no possibility is overlooked. To determine the number of rules, multiply the number of values for each condition by the number of values for every other condition. In Figure 9-4, we have two conditions, one with two values and one with three, so we need 2×3, or 6, rules. If we added a third condition with three values, we would need 2×3×3, or 18, rules.

When creating the table, alternate the values for the first condition, as we did in Figure 9-4 for type of employee. For the second condition, alternate the values but repeat the first value for all values of the first condition, then repeat the second value for all values of the first condition, and so on. You essentially follow this procedure for all subsequent conditions. Notice how we alternated the values of hours worked in Figure 9-4. We repeated "<40" for both values of type of employee, "S" and "H." Then we repeated "40," and then ">40."

Figure 9-5
Reduced decision table for payroll system example

Conditions/ Courses of Action	Rules			
	1	2	3	4
Employee type	S	H	H	H
Hours worked	–	<40	40	>40
Pay base salary	X			
Calculate hourly wage		X	X	X
Calculate overtime				X
Produce Absence Report		X		

4. *Define the actions for each rule.* Now that all possible rules have been identified, provide an action for each rule. In our example, we were able to figure out what each action should be and whether all of the actions made sense. If an action doesn't make sense, you may want to create an "impossible" row in the action stubs in the table to keep track of impossible actions. If you can't tell what the system ought to do in that situation, place question marks in the action stub spaces for that particular rule.

5. *Simplify the decision table.* Make the decision table as simple as possible by removing any rules with impossible actions. Consult users on the rules where system actions aren't clear and either decide on an action or remove the rule. Look for patterns in the rules, especially for indifferent conditions. We were able to reduce the number of rules in the payroll example from six to four, but often greater reductions are possible.

Let's look at an example from Hoosier Burger. The Mellankamps are trying to determine how they reorder food and other items they use in the restaurant. If they are going to automate the inventory control functions at Hoosier Burger, they need to articulate their reordering process. In thinking through the problem, the Mellankamps realize that how they reorder depends on whether the item is perishable. If an item is perishable, such as meat, vegetables, or bread, the Mellankamps have a standing order with a local supplier stating that a prespecified amount of food is delivered each weekday for that day's use and each Saturday for weekend use. If the item is not perishable, such as straws, cups, and napkins, an order is placed when the stock on hand reaches a certain predetermined minimum reorder quantity. The Mellankamps also realize the importance of the seasonality of their work. Hoosier Burger's business is not as good during the summer months when the students are off campus as it is during the academic year. They also note that business falls off during Christmas and spring breaks. Their standing orders with all their suppliers are reduced by specific amounts during the summer and holiday breaks. Given this set of conditions and actions, the Mellankamps put together an initial decision table (see Figure 9-6).

Figure 9-6
Complete decision table for Hoosier Burger's inventory reordering

Conditions/ Courses of Action	Rules											
	1	2	3	4	5	6	7	8	9	10	11	12
Type of item	P	N	P	N	P	N	P	N	P	N	P	N
Time of week	D	D	W	W	D	D	W	W	D	D	W	W
Season of year	A	A	A	A	S	S	S	S	H	H	H	H
Standing daily order	X				X				X			
Standing weekend order			X				X				X	
Minimum order quantity		X		X		X		X		X		X
Holiday reduction									X		X	
Summer reduction					X		X					

Type of item:
P = perishable
N = non-perishable

Time of week:
D = weekday
W = weekend

Season of year:
A = academic year
S = summer
H = holiday

Notice three things about Figure 9-6. First, notice how the values for the third condition have been repeated, providing a distinctive pattern for relating the values for all three conditions to each other. Every possible rule is clearly provided in this table. Second, notice we have 12 rules. Two values for the first condition (type of item) times two values for the second condition (time of week) times three values for the third condition (season of year) equals 12 possible rules. Third, notice how the action for nonperishable items is the same, regardless of day of week or time of year. For nonperishable goods, both time-related conditions are indifferent. Collapsing the decision table accordingly gives us the decision table in Figure 9-7. Now there are only seven rules instead of 12.

You have now learned how to draw and simplify decision tables. You can also use decision tables to specify additional decision-related information. For example, if the actions that should be taken for a specific rule are more complicated than one or two lines of text can convey, or if some conditions need to be checked only when other conditions are met (nested conditions), you may want to use separate, linked decision tables. In your original decision table, you can specify an action in the action stub that says "Perform Table B." Table B could contain an action stub that returns to the original table and the return would be the action for one or more rules in Table B. Another way to convey more information in a decision table is to use numbers that indicate sequence rather than Xs where rules and action stubs intersect. For example, for Rules 3 and 4 in Figure 9-7, it would be important for the Mellankamps to account for the summer reduction to modify the existing standing order for supplies. "Summer reduction" would be marked with a "1" for Rules 3 and 4 while "Standing daily order" would be marked with a "2" for Rule 3, and "Standing weekend order" would be marked with a "2" for Rule 4.

You have seen how decision tables can model the relatively complicated logic of a process. Decision tables are more useful than Structured English for complicated logic in that they convey information in a tabular rather than a linear, sequential format. As such, decision tables are compact; you can pack a lot of information into a small table. Decision tables also allow you to check for the extent to which your logic is complete, consistent, and not redundant. Despite the usefulness of Structured English and decision tables, there are still other techniques available for modeling process logic. The next such technique you will learn about is decision trees.

Figure 9-7

Reduced decision table for Hoosier Burger's inventory reordering

Conditions/ Courses of Action	Rules						
	1	2	3	4	5	6	7
Type of item	P	P	P	P	P	P	N
Time of week	D	W	D	W	D	W	–
Season of year	A	A	S	S	H	H	–
Standing daily order	X		X		X		
Standing weekend order		X		X		X	
Minimum order quantity							X
Holiday reduction					X	X	
Summer reduction			X	X			

MODELING LOGIC WITH DECISION TREES

A **decision tree** is a graphical technique that depicts a decision or choice situation as a connected series of nodes and branches. Decision trees were first devised as a management science technique to simplify a choice where some of the needed information is not known for certain. By relying on the probabilities of certain events, a management scientist can use a decision tree to choose the best course of action. Although this type of decision tree is beyond the scope of our text, we can use modified decision trees (without the probabilities) to diagram the same sorts of situations for which we used decision tables. Why introduce yet another diagramming technique to do what a decision table does? Both decision tables and decision trees are communication tools designed to make it easier for analysts to communicate with users. Deciding exactly which technique to use depends on various factors which we discuss in detail in the next section, after you have an understanding of decision trees.

As used in requirements structuring, decision trees have two main components: decision points, which are represented by nodes, and actions, which are represented by ovals. Figure 9-8 shows a generic decision tree. To read a decision tree, you begin at the root node on the far left. Each node is numbered, and each number corresponds to a choice; the choices are spelled out in a legend for the diagram. Each path leaving a node corresponds to one of the options for that choice. From each node, there are at least two paths that lead to the next step, which is either another decision point or an action. Finally, all possible actions are listed on the far right of the diagram in leaf nodes. Each rule is represented by tracing a series of paths from the root node, down a path to the next node, and so on, until an action oval is reached.

Look back at the decision tables we created for the payroll system logic (Figures 9-4 and 9-5). There are at least two ways to represent this same information as a decision tree. The first is shown in Figure 9-9. Here all of the choices are limited to two outcomes, either yes or no. However, looking at how the conditions are phrased in the decision tables, you remember that hours worked has three values, not two. You might argue that forcing a condition with three values into a set of conditions that have only yes or no available as values is somewhat artificial. To preserve the original logic of the decision situation, you can draw your decision tree as depicted in Figure 9-10. Here, there are only two conditions; the first condition has two values, and the second has three values, as is true in the decision table. We leave it as an exercise for the reader to diagram the logic of the situation depicted in Figures 9-6 and 9-7.

Decision tree: A graphical representation of a decision situation in which decision points (nodes) are connected together by arcs (one for each alternative on a decision) and terminate in ovals (the action which is the result of all of the decisions made on the path that leads to that oval).

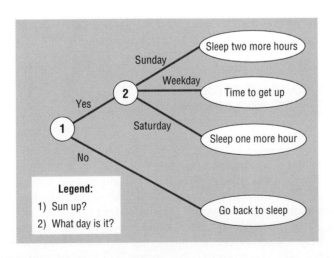

Figure 9-8
Generic decision tree

Figure 9-9
Decision tree representation of the decision logic in the decision tables in Figures 9-4 and 9-5, with only two choices per decision point

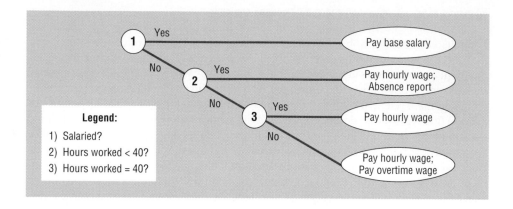

Figure 9-10
Decision tree representation of the decision logic in the decision tables in Figures 9-4 and 9-5, with multiple choices per decision point

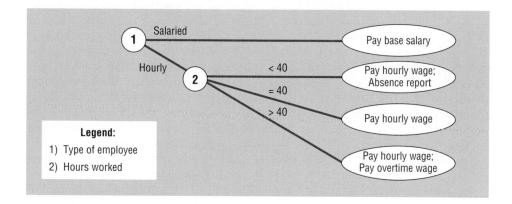

We have waited until now to make two important points about decision tables and decision trees. Once you have spent some time creating logic modeling aids such as these, be ready to refine them by drawing the diagrams again and again. As was the case with data flow diagrams, decision tables and decision trees benefit greatly from iteration. The second point is that you should always share your work with other team members and users to get feedback on the mechanical and content accuracy of your work. Other team members and users will often provide insight into issues you might have overlooked in describing the logic. For that reason, it is not uncommon for the analysis team leader to schedule a walkthrough at some point during the requirements structuring process.

DECIDING AMONG STRUCTURED ENGLISH, DECISION TABLES, AND DECISION TREES

How do you decide whether to use Structured English, decision tables, or decision trees when modeling process logic? On one level, the answer is to use whichever method you prefer and understand best. For example, some analysts and users prefer to see the logic of a complicated decision situation laid out in tabular form, as in a decision table; others will prefer the more graphical structure of a decision tree. Yet the issue actually extends beyond mere preferences. Just because you are very adept at using a hammer doesn't mean a hammer is the best tool for all home repairs—sometimes a screwdriver or a drill is the best tool. The same is true of logic modeling techniques: you have to consider the task you are performing and the purpose of the techniques in order to decide which technique is best. The relative advantages and disadvantages of Structured English, decision tables, and decision trees for different situations are presented in Tables 9-2 and 9-3.

Table 9-2 summarizes the research findings for comparisons of all three techniques. One study summarized in the table compared Structured English to decision tables and decision trees and analyzed the techniques for two different tasks (Vessey and Weber, 1986). The first task was determining the correct conditions and actions from a description of the problem, much the same situation analysts face when defining conditions and actions after an interview with a user. The study found that decision trees were the best technique to support this process as they naturally separate conditions and actions, making the logic of the decision rules more apparent. Even though Structured English does not separate conditions and actions, it was considered the second best technique for this task. Decision tables were the worst technique. The second task was converting conditions and actions to sequential statements, similar to what an analyst does when converting the stated conditions and actions to the sequence of pseudocode or a programming language. Structured English was the best technique for this task, as it is already written sequentially, but researchers found decision trees to be just as good. Decision tables were last again.

Both decision trees and decision tables do have at least one advantage over Structured English, however. Both decision tables and trees can be checked for completeness, consistency, and degree of redundancy. We checked all of our examples of decision tables for completeness when we made sure that each initial table included all possible rules. We knew the tables were complete when we multiplied the number of values for each condition to get the total number of possible rules. Following the other specific steps outlined earlier in the chapter will also help you check for a decision table's consistency and degree of redundancy. The same procedures can be easily adopted for decision trees. However, there are no such easy means to validate Structured English statements, giving decision tables and trees at least one advantage over Structured English.

TABLE 9-2 Criteria for Deciding among Structured English, Decision Tables, and Decision Trees

Criteria	Structured English	Decision Tables	Decision Trees
Determining conditions & actions	Second Best	Third Best	Best
Transforming conditions & actions into sequence	Best	Third Best	Best
Checking consistency & completeness	Third Best	Best	Best

TABLE 9-3 Criteria for Deciding between Decision Tables and Decision Trees

Criteria	Decision Tables	Decision Trees
Portraying complex logic	Best	Worst
Portraying simple problems	Worst	Best
Making decisions	Worst	Best
More compact	Best	Worst
Easier to manipulate	Best	Worst

Researchers have also compared decision tables to decision trees (Table 9-3). The pioneers of structured analysis and design thought decision tables were best for portraying complex logic while decision trees were better for simpler problems (Gane and Sarson, 1979). Others have found decision trees to be better for guiding decision making in practice (Subramanian et al., 1992), but decision tables have the advantage of being more compact than decision trees and easier to manipulate (Vanthienen, 1994). If more conditions are added to a situation, a decision table can easily accommodate more conditions, actions, and rules. If the table becomes too large, it can easily be divided into subtables, without the inconvenience of using flowchart-like tree connections used with decision trees. Creating and maintaining complex decision tables can be made easier with computer support (e.g., Prologa mentioned in Vanthienen, 1994).

SUMMARY

Logic modeling is one of the three key activities in the requirements structuring phase of systems analysis. There are various techniques available for modeling the decision logic in information system processes. One method, Structured English, is a special form of spoken English analysts use to illustrate the logic of processes depicted in data flow diagrams. Structured English is primarily a communication technique for analysts and users. Structured English dialect varies with analysts, but it must represent sequence, conditional statements, and repetition in information system processes.

Decision tables and decision trees are graphical methods for representing process logic. In decision tables, conditions are listed in the condition stubs, possible actions are listed in the action stubs, and rules link combinations of conditions with the actions that should result. A first pass at a decision table involves listing all possible rules that result from all values of the conditions listed. Second and subsequent passes reduce the complexity by eliminating rules that don't make sense and by combining rules with indifferent conditions. The same logic portrayed in a decision table can be portrayed in a decision tree but, in a decision tree, the conditions are represented by decision points and the values are represented by paths between decision points and ovals that contain actions.

Several research studies have compared Structured English, decision tables, and decision trees as techniques for representing decision logic. Most studies show that decision trees are the best for many criteria while decision tables are the worst on some criteria and the best on other criteria. Because there is no best technique to use for structuring requirements, an analyst must be proficient at all three techniques, as required by different situations.

KEY TERMS

Action stubs	Decision tree	Structured English
Condition stubs	Indifferent condition	
Decision table	Rules	

REVIEW QUESTIONS

1. Define each of the following terms:
   - a. Structured English
   - b. decision table
   - c. decision tree
   - d. event
   - e. state

2. What is the purpose of logic modeling? What techniques are used to model decision logic and what techniques are used to model temporal logic?

3. What is Structured English? How can Structured English be used to represent sequence, conditional statements, and repetition in an information systems process?

4. What is the difference between Structured English and pseudocode?

5. What are the steps in creating a decision table? How do you reduce the size and complexity of a decision table?

6. Explain the structure of a decision tree.

7. How do you know when to use Structured English, decision tables, or decision trees? Which is best for what situation?

8. What verbs are used in Structured English? What type of words are not used in Structured English?

9. What does the term "limited entry" mean in a decision table?

10. What is the formula that is used to calculate the number of rules a decision table must cover?

PROBLEMS AND EXERCISES

1. Match the following terms to the appropriate definitions.

   _____ rules

   _____ action stubs

   _____ condition stubs

   _____ indifferent condition

   - a. that part of a decision table listing the actions that result for a given set of conditions
   - b. that part of a decision table listing the conditions relevant to the decision
   - c. that part of a decision table specifying which actions are to be followed for a given set of conditions
   - d. in a decision table, a condition whose value does not affect the decision

2. Represent the decision logic in the decision table of Figure 9-5 in Structured English.

3. Look at the set of data flow diagrams created in Chapter 8 for Hoosier Burger's food ordering system.
   - a. Write Structured English to represent the logic in each process, at each level data flow diagram.
   - b. Represent the decision logic of one or more of the processes as decision tables.

4. Diagram the decision logic illustrated in the decision tables in Figures 9-6 and 9-7 as decision trees.

5. What types of questions need to be asked during requirements determination in order to gather the information needed for logic modeling? Give examples.

6. In one company the rules for buying personal computers are such that if the purchase is over $15,000.00, it has to go out for bid and the Request for Proposals must be approved by the Purchasing Department. If the purchase is under $15,000.00, the personal computers can simply be bought from any approved vendor; however, the Purchase Order must still be approved by the Purchasing Department. If the purchase goes out for bid, there must be at least three proposals received for the bid. If not, the RFP must go out again. If there still are not enough proposals, then the process can continue with the one or two vendors that have submitted proposals. The winner of the bid must be on an approved list of vendors for the company and, in addition, must not have any violations against them for affirmative action or environmental matters. At this point, if the proposal is complete, the Purchasing Department can issue a Purchase Order. Use Structured English to represent the logic in this process. Notice the similarities between the text in this question and format of your answer.

7. If you were going to develop a computer-based tool to help an analyst interview users and quickly and easily create and edit Structured English logic models, what type of tool would you build? What features would it have, and how would it work? Why?

8. Present the logic of the business process described in Problem and Exercise 6 in a decision table and then in a decision tree. For this example, how do these two techniques compare with one another? Why? How do they compare with the Structured English technique? Why? Do either of these techniques seem better suited to helping us diagnose problems and/or inefficiencies in the business process? Why or why not?

9. If you were going to develop a computer-based tool to help an analyst interview users and quickly and easily create and edit decision table and decision tree logic models, what type of tool would you build? What features would it have, and how would it work? Why? Would this type of tool be more or less useful than a tool built for this purpose which was based on Structured English? Why?

10. In a relatively small company that sells thin, electronic keypads and switches, the rules for selling products are such that sales representatives are assigned to unique regions of the country. Sales come either from cold calling, referrals, or current customers with new orders. A sizable portion of their business comes from referrals from larger competitors, who send their excess and/or "difficult" projects to this company. The company tracks these and, similarly, returns the favors to these competitors by sending business their way. The sales reps receive a 10% commission on purchases, not on orders, in their region. They can collaborate on a sale with reps in other regions and share the commissions, with 8% going to the "home" rep, and 2% going to the "visiting" rep. For any sales beyond the rep's previously stated and approved individual annual sales goals, he or she receives an additional 5% commission, an additional end-of-the-year bonus determined by management, and a special vacation for his or her family. Customers receive a 10% discount for any purchases over $100,000.00 per year, which are factored into the rep's commissions. In addition, the company focuses on customer satisfaction with the product and service, so there is an annual survey of customers in which they rate the sales rep. These ratings are factored into the bonuses such that a high rating increases the bonus amount, a moderate rating does nothing, and a low rating can lower the bonus amount. The company also wants to ensure that the reps close all sales. Any differences between the amount of orders and actual purchases is also factored into the rep's bonus amount. As best you can, present the logic of this business process first using Structured English, then using a decision table, and then using a decision

tree. Write down any assumptions you have to make. Which of these techniques is most helpful for this problem? Why?

11. The following is an example which demonstrates the rules of the tenure process for faculty at many universities. Present the logic of this business process first using Structured English, then using a decision table, and then using a decision tree. Write down any assumptions you have to make. Which of these techniques is most helpful for this problem? Why?

    A faculty member applies for tenure in his or her sixth year by submitting a portfolio summarizing his or her work. In rare circumstances he or she can come up for tenure earlier than the sixth year, but only if the faculty member has permission of the department chair and college dean. New professors, who have worked at other universities before taking their current jobs, rarely, if ever, come in with tenure. They are usually asked to undergo one "probationary" year during which they are evaluated and only can then be granted tenure. Top administrators coming in to a new university job, however, can often negotiate for retreat rights that enable them to become a tenured faculty member should their administrative post end. These retreat arrangements generally have to be approved by faculty. The tenure review process begins with an evaluation of the candidate's portfolio by a committee of faculty within the candidate's department. The committee then writes a recommendation on tenure and sends it to the department's chairperson who then makes a recommendation, and passes the portfolio and recommendation on to the next level, a college-wide faculty committee. This committee does the same as the department committee and passes its recommendation, the department's recommendation, and the portfolio on to the next level, a university-wide faculty committee. This committee does the same as the other two committees and passes everything on to the provost (or sometimes the acaemic vice-president). The provost then writes his or her own recommendation and passes everything to the president, the final decision maker. This process, from the time the candidate creates his or her portfolio until the time the president makes a decision, can take an entire academic year. The focus of the evaluation is on research, which could be grants, presentations, and publications, though preference is given for empirical research which has been published in top-ranked, refereed journals and where the publication makes a contribution to the field. The candidate must also do well in teaching and service (i.e., to the university, the community, or to the discipline) but the primary emphasis is on research.

12. An organization is in the process of upgrading microcomputer hardware and software for all employees. Hardware will be allocated to each employee in one of three packages. The first hardware package includes a standard microcomputer with a color monitor of moderate resolution and moderate storage capabilities. The second package includes a high-end microcomputer with high-resolution color monitor and a great deal of RAM and ROM. The third package is a high-end notebook-sized microcomputer. Each computer comes with a network interface card so that it can be connected to the network for printing and e-mail. The notebook computers come with a modem for the same purpose. All new and existing employees will be evaluated in terms of their computing needs (e.g., the types of tasks they perform, how much and in what ways they can use the computer). Light users receive the first hardware package. Heavy users receive the second package. Some moderate users will receive the first package and some will receive the second package, depending on their needs. Any employee who is deemed to be primarily mobile (e.g., most of the sales force) will receive the third package. Each employee will also be considered for additional hardware. For example, those who need scanners will receive them and those needing their own printers will receive them. A determination will be made regarding whether or not the user receives a color or black and white scanner, and whether or not they receive a slow or fast, or color or black and white printer. In addition, each employee will receive a suite of software,

including a word processor, spreadsheet, and presentation maker. All employees will be evaluated for their additional software needs. Depending on their needs, some will receive a desktop publishing package, some will receive a database management system (and some will also receive a developer's kit for the DBMS), and some will receive a programming language. Every 18 months those employees with the high-end systems will receive new hardware and then their old systems will be passed on to those who previously had the standard systems. All those employees with the portable systems will receive new notebook computers. Present the logic of this business process first using Structured English, then using a decision table, and then using a decision tree. Write down any assumptions you have to make. Which of these techniques is most helpful for this problem? Why?

13. Read the narratives below and follow the directions for each. If you discover that the narrative is incomplete, make up reasonable explanations to complete the story. Supply these extra explanations along with your answers.

   a. Samantha must decide which courses to register for this semester. She has a part-time job and she is waiting to find out how many hours per week she will be working during the semester. If she works 10 hours or less per week she will register for three classes, but if she works more than 10 hours per week she will register for only two classes. If she registers for two classes, she will take one class in her major area and one elective. If she registers for three classes, she will take two classes in her major area and one elective. Use both Structured English and a decision tree to represent this logic.

   b. Jerry plans on registering for five classes this semester: English composition, physics, physics lab, COBOL, and music appreciation. However, he is not sure if these classes are being offered this semester or if there will be timing conflicts. Also, two of the classes, physics and physics lab, must be taken together during the same semester. Therefore, if he can only register for one of them he will not take either class. If, for any reason, he cannot register for a class, he will identify and register for a different class to take its place that fits in his time schedule. Use a decision tree and a decision table that show all rules to represent this logic.

14. Mary is trying to decide what graduate programs she will apply to. She wants to stay in the southeast region of the United States, but if a program is considered one of the top 10 in the country she is willing to move to another part of the United States. Mary is interested in both the MBA and Master of MIS programs. An MBA program must have at least one well-known faculty member and meet her location requirements before she will consider applying to it. Additionally, any program she applies to must offer financial aid unless she is awarded a scholarship. Use Structured English, a decision tree, and a decision table to represent this logic.

15. At a local bank, loan officers must evaluate loan applications before approving or denying them. During this evaluation process, many factors regarding the loan request and the applicant's background are considered. If the loan is for less than $2,000, the loan officer checks the applicant's credit report. If the credit report is rated good or excellent, the loan officer approves the loan. If the credit report is rated fair, the officer checks to see if the applicant has an account at the bank. If the applicant holds an account, the application is approved; otherwise, the application is denied. If the credit report is rated poor, the application is denied. Loan applications for amounts between $2,000 and $200,000 are divided into four categories: car, mortgage, education, and other. For car, mortgage, and other loan requests, the applicant's credit report is reviewed and an employment check is made to verify the applicant's reported salary income. If the credit report rating is poor, the loan is denied. If the credit report rating is fair, good, or excellent and the salary income is verified, the loan is approved. If the salary income is not verifiable, the applicant is contacted and additional information is requested. In this case, the loan application along with the additional information is sent to the vice president for review and a

final loan decision. For educational loans, the educational institution the applicant will attend is contacted to determine the estimated cost of attendance. This amount is then compared to the amount of the loan requested in the application. If the requested amount exceeds the cost of attendance, the loan is denied. Otherwise, education loan requests for amounts between $2,000 and $34,999 are approved if the applicant's credit rating is fair, good, or excellent. Education loan applications requesting amounts from $35,000 to $200,000 are approved only if the credit rating is good or excellent. All loan applications for amounts greater than $200,000 are sent to the vice president for review and approval. Use Structured English, a decision tree, and a decision table to represent this logic.

FIELD EXERCISES

1. Choose a transaction that you are likely to encounter, perhaps ordering a cap and gown for graduation or ordering clothing from a mail order catalogue. Present the processes in this transaction using Structured English. Based on these examples, what appear to you to be the relative strengths and weaknesses of this technique versus decision tables or decision trees?

2. Why can't process logic simply be represented with regular written English? Research this issue in the library and write a position paper that explains the problems with representing procedure and action with the English language.

3. Explain the history of structured programming. How did it start? What was the basis for it? Why is it considered so important? How does structured programming fit within fourth-generation programming languages? To what extent is structured programming used in organizations with which you have come in contact?

4. Visit a shopping mall near you and observe the many transactions taking place in the various stores. What techniques presented in this chapter for modeling the logic of processes are most helpful for each of these various processes? Why? Are any of the modeling techniques robust enough to model all of these processes well? Why or why not?

REFERENCES

Booch, G. 1994. *Object-Oriented Analysis and Design, with Applications,* 2d ed. Redwood City, CA: The Benjamin/Cummings Publishing, Co., Inc.

Davis, W. S. 1983. *Systems Analysis and Design.* Reading, MA: Addison-Wesley Publishing Company.

Gane, C., and T. Sarson. 1979. *Structured Systems Analysis.* Englewood Cliffs, NJ: Prentice-Hall.

Subramanian, G. H., J. Nosek, S. P. Raghunathan, and S. S. Kanitkar. 1992. "A Comparison of the Decision Table and Tree." *Communications of the ACM* 35 (January): 89–94.

Vanthienen, J. 1994. "Technical Correspondence." *Communications of the ACM* 37 (February): 109–111.

Vessey, I., and R. Weber. 1986. "Structured Tools and Conditional Logic." *Communications of the ACM* 29 (January): 48–57.

Yourdon, E. 1989. *Managing the Structured Techniques.* Englewood Cliffs, NJ: Prentice-Hall.

Structuring System Requirements: Logic Modeling for the Customer Activity Tracking System

INTRODUCTION

The CATS project team continues to structure the requirements for the system by documenting the logic of processing rules and decisions that must be made within the system. These logic models will be validated during JAD sessions and walkthroughs. Probably the key decision in CATS is which product announcements should be sent to which customers. This case addresses how the project team represented this decision.

MATCHING PRODUCTS WITH CUSTOMERS

Frank Napier walked into Jorge Lopez's office. "Jorge," Frank said, "I'd like you to take a look at this."

"What is it, Frank?" Jorge asked. Jorge was reviewing some Structured English statements of process logic for BEC's Customer Activity Tracking System (CATS). "I've spent the morning looking at the Structured English statements you asked me to review. Most of this makes sense to me, but I think we need to schedule a walkthrough with Wendy Yoshimuro soon, before we go any further. So, what have you got there?"

"Yesterday I got the marketing information I had asked Wendy for. I've been trying to map out the logic in the process that matches customer profiles and music product profiles. Even though Wendy decided that we would send a customer just one reservation notice that covered all new releases in a given music category rather than a notice about particular artists, there's still a lot of information there, and the overall logic is pretty complicated. I started by looking at just three customer profile characteristics—income, taste in movies, and age—and how the three of them in combination can indicate a person's tastes in music. I started with only four music categories. There are so

many different kinds of music, some kinds filling very narrow niches. If I tried to put all of this information and all of the relationships...."

"Well, let me see what you have now. We can build on your past work and try to simplify the overall logic."

"Here's my first cut at a decision table," Frank said. He showed Jorge his notes. "I assigned values to each of the three customer characteristics I started out with. For income, I started with two categories: affluent and middle class. For movie tastes, I have four categories: adventure/action, romance, horror, and comedy. For age, there are three groupings: teenagers, young adults, and mature."

"How did you define each category?" Jorge asked.

"All of my information came from Wendy. Here's how I broke it down, based on the marketing categories Wendy uses:

Income:
    A = Affluent (> \$75,000 per year)
    M = Middle Class (\$30,000 to \$75,000)
Movie tastes:
    A = Adventure/Action (e.g., "Die Hard" movies)
    R = Romance (e.g., "Sleepless in Seattle")
    H = Horror (e.g., "Friday the Thirteenth" movies)
    C = Comedy (e.g., "Naked Gun" movies)
Age:
    T = Teenager (10 to 20)
    Y = Young adult (21 to 29)
    M = Mature (30 or older)."

"So how does this translate into a decision table?" Jorge asked.

"Since I have $2 \times 4 \times 3$ categories in this first cut, I need 24 different decision rules to cover all the possible combinations. That's what I have in my first decision table. The decision rules are based on information Wendy gave me in a memo and also from a procedure description of the music purchasing agent's job that

Wendy sent. The job description described what mix of music to purchase given the demographics of our members, and Wendy thought this might be relevant for matching customers and products, too.

"The four basic music categories I'm using are rock, AOR or adult-oriented radio, urban, and country. Rock is a broad category, ranging from Pearl Jam to the Rolling Stones, from Janis Joplin to the Breeders. AOR includes such performers as Michael Bolton, Mariah Carey, Jimmy Buffett, and Frank Sinatra. The urban music category is represented by such performers as Snoop Doggy Dogg, Ice-T, and N.W.A. Country is also a broad category which includes performers ranging from Garth Brooks to Patsy Cline, from Hank Williams Sr. to Reba McIntyre. Clearly, the final system will have to include narrower categories for both music products and personal tastes in movies. The narrower the categories, the more precise the mailings can be. Anyway, here's the decision table (Figure 1). We can also include categories of videos a member has rented and many other factors, but Wendy wanted to see what resulted from just these factors for now."

"Hmmmm, interesting," replied Jorge. "It looks as if the only group that would get all four new release music reservation notices would be affluent teenagers. They also look like the group that would be the most interested in urban music. Hardly any young adults or mature customers would be interested in urban music. How did you figure this out?"

"All of these decision rules are based on the studies of demographic data that Wendy collects and uses. Teenagers have the most disposable income, so affluent teenagers have even more. They also have eclectic musical tastes, so sending reservation notices for all new musical selections would have the biggest payoff with this group. This is kind of what the music clubs do. Maybe we could modify the 'BEC Membership In-

formation' form Wendy gave me during the original interview I did with her to include music preferences, but the added cost of sending all notices to this group with the most eclectic tastes does not seem that much. Mature customers, on the other hand, don't buy much prerecorded music and their tastes are narrower so, for this group, more selective notices mean better payoffs. Again, actual movie renting and buying behavior might be a better predictor of music interests than a one-time and possibly rather old membership form."

"What's the connection between movies and music?"

"Lots of movies these days rely on popular music from many different artists in their soundtracks. In fact, some soundtracks become big sellers at the record store. Remember that movie 'The Bodyguard'? The soundtrack was a big seller. Of course it didn't hurt that lots of the songs won Grammies."

"Interesting," said Jorge. "The more I look at this decision table, the more patterns I see."

"Right," said Frank. "In the second version of the table, I have only 12 rules [Figure 2]."

"And to make the entire decision process easier to understand on a more graphical level, I've prepared a decision tree that represents the decision logic in my second decision table [Figure 3]."

"Good work, Frank," Jorge replied. "But it looks as if there is a lot more work to do. Like you said, your musical categories are very broad."

"Yeah, you're right. I found out Broadway actually uses 25 different music categories."

"There has to be at least one more step," volunteered Jorge. "The announcements of new music releases also have to be categorized so that the customer receives a notice of a particular artist's new release based on the customer's profile. Remember, although we legally can't keep records about what

Figure 1
Complete decision table for deciding which music release announcements to send to which customers

Income	A	M	A	M	A	M	A	M	A	M	A	M	A	M	A	M	A	M	A	M	A	M	A	M
Movie tastes	A	A	R	R	H	H	C	C	A	A	R	R	H	H	C	C	A	A	R	R	H	H	C	C
Age	T	T	T	T	T	T	T	T	Y	Y	Y	Y	Y	Y	Y	Y	M	M	M	M	M	M	M	M
Rock notice	X	X	X		X	X	X	X	X	X	X		X	X	X	X						X		X
AOR notice	X		X	X	X		X	X	X	X	X	X		X	X	X	X	X	X	X			X	X
Urban notice	X	X	X		X	X	X						X	X							X			
Country notice	X		X	X	X		X		X			X	X	X		X		X		X	X	X		X

Figure 2
Reduced version of decision table from Figure 1

Income	A	A	M	M	M	M	M	M	A	A	A	A
Movie tastes	–	–	R	H	C	A	A	A	A	R	H	C
Age	T	M	–	–	–	T	Y	M	Y	Y	Y	Y
Rock notice	X			X	X	X	X		X	X	X	X
AOR notice	X	X	X			X		X	X	X	X	X
Urban notice	X			X		X					X	
Country notice	X	X	X						X	X	X	X

Figure 3
Decision tree representation of logic in Figure 2

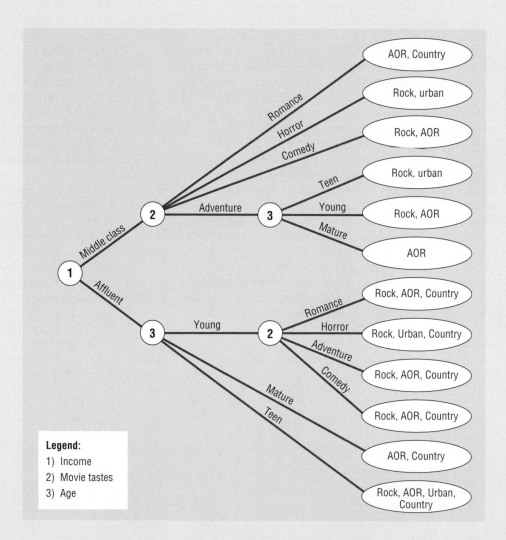

Legend:
1) Income
2) Movie tastes
3) Age

videos customers have bought, we can do this for music. And all of this has to be repeated for new video releases too."

"That's right," Frank replied. "I'm working on it. I'll add a few more factors, as you suggest, and then show the logic models to Jordan to see if she thinks I'm on the right track. Thanks for your help. By the way, as soon as you and the data analyst have a preliminary diagram for the CATS database, let me know and I'll be glad to give you feedback on that."

SUMMARY

Frank, Jorge, and Jordan, the core members of the CATS project team, are now well into some of the most challenging work of systems analysis: transforming what are generally imprecise and vague statements of what people want a system to do into clear and unambiguous models of system requirements. These models allow all interested parties at BEC to know exactly *what* CATS will do and what rules it will follow. Such clarity is necessary for systems design as well as for approval by the Systems Priority Board at the end of the analysis phase. The next BEC case will review some of the work in the last element of structuring requirements—data modeling.

CHAPTER

10

Structuring System Requirements:
Conceptual Data Modeling

After studying this chapter, you should be able to:

■ Concisely define each of the following key data-modeling terms: *entity type, attribute, multivalued attribute, relationship, degree, cardinality, business rule, associative entity,* and *trigger.*

■ Draw an entity-relationship (E-R) diagram to represent common business situations.

■ Explain the role of conceptual data modeling in the overall analysis and design of an information system.

■ Distinguish between unary, binary, and ternary relationships, and give an example of each.

■ Define four basic types of business rules in an E-R diagram.

■ Explain the role of CASE technology in the analysis and documentation of data required in an information system.

■ Relate data modeling to process and logic modeling as different views of describing an information system.

INTRODUCTION

In Chapters 8 and 9 you learned how to model and analyze two important views of an information system: (1) the flow of data between manual or automated steps and (2) the decision logic of processing data. None of the techniques discussed so far, however, has concentrated on the data that must be retained in order to support the data flows and processing described. For example, you learned how to show data stores, or *data at rest,* in a data flow diagram. The natural *structure* of data, however, was not shown. Data flow diagrams and various processing logic techniques show *how, where,* and *when* data are used or changed in an information system, but these techniques do not show the *definition, structure,* and *relationships* within the data. Data modeling develops this missing, and crucial, piece of the description of an information system.

In fact, some systems developers believe that a data model is the most important part of the statement of information system requirements. This belief is based on the following reasons. First, the characteristics of data captured during data modeling are crucial in the design of databases, programs, computer screens, and printed reports. For example, facts such as these—a data element is numeric, a product can be in only one product line at a time, a line item on a customer order can never be moved to another customer order, customer region name is limited to a specified set of values—are all essential pieces of information in ensuring data integrity in an information system.

Second, data rather than processes are the most complex aspects of many modern information systems and hence require a central role in structuring system requirements. Transaction processing systems can have considerable process complexity in validating data, reconciling errors, and coordinating the movement of data to various databases. These types of systems have been in place for years in most organizations; current systems development focuses more on management information systems (such as sales tracking), decision support systems (such as short-term cash investment), and executive support systems (such as product planning). MIS, DSS, and ESS are more data-intensive and require extracting data from various data sources. The exact nature of processing is also more ad hoc than with transaction processing systems, so the details of processing steps cannot be anticipated. Thus, the goal is to provide a rich data resource that might support any type of information inquiry, analysis, and summarization.

Third, the characteristics about data (such as length, format, and relationships with other data) are reasonably permanent. In contrast, the paths of data flow are quite dynamic. Who receives which data, the format of reports, and what reports are used change considerably and constantly over time. A data model explains the inherent nature of the organization, not its transient form. So, an information system design based on a data orientation, rather than a process or logic orientation, should have a longer useful life. Finally, structural information about data is essential for automatic generation of programs. For example, the fact that a customer order has many line items on it instead of just one line item affects the automatic design of a computer screen for entry of customer orders. Thus, although a data model specifically documents the file and database requirements for an information system, the business meaning, or semantics, of data included in the data model have broader impact on the design and construction of a system.

The most common format used for data modeling is entity-relationship (E-R) diagramming. A similar format used with object-oriented analysis and design methods is reviewed in Chapter 12. Data modeling using the E-R notation explains the characteristics and structure of data independent of how the data may be stored in computer memories. A data model using E-R notation is usually developed iteratively. Often IS planners use E-R notation to develop an enterprise-wide data model with very broad categories of data and little detail. Next, during the definition of a project, a specific E-R model is built to help explain the scope of a particular systems analysis and design effort. During requirements structuring, an E-R model represents conceptual data requirements for a particular system. Then, after system inputs and outputs are fully described during logical design, the conceptual E-R data model is refined before it is translated into a logical format (typically a relational data model) from which database definition and physical database design are done. Thus, you will use E-R diagramming in many systems development project steps, and most IS project members need to develop and read E-R diagrams. Therefore, mastery of the requirements structuring methods and techniques addressed in this chapter is critical to your success on a systems development project team.

CONCEPTUAL DATA MODELING

A **conceptual data model** is a representation of organizational data. The purpose of a conceptual data model is to show as many rules about the meaning and inter-relationships among data as are possible.

Conceptual data model:
A detailed model that captures the overall structure of organizational data while being independent of any database management system or other implementation considerations.

You typically do conceptual data modeling in parallel with other requirements analysis and structuring steps during systems analysis (see Figure 10-1). You collect the explanations of the business necessary for conceptual data modeling from information-gathering methods like interviewing, questionnaires, and JAD sessions. On larger systems development teams, a subset of the project team concentrates on data modeling while other team members focus attention on process or logic modeling. You develop (or use from prior systems development) a conceptual data model for the current system and build a conceptual data model that supports the scope and requirements for the proposed or enhanced system.

The work of all team members is coordinated and shared through the project dictionary or repository. As discussed in Chapter 4, this repository is often maintained by a common CASE tool, but some organizations still use manual documentation. Whether automated or manual, it is essential that the process, logic, and data model descriptions of a system be consistent and complete since each describes different but complementary views of the same information system. For example, the names of data stores on the primitive-level DFDs often correspond to the names of data

Figure 10-1
Systems development life cycle with analysis phase highlighted

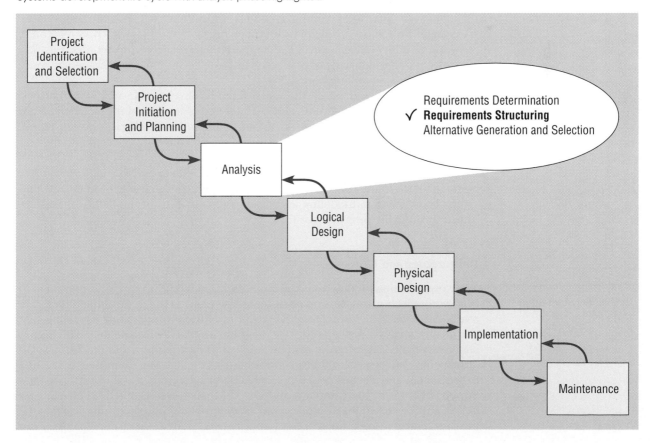

entities in entity-relationship diagrams, and the data elements associated with data flows on DFDs must be accounted for by attributes of entities and relationships in entity-relationship diagrams.

The Process of Conceptual Data Modeling

You typically begin the process of conceptual data modeling by developing a conceptual data model for the system being replaced, if a system exists. This is essential for planning the conversion of the current files or database into the database of the new system. Further, this is a good, but not a perfect, starting point for your understanding of the data requirements of the new system. Then, you build a new conceptual data model which includes all of the data requirements for the new system. You discovered these requirements from the fact-finding methods employed during requirements determination. Today, given the popularity of prototyping and other rapid development methodologies (see Chapter 13), these requirements often evolve through various iterations of a prototype, so the data model is constantly changing.

Conceptual data modeling is one kind of data modeling and database design carried out throughout the systems development process. Figure 10-2 shows the different kinds of data modeling and database design that go on during the whole systems development life cycle. The conceptual data modeling methods we discuss in this chapter are suitable for project identification and selection (including information systems planning which may lead to project identification), project initiation and planning, and analysis phases. These phases of the SDLC address issues of system scope, general requirements, and content—all independent of technical implementation. E-R diagramming is suited for this since E-R diagrams can be translated into a wide variety of technical architectures for data, such as relational, network, and hierarchical. An E-R data model evolves from project identification and selection through analysis as it becomes more specific and is validated by more detailed analysis of system needs.

In the logical design phase, the final E-R model developed in analysis is matched with designs for systems inputs and outputs and is translated into a format from which physical data storage decisions can be made in the physical design phase. During physical design, specific data storage architectures are selected and then, in implementation, files and databases are defined as the system is coded. Through the use of the project repository, a field in a physical data record can, for example, be traced back to the conceptual data attribute which represents it on an E-R diagram. Thus, the data modeling and design steps in each of the SDLC phases are linked through the project repository.

Deliverables and Outcomes

Most organizations today do conceptual data modeling using entity-relationship modeling which uses a special notation to represent as much meaning about data as possible. Thus, the primary deliverable from the conceptual data modeling step within the analysis phase is an E-R diagram, similar to Figure 10-3. This figure shows the major categories of data (rectangles on the diagram) and the business relationships between them (lines connecting rectangles). For example, Figure 10-3 describes that, for the business represented by this diagram, a SUPPLIER *sometimes* Supplies ITEMs to the company, and an ITEM is *always* Supplied by one to four SUPPLIERS. The fact that a supplier only sometimes supplies items implies that the business wants to keep track of some suppliers without designating what they can

Figure 10-2
Relationship between data modeling and the systems development life cycle

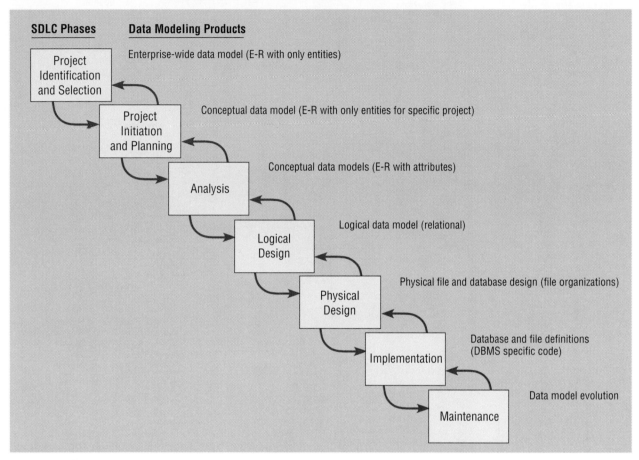

supply. This diagram includes two names on each line giving you explicit language to read a relationship in each direction. For simplicity, we will not typically include two names on lines in E-R diagrams in this book; however, this is a standard used in many organizations.

There may be as many as four E-R diagrams produced and analyzed during conceptual data modeling:

1. An E-R diagram that covers just the data needed in the project's application. (This allows you to concentrate on the data requirements of the project's application without being constrained or confused by unnecessary details.)

2. An E-R diagram for the application system being replaced. (Differences between this diagram and the first show what changes you have to make to convert databases to the new application.) This is, of course, not produced if the proposed system supports a completely new business function.

3. An E-R diagram that documents the whole database from which the new application's data is extracted. (Since many applications possibly share the same database or even several databases, this and the first diagram show how the new application shares the contents of more widely used databases.)

Figure 10-3
Sample conceptual data
model diagram

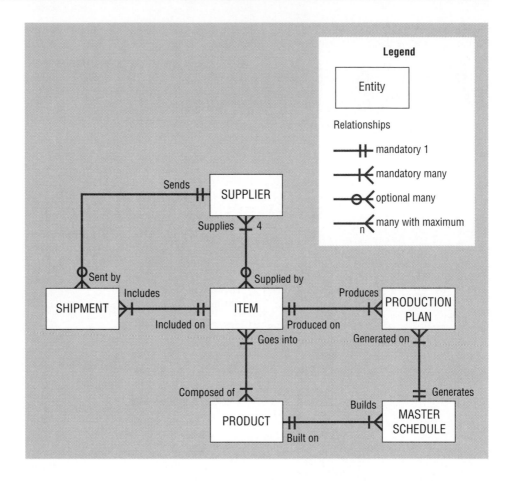

4. An E-R diagram for the whole database from which data for the application system being replaced is drawn. (Again, differences between this diagram and the third show what global database changes you have to make to implement the new application.) Even if there is no system being replaced, an understanding of the existing data systems is necessary to see where the new data will fit in or if existing data structures must change to accommodate new data.

The other deliverable from conceptual data modeling is a full set of entries about data objects to be stored in the project dictionary or repository. The repository is the mechanism to link data, process, and logic models of an information system. For example, there are explicit links between a data model and a data flow diagram. Some important links are briefly explained here.

- Data elements included in data flows also appear in the data model and vice versa. You must include in the data model any raw data captured and retained in a data store and a data model can include only data that has been captured or is computed from captured data. Since a data model is a general business picture of data, both manual and automated data stores will be included.

- Each data store in a process model must relate to business objects (what we will call data entities) represented in the data model. For example, in Figure 8-5, the Inventory File data store must correspond to one or several data objects on a data model.

Similar to what was shown in Figure 8-17, you can use an automated repository to verify these linkages.

GATHERING INFORMATION FOR CONCEPTUAL DATA MODELING

Requirements determination methods must include questions and investigations that take a data, not only a process and logic, focus. For example, during interviews with potential system users—during JAD sessions or within requirements questionnaires—you must ask specific questions in order to gain the perspective on data needed to develop a data model. In later sections of this chapter, we will introduce some specific terminology and constructs used in data modeling. Even without this specific data modeling language, you can begin to understand the kinds of questions that must be answered during requirements determination. These questions relate to understanding the rules and policies by which the area supported by the new information system operates. That is, a data model explains what the organization does and what rules govern how work is performed in the organization. You do not, however, need to know how or when data is processed or used to do data modeling.

You typically do data modeling from a combination of perspectives. The first perspective is generally called the *top-down approach.* This perspective derives the business rules for a data model from an intimate understanding of the nature of the business, rather than from any specific information requirements in computer displays, reports, or business forms. There are several very useful sources of typical questions that elicit the business rules needed for data modeling (see Aranow, 1989; Sandifer and von Halle, 1991a and 1991b). Table 10-1 summarizes a few key questions you should ask system users and business managers so that you can develop an accurate and complete data model. The questions in this table are purposely posed in business terms. In this chapter you will learn the more technical terms included in bold at the end of each set of questions. Of course, these technical terms do not mean much to a business manager, so you must learn how to frame your questions in business terms for your investigation.

You can also gather the information you need for data modeling by reviewing specific business documents—computer displays, reports, and business forms—handled within the system. This process of gaining an understanding of data is often called a *bottom-up approach.* These items will appear as data flows on DFDs and will show the data processed by the system and, hence, probably the data which must be maintained in the system's database. Consider, for example, Figure 10-4, which shows a customer order form used at Pine Valley Furniture. From this form, we determine that the following data must be kept in the database:

ORDER NO	CUSTOMER NO
ORDER DATE	NAME
PROMISED DATE	ADDRESS
PRODUCT NO	CITY-STATE-ZIP
DESCRIPTION	
QUANTITY ORDERED	
UNIT PRICE	

We also see that each order is from one customer, and an order can have multiple line items, each for one product. We will use this kind of understanding of an organization's operation to develop data models.

TABLE 10-1 Requirements Determination Questions for Data Modeling

1. *What are the subjects/objects of the business?* What types of people, places, things, materials, etc. are used or interact in this business, about which data must be maintained? How many instances of each object might exist?—**data entities and their descriptions**

2. *What unique characteristic (or characteristics) distinguishes each object from other objects of the same type?* Might this distinguishing feature change over time or is it permanent? Might this characteristic of an object be missing even though we know the object exists?—**primary key**

3. *What characteristics describe each object?* On what basis are objects referenced, selected, qualified, sorted, and categorized? What must we know about each object in order to run the business?—**attributes and secondary keys**

4. *How do you use this data?* That is, are you the source of the data for the organization, do you refer to the data, do you modify it, and do you destroy it? Who is not permitted to use this data? Who is responsible for establishing legitimate values for this data?—**security controls and understanding who really knows the meaning of data**

5. *Over what period of time are you interested in this data?* Do you need historical trends, current "snapshot" values, and/or estimates or projections? If a characteristic of an object changes over time, must you know the obsolete values?—**cardinality and time dimensions of data**

6. *Are all instances of each object the same?* That is, are there special kinds of each object that are described or handled differently by the organization? Are some objects summaries or combinations of more detailed objects?—**supertypes, subtypes, and aggregations**

7. *What events occur that imply associations between various objects?* What natural activities or transactions of the business involve handling data about several objects of the same or different type?—**relationships, and their cardinality and degree**

8. *Is each activity or event always handled the same way or are there special circumstances?* Can an event occur with only some of the associated objects, or must all objects be involved? Can the associations between objects change over time (for example, employees change departments)? Are values for data characteristics limited in any way?—**integrity rules, minimum and maximum cardinality, time dimensions of data**

Figure 10-4
Sample customer order

```
                      PVF CUSTOMER ORDER
       ORDER NO: 61384                        CUSTOMER NO:  1273

               NAME:              Contemporary Designs
               ADDRESS:           123 Oak St.
               CITY-STATE-ZIP:    Austin, TX 28384

       ORDER DATE: 11/04/1998    PROMISED DATE:  11/21/1998
```

PRODUCT NO	DESCRIPTION	QUANTITY ORDERED	UNIT PRICE
M128	Bookcase	4	200.00
B381	Cabinet	2	150.00
R210	Table	1	500.00

INTRODUCTION TO E-R MODELING

The basic entity-relationship modeling notation (Chen, 1976) uses three main constructs: data entities, relationships, and their associated attributes. The E-R model notation has subsequently been extended to include additional constructs by Chen and others; for example, see Teorey et al. (1986) and Storey (1991). Several different E-R notations exist, and many CASE tools support multiple notations. For simplicity, we have adopted one common notation for this book, the so-called crow's foot notation. If you use another notation in courses or work, you should be able to easily translate between notations.

An **entity-relationship data model** (or E-R model) is a detailed, logical representation of the data for an organization or for a business area. The E-R model is expressed in terms of entities in the business environment, the relationships or associations among those entities, and the attributes or properties of both the entities and their relationships. An E-R model is normally expressed as an **entity-relationship diagram** (or E-R diagram), which is a graphical representation of an E-R model. The notation we will use for E-R diagrams appears in Figure 10-5, and subsequent sections explain this notation.

> **Entity-relationship data model (E-R model):** A detailed, logical representation of the entities, associations, and data elements for an organization or business area.

> **Entity-relationship diagram (E-R diagram):** A graphical representation of an E-R model.

Entities

An entity (see the first question in Table 10-1) is a person, place, object, event, or concept in the user environment about which the organization wishes to maintain data. An entity has its own identity which distinguishes it from each other entity. Some examples of entities follow:

- Person: EMPLOYEE, STUDENT, PATIENT
- Place: STATE, REGION, COUNTRY, BRANCH
- Object: MACHINE, BUILDING, AUTOMOBILE, PRODUCT
- Event: SALE, REGISTRATION, RENEWAL
- Concept: ACCT, COURSE, WORK CENTER

There is an important distinction between entity *types* and entity *instances*. An **entity type** (sometimes called an *entity class*) is a collection of entities that share common properties or characteristics. Each entity type in an E-R model is given a name. Since the name represents a class or set, it is singular. Also, since an entity is an object, we use a simple noun to name an entity type. We use capital letters in naming an entity type and, in an E-R diagram, the name is placed inside a rectangle representing the entity:

> **Entity type:** A collection of entities that share common properties or characteristics.

An **entity instance** (or **instance**) is a single occurrence of an entity type. An entity type is described just once in a data model while many instances of that entity type may be represented by data stored in the database. For example, there is one EMPLOYEE entity type in most organizations, but there may be hundreds (or even thousands) of instances of this entity type stored in the database.

A common mistake made when you are just learning to draw E-R diagrams, especially if you already know how to do data flow diagramming, is to confuse data entities with sources/sinks or system outputs and relationships with data

> **Entity instance (instance):** A single occurrence of an entity type.

Figure 10-5
Entity-relationship notation

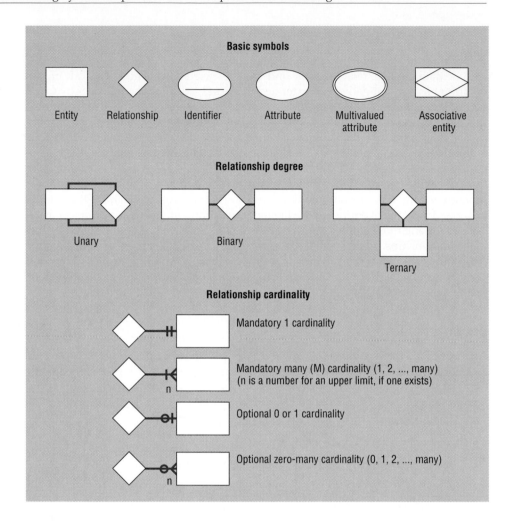

flows. A simple rule to avoid such confusion is that a true data entity will have many possible instances, each with a distinguishing characteristic, as well as one or more other descriptive pieces of data. Consider the entity types below that might be associated with a sorority expense system.

In this situation, the sorority treasurer manages accounts, and records expense transactions against each account. However, do we need to keep track of data about the Treasurer and her supervision of accounts as part of this accounting system? The Treasurer is the person entering data about accounts and expenses and making inquiries about account balances and expense transactions by category. Since there is only one Treasurer, TREASURER data does not need to be kept. On the other hand, if each account has an account manager (for example, a sorority officer) who is responsible for assigned accounts, then we may wish to have an ACCOUNT MANAGER entity type, with pertinent attributes as well as relationships to other entity types.

In this same situation, is an expense report an entity type? Since an expense report is computed from expense transactions and account balances, it is a data flow, not an entity type. Even though there will be multiple instances of expense reports over time, the report contents are already represented by the ACCOUNT and EXPENSE entity types.

Often when we refer to entity types in subsequent sections we will simply say entity. This is common among data modelers. We will clarify that we mean an entity by using the term entity instance.

Attributes

Each entity type has a set of attributes (see the third question in Table 10-1) associated with it. An **attribute** is a property or characteristic of an entity that is of interest to the organization (relationships may also have attributes, as we will see in the section on Relationships). Following are some typical entity types and associated attributes:

STUDENT: Student_ID, Student_Name, Address, Phone_Number, Major

AUTOMOBILE: Vehicle_ID, Color, Weight, Horsepower

EMPLOYEE: Employee_ID, Employee_Name, Address, Skill

We use an initial capital letter, followed by lowercase letters, and nouns in naming an attribute. In E-R diagrams, we can visually represent an attribute by placing its name in an ellipse with a line connecting it to the associated entity. Many CASE tools, to avoid placing a large number of symbols on a diagram, do not include attributes on an E-R diagram. Rather, the attributes of an entity (sometimes called its composition) are listed in the repository entry for the entity; then, each attribute may be separately defined as another object in the repository. This is similar to how the composition of a data flow is handled in Oracle's Designer/2000 (see Figure 8-18).

Candidate Keys and Identifiers

Every entity type must have an attribute or set of attributes that distinguishes one instance from other instances of the same type (see the second question in Table 10-1). A **candidate key** is an attribute (or combination of attributes) that uniquely identifies each instance of an entity type. A candidate key for a STUDENT entity type might be Student_ID.

Sometimes more than one attribute is required to identify a unique entity. For example, consider the entity type GAME for a basketball league. The attribute Team_Name is clearly not a candidate key, since each team plays several games. If each team plays exactly one home game against each other team, then the combination of the attributes Home_Team and Visiting_Team is a candidate key for GAME.

Some entities may have more than one candidate key. One candidate key for EMPLOYEE is Employee_ID; a second is the combination of Employee_Name and Address (assuming that no two employees with the same name live at the same address). If there is more than one candidate key, the designer must choose one of the candidate keys as the identifier. An **identifier** is a candidate key that has been selected to be used as the unique characteristic for an entity type. Bruce (1992) suggests the following criteria for selecting identifiers:

1. Choose a candidate key that will not change its value over the life of each instance of the entity type. For example, the combination of Employee_Name and Address would probably be a poor choice as a primary key for

Attribute: A named property or characteristic of an entity that is of interest to the organization.

Candidate key: An attribute (or combination of attributes) that uniquely identifies each instance of an entity type.

Identifier: A candidate key that has been selected as the unique, identifying characteristic for an entity type.

EMPLOYEE because the values of Address and Employee_Name could easily change during an employee's term of employment.

2. Choose a candidate key such that, for each instance of the entity, the attribute is guaranteed to have valid values and not be null. To insure valid values, you may have to include special controls in data entry and maintenance routines to eliminate the possibility of errors. If the candidate key is a combination of two or more attributes, make sure that all parts of the key will have valid values.

3. Avoid the use of so-called intelligent keys, whose structure indicates classifications, locations, and so on. For example, the first two digits of a key for a PART entity may indicate the warehouse location. Such codes are often modified as conditions change, which renders the primary key values invalid.

4. Consider substituting single-attribute surrogate keys for large composite keys. For example, an attribute called Game_ID could be used for the entity GAME instead of the combination of Home_Team and Visiting_Team.

For each entity, the name of the identifier is underlined on an E-R diagram. The following diagram shows the representation for a STUDENT entity type using E-R notation:

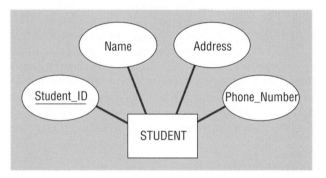

Multivalued Attributes

Multivalued attribute: An attribute that may take on more than one value for each entity instance.

A **multivalued attribute** may take on more than one value *for each entity instance.* Suppose that Skill is one of the attributes of EMPLOYEE. If each employee can have more than one skill, Skill is a multivalued attribute. During conceptual design, it is common to use a special symbol or notation to highlight multivalued attributes. Two ways of showing multivalued attributes are common. The first is to use a double-lined ellipse, so that the EMPLOYEE entity with its attributes is diagrammed as follows:

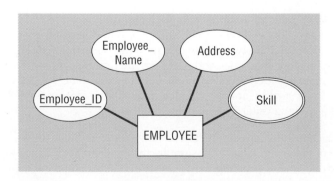

The second approach is to separate the repeating data into another entity, called a *weak* (or *attributive*) entity, and then using a relationship (relationships are discussed in the next section), link the weak entity to its associated regular entity. The approach also easily handles several attributes that repeat together, called a **repeating group.** For example, consider again an employee entity with multivalued attributes for data about each employee's dependents. In this situation, data such as dependent name, age, and relation to employee (spouse, child, parent, etc.) are multivalued attributes about an employee, and these attributes repeat together. We could show these multivalued attributes using the ellipse notation as

Repeating group: A set of two or more multivalued attributes that are logically related.

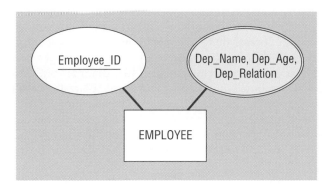

We can show this using an attributive entity, DEPENDENT, and a relationship, shown here simply by a line between DEPENDENT and EMPLOYEE. The crow's foot next to DEPENDENT means that there may be many DEPENDENTs for the same EMPLOYEE. Some E-R notations and CASE tools use a special symbol to signify a weak entity. Common notations are a double-line border on the entity box or a mark on the relationship line.

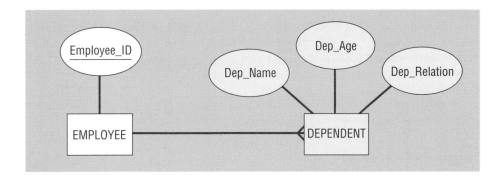

Relationships

Relationships are the glue that hold together the various components of an E-R model (see the fifth, seventh, and eighth questions in Table 10-1). A **relationship** is an association between the instances of one or more entity types that is of interest to the organization. An association usually means that event has occurred or that there exists some natural linkage between entity instances. For this reason, relationships are labeled with verb phrases. For example, a training department in a company is interested in tracking which training courses each of its employees has completed. This leads to a relationship (called Completes) between the EMPLOYEE and COURSE entity types that we diagram as follows:

Relationship: An association between the instances of one or more entity types that is of interest to the organization.

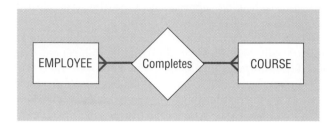

As indicated by the arrows, this is a many-to-many relationship: Each employee may complete more than one course, and each course may be completed by more than one employee. More significantly, we can use the Completes relationship to determine the specific courses that a given employee has completed. Conversely, we can determine the identity of each employee who has completed a particular course.

Many CASE tools, to avoid cluttering an E-R diagram with excess symbols, will not include the relationship diamond and simply place the verb phrase for the relationship name near the line (see Figure 10-3 for an example). We use both representations interchangeably in this book and, as noted earlier, we sometimes use two verb phrases so that there is an explicit name for the relationship in each direction. The standards you will follow will be determined by your organization.

CONCEPTUAL DATA MODELING AND THE E-R MODEL

The last section introduced the fundamentals of the E-R data modeling notation—entities, attributes, and relationships. The goal of conceptual data modeling is to capture as much of the meaning of data as is possible. The more details (business rules) about data that we can model, the better the system we can design and build. Further, if we can include all these details in a CASE repository, and if a CASE tool can generate code for data definitions and programs, then the more we know about data, the more code can be generated automatically. This will make system building more accurate and faster. More importantly, if we can keep a thorough repository of data descriptions, we can regenerate the system as needed as the business rules change. Since maintenance is the largest expense with any information system, the efficiencies gained by maintaining systems at the rule, rather than code, level drastically reduce the cost.

In this section, we explore more advanced concepts needed to more thoroughly model data and learn how the E-R notation represents these concepts.

Degree of a Relationship

Degree: The number of entity types that participate in a relationship.

The **degree** of a relationship (see question 7 in Table 10-1) is the number of entity types that participate in that relationship. Thus, the relationship Completes illustrated above is of degree two, since there are two entity types: EMPLOYEE and COURSE. The three most common relationships in E-R models are *unary* (degree one), *binary* (degree two), and *ternary* (degree three). Higher-degree relationships are possible, but they are rarely encountered in practice, so we restrict our discussion to these three cases. Examples of unary, binary, and ternary relationships appear in Figure 10-6.

Unary relationship (recursive relationship): A relationship between the instances of one entity type.

Unary Relationship   Also called a *recursive relationship*, a **unary relationship** is a relationship between the instances of one entity type. Two examples are shown in Figure 10-6. In the first example, Is_married_to is shown as a one-to-one relationship between instances of the PERSON entity type. That is, each person may be

Figure 10-6
Example relationships of different degrees

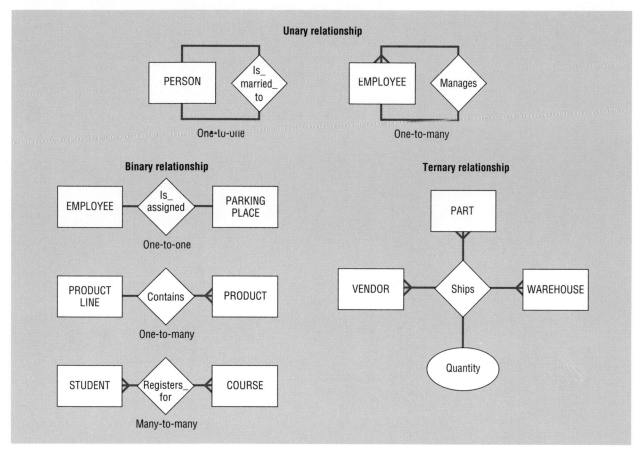

currently married to one other person. In the second example, Manages is shown as a one-to-many relationship between instances of the EMPLOYEE entity type. Using this relationship, we could identify (for example) the employees who report to a particular manager, or reading the Manages relationship in the opposite direction, who the manager is for a given employee.

Figure 10-7 shows an example of another common unary relationship, called a *bill-of-materials structure*. Many manufactured products are made of subassemblies, which in turn are composed of other subassemblies and parts, and so on. As shown in Figure 10-7a, we can represent this structure as a many-to-many unary relationship. In this figure, we use Has_components for the relationship name. The attribute Quantity, which is a property of the relationship, indicates the number of each component that is contained in a given assembly.

Two occurrences of this structure are shown in Figure 10-7b. Each diagram shows the immediate components of each item as well as the quantities of that component. For example, item X consists of item U (quantity 3) and item V (quantity 2). You can easily verify that the associations are in fact many-to-many. Several of the items have more than one component type (for example, item A has three immediate component types: V, X, and Y). Also, some of the components are used in several higher-level assemblies. For example, item X is used in both item A and item B. The many-to-many relationship guarantees, for example, that the

Figure 10-7
Bill-of-materials unary
relationship

(a) Many-to-many
relationship

(b) Two instances

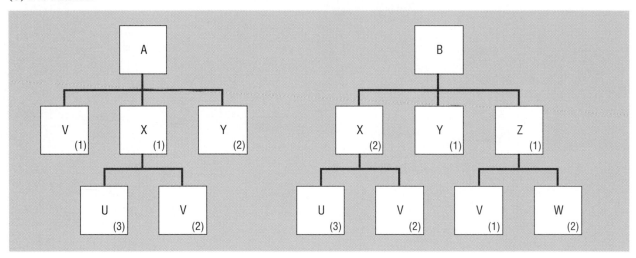

same subassembly structure of X is used each time item X goes into making some other item.

Binary relationship: A relationship between instances of two entity types. This is the most common type of relationship encountered in data modeling.

Binary Relationship   A **binary relationship** is a relationship between instances of two entity types and is the most common type of relationship encountered in data modeling. Figure 10-6 shows three examples. The first (one-to-one) indicates that an employee is assigned one parking place, and each parking place is assigned to one employee. The second (one-to-many) indicates that a product line may contain several products, and each product belongs to only one product line. The third (many-to-many) shows that a student may register for more than one course, and that each course may have many student registrants.

Ternary relationship: A simultaneous relationship among instances of three entity types.

Ternary Relationship   A **ternary relationship** is a *simultaneous* relationship among instances of three entity types. In the example shown in Figure 10-6, the relationship Ships tracks the quantity of a given part that is shipped by a particular vendor to a selected warehouse. Each entity may be a one or a many participant in a ternary relationship (in Figure 10-6, all three entities are many participants).

Note that a ternary relationship is not the same as three binary relationships. For example, Quantity is an attribute of the Ships relationship in Figure 10-6. Quantity cannot be properly associated with any of the three possible binary relationships among the three entity types (such as that between PART and VENDOR) because Quantity is the amount of a particular PART shipped from a particular VENDOR to a particular WAREHOUSE.

Cardinalities in Relationships

Suppose that there are two entity types, A and B, that are connected by a relationship. The **cardinality** of a relationship (see the fifth, seventh, and eighth questions in Table 11-1) is the number of instances of entity B that can (or must) be associated with each instance of entity A. For example, consider the following relationship for video movies:

Cardinality: The number of instances of entity B that can (or must) be associated with each instance of entity A.

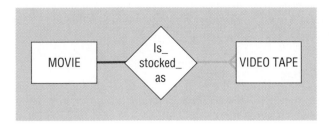

Clearly, a video store may stock more than one video tape of a given movie. In the terminology we have used so far, this example is intuitively a "many" relationship. Yet it is also true that the store may not have a single tape of a particular movie in stock. We need a more precise notation to indicate the *range* of cardinalities for a relationship. This notation was introduced in Figure 10-5, which you may want to review at this point.

Minimum and Maximum Cardinalities   The *minimum* cardinality of a relationship is the minimum number of instances of entity B that may be associated with each instance of entity A. In the preceding example, the minimum number of video tapes available for a movie is zero, in which case we say that VIDEO TAPE is an *optional participant* in the Is_stocked_as relationship. When the minimum cardinality of a relationship is one, then we say entity B is a *mandatory participant* in the relationship. The *maximum* cardinality is the maximum number of instances. For our example, this maximum is "many" (an unspecified number greater than one). Using the notation from Figure 10-5, we diagram this relationship as follows:

The zero through the line near the VIDEO TAPE entity means a minimum cardinality of zero, while the crow's foot notation means a "many" maximum cardinality.

Examples of three relationships that show all possible combinations of minimum and maximum cardinalities appear in Figure 10-8. A brief description of each relationship follows.

1. PATIENT Has PATIENT HISTORY (Figure 10-8a). Each patient has one or more patient histories (we assume that the initial patient visit is always

recorded as an instance of PATIENT HISTORY). Each instance of PATIENT HISTORY "belongs to" exactly one PATIENT.

2. EMPLOYEE Is_assigned_to PROJECT (Figure 10-8b). Each PROJECT has at least one assigned EMPLOYEE (some projects have more than one). Each EMPLOYEE may or (optionally) may not be assigned to any existing PROJECT, or may be assigned to several PROJECTs.

3. PERSON Is_married_to PERSON (Figure 10-8c). This is an optional 0 or 1 cardinality in both directions, since a person may or may not be married.

It is possible for the maximum cardinality to be a fixed number, not an arbitrary "many" value. For example, suppose corporate policy states that an employee may work on at most five projects at the same time. We could show this business rule by placing a 5 above or below the crow's foot next to the PROJECT entity in Figure 10-8b.

Associative Entities

As seen in the examples of the Ships relationship in Figure 10-6 and the Has_ components relationship of Figure 10-7, attributes may be associated with a many-to-many relationship as well as with an entity. For example, suppose that the organization wishes to record the date (month and year) when an employee completes each course. Some sample data follows:

Figure 10-8
Examples of cardinalities in relationships

(a) Mandatory cardinalities

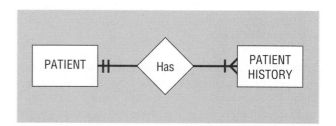

(b) One optional, one mandatory cardinality

(c) Optional cardinalities

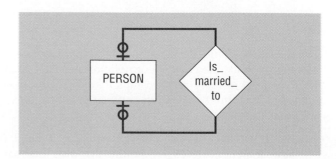

Employee_ID	Course_Name	Date_Completed
549-23-1948	Basic Algebra	March 1998
629-16-8407	Software Quality	June 1998
816-30-0458	Software Quality	Feb 1998
549-23-1948	C Programming	May 1998

From this limited data you can conclude that the attribute Date_Completed is not a property of the entity EMPLOYEE (since a given employee such as 549-23-1948 has completed courses on different dates). Nor is Date_Completed a property of COURSE, since a particular course (such as Software Quality) may be completed on different dates. Instead, Date_Completed is a property of the relationship between EMPLOYEE and COURSE. The attribute is associated with the relationship and diagrammed as follows:

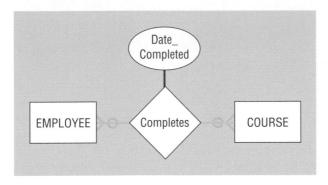

Since many-to-many and one-to-one relationships may have associated attributes, the E-R data model poses an interesting dilemma: is a many-to-many relationship actually an entity in disguise? Often the distinction between entity and relationship is simply a matter of how you view the data. An **associative entity** (sometimes called a *gerund*) is a relationship that the data modeler chooses to model as an entity type. Figure 10-9 shows the E-R notation for representing the Completes relationship as an associative entity. The diamond symbol is included within the entity rectangle as a reminder that the entity was derived from a relationship. The lines from CERTIFICATE to the two entities are not two separate binary relationships, so they do not have labels. Note that EMPLOYEE and COURSE have mandatory one cardinality since an instance of Completes must have an associated EMPLOYEE and COURSE. The implicit identifier of Completes is the combination of the identifiers of EMPLOYEE and COURSE, Employee_ID and Course_Name, respectively.

An example of the use of an associative entity for a ternary relationship appears in Figure 10-10. This figure shows an alternative (and equally correct) representation of the ternary Ships relationship shown in Figure 10-6. In Figure 10-10, the entity

Associative entity: An entity type that associates the instances of one or more entity types and contains attributes that are peculiar to the relationship between those entity instances; also called a gerund.

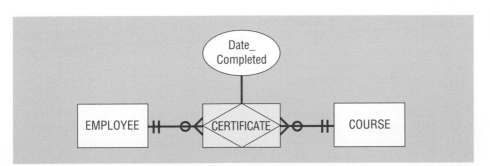

Figure 10-9
Example associative entity

Figure 10-10
SHIPMENT entity type
(an associative entity)

type (associative entity) SHIPMENT replaces the Ships relationship from Figure 10-6. Each instance of SHIPMENT represents a real-world shipment by a given vendor of a particular part to a selected warehouse. The Quantity of that shipment is an attribute of SHIPMENT. A Shipment_ID is assigned to each shipment and is the identifier of SHIPMENT, as shown in Figure 10-10.

One situation in which a relationship *must* be turned into an associative entity is when the associative entity has other relationships with entities besides the relationship which caused its creation. For example, consider the following E-R model which represents price quotes from different vendors for purchased parts stocked by Pine Valley Furniture:

Now, suppose that we also need to know which price quote is in effect for each part shipment received. This additional data requirement *necessitates* that the Quotes_price relationship be transformed into an associative entity, and this new situation is represented at the top of the next page.

In this case, PRICE QUOTE is not a ternary relationship. Rather, PRICE QUOTE is a binary many-to-many relationship (associative entity) between VENDOR and PART. In addition, each PART RECEIPT, based on Amount, has an applicable, negotiated Price. Each PART RECEIPT is for a given PART from a specific VENDOR, and the Amount of the receipt dictates the purchase price in effect by matching with the Quantity attribute. Since the PRICE QUOTE pertains to a given PART and given VENDOR, PART RECEIPT does not need direct relationships with these entities.

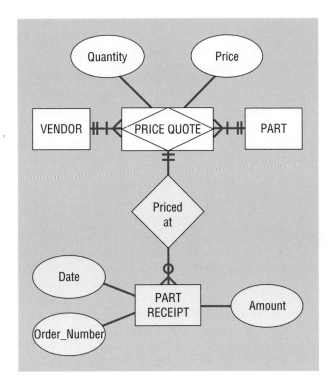

Summary of Conceptual Data Modeling with E-R Diagrams

The purpose of E-R diagramming is to capture the richest possible understanding of the meaning of data necessary for an information system or organization. Besides the aspects shown in this chapter, there are many other semantics about data that E-R diagramming can represent. Some of these more advanced capabilities are explained in McFadden, Hoffer, and Prescott (1999) and on the World Wide Web site for this book (http://hepg.awl.com/). You can also find some general guidelines for effective conceptual data modeling in Moody (1996). The following section presents one final aspect of conceptual data modeling: capturing the rules by which the organization operates.

BUSINESS RULES

Conceptual data modeling is a step-by-step process for documenting information requirements that is concerned with both the structure of data and with rules about the integrity of that data (see the eighth question in Table 10-1). **Business rules** are specifications that preserve the integrity of the logical data model. There are four basic types of business rules:

> **Business rules:**
> Specifications that preserve the integrity of a conceptual or logical data model.

1. *Entity integrity.* Each instance of an entity type must have a unique identifier that is not null.

2. *Referential integrity constraints.* Rules concerning the relationships between entity types.

3. *Domains.* Constraints on valid values for attributes.

4. *Triggering operations.* Other business rules that protect the validity of attribute values.

The entity-relationship model that we have described in this chapter is concerned primarily with the structure of data rather than with expressing business rules (although some elementary rules are implied in the E-R model). Generally the business rules are captured during requirements determination and stored in the CASE repository (described in Chapter 4) as they are documented. Entity integrity was described earlier in this chapter and referential integrity is described in Chapter 16 since it applies most to logical data modeling. In this section, we briefly describe two types of rules: domains and triggering operations. These rules are illustrated with a simple example from a banking environment, shown in Figure 10-11a. In this example, an ACCOUNT entity has a relationship (Is_for) with a WITHDRAWAL entity.

Domains

Domain: The set of all data types and values that an attribute can assume.

A **domain** is the set of all data types and ranges of values that attributes may assume (Fleming and von Halle, 1990). Domain definitions typically specify some (or all) of the following characteristics of attributes: data type, length, format, range, allowable values, meaning, uniqueness, and null support (whether an attribute value may or may not be null).

Figure 10-11b shows two domain definitions for the banking example. The first definition is for Account_Number. Since Account_Number is a primary key attribute, the definition specifies that Account_Number must be unique and also must not be null (these specifications are true of all identifiers). The definition specifies that the attribute data type is character and that the format is nnn-nnnn. Thus

Figure 10-11
Examples of business rules

(a) Simple banking relationship

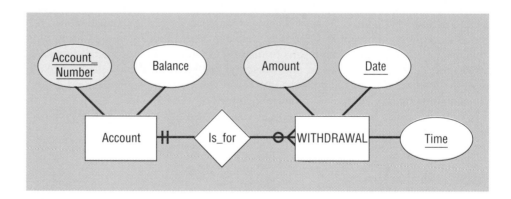

(b) Typical domain definitions

Name: Account_Number
Meaning: Customer account number in bank
Data type: Character
Format: nnn-nnnn
Uniqueness: Must be unique
Null support: Non-null

Name: Amount
Meaning: Dollar amount of transaction
Data type: Numeric
Format: 2 decimal places
Range: 0–10,000
Uniqueness: Nonunique
Null support: Non-null

(c) Typical triggering operation

User rule: WITHDRAWAL Amount may not exceed ACCOUNT Balance
Event: Insert
Entity Name: WITHDRAWAL
Condition: WITHDRAWAL Amount > ACCOUNT Balance
Action: Reject the insert transaction

any attempt to enter a value for this attribute that does not conform to its character type or format will be rejected, and an error message will be displayed.

The domain definition for the Amount attribute (dollar amount of the requested withdrawal) also may not be null, but is not unique. The format allows for two decimal places to accommodate a currency field. The range of values has a lower limit of zero (to prevent negative values) and an upper limit of 10,000. The latter is an arbitrary upper limit for a single withdrawal transaction.

The use of domains offers several advantages:

1. Domains verify that the values for an attribute (stored by insert or update operations) are valid.

2. Domains ensure that various data manipulation operations (such as joins or unions in a relational database system) are logical.

3. Domains help conserve effort in describing attribute characteristics.

Domains can conserve effort because we can define domains and then associate each attribute in the data model with an appropriate domain. To illustrate, suppose that a bank has three types of accounts, with the following identifiers:

Account Type	Identifier
CHECKING	Checking_Account_Number
SAVINGS	Savings_Account_Number
LOAN	Loan_Account_Number

If domains are not used, the characteristics for each of the three identifier attributes must be described separately. Suppose, however, that the characteristics for all three of the attributes are identical. Having defined the domain Account_Number once (as shown in Figure 10-11b), we simply associate each of these three attributes with Account_Number. Other common domains such as Date, Social_Security_ Number, and Telephone_Number also need to be defined just once in the model.

Triggering Operations

A **triggering operation** (or **trigger**) is an assertion or rule that governs the validity of data manipulation operations such as insert, update, and delete. The scope of triggering operations may be limited to attributes within one entity, or it may extend to attributes in two or more entities. Complex business rules may often be stated as triggering operations.

A triggering operation normally includes the following components:

1. *User rule:* a concise statement of the business rule to be enforced by the triggering operation

2. *Event:* the data manipulation operation (insert, delete, or update) that initiates the operation

3. *Entity name:* the name of the entity being accessed and/or modified

4. *Condition:* condition that causes the operation to be triggered

5. *Action:* action taken when the operation is triggered

Figure 10-11c shows an example of a triggering operation for the banking situation. The business rule is a simple (and familiar) one: the amount of an attempted withdrawal may not exceed the current account balance. The event of interest is an

Triggering operation (trigger): An assertion or rule that governs the validity of data manipulation operations such as insert, update, and delete.

attempted insert of an instance of the WITHDRAWAL entity type (perhaps from an automated teller machine). The condition is

Amount (of the withdrawal) > ACCOUNT Balance

When this condition is triggered, the action taken is to reject the transaction. You should note two things about this triggering operation: first, it spans two entity types; second, the business rule could not be enforced through the use of domains.

The use of triggering operations is an increasingly important component of database strategy. With triggering operations, the responsibility for data integrity lies within the scope of the database management system rather than with application programs or human operators. In the banking example, tellers could conceivably check the account balance before processing each withdrawal. Human operators would be subject to human error and, in any event, manual processing would not work with automated teller machines. Alternatively, the logic of integrity checks could be built into the appropriate application programs, but integrity checks would require duplicating the logic in each program. There is no assurance that the logic would be consistent (since the application programs may have been developed at different times by different people) or that the application programs will be kept up to date as conditions change.

As stated earlier, business rules should be documented in the CASE repository. Ideally, these rules will then be checked automatically by database software. Removing business rules from application programs and incorporating them in the repository (in the form of domains, referential integrity constraints, and triggering operations) has several important advantages:

1. Provides faster application development with fewer errors, since these rules can be generated into programs or enforced by the DBMS

2. Reduces maintenance effort and expenditures

3. Provides faster response to business changes

4. Facilitates end-user involvement in developing new systems and manipulating data

5. Provides for consistent application of integrity constraints

6. Reduces time and effort required to train application programmers

7. Promotes ease of use of a database

For a more thorough treatment of business rules, see McFadden, Hoffer, and Prescott (1999).

THE ROLE OF CASE IN CONCEPTUAL DATA MODELING

CASE tools provide two important functions in conceptual data modeling: (1) maintaining E-R diagrams as a visual depiction of structured data requirements and (2) linking objects on E-R diagrams to corresponding descriptions in a repository. Most CASE tools support one or more of several standard E-R diagramming notations, such as the crow's foot notation used in this text. Many tools do not support drawing ternary or higher relationships, so you may have to model these higher degree relationships as several binary relationships, even though this is not semantically correct.

Figure 10-12 lists the typical data model elements that are placed in the project dictionary or CASE repository during conceptual data modeling. A CASE tool will typically allow you to move directly to the repository entry for an object once you select it on an E-R diagram. The precise list of object characteristics will vary by CASE tool or the standard you use for a project dictionary. Figure 10-12, however, provides a basic set of repository contents used in almost any circumstance. Later data modeling and database design steps develop additional data model elements for the repository, as we will show in subsequent chapters.

AN EXAMPLE OF CONCEPTUAL DATA MODELING AT HOOSIER BURGER

Chapters 8 and 9 structured the process and logic requirements for a new inventory control system for Hoosier Burger. The data flow diagram and decision table (repeated here as Figures 10-13 and 10-14) describe requirements for this new system. The purpose of this system is to monitor and report changes in raw material inventory levels, and to issue material orders and payments to suppliers. Thus, the central data entity for this system will be an INVENTORY ITEM, corresponding to data store D1 in Figure 10-13.

Changes in inventory levels are due to two types of transactions: receipt of new items from suppliers and consumption of items from sales of products. Inventory is added upon receipt of new raw materials, for which Hoosier Burger receives a supplier

Figure 10-12
Typical conceptual data model elements in a project dictionary

Entity (major category of data)
Name	A short and a long name that uniquely label the entity
Description	Explanation so that it is clear what objects are covered by this entity
Alias	Alternative names used for this entity (that is, synonyms)
Primary key	Name(s) of attribute(s) that form the unique identifier for each instance of this entity
Attributes and repetition	List of attributes associated with this entity and the number of instances of each attribute for each entity instance
Abstraction	Indication of any superclasses or subclasses or composition of entity types involving this entity

Attribute (entity characteristic)
Name	A short and a long name that uniquely label the attribute
Description	Explanation of the attribute so that its meaning is clearly different from all other attributes
Alias	Alternative names used for this attribute (that is, synonyms)
Domain	The permitted values that this attribute may assume
Computation	If this is not raw data, the formula or method to calculate the attribute's value
Aggregation	Indication of any groupings of attributes involving this attribute (e.g., a month attribute as part of a date attribute)

Relationship (association between entity instances)
Name	A short and a long name that uniquely label the relationship
Description	Explanation of the relationship so that its meaning is clearly different from all other relationships
Degree	Names of entities involved in the relationship
Cardinality	The potential number of instances of each entity involved in the relationship
Insertion rules	Business rules that control the inclusion of entity instances in this relationship
Deletion rules	Business rules that control the elimination of entity instances from this relationship

Figure 10-13
Level-0 data flow diagram for Hoosier Burger's new logical inventory control system (same as Figure 8-16)

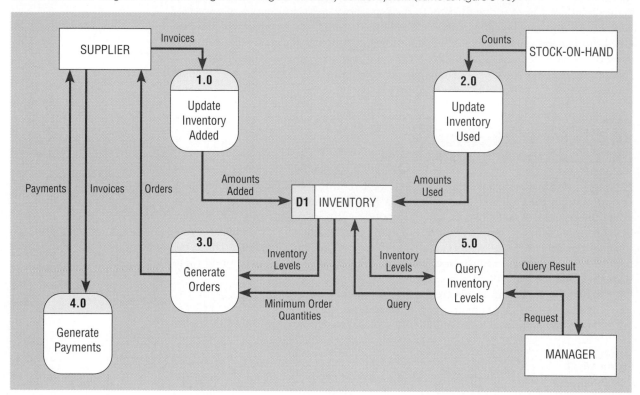

INVOICE (see Process 1.0 in Figure 10-13). Each INVOICE indicates that the supplier has sent a specific quantity of one or more INVOICE ITEMs, which correspond to Hoosier's INVENTORY ITEMs. Inventory is used when customers order and pay for PRODUCTs. That is, Hoosier makes a SALE for one or more SALE ITEMs, each of which corresponds to a food PRODUCT. Since the real-time customer order processing system is separate from the inventory control system, a source, STOCK ON-HAND on Figure 10-13, represents how data flows from the

Figure 10-14
Reduced decision table for Hoosier Burger's inventory reordering (Same as Figure 9-7)

Conditions/ Courses of Action	Rules						
	1	2	3	4	5	6	7
Type of item	P	P	P	P	P	P	N
Time of week	D	W	D	W	D	W	–
Season of year	A	A	S	S	H	H	–
Standing daily order	X		X		X		
Standing weekend order		X		X		X	
Minimum order quantity							X
Holiday reduction					X	X	
Summer reduction			X	X			

order processing to the inventory control system. Finally, since food PRODUCTs are made up of various INVENTORY ITEMs (and visa versa), Hoosier maintains a RECIPE to indicate how much of each INVENTORY ITEM goes into making one PRODUCT. From this discussion, we have identified the data entities required in a data model for the new Hoosier Burger inventory control system: INVENTORY ITEM, INVOICE, INVOICE ITEM, PRODUCT, SALE, SALE ITEM, and RECIPE. To complete the data model, we must determine necessary relationship between these entities as well as attributes for each entity.

The wording in the previous description tells us much of what we need to know to determine relationships:

- An INVOICE includes one or more INVOICE ITEMs, each of which corresponds to an INVENTORY ITEM. Obviously, an INVOICE ITEM cannot exist without an associated INVOICE, and over time there will be zero to many receipts, or INVOICE ITEMs, for an INVENTORY ITEM.

- Each PRODUCT has a RECIPE of INVENTORY ITEMs. Thus, RECIPE is an associative entity supporting a bill-of-materials type relationship between PRODUCT and INVENTORY ITEM.

- A SALE indicates that Hoosier sells one or more ITEM SALES, each of which corresponds to a PRODUCT. An ITEM SALE cannot exist without an associated SALE, and over time there will be zero to many ITEM SALES for a PRODUCT.

Figure 10-15 shows an E-R diagram with the entities and relationships described above. We include on this diagram two labels for each relationship, one to be read in either relationship direction (e.g., an INVOICE Includes one to many INVOICE ITEMS, and an INVOICE ITEM Is_included_on exactly one INVOICE). RECIPE, since it is an associative entity, also serves as the label for the many-to-many relationship between PRODUCT and INVENTORY ITEM. Now that we understand the entities and relationships, we must decide which data elements are associated with the entities and gerunds in this diagram.

You may wonder at this point why only the INVENTORY data store is shown in Figure 10-13 when there are seven entities and associative entities on the E-R

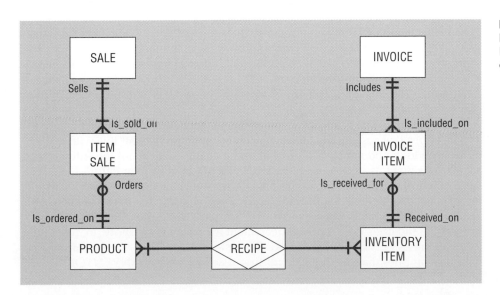

Figure 10-15
Preliminary E-R diagram for Hoosier Burger's inventory control system

Figure 10-16
Final E-R diagram for Hoosier Burger's inventory control system

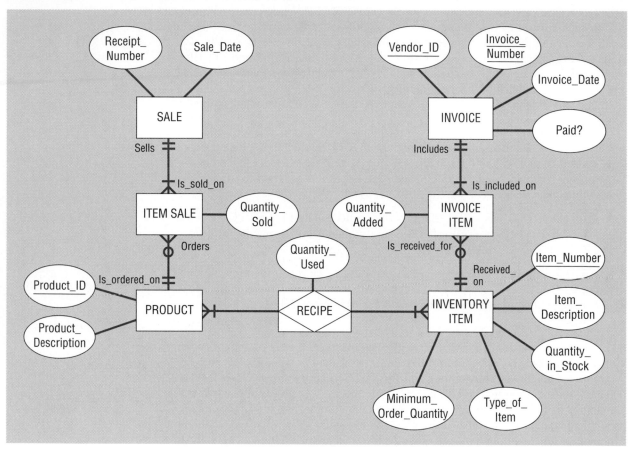

diagram. The INVENTORY data store corresponds to the INVENTORY ITEM entity in Figure 10-15. The other entities are hidden inside other processes for which we have not shown lower-level diagrams. In actual requirements structuring steps, you would have to match all entities with data stores: each data store represents some subset of an E-R diagram, and each entity is included in one or more data stores. Ideally, each data store on a primitive DFD will be an individual entity.

To determine data elements for an entity, we investigate data flows in and out of data stores that correspond to the data entity, and supplement this with a study of decision logic and temporal logic that use or change data about the entity. There are six data flows associated with the INVENTORY data store in Figure 10-13. The description of each data flow in the project dictionary or CASE repository would include the data flow's composition, which then tells us what data are flowing in or out of the data store. For example, the Amounts Used data flow coming from Process 2.0 indicates how much to decrement an attribute Quantity_in_Stock due to use of the INVENTORY ITEM to fulfill a customer sale. Thus, the Amounts Used data flow implies that Process 2.0 will first read the relevant INVENTORY ITEM record, then update its Quantity_in_Stock attribute, and finally store the updated value in the record. Structured English for Process 2.0 would depict this logic. Each data flow would be analyzed similarly (space does not permit us to show the analysis for each data flow).

The analysis of data flows for data elements is supplemented by a study of decision logic. For example, consider the decision table of Figure 10-14. One condition used to determine the process of reordering an INVENTORY ITEM involves the Type_of_Item. Thus, Process 3.0 in Figure 10-13 (to which this decision table relates) needs to know this characteristic of each INVENTORY ITEM, so this identifies another attribute of this entity.

Although we do not illustrate a state-transition diagram for this system, the analysis of such a chart could also reveal additional data requirements. For example, a state-transition diagram on an inventory item might show states of below reorder point, above reorder point, and projected above reorder point. This last state occurs when an invoice is received for a new shipment but before the shipment's quantity is verified. Such a state could imply the need for a new attribute on an INVENTORY ITEM to specify whether the Quantity_in_Stock is an actual value or an estimate.

After having considered all data flows in and out of data stores related to data entities, plus all decision and temporal logic related to inventory control, we derive the full E-R data model, with attributes, shown in Figure 10-16.

SUMMARY

We have presented the process and basic notation used to model the data requirements of an information system. We outlined the structuring of conceptual data models using the entity-relationship notation and also discussed how the components of a conceptual data model relate to data flows and data stores as well as states on a state-transition diagram.

Conceptual data modeling is based on certain constructs about the structure, not use, of data. These constructs include: entity, relationship, degree, and cardinality. A data model shows the relatively permanent business rules that define the nature of an organization. Rules define such characteristics of data as the legitimate domain of values for data attributes, the unique characteristics (identifier) of entities, the relationships between different entities, and the triggering operations that protect the validity of attributes during data maintenance.

A data model shows major categories of data, called entities, the associations or relationships between entities, and the attributes of both entities and relationships. A special type of entity called an associative entity is often necessary to represent a many-to-many relationship between entities. Entity types are distinct from entity instances. Each entity instance is distinguished from other instances of the same type by an identifier attribute (or attributes).

Relationships are the glue that hold a data model together. Three common relationship types are unary, binary, and ternary. The minimum and maximum number of entity instances that participate in a relationship represent important rules about the nature of the organization, as captured during requirements determination.

This chapter completes our coverage of the traditional techniques used to structure information system requirements. The next chapter, the last in the section on the analysis phase of the life cycle, addresses the selection among alternative directions for designing the new or replacement system.

K E Y   T E R M S

Associative entity
Attribute
Binary relationship
Business rules
Candidate key
Cardinality
Conceptual data model
Degree

Domain
Entity-relationship data
    model (E-R model)
Entity-relationship
    diagram (E-R diagram)
Entity instance (instance)
Entity type
Identifier

Multivalued attribute
Relationship
Repeating group
Ternary relationship
Triggering operation
    (trigger)
Unary relationship
    (recursive relationship)

R E V I E W   Q U E S T I O N S

1. Define each of the following terms:

   a. entity type
   b. business rule
   c. instance
   d. identifier
   e. relationship
   f. minimum cardinality

   g. attributive entity
   h. associative entity
   i. attribute
   j. degree
   k. trigger

2. Discuss why some systems developers believe that a data model is one of the most important parts of the statement of information system requirements.

3. Distinguish between the data modeling done during information systems planning, project initiation and planning, and analysis phases of the systems development life cycle.

4. What elements of a data flow diagram should be analyzed as part of data modeling?

5. Explain why a ternary relationship is not the same as three binary relationships.

6. When must a many-to-many relationship be modeled as an associative entity?

7. What is the significance of triggering operations business rules in the analysis and design of an information system?

8. Which of the following types of relationships can have attributes associated with them: one-to-one, one-to-many, many-to-many?

9. What are the linkages between data flow diagrams, decision tables, state-transition diagrams, and entity-relationship diagrams?

10. What is the degree of a relationship? Give an example of each of the relationship degrees illustrated in this chapter.

11. Give an example of a ternary relationship (different from any example in this chapter).

12. List the deliverables from the conceptual data modeling part of the analysis phase of the systems development process.

13. Explain the relationship between minimum cardinality and optional and mandatory participation.

14. List the ideal characteristics of an entity identifier attribute.

15. List the four types of E-R diagrams produced and analyzed during conceptual data modeling.

PROBLEMS AND EXERCISES

1. Match the following terms to the appropriate definitions.

   _____ entity type

   _____ alias

   _____ many-to-many relationship

   _____ domain

   _____ gerund

   a. set of all data types and range of values that an attribute can assume

   b. alternative name for an element of a data model

   c. binary relationship in which the maximum number of entity instances related to one instance of the other type of entity is greater than one

   d. another name for an associative entity

   e. collection of entities that share common properties

2. Assume that at Pine Valley Furniture each product (described by Product No., Description, and Cost) is comprised of at least three components (described by Component No., Description, and Unit of Measure) and components are used to make one or many products (that is, must be used in at least one product). In addition, assume that components are used to make other components and that raw materials are also considered to be components. In both cases of components being used to make products and components being used to make other components, we need to keep track of how many components go into making something else. Draw an E-R diagram for this situation and place minimum and maximum cardinalities on the diagram.

3. Much like Pine Valley Furniture's sale of products, stock brokerages sell stocks and the prices are continually changing. Draw an E-R diagram which takes into account the changing nature of stock price.

4. If you were going to develop a computer-based tool to help an analyst interview users and quickly and easily create and edit entity-relationship diagrams, what type of tool would you build? What features would it have, and how would it work? Why?

5. A software training program is divided into training modules and each module is described by module name and the approximate practice time. Each module sometimes has prerequisite modules. Model this situation of training programs and modules with an E-R diagram.

6. Each semester, each student must be assigned an advisor who counsels students about degree requirements and helps students register for classes. Students must register for classes with the help of an advisor, but if their assigned advisor is not available, they may register with any advisor. We must keep track of students, their assigned advisor, and with whom the student registered for the current term. Represent this situation of students and advisors with an E-R diagram.

7. Assume that entity PART has attributes Part_Number, Drawing_Number, Weight, Description, Storage_Location, and Cost. Which attributes are candidate keys? Why? Which attribute would you select for the identifier of PART? Why? Or do you think that you should create another attribute to be the identifier? Why or why not?

8. Consider the E-R diagram in Figure 10-9.
   a. What is the identifier for the COMPLETES associative entity?
   b. Now, assume that the same employee may take the same course multiple times, on different dates. Does this change your answer to part a? Why or why not?

9. Study the E-R diagram of Figure 10-17. Based on this E-R diagram, answer the following questions:

Figure 10-17
E-R diagram for Problem and Exercise 9

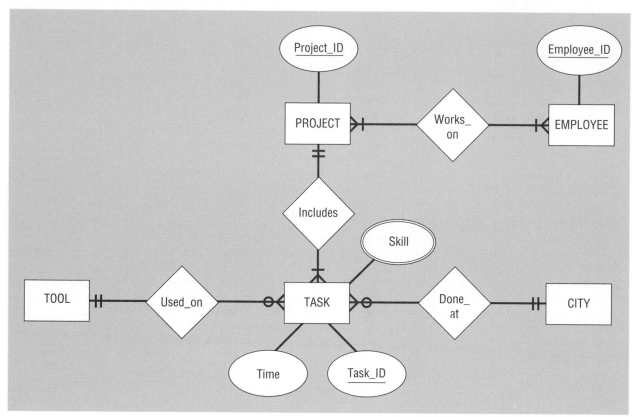

    a. How many PROJECTs can an employee work on?
    b. What is the degree of the Includes relationship?
    c. Are there any associative entities on this diagram? If so, name them.
    d. How else could the attribute Skill be modeled?
    e. Is it possible to attach any attributes to the Includes relationship?
    f. Could TASK be modeled as an associative entity?

10. For the entity-relationship diagram provided in Figure 10-18, draw in the relationship cardinalities and describe them. Describe any assumptions you must make about relevant business rules. Are there any changes or additions you would make to this diagram to make it better? Why or why not?

11. For the entity-relationship diagram provided in Figure 10-18, assume that this company decided to assign each sales representative to a small, unique set of customers; some customers can now become "members" and receive unique benefits; small manufacturing teams will be formed and each will be assigned to the production of a small, unique set of products; and each purchasing agent will be assigned to a small, unique set of vendors. Make the necessary changes to the entity-relationship diagram and draw and describe the new relationship cardinalities.

12. Obtain a copy of an invoice, order form, or bill used in one of your recent business transactions. Create an E-R diagram to describe your sample document.

13. Using Table 10-1 as a guide, develop the complete script (questions and possible answers) of an interview between analysts and users within the order entry function at Pine Valley Furniture.

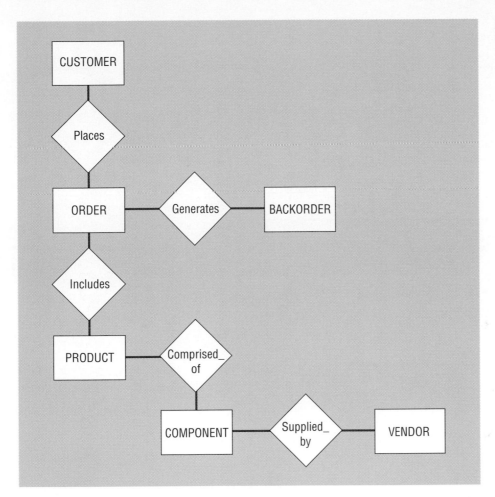

Figure 10-18
E-R diagram for Problem and
Exercises 10 and 11

14. An airline reservation is an association between a passenger, a flight, and a seat. Select a few pertinent attributes for each of these entity types and represent a reservation in an E-R diagram.

15. Choose from your own experiences with organizations and draw an E-R diagram for a situation that has a ternary relationship.

16. Consider the E-R diagram in Figure 10-19. Are all three relationships—Holds, Goes_on, and Transports—necessary (i.e., can one of these be deduced from the other two)? Are there reasonable assumptions which make all three relationships necessary? If so, what are these assumptions?

17. Draw an E-R diagram to represent the sample customer order in Figure 10-4.

18. In a real estate database, there is an entity called PROPERTY, which is a property for sale by the agency. Each time a potential property buyer makes a purchase offer on a property, the agency records the date, offering price, and name of the person making the offer.
    a. Represent the PROPERTY entity and its purchase offer attributes using the notation for multivalued attributes.
    b. Represent the PROPERTY entity and its purchase offer attributes using two entity types.
    c. Finally, assume the agency decides to also keep data about buyers and potential buyers, including their name, phone number, and address. Augment your answer to part b. above to accommodate this new entity type.

Figure 10-19
E-R diagram for Problem and Exercise 16

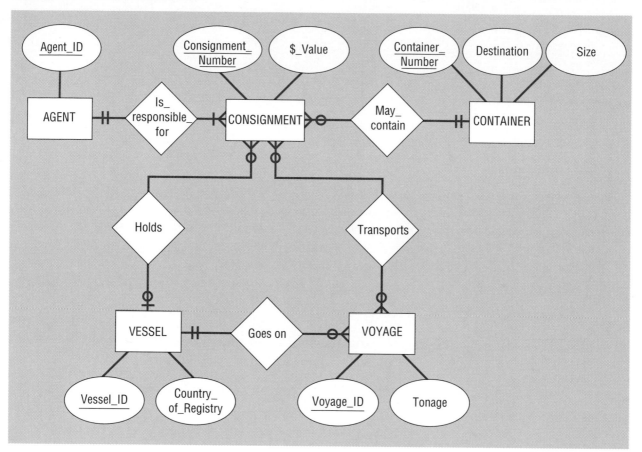

19. Consider the Is_married_to unary relationship in Figure 10-8c.
    a. Assume we wanted to know the date on which a marriage occurred. Augment this E-R diagram to include a Date_married attribute.
    b. Since sometimes persons remarry after the death of a spouse or divorce, redraw this E-R diagram to show the whole history of marriages (not just the current marriage) for persons. Show the Date_married attribute on this diagram.

20. Consider Figure 10-11.
    a. Write a domain integrity rule for Balance.
    b. Write a triggering operation business rule for the Balance attribute for the event of inserting a new ACCOUNT.

21. As best you can, describe the process logic and business rules underlying the entity-relationship diagrams from Problems and Exercises 10 and 11. How are entity-relationship diagrams similar to and different from the logic modeling techniques from the previous chapter (e.g., Structured English, decision tables, decision trees)? In what ways are these data and logic modeling techniques complimentary? What problems might be encountered if either data or logic modeling techniques were not performed well or not performed at all as part of the systems development process?

22. In the Purchasing Department at one company, each purchase request is assigned to a "case worker" within the Purchasing Department. This case worker follows the

purchase request through the entire purchasing process and acts as the sole contact person with the person or unit buying the goods or services. The Purchasing Department refers to its fellow employees buying goods and services as "customers." The purchasing process is such that purchase requests over $1,500.00 must go out for bid to vendors, and the associated Request for Bids for these large requests must be approved by the Purchasing Department. If the purchase is under $1,500.00, the product or service can simply be bought from any approved vendor, but the purchase request must still be approved by the Purchasing Department and they must issue a Purchase Order. For large purchases, once the winning bid is accepted, the Purchasing Department can issue a Purchase Order. List the relevant entities and attributes and draw an entity-relationship diagram for this business process. List whatever assumptions you must make to define primary keys, assess cardinality, and so on.

FIELD EXERCISES

1. Interview a friend or family member to elicit from them each of the entities, attributes, relationships, and relevant business rules they come into contact with at work. Use this information to construct and present to this person an entity-relationship diagram. Revise the diagram until it seems appropriate to you and to your friend or family member.

2. Visit an organization that provides primarily a service, such as a dry cleaners, and a company that manufactures a more tangible product. Interview employees from these organizations to elicit from them each of the entities, attributes, relationships, and relevant business rules that are commonly encountered by these companies. Use this information to construct entity-relationship diagrams. What differences and similarities are there between the diagrams for the service- and the product-oriented companies? Does the entity-relationship diagramming technique handle both situations equally well? Why or why not? What differences, if any, might there be in the use of this technique for a public agency?

3. Discuss with a systems analyst the role of conceptual data modeling in the overall systems analysis and design of information systems at his or her company. How, and by whom, is conceptual data modeling performed? What training in this technique is given? At what point(s) is this done in the development process? Why?

4. Ask a systems analyst to give you examples of unary, binary, and ternary relationships that they have heard of or dealt with personally at their company. Ask them which is the most common. Why?

5. Talk to MIS professionals at a variety of organizations and determine the extent to which CASE tools are used in the creation and editing of entity-relationship diagrams. Try to determine whether or not they use CASE tools for this purpose, what CASE tools are used, and why, when and how they use CASE tools for this. In companies that do not use CASE tools for this purpose, determine why not and what would have to change to have them use CASE tools.

6. Ask a systems analyst to give you a copy of the standard notation he or she uses to draw E-R diagrams. In what ways is this notation different from notation in this text? Which notation do you prefer and why? What is the meaning of any additional notation?

7. Ask a systems analyst in a manufacturing company to show you an E-R diagram for a database in that organization which contains bill-of-materials data. Compare that E-R diagram to the one in Figure 10-7. What are the differences between these diagrams and why?

REFERENCES

Aranow, E. B. 1989. "Developing Good Data Definitions." *Database Programming & Design* 2 (8) (August): 36–39.

Bruce, T. A. 1992. *Designing Quality Databases with IDEF1X Information Models.* New York, NY: Dorset House Publications.

Chen, P. P-S. 1976. "The Entity-Relationship Model—Toward a Unified View of Data." *ACM Transactions on Database Systems* 1 (March): 9–36.

Fleming, C. C., and B. von Halle. 1990. "An Overview of Logical Data Modeling." *Data Resource Management* 1 (1) (Winter): 5–15.

McFadden. F. R., J. A. Hoffer, and M. B. Prescott. 1999. *Modern Database Management.* 5th ed. Reading, MA: Addison Wesley Longman.

Moody, D. 1996. "The Seven Habits of Highly Effective Data Modelers." *Database Programming & Design* 9 (October): 57, 58, 60–62, 64.

Sandifer, A., and B. von Halle. 1991a. "A Rule by Any Other Name." *Database Programming & Design* 4 (2) (February): 11–13.

Sandifer, A., and B. von Halle. 1991b. "Linking Rules to Models." *Database Programming & Design* 4 (3) (March): 13–16.

Storey, V. C. 1991. "Relational Database Design Based on the Entity-Relationship Model." *Data and Knowledge Engineering* 7 (1991): 47–83.

Teorey, T. J., D. Yang, and J. P. Fry. 1986. "A Logical Design Methodology for Relational Databases Using the Extended Entity-Relationship Model." *Computing Surveys* 18 (2) (June): 197–221.

Structuring System Requirements: Conceptual Data Modeling for the Customer Activity Tracking System

INTRODUCTION

The third parallel requirements structuring activity in the analysis phase of the CATS project addresses developing a conceptual data model for the system. Jorge Lopez, one of the systems analysts on the project team, and Buffy Jarvis, a data analyst on loan to the team, are jointly responsible for developing the conceptual data model. Buffy specializes in conceptual data modeling in the data administration staff at BEC. She has reviewed the conceptual data models for the parts of the BEC databases used in the current systems with which CATS is likely to interact. Buffy and Jorge have developed a preliminary E-R data model for CATS and are ready for some feedback from other CATS project team members. We start this case near the end of a meeting Jorge and Buffy have had to prepare a revised E-R diagram consistent with the process and logic models.

CONCEPTUAL DATA MODELING FOR CATS

"Buffy, this has been a really good session. It looks like the estimate of five days of your time to work on this project was just about right. Having all the E-R models for various company databases available via the CASE tool has allowed you to answer most of my questions very quickly. After I get some feedback from Frank and Jordan, we ought to be able to finalize an E-R model of the central CATS system for discussion at the JAD later this month. I've really appreciated how you've been able to accommodate some different names for entities and attributes from the standard ones in the repository. I know our client also will appreciate this. Now, if we could only . . . ." A knock on Jorge's cubicle interrupts his last thought.

"Jorge . . . oh, I'm sorry, I didn't know you had someone with you," interjected Frank Napier. "I'll come back later."

"Frank, no problem. Buffy and I were about done," Jorge replied. "You remember Buffy Jarvis from our CATS orientation meeting? Buffy's the data analyst that's working with me on the E-R model for CATS."

"It's good to see you again, Buffy," replied Frank. "Have the two of you come up with a model you think works?"

Buffy took the lead. "Jorge thinks we are ready to get you and Jordan Pippen involved to see if our data model for central CATS is consistent with the process and logic modeling you've been doing. From what we see in the repository, we think the E-R model is fine, but we really need your feedback. You got a couple of minutes to take a quick look?"

"Sure. But, first tell me a little about how you developed your E-R model, which might help me to think about angles you may have missed," replied Frank.

"Buffy and I have tried to consider all the input we could. We started by reviewing the original CATS data model Jordan and Nancy Chen developed for the Baseline Project Plan (see Figure 1). We quickly discovered that it did not conform to the standards set by data administration for E-R models. You may recall from the company data modeling training you went through during your first few months at BEC that we are pretty particular about our standards. So we redrew the original E-R diagram with unique relationship names; two names for each relationship so it can be easily read in either direction; and singular nouns for each entity label. We also reversed the cardinality notation for associative entities, to conform to the notation used by our CASE tool. We talked through all

Figure 1
Entity-relationship diagram for the CATS project

of the relationships to see if their cardinalities made sense. Then, since I've learned a lot about CATS from the various activities in the requirements determination step, I just talked to Buffy about what CATS was and she was able to identify some additional entities and relationships. We didn't have specific forms or reports to look at, but simply in the process of my describing CATS, Buffy heard me mention business entities and rules, like there are three types of products—music, games, and video—and we can't legally keep track of video purchases and rentals. This led us to subtypes of the Product entity."

Buffy added, "Then we tried to match each of the entities with an entity from the consolidated data model we keep in data administration that cuts across all BEC systems. I was glad that Jordan and Nancy Chen had thought to identify some possible interacting systems in their request to the Systems Priority Board since this gave us some clues on where to look for matching entities. Also, the keyword search capability in the CASE tool was a big help. We found a match for many entities, but a few entities, like the profile- and reservation-related entities, were new. We then created CASE repository entries for each new CATS entity and, for entities in the consolidated model, we made sure that the CATS entity name was an alias. We still don't know if the CATS database will

physically have separate files for some of these entities, but at least we now know conceptually where the commonality is with existing database entities.

"Fortunately, since Jordan got me involved from the get-go on the project, you'll recall that I was able to give you, Jorge, and Jordan some ideas for questions to ask during the interviews and ways to analyze documents that emphasized data aspects of CATS. You all did a nice job of writing your interview notes to highlight data mentioned or shown to you in some document. I'm glad you decided to keep all your notes in a shared directory open to all CATS project team members on the LAN. Jorge and I read these notes, made a few phone calls to a couple of the interviewees to ask follow-up questions, and looked over several documents again; we were able to get a pretty good idea of the data requirements for CATS."

Jorge continued, "Then as the process and logic models were developed, we studied them to find data store and data flow contents and data elements used in Structured English. We studied decision tables, trees, and state-transition diagrams to see if additional data elements were mentioned. We then assigned all of these data elements to a data entity on our E-R diagram. We wanted to make sure, for example, that every data store was a subset of our data model, that every data element brought into CATS from a source was stored either in raw or aggregate form in the database, and that every data element sent out of CATS could be computed from data in the data model or data just passing through CATS. At this point, we were not concerned about how to access data as long as there were relationships in the data model that linked data needed in a process or logic step. We made a few adjustments this morning and were just about ready to send Jordan a note asking for some time at our next project status meeting to share our model with you and her. But, while you are here, we would appreciate a quick look at what we've developed." (Figure 2 contains this E-R diagram and Figure 3 is a listing of repository entries for this data model.)

"You can see a few significant changes right away," added Buffy. "First, we changed the name of the associative entity to Product Announcement to reflect the term used in most of the other CATS models; an attribute of the entity, Date Reserved, indicates whether the announcement turns into a reservation. Some DFDs refer to a Product Reservation data store, and that data store relates to this associative entity [see DFDs in the BEC case after Chapter 8].

"Second, we are able to tell what music products a customer buys or rents via the 'Is Purchased on' relationship between the Customer Transaction and the Music or Games Product entities. A customer may buy or rent a product that was announced even if the customer does not reserve the item. We thought some type of report about the number of these transactions

would be interesting. You might want to add that to a DFD somewhere. Unfortunately, we can't legally track what video products customers rent or buy, even if reserved, so we can associate a video item on a Customer Transaction only with a Product Profile. We made a rather critical decision here. A Customer Transaction could be associated with either a customer or a product, but not both, for a video product. We chose to make the transaction-product association vague through the Product Profile, rather than the customer-transaction association.

"Third, we thought the relationship between Customer Profile and Customer Transaction in the original E-R diagram was redundant since the same information could be found via the Describes and Buys relationships. Similarly, the relationship between Customer and Product Profile in the original E-R diagram is redundant. However, we added the 'Provides Product Info.' relationship, which could represent the decision rules on how to match customers to products.

"Finally, we included an Inventory associative entity to keep track of quantity on hand in each store. We saw that you had included an Inventory data store on one of your DFDs. This type of data is needed for the product ordering part of CATS. Given the way you show this on your DFD [Figure 4 from the BEC case after Chapter 8], I think that it is likely that this entity will, in fact, be a view into the database of the inventory control system, which indicates another interface between CATS and an existing system. Exactly how

Figure 2
Revised CATS E-R model

Figure 3
Repository for entities in CATS
E-R model

```
                    Designer/2000

          Report      : ENTITY RELATIONSHIP DIAGRAM DETAILS
          Filename    : a:fig113
          CDMODEL.lis
          Run by      : JGEORGE
          Report Date : 12-MAR-98 11:44am
          Total Pages : 5

          Parameter Values

          Application System : BEC
          Version            : 1
          Diagram            :
          Include Cardinality : True
```

```
12-MAR-98             Entity Relationship Diagram Details

Entity Name        Attributes              Relationships               To Entities
-----------        ----------              -------------               -----------
CUSTOMER           * customer name         buys              (1, 1)
                   * customer number (uid)  >- - - ------------<        CUSTOMER TRANSACTION
                   * customer street       (0, <null>)   sold to       (uid)
                   * telephone number
                   o credit card expiration date
                   o credit card number
                   o credit card type
                   o customer zip          described by      (1, <null>)
                   o social security number >- - - - ------------<      CUSTOMER PROFILE
                                            (0, <null>)   describes

                                            receives          (1, <null>)
                                            >- - - - - ------------<     PRODUCT ANNOUNCEMENT
                                            (0, <null>)   is sent to

                                            assigned to       (1, <null>)
                                            >-----------------             STORE
                                            (1, 1)        has assigned

CUSTOMER PROFILE   * customer category level (uid)  provides customer   (0, <null>)
                   * customer profile category       >- - - - - - - -<   PRODUCT PROFILE
                   (uid)                             (0, <null>)provides product in

                                                     describes       (0, <null>)
                                                     >- - - - - - - -<    CUSTOMER
                                                     (1, <null>)  described by
```

12-MAR-98   Entity Relationship Diagram Details

Entity Name	Attributes	Relationships	To Entities
CUSTOMER TRANSACTION	o transaction date (uid)		
		includes purchase (0, <null>) >- - - - - - - - - - - -< (0, <null>) is purchased on	MUSIC OR GAME PRODUCT
		is bought on (0, <null>) >- - - - - - - - - - - -< (0, <null>) includes	PRODUCT PROFILE
		sold to (0, <null>) >- - - - - - - - - - - - (1, 1) buys	CUSTOMER
		sold to (uid) (0, <null>) >- - - - - - - - - - - - (1, 1) buys	CUSTOMER
INVENTORY	* quantity in stock (uid)		
		contains (0, <null>) >- - - - - - - - - - - - (1, 1) held in	PRODUCT
		contains (uid) (0, <null>) >- - - - - - - - - - - - (1, 1) held in	PRODUCT
		belongs to (0, <null>) >- - - - - - - - - - - - (1, 1) has	STORE
		belongs to (uid) (0, <null>) >- - - - - - - - - - - - (1, 1) has	STORE
MUSIC OR GAME PRODUCT (sub-type)			
		is purchased on (0, <null>) >- - - - - - - - - - - -< (0, <null>) includes purchase o	CUSTOMER TRANSACTION

12-MAR-98   Entity Relationship Diagram Details

Entity Name	Attributes	Relationships	To Entities
PRODUCT	* product media type * product number (uid) * product title o date product is available	held in (1, 1) >- - - - - - - - - - - -< (0, <null>) contains	INVENTORY (uid)

Figure 3 *(continued)*

```
Entity Name          Attributes                      Relationships                               To Entities
-----------          ----------                      -------------                               -----------

PRODUCT ANNOUNCEMENT  * cats run number for           has profile                (0, <null>)
                        announcement                  >- - - - - - - - - - - <                    PRODUCT PROFILE
                      * date announcement sent         (0, <null>)      profiles
                      * date customer reserved
                        product                        announced by               (1, <null>)
                                                      >- - - - - - - - - - - <                    PRODUCT ANNOUNCEMENT
                                                       (0, <null>)      announces

                                                       is sent to                 (0, <null>)
                                                      >- - - - - - - - - - - <                    CUSTOMER
                                                       (1, <null>)      receives

PRODUCT ANNOUNCEMENT  * pcs code                       announces                  (0, <null>)
                                                      >- - - - - - - - - - - <                    PRODUCT
                                                       (1, <null>)      announced by

PRODUCT PROFILE       * product category name (uid)    provides product i         (0, <null>)
                      o superior product category     >- - - - - - - - - - - <                    CUSTOMER PROFILE
                                                       name (0, <null>) provides customer i

                                                       includes                   (0, <null>)
                                                      >- - - - - - - - - - - <                    CUSTOMER TRANSACTION
                                                       (0, <null>)      is bought on

                                                       profiles                   (0, <null>)
                                                      >- - - - - - - - - - - <                    PRODUCT
                                                       (0, <null>)      has profile

STORE                 * store manager name             has                        (1, 1)
                      * store number (uid)            - - - - - - - - - - - <                     INVENTORY
                                                       (0, <null>)      belongs to (uid)

                                                       has assigned               (1, 1)
                                                      - - - - - - - - - - - <                     CUSTOMER
                                                       (1, <null>)      assigned to

VIDEO PRODUCT
(sub-type)

12-MAR-98              Entity Relationship Diagram Details                                         Page 5 of 5

                                   Designer/2000
                       ENTITY RELATIONSHIP DIAGRAM DETAILS
                               End of Report
```

we'll implement this entity will be decided in a later project phase. One of the things I'd like to do for Jorge before we meet next is to take the entities we've identified and create a CRUD matrix showing which entities are Created in, Retrieved from, Updated by, and Deleted by which BEC system. This is the same type of matrix used in our information systems planning method. This will help to better understand the relationships between CATS and existing systems."

"All your changes make sense to me," replied Frank. "I was not sure, however, when I saw the original E-R diagram that the cardinalities next to the profile entities coming from Customer and Product, respectively, were right. I see you've kept these the same. What did you think about those cardinalities?"

"That gave us pause, too," interjected Jorge. "What we have tentatively decided, for example, is that a Customer Profile entity instance is a kind of atomic profile, that is, a single characteristic, like affluent income level. Thus, a customer has a set of these which describes that customer. Similarly, a product might be categorized as both jazz and R&B, which are individual Product Profile entity instances. So, the Describes relationship says that a customer has a set of profiles (a logical AND between the associated Customer Profile instances), and the 'Described by' relationship says which customers have that particular profile instance as one of their associated profiles. We think this gives us the greatest freedom in creating and tracking profiles of customers and products."

"You are right about flexibility, but I don't know what will happen when we have to process database queries and need to retrieve so many records to compose the total profile for a customer," said Frank.

Buffy responded, "Remember, an E-R model is only a conceptual picture of the database. When we normalize the data in logical database design and then pick data structures during physical database design, this conceptual picture of a customer's total profile as potentially several Customer Profile instances might be implemented all in one physical record. But, let's not deal with that until we better understand form and report design, processing volumes, and the other factors that affect physical database design."

"Okay, but why don't you make a note in the repository entry for the profile entities that this issue should be addressed during physical design. Who knows, none of us may be involved in this project then and we want to make sure the physical system designers know about this issue," Frank said. "I'll go back and look at the DFDs and associated Structured English to make sure that the process flows treat profile

data in data stores the same way you've represented them in the E-R diagram."

"Good idea about the repository note, Frank," replied Jorge. "I'll enter a note like that right away."

"Jorge and Frank, I've got a question for you," said Buffy. "Something you said before, Jorge, makes me wonder if we don't need a unary relationship on the Product Profile entity. The idea is that maybe there are hierarchical categories of products. For example, some people may have an interest in Jazz in general, so they'd like to know about any new jazz release. Others may be into fusion jazz, New Orleans jazz, big band jazz, or another specialty jazz category. The decision rules on which customer profile to match with what product profile could be adjusted to match aggregate or subordinate categories. This is exactly the kind of association a unary relationship can show. What do you think?"

"Buffy, that's the kind of creative idea someone with a data focus can provide," replied Jorge. "I'll call Wendy and Nancy and see what they think."

"What about the data requirements for the store-level CATS?" asked Frank. "Did you leave that off this data model because you think that will be a client database at the stores?"

"That is one possibility," responded Jorge. "We'll deal with that when we discuss alternative design strategies. Candidly, we've not thought much about the store CATS, yet. Could you give some thought to that before our next CATS staff meeting, when we hope to present this E-R model in a walkthrough with the whole team?"

"I'll be glad to. Besides the questions I've already asked, I don't see any other problems based on this quick review," responded Frank. "If you need any help working on business rules, besides those on the E-R diagram, just ask. I know we'll have to come back to this E-R diagram during logical design, once we design forms and reports and discover that users want some data we did not anticipate, but this level of work seems great for the analysis phase.

"Jorge, I had stopped by to confirm when we were going to meet about the study we are doing on CATS' impact on existing systems. I need to fit in a phone interview with one of the store managers Jordan talked to in Miami since he has some concerns about the store CATS system. Can we meet at 3:00 instead of 2:00 this afternoon?

"That's fine, and thanks for your reactions to our E-R model. See you at 3:00, your office, right?"

"Yep, my office. See you then, Jorge. Good to see you again, Buffy."

"Thanks for your help," replied Buffy. "See you at the staff meeting."

SUMMARY

You have seen in this and the prior two BEC cases how the CATS team members have structured the requirements for the system. Requirements structuring is based on the information in interview notes and other fact-gathering deliverables from requirements determination as well as on other models of the system, such as decision tables. Structuring requirements, like most systems development work, is quite iterative. As one analysis is done, this raises new issues not seen in other analyses, so the team must reanalyze deliverables they thought were complete. Eventually, all the pieces will come together at the end of the analysis phase into a design strategy for CATS, which is the subject of the next BEC case after Chapter 11.

11

Selecting the Best Alternative Design Strategy

After studying this chapter, you should be able to:

■ Describe the different sources of software.

■ Assemble the various pieces of an alternative design strategy.

■ Generate at least three alternative design strategies for an information system.

■ Select the best design strategy using both qualitative and quantitative methods.

■ Update a Baseline Project Plan based on the results of the analysis phase.

INTRODUCTION

You have now reached the point in the analysis phase where you are ready to transform all of the information you have gathered and structured into some concrete ideas about the nature of the design for the new or replacement information system. This is called the *design strategy*. From requirements determination, you know what the current system does and you know what the users would like the replacement system to do. From requirements structuring, you know what forms the replacement system's process flow, process logic, and data should take, at a logical level independent of any physical implementation. For example, every data flow from a system process to the external environment represents an on-line display, printed report, or business form or document that the system can produce, often for use by a human. Every data flow from a data store to a process implies a retrieval capability of the system's files and database. Most processes represent a capability of the system to transform inputs into outputs. And data flows from the environment to system processes indicate capabilities to capture data on on-line displays, or some batch method, to validate the data and protect access to the system from the environment and to route raw data to the appropriate processing points.

Thus, at this point in the systems development process you have a preliminary specification of what the new information system should do and you understand why a replacement system is necessary to fix problems in the current system and to respond to new needs and opportunities to use information. Actually, there still may be some uncertainty about the capabilities of a new system. This uncertainty is due to competing ideas from different users and stakeholders on what they would like the system to do and to existing alternatives for an implementation environment for the new system. To bring analysis to a conclusion, your job is to take these structured requirements and transform them into several competing design strategies, one of which will be pursued in the design phase of the life cycle.

Part of generating a design strategy is determining how you want to acquire the replacement system using a combination of sources inside and outside the organization. If you decide to proceed with development in-house, you will have to answer general questions about software, such as whether all of the software should be built in-house or whether some software components should be bought off-the-shelf or contracted to software development companies. You will have to answer general questions about hardware and system software, such as whether the new system will run on a mainframe platform, stand-alone personal computers, or on a client/server platform, and whether the system can run on existing hardware. It is also not too early to begin thinking about data conversion issues, which must be addressed as you move from your current system to the new one. You even have to start thinking about how much training will be required for users, and how easy or difficult the system will be to implement. You have to determine whether you can build and implement the system you desire given the funding and management support you can count on. And you have to address these concerns for each alternative you generate. These issues need to be addressed so that you can update the Baseline Project Plan with detailed activities and resource requirements for the next life cycle phase—logical design—and probably for the physical design phase as well. That is, in this step of the analysis phase you bring the current phase to a close, prepare a report and presentation to management concerning continuation of the project, and get ready to move the project into the design phases.

In this chapter, you will learn why you need to come up with alternative design strategies and about guidelines for generating alternatives. You will then learn about the different issues that must be addressed for each alternative. Once you have generated your alternatives, you will have to choose the best design strategy to pursue. We include a discussion of one technique that analysts and users often use to decide among system alternatives and to help them agree on the best approach for the new information system.

Throughout this chapter we emphasize the need for sound project management. Now that you have seen the various techniques and steps of the analysis phase, we outline what a typical analysis phase project schedule might look like and discuss the execution of the analysis phase and the transition from analysis to design.

SELECTING THE BEST ALTERNATIVE DESIGN STRATEGY

Design strategy: A high-level statement about the approach to developing an information system. It includes statements on the system's functionality, hardware and system software platform, and method for acquisition.

Selecting the best alternative system involves at least two basic steps: (1) generating a comprehensive set of alternative design strategies and (2) selecting the one that is most likely to result in the desired information system, given all of the organizational, economic, and technical constraints that limit what can be done. In a sense then, the most likely strategy is the best one. A system **design strategy** is an approach to developing the system. The strategy includes the system's functionality, hardware and system software platform, and method for acquisition. We use the term design strategy in this chapter rather than the term alternative system because, at the end of analysis, we are still quite a long way from specifying an actual system. This delay is purposeful since we do not want to invest in design efforts until there is agreement on which direction to take the project and the new system. The best we can do at this point is to outline rather broadly the approach we can take in moving from logical system specifications to a working physical system. The overall process of selecting the best system strategy and the deliverables from this step in the analysis process are discussed next.

The Process of Selecting the Best Alternative Design Strategy

As Figure 11-1 shows, there are three subphases to systems analysis: requirements determination, requirements structuring, and generating alternative system design strategies and selecting the best one. After the system requirements have been structured in terms of process flow, process logic (decision and temporal), and data, analysts again work with users to package the requirements into different system configurations. Shaping alternative system design strategies involves the following processes:

- Dividing requirements into different sets of capabilities, ranging from the bare minimum that users would accept (the required features) to the most elaborate and advanced system the company can afford to develop (which includes all the features desired across all users). Alternatively, different sets of capabilities may represent the position of different organizational units with conflicting notions about what the system should do.

- Enumerating different potential implementation environments (hardware, system software, and network platforms) that could be used to deliver the

Figure 11-1
Systems development life cycle with the analysis phase highlighted

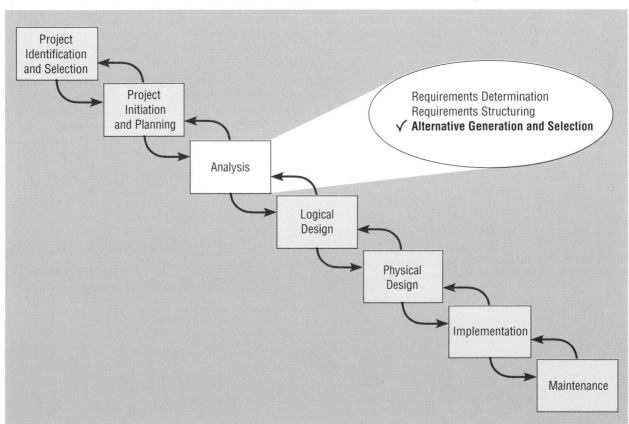

different sets of capabilities. (Choices on the implementation environment may place technical limitations on the subsequent design phase activities.)

- Proposing different ways to source or acquire the various sets of capabilities for the different implementation environments.

In theory, if there are three sets of requirements, two implementation environments, and four sources of application software, there would be twenty-four possible design strategies. In practice, some combinations are usually infeasible or uninteresting. Further, usually only a small number—typically three—can be easily considered. Selecting the best alternative is usually done with the help of a quantitative procedure. Analysts will recommend what they believe to be the best alternative but management (a combination of the steering committee and those who will fund the rest of the project) will make the ultimate decision about which system design strategy to follow. At this point in the life cycle, it is also certainly possible for management to end a project before the more expensive phases of design and implementation are begun if the costs or risks seem to outweigh the benefits, if the needs of the organization have changed since the project began, or if other competing projects appear to be of greater worth and development resources are limited.

Deliverables and Outcomes

The primary deliverables from generating alternative design strategies and selecting the best one are outlined in Table 11-1. The primary deliverable that is carried forward into design is an updated Baseline Project Plan detailing the work necessary to turn the selected design strategy into the desired replacement information system. Of course, that plan cannot be assembled until a strategy has been selected, and no strategy can be selected until alternative strategies have been generated and compared. Therefore, all three objects—the alternatives, the selected alternative, and the plan—are listed as deliverables in Table 11-1. Further, these three deliverables plus the supporting deliverables from requirements determination and structuring steps are necessary information to conduct systems design, so all of this information is carried in the project dictionary and CASE repository for reference in subsequent phases.

GENERATING ALTERNATIVE DESIGN STRATEGIES

In many cases, it may seem to an analyst that the solution to an organizational problem is obvious. Typically, the analyst is very familiar with the problem, having conducted an extensive analysis of it and how it has been solved in the past, or the analyst is very familiar with a particular solution that he or she attempts to apply to

---

TABLE 11-1 Deliverables for Generating Alternatives and Selecting the Best One

1. At least three substantively different system design strategies for building the replacement information system

2. A design strategy judged most likely to lead to the most desirable information system

3. A Baseline Project Plan for turning the most likely design strategy into a working information system

all organizational problems encountered. For example, if an analyst is an expert at using advanced database technology to solve problems, then there is a tendency for the analyst to recommend advanced database technology as a solution to every possible problem. Or if the analyst designed a similar system for another customer or business unit, the "natural" design strategy would be the one used before. Given the role of experience in the solutions analysts suggest, analysis teams typically generate at least two alternative solutions for every problem they work on.

A good number of alternatives for analysts to generate is three. Why three? Three alternatives can neatly represent both ends and the middle of a continuum or spectrum of potential solutions. One alternative represents the low end of the spectrum. Low-end solutions are the most conservative in terms of the effort, cost, and technology involved in developing a new system. In fact, low-end solutions may not involve computer technology at all, focusing instead on making paper flows more efficient or reducing the redundancies in current processes. A low-end strategy provides all the required functionality users demand with a system that is minimally different from the current system.

Another alternative represents the high end of the spectrum. High-end alternatives go beyond simply solving the problem in question and focus instead on systems that contain many extra features users may desire. Functionality, not cost, is the primary focus of high-end alternatives. A high-end alternative will provide all desired features using advanced technologies which often allow the system to expand to meet future requirements. Finally, the third alternative lies between the extremes of the low-end and high-end systems. Such alternatives combine the frugality of low-end alternatives with the focus on functionality of high-end alternatives. Midrange alternatives represent compromise solutions. There are certainly other possible solutions that exist outside of these three alternatives. Defining the bottom, middle, and top possibilities allows the analyst to draw bounds around what can be reasonably done.

How do you know where to draw bounds around the potential solution space? The analysis team has already gathered the information it needs to identify the solution space, but first that information must be systematically organized. There are two major considerations. The first is determining what the minimum requirements are for the new system. These are the mandatory features, any of which, if missing, make the design strategy useless. Mandatory features are those that everyone agrees are necessary to solve the problem or meet the opportunity. Which features are mandatory can be determined from a survey of users and other stakeholders who have been involved in requirements determination. You would conduct this survey near the end of the analysis phase after all requirements have been structured and analyzed. In this survey, stakeholders rate features discovered during requirements determination or categorize features on some desirable-mandatory scale, and an arbitrary breakpoint is used to divide mandatory from desired features. Some organizations will break the features into three categories: mandatory, essential, and desired. Whereas mandatory features screen out possible solutions, essential features are the important capabilities of a system which will serve as the primary basis for comparison of different design strategies. Desired features are those that users could live without but which are used to select between design strategies that are of almost equal value in terms of essential features. Features can take many different forms. Features might include

- Data kept in system files (for example, multiple customer addresses so that bills can be sent to addresses different from where we ship goods)

- System outputs (printed reports, on-line displays, transaction documents—for example, a paycheck or sales summary graph)

- Analyses to generate the information in system outputs (for example, a sales forecasting module or an installment billing routine)

- Expectations on accessibility, response time, or turnaround time for system functions (for example, on-line, real-time updating of inventory files)

The second consideration in drawing bounds around alternative design strategies is determining the constraints on system development. Constraints may exist on such factors as

- A date when the replacement system is needed

- Available financial and human resources

- Elements of the current system that cannot change

- Legal and contractual restrictions

- The importance or dynamics of the problem which may limit how the system can be acquired (for example, a strategically important system that uses highly proprietary data probably cannot be outsourced or purchased)

Remember, be impertinent and question whether stated constraints are firm; you may want to consider some design alternatives that violate constraints you consider to be flexible.

Both requirements and constraints must be identified and ranked in order of importance. The reason behind such a ranking should be clear. Whereas you can design a high-end alternative to fulfill every wish users have for a new system, you design low-end alternatives to fulfill only the most important wishes. The same is true of constraints. Low-end alternatives will meet every constraint; high-end alternatives will ignore all but the most daunting constraints.

ISSUES TO CONSIDER IN GENERATING ALTERNATIVES

The required functionality of the replacement system and the constraints that limit that functionality form the basis for the many issues that must be considered in putting together all of the pieces that comprise alternative design strategies. That is, most of the substantive debate about alternative design strategies hinges on the relative importance of system features. Issues of functionality lead, however, to other associated issues such as whether the system should be developed and run in-house, software and hardware selection, implementation, and organizational limitations such as available funding levels. This list is not comprehensive, but it does remind you that an information system is more than just software. Each issue must be considered when framing alternatives. We will discuss each consideration in turn, beginning with the outsourcing decision.

Outsourcing

Outsourcing: The practice of turning over responsibility of some to all of an organization's information systems applications and operations to an outside firm.

If another organization develops or runs a computer application for your organization, that practice is called **outsourcing.** Outsourcing includes a spectrum of working arrangements (*Business Week,* June 19, 1989; Moad, 1993). At one extreme is having a firm develop and run your application on their computers—all you do is supply input and take output. A common example of such an arrangement is a company that runs payroll applications for clients so that clients don't have to develop an independent in-house payroll system. Instead they simply provide employee payroll information to the company and, for a fee, the company returns completed paychecks, payroll accounting reports, and tax and other statements for employees. For many organizations, payroll is a very cost-effective operation when outsourced in this way. In another example of outsourcing arrangements, you hire a company to run your applications at your site on your computers. In some cases, an organization employing such an arrangement will dissolve some or all of its information systems unit and fire all of its information systems employees. Most of the time, though, the company brought in to run the organization's computing will hire many of the information systems unit employees.

Why would an organization outsource its information systems operations? As we saw in the payroll example, outsourcing may be cost-effective. If a company specializes in running payroll for other companies, it can leverage the economies of scale it achieves from running one very stable computer application for many organizations into very low prices. But why would an organization dissolve its entire information processing unit and bring in an outside firm to manage its computer applications? One reason may be to overcome operating problems the organization faces in its information systems unit. For example, the City of Grand Rapids, Michigan, hired an outside firm to run its computing 20 years ago in order to overcome personnel problems made difficult by union contracts and civil service constraints. Another reason for total outsourcing is that an organization's management may feel its core mission does not involve managing an information systems unit and that it might achieve more effective computing by turning over all of its operations to a more experienced, computer-oriented company. Kodak decided in the late 1980s that it was not in the computer applications business and turned over management of its mainframes to IBM and management of its personal computers to Businessland (Applegate and Montealegre, 1991).

Outsourcing is an alternative analysts need to be aware of. When generating alternative system development strategies for a system, you as an analyst should consult organizations in your area that provide outsourcing services. It may well be that at least one such organization has already developed and is running an application very close to what your users are asking for. Perhaps outsourcing the replacement system should be one of your alternatives. Knowing what your system requirements are before you consider outsourcing means that you can carefully assess how well the suppliers of outsourcing services can respond to your needs. However, should you decide not to consider outsourcing, you need to consider whether some software components of your replacement system should be purchased and not built.

Sources of Software

We can group organizations that produce software into four major categories: hardware manufacturers, packaged software producers, custom software producers, enterprise-wide solutions, and in-house developers.

Hardware Manufacturers At first it may seem counter-intuitive that hardware manufacturers would develop information systems or software. Yet hardware manufacturers are among the largest producers of software; for example, IBM is a leader in software development (Table 11-2). However, IBM actually develops relatively little application software (roughly 15 percent of their software revenue is from application software). Rather, IBM's leadership comes from its operating systems and utilities (like sort routines or database management systems) for the hardware it manufactures, as well as its middleware, the software that links one set of software services to another.

TABLE 11-2   The Top 10 U.S. Software Companies in the 1996 *Datamation* 100

Rank among Software Companies	Company	Revenues from Software, 1996
1	IBM	$12,911
2	Microsoft	9,435
3	Hitachi	5,487
4	Fujitsu	4,755
5	Computer Associates	3,157
6	NEC	2,310
7	Oracle	2,280
8	SAP	1,700
9	Novell	1,225
10	Digital	1,225

Notes: Revenue in millions. Market share is percent of *Datamation* 100 software revenues.
Adapted from *Datamation*, July, 1997.

Packaged Software Producers   The growth of the software industry has been phenomenal since its beginnings in the mid-1960s. Now, some of the largest computer companies in the world, as measured by the *Datamation* 100, are companies that produce software exclusively (see Table 11-2). Consulting firms, such as American Management Systems and Andersen Consulting, also rank in the top 40 packaged software producers.

Software companies develop what are sometimes called *prepackaged* or *off-the-shelf* systems. Microsoft's Project and Intuit's Quicken™, QuickPay™, and QuickBooks™ are popular examples of such software. The packaged software development industry serves many market segments. Their software offerings range from general, broad-based packages, such as general ledger, to very narrow, niche packages, such as software to help manage a day care center. Software companies develop software to run on many different computer platforms, from microcomputers to large mainframes. The companies range in size from just a few people to thousands of employees. Software companies consult with system users after the initial software design has been completed and an early version of the system has been built. The systems are then beta-tested in actual organizations to determine whether there are any problems with the software or if any improvements can be made. Until testing is completed, the system is not offered for sale to the public. Unfortunately, the software is sometimes put on the market before it is ready. Figure 11-2 describes the problems Ashton-Tate encountered when it released dBASE IV too soon.

Some off-the-shelf software systems cannot be modified to meet the specific, individual needs of a particular organization. Such application systems are sometimes called *turnkey systems.* The producer of a turnkey system will only make changes to the software when a substantial number of users ask for a specific change. Other off-the-shelf application software can be modified or extended, however, by the producer or by the user, to more closely fit the needs of the organization. Even though many organizations perform similar functions, no two organizations do the same thing in quite the same way. A turnkey system may be good enough for a certain level of performance but it will never perfectly match the way a given orga-

Figure 11-2
Ashton-Tate's dBASE
IV disaster

In October 1988, Ashton-Tate Corporation released its long-awaited version of dBASE IV (TM), the successor to its popular dBASE III (TM) database management system. dBASE IV was four times larger than dBASE III, with roughly 500,000 lines of code. Getting the program to operate on a standard IBM-compatible personal computer required ingenuity on the part of programmers. They had to figure out how to chop the program into pieces that could be swapped in and out of computer memory, a difficult task. The program was so complex, it outpaced Ashton-Tate's testing procedures at the time. The result: the company shipped a product containing thousands of errors. Customers complained dBASE IV was too slow and too likely to crash. Further, it lacked features customers were looking forward to having.

Ashton-Tate had once been considered one of the Big Three microcomputer software companies, along with Lotus Development Corp. and Microsoft Corp. In 1985, Ashton-Tate could boast of having 62.5% of the database market for microcomputers. In 1988, before the release of dBASE IV, Ashton-Tate controlled 43% of that market, but market share slipped to 35% in 1989 and to 30% in 1990. The company suffered through three quarterly losses in 1990, ending the year with a slight profit in the fourth quarter.

It took two years for Ashton-Tate to fix the problems with dBASE IV. They finally released a new version in the fall of 1990, two years after the fiasco. By that time, however, it was too late. They had lost many of their customers to fast-growing companies like Oracle Corp. To add to their problems, in December 1990, Ashton-Tate lost their copyright protection for their dBASE products. Ashton-Tate had sued rival Fox Software Inc. for copyright infringement. The judge in the case ruled that Ashton-Tate's products were initially based on a database system in the public domain, therefore invalidating the copyright protection they had for the products. Without such protection, Ashton-Tate had no right to sue Fox.

Ashton-Tate rewon their copyright protection for dBASE in 1991. That same year, however, the company was purchased by another rival, Borland International Inc.

*Sources: Zachary, G. P. "How Ashton-Tate Lost Its Leadership in PC Software Arena." Wall Street Journal, April 11, 1990, A1–A2.
Zachary, G. P. and Bulkeley, W. M. "Ashton-Tate Loses Flagship Software's Copyright Shield." Wall Street Journal, December 14, 1990, B1, B4.*

nization does business. A reasonable estimate is that off-the-shelf software can at best meet 70 percent of an organization's needs. Thus, even in the best case, 30 percent of the software system doesn't match the organization's specifications.

Custom Software Producers   If a company has a need for an information system but does not have the expertise or the personnel available to develop the system in-house and a suitable off-the-shelf system is not available, the company will likely consult a custom software company. Consulting firms, such as Price Waterhouse or EDS, will help a firm develop custom information systems for internal use. These firms employ people with expertise in the development of information systems. Their consultants may also have expertise in a given business area. For example, consultants who work with banks understand financial institutions as well as information systems. Consultants use many of the same methodologies, techniques, and tools that companies use to develop systems in-house. The 10 largest world-wide computer-services firms (based on revenues not only of custom software development but also outsourcing and other services) are listed in Table 11-3. Other large U.S. firms are ADP, TRW, First Data, and AT&T.

Enterprise Solutions Software   As mentioned in Chapter 1, more and more organizations are choosing complete software solutions, sometimes called enterprise solutions or enterprise resource planning systems, to support their operations and business processes. These software solutions consist of a series of integrated modules. The modules pertain to specific, traditional business functions, such as accounting, distribution, manufacturing, and human resources. The difference between the modules and traditional approaches is that the modules are integrated to focus on business processes rather than on business functional areas. Using enterprise software solutions, a firm can integrate all parts of a business process, such as order entry and filling, in a unified information system. All aspects of a single transaction, including receiving the order, picking goods in a warehouse, shipping, inventory adjustments, billing, and accounts receivable, occur seamlessly within a single information system, rather than in a series of disjointed, separate systems focused on business functional areas.

The benefits of the enterprise solutions approach include a single repository of data for all aspects of a business process and the flexibility of the modules. A single repository implies more consistent and accurate data, as well as less maintenance. The modules are very flexible because additional modules can be added as needed, once the basic system is in place. Added modules are immediately integrated into the existing system.

There are also disadvantages to enterprise solutions software. The systems are very complex, so implementation can take a long time to complete. Because the systems are complex, organizations typically do not have the necessary expertise in-house to implement the systems. Instead, they must rely on consultants or employees of the software vendor, and such expert help can be very expensive. In some cases, organizations must change how they do business in order to benefit from a migration to enterprise solutions.

TABLE 11-3   Top 10 Worldwide Services and Support Suppliers for 1996 ($ millions)

1996 Rank	Company	1996 Services & Support Revenue
1	IBM	$22,785
2	Electronic Data Systems	14,441
3	Hewlett-Packard	9,462
4	Digital Equipment	5,988
5	Computer Sciences	5,400
6	Andersen Consulting	4,878
7	Fujitsu	4,160
8	Cap Gemini Sogeti	4,104
9	Unisys	3,950
10	ADP	3,567

Notes: Revenues in millions. Adapted from *Datamation*, July 1, 1997

There are three major vendors of enterprise solution software. The best known is probably SAP AG, a German firm, known for its flagship product R/3. SAP stands for Systems, Applications, and Products in Data Processing. SAP AG was founded in 1972, but most of its growth has occurred since 1992. In 1996, SAP AG was the eighth largest supplier of software in the world (see Table 11-2). Another supplier of enterprise solution software is PeopleSoft, Inc., a U.S. firm founded in 1987. PeopleSoft began with enterprise solutions that focused on human resources management but has since expanded to cover financials, materials management, distribution, and manufacturing. The third vendor is The Baan Company, a Dutch firm founded in 1978. Baan's applications include manufacturing, finance, distribution and transportation, and service. The most recent offerings from all three vendors run on a client-server platform.

In-House Development   We have talked about three different types of external organizations that serve as sources of software, but in-house development remains an option. Of course, in-house development need not entail development of all of the software that will comprise the total system. Hybrid solutions involving some purchased and in-house software components are common. Table 11-4 compares the different software sources.

If you choose to acquire software from outside sources, this choice is made at the end of the analysis phase. Choosing between a package or external supplier will be driven by your needs, not by what the external party has to sell. As we will discuss, the results of your analysis study will define the type of product you want to buy and will make working with an external supplier much easier, productive, and worthwhile.

Choosing Off-the-Shelf Software

Once you have decided to purchase off-the-shelf software rather than write some or all of the software for your new system, how do you decide what to buy? There are several criteria to consider, and special criteria may arise with each potential software purchase. For each criterion, an explicit comparison should be made between the software package and the process of developing the same application in-house. The most common criteria are as follows:

TABLE 11-4   Comparison of Four Different Sources of Software Components

Producers	Source of Application Software?	When to Go to This Type Organization for Software	Internal Staffing Requirements
Hardware Manufacturers	Generally not	For system software and utilities	Varies
Packaged Software Producers	Yes	When supported task is generic	Some IS and user staff to define requirements and evaluate packages
Custom Software Producers	Yes	When task requires custom support and system can't be built internally	Internal staff may be needed, depending on application
In-House Developers	Yes	When resources and staff are available and system must be built from scratch	Internal staff necessary though staff size may vary

- Cost

- Functionality

- Vendor support

- Viability of vendor

- Flexibility

- Documentation

- Response time

- Ease of installation

These criteria are presented in no particular order. The relative importance of the criteria will vary from project to project and from organization to organization. If you had to choose two criteria that would always be among the most important, those two would probably be vendor viability and vendor support. You don't want to get involved with a vendor that might not be in business tomorrow. Similarly, you don't want to license software from a vendor with a reputation for poor support. How you rank the importance of the remaining criteria will very much depend on the specific situation in which you find yourself.

Cost involves comparing the cost of developing the same system in-house to the cost of purchasing or licensing the software package. You should include a comparison of the cost of purchasing vendor upgrades or annual license fees with the costs you would incur to maintain your own software. Costs for purchasing and developing in-house can be compared based on the economic feasibility measures outlined in Chapter 6 (for example, a present value can be calculated for the cash flow associated with each alternative). Functionality refers to the tasks the software can perform and the mandatory, essential, and desired system features. Can the software package perform all or just some of the tasks your users need? If some, can it perform the necessary core tasks? Note that meeting user requirements occurs at the end of the analysis phase because you cannot evaluate packaged software until user requirements have been gathered and structured. Purchasing application software is not a substitute for conducting the systems analysis phase; rather, purchasing software is part of one design strategy for acquiring the system identified during analysis.

As we said earlier, vendor support refers to whether and how much support the vendor can provide. Support occurs in the form of assistance to install the software, to train user and systems staff on the software, and to provide help as problems arise after installation. Recently, many software companies have significantly reduced the amount of free support they will provide customers, so the cost to use telephone, on-site, fax, or computer bulletin board support facilities should be considered. Related to support is the vendor's viability. You don't want to get stuck with software developed by a vendor that might go out of business soon. This latter point should not be minimized. The software industry is quite dynamic, and innovative application software is created by entrepreneurs working from home offices—the classic cottage industry. Such organizations, even with outstanding software, often do not have the resources or business management ability to stay in business very long. Further, competitive moves by major software firms can render the products of smaller firms outdated or incompatible with operating systems. One software firm we talked to while developing this book was struggling to survive just trying to make their software work on any supposedly IBM-compatible PC (given the infinite combination of video boards, monitors, BIOS chips, and other components). Keeping up with hardware and system software change may be more than a small firm can handle, and good off-the-shelf application software is lost.

Flexibility refers to how easy it is for you, or the vendor, to customize the software. If the software is not very flexible, your users may have to adapt the way they work to fit the software. Are they likely to adapt in this manner? Purchased software can be modified in several ways. Sometimes, the vendor will be willing to make custom changes for you, if you are willing to pay for the redesign and programming. Some vendors design the software for customization. For example, the software may include several different ways of processing data and, at installation time, the customer chooses which to initiate. Also, displays and reports may be easily redesigned if these modules are written in a fourth-generation language. Reports, forms, and displays may be easily customized using a process whereby your company name and chosen titles for reports, displays, forms, column headings, etc. are selected from a table of parameters you provide. You may want to employ some of these same customization techniques for in-house developed systems so that the software can be easily adapted for different business units, product lines, or departments.

Documentation includes the user's manual as well as technical documentation. How understandable and up-to-date is the documentation? What is the cost for multiple copies, if required? Response time refers to how long it takes the software package to respond to the user's requests in an interactive session. Another measure of time would be how long it takes the software to complete running a job. Finally, ease of installation is a measure of the difficulty of loading the software and making it operational.

Validating Purchased Software Information   One way to get all of the information you want about a software package is to collect it from the vendor. Some of this information may be contained in the software documentation and technical marketing literature. Other information can be provided upon request. For example, you can send prospective vendors a questionnaire asking specific questions about their packages. This may be part of a request for proposal (RFP) or request for quote (RFQ) process your organization requires when major purchases are made. Space does not permit us to discuss the topic of RFPs and RFQs here; you may wish to refer to purchasing and marketing texts if you are unfamiliar with such processes (additional references about RFPs and RFQs are found at the end of the chapter).

There is, of course, no replacement for actually using the software yourself and running it through a series of tests based on the criteria for selecting software. Remember to test not only the software but also the documentation, training materials, and even the technical support facilities. One requirement you can place on prospective software vendors as part of the bidding process is that they install (free or at an agreed-upon cost) their software for a limited amount of time on your computers. This way you can determine how their software works in your environment, not in some optimized environment they have.

One of the most reliable and insightful sources is other users of the software. Vendors will usually provide a list of customers (remember, they will naturally tell you about satisfied customers, so you may have to probe for a cross section of customers) and people who are willing to be contacted by prospective customers. And here is where your personal network of contacts, developed through professional groups, college friends, trade associations, or local business clubs, can be a resource; do not hesitate to find some contacts on your own. Such current or former customers can provide a depth of insight on use of a package at their organizations.

To gain a range of opinion about possible packages, you can use independent software testing and abstracting services that periodically evaluate software and collect user opinions. Such surveys are available for a fee either as subscription services or on demand (two popular services are Auerbach Publishers and DataPro);

occasionally, unbiased surveys appear in trade publications. Often, however, articles in trade publications, even software reviews, are actually seeded by the software manufacturer and are not unbiased.

If you are comparing several software packages, you can assign scores for each package on each criterion and compare the scores using the quantitative method we demonstrate at the end of the chapter for comparing alternative system design strategies.

Hardware and Systems Software Issues

The first question you need to ask yourself about hardware and system software is whether the new system that follows a particular design strategy can be run on your firm's existing hardware and software platform. System software refers to such key components as operating systems, database management systems, programming languages, code generators, and network software. To determine if current hardware and system software is sufficient, you should consider such factors as the age and capacity of the current hardware and system software, the fit between the hardware and software and your new application's goals and proposed functionality and, if some of your system components are off-the-shelf software, whether the software can run on the existing hardware and system software. The advantages to running your new system on the existing platform are persuasive:

1. Lower costs as little, if any, new hardware and system software has to be purchased and installed.

2. Your information systems staff is quite familiar with the existing platform and how to operate and maintain it.

3. The odds of integrating your new application system with existing applications are enhanced.

4. No added costs of converting old systems to a new platform, if necessary, or of translating existing data between current technology and the new hardware and system software you have to acquire for your system.

On the other hand, there are also very persuasive reasons for acquiring new hardware or system software:

1. Some software components of your new system will only run on particular platforms with particular operating systems.

2. Developing your system for a new platform gives your organization the opportunity to upgrade or expand its current technology holdings.

3. New platform requirements may allow your organization to radically change its computing operations, as in moving from mainframe-centered processing to a database machine or a client-server architecture.

As the determination of whether or not to acquire new hardware and system software is so context-dependent, providing platform options as part of your design strategy alternatives is an essential practice.

At this point, if you decide that new hardware or system software is a strong possibility, you may want to issue a request for proposal (RFP) to vendors. The RFP will ask the vendors to propose hardware and system software that will meet the requirements of your new system. Issuing an RFP gives you the opportunity to have vendors carry out the research you need in order to decide among various options. You can request that each bid submitted by a vendor contain certain information essential for you to decide on what best fits your needs. For example, you can ask for performance information related to speed and number of operations per second. You can ask about machine reliability and service availability and whether there is an installation nearby which you can visit for more information. You can ask to take part in a demonstration of the hardware. And of course the bid will include information on cost. You can then use the information you have collected in generating your alternative design strategies.

Implementation Issues

As you will see in Chapter 20, implementing a new information system is just as much an organizational change process as it is a technical process. Implementation involves more than installing a piece of software, turning it on, and moving on to the next software project. New systems often entail new ways of performing the same work, new working relationships, and new skills. Users have to be trained. Disruptions in work procedures have to be found and addressed. In addition, system implementation may be phased in over many weeks or even months. You must address the technical and social aspects of implementation as part of any alternative design strategy. Management and users will want to know how long the implementation will take, how much training will be required, and how disruptive the process will be.

Organizational Issues

One reason management is so interested in the outlook for implementation is that all of the concerns we listed previously cost management money. The longer the implementation process, the more training required; the more disruption expected, the more it will cost to implement the system. Implementation costs are just one cost management has to consider for the new system. Management must also consider the costs of the design process that precedes implementation and the cost of maintaining the system once implementation is over. Overall cost and the availability of funding is just one of the organizational issues to consider in developing alternative design strategies.

A second organizational issue is determining what management will support. Even if adequate funding is available, your organization's management may not be willing or able to support one or another of your alternatives. For example, if your new system differs dramatically from what the corporate office has determined is adequate or from the corporate standard computing environment, your local management may not be willing to support a system that will irritate the corporate office. Most organizations like to have a manageably small number of basic technologies since only a few choices on hardware and software platforms can be supported well. If your new system calls for high levels of cooperation across departments when current operations involve very little of such cooperation, your management may not be willing to support such a system. Your management may also have politically inspired reasons not to support your new system. For example, if your information systems unit reports to the organization's chief financial officer and your new system strengthens a rival department such as manufacturing, management may not support such a system because they prefer to continue the status quo whereby finance is stronger than manufacturing.

A third organizational issue is the extent to which users will accept the new system and use it as designed. A high-end, high-technology solution that represents a radical break in what users are familiar with may have less of a chance of acceptance than a system that is closer to what users know and use. On the other hand, acceptance of a high-end alternative will depend on the users. Some users may demand nothing less than what leading-edge technology can deliver.

These three organizational issues are not the only organizational issues you could, or should, consider. Your assessment of operational and political feasibility (see Chapter 6) which is updated during analysis may identify other organizational issues. Most likely, such organizational issues will affect all of the alternative design strategies you will develop, but it may be possible to offer a range of options in your alternatives that will allow management to make trade-offs between different approaches to various organizational issues. For example, management may be willing to support a system that requires making a little more funding available if it means a little less of a change in the status quo than you might believe is necessary.

DEVELOPING DESIGN STRATEGIES FOR HOOSIER BURGER'S NEW INVENTORY CONTROL SYSTEM

As an example of alternative generation and selection, let's look again at Hoosier Burger's inventory control system. Figure 11-3 lists ranked requirements and constraints for the enhanced information system being considered by Hoosier Burger. The requirements represent a sample of those developed from the requirements determination and structuring carried out in prior analysis steps. The system in question is an upgrade to the company's existing inventory system which was used as an example in Chapters 8, 9, and 10. As you remember, there were several steps to Bob Mellankamp's largely manual inventory control system (Figure 11-4).

Remember that when Bob receives invoices from suppliers, he records their receipt on an invoice log sheet, and he puts the actual invoices in his accordion file. Using the invoices, Bob records the amount of stock delivered on the stock logs,

Figure 11-3
Ranked system requirements and constraints for Hoosier Burger's inventory system

SYSTEM REQUIREMENTS (in descending priority)	SYSTEM CONSTRAINTS (in descending order)
1. Must be able to easily enter shipments into system as soon as they are received.	1. System development can cost no more than $50,000.
2. System must automatically determine whether and when a new order should be placed.	2. New hardware can cost no more than $50,000.
3. Management should be able to determine at any time approximately what inventory levels are for any given item in stock.	3. The new system must be operational in no more than six months from the start of the contract.
	4. Training needs must be minimal, i.e., the new system must be very easy to use.

Figure 11-4
The steps in Hoosier Burger's inventory control system

1. Meet delivery trucks before opening restaurant
2. Unload and store deliveries
3. Log invoices and file in accordion file
4. Manually add amounts received to stock logs
5. After closing, print inventory report
6. Count physical inventory amounts
7. Compare inventory reports totals to physical count totals
8. Compare physical count totals to minimum order quantities; if the amount is less, make order; if not, do nothing
9. Pay bills that are due and record them as paid

paper forms posted near the point of storage for each inventory item. The stock logs include minimum order quantities as well as spaces for posting the starting amount, amount delivered, and the amount used for each item. Amounts delivered are entered on the sheet when Bob logs stock deliveries; amounts used are entered after Bob has compared the amounts of stock used, according to a physical count, and according to the numbers on the inventory report generated by the food ordering system. You remember too that some Hoosier Burger items, especially perishable goods, have standing orders for daily (or Saturday) delivery.

The Mellankamps want to improve their inventory system so that new orders are immediately accounted for, so that the system can determine when new orders should be placed, and so that management can obtain accurate inventory levels at any time of the day, as we saw in Chapter 8. All three of these system requirements have been ranked in order of descending priority in Figure 11-3.

The constraints on developing an enhanced inventory system at Hoosier Burger are also listed in Figure 11-3, again in order of descending priority. The first two constraints cover costs for systems development and for new computer hardware. Development can cost no more than $50,000. New hardware can cost no more than $50,000. The third constraint involves time for development—Hoosier Burger wants the system to be installed and in operation in no more than six months from the beginning of the development project. Finally, Hoosier Burger would prefer that training for the system be simple; the new system must be designed so that it is easy to use. However, as this is the fourth most important constraint, the demands it makes are more flexible than those contained in the other three.

Any set of alternative solutions to Hoosier Burger's inventory system problems must be developed with the company's prioritized requirements and constraints in mind. Figure 11-5 illustrates how each of three possible alternatives meets (or exceeds) the criteria implied in Hoosier Burger's requirements and constraints. Alternative A is a low-end solution. It only meets the first requirement completely and partially satisfies the second requirement, but it does not meet the final one. However, Alternative A is relatively inexpensive to develop and requires hardware that is much less expensive than the largest amount Hoosier Burger is willing to pay. Alternative A also meets the requirements for the other two constraints: it will only take three months to become operational and users will require only one week of training. Alternative C is the high-end solution. Alternative C meets all of the requirements criteria. On the other hand, Alternative C violates two of the four constraints: development costs are high at $65,000 and time to operation is nine months. If Hoosier Burger really wants to satisfy all three of its requirements for its

Figure 11-5
Description of three alternative systems that could be developed for Hoosier Burger's inventory system

CRITERIA	ALTERNATIVE A	ALTERNATIVE B	ALTERNATIVE C
Requirements			
1. Easy real-time entry of new shipment data	Yes	Yes	Yes
2. Automatic reorder decisions	For some items	For all items	For all items
3. Real-time data on inventory levels	Not available	Available for some items only	Fully available
Constraints			
1. Cost to develop	$25,000	$50,000	$65,000
2. Cost of hardware	$25,000	$50,000	$50,000
3. Time to operation	Three months	Six months	Nine months
4. Ease of training	One week of training	Two weeks of training	One week of training

new inventory system, the company will have to pay more than it wants and wait longer for development. Once operational, however, Alternative C will take just as much time to train people to use as Alternative A. Alternative B is in the middle. This alternative solution meets the first two requirements, partially satisfies the third, and does not violate any of the constraints.

Now that three plausible alternative solutions have been generated for Hoosier Burger, the analyst hired to study the problem has to decide which one to recommend to management for development. Management will then decide whether to continue with the development project (incremental commitment) and whether the system recommended by the analyst is the system that should be developed.

SELECTING THE MOST LIKELY ALTERNATIVE

One method we can use to decide among the alternative solutions to Hoosier Burger's inventory system problem is illustrated in Figure 11-6. On the left, you see that we have listed all three system requirements and all four constraints from Figure 11-3. These are our decision criteria. We have weighted requirements and constraints equally; that is, we believe that requirements are just as important as constraints. We do not have to weigh requirements and constraints equally; it is certainly possible to make requirements more or less important than constraints. Weights are arrived at in discussions among the analysis team, users, and sometimes managers. Weights tend to be fairly subjective and, for that reason, should be determined through a process of open discussion to reveal underlying assumptions, followed by an attempt to reach consensus among stakeholders. We have also assigned weights to each individual requirement and constraint. Notice that the total of the weights for both requirements and constraints is 50. Our weights correspond with our prioritization of the requirements and constraints.

Figure 11-6
Weighted approach for comparing the three alternative systems for Hoosier Burger's inventory system

Criteria	Weight	Alternative A		Alternative B		Alternative C	
		Rating	Score	Rating	Score	Rating	Score
Requirements							
Real-time data entry	18	5	90	5	90	5	90
Auto reorder	18	3	54	5	90	5	90
Real-time data query	14	1	14	3	42	5	70
	50		158		222		250
Constraints							
Development costs	20	5	100	4	80	3	60
Hardware costs	15	5	75	4	60	4	60
Time to operation	10	5	50	4	40	3	30
Ease of training	5	5	25	3	15	5	25
	50		250		195		175
Total	100		408		417		425

The next step we have taken is to rate each requirement and constraint for each alternative, on a scale of 1 to 5. A rating of one indicates that the alternative does not meet the requirement very well or that the alternative violates the constraint. A rating of five indicates that the alternative meets or exceeds the requirement or clearly abides by the constraint. Ratings are even more subjective than weights and should also be determined through open discussion among users, analysts, and managers. The next step we have taken is to multiply the rating for each requirement and each constraint by its weight, and we have followed this procedure for each alternative. The final step is to add up the weighted scores for each alternative. Notice that we have included three sets of totals: for requirements, for constraints, and overall totals. If you look at the totals for requirements, Alternative C is the best choice, as it meets or exceeds all requirements. However, if you look only at constraints, Alternative A is the best choice, as it does not violate any constraints. When we combine the totals for requirements and constraints, we see that the best choice is Alternative C, even though it had the lowest score for constraints, as it has the highest overall score.

Alternative C, then, appears to be the best choice for Hoosier Burger. Whether Alternative C is actually chosen for development is another issue. The Mellankamps may be concerned that Alternative C violates two constraints, including the most important one, development costs. On the other hand, the owners (and chief users) at Hoosier Burger may so desire the full functionality Alternative C offers that they are willing to ignore the constraints violations. Or Hoosier Burger's management may be so interested in cutting costs they prefer Alternative A, even though its functionality is severely limited. What may appear to be the best choice for a systems development project may not always be the one that ends up being developed.

UPDATING THE BASELINE PROJECT PLAN

You will recall that the Baseline Project Plan was developed during project initiation and planning (see Chapter 6) to explain the nature of the requested system and the project to develop it. The plan includes (we presented this originally in Figure 6-10 and reproduce it here as Figure 11-7) a preliminary description of the system as requested, an assessment of the feasibility or justification for the system (the business case), and an overview of management issues for the system and project. It was this plan that was presented to a steering committee or other body who approved the commitment of funds to conduct the analysis phase just completed. Thus, it is time to report back (in written and oral form) to this group on the project's progress and to update the group on the findings from analysis. This group will make the final decision on the design strategy to be followed and approve the commitment of resources outlined from the logical (and possibly physical) design steps. Of course, this group could determine that the business case has not developed as originally thought and either stop or drastically redirect the project.

The outline of the Baseline Project Plan can still be used for the analysis phase status report. The updated plan will typically be longer as more is known on each topic. Further, the various process, logic, and data models are often included to make the system description more specific. Usually only high-level versions of the diagrams are included within section 2.0, and more detailed versions are provided as appendices.

Every section of the Baseline Project Plan Report is updated at this point. For example, section 1.0.B will now contain the recommendation for the design strategy chosen by the analysis team. Section 2.0.A provides the descriptions of the

Figure 11-7
Outline of Baseline Project Plan

BASELINE PROJECT PLAN REPORT

1.0 *Introduction*
   A. Project Overview—Provides an executive summary that specifies the project's scope, feasibility, justification, resource requirements, and schedules. Additionally, a brief statement of the problem, the environment in which the system is to be implemented, and constraints that affect the project are provided.
   B. Recommendation—Provides a summary of important findings from the planning process and recommendations for subsequent activities.

2.0 *System Description*
   A. Alternatives—Provides a brief presentation of alternative system configurations.
   B. System Description—Provides a description of the selected configuration and a narrative of input information, tasks performed, and resultant information.

3.0 *Feasibility Assessment*
   A. Economic Analysis—Provides an economic justification for the system using cost-benefit analysis.
   B. Technical Analysis—Provides a discussion of relevant technical risk factors and an overall risk rating of the project.
   C. Operational Analysis—Provides an analysis of how the proposed system solves business problems or takes advantage of business opportunities in addition to an assessment of how current day-to-day activities will be changed by the system.
   D. Legal and Contractual Analysis—Provides a description of any legal or contractual risks related to the project (e.g., copyright or nondisclosure issues, data capture or transferring, and so on).
   E. Political Analysis—Provides a description of how key stakeholders within the organization view the proposed system.
   F. Schedules, Timeline, and Resource Analysis—Provides a description of potential timeframe and completion date scenarios using various resource allocation schemes.

4.0 *Management Issues*
   A. Team Configuration and Management—Provides a description of the team member roles and reporting relationships.
   B. Communication Plan—Provides a description of the communication procedures to be followed by management, team members, and the customer.
   C. Project Standards and Procedures—Provides a description of how deliverables will be evaluated and accepted by the customer.
   D. Other Project-Specific Topics—Provides a description of any other relevant issues related to the project uncovered during planning.

---

competing strategies studied during alternative generation and selection, often including the types of comparison charts shown earlier in this chapter. Section 3.0 is typically significantly changed since you now know much better than you did during project initiation and planning what the needs of the organization are. For example, economic benefits which were intangible before may now be tangible. Risks, especially operational ones, are likely better understood.

Section 3.0.F will now show the actual activities and their durations during the analysis phase, as well as include a detailed schedule for the activities in the design phases and whatever additional details can be anticipated for later phases. Many Gantt charting packages can show actual progress versus planned activities. It is important to show in this section how well the actual conduct of the analysis phase matched the planned activities. This helps you and management understand how well the project is understood and how likely it is that the stated future schedule will occur. Those activities whose actual durations differed significantly from planned durations may be very useful to you in estimating future activity durations. For example, a longer than expected task to analyze a certain process on a DFD may suggest that the design of system features to support this process may take longer than originally anticipated.

Often the design phase activities will be driven by the capabilities chosen for the recommended design strategy. For example, you will place specific design activities on the schedule for such design deliverables as the following:

- Layout of each report and data input and display screens (the DFDs include data flows for each of these)

- Structuring of data into logical tables or files (the E-R diagrams identify what data entities are involved in this)

- Programs and program modules that need to be described (processes on DFD and process and temporal logic models explain how complicated these tasks will be)

- Training on new technologies to be used in implementing the system

Many design phase activities result in developing design specifications for one or more examples of the types of design deliverables listed previously.

Section 4.0 is also updated. It is likely that the project team needs to change as new skills are needed in the next and subsequent project phases. Also, since project team members are often evaluated after each phase, the project leader may request the reassignment of a team member who has not performed as required. The communication plan needs to be reassessed to see if other communication methods need to be employed (see Table 3-4 for a list of common communication methods). New standards and procedures will be necessary as the team discovers that some current procedures are inadequate for the new tasks. Section 4.0.D is often used to outline issues for management that have been discovered during analysis. Recall, for example, that we discussed in Chapter 7 how you might find redundancies and inconsistencies in job descriptions and the way people actually do their jobs. Since these issues must be resolved by management, and must be addressed before you can progress into detailed system design, now is the last time to call these issues to the attention of management.

As the project leader, you and other analysts also must ensure that the project workbook and CASE repository are completely up-to-date as you finalize the analysis phase. Since the project team composition will likely change and, as time passes, you forget facts learned in earlier stages, the workbook and repository are necessary to transfer information between phases. This is also a good time for the project leader to do a final check that all elements of project execution have been properly handled (see Table 3-5).

Besides the written Baseline Project Plan Report update, an oral presentation is typically made, and it may be at this meeting that a decision to approve your recommendations, redirect your recommendations, or kill the project is made. It is not uncommon for the analysis team to follow this project review meeting with a suitable celebration for reaching an important project milestone.

Before and After Baseline Project Plans for Hoosier Burger

Even though their Inventory Control System was relatively small, Hoosier Burger developed a Baseline Project Plan for the project. The plan included information for each area listed in the outline in Figure 11-7, parts of which are reproduced below. Now that the analysis phase of the life cycle has ended, the plan must be updated, and those updated sections are also reproduced below. The first item we will consider is the cost-benefit analysis prepared as part of Section 3.0.A, on economic analysis. Hoosier Burger's initial cost-benefit analysis for the inventory project is shown in Figure 11-8. The format is the same as you saw in Chapter 6.

The numbers in the spreadsheet are based in part on the constraints listed in Figure 11-3. Part of the worksheet the Mellankamps used to determine the values in the spreadsheet in Figure 11-8 is shown in Table 11-5. The Mellankamps estimated that the benefits of the new system could be quantified in two ways: first, instant entry of shipment data would lead to more accurate inventory data; second, Hoosier Burger would be less likely to run out of stock with an automatic order determination as part of the system. Savings from more accurate data amount to $1,500 per month or $18,000 per year; savings from fewer stockouts amount to $1,000 per month or $12,000 per year. As you can see from Figure 11-8, although a new inven-

Figure 11-8
Hoosier Burger's initial cost-benefit analysis for its Inventory Control System project

Hoosier Burger							
Economic Feasibility Analysis							
Inventory Control System							
				Year of Product			
	Year 0	Year 1	Year 2	Year 3	Year 4	Year 5	TOTALS
Net economic benefit	$0	$30,000	$30,000	$30,000	$30,000	$30,000	
Discount rate (12%)	1	0.8928571	0.7971939	0.7117802	0.6355181	0.5674269	
PV of benefits	$0	$26,786	$23,916	$21,353	$19,066	$17,023	
NPV of all BENEFITS	$0	$26,786	$50,702	$72,055	$91,120	$108,143	$108,143
One-time COSTS	($100,000)						
Recurring Costs	$0	($2,000)	($2,000)	($2,000)	($2,000)	($2,000)	
Discount rate (12%)	1	0.8928571	0.7971939	0.7117802	0.6355181	0.5674269	
PV of Recurring Costs	$0	($1,786)	($1,594)	($1,424)	($1,271)	($1,135)	
NPV of all COSTS	($100,000)	($101,786)	($103,380)	($104,804)	($106,075)	($107,210)	($107,210)
Overall NPV							$934
Overall ROI - (Overall NPV / NPV of all COSTS)							0.01

TABLE 11-5 Hoosier Burger's Initial Economic Analysis Worksheet

One-time costs: Development	$50,000
One-time costs: Hardware	$50,000
Recurring costs: Maintenance	$ 2,000 per year
Savings: Fewer stockouts due to automatic reordering	$12,000 per year
Savings: More accurate data from shipment logging	$18,000 per year
Intangible benefit: Better management information	

tory control system for Hoosier Burger would break even, it is not a very good investment, with only a 1% return, given a 12% discount rate.

Figure 11-9 shows the cost-benefit analysis after the analysis phase has ended, which appears in the updated Baseline Project Plan. Notice that developing the new system, represented by Alternative C, is now a better investment, with a 15% return. Yet the overall costs of Alternative C exceed the costs of the original estimation of the system. What happened?

Figure 11-9
Hoosier Burger's revised cost-benefit analysis for its Inventory Control System project

Hoosier Burger
Economic Feasibility Analysis
Inventory Control System

	Year 0	Year 1	Year 2	Year 3	Year 4	Year 5	TOTALS
				Year of Product			
Net economic benefit	$0	$39,000	$39,000	$39,000	$39,000	$39,000	
Discount rate (12%)	1	0.8928571	0.7971939	0.7117802	0.6355181	0.5674269	
PV of benefits	$0	$34,821	$31,091	$27,759	$24,785	$22,130	
NPV of all BENEFITS	$0	$34,821	$65,912	$93,671	$118,457	$140,586	$140,586
One-time COSTS	($115,000)						
Recurring Costs	$0	($2,000)	($2,000)	($2,000)	($2,000)	($2,000)	
Discount rate (12%)	1	0.8928571	0.7971939	0.7117802	0.6355181	0.5674269	
PV of Recurring Costs	$0	($1,786)	($1,594)	($1,424)	($1,271)	($1,135)	
NPV of all COSTS	($115,000)	($116,786)	($118,380)	($119,804)	($121,075)	($122,210)	($122,210)
Overall NPV							$18,377
Overall ROI - (Overall NPV / NPV of all COSTS)							0.15

Much of Figure 11-9 is the same as Figure 11-8. Recurring costs are the same; the discount rate is the same. What has changed, in addition to larger one-time costs, is that net benefits are now estimated to be larger than in Figure 11-8. Details on these new estimates are shown in Table 11-6. The Mellankamps re-estimated the savings from the new system, using more accurate data, and found they had been too optimistic. The expected savings from instantly logging new shipments of supplies were reduced from $18,000 per year to $15,000 per year. But the Mellankamps also found a new benefit: they realized that better management information, and its ready availability through a new query capability, could be quantified at about $1,000 per month. The Mellankamps did not just dream up the $1,000 per month savings estimate. They developed it from thinking about how timely, accurate management information would affect their ability to prepare reports as well as their ability to improve their operations through better inventory control. So even though Alternative C was more expensive to develop than the other alternatives, it actually resulted in a higher level of tangible benefits.

Figure 11-10 shows the part of the project schedule from the initial version of the Baseline Project Plan that applies to subsequent steps. Notice that the schedule covers only the design and implementation phases of the life cycle and that the schedule is very general. The physical design subphase is not broken down into its constituent parts. The task times in the schedule are also driven by two of the constraints listed in Figure 11-3. The entire schedule spans exactly six months of activity and training takes only one week. The estimates of how long each task should take to complete are all very rough.

Compare Figure 11-10 to Figure 11-11, the revised schedule that goes in the updated Baseline Project Plan. The schedule is more detailed and it more closely reflects the development time necessary for Alternative C. Training still takes only one week, but now that estimate is based on a clear understanding of the requirements of a particular system rather than based primarily on positive thinking. Also, the entire schedule now spans nine months, the time necessary to fully develop and implement Alternative C. Some design tasks in Figure 11-11 have been decomposed into four different subtasks, many of which can be worked on concurrently: interface design, designing the internals, physical database design, and data conversion. Note that even this schedule presents the project at a very high level. It would be typical in actual projects to show not only the major steps but also the individual activities needed to complete each step. For example, Interface design might be broken down into many steps for each display or report and for different activities, such as meetings with users to walkthrough the tentative designs.

We have shown you only two parts to the Hoosier Burger Baseline Project Plan for their Inventory Control System. Even for a project this small, a complete Baseline Project Plan would be too much to include in this book. From these examples,

TABLE 11-6 Hoosier Burger's Updated Economic Analysis Worksheet	
One-time costs: Development	$65,000
One-time costs: Hardware	$50,000
Recurring costs: Maintenance	$ 2,000 per year
Savings: Fewer stockouts due to automatic reordering	$12,000 per year
Savings: More accurate data from shipment logging	$15,000 per year
Savings: Better management information & availability	$12,000 per year

Figure 11-10
Hoosier Burger's initial schedule for its Inventory Control System project

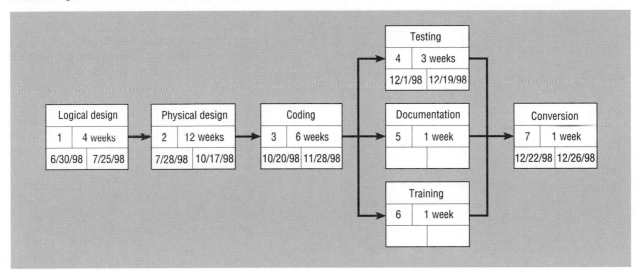

Figure 11-11
Hoosier Burger's revised schedule for its Inventory Control System project

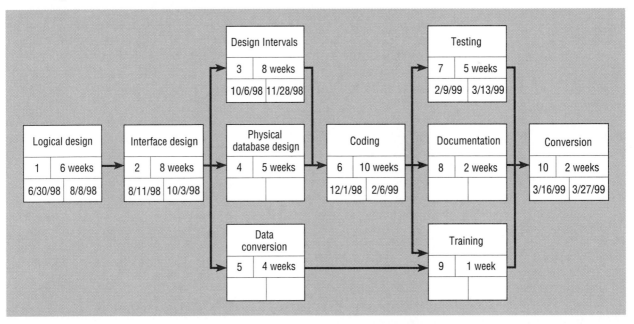

though, you should get a good general idea both of what an initial Baseline Project Plan contains and how it changes when a major life cycle phase, like analysis, ends.

SUMMARY

In the alternative generation and choice phase of systems analysis, you develop alternative solutions, or design strategies, to the organization's information system problem. A design strategy is a combination of system features, hardware and system software platform, and acquisition method that characterize the nature of the system and how it will be developed. A good number of alternative design strategies to develop is three, as three alternatives can represent the high-end, middle, and low-end of the spectrum of possible systems that can be built.

When developing design strategy alternatives, you must become aware of all of the possible options available. You must be aware of where you can obtain software that meets some or all of an organization's needs. You can obtain application (and system) software from hardware vendors, packaged software vendors, and custom software developers, as well as from internal systems development resources. You can even hire an organization to handle all of your systems development needs, called outsourcing. You must also know which criteria to use to be able to choose among off-the-shelf software products. These criteria include cost, functionality, vendor support, vendor viability, flexibility, documentation, response time, and ease of installation. You must also determine whether new hardware and system software are needed. Requests for proposals are one way you can collect more information about hardware and system software, their performance, and costs. In addition to software and hardware issues, you must consider implementation issues and broader organizational concerns, such as the availability of funding and management support.

Alternative design strategies are developed after a system's requirements and constraints have been identified and prioritized. Once developed, alternatives can be compared to each other through quantitative methods, but the actual decision may depend on other criteria, such as organizational politics.

Since generating and selecting alternative design strategies completes the analysis phase of the SDLC, the systems development project has reached a major milestone. Once an analysis of alternative design strategies is completed, you and other members of the analysis team will present your findings to a management steering committee and/or the client requesting the system change. In this presentation (both written and oral), you will summarize the requirements discovered, evaluate alternative design strategies and justify the recommended alternative as well as present an updated Baseline Project Plan for the project to follow if the committee decides to fund the next life cycle phase.

KEY TERMS

Design strategy
Outsourcing

REVIEW QUESTIONS

1. Define each of the following terms:

   a. outsourcing
   b. request for proposal (RFP)
   c. design strategy
   d. turnkey system

   e. custom software producer
   f. vendor support
   g. Baseline Project Plan

2. What are the deliverables from generating alternatives and selecting the best one?

3. Why generate at least three alternatives?

4. Describe the four sources of software.

5. How do you decide among various off-the-shelf software options? What criteria do you use?

6. What issues are considered when analysts try to determine whether new hardware or system software is necessary? What is an RFP and how do analysts use one to gather information on hardware and system software?

7. What issues other than hardware and software must analysts consider in preparing alternative system design strategies?

8. How do analysts generate alternative solutions to information systems problems?

9. How do managers decide which alternative design strategy to develop?

10. Which elements of a Baseline Project Plan might be updated during the alternative generation and selection step of the analysis phase of the SDLC?

11. What methods can a systems analyst employ to verify vendor claims about a software package?

12. What are enterprise resource planning systems? What are the benefits and disadvantages of such systems as a design strategy?

PROBLEMS AND EXERCISES

1. Match the following terms to the appropriate definitions.

_____ alternative generation and selection	a. statement of system features, hardware and software platform, and acquisition approach for a new system
_____ requirements structuring	b. process of collecting information about what the current system and what capabilities users and others want in a new information system
_____ requirements determination	c. process of organizing information about an information system using standard process, logic, and data modeling notations
_____ design strategy	d. process of developing choices for how to proceed with the design and implementation of an information system

2. Find the most current issue of *Datamation* that includes the most recent *Datamation* 100 listings. How much has the rank order of the top software companies changed compared to the list printed here? Read the issue and determine why your list is different from the list in this chapter. What changes are occurring in the computer industry that might affect this list?

3. Research how to prepare a Request for Proposal. Prepare an outline of an RFP for Hoosier Burger to use in collecting information on its new inventory system hardware.

4. Recreate the spreadsheet in Figure 11-6 in your spreadsheet package. Change the weights and compare the outcome to Figure 11-6. Change the rankings. Add criteria. What additional information does this "what if" analysis provide for you as a decision maker? What insight do you gain into the decision-making process involved in choosing the best alternative system design?

5. Prepare a list for evaluating computer hardware and system software that is comparable to the list of criteria for selecting off-the-shelf application software presented earlier.

6. The method for evaluating alternatives used in Figure 11-6 is called weighting and scoring. This method implies that the total utility of an alternative is the product of the weights of each criterion times the weight of the criterion for the alternative. What assumptions are characteristic of this method for evaluating alternatives? That is, what conditions must be true for this to be a valid method of evaluation alternatives?

7. Weighting and scoring (see Problem and Exercise 6) is only one method for comparing alternative solutions to a problem. Go to the library and find a book or articles on qualitative and quantitative decision making and voting methods and outline two other methods for evaluating alternative solutions to a problem. What are the pros and cons of these methods compared to the weighting and scoring method? Under weighting and scoring and the other alternatives you find, how would you incorporate the opinions of multiple decision makers?

8. Prepare an agenda for a meeting at which you would present the findings of the analysis phase of the SDLC to Bob Mellankamp concerning his request for a new inventory control system. Use information provided in Chapters 8–13 as background in preparing this agenda. Concentrate on which topics to cover, not the content of each topic.

9. Review the criteria for selecting off-the-shelf software presented in this chapter. Use your experience and imagination and describe other criteria that are or might be used to select off-the-shelf software in the "real world." For each new criterion, explain how use of this criterion might be functional (i.e., it is useful to use this criterion), dysfunctional, or both.

10. The owner of two pizza parlors located in adjacent towns wants to computerize and integrate sales transactions and inventory management within and between both stores. The point of sale component must be very easy to use and flexible enough to accommodate a variety of pricing strategies and coupons. The inventory management, which will be linked to the point of sale component, must also be easy to use and fast. The systems at each store must be linked so that sales and inventory levels can be determined instantly for each store and for both stores combined. The owner can allocate $40,000 for hardware and $20,000 for software and must have the new system operational in three months. Training must be very short and easy. Briefly describe three alternative systems for this situation and explain how each would meet the requirements and constraints. Are the requirements and constraints realistic? Why or why not?

11. Compare the alternative systems from Problem and Exercise 10 using the weighted approach demonstrated in Figure 11-6. Which system would you recommend? Why? Was the approach taken in this and Problem and Exercise 10 useful even for this relatively small system? Why or why not?

12. Suppose that an analysis team did not generate alternative design strategies for consideration by a project steering committee or client. What might the consequences be of having only one design strategy? What might happen during the oral presentation of project progress if only one design strategy is offered?

13. In the section on Choosing Off-the-Shelf Software there are eight criteria proposed for evaluating alternative packages. Suppose the choice was between alternative custom software developers rather than prewritten packages. What criteria would be appropriate to select and compare among competing bidders for custom development of an application? Define each of these criteria.

14. How might the project team recommending an enterprise resource planning design strategy justify its recommendation as compared to other types of design strategies?

FIELD EXERCISES

1. Consider the purchase of a new PC to be used by you at your work (or by you at a job that you would like to have). Describe in detail three alternatives for this new PC that represent the low, mid-, and high points of a continuum of potential solutions. Be sure that the low-end PC meets at least your minimum requirements and the high-end PC is at least within a reasonable budget. At this point, without quantitative analysis, which alternative would you choose?

2. For the new PC described above, developed ranked lists of your requirements and constraints as displayed in 11-6. Display the requirements and constraints, along with the three alternatives, in a diagram like the one displayed in Figure 11-6, and note how each alternative is rated on each requirement and constraint. Calculate scores for each alternative on each criterion and compute total scores. Which alternative has the highest score? Why? Does this choice fit with your selection in the previous question? Why or why not?

3. One of the most competitive software markets today is electronic spreadsheets. Pick three packages (for example, Microsoft Excel, Lotus 1-2-3, and Quattro Pro—but any three spreadsheet packages would do). Study how you use spreadsheet packages for school, work, and personal financial management. Develop a list of criteria important to you on which to compare alternative packages. Then contact each vendor and ask for the information you need to evaluate their package and company. Request a demonstration copy or trial use of their software. If they cannot provide a sample copy, then try to find a computer software dealer or club where you can test the software and documentation. Based on the information you receive and the software you use, rate each package using your chosen criteria. Which package is best for you? Why? Talk to other students and find out which package they rated as best. Why are there differences between what different students determined as best?

4. Interview businesspeople who participate in the purchase of off-the-shelf software in their organizations. Review with them the criteria for selecting off-the-shelf software presented in this chapter. Have them prioritize the list of criteria as they are used in their organization and provide an explanation of the rationale for the ranking of each criterion. Ask them to list and describe any other criteria that are used in their organization.

5. Obtain copies of actual Requests for Proposals used for information systems developments and/or purchases. If possible, obtain RFPs from public and private organizations. Find out how they are used. What are the major components of these proposals? Do these proposals seem to be useful? Why or why not? How and why are the RFPs different for the public versus the private organizations?

6. Contact an organization that has or is implementing an enterprise resource planning integrated application. Why did it choose this design strategy? How has it managed this development project differently from prior large projects? What organizational changes have occurred due to this design strategy? How long did the implementation last and why?

REFERENCES

Applegate, L. M., and R. Montealegre. 1991. "Eastman Kodak Company: Managing Information Systems Through Strategic Alliances." Harvard Business School case 9-192-030. Cambridge, MA: President and Fellows of Harvard College.

Harper, D. 1994. "Seek a Partner, Not a Vendor." *Industrial Distribution* 83 (April): 97.

Hartmann, C. R. 1993. "How to Write a Proposal." *D & B Reports* 42 (March-April): 62.

King, R. T., Jr., and J. E. Rigdon. 1994. "Hewlett Prints Computer Services in Big Capital Letters." *Wall Street Journal* (June 3): B8.

"Microcomputer Procurement Guidelines." 1994. *Public Works* 125 (April 15): G23 +.

Mikulski, F. A. 1993. *Managing Your Vendors: The Business of Buying Technology.* Englewood Cliffs, NJ: Prentice-Hall.

Moad, J. 1993. "Inside an Outsourcing Deal." *Datamation* 39 (February 15): 20–27.

"More Companies Are Chucking Their Computers." 1989. *Business Week* (June 19): 72–74.

Semich, J. W. "Is It Bye-Bye Borland?" *Datamation* 40 (June 15): 52–53.

Stein, M. 1993. "Don't Bomb Out When Preparing RFPs." *Computerworld* 27 (February 15): 102.

Zachary, G. P. 1990. "How Ashton-Tate Lost Its Leadership in PC Software Arena." *Wall Street Journal* (April 1): A1–A2.

Zachary, G. P., and W. M. Bulkeley. 1990. "Ashton-Tate Loses Flagship Software's Copyright Shield." *Wall Street Journal* (December 14): B1, B4.

Analysis: Selecting the Best Alternative Design Strategy for the Customer Activity Tracking System

INTRODUCTION

Frank Napier, Jordan Pippen, and Wendy Yoshimuro were meeting in Jordan's office to prepare for a preliminary analysis phase walkthrough meeting with Nancy Chen and Karen Gardner in preparation for the meeting with the Systems Priority Board (SPB). The walkthrough with the SPB would end the analysis phase of their Customer Activity Tracking System (CATS) project. Frank, Jordan, and Jorge had completed all of their work and had developed some alternative design strategies for CATS. Wendy, the marketing manager for U.S. Operations, had become so interested in CATS that she volunteered to be a part of the presentation team at the preliminary walkthrough, to show the strong user commitment to CATS.

PREPARING FOR THE PRELIMINARY CATS ANALYSIS WALKTHROUGH

"Frank," Jordan began, "You will start the meeting by presenting an overview of our three alternative system design strategies for CATS. Then Jorge, Wendy, and I will explain each of the alternative strategies, pointing out the good and bad points of each one."

"How are we going to organize that?" Wendy asked.

"I think the best way," Jordan answered, "is for Jorge and me to explain the information systems issues and for you to explain the functionality issues. After our overview of the alternatives, I will talk about the alternative we've selected and argue for its adoption."

"That's where I show the preliminary budget and schedule for the design phases," Frank said. "I'll also include a very preliminary budget and schedule for

implementation and maintenance. Jorge will be prepared to go over any of the requirements models we've developed, in case we get any questions about system details. Buffy Jarvis, from data administration, will be present to answer any questions about consistency with other databases. We'll have transparency masters made as backup, but Jorge will be able to show most of the charts on-line through a projection system tied to a PC running the CASE tool. Jorge is also coordinating a full-color computer-based slide show, for all of our presentation materials. We'll test all of this in our meeting with Nancy and Karen."

"You know this is the first time I've been involved in a systems development project at Broadway," Wendy stated. "Tell me again why both my boss, Nancy, and your boss, Karen, are involved in this meeting."

"Nancy has to decide if she is willing to lend the managerial and financial support it will take to complete the life cycle for CATS," Jordan responded. "Nancy is the one who has to pay for the development process. If she thinks what we are proposing is too expensive given the level of benefit we expect, she may cancel the whole project now. Design and implementation are more expensive than analysis, and Nancy may not want her area to take on that kind of expense right now. Karen, on the other hand, will have to decide where and if CATS as contemplated will fit into the overall information systems model for Broadway. For example, she will have to affirm to the SPB that CATS is compatible with the IS architecture and chosen platforms. She also has to decide if she is willing to let Frank, Jorge, and me continue on this project. It's possible one or more of us might get reassigned. Karen also has to think about the additional staffing demands for the design phase. We need to get both Karen and Nancy to buy into our ideas before we take them to the SPB for approval."

"Let's go over the material we've prepared once again, OK?" Wendy asked.

"No problem," replied Jordan. "That's why we're here. After all of our work in analysis, we've come up with three alternative design strategies for CATS. The first alternative is our high-end system—completely automated, all the bells and whistles, completely designed and implemented in-house so it meets our every need."

"And very expensive," Frank added.

"Our third alternative is our low-end system. Some of the work would be done manually, and functionality would be limited . . . ."

"But it's very cheap," Frank said.

"Yes," replied Jordan, "It's cheap. Anyway, the middle alternative is as middle-of-the-road as we could get on basic functionality, extra features . . . ."

"And cost," Frank said.

"Show me again the requirements and constraints lists," Wendy said.

"Here are the requirements [Figure 1], and here are the constraints [Figure 2]," said Frank.

"I recognize these requirements," Wendy said. "I helped Nancy put them together. This pretty much details the expected system functionality, right?"

"Yes, that's right," Jordan replied, "at least at a high level. You may not have seen the constraints

Figure 1
CATS requirements

1. Must create profile for each customer based on prior rental and purchase activity and demographic categories.

2. Must create profile for new releases of videos, games, and music.

3. Must match customer profiles to product profiles.

4. Must select customer/product matches most likely to lead to additional sales.

5. Must produce postcards about new products, addressed to customers matched with products.

6. Must be able to record reservation information that can be used to update BEC's inventory control system.

7. Must initiate shipment of reserved products to individual stores.

Figure 2
CATS constraints

1. New hardware expenditures must not exceed
   $10,000 per store.

2. Development costs must not exceed
   $385,000.

3. Disruption at store level must be
   minimal.

4. Successful pilot implementation must be
   operational within six months of the end
   of the design phase.

5. Total investment in training must not
   exceed one person day per store.

before, however. We developed this list working with Karen, although Nancy had a lot of input, too, especially about the costs involved."

"As you can see from the list, most of the constraints are monetary. But there is also an emphasis on how CATS will affect the stores," Jordan said.

"Where did that emphasis come from?" asked Wendy.

"Some of it is from Nancy, but it became clear to me in my meetings with store managers that they will not tolerate much disruption," Jordan replied. "Some of them are very skeptical about CATS. Oh, by the way, these lists are already prioritized from most to least important."

"Now here is how we estimate if each of the alternatives either meets or does not meet the requirements and stays faithful to or violates the constraints [Figure 3]. On this chart, our high-end system is Alternative 1, the middle-of-the-road system is Alternative 2, and Alternative 3 is the low-end system."

"Can you go over these alternatives for me one more time?" asked Wendy. "I want to think about them this time from Nancy's perspective."

"Sure," said Frank. "Alternative 1 is our own customized CATS, where we design and build the CATS so that it does everything Nancy and others have told us they want it to do, using state-of-the-art technology, from headquarters on down to the store level. We are

Figure 3
Alternative design strategies
for CATS

Criteria	Alternative 1	Alternative 2	Alternative 3
Requirements			
Customer profiles	Yes	Yes	Yes
Product profiles	Yes	Yes	Yes
Profile matching	Yes	Yes	Yes
Match selection	Yes	Yes	Yes
Generate cards	Yes	Yes	No
Track reservations	Yes	No	No
Initiate delivery	Yes	No	No
Constraints			
Hardware costs	$15K/store	$10K/store	$8K/store
Development costs	$500K	$400K	$300K
Store disruption	Medium	Low	Medium
Time to operation	12 months	6 months	6 months
Store training	Two days	One day	Two days

going to base the system at the store level on imaging, with CD-ROM storage. Eventually we'd like to have Broadway set up a node on the Internet so we can use e-mail instead of postcards and have samples of the video or music available on a bulletin board so customers could download it. Then they could skip the 800 number to make a reservation and just order the product directly over e-mail. They wouldn't have to send their credit card numbers over e-mail because we have them on file."

"So that's why this system violates every constraint," Wendy observed. "What about the middle system?"

"Alternative 2 is very interesting," Frank began. "I did some research and found a company doing a lot of what we want to do. They have a system that creates customer and product profiles, matches and selects profiles, and generates postcards. And the system is for sale. We'd have to do some customization, of course, and there is no tie-in to inventory control for tracking or initiating deliveries."

"What company is this?" Wendy asked.

"It's the TwoCat Petfood Company."

"What?" exclaimed Wendy.

"Yep, that's right. They have a really diverse line of cat foods and related products, and they are always developing new products. They do the same thing we want to do. They use data on loyal customers, create profiles, match those profiles with product profiles, all of the basic things we want. I heard about them from a friend at a local Association for Computing Machinery chapter meeting. We were talking about what

projects we were working on and she mentioned she received similar types of notices from this company for her cat, Memories. I think my friend is a candidate for a Broadway show soundtrack profile category, don't you? Anyhow, I called the company and got all the information; they even sent me a copy of the software to try."

"And the third alternative?"

"It will do the profile generation and matching, but it won't generate postcards. After the matching and selection, a report will be generated and sent to each store. The store will have to send postcards or call customers, keep track of reservations, and order product to fill their reservation needs," said Frank. "That's how we keep development costs down, by making some of the work manual and transferring it to the stores."

"That's why the cheapest alternative results in store disruption and more training time, too," said Jordan.

"OK," said Wendy. "What's our best alternative?"

"Here's how we determined it," said Frank, showing Wendy a spreadsheet output (Figure 4).

"We decided to make the requirements worth 60 percent of the choice, with constraints at 40 percent. We also decided to give weights of 10 to the four major requirements and the first two constraints. As both requirements and constraints are prioritized, the weights decrease in order after that. We determined these weights based on a survey we conducted during the JAD session. It was a small, but representative, sample. You can see that the high-end alternative, Al-

Figure 4
CATS alternatives evaluated and compared

Criteria	Weight	Alternative 1		Alternative 2		Alternative 3	
		Rating	Score	Rating	Score	Rating	Score
Requirements							
Customer Profiles	10	10	100	10	100	10	100
Product Profiles	10	10	100	10	100	10	100
Profile Matching	10	10	100	10	100	10	100
Profile Selection	10	10	100	10	100	10	100
Generate Cards	8	8	64	8	64	1	8
Track Reservations	6	6	36	1	6	1	6
Initiate Delivery	6	6	36	1	6	1	6
	60		536		476		420
Constraints							
Hardware Costs	10	5	50	10	100	10	100
Development	10	5	50	8	80	10	100
Store Disruption	8	4	32	8	64	4	32
Time to Operation	7	3	21	7	49	7	49
Store Training	5	2	10	5	25	2	10
	40		163		318		291
Total	100		699		794		711

ternative 1, did a great job on the requirements, but since it violated all of the constraints, Alternative 1 came in last among the three alternatives in terms of scores."

"Right," said Jordan. "Alternative 3 was last in terms of requirements. It fared OK for the constraints, and it would have done better, but there were problems with store disruption and training."

"So the winner is Alternative 2, the cat food system?" asked Wendy.

"Yep," said Frank, "TwoCat is our winner. The difference in scores is impressive in that Alternative 2 outscored the other two alternatives pretty well. We'll have a good bit of work to do to redesign some on-line displays, add some reports they don't have, and link this system into our other existing application portfolio. Next we just have to convince Nancy and Karen. Now, here is my budget and schedule for the design phase. Here is where you come in. . . ."

"Well, I'd like to stay and talk about the next step, but it's time for my appointment with one of our major suppliers who is probably waiting in my office. I need to go. By the way, would it help if I told him a little about our system? I've read a little about EDI,

electronic data interchange, and maybe some of the ordering functions within CATS could be handled through EDI. I'll send you an e-mail if he sees a possible connection. See you later."

SUMMARY

The analysis phase of the CATS project is about to come to a close. The CATS project team, along with several key stakeholders, have identified and evaluated alternative design strategies, deciding on the purchase of a software package from another company, TwoCat Petfood, as part of the recommended design strategy. Although TwoCat is not a software company, this does not matter since BEC is not looking for a software partner. Rather, Jordan Pippen and the other CATS team members expect to adapt the purchased software. In fact, TwoCat will sell BEC the source code for the software, which will facilitate BEC's customization. Thus, the CAT project must continue with subsequent design and implementation steps, although the purchased software will save considerable development time. The purchased software will provide most of the functionality BEC wants, and it is compatible with BEC's hardware and software platform.

The BEC Systems Priority Board (SPB) is impressed with the analysis done by the BEC team and the strong commitment from the client organization, evidenced by the integral role both Nancy Chen and Wendy Yoshimuro played in the analysis phase and the presentation of the design strategy and updated Baseline Project Plan. After gaining SPB approval, the CATS team is now ready to proceed to the design phases.

PART

IV

Blending Analysis and Design

Cambridge Technology Partners

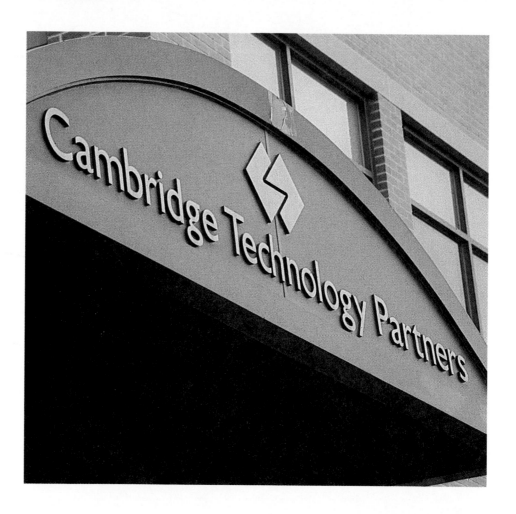

Building Systems On Time for a Fixed Cost

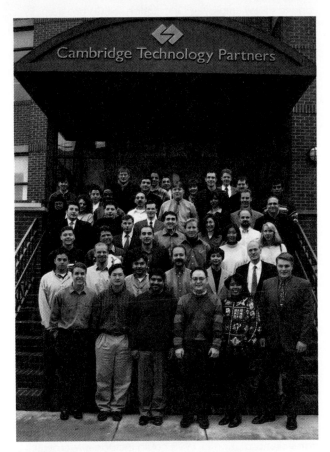

Cambridge Technology Partners (Cambridge) was founded in 1991 in Cambridge, Massachusetts. The firm is a consulting and systems integration company. By the end of 1997, Cambridge had grown to more than 3000 employees and 44 offices in over 14 countries. Revenues for 1996 were $272.9 million, a 52% increase over 1995 revenue. The company's stock is publicly traded and listed on the NASDAQ exchange.

Cambridge is unique in its approach to developing systems for clients. Historically, information systems development projects have been late, over budget, and have lacked the functionality originally envisioned for the systems. Cambridge, however, bucks this historical trend by building applications for a fixed price with a guaranteed delivery time. Cambridge is able to provide such guarantees because its consultants work with the client to carefully build consensus around the system and its capabilities throughout the development process. This consensus-building process is at the heart of all of Cambridge's client projects. A rapid application development (RAD)–specific example of this process is detailed in Chapter 13.

Cambridge relies on its core values in several areas of systems development. One area of focus is electronic commerce. Over half of Cambridge's current projects have an Internet component. Cambridge has also extended its core values to the fast-growing Enterprise Resource Planning (ERP) marketplace through its Enterprise Resource Solutions unit, which implements human resources, manufacturing, and financial solutions such as Peoplesoft, Oracle, and Baan.

Cambridge is able to grow rapidly because it is very successful in entering new markets. The company brings its unique set of differentiators to each service or market it enters. Cambridge applies its core values to the application development market to fundamentally reinvent the way information technology solutions are delivered.

- *Fast*: Cambridge completes projects quickly, while the solutions still have a strategic impact. Most projects are completed in only six to twelve months.

- *Right*: Cambridge develops the right (i.e., appropriate) application for its clients (to focus on the quick development of strategic and mission-critical applications).

- *Open Technology*: The Cambridge philosophy is using whatever technology is appropriate to develop the right solution for our client.

- *Guarantee Delivery*: Unlike most consulting firms, Cambridge shares the risk of projects with clients by guaranteeing delivery of each client's business solutions on time, and at a fixed price.

- *Business Case*: Cambridge will help clients determine the business case behind each solution prior to embarking on a project. The business case allows the client to gain executive buy-in for the effort and to keep the project in scope. A client has to have a business reason for developing a system, as opposed to a purely technological reason. The application should enable the client to possess some strategic advantage compared to its competitors, to enable it to "leapfrog" over the competition.

- *Behavioral Focus*: Sometimes an application cannot be successfully implemented because the firm's internal organization is an impediment or because the client has not been completely trained. Cambridge does not walk away until the client has been sufficiently trained and can operate the application appropriately.

Cambridge puts a heavy emphasis on maintaining and expanding its employees' skill sets. In addition to orientation workshops, Cambridge offers other training opportunities. Enterprise Learning, the overall training program at Cambridge, has two components: (1) professional training programs that focus on managerial skills and (2) technical training, where employees learn new skills through self-paced, computer-based training (CBT), or in the classroom. All employees are encouraged to participate in training that will maintain or improve the skills they need to perform their jobs or move into a new role. Cambridge assigns a Resource Manager to each employee who serves as a mentor throughout the employee's career at Cambridge, similar to the role of an advisor in college. Because a Cambridge employee can work on many projects with different project managers in a year, the RM program provides a consistent source of advice and supervision to ensure that employees receive support and guidance in determining career paths at Cambridge. All training programs are listed on Cambridge's Intranet site.

The guiding principles, the core values, the unique training policies, all add up to a unique corporate culture that the employees call the "Cambridge magic." The culture is one of high energy, where senior management is constantly thinking about how the firm can continue to reinvent itself and of what they can do for employees to make Cambridge a better place. Examples of the "Cambridge magic" include the "Recognize and Value Everyone" program where employees show their appreciation of others by giving them "RAVE" coupons which are accumulated and cashed in for merchandise twice per year.

To ensure that new employees become productive quickly, new hires from around the world travel to the Cambridge, Massachusetts, headquarters to attend Cambridge's New Employee Orientation (NEO) program. By conducting a monthly "boot camp" in Cambridge, the company maintains the consistency of their vision, corporate culture, and methodology.

Cambridge was a pioneer in client/server application development when the firm was formed in 1991. As the three-tier client/server architecture was a relatively new approach at that time, Cambridge custom-built most of the applications it deployed for clients and developed many of its own tools to assist in development, especially in the middleware area. In the early 1990s, Cambridge developers worked extensively on building interfaces to mainframe systems and the Unix platform with Macintosh clients.

As the client/server architecture became increasingly popular, Cambridge developers incorporated the steady stream of software tools available on the market. By 1994, as much as half of the development work was for the PC platform on the client side, although most of the mid-range servers remained Unix boxes. The development language of choice moved from C to C++.

Currently, Cambridge continues to be innovative in its use of information technology. Cambridge is "technology neutral" and strongly believes in using the right tool for the job; as such, the company uses a broad range of tools and technologies. An example of a configuration for a client solution in 1998 could include a Microsoft Windows NT server, PC workstations, Visual C++ front ends with object request brokers, and IBM MQSeries middleware. As the Internet continues to mature as a platform for commerce, Cambridge has increased its use of Java and Web-enabled middleware.

The RAD approach with the client/server focus that Cambridge started with in 1991 remains an important part of its business, but the firm now offers end-to-end business solutions including change implementation, business consulting, systems integration, network services, educational services, IT Strategy consulting, and expertise with the deployment of Enterprise Resource Planning (ERP) systems.

As information technology becomes more complex, and as the heterogeneity of the development and operating environments increases, Cambridge has responded by expanding the software toolkit its specialists use to solve client business problems. Yet, as Chief Technology Officer Sanjiv Gossain maintains, it is more important for Cambridge's employees to understand the fundamentals of information technology and of software engineering than to focus on individual software tools. Tools are im-

portant, but they change continually — understanding business processes and how information technology changes business helps developers choose the right tools for the job.

Cambridge Technology Partners is an example of how the nontraditional approach to information technology solutions for business can grow and flourish. With an emphasis on its people, and a unique set of core values that guide the company's work, Cambridge has enjoyed great success. Its pioneering efforts in rapid systems implementation and its deep technical expertise (originally in client/server, but now in a broad range of technologies including Internet, packaged applications, and more) have also been instrumental in its success.

An Overview of Part IV

Blending Analysis and Design

Even after over half a century of business computer applications, systems professionals are still creating new and improved methods for systems development. Recent increased cost and competitive pressures in business have caused organizations to seek ways of doing business that take less human effort (the largest source of costs) and reduce the cycle time from idea conception to implementation. Although no foolproof, "silver-bullet" methodology exists, two new methodologies show promise for improved systems development in at least some situations. These methodologies are object-oriented analysis and design (OOAD) and Rapid Application Development (RAD). Part IV explains these alternatives to the structured systems development approach, which has been emphasized so far in the text.

We choose to group these two, unrelated methodologies into one part of the text and, in particular, present them at this point in the text for three reasons. First, although clearly distinctive in approach, both OOAD and RAD draw on principles fundamental to all systems analysis and design approaches. Thus, it makes sense to cover them now while the essence of systems analysis is fresh in your minds. For example, the principles on which the static structure of objects is modeled are very similar to the principles of entity-relationship (ER) modeling. Also, some OOAD techniques, in particular, state-transition diagramming, have been used in structured methodologies to represent the logic of event-driven applications, especially on-line, real-time systems. Second, OOAD and RAD have several common traits: a strong focus on the business situation, extensive use of parallel development activities, and an orientation of reusing previously developed system components. Third, OOAD and RAD, significantly more than the structured methods covered so far, blend analysis and design steps together. Notice that we say that these steps are blended, not eliminated or avoided. Since the understanding of OOAD and RAD does not depend on a detailed knowledge of logical and physical design techniques, you will have no trouble understanding these approaches before Part V of the text. In fact, addressing OOAD and RAD now will help preview the logical and physical design activities to be presented in Part V.

Chapter 12 thoroughly covers OOAD. The field of OOAD is changing as rapidly as any in the systems development area, so we have been careful to present the most recent standards. In fact, the techniques and notations shown in Chapter 12 emerged from the leaders in the field while writing this chapter. The standard in OOAD is the Uniform Modeling Language (UML), developed by Grady Booch, Ivar Jacobson, and James Rumbaugh and the Rational Software Company. This standard is the culmination of a long project to bring together three previously competing styles of OOAD. The OOAD approach now has one widely accepted standard, which is what is presented in this chapter.

An object-oriented model, as you will learn in this chapter, is built around *objects*. As you shall see, an object *encapsulates* both data and *behavior*, implying that analysts can use the object-oriented approach for both data modeling and process modeling. By allowing a systems analyst to capture them together within a common representation, and by offering benefits such as *inheritance* and code reuse, the object-oriented modeling approach provides a powerful environment for developing complex systems. These principles of objects, encapsulation, behaviors, inheritance, and the like are the foundation for object-oriented systems development.

In Chapter 12 you will learn how to represent system requirements (use cases), the static and dynamic structure and behaviors of an information system (object and class models and state-transition diagrams, respectively), and the interaction between system components—objects (sequence diagrams). More techniques exist within UML, but these are the core techniques suitable for presentation in this text. In contrast to the SDLC, the object-oriented development life cycle is more like an onion than a waterfall. In the early stages (or core) of development, the model you build is abstract, focusing on external qualities of the application system. As the model evolves, it becomes more and more detailed, shifting the focus to how the system will be built and how it should function — system architecture, data structures, and algorithms. Important in this process is the concept that the model of a system evolves. A major benefit to OOAD is the continuity of modeling techniques across life cycle steps. As you discovered in Part III, although there are clear relationships between process, data, and logic modeling; structured techniques do not seamlessly fit together.

In Chapter 12 you will learn how to develop a requirements analysis model through use-case diagrams. A use-case diagram shows the interaction between external actors and actions performed within a system. You will also learn how to model the static structure of objects in the problem domain using class and object diagrams. Objects have both states (conditions during the life of an object) and behaviors (operations) which are encapsulated within. Associations exist between objects, just as relationships exist between entities in an entity-relationship diagram. Next, we introduce you to state diagrams for capturing the dynamic state transitions of an object. State transitions occur when events trigger changes in an object. Then you will see how to develop a dynamic model of interactions among objects using sequence diagrams. A sequence diagram shows the passing of messages between objects. Messages activate operations within objects, thus causing the system to perform needed functions. You will also see guidelines on transforming the analysis models to design models.

Chapter 12 explains several motivations and benefits of object-oriented modeling, which are:

- You are able to tackle more challenging problem domains.

- You can improve communication among yourself, users, other analysts, designers, and programmers.

- You are able to increase internal consistency across analysis, design, and programming activities.

- You are able to explicitly represent commonality among system components.

- You can build robust systems.

- You can reuse analysis, design, and programming results.

- You will be able to increase consistency among all the models developed during object-oriented analysis, design, and programming.

Since we say that OOAD blends analysis with design, you might wonder which diagrams belong to the analysis phase and which diagrams belong to the design phase. The answer is that, in general, the same type of diagram may apply to different phases. However, as you move from analysis to design, you need to refine the diagrams based on the requirements of the implementation environment. During design, you need to consider technical details relating to the target hardware, operating system, programming language, and database management system, and refine the models that you developed earlier. So, OOAD truly blends analysis with design through the evolution of techniques, rather than changing from one set of techniques to another.

Rapid Application Development (RAD) is an approach to developing information systems that promises better and cheaper systems and more rapid deployment by having systems developers and end users work together jointly in real-time to develop systems. As you will see in Chapter 13, RAD is not a single methodology but is more of a general strategy of developing information systems. As such, there are many different approaches to developing applications rapidly. Some are special life cycles, such as the Martin RAD life cycle. Others focus more on specific software tools and visual development environments that make the process of rapidly developing and deploying applications possible. Whatever strategy is taken, however, the goal remains the same: to rapidly analyze a business problem, to design a viable system solution through intense cooperation between users and developers, and to quickly get the finished application in the hands of users—saving time, money, and other resources in the process.

RAD relies on bringing together several systems development components that you have studied in this book. As you might have gathered from the definition, RAD depends on extensive user involvement. Much of end-user involvement takes place in the *prototyping* process, where users and analysts work together to design interfaces and reports for new systems. The prototyping is conducted in sessions that resemble traditional *Joint Application Development* (JAD) sessions. The primary difference is that in RAD, the prototype becomes the basis for the new system — the screens designed during prototyping become screens in the production system. This is accomplished through reliance on *integrated CASE tools,* which include *code generators* for creating bug-free code from the designs end users and analysts create during prototyping. The code includes the interfaces as well as the application programs that use them. Alternatively, RAD may employ visual development environments instead of CASE tools with code generators, but the benefits from rapid prototyping are the same. To further help speed the process, the *reuse* of templates, components, or previous systems described in the CASE tool repository is strongly encouraged.

Chapter 13 introduces two general approaches to RAD and discusses one specific RAD methodology. From the comparison of these three views of RAD, you will develop a good understanding of the principles that embody RAD. Unlike OOAD, there is no RAD standard; in fact, there is no effort underway to standardize RAD. Rather, RAD tends to be conducted with proprietary methodologies, owned by major information systems consulting firms. We have purposely selected the topics about RAD that will help you understand any particular RAD approach you encounter.

From the several approaches to RAD presented in Chapter 13, you will learn about keys to RAD success. These keys include:

- Prototyping tools, such as fourth-generation languages (4GLs) and visual development environments

- People well trained in the right skills, such as JAD, prototyping, and advanced tools

- A coherent methodology, which spells out the proper tasks to be done in the proper order

- The support and facilitation of management to garner all the attention needed to develop the right system quickly

- Avoiding classic systems development mistakes

- Applying systems development fundamentals (even when working with abbreviated and streamlined methods)

- Managing risks to avoid catastrophic setbacks

- Applying schedule-oriented practices

Chapter 13 reports several RAD success stories, which highlight the diverse situations in which RAD may be applied. These success stories come from aerospace, government, and financial services. These success stories point out that the primary advantage of RAD is obvious: information systems developed in as little as one-quarter the usual time. But shorter development cycles also mean cheaper systems, as fewer organizational resources need be devoted to develop any particular system. RAD also involves smaller development teams, which results in even more savings. Finally, because there is less time between the end of design and conversion, the new system is closer to current business needs and is therefore of higher quality than would be a similar system developed the traditional way. However, because of the shortcuts taken during RAD, it should be applied only in situations that require rapid deployment, where the system being developed is decoupled from other systems, the business model behind the system is relatively easy to discern, and system controls are not important.

We believe that you will find Part IV to be exciting. Although short, this section raises important challenges for systems analysis and design, and proposes systems development approaches that are receiving considerable attention in today's business climate.

CHAPTER

12

Object-Oriented Analysis and Design*

After studying this chapter, you should be able to:

■ Define the following key terms: *use case, object, class, state, behavior, operation, encapsulation, constructor operation, query operation, update operation, association, multiplicity, abstract class, concrete class, class-scope attribute, abstract operation, method, polymorphism, overriding, aggregation, composition, event, state transition,* and *sequence diagram.*

■ Describe the concepts and principles underlying the object-oriented approach.

■ Describe the activities in the different phases of the object-oriented development life cycle.

■ State the advantages of object-oriented modeling versus traditional systems development approaches.

■ Develop a requirements model using use-case diagrams.

■ Develop an object model of the problem domain using class diagrams.

■ Develop dynamic models using state and interaction diagrams.

■ Model real-world applications using UML diagrams.

INTRODUCTION

In Part III of this book you learned how to analyze the requirements for an information system using structured techniques. We introduced you to a variety of diagrams for modeling purposes, such as context diagrams, data flow diagrams, decision tables, and entity-relationship diagrams. With the traditional systems development life cycle and structured techniques, analysis and design are separate but overlapping steps, and different techniques are used for analysis and for design. You will learn about information system design issues and techniques in Part V. In this chapter, we will introduce you to the object-oriented model, which is becoming increasingly popular because of its ability to thoroughly represent complex relationships, as well as to represent data and data processing with a consistent notation. By a *consistent notation,* we mean that the same or compatible notation is

---

* This chapter was written by Professor Atish P. Sinha.

used throughout the systems development process. Thus, you can more easily blend analysis and design in an evolutionary process.

A model, as you already know, is an abstraction of the real world. It allows you to deal with the complexity inherent in a real-world problem by focusing on the essential and interesting features of an application. An object-oriented model, as you will learn in this chapter, is built around *objects.* An object *encapsulates* both data and *behavior*, implying that analysts can use the object-oriented approach for both data modeling and process modeling. By allowing a systems analyst to capture them together within a common representation, and by offering benefits such as *inheritance* and code reuse, the object-oriented modeling approach provides a powerful environment for developing complex systems. The principles of objects, encapsulation, inheritance, and *polymorphism* (discussed later) are the foundation for object-oriented systems development.

In this chapter you will also learn a wide variety of techniques that systems analysts use for object-oriented analysis and design. These techniques and associated notations are incorporated into a standard object-oriented language called the Uniform Modeling Language, or UML. This chapter is based on the UML standard. The techniques and notations within UML include

- *Use cases*, which represent the functional requirements, or the "what" of the system

- *Class diagrams*, which show the static structure of data and operations that act on the data

- *State diagrams*, which represent dynamic models of how objects change their states in response to events

- *Sequence diagrams*, which represent dynamic models of interactions between objects

You will also learn in this chapter how analysis and design activities are blended together in the object-oriented approach. You will learn the details of systems design beginning in Chapter 14.

OBJECT-ORIENTED DEVELOPMENT LIFE CYCLE

The object-oriented development life cycle, depicted in Figure 12-1, consists of progressively developing an object representation through three phases—analysis, design, and implementation—similar to the heart of the systems development life cycle explained in Chapter 1. In contrast to the SDLC, the object-oriented development life cycle is more like an onion than a waterfall. In the early stages (or core) of development, the model you build is abstract, focusing on external qualities of the application system. As the model evolves, it becomes more and more detailed, shifting the focus to how the system will be built and how it should function—system architecture, data structures, and algorithms. Ultimately, like any information system, the systems developer must generate code and database access routines. The emphasis in modeling should be on analysis and design, focusing on front-end conceptual issues, rather than back-end implementation issues, which unnecessarily restrict design choices (Rumbaugh et al., 1991).

The Process of Object-Oriented Analysis and Design

In the analysis phase, a model of the real-world application is developed showing its important properties. It abstracts concepts from the application domain and de-

Figure 12-1
Phases of object-oriented systems development cycle

scribes *what* the intended system must do, rather than *how* it will be done. The model specifies the functional behavior of the system, independent of concerns relating to the environment in which it is to be finally implemented. You need to devote sufficient time to clearly understand the requirements of the problem. The analysis model should capture those requirements completely and accurately. Remember that it is much easier and cheaper to make changes or fix flaws during analysis than during the later phases.

In the object-oriented design phase, you define *how* the application-oriented analysis model will be realized in the implementation environment. Jacobson (1992) cites three reasons for using object-oriented design. These three reasons are:

- The analysis model is not formal enough to be implemented directly in a programming language. To move seamlessly into the source code requires refining the objects by making decisions on what operations an object will provide, what the interobject communication should look like, what messages are to be passed, and so forth.

- The actual system must be adapted to the environment in which the system will actually be implemented. To accomplish that, the analysis model has to be transformed into a design model, considering different factors such as performance requirements, real-time requirements and concurrency, the target hardware and systems software, the DBMS and programming language to be adopted, and so forth.

- The analysis results can be validated using object-oriented design. At this stage, you can verify if the results from the analysis are appropriate for building the system, and make any necessary changes to the analysis model.

To develop the design model, you must identify and investigate the consequences that the implementation environment will have on the design (Jacobson et al., 1992). All strategic design decisions—such as how the DBMS is to be incorporated, how process communications and error handling are to be achieved, what component libraries are to be reused—are made. Next, you incorporate those decisions into a first-cut design model that adapts to the implementation environment. Finally, you formalize the design model to describe how the objects interact with one another.

Rumbaugh et al. (1991) separate the design activity into two stages: *system design* and *object design*. As the system designer, you propose an overall system architecture, which organizes the system into components called subsystems and provides the context to make decisions such as identifying concurrency; allocation of subsystems to processors and tasks; handling access to global resources; selecting the implementation of control in software; and more.

During object design, you build a design model by adding implementation details—such as restructuring classes for efficiency, internal data structures and algorithms to implement each class, implementation of control, implementation of associations, and packaging into physical modules—to the analysis model in accordance with the strategy established during system design. The application-domain object classes from the analysis model still remain, but they are augmented with computer-domain constructs, with a view toward optimizing important performance measures.

The design phase is followed by the implementation phase. In this phase, you implement the design using a programming language and/or a database management system. Translating the design into program code is a relatively straightforward process, given that the design model already incorporates the nuances of the programming language and/or the DBMS.

Deliverables and Outcomes

As with the structured modeling techniques you learned in Chapters 8 through 10, the deliverables from project activities using object-oriented modeling are diagrams and repository descriptions, which provide a full specification of the information system. A major characteristic of these diagrams is how tightly they are linked with each other. This is because all of the techniques and diagramming conventions for object-oriented modeling have been developed as a consistent set, rather than as relatively independent notations (as is true with the techniques of Chapters 8 through 10).

This consistency in notation yields certain outcomes for a systems development project using object-oriented modeling. Coad and Yourdon (1991b) identify several motivations and benefits of object-oriented modeling:

- The ability to tackle more challenging problem domains

- Improved communication among users, analysts, designers, and programmers

- Increased consistency among analysis, design, and programming activities

- Explicit representation of commonality among system components

- Robustness of systems

- Reusability of analysis, design, and programming results

- Increased consistency among all the models developed during object-oriented analysis, design, and programming

The last point needs further elaboration. In other modeling approaches, such as structured analysis and design, the models that are developed (e.g., data flow diagrams during analysis and structure charts during design) lack a common underlying representation and, therefore, are very weakly connected. In contrast to the abrupt and disjoint transitions that those approaches suffer from, the object-oriented approach provides a continuum of representation from analysis to design to implementation (Coad and Yourdon, 1991a), engendering a seamless transition from one model to another (Jacobson, 1992). For instance, moving from object-oriented analysis to object-oriented design entails expanding the analysis model with implementation-related details, not developing a whole new representation.

In this chapter, we show you how to analyze and design complex applications using the object-oriented approach. You will learn how to develop models by dealing with various aspects or views of a system. In general, each view will constitute multiple diagrams. We will show you how to draw those diagrams using a visual modeling language, described in the next section.

THE UNIFIED MODELING LANGUAGE

The Unified Modeling Language (UML) is "a language for specifying, visualizing, and constructing the artifacts of software systems, as well as for business modeling" (*UML Document Set*, 1997). It is a culmination of the efforts of three leading experts, Grady Booch, Ivar Jacobson, and James Rumbaugh, who have defined an object-oriented modeling language that is expected to become an industry standard in the near future. The UML builds upon and unifies the semantics and notations of the Booch (Booch, 1994), OOSE (Jacobson et al., 1992), and OMT (Rumbaugh et al., 1991) methods, as well as those of other leading methods.

The UML notation is useful for graphically depicting object-oriented analysis and design models. It not only allows you to specify the requirements of a system and capture the design decisions, but it also promotes communication among key persons involved in the development effort. A developer can use an analysis or design model expressed in the UML notation as a means to communicate with domain experts, users, and other stakeholders.

For representing a complex system effectively, it is necessary that the model you develop has a small set of independent views or perspectives. The UML allows you to represent multiple views of a system using a variety of graphical diagrams, such as the use-case diagram, class diagram, state diagram, sequence diagram, and collaboration diagram. The underlying model integrates those views so that the system can be analyzed, designed, and implemented in a complete and consistent fashion.

We will first show how to develop a use-case model during the requirements analysis phase. Next, we will show how to model the static structure of the system using class and object diagrams. You will then learn how to capture the dynamic aspects using state and interaction diagrams. Finally, we will provide a brief description of component and deployment diagrams, which are generated during the design and implementation phases.

USE-CASE MODELING

Jacobson et al. (1992) pioneered the application of use-case modeling for analyzing the functional requirements of a system. Because it focuses on *what* an existing system does or a new system should do, as opposed to *how* the system delivers or should deliver those functions, a use-case model is developed in the analysis phase of the object-oriented system development life cycle. Use-case modeling is done in the early stages of system development to help developers gain a clear understanding of the functional requirements of the system, without worrying about how those requirements will be implemented. The process is inherently iterative; developers need to involve the users in discussions throughout the model development process and finally come to an agreement on the requirements specification.

A use-case-driven design, in which use cases control the formation of all other models, promotes traceability among the different models. If user requirements change during the development life cycle, those changes are first made in the use case model. Changes to the use cases then dictate what changes need to be made in the other models. The models are therefore traceable; for example, you can trace a set of requirements specified in a use case to elements in the other analysis, design, and test models. It is also possible to trace backward; for instance, you could see what effects, if any, a design change has on the use-case model.

Actor: An external entity that interacts with the system (similar to an external entity in data flow diagramming).

A use-case model consists of actors and use cases. An **actor** is an external entity that interacts with the system (similar to an external entity in data flow diagramming). It is someone or something that exchanges information with the system. A **use case** represents a sequence of related actions initiated by an actor; it is a specific way of using the system (Jacobson et al., 1992). Note that there is a difference between an *actor* and a *user*. A user is anyone who uses the system. An actor, on the other hand, represents a role that a user can play. The actor's name should indicate that role. An actor is a type or class of users; a user is a specific instance of an actor class playing the actor's role. Note that the same user can play multiple roles. For example, if John Patton plays two roles, one as an instructor and the other as an advisor, we represent him as an instance of an actor called Instructor and as an instance of another actor called Advisor.

Use case: A complete sequence of related actions initiated by an actor; it represents a specific way of using the system.

Because actors are outside the system, you do not need to describe them in detail. The advantage of identifying actors is that it helps you to identify the use cases they carry out. For identifying use cases, Jacobson et al. (1992) recommend that you ask the following questions:

- What are the main tasks performed by each actor?

- Will the actor read or update any information in the system?

- Will the actor have to inform the system about changes outside the system?

- Does the actor have to be informed about unexpected changes?

Developing Use-Case Diagrams

Use cases help you to capture the functional requirements of a system. During the requirements analysis stage, the analyst sits down with the intended users of the system and makes a thorough analysis of *what* functions they desire from the system. These functions are represented as use cases. For example, a university registration system has a use case for class registration and another for student billing. These use cases, then, represent the typical interactions the system has with its users.

Use case diagram: A diagram that depicts the use cases and actors for a system.

In UML, a use-case model is depicted diagrammatically as in Figure 12-2. This **use-case diagram** is for a university registration system, which is shown as a box. Outside the box are four actors—Student, Registration Clerk, Instructor, and Bursar's Office—that interact with the system. An actor is shown using a stickman symbol with its name below. Inside the box are four use cases—Class registration, Registration for special class, Prereq courses not completed, and Student billing—which are shown as ellipses with their names underneath. These use cases are performed by the actors outside the system. Note that an actor does not necessarily have to be a human user. It could be anything, such as another system or a hardware device with which the system interacts or exchanges information.

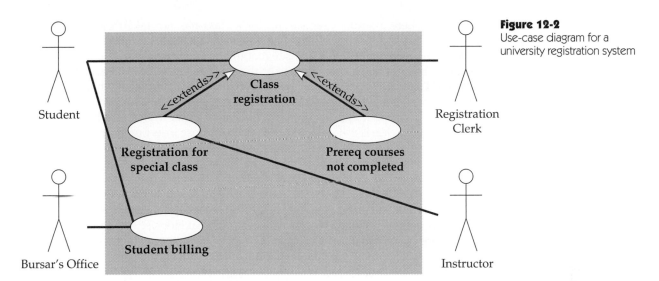

Figure 12-2
Use-case diagram for a
university registration system

A use case is always initiated by an actor. For example, Student billing is initiated by Bursar's Office. A use case can interact with actors other than the one that initiated it. The Student billing use case, although initiated by the Bursar's Office, interacts with the Student instances by mailing them tuition invoices. Another use case, Class registration, is carried out by two actors, Student and Registration Clerk. This use case performs a series of related actions aimed at registering a student for a class.

A use case represents a complete functionality. You should not represent an individual action that is part of an overall function as a use case. For example, although submitting a registration form and paying tuition are two actions performed by users (students) in the university registration system, we do not show them as use cases because they do not specify a complete course of events; each of these actions is executed only as part of an overall function or use case. You can think of Submit registration form as one of the actions of the Class registration use case, and Pay tuition as one of the actions of the Student billing use case. A use case, therefore, is a complete sequence of related actions performed by an actor and the system during a dialog (Jacobson et al., 1992).

Relationships Between Use Cases

A use case may participate in relationships with other use cases. We will describe two types of relationships: extends and uses. An *extends* relationship, shown as a line with a hollow triangle pointing toward the extended use case and labeled with the << extends>> symbol, extends a use case by adding new behavior or actions. In Figure 12-2, for example, the Registration for special class use case extends the Class registration use case by capturing the additional actions that need to be performed in registering a student for a special class. Registering for a special class requires prior permission of the instructor, in addition to the other steps carried out for a regular registration. You may think of Class registration as the *basic course*, which is always performed—independent of whether the extension is performed or not—and Registration for special class as an *alternative course*, which is performed only under special circumstances.

Another example of an extends relationship is that between the Prereq courses not completed and Class registration use cases. The former extends the latter in situations where a student registering for a class has not taken the prerequisite courses. In most cases, only Class registration would be performed, because students would have met the prerequisite requirements. However, in situations where a student has not taken one or more of the prerequisites, the Prereq courses not completed use case is performed, in addition to the Class registration use case. The extension use cases, Registration for special class and Prereq courses not completed, are inserted at appropriate points in the original use case. When the Class registration use case is initiated, it runs to each of those insertion points and checks if the conditions for extending the basic course are valid or not. If valid, the alternative course is performed; otherwise, the basic course continues till the next insertion point, or to its completion.

Figure 12-3 shows a use-case diagram for Hoosier Burger. Several actors and use cases can be identified. The actor that first comes to mind is Customer, which represents the class of all customers who order food at Hoosier Burger's; Order food is therefore represented as a use case. The other actor that is involved in this use case is Service Person. A specific scenario would represent a customer (an instance of Customer) placing an order with a service person (an instance of Service Person). At the end of each day, the manager of Hoosier Burger reorders supplies by calling suppliers. We represent this by a use case called Reorder supplies, involving the Manager and Supplier actors. A manager initiates the use case, which then sends requests to suppliers for various items.

Hoosier Burger also hires employees from time to time. We have therefore identified a use case called Hire employee, in which two actors, Manager and Applicant, are involved. When a person applies for a job at Hoosier Burger, the manager makes a hiring decision. Later, you will see how to capture all the details of interactions in this use case by drawing an interaction diagram.

Figure 12-3
Use-case diagram for a
Hoosier Burger's system

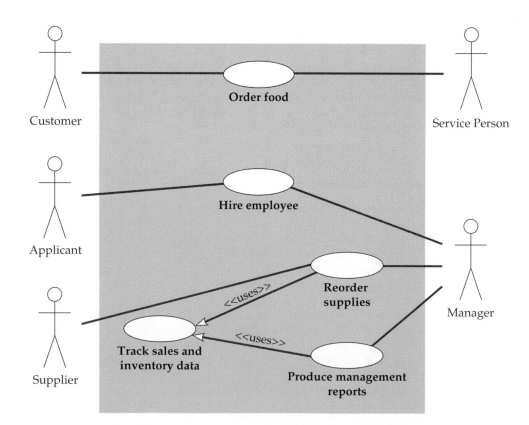

So far you have seen one kind of relationship, extends, between use cases. Another kind of relationship is uses, which arises when one use case *uses* another use case. A uses relationship is also shown diagrammatically as a line with a hollow triangle pointed toward the use case that is being used; the line is labeled with the << uses>> symbol. In Figure 12-3, for example, the uses relationship between the Reorder supplies and Track sales and inventory data use cases implies that the former uses the latter while executing. Simply put, when a manager reorders supplies, the sales and inventory data are tracked. The same data are also tracked when management reports are produced, so there is another uses relationship between the Produce management reports and Track sales and inventory data use cases.

The Track sales and inventory data is a generalized use case, representing the common behavior among the specialized use cases, Reorder supplies and Produce management reports. When Reorder supplies or Produce management reports is performed, the entire Track sales and inventory data is used. Note, however, that it is only used when one of the specialized use cases is performed. Such a use case, which is never performed by itself, is called an abstract use case (Eriksson and Penker,1998; Jacobson et al., 1992).

An Example of Use-Case Diagramming

Figure 12-4 shows a use-case model for different types of credit applications at a bank. The credit applications include those for home equity loans, home mortgage loans, auto loans, and credit cards. From the bank's perspective, therefore, the customers are home owners, home buyers, auto buyers, and credit card applicants. In the diagram, we have shown those different customer classes as actors—Home Owner, Home Buyer, Auto Buyer, and Credit Card Applicant—generalized into an actor called Customer, which represents the class of all customers. Each of the four relationships between a specialized actor and Customer, shown by a straight line with a hollow triangle pointing toward the more general actor, is a generalization relationship (see discussion later in this chapter on class generalization).

To process any type of loan or credit card application, the bank needs to check the applicant's credit history, based on a report from the credit bureau. We, therefore, have a generalized use case called Credit history check, which is used by three use cases relating to credit applications, that is, Home mortgage loan, Auto loan, and Credit card. The Home assessment use case models the common behavior among the Home mortgage loan and Home equity loan use cases; for both types of loans, the bank summons an assessor to assess the property value before making a decision.

If you are not quite sure about whether to employ *extends* or *uses* to model a given relationship between two use cases, consider the following criteria suggested by Jacobson. If the intent is to model an extension to, or a variation of, a complete use case that exists in its own right, employ extends. In Figure 12-2, for example, Class registration is a complete use case. It is totally independent of the extension use cases—Registration for special class and Prereq courses not completed—that were inserted to model alternatives to its basic behavior. If the intent on the other hand is to factor the common behavior among two or more use cases into a single generalized use case, then you should employ the uses relationship. The common behavior described by the generalized use case must be inserted into a specialized use case to complete it. For example, to carry out the Home equity loan or Home mortgage loan use case (see Figure 12-4), the Home assessment use case must be performed, too.

While a use-case diagram shows all the use cases in the system, it does not describe how those use cases are carried out by the actors. The contents of a use case are normally described in plain text. While describing a use case, you should focus on its external behavior, that is, how it interacts with the actors, rather than how the

Figure 12-4
Use-case diagram for a bank lending system

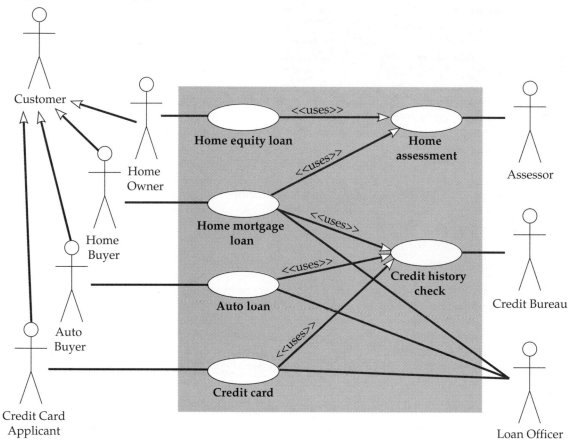

use case is performed inside the system (Eriksson and Penker, 1998). For example, we can describe the Class registration use case as follows:

1. A student completes a registration form by entering the following information:
   courseNumber
   sectionNumber
   term
   year

2. The student then takes the completed registration form to his or her advisor for signature. After checking the entries, the advisor signs the form.

3. The student then submits the form to a clerk at the registration office, who then enters the information into the computer.

4. The clerk provides the student with a computer printout of the classes in which he or she is successfully registered.

Note that the description includes the following three components:

1. The objective of the use case, which is to register the student for a class

2. The actor (Student) that initiates the use case

3. The exchange of information between the actors (Student and Registration Clerk) and the use case

In this section, we have shown how to develop a use-case model that captures the functional requirements of a system. A use-case diagram is an invaluable vehicle for communication between developers and end users. It also promotes modifiability, by allowing you to easily trace the effects of changes you make in the use-case model on other models (discussed in subsequent sections).

OBJECT MODELING: CLASS DIAGRAMS

In this section, we show how to develop object models by drawing class diagrams. We describe the main concepts and techniques involved in object modeling, including: objects and classes; encapsulation of attributes and operations; association, generalization, and aggregation relationships; cardinalities and other types of constraints; polymorphism; and inheritance. We show how you can develop class diagrams, using the UML notation, to provide a logical view of the system being modeled.

Representing Objects and Classes

In the object-oriented approach, we model the world in objects. Before applying the approach to a real-world problem, therefore, we need to understand what an object really is. An **object** is an entity that has a well-defined role in the application domain, and has state, behavior, and identity. An object is a concept, abstraction, or thing that makes sense in an application context (Rumbaugh et al., 1991). An object could be a tangible or visible entity (e.g., a person, place, or thing); it could be a concept or event (e.g., Department, Performance, Marriage, Registration, etc.); or it could be an artifact of the design process (e.g., User Interface, Controller, Scheduler, etc.).

Object: An entity that has a well-defined role in the application domain, and has state, behavior, and identity.

An object has a state and exhibits behavior, through operations that can examine or affect its state. The **state** of an object encompasses its properties (attributes and relationships) and the values those properties have, and its **behavior** represents how an object acts and reacts (Booch, 1994). An object's state is determined by its attribute values and links to other objects. An object's behavior depends on its state and the operation being performed. An operation is simply an action that one object performs upon another in order to get a response. You can think of an operation as a service provided by an object (supplier) to its clients. A client sends a message to a supplier, which delivers the desired service by executing the corresponding operation.

State: Encompasses an object's properties (attributes and relationships) and the values those properties have.

Behavior: Represents how an object acts and reacts.

Consider the example of a student, Mary Jones, represented as an object. The state of this object is characterized by its attributes, say, name, date of birth, year, address, and phone, and the values these attributes currently have. For example, name is "Mary Jones," year is "junior," and so on. Its behavior is expressed through operations such as calc-gpa, which is used to calculate a student's current grade point average. The Mary Jones object, therefore, packages both its state and its behavior together.

All objects have an identity; that is, no two objects are the same. For example, if there are two Student instances with the same name and date of birth, they are essentially two different objects. Even if those two instances have identical values for all the attributes, the objects maintain their separate identities. At the same time, an object maintains its own identity over its life. For example, if Mary Jones gets married and changes her name, address, and phone, she will still be represented by the same object.

The term "object" is sometimes used to refer to a group of objects, rather than an individual object. The ambiguity can be usually resolved from the context. In the strict sense of the term, however, "object" refers to an individual object, not to a class of objects. That is the interpretation we follow in this text. If you want to eliminate any possible confusion altogether, you can use "object instance" to refer to an individual object, and **object class** (or simply **class**) to refer to a set of objects that share a common structure and a common behavior (just as we used entity type and entity instance in Chapter 3). In our example, therefore, *Mary Jones* is an object instance, while Student is an object class.

You can depict the classes graphically in a class diagram as in Figure 12-5a. A **class diagram** shows the static structure of an object-oriented model: the object classes, their internal structure, and the relationships in which they participate. In UML, a class is represented by a rectangle with three compartments separated by horizontal lines. The class name appears in the top compartment, the list of attributes in the middle compartment, and the list of operations in the bottom compartment of a box. The figure shows two classes, Student and Course, along with their attributes and operations.

The Student class is a group of Student objects that share a common structure and a common behavior. All students have in common the properties of name, date of birth, year, address, and phone. They also exhibit common behavior by sharing the calc-age, calc-gpa, and register-for(course) operations. A class, therefore, provides a template or schema for its instances. Each object knows to which class it belongs; for example, the Mary Jones object knows that it belongs to the Student

Object class (class): A set of objects that share a common structure and a common behavior.

Class diagram: Shows the static structure of an object-oriented model: the object classes, their internal structure, and the relationships in which they participate.

Figure 12-5
UML class and object diagrams

(a) Class diagram showing two classes

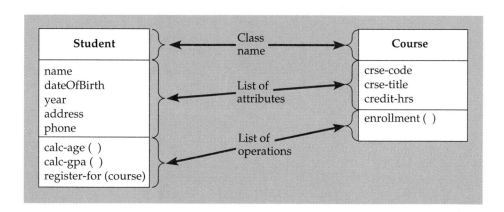

(b) Object diagram with two instances

class. Objects belonging to the same class may also participate in similar relationships with other objects; for example, all students register for courses and, therefore, the Student class can participate in a relationship called "registers-for" with another class called Course (see the later section on Association).

An **object diagram**, also known as instance diagram, is a graph of instances that are compatible with a given class diagram. In Figure 12-5b, we have shown an object diagram with two instances, one for each of the two classes that appear in Figure 12-5a. A static object diagram is an instance of a class diagram, providing a snapshot of the detailed state of a system at a point in time (*UML Notation Guide*, 1997).

> **Object diagram:** A graph of instances that are compatible with a given class diagram.

In an object diagram, an object is represented as a rectangle with two compartments. The names of the object and its class are underlined and shown in the top compartment using the following syntax. objectname : classname. The object's attributes and their values are shown in the second compartment. For example, we have an object called Mary Jones which belongs to the Student class. The values of the name, dateOfBirth, and year attributes are also shown. Attributes whose values are not of interest to you may be suppressed; for example, we have not shown the address and telephone attributes for Mary Jones. If none of the attributes are of interest, the entire second compartment may be suppressed. The name of the object may also be omitted, in which case the colon should be kept with the class name as we have done with the instance of Course. If the name of the object is shown, the class name, together with the colon, may be suppressed.

An **operation**, such as calc-gpa in Student (see Figure 12-5a), is a function or a service that is provided by all the instances of a class. It is only through such operations that other objects can access or manipulate the information stored in an object. The operations, therefore, provide an external interface to a class; the interface presents the outside view of the class without showing its internal structure or how its operations are implemented. This technique of hiding the internal implementation details of an object from its external view is known as **encapsulation** or information hiding (Booch, 1994; Rumbaug et al., 1991). So while we provide the abstraction of the behavior common to all instances of a class in its interface, we encapsulate within the class its structure and the secrets of the desired behavior.

> **Operation:** A function or a service that is provided by all the instances of a class.

> **Encapsulation:** The technique of hiding the internal implementation details of an object from its external view.

Types of Operations

Operations can be classified into three types, depending on the kind of service requested by clients: (1) constructor, (2) query, and (3) update (*UML Notation Guide*, 1997). A **constructor operation** creates a new instance of a class. For example, you can have an operation called create-student within Student that creates a new student and initializes its state. Such constructor operations are available to all classes and are therefore not explicitly shown in the class diagram.

> **Constructor operation:** An operation that creates a new instance of a class.

A **query operation** is an operation without any side effects; it accesses the state of an object but does not alter the state (Fowler, 1997; Rumbaugh et al., 1991). For example, the Student class can have an operation called get-year (not shown), which simply retrieves the year (freshman, sophomore, junior, or senior) of the Student object specified in the query. Note that there is no need to explicitly show a query such as get-year in the class diagram since it retrieves the value of an independent, base attribute. Consider, however, the calc-age operation within Student. This is also a query operation because it does not have any side effects. Note that the only argument for this query is the target Student object. Such a query can be represented as a derived attribute (Rumbaugh et al., 1991); for example, we can represent "age" as a derived attribute of Student. Because the target object is always an implicit argument of an operation, there is no need to show it explicitly in the operation declaration.

> **Query operation:** An operation that accesses the state of an object but does not alter the state.

Update operation: An operation that alters the state of an object.

An **update operation** has side effects; it alters the state of an object. For example, consider an operation of Student called promote-student (not shown). The operation promotes a student to a new year, say, from junior to senior, thereby changing the Student object's state (value of the year attribute). Another example of an update operation is register-for(course), which, when invoked, has the effect of establishing a connection from a Student object to a specific Course object. Note that, in addition to having the target Student object as an implicit argument, the operation has an explicit argument called "course," which specifies the course for which the student wants to register. Explicit arguments are shown within parentheses.

Representing Associations

Association: A relationship between object classes.

Parallel to the definition of a relationship for the E-R model (see Chapter 10), an **association** is a relationship among object classes. As in the E-R model, the degree of an association relationship may be one (unary), two (binary), three (ternary), or higher (*n*-ary). In Figure 12-6, we illustrate how the object-oriented model can be used to represent association relationships of different degrees. An association is

Figure 12-6
Examples of association relationships of different degrees

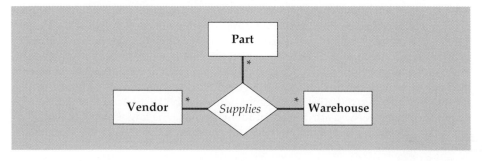

shown as a solid line between the participating classes. The end of an association where it connects to a class is called an **association role** (*UML Notation Guide*, 1997). Each association has two or more roles. A role may be explicitly named with a label near the end of an association (see the "manager" role in Figure 12-6a). The role name indicates the role played by the class attached to the end near which the name appears. Use of role names is optional. You can specify role names in place of or, in addition to, an association name.

Association role: The end of an association where it connects to a class.

Figure 12-6a shows two unary relationships, *Is-married-to* and *Manages*. At one end of the *Manages* relationship, we have named the role as Manager, implying that an employee can play the role of a manager. We have not named the other roles, but we have named the associations. When the role name does not appear, you may think of the role name as being that of the class attached to that end (Fowler, 1997). For example, you may call the role for the right end of the *Is-assigned* relationship in Figure 12-6b Parking Place.

Each role has a **multiplicity**, which indicates how many objects participate in a given association relationship. In a class diagram, a multiplicity specification is shown as a text string representing an interval (or intervals) of integers in the following format: lower-bound..upper-bound. The interval is considered to be closed, which means that the range includes both the lower and upper bounds. For example, a multiplicity of 2..5 denotes that a minimum of 2 and a maximum of 5 objects can participate in a given relationship. Multiplicities, therefore, are nothing but cardinality constraints, which you saw in Chapter 3. In addition to integer values, the upper bound of a multiplicity can be a star character (*), which denotes an infinite upper bound. If a single integer value is specified, it means that the range includes only that value.

Multiplicity: Indicates how many objects participate in a given relationship.

The most common multiplicities in practice are 0..1, *, and 1. The 0..1 multiplicity indicates a minimum of 0 and a maximum of 1 (optional one), while * (or equivalently, 0..*) represents the range from 0 to infinity (optional many). A single 1 stands for 1..1, implying that exactly one object participates in the relationship (mandatory one).

The multiplicities for both roles in the *Is-married-to* relationship are 0..1, indicating that a person may be single or married to one person. The multiplicity for the manager role in the *Manages* relationship is 0..1 and that for the other role is *, implying that an employee may be managed by only one manager, but a manager may manage many employees.

Figure 12-6b shows three binary relationships: *Is-assigned* (one-to-one), *Contains* (one-to-many), and *Registers-for* (many-to-many). A binary association is inherently bidirectional, though in a class diagram, the association name can be read in only one direction (Rumbaugh et al., 1991). For example, the *Contains* association is read from Product Line to Product. (Note: As in this example, you may show the direction explicitly by using a solid triangle next to the association name.) Implicit, however, is an inverse traversal of *Contains*, say, *Belongs-to*, which denotes that a product belongs to a particular product line. Both directions of traversal refer to the same underlying association; the name simply establishes a direction.

The diagram for the *Is-assigned* relationship shows that an employee is assigned a parking place or not assigned at all (optional one). Reading in the other direction, we say that a parking place has either been allocated for a single employee or not allocated at all (optional one again). Similarly, we say that a product line contains many products, but at least one, whereas a given product belongs to exactly one product line (mandatory one). The diagram for the third binary association states that a student registers for multiple courses, but it is possible that he or she does not register at all, and a course, in general, has multiple students enrolled in it (optional many in both directions).

In Figure 12-6c, we show a ternary relationship called *Supplies* among Vendor, Part, and Warehouse. As in an E-R diagram, we represent a ternary relationship using a diamond symbol and place the name of the relationship there. The relationship is many-to-many-to-many; it cannot be replaced by three binary relationships without loss of information.

The class diagram in Figure 12-7a shows binary associations between Student and Faculty, between Course and Course Offering, between Student and Course Offering, and between Faculty and Course Offering. The diagram shows that a student may have an advisor, while a faculty member may advise up to a maximum of 10 students. Also, while a course may have multiple offerings, a given course offering is scheduled for exactly one course. UML allows you to numerically specify any multiplicity. For example, the diagram shows that a course may be taught by one or two instructors (1,2). You can specify a single number (e.g., 2 for the members of a bridge team), a range (e.g., 11..13 for the players of a soccer team who participated in a particular game), or a discrete set of numbers and ranges (e.g., 3, 5, 7 for the number of committee members, and 20..32, 35..40 for the workload in hours per week of the employees of a company).

Figure 12-7a also shows that a faculty member plays the role of an instructor, as well as that of an advisor. While the advisor role identifies the Faculty object associated with a Student object, the advisees role identifies the set of Student objects associated with a Faculty object. We could have named the association, say, *Advises*, but, in this case, the role names are sufficiently meaningful to convey the semantics of the relationship.

Figure 12-7b shows another class diagram for a customer order. The corresponding object diagram is presented in Figure 12-8; it shows some of the instances of the classes and the links among them. (Note: Just as an instance corresponds to a

Figure 12-7
Examples of binary association relationships

(a) University example

(b) Customer order example

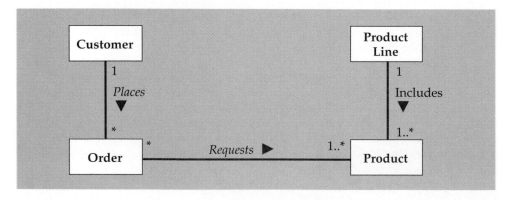

Figure 12-8
Object diagram for customer order example

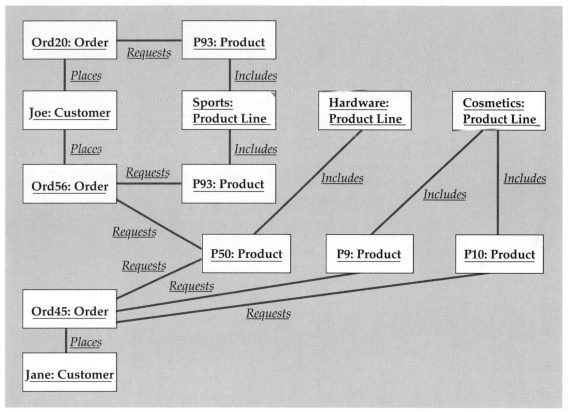

class, a link corresponds to a relationship.) In this example, we see the orders placed by two customers, Joe and Jane. Joe has placed two orders, Ord 20 and Ord 56. In Ord 20, Joe has ordered product P93 from the sports product line. In Ord 56, he has ordered the same sports product again, as well as product P50 from the hardware product line. Notice that Jane has ordered the same hardware product as Joe, in addition to two other products (P9 and P10) from the cosmetics product line.

Representing Association Classes

When an association itself has attributes or operations of its own, or when it participates in relationships with other classes, it is useful to model the association as an **association class** (just as we used an "associative entity" in Chapter 10). For example, in Figure 12-9a, the attributes term and grade really belong to the many-to-many association between Student and Course. The grade of a student for a course cannot be determined unless both the student and the course are known. Similarly, to find the term(s) in which the student took the course, both student and course must be known. The checkEligibility operation, which determines if a student is eligible to register for a given course, also belongs to the association, rather than to any of the two participating classes. We have also captured the fact that, for some course registrations, a computer account is issued to a student. For these reasons, we model Registration as an association class, having its own set of features and an association with another class (Computer Account). Similarly, for the unary *Tutors* association, beginDate and numberOfHrs (number of hours tutored) really belong to the association, and, therefore, appear in a separate association class.

Association class: An association which has attributes or operations of its own, or which participates in relationships with other classes.

Figure 12-9
Association class and link object

(a) Class diagram showing association classes

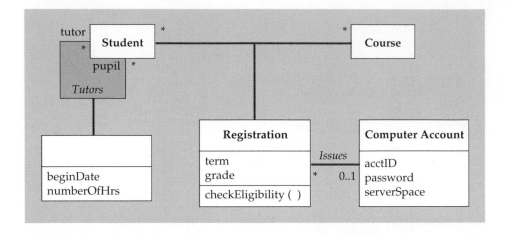

(b) Object diagram showing link objects

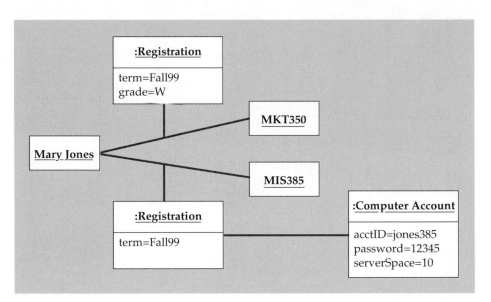

You have the option of showing the name of an association class on the association path, or the class symbol, or both. When an association has only attributes, but does not have any operations or does not participate in other associations, the recommended option is to show the name on the association path, but to omit it from the association class symbol, to emphasize its "association nature" (*UML Notation Guide*, 1997). That is how we have shown the *Tutors* association. On the other hand, we have displayed the name of the Registration association—which has two attributes and one operation of its own, as well as an association called *Issues* with Computer Account—within the class rectangle to emphasize its "class nature."

Figure 12-9b shows a part of the object diagram representing a student, Mary Jones, and the courses she has registered for in the Fall 1999 term: MKT350 and MIS385. Corresponding to an association class in a class diagram, link objects are present in an object diagram. In this example, there are two link objects (shown as :Registration) for the Registration association class, capturing the two course registrations. The diagram also shows that for the MIS385 course, Mary Jones has been issued a computer account with an ID, a password, and a designated amount of space on the server. She still has not received a grade for this course, but, for the MKT350 course, she received a grade of W because she withdrew from the course.

Figure 12-10 shows a ternary relationship among the Student, Software, and Course classes. It captures the fact that students use various software tools for different courses. For example, we could store the information that Mary Jones used Microsoft Access and Oracle for the Database Management course, Rational Rose and Visual C++ for the Object-Oriented Modeling course, and Level5 Object for the Expert Systems Course. Now suppose we want to estimate the number of hours per week Mary will spend using Oracle for the Database Management course. This process really belongs to the ternary association, and not to any of the individual classes. Hence we have created an association class called Log, within which we have declared an operation called estimateUsage. In addition to this operation, we have specified three attributes that belong to the association: beginDate, expiryDate, and hoursLogged.

Representing Derived Attributes, Derived Associations, and Derived Roles

A derived attribute, association, or role is one that can be computed or derived from other attributes, associations, and roles, respectively (the concept of a derived attribute was introduced in Chapter 3). A derived element (attribute, association, or role) is shown by placing a slash (/) before the name of the element. For instance, in Figure 12-11, age is a derived attribute of Student, because it can be calculated from the date of birth and the current date (the calculation is shown on this diagram within braces below the Student object class). Also, the *Takes* relationship between Student and Course is derived, because it can be inferred from the *Registers-for* and *Scheduled-for* relationships. By the same token, participants is a derived role because it can be derived from other roles.

Representing Generalization

In the object-oriented approach, you can abstract the common features (attributes and operations) among multiple classes, as well as the relationships they participate in, into a more general class. This is known as *generalization*. The classes that

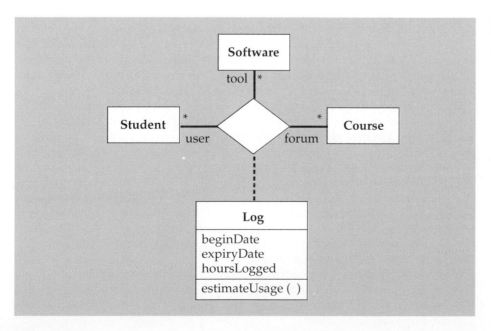

Figure 12-10
Ternary relationship with association class

Figure 12-11
Derived attribute, association, and role

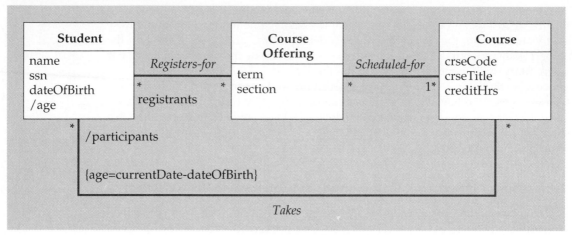

are generalized are called subclasses, and the class they are generalized into is called a superclass.

Consider the example shown in Figure 12-12a. There are three types of employees: hourly employees, salaried employees, and consultants. The features that are shared by all employees: empName, empNumber, address, dateHired, and printLabel, are stored in the Employee superclass, while the features that are peculiar to a particular employee type are stored in the corresponding subclass (e.g., hourlyRate and computeWages of Hourly Employee). A generalization path is shown as a solid line from the subclass to the superclass, with a hollow triangle at the end of, and pointing toward, the superclass. You can show a group of generalization paths for a given superclass as a tree with multiple branches connecting the individual subclasses, and a shared segment with a hollow triangle pointing toward the superclass. In Figure 12-12b, for instance, we have combined the generalization paths from Outpatient to Patient, and from Resident Patient to Patient, into a shared segment with a triangle pointing toward Patient.

You can indicate the basis of a generalization by specifying a discriminator next to the path. A discriminator (corresponding to the subtype discriminator defined in Chapter 4) shows which property of an object class is being abstracted by a particular generalization relationship (Rumbaugh et al., 1991). You can discriminate on only one property at a time. For example, in Figure 12-12a, we discriminate the Employee class on the basis of employment type (hourly, salaried, consultant). To discriminate a group of generalization relationships, as in Figure 12-12b, we need to specify the discriminator only once. Although we discriminate the Patient class into two subclasses, Outpatient and Resident Patient, based on residency, we show the discriminator label only once next to the shared line.

An instance of a subclass is also an instance of its superclass. For example, in Figure 12-12b, an Outpatient instance is also a Patient instance. For that reason, a generalization is also referred to as an *Is-a* relationship. Also, a subclass inherits all the features from its superclass. For example, in Figure 12-12a, in addition to its own special features—hourlyRate and computeWages—the Hourly Employee subclass inherits empName, empNumber, address, dateHired, and printLabel from Employee. An instance of Hourly Employee will store values for the attributes of Employee and Hourly Employee, and, when requested, will apply the printLabel and computeWages operations.

Figure 12-12
Examples of generalization, inheritance, and constraints

(a) Employee superclass with three subclasses

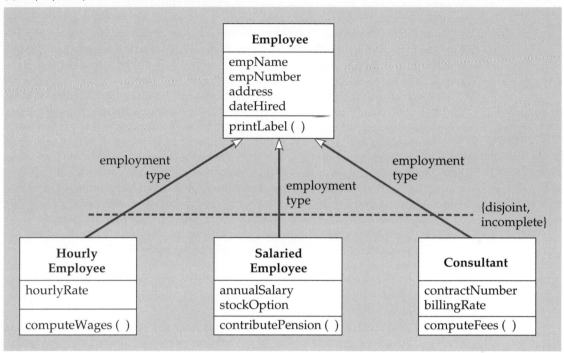

(b) Abstract Patient class with two concrete subclasses

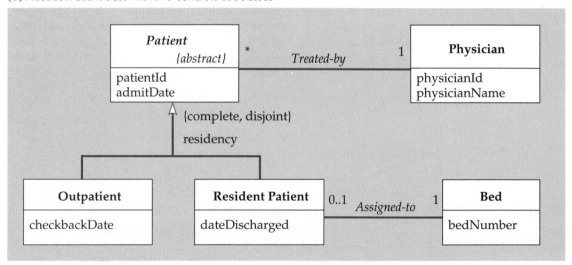

Generalization and inheritance are transitive across any number of levels of a superclass/subclass hierarchy. For instance, we could have a subclass of Consultant called Computer Consultant, which would inherit the features of Employee and Consultant. An instance of Computer Consultant would be an instance of Consultant and, therefore, an instance of Employee, too. Employee is an ancestor of Computer Consultant, while Computer Consultant is a descendant of Employee; these terms are used to refer to generalization of classes across multiple levels (Rumbaugh et al., 1991).

Inheritance is one of the major advantages of using the object-oriented model. It allows code reuse: there is no need for a programmer to write code that has already been written for a superclass. The programmer only writes code that is unique to the new, refined subclass of an existing class. In actual practice, object-oriented programmers typically have access to large collections of class libraries in their respective domains. They identify those classes that may be reused and refined to meet the demands of new applications. Proponents of the object-oriented model claim that code reuse results in productivity gains of several orders of magnitude.

Notice that in Figure 12-12b the *Patient* class is in italics, implying that it is an abstract class. An **abstract class** is a class that has no direct instances, but whose descendants may have direct instances (Booch, 1994; Rumbaugh, et al., 1991). (Note: You can additionally write the word *abstract* within braces just below the class name. This is especially useful when you generate a class diagram by hand.) A class that can have direct instances (e.g., Outpatient or Resident Patient) is called a **concrete class**. In this example, therefore, Outpatient and Resident Patient can have direct instances, but *Patient* cannot have any direct instances of its own.

The *Patient* abstract class participates in a relationship called *Treated-by* with Physician, implying that all patients, outpatients and resident patients alike, are treated by physicians. In addition to this inherited relationship, the Resident Patient class has its own special relationship called *Assigned-to* with Bed, implying that only resident patients may be assigned to beds. So, in addition to refining the attributes and operations of a class, a subclass can also specialize the relationships in which it participates.

In Figure 12-12, the words "complete" and "disjoint" have been placed within braces, next to the generalization. They indicate semantic constraints among the subclasses (*complete* corresponds to total specialization in the EER notation, whereas *incomplete* corresponds to partial specialization). In UML, a comma-separated list of keywords is placed either near the shared triangle as in Figure 12-12b, or near a dashed line that crosses all of the generalization lines involved as in Figure 12-12a (*UML Notation Guide*, 1997). Any of the following UML keywords may be used: overlapping, disjoint, complete, and incomplete. According to the *UML Notation Guide* (1997), the definition of these terms are:

- *Overlapping*: A descendant may be descended from more than one of the subclasses (same as the overlapping rule in EER diagramming).

- *Disjoint*: A descendant may not be descended from more than one of the subclasses (same as the disjoint rule in EER diagramming).

- *Complete*: All subclasses have been specified (whether or not shown). No additional subclasses are expected (same as the total specialization rule in EER diagramming).

- *Incomplete*: Some subclasses have been specified, but the list is known to be incomplete. There are additional subclasses that are not yet in the model (same as the partial specialization rule in EER diagramming).

Both the generalizations in Figures 12-12a and 12-12b are disjoint. An employee can be an hourly employee, a salaried employee, or a consultant, but cannot, say, be both a salaried employee and a consultant. Similarly, a patient can be an outpatient or a resident patient, but not both. The generalization in Figure 12-12a is incomplete, specifying that an employee may not belong to any of the three types. In such a case, an employee will be stored as an instance of Employee, a concrete class. In contrast, the generalization in Figure 12-12b is complete, implying that a patient has

Abstract class: A class that has no direct instances, but whose descendants may have direct instances.

Concrete class: A class that can have direct instances.

to be either an outpatient or a resident patient, and nothing else. For that reason, *Patient* has been specified as an abstract class.

In Figure 12-13, we show an example of an overlapping constraint. The diagram shows that research assistants and teaching assistants are graduate students. The overlapping constraint indicates that it is possible for a graduate student to serve as both a research assistant and a teaching assistant. For example, Sean Bailey, a graduate student, has a research assistantship of 12 hours per week and a teaching assistantship of 8 hours per week. Also notice that Graduate Student has been specified as a concrete class so that graduate students without an assistantship can be represented. The ellipsis marks (. . .) under the generalization line based on the "level" discriminator does not represent an incomplete constraint. It simply indicates that there are other subclasses in the model that have not been shown in the diagram. For example, although Undergrad Student is in the model, we have opted not to show it in the diagram since the focus is on assistantships. You may also use ellipsis marks when there are space limitations.

In Figure 12-14, we represent both graduate and undergraduate students in a model developed for student billing. The calc-tuition operation computes the tuition a student has to pay; this sum depends on the tuition per credit hour (tuitionPerCred), the courses taken, and the number of credit hours (creditHrs) for each of those courses. The tuition per credit hour, in turn, depends on whether the student is a graduate or an undergraduate student. In this example, that amount is $300 for all graduate students and $250 for all undergraduate students. To denote that, we have underlined the tuitionPerCred attribute in each of the two subclasses, along with its value. Such an attribute is called a **class-scope attribute**, which specifies a value common to an entire class, rather than a specific value for an instance (Rumbaugh et al., 1991).

You can specify an initial default value of an attribute using an equals sign (=) after the attribute name. This is the initial attribute value of a newly created object instance. For example, in Figure 12-14, the creditHrs attribute has an initial value of 3, implying that when a new instance of Course is created, the value of creditHrs is set to 3 by default. You can write an explicit constructor operation to modify the

Class-scope attribute: An attribute of a class which specifies a value common to an entire class, rather than a specific value for an instance.

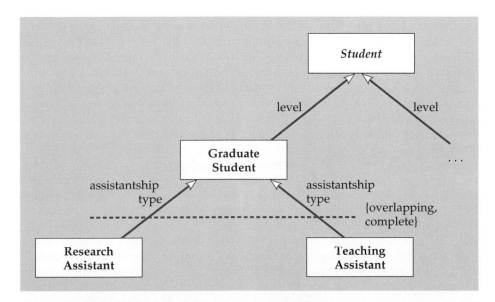

Figure 12-13
Example of overlapping constraint

Figure 12-14
Polymorphism, abstract operation, class-scope attribute, and ordering

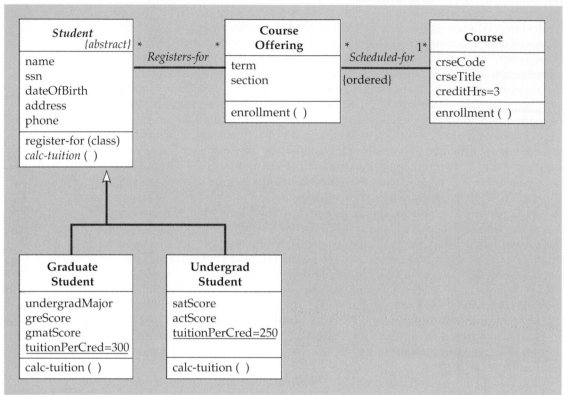

initial default value. The value may also be modified later through other operations. The difference between an initial value specification and a class-scope attribute is that while the former allows the possibility of different attribute values for the instances of a class, the latter forces all the instances to share a common value.

In addition to specifying the multiplicity of an association role, you can also specify other properties, for example, if the objects playing the role are ordered or not. In the figure, we placed the keyword constraint "{ordered}" next to the Course Offering end of the *Scheduled-for* relationship to denote the fact that the offerings for a given course are ordered into a list—say, according to term and section. It is obvious that it makes sense to specify an ordering only when the multiplicity of the role is greater than one. The default constraint on a role is "{unordered};" i.e., if you do not specify the keyword "{ordered}" next to the role, it is assumed that the related elements form an unordered set. For example, the course offerings are not related to a student who registers for those offerings in any specific order.

The Graduate Student subclass specializes the abstract Student class by adding three attributes—undergradMajor, greScore, and gmatScore—and by refining the inherited *calc-tuition* operation. Notice that the operation is shown in italics within the Student class, indicating that it is an abstract operation. An **abstract operation** defines the form or protocol of the operation, but not its implementation (Rumbaug et al., 1991). In this example, the Student class defines the protocol of the *calc-tuition* operation, without providing the corresponding **method** (the actual implementation of the operation). The protocol includes the number and types of the arguments, the result type, and the intended semantics of the operation. The two concrete subclasses, Graduate Student and Undergrad Student, supply their own

Abstract operation: Defines the form or protocol of the operation, but not its implementation.

Method: The implementation of an operation.

implementations of the calc-tuition operation. Note that because these classes are concrete, they cannot store abstract operations.

It is important to note that although the Graduate Student and Undergraduate Student classes share the same calc-tuition operation, they might implement the operation in quite different ways. For example, the method that implements the operation for a graduate student might add a special graduate fee for each course the student takes. The fact that the same operation may apply to two or more classes in different ways is known as **polymorphism,** a key concept in object-oriented systems (Booch, 1994; Rumbaugh et al., 1991). The enrollment operation in Figure 12-14 illustrates another example of polymorphism. While the enrollment operation within Course Offering computes the enrollment for a particular course offering or section, an operation with the same name within Course computes the combined enrollment for all sections of a given course.

> **Polymorphism:** The same operation may apply to two or more classes in different ways.

Interpreting Inheritance and Overriding

We have seen how a subclass can augment the features inherited from its ancestors. In such cases, the subclass is said to use *inheritance for extension*. On the other hand, if a subclass constrains some of the ancestor attributes or operations, it is said to use *inheritance for restriction* (Booch, 1994; Rumbaug et al., 1991). For example, a subclass called Tax-Exempt Company may suppress or block the inheritance of an operation called compute-tax from its superclass, Company.

The implementation of an operation can also be overridden. **Overriding** is the process of replacing a method inherited from a superclass by a more specific implementation of that method in a subclass. The reasons for overriding include extension, restriction, and optimization (Rumbaugh et al., 1991). The name of the new operation remains the same as the inherited one, but it has to be explicitly shown within the subclass to indicate that the operation is overridden.

> **Overriding:** The process of replacing a method inherited from a superclass by a more specific implementation of that method in a subclass.

In *overriding for extension*, an operation inherited by a subclass from its superclass is extended by adding some behavior (code). For example, a subclass of Company called Foreign Company inherits an operation called compute-tax, but extends the inherited behavior by adding a foreign surcharge to compute the total tax amount.

In *overriding for restriction*, the protocol of the new operation in the subclass is restricted. For example, an operation called place-student(job) in Student may be restricted in the International Student subclass by tightening the job argument (see Figure 12-15). While students in general may be placed in all types of jobs during the summer, international students may be limited to only on-campus jobs because of visa restrictions. The new operation overrides the inherited operation by tightening the job argument, restricting its values to only a small subset of all possible jobs. This example also illustrates the use of multiple discriminators. While the basis for one set of generalizations is a student's "level" (graduate or undergraduate), that for the other set is his or her "residency" status (United States or international).

In *overriding for optimization*, the new operation is implemented with improved code by exploiting the restrictions imposed by a subclass. Consider, for example, a subclass of Student called Dean's List Student, which represents all those students who are on the Dean's list. To qualify for the Dean's list, a student must have a grade point average (gpa) greater than or equal to 3.50. Suppose Student has an operation called mailScholApps, which mails applications for merit- and means-tested scholarships to students who have a gpa greater than or equal to 3.00, and whose family's total gross income is less than $20,000. The method for the operation in Student will have to check both conditions, whereas the method for the same operation in the Dean's List Student subclass can improve upon the speed of

Figure 12-15
Overriding inheritance

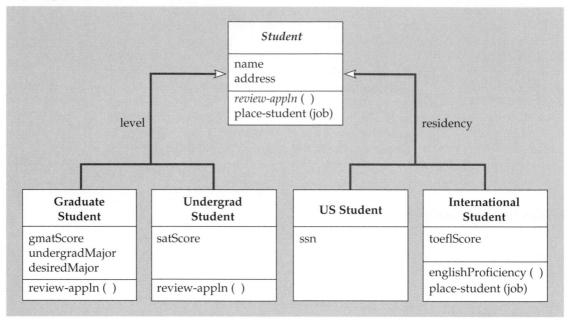

execution by removing the first condition from its code. Consider another operation called findMinGpa, which finds the minimum gpa among the students. Suppose the Dean's List Student class is sorted in ascending order of the gpa, but the Student class is not. The method for findMinGpa in Student must perform a sequential search through all the students. In contrast, the same operation in Dean's List Student can be implemented with a method that simply retrieves the gpa of the first student in the list, thereby obviating the need for a time-consuming search.

Representing Multiple Inheritance

So far you have been exposed to single inheritance, where a class inherits from only one superclass. But sometimes, as we saw in the example with research and teaching assistants, an object may be an instance of more than one class. This is known as **multiple classification** (Fowler, 1997; *UML Notation Guide*, 1997). For instance, Sean Bailey, who has both types of assistantships, has two classifications: one as an instance of Research Assistant and the other as an instance of Teaching Assistant. Multiple classification, however, is discouraged by experts. It is not supported by the ordinary UML semantics and many object-oriented languages.

Multiple classification: An object is an instance of more than one class.

To get around the problem, we can use multiple inheritance, which allows a class to inherit features from more than one superclass. For example, in Figure 12-16, we have created Research & Teaching Assistant, which is a subclass of both Research Assistant and Teaching Assistant. All students who have both research and teaching assistantships may be stored under the new class. We may now represent Sean Bailey as an object belonging to only the Research & Teaching Assistant class, which inherits features from both its parents, such as researchHrs and assignProject(proj) from Research Assistant and teachingHrs and assignCourse(crse) from Teaching Assistant.

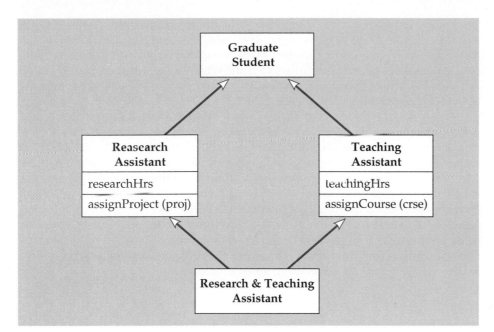

Figure 12-16
Multiple inheritance

Representing Aggregation

An **aggregation** expresses a *Part-of* relationship between a component object and an aggregate object. It is a stronger form of association relationship (with the added "part-of" semantics) and is represented with a hollow diamond at the aggregate end. For example, Figure 12-17 shows a personal computer as an aggregate of CPU (up to four for multiprocessors), hard disks, monitor, keyboard, mouse, and other objects. Note that aggregation involves a set of distinct object instances, one of which contains or is composed of the others. For example, a Personal Computer object is related to (consists of) CPU objects, one of its parts. In contrast, generalization relates object classes: an object (e.g., Mary Jones) is simultaneously an instance of its class (e.g., Graduate Student) and its superclass (e.g., Student). Only one object (e.g., Mary Jones) is involved in a generalization relationship. This is why multiplicities are indicated at the ends of aggregation lines, whereas there are no multiplicities for generalization relationships.

Aggregation: A *part-of* relationship between a component object and an aggregate object.

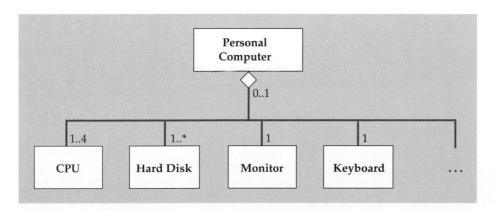

Figure 12-17
Example of aggregation

Figure 12-18a shows an aggregation structure of a university. The object diagram in Figure 12-18b shows how Riverside University, a University object instance, is related to its component objects, which represent administrative units (e.g., Admissions, Human Resources, etc.) and schools (e.g., Arts and Science, Business, etc.). A school object (e.g., Business), in turn, comprises several department objects (e.g., Accounting, Finance, etc.).

Notice that the diamond at one end of the relationship between Building and Room is not hollow, but solid. A solid diamond represents a stronger form of aggregation, known as composition (Fowler, 1997; *UML Notation Guide*, 1997). In **composition,** a part object belongs to only one *whole* object; for example, a room is part of only one building. Therefore, the multiplicity on the aggregate end may not exceed one. Parts may be created after the creation of the whole object; for example, rooms may be added to an existing building. However, once a part of a composition is created, it lives and dies with the whole; deletion of the aggregate object cascades to its components. If a building is demolished, for example, so are all its rooms. However, it is possible to delete a part before its aggregate dies, just as it is possible to demolish a room without bringing down a building.

Composition: A part object that belongs to only one whole object, and that lives and dies with the whole.

Figure 12-18
Aggregation and composition

(a) Class diagram

(b) Object diagram

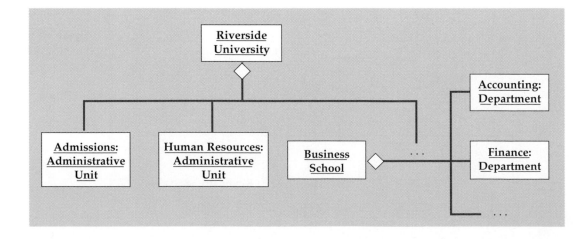

BUSINESS RULES

In the examples provided in this chapter, we captured many business rules as constraints—implicitly, as well as explicitly—on classes, instances, attributes, operations, relationships, etc. For example, you saw how to specify cardinality constraints and ordering constraints on association roles. You also saw how to represent semantic constraints (e.g., overlapping, disjoint, etc.) among subclasses. Many of the constraints that were discussed so far in this chapter were imposed by including a set of UML keywords within braces—for example, {disjoint, complete} and {ordered}—and placing them close to the elements the constraints apply to. For example, in Figure 12-14, we expressed a business rule that offerings for a given course are ordered. But if you cannot represent a business rule using such a predefined UML constraint, you can define the rule in plain English, or in some other language such as formal logic.

When you have to specify a business rule involving two graphical symbols (such as those representing two classes or two associations), you can show the constraint as a dashed arrow from one element to the other, labeled by the constraint name in braces (*UML Notation Guide,* 1997). In Figure 12-19, for example, we have stated the business rule that the chair of a department must be a member of the department by specifying the *Chair-of* association as a subset of the *Member-of* association.

When you have to specify a business rule involving three or more graphical symbols, you can show the constraint as a note and attach the note to each of the symbols by a dashed line (*UML Notation Guide,* 1997). In Figure 12-19, we have captured the business rule that "each faculty member assigned to teach a section of a course must be qualified to teach that course" within a note symbol. Because this constraint involves all the three association relationships, we have attached the note to each of the three association paths.

DYNAMIC MODELING: STATE DIAGRAMS

You have seen how to model the static structure of a system using class diagrams. In this section, we show you how to model the dynamic aspects of a system from the

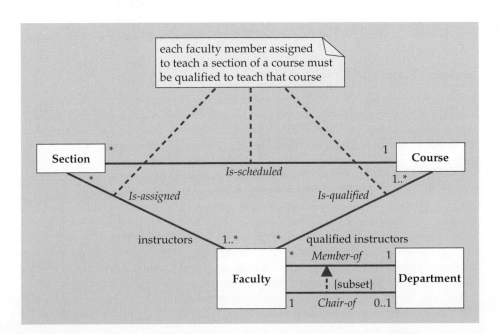

Figure 12-19
Representing business rules

perspective of state transitions. In UML, state transitions are shown using state diagrams. A state diagram depicts the various state transitions or changes an object can experience during its lifetime, along with the events that cause those transitions.

From the perspective of dynamic modeling, a *state* is a condition during the life of an object during which it satisfies some condition(s), performs some action(s), or waits for some event(s) (*UML Notation Guide*, 1997). The state changes when the object receives some event; the object is said to undergo a **state transition**. The state of an object depends on its attribute values and links to other objects.

An **event** is something that takes place at a certain point in time. It is a noteworthy occurrence that triggers a state transition. Some examples of events are: a customer places an order; a student registers for a class; a person applies for a loan; and a company hires a new employee. For the purpose of modeling, an event is considered to be instantaneous, though, in reality, it might take some time. A state, on the other hand, spans a period of time. An object remains in a particular state for some time before transitioning to another state. For example, an Employee object might be in the Part-time state (as specified in its employment-status attribute) for a few months, before transitioning to a Full-time state, based on a recommendation from the manager (an event).

Not all attributes are important in determining the state of an object. For example, the address and phone attributes of a Student object may not be important. When a student changes apartments, the object does not undergo any state transition. (If, however, for the purposes of your model, you want to classify a student as being in one of two states, On-campus or Off-campus, then address could be an important attribute.) In determining the state of an object, only those attributes that affect its gross behavior are considered to be important.

The other thing to note is that the state of an object does not change whenever an attribute changes its value. For example, from a bank's perspective, the fluctuations in a customer's monthly debt payments will not normally trigger state transitions. However, if the debt-to-income ratio exceeds a certain threshold (say, 45 percent) after some event—say, the purchase of a new yacht—then the Customer object may transition from a Low-risk state to a High-risk state. Within a given state, an object's gross behavior will remain qualitatively the same in response to an event, while the behavior could be quite different in another state (Rumbaugh et al., 1991). For example, the bank's lending procedures for all low-risk customers are more or less the same, but the procedures could be very different for high-risk customers.

Modeling States and State Transitions

In UML, a state is shown as a rectangle with rounded corners. In Figure 12-20, for example, we have shown different states of a Student object, such as Inquiry, Applied, Approved, Rejected, etc. This **state diagram** shows how the object transitions from an initial state (shown as a small, solid, filled circle) to other states, when certain events occur or when certain conditions are satisfied. When a new Student object is created, it is in its initial state. The event that created the object, inquires, transitions it from the initial state to the Inquiry state. When a student in the Inquiry state submits an application for admission, the object transitions to the Applied state. The transition is shown as a solid arrow from Inquiry (the source state) to Applied (the target state), labeled with the name of the event, submits application.

A transition may be labeled with a string consisting of the event name, parameters of the event, guard condition, and action expression. A transition, however, does not have to show all the elements; it only shows those that are relevant to the transition. For example, we label the transition from Inquiry to Applied with simply the event name. But, for the transition from Applied to Approved, we show the

---

State transition: Changes in the attributes of an object or in the links an object has with other objects.

Event: Something that takes place at a certain point in time; it is a noteworthy occurrence that triggers a state transition.

State diagram: A model of the states of an object and the events that cause the object to change from one state to another.

Figure 12-20
State diagram for the Student object

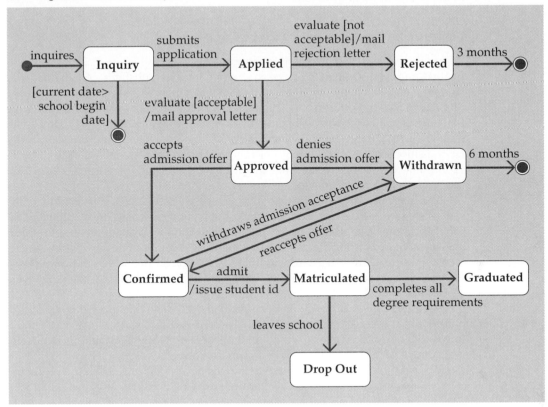

event name (evaluate), the guard condition (acceptable), and the action taken by the transition (mail approval letter). It simply means that an applicant is approved for admission if the admissions office evaluates the application and finds it acceptable. If acceptable, a letter of approval is mailed to the student. The guard condition is shown within square brackets, and the action is specified after the "/" symbol.

If the evaluate event results in a not-acceptable decision (another guard condition), a rejection letter is mailed (an action) and the Student object undergoes a state transition from the Applied to the Rejection state. It remains in that state for three months, before reaching the final state. In the diagram, we have shown an elapsed-time event, three months, indicating the amount of time the object waits in the current state before transitioning. The final state is shown as a bull's eye: a small, solid, filled circle surrounded by another circle. After transitioning to the final state, the Student object ceases to exist.

Notice that the Student object may transition to the final state from two other states: Inquiry and Withdrawn. For the transition from Inquiry, we have not specified any event name or action, but we have shown a guard condition, current date > school begin date. This condition implies that the Student object ceases to exist beyond the first day of school unless, of course, the object has moved in the meantime from the Inquiry state to some other state.

The state diagram shown in Figure 12-20 captures all the possible states of a Student object, the state transitions, the events or conditions that trigger those transitions, and the associated actions. For a typical student, it captures the student's sojourn through college, right from the time when he or she expressed an interest in the college until graduation.

Diagramming Substates and Decomposing Events

We can expand a state or an event to show more details. In Figure 12-21, we have expanded the Matriculated state of a student into its substates. A matriculated student could be in any one of the substates: Freshman, Sophomore, Junior, or Senior. The initial state transitions automatically to the Freshman state, indicating the first substate of a matriculated student. When the student completes the freshman requirements, a transition fires and moves the object to the Sophomore state. Similar transitions move the Student object through the subsequent substates. Figure 12-21 is an example of a nested state diagram, where the substates are nested within the general state, Matriculated.

The diagram captures a further substate called Probation. The transition to this state is shown as an arrow from the enclosing rectangle, which represents the Matriculated state. What that means is that the transition to Probation could fire from any substate of Matriculated, whether it be Freshman, Sophomore, Junior, or Senior. However, there is a guard condition on the transition, which indicates that a matriculated student is placed on probation only when his or her grade point average falls below 2.0.

A Student object in the Probation state could go back to its previous state if the gpa equals or exceeds 2.0 after the next term (represented by an arrow from Probation to the outer rectangle). Otherwise, the object transitions to the Expelled state, indicating that the student is expelled from the college.

An event can also be expanded in a lower level diagram. In Figure 12-22, the *accepts admission offer* event shown in the high-level diagram of Figure 12-20 has been

Figure 12-21
Nested state diagram for Matriculated state of Student object

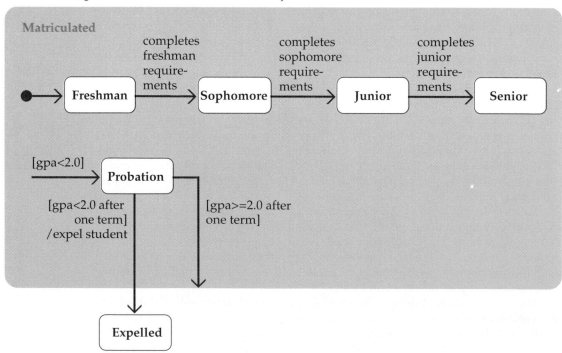

Figure 12-22
Nested state diagram for the accepts admission offer event

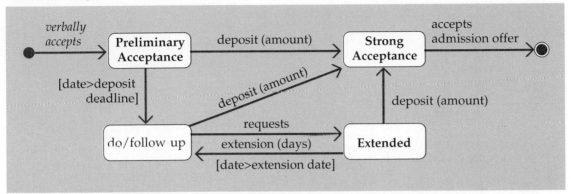

refined to show its fine structure. When a student verbally accepts the admission offer, the corresponding Student object transitions to the Preliminary Acceptance state. When the student deposits an amount of money, the object transitions to the Strong Acceptance state. If the deposit is not made by a given deadline, the object enters another state, which we have not named. Instead, we have shown the activity performed in that state, which is to follow up with the student.

An activity is an operation that is performed when an object is in a certain state. An ongoing activity is labeled by the keyword "do" followed by the "/" sign. It could be a continuous operation such as displaying the balance on a cash register, or it could be a sequential operation such as processing a customer order. This type of activity takes time to complete and can be interrupted by other events. On the other hand, an entry or an exit activity is an atomic operation performed on entry to or exit from a state.

After the follow up, if the student requests an extension for paying the deposit, the object enters the Extended state. Note that the requests extension event has an argument or parameter called "days," which indicates the number of days for which the extension is requested. You can attach multiple arguments to an event. If the student deposits the amount by the extension date, then the object transitions to the Strong Acceptance state. From there, it reaches the Confirmed state, which is implicitly represented by labeling the final state with the name of the top-level event, accepts admission offer.

A State Transition Diagram for Hoosier Burger

In Figure 12-23, we have shown how an object, representing a customer order at Hoosier Burger, dynamically changes states. When a customer places an order, a new Order object is created and the register is reset. The object enters the Checking state and it remains in that state until all the items have been checked. The state is shown with two compartments. The top compartment indicates the name of the state and the bottom one shows the activities associated with the state.

The transition from Checking back to itself is a self-transition. It fires every time the customer orders the next item. The entry activity, calculate line total, is performed on entry to the Checking state. This activity is performed even for the self-transition, capturing the fact that a new line total has to be calculated for each order line. The display line total is a continuous operation; it displays all the line totals for the order.

When all the items are checked, the Order object enters the Checked state. On entry, the total for the entire order is calculated, and the register displays that

Figure 12-23
State diagram for the Order object in Hoosier Burger's system

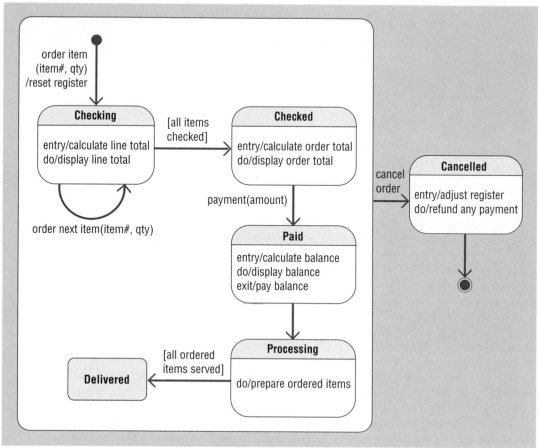

figure. When the customer pays, the object enters the Paid state, and the balance to be paid back to the customer is calculated and displayed. On exit from this state, the balance is paid back to the customer and the order enters the Processing state. The transition arrow is shown without an event name to indicate that the transition automatically fires when the activites in the source state (Paid) are completed. While in the Processing state, all the order items are prepared. Finally, when all the items have been served, the Order object transitions to the Delivered state.

Notice that there is a transition arrow from the outer rectangle surrounding the different order states to a state called Cancelled. That captures the transition from any of those states to the Cancelled state in the event that the customer cancels the order. Showing a common transition this way makes the diagram much simpler than showing a separate transition from each of the states.

In general, an action associated with an event can be modeled as an action or as entry activity; both are atomic operations. For example, we have shown adjust register as an entry activity within the Cancelled state, but we could have just as well represented it as an action associated with the cancel order event. Sometimes, however, you have to choose one over the other. The calculate line total operation is shown as an entry activity within the Checking state. This operation will be performed for both transitions entering the state. On the other hand, we represented reset register as an action associated with the order item event, because this operation is performed only when the first item is ordered, not for subsequent items (shown by the self-transitions).

Summary of State Transition Digramming

In this section, we showed examples of various state diagrams. Remember that a state diagram captures the states of a single class of objects. To develop a dynamic model for an application, you need to combine all the state diagrams you have drawn for different object classes. In such a model, the interaction among the component state diagrams are shown via shared events.

DYNAMIC MODELING: SEQUENCE DIAGRAMS

In this section we will show how to design some of the use cases we identified earlier in the analysis phase. A use-case design describes how each use case is performed by a set of communicating objects (Jacobson et al., 1992).

In UML, an interaction diagram is used to show the pattern of interactions among objects for a particular use case. There are two types of interaction diagrams: *sequence diagrams* and collaboration diagrams (*UML Notation Guide*, 1997). Both of them express similar information, but they do so in different ways. While sequence diagrams show the explicit sequencing of messages, collaboration diagrams show the relationship among objects. We will show you how to design use cases using sequence diagrams.

Components of a Sequence Diagram

A **sequence diagram** depicts the interactions among objects during a certain period of time. Because the pattern of interactions varies from one use case to another, each sequence diagram shows only the interactions pertinent to a specific use case. It shows the participating objects by their lifelines, and the interactions among those objects—arranged in time sequence—by the messages they exchange with one another.

A sequence diagram may be presented either in a generic form or in an instance form. The generic form shows all possible sequences of interactions, that is, the sequences corresponding to all the scenarios of a use case. For example, a generic sequence diagram for the Class registration use case (see Figure 12-2) would capture the sequence of interactions for every valid scenario of that use case. The instance form, on the other hand, shows the sequence for only one scenario. A scenario in UML refers to a single path, among possibly many different paths, through a use case (Fowler, 1997). A path represents a specific combination of conditions within the use case. In Figure 12-24, we have shown a sequence diagram, in instance form, for a scenario where a student registers for a course that specifies one or more prerequisite courses as requirements.

The vertical axis of the diagram represents time and the horizontal axis represents the various participating objects. Time increases as we go down the vertical axis. The diagram has six objects, from an instance of Registration Window on the left, to an instance of Registration called "a New Registration" on the right. The ordering of the objects has no significance. However, you should try to arrange the objects in such a way that the diagram is easy to read and understand. Each object is shown as a vertical dashed line called the lifeline; the lifeline represents the object's existence over a certain period of time. An object symbol—a box with the object's name underlined—is placed at the head of each lifeline.

A thin rectangle, superimposed on the lifeline of an object, represents an activation of the object. An **activation** shows the time period during which the object performs an operation, either directly or through a call to some subordinate operation. The top of the rectangle, which is at the tip of an incoming message, indicates the initiation of the activation, and the bottom its completion.

Sequence diagram:
Depicts the interactions among objects during a certain period of time.

Activation: The time period during which an object performs an operation.

Figure 12-24
Sequence diagram for a class registration scenario with prerequisites

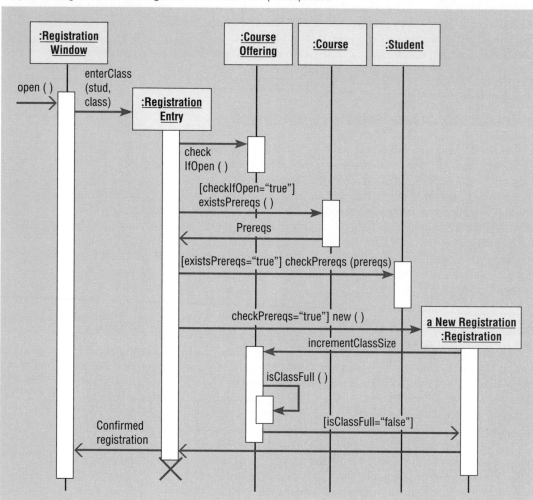

Objects communicate with one another by sending messages. A message is shown as a solid arrow from the sending object to the receiving object. For example, the checkIfOpen message is represented by an arrow from the Registration Entry object to the Course Offering object. Normally the arrow is drawn horizontally, but, in some situations (discussed later), you may have to draw a sloping message line.

Messages could be of different types (Eriksson and Penker, 1998; *UML Notation Guide*, 1997). Each type is indicated in a diagram by a particular type of arrowhead. A **synchronous message**, shown as a full, solid arrowhead, is one where the caller has to wait for the receiving object to complete executing the called operation before it itself can resume execution. An example of a synchronous message is checkIfOpen. When a Registration Entry object sends this message to a Course Offering object, the latter responds by executing an operation called checkIfOpen (same name as the message). After the execution of this operation is completed, control is transferred back to the to the calling operation within Registration Entry with a return value, "true" or "false."

Synchronous message: A type of message in which the caller has to wait for the receiving object to finish executing the called operation before it can resume execution itself.

A synchronous message always has an associated return message. The message may provide the caller with some return value(s), or simply acknowledge to the caller that the operation called has been successfully completed. We have not shown the return for the checkIfOpen message; it is implicit. We have explicitly shown the return for the existsPrereqs message from Registration Entry to Course. The tail of the return message is aligned with the base of the activation rectangle for the exists-Prereqs operation. The message returns the list of prerequisites, if any, for the course in question. Return messages, if shown, unnecessarily clutter the diagram; you may just show the ones that help in understanding the sequence of interactions.

A **simple message** simply transfers control from the sender to the recipient without describing the details of the communication. In a diagram, the arrowhead for a simple message is drawn as a transverse tick mark. As we have seen, the return of a synchronous message is a simple message. The "open" message in Figure 12-24 is also a simple message; it simply transfers control to the Registration Window object.

An **asynchronous message**, shown as a half arrowhead in a sequence diagram, is one where the sender does not have to wait for the recipient to handle the message. The sender can continue executing immediately after sending the message. Asynchronous messages are common in concurrent, real-time systems, where several objects operate in parallel. We do not discuss asynchronous messages further in this chapter.

Simple message: A message that transfers control from the sender to the recipient without describing the details of the communication.

Asynchronous message: A message in which the sender does not have to wait for the recipient to handle the message.

Designing a Use Case with a Sequence Diagram

Let us now see how we can design use cases. We will draw a sequence diagram for an instance of the class registration use case, one in which the course has prerequisites. A description of this scenario is provided below.

1. Registration Clerk opens the registration window and enters the registration information (student and class).

2. Check if the class is open.

3. If the class is open, check if the course has any prerequisites.

4. If the course has prerequisites, then check if the student has taken all of those prerequisites.

5. If the student has taken those prerequisites, then register the student for the class, and increment the class size by one.

6. Check if the class is full; if not, do nothing.

7. Display the confirmed registration in the registration window.

The diagram of Figure 12-24 shows the sequence of interactions for this scenario. In response to the "open" message from Registration Clerk (external actor), the registration window pops up on the screen and the registration information is entered. This creates a new Registration Entry object, which then sends a checkIf-Open message to the Course Offering object (representing the class the student wants to register for). There are two possible return values: true or false. In this scenario, the assumption is that the class is open. We have therefore placed a *guard condition*, checkIfOpen = "true," on the message existsPrereqs. The guard condition ensures that the message will be sent only if the class is open. The return value is a list of prerequisites; the return is shown explicitly in the diagram.

For this scenario, the fact that the course has prerequisites is captured by the guard condition, existsPrereqs = "true." If this condition is satisfied, the Registration

Entry object sends a checkPrereqs message, with "prereqs" as an argument, to the Student object to determine if the student has taken those prerequisites. If the student has taken all the prerequisites, the Registration Entry object creates an object called a New Registration, which denotes a new registration.

Next, a New Registration sends a message called incrementClassSize to Course Offering in order to increase the class size by one. The incrementClassSize operation within Course Offering then calls upon isClassFull, another operation within the same object; this is known as self-delegation (Fowler, 1997). Assuming that the class is not full, the isClassFull operation returns control to the calling operation with a value of "false." Next, the incrementClassSize operation completes and relinquishes control to the calling operation within a New Registration.

Finally, on receipt of the return message from a New Registration, the Registration Entry object destroys itself (the destruction is shown with a large X) and sends a confirmation of the registration to the registration window. Note that Registration Entry is not a persistent object; it is created on the fly to control the sequence of interactions and is deleted as soon as the registration is completed. In between, it calls several other operations within other objects by sequencing the following messages: checkIfOpen, existsPrereqs, checkPrereqs, and new. Hence Registration Entry may be viewed as a control object (Jacobson et al., 1992).

Apart from the Registration Entry object, "a New Registration" is also created during the time period captured in the diagram. The messages that created these objects are represented by arrows pointing directly toward the object symbols. For example, the arrow representing the message called "new" is connected to the object symbol for "a New Registration." The lifeline of such an object begins when the message that creates it is received (the dashed vertical line is hidden behind the activation rectangle).

As we discussed before, the Registration Entry object is destroyed at the point marked by X. The lifeline of this object, therefore, extends from the point of creation to the point of destruction. For objects that are neither created nor destroyed during the time period captured in the diagram—e.g., Course Offering, Course, and Student—the lifelines extend from the top to the bottom of the diagram.

Figure 12-25 shows the sequence diagram for a slightly different scenario, where a student registers for a course without any prerequisites. Notice that the guard condition to be satisfied for creating a New Registration, existsPrereqs = "false," is different from that in the previous scenario. Also, because there is no need to check if the student has taken the prerequisites, there is no need to send the checkPrereqs message to Student. The Student object, therefore, does not participate in this scenario.

There is another difference between this scenario and the previous one. In this scenario, when the incrementClassSize operation within Course Offering calls isClassFull, the value returned is "true." Before returning control to a New Registration, the incrementClassSize operation self delegates again, this time calling setStatus to set the status of the class to "closed."

Both of the sequence diagrams we have seen so far are in instance form. In Figure 12-26, we present a sequence diagram in generic form. This diagram encompasses all possible combinations of conditions for the "Prereq courses not completed" use case (see Figure 12-2). Because this use case is an extension to the Class registration use case, we have not shown the Registration Window object. It is assumed that the Registration Entry object has already been created by the original use case. To improve understandability, we have provided textual description in the left margin. You may provide such description in either the left or the right margin, but try to align the text horizontally with the corresponding element in the diagram. The contents of the use case are described on the following page.

Figure 12-25
Sequence diagram for a class registration scenario without prerequisites

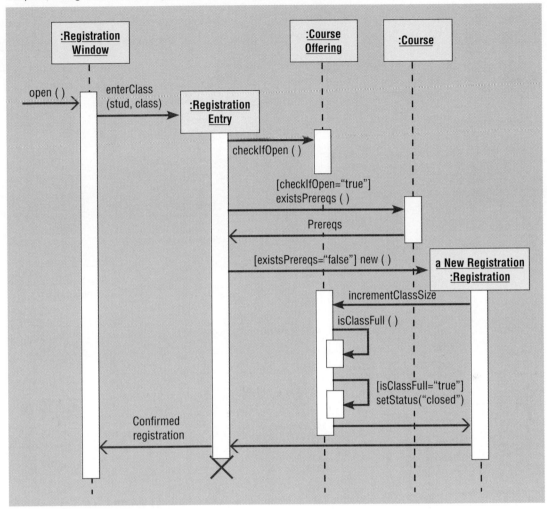

1. If the student has not taken one or more of the prerequisites for the course he or she wants to register for, check if the student has been granted a waiver for each of those prerequisites.

2. If waiver was not granted for one or more of the prerequisites not taken, then check if the student tested out each of those prerequisites by taking an exam.

3. If the student did not test out for any of those prerequisites, then deny registration. Otherwise, register the student for the class and provide a confirmation.

Because this use case extension pertains only to those registration situations where a student has not taken the prerequisite courses, we have placed a guard condition, checkPrereqs = "false," on the checkWaiver message from Registration Entry to Student. This message invokes the checkWaiver operation within Student to find if the student has been granted waivers on all the prerequisites he or she has not taken. Note that the operation has to be applied to each of the prerequisites not taken. The iteration is described in the text on the left margin.

Figure 12-26

A generic sequence diagram for the "Prereq courses not completed" use case

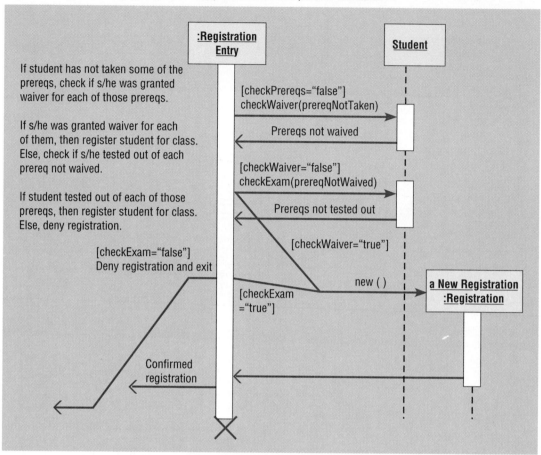

The diagram also exhibits branching, with multiple arrows leaving a single point. Each branch is labeled by a guard condition. The first instance of branching is based on the value returned by the checkWaiver operation. If checkWaiver = "true," the system creates a New Registration object, bypassing other operations. If checkWaiver = "false"—meaning that some of the prerequisites in question were not waived—Registration Entry sends another message, checkExam, to Student to check if he or she tested out of each of the prerequisite courses not waived.

There is another instance of branching at this point. If checkExam = "false," Registration Entry sends a message (to Registration Window), denying the registration and exiting the system. We have deliberately bent the message line downward to show that none of the other remaining interactions takes place. If checkExam = "true," then a New Registration is created.

A Sequence Diagram for Hoosier Burger

In Figure 12-27, we show another sequence diagram, in generic form, for Hoosier Burger's "Hire employee" use case (see Figure 12-3). The description of the use case is given on the following page.

Figure 12-27
Sequence diagram for Hoosier Burger's Hire employee use case

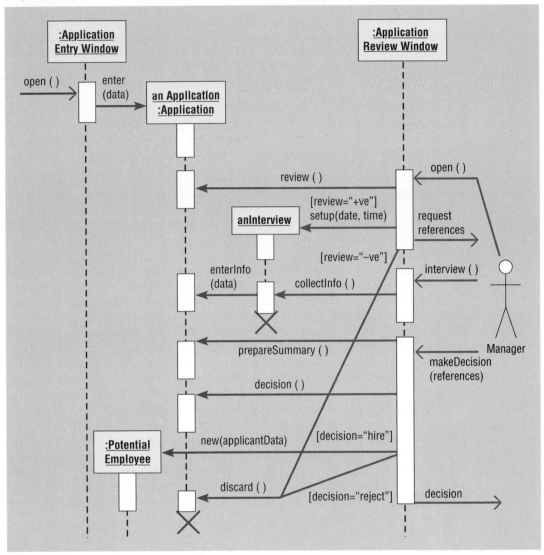

1. On receipt of an application for a job at Hoosier Burger, the data relating to the applicant is entered through the application entry window.

2. The manager opens the application review window and reviews the application.

3. If the initial review is negative, the manager discards the application and conveys the rejection decision to the applicant. No further processing of the application is involved.

4. If the initial review is positive, then the manager sets up a date and time to interview the applicant. The manager also requests the references specified in the application for recommendation letters.

5. The manager interviews the candidate and enters the additional information gathered during the interview into the application file.

6. When the recommendation letters come in, the manager is ready to make a decision. First, he or she prepares a summary of the application. Based on the summary, he or she then makes a decision. If the decision is to reject the candidate, the application is discarded and the decision is conveyed to the applicant. The processing of the application comes to an end.

7. If the decision is to hire the candidate, a potential employee file is created and all relevant information about the candidate (e.g., name, social security number, birthdate, address, phone, etc.) is entered into this file. The hiring decision is conveyed to the applicant.

In the sequence diagram for this use case, we have explicitly shown Manager as an external actor. The branching after the return value from the review message is received represents the two options Manager has. If review = "+ve," then an object called "an Interview" is created through the setup message shown in the upper branch. We have shown the arguments to the message—date and time—because their values are required to set up an interview. Notice that if review = "–ve" (lower branch), the discard message is sent to destroy the Application. The operations in between, for example, enterInfo, prepareSummary, etc., are completely bypassed.

Note that within the "an Interview" object created by the setup operation, there is another operation called collectInfo, which is invoked when the object receives the collectInfo message from Application Review Window. The operation collects all the relevant information during the interview, and enters this information into an Application. After "an Interview" receives a successful return message (not shown) from "an Application," it self destructs, as there is no need for it anymore.

Next, Manager sends a makeDecision message, which invokes a corresponding operation within Application Review Window. This operation first sends a prepareSummary message to an "Application," followed by another called "decision" to the same object. There is branching again at this point, depending on the return value. If decision = "hire," then a message called "new" is sent to create an instance of Potential Employee, which stores the relevant applicant data. If decision = "reject," the discard operation destroys "an Application." In either case, the decision is conveyed to the applicant.

Summary of Sequence Diagrams

In this section, we showed you how to design use cases by drawing sequence diagrams. A sequence diagram is an invaluable tool for specifying and understanding the flow of control. When coding the system, sequence diagrams help you to effectively and easily capture the dynamic aspects of the system by implementing the operations, messages, and the sequencing of those messages in the target programming language.

ANALYSIS VERSUS DESIGN

We have introduced you to a variety of diagramming techniques for capturing different aspects of a system. At the beginning of the chapter, we also described the activities involved in the various phases of the object-oriented development life cycle.

You might wonder which diagrams belong to the analysis phase and which diagrams belong to the design phase. The answer is that, in general, the same type of diagram may apply to different phases. However, as you move from analysis to design, you need to refine the diagrams based on the requirements of the implementation environment. During design, you need to consider technical details relating to the target hardware, operating system, programming language, and database management system, and refine the models that you developed earlier accordingly.

All the diagrams you have seen so far are useful for analyzing a system. Use-case diagrams help you to generate a requirements analysis model, which captures the functionalities of the system as seen by external actors. Class diagrams help you to analyze the objects in the problem domain (business objects) and describe their static structure. During analysis, you model the dynamic aspects of the system using state and interaction diagrams.

When you move to design, you start with the existing set of analysis models and keep adding technical details. For example, you might add several interface classes to your class diagrams to model the windows that you will later implement using a GUI development tool. You would define all the operations in detail, specifying the procedures, signatures, and return values completely. If you decide to use a relational DBMS, you need to map the object classes and relationships to tables, primary keys and foreign keys. The models generated during the design phase will therefore be much more detailed than the analysis models.

Eriksson and Penker (1998) identify the following activities that are typical during design:

- Designing the architecture of the system in terms of functional *packages,* such as those for user interface, database storage and retrieval, and communication

- Modeling concurrent processes by using active classes, multiple threads of control, asynchronous messages, etc.

- Designing user interfaces

- Identifying class libraries and components that could be reused

- Mapping the classes to constructs in the chosen DBMS for storage and retrieval

- Designing mechanisms for handling faults and errors

- Allocation of classes to source code and executable code components

These design activities parallel those performed using the structured methodologies, many of which will be explained in more detail starting in Chapter 14. For example, you will see how to map an E-R model into a relational database representation in Chapter 16.

Figure 12-28 shows a three-layered architecture, consisting of a User Interface package, a Business Objects package, and a Database package. The **packages** represent different generic subsystems of an information system. The dashed arrows represent the dependencies among the packages. For example, the User Interface package depends on the Business Objects package; the packages participate in a client-supplier relationship. If you make changes to some of the business objects, the interface (e.g., screens) might change.

A package consists of a group of classes. Classes within a package are cohesive, that is, they are tightly coupled. The packages themselves should be loosely coupled so that changes in one package do not affect the other packages a great deal. In the architecture of Figure 12-28, the User Interface package contains all the

Package: A set of cohesive, tightly coupled classes representing a subsystem.

Figure 12-28
An example of UML Packages
and dependencies

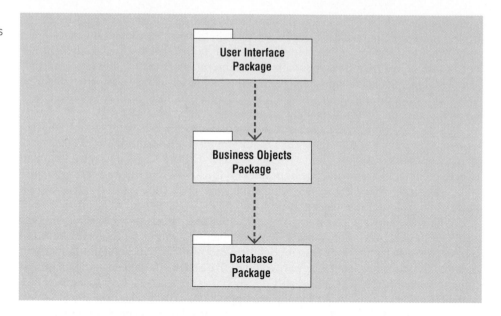

windows, the Business Objects package contains the problem domain objects that you identified during analysis, and the Database package contains a Persistence class for data storage and retrieval. In the university registration system that we considered earlier, the User Interface package could include Microsoft Windows class libraries for developing different types of Windows. The Business Objects package would include all the domain classes, such as Student, Course, Course Offering, Registration, etc. If you are using an SQL server, the classes in the Database package would contain operations for data storage, retrieval, and update (all using SQL commands).

During design, you would also refine the other analysis models. For example, you may need to show the interaction between a new window object you introduced during design and the other existing objects in a sequence diagram. Also, once you have selected a programming language, for each of the operations shown in the sequence diagram, you should provide the exact names that you would be using in the program, along with the names of all the arguments.

In addition to the types of diagrams you have seen so far, there are two other types of diagrams—component diagrams and deployment diagrams—that are pertinent during the design phase. A **component diagram** shows the software components or modules and their dependencies. For example, you can draw a component diagram showing the modules for source code, binary code, and executable code and their dependency relationships. Figure 12-29 shows a component diagram for the university registration system. In this figures, three software components have been identified: Class Scheduler, Class Registration, and GUI (graphical user interface). The small circles in the diagram represent interfaces. The "registration" interface, for example, is used to register a student for a class, and the schedule update interface is used for updating a class schedule. We have also shown two dependencies. The GUI component depends on the features of the registration interface. The Class Registration component depends on the existing class schedule, which is retrieved via the schedule retrieval interface.

Another type of diagram, a deployment diagram (not illustrated), shows how the software components, processes, and objects are deployed into the physical architecture of the system. It shows the configuration of the hardware units (e.g.,

Component diagram:
Shows the software components or modules and their dependencies.

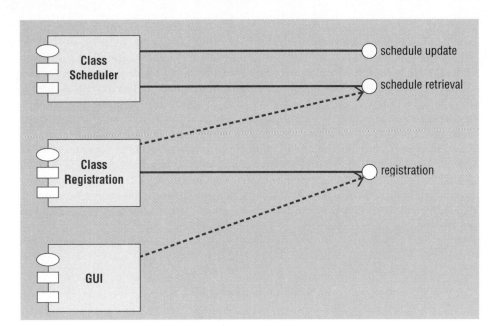

Figure 12-29
A component diagram for class registration

computers, communication devices, etc.) and how the software (components, objects, etc.) is distributed across the units. For example, a deployment diagram for the university registration system might show the topology of nodes in a client-server architecture, and the deployment of the Class Registration component to a Windows NT Server and of the GUI component to client workstations.

When the design phase is complete, you move on to the implementation phase where you code the system. If you are using an object-oriented programming language, translating the design models to code should be relatively straightforward. Programming of the system is followed by testing. The system is developed after going through multiple iterations, with each new iteration providing a better version of the system. The models that you developed during analysis, design, and implementation are navigable in both directions. You should be able to easily trace how a class defined during analysis is coded in the implementation phase. Similarly, you should be able to reverse engineer from a piece of code into the corresponding object class.

SUMMARY

In this chapter, we introduced you to the object-oriented modeling approach, which is becoming increasingly popular because it allows you to thoroughly model a real-world application—both in terms of its data and processes—using a common underlying representation. We described the activities involved in the different phases of the object-oriented development life cycle, and emphasized the seamless nature of the transitions that an object-oriented model undergoes as it evolves through the different phases, from analysis to design to implementation. This is in sharp contrast to other modeling approaches, such as structured analysis and design, which lack a common underlying representation and, therefore, suffer from abrupt and disjoint model transitions.

We showed how to develop different types of models using the Unified Modeling Language (UML) notation. You saw how to develop a requirements analysis model through use-case diagrams. A use-case diagram shows the interaction between external actors and actions performed within a system. You then saw how to model the static structure of objects in the problem domain using class diagrams. Objects have both states (conditions during the life of an object) and behavior (operations) which are encapsulated within. Associations exist between objects, just as relationships exist between entities in an entity-relationship diagram. Next, we introduced state diagrams for capturing the dynamic state transitions of an object. State transitions occur when events trigger changes in an object. We also showed how to develop a dynamic model of interactions among objects using sequence diagrams. A sequence diagram shows the passing of messages between objects. Messages activate operations within objects, thus causing the system to perform needed functions. We provided guidelines on transforming the analysis models to design models, and introduced other diagramming techniques that are useful during design.

KEY TERMS

Abstract class	Composition	Package
Abstract operation	Concrete class	Polymorphism
Activation	Constructor operation	Query operation
Actor	Encapsulation	Sequence diagram
Aggregation	Event	Simple message
Association	Method	State
Association class	Multiple classification	State diagram
Association role	Multiplicity	State transition
Asynchronous message	Object	Synchronous message
Behavior	Object class (class)	Update operation
Class diagram	Object diagram	Use case
Class-scope attribute	Operation	Use-case diagram
Component diagram	Overriding	

REVIEW QUESTIONS

1. Define each of the following terms:

   a. actor
   b. use case
   c. object class
   d. state
   e. behavior
   f. encapsulation
   g. operation
   h. method
   i. constructor operation
   j. query operation

   k. update operation
   l. abstract class
   m. multiplicity
   n. class-scope attribute
   o. association class
   p. polymorphism
   q. overriding
   r. composition
   s. event
   t. state transition

2. Contrast the following terms:

   a. actor; use case

   b. extends relationship; uses relationship

   c. object class; object

   d. attribute; operation

   e. state; behavior

   f. operation; method

   g. query operation; update operation

   h. abstract class; concrete class

   i. class diagram; object diagram

   j. association; aggregation

   k. generalization; aggregation

   l. aggregation; composition

   m. overriding for extension; overriding for restriction

   n. state; event

   o. event; action

   p. entry action; exit action

   q. state diagram; sequence diagram

   r. generic sequence diagram; instance sequence diagram

   s. synchronous message; asynchronous message

3. State the activities involved in each of the following phases of the object-oriented development life cycle: object-oriented analysis, object-oriented design, and object-oriented implementation.

4. Compare and contrast the object-oriented analysis and design models with the structured analysis and design models.

5. State the conditions under which the "extends" relationship should be used between use cases.

6. State the conditions under which the "uses" relationship should be used between use cases.

7. Give an example of an abstract use case. Your example should involve at least two other use cases and show how they are related to the abstract use case.

8. State the conditions under which a designer should model an association relationship as an association class.

9. Using a class diagram, give an example for each of the following types of relationships: unary, binary, and ternary. Specify the multiplicities for all the relationships.

10. Add role names to the association relationships you identified in Review Question 9.

11. Add operations to some of the classes you identified in Review Question 9.

12. Give an example of generalization. Your example should include at least one superclass and three subclasses, and a minimum of one attribute and one operation for each of the classes. Indicate the discriminator and specify the semantic constraints among the subclasses.

13. If the diagram you developed for Review Question 12 does not contain an abstract class, extend the diagram by adding an abstract class that contains at least one abstract operation. Also, indicate which features of a class are inherited by other classes.

14. Using (and, if necessary, extending) the diagram from your solution to Review Question 13, give an example of polymorphism.

15. Give an example of aggregation. Your example should include at least one aggregate object and three component objects. Specify the multiplicities at each end of all the aggregation relationships.

16. Give an example of state transition. Your example should show how the state of the object undergoes a transition based on some event.

PROBLEMS AND EXERCISES

1. Match the following terms to the appropriate definitions:

   _____ concrete class   a. operation applied in different ways

   _____ abstract operation   b. form, not implementation

   _____ aggregation   c. direct instances

   _____ overriding   d. belongs to only one whole object

   _____ polymorphism   e. method replacement

   _____ association class   f. part-of relationship

   _____ composition   g. a set of objects

   _____ object class   h. equivalent to associative entity

   _____ abstract use case   i. an object performs an operation

   _____ event   j. a noteworthy occurrence

   _____ activation   k. not performed by itself

2. The use-case diagram shown in Figure 12-2 captures the student billing function, but does not contain any function for accepting tuition payment from students. Revise the diagram to capture this functionality. Also, express some common behavior among two use cases in the revised diagram by using "uses" relationships.

3. Suppose that the employees of the university are not billed for tuition. Their spouses do not get a full tuition waiver, but pay for only 25 percent of the total tuition. Extend the use-case diagram of Figure 12-2 to capture these situations.

4. An auto rental company wants to develop an automated system that would handle car reservations, customer billing, and car auctions. Usually a customer reserves a car, picks it up, and then returns it after a certain period of time. At the time of pick up, the customer has the option to buy or waive collision insurance on the car. When the car is returned, the customer receives a bill and pays the specified amount. In addition to renting out cars, every six months or so, the auto rental company auctions the cars that have accumulated over 20,000 miles. Draw a use-case diagram for capturing the requirements of the system to be developed. Include an abstract use case for capturing the common behavior among any two use cases. Extend the diagram to capture corporate billing, where corporate customers are not billed directly; rather, the corporations they work for are billed and payments are made sometime later.

5. Draw a use-case diagram for the faculty tenure application and review problem as follows: A faculty member applies for tenure in his or her sixth year by submitting a portfolio summarizing his or her work. In rare circumstances he or she can come up for tenure earlier than the sixth year, but only if the faculty member has permission of the department chair and college dean. New professors, who have worked at other universities before taking their current jobs, rarely, if ever, come in with tenure. They are usually asked to undergo one "probationary" year during which they are evaluated and only can then be granted tenure. Top administrators coming in to a new university job, however, can often negotiate for retreat rights that enable them to become a tenured faculty member should their administrative post end. These retreat arrangements generally have to be approved by faculty. The tenure review process begins with an evaluation of the candidate's portfolio by a committee of faculty within the candidate's department. The committee then writes a recommendation on tenure and sends it to the department's chairperson who then makes a recommendation, and passes the portfolio and recommendation on to the

next level, a college-wide faculty committee. This committee does the same as the department committee and passes its recommendation, the department's recommendation, and the portfolio on to the next level, a university-wide faculty committee. This committee does the same as the other two committees and passes everything on to the provost. The provost then writes his or her own recommendation and passes everything to the president, the final decision maker. This process, from the time the candidate creates his or her portfolio until the time the president makes a decision, can take an entire academic year. The focus of the evaluation is on research, which could be grants, presentations, and publications, though preference is given for empirical research that has been published in top-ranked, refereed journals and where the publication makes a contribution to the field. The candidate must also do well in teaching and services (i.e., to the university, community, or to the discipline) but the primary emphasis is on research.

6. Draw a class diagram for the system to be developed for the auto rental company explained in Problem and Exercise 4. The diagram should identify all the relevant classes from the problem domain, such as cars, customers, etc., and show their attributes and operations, as well as the relationships among the classes. In drawing the diagram, you can make any assumptions, as long as they are realistic.

7. Draw a class diagram, showing the relevant classes, attributes, operations, and relationships, for each of the following situations (if you believe that you need to make additional assumptions, clearly state them for each situation):

   a. A company has a number of employees. The attributes of Employee include employeeId (primary key), name, address, and birthdate. The company also has several projects. Attributes of Project include projectName and startDate. Each employee may be assigned to one or more projects, or may not be assigned to a project. A project must have at least one employee assigned, and may have any number of employees assigned. An employee's billing rate may vary by project, and the company wishes to record the applicable billing rate for each employee when assigned to a particular project. At the end of each month, the company mails a check to each employee who has worked on a project during that month. The check amount is based on the billing rate and the hours logged for each project assigned to the employee.

   b. A university has a large number of courses in its catalog. Attributes of Course include courseNumber (primary key), courseName, and Units. Each course may have one or more different courses as prerequisites, or may have no prerequisites. Similarly, a particular course may be a prerequisite for any number of courses, or may not be a prerequisite for any other course. The university adds or drops a prerequisite for a course only when the director for the course makes a formal request to that effect.

   c. A laboratory has several chemists who work on one or more projects. Chemists also may use certain kinds of equipment on each project. Attributes of Chemist include name and phoneNo. Attributes of Project include projectName and startDate. Attributes of Equipment include serialNo and cost. The organization wishes to record assignDate—that is, the date when a given equipment item was assigned to a particular chemist working on a specified project—as well as totalHours, that is, the total number of hours the chemist has used the equipment for the project. The organization also wants to track the usage of each type of equipment by a chemist. It does so by computing the average number of hours the chemist has used that equipment on all assigned projects. A chemist must be assigned to at least one project and one equipment item. A given equipment item need not be assigned, and a given project need not be assigned either a chemist or an equipment item.

   d. A college course may have one or more scheduled sections, or may not have a scheduled section. Attributes of Course include courseID, courseName, and units. Attributes of Section include sectionNumber and semester. The value of sectionNumber is an integer (such as 1 or 2), which distinguishes one section from another for the same course, but does not uniquely identify a section. There is an operation called findNumSections, which finds the number of sections offered for a given course in a given semester.

e. A hospital has a large number of registered physicians. Attributes of Physician include physicianId (primary key) and specialty. Patients are admitted to the hospital by physicians. Attributes of Patient include patientId (primary key) and patientName. Any patient who is admitted must have exactly one admitting physician. A physician may optionally admit any number of patients. Once admitted, a given patient must be treated by at least one physician. A particular physician may treat any number of patients, or may not treat any patients. Whenever a patient is treated by a physician, the hospital wishes to record the details of the treatment, by including the date, time, and results of the treatment.

8. A student, whose attributes include studentName, Address, phone, and age, may engage in multiple campus-based activities. The university keeps track of the number of years a given student has participated in a specific activity and, at the end of each academic year, mails an activity report to the student showing his participation in various activities. Draw a class diagram for this situation.

9. Draw a class diagram for some organization that you are familiar with—boy scouts/girl scouts, sports team, etc. In your diagram, indicate names for at least four association roles.

10. Draw a use-case diagram, as well as a class diagram, for the following situation (state any assumptions you believe you have to make in order to develop a complete diagram): Stillwater Antiques buys and sells one of a kind antiques of all kinds (for example, furniture, jewelry, china, and clothing). Each item is uniquely identified by an item number, and is also characterized by a description, asking price, condition, and open-ended comments. Stillwater works with many different individuals, called clients, who sell items to and buy items from the store. Some clients only sell items to Stillwater, some only buy items, and some others both sell and buy. A client is identified by a client number, and is also described by a client name and client address. When Stillwater sells an item in stock to a client, the owners want to record the commission paid, the actual selling price, sales tax (tax of zero indicates a tax-exempt sale), and date sold. When Stillwater buys an item from a client, the owners want to record the purchase cost, date purchased, and condition at time of purchase.

11. Draw a use-case diagram, as well as a class diagram, for the following situation (state any assumptions you believe you have to make in order to develop a complete diagram): The H. I. Topi School of Business operates international business programs in ten locations throughout Europe. The School had its first of 9000 graduates in 1965. The School keeps track of each graduate's student number, name, country of birth, current country of citizenship, current name, current address, and the name of each major the student completed (each student has one or two majors). In order to maintain strong ties to its alumni, the School holds various events around the world. Events have a title, date, location, and type (for example, reception, dinner, or seminar). The School needs to keep track of which graduates have attended which events. For an attendance by a graduate at an event, a comment is recorded about information School officials learned from that graduate at that event. The School also keeps in contact with graduates by mail, e-mail, telephone, and fax interactions. As with events, the School records information learned from the graduate from each of these contacts. When a School official knows that he or she will be meeting or talking to a graduate, a report is produced showing the latest information about that graduate and the information learned during the past two years from that graduate from all contacts and events the graduate attended.

12. Draw a class diagram for the following problem. A nonprofit organization depends on a number of different types of persons for its successful operation. The organization is interested in the following attributes for all of these persons: social security number (ssn), name, address, and phone. There are three types of persons who are of greatest interest: employees, volunteers, and donors. In addition to the attributes for a person, an employee has an attribute called dateHired, and a volunteer has an attribute called skill. A donor is a person who has donated one or more items to the organization. An item, specified by a name, may have no donors, or one or more donors. When an item is donated, the organization records its price, so that at the end of the year, it can identify the top 10 donors.

    There are persons other than employees, volunteers, and donors who are of interest to the organization, so that a person need not belong to any of these three groups. On the other hand, at a given time a person may belong to two or more of these groups (for example, employee and donor).

13. A bank has three types of accounts: checking, savings, and loan. Following are the attributes for each type of account:
    CHECKING: Acct_No, Date_Opened, Balance, Service_Charge
    SAVINGS: Acct_No, Date_Opened, Balance, Interest_Rate
    LOAN: Acct_No, Date_Opened, Balance, Interest_Rate, Payment
    Assume that each bank account must be a member of exactly one of these subtypes. At the end of each month the bank computes the balance in each account and mails a statement to the customer holding that account. The balance computation depends on the type of the account. For example, a checking account balance may reflect a service charge, whereas a savings account balance may include an interest amount. Draw a class diagram to represent the situation. Your diagram should include an abstract class, as well as an abstract operation for computing balance.

14. An organization has been entrusted with developing a Registration and Title system that maintains information about all vehicles registered in a particular state. For each vehicle that is registered with the office, the system has to store the name, address, telephone number of the owner, the start date and end date of the registration, plate information (issuer, year, type, and number), sticker (year, type, and number), and registration fee. In addition, the following information is maintained about the vehicles themselves: the number, year, make, model, body style, gross weight, number of passengers, diesel-powered (yes/no), color, cost, and mileage. If the vehicle is a trailer, diesel-powered and number of passengers are not relevant. For travel trailers, the body number and length must be known. The system needs to maintain information on the luggage capacity for a car, maximum cargo capacity and maximum towing capacity for a truck, and horsepower for a motorcycle. The system issues registration notices to owners of vehicles whose registrations are due to expire after two months. When the owner renews the registration, the system updates the registration information on the vehicle.
    a. Develop a static object model by drawing a class diagram that shows all the object classes, attributes, operations, relationships, and multiplicities. For each operation, show its argument list.
    b. Draw a state diagram that captures all the possible states of a Vehicle object, right from the time the vehicle was manufactured until it goes to the junkyard. In drawing the diagram, you may make any necessary assumptions, as long as they are realistic.
    c. Select any state or event from the high-level state diagram that you have drawn and show its fine structure (substates and their transitions) in a lower-level diagram.
    d. One of the use cases for this application is "Issue registration renewal notice," which is performed once every day. Draw a sequence diagram, in generic form, showing all possible object interactions for this use case.

15. Draw a state diagram showing all the states and transitions of a Car object for the auto rental system described in Problem and Exercise 4. The diagram should show the events that cause the transitions, along with any associated actions. If necessary, show the activities associated with a state.

16. One of the use cases for the auto rental system in Problem and Exercise 4 is "Car reservation." Draw a sequence diagram, in instance form, to describe the sequence of interactions for each of the following scenarios of this use case:
    a. Car is available during the specified time period.
    b. No car in the desired category (e.g., compact, midsize, etc.) is available during the specified time period.

FIELD EXERCISES

1. Interview a friend or family member to elicit from them common examples of superclass/subclass relationships. You will have to explain the meaning of this term and provide a common example, such as: PROPERTY: RESIDENTIAL, COMMERCIAL; or BONDS: CORPORATE, MUNICIPAL. Use the information they provide to construct a class diagram segment and present it to this person. Revise if necessary until it seems appropriate to you and your friend or family member.

2. Visit two local small businesses, one in the service sector and one in manufacturing. Interview employees from these organizations to obtain examples of both superclass/subclass relationships and operational business rules (such as "a customer can return merchandise only if they have a valid sales slip"). In which of these environments is it easier to find examples of these constructs? Why?

3. Ask a database administrator or database or systems analyst in a local company to show you an EER (or E-R) diagram for one of the organization's primary databases. Translate this diagram into a class diagram.

4. Interview a systems analyst in a local company which uses object-oriented programming and system development tools. Ask to see any analysis and design diagrams they have drawn of the database and applications. Compare these diagrams to the ones in this chapter. What differences do you see? What additional features and notations are used and what are their purpose?

REFERENCES

Booch, G. 1994. *Object-Oriented Analysis and Design with Applications*. 2nd. ed. Redwood City, CA: Benjamin/Cummings.

Coad, P., and E. Yourdon. 1991a. *Object-Oriented Analysis*. 2nd. ed. Englewood Cliffs, NJ: Prentice-Hall.

Coad, P., and E. Yourdon. 1991b. *Object-Oriented Design*. Englewood Cliffs, NJ: Prentice-Hall.

Eriksson, H., and M. Penker. 1998. *UML Toolkit*. New York: John Wiley.

Fowler, M. 1997. *UML Distilled: Applying the Standard Object Modeling Language*. Reading, MA: Addison-Wesley.

Jacobson, I., M., Christerson, P. Jonsson, and G. Overgaard. 1992. *Object-Oriented Software Engineering: A Use-Case Driven Approach*. Reading, MA: Addison-Wesley.

Rumbaugh, J., M. Blaha, W. Premerlani, F. Eddy, and W. Lorensen. 1991. *Object-Oriented Modeling and Design*. Englewood Cliffs, NJ: Prentice-Hall.

UML Document Set. 1997. Version 1.0 (January). Santa Clara: Rational Software Corp.

UML Notation Guide. 1997. Version 1.0 (January). Santa Clara: Rational Software Corp.

Rapid Application Development

After studying this chapter, you should be able to:

■ Explain the Rapid Application Development (RAD) approach and how it differs from traditional approaches to information systems development.

■ Describe the system development components essential to RAD.

■ Discuss the conceptual pillars that support the RAD approach.

■ Explain the advantages and disadvantages of RAD as an exclusive systems development methodology.

INTRODUCTION

RAD [Rapid Application Development] has been demonstrated in many projects to be so superior to traditional development that it seems irresponsible to continue to develop systems the old way.

James Martin, 1991

James Martin is generally credited with inventing Rapid Application Development, or RAD, so it should be no surprise that he so enthusiastically supports the concept, as the above quote shows. Not everyone shares his enthusiasm, however, as you will see. In this chapter, you will learn about RAD: what it is, the components it relies on to succeed, software tools that can support RAD, and Martin's four-phase RAD life cycle. You will also see an example of a RAD methodology developed by a consulting firm, Cambridge Technology Partners. There are many different RAD approaches; in fact, most consulting firms and many corporations have defined their own RAD methodologies. The ones used by information system consulting firms are often proprietary, so we cannot discuss them here. So that you can understand any RAD methodology you might encounter, we concentrate on the concepts of RAD and use several specific publicly known RAD approaches as examples. We end the chapter with examples of how the RAD approach can pay off handsomely and the advantages and disadvantages of RAD.

The topic of RAD is very extensive, and like object-oriented analysis and design (see Chapter 12), this chapter introduces you only to the major principles of RAD. To conduct a project with RAD requires applying skills and concepts discussed elsewhere in this text (such as interviewing, designing screens and reports, and using automated tools for systems development); thus, this is not a self-contained chapter on how to conduct an information systems development project via RAD. By carefully studying this chapter, you will, however, be able to see how to apply the skills learned in other parts of this text within the RAD approach.

RAPID APPLICATION DEVELOPMENT

Rapid Application Development (RAD): Systems development methodology created to radically decrease the time needed to design and implement information systems. RAD relies on extensive user involvement, Joint Application Design sessions, prototyping, integrated CASE tools, and code generators.

Rapid Application Development (RAD) is an approach to developing information systems which promises better and cheaper systems and more rapid deployment by having systems developers and end users work together jointly in real-time to develop systems. RAD grew out of the convergence of two trends: the increased speed and turbulence of doing business in the late 1980s and early 1990s, and the ready availability of high-powered computer-based tools to support systems development and easy maintenance. As the conditions of doing business in a changing, competitive global environment became more turbulent, management in many organizations began to question if it made sense to wait two to three years to develop systems (in a methodical, controls-rich process) that would be obsolete upon completion. On the other hand, CASE tools and prototyping software were diffusing throughout organizations, making it relatively easy for end users to see what their systems would look like before they were completed. Why not use these tools to more productively address the problems of developing systems in a rapidly changing business environment? And so RAD was born.

The creation of RAD did not lead to its immediate adoption, however. To some, RAD was not an approach that could be taken seriously for enterprisewide information systems. But increasing disenchantment with traditional systems development methods and the long development times associated with them led more and more firms to seriously consider RAD. The ready availability of increasingly powerful software tools created to support RAD also increased interest in this approach. RAD is becoming more and more a legitimate way to develop information systems, as evidenced by Cambridge Technology Partners' estimate that the demand for their RAD business increases at a rate of 80–90 percent per year (Classe, 1996).

The Process of Developing an Application Rapidly

As you will see in this chapter, RAD is not a single methodology but is instead a general strategy of developing information systems. As such, there are many different approaches to developing applications rapidly. Some are special life cycles, such as the Martin RAD life cycle, which will be introduced soon. Others focus more on specific software tools and visual development environments that enable the process of rapidly developing and deploying applications. Whatever strategy is taken, however, the goal remains the same: to rapidly analyze a business problem, design a viable system solution through intense cooperation between users and developers, and to quickly get the finished application in the hands of users, saving time, money, and other resources in the process.

As Figure 13-1 shows, the same phases that are followed in the traditional SDLC are also followed in RAD, but the phases are shortened and combined with each other to produce a more streamlined development technique. Planning and design phases in RAD are shortened by focusing work on system functional and user interface requirements at the expense of detailed business analysis and concern for system performance issues. Also, usually RAD looks at the system being developed in isolation from other systems, thus eliminating the time-consuming

Figure 13-1
RAD systems development life cycle compared to standard SDLC

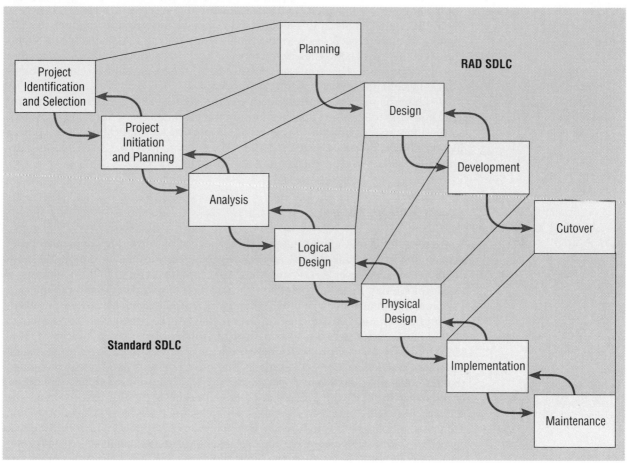

activities of coordinating with existing standards and systems during design and development. The emphasis in RAD is generally less on the sequence and structure of processes in the life cycle and more on doing different tasks in parallel with each other and on using prototyping extensively. Notice also that the iteration in the RAD life cycle is limited to the design and development phases. This is where the bulk of the work in a RAD approach takes place. Although it is possible in RAD for there to be a return to planning once design has begun, it is rarely done. Similarly, although it is possible to return to development from the cutover phase, RAD is designed to minimize iteration at this point in the life cycle. The high level of user commitment and involvement throughout RAD implies that the system which emerges should be more readily accepted by the user community (and hence more easily implemented during cutover) than would be a system developed using traditional techniques.

Deliverables and Outcomes

The deliverables and outcomes of RAD are the same as for the traditional SDLC: a systems development plan, which includes the application being developed; a description of user and business process requirements for the application; logical and physical designs for the application; and the application's construction and implementation, with a plan for its continued maintenance and support. Whereas the traditional SDLC is indifferent as to the specific tools and techniques used to create and modify each of the deliverables listed above, RAD puts a heavy emphasis on the use of computer-based tools to support as much of the development process as possible. This emphasis on speed and the tools that make it possible is what sets RAD apart from traditional approaches.

In the next section, we describe the components most useful to a successful RAD effort. This is followed by sections on the foundations of the RAD approach, on the tools and techniques designed to support rapid application development and shortening project schedules, on situations where RAD has been successfully employed, and on the advantages and disadvantages of RAD.

COMPONENTS OF RAD

To succeed, RAD relies on bringing together several systems development components found in this book. As you might have gathered from the definition, RAD depends on extensive user involvement. End users are involved from the beginning of the development process, where they participate in application planning; through requirements determination, where they work with analysts in system prototyping; and design and implementation, where they work with system developers to validate final elements of the system's design. Much of end-user involvement takes place in the *prototyping* process, where users and analysts work together to design interfaces and reports for new systems. The prototyping is conducted in sessions that resemble traditional *Joint Application Design (JAD)* sessions. The primary difference is that in RAD, the prototype becomes the basis for the new system—the screens designed during prototyping become screens in the production system. This is accomplished through reliance on *integrated CASE tools* which include *code generators* for creating code from the designs end users and analysts create during prototyping. The code includes the interfaces as well as the application programs that use them. Alternatively, RAD may employ visual development environments instead of CASE tools with code generators, but the benefits from rapid prototyping are the same. In many cases, the basis for the production system is being built even as users are talking about the system during development workshops. In many cases, end users can get hands-on experience with the developing system before the design workshops are over. To further help speed the process, the reuse of templates, components, or previous systems described in the CASE tool repository is strongly encouraged.

APPROACHES TO RAD

Martin suggests there are four important supporting components or "pillars" of RAD. The first consists of software development tools. Tools alone, however, are not enough to make RAD work (see Figure 13-2). Tools are necessary but not sufficient. According to Martin, the other three pillars of RAD are people, who must be trained in the right skills; a coherent methodology, which spells out the proper tasks to be done in the proper order; and the support and facilitation of management (Martin, 1991).

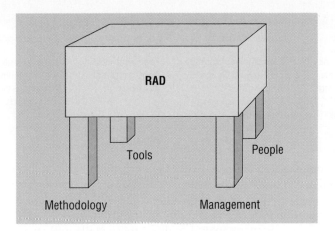

Figure 13-2
Martin's four necessary pillars for the RAD approach

Martin suggests that no information systems organization should be converted to the RAD approach overnight. Instead, a small group of well-trained and dedicated professionals, called a RAD cell, should be created to demonstrate the viability of RAD through pilot projects. Over time, the cell can grow, gradually adding more people, skills, and projects, until RAD is the predominant approach of the information systems unit.

Steve McConnell (1996) presents another approach to rapid development. Underlying his approach are the sound if somewhat conservative management practices of careful planning, efficient use of time, and the humane use of human resources. McConnell suggests his own set of four pillars fundamental to a successful RAD approach: avoiding classic mistakes, applying development fundamentals, managing risks to avoid catastrophic setbacks, and applying schedule-oriented practices (see Figure 13-3). McConnell lists 36 different classic development mistakes, 10 of which are included in Table 13-1. It should be pointed out that McConnell's classic mistakes apply to all systems development projects, not just RAD projects. Most of the mistakes listed in Table 13-1 are easily understood from their brief descriptions, such as unrealistic expectations, insufficient planning, and overestimated savings from new tools or methods. Some of the remaining items need additional explanation.

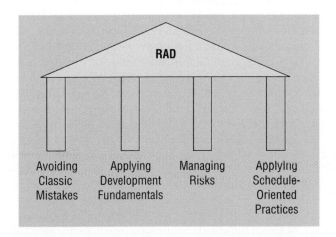

Figure 13-3
McConnell's four necessary pillars for the RAD approach

TABLE 13-1 Ten of McConnell's 36 Classic Development Mistakes

People-Related	Process-Related	Product-Related	Technology-Related
1. Weak personnel	1. Insufficient planning	1. Feature creep	1. Silver-bullet syndrome
2. Adding people to a project late	2. Overly optimistic schedules	2. Requirements gold-plating	2. Overestimated savings from new tools or methods
3. Unrealistic expectations	3. Planning to catch up later		

Under people-related mistakes, weak personnel refers to employees that are not as well trained in the skills necessary to a particular project. Weak has nothing to do with the employees' personalities or physical abilities. Since skills such as prototyping, fourth-generation language programming, and interaction with end users are needed for RAD, an excellent analyst without these skills will struggle on a RAD project. The second people-related mistake, adding people late to a project, may not seem like a mistake. Common sense would dictate that additional people should add to productivity, as the remaining work can now be divided among more people, leaving each person with less to do in the same amount of time. But as Brooks (1995) convincingly argued, adding more people also adds more need for coordination among all the people on the project, new and old. Adding more people actually ends up reducing productivity on a project. Brooks also identified the problem called the silver-bullet syndrome. The silver-bullet syndrome occurs when developers believe a new and usually untried technology is all that is needed to cure the ills of any development project. In application development, however, there is no silver bullet. No one technology can solve every problem, and those who believe it will be disappointed.

Two other mistakes from the list that need additional explanation are both product-related mistakes: feature creep and requirements gold-plating. Feature creep refers to the tendency of system requirements to change over the lifetime of the development project. It's called feature creep because more and more features that were not in the original specifications for the application "creep in" during the development process. The average project may see a 25 percent change in requirements, all of which can have a negative impact on keeping the project on schedule and containing project costs. Changes to an application typically cost 50 to 200 times less if they are made during requirements determination rather than during the physical design process. Requirements gold-plating means an application may have more requirements than it needs, even before the development project begins. Many of these requirements can be extreme and complex and not really necessary.

McConnell's second pillar is development fundamentals. Many of these fundamentals are stressed in other parts of this text and include such practices as proper project estimating, scheduling, planning, and tracking; measuring software quality and productivity; managing system requirements; engaging in good design techniques; and assuring quality. The third pillar is managing risk, a topic discussed in Chapters 2 and 3. Once the first three pillars have been successfully built, you have reached what McConnell calls "efficient development." Without efficient development, achieving the reduced schedules necessary for rapid development will be more difficult. Once achieved, however, you can go on to develop the fourth pillar: schedule-oriented practices, designed to improve development speed, reduce schedule risk, and make progress visible. McConnell lists over 25 best schedule-oriented practices in his book, everything from outsourcing to using a spiral life cycle to staged delivery. Many of his schedule-oriented practices are focused on choosing the appropriate software tools and life cycle approaches, both of which are discussed in more detail in the next sections.

Software Tools for RAD

There are many different software tools that can be successfully used to support the RAD approach. Remember that there is no silver bullet for software development, and that includes software tools that support RAD. Some tools will work better for certain applications than others, and developers need to have a good understanding of the limits as well as the possibilities of any development environment they decide to use.

We have previously mentioned how integrated CASE tools can be used to support RAD. Such CASE tools should have prototyping facilities as well as code generators in order to provide the best level of support. An example of a CASE tool with these capabilities is COOL:Gen from Sterling Software (formerly Texas Instruments Software's Composer). COOL:Gen allows developers and users to work together closely to design windows and navigation paths between them (see Figure 13-4). It generates code in several languages, including C and C++.

Other software tools that can support RAD are types of visual development environments (see Chapter 4). Visual development environments are based on different underlying programming languages and allow developers to design windows and manipulate different aspects of graphical user interfaces (GUIs), such as push buttons and list boxes. Examples include Microsoft's Visual Basic, based on the Basic programming language; Borland's Delphi, based on object-oriented Pascal (see Figure 13-5); and PowerSoft's PowerBuilder. These are by no means the only development environments that can support RAD but are listed here only as examples of the many tool sets available.

Martin's RAD Life Cycle

Recall that Martin listed tools as just one of his four pillars necessary for RAD. Another pillar he listed was methodology. For methodology, Martin developed a specific RAD life cycle, which contains the basic phases of any RAD life cycle (see Figure 13-1)—planning, design, development, and cutover—although he calls the phases requirements planning, user design, construction, and cutover (see Figure 13-6).

Figure 13-4
Example CASE tool used during RAD: COOL:Gen™ from Sterling Software

Figure 13-5
Example visual development
environment used during
RAD: Borland's Delphi

Figure 13-6
Martin's four-phase RAD
life cycle

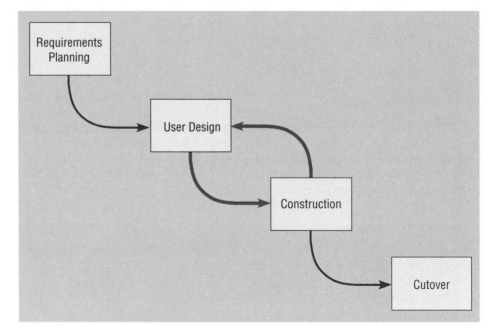

Requirements planning incorporates elements of the traditional planning and
analysis phases. During this phase, high-level managers, executives, and knowledgeable end users determine system requirements, but the determination is done
in the context of a discussion of business problems and business areas. Once specific systems have been identified for development, users and analysts conduct a
joint requirements planning workshop to reach agreement on system requirements. The overall planning process is not all that much different from planning in
the traditional SDLC.

During user design, end users and information systems professionals participate in JAD workshops, where those involved use integrated CASE tools to support the rapid prototyping of system design. Users and analysts work closely and

quickly to create prototypes that capture system requirements and that become the basis for the physical design of the system being developed. Users sign off on the CASE-based design — there are no paper-based specifications. Because user design ends with agreement on a computer-based design, the gap between the end of design and the handing over of the new system to users might only take three months instead of the usual 18.

In construction, the same information systems professionals who created the design now generate code using the CASE tools' code generator. End users also participate, validating screens and other aspects of the design as the application system is being built. Construction can be combined with user design into one phase for smaller systems.

Cutover means delivery of the new system to its end users. Because the RAD approach is so fast, planning for cutover must begin early in the RAD process. Cutover involves many of the traditional activities of implementation, including testing, training users, dealing with organizational changes, and running the new and old systems in parallel, but all of these activities occur on an accelerated basis.

According to Martin, RAD can produce a system in six months that would take 24 months to produce using the traditional systems development life cycle.

A Specific RAD Life Cycle

Many firms have adopted Rapid Application Development as one of the approaches they use for in-house systems development. Many consulting firms, such as Cambridge Technology Partners (CTP), headquartered in Cambridge, MA, have adopted the RAD approach for developing systems for their clients. The Cambridge life cycle, as shown in Figure 13-7, is very similar to James Martin's RAD life cycle. Cambridge divides Martin's requirements planning phase into two stages, scope and rapid solutions workshop. Both life cycles have one phase called design. Cambridge's development phase is similar to Martin's construction, and their rollout phase parallels Martin's cutover. Each of these phases is discussed in more detail below.

As is the case for RAD in general, the Cambridge RAD methodology uses an iterative, prototyping approach to the design and development of application systems. One goal of this methodology is to continuously expand and refine the prototype using constant feedback from the end users. This process, based on extensive end user involvement, ensures the delivery of information systems that meet or exceed user needs and expectations.

The first phase in the Cambridge RAD life cycle is scope, which involves a series of facilitated, cross-functional meetings with executives, end users, and technical specialists. These nontechnical meetings are focused on end-user needs and the business drivers for change. The process relies on building consensus, building the business case, and communicating among all involved parties within the organization. At the

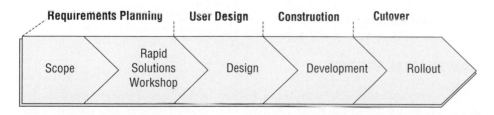

Martin's Four RAD Life Cycle Phases

Requirements Planning   User Design   Construction   Cutover

Scope | Rapid Solutions Workshop | Design | Development | Rollout

Figure 13-7
Cambridge Technology Partners' RAD life cycle

end of the scope phase, Cambridge's analysts have developed a set of deliverables that includes: business goals, critical success factors, a cost-benefit analysis of the proposed application, an analysis of the fit between the application and the client's business processes, and a joint implementation plan.

The second phase, the rapid solutions workshop, is an intensive three-week process in which a team made up of Cambridge analysts and client representatives work together full-time to develop a prototype system. The rapid solutions workshop drastically reduces requirements definition time. During the workshop, the team develops a working prototype that illustrates a representative part of the application. The joint client and Cambridge team works toward establishing a vision and end-user scenarios for the prototype. The initial prototype becomes the basis for the application but can necessarily represent only an illustrative part of the larger, more complex application. The initial design and momentum generated during the workshop helps keep the client's design and development process on track throughout later phases of the life cycle.

The next two phases in Cambridge's RAD life cycle are design and development. One primary goal of this part of the methodology is the continual refinement and expansion of the original prototype, through constant feedback from users. The design and development phases illustrate the iterative nature of the work being done, as end users and analysts work together to modify the application during its development. During the design phase, Cambridge typically divides the design team into two subteams: the user design team and the technical design team. The user design team continues to gather functional and interface specifications for the complete application from the users. This information is the starting point for the technical design, and often serves to deter users from specifying unreasonable requirements. The result is a system design that is technically feasible, meets the fundamental needs of the users, and provides the business benefit required. As the Cambridge RAD approach is comprehensive and user-driven, Cambridge teams work to satisfy user requirements as much as technically possible. User requirements serve as the basis for the technical architecture of the application and work to refine the technical design, but at the same time, the technical design serves to limit user requests that are not feasible, given the design. This tight relationship between technical design and user requirements also illustrates the iterative nature of the process. The ability of Cambridge teams to prioritize system functionality is one of the reasons Cambridge has been so successful with its RAD methodology.

During development, the requirements defined in previous phases are made operational. The client's business managers and information technology staff are involved in the development process for checkpoints and functionality status reviews. Checkpoints and reviews allow the user representatives and information technology staff to verify that the application is being implemented as specified. Throughout the development process, the application development staff performs rigorous unit testing, quality assurance, and usability testing.

The final phase, rollout, has two parts, preparation and execution. During rollout preparation, the development staff conducts conversion strategy, conversion program design, and the development of conversion programs. Rollout execution involves the complete installation of the application in the production environment for the extended user community.

RAD SUCCESS STORIES

When used successfully, the results of RAD can be dramatic. Here are three stories about successful use of the RAD approach. The first story is an illustration of the

Cambridge Technology Partners' RAD methodology. The other two stories focus on the use of a particular software tool suite, Borland's Delphi. Both of the Delphi stories are based on postings to the Delphi Web pages (see References at the end of the chapter).

An Example from Cambridge Technology Partners

Cambridge Technology Partners, whose RAD methodology we reviewed earlier, has made RAD the basis of its highly successful business, which is typically initiated with a scope and a rapid solutions workshop (Harrar, 1993). Using their RAD approach, Cambridge Technology was able to develop a decision support system for Hughes Space and Communications Company in about half the time the traditional systems development methodology would have demanded.

As we have seen, the Cambridge RAD approach involves several phases. During scope, consultants spent two to three days identifying which of Hughes Space and Communications's applications would be suitable to a RAD approach. A team from CTP then spent two weeks at the client's site, gathering information and observing the client's information systems operations. As part of the rapid solutions workshop, a client team from Hughes spent a week at the CTP offices in Massachusetts. The Hughes team was given a very real incentive to cooperate: at the end of their week, the team had to give a presentation of their newly developed system to their own high-level managers.

For Hughes Space and Communications Company, Cambridge Technology was able to create a complex decision support system prototype in three weeks, the usual time for a rapid solutions workshop. The system integrated data from four databases that were previously thought to be unintegratable. After getting approval on the design, Cambridge went on to complete the design phase in less than two months. Ten months later, after completing all aspects of development, Hughes launched the production application. Hughes estimated that developing the same system in-house would have taken them at least two years. Hughes liked the RAD approach so much they had CTP develop three more systems and then train the Hughes information systems people to conduct the workshops back at Hughes' offices in El Segundo, California.

RAD Success with Borland's Delphi

Two RAD success stories with Borland's Delphi, one from the U.S. government and one from the financial business sector, suggest the broad applicability of the RAD approach.

U.S. Navy Fleet Modernization   The U.S. Navy has as an ongoing challenge: the modernization of its fleet as well as its maintenance. Modernization has become especially crucial as the Navy has downsized from a fleet of almost 600 ships in the 1980s to just 260 in 1997. The Navy wanted to upgrade its fleet modernization management system at the same time it was renovating the fleet. The requirement was to move from three character-based systems to a unified, GUI-based system based on a single database. The Fleet Modernization program chose Delphi to build the new system. Two aspects of Delphi that were attractive to the Navy were its support of rapid prototyping and the promise of reuse of components in the object-oriented Pascal environment. The final system was developed with Delphi using a RAD approach in six months, an estimated savings of 50 percent. The Navy estimates the new system resulted in immediate savings of 20 percent per year due to reduced maintenance costs.

First National Bank of Chicago First National Bank of Chicago is one of the 10 largest banks in the United States, with assets of over $122 billion. In October 1994, the Bank was awarded a bid to develop a new Electronic Federal Tax Payment System, intended to foster faster tax withholdings and eliminate all paper in the process. The contract, signed by a joint venture of the Bank with Mercantile Bank of St. Louis, specified exacting system requirements and very short deadlines. The venture chose Delphi for the job. The use of Delphi enabled rapid development and rapid prototyping of a GUI front-end to the system.

At one point, over 125 programmers organized into several teams were working on the project. Fifteen to twenty developers worked on the GUI front-end. Rapid prototyping for requirements elicitation allowed coding to begin in May 1995, only seven months after the contract was awarded. The system was completed and ready for testing in March 1996, only 10 months later. After three months of certification testing, the system went live in July 1996. The size of the database used in the Electronic Federal Tax Payment System is not trivial at 225 tables, with 250 million rows and 55 gigabytes in size. By the year 2000, there will be 500 million rows maintained on-line. RAD techniques, with Delphi's support, allowed the project to come in on time and on budget, despite the extensive requirements and short deadlines specified in the contract.

ADVANTAGES AND DISADVANTAGES OF RAD

As these success stories show, the primary advantage of RAD is obvious: information systems developed in as little as one-quarter the usual time. But shorter development cycles also mean cheaper systems, as fewer organizational resources need be devoted to develop any particular system. Martin (1991) points out that RAD also involves smaller development teams, which results in even more savings. Finally, because there is less time between the end of design and conversion, the new system is closer to current business needs and is therefore of higher quality than would be a similar system developed the traditional way.

Others point out, however, that although RAD works, it only works well for systems that have to be developed quickly (Gibson and Hughes, 1994). Such systems include those that are developed in response to quickly changing business conditions, perceived opportunities to gain a competitive edge by moving quickly in a market or industry, or new government regulations. If speed is a goal, however, then other aspects of an application must oftentimes be sacrificed (McConnell, 1996). In general, in a systems development effort, you can obtain two of three key characteristics of the development effort—speed, cost, and quality—but never all three. If hard-and-fast goals for speed and cost are set, quality of the final application will suffer. Similarly, if you must achieve a certain level of quality and you must do so in a fixed amount of time, the cost will be greater than it might otherwise have been. Finally, if you have set goals for cost and quality, you will take longer to develop the application than you might have wanted originally.

It should also be pointed out that taking too much time to develop a system can actually have a negative effect on the quality of the system. Too much time between the initial requirements determination and the delivery of the completed system adds many complications to the overall development process. It will be more difficult to accurately estimate requirements at the time the system will be delivered because business conditions will have changed so much during the intervening time. Although predicting the future is always difficult, predicting the near-term future is more certain than predicting a future that is three to five years away. Changing business conditions will also make it easier for system owners and developers to become side-tracked during the development process. Finally, too much time between the beginning and end of a project almost guarantees problems with feature creep, again due to changing business conditions. The key, then, is finding the right balance between time to completion and quality. Too much time can be just as bad as too little.

While RAD is the methodology of choice for all systems development, RAD's emphasis on what a system does and how it does it implies that essential information about the business models and processes is not included. In its highly accelerated analysis and design phases, RAD leaves little room for understanding the business area, what it does, what its functions are and who performs them, or what the people in the business area do in their jobs. The greater the reliance on RAD, the greater the risk that many systems will be out of alignment with the business.

Another drawback of RAD has to do with the very thing that makes it so attractive as a systems development methodology: its speed. Because the RAD process puts such an emphasis on speed, many important software engineering concepts, such as interface consistency, programming standards, module reuse, scalability, and systems administration, are overlooked (Bourne, 1994). For example:

- *Consistency*   In their efforts to quickly paint screens, RAD analysts often ignore the need to be consistent both within an application and across a suite of related applications. Areas of concern include window size and color, consistent format masks, and using the same error message for the same offense.

- *Programming standards*   Documentation standards and data naming standards should be established early in RAD or it may be difficult to implement them later.

- *Module reuse*   Many times during prototyping, analysts forget that similar screen or report designs may have already been created. Often in RAD there is no mechanism in place that allows analysts to easily determine whether modules that can be reused are already in existence.

- *Scalability*   If the system designed during RAD is useful, its use will gradually spread beyond those initial users who helped build it. Developers should build such growth into their initial system. Scalability also applies to hardware; system scope; the number, type, and users of reports; growth in the software team developing and maintaining the system as it grows; user training as system use expands; and security.

- *Systems administration*   System administration is typically ignored altogether during RAD, as the emphasis is usually on the excitement of seeing a new application system develop before users' eyes. Important system administration issues include database maintenance and reorganization, backup and recovery, distribution or installation of application updates, and scheduling and implementing planned system downtime and restarts.

Although RAD can reduce a project's cost, because fewer resources and less time go into the overall development effort, there are ways RAD can end up increasing costs. RAD is reliant on high levels of user commitment and participation, so it is crucial that key members of the user community be involved during the entire RAD process. The problem is that key users have their own work to do. Pulling key individuals away from their own work can come at a high cost to the organization. If the key user can't do his or her job because of a RAD effort, the organization must either wait for the user to get back to the job or find another way to accomplish the same work. Neither solution is optimal and the organization may ultimately suffer. Again, a suitable balance has to be found between a key user's commitment to his or her job and to the RAD effort.

Table 13-2 Advantages & Disadvantages of RAD

Advantages	Disadvantages
Dramatic time savings during the system development effort.	More speed and lower cost may lead to lower overall system quality (e.g., due to lack of attention to internal controls).
Can save time, money, and human effort.	Danger of misalignment of system developed via RAD with the business due to missing information on underlying business processes.
Tighter fit between user requirements and system specifications.	May have inconsistent internal designs within and across systems.
Works especially well where speed of development is important, as with rapidly changing business conditions or where systems can capitalize on strategic opportunities.	Possible violation of programming standards related to inconsistent naming conventions and insufficient documentation.
Ability to rapidly change system design as demanded by users.	Difficulties with module reuse for future systems.
System optimized for users involved in RAD process.	Lack of scalability designed into the system.
Concentrates on essential system elements from user viewpoint.	Lack of attention to later systems administration built into the system (e.g., not integrated into overall enterprise data model and missing system recovery features).
Strong user stake and ownership of system.	High costs of commitment on the part of key user personnel.

Clearly, RAD is a powerful approach to information systems development, with the potential for many payoffs. Just as clearly, there are risks associated with using RAD, especially for every systems development project in an organization's portfolio of projects. The relative advantages and disadvantages of the RAD approach are summarized in Table 13-2.

SUMMARY

Rapid Application Development (RAD) is an alternative to the traditional systems development life cycle. All of the phases of the traditional life cycle are included in RAD, but the phases are executed at an accelerated rate. RAD relies on heavy user involvement, Joint Application Development sessions, prototyping, integrated CASE tools, and code generators to design and implement systems quickly. The abbreviated RAD life cycle, as defined by James Martin, begins with requirements planning, followed by user design, construction, and cutover.

The primary advantage of RAD is the quick development of systems, but quick development may also lead to cost savings and higher quality systems. RAD does have drawbacks: with its emphasis on developing systems quickly, the detailed business models that underlie information systems are often neglected, leading to the risk that systems may be out of alignment with the overall business. Similarly, the speed of development may lead to analysts overlooking systems engineering concepts such as consistency, programming standards, module reuse, scalability, and systems administration. If applied successfully, however, RAD may result in dramatic savings and improved performance. Systems may be designed and implemented in one-quarter to one-half the time needed for the traditional life cycle approach.

KEY TERMS

Rapid Application Development (RAD)

REVIEW QUESTIONS

1. Define each of the following terms:
   a. prototyping
   b. JAD
   c. Rapid Application Development
   d. user design
   e. requirements planning
2. List and briefly define the four phases of RAD, as defined by James Martin.
3. List and briefly explain two different views for the four pillars of RAD.
4. Explain the systems development components essential to RAD.
5. What trends in information systems encouraged the invention of the RAD approach to systems development?
6. Explain the concept of scalability and its influence on systems development.
7. List the major phases of the RAD life cycle used by Cambridge Technology Partners and briefly explain them.
8. Compare the Martin and Cambridge Technology Partners RAD approaches.
9. Explain the advantages and disadvantages of RAD.
10. Given the relative advantages and disadvantages of RAD, why would a systems development group follow the RAD approach for a project? When is the best time to use RAD and when is the best time to use a more traditional method?
11. What is the role of JAD in Rapid Application Development?

PROBLEMS AND EXERCISES

1. Match the following terms to the appropriate definitions:

   _____ RAD

   _____ prototyping

   _____ code generation

   a. process that allows the automatic writing of programs from system specifications

   b. iterative process of revising a system through close work between an analyst and users

   c. systems development methodology that relies on heavy user involvement, JAD, prototyping, and CASE

2. Compare RAD and prototyping. How are these methodologies different from one another? In what ways are they similar?
3. How might RAD be used in conjunction with the structured systems development life cycle? Are RAD and the SDLC totally different approaches or could they complement each other?

4. What types of tools are necessary to do RAD? Is it possible to do RAD without fourth-generation languages and other tools?

5. One of the criticisms of RAD is that RAD may cause a system to be out of alignment with the direction of the business. Explain how this may occur and suggest what might be done to overcome this potential hazard of RAD.

6. The example of the use of RAD by Cambridge Technology Partners involves the development of a decision support system (DSS). Do you think RAD could be applied to other types of systems besides DSSs? Why or why not? Are the criticisms of RAD outlined in this chapter more or less important depending on the type of information system being developed?

7. Consider Figure 13-1. From what you read in this chapter, answer the following questions:

    a. How does the RAD planning phase differ from the corresponding SDLC phases?

    b. How does the RAD design phase differ from the corresponding SDLC phases?

    c. How does the RAD development phase differ from the corresponding SDLC phases?

    d. How does the RAD cutover phase differ from the corresponding SDLC phases?

8. Describe the characteristics of a situation requiring a new information system that would be ideal for the use of the RAD approach.

9. Consider Figures 13-2 and 13-3. Which of these two viewpoints on the essential pillars for RAD helps you the most to understand the keys to successful application of RAD? Why?

10. Consider Table 13-1. Explain what you would do during RAD to avoid the following classic development mistakes:

    a. Unrealistic expectations

    b. Insufficient planning

    c. Overly optimistic schedules

FIELD EXERCISES

1. Electronic Data Systems (EDS) uses a form of RAD which they call SLC–RISE (Systems Life Cycle–Rapid Iterative Systems Engineering). Contact a systems analyst at EDS or at a client organization and investigate the impact of this methodology on systems development projects. Have all systems professionals in the client organization embraced RISE? What does the RISE methodology do to address some of the potential RAD hazards outlined in this chapter?

2. Contact an organization that has done a RAD-based systems development project. Investigate why they chose that project using RAD as opposed to some other methodology also used in their organization. Explain what factors that organization considers when deciding to conduct a project using a RAD or an SDLC methodology. What factors do they consider contribute to the success of a RAD-based project?

3. If you have access to a CASE tool as part of your course, study the features that might be helpful in support of RAD. Which components of the CASE tool would be helpful in which RAD life cycle phases? What capabilities are missing? If you do not have access to a CASE tool, contact an organization that uses a CASE tool and

investigate how they use that tool in RAD or to accomplish some of the goals of RAD. Document your findings in a report.

4. Visit the Borland Delphi Web site (http://netserv.borland.com/delphi/cases) and other Web sites to find additional RAD success stories. From these stories or cases, what do you personally conclude are the keys to successful use of the RAD approach? Why?

REFERENCES

Borland Delphi Website, *http://netserv.borland.com/delphi/cases.*

Bourne, K.C. 1994. "Putting Rigor Back in RAD."' *Database Programming & Design* 7(8):25–30.

Brooks, F.P., Jr. 1995. *The Mythical Man-Month, Anniversary Edition.* Reading, MA: Addison-Wesley.

Classe, A. 1996. "Rapid Reaction." *ComputerWeekly* (Jan. 25) located on Web page *http://www.computerweekly.co.uk/cwhome.asp.*

Gibson, M.L. and C.T. Hughes, 1994. *Systems Analysis and Design: A Comprehensive Methodology with CASE.* Danvers, MA: Boyd & Fraser Publishing Company.

Harrar, G. 1993. "Welcome to IS Boot Camp." *Forbes ASAP* 152(10):112–118.

Martin, J. 1991. *Rapid Application Development.* New York: Macmillan Publishing Company.

McConnell, S. 1996. *Rapid Development.* Redmond, WA: Microsoft Press.

PART

V

Logical and Physical Design

IVI Publishing

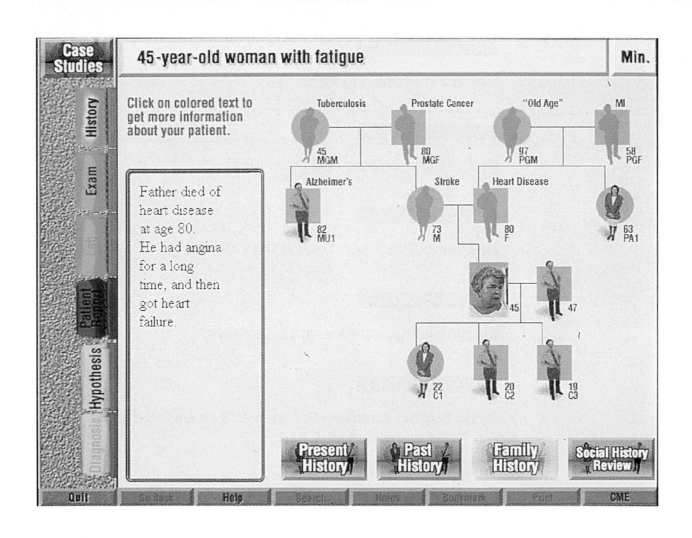

Creating a Conversation Between Computer and User

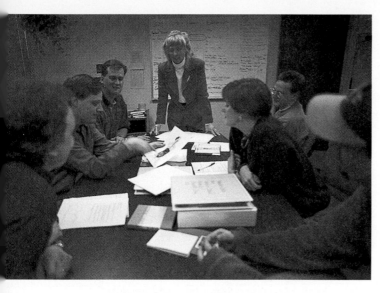

IVI Publishing was formed in 1991 to publish interactive multimedia software titles, initially on CD-ROM, with a focus on health and medical information. IVI had dozens of award-winning products and was the leading publisher of health and medical information for professionals (for example, doctors) and consumers. IVI had approximately 100 employees, a relatively flat organizational structure, and a team-based approach.

For professionals, IVI produced *PrimePractice,* a quarterly interactive magazine which provides continuing education to primary care physicians. IVI developed this software with Mayo Clinic doctors and the appropriate accrediting agencies so that doctors can receive continuing medical education credit for using the soft-

ware. For adult consumers, IVI and the Mayo Clinic produced a line of interactive CD-ROMs, including *Family Health Book, The Total Heart, Sports Health and Fitness,* and *Family Pharmacist.* For children, IVI produced *Anna Tommy* and *Safety Monkey* (also with the Mayo Clinic) as well as *What Is a Belly Button?, Welcome to Body Land,* and *The Virtual Body* (with Time-Life).

IVI is as innovative in their business processes as they are with their products. They are continually trying to improve their internal business processes. They completed a business process reengineering project which involved a team of 17 people who focused on completely redesigning the software design process for their products. As a result of this reengineering process, they produced a "Clean Plate" document which describes their new streamlined software design process. IVI previously took nine months to complete a new product. The length of the new software development process—including software design, building, and testing—is shorter than the previous process by one third.

Whereas other software publishers have one person design a new product alone, literally in a vacuum with no input from other designers or users, IVI used a team approach. An executive producer sponsors a new product project and a senior designer is assigned as the project leader. The senior designer consults with system engineers, artists, graphic designers, a product manager from marketing, content experts (for example, doctors), and users to design the new software. The core team then works with a professional facilitator to conduct extensive user testing in a special laboratory environment with computers and audio/visual recording equipment. IVI often conducted such product testing in separate cities for a demographic sampling of various users' reactions to new products, features, and functionality.

To support this collaborative design approach, each project was assigned to a large dedicated collaborative workroom equipped with personal computers and peripherals, whiteboards, noteboards, conference tables and chairs, and phones. IVI also supported individual workspaces in addition to these team rooms. IVI had many of these collaborative workrooms, with seven such rooms in one wing of the building alone. Project team members commonly spent several hours a day in the workroom collaborating on their project.

The innovation of IVI's business processes is matched by the innovation of their design philosophy. Dori Pelz-Sherman, senior designer, explains that while pure graphic designers provide useful input into the interactive software design process, graphic design skills do not necessarily transfer well to the interactive software design process. Designers like Pelz-Sherman are described as "conceptual interactive designers." They have to be concerned not only about the aesthetics of the software but also about whether or not the software is functional, easily understood, and useful. Pelz-Sherman believes that, for interactive software, the designer must get into the head of the user and create interfaces that lighten the "cognitive load." Content of the software must drive the visuals. She constantly asks herself, "What is the point of this software? What will the user want and need to do with it, and how?"

While print conventions have taken over 500 years to evolve, interactive software is very new. Pelz-Sherman argues that in the most closely related discipline, graphic design, designers have been trained almost exclusively in the fine arts and have had little experience or training with the analysis and presentation of data, cognitive science, or user-machine interactivity. She cites the work of Wurman who has argued that the graphic design profession bestows awards for appearance rather than for understandability. She borrows a line from Wurman that there are no Oscars, Emmys, or Tonys for making graphics comprehensible.

Pelz-Sherman represents a new breed of designer at IVI. She has an undergraduate double major in Visual Arts and English, with a teaching degree for both areas and a master's degree in Design and Instructional Technology at San Diego State University. Because programs in interactive software design are so rare, she customized an advanced degree by combining coursework in instructional design, computing, graphic design, and psychology.

IVI Chief Executive Officer Ron Buck has said that he would like people to think of IVI for the way they work rather than for what they produce. Given the success of IVI's products and its innovative management practices, IVI is likely to be remembered equally for their software products, business processes, and management practices.

An Overview of Part V

Logical and Physical Design

Part III covered the activities necessary to determine and structure information system requirements. Then in Part IV we showed you how to use two newer systems development approaches, object orientation and Rapid Application Development (RAD), to produce system specifications. For both object orientation and RAD, which rather seamlessly combine analysis with design, you got a taste of logical and physical design issues. In this part of the text, we cover these important areas in depth.

Logical design is often the first phase of the systems development life cycle in which you and the user develop a concrete understanding of how the system will operate. Although you may have developed prototypes for selected system functions, it is during logical design that you define the "look and feel" of all system inputs, outputs, and interfaces and dialogues. Also, during logical design you supplement the conceptual data model from the analysis phase with new data requirements. These are identified as you design system inputs and outputs and then transform all data requirements into a new type of data model, the relational database model.

As depicted in Figure 1, logical design includes the following steps:

- *Designing forms (hard copy and computer displays) and reports,* which describe how data will appear to users in system inputs and outputs

- *Designing interfaces and dialogues,* which describe the pattern of interaction between system users and software

- *Designing logical databases,* which describe a standard structure for the database of a system that is easy to implement in a variety of database technologies

Logical design is tightly linked to previous systems development phases, especially analysis. For example, every system input and output you develop during logical design will appear as a data flow between a manual and automated process or between a source/sink and an automated process in data flow diagrams. In fact, you must develop a form or report design for every data flow between a user and the system. Also, the E-R diagram from conceptual data modeling is the typical starting point for logical data modeling. Because you often discover additional data requirements from prototypes of the system's inputs and outputs, logical data modeling is not simply a transformation process from the E-R data model. In addition, the events on a state-transition diagram which correspond to user actions (for

Figure 1

Steps in Logical Design

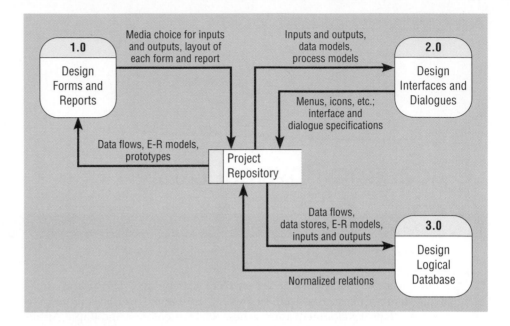

example, cancel an order) prescribe menu selections, buttons, or commands on computer displays.

The three subphases of logical design are not necessarily sequential. The logical design of system inputs and outputs, interfaces, and databases interact to identify flaws and missing elements. Thus, the project dictionary or CASE repository becomes an active and evolving component of system development management during logical design. It is only when each logical design element (forms and reports, interface and dialogue, and logical database) is consistent with others and satisfactory to the end user that you know logical design is complete.

In Chapter 14 you will learn the principles and guidelines for usable system inputs and outputs. Your overall goal in formatting the presentation of data to users should be usability: helping users of all types to use the system efficiently, accurately, and with satisfaction. The achievement of these goals can be greatly improved if you follow certain guidelines on the way to present data on business forms, visual display screens, printed documents, and other kinds of media.

Fortunately, there has been considerable research on how to present data to users, and Chapter 14 summarizes and illustrates the most useful of these guidelines. You will see how to place titles on system inputs and outputs, how and when to highlight data for users, how to effectively use color, how to display textual data, how to organize lists and tables for readability and use, and how to design graphical output formats. You will also understand how poor design of data input and output can bias users' understanding of data. The material in Chapter 14 applies to both graphical user interface environments, like Microsoft Windows or Apple Macintosh, as well as character-based systems.

Chapter 15 addresses principles you should follow in tying all the system inputs and outputs together into an overall pattern of interaction between users and the system. System interfaces and dialogues form a conversation that provides users access to and navigation between each system function. Chapter 15 discusses the principles of building on-line systems in which users interact directly with the application system. One choice you must make is the style of interaction: command language, menus, forms, objects or icons, and natural language. You must also choose among alternative hardware, such as a keyboard, mouse, or graphics tablet. We will briefly review when to use each of these interaction styles and hardware.

As part of system interface design, there are additional choices you must make about how a user can enter, edit, and display data during data entry. The choices include providing for cursor control, editing characters, exiting system tasks, and providing help to users. Central to all interfaces is providing user feedback. You must choose the type of status information, prompting messages, and error and warning indications. We also review various controls that you can include in the interface design to improve data entry accuracy. All of these interface elements must be designed during the logical design process.

One of the specifications that you must provide to those who will program an on-line information system is the sequence of on-line forms and when each is displayed. Guidelines for consistency, shortcuts, reversal of actions, and control will help you decide on usable dialogues. Dialogue diagramming is a graphical tool that specifies which on-line form is accessible from a given form.

Principles of good interface and dialogue design apply in almost every computer environment. Graphical user interface (GUI) environments, however, present special issues since they permit so many variations and options. Although GUI forms, reports, and dialogues are illustrated throughout Chapters 14 and 15, Chapter 15 closes with a review of special interface design topics and design guidelines for a GUI environment.

Data make up a core system element that is studied in all systems development methodologies. You have seen how data flow diagrams (DFDs) and E-R diagrams are used to depict the data requirements of a system. Both of these diagrams are very flexible and give you considerable latitude in how you represent data. For example, you can use one or many data stores with a process in a DFD. E-R diagrams provide more structure, but an entity can still be either very detailed or rather aggregate. During the data modeling subphase of logical design, discussed in Chapter 16, you define data in its most fundamental form, called normalized data. *Normalization* is a well-defined method of identifying relationships between each data attribute and representing all the data so that they cannot logically be broken down into more detail. The goal is to rid the data design of unwanted anomalies which would make a database susceptible to errors and inefficiencies.

Normalization is driven by the concept of functional dependencies, which are atomic relationships among data. In Chapter 16 you will learn about the relationship between functional dependencies and different normal forms and how to transform unnormalized data into well-structured data called *relations*. Also, you will learn how to identify functional dependencies in system inputs and outputs and how to translate these and E-R models into relations. You will also learn how to merge the relations that represent several system inputs and outputs and an E-R diagram into one consolidated set of relations, which will then be the basis for physical database design.

The deliverables of logical design include detailed, functional specifications for system inputs, outputs, interfaces, dialogues, and databases. Often these elements are represented in prototypes, or working versions. The project dictionary or CASE repository is updated to include each form, report, interface, dialogue, and relation design. Due to considerable user involvement in reviewing prototypes and specifications during logical design, and due to the fact that logical and physical design phases can be scheduled with considerable overlap in the project baseline plan, there often is not a formal review milestone or walkthrough after the logical design phase. If prototyping is not done, however, then you should conduct a logical design walkthrough similar to the walkthrough at the end of the analysis phase.

Chapters 14, 15, and 16 each conclude with a case from Broadway Entertainment Company (BEC). These cases illustrate the development of the Customer Activity Tracking System (CATS) as specific inputs, outputs, dialogues, and databases are specified.

The project team often expands during the physical design phase to include a variety of specialists in areas such as databases, computer security, data networks, systems controls and audits, programming, and development environments. The purpose of physical design is to specify all the technological characteristics of the system so that those involved in the implementation phase can concentrate on building the system, not on deciding how the system should be built. Prior phases dealt with what the system should do and how the system should look to the user. In contrast, physical design specifies the structures for data and programs that will make the system work efficiently and securely, including considerations for the location of data and data processing on a computer network.

As depicted in Figure 2, physical design includes these steps:

- *Designing physical files and databases*—describes how data will be stored and accessed in secondary computer memory and how the quality of data will be ensured

- *Designing system and program structures*—describes the various programs and program modules that correspond to the data flow diagrams and other documentation developed in prior life cycle stages

- *Designing distributed processing strategies*—describes how your system will make data and processing available to users on computer networks within the capabilities of existing computer networks

Physical design is tightly linked to previous systems development phases, especially analysis and logical design. For example, data flow diagrams outline all the various processing steps required in the system. These steps must be transformed into programs and program modules, traditionally described as hierarchies of processing units rather than in flow diagrams. Programs will accept or produce data

Figure 2
Steps in Physical Design

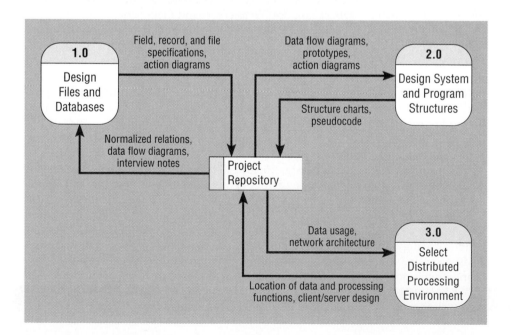

through the forms and reports designed during logical design. In physical design, the functional capabilities of system inputs, outputs, and dialogues are specified within the constraints of the implementation tools. Finally, physical file and database design uses the normalized relations developed in logical data modeling.

As with prior life cycle phases, it is possible that during physical design you will discover inadequacies or errors in the logical design. So, iteration back to previous phases to gather additional information or to fill in gaps in the design is quite possible. Since physical design is the last life cycle phase before implementation, this is your last chance to make sure the system design is complete and consistent— before the cost to correct mistakes escalates. You will also generate new information to be stored in the CASE repository or project dictionary.

The three subphases of physical design are not necessarily sequential. The physical design of files and databases and the physical design of distributed processing methods interact to identify flaws and missing elements in each other. Furthermore, the references to physical data elements in program design charts and the physical structure of files and databases must be consistent. Finally, for a program module that accesses files, the logic of how the data will be accessed must match the storage and file structure capabilities provided in the file design. Thus, the project dictionary or CASE repository remains an active and evolving centralized data source for the management of system development during physical design.

During the design of physical files and databases, the subject of Chapter 17, you will learn about the wide variety of decisions that you must make in order to create efficient data storage and accessing methods. Your overall goal in designing files and databases is to balance the costs to store, access, and maintain data in secondary computer memory such as hard disks. Because there are so many options available, and the options you have depend on the environment in which the system will be built, this chapter reviews only the general decisions you will have to make.

File and database design is presented in a bottom-up fashion in Chapter 17. First you learn about how to translate attributes, or columns, from normalized relations into physical data field specifications; the choice of data types and coding schemes is emphasized. Next, we review issues in the formation of records, including reasons why you might want to violate data normalization in order to improve data processing performance. Then, you will study the pros and cons of various methods for arranging records within a computer file, called file organizations. This is followed by an overview of the database design choices you must make, including the selection of the appropriate architecture for a database and the associated database management system. One of the most important decisions made during the design of files and databases is the choice of indexes for providing rapid access to data based on content; the chapter provides guidelines for choosing indexes.

Central to the design of data storage and access is controlling the integrity of data as they are captured and stored. Chapter 17 covers controls on fields, such as range checks and default values, which help to create accurate data. Contamination and even destruction of data are inevitable in complex, modern information systems; you will therefore also learn about methods to recover data after a failure has occurred.

Next, Chapter 18 addresses techniques and principles you should use in the structuring of systems and programs to give programs an easily understood and maintainable form. You need to transform the sequential flow of data between processes in data flow diagrams (a conceptual design notation), into hierarchical structures that can guide programmers in building programs. Program structure is typically represented as a hierarchy of main and iteratively subordinate modules. A chart showing such a hierarchical structure is called a structure chart, and Chapter 18 reviews the notation used in these charts.

Chapter 18 shows you how to translate data flow diagrams into structure charts for different types of systems. Once program modules are shown in their hierarchical relationship with one another, the processing logic in each module must be specified. This processing logic is outlined in a generic language called pseudocode, which can be translated easily into any programming language. Thus, the physical system and program specifications developed in this step can be translated into a variety of development environments, or even a mixed environment if parts of the system will be implemented in different platforms. Nassi-Shneiderman diagramming, a popular alternative notation, is also introduced, since some organizations prefer this notation over pseudocode.

Developing well-structured programs is guided by two principles, *coupling* and *cohesion*. In Chapter 18 you will learn more about these principles and how to identify their different forms and the desirable and undesirable properties of these different forms. Chapter 18 gives you both the notations and the principles to apply as you transform the logical design of the system into its physical program structure.

Most modern information systems are shared systems: they are used by several or many people who work at geographically dispersed locations. Special issues arise in such distributed processing environments not present in stand-alone or single-user systems; Chapter 19 addresses these special issues. In most cases, the design of an individual information system does not change the basic design of computer networks in an organization. As the system's designer, you must be aware of the options you have within existing networks so that you can design your system for efficiency and integrity. Thus, Chapter 19 concentrates on the issues involved in designing an information system in a distributed processing environment, not on the design of telecommunications networks.

A common platform for modern systems is local area networks (LANs). Chapter 19 reviews several forms of networks, including different types of client/server networks, and highlights how systems are built differently for each network environment. Since many organizations support both file server and client/server networks, the chapter provides guidelines on when each is applicable so that you can choose the right network for your application.

Distributed systems mean that potentially both data and programs can be handled on multiple, linked computers. A fundamental question is where to locate data in a network of computers. Options for distributing data are compared in Chapter 19 so that you know which factors to consider when addressing a data distribution decision. In data distribution, you allocate whole or parts of files to secondary memory media at different computers. The goal is to locate data as close as possible to where they are needed, with a controlled amount of redundancy. As usual, you are trying to balance data storage, accessing, and maintenance costs.

The chapter concludes with an overview of the evolving alternatives for distribution of data processing functions in a computer network. It is shown that three general components of systems—data presentation, data analysis, and data management—can be placed in various combinations on local PCs, server computers, or both. The features of six different combinations of locating these system functions are compared so that you can understand the relative merits and risks of each.

Chapters 17, 18, and 19 each concludes with a case from Broadway Entertainment Company (BEC). These cases illustrate the development of the Customer Activity Tracking System (CATS) as physical files, databases, and programs are designed. The BEC case following Chapter 19 raises issues related to data privacy and ethics confronting organizations that store extensive data about customers in their information systems.

Designing Forms and Reports

After studying this chapter, you should be able to:

- Explain the process of designing forms and reports and the deliverables for their creation.

- Describe and contrast the differences between internal information, external information, and turnaround documents.

- Apply the general guidelines for formatting forms and reports.

- Use color and know when color improves the usability of information.

- Format text, tables, and lists effectively.

- Describe how the formatting of information can bias users' understanding.

- Explain how to assess usability and describe how variations in users, tasks, technology, and environmental characteristics influence the usability of forms and reports.

INTRODUCTION

In this chapter, you will learn guidelines to follow when designing forms and reports. In general, forms are used to present or collect information on a single item such as a customer, product, or event. Forms can be used for both input and output. Reports, on the other hand, are used to convey information on a collection of items. Form and report design is a key ingredient for successful systems. As users often equate the quality of a system to the quality of its input and output methods, you can see that the design process for forms and reports is an especially important activity. And since information can be collected and formatted in many ways, gaining an understanding of the dos and don'ts and the trade-offs between various formatting options is a useful skill for all systems analysts.

In the next section, the process of designing forms and reports is briefly described and we also provide guidance on the deliverables produced during this process. Guidelines for formatting information are then provided which serve as the building blocks for designing all forms and reports. This is followed by a short discussion on how information can be presented in order to bias understanding.

The final major section describes methods for assessing the usability of form and report designs.

DESIGNING FORMS AND REPORTS

This is the first chapter focusing on logical design within the systems development life cycle (see Figure 14-1). In this chapter, we describe issues related to the design of system inputs and outputs—forms and reports. In Chapter 15, we focus on the logical design of dialogues and interfaces, which are how users interact with systems. Due to the highly related topics and guidelines in these two chapters, they form one conceptual body of guidelines and illustrations that jointly guide the design of all aspects of system inputs and outputs. Chapter 16 focuses on logical database design. In each of these chapters, your objective is to gain an understanding of how you can transform information gathered during analysis into a coherent design. Although all logical design issues are related, topics discussed in this chapter on designing forms and reports are especially relative to those in the following chapter—the design of dialogues and interfaces.

   System inputs and outputs—forms and reports—were identified during requirements structuring. The kinds of forms and reports the system will handle were established as part of the design strategy formed at the end of the analysis

Figure 14-1
Systems development life cycle with logical design phase highlighted

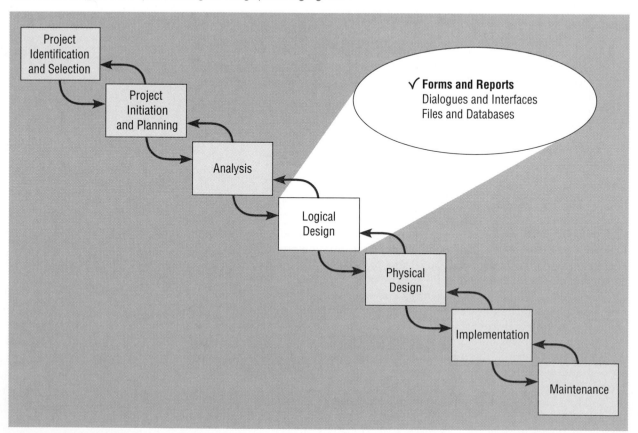

phase of the systems development process. During analysis, however, you may not have been concerned with the precise appearance of forms and reports, only with which ones needed to exist and what their contents were. You may have distributed prototypes of forms and reports which emerged during analysis as a way to confirm requirements with users. Forms and reports are integrally related to various diagrams developed during requirements structuring. For example, every input form will be associated with a data flow entering a process on a DFD, and every output form or report will be a data flow produced by a process on a DFD. This means that the contents of a form or report correspond to the data elements contained in the associated data flow. Further, the data on all forms and reports must consist of data elements in data stores and on the E-R data model for the application, or must be computed from these data elements. (In rare instances, data simply go from system input to system output without being stored within the system.) It is common that, as you design forms and reports, you will discover flaws in DFDs and E-R diagrams; the project dictionary or CASE tool repository, therefore, continues to be the central and constantly updated source of all project information.

If you are unfamiliar with computer-based information systems, it will be helpful to clarify exactly what we mean by a form or report. A **form** is a business document containing some predefined data and often includes some areas where additional data are to be filled in. Most forms have a stylized format and are usually not in a simple row and column format. Examples of business forms are product order forms, employment applications, and class registration sheets. Traditionally, forms have been displayed on a paper medium, but today video display technology allows us to duplicate the layout of almost any printed form, including an organizational logo or any graphic, on a video display terminal. Forms displayed on a video display may be used for data display or data entry. Additional examples of forms are an electronic spreadsheet, computer sign-on or menu, and an ATM transaction layout.

A **report** is a business document containing only predefined data; it is a passive document used solely for reading or viewing. Examples of reports are invoices, weekly sales summaries by region and salesperson, and a pie chart of population by age categories. We usually think of a report as printed on paper, but it may be printed to a computer file, a visual display screen, or some other medium such as microfilm. Often a report has rows and columns of data, but a report may consist of any format—for example, mailing labels. Frequently, the differences between a form and a report are subtle. A report is only for reading and often contains data about multiple unrelated records in a computer file. On the other hand, a form typically contains data from only one record or is, at least, based on one record, such as data about one customer, one order, or one student. The guidelines for the design of forms and reports are very similar.

Form: A business document that contains some predefined data and may include some areas where additional data are to be filled in. An instance of a form is typically based on one database record.

Report: A business document that contains only predefined data; it is a passive document used solely for reading or viewing. A report typically contains data from many unrelated records or transactions.

The Process of Designing Forms and Reports

Designing forms and reports is a user-focused activity that typically follows a prototyping approach (see Figure 1-9). First, you must gain an understanding of the intended user and task objectives by collecting initial requirements during requirements determination. During this process, several questions must be answered. These questions attempt to answer the "who, what, when, where, and how" related to the creation of all forms or reports (see Table 14-1). Gaining an understanding of these questions is a required first step in the creation of any form or report.

For example, understanding who the users are—their skills and abilities—will greatly enhance your ability to create an effective design. In other words, are your users experienced computer users or novices? What is their educational level,

TABLE 14-1 Fundamental Questions when Designing Forms and Reports

1. Who will use the form or report?

2. What is the purpose of the form or report?

3. When is the form or report needed and used?

4. Where does the form or report need to be delivered and used?

5. How many people need to use or view the form or report?

business background, and task-relevant knowledge? Answers to these questions will provide guidance for both the format and content of your designs. Also, what is the purpose of the form or report? What task will users be performing and what information is needed to complete this task? Other questions are also important to consider. Where will the users be when performing this task? Will users have access to on-line systems or will they be in the field? Also, how many people will need to use this form or report? If, for example, a report is being produced for a single user, the design requirements and usability assessment will be relatively simple. A design for a larger audience, however, may need to go through a more extensive requirements collection and usability assessment process.

After collecting the initial requirements, you structure and refine this information into an initial prototype. Structuring and refining the requirements are completed independently of the users, although you may need to occasionally contact users in order to clarify some issue overlooked during analysis. Finally, you ask users to review and evaluate the prototype. After reviewing the prototype, users may accept the design or request that changes be made. If changes are needed, you will repeat the construction-evaluate-refinement cycle until the design is accepted. Usually, several iterations of this cycle occur during the design of a single form or report. As with any prototyping process, you should make sure that these iterations occur rapidly in order to gain the greatest benefits from this design approach.

The initial prototype may be constructed in numerous environments. The obvious choice is to use a CASE tool or the standard development tools used within your organization. Often, initial prototypes are simply mock screens that are not working modules or systems. Mock screens can be produced from a word processor, computer graphics design package, or electronic spreadsheet. It is important to remember that the focus of this phase within the SDLC is on the *design*—content and layout. How specific forms or reports are implemented (for example, the programming language or screen painter code) is left to later phases. Nonetheless, tools for designing forms and reports are rapidly evolving. In the past, inputs and outputs of all types were typically designed by hand on a coding or layout sheet. For example, Figure 14-2 shows the layout of a disk operating system (DOS) shell program using a coding sheet.

Although coding sheets are still used, their importance has diminished due to significant changes in system operating environments and the evolution of automated design tools. Prior to the creation of graphical operating environments, for example, analysts designed many inputs and outputs that were 80 columns (characters) by 25 rows, the standard dimensions for most video displays. These limits in screen dimensions are radically different in graphical operating environments such as Microsoft's Windows® where font sizes and screen dimensions can often be changed from user to user. Consequently, the creation of new tools and develop-

Figure 14-2
Designing a screen layout using a coding sheet

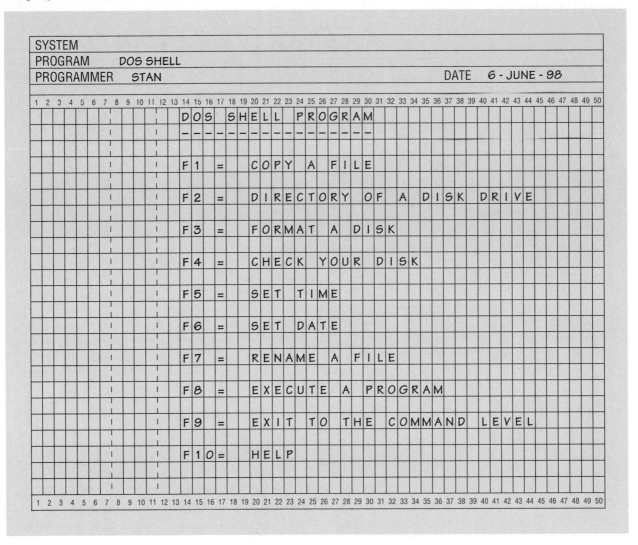

ment environments was needed to help analysts and programmers develop these graphical and flexible designs. Figure 14-3 shows an example of the same DOS shell screen as designed in Microsoft's Visual Basic®. Note the variety of fonts, sizes, and highlighting that was used. Needless to say, on-line graphical tools for designing forms and reports are rapidly becoming the de facto standard in most professional development organizations.

Deliverables and Outcomes

Each SDLC phase helps you to construct a system. In order to move from phase to phase, each phase produces some type of deliverable that is used in a later phase or activity. For example, within the project initiation and planning phase of the SDLC, the Baseline Project Plan serves as input to many subsequent SDLC activities. In the case of designing forms and reports, design specifications are the major

Figure 14-3
Designing a form using
Microsoft's Visual Basic®

deliverables and are inputs to the system implementation phase. Design specifications have three sections:

1. Narrative overview

2. Sample design

3. Testing and usability assessment

The first section of a design specification contains a general overview of the characteristics of the target users, tasks, system, and environmental factors in which the form or report will be used. The purpose is to explain to those who will actually develop the final form why this form exists and how it will be used so that they can make the appropriate implementation decisions. In this section, you list general information and the assumptions that helped shape the design. For example, Figure 14-4 shows an excerpt of a design specification for a Customer Account Status form for Pine Valley Furniture. The first section of the specification, Figure 14-4a, provides a narrative overview containing the relevant information to developing

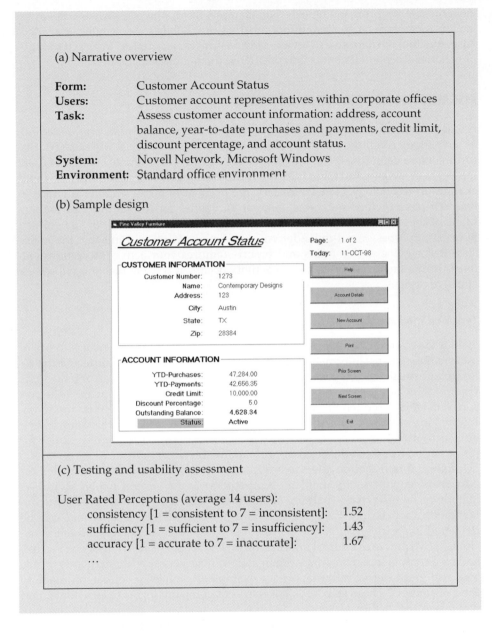

Figure 14-4
Design specification for the
design of forms and reports

(a) Narrative overview

(b) Sample design

(c) Testing and usability
assessment

(a) Narrative overview

Form:	Customer Account Status
Users:	Customer account representatives within corporate offices
Task:	Assess customer account information: address, account balance, year-to-date purchases and payments, credit limit, discount percentage, and account status.
System:	Novell Network, Microsoft Windows
Environment:	Standard office environment

(b) Sample design

(c) Testing and usability assessment

User Rated Perceptions (average 14 users):
consistency [1 = consistent to 7 = inconsistent]:   1.52
sufficiency [1 = sufficient to 7 = insufficiency]:   1.43
accuracy [1 = accurate to 7 = inaccurate]:   1.67
...

and using the form within PVF. The overview explains the tasks supported by the form, where and when the form is used, characteristics of the people using the form, the technology delivering the form, and other pertinent information. For example, if the form is delivered on a visual display terminal, this section would describe the capabilities of this device, such as whether it has a touch screen and whether color and a mouse are available.

In the second section of the specification, Figure 14-4b, a sample design of the form is shown. This design may be hand-drawn using a coding sheet although, in most instances, it is developed using CASE or standard development tools. Using actual development tools allows the design to be more thoroughly tested and assessed. The final section of the specification, Figure 14-4c, provides all testing and usability assessment information. Procedures for assessing designs are described later in the chapter. Some specification information may be irrelevant when designing some forms and reports. For example, the design of a simple Yes/No selection form may be so straightforward that no usability assessment is needed. Also, much of the narrative overview may be unnecessary unless intended to highlight some exception that must be considered during implementation.

FORMATTING FORMS AND REPORTS

A wide variety of information can be provided to users of information systems and, as technology continues to evolve, a greater variety of data types will be used. Unfortunately, a definitive set of rules for delivering every type of information to users has yet to be defined and these rules are continuously evolving along with the rapid changes in technology. Nonetheless, a large body of human-computer interaction research has provided numerous general guidelines for formatting information. Many of these guidelines will undoubtedly apply to the formatting of all evolving information types on yet-to-be-determined devices. Keep in mind that the mainstay of designing usable forms and reports requires your active interaction with users. If this single and fundamental activity occurs, it is likely that you will create effective designs.

Types of Information

Internal information: Information that is collected, generated, or consumed within an organization.

Within the context of building information systems, there are two general types of information: internal information and external information. **Internal information** refers to information that is collected, generated, or consumed within an organization. Examples include lengthy reports summarizing business activity, such as salesperson or machine productivity, production scrap rates, forecasting trends, and so on. Internal information can also consist of simple informational reports summarizing daily activities, such as a sales contact report that a salesperson might produce for his or her boss or the forms used to collect daily travel expenditures.

External information: Information that is collected from or created for individuals and groups external to an organization.

External information refers to information that is collected from or created for customers, suppliers, stockholders, competitors, or the general public. Examples include receipts, invoices, packing slips, checks, quarterly reports, product documentation, and so on. Like internal information, external information can be delivered in a variety of formats and media. For example, an automated teller machine (ATM) produces external information on both paper (e.g., a transaction receipt) and on a computer display. Many organizations have very specific standards for the formatting of external information, for example, to convey a consistent image to their customers. These standards cover use of company logos, colors, fonts, and paper size and quality.

Turnaround document: Information that is delivered to an external customer as an output that can be returned to provide new information as an input to an information system.

A hybrid type of information that is both internal and external is called a **turnaround document.** A turnaround document is produced by a system as an output that may also "turn around" and return to the organization as an input. An example of a turnaround document is a warranty card for a Pine Valley Furniture product, shown in Figure 14-5. The bottom half of the card explains the product warranty to the customer. The top portion is a detachable registration card that must be returned to Pine Valley to register a purchase. This form has pre-printed system-generated information that a customer must verify and return to PVF. The customer also adds new information (e.g., name and address). The verified and new information then serves as an input to PVF's customer warranty tracking system. Other common examples of turnaround documents are credit card and utility bills.

Some turnaround documents within high-volume transaction-based systems can contain computer-readable information such as a bar code (Figure 14-6a) or

Figure 14-5
An example of a turnaround document (Pine Valley Furniture)

computer-readable text and numbers that are read using an optical or magnetic ink character reader. For example, the bottom of most bank checks contain computer-readable account information (Figure 14-6b) that is read by an optical character reader as input into a check-processing system. The keyless processing of computer-readable information not only speeds processing and customer service but also significantly reduces data entry errors.

You can format internal and external information in a variety of ways. For example, when producing a document using a preprinted form, only the unique data for the form is printed onto the paper. This is similar to how information can be typed onto a preprinted form using a typewriter (see Figure 14-7 for an example of a preprinted form). Alternatively, laser and page printers now make it possible to generate the headings and labels of a form or report along with the data when displayed or printed. This alternative allows you to print on normal paper stock, and

Figure 14-6
Keyless data entry options

(a) Bar code

(b) Optical character
recognition

special forms do not have to be kept in inventory only to become obsolete when requirements or design change. Different methods of producing standard forms and
reports will, of course, influence the cost of producing information. Cost concerns
are beyond the scope of our discussion, but these costs are primarily influenced by
the type of media used. The types of media for displaying system-generated information is also beyond the scope of our discussion; see Alter (1999) for a review of
this topic.

A variety of media can be used to deliver system information. From a design
perspective, you must determine whether users will interact directly with the system—the information will be available on-line—or whether information will be
collected and provided on paper—that is, on hard copy. Another distinction, and
the one we are focusing on here, is whether system information is processed on-
line or in batch.

On-line processing: The collection and delivery of the
most recent available information, typically through an
on-line workstation.

On-line processing refers to the collection and delivery of the most recent available information, typically through an on-line workstation. On-line processing is
preferred under the following conditions:

1. Access to or capture of the information occurs randomly.

2. The format and type of information are not consistent (for example, an ad
   hoc query).

3. Information is continuously changing and the most current information is
   needed for proper processing and decision making.

Figure 14-7
Example of a pre-printed form

Application For Employment	Pine Valley Furniture

Personal Information

Name:	Date:
Social Security Number:	
Home Address:	
City, State, Zip	
Home Phone:	Business Phone:
U.S. Citizen?	If Not Give Visa No. & Expiration:

Position Applying For

Title:	Salary Desired:
Referred By:	Date Available:

Education

High School (Name, City, State):	
Graduation Date:	
Business or Technical School:	
Dates Attended:	Degree, Major:
Undergraduate College:	
Dates Attended:	Degree, Major:
Graduate School:	
Dates Attended:	Degree, Major:

References

Form #2019
Last Revised: 9/15/98

4. Users are in locations where there is easy access to an information system or a remotely connected terminal.

Any one or all of these criteria suggest that information be processed on-line. There are many other factors—user characteristics, task, technological, and physical environment—that can also influence your design decisions (see below).

Batch processing, on the other hand, refers to the input or output of system information on a predetermined and specific time interval. This means that information collected or generated through batch processing has a shelf life of a limited time period whereas on-line processing always represents the most recent available information. Note, however, that batch processing can be collected and delivered both on-line or on hard copy. For example, when viewing an *on-line* batch processing report, users would access a static textual or graphical report from a terminal or workstation. In this case, the display is on-line, but the data are not current. Alternatively, a *hard copy* batch processing report would simply be a system output produced on some type of media such as a printer. For batch output, it is important to know both the date (and possibly time) the output is produced as well as when the data were current. For example, a system might produce a month-end sales report on the 10th of the following month.

Batch processing is preferred under the following conditions:

1. Access to information occurs regularly.

2. The format and type of information are consistent.

3. Information is stable for some time period and/or the users' informational needs do not require the most up-to-date information for effective decision making or task performance.

4. Users are in locations where access to an on-line information system or remotely connected terminal is not possible or extremely difficult.

Other factors to consider when choosing on-line versus batch processing relate to information control—assuring that only approved users have access to specific information. The most secure method of delivering information is using on-line delivery that requires a password for viewing. For hard copy information, routing slips and internal and external mail systems are used to help control unauthorized access to confidential outputs. Now that you understand how information can be processed and delivered, we will next focus on information formatting issues.

General Formatting Guidelines

Over the past several years, industry and academic researchers have spent considerable effort investigating how information formatting influences individual task performance and perceptions of usability. Through this work, several guidelines for formatting information have emerged (see Table 14-2). These guidelines reflect some of the general truths that apply to the formatting of most types of information (for more information, the interested reader should see the books by Shneiderman, 1992; Carroll, 1991; and Norman, 1991).

The differences between a well-designed form or report and one that is poorly designed will often be obvious to you. For example, Figure 14-8a shows a poorly designed form for viewing a current account balance for a PVF customer. Figure 14-8b (page 2 of 2) is a better design incorporating several general guidelines from Table 14-2.

The first major difference between the two forms has to do with the title. The title on Figure 14-8a is ambiguous whereas the title on Figure 14-8b clearly and specifically describes the contents of the form. The form in Figure 14-8b also includes

TABLE 14-2 General Guidelines for the Design of Forms and Reports

Meaningful Titles:

Clear and specific titles describing content and use of form or report

Revision date or code to distinguish a form or report from prior versions

Current date which identifies when the form or report was generated

Valid date which identifies on what date (or time) the data in the form or report were accurate

Meaningful Information:

Only needed information should be displayed

Information should be provided in a manner that is usable without modification

Balanced Layout:

Information should be balanced on the screen or page

Adequate spacing and margins should be used

All data and entry fields should be clearly labeled

Easy Navigation:

Clearly show how to move forward and backward

Clearly show where you are (e.g., page 1 of 3)

Notify user when on the last page of a multipaged sequence

Adapted from Dumas, 1988.

the date on which the form was generated so that, if printed, it will be clear to the reader when this occurred. Figure 14-8a displays information that is extraneous to the intent of the form—viewing the current account balance—and provides information that is not in the most useful format for the user. For example, Figure 14-8a provides all customer data as well as account transactions and a summary of year-to-date purchases and payments. The form does not, however, provide the current outstanding balance of the account without making a manual calculation. The layout of information between the two forms also varies in balance and information density. Gaining an understanding of the skills of the intended system users and the tasks they will be performing is invaluable when constructing a form or report. By following these general guidelines, your chances of creating effective forms and reports will be enhanced. In the next sections we will discuss specific guidelines for highlighting information, using color, displaying text, and presenting numeric tables and lists.

Highlighting Information

As display technologies continue to improve, there will be a greater variety of methods available to you for highlighting information. Table 14-3 provides a list of the most commonly used methods for highlighting information. Given this vast array of options, it is more important than ever to consider how highlighting can be used to enhance an output and not prove a distraction. In general, highlighting should be used sparingly to draw the user to or away from certain information and to group together related information. There are several situations when highlighting can be a valuable technique for conveying special information:

- Notifying users of errors in data entry or processing

- Providing warnings to users regarding possible problems such as unusual data values or an unavailable device

Figure 14-8
Contrasting customer
information forms (Pine
Valley Furniture)

(a) Poorly designed form

(b) Improved design
for form

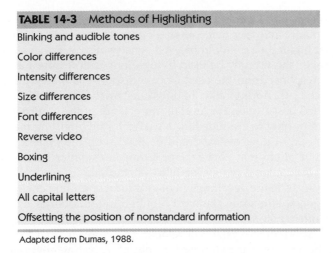

TABLE 14-3   Methods of Highlighting

Blinking and audible tones

Color differences

Intensity differences

Size differences

Font differences

Reverse video

Boxing

Underlining

All capital letters

Offsetting the position of nonstandard information

Adapted from Dumas, 1988.

- Drawing attention to keywords, commands, high priority messages, and data that have changed or gone outside normal operating ranges

Additionally, many highlighting techniques can be used singularly or in tandem, depending upon the level of emphasis desired by the designer. Figure 14-9 shows a form where several types of highlighting are used. In this example, boxes clarify different categories of data; capital letters and different fonts distinguish labels from actual data; and intensity is used to draw attention to important data.

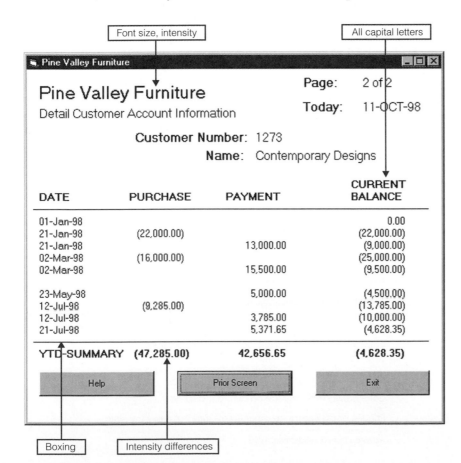

Figure 14-9
Customer account status display using various highlighting techniques (Pine Valley Furniture)

Much research has focused on the effects of varying highlighting techniques on task performance and user perceptions. A general guideline resulting from this research is that highlighting should be used conservatively. For example, blinking and audible tones should only be used to highlight critical information requiring an immediate response from the user. Once a response is made, these highlights should be turned off. Additionally, highlighting methods should be consistently used and selected based upon the level of importance of the emphasized information. It is also important to examine how a particular highlighting method appears on all possible output devices that could be used with the system. For example, some color combinations may convey appropriate information on one display configuration but wash out and reduce legibility on another.

Recent advances in the development of graphical operating environments have provided designers with some standard highlighting guidelines. However, these guidelines are often quite vague and are continuously evolving, leaving a great deal of control in the hands of the systems developer. Therefore, in order for organizations to realize the benefits of using standard graphical operating environments—such as reduced user training time and interoperability among systems—you must be disciplined in how you use highlighting.

Color versus No-Color

Color is a powerful tool for the designer in influencing the usability of a system. When applied appropriately, color provides many potential benefits to forms and reports, summarized in Table 14-4. As the use of color displays became widely available during the 1980s, a substantial amount of color versus no-color research was conducted. The objective of this research was to gain a better understanding of the effects of color on human task performance (see, for example, Benbasat, Dexter, and Todd, 1986).

The general findings from this research were that the use of color had positive effects on user task performance and perceptions when the user was under time constraints for the completion of a task. Color was also beneficial for gaining greater understanding from a display or chart. An important conclusion from this research

TABLE 14-4 Benefits and Problems from Using Color

Benefits from Using Color:

Soothes or strikes the eye.

Accents an uninteresting display.

Facilitates subtle discriminations in complex displays.

Emphasizes the logical organization of information.

Draws attention to warnings.

Evokes more emotional reactions.

Problems from Using Color:

Color pairings may wash out or cause problems for some users (e.g., color blindness).

Resolution may degrade with different displays.

Color fidelity may degrade on different displays.

Printing or conversion to other media may not easily translate.

Adapted from Shneiderman, 1992.

was that color was *not* universally better than no-color. *The benefits of color only seem to apply if the information is first provided to the user in the most appropriate presentation format.* That is, if information is most effectively displayed in a bar chart, color can be used to enhance or supplement the display. If information is displayed in an inappropriate format, color has little or no effect on improving understanding or task performance.

There are also several problems associated with using color, also summarized in Table 14-4. Most of these dangers are related more to the technical capabilities of the display and hard copy devices than misuse. However, color blindness is a particular user issue that is often overlooked in the design of systems. Shneiderman (1992) reports that approximately eight percent of the males in the European and North American communities have some form of color blindness. He suggests that you first design video displays for monochrome and allow color (or better yet, a flexible palette of colors) to be a user-activated option. He also suggests that you limit the number of colors and where they are applied, using color primarily as a tool to assist in the highlighting and formatting of information.

Displaying Text

In business-related systems, textual output is becoming increasingly important as text-based applications such as electronic mail, bulletin boards, and information services (e.g., Dow Jones) are more widely used. The display and formatting of system help information, which often contains lengthy textual descriptions and examples, is one example of textual data which can benefit from following a few simple guidelines that have emerged from past research (see Table 14-5). The first guideline is simple: you should display text using common writing conventions such as mixed upper and lower case and appropriate punctuation. If space permits, text should be double-spaced and, minimally, a blank line should be placed between each paragraph. You should also left-justify text with a ragged right margin—research shows that a ragged right margin makes it easier to find the next line of text when reading than when text is both left- and right-justified.

When displaying textual information, you should also be careful not to hyphenate words between lines or use obscure abbreviations and acronyms. Users may not know whether the hyphen is a significant character if it is used to continue words across lines. Information and terminology that are not widely understood by the intended users may significantly influence the usability of the system. Thus, you should use abbreviations and acronyms only if they are significantly shorter than the full text and are commonly known by the intended system users. Figure 14-10 shows two versions of a help screen from an application systems at PVF. Figure 14-10a shows many violations of the general guidelines for displaying text whereas 14-10b

TABLE 14-5 Guidelines for Displaying Text	
Case	Display text in mixed upper and lower case and use conventional punctuation.
Spacing	Use double spacing if space permits. If not, place a blank line between paragraphs.
Justification	Left-justify text and leave a ragged right margin.
Hyphenation	Do not hyphenate words between lines.
Abbreviations	Use abbreviations and acronyms only when they are widely understood by users and are significantly shorter than the full text.

Adapted from Dumas, 1988.

Figure 14-10
Contrasting the display of textual help information

(a) Poorly designed form

(b) Improved design for form

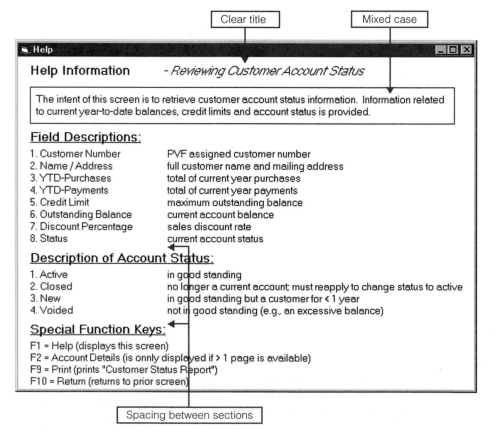

shows the same information but follows the general guidelines for displaying text. Formatting guidelines for the *entry* of text and alphanumeric data is also a very important topic. These guidelines are presented in Chapter 15, *Designing Interfaces and Dialogues,* where we focus on issues of human-computer interaction.

Designing Tables and Lists

Unlike textual information, where context and meaning are significantly derived through reading, the context and meaning of tables and lists are significantly derived from the format of the information. Consequently, the usability of information displayed in tables and alphanumeric lists is likely to be much more influenced by effective layout than most other types of information display. As with the display of textual information, tables and lists can also be greatly enhanced by following a few simple guidelines. These are summarized in Table 14-6.

Figure 14-11 displays two versions of a form design from a Pine Valley Furniture application system that displays customer year-to-date transaction information in a table format. Figure 14-11a displays the information without consideration of the guidelines presented in Table 14-6 and Figure 14-11b (only page 2 of 2 is shown) displays this information after consideration of these guidelines.

One key distinction between these two display forms relates to labeling. The information reported in Figure 14-11b has meaningful labels that more clearly stand out as labels compared to the display in Figure 14-11a. Transactions are sorted by date and numeric data are right-justified and aligned by decimal point in Figure 14-11b,

---

TABLE 14-6 General Guidelines for Displaying Tables and Lists

Use meaningful labels:

All columns and rows should have meaningful labels.

Labels should be separated from other information by using highlighting.

Re-display labels when the data extend beyond a single screen or page.

Formatting columns, rows, and text:

Sort in a meaningful order (e.g., ascending, descending, or alphabetic).

Place a blank line between every five rows in long columns.

Similar information displayed in multiple columns should be sorted vertically (that is, read from top to bottom, not left to right).

Columns should have at least two spaces between them.

Allow white space on printed reports for user to write notes.

Use a single typeface, except for emphasis.

Use same family of typefaces within and across displays and reports.

Avoid overly fancy fonts.

Formatting numeric, textual, and alphanumeric data:

Right-justify *numeric data* and align columns by decimal points or other delimiter.

Left-justify *textual data.* Use short line length, usually 30–40 characters per line (this is what newspapers use, and it is easier to speed read).

Break long sequences of *alphanumeric data* into small groups of three to four characters each.

Adapted from Dumas, 1988.

Figure 14-11
Contrasting the display of
tables and lists (Pine Valley
Furniture)

(a) Poorly designed form

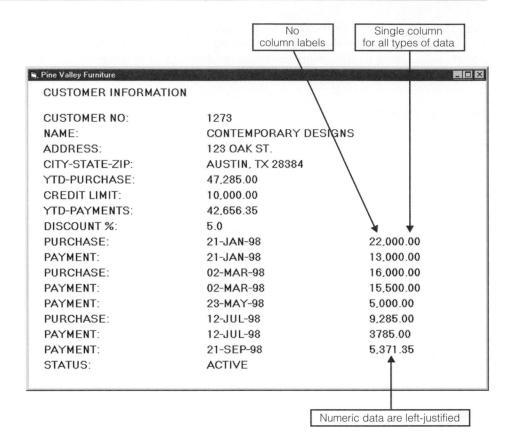

which helps to facilitate scanning. Adequate space is left between columns, and blank lines are inserted after every five rows in Figure 14-11b to help ease the finding and reading of information. Such spacing also provides room for users to annotate data that catch their attention. Taken together, using a few simple rules significantly enhanced the layout of the information for the user.

Most of the guidelines in Table 14-6 are rather obvious, but this and other tables serve as a quick reference to validate that your form and report designs will be usable. It is beyond our scope here to discuss each of these guidelines, but you should read each carefully and think about why each is appropriate. For example, why should labels be repeated on subsequent screens and pages (the third guideline in Table 14-6)? One explanation is that pages may be separated or copied and the original labels will no longer be readily accessible to the reader of the data. Why should long alphanumeric data (see the last guideline) be broken into small groups? (If you have a credit card or bank check, look at how your account number is displayed.) Two reasons are that the characters will be easier to remember as you read and type them, and there will be a natural and consistent place to pause when you speak them over the phone; for example, when you are placing a phone order for products in a catalog.

A fundamental choice when you design the display of numeric information is to determine whether a table or a graph should be used. A considerable amount of research focusing on this topic has been conducted (see, for example, Jarvenpaa and Dickson, 1988, for very specific guidelines on the use of tables and graphs). In general, this research has found that tables are best when the user's task is related to finding an individual data value from a larger data set whereas line and bar graphs are more appropriate for gaining an understanding of data changes over

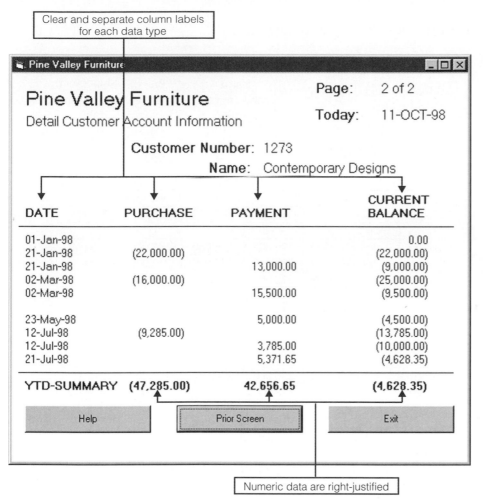

Clear and separate column labels for each data type

Figure 14-11 *(continued)*

(b) Improved design for form

Numeric data are right-justified

time (see Table 14-7). For example, if the marketing manager for Pine Valley Furniture needed to review the actual sales of a particular salesperson for a particular quarter, a tabular report like the one shown in Figure 14-12 would be most useful. This report has been annotated to emphasize good report design practices. The

TABLE 14-7 Guidelines for Selecting Tables vs. Graphs
Use Tables for
Reading individual data values
Use Graphs for
Providing a quick summary of data
Detecting trends over time
Comparing points and patterns of different variables
Forecasting activities
Reporting vast amounts of information when relatively simple impressions are to be drawn

Adapted from Jarvenpaa and Dickson, 1988.

Figure 14-12
Tabular report illustrating numerous design guidelines (Pine Valley Furniture)

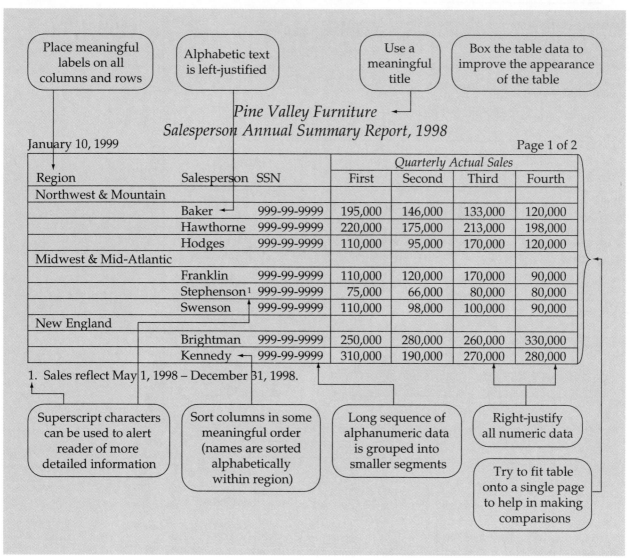

report has both a printed date as well as a clear indication, as part of the report title, of the period over which the data apply. There is also sufficient white space to provide some room for users to add personal comments and observations. Often, to provide such white space, a report must be printed in landscape, rather than portrait, orientation. Alternatively, if the marketing manager wished to compare the overall sales performance of each sales region, a line or bar graph would be more appropriate (see Figure 14-13). As with other formatting considerations, the key determination as to when you should select a table or a graph is the task being performed by the user.

FORMATTING INFORMATION TO AVOID BIAS

A goal of this chapter is to help you understand how to select appropriate formats for conveying information on forms and reports. Unfortunately, this understanding is not widely held. For example, there are countless examples of unintended (or intended) biasing of information displayed on television or reported in the popular press. For example, in many automobile advertisements, bar charts are used with biased scales to project greater (or fewer) differences (depending upon their objective!) among products. As a designer of information systems, how you format information can have a tremendous influence on how information is perceived by users. In this section, we discuss information bias as it relates to the design of forms and reports. For a more general and somewhat humorous examination of information bias, see Huff's classic book *How to Lie with Statistics.*

There are several ways in which the format of output can bias user perceptions. Information biasing is often unavoidable and not necessarily a bad thing. It is simply the result of how the format of data can have intentional or unintentional influence on users. As a designer of system output, your role is to understand the sources of bias so that you can design outputs to either minimize their effects on users or to provide users with the ability to review information in order to gain an objective understanding of their data.

Bias can be introduced by both the type and format of the information provided. Sources of bias can include

1. Providing information (table or graph) that does not match the user's task

2. Providing charts that contain too many items

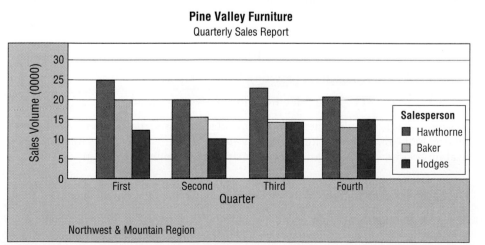

Figure 14-13
Graphs for comparison

(a) Line graph

(b) Bar graph

3. Using colors and highlighting improperly

4. Providing charts that use improper scaling

Providing tables and graphs that do not directly match the user's task is a common source of bias. An example of this is to provide a user with information in a table that might best be delivered as a graph. A more subtle example of introducing bias would be through the use of sorting. For example, suppose that a manager makes customer support assignments for support personnel based upon criteria such as hours worked or years of experience. If a report is produced listing support personnel sorted on some other criteria (for example, alphabetically by last name) it may be difficult for the manager to make the proper assignments.

A related source of bias is to include too much information on a graph or report so that finding the important information is too difficult. For example, too many lines, bars, data items, labels, and fonts can obscure the task-relevant information from the user. In these instances, users can experience information overload which often puts unwanted variance into a user's task performance. On the other hand, information can be summarized to such a point that distinctions between items are impossible to make or are irrelevant. Additionally, the improper or inconsistent use of color and highlighting can draw a user's attention away from important task-relevant information.

Another source of bias that is regularly found in output from the mass media, as well as from information systems, relates to information scaling. Information scaling refers to the range of values reported on a graph or table. For example, the scales for graphs should typically begin at zero and end with some value near, but greater than, the maximum value on the graph (see Figure 14-14a). To bias users' perceptions that there are greater differences between items on a graph than there really are can be done by setting the bottom of the scale to greater than zero (see Figure 14-14b). Alternatively, less variance between items can be implied by setting the top end of the scale much greater than any of the items' top end on the graph maximum value (see Figure 14-14c). Although the same data were used to construct the three graphs in the figure, the use of different scales suggests very different meanings to users. Making unusual adjustments to the high and low scales for graphs and tables is a commonly used biasing technique when advertising many products. Such techniques can also be used to bias system output.

ASSESSING USABILITY

There are many factors to consider when you design forms and reports. The objective for designing forms, reports, and all human-computer interactions is **usability.** Usability typically refers to the following three characteristics:

1. *Speed.* Can you complete a task efficiently?

2. *Accuracy.* Does the output provide what you expect?

3. *Satisfaction.* Do you like using the output?

In other words, usability means that your designs assist, not hinder, user performance. In the remainder of this section, we describe numerous factors that influence usability and several techniques for assessing the usability of a design.

Usability Success Factors

Research and practical experience have found that design consistency is the key ingredient in designing usable systems. Consistency significantly influences users'

Normal Scale
Bottom of Scale = 0
Top of Scale = near maximum value

Figure 14-14
How scaling can bias the
meaning of information

(a) No bias in scaling

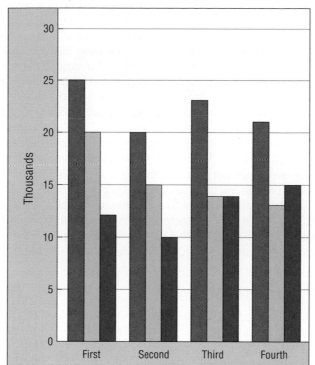

Biased Scale
Bottom of Scale = 10,000
Top of Scale = near maximum value

Biased Scale
Bottom of Scale = 0
Top of Scale = too much greater than maximum value

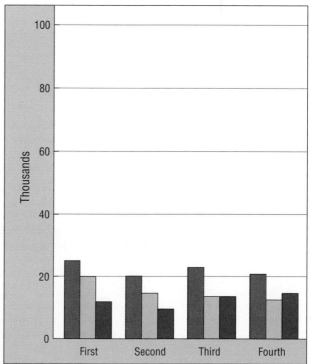

(b) Nonzero bottom of scale

(c) Too high top of scale

ability to gain proficiency when interacting with a system. Consistency means, for example, that titles, error messages, menu options, and other design elements appear in the same place and look the same on all forms and reports. Consistency also means that the same form of highlighting has the same meaning each time it is used and that the system will respond in roughly the same amount of time each time a particular operation is performed. Other important factors found to be important include efficiency, ease (or understandability), format, and flexibility. Each of these usability factors, with associated guidelines, is described in more detail in Table 14-8.

When designing outputs, you must also consider the context in which the screens, forms, and reports will be used. As mentioned, numerous characteristics play an important role in shaping a system's usability. These characteristics are related to the intended users and task being performed in addition to the technological, social, and physical environment in which the system and outputs are used. Table 14-9 lists several factors in which variations in any item may influence the usability of a design. Your role is to gain a keen awareness of these factors so that your chances of creating highly usable designs are increased.

Measures of Usability

User friendliness is a term often used, and misused, to describe system usability. Although the term is widely used, it is too vague from a design standpoint to provide adequate information because it means different things to different people. Consequently, most development groups use several methods for assessing usability, including these considerations (Shneiderman, 1992):

- Time to learn
- Speed of performance

TABLE 14-8   General Design Guidelines for Usability of Forms and Reports

Usability Factor	Guidelines for Achievement of Usability
Consistency	Consistent use of terminology, abbreviations, formatting, titles, and navigation within and across outputs. Consistent response time each time a function is performed.
Efficiency	Formatting should be designed with an understanding of the task being performed and the intended user. Text and data should be aligned and sorted for efficient navigation and entry. Entry of data should be avoided where possible (e.g., computing rather than entering totals).
Ease	Outputs should be self-explanatory and not require users to remember information from prior outputs in order to complete tasks. Labels should be extensively used, and all scales and units of measure should be clearly indicated.
Format	Information format should be consistent between entry and display. Format should distinguish each piece of data and highlight, not bury, important data. Special symbols, such as decimal places, dollar signs, and +/− signs should be used as appropriate.
Flexibility	Information should be viewed and retrieved in a manner most convenient to the user. For example, users should be given options for the sequence in which to enter or view data and for use of shortcut keystrokes, and the system should remember where the user stopped during the last use of the system.

TABLE 14-9	Characteristics for Consideration When Designing Forms and Reports
Characteristic	**Consideration for Form and Report Design**
User	Issues related to experience, skills, motivation, education, and personality should be considered.
Task	Tasks differ in amount of information that must be obtained from or provided to the user. Task demands such as time pressure, cost of errors, and work duration (fatigue) will influence usability.
System	The platform on which the system is constructed will influence interaction styles and devices.
Environment	Social issues such as the users' status and role should be considered in addition to environmental concerns such as lighting, sound, task interruptions, temperature, and humidity. The creation of usable forms and reports may necessitate changes in the users' physical work facilities.

Adapted from Norman, 1991.

- Rate of errors
- Retention over time
- Subjective satisfaction

In assessing usability, you can collect information by observation, interviews, keystroke capturing, and questionnaires. Time to learn simply reflects how long it takes the average system user to become proficient using the system. Equally important is the extent to which users remember how to use inputs and outputs over time. The manner in which the processing steps are sequenced and the selection of one set of keystrokes over others can greatly influence learning time, the user's task performance, and error rates. For example, the most commonly used functions should be quickly accessed in the fewest number of steps (for example, pressing one key to save your work). Additionally, the layout of information should be consistent, both *within and across* applications, whether the information is delivered on a screen display or hard copy report.

SUMMARY

We present this chapter first in a sequence of three chapters on logical system design topics since it focuses on a primary product of information systems: designing forms and reports. As organizations move into more complex and competitive business environments with greater diversity in the workforce, the quality of the business processes will determine success. One key to designing quality business processes is the delivery of the right information to the right people, in the right format, at the right time. The design of forms and reports concentrates on this goal. A major difficulty of this process comes from the great variety of information-formatting options available to designers.

We saw in this chapter that information can take three general forms: internal—for use within the organization; external—for distribution to customers, suppliers, and other parties outside the organization; and turnaround—documents which are produced for outside parties and returned as input to an internal system. Information processing can occur at pre-determined and regular times after sufficient data are collected, called batch processing, or it can be created or entered at user request, called on-line processing.

Specific guidelines should be followed when designing forms and reports. These guidelines, proven over years of experience with human-computer interaction, help you to create professional, usable systems. The chapter presented a variety of guidelines covering use of titles, layout of fields, navigation between pages or screens, highlighting data, use of color, format of text and numeric data, appropriate use and layout of tables and graphs, avoiding bias in information display, and achieving usable forms and reports.

Form and report designs are created through a prototyping process. Once created, designs may be stand-alone or integrated into actual working systems. The purpose, however, is to show users what a form or report will look like when the system is implemented. The outcome of this activity is the creation of a specification document where characteristics of the users, tasks, system, and environment are outlined along with each form and report design. Performance testing and usability assessments may also be included in the design specification.

The goal of form and report design is usability. Usability means that users can use a form or report quickly, accurately, and with high satisfaction. To be usable, designs must be consistent, efficient, self-explanatory, well-formatted, and flexible. These objectives are achieved by applying a wide variety of guidelines concerning such aspects as navigation, use of highlighting and color, display of text, tables, and lists.

K E Y   T E R M S

Batch processing	Internal information	Turnaround document
External information	On-line processing	Usability
Form	Report	

R E V I E W   Q U E S T I O N S

1. Define each of the following terms:
   a. batch processing
   b. external information
   c. internal information
   d. on-line processing
   e. turnaround document

2. Contrast the following terms:
   a. batch processing, on-line processing
   b. external information, internal information, turnaround document
   c. form, report

3. Describe the prototyping process of designing forms and reports. What deliverables are produced from this process? Are these deliverables the same for all types of system projects? Why or why not?

4. To which initial questions must the analyst gain answers in order to build an initial prototype of a system output?

5. Describe what is meant by the term internal information and provide at least three examples (not already used in this chapter) in your answer.

6. Describe what is meant by the term external information and provide at least three examples (not already used in this chapter) in your answer.

7. Describe what is meant by the term turnaround document and provide at least three examples (not already used in this chapter) in your answer.

8. What factors make the delivery of on-line information most practical? What factors make the delivery of batch processing most practical?

9. When can highlighting be used to convey special information to users?

10. Discuss the benefits, problems, and general design process for the use of color when designing system output.

11. How should textual information be formatted on a help screen?

12. What type of labeling can you use in a table or list to improve its usability?

13. What column, row, and text formatting issues are important when designing tables and lists?

14. Describe how numeric, textual, and alphanumeric data should be formatted in a table or list.

15. Using examples, discuss four ways in which the type and format of information can bias its meaning.

16. Provide some examples where variations in user, task, system, and environmental characteristics might impact the design of system forms and reports.

PROBLEMS AND EXERCISES

1. Match the following terms to the appropriate definitions.

   _____ form
   _____ balance
   _____ report
   _____ highlighting

   a. a way to draw attention to or away from data in output
   b. type of output that typically lists and summarizes data from several unrelated database records
   c. a characteristic of output which includes minimal density of information in the output
   d. type of output that typically lists data associated with one database record

2. Imagine that you are to design a budget report for a colleague at work using a spreadsheet package. Following the prototyping discussed in the chapter (see also Figure 1-9), describe the steps you would take to design a prototype of this report.

3. Consider a system that produces budget reports for your department at work. Alternatively, consider a registration system that produces enrollment reports for a department at a university. For whichever system you choose, answer the following design questions. Who will use the output? What is the purpose of the output? When is the output needed and when is the information that will be used within the output available? Where does the output need to be delivered? How many people need to view the output?

4. Imagine the worst possible reports from a system. What is wrong with them? List as many problems as you can. What are the consequences of such reports? What could go wrong as a result? How does the prototyping process help guard against each problem?

5. How many turnaround documents have you encountered in the past 30 days at work, home, school, or from any other organization? List what you like and dislike about these documents. Using one of these documents, describe how it could be improved.

6. Imagine a moderately sized flower shop. List as many internal and external informational items as you can for this business. Which of the internal information items should be delivered to users as on-line and/or hard copy reports? Will there be any turnaround documents? If so, describe.

7. Consider your answer for the previous question about the flower shop. Use the relevant criteria in this chapter to determine whether the output should be processed on-line or in batch.

8. Imagine an output display form for a hotel registration system. Using a software package for painting and/or drawing, such as MacPaint, Paintbrush, or Corel Draw, follow the design suggestions in this chapter and design this form entirely in black and white. Save the file and then, following the color design suggestions in this chapter, redesign the form using color. Based on this exercise, discuss the relative strengths and weaknesses of each output form.

9. Consider reports you might receive at work (e.g., budgets or inventory reports) or at a university (e.g., grade reports or transcripts). Evaluate the usability of these reports in terms of speed, accuracy, and satisfaction. What could be done to improve the usability of these outputs?

10. List the PC-based software packages you like to use. Describe each package in terms of the following usability characteristics: time to learn, speed of performance, rate of errors by users, retention over time, and subjective satisfaction. Which of these characteristics has led to your wanting to continue to use this package?

11. Given the guidelines presented in this chapter, identify flaws in the design of the Report of Customers shown below. What assumptions about users and tasks did you make in order to assess this design? Redesign this report to correct these flaws.

Report of Customers – 26-Oct-99

Cust-ID	Organization
AC-4	A.C. Nielson Co.
ADTRA-20799	Adran
ALEXA-15812	Alexander & Alexander, Inc.
AMERI-1277	American Family Insurance
AMERI-28157	American Residential Mortgage
ANTAL-28215	Antalys
ATT-234	AT&T Residential Services
ATT-534	AT&T Consumer Services
. . .	
DOLE-89453	Dole United, Inc.
DOME-5621	
DO-67	Doodle Dandies
. . .	
ZNDS-22267	Zenith Data System

12. Review the guidelines for attaining usability of forms and reports in Table 14-8. Consider an on-line form you might use to register a guest at a hotel. For each usability factor, list two examples of how this form could be designed to achieve that dimension of usability. Use examples other than those mentioned in Table 14-8.

FIELD EXERCISES

1. Find your last grade report. Given the guidelines presented in this chapter, identify flaws in the design of this grade report. Redesign this report to correct these flaws.

2. As stated in the chapter, most forms and reports are designed for contemporary information systems by using software to prototype output. Packages like Visual Basic, PowerBuilder, and Paradox for Windows have very sophisticated output design modules. Gain access to such a tool at your university or where you work and study all the features the software provides for the design of printed output. Write a report that lists and explains all the features for layout, highlighting, summarizing data, etc.

3. Investigate the display uses in another field (e.g., aviation). What types of forms and reports are used in this field? What standards, if any, are used to govern the use of these outputs?

4. Interview a variety of people you know about the different types of forms and reports they use in their jobs. Ask to examine a few of these documents and answer the following questions for each one:
   a. Do they provide internal or external information (or both)? Are any turnaround documents?
   b. Which are processed on-line, which are processed in batch?
   c. What types of tasks does each support and how is it used?
   d. What types of technologies and devices are used to deliver each one?
   e. Assess the usability of each form or report. Is each usable? Why or why not? How could each be improved?

5. Scan the annual reports from a dozen or so companies for the past year. These reports can usually be obtained in a university library. Describe the types of information and the ways that information has been presented in these reports. How have color and graphics been used to improve the usability of information? Describe any instances where formatting has been used to hide or enhance the understanding of information.

6. Choose a PC-based package you like to use and choose one that you don't like to use. Interview other users to determine their evaluations of these two packages. Ask each individual to evaluate each package in terms of the usability characteristics described in the previous question. Is there a consensus among these evaluations, or do the respondents' evaluations differ from each other or from your own evaluations? Why?

REFERENCES

Alter, S. 1999. *Information Systems: A Management Perspective.* 3/e. Reading, MA: Addison-Wesley

Benbasat, I., A. S. Dexter, and P. Todd. 1986. "The Influence of Color and Graphical Information Presentation in a Managerial Decision Simulation." *Human-Computer Interaction* 2: 65–92.

Carroll, J. M. 1991. *Designing Interaction.* Cambridge: Cambridge University Press.

Dumas, J. S. 1988. *Designing User Interfaces for Software.* Englewood Cliffs, NJ: Prentice-Hall.

Huff, D. 1954. *How to Lie with Statistics*. New York, NY: W. W. Norton.

Jarvenpaa, S. L., and G. W. Dickson. 1988. "Graphics and Managerial Decision Making: Research Based Guidelines." *Communications of the ACM* 31 (6): 764–74.

Norman, K. L. 1991. *The Psychology of Menu Selection*. Norwood, NJ: Ablex.

Shneiderman, B. 1992. *Designing the User Interface: Strategies for Effective Human-Computer Interaction*. Reading, MA: Addison-Wesley.

Logical Design: Designing a Customer Reservation Report

INTRODUCTION

In this case in the design of the Customer Activity Tracking System (CATS), we have been following the activities of Frank Napier, a systems analyst on the project. It is at this point that system outputs—screens, forms and reports—are being designed. Even though BEC has chosen prewritten software for CATS, outputs must be designed to verify that those in the package are adequate and to satisfy those requirements not provided in the package. The focus of this case is the customer-product assignment report, one of several reservation reports that is integral to the successful implementation of CATS. The customer-product assignment report is sent electronically to each store over BEC's private communications network and lists which customers have reserved which products. The report is stored on the file server at a store and a notification that a new report was sent is automatically displayed by the daily start-up routine from the store manager's personal computer. The report can be printed or used on-line. A store manager or other store personnel uses the report to notify customers that the product has arrived at the store and is available for purchase.

INITIATING THE DESIGN

During a recent meeting, Jordan Pippen explained Frank's next project assignment.

"Frank, the customer-product assignment report, or what I like to call the CPA report, is a very important component in the system. The CPA report is sent over the BEC network to each store from BEC headquarters and contains the customer-product reservation information generated by CATS. The report is sent to arrive the day the store receives a new product shipment and lists each reservation in a format that makes it easy for the store to call customers to let them know the products they reserved are in the store. Other

reservation reports serve other purposes, like helping the store set aside the right quantity of product to cover reservations. The information in the CPA report must be delivered to stores in a timely manner and in a format that makes it easy for personnel to do their job. The store must be able to track who needs to be called and who has been contacted. The CPA report will be an important way stores will interface with CATS. How our stores view the system will be significantly influenced by the usability of the CPA report."

"Wow," said Frank, "this *is* an important report. Is there anything special you want me to do during the design?"

"No, not really," said Jordan. "The strength of our design methodology is that it works fine for the design of both routine and high-profile outputs, such as the CPA report. Yet, you should give some thought to which clients you want to work with during the design and usability assessment process. We must get the right people involved in this one and then thoroughly understand how they will use the report."

"OK, I will get on it," replied Frank as he returned to his office.

DESIGNING THE CUSTOMER-PRODUCT ASSIGNMENT REPORT

After arriving back at his office, Frank reviewed the BEC output design methodology and was reminded that his first task was to answer several questions, questions that form the basis of the design. A summary of his work is shown in Figure 1. These questions and associated answers, along with his understanding of the information needed in the report, oriented Frank to his task. The next step was to identify individuals to help him design and assess the report. He remembered that Jordan had recently met with the managers of seven BEC retail stores with the highest sales figures. He thought, "Maybe those should be the users that I work with on this design?" After checking with

Figure 1
Fundamental questions and
answers to the design of the
customer reservation report

QUESTIONS	ANSWERS
Who will use the output?	All store managers and sales representatives
What is the purpose of the output?	Provide a list of customers with reservations Matching customers with inventory Provide a way for store to track contacts with customers concerning reservations
When is the output needed and used?	Needed (used) on (after) product delivery to store
Where does the output need to be delivered?	To each BEC store
How many people need to view the output?	The store manager and several sales representatives at each of several hundred stores in U.S.

Jordan for approval, he crafted an intracompany memo to these managers requesting their involvement in the design of the CPA report (Figure 2). The memo was routed to each manager via BEC's electronic mail system. He also asked Nancy Chen (VP of U.S. Operations) and Wendy Yoshimuro (marketing manager responsible for CATS) to serve as design and usability reviewers. Nancy, Wendy, and all store managers agreed to participate.

The process Frank followed in the design of the CPA report is based on BEC's prototyping methodology (see Figure 3). At this stage, users will not be working with the report since it will be delivered electronically to the stores, but they will see copies of sample reports on which they can base reactions. Having several different users actually interact with a system before implementation can be awkward and misleading for the users which is why a passive prototyping process is used. Assuring that the report is delivered conveniently to users will be done during final system acceptance testing after all CATS modules have been implemented.

Using the available information from analysis and talking with design participants, an initial design was developed (step 1) from the Developer/2000 CASE tool used at BEC (see Figure 4). Frank did this for two main reasons. First, the report could be linked to the rest of the CATS project repository for consistency among process, data, and interface models that show structured requirements. Second, from the report design the CASE tool could generate the necessary program code for the report for a variety of development platforms. The CPA report is one variation of the Reservation Report shown on DFDs for CATS (see Figure 4 in the BEC case after Chapter 8). Thus, the repository information about the composition of the

Reservation Report and other subflows on more detailed DFDs was a good starting point for Frank.

Most of the fields used to construct the prototype were already stored in the Developer/2000 CASE repository, so standards for the formatting of fields and their expected length were already established. An exception to this was the reservation code field; this was a new field and not yet represented in the repository. The intent of the field is to uniquely identify customers, products, and stores and, in essence, this field could be the concatenation of three fields—customer, product, and store identifiers. This would, however, be an extremely long field. Since the customer must report the contents of this field to a phone operator in order to make a reservation, Frank decided to make this field a relatively short five-character, alphanumeric sequence number. The actual selection of the field format is a physical design and implementation issue that will be finalized later in the project.

The initial design was sent to all design participants with clear assessment instructions (step 2) and a firm date for critiquing the design. To ease the review process, each participant was also given a design review form with a check-box for either approving the design or recording change requests (Figure 5). In this way, during the second step of the prototyping methodology, each participant has the opportunity to critique the design and suggest changes. During step 3, Frank's role is to collect all participant critiques and consolidate the feedback into an overall evaluation report. The conclusions from this report can lead to either of the following choices:

1. Refine the design based upon the collective feedback of the participants and return to step 1.

2. Finalize the design specification (step 4).

Figure 2
Memorandum requesting participation in the design of the customer-product assignment report

Memorandum

To: Selected BEC Store Managers, Nancy Chen, Wendy Yoshimuro

CC: Jordan Pippen

From: Frank Napier

Date: June 21, 1998

Subject: Request for help with an aspect of the Customer Activity Tracking System

As most of you are aware, BEC is actively working on the design of a new system, CATS, that will revolutionize the way in which we serve our customers. An important component of this system is a report summarizing the store-level reservations of customers and products. This report is called the customer-product assignment (CPA) report.

Due to your keen interest in this project and your awareness of the needs of the retail stores, you are being asked to participate in the design of this report. In order to move as quickly as possible, we must have your agreement to participate within one week (sooner if possible!).

See the attached document (an embedded object), The BEC Methodology for Designing Interfaces, Forms, and Reports, to get a better understanding of your role in this design process. I expect that this entire project will require less than 2 hours of your time.

Please respond to this request by either return e-mail, or by simply marking your decision below and faxing this sheet back to me at headquarters.

Check one:
☐ I agree to participate on the CPA report design team.
☐ I am sorry, but I won't be able to participate at this time.

_____   _____
Name (print)   Name (sign)

enclosure· The BEC Methodology for Designing Interfaces, Forms, and Reports

Figure 3
BEC's prototyping methodology for designing interfaces, forms, and reports

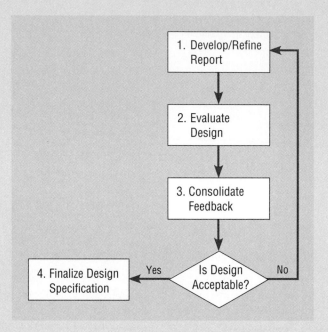

Figure 4
Initial design of the customer-product assignment report

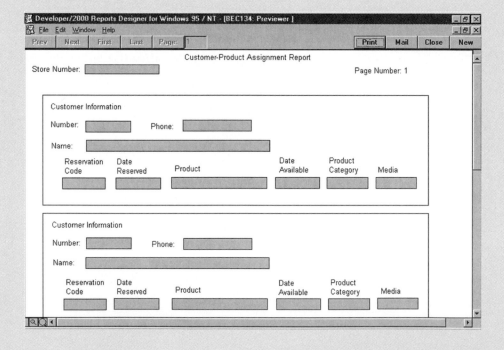

This means that if participants suggest changes, Frank must consolidate these changes into a revised design specification, sometimes resolving differences between conflicting suggestions. Using this feedback, he can then refine the design and repeat the evaluation and consolidation process until the design is accepted.

After three rounds, the design was accepted by the panel of users. During these iterations as well as during the usability assessment process, several changes to the original design were made. A final version of the report is shown in Figure 6, which highlights the differences between the initial and final

Figure 5
Design review form for the customer-product assignment report

Broadway Entertainment Company
Report Assessment Form

Name: Brett Williams

Location: Norman, OK – store #4

Report: CPA   Version: 1

☐ I accept the current design.
☒ I request that the following changes be considered.

- -

Importance (circle one)	*Description of Change*
Low Med High	
1 ----- (2) ----- 3	1. Need more descriptive wording for the media field – I suggest using word 'format' instead
1 ------ 2 ------ 3	2.
1 ------ 2 ------ 3	3.
1 ------ 2 ------ 3	4.
1 ------ 2 ------ 3	5.
1 ------ 2 ------ 3	6.
1 ------ 2 ------ 3	7.
1 ------ 2 ------ 3	8.
1 ------ 2 ------ 3	9.
1 ------ 2 ------ 3	10.

Figure 6
Final design of the customer-product report highlighting changes between the initial and final design

versions. Frank's next activity was to assess the usability of the report.

ASSESSING DESIGN USABILITY

The last major activity in the design of the CPA report was to assess its usability. When assessing design usability, BEC's methodology suggests that the following factors be considered:

- Time to learn
- Speed of performance
- Rate of errors
- Retention over time
- Subjective satisfaction

Since the report did not take users a significant amount of time to learn to use and since the report would be used daily, Frank determined that the most reasonable usability factors to assess for this report would be speed of performance, rate of errors, and subjective satisfaction. To make this assessment, he constructed a new sample report with fictitious customers and data. This report contained products of every category and combination. The length of the report was determined

by examining information collected during analysis. Frank's objective was to construct a report representative of those likely to be created by the actual system.

Next, he constructed a series of report evaluation questions about the content. These questions were recorded on a formal questionnaire that included questions related to three areas: background information on the person doing the assessment, objective questions of report comprehension, and user perceptions (see Figure 7 for questions excerpted from these three sections). Using both the sample report and evaluation questionnaire, Frank was now ready to assess the usability of the CPA report design. To do this, he identified a representative cross section of potential system users (both store managers and sales representatives, as identified in Figure 1). He then gave both the report and evaluation questions to these users, recording the number of errors and the speed with which each could complete the series of questions. To get a representative sample of potential system users, he visited several BEC stores across the country to collect usability data. Frank did not take special trips for these assessments only but conducted the assessment of the CPA report design along with other system components during these visits. In addition to questions related to report information, he also asked a standard set of questions related to user perceptions about the

Figure 7
Sections of the usability questionnaire to assess the customer-product assignment report

Report Evaluation Questionnaire

Background Information:

1. Name (print): _____ 2. Location (store number): _____
3. How long have you worked for BEC? _____ _____
4. Your current title:
   ☐ Store Manager
   ☐ Sales Representative
   ☐ Other _____

Report Evaluation: Use the information on the attached report to answer the following
questions.

1. Record current time now: _____ am/pm (circle one)
2. Check the customer names that have reserved a copy of Jimmy Buffet's "Fruit Cakes"
   compact disk.
   _____ Bill Jones   _____ Dana Merry
   _____ Janet Jones   _____ Billy Dolan
   _____ Anita Rosenburg   _____ Larry Mueller

8. Match customers to the products they reserved.
   _____ Babe Harnett   a. Revenge of the Nerds XI—video
   _____ Tina Albright   b. Yawni—"I Need to Take a Nap"—music CD
   _____ Bill Bixby   c. Cruise Control—Game
                               d. Snoop Doggy Dogg—music CD

Perceptions of Report Format:

1. Rate the consistency and dependability of the information on the report.
   inconsistent   1   2   3   4   5   6   7   consistent
   insufficient   1   2   3   4   5   6   7   sufficient
2. Rate the ability of the report to accurately transmit information.
   inaccurate   1   2   3   4   5   6   7   accurate
   insufficient   1   2   3   4   5   6   7   sufficient

6. Please note any other thing you think we should know about using this report (e.g.,
   were all fields clearly labeled?):
   _____
   _____
   _____

reports. These questions were used to collect qualitative information and to assess overall user satisfaction. Additionally, background information was used to segment the data in order to compare the evaluations of long-term employees with new employees, managers with sales representatives, and so on.

SUMMARY

Here we described how the customer-product assignment report was designed and assessed within the Customer Activity Tracking System at Broadway Entertainment Company. It should be clear from this description that the design of even a single report requires both technical and interpersonal skills in addition to a lot of hard work. In the course of the design and assessment process, the systems analyst not only managed the prototyping development process but also interacted with many BEC employees from numerous levels and functions. The success of this design effort likely resulted from a combination of strong interpersonal and technical skills.

15

Designing Interfaces
and Dialogues

After studying this chapter, you should be able to:

- Explain the process of designing interfaces and dialogues and the deliverables for their creation.

- Contrast and apply several methods for interacting with a system.

- List and describe various input devices and discuss usability issues for each in relation to performing different tasks.

- Describe and apply the general guidelines for designing interfaces and specific guidelines for layout design, structuring data entry fields, providing feedback, and system help.

- Choose between various mechanisms for providing system security through a system's interface.

- Design human-computer dialogues, including the use of dialogue diagramming.

- Design graphical user interfaces.

INTRODUCTION

In this chapter, you learn about system interface and dialogue design. Interface design focuses on how information is provided to and captured from users; dialogue design focuses on the sequencing of interface displays. Dialogues are analogous to a conversation between two people. The grammatical rules followed by each person during a conversation are analogous to the interface. Thus, the design of interfaces and dialogues is the process of defining the manner in which humans and computers exchange information. A good human-computer interface provides a uniform structure for finding, viewing, and invoking the different components of a system. This chapter complements Chapter 14 which addressed design guidelines for the content of forms and reports. In Chapter 15, you will learn about navigation between forms, alternative ways for users to cause forms and reports to appear, and how to supplement the content of forms and reports with user help and error messages, among other topics.

In the next section, the process of designing interfaces and dialogues and the deliverables produced during this activity are described. This is followed by a section that describes interaction methods and devices. Next, interface design is described. This discussion focuses on layout design, data entry, providing feedback, and designing help. Since system security is an important part of interface design, a brief discussion of how to build user access controls follows. The last section examines techniques for designing human-computer dialogues.

DESIGNING INTERFACES AND DIALOGUES

This is the second chapter that focuses on logical design within the systems development life cycle (see Figure 15-1). In Chapter 14, you learned about the design of forms and reports. As you will see, the guidelines for designing forms and reports also apply to the design of human-computer interfaces. Chapter 16 focuses on the logical design of system files and databases. The specific ordering of when you *should* design forms and reports, interfaces and dialogues, or databases is open to some debate. Our sequence was chosen because each topic builds on prior ones. Yet, within organizations, the order of these activities is not sequential but likely to be done in an iterative or parallel fashion.

The Process of Designing Interfaces and Dialogues

Similar to designing forms and reports, the process of designing interfaces and dialogues is a user-focused activity. This means that you follow a prototyping

Figure 15-1
Systems development life cycle with logical design phase highlighted

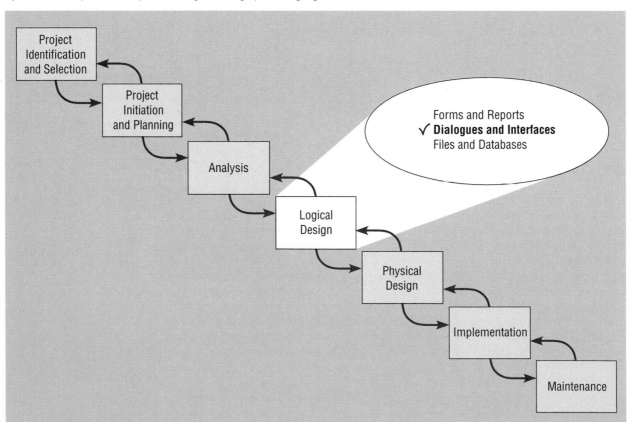

methodology of iteratively collecting information, constructing a prototype, assessing usability, and making refinements. To design usable interfaces and dialogues, you must answer the same who, what, when, where, and how questions used to guide the design of forms and reports (see Table 14-1). Thus, this process parallels that of designing forms and reports.

Deliverables and Outcomes

The deliverable and outcome from system interface and dialogue design is the creation of a design specification. This specification is also similar to the specification produced for form and report designs—with one exception. Recall that design specifications in Chapter 14 had three sections (see Figure 14-4):

1. Narrative overview

2. Sample design

3. Testing and usability assessment

For interface and dialogue designs, one additional subsection is included: a section outlining the dialogue sequence—the ways a user can move from one display to another. Later in the chapter you will learn how to design a dialogue sequence by using dialogue diagramming and state-transition diagramming. An outline for a design specification for interfaces and dialogues is shown in Figure 15-2.

Figure 15-2
Specification outline for the design of interfaces and dialogues

Design Specification

1. Narrative overview
   a. Interface/Dialogue Name
   b. User Characteristics
   c. Task Characteristics
   d. System Characteristics
   e. Environmental Characteristics

2. Interface/Dialogue Designs
   a. Form/Report Designs
   b. Dialogue Sequence Diagram(s) and Narrative Description

3. Testing and Usability Assessment
   a. Testing Objectives
   b. Testing Procedures
   c. Testing Results
      i) Time to Learn
      ii) Speed of Performance
      iii) Rate of Errors
      iv) Retention Over Time
      v) User Satisfaction and Other Perceptions

INTERACTION METHODS AND DEVICES

Interface: A method by which users interact with information systems.

The human-computer **interface** defines the ways in which users interact with an information system. All human-computer interfaces must have an interaction style and use some hardware device(s) for supporting this interaction. In this section we therefore describe various interaction methods and guidelines for designing usable interfaces.

Methods of Interacting

When designing the user interface, the most fundamental decision you make relates to the methods used to interact with the system. Given that there are numerous approaches for designing the interaction, we briefly provide a review of those most commonly used.[1] Our review will examine the basics of five widely used styles: command language, menu, form, object, and natural language. We will also describe several devices for interacting, focusing primarily on their usability for various interaction activities.

Command language interaction: A human-computer interaction method where users enter explicit statements into a system to invoke operations.

Command Language Interaction   In **command language interaction,** the user enters explicit statements to invoke operations within a system. This type of interaction requires users to remember command syntax and semantics. For example, to copy a file named PAPER.DOC from one storage location (C:) to another (A:) using Microsoft's disk operating system (DOS), a user would type
COPY C:PAPER.DOC A:PAPER.DOC
    Command language interaction places a substantial burden on the user to remember names, syntax, and operations. Most newer or large-scale systems no longer rely entirely on a command language interface. Yet, command languages are good for experienced users, for systems with a limited command set, and for rapid interaction with the system.
    A relatively simple application such as a word processor may have hundreds of commands for such operations as saving a file, deleting words, canceling the current action, finding a specific piece of data, or switching between windows. Some of the burden of assigning keys to actions has been taken off your shoulders through the development of user interface standards such as the Macintosh and Microsoft Windows (Apple, 1987; IBM, 1991). For example, Figure 15-3a shows the help screen from Microsoft Word describing the function key commands, and Figure 15-3b shows the same screen for Microsoft Excel. Note how many of the same keys have been assigned the same function. Also note that designers still have great flexibility in how they interpret and implement these standards. This means that you still need to pay attention to usability factors and conduct formal assessments of designs. Any application may adopt the CUA function key standard, as appropriate for the functionality of that application.

Menu interaction: A human-computer interaction method where a list of system options is provided and a specific command is invoked by user selection of a menu option.

Menu Interaction   A significant amount of interface design research has stressed the importance of a system's ease of use and understandability. **Menu interaction** is a means by which many designers have accomplished this goal. A menu is simply a list of options; when an option is selected by the user, a specific command is invoked, or another menu is activated. Menus have become the most widely used interface method because the user only needs to understand simple signposts and route options to effectively navigate through a system.

---

[1]Readers interested in learning more about interaction methods are encouraged to see the books by Dumas (1988), Norman (1991), or Shneiderman (1992).

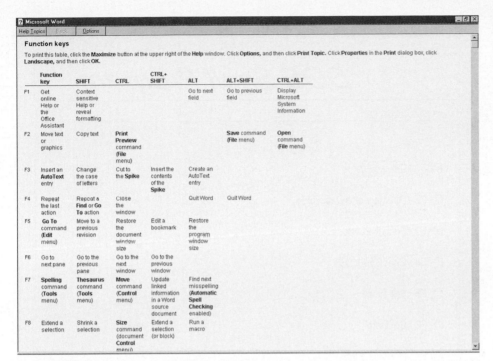

Function keys

To print this table, click the **Maximize** button at the upper right of the **Help** window. Click **Options**, and then click **Print Topic**. Click **Properties** in the **Print** dialog box, click **Landscape**, and then click **OK**.

Function key	SHIFT	CTRL	CTRL+ SHIFT	ALT	ALT+SHIFT	CTRL+ALT
F1 Get online Help or the Office Assistant	Context sensitive Help or reveal formatting			Go to next field	Go to previous field	Display Microsoft System Information
F2 Move text or graphics	Copy text	**Print Preview** command (**File** menu)			**Save** command (**File** menu)	**Open** command (**File** menu)
F3 Insert an **AutoText** entry	Change the case of letters	Cut to the **Spike**	Insert the contents of the **Spike**	Create an AutoText entry		
F4 Repeat the last action	Repeat a **Find** or **Go To** action	Close the window		Quit Word	Quit Word	
F5 **Go To** command (**Edit** menu)	Move to a previous revision	Restore the document window size	Edit a bookmark	Restore the program window size		
F6 Go to next pane	Go to the previous pane	Go to the next window	Go to the previous window			
F7 **Spelling** command (**Tools** menu)	**Thesaurus** command (**Tools** menu)	**Move** command (**Control** menu)	Update linked information in a Word source document	Find next misspelling (**Automatic Spell Checking** enabled)		
F8 Extend a selection	Shrink a selection	**Size** command (document **Control** menu)	Extend a selection (or block)	Run a macro		

Function keys in Microsoft Excel

Function key	SHIFT	CTRL	ALT	CTRL+ SHIFT	ALT+ SHIFT
F1 Display Help or the Office Assistant	**What's This?**		Insert a chart sheet		Insert a new worksheet
F2 Edit the active cell	Edit a cell comment		**Save As** command		**Save** command
F3 Paste a name into a formula	Paste a function into a formula	Define a name		Create names by using row and column labels	
F4 Repeat the last action	Repeat the last **Find (Find Next)**	Close the window	Exit		
F5 **Go To**	Display the **Find** dialog box	Restore the window size			
F6 Move to the next pane	Move to the previous pane	Move to the next workbook window		Move to the previous workbook window	
F7 **Spelling** command		Move the window			
F8 Extend a selection	Add to the selection	Resize the window	Display the **Macro** dialog box		
F9 Calculate all sheets in all open workbooks	Calculate the active worksheet	Minimize the workbook			
F10 Make the menu bar active	Display a shortcut menu	Maximize or restore the workbook window			

Menus can differ significantly in their design and complexity. The variation of their design is most often related to the capabilities of the development environment, the skills of the developer, and the size and complexity of the system. For smaller and less complex systems with limited system options, you may use a single menu or a linear sequence of menus. A single menu has obvious advantages over a command language but may provide little guidance beyond invoking the command. A single menu for a DOS shell program is shown in Figure 15-4.

Figure 15-4
Single-level menu for disk operating system application

For large and more complex systems, you can use menu hierarchies to provide navigation between menus. These hierarchies can be simple tree structures or variations wherein children menus have multiple parent menus or which allow multilevel traversal. Variations as to how menus are arranged can greatly influence the usability of a system. Figure 15-5 shows a variety of ways in which menus can be structured and traversed. An arc on this diagram signifies the ability to move from one menu to another. Although more complex menu structures provide greater user flexibility, they may also confuse users about exactly where they are in the system. Structures with multiple parent menus also require the application to remember which path has been followed so that users can correctly backtrack.

Pop-up menu: A menu positioning method that places a menu near the current cursor position.

There are two common methods for positioning menus. In a **pop-up menu** (also called a dialogue box), menus are displayed near the current cursor position so users don't have to move the position or their eyes to view system options (Figure 15-6a). A pop-up menu has a variety of potential uses. One is to show a list of commands relevant to the current cursor position (for example, delete, clear, copy, or validate current field). Another is to provide a list of possible values (from a

Figure 15-5
Various types of menu configurations (Adapted from Shneiderman, 1992)

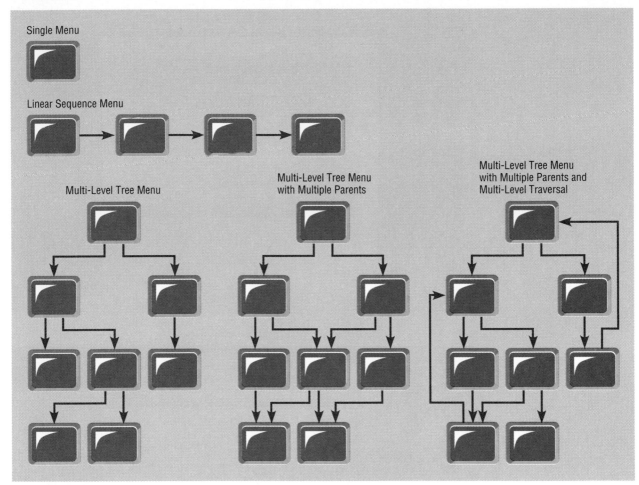

look-up table) to fill in for the current field. For example, in a customer order form, a list of current customers could pop up next to the customer number field so the user can select the correct customer without having to know the customer's identifier. In a **drop-down menu,** menus drop down from the top line of the display (Figure 15-6b). Drop-down menus have become very popular in recent years because they provide consistency in menu location and operation among applications and efficiently use display space. Most advanced operating environments such as Microsoft Windows, Macintosh, and the Unix graphical operating environment called X-Windows provide a combination of both pop-up and drop-down menus.

When designing menus, there are several general rules that should be followed and these are summarized in Table 15-1. For example, each menu should have a meaningful title and be presented in a meaningful manner to users. A menu option of Quit, for instance, is ambiguous—does it mean return to the previous screen, exit the program, or exit to DOS? To more easily see how to apply these guidelines, Figure 15-7 contrasts a poorly designed menu with a menu following the menu design guidelines. Annotations on the two parts of this figure highlight poor and improved menu interface design features.

Many advanced programming environments provide powerful tools for designing menus. For example, Microsoft's Visual Basic allows you to quickly design a menu structure using a menu design facility. Figure 15-8a shows the design form,

Drop-down menu: A menu positioning method that places the access point of the menu near the top line of the display; when accessed, menus open by dropping down onto the display.

Figure 15-6
Menus from Microsoft Word 97

(a) Pop-up menu

(b) Drop-down menu

Menu Design Window, in which a menu structure is defined. Figure 15-8b shows how the menu looks to a user within the actual information system. To build a menu you only need to type the words that will represent each item on the menu. With the use of a few easily invoked options, you can also assign shortcut keys to menu items, connect help screens to individual menu items, define submenus, and set usage properties. Usage properties, for example, include the ability to dim the

TABLE 15-1   Guidelines for Menu Design

Wording	• Each menu should have a meaningful title
	• Command verbs should clearly and specifically describe operations
	• Menu items should be displayed in mixed upper- and lower-case letters and have a clear, unambiguous interpretation
Organization	• A consistent organizing principle should be used that relates to the tasks the intended users perform; for example, related options should be grouped together and the same option should have the same wording and codes each time it appears
Length	• The number of menu choices should not exceed the length of the screen
	• Submenus should be used to break up exceedingly long menus
Selection	• Selection and entry methods should be consistent and reflect the size of the application and sophistication of the users
	• How the user is to select each option and the consequences of each option should be clear (e.g., whether another menu will appear)
Highlighting	• Highlighting should be minimized and used only to convey selected options (e.g., a check mark) or unavailable options (e.g., dimmed text)

Adapted from Dumas, 1988.

color of a menu item while a program is running to indicate that a function is currently unavailable. Menu building tools allow a designer to quickly and easily prototype a design that will look exactly as it will in the final system.

Form Interaction   The premise of **form interaction** is to allow users to fill in the blanks when working with a system. Form interaction is effective for both the input and presentation of information. An effectively designed form includes a self-explanatory title and field headings, has fields organized into logical groupings with distinctive boundaries, provides default values when practical, displays data in appropriate field lengths, and minimizes the need to scroll windows (Shneiderman, 1992). You saw many other design guidelines for forms in Chapter 14. Form interaction is the most commonly used method for data entry and retrieval in business-based systems. Figure 15-9 shows a form from David Letterman's World Wide Web site on the Internet. Using interactive forms, organizations can easily provide all types of information to Web surfers.

Form interaction: A highly intuitive human-computer interaction method whereby data fields are formatted in a manner similar to paper-based forms.

Object-Based Interaction   The most common method for implementing **object-based interaction** is through the use of icons. **Icons** are graphic symbols that look like the processing option they are meant to represent. Users select operations by pointing to the appropriate icon with some type of pointing device. The primary advantages to icons are that they take up little screen space and can be quickly understood by most users. An icon may also look like a button which, when selected or depressed, causes the system to take an action relevant to that form, such as cancel, save, edit a record, or ask for help. For example, Figure 15-10 illustrates an icon-based interface when entering Microsoft Visual Basic.

Object-based interaction: A human-computer interaction method where symbols are used to represent commands or functions.

Icon: Graphical pictures that represent specific functions within a system.

Natural Language Interaction   A branch of artificial intelligence research studies techniques for allowing systems to accept inputs and produce outputs in a conventional language like English. This method of interaction is referred to as **natural language interaction.** Presently, natural language interaction is not as viable an interaction style as other methods presented. Current implementations can be tedious,

Natural language interaction: A human-computer interaction method whereby inputs to and outputs from a computer-based application are in a conventional speaking language such as English.

Figure 15-7
Contrasting menu designs

(a) Poor menu design

(b) Improved menu design

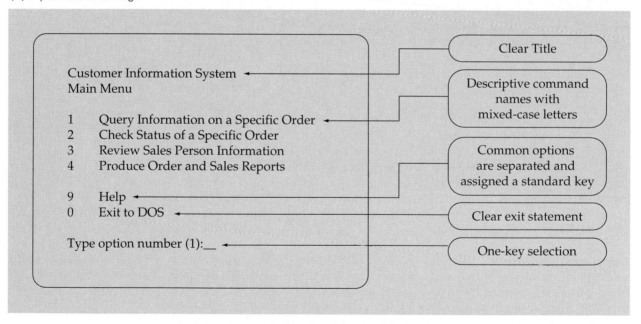

frustrating, and time-consuming for the user and are often built to accept input in narrowly constrained domains (e.g., database queries). Natural language interaction is being applied within both keyboard and voice entry systems.

Hardware Options for System Interaction

In addition to the variety of methods used for interacting with a system, there is also a growing number of hardware devices employed to support this interaction (see Table 15-2 for a list of interaction devices along with brief descriptions of the

Figure 15-8
Menu building within a
graphical user interface
environment

(a) Menu design window

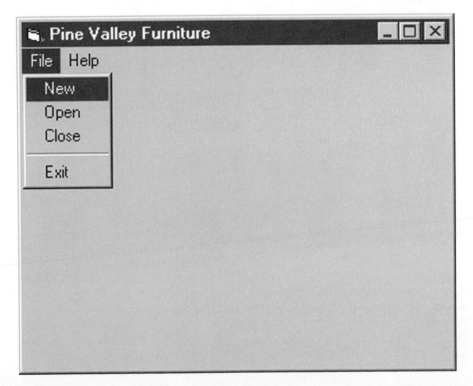

(b) Menu design as viewed
by user

Figure 15-9
Example of form interaction in the Netscape Navigator™ World Wide Web browser (Copyright 1998 Netscape Communications Corp. Used with permission. All Rights Reserved. This electronic file or page may not be reprinted or copied without the express written permission of Netscape.)

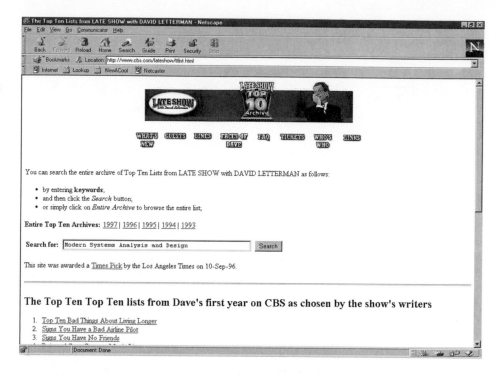

Figure 15-10
Icon-based interface for beginning a new session in Microsoft Visual Basic

typical usage of each). The most fundamental and widely used is the keyboard, which is the mainstay of most computer-based applications for the entry of alphanumeric information. Keyboards vary, from the typewriter kind of keyboards used with personal computers to special-function keyboards on point-of-sale or shop floor devices. The growth in graphical user environments, however, has spurred the broader use of pointing devices such as mice, joysticks, trackballs, and graphics

TABLE 15-2 Common Devices for Interacting with an Information System

Device	Description and Primary Characteristics or Usage
Keyboard	Users push an array of small buttons that represent symbols which are then translated into words and commands. Keyboards are widely understood and provide considerable flexibility for interaction.
Mouse	A small plastic box that users push across a flat surface and whose movements are translated into cursor movement on a computer display. Buttons on the mouse tell the system when an item is selected. A mouse works well on flat desks but may not be practical in dirty or busy environments, such as a shop floor or check-out area in a retail store. Newer pen-based mice provide the user with more of the feel of a writing implement.
Joystick	A small vertical lever mounted on a base that steers the cursor on a computer display. Provides similar functionality to a mouse.
Trackball	A sphere mounted on a fixed base that steers the cursor on a computer display. A suitable replacement for a mouse when work space for a mouse is not available.
Touch Screen	Selections are made by touching a computer display. This works well in dirty environments or for users with limited dexterity or expertise.
Light Pen	Selections are made by pressing a pen-like device against the screen. A light pen works well when the user needs to have a more direct interaction with the contents of the screen.
Graphics Tablet	Moving a pen-like device across a flat tablet steers the cursor on a computer display. Selections are made by pressing a button or by pressing the pen against the tablet. This device works well for drawing and graphical applications.
Voice	Spoken words are captured and translated by the computer into text and commands. This is most appropriate for users with physical challenges or when hands need to be free to do other tasks while interacting with the application.

tablets. The creation of notebook and pen-based computers which have trackballs, joysticks, or pens attached directly to the computer has also brought renewed interest to the usability of these various devices.

Research has found that each device has its strengths and weaknesses which must guide your selection of the appropriate devices to aid users in their interaction with an application. The selection of devices users will use for interaction must be made during logical design since different interfaces require different devices. Table 15-3 summarizes much of the usability assessment research by relating each device to various types of human-computer interaction problems. For example, for many applications keyboards do not give users a precise feel for cursor movement, do not provide direct feedback on each operation, and can be a slow way to enter data (depending on the typing skill of the user). Another means to gain an understanding of device usability is to highlight which devices have been found most useful for completing specific tasks. The results of this research are summarized in Table 15-4. The rows of this table list common user-computer interaction tasks, and the columns show three criteria for evaluating the usability of the different devices. After reviewing these three tables, it should be evident that no device is perfect and that some are more appropriate for performing some tasks than others. To design the most effective interfaces for a given application, you should understand the capabilities of various interaction methods and devices.

DESIGNING INTERFACES

Building on the information provided in Chapter 14 on the design of content for forms and reports, in this section we discuss issues related to the design of interface layouts. This discussion provides guidelines for structuring and controlling data

TABLE 15-3   Summary of Interaction Device Usability Problems

Device	Problem						
	Visual Blocking	User Fatigue	Movement Scaling	Durability	Adequate Feedback	Speed	Pointing Accuracy
Keyboard	□	□	■	□	■	■	□
Mouse	□	□	■	□	■	□	□
Joystick	□	□	■	□	■	□	■
Trackball	□	□	■	■	■	□	□
Touch Screen	■	■	□	■	□	□	■
Light Pen	■	■	□	□	□	□	■
Graphics Tablet	□	□	■	□	■	□	□
Voice	□	□	■	□	■	□	■

Adapted from Blattner & Schultz, 1988.

Key:

□ = little or no usability problems
■ = potentially high usability problems for some applications
Visual Blocking = extent to which device blocks display when using
User Fatigue = potential for fatigue over long use
Movement Scaling = extent to which device movement translates to equivalent screen movement
Durability = lack of durability or need for maintenance (e.g., cleaning) over extended use
Adequate Feedback = extent to which device provides adequate feedback for each operation
Speed = cursor movement speed
Pointing Accuracy = ability to precisely direct cursor

TABLE 15-4   Summary of General Conclusions from Experimental Comparisons of Input Devices in Relation to Specific Task Activities
(Adapted from Blattner & Schultz, 1988)

Task	Most Accurate	Shortest Positioning	Most Preferred
Target Selection	trackball, graphics tablet, mouse, joystick	touch screen, light pen, mouse, graphics tablet, trackball	touch screen, light pen
Text Selection	mouse	mouse	—
Data Entry	light pen	light pen	—
Cursor Positioning	—	light pen	—
Text Correction	light pen, cursor keys	light pen	light pen
Menu Selection	touch screen	—	keyboard, touch screen

Key:

Target Selection = moving the cursor to select a figure or item
Text Selection = moving the cursor to select a block of text
Data Entry = entering information of any type into a system
Cursor Positioning = moving the cursor to a specific position
Text Correction = moving the cursor to a location to make a text correction
Menu Selection = activating a menu item
— = no clear conclusion from the research

entry fields, providing feedback, and designing on-line help. Effective interface design requires that you gain a thorough understanding of each of these concepts.

Designing Layouts

To ease user training and data recording, you should use standard formats for computer-based forms and reports similar to paper-based forms and reports for recording or reporting information. A typical paper-based form for reporting customer sales activity is shown in Figure 15-11. This form has several general areas common to most forms:

- Header information

- Sequence and time-related information

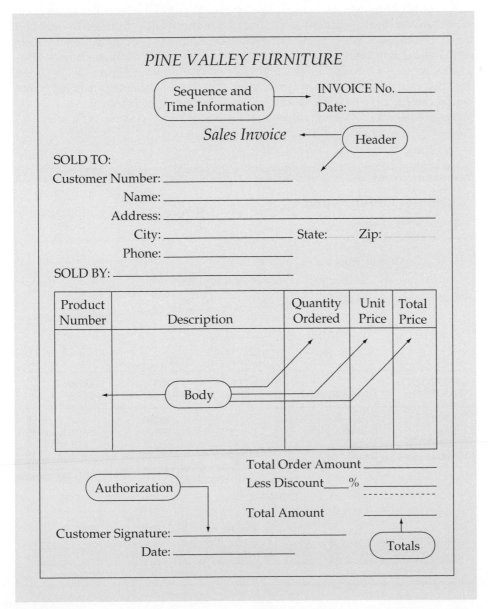

Figure 15-11
Paper-based form for reporting customer sales activity
(Pine Valley Furniture)

- Instruction or formatting information

- Body or data details

- Totals or data summary

- Authorization or signatures

- Comments

In many organizations, data is often first recorded on paper-based forms and then later recorded within application systems. When designing layouts to record or display information on paper-based forms, you should try to make both as similar as possible. Additionally, data entry displays should be consistently formatted across applications to speed data entry and reduce errors. Figure 15-12 shows an equivalent computer-based form to the paper-based form shown in Figure 15-11.

Another concern when designing the layout of computer-based forms is the design of between-field navigation. Since you can control the sequence for users to move between fields, standard screen navigation should flow from left to right and top to bottom just as when you work on paper-based forms. For example, Figure 15-13 contrasts the flow between fields on a form used to record business contacts. Figure 15-13a uses a consistent left to right, top to bottom flow. Figure 15-13b uses a flow that is nonintuitive. When appropriate, you should also group data fields into logical categories with labels describing the contents of the category. Areas of the screen not used for data entry or commands should be inaccessible to the user.

Figure 15-12
Computer-based form reporting customer sales activity (Pine Valley Furniture)

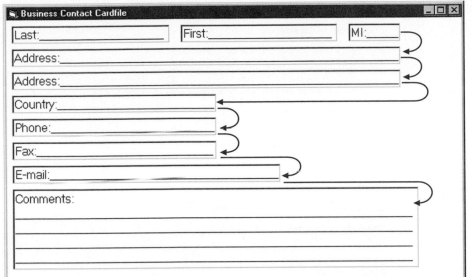

Figure 15-13
Contrasting the navigation flow within a data entry form

(a) Proper flow between data entry fields

(b) Poor flow between data entry fields

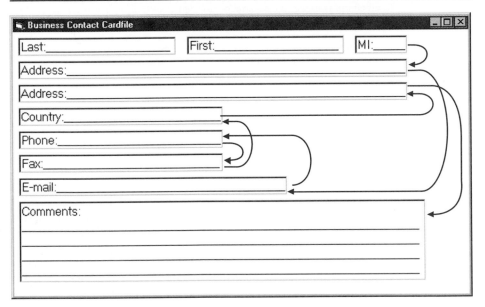

When designing the navigation procedures within your system, flexibility and consistency are primary concerns. Users should be able to freely move forward and backward or to any desired data entry fields. Users should be able to navigate each form in the same way or in as similar a manner as possible. Additionally, data should not *usually* be permanently saved by the system until the user makes an explicit request to do so. This allows the user to abandon a data entry screen, back up, or move forward without adversely impacting the contents of the permanent data.

Consistency extends to the selection of keys and commands. Each key or command should have only one function and this function should be consistent throughout the entire system and across systems, if possible. Depending upon the application, various types of functional capabilities will be required to provide smooth navigation and data entry. Table 15-5 provides a list of the functional requirements for providing smooth and easy navigation within a form. For example,

TABLE 15-5 Data Entry Screen Functional Capabilities

Cursor Control Capabilities:

Move the cursor forward to the next data field

Move the cursor backward to the previous data field

Move the cursor to the first, last, or some other designated data field

Move the cursor forward one character in a field

Move the cursor backward one character in a field

Editing Capabilities:

Delete the character to the left of the cursor

Delete the character under the cursor

Delete the whole field

Delete data from the whole form (empty the form)

Exit Capabilities:

Transmit the screen to the application program

Move to another screen/form

Confirm the saving of edits or go to another screen/form

Help Capabilities:

Get help on a data field

Get help on a full screen/form

Adapted from Dumas, 1988.

a functional and consistent interface will provide common ways for users to move the cursor to different places on the form, editing characters and fields, moving among form displays, and obtaining help. These functions may be provided by keystrokes, mouse or other pointing device operations, or menu selection or button activation. It is possible that, for a single application, all functional capabilities listed in Table 15-5 may not be needed in order to create a flexible and consistent user interface. Yet, the capabilities that are used should be consistently applied to provide an optimal user environment. As with other tables in Chapters 14 and 15, Table 15-5 can serve as a checklist for you to validate the usability of user interface designs.

Structuring Data Entry

Several rules should be considered when structuring data entry fields on a form (see Table 15-6). The first is simple, but often violated by designers. To minimize data entry errors and user frustration, *never* require the user to enter information which is already available within the system or information that can be easily computed by the system. For example, never require the user to enter the current date and time, since each of these values can be easily retrieved from the computer system's internal calendar and clock. By allowing the system to do this, the user simply confirms that the calendar and clock are working properly.

Other rules are equally important. For example, suppose that a bank customer is repaying a loan on a fixed schedule with equal monthly payments. Each month when a payment is sent to the bank, a clerk needs to record that the payment has been received into a loan processing system. Within such a system, default values

TABLE 15-6   Guidelines for Structuring Data Entry Fields

Entry	Never require data that are already on-line or that can be computed; for example, do not enter customer data on an order form if that data can be retrieved from the database, and do not enter extended prices which can be computed from quantity sold and unit prices.
Defaults	Always provide default values when appropriate; for example, assume today's date for a new sales invoice, or use the standard product price unless overridden
Units	Make clear the type of data units requested for entry; for example, indicate quantity in tons, dozens, pounds, etc.
Replacement	Use character replacement when appropriate; for example, allow the user to look up the value in a table or automatically fill in the value once the user enters enough significant characters.
Captioning	Always place a caption adjacent to fields; see Table 15-7 for caption options.
Format	Provide formatting examples when appropriate; for example, automatically show standard embedded symbols, decimal points, credit symbol, or dollar sign.
Justify	Automatically justify data entries; numbers should be right-justified and aligned on decimal points, and text should be left-justified.
Help	Provide context-sensitive help when appropriate; for example, provide a hot key, such as the F1 key, that opens the help system on an entry that is most closely related to where the cursor is on the display.

Adapted from Dumas, 1988.

for fields should be provided whenever appropriate. This means that *only* in the instances where the customer pays *more or less* than the scheduled amount should the clerk have to enter data into the system. In all other cases, the clerk would simply verify that the check is for the default amount provided by the system and press a single key to confirm the receipt of payment.

When entering data, the user should also not be required to specify the dimensional units of a particular value. For example, a user should not be required to specify that an amount is in dollars or that a weight is in tons. Field formatting and the data entry prompt should make clear the type of data being requested. In other words, a caption describing the data to be entered should be adjacent to each data field. Within this caption, it should be clear to the user what type of data is being requested. As with the display of information, all data entered onto a form should automatically justify in a standard format (e.g., date, time, money). Table 15-7

TABLE 15-7   Options for Entering Text

Options	Example
Line caption	Phone Number ( ) -
Drop caption	( ) - / Phone Number
Boxed caption	Phone number
Delimited characters	( ) - / Phone Number
Check-off boxes	Method of payment (check one) □ Check □ Cash □ Credit card: Type

illustrates a few options appropriate for printed forms. For data entry on video display terminals, you should highlight the area in which text is entered so that the exact number of characters per line and number of lines are clearly shown. You can also use check boxes or radio buttons to allow users to choose standard textual responses. And, you can use data entry controls to ensure that the proper type of data (alphabetic or numeric, as required) are entered. Data entry controls are discussed next.

Controlling Data Input

One objective of interface design is to reduce data entry errors. As data are entered into an information system, steps must be taken to ensure that the input is valid. As a systems analyst, you must anticipate the types of errors users may make and design features into the system's interfaces to avoid, detect, and correct data entry mistakes. Several types of data errors are summarized in Table 15-8. In essence, data errors can occur from appending extra data onto a field, truncating characters off a field, transcripting the wrong characters into a field, or transposing one or more characters within a field. Systems designers have developed numerous tests and techniques for catching invalid data before saving or transmission, thus improving the likelihood that data will be valid (see Table 15-9 which summarizes these techniques). These tests and techniques are often incorporated into both data entry screens and intercomputer data transfer programs.

Practical experience has also found that correcting erroneous data is much easier to accomplish before it is permanently stored in a system. On-line systems can notify a user of input problems as data are being entered. When data are processed on-line as events occur, it is much less likely that data validity errors will occur and not be caught. In an on-line system, most problems can be easily identified and resolved before permanently saving data to a storage device using many of the techniques described in Table 15-9. However, in systems where inputs are stored and entered (or transferred) in batch, the identification and notification of errors is more difficult. Batch processing systems can, however, reject invalid inputs and store them in a log file for later resolution.

Most of the tests and techniques shown in Table 15-9 are widely used and straightforward. Some of these tests can be handled by data management technologies, such as a database management system (DBMS), to ensure that they are applied for all data maintenance operations. If a DBMS cannot perform these tests, then you must design the tests into program modules. An example of one item that is a bit sophisticated, self-checking digits, is shown in Figure 15-14. The figure provides a description and an outline of how to apply the technique as well as a short example. The example shows how a check digit is added to a field before data entry or transfer. Once entered or transferred, the check digit algorithm is again applied to the field to "check" whether the check digit received obeys the calculation. If it does, it is likely (but not guaranteed, since two different values could yield the same check digit) that no data transmission or entry error occurred. If not equal, then some type of error occurred.

TABLE 15-8	Sources of Data Errors
Data Error	**Description**
Appending	Adding additional characters to a field
Truncating	Losing characters from a field
Transcripting	Entering invalid data into a field
Transposing	Reversing the sequence of one or more characters in a field

TABLE 15-9   Validation Tests and Techniques to Enhance the Validity of Data Input

Validation Test	Description
Class or Composition	Test to assure that data are of proper type (e.g., all numeric, all alphabetic, alphanumeric)
Combinations	Test to see if the value combinations of two or more data fields are appropriate or make sense (e.g., does the quantity sold make sense given the type of product?)
Expected Values	Test to see if data Is what is expected (e.g., match with existing customer names, payment amount, etc.)
Missing Data	Test for existence of data items in all fields of a record (e.g., is there a quantity field on each line item of a customer order?)
Pictures/Templates	Test to assure that data conform to a standard format (e.g., are hyphens in the right places for a student ID number?)
Range	Test to assure data are within proper range of values (e.g., is a student's grade point average between 0 and 4.0?)
Reasonableness	Test to assure data are reasonable for situation (e.g., pay rate for a specific type of employee)
Self-Checking Digits	Test where an extra digit is added to a numeric field in which its value is derived using a standard formula (see Figure 15-14)
Size	Test for too few or too many characters (e.g., is social security number exactly nine digits?)
Values	Test to make sure values come from set of standard values (e.g., two-letter state codes)

Description	Techniques where extra digits are added to a field to assist in verifying its accuracy
Method	1. Multiply each digit of a numeric field by a weighting factor (e.g., 1,2,1,2,...). 2. Sum the results of weighted digits. 3. Divide sum by modulus number (e.g., 10). 4. Subtract remainder of division from modulus number to determine check digit. 5. Append check digits to field.
Example	Assume a numeric part number of: 12473 1–2. Multiply each digit of part number by weighting factor from right to left and sum the results of weighted digits: $\begin{array}{ccccc} 1 & 2 & 4 & 7 & 3 \\ \times 1 & \times 2 & \times 1 & \times 2 & \times 1 \\ \hline 1 + & 4 + & 4 + & 14 + & 3 = 26 \end{array}$ 3. Divide sum by modulus number. $26/10 = 2$ remainder 6 4. Subtract remainder from modulus number to determine check digit. check digit = $10 - 6 = 4$ 5. Append check digits to field. Field value with appended check digit = 124734

Figure 15-14
Using check digits to verify data correctness

In addition to validating the data values entered into a system, controls must be established to verify that all input records are correctly entered and that they are only processed once. A common method used to enhance the validity of entering batches of data records is to create an audit trail of the entire sequence of data entry, processing, and storage. In such an audit trail, the actual sequence, count, time, source location, human operator, and so on are recorded into a separate transaction log in the event of a data input or processing error. If an error occurs, corrections can be made by reviewing the contents of the log. Detailed logs of data inputs are not only useful for resolving batch data entry errors and system audits but also serve as a powerful method for performing backup and recovery operations in the case of a catastrophic system failure. These types of file and database controls are discussed further in Chapter 17.

Providing Feedback

When talking with a friend, you would be concerned if he or she did not provide you with feedback by nodding and replying to your questions and comments. Without feedback, you would be concerned that he or she was not listening, likely resulting in a less than satisfactory experience. Similarly, when designing system interfaces, providing appropriate feedback is an easy method for making a user's interaction more enjoyable; not providing feedback is a sure way to frustrate and confuse. System feedback can consist of three types:

1. Status information

2. Prompting cues

3. Error or warning messages

Status Information   Providing status information is a simple technique for keeping users informed of what is going on within a system. For example, relevant status information such as displaying the current customer name or time, placing appropriate titles on a menu or screen, or identifying the number of screens following the current one (e.g., Screen 1 of 3) all provide needed feedback to the user. Providing status information during processing operations is especially important if the operation takes longer than a second or two. For example, when opening a file you might display "Please wait while I open the file" or, when performing a large calculation, flash the message "Working . . ." to the user. Further, it is important to tell the user that besides working, the system has accepted the user's input and the input was in the correct form. Sometimes it is important to give the user a chance to obtain more feedback. For example, a function key could toggle between showing a "Working . . ." message and giving more specific information as each intermediate step is accomplished. Providing status information will reassure users that nothing is wrong and make them feel in command of the system, not vice versa.

Prompting Cues   A second feedback method is to display prompting cues. When prompting the user for information or action, it is useful to be specific in your request. For example, suppose a system prompted users with the following request:
READY FOR INPUT:_____
With such a prompt, the designer assumes that the user knows exactly what to enter. A better design would be specific in its request, possibly providing an example, default values, or formatting information. An improved prompting request might be as follows:
Enter the customer account number (123-456-7):_____-_____-__

Errors and Warning Messages   A final method available to you for providing system feedback is using error and warning messages. Practical experience has found that a few simple guidelines can greatly improve their usefulness. First, messages should be specific and free of error codes and jargon. Additionally, messages should never scold the user and should attempt to guide the user toward a resolution. For example, a message might say "No Customer Record Found for That Customer ID. Please verify that digits were not transposed." Messages should be in user, not computer, terms. Hence, such terms as "end of file," "disk I/O error," or "write protected" may be too technical and not helpful for many users. Multiple messages can be useful so that a user can get more detailed explanations if wanted or needed. Also, error messages should appear in roughly the same format and placement each time so that they are recognized as error messages and not as some other information. Examples of good and bad messages are provided in Table 15-10. Using these guidelines, you will be able to provide useful feedback in your designs. A special type of feedback is answering help requests from users. This important topic is described next.

Providing Help

Designing how to provide help is one of the most important interface design issues you will face. When designing help, you need to put yourself in the user's place. When accessing help, the user likely does not know what to do next, does not understand what is being requested, or does not know how the requested information needs to be formatted. A user requesting help is much like a ship in distress, sending an SOS. In Table 15-11, we provide our SOS guidelines for the design of system help: Simplicity, Organize, and Show. Our first guideline, *simplicity*, suggests that help messages should be short, to the point, and use words that enable understanding. This leads to our second guideline, *organize*, which means that help messages should be written so that information can be easily absorbed by users. Practical experience has found that long paragraphs of text are often difficult for people to understand. A better design organizes lengthy information in a manner easier for users to digest through the use of bulleted and ordered lists. Finally, it is often

TABLE 15-10   Examples of Poor and Improved Error Messages

Poor Error Messages	Improved Error Messages
ERROR 56 OPENING FILE	The file name you typed was not found. Press F2 to list valid file names.
WRONG CHOICE	Please enter an option from the menu.
DATA ENTRY ERROR	The prior entry contains a value outside the range of acceptable values. Press F9 for list of acceptable values.
FILE CREATION ERROR	The file name you entered already exists. Press F10 if you want to overwrite it. Press F2 if you want to save it to a new name.

TABLE 15-11   Guidelines for Designing Usable Help

Guideline	Explanation
Simplicity	Use short, simple wording, common spelling, and complete sentences. Give users only what they need to know, with ability to find additional information.
Organize	Use lists to break information into manageable pieces.
Show	Provide examples of proper use and the outcomes of such use.

useful to explicitly *show* users how to perform an operation and the outcome of procedural steps. Figure 15-15 contrasts the designs of two help screens, one employing our guidelines and one that does not.

Many commercially available systems provide extensive system help. For example, Table 15-12 lists the range of help available in a popular electronic spreadsheet. Many systems are also designed so that users can vary the level of detail provided. Help may be provided at the system level, screen or form level, and individual field level. The ability to provide field level help is often referred to as "context-sensitive" help. For some applications, providing context-sensitive help for all system options is a tremendous undertaking that is virtually a project in it-

Figure 15-15
Contrasting help screens

(a) Poorly designed help display

(b) Improved design for help display

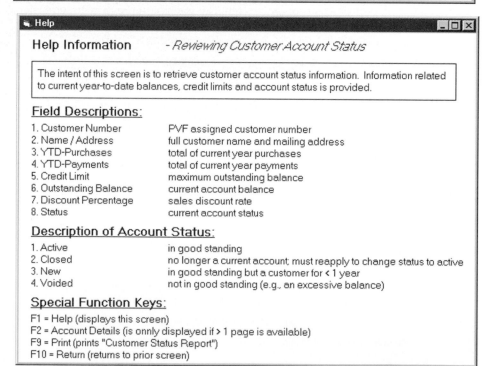

TABLE 15-12 Types of Help

Type of Help	Example of Question
Help on Help	How do I get help?
Help on Concepts	What is a customer record?
Help on Procedures	How do I update a record?
Help on Messages	What does "Invalid File Name" mean?
Help on Menus	What does "Graphics" mean?
Help on Function Keys	What does each Function key do?
Help on Commands	How do I use the "Cut" and "Paste" commands?
Help on Words	What do "merge" and "sort" mean?

Adapted from Dumas, 1988.

self. If you do decide to design an extensive help system with many levels of detail, you must be sure that you know exactly what the user needs help with, or your efforts may confuse users more than help them. After leaving a help screen, users should always return back to where they were prior to requesting help. If you follow these simple guidelines, you will likely design a highly usable help system.

As with the construction of menus, many programming environments provide powerful tools for designing system help. For example, Microsoft's Help Compiler allows you to quickly construct hypertext-based help systems. In this environment, you use a text editor to construct help pages that can be easily linked to other pages containing related or more specific information. Linkages are created by embedding special characters into the text document that make words hypertext buttons—that is, direct linkages—to additional information. The Help Compiler transforms the text document into a hypertext document. For example, Figure 15-16 shows a hypertext-based help screen from Netscape Navigator™. Hypertext-based help

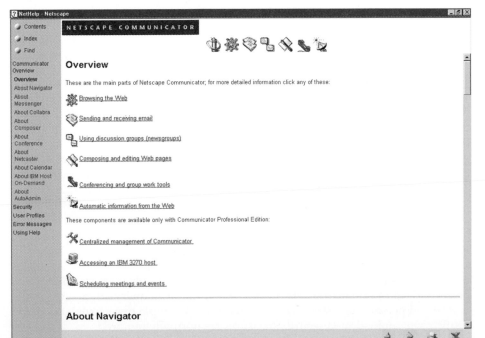

Figure 15-16
Hypertext-based help system from Netscape Navigator™ (Copyright 1998 Netscape Communications Corp. Used with permission. All Rights Reserved. This electronic file or page may not be reprinted or copied without the express written permission of Netscape.)

systems have become the standard environment for most commercial Windows-based applications. This has occurred for two primary reasons. First, standardizing system help across applications eases user training. Second, hypertext allows users to selectively access the level of help they need, making it easier to provide effective help for both novice and experienced users within the same system.

CONTROLLING USER ACCESS

Corporations and government agencies are putting more and more sensitive data on computers. As the number and sophistication of user access paths to the data increase, those data become vulnerable to unwanted access or corruption. A recent survey of computer security professionals estimates the annual losses from computer abuse at over $500,000,000 nationally. Among the survey respondents, the average installation experienced losses of over $100,000 and 365 person-hours per year (Bloombecker, 1989). Part of your job during interface design is to decide which forms of user access controls are necessary and make your choice or advise other system developers on which mechanisms will be most effective in securing the application.

You have several techniques available to control user access:

1. Views or subschemas: Restrict user views of a database

2. Authorization rules: Restrict user access and activities within a system

3. Encryption procedures: Encode data in an unrecognizable form

4. Authentication schemes: Identify users with certainty so that other security mechanisms can work

In essence, since an interface defines how users are able to create, read, update, or delete data, security controls should be designed into an interface when it is initially designed. Experience has shown that if designed separately from the rest of the interface, security procedures are usually cumbersome and less effective.

Views

View: A subset of the database that is presented to one or more users.

One form of user access control for system interfaces is to provide a customized version of the systems data to the user. A **view** is a subset of the database that is presented to one or more users. As long as the user can access data only through the system, they will be able to use only the data, raw or summarized, available in the view supported by the parts of the system they are authorized to use. Many database management systems include this concept. If not, it is possible to achieve the same effect through controls on access to specific programs and use of other mechanisms described below. Since views are commonly covered in database management texts (McFadden, Hoffer, and Prescott, 1999), we do not illustrate this control here.

Although views promote security by restricting user access to limited data, views are not adequate security measures, as unauthorized persons may gain knowledge of or access to a particular view. Also, several persons may share a particular view; all may have authority to read the data but only a restricted few may be authorized to update the data. Finally, with high-level query languages, an unauthorized person may gain access to data through simple experimentation. As a result, more sophisticated security measures are normally required.

Authorization Rules

Controls incorporated in an application or system software that restrict access to data and also restrict the actions that people may take when data are accessed are called **authorization rules.** For example, a person who can supply a particular password may be authorized to gain access to a system and read any record in a database but cannot necessarily modify any of those records.

Fernandez, Summers, and Wood (1981) have developed a conceptual model for authorization rules within database environments. Their model expresses authorization rules in the form of a table (or matrix) that includes subjects, objects, actions, and constraints. Each row of the table indicates that a particular subject is authorized to take a certain action on an object in the database, perhaps subject to some constraint. An example of such an authorization matrix is shown in Figure 15-17. This table contains several entries pertaining to records in an accounting database. The first row in the table indicates that anyone in the Sales Department is authorized to insert a new customer record in the database, provided that the customer's credit limit does not exceed $5,000. The last row indicates that the program AR4 is authorized to modify order records without restriction. Owners of data along with data and system administration are responsible for determining authorization rules.

Authorization rules: Controls incorporated to restrict access to systems and data and also to restrict the actions that people may take once in the system.

Encryption Procedures

For highly sensitive data (such as company financial data), data encryption can be used. Encryption is the coding (or scrambling) of data so that they cannot be read by humans (see Chapter 17). Special hardware and software can be purchased to encrypt data so that users cannot read stored data except through the authorized use of decoding mechanisms. Some DBMS products include encryption routines that automatically encode sensitive data when they are stored or transmitted over communications channels. For example, encryption is commonly used in electronic funds transfer (EFT) systems. Any system that provides encryption facilities must also provide complementary routines for decoding the data. These decoding routines must, of course, be protected by adequate security, or else the advantages of encryption are lost.

Authentication Schemes

A longstanding problem in computer circles is how to positively identify persons who are trying to gain access to a computer or its resources. Passwords cannot, of themselves, ensure the security of a computer and its databases because they give no indication of who is trying to gain access. For systems that involve highly sensitive data or perform functions initiated by a select group of people, it is important

SUBJECT	OBJECT	ACTION	CONSTRAINT
Sales Dept.	Customer record	Insert	Credit limit ≤ $5,000
Order Trans.	Customer record	Read	None
Terminal 12	Customer record	Modify	Balance due only
Accounting Dept.	Order record	Delete	None
Luke Skywalker	Order record	Insert	Order amt < $2,000
Program AR4	Order record	Modify	None

Figure 15-17
Authorization matrix

to design mechanisms into the system interface to ensure that only authorized people are using the system.

The computer industry is developing devices and techniques to positively identify any prospective user. The most promising of these appear to be **biometric devices** which measure or detect personal characteristics such as fingerprints, voice prints, retina prints, or signature dynamics. To implement this approach, several companies have developed a **smart card**—a thin plastic card, the size of a credit card, with an embedded microprocessor and memory. An individual's unique biometric data (such as fingerprints) are stored permanently on the card. To access a computer, the user inserts the card into a device that reads the person's unique biometric data from the smart card. A second device reads the user's actual characteristics and compares this data with the data stored on the smart card. The two must match to gain computer access. A lost or stolen card would be useless to another person, since the biometric data would not match.

In this and the prior sections, we have described a wide variety of issues—from how to structure data entry fields to how to be sure human-system interactions are legitimate—relevant to the design of system interfaces. Designing useful interfaces requires that you effectively apply numerous guidelines and pay careful attention to issues of usability. Doing this will ensure that information is clearly laid out, data entry fields are effectively designed, and appropriate amounts of feedback and help are provided. After completing interface design, you will have available individual displays to support specific tasks, such as user sign-on, entry of a customer order, or selection of a particular reporting option. The next step is to design the sequencing of, or navigation between, these displays. This process is the topic of the next section—designing dialogues.

DESIGNING DIALOGUES

The process of designing the overall sequences that users follow to interact with an information system is called dialogue design. A **dialogue** is the sequence in which information is displayed to and obtained from a user. As the designer, your role is to select the most appropriate interaction methods and devices (described above) and to define the conditions under which information is displayed and obtained from users. There are three major steps:

1. Designing the dialogue sequence

2. Building a prototype

3. Assessing usability

There are a few general rules that should be followed when designing a dialogue and they are summarized in Table 15-13. For a dialogue to have high usability, it must be consistent in form, function, and style. All other rules regarding dialogue design are mitigated by the consistency guideline. For example, the effectiveness of how well errors are handled or feedback is provided will be significantly influenced by consistency in design. If the system does not consistently handle errors, the user will often be at a loss as to why certain things happen.

One example of these guidelines concerns removing data from a database or file (see the Reversal entry in Table 15-13). It is good practice to display the information that will be deleted before making a permanent change to the file. For example, if the customer service representative wanted to remove a customer from the database, the system should ask only for the customer ID in order to retrieve the correct customer account. Once found, and before allowing the confirmation of the

Biometric device: An instrument that detects personal characteristics such as fingerprints, voice prints, retina prints, or signature dynamics.

Smart card: A thin plastic card the size of a credit card with an embedded microprocessor and memory.

Dialogue: The sequence of interaction between a user and a system.

TABLE 15-13 Guidelines for the Design of Human-Computer Dialogues

Guideline	Explanation
Consistency	Dialogues should be consistent in sequence of actions, keystrokes, and terminology (e.g., the same labels should be used for the same operations on all screens, and the location of the same information should be the same on all displays).
Shortcuts and Sequence	Allow advanced users to take shortcuts using special keys (e.g., CTRL-C to copy highlighted text). A natural sequence of steps should be followed (e.g., enter first name before last name, if appropriate).
Feedback	Feedback should be provided for every user action (e.g., confirm that a record has been added, rather than simply putting another blank form on the screen).
Closure	Dialogues should be logically grouped and have a beginning, middle, and end (e.g., the last in the sequence of screens should indicate that there are no more screens).
Error Handling	All errors should be detected and reported; suggestions on how to proceed should be made (e.g., suggest why such errors occur and what user can do to correct the error). Synonyms for certain responses should be accepted (e.g., accept either "t," "T," or "TRUE").
Reversal	Dialogues should, when possible, allow the user to reverse actions (e.g., undo a deletion); data should not be destructed without confirmation (e.g., display all the data for a record the user has indicated is to be deleted).
Control	Dialogues should make the user (especially an experienced user) feel in control of the system (e.g., provide a consistent response time at a pace acceptable to the user).
Ease	Dialogues should be simple for users to enter information and navigate between screens (e.g., provide means to move forward, backward, and to specific screens, such as first and last).

Adapted from Shneiderman, 1992.

deletion, the system should display the account information. For actions making permanent changes to system data files and when the action is not commonly performed, many system designers use the *double-confirmation* technique where the users must confirm their intention twice before being allowed to proceed.

Designing the Dialogue Sequence

Your first step in dialogue design is to define the sequence. In other words, you must first gain an understanding of how users might interact with the system. This means that you must have a clear understanding of user, task, technological, and environmental characteristics when designing dialogues. Suppose that the marketing manager at Pine Valley Furniture (PVF) wants sales and marketing personnel to be able to review the year-to-date transaction activity for any PVF customer. After talking with the manager, you both agree that a typical dialogue between a user and the Customer Information System for obtaining this information might proceed as follows:

1. Request to view individual customer information
2. Specify the customer of interest
3. Select the year-to-date transaction summary display
4. Review customer information
5. Leave system

As a designer, once you understand how a user wishes to use a system, you can then transform these activities into a formal dialogue specification.

Dialogue diagramming:
A formal method for designing and representing human-computer dialogues using box and line diagrams.

A formal method for designing and representing dialogues is **dialogue diagramming.** Dialogue diagrams have only one symbol, a box with three sections; each box represents one display (which might be a full screen or a specific form or window) within a dialogue (see Figure 15-18). The three sections of the box are used as follows:

1. *Top:* Contains a unique display reference number used by other displays for referencing it

2. *Middle:* Contains the name or description of the display

3. *Bottom:* Contains display reference numbers that can be accessed from the current display

All lines connecting the boxes within dialogue diagrams are assumed to be bi-directional and thus do not need arrowheads to indicate direction. This means that users are allowed to always move forward and backward between adjacent displays. If you desire only unidirectional flows within a dialogue, arrowheads should be placed on one end of the line. Within a dialogue diagram, you can easily represent the sequencing of displays, the selection of one display over another, or the repeated use of a single display (e.g., a data entry display). These three concepts—sequence, selection, and iteration—are illustrated in Figure 15-19.

Continuing with our PVF example, Figure 15-20 shows a partial dialogue diagram for processing the marketing manager's request. In this diagram, the analyst placed the request to view year-to-date customer information within the context of the overall Customer Information System. The user must first gain access to the system through a log-on procedure (item 0). If log-on is successful, a main menu is displayed that has four items (item 1). Once the user selects the Individual Customer Information (item 2), control is transferred to the Select Customer display (item 2.1). After a customer is selected, the user is presented with an option to view customer information four different ways (item 2.1.1). Once the user views the customer's year-to-date transaction activity (item 2.1.1.2), the system will allow the user to back up to select a different customer, back up to the main menu, or exit the system (see bottom of item 2.1.1.2).

Building Prototypes and Assessing Usability

Building dialogue prototypes and assessing usability are often optional activities. Some systems may be very simple and straightforward. Others may be more complex but are extensions to existing systems where dialogue and display standards have already been established. In either case, you may not be required to build prototypes and do a formal assessment. However, for many other systems, it is critical that you build prototype displays and then assess the dialogue; this can pay numerous divi-

Figure 15-18
Sections of a dialogue diagramming box

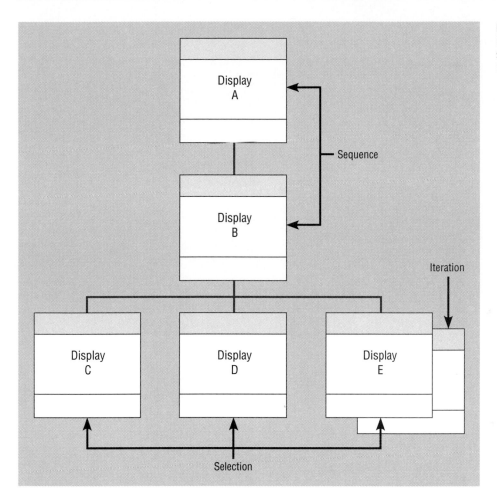

Figure 15-19
Dialogue diagram illustrating sequence, selection, and iteration

dends later in the systems development life cycle (for example, it may be easier to implement a system or train users on a system they have already seen and used).

   Building prototype displays is often a relatively easy activity for you to perform when using CASE tools or many of the graphical development environments such as Microsoft's Visual Basic or Visual C. Recall that Chapter 4 extensively describes the use of CASE for the design of system displays and interfaces. Some systems development environments include easy-to-use input and output (form, report, or window) design utilities. There are also several tools called "Prototypers" or "Demo Builders" that allow you to quickly design displays and show how an interface will work within a full system. These demo systems allow users to enter data and move through displays as if using the actual system. Such activities are not only useful for you to show how an interface will look and feel, they are also useful for assessing usability and for performing user training long before actual systems are completed. In the next section, we extend our discussion of interface and dialogue design to consider issues specific to graphical user interface environments.

Designing Interfaces and Dialogues in Graphical Environments

Graphical user interface (GUI) environments are rapidly growing in popularity. Although all of the interface and dialogue design guidelines presented previously apply to designing GUIs, there are additional issues that are unique to these environments that must be considered. Here, we briefly discuss some of these issues.

Figure 15-20
Dialogue diagram for the Customer Information System (Pine Valley Furniture)

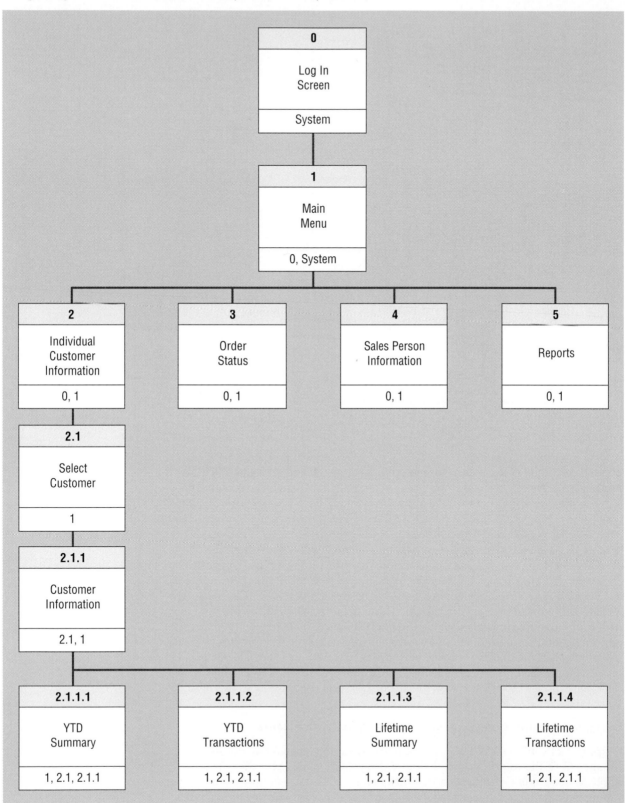

Graphical Interface Design Issues   When designing GUIs for an operating environment such as Microsoft Windows or for the Macintosh, there are numerous factors to consider. Some factors are common to all GUI environments while others are specific to a single environment. We will not, however, discuss the subtleties and details of any single environment. Instead, our discussion will focus on a few general truths that experienced designers mention as critical to the design of usable GUIs (for more information on GUI design, see the books by Porter, 1993, and May, 1991). In most discussions of GUI programming, two rules repeatedly emerge as comprising the first step to becoming an effective GUI designer:

1. *Become an expert user of the GUI environment.*

2. *Understand the available resources and how they can be used.*

The first step should be an obvious one. The greatest strength of designing within a standard operating environment is that *standards* for the behavior of most system operations have already been defined. For example, how you cut and paste, set up your default printer, design menus, or assign commands to functions have been standardized both within and across applications. This allows experienced users of one GUI-based application to easily learn a new application. Thus, in order to design effective interfaces in such environments, you must first understand how other applications have been designed so that you will adopt the established standards for "look and feel." Failure to adopt the standard conventions in a given environment will result in a system that will likely frustrate and confuse users.

The second rule—gaining an understanding of the available resources and how they can be used—is a much larger undertaking. For example, within Windows you can use menus, forms, and boxes in many ways. In fact, the flexibility with which these resources *can be used* versus the established standards for how most designers *actually use* these resources makes design especially challenging. For example, you have the ability to design menus using all upper-case text, putting multiple words on the top line of the menu, and other non-standard conventions. Yet, the standards for menu design require that top-level menu items consist of one word and follow a specific ordering. Numerous other standards for menu design have also been established (see Figure 15-21 for illustrations of many of these standards). Failure to follow standard design conventions will likely prove very confusing to users.

In GUIs, information is requested by placing a window (or form) on the visual display screen. Like menu design, forms can also have numerous properties that can be mixed and matched (see Table 15-14). For example, properties about a form determine whether a form is resizable or movable after being opened. Since properties define how users can actually work with a form, the effective application of properties is fundamental to gaining usability. This means that, in addition to designing the layout of a form, you must also define the "personality" of the form with its characteristic properties. Fortunately, numerous GUI design tools have been developed that allow you to "visually" design forms and interactively engage properties. Interactive GUI design tools have greatly facilitated the design and construction process.

In addition to the issues related to interface design, the sequencing of displays turns out to be a bit more challenging in graphical environments. This topic is discussed next.

Dialogue Design Issues in a Graphical Environment   When designing a dialogue, your goal is to establish the sequence of displays (full screens or windows) that users will encounter when working with the system. Within many GUI environments, this process can be a bit more challenging due to the GUI's ability to suspend activities (without resolving a request for information or exiting the application

Figure 15-21
Highlighting graphical user
interface design standards

altogether) and switch to another application or task. For example, within Microsoft Word, the spell checker executes independently from the general word processor. This means that you can easily jump between the spell checker and word processor without exiting either one. Conversely, when selecting the print operation, you must either initiate printing or abort this request before returning to the word processor. This is an example of the concept of "modality" described in Table 15-14. Thus, Windows-type environments allow you to create forms that either *require* the user to resolve a request before proceeding (print example) or *selectively choose* to resolve a request before proceeding (the spell checker). Creating dialogues that allow the user to jump from application to application or from module to module within a given application requires that you carefully think through the design of dialogues.

One easy way to deal with the complexity of designing advanced graphical user interfaces is to require users to *always* resolve all requests for information before proceeding. For such designs, the dialogue diagramming technique is an adequate design tool. This, however, would make the system operate in a manner similar to a traditional non-GUI environment where the sequencing of displays is tightly controlled. The drawback to such an approach would be the failure to capitalize on the task-switching capabilities of these environments. Thus, if you want to allow users to selectively perform some functions or to selectively switch between tasks, a more powerful design tool may be needed. One tool that is often applied to this problem is the state-transition diagram (STD), introduced in Chapter 12. STDs can be used

TABLE 15-14   Common Properties of Windows and Forms in a Graphical User Interface Environment that can be Active or Inactive

Property	Explanation
Modality	Requires users to resolve the request for information before proceeding (e.g., need to cancel or save before closing a window).
Resizable	Allows users to resize a window or form (e.g., to make room to see other windows also on the screen).
Movable	Allows users to move a window or form (e.g., to allow another window to be seen).
Maximize	Allows users to expand a window or form to a full screen in size (e.g., to avoid distraction from other active windows or forms).
Minimize	Allows users to shrink a window or form to an icon (e.g., to get the window out of the way while working on other active windows).
System Menu	Allows a window or form to also have a system menu to directly access system-level functions (e.g., to save or copy data).

Adapted from Wagner, 1994.

to model dialogues where displays are selectively suspended and activated by the user. For example, Figure 15-22 shows a simple STD that models the various states a spell checker encounters when in use.

Recall that the first step when designing a STD is to identify all possible states for a given object or process. In the case of the spell checker, it can have the following states:

1. Closed (not loaded)

2. Open, but idle (waiting to check)

3. Open and checking

Further, several events or transitions occur that move the spell checker from one state to another. The first transition (labeled 1) loads the spell checker. In other words, this represents a user's request to activate the spell-checking system by

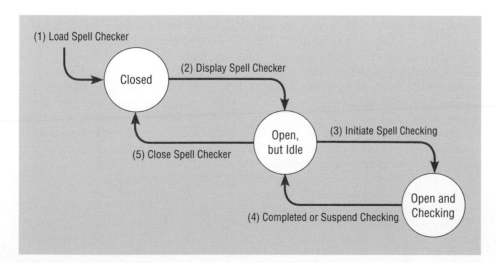

Figure 15-22
State-transition diagram for spell checker

selecting the appropriate command within the word processor. As the spell checker can be activated at virtually any time within the system, it would be difficult if not impossible to model all possible display sequences using normal dialogue diagramming techniques.

The second transition occurs when the spell checker moves from the "Closed" state to the "Open, but Idle" state, referred to as the "Display spell checker" transition (labeled 2). At this point, the spell checker can be requested to "Initiate Spell Checking" (labeled 3), left idle, or closed (labeled 5). If spell checking is initiated, the spell checker moves into its final unique state, "Open and Checking." As before, the user has the option to suspend checking or wait for the spell checking to be completed (labeled 4). When either of these transitions occur, the spell checker will return to the "Open, but Idle" state. From there, the spell checker can be closed (labeled 5) or reinitiated. For each state, or transformations between states, a specific display, dialogue box, or request must be designed. The sequencing of these displays and dialogue boxes will be guided by the STD. This means that it is only through a clear understanding of all possible states, and the transitions that make them change, that a complete dialogue specification can be designed for most multi-windowing GUI applications.

In summary, designing dialogues in environments where the sequence between displays cannot be predetermined offers significant challenges to the designer. In fact, the focus of object-oriented systems analysis and design, a much more advanced design approach, is to provide designers with tools and techniques for modeling systems employing these concepts (see Chapter 12).

SUMMARY

In this chapter, our focus was to acquaint you with the process of designing human-computer interfaces and dialogues. Understanding the characteristics of various interaction methods (command language, menu, form, object, natural language) and devices (keyboard, mouse, joystick, trackball, touch screen, light pen, graphics tablet, voice) is a fundamental skill you must master. No single interaction style or device is the most appropriate in all instances: each has its strengths and weaknesses. You must consider characteristics of the intended users, the tasks being performed, and various technical and environmental factors when making design decisions.

The chapter also reviewed design guidelines for computer-based forms. You learned that most forms have a header, sequence or time-related information, instructions, a body, summary data, authorization, and comments. Users must be able to move the cursor position, edit data, exit with different consequences, and obtain help. Techniques for structuring and controlling data entry were presented along with guidelines for providing feedback, prompting, and error messages. A simple, well-organized help function that shows examples of proper use of the system should be provided. A variety of help types were reviewed. A final topic of interface design focused on controlling user access to systems and data. This discussion presented four techniques: views, authorization rules, encryption procedures, and authentication schemes.

Next, guidelines for designing human-computer dialogues were presented including a description of dialogue diagramming. These guidelines are consistency, allowing for shortcuts, providing feedback and closure on tasks, handling errors, allowing for operations reversal, giving the user a sense of control, and ease of navigation. Designing dialogues and procedures for assessing their usability were also reviewed. Finally, several interface and dialogue design issues were described within the context of designing graphical user interfaces. These included the need to follow standards to provide the capabilities of modality, resizing, moving, maximizing and minimizing windows, and to offer a system menu choice. This discussion highlighted how concepts presented earlier in the chapter can be applied or augmented in these emerging environments.

Our goal was to provide you with a foundation for building highly usable human-computer interfaces. As more and more development environments provide rapid prototyping tools for the design of interfaces and dialogues, many complying to common interface standards, the difficulty of designing usable interfaces will be reduced. However, you still need a solid understanding of the concepts presented in this chapter in order to succeed. Learning to use a computer system is like learning to use a parachute—if a person fails on the first try, odds are he or she won't try again (Blattner & Schultz, 1988). If this analogy is true, it is important that a user's first experience with a system be a positive one. By following the design guidelines outlined in this chapter, your chances of providing a positive first experience to users will be greatly enhanced.

KEY TERMS

Authorization rules
Biometric device
Command language
   interaction
Dialogue
Dialogue diagramming

Drop-down menu
Form interaction
Icon
Interface
Menu interaction

Natural language
   interaction
Object-based interaction
Pop-up menu
Smart card
View

REVIEW QUESTIONS

1. Define each of the following terms:

   a. dialogue
   b. drop-down menu
   c. icon
   d. pop-up menu
   e. authorization rules
   f. smart card
   g. view

2. Contrast the following terms:

   a. dialogue, interface
   b. command language interaction, form interaction, menu interaction, natural language interaction, object-based interaction
   c. drop-down menu, pop-up menu
   d. authorization rules, biometric device, view

3. Describe the process of designing interfaces and dialogues. What deliverables are produced from this process? Are these deliverables the same for all types of system projects? Why or why not?

4. Describe five methods of interacting with a system. Is one method better than all others? Why or why not?

5. Describe several input devices for interacting with a system. Is one device better than all others? Why or why not?

6. Describe the general guidelines for the design of menus. Can you think of any instances when it would be appropriate to violate these guidelines?

7. List and describe the general sections of a typical business form. Do computer-based and paper-based forms have the same components? Why or why not?

8. List and describe the functional capabilities needed in an interface for effective entry and navigation. Which capabilities are most important? Why? Will this be the same for all systems? Why or why not?

9. Describe the general guidelines for structuring data entry fields. Can you think of any instances when it would be appropriate to violate these guidelines?

10. Describe four types of data errors.

11. Describe the methods used to enhance the validity of data input.

12. Describe the types of system feedback. Is any form of feedback more important than the others? Why or why not?

13. Describe the general guidelines for designing usable help. Can you think of any instances when it would be appropriate to violate these guidelines?

14. Describe four ways to control user access to a system or data.

15. What steps do you need to follow when designing a dialogue? Of the guidelines for designing a dialogue, which is most important? Why?

16. Describe the properties of windows and forms in a graphical user interface environment. Which property do you feel is most important? Why?

PROBLEMS AND EXERCISES

1. Match the following terms to the appropriate definitions.

   _____ interface

   _____ command language interaction

   _____ menu interaction

   _____ object-based interaction

   _____ natural language interaction

   _____ dialogue

   _____ drop-down menu

   a. human-computer interaction method where a list of system options is provided and, if selected, each option invokes a command

   b. menu positioning method that places the access point of the menu near the top line of the display; when accessed, menus open by dropping down onto the display

   c. human-computer interaction method where symbols are used to represent commands or functions

   d. method by which users interact with information systems

   e. human-computer interaction method where explicit statements are entered into a system to invoke operations

   f. sequence of interaction between a user and a system

   g. human-computer interaction method where inputs to and outputs from a computer-based application are in a conventional speaking language such as English

2. Consider software applications that you regularly use that have menu interfaces, whether they be PC- or mainframe-based applications. Evaluate these applications in terms of the menu design guidelines outlined in Table 15-1.

3. Consider the design of a registration system for a hotel. Following design specification items in Figure 15-2, briefly describe the relevant users, tasks, and displays involved in such a system.

4. Imagine the design of a system used to register students at a university. Discuss the user, task, system, and environmental characteristics (see Table 14-9) that should be considered when designing the interface for such a system.

5. For each of the following interaction methods recall a software package that you have used recently: command language, menus, and objects. What did you like and dislike about each package? What were the strengths and weaknesses of each? Which type do you prefer for which circumstances? Which type do you believe will become most prevalent? Why?

6. Briefly describe several different business tasks that are good candidates for form-based interaction within an information system.

7. List the physical input devices described in this chapter that you have seen or used. For each device, briefly describe your experience and provide your personal evaluation. Do your personal evaluations parallel the evaluations provided in Tables 15-3 and 15-4?

8. Propose some specific settings where natural language interaction would be particularly useful and explain why.

9. Examine the help systems for some software applications that you use. Evaluate each using the general guidelines provided in Table 15-11.

10. Design one sample data entry screen for a hotel registration system using the data entry guidelines provided in this chapter (see Table 15-6). Support your design with arguments for each of the design choices you made.

11. Describe some typical dialogue scenarios between users and a hotel registration system. For hints, reread the section in this chapter that provides sample dialogue between users and the Customer Information System at Pine Valley Furniture.

12. Represent the dialogues from the previous question through the use of dialogue diagrams.

FIELD EXERCISES

1. Research the topic "natural language" at your library. Determine the status of applications available with natural language interaction. Forecast how long it will be before natural language capabilities are prevalent in information systems use.

2. Examine two PC-based graphical user interfaces (e.g., Microsoft's Windows and Macintosh). If you do not own these interfaces, you are likely to find them at your university, workplace, or at a computer retail store. You may want to supplement your hands-on evaluation with recent formal evaluations published in magazines such as *PC Magazine*. In what ways are these two interfaces similar and different? Are these interfaces intuitive? Why or why not? Is one more intuitive than the other? Why or why not? Which interface seems easier to learn? Why? What types of system requirements does each interface have, and what are the costs of each interface? Which do you prefer? Why?

3. Interview a variety of people you know about the various ways they interact, in terms of inputs, with systems at their workplaces. What types of technologies and devices are used to deliver these inputs? Are the input methods and devices easy to

use and do they help these people complete their tasks effectively and efficiently? Why or why not? How could these input methods and devices be improved?

4. Interview systems analysts and programmers in an organization where graphical user interfaces are used. Describe the ways that these interfaces are developed and used. How does the use of such interfaces enhance or complicate the design of interfaces and dialogues?

REFERENCES

Apple. 1987. *Human Interface Guidelines: The Apple Desktop Interface.* Reading, MA: Addison-Wesley.

Blattner, M., and E. Schultz. 1988. "User Interface Tutorial." Presented at the 1988 Hawaii International Conference on System Sciences, Kona, Hawaii, January, 1988.

Bloombecker, J. J. 1989. "Short-Circuiting Computer Crime." *Datamation* 55 (Oct. 1): 71–72.

Dumas, J. S. 1988. *Designing User Interfaces for Software.* Englewood Cliffs, NJ: Prentice-Hall.

Fernandez, E. B., R. C. Summers, and C. Wood. 1981. *Database Security and Integrity.* Reading, MA: Addison-Wesley.

IBM. 1991. *Systems Application Architecture: Common User Access Guide to User Interface.* IBM Document SC34-4289-00. October.

May, J. C. 1991. *Extending the Macintosh Toolbox: Programming Menus, Windows, Dialogues, and More.* Reading, MA: Addison-Wesley.

McFadden, F. R., J. A. Hoffer., and M. B. Prescott. 1999. *Modern Database Management,* 5th ed. Reading, MA: Addison Wesley Longman.

Norman, K. L. 1991. *The Psychology of Menu Selection.* Norwood, NJ: Ablex.

Porter, A. 1993. *C++ Programming for Windows.* Berkeley, CA: Osborne McGraw-Hill.

Shneiderman, B. 1992. *Designing the User Interface: Strategies for Effective Human-Computer Interaction.* Reading, MA: Addison-Wesley.

Wagner, R. 1994. "A GUI Design Manifesto." *Paradox Informant* 5 (June): 36–42.

Logical Design: Designing the Customer Reservation Interface and Dialogue

INTRODUCTION

In this Broadway Entertainment Company (BEC) case, we review the activities that occurred during the design of an important custom interface to the Customer Activity Tracking System (CATS). Specifically, we focus on the activities of one systems analyst, Frank Napier, during the creation of the on-line customer-product reservation confirmation module within CATS. This interface occurs where a BEC telephone reservation clerk confirms a customer reservation request after the customer receives a postcard notifying him or her of a new product release.

DESIGNING THE CUSTOMER RESERVATION INTERFACE AND DIALOGUE

After completing the design of the customer-product assignment report (see BEC case after Chapter 14), Frank Napier was assigned to develop an initial design of the interface and dialogue for recording customer product reservations within CATS. This custom dialogue, not provided in the purchased software, was to be only a very small piece of CATS, but it must be consistent with the overall style for CATS. CATS uses a graphical user interface with a fairly strict navigation path. Buttons on each on-line form rather than general menus are used to move from form to form. Forms are used to capture data to enter into the CATS database. Each reservation clerk will work from a personal computer equipped with a color monitor, keyboard, and mouse.

BEC's system development methodology requires that Frank first gain an understanding of the data and process requirements for making reservations. To do this, he reviewed the data flow diagrams, entity-relationship models, data element list, and designs of system outputs. In essence, he reviewed all relevant analysis and design information concerning customers placing reservations for products. From this review, he concluded that the dialogue flow for recording the reservation within CATS would take the following five steps:

1. A customer receives a notification postcard containing a product description, date of availability, and reservation code (the product/customer/store code).

2. If a customer desires to make a product reservation, he or she calls BEC to confirm the reservation.

3. To record the reservation, a BEC telephone clerk requests the reservation code from the customer; this code is entered into a CATS module.

4. After entering the reservation code, the information system displays customer and product information; this information will be visually inspected for correctness by the clerk through questions and answers with the customer.

5. After verifying the information correctness, the clerk will confirm the reservation, thank the customer, and hang up the telephone call.

After outlining the flow and sequence of the reservation recording process, Frank outlined the sequence of on-line forms using dialogue diagramming (Figure 1). The dialogue diagram contained three forms in its sequence. Form 1, Reservation Code Entry, equates to step 3. Form 2, Information Verification, equates to step 4 while Form 3, Reservation Confirmation, equates to step 5 in the sequence. For each form, the dialogue diagram shows that the user is able to back up to the previous form. Also, after Reservation Confirmation (Form 3), the user is taken back to Form 1, Reservation Code Entry. In other words, after a reservation confirmation, the clerk will be ready to take another reservation.

Figure 1
Dialogue diagramming for
the customer product
reservation sequence

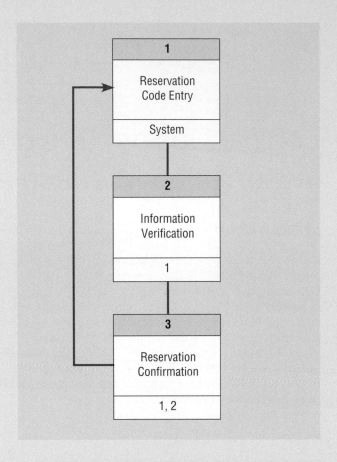

After designing the dialogue flow, Frank's next step was to design prototypes of each form in the sequence. The BEC systems development group uses a variety of tools for prototyping including CASE and visual interface design tools. The CATS design team decided to use Microsoft's Visual Basic for Windows to design the prototype because display forms can be easily constructed and compiled into a working prototype. These prototypes can then be distributed to users and others within the design team to assess system usability and completeness.

Figure 2 shows the initial prototype design for Form 1, Reservation Code Entry. This form contains a single field for entering the reservation code and three selection buttons: OK, Help, and Quit. Frank also defined a picture statement for the reservation code field to restrict it to a five-character, alphanumeric value with a dash between the third and fourth characters. Using a picture statement on data entry fields is one easy way to help users enter correct values.

Until any of the buttons is pushed, the reservation clerk can edit the reservation code using normal Windows field editing functions. Selecting the OK button (or pressing the Enter key) will advance the sequence

of the dialogue to Form 2. In this initial design, Frank does not deal with data entry errors (in this case, an improper reservation code); these will be designed after evaluating the usability of the basic design. Selecting Help will invoke the help system (also not yet designed), and Quit will terminate the execution of the reservation system. Under the OK button, Frank added two lines of Basic language programming code to "unload" the current form (Cats1) and to "show" the second form in the sequence (Cats2) when executing the prototype (see Figure 3). Thus, when the application is compiled, users can use a mouse to press the OK button to move to Form 2, Information Verification. This means that the prototype can be easily made to behave in a manner consistent with the actual system implementation, greatly improving the usefulness of any usability assessment activities.

As described, Form 2, Information Verification, contains both customer and product information (Figure 4). All of this information is retrieved from the CATS database based on the reservation code. The customer data fields may be updated (except for the Customer Number field), if necessary. This form also has three buttons: Record, Help, and Cancel. Choosing Record

Figure 2
Reservation code entry
form prototype

Figure 3
Visual Basic programming
code attached to the OK
button to unload Form 1 and
display Form 2

Figure 4
Information verification
form prototype

or pressing the Enter key advances the sequence of the dialogue to Form 3 while pressing the Cancel button returns the user to Form 1. As with the prior form, Frank programmed the Record button to load Form 3,

Reservation Confirmation. This time, however, he did not program the system to unload Form 2 but simply to overlay Form 3 on top of Form 2 (Figure 5). After Form 3 is displayed, a user can confirm the reservation

Figure 5
Reservation confirmation
form prototype

Figure 6
One-to-one mapping of dialogue diagramming sequence to prototype form designs

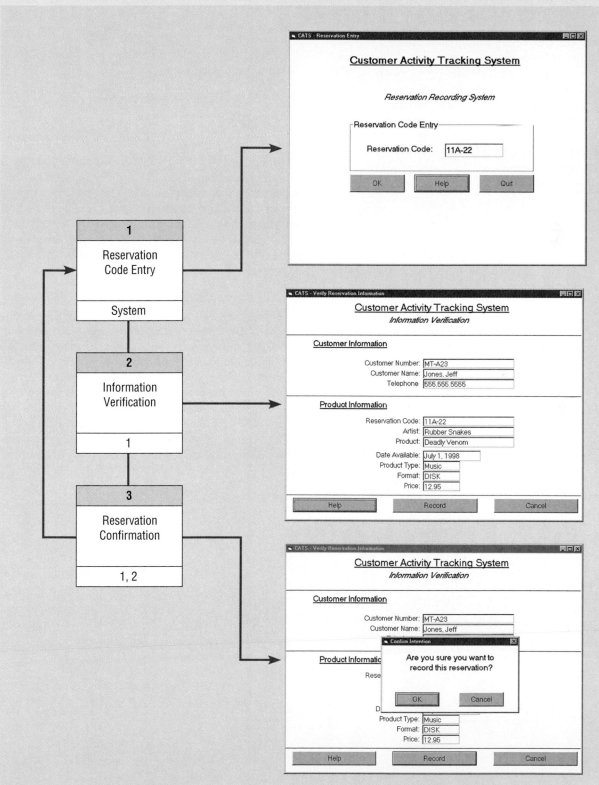

by selecting the OK button, or cancel the reservation request and return to Form 2 by selecting the Cancel button. Since Form 3 is a window, the reservation clerk can move this confirmation box to anywhere on the display screen. Again, Frank programmed the selection buttons so that the prototype would behave in a manner consistent with the design represented in the dialogue diagram.

In summary, the customer-product reservation dialogue sequence contains three forms. Each form has a one-to-one mapping with dialogue sequence and movement between each form controlled by selection buttons (see Figure 6).

SUMMARY

After completing the dialogue and form design process, Frank assessed the design's usability. As he had done with system outputs, Frank first contacted several store managers and arranged to have them use the dialogue on the PCs in their stores. After consolidating some comments from these potential users, he developed new form layouts and a hard copy script of sample forms which he distributed to a cross section of potential users. He prepared a questionnaire that captured user background data, responses to comprehension questions, and satisfaction perceptions (see Figure 7 from the BEC installment after Chapter 14). Comprehension tasks involved responding to which buttons to press to perform a certain navigation activity, the meaning of fields on the form, and how to undo data already entered.

From this survey Frank discovered several improvements were needed:

- More descriptive button labels

- More specific form titles

- Color coding fields which are read-only

- Changes to the information verification and confirmation forms to handle declining a reservation

Frank realized that these were initial form designs since he would have to add additional functions (like pop-up lists to look up valid field values) to support modifying and deleting reservations (inevitable when customers changed their minds). Also, he would have to design such elements as help displays, error messages, shortcut keystrokes, and more methods to undo data entries before the dialogue and interface were complete. In addition, the reservation interface must be integrated into the total interface available to each telephone clerk. However, a reaction to an initial design was important before more detailed work was completed. Fortunately, both potential users and development colleagues enthusiastically praised Frank's efforts at initial dialogue and interface designs. Nevertheless, Frank knew that much more work was required to translate the form prototypes into an operational system. He was, however, reassured that BEC's system development methodology would help guide him through the additional work that remains to be done.

16

Designing Databases: Logical Data Modeling

After studying this chapter, you should be able to:

- Concisely define each of the following key logical data modeling terms: *relation, functional dependency, foreign key,* and *normalization.*

- Explain the role of logical data modeling in the overall analysis and design of an information system.

- Describe four steps in logical data modeling.

- Be able to represent unary, binary, and ternary relationships in the relational data model.

- Give concise definitions of first, second, and third normal forms.

- Merge normalized relations from separate user views into a consolidated set of normalized relations.

- Transform an entity-relationship (E-R) diagram into an equivalent set of normalized relations.

INTRODUCTION

In Chapter 10 you learned how to describe the data requirements of an information system using a graphical notation, the entity-relationship (E-R) data model. You used E-R data models to represent a conceptual view of organizational data independent of any particular database processing technology. Further, you learned how to use E-R diagramming to represent data about an organization based on business rules and policies rather than on specific information processing requirements. Although we concentrated on representing the nature of data in an organization, we did not concern ourselves with guidelines on what were good or poor data models. We address this important topic in this chapter.

In Chapter 16 you learn more about structuring the description of data through logical data modeling. Logical data modeling has three purposes. First, in logical data modeling you use the *normalization* process which results in a structure for data that has some very desirable properties. These properties help you represent data in more stable structures that are not likely to change over time and that have minimal redundancy. If you were to implement the database for an information system from normalized data, database processing would be simple, generally efficient, and less susceptible to problems, or *anomalies,* during data maintenance.

The second purpose of logical data modeling is to develop a data model from which we can do physical database design. Since most information systems today use relational database management systems, logical data modeling usually produces a relational database model. It is possible to produce network, hierarchical, or object-oriented data models from logical data modeling, but we cover only the most typical situation in this chapter. In fact, we suggest that even if network or hierarchical technologies are used, you still should do logical data modeling to produce relations. You can then translate these relations into the target data model during physical database design. Here we will present the basic principles of the relational database model and will show you how to develop relational models from E-R models.

The final purpose of logical data modeling is to develop a data model that reflects the actual data requirements that exist in the forms (hard copy and computer displays) and reports of an information system. Thus, logical data modeling occurs after or concurrent with the design of system externals and outputs. Logical data modeling includes a *bottom-up* process of deriving relations from specific forms and reports, or what are called user views of an information system. We will show how to do this bottom-up logical design and then describe how to integrate or merge separate relations for individual forms and reports into a consolidated logical data model. Then we will illustrate how to translate an E-R model into relational form so that the conceptual data model can be compared with the logical data model and differences resolved.

Familiarity with the concepts and terminology introduced in Chapter 10 is essential for reading and understanding the contents of Chapter 16 (you may want to review Chapter 10 now). Once you master the conceptual and logical data modeling techniques explained in Chapters 10 and 16, you will likely design normalized data into entity-relationship diagrams. Thus, although we introduce conceptual and logical data modeling as separate topics, sometimes these project activities are combined into one data modeling project step.

LOGICAL DATA MODELING

Logical database model:
A description of data using a notation which corresponds to a data organization used by a database management system.

A **logical data model** describes data using a notation which corresponds to a data organization used by a database management system. The most common style for a logical data model is the *relational database model.*

You typically do logical data modeling in parallel with other systems design steps (see Figure 16-1). Thus, you collect the detailed specifications of data necessary for logical data modeling as you design system inputs and outputs. Logical data modeling is driven not only from the previously developed E-R data model for the application but also from form and report layouts. You study data elements on these system inputs and outputs and identify inter-relationships among the data. As with conceptual data modeling, the work of all systems development team members is coordinated and shared through the project dictionary or repository. Increasingly, this repository is maintained by a common CASE tool although some organizations still use manual documentation. In either case, it is essential that the process, logic, system input, system output, and data model descriptions of a system be consistent and complete since each describes different views of the same information system.

Figure 16-1
Systems development life cycle with logical design phase highlighted

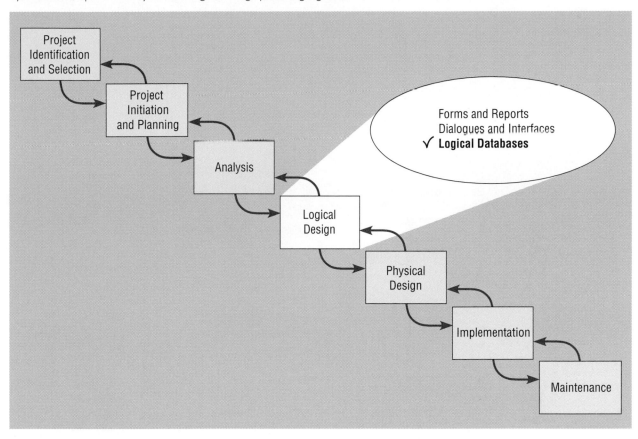

The Process of Logical Data Modeling

Figure 16-2 shows that data modeling occurs in the project planning, analysis, and logical design steps of the systems development process. In this chapter we discuss methods which help you finalize a data model during the logical design phase. Data modeling during project planning and analysis is done using entity-relationship modeling which uses a special notation to represent as much meaning about data as possible. In logical design you use a process called normalization, which is a way to build a data model that has some desirable properties of simplicity, non-redundancy, and maintenance. We will discuss normalization later within the context of developing a relational database model. We develop only the fundamentals of logical data modeling in this chapter. The interested reader is referred to McFadden, Hoffer, and Prescott (1999) for a more thorough treatment of techniques for logical data modeling.

There are four key steps in logical data modeling:

1. Develop a logical data model for each known user view (form and report) for the application using normalization principles.

2. Combine all normalized user views into one consolidated logical data model; this step is called *view integration.*

Figure 16-2
Relationship between data modeling and the systems development life cycle

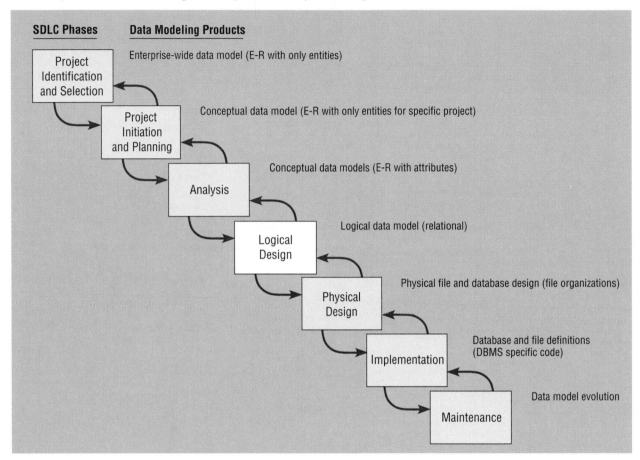

3. Translate the conceptual E-R data model for the application, developed without explicit consideration of specific user views, into normalized relations.

4. Compare the consolidated logical data model with the translated E-R model and produce, through view integration, one final logical data model for the application.

We will show how to do each of these steps in this chapter.

Deliverables and Outcomes

During logical data modeling, you must account for every data element on a system input or output—form or report—and on the E-R model in the logical data model. Each data element (like customer name, product description, or purchase price) must be a piece of raw data kept in the system's database or else, in the case of a data element on a system output, the element can be derived from data in the database. Figure 16-3 (on pages 604–605) illustrates the outcomes from the four-step logical data modeling process listed above. Figures 16-3a and 16-3b (step 1) contain two sample system outputs for a customer order processing system in

Pine Valley Furniture. Normalized relations are listed below each output diagram. Each relation is named and its attributes are listed within parentheses. The primary key attribute is indicated by an underline, and an attribute of a relation which is the primary key of another relation is indicated by a dashed underline. Figure 16-3c (step 2) shows the result of integrating these two separate sets of normalized relations. Figure 16-3d (step 3) shows an E-R diagram for a customer order processing application that might be developed during conceptual data modeling along with equivalent normalized relations. Finally, Figure 16-3e (step 4) shows a set of normalized relations that would result from reconciling the logical data models of Figures 16-3c and 16-3d. Normalized relations like those in Figure 16-3e are the primary deliverable from logical data modeling.

Updating the CASE repository or project dictionary is the second output from logical data modeling. Figure 10-12 listed the typical project dictionary entries from conceptual data modeling and Figure 16-4 (on page 606) shows the additional entries made during logical data modeling. Since some of this information is collected during design of system externals and outputs, you make some of these entries during other logical design steps. A key difference between conceptual and logical data modeling is that you have structured data requirements during logical data modeling into relations, rather than entities. Because of normalization, there is not necessarily a one-to-one correspondence between entities and relations. Also, as we will see, relationships are not explicitly represented in relations but are shown indirectly by using common attributes (*foreign keys*) in associated relations. Thus, you do not add new relationship information during logical database design. Any new relationships discovered during logical data modeling, however, would be added into the conceptual data model and the project dictionary would be updated. Relationship information is useful in physical database and computer program design, which we will illustrate in later chapters.

It is important to remember that relations do not correspond to computer files. The project dictionary still contains a logical description of data at this point. In physical database design (Chapter 17), we show how relations are transformed into the design for physical computer files.

Since the relational data model is central to our discussion of logical data modeling, the next section introduces this data model.

RELATIONAL DATABASE MODEL

The **relational database model** (Codd, 1970) represents data in the form of tables or relations. You need only a few simple concepts to describe the relational model, and it is easily understood and used by those unfamiliar with the underlying theory.

A **relation** is a named, two-dimensional *table* of data. Each relation (or table) consists of a set of named *columns* and an arbitrary number of unnamed *rows*. Each column in a relation corresponds to an attribute of that relation. Each row of a relation corresponds to a record that contains data values for an entity.

Figure 16-5 shows an example of a relation named EMPLOYEE1. This relation contains the following attributes describing employees: Emp_ID, Name, Dept, and Salary. There are five rows in the table, corresponding to five employees.

You can express the *structure* of a relation by a shorthand notation in which the name of the relation is followed (in parentheses) by the names of the attributes in the relation. The primary key attribute is underlined. For example, you would express EMPLOYEE1 as follows:

EMPLOYEE1(Emp_ID,Name,Dept,Salary)

Relational database model: A data model that represents data in the form of tables or relations.

Relation: A named, two-dimensional table of data. Each relation consists of a set of named columns and an arbitrary number of un-named rows.

Figure 16-3
Simple example of logical
data modeling

(a) Highest volume customer
query screen

```
HIGHEST VOLUME CUSTOMER

ENTER PRODUCT ID.:        M 128
START DATE:               11/01/1998
END DATE:                 12/31/1998
- - - - - - - - - - - - - - - - - - - - -
CUSTOMER ID.:             1256
NAME:                     Commonwealth Builder
VOLUME:                   30
```

This inquiry screen shows the customer with the largest volume total sales of a specified product during an indicated time period.

Relations:
    CUSTOMER (Customer ID, Name)
    ORDER (Order_Number, Customer ID, Order_Date)
    PRODUCT (Product ID)
    LINE ITEM (Order_Number, Product_ID, Order_Quantity)

(b) Backlog summary report

```
                                                        PAGE 1

                    BACKLOG SUMMARY REPORT
                        11/30/1998

                                    BACKLOG
                    PRODUCT ID      QUANTITY
                       B381            0
                       B975            0
                       B985            6
                       E125           30
                        ⋮
                       M128            2
                        ⋮
```

This report shows the unit volume of each product that has been ordered less that amount shipped through the specified date.

Relations:
    PRODUCT (Product_ID)
    LINE ITEM (Product_ID, Order_Number, Order_Quantity)
    ORDER (Order_Number, Order_Date)
    SHIPMENT (Product_ID, Invoice_Number, Ship_Quantity)
    INVOICE (Invoice_Number, Invoice_Date)

CUSTOMER (<u>Customer_ID</u>, Name)
PRODUCT (<u>Product_ID</u>)
INVOICE (<u>Invoice_Number</u>, Invoice_Date)
ORDER (<u>Order_Number</u>, <u>Customer_ID</u>, Order_Date)
LINE ITEM (<u>Order_Number</u>, <u>Product_ID</u>, Order_Quantity)
SHIPMENT (<u>Product_ID</u>, <u>Invoice_Number</u>, Ship_Quantity)

(c) Integrated set of relations

(d) Conceptual data model
and transformed relations

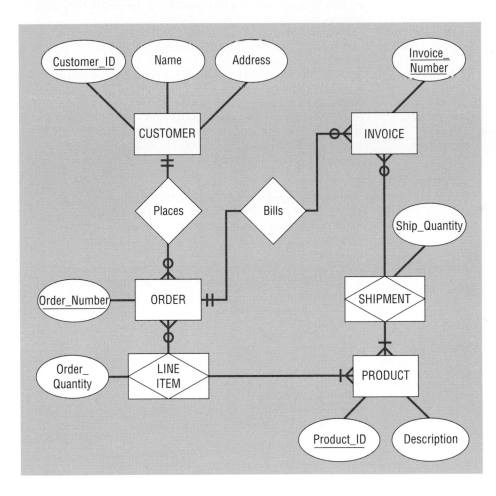

Relations:
 CUSTOMER (<u>Customer_ID</u>, Name, Address)
 PRODUCT (<u>Product_ID</u>, Description)
 ORDER (<u>Order_Number</u>, Customer_ID, Order_Date)
 LINE ITEM (<u>Order_Number</u>, <u>Product_ID</u>, Order_Quantity)
 INVOICE (<u>Invoice_Number</u>, Order_Number)
 SHIPMENT (<u>Invoice_Number</u>, <u>Product_ID</u>, Ship_Quantity)

CUSTOMER (<u>Customer_ID</u>, Name, Address)
PRODUCT (<u>Product_ID</u>, Description)
ORDER (<u>Order_Number</u>, Customer_ID, Order_Date)
LINE ITEM (<u>Order_Number</u>, <u>Product_ID</u>, Order_Quantity)
INVOICE (<u>Invoice_Number</u>, Order_Number, Invoice_Date)
SHIPMENT (<u>Invoice_Number</u>, <u>Product_ID</u>, Ship_Quantity)

(e) Final set of normalized
relations

Figure 16-4

Typical data model elements added to a project dictionary during logical data modeling

RELATION	
Name	A label for the relation; may correspond to an entity name if the meaning of the relation is the same as some entity from the conceptual data model
Description	Explanation so that it is clear which objects are covered by this relation; clarifies relationship of this relation to any entities from the conceptual data model
Attributes and null restrictions	List of attributes included in this relation and for each a statement of whether the attribute may be null (i.e., have no value) for this relation
Primary key	Name(s) of attribute(s) that form the unique identifier for each row of this relation
Foreign keys and referential integrity restrictions	Name of each attribute that is a cross reference to a primary key in another relation; for each foreign key, a statement of the relationship between a value of the foreign key attribute in this relation and values for this attribute found in the associated relation in which this attribute is the primary key
ATTRIBUTE	
Name	A name that uniquely labels the attribute; this would be an attribute name already entered from conceptual data modeling, and the other information about this attribute (like description and domain) would be updated, if necessary
Data type	A specification of the natural format of the attribute (such as alphanumeric, integer, date) as well as a maximum length, if appropriate

Figure 16-5

EMPLOYEE1 relation with sample data

EMPLOYEE1

Emp_ID	Name	Dept	Salary
100	Margaret Simpson	Marketing	42,000
140	Allen Beeton	Accounting	39,000
110	Chris Lucero	Info Systems	41,500
190	Lorenzo Davis	Finance	38,000
150	Susan Martin	Marketing	38,500

Properties of Relations

We have defined relations as two-dimensional tables of data; however, not all tables are relations. Relations have several properties that distinguish them from nonrelational tables:

1. *Entries in columns are atomic.* An entry at the intersection of each row and column is *atomic* (or single-valued).

2. *Entries in columns are from the same domain.* In a relation, all entries in a given column are drawn from the same domain of values.

3. *Each row is unique.* No two rows in a relation are identical. Uniqueness is guaranteed since the relation has a nonnull primary key.

4. *The sequence of columns (left to right) is insignificant.* The columns of a relation can be interchanged without changing the meaning or use of the relation.

5. *The sequence of rows (top to bottom) is insignificant.* As with columns, the rows of a relation may be interchanged or stored in any sequence. Users may view the rows of a relation in different logical sequences.

Well-Structured Relations

To prepare for our discussion of normalization, we need to address the following question: What constitutes a well-structured relation? Intuitively, a **well-structured relation** contains a minimum amount of redundancy and allows users to insert, modify, and delete the rows in a table without errors or inconsistencies. EMPLOYEE1 (Figure 16-5) is such a relation. Each row of the table contains data describing one employee, and any modification to an employee's data (such as a change in salary) is confined to one row of the table.

In contrast, EMPLOYEE2 (Figure 16-6) contains data about employees and the courses they have completed. Each row in this table is unique for the combination of Emp_ID and Course, which becomes the primary key for the table. This is not a well-structured relation. If you examine the sample data in the table, you will notice a considerable amount of redundancy. For example, the Emp_ID, Name, Dept, and Salary appear in two separate rows for employees 100, 110, and 150. Consequently, if the salary for employee 100 changes, we must record this fact in two rows (or more, for some employees).

Redundancies in a table may result in errors or inconsistencies (called **anomalies**) when a user attempts to update the data in the table. Three types of anomalies are possible: insertion, deletion, and modification.

1. *Insertion anomaly.* Suppose that you need to add a new employee to EMPLOYEE2. Since the primary key for this relation is the combination of Emp_ID and Course you must supply values for both Emp_ID and Course (since primary key values cannot be null or nonexistent). This is an anomaly, since the user should be able to enter employee data without supplying course data.

2. *Deletion anomaly.* Suppose that the data for employee number 140 is deleted from the table. This will result in losing the information that this employee completed a course (Tax Acc) on 12/8/1999. In fact, it results in losing all the information about this course.

3. *Modification anomaly.* Suppose that employee number 100 gets a salary increase. You must record the increase in each of the rows for that employee (two occurrences in Figure 16-6), otherwise the data will be inconsistent.

Well-structured relation: A relation that contains a minimum amount of redundancy and allows users to insert, modify, and delete the rows in a table without errors or inconsistencies.

Anomalies: Errors or inconsistencies that may result when a user attempts to update a table that contains redundant data. There are three types of anomalies: insertion, deletion, and modification anomalies.

Figure 16-6
Relation with redundancy

EMPLOYEE2

Emp_ID	Name	Dept	Salary	Course	Date_Completed
100	Margaret Simpson	Marketing	42,000	SPSS	6/19/1999
100	Margaret Simpson	Marketing	42,000	Surveys	10/7/1999
140	Alan Beeton	Accounting	39,000	Tax Acc	12/8/1999
110	Chris Lucero	Info Systems	41,500	SPSS	1/12/1999
110	Chris Lucero	Info Systems	41,500	C++	4/22/1999
190	Lorenzo Davis	Finance	38,000	Investments	5/7/1999
150	Susan Martin	Marketing	38,500	SPSS	6/19/1999
150	Susan Martin	Marketing	38,500	TQM	8/12/1999

These anomalies indicate that EMPLOYEE2 is not a well-structured relation. The problem with this relation is that it contains data about two entities: EMPLOYEE and COURSE. You will use normalization to divide EMPLOYEE2 into two relations. One of the resulting relations is EMPLOYEE1 (Figure 16-5). The other we will call EMP COURSE, which appears with sample data in Figure 16-7. The primary key of this relation is the combination of Emp_ID and Course, and we underline these attribute names in Figure 16-7 to highlight this fact. Examine Figure 16-7 to verify that EMP COURSE is free of the types of anomalies described previously and is therefore well-structured.

CONCEPTS OF NORMALIZATION

Normalization: The process of converting complex data structures into simple, stable data structures.

We have presented an intuitive discussion of well-structured relations; however, we need formal definitions of such relations, together with a process for designing them. **Normalization** is a process for converting complex data structures into simple, stable data structures (see Dutka and Hanson, 1989, for a thorough explanation of normalization and a wide variety of normal forms). For example, we used the principles of normalization to convert the EMPLOYEE2 table with its redundancy to EMPLOYEE1 (Figure 16-5) and EMP COURSE (Figure 16-7).

Steps in Normalization

Normal form: A state of a relation that can be determined by applying simple rules regarding dependencies to that relation.

Normalization can be accomplished in stages, each of which corresponds to a normal form (see Figure 16-8). A **normal form** is a relation state that can be determined by applying simple rules regarding dependencies (or relationships between attributes) to that relation. Many normal forms, each of which rids a data model of anomalies, have been identified. Space does not permit a thorough treatment of all commonly used normal forms (see McFadden, Hoffer, and Prescott, 1999). We concentrate here on the three most frequently used:

1. *First normal form (1NF).* Any repeating data have been removed, so there is a single value at the intersection of each row and column of the table.

2. *Second normal form (2NF).* Nonkey attributes require the whole key for identification (what we will call *full functional dependency*).

3. *Third normal form (3NF).* Nonkey attributes do not depend on other nonkey data elements (what we will call no *transitive dependencies*).

Figure 16-7
EMP COURSE relation

EMP COURSE

Emp_ID	Course	Date_Completed
100	SPSS	6/19/1999
100	Surveys	10/7/1999
140	Tax Acc	12/8/1999
110	SPSS	1/22/1999
110	C++	4/22/1999
190	Investments	5/7/1999
150	SPSS	6/19/1999
150	TQM	8/12/1999

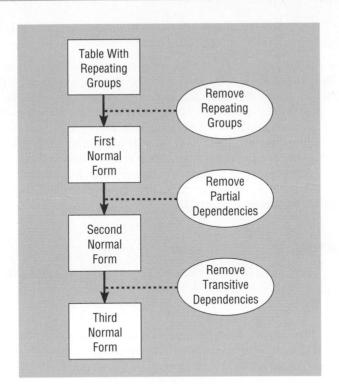

Figure 16-8
Steps in normalization

Thus, the result of normalization is that every nonkey attribute depends upon the whole primary key and nothing but the primary key.

Functional Dependence and Keys

Normalization is based on the analysis of functional dependence. A **functional dependency** is a particular relationship between two attributes. For any relation R, attribute B is *functionally dependent* on attribute A if, for every valid instance of A, that value of A uniquely determines the value of B (Dutka and Hanson, 1989). The functional dependence of B on A is represented by an arrow, as follows: A→B (for example, Emp_ID→Name in the relation of Figure 16-5). Functional dependence does not imply mathematical dependence—that the value of one attribute may be computed from the value of another attribute; rather, functional dependence of B on A means that there can be only one value of B for each value of A. Thus, for a given Emp_ID value, there can be only one Name value associated with it; the value of Name, however, cannot be derived from the value of Emp_ID.

An attribute may be functionally dependent on two (or more) attributes, rather than on a single attribute. For example, consider the relation EMP COURSE (Emp_ID,Course,Date_Completed) shown in Figure 16-7. We represent the functional dependency in this relation as follows: Emp_ID,Course→Date_Completed.

Common examples of functional dependencies are the following:

1. SSN→Name,Address,Birthdate: A person's name, address, and birth date are functionally dependent on that person's Social Security number.

2. VIN→Make,Model,Color: The make, model, and color of a vehicle are functionally dependent on the vehicle identification number.

Functional dependency:
A particular relationship between two attributes. For any relation R, attribute B is functionally dependent on attribute A if, for every valid instance of A, that value of A uniquely determines the value of B. The functional dependence of B on A is represented as A→B.

3. ISBN→Title: The title of a book is functionally dependent on the book's international standard book number (ISBN).

You should be aware that the instances (or sample data) in a relation do not prove that a functional dependency exists. Only knowledge of the problem domain, obtained from a thorough requirements analysis, is a reliable method for identifying a functional dependency. However, you can use sample data to demonstrate that a functional dependency does *not* exist between two or more attributes. For example, consider the sample data in the relation EXAMPLE(A,B,C,D), shown in Figure 16-9. The sample data in this relation proves that attribute B is not functionally dependent on attribute A since A does not uniquely determine B (two rows with the same value of A have different values of B). You should examine Figure 16-9 to eliminate other possible functional dependencies based on the sample data.

First Normal Form

First normal form (1NF):
A relation that contains no repeating data.

A relation is in **first normal form (1NF)** if it contains no repeating data. Recall that the first property of a relation is that the value at the intersection of each row and column is atomic. A table that contains multivalued attributes or repeating data is not a relation.

Figure 16-10 shows a table with repeating data. Figure 16-6 shows one simple way of removing the repeating data from the table in Figure 16-10. A table with repeating data can be converted to a relation in first normal form by extending the data in each column to fill cells that are empty because of the repeating data structures. Another, and better, way of removing the repeating data in Figure 16-10 is to separate the employee data from the employee-course data, which has been done in Figures 16-5 and 16-7. This second approach also happens to address the characteristic of second normal form, which we define next.

Figure 16-9
EXAMPLE relation

EXAMPLE

A	B	C	D
X	U	X	Y
Y	X	Z	X
Z	Y	Y	Y
Y	Z	W	Z

Figure 16-10
Table with repeating data

EMPLOYEE2

Emp_ID	Name	Dept	Salary	Course	Date_Completed
100	Margaret Simpson	Marketing	42,000	SPSS	6/19/1999
				Surveys	10/7/1999
140	Alan Beeton	Accounting	39,000	Tax Acc	12/8/1999
110	Chris Lucero	Info Systems	41,500	SPSS	1/12/1999
				C++	4/22/1999
190	Lorenzo Davis	Finance	38,000	Investments	5/7/1999
150	Susan Martin	Marketing	38,500	SPSS	6/19/1999
				TQM	8/12/1999

Second Normal Form

A relation is in **second normal form (2NF)** if it is in first normal form and every nonkey attribute is fully functionally dependent on the primary key. Thus no nonkey attribute is functionally dependent on part, but not all, of the primary key. A relation that is in first normal form will be in second normal form if any one of the following conditions apply:

1. The primary key consists of only one attribute (such as the attribute Emp_ID in relation EMPLOYEE1).

2. No nonkey attributes exist in the relation.

3. Every nonkey attribute is functionally dependent on the full set of primary key attributes.

EMPLOYEE2 (Figure 16-6) is an example of a relation that is not in second normal form. The shorthand notation for this relation is
EMPLOYEE2(Emp_ID,Name,Dept,Salary,Course,Date_Completed).
The functional dependencies in this relation are the following:
Emp_ID→Name,Dept,Salary
Emp_ID,Course→Date_Completed
The primary key for this relation is the composite key Emp_ID,Course. Therefore, the nonkey attributes Name, Dept, and Salary are functionally dependent on only Emp_ID but not on Course. A **partial functional dependency** exists when one or more nonkey attributes (such as Name) are functionally dependent on part, but not all, of the primary key.

The partial functional dependency in EMPLOYEE2 creates redundancy in that relation, which results in anomalies when the table is updated. We described the anomalies in EMPLOYEE2 in the previous section on Well-Structured Relations, so we do not repeat the discussion here.

To convert a relation to second normal form, you decompose the relation into new relations using the attributes, called determinants, that determine other attributes; the determinants are the primary keys of these relations. EMPLOYEE2 is decomposed into the following two relations:

1. EMPLOYEE1(Emp_ID,Name,Dept,Salary) This relation satisfies the first second normal form condition (sample data is shown in Figure 16-5).

2. EMP COURSE(Emp_ID,Course,Date_Completed) This relation satisfies second normal form condition three (sample data appear in Figure 16-7).

Examine these new relations to verify that they are free of the anomalies associated with EMPLOYEE2.

Third Normal Form

A relation is in **third normal form (3NF)** if it is in second normal form and no transitive dependencies exist. A **transitive dependency** in a relation is a functional dependency between two (or more) nonkey attributes. For example, consider the relation
SALES(Customer_ID,Customer_Name,Salesperson,Region) (sample data for this relation are shown in Figure 16-11a).

Second normal form (2NF): A relation is in second normal form if it is in first normal form and every nonkey attribute is fully functionally dependent on the primary key. Thus no nonkey attribute is functionally dependent on part (but not all) of the primary key.

Partial functional dependency: A dependency in which one or more nonkey attributes are functionally dependent on part, but not all, of the primary key.

Third normal form (3NF): A relation is in third normal form if it is in second normal form and no transitive dependencies exist.

Transitive dependency: A functional dependency between two (or more) nonkey attributes in a relation.

Figure 16-11
Removing transitive
dependencies

(a) Relation with transitive
dependency

SALES

Customer_ID	Customer_Name	Salesperson	Region
8023	Anderson	Smith	South
9167	Bancroft	Hicks	West
7924	Hobbs	Smith	South
6837	Tucker	Hernandez	East
8596	Eckersley	Hicks	West
7018	Arnold	Faulb	North

(b) Relations in 3NF

SALES1

Customer_ID	Customer_Name	Salesperson
8023	Anderson	Smith
9167	Bancroft	Hicks
7924	Hobbs	Smith
6837	Tucker	Hernandez
8596	Eckersley	Hicks
7018	Arnold	Faulb

SPERSON

Salesperson	Region
Smith	South
Hicks	West
Hernandez	East
Faulb	North

The following functional dependencies exist in the SALES relation:

1. Customer_ID→Customer_Name,Salesperson,Region (Customer_ID is the primary key.)

2. Salesperson→Region (Each salesperson is assigned to a unique region.)

Notice that SALES is in second normal form since the primary key consists of a single attribute (Customer_ID). However, there is a transitive dependency: Region is functionally dependent on Salesperson and Salesperson is functionally dependent on Customer_ID. As a result, there are update anomalies in SALES.

1. *Insertion anomaly.* A new salesperson (Robinson) assigned to the North region cannot be entered until a customer has been assigned to that salesperson (since a value for Customer_ID must be provided to insert a row in the table).

2. *Deletion anomaly.* If customer number 6837 is deleted from the table, we lose the information that salesperson Hernandez is assigned to the East region.

3. *Modification anomaly.* If salesperson Smith is reassigned to the East region, several rows must be changed to reflect that fact (two rows are shown in Figure 16-11a).

These anomalies arise as a result of the transitive dependency. The transitive dependency can be removed by decomposing SALES into the two relations, based on the two determinants, shown in Figure 16-11b. These relations are the following:
SALES1(Customer_ID,Customer_Name,Salesperson)
SPERSON(Salesperson,Region).

Foreign key: An attribute that appears as a nonkey attribute in one relation and as a primary key attribute (or part of a primary key) in another relation.

Note that Salesperson is the primary key in SPERSON. Salesperson is also a foreign key in SALES1. A **foreign key** is an attribute that appears as a nonkey attribute in one relation (such as SALES1) and as a primary key attribute (or part of a primary key) in another relation. You designate a foreign key by using a dashed underline.

One business rule we did not discuss earlier is called referential integrity. **Referential integrity** specifies that the value of an attribute in one relation depends on the value of the same attribute in another relation. A foreign key must satisfy referential integrity, as must any part of a composite key that refers to a primary key in another table. Referential integrity is one of the most important types of business rules implied by the relational model.

The relations in Figure 16-11b are now in third normal form, since no transitive dependencies exist. You should verify that the anomalies that exist in SALES are not present in SALES1 and SPERSON.

Referential integrity: An integrity constraint specifying that the value (or existence) of an attribute in one relation depends on the value (or existence) of an attribute in the same or another relation.

TRANSFORMING E-R DIAGRAMS INTO RELATIONS

As mentioned earlier, normalization is a bottom-up process. Normalization produces a set of well-structured relations that contain all of the data mentioned in system externals and outputs. Normalization is grounded in specific information requirements developed in other logical design steps. Since these specific information requirements may not represent all future information needs or all business rules, the E-R diagram you developed in conceptual data modeling is another source of insight into possible information requirements for a new application system. To compare the conceptual data model and the normalized relations developed so far, your E-R diagram must be transformed into relational notation, normalized, and then merged with the existing normalized relations.

Transforming an E-R diagram into normalized relations and then merging all the relations into one final, consolidated set of relations can be accomplished in four steps. These steps are summarized briefly here, and then steps 1, 2, and 4 are discussed in detail in the remainder of this chapter.

1. *Represent entities.* Each entity type in the E-R diagram is represented as a relation in the relational data model. The identifier of the entity type becomes the primary key of the relation, and other attributes of the entity type become nonkey attributes of the relation.

2. *Represent relationships.* Each relationship in an E-R diagram must be represented in the relational model. How we represent a relationship depends on its nature. For example, in some cases we represent a relationship by making the primary key of one relation a foreign key of another relation. In other cases, we create a separate relation to represent a relationship.

3. *Normalize the relations.* The relations that are created in Steps 1 and 2 may have unnecessary redundancy and may be subject to anomalies when they are updated. So, we need to normalize these relations to make them well-structured.

4. *Merge the relations.* So far in logical data modeling we have created various relations from both a bottom-up normalization of user views and from transforming one or more E-R diagrams into sets of relations. Across these different sets of relations, there may be redundant relations (two or more relations that describe the same entity type) that must be merged and re-normalized to remove the redundancy.

Represent Entities

Each regular entity type in an E-R diagram is transformed into a relation. The primary key (or identifier) of the entity type becomes the primary key of the corresponding relation. You should check to make sure that this key satisfies the following two properties:

1. The value of the key must uniquely identify every row in the relation.

2. The key should be nonredundant; that is, no attribute in the key can be deleted without destroying its unique identification.

Some entities may have keys that include the primary keys of other entities. For example, an EMPLOYEE DEPENDENT may have a Name for each dependent but, to form the primary key for this entity, you must include the Employee_ID attribute from the associated EMPLOYEE entity. Such an entity whose primary key depends upon the primary key of another entity is called a weak entity.

Each nonkey attribute of the entity type becomes a nonkey attribute of the relation. The relations that are formed from entity types may be modified as relationships are represented.

Representation of an entity as a relation is straightforward. Figure 16-12a shows the CUSTOMER entity type for Pine Valley Furniture Company. The corresponding CUSTOMER relation is represented as follows:

CUSTOMER(Customer_ID,Name,Address,City_State_ZIP,Discount)

In this notation, the entity type label is translated into a relation name. The identifier of the entity type is listed first and underlined. All nonkey attributes are listed after the primary key. This relation is shown as a table with sample data in Figure 16-12b.

Represent Relationships

The procedure for representing relationships depends on both the degree of the relationship—unary, binary, ternary—and the cardinalities of the relationship.

Binary 1:N and 1:1 Relationships   A binary one-to-many (1:N) relationship in an E-R diagram is represented by adding the primary key attribute (or attributes) of the

Figure 16-12

Transforming an entity type to a relation

(a) E-R diagram

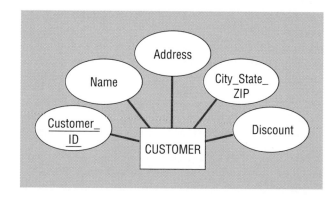

(b) Relation

CUSTOMER

Customer_ID	Name	Address	City_State_ZIP	Discount
1273	Contemporary Designs	123 Oak St.	Austin, TX 38405	5%
6390	Casual Corner	18 Hoosier Dr.	Bloomington, IN 45821	3%

entity on the one-side of the relationship as a foreign key in the relation that is on the many-side of the relationship.

Figure 16-13a, an example of this rule, shows the Places relationship (1:*N*) linking CUSTOMER and ORDER at Pine Valley Furniture Company. Two relations, CUSTOMER and ORDER, were formed from the respective entity types. Customer_ID, which is the primary key of CUSTOMER (on the one-side of the relationship) is added as a foreign key to ORDER (on the many-side of the relationship).

Figure 16-13
Representing a 1:*N* relationship

(a) E-R diagram

(b) Relations

CUSTOMER

Customer_ID	Name	Address	City_State_ZIP	Discount
1273	Contemporary Designs	123 Oak St.	Austin, TX 38405	5%
6390	Casual Corner	18 Hoosier Dr.	Bloomington, IN 45821	3%

ORDER

Order_Number	Order_Date	Promised_Date	Customer_ID
57194	3/15/9X	3/28/9X	6390
63725	3/17/9X	4/01/9X	1273
80149	3/14/9X	3/24/9X	6390

One special case under this rule was mentioned in the previous section. If the entity on the many-side needs the key of the entity on the one-side as part of its primary key (this is a so-called weak entity), then this attribute is added not as a nonkey but as part of the primary key.

For a binary or unary one-to-one (1:1) relationship between two entities A and B (for a unary relationship, A and B would be the same entity type), the relationship can be represented by any of the following choices:

1. Adding the primary key of A as a foreign key of B

2. Adding the primary key of B as a foreign key of A

3. Both of the above

Binary and Higher Degree *M:N* Relationships   Suppose that there is a binary many-to-many (*M:N*) relationship or a gerund between two entity types A and B. For such a relationship or gerund, we create a separate relation C. The primary key of this relation is a composite key consisting of the primary key for each of the two entities in the relationship. Any nonkey attributes that are associated with the *M:N* relationship or gerund are included with the relation C.

Figure 16-14a, an example of this rule, shows the Requests relationship (*M:N*) between the entity types ORDER and PRODUCT for Pine Valley Furniture Company. Figure 16-14b shows the three relations (ORDER, PRODUCT, and ORDER LINE) that are formed from the entity types and the Requests relationship. First, a relation is created for each of the two entity types in the relationship (ORDER and PRODUCT). Then a relation (called ORDER LINE in Figure 16-14b) is created for the Requests relationship. The primary key of ORDER LINE is the combination (Order_Number,Product_ID), which are the respective primary keys of ORDER and PRODUCT. The nonkey attribute Quantity_Ordered also appears in ORDER LINE.

Occasionally, the relation created from an *M:N* relationship requires a primary key that includes more than just the primary keys from the two related relations. Consider, for example, the following situation:

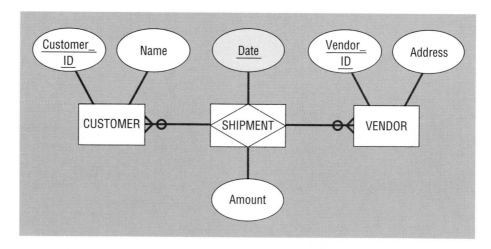

In this case, Date must be part of the key for the SHIPMENT relation to uniquely distinguish each row of the SHIPMENT table, as follows:

SHIPMENT(Customer_ID,Vendor_ID,Date,Amount)

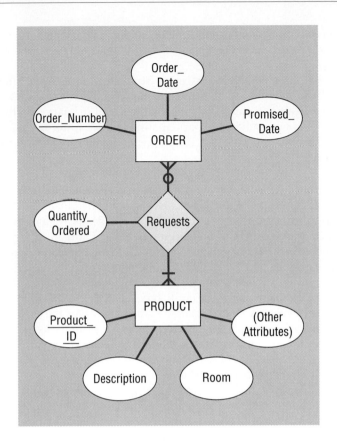

Figure 16-14
Representing an *M:N*
relationship

(a) E-R diagram

ORDER

(b) Relations

Order_Number	Order_Date	Promised_Date
61384	2/17/1999	3/01/1999
62009	2/13/1999	2/27/1999
62807	2/15/1999	3/01/1999

ORDER LINE

Order_Number	Product_ID	Quantity_Ordered
61384	M128	2
61384	A261	1

PRODUCT

Product_ID	Description	(Other Attributes)
M128	Bookcase	—
A261	Wall unit	—
R149	Cabinet	—

If each shipment has a separate nonintelligent key, say a shipment number, then Date becomes a nonkey and Customer_ID and Vendor_ID become cross reference keys, as follows:

SHIPMENT(Shipment_Number,Customer_ID,Vendor_ID,Date,Amount)

In some cases, there may be a relationship among three or more entities. In such cases, we create a separate relation that has as a primary key the composite of the primary keys of each of the participating entities (plus any necessary additional key elements). This rule is a simple generalization of the rule for a binary M:N relationship.

Unary Relationship   To review, a *unary* relationship is a relationship between the instances of a single entity type, which are also called *recursive relationships*. Figure 16-15 shows two common examples. Figure 16-15a shows a one-to-many relationship named Manages that associates employees of an organization with another employee who is their manager. Figure 16-15b shows a many-to-many relationship that associates certain items with their component items. This relationship, introduced in Chapter 10, is called a *bill-of materials structure.*

For a unary 1:N relationship, the entity type (such as EMPLOYEE) is modeled as a relation. The primary key of that relation is the same as for the entity type. Then a foreign key is added to the relation that references the primary key values. A **recursive foreign key** is a foreign key in a relation that references the primary key values of that same relation. We can represent the relationship in Figure 16-15a as follows:

EMPLOYEE(Emp_ID,Name,Birthdate,Manager_ID)

In this relation, Manager_ID is a recursive foreign key that takes its values from the same domain of worker identification numbers as Emp_ID.

For a unary M:N relationship, we model the entity type as one relation. Then we create a separate relation to represent the M:N relationship. The primary key of this new relation is a composite key that consists of two attributes (which need not have the same name) that both take their values from the same primary key domain. Any attribute associated with the relationship (such as Quantity in Figure 16-15b) is included as a nonkey attribute in this new relation. We can express the result for Figure 16-15b as follows:

ITEM(Item_Number,Name,Cost)
ITEM-BILL(Item_Number,Component_Number,Quantity)

IS-A Relationship (Class-Subclass)   IS-A relationships are explained in an article on this textbook's Web site. The relational data model does not directly support class-subclass (or IS-A) relationships. We use the following rules to represent IS-A relationships:

1. Create a separate relation for the class and for each of the subclasses.

2. The table (relation) for the class consists only of the primary key and the attributes that are common to all of the subclasses.

3. The table for each subclass contains only its primary key and the columns unique to that subclass.

4. The primary keys of the class and each of the subclasses are from the same domain, but do not have to have the same names.

An IS-A relationship (with two subclasses for different types of rental properties) appears in the E-R diagram of Figure 16-16a, and the relations that are derived by applying the rules are shown in Figure 16-16b. Notice that there are three relations: PROPERTY, BEACH, and MOUNTAIN. The primary key of

Recursive foreign key: A foreign key in a relation that references the primary key values of that same relation.

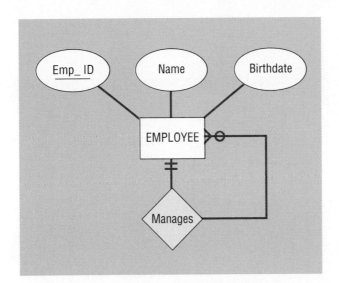

Figure 16-15
Two unary relationships

(a) EMPLOYEE with Manages
relationship (1:*N*)

(b) Bill-of-materials structure
(*M:N*)

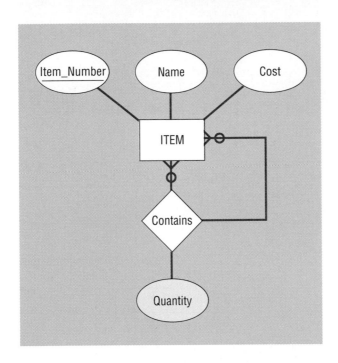

each of these relations is the composite key (Street_Address,City_State_ZIP). Although the primary key of a subclass does not have to have the same name as the primary key of the class as in this example, they must be from the same domain.

The PROPERTY relation contains those descriptors (or nonkey attributes) that are common to both subclasses: Number_of_Rooms and Typical_Rent. The relations BEACH and MOUNTAIN (representing the subclasses) have the same primary key as PROPERTY. Each relation contains an attribute, however, that is unique to the subclass (Blocks_to_Beach for BEACH, Skiing for MOUNTAIN). We can form a subclass with its inherited attributes by combining the subclass relation with the class relation. This is called joining in relational terminology.

Figure 16-16
Representing IS-A relationships

(a) E-R diagram

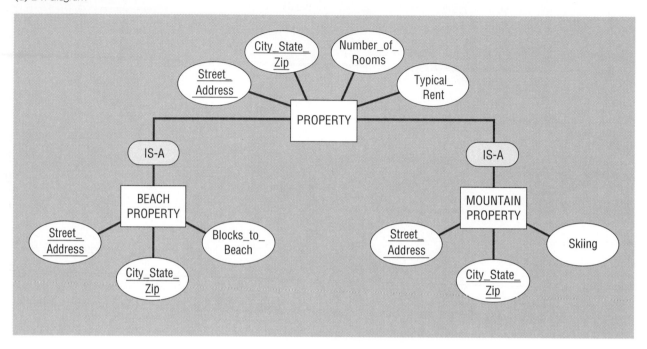

(b) Relations

PROPERTY

Street_Address	City_State_ZIP	Number_of_Rooms	Typical_Rent
120 Surf Dr.	Honolulu, HI 99987	3	500
100 Mogul Dr.	Jackson, WY 89204	3	250

BEACH

Street_Address	City_State_ZIP	Blocks_to_Beach
120 Surf Dr	Honolulu, HI 99987	2

MOUNTAIN

Street_Address	City_State_ZIP	Skiing
100 Mogul Dr.	Jackson, WY 89204	N

Summary of Transforming E-R Diagrams to Relations

We have now described how to transform E-R diagrams to relations. Table 16-1 lists the rules discussed in this section for transforming entity-relationship diagrams into equivalent relations. After this transformation, you should check the resulting relations to determine whether they are in third normal form and, if necessary, perform normalization as described earlier in the chapter.

TABLE 16-1   E-R to Relational Transformation

E-R Structure	Relational Representation
Regular entity	Create a relation with primary key and nonkey attributes
Weak entity	Create a relation with a composite primary key (which includes the primary key of the entity on which this entity depends) and nonkey attributes
Binary or unary 1:1 relationship	Place the primary key of either entity in the relation for the other entity or do this for both entities
Binary 1:*M* relationship	Place the primary key of the entity on the one-side of the relationship as a foreign key in the relation for the entity on the many-side
Binary or unary *M:N* relationship or gerund	Create a relation with a composite primary key using the primary keys of the related entities, plus any nonkey attributes of the relationship or gerund
Binary or unary *M:N* relationship or gerund with additional key(s)	Create a relation with a composite primary key using the primary keys of the related entities and additional primary key attributes associated with the relationship or gerund, plus any nonkey attribute of the relationship or gerund
Binary or unary *M:N* relationship or gerund with its own key	Create a relation with the primary key associated with the relationship or gerund, plus any nonkey attributes of the relationship or gerund and the primary keys of the related entities (as nonkey attributes)
IS-A relationship	Create a relation for the superclass which contains the primary key and all nonkey attributes in common with all subclasses, plus create a separate relation for each subclass with the same primary key (with the same or a local name) but with only the nonkey attributes related to that subclass

MERGING RELATIONS

As part of the logical data modeling process, normalized relations likely have been created from a number of separate E-R diagrams and various user views. Some of the relations may be redundant—they may refer to the same entities. If so, you should merge those relations to remove the redundancy. This section describes merging relations or *view integration,* which is the last step in the logical data modeling process defined earlier in the chapter.

An Example of Merging Relations

Suppose that modeling a user view or transforming an E-R diagram results in the following 3NF relation:

EMPLOYEE1(Emp_ID,Name,Address,Phone)

Modeling a second user view might result in the following relation:

EMPLOYEE2(Emp_ID,Name,Address,Jobcode,Number_of_Years)

Since these two relations have the same primary key (Emp_ID) and describe the same entity, they should be merged into one relation. The result of merging the relations is the following relation:

EMPLOYEE(Emp_ID,Name,Address,Phone,Jobcode,Number_of_Years)

Notice that an attribute that appears in both relations (such as Name in this example) appears only once in the merged relation.

View Integration Problems

When integrating relations, you must understand the meaning of the data and must be prepared to resolve any problems that may arise in that process. In this section, we describe and briefly illustrate four problems that arise in view integration: *synonyms, homonyms, transitive dependencies,* and *class/subclass relationships.*

Synonyms   In some situations, two or more attributes may have different names but the same meaning, as when they describe the same characteristic of an entity. Such attributes are called **synonyms.** For example, Emp_ID and Employee_Number may be synonyms.

> **Synonyms:** Two different names that are used to refer to the same data item (for example, *car* and *automobile*).

When merging the relations that contain synonyms, you should obtain, if possible, agreement from users on a single standardized name for the attribute and eliminate the other synonym. Another alternative is to choose a third name to replace the synonyms. For example, consider the following relations:

> STUDENT1(Student_ID,Name)
> STUDENT2(Matriculation_Number,Name,Address)

In this case, the analyst recognizes that both the Student_ID and Matriculation_Number are synonyms for a person's social security number and are identical attributes. One possible resolution would be to standardize on one of the two attribute names, such as Student_ID. Another option is to use a new attribute name, such as SSN, to replace both synonyms. Assuming the latter approach, merging the two relations would produce the following result:

> STUDENT(SSN,Name,Address)

Often when there are synonyms, there is a need to allow some system users to refer to the same data by different names. Users may need to use familiar names that are consistent with terminology in their part of the organization. An **alias** is an alternative name used for an attribute. Many database management systems and CASE repositories allow the definition of an alias that may be used interchangeably with the primary attribute label.

> **Alias:** An alternative name given to an attribute.

Homonyms   In other situations, a single attribute, called a **homonym,** may have more than one meaning or describe more than one characteristic. For example, the term *account* might refer to a bank's checking account, savings account, loan account, or other type of account; therefore, *account* refers to different data, depending on how it is used.

> **Homonym:** A single name that is used for two or more different attributes (for example, the term *invoice* to refer to both a customer invoice and a supplier invoice).

You should be on the lookout for homonyms when merging relations. Consider the following example:

> STUDENT1(Student_ID,Name,Address)
> STUDENT2(Student_ID,Name,Phone_Number,Address)

In discussions with users, the systems analyst may discover that the attribute Address in STUDENT1 refers to a student's campus address while in STUDENT2 the same attribute refers to a student's home address. To resolve this conflict, we would probably need to create new attribute names and the merged relation would become

> STUDENT(Student_ID,Name,Phone_Number,Campus_Address,
>   Permanent_Address)

Transitive Dependencies   When two 3NF relations are merged to form a single relation, *transitive dependencies* may result. For example, consider the following two relations:

> STUDENT1(Student_ID,Major)
> STUDENT2(Student_ID,Advisor)

Since STUDENT1 and STUDENT2 have the same primary key, the two relations may be merged:

STUDENT(Student_ID,Major,Advisor)

However, suppose that each major has exactly one advisor. In this case, Advisor is functionally dependent on Major:

Major→Advisor

If the above dependency exists, then STUDENT is in 2NF but not 3NF, since it contains a transitive dependency. The analyst can create 3NF relations by removing the transitive dependency (Major becomes a foreign key in STUDENT):

STUDENT(Student_ID,Major)

MAJOR ADVISOR(Major,Advisor)

Class/Subclass (IS-A)   Class/subclass relationships (defined in an article on this textbook's Web site) may be hidden in user views or relations. Suppose that we have the following two hospital relations:

PATIENT1(Patient_ID,Name,Address)

PATIENT2(Patient_ID,Room_Number)

Initially, it appears that these two relations can be merged into a single PATIENT relation. However, suppose that there are two different types of patients: inpatients and outpatients. PATIENT1 actually contains attributes common to *all* patients. PATIENT2 contains an attribute (Room_Number) that is a characteristic only of inpatients. In this situation, you should create *class/subclass (IS-A)* relationships for these entities:

PATIENT(Patient_ID,Name,Address)

INPATIENT(Patient_ID,Room_Number)

OUTPATIENT (Patient_ID,Date_Treated)

For an extended discussion of view integration in database design, see Navathe, et al. (1986).

LOGICAL DATA MODELING FOR HOOSIER BURGER

In Chapter 10 we developed a conceptual data model, an E-R model, for a new inventory control system at Hoosier Burger. That E-R diagram is repeated here as Figure 16-17. In this section we show how this E-R model is translated into normalized relations and how to normalize and then merge the relations for a new report with the relations from the E-R model.

In this E-R model, four entities exist independently of other entities: SALE, PRODUCT, INVOICE, and INVENTORY ITEM. Given the attributes shown in Figure 16-17, we can represent these entities in the following four relations:

SALE(Receipt_Number,Sale_Date)

PRODUCT(Product_ID,Product_Description)

INVOICE(Vendor_ID,Invoice_Number,Invoice_Date,Paid?)

INVENTORY ITEM(Item_Number,Item_Description,Quantity_in_Stock,
      Minimum_Order_Quantity,Type_of_Item)

The entities ITEM SALE and INVOICE ITEM as well as the associative entity RECIPE each have composite primary keys taken from the entities to which they relate, so we can represent these three entities in the following three relations:

ITEM SALE(Receipt_Number,Product_ID,Quantity_Sold)

INVOICE ITEM(Vendor_ID,Invoice_Number,Item_Number,Quantity_Added)

RECIPE(Product_ID,Item_Number,Quantity_Used)

Since there are no many-to-many, one-to-one, IS-A, or unary relationships, we have now represented all the entities and relationships from the E-R model. Also, each of

Figure 16-17

Final E-R diagram for Hoosier Burger's inventory control system

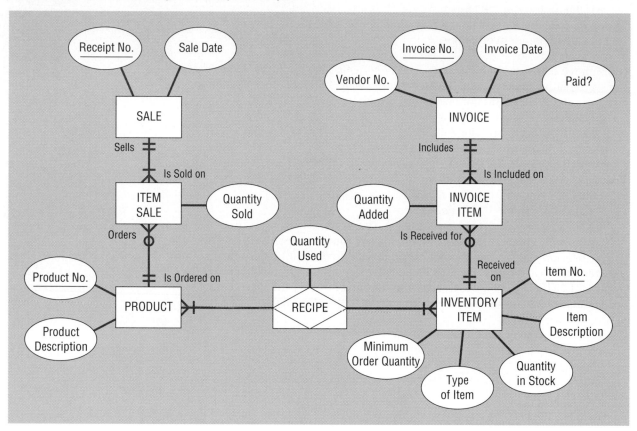

the above relations is in 3NF since all attributes are simple, all nonkeys are fully dependent on the whole key, and there are no dependencies between nonkeys in the INVOICE and INVENTORY ITEM relations.

Now suppose that Bob Mellankamp wanted an additional report which was not previously known by the analyst who designed the inventory control system for Hoosier Burger. A rough sketch of this new report, listing usage of inventory items in both regular item sales and Hoosiers in a Hurry meal sales, appears in Figure 16-18. A Hoosiers in a Hurry meal is a special, predefined package of several products, such as a hamburger, regular fries, and a medium drink. The combination of products in a Hoosiers in a Hurry meal is not the same concept as a RECIPE; in fact, each product within A Hoosiers in a Hurry meal has a recipe.

This report contains data about several relations already known to the analyst, including

SALE(Receipt_Number,Sale_Date)
PRODUCT(Product_ID,Product_Description)
INVENTORY ITEM(Item_Number,Item_Description)
ITEM SALE(Receipt_Number,Product_ID,Quantity_Sold)
RECIPE(Product_ID,Item_Number,Quantity_Used)

Even though data such as Receipt_Number and Quantity_Used are not on the report, the analyst realizes that these data are needed to identify relations or to compute data

INVENTORY USAGE REPORT   Page x of n
for Sales *Date 1–Date 2*   *Date Printed*

Figure 16-18
Hoosier Burger inventory
usage report

REGULAR PRODUCT_ID	DESCRIPTION	DATE USED	CONSUMPTION		
			REGULAR	HOOSIER	TOTAL
xxx		aaa	—	—	—
		bbb	—	—	—
		ccc	—	—	—
		⋮	⋮	⋮	⋮
yyy		—	—	—	—
		—	—	—	—
		—	—	—	—
		⋮	⋮	⋮	⋮
⋮					

on the report. Since the five relations show no new relations or attributes, the current normalized logical data model is so far sufficient to cover the new report.

The analyst recognizes, however, that Hoosiers in a Hurry meals do not actually have recipes as only individual products have recipes. Thus, the RECIPE relation does not really help to compute the amount of inventory used for Hoosiers in a Hurry consumption, whereas these are products with a product number. Consequently, the analyst realizes that there are really two kinds (subclasses) of products: regular products and Hoosiers in a Hurry products, and that there is a many-to-many relationship between Hoosiers in a Hurry and regular products. Thus, the analyst defines two subclass PRODUCT relations and adds a new relation to represent the relationship between them, as follows:

REGULAR PRODUCT(Regular Product_ID)
HOOSIER PRODUCT(Hoosier Product_ID)
MEAL(Hoosier Product_ID,Regular_Product_ID,Meal_Quantity)

where Meal_Quantity is the number of a particular regular product used in a particular Hoosiers in a Hurry meal.

The analyst then recognizes that the RECIPE relation should be changed to capture the fact that only regular products have a recipe, as follows:

RECIPE(Regular_Product_ID,Item_Number,Quantity_Used)

The final set of relations, after considering this new report and merging relations for it with those identified before, look like this:

SALE(Receipt_Number,Sale_Date)
PRODUCT(Product_ID,Product_Description)
REGULAR PRODUCT(Regular_Product_ID)
HOOSIER PRODUCT(Hoosier_Product_ID)
MEAL(Hoosier_Product_ID,Regular_Product_ID,Meal_Quantity)
INVOICE(Vendor_ID,Invoice_Number,Invoice_Date,Paid?)
INVENTORY ITEM(Item_Number,Item_Description,Quantity_in_Stock,
    Minimum_Order_Quantity,Type_of_Item)
INVOICE ITEM(Vendor_ID,Invoice_Number,Item_Number,Quantity_Added)
ITEM SALE(Receipt_Number,Product_ID,Quantity_Sold)
RECIPE(Regular_Product_ID,Item_Number,Quantity_Used)

The updated E-R model for these relations appears in Figure 16-19.

When comparing this list of ten relations with the E-R diagram, we note that the ten relations correspond to the ten entities and associative entities in Figure 16-19. If there had been any *M:N* relationships on the E-R diagram, these, too, would have

Figure 16-19

E-R diagram corresponding to normalized relations of Hoosier Burger's inventory control system

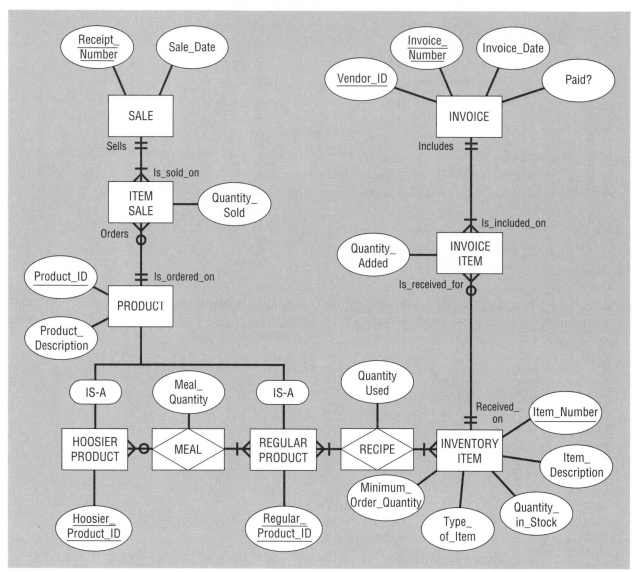

been represented by a relation, which would contain only the primary keys of the related entities. Also note in Figure 16-19 that there is a relationship, the MEAL gerund, connecting two subclass entities. The list of ten relations, with the E-R diagram as a visual representation, now becomes input to physical file and database design, which is the topic of the next chapter.

SUMMARY

In this chapter, we have presented the process and techniques used to structure the logical data requirements of an information system. Logical data modeling uses the relational data model to represent data requirements as tables of data in which every cell has an atomic value. We also showed how to transform conceptual data models between entity-relationship and relational notations.

The data normalization process transforms unnormalized relations identified from E-R diagrams into first, second, and third normal forms. Normalization develops a structure for data requirements that has desirable properties which avoid insertion, deletion, and maintenance anomalies in data. Normalization is based on functional dependencies between attributes, in which a relation in third normal form has each nonkey attribute dependent on the full primary key, and nothing but this key, of its relation.

In addition, we showed how to merge relations developed from separate E-R diagrams or normalization activities into consolidated, normalized relations. We discussed how to handle issues of synonyms, homonyms, transitive dependencies, and IS-A relationships during relation merging. Such a consolidated set of normalized relations, along with updating the project dictionary, are the deliverables from logical data modeling.

Logical data modeling is based on certain constructs about the structure of data. These constructs include relation, functional dependency, primary key, foreign key, and referential integrity. Logical data modeling is grounded in specific data requirements (forms and reports), but the final steps reconcile the structure of data found in specific system externals and outputs with the view of data portrayed in a conceptual data model.

This chapter completes our coverage of the logical design of an information system. The chapters in the following section address the techniques necessary for the physical design of an information system. Chapter 17 begins by discussing physical database design, which follows directly from the results demonstrated in this chapter on logical data modeling.

KEY TERMS

Alias	Normal form	Relational database model
Anomalies	Normalization	Second normal form (2NF)
First normal form (1NF)	Partial functional	Synonyms
Foreign key	dependency	Third normal form (3NF)
Functional dependency	Recursive foreign key	Transitive dependency
Homonym	Referential integrity	Well-structured relation
Logical data model	Relation	

REVIEW QUESTIONS

1. Define each of the following terms:
   a. functional dependency
   b. normalization
   c. relation
   d. primary key
   e. foreign key
   f. anomalies
   g. first normal form
   h. second normal form
   i. third normal form

2. What is the purpose of normalization?

3. What is the role of a conceptual data model during logical database design?

4. List five properties of relations.

5. What do you need to know about an information system to do logical data modeling?

6. What are the two major deliverables from logical data modeling?

7. What problems can arise during view integration or merging relations?

8. How are relationships between entities represented in the relational data model?

9. How do you represent a 1:M unary relationship in a relational database model?

10. How do you represent a M:N ternary relationship in a relational database model?

11. What is the relationship between the primary key of a relation and the functional dependencies among all attributes within that relation?

12. Describe four steps in logical data modeling.

13. Describe the deliverables from logical data modeling.

14. What are the two general sources of inputs to logical data modeling?

15. How is a foreign key represented in relational notation?

16. How are relationships represented in relational notation?

17. List three types of anomalies that may arise during normalization.

18. Can instances of a relation (sample data) prove the existence of a functional dependency? Why or why not?

PROBLEMS AND EXERCISES

1. Match the following terms to the appropriate definitions.

_____ view integration

_____ third normal form

_____ referential integrity

_____ homonym

_____ relation

_____ functional dependency

_____ transitive dependency

a. named two-dimensional table of data

b. state of a relation that does not have transitive dependencies

c. functional dependency between two (or more) non-key attributes in a relation

d. process of merging relations developed from a conceptual data model with those from different user views

e. particular relationship between two attributes

f. name used for several different attributes

g. requirement that the value of an attribute come from the domain of another attribute

2. Assume that in Pine Valley Furniture products are comprised of components, products are assigned to salespersons, and components are produced by vendors. Also assume that in the relation
PRODUCT(Prodname,Salesperson,Compname,Vendor)
Vendor is functionally dependent on Compname and Compname is functionally dependent on Prodname. Eliminate the transitive dependency in this relation and form 3NF relations.

3. Draw an E-R diagram for the situation described in Problem and Exercise 2. Transform the E-R diagram into a set of 3NF relations.

4. In this chapter we emphasize the importance of well-structured relations and normalization of data. In practice, however, information systems designers often choose to unnormalize relations when creating files. Why do you think this is done? (*Hint:* Remember, normalization is done during logical data modeling and files are designed during physical file and database design.)

5. Transform the E-R diagram of Figure 10-11 into a set of 3NF relations.

6. Transform the E-R diagram of Figure 10-3 into a set of 3NF relations. Make up a primary key and one or more nonkeys for each entity.

7. Transform the E-R diagram at the bottom of this page into a set of 3NF relations.

8. Consider the list of individually 3NF relations below. These relations were developed from several separate normalization activities.
   PATIENT(Patient_ID,Room_Number,Admit_Date,Address)
   ROOM(Room_Number,Phone,Daily_Rate)
   PATIENT(Patient_Number,Treatment_Description,Address)
   TREATMENT(Treatment_ID,Description,Cost)
   PHYSICIAN(Physician_ID,Name,Department)
   PHYSICIAN(Physician_ID,Name,Supervisor_ID)

   a. Merge these relations into a consolidated set of 3NF relations. Make and state whatever assumptions you consider necessary to resolve any potential problems you identify in the merging process.
   b. Draw an E-R diagram for your answer to part (a).

9. Develop a set of 3NF relations for the customer account information screen display shown in Figure 14-11b.

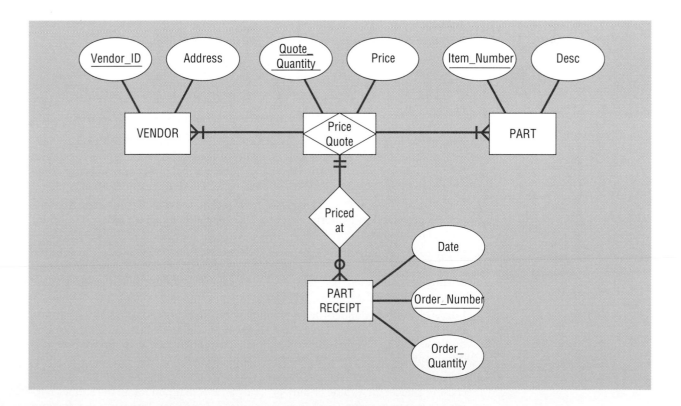

10. Consider the following 3NF relations about a sorority or fraternity:
    MEMBER(Member_ID,Name,Address,Dues_Owed)
    OFFICE(Office_Name,Officer_ID,Term_Start_Date,Budget)
    EXPENSE(Ledger_Number,Office_Name,Expense_Date,Amt_Owed)
    PAYMENT(Check_Number,Expense_Ledger_Number,Amt_Paid)
    RECEIPT(Member_ID,Receipt_Date,Dues_Received)
    COMMITTEE(Committee_ID,Officer_in_Charge)
    WORKERS(Committee_ID,Member_ID)
    a. Foreign keys are not indicated in these relations. Decide which attributes are foreign keys and justify your decisions.
    b. Draw an E-R diagram for these relations, using your answer to part (a).
    c. Explain the assumptions you made about cardinalities in your answer to part (b). Explain why it is said that the E-R data model is more expressive or more semantically rich than the relational data model.

11. Consider the following functional dependencies:
    Applicant_ID→Applicant_Name
    Applicant_ID→Applicant_Address
    Position_ID→Position_Title
    Position_ID→Date_Position_Opens
    Position_ID→Department
    Applicant_ID + Position_ID→Date_Applied
    Applicant_ID + Position_ID + Date_Interviewed→
    a. Represent these attributes with 3NF relations. Provide meaningful relation names.
    b. Represent these attributes using an E-R diagram. Provide meaningful entity and relationship names.

12. Develop 3NF relations for the E-R diagram you drew for Problem and Exercise 2 in Chapter 10.

13. Develop 3NF relations for the E-R diagram you drew for Problem and Exercise 22 in Chapter 10.

14. Transform the E-R diagram of Figure 10-16 into a set of 3NF relations.

FIELD EXERCISES

1. Find in the literature discussions of additional normal forms other than first, second, and third normal forms. Describe each of these additional normal forms and give examples of each. How are these additional normal forms different from those presented in this chapter? What additional benefit does their use provide?

2. Find a form or report from a business organization. Draw an E-R diagram from the entities presented in the form or report. Transform the diagram into a set of third normal form relations.

3. Interview data analysts in organizations where normalization is done. Describe the ways that they conduct normalization. What problems do they encounter when conducting normalization? Do they ever unnormalize relations when creating files? Why or why not?

4. Interview systems builders in a few different business organizations. Is logical data modeling done? Why or why not? If so, what are the steps taken and how closely do these fit with the steps described in this chapter? If not, what are the potential disadvantages of skipping or shortening this process?

5. Consider a recent interaction with an organization (e.g., paying a utility bill, purchasing a ticket for a game or movie). Draw an E-R diagram for all the entities relevant to this transaction (even indirectly involved entities). Transform the diagram into a set of third normal form relations.

REFERENCES

Codd, E. F. 1970. "A Relational Model of Data for Large Relational Databases." *Communications of the ACM* 13 (June): 77–87.

Dutka, A. F., and H. H. Hanson, 1989. *Fundamentals of Data Normalization.* Reading, MA: Addison-Wesley.

McFadden, F. R., J. A. Hoffer, and M. B. Prescott. 1999. *Modern Database Management,* 5th edition. Reading, MA: Addison Wesley Longman.

Navathe, S., R. Elmasri, and J. Larson. 1986. "Integrating User Views in Database Design." *Computer* (Jan.): 50–62.

Logical Design: Designing the Logical Database

INTRODUCTION

In this last BEC case for the logical design phase of the Customer Activity Tracking System (CATS) project, we follow the activities of Jorge Lopez, a systems analyst on the project, and Buffy Jarvis, a data analyst on loan to the team. In addition, we track the overall progress of the CATS project as the team makes the transition from logical to physical design. In particular, this BEC case shows how Jorge and Buffy developed the logical data model for the CATS project. This consolidated relational database model shows all functional aspects of the CATS databases, except for those dimensions which relate to the features of the database management system to be used for CATS. Jorge and Buffy developed the normalized relations from the final CATS E-R model derived during conceptual database design and supplemented this with more data details discovered during other logical design steps. These normalized relations will be input to physical file and database design when the CATS team decides if and how they will change the data structures of the purchased system.

TRANSFORMING THE E-R MODEL

"Jorge, you are really catching on to data modeling," observes Buffy Jarvis as she reviews the preliminary work Jorge Lopez has done to prepare normalized relations. "The relations appear to be normalized, but why don't you review for me how you developed these relations."

"The CASE tool was a big help," responded Jorge. "Since the E-R model we prepared was in the repository (Figures 1 and 2), I simply had the CASE tool use its built-in rules for transforming an E-R model into relations—you know, rules like each entity becomes a relation, each many-to-many relationship becomes a relation, and how foreign keys are assigned. You'll remember, we updated the E-R model since conceptual

design when we discovered that the 'Superior product category name' attribute represented a unary relationship between product profiles (see the has Superior relationship in Figure 1). I thought this E-R diagram would be a good starting point."

Jorge continued, "Then I looked over the relations for the E-R diagrams (see Figure 3). Notice the foreign key STORE_ID in the CUSTOMER relation, the unary relation on the PRODUCT PROFILE entity appears as a foreign key in the PRODUCT_PROFILE relation, and the relation PRODUCT_FOR_CUSTOMER with a compound primary key for the many-to-many 'provides customer info for' relationship. As you can see, there are some relations, like the ones for the subclasses of products and the one for customer profile, with only primary key attributes; I still need to investigate why we don't have any nonkey attributes for those relations yet."

"I didn't worry about field data types yet, although I understand we'll need to make some basic decisions on data types before the end of logical design. And the primary and foreign keys imply referential integrity constraints, which we will also have to decide how to implement during physical design."

"Next, since an E-R model is not necessarily normalized, I checked the functional dependencies within each relation. Since there were no multivalued attributes on the E-R model, I knew we were in first normal form. I then used that guideline you told me one day: make sure that each nonkey is 'fully dependent on the whole key and nothing but the key, so help me Codd.' This guideline covers both second and third normal forms. Generally, I found no normal form violations but, Buffy, should we do something about the relationship between zip code and city and state in the CUSTOMER relation? Clearly there is a relationship here."

Buffy replied, "I think just about every project that deals with addresses faces this question. You are right, zip code determines state and city, and even restricts valid values for street. However, as a company,

Figure 1
Updated CATS E-R model
from conceptual data
modeling

we have not implemented a standard zip code table for all systems, so I suggest we ignore this functional dependency for CATS.

"As you said, our CASE tool created VIDEO_PRODUCT and MUSIC_OR_GAME_PRODUCT relations for the IS-A relationships in the E-R diagram. This is fine for now. If these subclass relations do not carry any data in addition to what any PRODUCT does, we may not actually create tables for these relations, but we'll decide that in physical design, too. Jorge, what did you do next?"

CREATING NORMALIZED RELATIONS FOR SYSTEM INPUTS AND OUTPUTS

"Next I took each report and on-line form in the system and made sure that each field was contained in or could be computed from data in the E-R model. Not surprisingly, I found numerous examples of data in these system inputs and outputs, or what you call user views, that we had not anticipated during conceptual design. For example, here is the first analysis I've done—the customer-product assignment (CPA) report that indicates which customers have reserved which products (see Figure 4) for pick-up at a particular store. You may recall, Buffy, that this report is generated from central CATS and sent as an electronic document to the store CATS. Thus, the system design

does not require that any of this data be part of the store CATS database. Consequently, a field like Contact Date is really just a label printed on the report for use by the store personnel, not a database field. What I did was create a list of fields on this report and the functional dependencies between them (see Figure 5) to see if the central CATS database was sufficient to produce this report. I used, where possible, the field names generated from the CASE tool to avoid creating synonyms. I'll bet that when I look at other reports and forms I'll find some nonkey attributes for the relations with only primary key attributes."

"This looks good, Jorge," said Buffy. "It looks like the CUSTOMER relation generated from the E-R model is complete since all of the attributes dependent on CUST_ID are in this relation. And the necessary changes to the PRODUCT relation seem pretty straightforward because we can just add the PROD_ARTIST and PROD_PRICE attributes to the relation since these attributes also depend on PROD_ID. But what does the last functional dependency mean? RESERVATION_CONFIRMATION was not in the E-R model, and RESERVATION_DATE was."

"Yes, that's the one area I've been wondering about, too," replied Jorge. "First, let me explain what this last functional dependency represents. I included it since only announcements that have been confirmed are on the report, so CATS has to know the confirmation status for each product announcement to a customer. The PCS_CODE stands for this announcement.

Figure 2
Repository reports for final CATS E-R data model

```
                    Designer/2000

        Report      : ENTITY RELATIONSHIP DIAGRAM DETAILS
        Filename    : a:fig152    CDMODEL.lis
        Run by      : JGEORGE
        Report Date : 12-MAR-98 11:32am
        Total Pages : 5

        Parameter Values

        Application System : BEC
        Version            : 1
        Diagram            :
        Include Cardinality : True


12-MAR-98        Entity Relationship Diagram Details           Page 2 of 5

Entity Name      Attributes                Relationships            To Entities
-----------      ----------                -------------            -----------
CUSTOMER         * customer name           buys           (1, 1)
                 * customer number (uid)   - - - - - - - - - - - - -<   CUSTOMER TRANSACTION
                 * customer street         (0, <null>)   sold to (uid)
                 * telephone number
                 o credit card expiration date
                 o credit card number
                 o credit card type        described by     (1, <null>)
                 o customer zip            > - - - - - - - - - - - - -<   CUSTOMER PROFILE
                 o social security number  (0, <null>)   describes

                                           receives         (1, <null>)
                                           > - - - - - - - - - - - - -<   PRODUCT ANNOUNCEMENT
                                           (0, <null>)   is sent to

                                           assigned to      (1, <null>)
                                           > - - - - - - - - - - - - -<   STORE
                                           (1, 1)        has assigned

CUSTOMER PROFILE * customer category level (uid)  provides customer  (0, <null>)
                 * customer profile category       > - - - - - - - - - - - - -<   PRODUCT PROFILE
                   (uid)                   (0, <null>)   provides product in

                                           describes        (0, <null>)
                                           > - - - - - - - - - - - - -<   CUSTOMER
                                           (1, <null>)   described by


12-MAR-98        Entity Relationship Diagram Details           Page 3 of 5

Entity Name      Attributes                Relationships            To Entities
-----------      ----------                -------------            -----------
CUSTOMER TRANSACTION  o transaction date (uid)   includes purchase   (0, <null>)
                                           > - - - - - - - - - - - - -<   MUSIC OR GAME PRODUCT
                                           (0, <null>)   is purchased on
```

INVENTORY
* quantity in stock (uid)

```
is bought on          (0, <null>)           PRODUCT PROFILE
>- - - - - - - - - - - -<
(0, <null>)           includes

sold to               (0, <null>)           CUSTOMER
>- - - - - - - - - - - -
(1, 1)                buys

sold to (uid)         (0, <null>)           CUSTOMER
>- - - - - - - - - - - -
(1, 1)                buys

contains              (0, <null>)           PRODUCT
>- - - - - - - - - - - -
(1, 1)                held in

contains (uid)        (0, <null>)           PRODUCT
>- - - - - - - - - - - -
(1, 1)                held in

belongs to            (0, <null>)           STORE
>- - - - - - - - - - - -
(1, 1)                has

belongs to (uid)      (0, <null>)           STORE
>- - - - - - - - - - - -
(1, 1)                has
```

MUSIC OR GAME PRODUCT
(sub-type)

```
is purchased on       (0, <null>)           CUSTOMER TRANSACTION
>- - - - - - - - - - - -<
(0, <null>)includes purchase o
```

12-MAR-98   Entity Relationship Diagram Details

Entity Name	Attributes	Relationships	To Entities
PRODUCT	* product media type * product number (uid) * product title	held in `>- - - - - - - -<` (0, <null>) contains	(1, 1) INVENTORY (uid)
	o date product is available	has profile `>- - - - - - - -<` (0, <null>) profiles	(0, <null>) PRODUCT PROFILE
		announced by `>- - - - - - - -<` (0, <null>) announces	(1, <null>) PRODUCT ANNOUNCEMENT
PRODUCT ANNOUNCEMENT	* cats run number for announcement * date announcement sent	is sent to `>- - - - - - - -<` (1, <null>) receives	(0, <null>) CUSTOMER

Figure 2 (continued)

```
                                                                              Page 5 of 5

              Attributes              Relationships                    To Entities

              * date customer reserved
                product
              * pcs code              announces              (0, <null>)    PRODUCT
                                      >------ - - - - - - - <
                                      announced by           (1, <null>)

PRODUCT PROFILE  * product category name (uid)   has subordinate  (0, <null>)  PRODUCT PROFILE
                 o superior product category     >- - - - - - - - <
                   name                           has superior     (0, 1)

                                      has superior            (0, 1)         PRODUCT PROFILE
                                      >- - - - - - - - - - <
                                      has subordinate         (0, <null>)

                                      provides product i      (0, <null>)    CUSTOMER PROFILE
                                      >- - - - - - - - <
                                      (0, <null>)provides customer i

                                      includes                (0, <null>)    CUSTOMER TRANSACTION
                                      >- - - - - - - - <
                                      is bought on            (0, <null>)

                                      profiles                (0, <null>)    PRODUCT
                                      >- - - - - - - - <
                                      has profile             (0, <null>)


12-MAR-98            Entity Relationship Diagram Details                  Page 5 of 5

Entity Name   Attributes            Relationships                    To Entities
-----------   ----------            -------------                    -----------

STORE         * store manager name  has                     (1, 1)         INVENTORY
              * store number (uid)  - - - - - - - <                         (uid)
                                    belongs to              (0, <null>)

                                    has assigned            (1, 1)         CUSTOMER
                                    - - - - - - - <
                                    assigned to             (1, <null>)

VIDEO PRODUCT
(sub-type)


                        Designer/2000 Report :  cdmodel

                      ENTITY RELATIONSHIP DIAGRAM DETAILS

                                End of Report
```

```
STORE (STORE_ID, STORE_MRG_NAME)
PRODUCT (PROD_ID, PROD_TITLE, PROD_MEDIA, PROD_DATE_AVAILABLE)
VIDEO_PRODUCT (VIDEO_PROD_ID)
MUSIC/GAME_PRODUCT (MUSIC/GAME_PROD_ID)
CUSTOMER (CUST_ID, STORE_ID, CUST_NAME, CUST_STREET, CUST_CITY, CUST_STATE,
    CUST_ZIP, CUST_PHONE, CUST_CARD_TYPE, CUST_CARD_NO, CUST_CARD_EXPIRES, SSN)
INVENTORY (STORE_ID, PROD_ID, QTY_IN_STOCK)
PRODUCT_ANNOUNCEMENT (PROD_ID, CUST_ID, ANNOUNCE_DATE, RUN_NUMBER,
    RESERVATION_DATE, PCS_CODE)
CUSTOMER_TRANSACTION (CUST_TRAN_ID, CUST_ID, CUST_TRAN_DATE)
PURCHASE (CUST_TRAN_ID, MUSIC/GAME_PROD_ID)
CUSTOMER_PROFILE (CUST_PROF_CATEGORY, CUST_PROF_CAT_LEVEL)
PRODUCT_PROFILE (PROD_PROF_CATEGORY, PROD_PROF_SUPERIOR_CAT)
PRODUCT_FOR_CUSTOMER (CUST_PROF_CATEGORY, CUST_PROF_CAT_LEVEL, PROD_PROF_CATEGORY)
CUSTOMER_PROFILE_TRAN(CUST_PROF_CATEGORY, CUST_PROF_CAT_LEVEL, CUST_TRAN_ID)
PRODUCT_PROFILE_TRAN(PROD_PROF_CATEGORY, CUST_TRAN_ID)
```

(Note: Primary keys are underlined and foreign keys are in italics.)

Figure 3
Normalized relations from E-R model

Figure 4
Customer-product assignment (CPA) report

```
CUST_ID  →  CUST_NAME, CUST_PHONE, STORE_ID
PROD_ID  →  PROD_ARTIST, PROD_TITLE, PROD_MEDIA, PROD_DATE_AVAILABLE, PROD_PRICE
PCS_CODE →  RESERVATION_CONFIRMATION, CUST_ID, PROD_ID
```

Figure 5
Functional dependencies for customer-product assignment (CPA) report

"What I further concluded is that until a customer confirms an announcement, the RESERVATION_DATE is null (empty). Once customers call to confirm the reservation, the date they call is automatically put in this field. Thus, RESERVATION_CONFIRMATION represents this logical status of the RESERVATION_DATE field. What I propose we do is simply use the RESERVATION_DATE attribute, treating a null value as an unconfirmed reservation.

"Further, what this functional dependency says is that if we know a PCS_CODE, which is unique for each announcement of a new product release to a customer, then there is only one possible value for whether that customer has confirmed the reservation of that product associated with that PCS_CODE. The PCS_CODE was included in the PRODUCT_ANNOUNCEMENT relation as a nonkey. I think that PCS_CODE may also be a candidate key for this relation, and maybe we ought to make it the primary key instead of the compound key previously chosen. Then PROD_ID and CUST_ID will be foreign keys. Remember, the PCS_CODE stands for a product/customer/store combination. The store is the one to which the customer is assigned, so we don't need to keep that attribute in this relation. What do you think about these changes?"

Buffy thought for a moment before replying. "What you say makes sense, but I don't think you've gone far enough. What do we do with ANNOUNCE_DATE in the PRODUCT_ANNOUNCEMENT relation? It seems that ANNOUNCE_DATE may actually depend on RUN_NUMBER, since this is the date CATS produces an announcement. Maybe there is a transitive dependency here since the conceptual data modeling did not identify a RUN entity. All of the announcements generated from the same run will have the same ANNOUNCE_DATE, won't they? Is it possible that CATS might announce the same product to the same customer for the same store on more than one occasion, so PCS_CODE cannot identify a unique RUN_NUMBER? Jorge, am I getting confused here?"

"No, I think you are asking some very good and very tough questions, some of which I asked myself," said Jorge. "I went back to the on-line interview notes to see what was said about PCS_CODE and RUN_NUMBER. It really helped that we decided to store those interview notes as word processing documents indexed by AskSAM, a text DBMS. That made it a lot easier to search through all the notes for certain keywords. I couldn't find any insights, however. Let's see if we can get hold of Wendy Yoshimuro (the marketing manager responsible for CATS) on the phone and try to resolve this."

Jorge used a programmed speed dial button on his speaker phone to call Wendy. Fortunately, Wendy was in and confirmed to Jorge and Buffy that her intent was that BEC would give a customer only one announce-

ment for a given product, as the product was being released. There would be no second announcement.

Jorge summarized his conclusions after this phone call. "Well, I think we can now finalize the changes to the normalized relations due to the CPA report. We'll make PCS_CODE the primary key of the PRODUCT_ANNOUNCEMENT relation; we'll use the ANNOUNCE_DATE attribute to know whether to generate an entry for the CPA report; and we'll create a RUN relation to hold the ANNOUNCE_DATE, using RUN_NUMBER as a foreign key in PRODUCT_ANNOUNCEMENT to tie these data together. Does this seem right, Buffy?" (Figure 6 shows the new set of normalized relations.)

"As I said earlier, you really are getting the hang of data modeling," responded Buffy. "That seems to me to be exactly what we should do. Next, you can have the CASE tool reverse engineer a new E-R data model from the revised normalized relations. If I had more time we could go through all the other outputs and inputs you've analyzed, but it looks like you know what you are doing. I'll take a look at your final product when we do a team-level walkthrough of the logical design for the interim report Jordan said she wants to produce for the Systems Priority Board. Call me or send me an e-mail if you want me to look at any particular changes."

THE TRANSITION TO PHYSICAL DESIGN

Buffy continued, "I really like Jordan's idea of this status report, even though we don't owe the SPB anything until the end of physical design. I think it gives the SPB a chance to informally check our work and gives them a chance to execute their overseers' role. Based on what you've done so far, Jorge, do you see

Figure 6
Revised normalized relations based on functional dependency analysis of the CPA report

```
STORE (STORE_ID, STORE_MRG_NAME)
PRODUCT (PROD_ID, PROD_TITLE, PROD_MEDIA, PROD_DATE_AVAILABLE, PROD_ARTIST,
    PROD_PRICE)
VIDEO_PRODUCT (VIDEO_PROD_ID)
MUSIC/GAME_PRODUCT (MUSIC/GAME_PROD_ID)
CUSTOMER (CUST_ID, STORE_ID, CUST_NAME, CUST_STREET, CUST_CITY, CUST_STATE,
    CUST_ZIP, CUST_PHONE, CUST_CARD_TYPE, CUST_CARD_NO, CUST_CARD_EXPIRES, SSN)
INVENTORY (STORE_ID, PROD_ID, QTY_IN_STOCK)
PRODUCT_ANNOUNCEMENT (PCS_CODE, PROD_ID, CUST_ID, RUN_NUMBER, RESERVATION_DATE)
RUN (RUN_NUMBER, ANNOUNCE_DATE)
CUSTOMER_TRANSACTION (CUST_TRAN_ID, CUST_ID, CUST_TRAN_DATE)
PURCHASE (CUST_TRAN_ID, MUSIC/GAME_PROD_ID)
CUSTOMER_PROFILE (CUST_PROF_CATEGORY, CUST_PROF_CAT_LEVEL)
PRODUCT_PROFILE (PROD_PROF_CATEGORY, PROD_PROF_SUPERIOR_CAT)
PRODUCT_FOR_CUSTOMER (CUST_PROF_CATEGORY, CUST_PROF_CAT_LEVEL, PROD_PROF_CATEGORY)
CUSTOMER_PROFILE_TRAN(CUST_PROF_CATEGORY, CUST_PROF_CAT_LEVEL, CUST_TRAN_ID)
PRODUCT_PROFILE_TRAN(PROD_PROF_CATEGORY, CUST_TRAN_ID)
```

(*Note:* Primary keys are underlined and foreign keys are in italics.)

any need to recommend to Jordan any changes in the project schedule?"

"No, but I was wondering what else we'll need to know for physical database design. I want to make sure that the CASE repository and other notes contain all the information we'll need when we have to make final, physical design decisions."

"I'm glad you are looking ahead. I wanted to talk about exactly this point at our next weekly project team meeting. Briefly, you'll want to review interview notes and other documentation to make sure we know attribute formats and lengths, validation rules on each attribute (like a range of permitted values), the number of instances of each relation, what relations are used together for each report and form, and how frequently different processes that update or retrieve from the database occur. DFDs will tell us which data stores are used together, and these data stores must be mapped to relations. Hopefully the description of processes tells us how frequently certain activities occur. We may need to put together a questionnaire to send to selected CATS users to capture some of this information if we don't already have these details. The whole point is that we want to match the capabilities of the DBMS with the characteristics of the CATS operating environment. So far we have concentrated on what we wanted CATS to do; now it's time to consider how efficiently CATS has to work.

"It's so important that we deal with issues in the incremental fashion dictated by the systems development methodology. Otherwise, we have more to deal with than we can handle. The methodology allows us to deal with issues step-by-step, delaying costly decisions as long as possible. But, I think we are just about ready to make the critical physical design decisions, including database design."

SUMMARY

The CATS project team is in the final stages of the logical design phase of BEC's systems development process. As indicated in this case, new functional specifications have been developed during logical design, but the previous analysis information is still referenced and will continue to be useful during physical design. The amount of information about the CATS project is becoming overwhelming. Without automated tools, like a CASE tool and project management software, coordination across team members and across models and specifications would be too laborious and would likely become inaccurate. The team must ensure that every report, form, relation, process, data store, and so forth are complete and consistent with one another before physical system design can begin. Physical design is the last point at which CATS will be abstract, as implementation will begin to make CATS real and very costly to change if design errors are found. Thus, the work done by Jorge Lopez, Buffy Jarvis, and other team members will be carefully coordinated before moving into the next systems development phase.

Designing Physical Files and Databases

After studying this chapter, you should be able to:

- Define each of the following key physical file and database terms: *null value, pointer, record, page, file, file organization, index, database,* and *database management system.*

- Define six types of data files maintained by information systems.

- Choose storage formats (data types, coding schemes, display patterns, etc.) for attributes from a logical data model.

- Select controls on fields and files that will improve data accuracy and protect data from loss, contamination, or abusive use.

- Translate a relational data model into efficient storage structures for database processing, including knowing when to denormalize the logical data model.

- Choose among alternative methods of representing and handling missing data.

- Explain when to use different types of file organizations to store computer files.

- Calculate file sizes and estimate the amount of secondary computer memory required to store an application's data.

- Describe the purpose of indexes and the important considerations in selecting attributes to be indexed.

INTRODUCTION

In Chapters 10 and 16 you learned how to describe and model organizational data during the analysis and logical design phases of the systems development process. The processes and notations shown in those chapters were technology independent. That is, we use the processes and notations of E-R diagrams and normalization to develop abstractions of organizational data that capture the meaning of data; however, these notations do not explain *how* data will be processed or stored. The purpose of physical file and database design is to translate the logical description of data into the technical specifications for storing data. Systems analysts develop these specifications jointly with programmers, database analysts and administrators, data security staff, and other IS technical specialists. Beginning with this chapter, we turn our attention to issues of processing and storage efficiency, since prior development stages have structured the business information requirements as thoroughly and accurately as possible.

Physical file and database design has two main purposes:

1. You must translate relations from a logical data model into a technical design. This design includes choosing storage formats for each attribute, grouping attributes from one or more relations into one or more physical computer records, choosing organizations for the contents of each file of records, and designing methods to access data in and between files.

2. You must choose data storage technologies that will be used to help manage data. These technologies include various operating system functions, called access methods, and database management systems. These different technologies follow certain architectures, each of which is best suited for different data processing situations.

It is important to remember that physical file and database design does not include implementing (i.e., creating and loading data into) files and databases. Physical design produces the technical specifications that programmers and others involved in system construction will use during the implementation phase of systems development to create and populate files, file organizations, and databases.

PHYSICAL FILE AND DATABASE DESIGN

Physical file and database design is a natural, succeeding step after logical data modeling, which is why these are sequential chapters (see Figures 17-1 and 17-2). As in logical design, the three steps of the physical design phase—physical file and database design, program and system structure design, and distributed system design—are typically conducted in parallel because of the overlap of issues addressed. For example, in Chapter 19 we discuss the design of distributed databases. Thus, you will use together the concepts and skills you learn in Chapters 17–19.

The Process of Physical File and Database Design

In most situations, many physical data storage decisions are implicit or eliminated when you choose the data management technologies to use with the application you are designing. Since many organizations have standards for operating systems, database management systems, and data access languages, you must deal only with those choices not implicit in the given technologies. For example, many relational database management systems (DBMSs) give you little if any choice on the way to arrange records within computer files. In addition, computer center staff or systems programmers may have selected such parameters as virtual memory page sizes, which will affect data retrieval performance; these cannot be changed for individual applications. Thus, we will cover only those decisions you will make most frequently, plus a few selected decisions fundamental to your interactions with other systems developers making these decisions.

The goal of physical design, in general, and physical file and database design, in particular, is data processing efficiency. In other words, prior SDLC stages concen-

Figure 17-1
Systems development life cycle with physical design phase highlighted

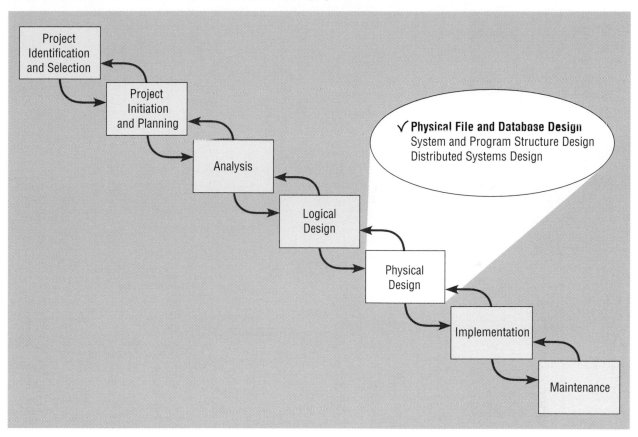

trated on "doing the right things," whereas physical design focuses on "doing the right things right." Today, with ever-decreasing costs for computer technology per unit of measure (both speed and space measures), it is typically very important for you to develop a physical system design that will minimize the time required by users to interact with the system. This means shortening data retrieval time and computer job turnaround time. Thus, we will concentrate on how to make processing of physical files and databases efficient, with less attention on efficient use of space.

Designing physical files and databases requires certain information that should have been collected and produced during prior SDLC phases. The information needed for physical file and database design includes these requirements:

- Normalized relations, including volume estimates

- Definitions of each attribute

- Descriptions of where and when data are used: entered, retrieved, deleted, and updated (including frequencies)

- Expectations or requirements for response time and data integrity

- Descriptions of the technologies used for implementing the files and database so that the range of required decisions and choices for each is known

Figure 17-2
Relationship between data modeling and the systems development life cycle

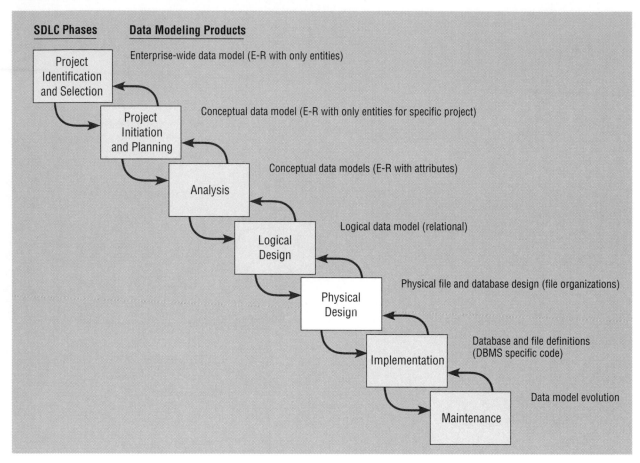

In physical file and database design you will make a number of critical decisions that will affect the integrity and performance of the application system. These key decisions include the following:

1. Choosing the storage format (called *data type*) for each attribute from the logical data model; the format is chosen to minimize storage space and to maximize data integrity. Data type involves choosing length, coding scheme, number of decimal places, minimum and maximum values, and potentially many other parameters for each attribute.

2. Grouping attributes from the logical data model into physical records (in general, this is called selecting a *stored record*, or *data, structure*).

3. Arranging related records in secondary memory (hard disks and tapes) so that individual and groups of records can be stored, retrieved, and updated rapidly (called *file organizations*). Consideration must be given also to protecting data and recovering data after errors are found.

4. Selecting media and structures for storing data to make access more efficient. The choice of media affects the utility of different file organizations. If you are using a database management system, this step involves selecting options for

random and sequential data retrieval as well as implementing relationships between entities and relations. The primary structure used today to make access to data more rapid is primary and secondary key indexes.

In this chapter we will address the factors that must be considered in making each of these decisions.

Deliverables and Outcomes

The deliverables from physical file and database design are a set of specifications that a programmer or database analyst will use to define the format and structure of data in secondary computer storage (usually hard disks). You are defining the structure of files recognized by system software, such as database management systems and operating systems. For many modern systems, these specifications would contain all the information needed to write or generate SQL (a standard relational database language) data definition statements. In other cases, these specifications would allow a COBOL, C, or C++ programmer to write data definitions. The specifications may be in the form of a pseudocode, but often the specifications are provided in the target language. The statements are not, however, executed to allocate space in secondary computer memory. Since data analysts and programmers often have to enter the code and verify specifications provided from several analysts or even several projects, specifications are often combined across different projects or major parts of a project before file and database implementation occurs.

The CASE repository or manual project dictionary is the natural place to store all of these specifications. Figure 17-3 lists the typical elements added to a project dictionary or repository during physical file and database design. For example, you would enter a specific data type for each attribute (called a field in physical design) object. Although a general data type may have been entered during logical design (for example, alphanumeric), it is during physical design that you finally decide whether an alphanumeric field is of fixed or variable length, what its maximum length is, and which unit of measure numeric values will represent. You would also enter specifications for how a field might be coded or formatted to more compactly represent longer, sparse sets of values. You group fields to form physical records and state rules—called referential integrity—to specify which fields must have matching values in different records (for example, the customer number in an order record must match a customer number field in a customer record). For each file, you must specify on what medium and device the file will be stored and the organization of records within the file. And you must indicate which files constitute each database and what structures will be used to link together the different files in a database.

We take a bottom-up approach to reviewing physical file and database design. Thus, we begin the physical design phase by addressing the design of physical fields for each attribute in a logical data model.

DESIGNING FIELDS

A **field** is the smallest unit of application data recognized by system software, such as a programming language or database management system. An attribute from a logical data model may be represented by several fields. For example, a student name attribute in a normalized student relation might be represented as three fields: last name, first name, and middle initial. Each field requires a separate definition when the application system is implemented.

Field: The smallest unit of named application data recognized by system software.

Figure 17-3

Typical data specifications added to a project dictionary during physical file and database design

FIELD	
Name	A name, in the format accepted by the DBMS, that uniquely labels the field; logical data model attribute and field names must be matched. *Example*: Qty_on_Hand for the quantity in stock of an inventory item.
Data type	Computer storage format, including length. *Example*: Two-byte numeric.
Unit of measure	The units represented by the value of the field. *Example*: Inches, pounds, dollars.
Coding	Abbreviations used for each possible real-world field value. *Example*: States represented by standard two-character abbreviation.
Data integrity rules	Specifications of the limitations on what constitutes a legitimate value. *Example*: A default value of 0 for Qty_on_Hand or a range from 0 to .25 for any price discount value.
Maintenance controls	Indication if value is allowed to change once it is entered. *Example*: Invoice data cannot change once the invoice is created.
Missing data procedures	Specifications of how to handle a missing value for the field when records in which the field appear are processed. *Example*: Ignore the field or use an average of other instances in the field.
Formula	For a calculated field, the equation used to compute the value for the field. *Example*: Extended price is unit price times quantity sold.
Check digit	If used, specifications for how certain digits within the field are mathematically related to other digits. *Example*: Adding to the end of a field the remainder after dividing the field value by 43.
Referential integrity	Specifications if values for the field must match values in a field in another record. *Example*: The customer number field value in a customer order must match a customer number field value in a customer record.
Ownership	Who is responsible for the meaning of this field and methods which access and update its value. *Example*: Storeroom manager is responsible for the accuracy of Qty_on_Hand.
RECORD TYPE	
Fields	List of fields that appear in record. *Example*: Item_Number, Description, and Qty_on_Hand for an inventory item record.
Structural data	Specification of any structural data necessary to interpret the format of a record. *Example*: Pointers and other data about the location of variable-length fields within the record.
Retention	Specification of how long the record is to be kept in a data file before it is purged or archived. *Example*: Retain an inactive customer record for two years after the most recent sales transaction.

In general, you will represent each attribute from each normalized relation as one or more fields. The basic decisions you must make in specifying each field concern the type of data (or storage type) used to represent the field, data integrity controls, and how to handle missing values for the field.

FILE	
Name and location	Label for file and the medium and device to which the file is allocated. *Example*: CUSTOMER file located on hard disk drive D:.
Record(s)	Specification of which record types are stored in the file; if only certain records of a given record type are included, then the logic of which records are included is provided. *Example*: The file contains records for two types, both IN_PATIENT and OUT_PATIENT; and the first field of each record indicates which type record it is.
Primary key	The field or combination of fields that will serve as the unique identifier of each record in the file. *Example*: Item_Number for an inventory item file.
Indexes	Which fields are indexed and whether the index is a primary or secondary key index. *Example*: Inventory items are indexed by the Finish field which is a secondary key (since more than one item can have the same finish).
Record blocking factor	Number of records per page or record block. *Example*: Ten ITEM records will be stored in each secondary memory page, and records cannot span page boundaries.
Retention and backup	How long the file is kept before it is purged or archived; procedures for file backup. *Example*: The ITEM file is backed up daily and the daily sales transaction file is kept for seven days, in case item data must be restored due to damage.
File organization	Operating system access method and file or database system method for arranging records within the file. *Example:* ITEM file will be stored as a hashed file based on Item_Number.
Controls	Specifications of audit trail or image files and encryption method. *Example:* File contents will be scrambled using a standard encryption procedure.
DATABASE	
Files	The files which are included in the database and their location in secondary memory. *Example:* The ITEM, CUSTOMER, ORDER, and LINE_ITEM files form the order entry database, stored in subdirectory F:\ENTRY.
Architecture	Type of database structure used to organize files. *Example:* The order entry database is managed by a relational DBMS.
Relationships	Mechanisms used to link files together. *Example:* In a network or hierarchical database, what types of pointers are used to link records in different files.

Choosing Data Types and Data Representations

A **data type** is a detailed coding scheme recognized by system software for representing organizational data. The bit pattern of the coding scheme is usually transparent to you, but the space to store data and the speed required to access data are of consequence in the physical file and database design. The specific file or database management software you will use with your system will dictate which choices are available to you. For example, Table 17-1 lists the data types available in many SQL systems. Additional data types might be available for currency, variable-length

Data type: A detailed coding scheme recognized by system software for representing organizational data.

TABLE 17-1   Typical SQL Data Types

Data Type	Description
DECIMAL(m,n)	Signed numbers, where m is the total number of digits and n is the number of digits to the right of the decimal point
INTEGER	Large (up to 11 digits) positive or negative whole numbers
SMALLINT	Small (5 or 6 digits) positive or negative whole numbers (requires less storage space than INTEGER)
FLOAT(m,n)	Whole and fractional numbers represented in scientific notation, where m is the total number of digits and n is the number of digits to the right of the decimal point
CHAR(n)	Alphanumeric, where n is the maximum length
DATE	Calendar date, using several different styles
LOGICAL	True or false

alphanumeric data where only the required space is used (often called a memo field), and time.

Selecting a data type involves four objectives which will have different relative importances for different applications:

1. Minimize storage space

2. Represent all possible values

3. Improve data integrity

4. Support all data manipulations

You want to choose a data type for a field that can, in the minimal amount of space, represent every possible value for the associated attribute and for which you can do the required data manipulations. For example, suppose a quantity sold field can be represented by a SMALLINT data type. Some SQL systems will automatically assign the SMALLINT data type to the temporary field which is the sum of the quantity sold values. Since it is possible that the sum may have more digits than each component field, SMALLINT may not be of sufficient size for this field. Further, you want a data type that will restrict users from entering inappropriate values. For example, a numeric data type is stronger than an alphanumeric one and will reject entry of alphabetic values. In SQL, a SMALLINT data type might be sufficient for a quantity on hand attribute for most organizations but it does not, by itself, restrict negative numbers, which may be invalid.

Be careful—the data type must be suitable for the life of the application, otherwise maintenance will be required. Thus, it is advisable that you choose data types for future needs, anticipating growth.

To illustrate supporting data manipulations, consider an invoice date attribute. Two possible data types for this field would be DATE and CHAR(6); in CHAR(6) the date would be 6 digits as MMDDYY. Besides evaluating how much space is required for a DATE versus a CHAR(6) data type, for example, you would also want to know if there will ever be any date arithmetic done on invoice date. Most systems that support a date data type will allow subtraction and addition of dates with each other and with constants.

Some implementation platforms will support more advanced data types. Newer data types include voice, image or graphic, video, and user-defined. There is growing recognition that business applications require a more diverse set of data rather than just numbers and characters, so the data types supported are significantly improving.

Calculated Fields   It is common that a logical data model will include attributes which are mathematically related to other data. For example, an invoice may include a total due field, which represents the sum of the amount due on each item on the invoice. A field which can be derived from other database fields is called a **calculated field** (or a computed or derived field). Some implementation environments allow you to explicitly define calculated fields as a special data type. You would then usually be prompted to enter the formula for the calculation; the formula can involve other fields from the same record and possibly fields from records in related files.

> **Calculated field:** A field which can be derived from other database fields. Also called computed or derived field.

In general, data storage technologies provide three ways to handle a calculated field:

1. You cannot represent the calculated field, but you must compute it on a record-by-record basis in each program that needs the computed value.

2. You may store the calculated field in the file as you would any other field so that it need not be recalculated every time it is needed (it must be recalculated only if the data it depends on changes), but use "extra" storage space to save the computational time.

3. You may virtually store the calculated field, but the data management technology actually stores only the formula in the data definitions and not the computed value. The data management technology transparently recalculates the field value at run time, giving you the impression it was retrieved.

The third option, if available, is usually the most desirable. It requires the consumption of the least storage space and the computational time is usually negligible. The second option allows the calculated field to be processed like any other field, which is desirable, but it does require redundant storage. For some systems, you define calculated fields not as part of record definitions but as fields on forms or reports. This is similar to the first option, but the database management system generates the code to do the calculations.

Coding and Compression Techniques   Some attributes have very sparse domains. For example, although a six-digit field (five numbers plus sign) can represent numbers -99999 to 99999, maybe only 100 positive values within this range will ever exist. Thus, a SMALLINT data type does not adequately restrict the permissible values, and storage space for five digits plus sign is wasteful. To more efficiently use space, you can define a field for an attribute so that the possible attribute values are not represented literally but rather are abbreviated. For example, suppose in Pine Valley Furniture each product has a finish attribute, with possible values Birch, Walnut, Oak, and so forth. To store this attribute as a character string might require 12, 15, or even 20 bytes to represent the longest finish character string value. Suppose that even a liberal estimate is that Pine Valley Furniture will never have more than 25 finishes. Thus, a single alphabetic or alphanumeric character would be more than sufficient. In the case of such coding, a separate code look-up table is created which matches each code value with the associated real-world value, as illustrated in Figure 17-4. On all user interfaces the real-world values are shown, but the internal storage is minimized to the length of the coded value in each product record, at the expense of minimal space for a look-up table and the (negligible) cost for the look-up. This look-up operation may be directly supported by the data

Figure 17-4
Example code look-up table (Pine Valley Furniture)

PRODUCT FILE   FINISH LOOK-UP TABLE

Product Number	Description	Finish	...
B100	Chair	C	
B120	Desk	A	
M128	Table	C	
T100	Bookcase	B	
⋮	⋮	⋮	

Code	Value
A	Birch
B	Maple
C	Oak
⋮	⋮

management software or may have to be handled by application software. A further advantage is that the dense code (no wasted values) reduces the likelihood of incorrect data entry since each entered value must correspond with an entry in the code table. Thus, we not only reduce storage space but also increase integrity, which helps to achieve two of the physical file and database design goals. Codes also have disadvantages. If used in system inputs and outputs, they can be more difficult for users to remember, and programs must be written to decode fields if codes will not be displayed.

Data compression technique: Pattern matching and other methods which replace repeating strings of characters with codes of shorter length.

Data compression techniques reduce data storage requirements by looking for patterns in data and then coding frequently appearing patterns with fewer bits. A popular technology that uses data compression techniques is WinZip® from Nico Mak Computing, Inc., which compresses MS-DOS files.

Selection of Primary Key Values   Sometimes proper primary keys have not been chosen prior to the physical design phase. The relations resulting from logical data modeling may have primary keys that violate the principles for formulating primary keys. The result of applying the guidelines for key design described in Chapter 10 is typically a value that has no real-world meaning, a so-called nonintelligent key. For example, a product relation in third normal form may have a primary key of product number; if this attribute changes value over time, is null, or indicates location or classification of products, then it is not a good selection for the primary key. Consider an intelligent product number of M128 (where M indicates the line of product, for example, modern). In this case, it would be better to create a Product_ID primary key, with a new system assigned value for each record as it is added to the file. The intelligent product number would also be stored, but only as a regular attribute.

Controlling Data Integrity

We have already explained that data typing helps control data integrity by limiting the possible range of values for a field. In this section, we discuss several additional physical file and database design options you might use to ensure higher-quality data. This discussion supplements the coverage of validation tests and techniques from Chapter 15 (see Table 15-9). Although these controls can be imposed within application code, it is better to include these as part of the file and database definitions so that the controls are guaranteed to be applied all the time as well as uniformly for all programs. There are five popular data integrity control methods: default values, picture statement, range control, referential integrity, and null value controls.

Default Value   Some attributes are such that a large percentage of the instances of that attribute have a common value. For example, the city and state of most customers for a particular retail store will likely be the same as the store's city and state. A **default value** is the value a field will assume unless an explicit value is entered for the field. Assigning a default value to a field can reduce data entry time (the field can simply be skipped during data entry) and helps to reduce data entry errors, such as typing 'IM' instead of 'IN' for Indiana.

Default value: A value a field will assume unless an explicit value is entered for that field.

Picture Control   Some data must follow a specified pattern. A **picture (or template)** is a pattern of codes that restricts the width and possible values for each position within a field. For example, a product number at Pine Valley Furniture is four alphanumeric characters—the first is alphabetic and the next three are numeric—defined by a picture of A999 where A means that only alphabetic characters are accepted and 9 means that only numeric digits are accepted. Thus, M128 is an acceptable value but 3128 or M12H would be unacceptable.

Picture (or template): A pattern of codes that restricts the width and possible values for each position of a field.

A picture may specify that certain special characters appear in certain positions within a field during display. For example, for the bank account example, a template might specify a hyphen between the second and third and between the sixth and seventh digits. A picture helps to not only visually format data for easy inspection of correctness but also allows the computer software to check that individual digits are not skipped during entry. Consider a picture of

$$\$999,999.00$$

for an integer field. This picture could be used during data entry to confirm to the user that the entered data is in dollars, the proper placement of digits is within a limit of six significant digits (even though an integer data type might support a much larger number), and that values must be in whole dollars. Other types of picture controls can be used to specify the following choices:

- How to show negative numbers

- Whether to suppress showing leading zeros

- Whether a floating currency symbol should appear immediately to the left of the most significant digit

- Justification of the value within the space for the field display

Range Controls   Both numeric and alphabetic data may have a limited set of permissible values. For example, a field for the number of product units sold may have a lower bound of 0 and a field which represents the month of a product sale may be limited to the values JAN, FEB, and so forth.

Although a significant help in ensuring data integrity, range and other data integrity controls must be used with caution because the world changes and such restrictions may themselves change. For example, should the value PR be accepted for a U.S. state? Or must all years begin with 19? Many systems that support range and other controls will allow you to update these controls as long as no field values violate the new restrictions. Furthermore, if you have implemented integrity controls as "hard code" in programs rather than through data definitions, it may be very cumbersome and expensive to update the restrictions.

Referential Integrity   The term referential integrity was defined in Chapter 16 as limiting values for a given attribute to the existing values of another attribute in the data model. The most common example of this is cross referencing between relations. For example, consider the pair of relations in Figure 17-5a. In this case, the values for the foreign key Customer_ID field within a customer order must be limited to the set of Customer_ID values from the customer relation; we would not

Figure 17-5
Examples of referential
integrity field controls

(a) Referential integrity
between relations

(b) Referential integrity within
a relation

CUSTOMER (**Customer_ID**, Cust_Name, Cust_Address,...)

CUST_ORDER (Order_ID, **Customer_ID**, Order_Date,...)

    and Customer_ID may not be null since every order must be for some
    existing customer

EMPLOYEE (**Employee_ID**, **Supervisor_ID**, Empl_Name,...)

    and Supervisor_ID may be null since not all employees have supervisors

want to accept an order for a nonexisting or unknown customer. Referential integrity may be useful in other instances. Consider the employee relation example in Figure 17-5b. In this example, the employee relation has a field of Supervisor_ID. This field refers to the Employee_ID of the employee's supervisor and should have referential integrity on the Employee_ID field within the same relation. Note in this case that since some employees do not have supervisors, this is a weaker referential integrity constraint because the value of a Supervisor_ID field may be empty.

Referential integrity acts like a dynamic table (in this case, file) look-up. Whereas a range control limits a field to those values found in a table defined when the files and databases were created, referential integrity says that a field is limited to those values currently in some field in the database. Since it is cross references between relations that hold a relational database together, it is usually critical that all possible referential integrity controls be defined in relational databases.

Note that referential integrity guarantees that only some existing cross reference value is used, not that it is the correct one. This is why visual checks are still usually applied. For example, when entering a customer order, it is advisable to not only enforce referential integrity on the Customer_ID field but also to retrieve the associated customer data and display them for visual verification by the data entry person.

Null Value Control   It is not uncommon that when it is time to enter data—for example, a new customer—you might not know the customer's phone number. The question is whether a customer, to be valid, must have a value for this field. The answer for *this* field is probably no, since most data processing can continue without knowing the customer's phone number. It is possible that a customer's phone number might be unknown when the customer record is created, but it may not be allowed to be unspecified when you are ready to ship product to the customer. On the other hand, you must always know a value for the Customer_ID field. Due to referential integrity, you cannot enter any customer orders for this new customer without knowing an existing Customer_ID value, and customer name is essential for visual verification of correct data entry.

Null value: A special field value, distinct from 0, blank, or any other value, that indicates that the value for the field is missing or otherwise unknown.

A **null value** is a special field value, distinct from 0, blank, or any other value, that indicates that the value for the field is missing or otherwise unknown. Usually when you apply a referential integrity restriction on a field, it implies that the field may not be null or empty; the example in Figure 17-5b illustrates that this is not always the case. In addition, you should also specify whether nonkey fields such as the customer name field of a customer record may be null.

Handling Missing Data

When a field may be null, there is a question of how to handle null values in processing data. For example, suppose a customer zip code field is null and a report summarizes total sales by month and zip code. How should sales to customers with unknown zip codes be handled? Or what if monthly total sales for some product is missing for a given month? How should a sales forecasting routine cope with this missing data? During physical file and database design you must specify how your system is to handle missing data for each field.

Two options for handling or preventing missing data have already been mentioned: using default values and not permitting missing (null) values. Both of these methods bias some results since neither may accurately depict the true state of the organization. Certainly preventing missing data to the extent possible minimizes the ramifications of data inaccuracies. But some missing data is inevitable. According to Babad and Hoffer (1984), other possible methods for handling missing data are the following:

1. Substitute an estimate of the missing value. For example, for monthly product sales, use a formula involving the mean of monthly sales for that product indexed by total sales for that month across all products. Such estimates must be marked so that users know that these are not actual values.

2. Track missing data so that special reports and other system elements cause people to quickly resolve unknown values. This method allows data to be entered promptly in a system yet calls attention to the missing data in order to expedite finding the missing values.

3. Perform sensitivity testing so that missing data are ignored unless knowing a value might significantly change results; if, for example, total monthly sales for a particular salesperson are almost over a threshold that would make a difference in that person's compensation. This is the most complex of the methods mentioned and hence requires the most sophisticated programming to implement.

Missing data are a fact of information systems. Yet, in practice, explicit methods for handling missing data are often overlooked during physical file and database design. Ignoring missing data may, however, cause misrepresentation of the organization's state and result in bad decisions.

DESIGNING PHYSICAL RECORDS

In logical data modeling you grouped into a relation those attributes which concern some unifying business concept, such as a customer, product, or employee. In contrast, a **physical record** is a group of fields stored in adjacent memory locations and retrieved together as a unit. The design of a physical record involves choosing the sequence and grouping of fields into adjacent storage locations to achieve two goals: efficient use of secondary storage and data processing speed.

One consideration when designing physical data records is conserving secondary memory space. Computer operating systems actually read data from hard disks in units called pages. A **page** is the amount of data read or written in one secondary memory input or output operation. (With magnetic tapes, the equivalent concept is a *record block.*) The page size is fixed by system programmers and is selected to most efficiently use RAM across all applications. Depending on the computer system, a physical record may or may not be allowed to span two pages. Thus, if page length is not an integer multiple of the physical record length, wasted space may occur at the end of a page. For example, consider a physical record containing fields whose total length is 1,034 bytes. If a page is 2,000 bytes and the file management software does not allow physical records to span pages, then there would be only one record per page, with 966 wasted bytes per page. The number

Physical record: A group of fields stored in adjacent memory locations and retrieved together as a unit.

Page: The amount of data read or written in one secondary memory (disk) input or output operation. For I/O with a magnetic tape, the equivalent term is *record block.*

Blocking factor: The number of physical records per page.

of records per page is called the **blocking factor.** If storage space is scarce and physical records cannot span pages, you should consider creating multiple physical records from one logical relation so that wasted storage space is minimized.

A second and often more important consideration when selecting a physical record design is efficient data processing. Data are most efficiently processed when the needed data are stored close to one another in secondary memory, thus minimizing the number of input/output (I/O) operations that must be performed.

Record partitioning: The process of splitting logical records into separate physical segments based on affinity of use.

Record partitioning is the process of splitting normalized relations into separate physical segments based on affinity of use. Each segment is a separate physical record, stored with other like segments in a separate physical file. For example, consider patient data in Figure 17-6. In this figure, the logical record has been broken into two segments. The primary segment contains fields used in almost every retrieval of patient data. The secondary segment contains data used on an intermittent basis. The result is very short primary segments, so there will be many primary segments per page. Since many primary segments can be read in one I/O operation, total I/O time for many processing functions is minimized. Other examples of partitioning might include splitting a product record into separate segments with each containing only engineering, accounting or marketing data, or dividing customer account data by geographical region.

Partitioning is a deliberate form of denormalization—defining physical records not in third or higher normal forms. Denormalization also includes joining attributes from several relations together to avoid the cost of accessing several files instead of one. For example, at the cost of redundantly storing the customer data, you could store customer and customer order data in one physical record to avoid retrieving two separate records. Since the relative benefits of denormalization may change with new technology, you must maintain the normalized relations in the project dictionary so that the decision to denormalize can be readdressed as new technology is introduced.

Denormalization can create some of the problems (anomalies) that normalization, as discussed in Chapter 16, is designed to avoid. As Finkelstein (1988) points out, denormalization can increase the chance of errors and inconsistencies and can force reprogramming systems if business rules change. Further, denormalization optimizes certain data processing at the expense of others, so if the frequencies of different processing activities change, the benefits of denormalization may no longer exist.

Various forms of denormalization can be done and there are no hard-and-fast rules for deciding when to denormalize data. Rodgers (1989) discusses the general trade-offs. You should consider denormalization in the following situations

Figure 17-6
Example of record partitioning

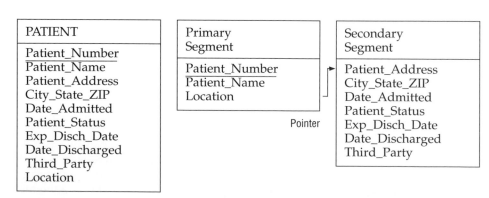

Logical record   Physical record segments

(Figure 17-7 shows examples of normalized and denormalized relations for each of these three situations):

1. *Two entities with a one-to-one relationship.* Even if one of the entities is an optional participant, if the matching entity exists most of the time, then it may be wise to combine these two relations into one record definition. Figure 17-7a shows student data with optional data from a standard scholarship application a student may complete. In this case, one record could be formed with four fields from the STUDENT and SCHOLARSHIP APPLICATION FORM normalized relations. (*Note:* In this case, fields from the optional entity must have null values allowed.)

2. *A many-to-many relationship (gerund) with nonkey attributes.* Rather than joining three files to extract data from the two entities in the relationship, it may be advisable to combine attributes from one of the entities into the record representing the many-to-many relationship, thus avoiding one join in many data access modules. Figure 17-7b shows price quotes for different items from different vendors. In this case, fields from ITEM and PRICE QUOTE relations might be combined into one record to avoid having to join all three files together. (*Note:* This may create considerable duplication of data—in the example, the ITEM fields, such as DESCRIPTION, would repeat for each price quote—and excessive updating if duplicated data changes.)

3. *Reference data.* Reference data exists in an entity on the one-side of a one-to-many relationship, and this entity participates in no other database relationships. You should seriously consider merging the two entities in this situation into one record definition when there are few instances of the entity on the many-side for each entity instance on the one-side. See Figure 17-7c in which several ITEMs have the same STORAGE INSTRUCTIONS and STORAGE INSTRUCTIONS only relate to ITEMs. In this case, the storage instruction data could be stored in the ITEM records creating, of course, redundancy and the potential for extra data maintenance.

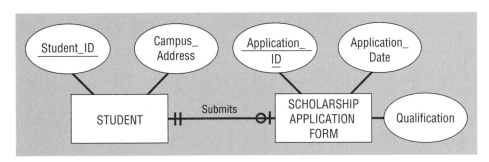

Figure 17-7
Possible denormalization situations

(a) Two entities with one-to-one relationship

Normalized relations:
  STUDENT (Student_ID, Campus_Address, Application_ID)
  APPLICATION (Application_ID, Application_Date, Qualifications, Student_ID)

Denormalized relation:
  STUDENT (Student_ID, Campus_Address, Application_Date, Qualifications)

  and Application_Date and Qualifications may be null

(*Note:* We assume Application_ID is not necessary when all fields are stored in one record, but this field can be included if it is required application data.)

(continues)

Figure 17-7 *(continued)*

(b) A many-to-many relationship with nonkey attributes

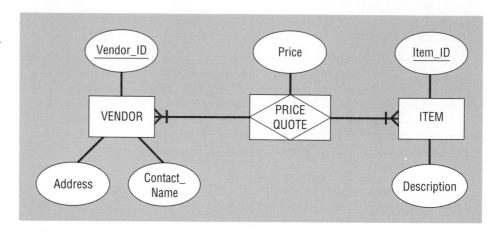

Normalized relations:
    VENDOR (<u>Vendor_ID</u>, Address, Contact_Name)
    ITEM (<u>Item_ID</u>, Description)
    PRICE QUOTE (<u>Vendor_ID</u>, <u>Item_ID</u>, Price)

Denormalized relations:
    VENDOR (<u>Vendor_ID</u>, Address, Contact_Name)
    ITEM-QUOTE (<u>Vendor_ID</u>, <u>Item_ID</u>, Description, Price)

(c) Reference data

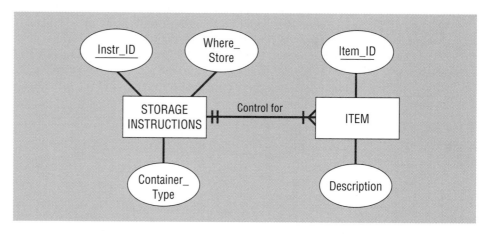

Normalized relations:
    STORAGE (<u>Instr_ID</u>, Where_Store, Container_Type)
    ITEM (<u>Item_ID</u>, Description, <u>Instr_ID</u>)

Denormalized relation
    ITEM (<u>Item_ID</u>, Description, Where_Store, Container_Type)

Handling Fixed-Length Fields

Designing a physical record is easier if every field is of fixed length. In the case of fixed-length fields, a positional technique is most often used to place and find fields. This technique is illustrated in Figure 17-8. With this technique, character fields have trailing blanks and numeric fields have leading zeros to make all instances of a given field the same length. In this scheme, we know that the fifth field is always offset from the beginning of the record by a known displacement, which is the

Figure 17-8
Positional field format
technique

ELWAYbbbbbbbJbRbbQBbbb83

sum of the lengths of the preceding fields. Further, since every record has the same fields, each record has the same length. Thus, it is easy to find the position of the mth field in the nth record in this way:

$$\text{address of beginning of file} + (n-1)*\text{record length} + \text{sum (length}_i)$$
$$i = 1 \text{ to } m - 1$$

where length$_i$ is the length of field i. Other techniques are used and the interested reader can refer to database and data structure texts for explanations of alternatives.

Handling Variable-Length Fields

A variable-length field, such as a memo field, makes the location of a particular field and of a particular record irregular. That is, depending on which records exist and the precise values for fields, different records and fields will be in different locations. A common way you can handle variable-length fields is to break the relation into a fixed-length physical record containing all of the fixed-length fields and one or more variable-length physical records. You design the fixed-length record as described previously. You can then allocate each variable-length field to a separate file. This is the automatic physical record design technique used by most microcomputer DBMSs that support a memo field. Other techniques for handling variable-length fields are addressed in many data structure texts.

DESIGNING PHYSICAL FILES

A **physical file** is a named portion of secondary memory (a magnetic tape or hard disk) allocated for the purpose of storing physical records. Some computer operating systems allow a physical file to be split into separate pieces. If this occurs, it will be transparent to you as the file designer and is the result of the operating system trying to use every page of secondary memory. In subsequent sections, we will assume that a physical file is not split and each record has the same structure.

Physical file: A named set of contiguous records.

Before we present the principles and options for designing files, it is worthwhile reviewing the various types of files that might exist in a system, each of which requires a design.

Types of Files

Table 17-2 lists and defines the six different types of files associated with a typical information system, along with considerations for the design of each. During physical file and database design you must anticipate the need for each of these files and design the structure of each. The nuances of each file are beyond the scope of our discussion, but the following sections review general principles of file design that can apply to each file type. In subsequent examples we will exclusively use data files since these are the types of files on which you typically concentrate most attention during physical file and database design.

TABLE 17-2	Types of Files
Type of File	**Description**
Data File (also called Master File)	A file that contains business data related to the conceptual and logical data models for applications. The file is permanent but the contents change. Data files should be designed for both random and sequential processing speed and storage efficiency and to accommodate changes in size. *Example:* customer file or invoice file.
Look-Up Table File	A list of reference data used to validate field values in one or more data files. Such files are usually static and should be designed for rapid data retrieval of individual entries. *Example:* list of valid product finishes.
Transaction File	A temporary file of data about the day-to-day activities of an organization. This file may hold data until they can be processed to update data files or the file may be retained in case the data must be reused. Transaction files are usually designed for rapid sequential processing. *Example:* all the ATM transactions for a given day.
Work File	A temporary file in which intermediate results are held. A temporary file is automatically deleted once no longer needed and recreated when again needed. Work file design is unique to the uses of that file. *Example:* a sorted list of customer and customer order data needed to produce a report.
Protection File (also called an Audit Trail)	A file used to restore other files in the case that the other files are damaged. This type of file may include before or after images of data file records so old values can be restored. This type of file is usually designed for rapid sequential processing. *Example:* a backup copy of a customer file.
History File	A file which contains data that are no longer current but which are needed to show what the state of the organization was at some prior point in time. History files are usually designed for efficient storage space. *Example:* a bank account file showing account balances at the end of the prior business day.

Pointer

All files are organized by using two basic constructs to link one piece of data with another piece of data: sequential storage and pointers. With sequential storage one field or record is stored right after another field or record. As illustrated in Figure 17-6, various circumstances can occur when the sequential storage of data must be broken and we need to know where the "next" field of data is. A **pointer** is a field of data that can be used to locate a related field or record of data. In most cases, a pointer contains the address of the associated data. For example, in Figure 17-6, a pointer is used to link each primary segment to its associated secondary segment. Pointers are used in many different contexts in physical file and database design.

Pointer: A field of data that can be used to locate a related field or record of data.

Access Methods

All I/O operations are ultimately handled by the data management portion of the computer's operating system. Each operating system supports one or more different algorithms for storing and retrieving data and these algorithms are called **access methods.** Your understanding of the access methods on the target computer system is fundamental to designing data files for an application.

Access method: An operating system algorithm for storing and locating data in secondary memory.

There are basically two types of access methods: relative and direct. A relative access method supports accessing data as an offset from the most recently referenced point in secondary memory. A sequential access method is a special case of this type since the "next" record begins the distance of one record from the beginning of the current record. In general, a relative access method supports finding the nth record from the current position or from the beginning of the file. A direct access method uses some calculation to generate the beginning address of a record. The simplest form of a direct method is to tell the access method to go to a particular disk address. Another variation is to provide a record's primary key and the direct access method determines where this record should be located. We will discuss this access method under the more inclusive concept of file organizations in the next section.

It is rare that you will directly use the operating system's access methods. Rather, you will more likely use the data organizations supported by a programming language or database or file management system. These data arrangements are called file organizations, which we discuss next.

File Organizations

A **file organization** is a technique for physically arranging the records of a file on secondary storage devices. In choosing a file organization for a particular file, you should consider seven important factors:

1. Fast data retrieval

2. High throughput for processing transactions

3. Efficient use of storage space

4. Protection from failures or data loss

5. Minimizing need for reorganization

6. Accommodating growth

7. Security from unauthorized use

File organization: A technique for physically arranging the records of a file on secondary storage devices.

Often these objectives conflict, and you must select an organization for each file that provides a reasonable balance among the criteria within the resources available.

Literally hundreds of different file organizations and variations have been created but we will outline the basics of three families of file organizations used in most file management environments: sequential, indexed, and hashed (see Figure 17-9). You will need to understand the particular variations of each method available in the environment for which you are designing files.

Sequential File Organizations   In a **sequential file organization,** the records in the file are stored in sequence according to a primary key value (see Figure 17-9a). To locate a particular record, a program must normally scan the file from the beginning until the desired record is located. A common example of a sequential file is the alphabetical list of persons in the white pages of a phone directory (ignoring any index that may be included with the directory). Sequential files are very fast if you want to process records sequentially but they are essentially impractical for random record retrievals. Deleting records can cause wasted space or the need to compress the file. Adding records requires rewriting the file, at least from the point of insertion. Updating a record may also require rewriting the file, unless the file organization supports rewriting over the updated record only. Moreover, only one sequence can be maintained without duplicating the records.

Sequential file organization: The records in the file are stored in sequence according to a primary key value.

Indexed File Organizations   In an **indexed file organization,** the records are either stored sequentially or non-sequentially and an index is created that allows the application software to locate individual records (see Figure 17-9b). Like a card catalog in a library, an **index** is a table that is used to determine the location of rows in a file that satisfy some condition. Each entry matches a key value with one or more records. An index can point to unique records (a primary key index, such as on the

Indexed file organization: The records are either stored sequentially or nonsequentially and an index is created that allows software to locate individual records.

Index: A table or other data structure used to determine the location of rows in a file that satisfy some condition.

Figure 17-9
Comparison of file
organizations

(a) Sequential

(b) Indexed

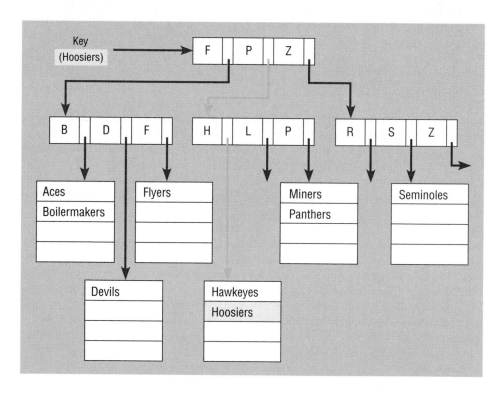

Secondary key: One or a
combination of fields for which
more than one record may
have the same combination
of values.

Product_ID field of a product record) or to potentially more than one record. An
index that allows each entry to point to more than one record is called a **secondary
key** index. Secondary key indexes are important for supporting many reporting requirements and for providing rapid ad hoc data retrieval. An example would be an
index on the Finish field of a product record.

The example in Figure 17-9b illustrates that indexes can be built on top of indexes, creating a hierarchical set of indexes. This may be desirable since an index
itself is a file and, if it is very large, it too can be organized by indexing the index.

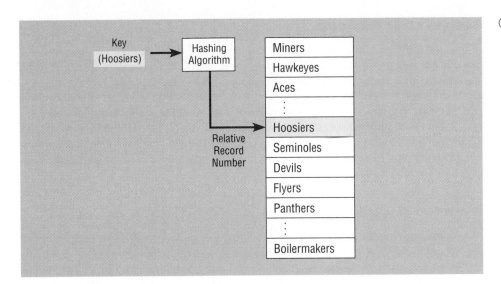

Each index entry in Figure 17-9b has a key value and a pointer to another index or to a data record. For example, to find the record with key "Hoosiers", the file organization would start at the top index and take the pointer after the entry P, which points to another index for all keys that begin with the letter G through P in the alphabet. Then the software would follow the pointer after the H in this index, which represents all those records with keys that begin with the letters G through H. Eventually, the search through the indexes either locates the desired record or indicates that no such record exists. See McFadden, Hoffer, and Prescott (1999) for a thorough treatment of the most popular indexing methods.

The main disadvantages to indexed file organizations are the extra space required to store the indexes and the extra time required to access and maintain indexes. Usually these disadvantages are more than offset by the advantages. Since the index is kept in sequential order, both random and sequential processing are practical. Also, since the index is separate from the data, you can build multiple index structures on the same data file (just as in the library where there are multiple indexes on author, title, subject, and so forth). With multiple indexes, software may rapidly find records that have compound conditions, such as finding books by Tom Clancy on espionage. Also, since the raw data can be stored nonsequentially, data addition, deletion, and modification may be easy. Depending on how the indexes are managed, however, the file may need to be reorganized after many updates. Two popular variations on indexed file organizations are distinguished by this last factor: indexed sequential access method, ISAM, files must be periodically reorganized and virtual storage access method, VSAM, files are dynamically reorganized with negligible overhead.

Hashed File Organizations   In a **hashed file organization,** the address of each record is determined using a hashing algorithm (see Figure 17-9c). A **hashing algorithm** is a routine that converts a primary key value into a record address. Although there are several variations of hashed files, in most cases the records are located nonsequentially as dictated by the hashing algorithm. Thus, sequential data processing is impractical. On the other hand, retrieval of random records is very fast. There are issues in the design of hashing file organizations, such as how to handle two primary keys that translate into the same address, but again, these issues are beyond our scope (see McFadden, Hoffer, and Prescott (1999) for a thorough discussion).

Hashed file organization:
The address for each record is determined using a hashing algorithm.

Hashing algorithm: A routine that converts a primary key value into a relative record number (or relative file address).

Summary of File Organizations

The three families of file organizations cover most of the file organizations you will have at your disposal as you design physical files and databases. Other more basic data structures, such as linked lists and chains, are typically used by operating systems and file management software. Unless you are building a system without the aid of modern system software, you will not deal with these structures directly.

Table 17-3 summarizes the comparative features of sequential, indexed, and hashed file organizations. You can use this table to help choose a file organization by matching the file characteristics and file processing requirements with the features of the file organization.

Designing Controls for Files

When you design files and databases, it is important to decide how you will protect them from destruction or contamination. Certainly the field data integrity controls discussed earlier in the chapter help, but you can use other techniques to protect the whole file. Two frequently used techniques are backup procedures and encryption.

File Backup Procedures   Before the system is written, you should decide how and how often each file will be backed up. The easiest approach is to specify that all files will be periodically copied onto a separate electronic medium and stored off site from the current versions. Since a total backup of all files may be time-consuming and each file has a different volatility, some files may need to be backed up more frequently than others. Although frequent backups can be expensive in lost computer time and media, you have to reconstruct less work to restore a file if it is damaged. You must also decide how many backup versions need to be retained.

TABLE 17-3   Comparative Features of Different File Organizations

Factor	Sequential	Indexed	Hashed
		File Organization	
Storage Space	No wasted space	No wasted space for data, but extra space for index	Extra space may be needed to allow for addition and deletion of records
Sequential Retrieval on Primary Key	Very fast	Moderately fast	Impractical
Random Retrieval on Primary Key	Impractical	Moderately fast	Very fast
Multiple Key Retrieval	Possible, but requires scanning whole file	Very fast with multiple indexes	Not possible
Deleting Records	Can create wasted space or require reorganizing	If space can be dynamically allocated, this is easy, but requires maintenance of indexes	Very easy
Adding Records	Requires rewriting file	If space can be dynamically allocated, this is easy, but requires maintenance of indexes	Very easy, except multiple keys with same address require extra work
Updating Records	Usually requires rewriting file	Easy, but requires maintenance of indexes	Very easy

Legal reasons or an estimate of how long it might take to discover an error in a file may dictate the age of the oldest file.

Recovery from file failure can be done by two methods, only one of which, forward recovery, requires a file backup (see Figure 17-10). In **forward recovery** (Figure 17-10a) you restore the most recent correct copy of the file and rerun all maintenance (and possibly display and reporting) activity against the file input since the time of the backup copy. In **backward recovery** (Figure 17-10b) you take the current state of the file, assuming the file is usable, and backout (undo) each transaction to a point at which the file is correct, then rerun all the transactions up to the current point. A database administrator can be very helpful in deciding which of these approaches makes sense for the files involved in the application you are designing. For a shared database managed by a database management system, backup procedures may already be specified, and you have no decision to make in support of your individual application.

The file which contains a chronological history of changes and accesses to a file or database is called an **audit trail**. An audit trail (and related files like a transaction log) might contain images of records before or after modification, copies of transaction data, and other identifying information useful in tracing problems found in files and databases (see Figure 17-11). An audit trail can be used to rebuild damaged files and can also be used to test whether file update procedures are working correctly. The audit trail can be inspected by computer auditors to see if the results of sampled transactions are correct or to trace a chain of data updates to discover where erroneous data were introduced when contaminated data are discovered.

Figure 17-11a illustrates a simple situation of maintenance and retrieval of ON_HAND inventory data in an ITEM file. An analysis of the audit trail entries indicates that some type of data maintenance error occurred during the second file update operation, since the ON_HAND after image of 60 and the transaction

Forward recovery (rollforward): An approach to rebuilding a file in which one starts with an earlier version of the file and either reruns prior transactions or replaces a record with its image after each transaction.

Backward recovery (rollback): An approach to rebuilding a file in which before images of changed records are restored to the file in reverse order until some earlier state is achieved.

Audit trail: A list of changes to a data file which allows business transactions to be traced. Both the updating and use of data should be recorded in the audit trail, since the consequences of bad data should be discovered and corrected.

Figure 17-10
File recovery approaches

(a) Forward recovery

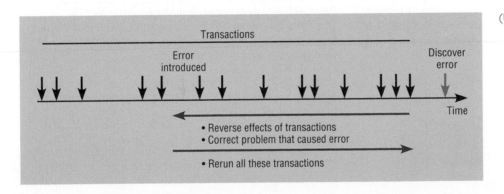

(b) Backward recovery

operation do not agree. In this case, the audit trail not only helps us identify where the problem occurred but it may also be used to reprocess transactions once the problem is corrected. Further, the audit trail also identifies retrieval activity (transaction R1) after the error is introduced. We could use this information to notify the system user associated with this retrieval that he or she is working with erroneous data. Figure 17-11b lists and defines some possible contents for each audit trail entry. The information in each audit trail entry is used to diagnose the possible source of the data contamination as well as which business areas might be affected by bad data. Since software is written by humans (even the logic of generated code was designed by a programmer), application software is fallible. Thus, systems should be tested periodically for accuracy, and an audit trail is an effective mechanism to help in this testing and in restoring data to an uncontaminated state.

Encryption   Security of file contents is an important issue for some applications, often when financial, personal, or proprietary data are involved. Although various schemes for security may be in place, one security mechanism for an individual file

Figure 17-11
Audit trail controls on a file

(a) Sample audit trail

(b) Possible audit trail contents

AUDIT TRAIL DATA	EXPLANATION
Transaction identifier	Primary key value for each audit trail file record
Transaction value	The value in the transaction. For a numeric field, this may be the value by which the existing field value is changed. For an alphanumeric field, this will be the new field value
Before or after image	The value of the field before or after the change is made
Type of operation	The type of data operation logged: retrieval, insertion, deletion, modification
Date/Time stamp	A unique indication of when the transaction occurred
Program name	The name and version number of the computer program initiating the transaction
User/Device	The user name or computer device from which the transaction was initiated

is encryption. **Encryption** is the coding or scrambling of data so that they cannot be read by humans. A person or a software program must know how to descramble the data to make them readable. Since the encryption scheme is usually more difficult to subvert than other security measures, encryption is considered the soundest form of data security. Either the operating system or data management software may provide an encryption algorithm and encryption can be done by computer chips; if not, you can build an encryption routine yourself using a function like a hashing algorithm or random number generator. Of course, the encryption algorithm itself must be secured. The U.S. federal government is attempting to standardize an encryption chip, the Clipper chip, so that federal authorities will have a way to decode any computer-encrypted data. Encryption is not always allowed. For example, since some foreign governments (e.g., France) forbid the transmission of encrypted data across national borders, companies doing business in these countries cannot use encryption to protect data files transported in and out of the country.

Encryption: The coding (or scrambling) of data so that they cannot be read by humans.

Calculating File Size

Sometimes it is necessary to calculate the potential sizes of data files. There are two purposes for calculating the total amount of space a file might consume. First, in some computer environments, you must request a fixed amount of space for each file, and you want to ask for enough but not too much. Second, there may be an issue of whether enough space exists, or you may need to determine the size of a hard disk needed for an application.

The size of a file depends on the following specifications:

- Data type of each field and structure of records

- Media (magnetic tape, floppy diskette, or hard disk)

- Page sizes (and, hence, blocking factors)

- File organization

The data types and record structures determine how much raw data space is required. The medium dictates how data is generally laid out. For example, floppy disks come in different capacities and use a sector as the basic physical storage unit (similar to a page). The page size and whether records can span pages for hard disks, as discussed earlier, influence the use and waste of space. Finally, the file organization determines the need for overhead data besides the raw data.

Because there are so many options, it is not feasible to illustrate all possible situations you might face. To understand all parameters, you should refer to reference manuals for the hardware and operating system that you are designing for.

As a hypothetical example of the general approach to calculating file size, consider the hashed file in Figure 17-12. This hard disk file was designed to accommodate a maximum of 172 records of 240 bytes each. Assume that space for the file cannot be dynamically allocated, so the space for the maximum file size must be assigned at once. The records are grouped into blocks of 4 records each, for a total of 43 blocks (172/4). This is done to create a number of blocks which corresponds to a prime number (a typical basis for a hashing algorithm). The prime number, 43 in this case, is used in the hashing algorithm called division hashing. In division hashing, the primary key is divided by the prime number and the remainder is the record's address (block number, from 0 to 42). Assuming that records (and also blocks) may span page boundaries, we are not concerned with page size in this example. But, hard disks have tracks, and let us assume that records (and also blocks) may not span track boundaries. In this example, a track is 4,000 bytes. Visually we

Figure 17-12
Example hash file layout and size

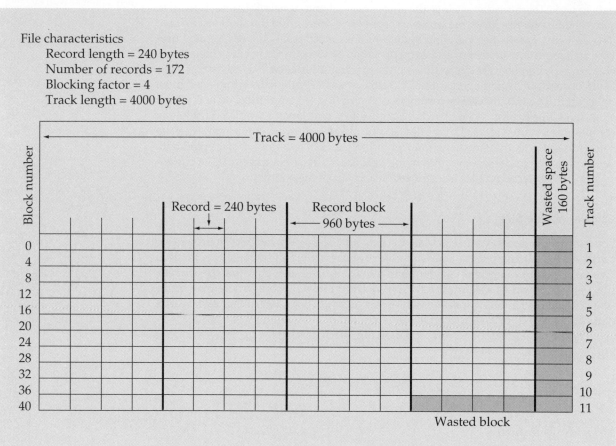

File characteristics
    Record length = 240 bytes
    Number of records = 172
    Blocking factor = 4
    Track length = 4000 bytes

see from the layout that we can fit 16 records per track and need 11 tracks, or 44,000 bytes, for this file. Within each track, 160 bytes are wasted due to the restriction on record spanning tracks, and an additional record block of 960 bytes is not needed in the last track. Thus, there are 1,600 (10*160) plus 960 bytes wasted, or 1,760 bytes, or roughly 4 percent of the allocated space is wasted.

DESIGNING DATABASES

Database management system (DBMS): Software that is used to create, maintain, and provide controlled access to user databases.

Most modern information systems utilize database technology, called database management systems (DBMSs), for data storage and retrieval. A **database management system (DBMS)** is the software that sits between application programs and the operating system and extends the capabilities of the operating system for organizing data. Technologies such as IMS and DB2 on IBM mainframes, Ingres and Oracle on minicomputers (and other environments), Sybase SQL Server on client/server networks, and Paradox for Windows on personal computers provide a wide range of data storage and accessing options.

Recall that a database is a collection of logically related data, designed to meet the information needs of multiple users in an organization. A more operational definition for our purpose is that a database is a set of inter-related files. The relationship between files is due to relationships identified in the conceptual and logical data models. The relationships imply access paths between data. For example, consider Figure 17-13 for Hoosier Burger's inventory control system (you may also want to refer to the normalized relations located in Chapter 16 on page 626). To discover whether you have enough inventory in stock to fill a large order, this data model says that you could actually trace an item sale through product data, then through recipe data to inventory item data.

Choosing Database Architectures

There are different styles of database management systems, each characterized by the way data are defined and structured, called database architectures. Deciding

Figure 17-13

Final E-R diagram for Hoosier Burger's inventory control system

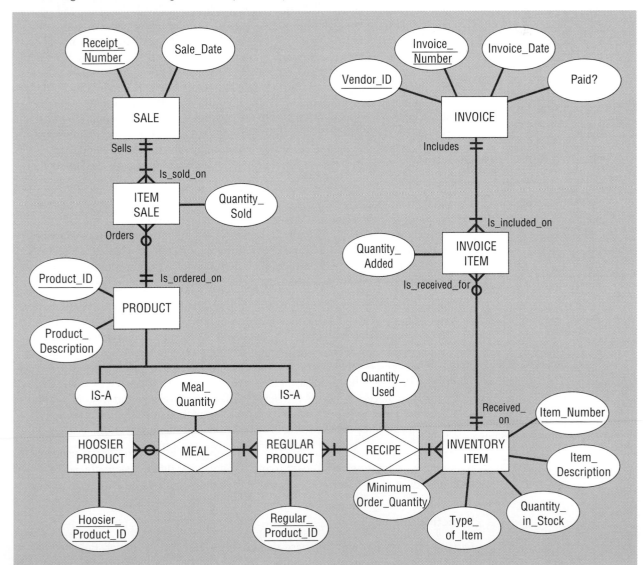

which database architecture best suits your database is fundamental to database design. A particular database management system supports one of four different architectures. Figure 17-14 compares these four architectures:

1. *Hierarchical database model:* In this model, files are arranged in a top-down structure that resembles a tree or genealogy chart. The top file is called the root, the bottom files are called leaves, and intermediate files have one parent, or owner, file and one or several children files. Among the oldest of the database architectures, many hierarchical databases exist in larger organizations. This technology is best applied when the conceptual data model also resembles a tree and when most data access begins with the same file. Hierarchical database technology is used for high-volume transaction processing and MIS applications. Few new databases are developed with hierarchical DBMSs since newer applications tend to have broader needs than simply transaction processing or summarization of transaction data.

2. *Network database model:* In this model, each file may be associated with an arbitrary number of files. Although very flexible as any relationships can be implemented, the form of implementation, usually using pointers between related records in different files, creates significant overhead in storage space and maintenance time. Network model systems are still popular on powerful mainframes and for high-volume transaction processing applications. Since the database designer has such detailed control over data organizations, it is possible to design highly optimized databases with network systems. Network systems support a wider variety of processing requirements than do hierarchical database systems, but network systems still require significant programming and database design knowledge and time, and hence are used primarily in those organizations with significant expertise with such technologies.

3. *Relational database model:* The most common database model for new systems, this model defines simple tables for each relation and many-to-many relationship. Cross-reference keys link the tables together, representing the relationships between entities. Primary and secondary key indexes provide rapid access to data based upon qualifications. Most new applications are built using relational DBMSs, and many relational DBMS products exist.

4. *Object-oriented database model:* In this model, attributes and methods that operate on those attributes are encapsulated in structures called object classes. Relationships between object classes are shown, in part, by nesting or encapsulating one object class within another. New object classes are defined from more general object classes. A major advantage of this data model is that complex data types like graphics, video, and sound are supported as easily as simpler data types. This is the newest DBMS technology and larger organizations are gaining experience with it by selectively using it when complex data or event-driven programming is appropriate for the application.

Since relational databases are the most common kind of database used today, we will cover the most significant relational database design issue, the selection of indexes.

Selecting Indexes

During physical file and database design you must choose which fields to use to create indexes. As mentioned earlier in the chapter, indexes can be created for both primary and secondary keys. When using indexes, there is a trade-off between

Figure 17-14
Database architectures

(a) Hierarchical

(b) Network

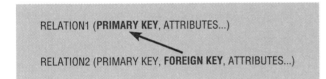

RELATION1 (**PRIMARY KEY**, ATTRIBUTES...)

RELATION2 (PRIMARY KEY, **FOREIGN KEY**, ATTRIBUTES...)

(c) Relational

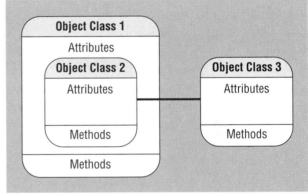

(d) Object-Oriented

improved performance for retrievals and degrading performance for inserting, deleting, and updating the records in a file. Thus, indexes should be used generously for databases intended primarily to support data retrievals, such as for decision support applications. Because they impose additional overhead, indexes should be used judiciously for databases that support transaction processing and other applications with heavy updating requirements (Gibson et al., 1989).

Following are some guidelines for choosing indexes for relational databases.

1. Specify a unique index for the primary key of each table (file). This selection ensures the uniqueness of primary key values and speeds retrieval based on those values. Random retrieval based on primary key value is common for answering multi-table queries and for simple data maintenance tasks.

2. Specify an index for foreign keys used in joining tables. As in point 1, this speeds processing multiple-table queries.

3. Specify an index for nonkey fields that are referred to in qualification, sorting, and grouping commands for the purpose of retrieving data.

To illustrate the use of these rules, consider the following relations for Pine Valley Furniture Company:

PRODUCT (Product_Number, Description, Finish, Room, Price)

ORDER (Order_Number, Product_Number, Quantity)

You would normally specify a unique index for each primary key: Product_Number in PRODUCT and Order_Number in ORDER. Other indexes would be assigned based on how the data are used. For example, suppose that there is a system module that requires PRODUCT and PRODUCT_ORDER data for products with a price below $500, grouped by Product_Number. To speed up this retrieval, you could consider specifying indexes on the following nonkey attributes:

1. Price in PRODUCT since it satisfies rule 3.

2. Product_Number in ORDER since it satisfies rule 2.

Since users may direct a potentially large number of different queries against the database, especially for a system with a lot of ad hoc queries, you will probably have to be selective in specifying indexes to support the most common or frequently used queries.

Selecting indexes is arguably the most important physical database design decision, but it is not the only way you can improve the performance of a database. Other ways address such issues as reducing the costs to relocate records, optimizing the use of extra or so-called free space in files, and optimizing query processing algorithms (Viehman, 1994).

Representing Data Volume

For making some database design decisions (such as calculating file sizes) and for developing data access strategies, it is advisable to create diagrams that show the volume of data. As an analyst, you may not be responsible for finalizing database designs; rather, this may be the job of a database analyst who has specialized skills and intimate knowledge of the DBMS features used for the application. In either case, you are responsible for outlining the need for data based on your knowledge of the application. Thus, you are in a better position than database specialists to determine the volume of data your application must handle.

To size files and to choose physical database structures like file organizations, you need to know how many records to expect for each file. A starting point for this is illustrated in Figure 17-15, which shows a variation of an E-R diagram, indicating the number of occurrences of each entity with ratios that help you estimate the number of occurrences. Similar to Figure 17-13, this figure omits relationship names and attributes and the number of instances of each entity is added. You might develop such a chart by starting with any entity for which you know the volume of instances. Using information collected during analysis, you can then estimate ratios and other volumes. For example, if you knew that Hoosier Burger has 30 products on the menu board, and that roughly 20 percent of the products are Hoosier products, then there are approximately 6 Hoosier products and 24 Regular products. Also, since your study of past accounting records shows that Hoosier Burger generates approximately 1,200 sales a day for seven days a week, and one month of sales data will be kept on-line, then there will be approximately 1200*7*31, or 260,400 SALE records. With an average of three items on each sale, there will be roughly 781,200 ITEM SALE records.

Your role as a systems analyst is to provide as much information as possible about data volume and usage in a useful format so that database specialists (analysts and administrators) can create the final, technical designs which will make database processing and storage most efficient. As with telecommunications, detailed

Figure 17-15
Data volume chart

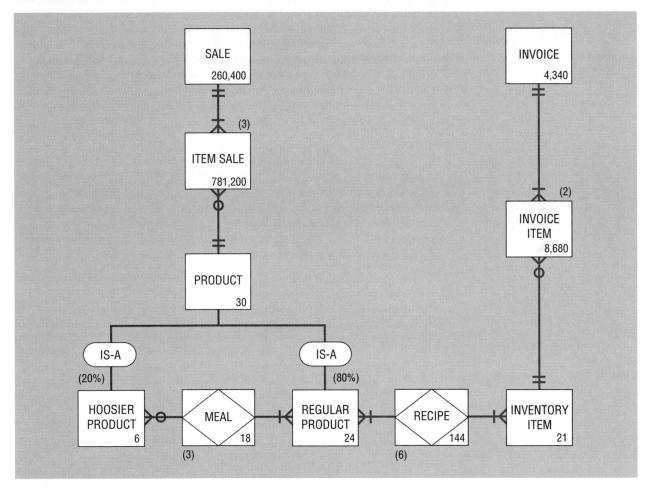

database design is typically done by these specialists, but your role of translating the system requirements into clear specifications for data is invaluable in the total process. In organizations that do not have database specialists, the final decisions on database design will rest with you. Thus, you should study the field of database design to either communicate effectively with specialists or to do database design when specialists are not available.

CASE IN DATABASE DESIGN

There are integrated and stand-alone CASE tools which can be useful during physical file and database design in four ways:

1. By storing the results of file and database design in a repository which shows how logical data attributes, relations, and entities map into physical data structures.

2. By generating file (like COBOL Data Division) or database (like SQL) definition code. This function saves considerable time in the implementation phase

of the life cycle and ensures that the data definitions comply with the design. Figure 17-16 shows a typical example of generated SQL database defintion code from an E-R diagram and attribute definitions in the repository of a CASE tool. Figure 17-16a shows a simple E-R diagram and Figure 17-16b shows SQL code generated from this E-R diagram and the descriptions (not shown) of the entities and attributes associated with this E-R model. Often a CASE tool can generate to several different SQL dialects associated with different SQL-based DBMSs. As the database evolves, analysts can simply change the E-R model and attribute repository entries, and the CASE tool will generate the new database definition code.

3. By reverse engineering existing file and database definitions for elements of current systems that will be reused in the new application. Often the structure of data is not obvious in existing, or legacy, systems. Reverse data engineering tools are very sophisticated (akin to an expert system), and can analyze the data definitions as well as program code to surmise functional dependencies and other information necessary to develop a data model of existing data. These descriptions are then combined with the descriptions of the new data in the CASE repository for generation of the new data structures.

4. By assisting in making file and database design decisions. There are some CASE tools and stand-alone analysis tools, like the IBM Database Design Aid, that will analyze data characteristics (sizes and volumes) along with usage patterns and suggest a good or optimal set of secondary key indexes. Such tools can be of great assistance when the database has tens or hundreds of

Figure 17-16
CASE tool SQL database definition code generation

(a) Sample E-R diagram

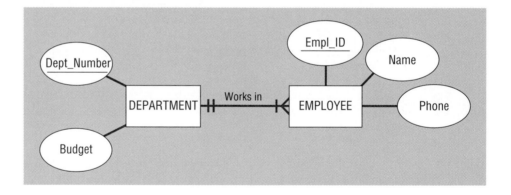

(b) Generated SQL code

```
CREATE TABLE DEPARTMENT
(
    DEPT_NUMBER   SMALLINT              NOT NULL,
    BUDGET        DECIMAL (8,2)
);

CREATE UNIQUE INDEX DEPT_INDEX ON DEPARTMENT (DEPT_NO);

CREATE TABLE EMPLOYEE
(
    EMPL_ID       SMALLINT              NOT NULL,
    NAME          CHAR(20)                    ,
    PHONE         INT                         ,
    DEPT_NUMBER   SMALLINT              NOT NULL,

    FOREIGN KEY (DEPT_NUMBER) REFERENCES DEPARTMENT
);

CREATE UNIQUE INDEX EMPL_INDEX ON EMPLOYEE (EMPL_ID);
```

files and hundreds of database access modules—which would not be atypical of major application systems.

SUMMARY

We have presented a wide range of concepts and techniques you will need for designing computer files and databases during the physical design phase of the systems development life cycle. Because of the technical and often technology-specific nature of physical design, you will often assist or provide information to specialists who will actually design the physical file and database.

Physical file and database design takes, as input, the normalized relations from logical data modeling as well as other models that explain how data in files and databases will be accessed. You must have a basic understanding of the capabilities of the data management technology used with the system since your design options may be limited by the technology's capabilities. The deliverables are specifications that can be given to programmers and data management specialists who will write the code to define file and database structures.

Physical file and database design involves designing fields, records, files, and databases. Designing a field includes selecting a data type, coding and compression methods to reduce storage space and improve data accuracy, the format for primary keys, and data integrity controls to ease data entry and reduce errors. The chapter also discussed several techniques for handling missing fields, a common situation for many application systems.

Designing physical records involves grouping fields together based on a shared primary key and an affinity of usage. Records are also designed to minimize wasted space in secondary memory storage units, called pages. You also learned that record partitioning and denormalization are two approaches to creating efficient record structures. The techniques for handling fixed-length and variable-length records use constructs such as sequential storage and pointers to arrange fields within a record.

There are six types of physical files: data, look-up table, transaction, work, temporary, and history. Most of the effort in physical file and database design focuses on data files, but the need for and structure of each of these files must be handled during this life cycle step. Operating systems handle the physical input/output operations with files using relative and direct access methods. File and database management software use these basic access methods to create file organizations that can support a variety of data accessing needs. File organizations are grouped into three general families: sequential, indexed, and hashing. The most common file organization in use today is indexed, so the selection of primary and secondary keys for indexes is one of the major physical file and database design choices. The performance of different file organizations varies by such factors as storage space consumed, speed of sequential or random record retrieval, and speed for adding, deleting, and updating records. Some file organizations are specifically designed to rapidly find data based on multiple-key selection statements, such as are supported in most relational database query languages.

Designing files also includes selecting strategies for file backup and security (such as data encryption). Another file design task is estimating file size so that suitable secondary memory space can be allocated for the application you are designing. The estimation of file size depends on the storage medium, field data types, record structures, volume of data, secondary memory page or record block sizes, and file organizations you choose.

Designing databases presents additional physical file and database design issues. Files must be designed within the capabilities of the database environment, including the database management system, the data definition and data manipulation languages used in the application, and the data dictionary. Four database architectures are available to you: hierarchical, network, relational, and object-oriented, with relational being the norm for modern systems. The database design decision of greatest import in relational environments is selecting primary and secondary key indexes.

Physical file and database design also includes documenting the number of instances of each entity from the logical and conceptual data models. Information about data volume and usage are important parameters for making a variety of file and database design decisions.

CASE tools can help in physical file and database design by storing the results of file and database design in a CASE repository, generating file (like COBOL Data Division) or database (like SQL) definition code, reverse engineering existing file and database definitions for elements of current systems that will be reused in the new application, and assisting in making file and database design decisions (such as index selection).

Physical file and database design is one of three parallel steps in the physical design phase of the systems development life cycle. Program and distributed system design are the other two steps and are the subjects of the following two chapters.

KEY TERMS

Access method
Audit trail
Backward recovery
Blocking factor
Calculated field
Data compression
  technique
Data type
Database management
  system (DBMS)

Default value
Encryption
Field
File organization
Forward recovery
Hashed file organization
Hashing algorithm
Index
Indexed file organization
Null value

Page
Physical file
Physical record
Picture (or template)
Pointer
Record partitioning
Secondary key
Sequential file
  organization

REVIEW QUESTIONS

1. Define each of the following terms:

   a. data type
   b. file organization
   c. index
   d. check digit
   e. page

   f. hashing algorithm
   g. null value
   h. pointer
   i. record
   j. page

2. List and describe six types of files found in information systems.

3. Describe the inputs to physical file and database design.

4. Describe the deliverables from physical file and database design.

5. In what way does the choice of a data type for a field help to control the integrity of that field?

6. Explain the term referential integrity. Do only foreign keys have referential integrity? Why or why not?

7. How can missing data be handled for a field?

8. What is the difference between how a range control statement and a referential integrity control statement are handled by a file management system?

9. What is the purpose of record partitioning and denormalization? Why might you not want to create one file for each relation in a logical data model?

10. What techniques can be used to keep track of where variable-length fields are in a physical record?

11. What factors influence the decision to create an index on a field?

12. Describe three methods commonly used to handle storage of calculated fields.

13. Explain the purpose of data compression techniques.

14. What are the goals of designing physical records?

15. What are the seven factors that should be considered in selecting a file organization?

16. Explain the differences between forward and backward file recovery techniques.

17. List and briefly describe the four major database architectures.

P R O B L E M S   A N D   E X E R C I S E S

1. Match the following terms to the appropriate definitions.

_____ backward recovery	a. an approach to locating and storing records based on searching a table of keys and locations for the associated record(s) with that key value
_____ forward recovery	b. use of a backup file and a transaction log to restore a damaged file to an uncontaminated state
_____ data compression technique	c. a way to get rid of unnecessary and redundant data in a file or field
_____ sequential file organization	d. use of an algorithm to convert a key value into the location where a record is stored
_____ indexed file organization	e. use of a log of records before images to restore an erroneous file to a prior state before reprocessing transactions
_____ hashed file organization	f. location of records one right after another

2. On page 626 of Chapter 16 a list of normalized relations for Hoosier Burger's inventory control system appears. Choose data types for the fields in these relations based on figures about this database shown throughout the book.

3. Explain the four criteria that influence the choice of a data type for a field and give examples of how each criterion is applied.

4. Suppose you were designing a file of student records for your university's placement office. One of the fields that would likely be in this file is the student's major. Develop a coding scheme for this field that achieves the objectives outlined in this chapter for field coding.

5. In Problem and Exercise 7 in Chapter 16 you developed normalized relations for a particular E-R data model. Choose primary keys for the files that would hold the

data for these relations. Did you use attributes from the relations for primary keys or did you design new fields? Why or why not?

6. Suppose you created a file for each relation in your answer to Problem and Exercise 7 from Chapter 16. If the following queries represented the complete set of accesses to this database, suggest and justify what primary and secondary key indexes you would build.

   a. For each PART in Item_Number order list in Vendor_ID sequence all the vendors and their associated prices for that part.
   b. List all PART RECEIPTs including related PART fields for all the parts received on a particular day.
   c. For a particular VENDOR, list all the PARTs and their associated prices that VENDOR can supply.

7. The following questions involve the construction of check digits for the account numbers with a local telephone company. The account number is the telephone number, not including area code.

   a. What are the first seven prime numbers?
   b. Suppose that the check digits on the account number are calculated by summing the multiplications of each telephone number digit by the associated prime number starting with the right-most digit (that is, in the telephone number 555-6789 the 9 would be multiplied by the first prime number, the 8 by the second prime number, and so forth). The check digit is the three least significant digits in the result of this formula. What would be the check digits for the above telephone number?

8. Suppose you were designing a default value for the age field in a student record at your university. What possible values would you consider and why? How might the default vary by other characteristics about the student, such as school within the university or degree sought?

9. The following questions concern the use of null values for a field.

   a. When a student has not chosen a major at a university, the university often enters a value of "Undecided" for the major field. Is "Undecided" a default value or a way to represent the null value?
   b. What problems might allowing a null value for the field PERMANENT ADDRESS cause for processing student records at a university?

10. Assume that you have a hard disk file designated to accommodate a maximum of 1,000 records of 240 bytes each and all other factors are similar to those described in the example related to Figure 17-12. How many bytes will be needed for this file?

11. Consider the E-R diagram for Hoosier Burger in Figure 17-13.

    a. Represent this data model as a set of 3NF relations.
    b. Suggest physical record structures for these relations. Which relations might be denormalized in order to speed up frequent data-processing steps, such as entering sales transactions, generating an order to the kitchen, and handling the receipt of new inventory?
    c. Would a hierarchical database architecture be suitable for this database? Why or why not?
    d. For each of the attributes of the INVOICE entity, develop each of the field data specifications found in Figure 17-3.
    e. Which, if any, of the attributes on this E-R diagram should be represented using a code look-up table? Why?

12. Explain whether pointers should be used to implement referential integrity.

13. Consider Figure 17-7b. Explain a query which would likely be processed more quickly using the denormalized relations rather than the normalized relations.

FIELD EXERCISES

1. Find out what database management systems are available at your university for student use. Investigate which data types these DBMSs support. Compare these DBMSs based upon data types supported and suggest which types of applications each DBMS is best suited for based on this comparison.

2. Contact someone in the data center at your school, university, or place of work. Find out how frequently they back up files on different computers or file servers. Why do they back up with that frequency? Where do they keep these files and for how long are the backup files kept?

3. Investigate data compression products, such as WinZip from Nico Mak Computing, and PKZIP by PKWARE. Gather information from popular press articles found in the library, directly from the software writers, or from hands-on testing. What products are available? Are they useful? Are they reliable? How much do they cost? Do they seem to be worthwhile given the costs and benefits? Why or why not? What is the extent of use in the market of these data compression products?

4. Investigate data encryption techniques presented in the academic research literature. What is the state of the art in data encryption? What seem to be the strengths and weaknesses of these techniques? What applications do you foresee for data encryption in the future?

5. Investigate object-oriented database products. Gather information from popular press articles found in the library, directly from the software writers, or from hands-on testing. What products are available? Are they useful? How much do they cost? Do they seem to be worthwhile given the costs and benefits? Why or why not? For what types of applications are object-oriented databases being used? Do you foresee that object-oriented databases will replace other types of databases discussed in this chapter? Why or why not?

REFERENCES

Babad, Y. M., and J. A. Hoffer. 1984. "Even No Data Has a Value." *Communications of the ACM* 27 (Aug.):748–56.

Finkelstein, R. 1988. "Breaking the Rules Has a Price." *Database Programming & Design* 1 (June):11–14.

Gibson, M., C. Hughes, and W. Remington. 1989. "Tracking the Trade-Offs with Inverted Lists." *Database Programming & Design* 2 (Jan.):28–34.

McFadden, F. R., J. A. Hoffer, and M. B. Prescott. 1999. *Modern Database Management.* 5th Edition. Reading, MA: Addison Wesley Longman.

Rodgers, U. 1989. "Denormalization: Why, What, and How?" *Database Programming & Design* 2(12) (Dec.):46–53.

Viehman, P. 1994. "24 Ways to Improve Database Performance." *Database Programming & Design* 7(2) (Feb.):32–41.

Physical Design: Designing Files and Databases

INTRODUCTION

As with other elements of the logical and physical design of the Customer Activity Tracking System (CATS), the project team continues with a complete design effort even though the chosen strategy is to use packaged software as much as possible. The design effort is important to identify what BEC wants from CATS. In the final stages of design, the team will decide if the package needs to be modified to meet the detailed needs of CATS or if the specifications for CATS need to be changed to fit the capabilities of the package or if a combination of both of these modifications is required. Frank Napier, an analyst on the CATS team, and Buffy Jarvis, a data analyst assigned to help the CATS team, are reviewing several issues related to tuning the performance of the physical files and database and identifying how the data in CATS relate to data in other BEC systems. These are some of the issues the CATS team is addressing during file and database design.

CATS RELATIONSHIP WITH EXISTING FILES AND DATABASES

"Hi, Buffy, come on in," Frank Napier greets Buffy Jarvis at the entrance to Frank's cubicle. "Thanks for stopping by between appointments. Please sit down. I'm anxious to see what you discovered from your analysis of existing BEC files." Buffy has been studying the attributes in the normalized relations developed from the logical data modeling step in the CATS project (see Figure 6 in the BEC case at the end of Chapter 16). The purpose of this analysis is to determine what data identified for CATS already exist in other BEC files and databases. This will be used to decide what data CATS must capture itself and what will simply be fed from other systems.

"Frank, I think I've discovered everything we'll need to know to make some decisions on data sourc-

ing," responds Buffy. "In many ways, we got lucky, Frank. I called the head of information systems at TwoCat Petfood, the supplier of the package we intend to use for CATS. I found out that their system is written in Paradox for Windows, a popular PC relational DBMS package, and all of the data is stored in Paradox tables. It's written as a simple LAN application, but they were smart enough to build a lot of controls into it. We don't currently use Paradox, but we knew we'd have to get a LAN license for it.

"The TwoCat package is written to use the LAN server as a shared hard disk, with each workstation addressing the server just like it would a local hard drive. This is about the simplest kind of LAN database environment, what people call a file server environment. It allows data to be shared by several users, but each user is running a separate copy of the database management system. As you know, BEC decided several years ago to use an SQL database system called Sybase SQL Server™, which is a lot more sophisticated than Paradox. We've been building all our new systems under Sybase and converting older systems as it made sense. Sybase allows us to design programs to be run on workstations for all data capture, analysis, and presentation functions, but all data management functions are done at the server. This has proven to be a great way for us to decouple various components of systems, giving us greater flexibility to use the latest technology for each application we build yet still have central management of data. It has also allowed us to minimize network traffic, a big plus for a company our size.

"At first I was concerned that we'd have to write a lot of bridge routines to regularly transfer data between our current BEC files managed by SQL Server and CATS, but then I saw an article in *PC Week* about a product called SQL Link® from Borland, the vendor for Paradox. What SQL Link would allow us to do is access the SQL files in Sybase as if they were Paradox files. Thus, whenever CATS needs data we already have under SQL Server, we'll just need to define the path to it and a Paradox application can access it without much modification. This is going to save us a lot of time in installing the package since the source code can generally stay the same and we won't have to convert data; this will make it easier to get final approval from management for the implementation phase.

"What we will end up with is a database environment that will look something like this (Buffy quickly sketches a drawing on the whiteboard on Frank's office wall; see Figure 1). As far as the Paradox programs are concerned, all the data appear to be in Paradox tables on the server. When a query requires data from a Sybase table, SQL Link will send a request to the server which will return a table to the PC which Paradox will then join with Paradox tables. Although CATS will be able to use and maintain data housed in Sybase databases, CATS will still run as a Paradox application. This means that the PC workstations will do all the work. From the analysis I've done, most of the CATS data are in existing Sybase tables. Eventually we'll want to recode the package into a language that can allow Sybase to do as much work as possible, but at least we can make the package work now in our environment. As you can imagine, I was quite relieved to reach this conclusion. This has really simplified satisfying our data sourcing requirements in order to get CATS up and running soon."

"This sounds like one of your advertisements for using standards, Buffy." Frank said with just a hint of sarcasm. "Okay, so we can get to existing data, but where are the data?"

Buffy continued, "Then what I did was prepare a table listing all of the relations and selected attributes from the normalized relations for CATS and where these items are in our Sybase corporate database. I also included what I would suggest we do in terms of data sourcing for CATS (Buffy hands Frank a copy of Table 1). For example, let's look at the STORE relation.

This relation is a simple subset of the standard BEC Sybase database table of the same name. I don't see where CATS will interfere with this Sybase table in any way, so I think that CATS ought to use the existing database table. We ought to make this a read-only table to CATS, and we can disable the STORE data maintenance functions in the package. The same is true for PRODUCT, CUSTOMER, INVENTORY, CUSTOMER_ TRANSACTION, and PURCHASE. In each of these cases, CATS just wants to use a subset of attributes in existing Sybase tables.

"The PURCHASE table does require some minor modification. Implicitly this relation in CATS means a purchase generated from a reservation. Since the idea of a reservation is new, our Point of Sale (POS) system and the corporate sales tracking system don't have any field to record this. I've prepared a change request for these systems to add this field and to modify the POS to record a reservation sale.

"I've looked at the statistics you, Jorge, and Jordan gave me about the frequency of various CATS accesses to the data, and I see no reason to separate the CATS processing from the other activity against this database. The bulk of the activity in CATS is handling reservations, and that will require real-time access to the Sybase CUSTOMER and PRODUCT tables; the rest of CATS is a minimally extra load on Sybase. Thus, it would not be wise to try to maintain two copies of these files, with one copy strictly for CATS use. So, what I am recommending is that we use existing Sybase tables, appropriately modified, when a table exists."

Frank interjected, "Now, what about the relations and fields that are new for CATS? Can we just use the Paradox tables found in the TwoCat package?"

Buffy replied, "To some degree, but it depends on the relation. Let's take a look at the PRODUCT_ ANNOUNCEMENT relation (see Table 1). The TwoCat package has such a table, but it does not use a code like our PCS_CODE. There is, of course, a primary

Figure 1
BEC database environment
with Paradox and Sybase

Queries and data
to update tables

Paradox tables and
Sybase tables translated
into Paradox format

Client PC running
CATS, Paradox,
and SQL Link

LAN server
running SQL Link
and Sybase DBMS

CATS Paradox
Tables

BEC Sybase
Tables

TABLE 1   Sources of CATS Data

CATS Data	Source(s)	Recommendation
STORE	standard STORE relation	Use standard relation
PRODUCT	standard PRODUCT relation	Use standard relation
VIDEO_PRODUCT	standard VIDEO_PRODUCT relation	Use standard relation
MUSIC/GAME_PRODUCT	standard MUSIC/GAME_ PRODUCT relation	Use standard relation
CUSTOMER	standard CUSTOMER relation	Use standard relation
INVENTORY	standard INVENTORY relation	Use standard relation

PRODUCT_ANNOUNCEMENT
  PCS_CODE
 	
  RUN_NUMBER
  ANNOUNCE_DATE
	package
	  8 alphanumerics
	    (99XXXXXX)
	  S (small integer)
	  DATE
		Modify package to accept our PCS code; use Paradox table, but add indexes on RUN_NUMBER and ANNOUNCE_DATE

RUN	does not exist	Combine into PRODUCT_ANNOUNCEMENT table
CUSTOMER_TRANSACTION	standard CUSTOMER_ TRANSACTION relation	Use standard relation
PURCHASE	standard PURCHASE relation	Use standard relation; modify standard relation to indicate reservation purchase

CUSTOMER_PROFILE
  CUST_PROF_CATEGORY
  CUST_PROF_CAT_LEVEL
	package	Modify package with new data integrity controls for these two fields; use Paradox table

PRODUCT_PROFILE
  PROD_PROF_CATEGORY
  PROD_PROF_SUPERIOR_CAT
	package	Modify package with new data integrity controls for these two fields; use Paradox table

PRODUCT_FOR_CUSTOMER	package	No changes to package; use Paradox table
CUSTOMER_PROFILE_TRAN	package	No changes to package; use Paradox table
PRODUCT_PROFILE_TRAN	package	No changes to package; use Paradox table
PRODUCT_FOR_CUSTOMER	package	No changes to package; use Paradox table

key for the file; we'll just need to change the field's definition, and my contact at TwoCat said this is pretty easy to do. What I suggest for a primary key is an 8-character alphanumeric, with the first two characters being the last two digits of the year in which we send the announcement to the customer. This will give us 26^6, or roughly 309 million, announcements per year. From the estimates that you sent me on transaction volumes, this should be sufficient for at least five years. By then, CATS will need a major overhaul, and the format of the PCS_CODE could be addressed then.

"The CUSTOMER_PROFILE, PRODUCT_PROFILE, and PRODUCT_FOR_CUSTOMER tables can be used straight out of the package. The only thing we'll need to do is modify what Paradox calls validity checks on

some of the fields. Validity checks control the range of possible values and table look-ups for lists of legal values, like the allowable values for CUST_PROF_ CATEGORY. Not surprisingly, TwoCat uses different categories and levels than we plan to use, but the concept is the same. The format of these fields in the package will be fine."

"What about the RUN_NUMBER field in PRODUCT_ANNOUNCEMENT and the RUN relations?" asked Jorge. "Your table says these are new for us?"

"Yes, interestingly, TwoCat designed their system to run daily, so they did not need a run concept. They just store the date of the announcement as part of the PRODUCT_ANNOUNCEMENT table. I think we ought to do the same. This violates normalization, but I think this would be an appropriate situation to denormalize. Almost every time any PRODUCT_ANNOUNCEMENT data are used, so is the ANNOUNCE_DATE. Thus, the system would be doing a lot of joining of these two tables. Also, AN-NOUNCE_DATE is not a very large field, so even though there are potentially a very large number of PRODUCT_ANNOUNCEMENT records each with the same date, we won't be storing much extra data. We should create a secondary key on ANNOUNCE_DATE as well as RUN_NUMBER, which TwoCat did not do for their system. We do summaries of announcements by both RUN_NUMBER and ANNOUNCE_DATE, so these indexes will speed those processes."

"Okay, that makes sense. Did you look at all the integrity rules, file organizations, backup procedures, and indexes used throughout the package—do we need to make any other modifications for CATS?" asked Frank. "We seem to be a lot bigger operation than TwoCat, so we might need more tuning of the database."

"Good questions, Frank. That must have been a fine database course you took at the University of Western Florida. You new guys think you have all the answers," chided Buffy. "Actually, I have looked over those aspects of the TwoCats system and I have only a few changes to recommend, but several are significant. First, Paradox, as opposed to Sybase, does not do any automatic logging of transactions or keep audit trails so files can be rebuilt in case of damage. Since CATS will be installed as a Paradox application running on each client PC, we'll need to modify the package to write these additional files. Second, TwoCats put a manual backup option into the main system menu. I think we'll want to create a batch procedure that will automatically run every night to back up the PRODUCT_ANNOUNCEMENT table, and every week

back up the whole database. Third, Paradox does not allow encryption of tables, and I don't see a need for that in this system. Finally, I looked at the statistics on data usage you sent me and I have identified some additional fields for indexing, since we have designed some new on-line and batch reports that the TwoCat system does not produce. The report programs will be easy to write, but production of the reports will go faster with some additional indexes. I've placed these changes in the CATS repository as notes, so whoever defines the Paradox tables in our environment will know to create these other indexes."

Frank then said, "Buffy, another fine job. I'll brief Jorge on your ideas and we'll check them against the program module plan we are currently developing. Again, we want to see how well our methods for system design match with the package's design. You've helped on the data side, and we need to do some work on the processing side. Thanks again for your help. Thanks for stopping by on your way to the Sybase training session you are leading for end users. See you at next Monday's team meeting."

SUMMARY

This Broadway Entertainment Company case has shown a part of the analysis of physical file and database issues during the CATS project. Some unique issues arose since CATS will adopt a software package where possible, and this package needs to fit into the overall Sybase LAN data environment at BEC. Besides the data aspects of CATS, the project team must match the data processing requirements of CATS with those of the package. We will see an example of program design in the next BEC case.

CHAPTER

18

Designing the Internals:
Program and Process Design

After studying this chapter, you should be able to:

■ Draw and explain a structure chart.

■ Develop both transform-centered and transaction-centered information system designs.

■ Turn a data flow diagram into a structure chart using transform analysis.

■ Refine an initial system design into a more detailed design.

■ Explain and apply the guidelines for good program design.

■ Differentiate between the five types of coupling and apply these in program design.

■ Differentiate between the seven types of cohesion and apply these in program design.

■ Represent the processing logic inside program modules using pseudocode and Nassi-Shneiderman diagrams.

INTRODUCTION

Once you know what the input, output, interface, dialogue, and database for an information system are, you can design the inside of the system, the part that will make the interface operable, generate output, and access and update the organization's databases. In this chapter, you will learn about designing a system's "internals." We will begin at an abstract level, taking what we already know about a system's processes, in the form of documented data flow diagrams, and converting them to *structure charts*. Structure charts graphically represent system designs. You will learn how to draw structure charts and how to derive them from data flow diagrams. Just as most CASE tools support the creation and revision of data flow diagrams and screen and report design, most CASE tools also support the creation and revision of structure charts.

The structure charts you create will form the basis for the structure of the system you design and build. Decisions you make at this point will heavily influence the overall design and implementation of your information system. Therefore, you need to be aware of what constitutes a *good* system design. You will learn about good design and some guidelines that will help you achieve it. The primary goal behind good design is to make your system easy to read and easy to maintain. The primary way the structured systems development techniques you have been studying promote good design is through the division of problem solutions into smaller and smaller pieces. The smaller the piece, or *module,* the easier it is to program, to read, and to revise due to changing business conditions. Modularization, then, promotes ease of coding and maintenance. On the other hand, modularization is not simply a reflection of size—it is also a reflection of function, that is, what a particular piece of a system is supposed to do. One guideline for good design, then, is to maximize *cohesion,* the extent to which a part of the system is designed to perform one and only one function. Modules that perform a single task are easier to write and maintain than those that perform many varied tasks. As modularization also involves how different parts of the system work in conjunction with each other, another guideline for good design is to minimize *coupling,* the extent to which different parts of the system are dependent on each other. The processing logic represented by each system module needs to become an explicit part of the system specifications you will pass on to programmers for coding, so you will also learn how to represent processing logic as *pseudocode* and as Nassi-Shneiderman diagrams.

DESIGNING THE INTERNALS

Chapters 17, 18, and 19 all focus on the physical design phase in the systems development life cycle (see Figure 18-1). In this chapter, you will learn how to design computer programs and processes contained in information systems. Processes take incoming data and transform them or route them to other locations in the information system. In designing programs and processes, however, you will not immediately begin to write computer code. Coding doesn't begin until the implementation phase. The focus in designing the internals is to turn the previously defined relationships among data, processing, and output into a detailed blueprint programmers can use as a guide to writing programs once implementation begins.

The Process of Designing the Internals

You begin designing internals armed with a great deal of information about the system chosen for development and implementation. With the exception of the detailed physical file and database design, most of that information is at a logical level. For the processes that have been identified as part of the system, the information takes the form of data flow diagrams and mostly textual descriptions of what each process is supposed to accomplish. Your job now is to take the logical information and turn it into a blueprint for the physical information system that will be programmed.

Deliverables and Outcomes

There are two primary outcomes of the physical design process for the system's internals: a set of structure charts and a set of physical design specifications for each separate part of the system. In addition to providing the functional descriptions for each part of the system, you must also provide information about input received and output generated for each program and its component parts. Table 18-1 provides more detailed information on the deliverables from designing the system internals.

Figure 18-1
The systems development life cycle with physical design phase highlighted

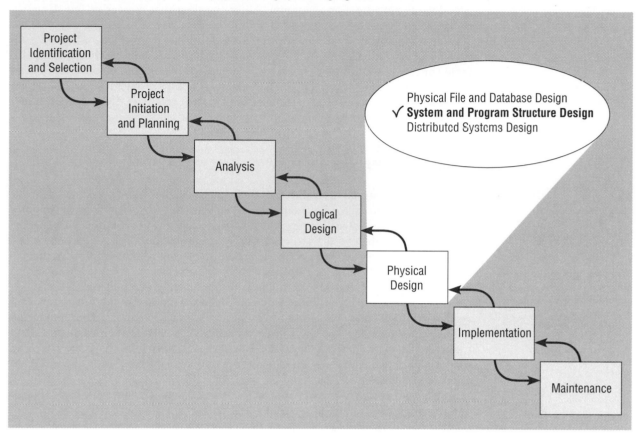

TABLE 18-1   Deliverables from the Design of System Internals

1. Structure Charts
   a. Fully factored structure charts
   b. Complete descriptions of data couples and flags

2. Module Specifications
   a. Input specifications
      1. Database specifications
      2. Other input specifications
         a. On-line or batch
         b. Files
         c. Other modules
   b. Processing specifications
      1. Pseudocode
      2. Nassi-Shneiderman charts
   c. Output specifications
      1. Database and file update specifications
      2. Print or on-line specifications
      3. Other modules

The specifications for input to and output from the database will come from the physical database description, often in the form of pseudocode or a special pseudocode called action diagrams. All of the data that appear in the structure charts should have already been defined in the database or in input form designs. Specifications for modules that capture system inputs or produce system outputs may be in narrative form since the processing logic of these modules is usually quite simple. If input modules also include procedures to validate data, handle errors in the data, or capture different data depending on the data that are input, then pseudocode can also be used to explain these system modules. These specifications will be supplemented by the actual form, report, and dialogue designs.

STRUCTURE CHARTS

Just as you can diagram how information flows through a system and how data entities are related to each other, you can also diagram how the various program parts of an information system are physically organized. The most common architecture for representing the physical structure of a system is hierarchical. A hierarchy looks like an inverted tree or organization chart with one root or main routine at the top and multiple levels of other modules nested underneath. A **structure chart** shows how an information system is organized in a hierarchy of components, called modules. The purpose of a structure chart is to show graphically how the parts of a system or program are related to each other, in terms of passing data and in terms of the basic components of structured programming: sequence, selection, and repetition. A structure chart redefines the flow and processing of data from data flow diagrams into a structure of system components that follow certain principles of good program design.

> **Structure chart:** Hierarchical diagram that shows how an information system is organized.

Structure charts are used to show the breakdown of a system into programs and the internal structure of programs written in third- and fourth-generation languages. The structure of programs written in newer object-oriented or event-driven programming languages is usually depicted by state-transition diagrams and Structured English, which we discussed in Chapters 12 and 9, respectively.

A **module** is a relatively small unit of a system that is defined by its function. Modules are self-contained system components. As much as possible, all of the computer instructions contained in a module should contribute to the same function. Modules are executed as units and, in most instances, have a single point of entry and a single point of exit. Standard programming terms used to identify modules include COBOL sections, paragraphs, or subprograms, and subroutines in BASIC or FORTRAN. For object-oriented programming languages, a module would roughly be a method. A computer program is typically made up of several modules. Modules may also represent separately compiled programs, subprograms, or identifiable internal procedures.

> **Module:** A self-contained component of a system, defined by function.

In a structure chart, there is a single coordinating module at the root and on the next level are modules that the coordinating module calls. For on-line systems, you can think of the root as the main menu and each of the subordinate modules as the main menu options. Each of the modules that report to the coordinating module may call additional modules in the next row down. A module calls another, lower-level module when the subordinate module is needed to perform its function. Modules at the lowest levels do not call any other modules; instead they only perform specific tasks. Middle-level modules act as coordinating modules for those lower-level modules they control but may perform some processing as well. In a structure chart, each module is represented as a rectangle containing a descriptive name of its function (see Figure 18-2). Each module name should concisely and ac-

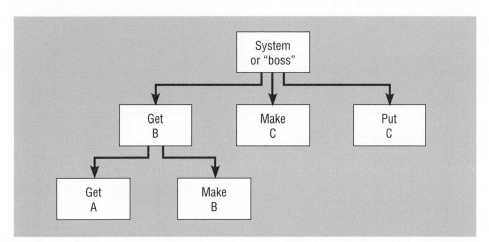

Figure 18-2
An illustration of the
hierarchy of a structure chart

curately reflect what that module does. When naming modules, you should avoid names that include conjunctions as conjunctions indicate that the module performs more than a single function. Modules that seem to need compound names would probably be better represented as multiple modules. Modules are called in order from left to right.

Modules in a structure chart communicate with each other through passing parameters. These parameters take the form of data, represented as data couples and flags. A **data couple** shows data being exchanged between two modules. Data couples are drawn as circles with arrows coming out of them (see Figure 18-3a). The arrow indicates the direction of movement of the data couple between modules. A data couple's circle is not filled in. A data couple is usually a single data element, although it can also be a data structure or even an entire record. A **flag** shows control data, or a message, being passed between modules. You represent a flag (also called a control flag) using the same symbol as a data couple except that you fill in the circle. A flag represents information the system needs for processing; a flag itself is never processed. For example, a flag may carry a message such as "End of file" or "Value out of range." A flag should never represent one module telling another module what to do, such as "Write EOF message."

You use special symbols with modules to indicate specific types of processing or special types of modules. A diamond shape at the bottom of a module means that only one of the subordinates attached to the diamond will be called; other modules, called each time, are not attached to the diamond. The diamond indicates there is a conditional statement in the module's code that determines which subordinate module to call (see Figure 18-3b). The diamond is how we show selection in structure charts. If a module's subordinates are called over and over again until some terminal condition, a curved line is drawn through the arrows connecting the module to these subordinates to indicate repetition (see Figure 18-3c). Again, other subordinates may be called only once and, hence, the curved line does not intersect the connection to these modules. If a module is predefined, meaning that its function is dictated by some preexisting part of the system, then you represent the module with a vertical bar drawn down each side (see Figure 18-3d). For example, a predefined module may already exist because it is part of the operating system or because its function is dictated by some piece of hardware necessary for the system to work. Predefined modules are most commonly found on the very bottom layer of a structure chart because the types of functions they perform deal with such things as reading raw data from the original source or printing to a specific type of printer.

Data couple: A diagrammatic representation of the data exchanged between two modules in a structure chart.

Flag: A diagrammatic representation of a message passed between two modules.

Figure 18-3
Special symbols used in structure charts

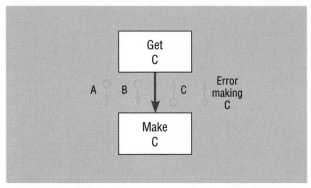

(a) Data couples and control flag

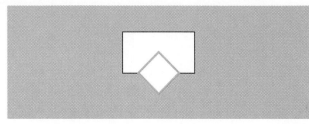

(b) Conditional call of subordinates

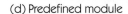

(c) Repetitive calls of subordinates

(d) Predefined module

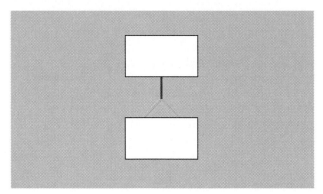

(e) Embedded module

In Figure 18-3e, the special symbol connecting the two modules is called a "hat." A hat means that the function in the subordinate module is important logically to the system, but so few lines of code are needed to perform the function that the code itself is actually contained in the superior module. For example, a university registrar's system will definitely contain code for calculating a student's grade point average (GPA). A module that calculates GPA will be a central transform to a registrar's system, so it will appear on a structure chart as a separate module. However, to calculate GPA takes only a few lines of code, not enough to really merit a separate module. The Calculate GPA module, then, appears on the structure chart as a separate module logically, but the actual code needed for the function will be contained in the boss module.

Structure charts are read from left to right, and the order in which modules are called is determined not so much by the placement of the modules as it is by the placement of the arrows connecting the modules. Look at Figure 18-4a. The arrows connecting the modules do not overlap. The system module first calls the Get Valid

Figure 18-4
How to read a structure chart

(a) Nonoverlapping arrows

(b) Overlapping arrows

A module. Get Valid A first calls the module Read A which executes its function and returns the data couple A to its coordinating module, often called the boss module. A is then passed to Validate A which returns the data couple Valid A. Control is returned to Get Valid A which then returns the data couple Valid A and control to the boss module. A similar set of steps occurs in connection with the data couple Valid B. Next, Valid A and Valid B are passed to Make C which returns the data couple C and control to the system module. Finally, the system module calls Put C and passes C to the module.

Now look at Figure 18-4b. Here the system designer has decided that the Validate B module is redundant and that the validation process implemented in the module Validate A works just as well for validating B. Therefore, there is only one validation module, called Validate data. Processing continues here as in the structure chart described previously. Notice, however, that the arrows leaving the module Get Valid B now cross over each other. The left-most arrow that leaves the module points to Read B, and the right-most arrow points to Validate data. Read B is called first, as the arrow that points to it is the left-most arrow leaving Get Valid B. Validate data is called next. You can also tell the order in which the modules are called by reading the labels—you can't validate B until you have read it into the system.

Once you understand all of the different symbols that make up structure charts, you can begin to use them to represent program designs. When you begin drawing structure charts, you can actually begin with data flow diagrams, converting DFDs to structure charts. *Transform analysis* and *transaction analysis* are two structured methods you can use to convert DFDs to structure charts. Transform analysis and transaction analysis are discussed in more detail later. But before you can use transaction analysis or transform analysis, you have to be able to distinguish between transaction-centered systems and transform-centered systems.

TRANSACTION-CENTERED AND TRANSFORM-CENTERED DESIGNS

Transaction-centered system: An information system that has as its focus the dispatch of data to their appropriate locations for processing.

Information systems (or parts of an IS) are typically either transaction-centered or transform-centered. In a **transaction-centered system,** the system's primary function is to send data to their proper destinations within a more general system. Data come into the central module of the system, the transaction center, and they are dispatched to their proper locations based on their data type. An example of a transaction-centered system is a bank system designed to process banking transactions (see Figure 18-5). Coming into the transaction center would be all kinds of banking transactions: deposits to checking, deposits to savings, withdrawal from checking, withdrawal from savings, car loan payments, and so on. Within the transaction center, the data are evaluated and dispatched, depending on their type. Deposits to checking would take one path, withdrawals from checking another path, car loan payments yet another path. Each path leads to modules designed for processing that particular type of transaction. For on-line systems, each path is a menu choice leading to the part of the system handling that type of transaction. Processes along a transaction path often have user interactions.

Transform-centered system: An information system that has as its focus the derivation of new information from existing data.

A **transform-centered system** has as its central function the derivation of new data values from existing data values. An example is converting student grades and class hours to grade point average. Another example is calculating a mortgage payment from an interest rate, compounding period, and principal. In transform-centered systems, the derivation of new data, or the transformation, tends to be the core of the system. As such, transformations are often transparent to users; once the transformation is initiated, there is little if any interaction with users until the transformation is complete. The structure charts in Figure 18-4 are transform-centered designs. The module or modules that represent the core, in this case Make C, are

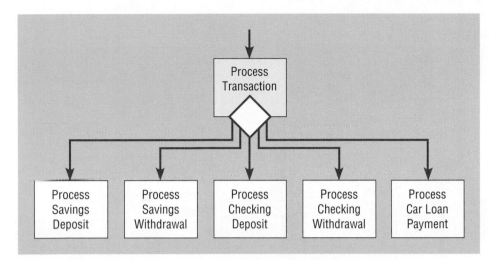

Figure 18-5
A transaction-centered
system design

called the **central transform.** The modules that perform the task of bringing data into the system are called **afferent** modules. Afferent modules are arranged in groups referred to as afferent branches. The modules that perform tasks associated with the output of the transformed data are called **efferent** modules, which are arranged in efferent branches. Transaction-centered systems would also have afferent and efferent modules and branches.

As should be obvious from Figures 18-4 and 18-5, the type of design determines how a system's structure chart is constructed. You should be able to look at a data flow diagram and determine if what is represented is transform-centered or transaction-centered. In a transform-centered design, there are one or more data flows that converge on a single area of the system where they arc "transformed." The area of transformation may consist of one or several processes. The transformed or derived data then flow away in one or more streams (see Figure 18-6). In a transaction-centered design, the data flows converge on a single process and then flow away along many different paths (see Figure 18-7). The single point of

Central transform: The area of a transform-centered information system where the most important derivation of new information takes place.

Afferent module: A module of a structure chart related to input to the system.

Efferent module: A module of a structure chart related to output from the system.

Figure 18-6
A central transform in a data flow diagram

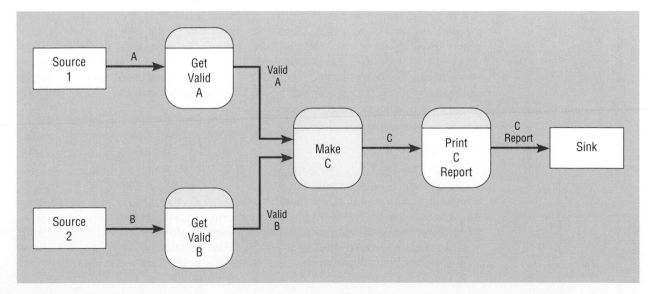

Figure 18-7
A transaction center in a data flow diagram

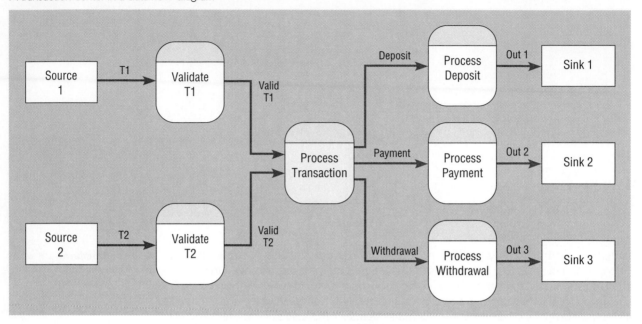

Transform analysis: The process of turning data flow diagrams of a transform-centered system into structure charts.

distribution in the system is the transaction center. It is also certainly possible to have a transaction-based system that has a transform center and a transform-based system that includes a transaction center. In the next section, you will learn how to start with a data flow diagram and proceed to a refined structure chart which reflects the system design as contained in the DFD. For transform-centered designs, this process is called **transform analysis.**

TRANSFORM ANALYSIS

The goal of transform analysis is to convert a transform-centered data flow diagram into a structure chart that remains faithful to the system description contained in the DFD. Transform analysis is not an algorithm: it is a structured process, but you are left with some discretion. One choice you make in the process is which level data flow diagram to convert to a structure chart. In some cases, you will want to start with a level-0 diagram; in other situations, you will want to start at a more detailed level. If you find as you proceed that you need more detail, then switch to a more detailed DFD (Page-Jones, 1980). The transform analysis process has two main parts: top-level design and detailed design.

Top-Level Design

The goal of top-level design is to create a structure chart that captures the essence of the afferent central transform and efferent processes in a DFD. Let's begin with Figure 18-6. We already know that the system here is transform-centered. The first thing we need to do is find the central transform. One way to find the central transform is to trace each afferent flow forward until it disappears and to trace each efferent flow backward until it disappears. The point at which all the flows disappear is the central transform. Sometimes this point consists of more than one process. In such a case, each process should become a separate high-level module in your initial structure chart. You want to identify the central transform because it contains the essential elements of your system where data input streams are transformed into data output streams. In the DFD in Figure 18-6, we see that the data flows Valid A and Valid B converge on the process Make C. This process would seem to be the central transform: the afferent data flows converge on it and the name indicates new data will be derived from existing data. To provide added evidence that Make C is the central transform, we can also look at the process that follows, Print C Report. A process that prints a report would most likely not derive any new data as its primary purpose is to format the information necessary for the report and print it. It seems, then, that Make C is indeed our central transform. Figure 18-8 shows the data flow diagram with the central transform circled.

The next step is to find a boss or coordinating module. Generally, coordinating modules are not evident in a data flow diagram. DFDs map the flow of information through a system, and while such a mapping is very useful in identifying key data and processes in a system, there is no one-to-one correspondence between the processes in a DFD and the modules in a structure chart. Many modules necessary for an information system must be created by the analyst. The coordinating module must almost always be created. For the DFD in Figure 18-8, we must create a coordinating module.

Now that we have identified a central transform and added a coordinating module, it is a straightforward process to identify the afferent and efferent flows. In Figure 18-8, we see there are two afferent flows, from Source 1 through Get Valid A to the central transform, and from Source 2 through Get Valid B to the central transform. The data flowing into the central transform are Valid A and Valid B. There is only one efferent branch, leaving Make C and ending at the Sink. Now that we have identified the central transform and the data flowing in and out of it, we have enough information to draw a top-level structure chart that represents the system's initial design (see Figure 18-9).

Notice that the structure chart in Figure 18-9 has two levels in its hierarchy, one for the coordinating module, and one for the main modules in each of the system's

Figure 18-8
The data flow diagram from Figure 18-6 with the central transform circled

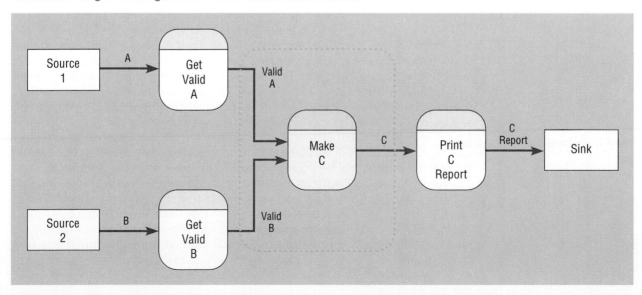

Figure 18-9

The top-level structure chart
derived from the data flow
diagram in Figure 18-8

primary branches: the two afferent branches, the central transform, and the efferent branch. We have now defined the basic structure of our information system. Now we want to refine the design. To do that, we need to go back to the original data flow diagram.

Detailed Design

In order to refine the structure chart we created for Figure 18-9, we need to further develop the afferent and efferent branches and, if necessary, the central transform. In this particular example, the central transform needs no further elaboration as it performs a single function, namely making C from Valid A and Valid B. We must, however, account for the data flows that bring A and B into the system and validate them. In both cases, the data are read into the system from outside sources and validated. We can represent these actions with two modules for each afferent flow, one module for reading the data and the other for validating them. Figure 18-10 shows how the fully developed afferent flows would look.

Now we turn our attention to the efferent branch. We see from Figure 18-8 that the derived data C are processed by the module Print C Report. The C Report then flows to a sink. The print process implies two modules, one for formatting the report and one for printing the report. The module for formatting must be inferred, much as the coordinating module was. We know that to turn data into a report, the data must be formatted in a particular way so that they are printed in the right places, and the report will need to have headings and page numbers and other information. On the structure chart, therefore, we will want to include a separate module for formatting the report. Once we add the formatting and printing modules subordinate to the Put C module, we have finished our first refinement (see Figure 18-11).

Any additional refinements to this particular structure chart will be in the form of design improvements. For example, we might want to consider having the modules Get Valid A and Get Valid B share the same validation module, much as we did in Figure 18-4b. Later in this chapter, you will learn about additional design guidelines that will affect how you further refine and improve your structure charts. (For an excellent example of how refining a structure chart improves its design and dramatically changes how it looks, see Chapter 10 in Yourdon and Constantine, 1979.)

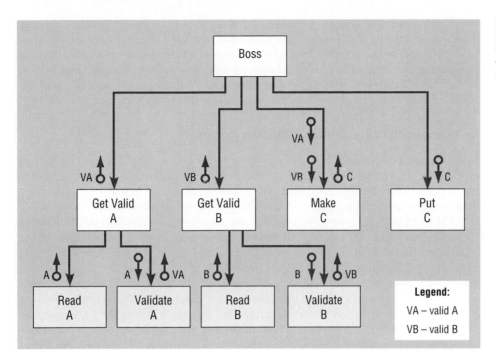

Figure 18-10
First refinement—the structure chart from Figure 18-9 with both afferent branches refined

Figure 18-11
Complete first refinement of the structure chart from Figure 18-9

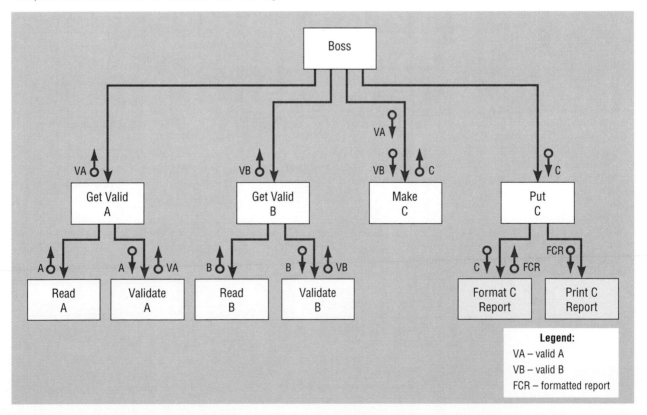

The example we have presented is a simple one. System and program design has many more complexities than we have presented here, so we refer you to software engineering and other systems development texts which treat transform analysis and program design in much more detail (see, for example, Adams, Powers, and Owles, 1985). The example we present next, from Pine Valley Furniture, is also relatively simple but it introduces transform analysis in a more typical business context.

An Example: PVF's Purchasing Fulfillment System

The data flow diagram for Pine Valley Furniture's Purchasing Fulfillment System is reproduced in Figure 18-12. Using the Purchasing Fulfillment System as an example, we will demonstrate how to use transform analysis to convert the data flow diagram into a structure chart useful for beginning the physical design process.

The first step is to identify the area of central transformation. If we look at the data flow diagram for the Purchasing Fulfillment System, we see that some transformation actually occurs in each process. What we want to do, however, is identify the most important or central transformations. Process 1.0 is a transform, where production capacities are turned into material forecasts. However, Process 1.0 is not a central transform as it involves a single input and a single output, and the data generated by Process 1.0 must be transformed again before they are useful to the ordering process. Process 6.0 is not considered the central transform because it primarily uses existing data to prepare orders and derives very little new data. Process 6.0 is an assembly point for much of the data created by the system. Process 4.0 is not the central transform either. In fact, very little transformation takes place in Process 4.0, as the primary function of this process is to select a preferred supplier based on information about suppliers and criteria that guide the selection. Process

Figure 18-12
PVF Purchasing Fulfillment
System data flow diagram

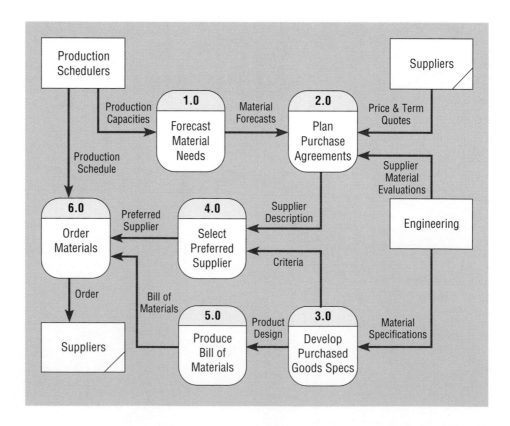

5.0 is a transform, as it takes product designs and converts them to bills of materials but, like Process 1.0, Process 5.0 has only one input and one output. That leaves us with Processes 2.0 and 3.0 as potential central transforms. Notice that, in determining the central transform, we have worked our way inward from the periphery of the DFD. We reasoned through each process' function and eliminated those that were either not transforms or were simple one-input, one-output processes.

For this system, by process of elimination, the area of central transformation encompasses the remaining two processes: 2.0: Plan Purchase Agreements, and 3.0: Develop Purchased Goods Specs. Process 2.0 has three inputs, making it central to processing early in the system. Process 3.0 has only one input but it generates two outputs that are necessary for Processes 4.0 and 5.0 to perform their functions. Why did we choose both processes as the central transform? Why wasn't it just Process 2.0 or Process 3.0? The answer lies in the structure of the DFD. Processes 2.0 and 3.0 are independent of each other—notice there are no direct data flows between them. Both processes serve as starting points for streams of transformed data that eventually become inputs to the assembly point for all of the system's tranformed data, Process 6.0. Figure 18-13 shows the data flow diagram for the Purchasing Fulfillment System with the area of central transform circled.

Now that we have identified the central transforms, we have to create a coordinating module, as no coordinating process is evident on the DFD. In our top-level structure chart, the coordinating module will be at the root of the hierarchy. Each process of the central transform will be a coordinating module at the next level. We have two central transform modules in this example because the processes we identified are independent of each other. Now that we have created a coordinating module and established the central transform in the top-level

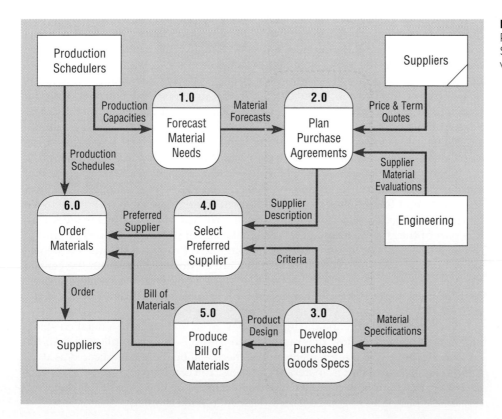

Figure 18-13
PVF Purchasing Fulfillment System data flow diagram with central transform circled

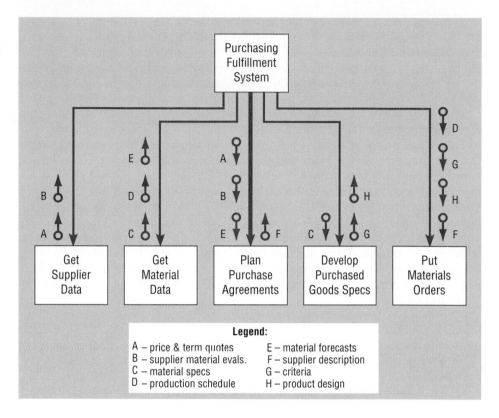

Legend:
A – price & term quotes   E – material forecasts
B – supplier material evals.   F – supplier description
C – material specs   G – criteria
D – production schedule   H – product design

structure chart (see Figure 18-14), we can focus on the main afferent and efferent flows in the system. The efferent flow is the easiest to identify here as it consists solely of outputting the materials order. To identify the afferent branches, we have to look carefully at the data flowing into Processes 2.0 and 3.0 on the data flow diagram. There are three inflows of data into Process 2.0: Material Forecasts from Process 1.0, Price & Term Quotes from Suppliers, and Supplier Material Evaluations from Engineering. Process 3.0 has a single input: Material Specifications from Engineering. As the inputs to Processes 2.0 and 3.0 are either about the suppliers or the material, we can identify two afferent branches, organized by entity: Get Supplier Data, and Get Material Data. Now that we have identified all of the highest-level modules in the chart, we need to identify the data couples that are input to and output from each of these modules. The now complete top-level structure chart for the Purchasing Fulfillment System is shown in Figure 18-14. Notice that Process 1.0 is not shown on the structure chart at this level because it is part of the afferent branch that gets material data. Process 1.0 will be shown in our refinements of the structure chart. Similarly, Processes 4.0 and 5.0 are not shown on the structure chart because they are all downstream from the central transforms and so are actually part of the efferent branch that produces orders. Both of these processes will also be shown in further refinements of the structure chart.

The next step is to refine the top-level design so that we have a detailed structure chart. As the data flow diagram in Figure 18-13 is more complicated than the DFD in Figure 18-8, the refinement process here will be more complicated as well. Refining a structure chart is an iterative process. You continue to improve the structure chart based on how complete, internally consistent, and correct it is. You also rely on the principles of good design we list later in the chapter.

Our starting point is our top-level structure chart. Working left to right, we begin with the afferent branches. We have identified two data couples representing supplier data and three data couples representing material data. We need to account for each data couple in our elaboration of the afferent branches. Figure 18-15 shows one possible refinement of the afferent branches. Notice that we have added two modules that are subordinate to Get Supplier Data. Each module is responsible for the task of obtaining a data couple that has to do with suppliers. The same logic is used for further elaboration of the Get Material Data module. Three subordinate modules have been introduced, each given the task of obtaining a particular data couple associated with material. One of these subordinate modules, Get Material Forecasts, has been assigned two subordinate modules of its own, one for obtaining production capacities and one for transforming production capacities into material forecasts. This latter module effectively represents the action of Process 1.0 in the data flow diagram in Figure 18-13.

Our next task is to refine the central transforms. Neither central transform needs any further elaboration. Both are shown in Figure 18-16. Notice that all the data couples the transforms use have already been obtained by the system and that each transform returns the same data couples as are on the corresponding DFD.

Figure 18-15
Refined afferent branches for the PVF Purchasing Fulfillment System structure chart

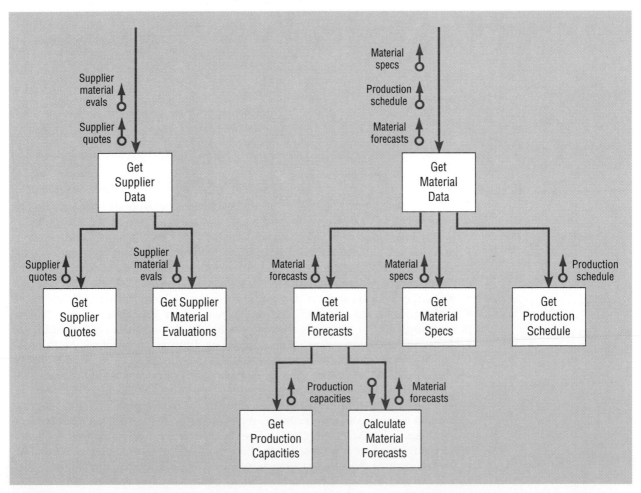

Figure 18-16

Refined central transforms and efferent branch for the PVF Purchasing Fulfillment System structure chart

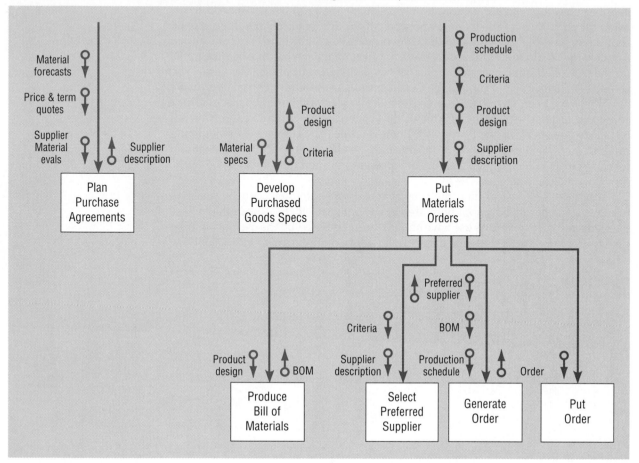

We are now ready to focus on the efferent branch Put Materials Orders. As you can see from the DFD in Figure 18-13, Process 6.0 needs three inputs, Bill of Materials, Preferred supplier, and Production schedule. We have already obtained Production schedule in the Get Material Data afferent branch. We need to get the other two inputs to produce and send orders, but we notice from the DFD that the other inputs are generated by Processes 4.0 and 5.0, respectively. We have decided to make the modules that correspond to Processes 4.0 and 5.0 subordinate to the Put Materials Orders module. The inputs needed by Processes 4.0 and 5.0 are passed down to Put Materials Orders, which calls the modules corresponding to each process and passes down the needed data. Process 5.0 becomes the Produce Bill of Materials module and Process 4.0 becomes the Select Preferred Supplier module. Produce Bill of Materials generates the bill of materials (BOM) data couple, and Select Preferred Supplier generates the Preferred Supplier data couple. Now we have all the inputs we need for our Process 6.0, Order Materials. That part of Process 6.0 that generates orders is represented by the Generate Order module subordinate to Put Materials Orders. The finished order is returned to Put Materials Order from where it is passed to the final module, Put Order. Figure 18-16 shows the refinement of the efferent branch as we have described it, and Figure 18-17 shows the overall shape of the entire structure chart we have constructed.

Figure 18-17
Complete refined structure chart for the PVF Purchasing Fulfillment System

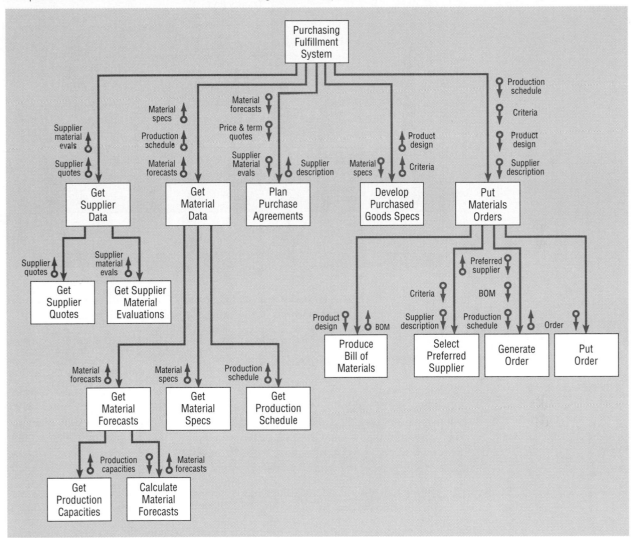

TRANSACTION ANALYSIS

Transaction analysis is similar to transform analysis in that you begin with a DFD and use it as the basis for a structure chart. The primary difference in the procedures is that, as the name implies, you focus on the transaction center in transaction analysis, instead of focusing on the central transform. The transaction center is shown as a high-level module with a diamond-shaped symbol to indicate choice (see Figure 18-3b). Each transaction type is represented as a module at the next level in the structure chart. The transaction center module does nothing more than recognize the type of transaction coming in and route it to the appropriate transaction module at the next level. The actual process of transactions is done at the third level, where specific processing actions are performed. A generic transaction-centered structure chart is shown in Figure 18-18. In creating a top-level structure chart for a transaction-centered system, you would identify and represent the

Transaction analysis: The process of turning data flow diagrams of a transaction-centered system into structure charts.

Figure 18-18
Generic transaction-centered
structure chart

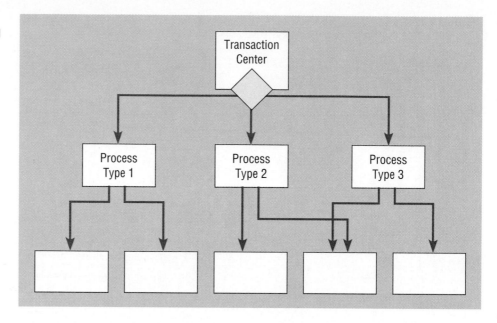

transaction center and each major transaction type. During refinement, you would identify and represent the modules at the third and subsequent levels.

GUIDELINES OF GOOD DESIGN

As we said earlier in this chapter, further refinement of a structure chart is influenced by a set of guidelines for good design (see Page-Jones, 1980, for a much more extensive discussion of good design guidelines). The goal of good design is to produce a system that is easy to read, easy to code, and easy to maintain. The system designs that result from adherence to the guidelines are considered good because these systems meet the overall goals of systems design:

1. The system should be modular; that is, the system should be organized hierarchically into several smaller units.

2. Each module should control the functions of a reasonable number of subordinate modules at the next hierarchical level.

3. Modules should be relatively independent of each other in that no module's function should rely on the internal workings of other modules; therefore, the amount of communication between modules can be kept to a minimum.

4. Each module should be of reasonable size.

5. To the greatest extent possible, each module should perform one and only one function.

6. The code within each module should be as generic as possible so that each module can be used as often as possible within a system.

Each of these system design goals corresponds to a guideline of good design, as follows:

1. *Factoring:* Factor, or decompose, a system into smaller and smaller parts. (Use the guidelines for Reasonable Size and Cohesion to help you decide when to stop factoring.)

2. *Span of Control:* In general, no superordinate module should control more than seven subordinate modules.

3. *Coupling:* Minimize the extent to which modules are dependent on each other and, by so doing, minimize the amount of communication between modules. In the best case, communication should only be through passing data elements and informational flags.

4. *Reasonable Size:* In general, modules should be limited to between 50 and 100 lines of code. The more reasonable the size, the easier the module is to read.

5. *Cohesion:* To the greatest extent possible, all instructions within a module should pertain to the same function. You should be able to accurately describe the function that a module performs in just a few words, with no "ands" or "ors" in the name.

6. *Shared Use:* Especially at the lower levels of a system design, subordinate modules should be called by multiple superordinate modules.

We have already seen several examples of good design guidelines in this chapter as we have been creating and refining structure charts. Although we did not call it factoring, we were factoring when we took a module in a structure chart and decomposed it into several more modules at the next level. Look, for example, at Figures 18-11 and 18-15 through 18-17 where we were refining afferent and efferent branches in structure charts. In refining our structure charts, we also adhered to the guideline of span of control. The highest number of modules any module controlled in Figure 18-17 was five, and that was the coordinating module. We used the guideline of shared use back in Figure 18-4b when we decided to have a single module, Validate Data, called by two different superordinate modules, Get Valid A and Get Valid B.

Reasonable size is not something we can show in a structure chart. The idea behind reasonable size is to make a module small enough so that how it works can be readily understood by the programmer who has to modify it. Coupling can be shown in a structure chart through the passing of data couples and flags between modules. Coupling is evident throughout the structure charts we have created in this chapter. Whether or not the coupling you have seen is good coupling is a different question. In fact, there are actually five different types of coupling, some good, some not so good (Page-Jones, 1980), and we will provide definitions and examples of all of them in the next section. Similarly, cohesion can be shown in a structure chart through the way modules are named. Note that there are good and not so good forms of cohesion, and to distinguish between good and not so good requires a little more information. We will discuss the seven types of cohesion after we finish with coupling.

FIVE TYPES OF COUPLING

The extent to which modules are interdependent is called *coupling.* Ideally, you want to minimize interdependence among modules. The more dependent one module is on another, the more chance there is for error, as a mistake in one module is no longer confined to that module but also affects another module. Also, programmers who modify information systems have a much more difficult job to do if the code inside one module is dependent on the code in other modules for performing its function. Changing the code in one module may then cause unwanted or unexpected changes in other modules that are dependent on it. Keeping modules as independent as possible makes life easier for everyone involved and makes for a better information system.

Despite its desirability, it is not always possible in practice to minimize coupling. Five different types of coupling have been identified (Page-Jones, 1980), and we present them in order from best to worst.

1. *Data Coupling:* This is the best kind of coupling, as the modules in question are so independent of each other that they can communicate only through passing data elements or informational flags. Neither module has any idea about what goes on inside the other module, which is as it should be. Look at Figure 18-19. The superordinate module has no need to know what goes on inside Calculate New Balance. All the superordinate module needs to know is what data to pass to its subordinate. Similarly, the subordinate module has no need to know what all goes on inside its superordinate module—it only needs to know what data it requires and what data it returns.

2. *Stamp Coupling:* In stamp coupling, data are passed in the form of data structures or entire records. Stamp coupling is not quite as good as data coupling because using data structures instead of data elements tends to make the system more complicated than it needs to be. A change in a data structure will affect all modules that use it, even if the modules do not use the same parts of the structure. Stamp coupling makes modules more dependent on each other since, in order to avoid errors, modules must have some knowledge of the internal workings of other modules that use the same data structure. Stamp coupling exposes modules to more data than they need, which can result in problems for the system. Figure 18-20 presents an example of stamp coupling. The example is similar to Figure 18-19, except that we have substituted the data structure CUSTOMER RECORD for the data element Current balance. Clearly, the entire customer record is much more data than the module Calculate New Balance needs. Data structure CUSTOMER RECORD is then used again by the process Format Customer Bill. Once again, CUSTOMER RECORD contains too much data for the process. It would be better for both subordinate modules, and for the system, if only the relevant data elements were passed, instead of the entire record.

3. *Control Coupling:* When one module passes control information to another module, the two are said to be control-coupled. The control information, which may appear as a flag on a structure chart, tells the receiving module what actions it should perform. Obviously, for such control information to be passed, the sending module must know a great deal about the inner workings

Figure 18-19
Example of data coupling

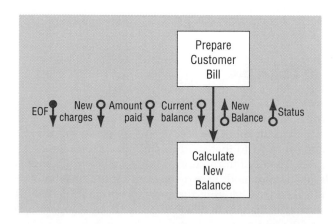

of the receiving module. In such a case, the modules in question are far too interdependent. An example of control coupling is in Figure 18-21. Notice that the flag's label starts with a verb, indicating some control information is being passed. Control information may also be passed from a subordinate to a superordinate module. Such a practice is referred to as an inversion of authority because the subordinate is telling the boss what to do.

4. *Common Coupling:* When two modules refer to the same global data area, they are common-coupled. Global data areas are possible in several computer languages, such as FORTRAN (common block) and COBOL (the data division is global to any paragraph in the procedure division). The main reason common coupling is undesirable is because of the tremendous opportunity for errors to spread throughout the system. An error in any module using the global data area can show up in any other module using the same area. The level of module interdependence becomes quite high.

5. *Content Coupling:* By far the worst type of coupling, content coupling, involves one module directly referring to the inner workings of another module. For example, one module may alter data in a second module or change a statement coded into another module. In content coupling, modules are tightly intertwined. There is no semblance of independence. Fortunately, most higher-level languages have no provisions for creating content coupling.

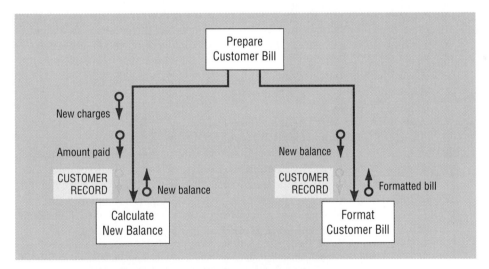

Figure 18-20
Example of stamp coupling

Figure 18-21
Example of control coupling

SEVEN TYPES OF COHESION

The extent to which all instructions in a module relate to a single function is called *cohesion*. In a truly cohesive module, all of the instructions in the module pertain to performing a single, unified task. You want to maximize cohesion in modules. Maximally cohesive modules also tend to be the most loosely coupled, so achieving high levels of cohesion in your system design also helps you minimize coupling. If a module is designed to perform one and only one function, then it has no need to know about the interior workings of other modules. The cohesive module only needs to take the data it is passed, act on them, and pass its output on to its superordinate module. Seven types of cohesion have been identified (Page-Jones, 1980) and we will discuss them in order of best to worst.

1. *Functional Cohesion:* A functionally cohesive module is the most desirable type in that all instructions contained in the module pertain to a single function or task. Many times, the name of a module will indicate that it is functionally cohesive, e.g., Maintain proper temperature for steel furnace, Calculate interest rate, or Select supplier.

2. *Sequential Cohesion:* If a module is sequentially cohesive, the instructions inside of it are related to each other through the data that are input rather than through the task being performed. In sequential cohesion, the first instruction acts on the data that are passed in, and the second instruction uses the output of the first instruction as its input. The output of the second instruction then becomes input for the third instruction, the output of the third instruction becomes input for the fourth, and so on. Sequence, or the ordering of events, is very important in sequential cohesion. Let's look at a nonsystems example.
   CUT DOWN TREE
   CUT TREE INTO PLANKS
   PLANE PLANKS
   SAND PLANKS
   SAW PLANKS TO SPECIFICATIONS
   PUT PLANKS TOGETHER TO MAKE DOOR
   A living tree is the initial input for this set of instructions. The cut-down tree is the input to the second instruction where the tree is made into planks. The raw planks are the input for the next instruction where the planks are planed. Planed planks are the input for the next instruction where the planks are sanded. This pattern of processing continues until we end up with a wooden door. Information system modules follow a similar pattern of logic.

3. *Communicational Cohesion:* In a module that has communicational cohesion, the activities are also related to each other by the data that the module uses, but here sequence is not important. Each instruction in a communicational module acts on the same input data or is concerned with the same output data. An example of communicational cohesion is in Figure 18-22a. The module Find Part Details is so vague that it tips you off to the module as not being functionally cohesive. The module is designed to use part # as input to find a part's name, cost, and supplier. Sequence is not important as it does not matter whether name, cost, or supplier are found first or last. Page-Jones (1980) states that a communicationally cohesive module is easier to understand and maintain if it is split into two functionally cohesive modules, as is the case in Figure 18-22b.

4. *Procedural Cohesion:* As we progress further in the list of the different types of cohesion, we get further away from functional cohesion. Modules exhibiting these kinds of cohesion become more and more difficult to maintain. In

Figure 18-22
Examples of communicational cohesion

(a) Example of a communicational cohesion module

(b) Example of a communicationally cohesive module split into two functionally cohesive modules

procedural cohesion, the instructions in a module are related to each other through flow of control. Instructions have to be carried out in a specific order, so sequence is important. The instructions in a procedurally cohesive module are generally more related to activities in other modules than they are to each other. A nonsystems example of procedural cohesion would be the following set of instructions:

> PICK UP THE NEWSPAPER
> CHECK MAILBOX FOR YESTERDAY'S MAIL
> PUT NEWSPAPER AND MAIL IN BOX
> WATER PLANTS
> CHECK ON WATER AND FOOD FOR DOGS
> MAKE SURE DOORS ARE LOCKED BEFORE LEAVING

You might leave a set of instructions like this for someone who is watching your house while you are away on vacation. Although it might seem that the order of some of the instructions can be interchanged, there is a logic to the order as presented. The instructions are written in the order they would be followed if the person watching your house started at the street, entered the house, checked on the dogs in the backyard, and then locked up before leaving.

5. *Temporal Cohesion:* In a temporally cohesive module, the instructions are also related to each other through the flow of control, but sequence does not matter. The only reason the instructions are in the module at all is that they occur at about the same point in time, hence the name temporal. The classic example of a temporally cohesive module is one that contains instructions for initializing a whole host of variables, counters, switches, and so on, throughout the system. Such a module is related to several other modules, making it very difficult to change the timing of a particular initialization step without affecting other modules that rely on the other instructions in the initialization module.

6. *Logical Cohesion:* In a logically cohesive module, the instructions are hardly related to each other at all. A logically cohesive module consists of several sets of instructions, but the particular set that is executed is determined from outside the module. Typically, a flag that specifies what is to be done is passed in from the outside. A nonsystems example is the following:

> EAT AT A RESTAURANT
> EAT AT YOUR DESK

EAT AT HOME
SKIP LUNCH

According to Page-Jones, people write logically cohesive modules to overlap parts of functions that have the same lines of code or the same buffers. Maintenance is very difficult.

7. *Coincidental Cohesion:* Coincidental cohesion is the worst type because the instructions have no relationship to each other at all. As with logical cohesion, a flag from outside is generally sent in to tell the coincidentally cohesive module what to do. Such modules are the result of haphazard factoring, attempts to save time in design or programming, or bad fixes to existing code. Fortunately, modules that suffer from coincidental cohesion are rare.

Page-Jones (1980) has developed a useful diagram for keeping the different types of cohesion straight (Figure 18-23). Using his decision tree, first ask whether the module is performing a single function. If so, the module is functionally cohesive. If not, ask what connects the activities inside the module. If the connection is data, ask whether sequence is important. If sequence is important, you have sequential cohesion; if not, you have communicational. If it is the flow of control that connects the activities in a module, ask whether sequence is important. If it is, you have procedural cohesion; if not, you have temporal. Finally, if neither data nor control relates the activities in a module to each other, ask whether the activities are in the same general category. If they are, you have logical cohesion; if not, you have coincidental cohesion, the worst type, and the farthest from functional cohesion you can get.

We should make two more points before leaving the topic of cohesion. The first point relates to naming conventions. If a module is truly functionally cohe-

Figure 18-23

A decision tree that helps distinguish among the seven types of cohesion (Adapted from Page-Jones, 1980)

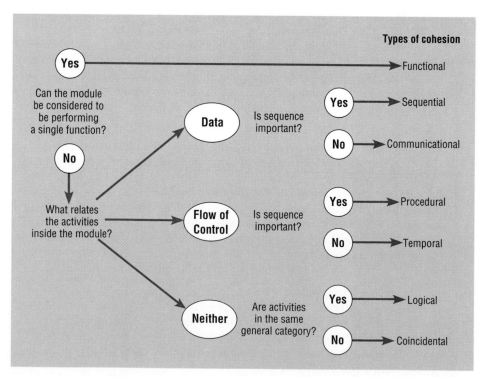

sive, its function can be summed up in a name made up of a single imperative verb and a concise direct object, such as READ STUDENT MASTER FILE, CALCULATE GPA, and PRINT DEAN'S LIST REPORT. Modules with sequential or communicational cohesion will usually include "and" in their names, indicating that they perform more than one function. As you go further down the list of types of cohesion, names that capture what modules do become more general and less understandable. The second point we should make is that the functions modules perform differ according to the level you are considering in your structure chart. As we said previously, coordinating modules, at the root and at the first level of modules in the structure chart, are primarily concerned with decision functions, that is, deciding which modules to call and which parameters to pass and when. The modules at the very bottom of the chart have no decision responsibilities. They simply take inputs, perform their functions, and return output to the modules that called them. Modules in the middle of the chart, then, have a mixture of decision responsibility and task performance responsibility. How you show the details of what a module does is the subject of the next section.

SPECIFYING THE CONTENTS OF MODULES

So far, we have concentrated on depicting a system's hierarchical design in the form of a structure chart. We have focused on transforming a DFD into a structure chart and on refining the initial design using factoring and five other guidelines for good design. If you were a practicing systems analyst, you would have a pretty good overall design at this point. You already know which modules to include in your system and the specifics of how they communicate with each other through the passing of data and informational flags. You have a pretty good idea of what goes on inside each module, but now you must turn your attention to describing the specific instructions contained in each module. We will look at two ways to describe the contents of each module: pseudocode and Nassi-Shneiderman diagrams. Both methods rely on representing the three basic parts of structured programming: sequence, conditional statements, and iterative statements (Bohm and Jacopini, 1966). Pseudocode and Nassi-Shneiderman diagrams both perform the same task, which is representing the contents of system modules. A variation of pseudocode, developed for showing the logic of file and database accesses, is action diagramming. Action diagramming is described in some database management texts and is used with some CASE tools.

Pseudocode

In Chapter 10, you learned about representing the logic of a data flow diagram process with Structured English. In design, a more exact representation of processing logic is required, as programmers will use these representations as specifications for coding. Representing program code as text is the purpose of **pseudocode.** Think of pseudocode as "almost code," a personalized way to describe a computer program and all of its steps using a language that is not quite a programming language but not quite English either. Pseudocode serves two functions:

Pseudocode: A method for representing the instructions in a module with language very similar to computer programming code.

1. It helps an analyst think in a structured way about the task a module is designed to perform.

2. It acts as a communication tool between the analyst, who understands what the module needs to do, and the programmer, who must write the code to make the module perform appropriately.

Every analyst develops his or her own version of pseudocode, so there is no one right way to write it. However, some organizations have standardized on a version of pseudocode and require its use. Whether its origin is personal or standard, all pseudocode must have a way to represent at least sequence, conditional statements, and iteration. The actual form pseudocode takes will depend on the programming languages the analyst knows best. For example, a COBOL-based representation of sequence might be as follows:

```
OPEN INPUT CUSTOMER-MASTER-FILE
OUTPUT CUSTOMER-BILLING-FILE
PERFORM PROCEDURE-INITIALIZE-FIELDS
READ CUSTOMER-MASTER-FILE
AT END MOVE "Y" TO WS-END-OF-FILE-SWITCH
```

A conditional statement based on Pascal might be represented in this way:

```
if A>B
then
        writeln('A is greater')
else writeln('B is greater')
```

Iteration can be represented as either do-while or do-until loops, as illustrated with the following, again based on Pascal:

```
begin
    read(k);
    while k > 0
        do k:= k + 1;
    writeln(k)
end.

begin
    read(k);
    repeat
        k := k + 1
    until k <= 0;
    writeln(k)
end.
```

The format and phrasing of pseudocode is not as important as the information it conveys. The point in using pseudocode in this phase of the life cycle is to provide the programmers who will write the code with a specific description of the contents of each module. Figure 18-24 shows what the pseudocode description of the module Calculate New Balance from Figure 18-19 could be like.

Notice in Figure 18-24 that the name of the module is specified, as are the data passed in and out of the module. Notice also that indentation is used to call attention to the nested conditional statements and the contents of the do-until loop. Finally, notice that the data couple Status is assigned an integer value. The meanings of the integers are explained in a note at the end of the pseudocode.

Nassi-Shneiderman Diagrams

Dissatisfied with logic flow charting techniques and the problems of using them in structured programming, Nassi and Shneiderman developed their own flow

Figure 18-24
Pseudocode description
of Calculate New Balance
module

```
Module name: Calculate New Balance
Receives: Current-balance, New-charges, Amount-paid, EOF
Returns: New-balance, Status

Set New-balance, Status to 0
Read Current-balance, New-charges, Amount-paid, EOF
Repeat
   New-balance = Current-balance + New-charges – Amount-paid
   Beginif
      If New-balance < 0
      Then Status = 1
      Else
         Beginif
         If New-balance = 0
         Then Status = 2
         Else Status = 3
         Endif
   Endif
   Return New-balance, Status
Until EOF = YES
```

(*Note:* The data couple Status has three values, 1, 2, and 3. The value 1 corresponds to "credit," 2 to "nothing due," 3 to "amount due.")

charting techniques for structured programming (1973). Rather than depend on multiple flow charting symbols to represent the basic constructs of structured programming, Nassi and Shneiderman developed their own symbols, shown in Figure 18-25. The diagrams that result from using these symbols are called Nassi-Shneiderman charts. As the figure shows, there are specific symbols for conditional

Figure 18-25
Basic symbols in Nassi-
Shneiderman charts

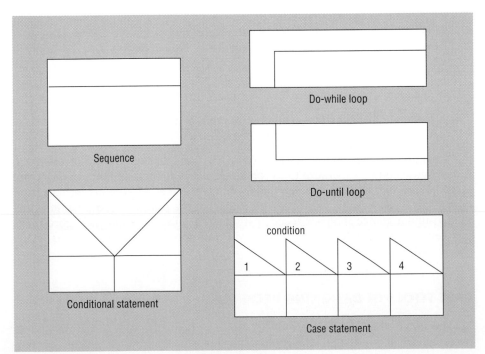

Figure 18-26

The contents of the module Calculate New Balance in the form of a Nassi-Shneiderman chart

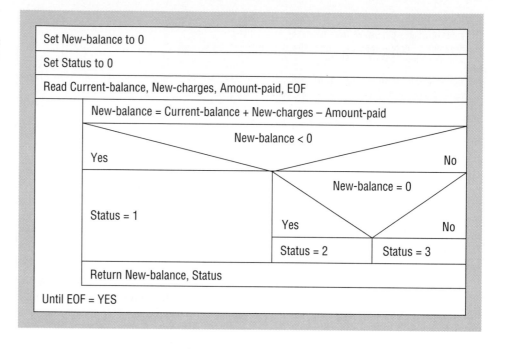

statements, do-while loops, do-until loops, and for sequential statements. There is also a special symbol for case statements.

There are a few rules for using Nassi-Shneiderman charts (Schneyer, 1984):

1. The charts are always rectangular in form.

2. Nassi-Shneiderman charts always start at the top.

3. Movement through the chart is always top to bottom, except at the end of a loop. If the end of a loop has been reached but the exit condition has not been satisfied, movement begins again at the beginning of the same loop. Loops can only be exited through the horizontal bar of the L-shape.

4. Never cross vertical lines.

5. A rectangle can only be exited in one direction at any given time.

6. A rectangle that contains no other lines is either a single instruction (sequence) or another Nassi-Schneideman chart.

Using these rules, follow the flow of instructions through Figure 18-26, which is the pseudocode from Figure 18-24 converted to a Nassi-Shneiderman chart. Once you have learned the different symbols, one glance at a Nassi-Shneiderman chart should give you a more immediate idea of what the diagrammed program does than a similar glance at a pseudocode listing. For example, looking at Figure 18-26, you can tell immediately that there is a do-until loop and two conditional statements in the module.

CASE TOOLS IN DESIGNING PROGRAMS

As shown in this chapter, the design of programs through structure charts, pseudocode, and Nassi-Shneiderman diagrams is an analyst-led process of tran-forming DFDs into program designs. During this manual process, you can use CASE tools for their diagramming capabilities, like an intelligent drawing package, and for maintaining the program designs as part of the project repository. A CASE drawing tool will contain the special symbols of structure charts, for example, and will know to place data couples and control flags along the lines connecting modules. As with other diagrams, each symbol on a structure chart (module, data couple, and control flag) is an object in the repository, and the relationships between objects shown on the diagrams are also maintained in words within the repository, for reporting purposes. Analysis functions of the CASE tool can check that diagrams are complete, consistent, and that they follow rules for drawing that type of diagram.

Figure 18-27 shows an excerpt of a system design represented in Oracle's Designer/2000 CASE tool. These diagrams represent part of a simple library information system. Figure 18-27a contains the level-0 DFD for the entire system and Figure 18-27b shows a simple level-1 diagram for process 2, Checkout and Return Books. The five processes of this DFD were transformed into the structure chart in Figure 18-27c.

The Main module in Figure 18-27c represents the initial, sign-on module of the system. This structure chart shows that a sign-on screen would be displayed and the user would enter a UserID to be validated as a legitimate user of the system. The User Menu connector points to another structure chart not shown. Finally, a Library Main Menu transaction module routes the user to the function he or she wants to perform. Each function is shown on another structure chart, with the connector pointing to that chart. Two of these other structure charts correspond to processes 1.2.1 (Checkout Books) and 1.2.2 (Return Books) from Figure 18-27b. The structure chart for Checkout Books 1.6 appears in Figure 18-27d. The Checkout Books module coordinates the display of a pertinent screen and then controls calling other modules for the various functions necessary to check out a book.

Figure 18-27
Example CASE tool usage for program structure design

(a) Level-0 DFD for library system

Figure 18-27 *(continued)*
Example CASE tool usage for program structure design

(b) Level-1 DFD for Checkout and Return Books process

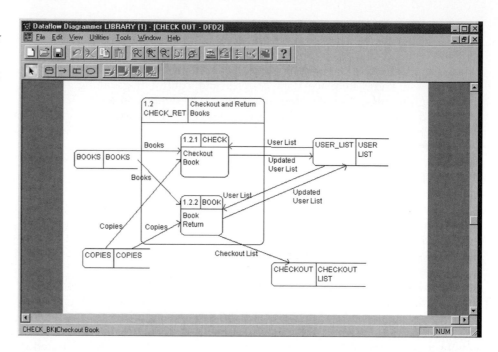

(c) Structure chart for level-0 DFD

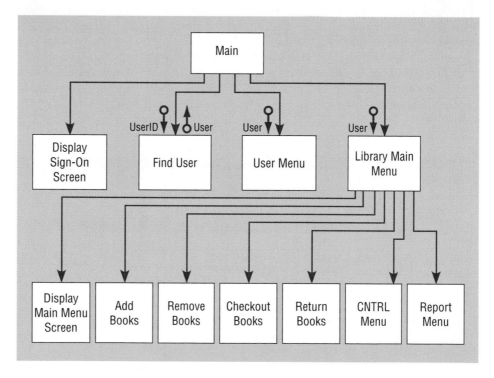

Figures 18-27e, 18-27f, and 18-27g show the repository entries for the Main, Library Main Menu, and Checkout Books modules, respectively. In these figures you can see how pseudocode is used to describe the logic within that module. The Location information within each module entry lists what other modules that module is called by or calls and the data couples and control flags passed between pairs of modules.

(d) Structure chart for
Checkout Books section
of system

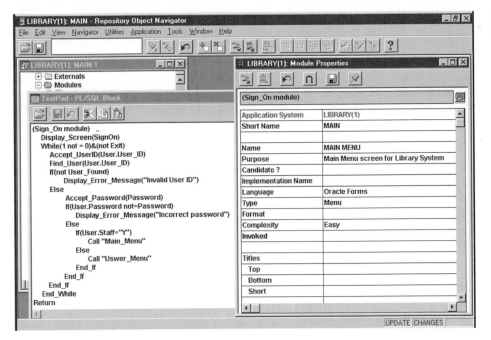

(e) Repository entry for
Main module

(continues)

SUMMARY

In physical information systems design, designers must be concerned with the system's input, output, databases, and programs' physical specifications. Designers must consider what each component will look like and how it will be physically implemented in the new system. In this chapter, we have focused on physical program design. You have learned how to draw structure charts, and you have learned how structure charts are a useful diagramming tool for representing a system's program components and their inter-relations.

Structure charts can represent both transform-centered and transaction-centered system designs. In a transform-centered design, the primary activity of the system

Figure 18-27 *(continued)*
Example CASE tool usage for
program structure design

(f) Repository entry for
Library Main Menu module

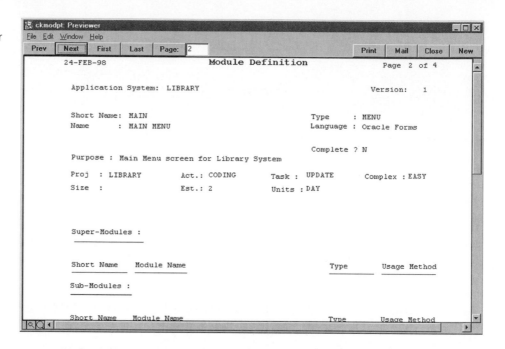

(g) Repository entry for
Checkout_Books module

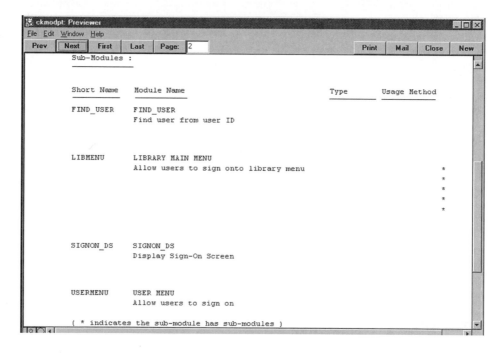

is to derive new data from existing data or to transform existing data into new data. In a transaction-centered design, the primary activity is to dispatch transactions to their proper destinations, where they are further processed. Transform-centered designs can be derived from data flow diagrams using a process called transform analysis.

The first step in transform analysis is to find the area of central transform, where the most important transformations of data take place. Once the central transforms have been identified, the second step is to either find or infer a coordinating module for the top of the structure chart. The third step is to identify the primary afferent (input) and efferent (output) data flows. The fourth step in transform analysis is to draw a top-level structure chart, using the information you uncovered in the first three steps. The top-level structure chart has only two hierarchical levels, one for the coordinating module and one for the primary modules for the afferent and efferent branches and for the central transforms. The fifth step is to further refine the structure chart until the origin of data entering the system, the functions of the central transforms, and the final disposition of the system's outputs have all been satisfactorily accounted for. Transform analysis is an iterative process, so the fifth step may well be the most involved and take the most effort.

The factoring of modules that you undertake to refine a structure chart is the first of six guidelines you can use to help ensure good systems designs. Other guidelines are to limit the number of subordinate modules to no more than seven per boss module; to minimize the interdependence of modules (coupling); to limit the number of lines of code in a module to a reasonable number; to maximize the extent to which all instructions in a module are related to a single function or task (cohesion); and to design some modules, especially at lower levels, so that they may be called by more than one superordinate module. There are five types of coupling and seven types of cohesion. Analysts should be able to identify the various types of coupling and cohesion so that they can recognize the less desirable forms and understand what it takes to convert the less desirable to the preferred forms.

Once the analyst has determined the overall design of an information system, he or she must describe the contents of the individual modules that make up the system. Two methods for describing module contents are pseudocode, a textual way of representing program instructions that is similar to a programming language, and Nassi-Shneiderman charts, a form of program logic flow charting for structured programming. Analysts must also provide specifications for the data input by each module and their sources, as well as specifications for the output the system generates.

CASE tools help analysts in program structuring. The drawing component of a CASE tool will maintain the structure chart diagram and analyze it for completeness, consistency, and structural errors. Each object on a structure chart is linked to a repository entry. An entry for a module can contain pseudocode to explain the logic which must be programmed to implement that module.

KEY TERMS

Afferent module	Module	Transaction-centered system
Central transform	Pseudocode	Transform analysis
Data couple	Structure chart	Transform-centered system
Efferent module	Transaction analysis	
Flag		

REVIEW QUESTIONS

1. Define each of the following terms:
   a. structure chart
   b. module
   c. coordinating module
   d. central transform
   e. transform analysis
   f. transaction-centered system

2. What is a structure chart's role in physical information system design?

3. What is the difference between a data couple and a flag?

4. What does a diamond mean in a structure chart? What does a hat in a structure chart mean? What is a predefined module? How do you represent repetition in a structure chart?

5. What is the difference between a transform-centered system and a transaction-centered system? Give an example of each.

6. What is transform analysis? What is its goal?

7. Explain how to use transform analysis to create a top-level structure chart from a data flow diagram.

8. Explain how to refine a top-level structure chart.

9. Explain the six guidelines to good design.

10. Distinguish among the five types of coupling. How are five categories of coupling useful to a systems analyst?

11. Distinguish among the seven types of cohesion. How are seven categories of cohesion useful to a systems analyst?

12. What are the key differences between pseudocode and Nassi-Shneiderman charts?

PROBLEMS AND EXERCISES

1. Match the following terms to the appropriate definitions.

   _____ afferent
   _____ efferent
   _____ flag
   _____ coupling
   _____ cohesion
   _____ pseudocode

   a. diagrammatic representation of a message passed between two modules
   b. extent to which modules are interdependent
   c. output
   d. input
   e. representing the instructions in a module with language similar to code
   f. extent to which all instructions in a module relate to a single function

2. Using transform analysis, convert the level-0 data flow diagram for Hoosier Burger's food ordering system (see Figure 8-5) to a refined structure chart.

3. Using transform analysis, convert the level-0 data flow diagram for Hoosier Burger's inventory control system (see Figure 8-16) to a refined structure chart.

4. Study Figure 18-17, the complete refined structure chart for Pine Valley Furniture's Purchasing Fulfillment System. How many different types of coupling can you iden-

tify in the structure chart? If you find evidence of more types of coupling than simple data coupling, how can you convert all types of coupling to data coupling? How many different types of cohesion are represented by the structure chart's functions? If you find evidence of more types than simple functional cohesion, what can you suggest to convert all types of cohesion to functional cohesion?

5. Represent the processing logic of each module in Figure 18-15 (or 18-16) using pseudocode.

6. Represent the processing logic of each module in Figure 18-15 (or 18-16) using Nassi-Shneiderman charts.

7. Compare the pseudocode and Nassi-Shneiderman charts you created in Problems and Exercises 5 and 6 (for either Figure 18-15 or Figure 18-16). Which type of representation is the clearest? Which works best for you? Explain why.

8. Starting with Figure 18-12 (Pine Valley Furniture's Purchasing Fulfillment System), use a CASE tool to convert the data flow diagram to a complete, refined structure chart.

9. A module of a payroll system calculates the overtime pay for employees. Employees who work over 40 hours in a one-week period are paid their base salary rate for hours 1 through 40 plus one and a half times their base salary rate for every additional hour. However, if the employee data indicate that an employee worked over 70 hours in a one-week period, the record is flagged, an overtime calculation is not made, and an error message is printed. Represent the processing logic of this module using pseudocode and Nassi-Shneiderman charts.

10. Using transform analysis, convert the level-0 data flow diagram created for Problem and Exercise 14 in Chapter 8 to a refined structure chart.

11. Using transform analysis, convert the level-0 data flow diagram created for Problem and Exercise 15 in Chapter 8 to a refined structure chart.

12. Using transform analysis, convert the level-0 data flow diagram created for Problem and Exercise 16 in Chapter 8 to a refined structure chart.

FIELD EXERCISES

1. Interview a systems analyst about the physical design process where the analyst works. What specific design methodology does the analyst's organization follow? What are the roles of structure charts and transform analysis in the methodology? Does the methodology prescribe pseudocode or Nassi-Shneiderman charts?

2. Look for an Internet USENET discussion group on systems design. Follow the discussion for several weeks and document what you have learned in a journal to be turned in to your instructor.

3. Research the principles of good design for information systems and for some other artifact that people design and build, such as bridges, computer peripherals, furniture, or cars. Prepare a report on the principles of good design for information systems and for whatever else you have chosen to study. How are the principles different? How are they similar?

4. Research the physical information design process in Japan and in Europe. How do these processes compare to what you have learned here about North American practice? How are the processes similar? How are they different?

REFERENCES

Adams, D. R., M. J. Powers, and V. A. Owles. 1985. "Computer Information Systems Development: Design and Implementation." Cincinnati, OH: South-Western Publishing Co.

Bohm, C., and I. Jacopini. 1966. "Flow Diagrams, Turing Machines, and Languages with Only Two Formation Rules." *Communications of the ACM* 9 (May): 366–71.

Nassi, I., and B. Shneiderman. 1973. "Flowchart Techniques for Structured Programming." *ACM SIGPLAN Notices* 8(8) (Aug.): 12–26.

Page-Jones, M. 1980. *The Practical Guide to Structured Systems Design.* New York, NY: Yourdon Press.

Schneyer, R. 1984. *Modern Structured Programming: Program Logic, Style, and Testing.* Santa Cruz, CA: Mitchell Publishing Inc.

Yourdon, E., and L. L. Constantine. 1979. *Structured Design.* Englewood Cliffs, NJ: Prentice-Hall.

Designing the Internals: Program and Process Design

INTRODUCTION

The Customer Activity Tracking System (CATS) team is progressing on schedule. Considerable documentation has been generated about what CATS should do, but not much has been specified on how CATS will be structured. Since BEC will purchase a large portion of CATS, the purchased functions only need to be checked against BEC's unique requirements to determine whether the structure of the package is sufficient. The in-store component of CATS, however, is not in the package and must be added on. Thus, the in-store processes, identified in analysis, must be transformed into a software design so the BEC programmers can build this portion. This case includes a discussion between Jordan Pippen, the CATS project leader, and Frank Napier, a systems analyst on the CATS team, as they review structure charts generated for the in-store portion of CATS.

TRANSFORM ANALYSIS FOR IN-STORE CATS

"Everything is coming together," Jordan Pippen told Frank Napier. "I am really pleased at the progress we have been making. Using the TwoCats system as the basis for our corporate Customer Activity Tracking System (CATS) was a good choice."

"It doesn't help that much with our in-store component, though," Frank replied. "We still have to pretty much grow our own on that one."

"So," Jordan answered. "How much progress have you made in coming up with a program design for the in-store component?"

"I've done a rough draft on the structure chart. Want to see it? I thought you might ask about it, so I brought my work with me."

"Yeah, now would be a good time—I have a couple of minutes before my next meeting."

"OK, good," Frank said, pulling out some printouts. "Here's what I've been working on. I started with the data flow diagram we drew for the in-store component of CATS (Figure 1). You can see that there are four processes, one for updating store inventory, one for updating product reservations, one for recording customer purchases, and one for generating the CATS success report.

"I had to figure out which one of these processes was the central transform. That wasn't a straight-forward decision. But after analyzing the data flows coming into the system, it seemed to me that everything pointed to the fourth process, Produce Success Evaluation Report. Start at Process 2.4 and trace back those two data flows that enter it, New Reservations, and Store Transactions. All of the activity in the system, except for the activity surrounding Update Store Inventory, is focused on populating and updating the two data stores that are the sources of New Reservations and Store Transactions."

"Hmmmm, I'm not so sure," Jordan replied. "Are you sure this process is the central transform? All Process 2.4 does is produce a report. There's not much transformation going on there. And look at these other processes. They aren't really transforms either. Processes 2.1 and 2.2 update data stores; Process 2.3 simply records store transactions. In fact, it doesn't even look like Process 2.1 is part of this system at all. The in-store CATS system never uses any of the data in the store inventory records. Isn't there already a system in place that updates the inventory for each store as shipments arrive? And now that I think about it, Process 2.3 shouldn't be in our system either. The point-of-sale system we run at all of our stores automatically captures each transaction."

Looking slightly discouraged, Frank responded, "Yes, I think you're right. I guess I didn't look at the DFD that carefully, I was so focused on transform analysis. Processes 2.1 and 2.3 don't really belong in our system. We included Process 2.1 in the in-store

Figure 1
DFD of CATS in-store
component

CATS system because the process will have to take reservation purchases into consideration for updating inventory, but that inventory update system is already in place. I need to find out who is responsible for maintaining the store inventory update system. I'll have to work with that person so that we're sure the reservation purchases our in-store CATS system generates are taken into consideration."

"You're going to have to do the same thing with Process 2.3, Frank," Jordan added. "That process is just not in our system. But this DFD does point to some changes that will have to be made. The point-of-sale system will have to be modified so that it can record a purchase as a reservations purchase. Also, we need a process on our DFD that can extract reservation purchase data from the Store Transactions data store, even if that process is really just a single query. Why don't you redraw the DFD so that the inventory update system is an external entity that receives the reservation purchases data flow and so that Process 2.3 is replaced with an extraction process?"

"How about this?" Frank asked, redrawing the DFD as he spoke (see Figure 2).

"Meanwhile," Jordan said, "You've still got a DFD with no real central transform. So this is a transaction-centered system, even though there is no obvious transaction center. The system is linked together by the data stores."

"Another reason to see this as transaction-centered is timing." Frank stated. "Is there any reason to believe

these three processes have to be performed in order or at the same time? When is the CATS success report generated?"

"It's projected to be a daily report," Jordan responded, "Although I guess it could be generated on demand. Look at this process—Update Product Reservations. One of the events that triggers it is the reservation report from Central CATS. We need to find out how often and when the Central CATS reservation report is generated. I bet it's out of synch with generating the CATS success report. And how often do we want to run this purchase data extraction process?"

"I think your idea of making this system transaction-centered is right. Because of the timing differences, this system seems ideally suited to be menu-based. We end up with one transaction module for two of the processes on the revised DFD, Update Product Reservations and Generate CATS Success Report. That pretty much gives us a first-cut transaction-centered design," Frank said (see Figure 3).

"What about Process 2.1, Extract Reservations Purchase Data?" Jordan asked. "Did you forget that?"

"No," Frank said, "I didn't forget it. Both of the other processes need the reservations purchases data in order to function, so it seems to me that we should make Process 2.1 subordinate to both of the other modules. When a user calls for a product reservation update or calls for the CATS report to be generated, then the main module for whatever the user chooses

Figure 2
Revised DFD of CATS in-store component

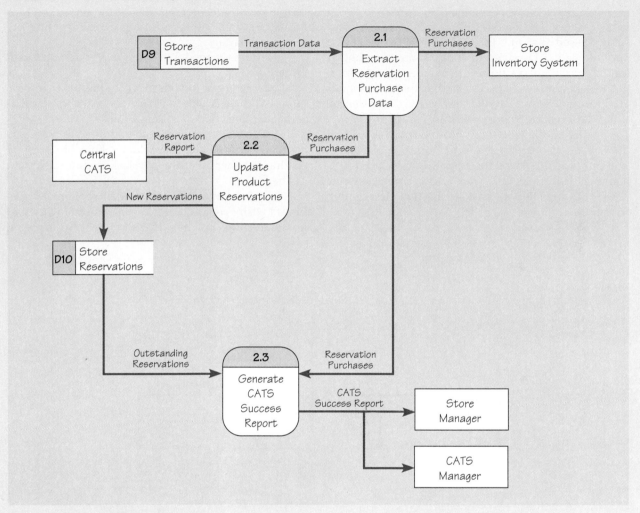

Figure 3
First-cut transaction-centered structure chart for the CATS in-store component

calls Process 2.1. So we'll show Process 2.1 on the refined structure chart."

"OK, I see. Now let's refine this," Jordan said.

"First we'll add modules that we need for a transaction-based system," Frank replied. "So we have a module called Display Function Menu and another called Accept Valid Choice. Then under Update Product Reservations we'll need a module that corresponds to Process 2.1 and another for getting the Central CATS Reservation Report, like this (Figure 4)."

"Add another subordinate module for adding new reservations," Jordan said, "and we're done at the subordinate level for updating product reservations. Now let's draw an arrow from Generate CATS Success Report back to Extract Reservation Purchase. . . ."

"Good—reuse."

"And then add a module responsible for getting the reservations still outstanding. Now we add a couple of modules for producing the report, one for formatting and one for printing or transmitting it," continued Jordan.

"Hey, this is good, I like how this ended up," said Frank.

"Now go back to your office and refine this some more. And then you're ready to create the Nassi-Schneiderman charts," Jordan smiled.

"I want to work with some other team members on that," Frank said. "You know how big a chore putting together all of the physical specs for a system can be."

"Oh, I know, all right," Jordan replied. "Sometimes I wish I could do more of that kind of work and less managing, but hey, that's my job. Speaking of

Figure 4

First refinement of the transaction-centered structure chart for the CATS in-store component which, I'm late for my meeting—gotta run. Keep me posted, Frank."

And Jordan practically ran out of her office.

SUMMARY

The specifications for the in-store portion of CATS are taking shape. The project team is in a transition within the project. They are moving from a functional to a technical perspective and soon will be turning work over to new members of the team responsible for building CATS. Thus, whereas the functional specifications were for communications within the group and with clients, the program specifications are guidelines to the programmers. The programmers may not have sufficient time to review all of the repository, so the structure charts need to capture just what they need to know in order to write program modules. Frank's work is very detailed and critical to the continued success of the project. We will see in the next BEC case that, even with all the analysis and study done during the project, unanticipated issues can arise. Each project is unique and presents new challenges to systems developers and to the organization.

Designing Distributed Systems

After studying this chapter, you should be able to:

- Define the key terms client/server architecture, local area network, distributed database, and middleware.

- Choose between file server and other client/server architectures for an application, based on the relative advantages of each.

- Distinguish between file server and client/server environments, and contrast how each is used in a local area network.

- Describe and apply four major strategies for distributing data in distributed systems.

- Describe alternative designs for distributed systems and their trade-offs.

INTRODUCTION

The advances in personal computer technology and the rapid evolution of graphical user interfaces, networking, and communications are changing the way today's computing systems are being used to meet ever more demanding business needs. In many organizations, previous stand-alone personal computers are being linked together to form networks that support workgroup computing (this process is sometimes called *upsizing*). At the same time, other organizations (or even the same organization) are migrating mainframe applications to personal computers, workstations, and networks (this process is sometimes called *downsizing*) to take advantage of the greater cost-effectiveness of these environments. Now, organizations are using the World Wide Web for delivering applications to internal users and customers. In short, as technology continues to evolve, users are increasingly capable of interconnecting various types of computers, efficiently and transparently, to distribute data and applications within and across organizations.

A variety of new opportunities and competitive pressures are driving the trend toward these technologies. Corporate restructuring—mergers, acquisitions, consolidations—makes it necessary to connect or replace existing stand-alone applications. Similarly, corporate downsizing has caused individual managers to have a broader span of control, thus requiring access to a wider range of data, applications, and people. Applications are being downsized from expensive mainframes to networked microcomputers and workstations (possibly with a mainframe as a server) that are much more cost-effective and scalable, and can also be more user-friendly. However, data traffic congestion on traditional local area networks (LANs) with a simple file server architecture can cause serious performance problems. Thus, how distributed systems are designed and configured can have obvious ramifications for day-to-day organizational activities and the success of an information system.

In this chapter we describe several technologies that are being used to upsize, downsize, and distribute information systems and data. These technologies are LAN-based DBMSs, client/server DBMSs, and distributed databases. The capabilities and issues surrounding these technologies are the foundation for understanding how to migrate single processor applications and designs into a multiprocessor, distributed computing environment. As you will learn, deciding to design a new information system as a distributed system must be made prior to implementation. For example, in order to effectively share data across locations, you must consider trade-offs between various designs for distributing data. Choosing a design without considering how data will be created, shared, updated, and destroyed across locations may significantly reduce overall system throughput and organizational effectiveness.

DESIGNING DISTRIBUTED SYSTEMS

In this section we will briefly discuss the process and deliverables when designing distributed systems. Given the direction of organizational change and technological evolution, it is likely that most future systems development efforts will need to consider the issues surrounding the design of distributed systems.

The Process of Designing Distributed Systems

This is the last chapter in the text dealing with physical design issues within the systems development life cycle (see Figure 19-1). In the previous chapters on physical design, specific techniques for representing and refining modules of processes and data were presented. In this chapter, however, no specific techniques will be presented on how to design distributed systems since no generally accepted techniques exist. Alternatively, we will focus on increasing your awareness of common environments for deploying distributed systems and the issues you will confront surrounding their design and implementation. You will learn about the trade-offs between different ways to deal with distributed systems design, and should be able to apply this understanding when you design multiuser, distributed systems.

Designing distributed systems is much like designing single-location systems. The primary difference is that because a system will be distributed over two or more locations, numerous design issues must be considered due to their influence on the reliability, availability, and survivability of the system when it is implemented. Because distributed systems have more components than a single-location system—that is, more processors, networks, locations, data, and so on—there are more potential places for a failure to occur. Consequently, various strategies can be used when designing and implementing distributed systems. For example, replicating all data elements across all distributed sites will enhance the *reliability* that a given piece of information will be available at a given time, and enhance the overall system *survivability* if a single node has a catastrophic failure. Yet, replicating all data elements at all sites may result in not having the latest information at a given site since it may not be possible to simultaneously

Figure 19-1
Systems development life cycle with physical design phase highlighted

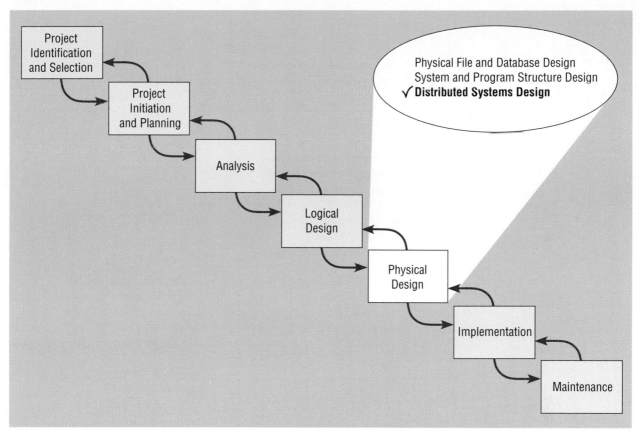

update changes to all locations. Such a design is somewhat low on the *availability* dimension.

Thus, when designing distributed systems, you will need to consider numerous trade-offs that will influence reliability, survivability, and availability. To create effective designs, you need to understand the characteristics of the commonly used architectures for supporting distributed systems and sharing data. In other words, you must decide whether you want to partition data and processing across single or multiple sites and, if you do, what trade-offs to make.

Deliverables and Outcomes

When designing distributed systems, the deliverable is a document that will consolidate the information that must be considered when implementing a physical distributed system design. Figure 19-2 lists the types of information that must be considered when implementing a distributed system. In general, the information that must be considered when designing a distributed system is the site, processing, and data information for *each* location (or processor) in a distributed environment. Specifically, information related to physical distances between locations, counts and usage patterns by users, building and location infrastructure issues, personnel capabilities, data usage (use, create, update, or destroy), and local organizational processes must be described. Additionally, the pros and cons of various

Figure 19-2
Outcomes and deliverables from designing distributed systems

1. Description of Site (for each site)
   a. geographical information
   b. physical location
   c. infrastructure information
   d. personnel characteristics (education, technical skills, etc.)
   e. ...

2. Description of Data Usage (for each site)
   a. data elements used
   b. data elements created
   c. data elements updated
   d. data elements deleted

3. Description of Business Process (for each site)
   a. list of processes
   b. description of processes

4. Contrasts of Alternative IS Architectures for Site, Data, and Process Needs (for each site)
   a. pros and cons of no technological support
   b. pros and cons of non-networked, local system
   c. pros and cons of various distributed configurations
   d. ...

implementation solutions for each location should be reviewed. The collection of this information, in conjunction with the physical design information already developed, will provide the basis for implementing the information system in the distributed environment. Note, however, that our discussion assumes that any required network infrastructure is already in place. In other words, we focus only on those issues in which you will likely have a choice.

DESIGNING SYSTEMS FOR LOCAL AREA NETWORKS

Personal computers and workstations can be used as stand-alone systems to support local applications. However, organizations have discovered that if data are valuable to one employee, they are probably also valuable to other employees in the same workgroup or in other workgroups. By interconnecting their computers, workers can exchange information electronically and can also share devices such as laser printers that are too expensive to be used by only a single user.

A **local area network (LAN)** supports a network of personal computers, each with its own storage, that are able to share common devices and software attached to the LAN. Each PC and workstation on a LAN is typically within 100 feet of the others, with a total network cable length of under 1 mile. At least one computer (a microcomputer or larger) is designated as a file server, where shared databases and applications are stored. The LAN modules of a DBMS, for example, add concurrent access controls, possibly extra security features, and query or transaction

Local area network (LAN):
The cabling, hardware, and software used to connect workstations, computers, and file servers located in a confined geographical area (typically within one building or campus).

queuing management to support concurrent access from multiple users of a shared database.

File Servers

In a basic LAN environment (see Figure 19-3), all data manipulation occurs at the workstations where data are requested. One or more file servers are attached to the LAN. A **file server** is a device that manages file operations and is shared by each client PC that is attached to the LAN. In a file server configuration, each file server acts as an additional hard disk for each client PC. For example, your PC might recognize a logical F: drive, which is actually a disk volume stored on a file server on the LAN. Programs on your PC refer to files on this drive by the typical path specification, involving this drive and any directories, as well as the file name.

When using a DBMS in a file server environment, each client PC is authorized to use the DBMS application program on that PC. Thus, there is one database on the file server and many concurrently running copies of the DBMS on each active PC. The primary characteristic of a client-based LAN is that all data manipulation is performed at the client PC, not at the file server. The file server acts simply as a shared data storage device and is an extension of a typical PC. It also provides additional resources (e.g., disk drives, shared printing), collaborative applications (e.g., electronic mail), in addition to the shared data. Software at the file server only queues access requests; it is up to the application program at each client PC, working with the copy of the DBMS on that PC, to handle all data management functions. This means that in an application that wants to view a single customer account record in a database stored on the server, the file containing all customer account records will be sent over the network to the PC. Once at the PC, the file will

File server: A device that manages file operations and is shared by each client PC attached to a LAN.

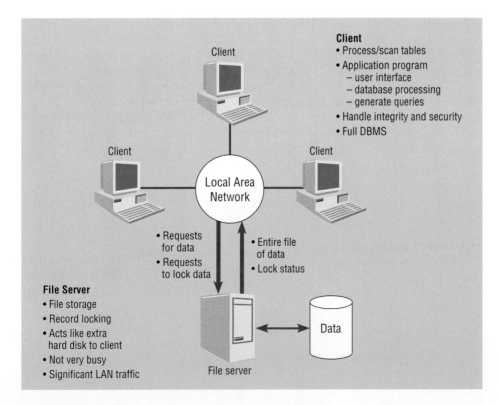

Figure 19-3
File server model

be searched to find the desired record. Additionally, data security checks and file and record locking are done at the client PCs in this environment, making multiuser application development a relatively complex process.

Limitations of File Servers

There are three limitations when using file servers on local area networks:

1. Excessive data movement

2. Need for powerful client workstation

3. Decentralized data control

First, when using a file server architecture, considerable data movement is generated across the network. For example, when an application program running on a client PC in Pine Valley Furniture wants to access the Birch products, the whole Product table is transferred to the client PC; then, the table is scanned at the client to find the few desired records. Thus, the server does very little work, the client is busy with extensive data manipulation, and the network is transferring large blocks of data (see Figure 19-4). Consequently, a client-based LAN places a considerable burden on the client PC to carry out functions that have to be performed on all clients and creates a high network traffic load.

Second, since each client workstation must devote memory to a full version of the DBMS, there is less room on the client PC to rapidly manipulate data in high-speed random access memory (RAM). Often, data must be swapped between RAM and a relatively slower hard disk when processing a particularly large database. Further, because the client workstation does most of the work, each client must be rather powerful to provide a suitable response time. File server-based architectures also benefit from having a very fast hard disk and cache memory in both clients and the server to enhance their ability to transfer files to and from the network, RAM, and hard disk.

Third, and possibly most important, the DBMS copy in each workstation must manage the shared database integrity. In addition, each application program must recognize, for example, locks on data and take care to initiate the proper locks. A lock is necessary to stop users from accessing data that are in the process of being updated. Thus, application programmers must be rather sophisticated to understand various subtle conditions that can arise in a multiple-user database environment. Programming is more complex since you have to program each application with the proper concurrency, recovery, and security controls.

Figure 19-4
File servers transfer entire files when data are requested from a client

DESIGNING SYSTEMS FOR A CLIENT/SERVER ARCHITECTURE

A recent improvement in LAN-based systems is the **client/server architecture** in which application processing is divided (not necessarily evenly) between client and server. The client workstation is most often responsible for managing the user interface, including presenting data, and the database server is responsible for database storage and access such as query processing. The typical client/server architecture is illustrated in Figure 19-5. Variations on the basic client/server design are discussed later in the chapter.

In the typical client/server architecture, all database recovery, security, and concurrent access management is centralized at the server, whereas this is the responsibility of each user workstation in a simple LAN. These central DBMS functions are often called a **database engine** in a client/server environment. Some people refer to the central DBMS functions as the back-end functions whereas client-based delivery of applications to users using PCs and workstations are called front-end applications. Further, in the client/server architecture, the server executes all requests for data so that only data that match the requested criteria are passed across the network to client stations. This is a significant advantage of client/server over simple file server-based designs. Since the server provides all shared database services, this leaves the **client** software to concentrate on user interface and data manipulation functions. The trade-off is that the server must be more powerful than the server in a file server environment.

An application built using the client/server architecture is also different from a centralized database system on a mainframe. The primary difference is that each client is an *intelligent* part of the application processing system. In other words, the application program executed by a user is running on the client, not on the server. The application program handles all interactions with the user and local devices (printer, keyboard, screen, etc.). Thus, there is a division of duties between the server (database engine) and the client: the database engine handles all database access and control functions and the client handles all user interaction and data manipulation functions. The client PC sends database commands to the database engine for processing. Alternatively, in a mainframe environment, all parts of the information system are managed and executed by the central computer.

Another advantage of client/server architectures is the ability to decouple the client environment from the server environment. Clients can consist of multiple types

Client/server architecture: A LAN-based computing environment in which a central database server or engine performs all database commands sent to it from client workstations, and application programs on each client concentrate on user interface functions.

Database engine: The (back-end) portion of the client/server database system running on the server and providing database processing and shared access functions.

Client: The (front-end) portion of the client/server database system that provides the user interface and data manipulation functions.

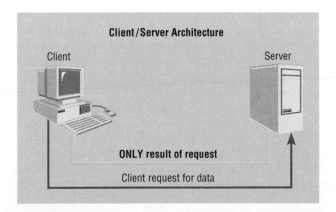

Figure 19-5
Client/server architecture transfers only the required data after a request from a client

Application program inter-face (API): Software which allows a specific front-end program development platform to communicate with a particular back-end database engine, even when the front-end and back-end were not built to be compatible.

(for example, different computers, operating systems, and application programs) which means that the client can be running any application system that can generate the proper commands (often SQL) to request data from the server. For example, the application program might be written in Quattro Pro, dBASE IV, a report writer, a sophisticated screen painter, or any fourth-generation language that has an **application program interface,** or API, for the database engine. The database engine might be DB2 on an IBM mainframe or midrange computer, or Sybase or Oracle running on a variety of platforms. An API calls library routines that transparently route SQL commands from the front-end client application to the database server. An API might work with existing front-end software, like a third-generation language or custom report generator, and it might include its own facilities for building applications. When APIs exist for several program development tools, then you have considerable independence to develop client applications in the most convenient front-end programming environment, yet still draw from a common server database. With some APIs, it is possible to access data from both the client and server in one database operation, as if the data were in one location managed by one DBMS.

Client/Server Advantages and Cautions

There are several significant benefits that can be realized by adopting a client/server architecture:

1. It allows companies to leverage the benefits of microcomputer technology. Today's workstations deliver impressive computing power at a fraction of the costs of mainframes.

2. It allows most processing to be performed close to the source of processed data, thereby improving response times and reducing network traffic.

3. It facilitates the use of graphical user interfaces (GUIs) and visual presentation techniques commonly available for workstations.

4. It allows for and encourages the acceptance of open systems.

Many other vendors of relational DBMSs and other LAN-based technologies are attempting to migrate their products into the client/server environment. However, products which were not designed from the beginning under a client/server architecture may have problems adapting to this new environment (see Radding, 1992, for a discussion of such issues). This is because new issues and new spins on old issues arise in this new environment. These issues and areas include compatibility of data types, query optimization, distributed databases, data administration of distributed data, CASE tool code generators, cross operating system integration, and more. In general, there is a lack of tools for systems design and performance monitoring in a client/server environment. As versions of different front- and back-end tools change, problems may arise with compatibility, until the API evolves, and these problems must be handled directly by the programmer, not by development tools.

Now that you have an understanding of the general differences between file server and client/server architectures, we will next discuss how data can be managed within a distributed environment. After discussing data management options, we will present several design alternatives for distributed systems. All LAN-based distributed system designs are implemented using some configuration of the general file server or client/server architectures and data management options.

MANAGING DATA IN DISTRIBUTED SYSTEMS

When an organization is geographically dispersed, it may choose to store its databases on a central computer and make this data available over telecommunications lines to multiple users. More recently, organizations are choosing to distribute data among a network of local computers. A **distributed database** is a single logical database that is physically spread across computers in multiple locations that are connected by a data communications network. We emphasize that a distributed database is truly a database, not a loose collection of files. The network must allow the users to share the data; thus a user (or program) at location A must be able to access and perhaps update data at location B. The sites of a distributed system may be distributed over a large area such as the United States or the world, or over a small area such as a building or campus. The computers may range from micros to large-scale computers or even supercomputers.

Distributed database: A single logical database that is spread across computers in multiple locations which are connected by a data communications link.

Objectives and Trade-Offs

A major objective of distributed databases is to provide easy access to data for users at many different locations. To meet this objective, the distributed database system must provide what is called location transparency. **Location transparency** means that a user (or user program) requesting data need not know at which site these data are located. Any request to retrieve or update data at a nonlocal site is automatically forwarded by the system to that site. Ideally, the user is unaware of the distribution of data, and all data in the network appear as a single logical database. Distributed databases have several advantages and disadvantages that are summarized in Table 19-1. Advantages include greater system reliability, data integrity and control modularity, and faster user response. Disadvantages include greater cost, complexity, processing overhead, and increased security concerns. Whether distributed databases are appropriate for a particular organization or application will depend upon the balancing of these factors.

Location transparency: A design goal for a distributed database which says that a user (or user program) requesting data need not know at which site those data are located.

TABLE 19-1   Advantages and Disadvantages of Distributed Databases

Advantages of Distributed Databases:

1. Increased system reliability due to redundancy

2. Local control of data, which tends to promote improved data integrity and administration

3. Modular growth of applications and databases without disruption to existing users

4. Lower communication costs by reducing communication traffic

5. Faster response since most applications use data at a local site

Disadvantages of Distributed Databases:

1. Software cost and complexity, since more complex software is required for a distributed environment

2. Processing overhead to exchange messages among the sites

3. Data integrity, which is more difficult to control with multiple and dispersed copies of data

4. Slow response if the data and application software are not distributed properly according to their usage

Options for Distributing a Database

Given that there are various options for distributing databases, a fundamental question is how should you distribute data for one or several applications among the sites (or nodes) of a distributed network? Research and practical experience have found that there are four basic strategies you can follow for distributing databases:

1. Data replication

2. Horizontal partitioning

3. Vertical partitioning

4. Combinations of 1, 2, and 3

We will explain and illustrate each approach using relational databases.

Suppose that a bank has numerous branches located throughout a state. One of the relations in the bank's database is the Customer relation. The format for an abbreviated version of this relation is shown in Figure 19-6. For simplicity, the sample data in the relation apply to only two of the branches (Lakeview and Valley). The primary key in this relation is account number (ACCT NO.). BRANCH NAME is the name of the branch where customers have opened their accounts and, therefore, where they presumably perform most of their transactions.

Data Replication   One option for data distribution is to store a separate copy of the database at each of two or more sites. The Customer relation in Figure 19-6 could be stored at both Lakeview and Valley, for example. If a copy is stored at every site, we have the case of full replication. The advantages and disadvantages of data replication are summarized in Table 19-2. In short, data replication enhances system reliability and system response but requires increased data storage, processing complexity, and cost. These issues are especially acute when each copy of the data must be constantly identical. Newer technologies, called replication database server systems, are reducing the cost of replicated data when users can tolerate some lack of synchronization across copies of data. Given its trade-offs, full data replication is favored for data where most transactions are read-only and where the data are relatively static, such as catalogs, telephone directories, train schedules, and so on. CD-ROM storage technology has promise as an economical medium for replicated databases.

Horizontal partitioning:
Distributing the rows of a table into several separate tables.

Horizontal Partitioning   With **horizontal partitioning,** some of the rows of a table (or relation) are put into a base relation at one site and other rows are put into a base relation at another site. More generally, the rows of a relation are distributed to many sites. The advantages and disadvantages of horizontal partitioning are summarized in Table 19-3. Horizontal partitioning has the advantages of greater

Figure 19-6
Customer relation for a bank

ACCT NO.	CUSTOMER NAME	BRANCH NAME	BALANCE
200	Jones	Lakeview	1000
324	Smith	Valley	250
153	Gray	Valley	38
426	Dorman	Lakeview	796
500	Green	Valley	168
683	McIntyre	Lakeview	1500
252	Elmore	Lakeview	330

TABLE 19-2 Advantages and Disadvantages of Data Replication

Advantages of Data Replication:

1. Reliability: If one of the sites containing the relation (or database) fails, a copy can always be found at another site.

2. Fast response: Each site that has a full copy can process queries locally, so queries can be processed rapidly.

Disadvantages of Data Replication:

1. Storage requirements: Each site that has a full copy must have the same storage capacity that would be required if the data were stored centrally.

2. Complexity and cost of updating: Whenever a relation is updated, it must be updated at each of the sites that holds a copy, which requires careful coordination.

processing efficiency and security but is susceptible to inconsistent data access speeds and backup vulnerability due to the need to join data from multiple sites.

An example of horizontal partitioning within the Customer relation is shown in Figure 19-7. Each row is now located at its "home" branch. If a customer, in fact, conducts most of his or her transactions at the home branch, such transactions are processed locally and response times are minimized. When a customer initiates a transaction at another branch, the transaction must be transmitted to the home branch for processing and the response transmitted back to the initiating branch (this is the normal pattern for persons using automated teller machines, or ATMs). If a customer's usage pattern changes (perhaps because of a move), the system may be able to detect this change and dynamically move the record to another location where most transactions are being initiated. Thus, horizontal partitions are usually used when an organizational function is distributed, but each site is concerned with only a subset of the entity instances (frequently based on geography).

Vertical Partitioning With the **vertical partitioning** approach, some of the columns of a relation are moved into a base relation at one of the sites while other columns are moved into a base relation at another site (more generally, columns may be moved to several sites). The relations at each of the sites must share a common key so that the original table can be reconstructed.

Vertical partitioning: Distributing the columns of a table into several separate tables.

TABLE 19-3 Advantages and Disadvantages of Horizontal Partitioning

Advantages of Horizontal Partitioning:

1. Efficiency: Data are stored close to where they are used and separate from other data used by other users or applications.

2. Local optimization: Data can be stored to optimize performance for local access.

3. Security: Data not relevant to usage at a particular site are not made available.

Disadvantages of Horizontal Partitioning:

1. Inconsistent access speed: When data from several partitions are required, the access time can be significantly different from local-only data access.

2. Backup vulnerability: Since data are not replicated, when data at one site become inaccessible or damaged, usage cannot switch to another site where a copy exists; data may be lost if proper backup is not performed at each site.

Figure 19-7
Horizontal partitions

ACCT NO.	CUSTOMER NAME	BRANCH NAME	BALANCE
200	Jones	Lakeview	1000
426	Dorman	Lakeview	796
683	McIntyre	Lakeview	1500
252	Elmore	Lakeview	330
(a) Lakeview Branch			

ACCT NO.	CUSTOMER NAME	BRANCH NAME	BALANCE
324	Smith	Valley	250
153	Gray	Valley	38
500	Green	Valley	168
(b) Valley Branch			

To illustrate vertical partitioning, we use an application for a manufacturing company. A Part relation with PART NO. as the primary key is shown in Figure 19-8. Some of these data are used primarily by manufacturing while others are used mostly by engineering. The data are distributed to the respective departmental computers using vertical partitioning, as shown in Figure 19-9. Each of the partitions shown in Figure 19-9 is obtained by taking selected columns of the original relation. The original relation in turn can be obtained by joining the partitions into a single table.

Combinations for Data Distribution To complicate matters further, there are almost unlimited combinations of the preceding strategies. Some data may be stored centrally while other data are replicated at the various sites. Also, for a given relation, both horizontal and vertical partitions may be desirable for data distribution. Figure 19-10 is an example of a combination strategy which shows the following:

1. Engineering parts, Accounting, and Customer data are each centralized at different locations.

2. Standard parts data is partitioned horizontally among the three locations.

3. The Standard price list is replicated at all three locations.

The overriding principle in distributed database design as part of designing distributed applications is that data should be stored at the sites where they will be accessed most frequently. Other considerations, such as security, data integrity, and cost, are also likely to be important.

Figure 19-8
Part relation

PART NO.	NAME	COST	DRAWING NO.	QTY ON HAND
P2	Cap	100	123-7	20
P7	Lead	550	621-0	100
P3	Spring	48	174-3	0
P1	Clip	220	416-2	16
P8	Body	16	321-0	50
P9	Gripper	75	400-1	0
P6	Eraser	125	129-4	200

PART NO.	DRAWING NO.
P2	123-7
P7	621-0
P3	174-3
P1	416-2
P8	321-0
P9	400-1
P6	129-4

(a) Engineering

PART NO.	NAME	COST	QTY ON HAND
P2	Cap	100	20
P7	Lead	550	100
P3	Spring	48	0
P1	Clip	220	16
P8	Body	16	50
P9	Gripper	75	0
P6	Erase	125	200

(b) Manufacturing

Figure 19-9
Vertical partitioning of Part relation

Distributed systems, because they permit multiple users to concurrently use data, raise special issues on data integrity controls. With concurrent processing involving updates, a database without **concurrency control** will be compromised. Concurrency controls refer to techniques that prevent loss of data integrity due to interference between users in a multi-user environment. There are many techniques that database administrators can utilize to enforce concurrency control. Since this topic involves issues beyond general system design, the interested reader is encouraged to see McFadden, Hoffer, and Prescott, (1999) for a detailed discussion of concurrency control techniques and related issues.

Concurrency control:
A method for preventing loss of data integrity due to interference between users in a multi-user environment.

Figure 19-10
Data distribution strategies

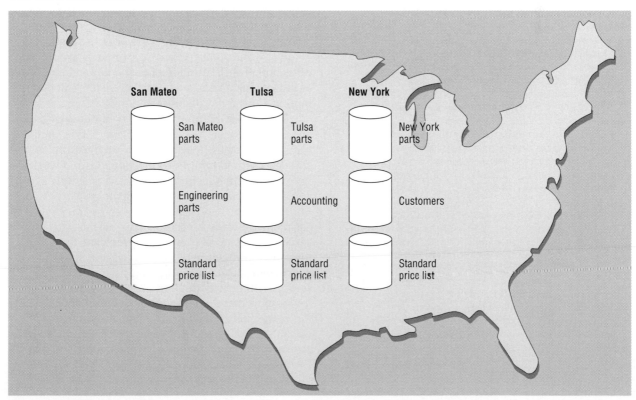

ALTERNATIVE DESIGNS FOR DISTRIBUTED SYSTEMS

A clear trend in physical systems design is to move away from central mainframe systems and stand-alone PC applications to some form of system that distributes data and processing across multiple computers. Figure 19-11 represents these trends, including the trend that simple file server use has flattened or slightly declined in recent years. The excerpt in the box "Can a Client/Server Environment Replace a Mainframe?" characterizes what many organizations are attempting to do and the success of these efforts with existing technology.

One result of this increased interest in distributing system functions is that new forms of distributed processing are being developed, increasing your choices as a systems analyst for the design of new systems. In this section, we briefly review the major differences between two common types of network computing environments introduced earlier, file servers and database servers. In the following section, we discuss the trade-offs among newer ways to separate processing between clients and servers that are giving you greater options. Remember, development tools, such as CASE environments, are still relatively immature in generating code for systems in the wide variety of distributed processing options available to you, so be prepared to have significant portions of systems coded by hand if you choose some of the more advanced options.

Choosing Between File Server and Client/Server Architectures

Both file server and client/server architectures use personal computers and workstations and are interconnected using a LAN. Yet, a file server architecture is very different from a client/server architecture. A file server architecture supports only the distribution of data whereas the client/server architecture supports both the distribution of data and the distribution of processing. This is an important distinction that has ramifications for systems design.

Table 19-4 summarizes some of the key differences between file server and client/server architectures. Specifically, a file server architecture is the simplest method for interconnecting PCs and workstations. In this architecture, the file server simply acts as a shared storage device for all clients on the network. Entire programs and databases must be transferred to each client when accessed. This means that a file server architecture is most appropriate for applications that are relatively small in size with little or no concurrent data access by multiple users. The file server architecture has been found to be very effective for systems that do not require the simultaneous sharing of the same data and when the size of the applications "served" to workstations are relatively small in size and infrequently used. For example, numerous LAN-based electronic mail packages run exceptionally well in a file server environment.

Can a Client/Server Environment Replace a Mainframe?

Chase Manhattan Bank conducted a test for the possible conversion of a mainframe decision support application, the Affluent Database, to a Sybase SQL Server Unix application. This database contains 3 gigabytes of storage, with data on two million customers, 2.9 million accounts, and 1.6 million households. The server in the test was a Sun SPARC Server 10. Clients were AT&T Global Information Solution PCs, some running DOS and some running OS/2. Microsoft Access®, QBE Vision® from Coromandel Industries, and Lotus Approach® were chosen as the GUI front ends. Data were transferred from the IBM DB2 mainframe database using Platinum Technology's Platinum Migration Utility. A side-by-side comparison was done of identical queries running on the previous mainframe and the new client/server systems. Queries in the client/server environment were tuned to achieve the greatest possible performance, given that the existing mainframe application had already been similarly tuned. The results showed that simple queries and on-line transactions processed equally as quickly on the server as on the mainframe, but that complex queries took much longer in the client/server. Part of this can be explained by the newness of the technology. The front-end and server software are not as mature, and have not been optimized over repeated updates as has the mainframe software. Also, more problems arose in the client/server environment, in part because of the difficulties of getting software from multiple vendors to work smoothly together. The test showed that the migration of a DSS from a mainframe to a client/server environment was possible, but that performance is less predictable and reliable in a client/server environment.

(Adapted from Rideout, 1994)

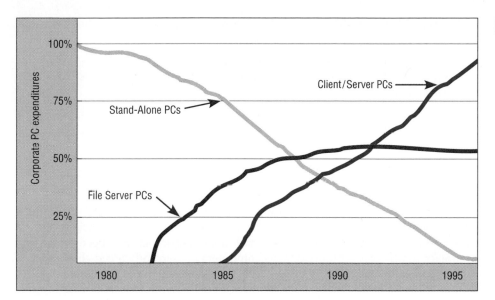

Figure 19-11
Trends in distributed systems

Alternatively, a client/server architecture overcomes many of the limitations of the file server architecture since both client and server share the processing workload of a task and only transfer needed information. This characteristic has resulted in having many organizations migrate very large applications with extensive data sharing requirements to client/server environments. In fact, client/server computing has become the workhorse architecture for many organizations where multiple clients are likely to be concurrently working with the same data. Also, if the systems and databases are relatively large in size, the client/server architecture is preferred because of the client and server's ability to distribute the work and to transfer only needed information (e.g., only a record if that is all that is needed rather than an entire database as in a file server environment).

Advanced Forms of Client/Server Architectures

The client/server vendors are evolving into architectures that represent variations in the way different application system functions are distributed between client

TABLE 19-4   Several Differences between File Server and Client/Server Architectures

Characteristic	File Server	Client/Server
Processing	Client only	Both client and server
Concurrent Data Access	Low—managed by each client	High—managed by server
Network Usage	Large file and data transfers	Efficient data transfers
Database Security and Integrity	Low—managed by each client	High—managed by server
Software Maintenance	Low—software changes just on server	Mixed—some new parts must be delivered to each client
Hardware and System Software Flexibility	Client and server decoupled and can be mixed	Need for greater coordination between client and server

and server computers. These variations are based on the concept that there are three general components to any information system:

1. *Data management:* These functions manage all interaction between software and files and databases, including data retrieval/querying, updating, security, concurrency control, and recovery.

2. *Data presentation:* These functions manage just the interface between system users and the software, including the display and printing of forms and reports and possibly validating system inputs.

3. *Data analysis:* These functions transform inputs into outputs, including simple summarization to complex mathematical modeling like regression analysis.

Different client/server architectures distribute, or partition, each of these functions to one or both of the client or server computers, and more increasingly, into a third computer referred to as the **application server.** In fact, it is becoming commonplace to use three or more distinct computers in many advanced client/server architectures (see Askren, 1996; Kara, 1997). This evolution in client/server computing has resulted in two new terms, **three-tiered client/server** and **middleware,** to represent this evolution. Three-tiered client/server combines three logical and distinct applications—data management, presentation, and analysis—into a single information system application. Middleware brings together distinct hardware, software, and communication technologies in order to create a three-tiered client/server environment.

A typical use of middleware is shown in Figure 19-12. This figure shows how client applications can access databases on database servers. Open DataBase Con-

Application server:
A computing server where data analysis functions primarily reside.

Three-tiered client/server:
Advanced client/server architectures in which there are three logical and distinct applications—data management, presentation, and analysis—which are combined to create a single information system.

Middleware: A combination of hardware, software, and communication technologies that bring together data management, presentation, and analysis into a three-tiered client/server environment.

Figure 19-12
ODBC middleware environment

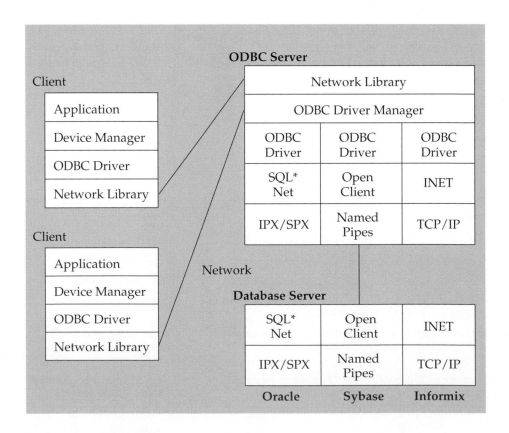

nectivity (ODBC) is a Microsoft standard for database middleware. ODBC drivers, residing on both client and server computers, allow, for example, an Access query to retrieve data stored in an Oracle database as if they were in an Access database. By referring to a different ODBC driver, the Access database could reference data in an Informix database using the same query.

There are three primary reasons for creating three-tiered client/server architectures (Stevens, 1996). First, applications can be partitioned in a way that best fits the organizational computing needs. For example, in a traditional two-tiered client/server system, the application (data analysis) resides on the client, which would access information like customer data from a database server. In a three-tiered architecture, data analysis can reside on a powerful application server, resulting in substantially faster response times for users. In addition, a three-tiered architecture provides greater flexibility by allowing the partitioning of applications in different ways for different users in order to optimize performance. For example, the New York State Department of Motor Vehicles has a licensing and vehicle-registering system that uses a three-tiered architecture across its 120 branch offices. The larger of these offices have their own application servers while the smaller branches, in groups of three or four, dial into a shared application server. According to Jeff Deal, computer analyst at the New York State Department of Motor Vehicles, the time to complete a transaction has dropped from about 30 seconds to 2 or 3 seconds (Stevens, 1996)!

A second advantage of three-tiered architecture is that since most or all of the data analysis is contained in the application server, making global changes or customizing processes for individual users is relatively easy. This allows developers to easily create custom versions of large-scale systems without creating a completely separate system. Finally, because the data analysis is separate from the user interface, it is a lot easier to change one or both without having a major maintenance effort. By separating the data analysis from the data presentation (the user interface), either can be changed independently without affecting the other—greatly simplifying system maintenance. The combinations of these three benefits—application partitioning, easier customization, and easier maintenance—are driving many organizations to adopt this powerful alternative to standard client/server computing.

Given the flexibility of placing data management, presentation, and analysis on two or more separate machines, there are countless possible architectures. In practice, however, only six possible configurations have emerged (see Figure 19-13). Technology exists to allow you to develop an application using any of these six architectures; although automated development tools do not yet have equal code-generation capabilities for each.

Distributed Presentation   The distributed presentation form of client/server (Figure 19-13a) is used to freshen up the delivery of existing server-based applications to distributed clients. Often the server is a mainframe, and the existing mainframe code is not changed. Without the client presentation support, users must interact directly with mainframe programs, often using character-based interfaces and whatever response time the server supports. In this client/server architecture, technologies called "screen scrappers" work on the client machines to simply reformat the same data handled by the server forms and reports. The result is more appealing and has easier-to-use interfaces without destroying or having to rewrite legacy systems. Network traffic is limited to transmitting data only on the forms and reports. Distributed presentation is limited to the functionality of existing forms and reports and, when these change, the presentation modules on both the clients and server must change, so there is double maintenance. Thus, this approach may be very costly if the user interface designs frequently change. Client

Figure 19-13
Types of client/server
architectures

(a) Distributed presentation

FUNCTION	CLIENT	SERVER
Data management		All data management
Data analysis		All data analysis
Data presentation	Data for presentation on server are reformatted for presentation to user	Data delivered to client using server presentation technologies

(b) Remote presentation

FUNCTION	CLIENT	SERVER
Data management		All data management
Data analysis		All data analysis
Data presentation	Data from analysis on server are formatted for presentation to user	

(c) Remote data
management

FUNCTION	CLIENT	SERVER
Data management		All data management
Data analysis	Raw data from server are retrieved and analyzed	
Data presentation	All data presentation	

environments (e.g., Microsoft Windows, Apple, and UNIX X-Windows) can be mixed, which may open access to mainframe data to a wider group of users.

Remote Presentation   The remote presentation style of client/server architecture (Figure 19-13b) places all data presentation functions on the client machine so that software on the client has total responsibility for formatting data. This architecture gives you greater flexibility compared to the distributed presentation style since the presentation on the client will not be constrained by having to be compatible with that on the server. There will be less maintenance since only software on the client needs to change when users want forms and reports to be reorganized or new content added. There may be more network traffic than with distributed presentation since the client must extensively interact with the server to receive all the needed data.

Remote Data Management   The remote data management form of client/server architecture (Figure 19-13c) places all software on the client except for the data management functions. This form is the closest to what we have called client/server earlier in the chapter. Network traffic is higher than in the previous two options since all data needed for analysis, not just for presentation, must be transferred to clients. However, you now have the flexibility to use any software, like PC-based spreadsheets, for analysis. Further, the analysis processing is done on the less expensive client machine. The database is still shared but centrally controlled, which is simpler than some of the subsequent architectures we will discuss. If you want to change the analysis code, you have to make sure that each copy is changed. A

FUNCTION	CLIENT	SERVER
Data management		All data management
Data analysis	Selective data from server retrieved and analyzed	Selective data from server retrieved and analyzed, then transmitted to client
Data presentation	All data presentation, from analyses on both server and client	

Figure 19-13 (continued) Types of client/server architectures

(d) Distributed function

FUNCTION	CLIENT	SERVER
Data management	Local data management	Shared management of data on server
Data analysis	Data retrieved from both client and server for analysis	
Data presentation	All data presentation	

(e) Distributed database

FUNCTION	CLIENT	SERVER
Data management	Local data management	Shared management of data on server
Data analysis	Data retrieved from both client and server for analysis	Data retrieved from server for analysis, then sent to client for further analysis and presentation
Data presentation	All data presentation	

(f) Distributed processing

mixed client environment may be more difficult to support than in the previous architectures since you must learn multiple analysis programming environments, not just those for presentation tools.

Distributed Function   The distributed function client/server architecture (Figure 19-13d) splits analysis functions between the client and server, leaving all presentation on the client and all data management on the server. This architecture allows analysis to be located on the most cost-efficient machine; for example, analysis that requires superior numerical calculations can be done on the server, which might be a supercomputer. Also, analysis functions that require extensive data access can be located on the server in order to reduce network traffic. This is a very difficult environment in which to develop, test, and maintain software due to the potential for considerable coordination between analysis functions on both client and server.

Distributed Database   The distributed database client/server architecture (Figure 19-13e) places all functionality on the client, except data storage and management which is divided between client and server. Technologies like Microsoft Access on a client running ODBC middleware into an Oracle or Sybase server support this client/server architecture. In this case, data can be located at an optimal site but, given today's technologies, usually only the data on the server is shared across all clients. Client programs can mix calls to local and server data, possibly even within the same query. Concepts of vertical and horizontal partitioning of data can be used to decide what data to locate on each client or on the server. Although possible today, this is a very unstable architecture since it requires considerable compatibility and communication between software on the client and server, which may never have been meant to be compatible. Thus, organizations attempting to implement this architecture tend to standardize on a limited set of development tools to simplify distributed system design and implementation. Also, a decision to locate data on a client may make it difficult or impossible to share this data with remote or mobile computers.

Distributed Processing   The distributed processing client/server architecture (Figure 19–13f) combines the best features of distributed function and distributed database by splitting both of these across client and server, with presentation functions under the exclusive responsibility of the client machine. This permits even greater flexibility since analysis functions and data both can be located wherever it makes the most sense. Complexity is actually less than with the distributed database architecture since analysis and database functions on the same machine can be very compatible.

As the designer of information systems, you have more choices available to you today than ever before. You must weigh the factors discussed above and outlined in Table 19-4 to determine a distributed system design that will be most beneficial to the organization. As with other physical design decisions, organizational standards may limit your choices, and you will make such application design decisions in cooperation with other system professionals. You, however, are in the best position to understand user requirements and to be able to estimate the ramifications of distributed system design decisions on response time and other factors for the user.

SUMMARY

We have covered in this chapter various issues and technologies involved in the sharing of systems and data by multiple people across space and time in distributed systems. You learned about the client/server architecture which is being used in both network personal computers and workstations (upsizing) and to replace older mainframe applications (downsizing). Components of the client/server architecture, including local area networks, database servers, application programming interfaces, and application development tools were described.

Two common types of local area network-based architectures—file server and client/server—were compared. It was shown that the newer client/server technologies have significant advantages over the older file servers. These advantages include less network traffic, greater flexibility to develop applications in convenient environments, and a more sensible distribution of queries to form a cooperative computing situation.

We saw that a distributed database is a single logical database spread across computers in multiple locations connected by a data communications network. The network must allow the users to share the data as transparently as possible. There are numerous advantages to distributed databases. The most important of these are the following: increased reliability and availability of data, local control by users over "their" data, modular (or incremental) growth, reduced communication costs, and faster response to requests for data. There are also several costs and disadvantages of distributed databases: software is more costly and complex, processing overhead often increases, maintaining data integrity is often more difficult, and if data is not distributed properly, response to requests for data may be very slow. Both the advantages and disadvantages should be weighed by an organization that is considering distributed database management.

There are several options for distributing data in a network: data replication, horizontal partitioning, vertical partitioning, and combinations of these approaches. With data replication, a separate copy of the database (or part of the database) is stored at each of two or more sites. Data replication can result in improved reliability and faster response; however, additional storage capacity is required and it may be difficult to keep the data updated at each of the sites. With horizontal partitioning, some of the rows of a relation are placed at one site while other rows are placed in a relation at another site (or several sites). On the other hand, with vertical partitioning, the columns of a relation are distributed among different sites. The objectives of data partitioning include improved performance and security.

We also outlined in this chapter the evolution of distributed systems and three-tiered client/server technologies that are giving you more options for distributed system design. These client/server architectures—distributed presentation, remote presentation, remote data management, distributed function, distributed database, and distributed processing—are supported by some CASE tool code generators, but CASE tool support may be limited. Thus, the decision to use very sophisticated distributed processing environments must consider the potential for considerable human support for both programming and training as well as the availability of middleware to allow software and hardware on each tier to interact.

We did not have the space in this chapter to address several additional issues concerning distributed systems. Many of these issues are handled by other systems professionals, such as database administrators, telecommunications experts, and computer security specialists. Systems analysts must work closely with other professionals to build sound distributed systems.

KEY TERMS

Application program interface (API)	Concurrency control	Local area network (LAN)
Application server	Database engine	Location transparency
Client	Distributed database	Middleware
Client/server architecture	File server	Three-tiered client/server
	Horizontal partitioning	Vertical partitioning

REVIEW QUESTIONS

1. Define each of the following terms:
   a. application program interface (API)
   b. application server
   c. client
   d. client/server architecture
   e. concurrency control
   f. database engine
   g. distributed database
   h. file server
   i. horizontal partitioning
   j. location transparency
   k. middleware
   l. three-tiered client/server

2. Contrast the following terms.
   a. file server, client/server architecture, local area network
   b. horizontal partitioning, vertical partitioning, data replication
   c. distributed database, database engine
   d. data management, data analysis, data presentation
3. Describe the limitations of a file server architecture.
4. Describe the advantages of a client/server architecture.
5. Explain the relative advantages and disadvantages of distributed databases.
6. What are the advantages and disadvantages of replicated databases?
7. What are the advantages and disadvantages of partitioned databases?
8. What are the major advantages and issues of the client/server architecture?
9. Summarize the six possible architectures for client/server systems.
10. Summarize the reasons for a three-tiered client/server architecture.
11. Explain the role of middleware in client/server computing.

PROBLEMS AND EXERCISES

1. Match each of the following terms with the most appropriate definition:

   _____ file server   a. rows of a table are distributed to nodes
   _____ concurrency control   b. user is unaware that data are distributed to several nodes
   _____ horizontal partition   c. technique used to prevent data integrity errors
   _____ location transparency d. one logical database allocated to several physical nodes
   _____ distributed database   e. allows PCs to share data and resources on a LAN

2. Under what circumstances would you recommend that a file server approach, as opposed to a client/server approach, be used for a distributed information system application? What warnings would you give the prospective user for this file server approach? What factors would have to change for you to recommend the move to a client/server approach?

3. A supplier of water pumps and filtration systems has one warehouse and sales outlets in several towns in the region. The warehouse is used strictly to store the various products and ship them to the sales outlets in predetermined monthly deliveries and upon specialized requests. In response to the owners' wish to employ a distributed database, recommend one of the options discussed in this chapter (e.g., data replication, horizontal or vertical partitioning, combination) and provide your rationale.

4. A bank has one main office and five branch office locations. Design a series of database tables that employ data replication, horizontal, and/or vertical partitioning for sharing data between the main office and branches. Define at least 10 separate data attributes for these tables. Provide a definition for your attributes that describes their meaning and list all assumptions about the bank and your data to help clarify your design.

5. Develop a table that summarizes the comparative capabilities of the six client/server architectures. You might start with Table 19-4 for some ideas.

6. Suppose you are responsible for the design of a new order entry and sales analysis system for a national chain of auto part stores. Each store has a PC that supports office functions. The company also has regional managers who travel from store to store working with the local managers to promote sales. There are four national offices for the regional managers, who each spend about one day a week in their office and four on the road. Stores place orders to replenish stock on a daily basis, based on sales history and inventory levels. The company uses high-speed dial-in lines and modems to attach store PCs into the company's main computer. Each regional manager has a laptop computer with a modem and a network connection for times when the manager is in the office. Would you recommend a client/server distributed system for this company and, if so, which architecture would you recommend? Why?

7. The Internet is a network of networks. Using the terminology of this chapter, what type of distributed network architecture is used on the Internet?

8. Suppose you were designing applications for a standard file server environment. One issue discussed in the chapter for this distributed processing environment is that the application software on each client PC must share in the responsibilities for data management. One data management problem that can arise is that applications running concurrently on two clients may want to update the same data at the same time. What could you do to manage this potential conflict? Is there any way this conflict might result in both PCs making no progress (in other words, going into an infinite loop)? How might you avoid such problems?

9. An extension of the three-tiered client/server architecture is the n-tiered architecture, in which there are many specialized application servers. Extend the reasons for the three-tiered architecture to an n-tiered architecture.

10. You read in this chapter about the advantages of client/server architecture. What operational and management problems can client/server create? Considering both the advantages and disadvantages of client/server, suggest the characteristics of an application that could be implemented in a client/server architecture.

11. Obtain access to a typical PC database management system, such as Microsoft Access. What steps do you have to follow to link an Access database to a database on a server? Do any of these steps change depending on the database management system on the server?

FIELD EXERCISES

1. Visit an organization that has installed a local area network (LAN). Explore the following questions:
   a. Inventory all application programs that are delivered to client PCs using a file server architecture. How many users use each application? What are their professional and technical skills? What business processes are supported by the application? What data are created, read, updated, or destroyed in each application? Could the same business processes be performed without using technology? If so, how? If not, why not?
   b. Inventory all application programs that are delivered to client PCs using a client/server architecture. How many users use each application? What are their professional and technical skills? What business processes are supported by the application? What data are created, read, updated, or destroyed in each application? Could the same business processes be performed without using technology? If so, how? If not, why not?

2. Visit an organization that has installed a distributed database. Explore the following questions:

   a. Is this truly a distributed database? If so, how are the data distributed: replication, horizontal partitioning, vertical partitioning?
   b. What commercial distributed DBMS software products are used? What are the advantages, disadvantages, and problems with this system?
   c. To what extent does this system provide location transparency?
   d. What are the organization's plans for future evolution of this system?

3. Scan the literature and determine the various local area network operating systems available. Describe the relative strengths and weaknesses of these systems. Do these systems seem to be adequate for distributed information system needs in organizations? Why or why not? Determine the current sales volume and approximate market shares for these systems. Why are they selling so well?

4. In this chapter file servers were described as one way of providing information to users of a distributed information system. What file servers are available and what are their relative strengths and weaknesses and costs? What other types of servers are available and/or for what other uses are file servers employed (e.g., print servers)?

5. Examine the capabilities of a client/server API environment. List and describe the types of client-based operations that you can perform with the API. List and describe the types of server-based operations that you can perform with the API. How are these operations the same/different?

REFERENCES

Askren, S. 1996. "Building Multi-Tier Apps Is About To Get Easier." *Client/Server Computing,* April: 61–64.

Kara, D. 1997. "Why Partition?" *Application Development Trends,* May: 38–46.

McFadden, F. R., J. A. Hoffer, and M.B. Prescott. 1999. *Modern Database Management,* 5th ed. Reading, MA: Addison Wesley Longman.

Radding, A. 1992. "DBAs Find Tools Gap in C/S." *Software Magazine.* Client/Server Special Section 12 (16) (November), 33–38.

Rideout, R. 1994. "Banking on Client/Server." *DBMS* 7(9) (August): 57–62.

Stevens, L. 1996. "Consider Three-Tier Client/Server." *Datamation,* February 15: 61–64.

Data Privacy Within CATS

INTRODUCTION

In a recent interview with *Video Entrepreneur Magazine*, Nigel Broad, chairman of BEC, described his road to success through the creation of his video and music empire. He stressed BEC's ability to be more innovative than their competition as their major competitive advantage. This spurred the interviewer to ask Nigel for an example of an innovative project that was currently underway at BEC so that she could provide the reader with an example of such leading-edge thinking. After pausing a moment to collect his thoughts, Nigel described the Customer Activity Tracking System (CATS).

DATA PRIVACY ISSUES ARISE

During this exchange Nigel explained, "CATS will allow us to really understand and, consequently, serve our customers. We will know what they like and don't like. Although such information on general consumer buying patterns has been readily available for years, CATS will be the first such system for home entertainment." He continued, "With appropriate modeling and analysis, we will be able to very accurately predict the likelihood of a given customer to purchase or rent a specific movie, music CD or cassette, or video game. This will ensure that we have in stock exactly what people want when they enter our stores. Again, we will have this for *each* customer, not just an aggregate view of the overall patterns at a particular store. This will be very powerful information for our marketing people. To take this a bit further, we could combine the CATS data with general consumer buying information on a particular customer and be able to construct a very accurate understanding of each customer. We will know what they drive, where they live, what they eat, how much they earn, and, most importantly for our business, what they like to do with their leisure time."

The interviewer found this to be a very interesting development in the conversation so she followed up the description of CATS with a few questions. "Mr. Broad, could you discuss some of the ethical ramifications of constructing such profiles you have considered and the steps BEC is going to follow to assure the accuracy of this data and to protect the privacy of your customers?"

Nigel was lucky that this was a phone interview, due to the crimson tint his face took on while listening to the interviewer's question. This topic was not something he, nor to his knowledge anyone at BEC, had yet considered. Caught off guard, Nigel took a moment before answering. He began by first assuring the interviewer that BEC had a fundamental obligation to protect the privacy of their customers and that federal laws prohibited tracking the actual movie titles rented by each customer. He continued, "CATS is being created only to provide better service to our customers. In no way will we invade the privacy of anyone. Precautions will be taken to assure information validity. Additionally, each customer's profile will be guarded like the 'Crown Jewels'."

After the interview, Nigel felt a bit uneasy, not really knowing what was being done to assure data validity and to protect the privacy of individuals. But, he believed what he had told the interviewer; BEC *did* have an obligation to protect the privacy of their customers. To follow through on his belief, his next action was to contact Karen Gardner, director of MIS.

"Karen, I have been thinking about CATS," Nigel began. "How are we going to protect the privacy of each individual's profile from falling into the wrong hands? I mean, analyzing a customer's long-term buying patterns is going to be very revealing about how a given customer spends his or her leisure time. I understand that this is exactly why we want CATS, and what we need it to do, but are we taking adequate steps to protect the privacy of each individual?"

Karen responded, "Nigel, your questions are certainly good ones. In fact, Dwight Ford, our legal

TABLE 1 Data Privacy Questions Regarding Customer Profiles

1. Can the details of individual customer profiles be viewed or can data only be viewed in aggregate?

2. Who can access customer profile information? Do we need security access levels for viewing less aggregate data as we do in personnel databases?

3. What security mechanisms should be followed to secure the customer profile information?

4. Can customers view their profiles and, if so, what mechanisms should be followed to allow customers to access, validate, or even modify their data?

5. Does BEC have an obligation to tell customers that a profile has been created on them?

6. Should BEC combine CATS data with other consumer databases (such as shopping data or even driver's license data) to get a more detailed and revealing profile of customers?

7. Should BEC sell customer profile data to other companies and, if so, in what form should the data be made available? Should customers be informed about this?

counsel, raised a similar query when we initially reviewed the CATS proposal. What I've discovered is that most BEC information systems employees are members of one of the industry's professional societies. As a member, you are asked to follow a code of ethics that includes protecting the privacy of others [see Figure 2-10 for the code of ethics for one such society]. However, other than that, we haven't talked about securing the contents of customer profiles beyond normal security mechanisms. But I think that this is an important issue. How should we proceed?"

Over the next few days, Nigel and Karen met and outlined several questions that both felt needed to be resolved before implementing CATS. Nigel intended to pose these questions to BEC managers and the Board of Directors (see Table 1). The answers to these questions would help shape how customer profiles would be accessed and secured, clearly important issues for both BEC and their customers.

SUMMARY

Strong customer relationships begin with trust, and Nigel Broad believes that trust is fundamental to BEC's continued growth. Furthermore, Nigel feels a social responsibility to maintain the highest ethical standards in the face of intense competition. Confronting ethical issues is relatively new in the systems development field, and BEC has little experience to draw on to decide how to handle consumer data privacy in CATS. The questions in Table 1 are only a start at clarifying the obligation BEC has for protecting the rights of customers, employees, suppliers, and other stakeholders.

Implementation and Maintenance

Albertson's, Inc.

Organizational and Human Issues in the Implementation of Business Reengineering

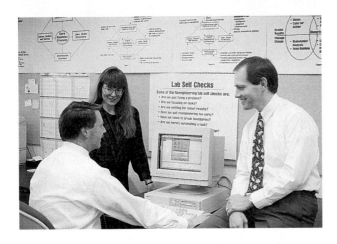

Albertson's, Inc., is one of the largest retail food and drug chains with well over 900 retail stores in 22 states throughout the west, midwest, and southern United States. For an organization as large as Albertson's, operating effectively and efficiently is not a trivial task. To be more productive, they develop information systems that satisfy real user needs, solve real problems, and support business processes well.

As have other forward-thinking organizations, Albertson's realized that their information systems solutions were too frequently only incremental changes to current business processes. They wanted to help systems development people and users stop thinking about their work in traditional, routine ways. They wanted to have employees be able to step back from their work, critically analyze it, and figure out how to do it better, even if it meant doing it in dramatically differ-ent ways. They decided to learn more about business process reengineering by visiting other organizations. Albertson's management has adapted some of the reengineering techniques they saw and launched their own reengineering efforts, but in a unique way.

Albertson's houses their reengineering effort in specially created meeting rooms called "labs." These labs are equipped with PCs and printers connected to the organization's network, electronic whiteboards, conference tables and chairs; the walls are nearly covered with regular whiteboards. There are currently six different labs in a variety of sizes. One lab is a spacious 22' × 22', though there are other smaller labs.

Albertson's brings together in a lab a core group of two to six relevant stakeholders for a particular project, including systems developers, users, and managers, and dedicates them to the project for anywhere from four to eight weeks. This is their only task and their primary place of work; they must temporarily reassign their normal duties to other employees. Albertson's commonly brings in additional members to the teams as they are needed. The teams use various methodologies such as interviewing, Joint Application Design, and group problem-solving techniques to elicit information and solve problems.

Albertson's believes that a key ingredient of the lab approach is bringing together the key people for a project, even if it means bringing in people direct from the retail stores, a district manager, a foreman, or a store manager. Once in the lab, hierarchy, job titles, and status are abandoned as the team slowly breaks down hierarchical and discipline-based barriers and builds camaraderie and trust. In addition, they are free from distractions and interruptions in the lab.

The physical and structural changes resulting from the lab approach lead to psychological changes in the participants. The lab approach helps them to achieve their goals, to develop real solutions to real problems, to think outside the box, and to imagine, if they could do anything to solve their particular problem or improve their particular process, what they could do.

During Albertson's first lab, senior managers addressed the fundamental strategic question, "What should the company really be doing and where should it really be heading?" They critically analyzed the Hammer and Champy book, *Reengineering the Corporation,* and applied it to their company. In this trial experience with the lab they learned a lot about the company and how to refine and best use the lab approach. It worked so well and was liked so much that they quickly built more labs and applied the approach to other problems.

Hadley Wagner, vice president of Information Systems, says that as a result of using the lab approach, they are now much closer to providing real solutions to real problems than they were before using the labs. He admits that, like so many other companies, they were simply "automating" traditional business processes when building information systems. He adds that they now garner much higher levels of commitment to new systems by users and managers because they are now very heavily involved and invested in the process of designing and building the new system and enhancing the business process.

Craig Olsen, senior vice president and chief financial officer, says that the return on investment in the labs is huge. First, the investment in the labs themselves is minuscule. Then considering the salaries of a half dozen people working for two to three months and adding in their travel expenses, the total investment is still relatively small. Further, this investment is far outweighed by the savings and revenue from the solutions that teams generate and implement. For example, one team determined a much more cost-effective way to transfer goods to stores. This also will ultimately result in better service, better product, improved customer satisfaction, and increased revenue. Surprisingly, teams frequently hit home runs like this. In Olsen's mind there is no question about the payback on the labs.

The labs do have some potential challenges. It is difficult to break down the barriers between people and build trust among the team members. In addition, because the participants are so motivated, there are differences of opinion and even arguments at times. Participants can also become frustrated when the rest of the organization cannot move as quickly and easily as the team would like it to. To address these and other concerns, Albertson's will temporarily bring into a new team a person from a previous team who will serve as a mentor. An additional potential challenge is that there often are some language differences among people from different levels and functional areas within the organization. As a result, part of the methodology is to build a project term dictionary. This helps everyone to better interpret and understand each other.

Albertson's learns more about the labs and improves the process with each new team. Given their success thus far, they plan to build more labs in other locations and to apply the lab approach to other types of business problems and processes. They like what the labs have helped them to do thus far and they want to empower even more employees to develop real solutions to solve real problems, to break out of tradition and incremental change, and to effect revolutionary, purposeful, strategic change.

An Overview of Part VI

Implementation and Maintenance

Implementation and maintenance are the last two phases of the systems development life cycle. The end of implementation typically brings your responsibilities for a system to a close, but others will continue to work with the system to support and maintain it until it is replaced by another system. The purpose of implementation is to build a properly working system and to install it in the organization, replacing old systems and work methods. Implementation also includes finalizing all system and user documentation, thoroughly training users and others to effectively use the new system, and preparing support systems to assist users as they encounter difficulties. The purpose of maintenance is to fix and enhance the system to respond to problems and changing business conditions. Maintenance work also includes activities from all systems development phases and usually eventually leads to a decision to abandon a system and build a replacement, starting the cycle over again.

As depicted in Figure 1, implementation includes the following phases:

- *Writing computer software*—for a systems analyst, this may mean actually writing code or monitoring coding done by programmers to ensure that programs meet design specifications

- *Testing software*—involves using test data and scenarios to verify that each component and the whole system work under normal and abnormal circumstances

- *Converting from the old to the new system*—includes not only installing the new system in organizational sites but also dealing with personal and organizational resistance to the change that the new system causes

- *Documenting the system*—includes reviewing all project dictionary or CASE repository entries for completeness as well as finalizing all user documentation, such as user guides, reference cards, and tutorials

- *Training users and others*—may include a variety of human and computer-assisted sessions as well as tools to explain the purpose and use of the system

- *Designing support procedures*—ensures that users can obtain the assistance they need as questions and problems arise

Implementation also includes the close-down of the project, including evaluating personnel, reassigning staff, assessing the success of the project, and turning all resources over to those who will support and maintain the system. Thus,

Figure 1
Steps in implementation

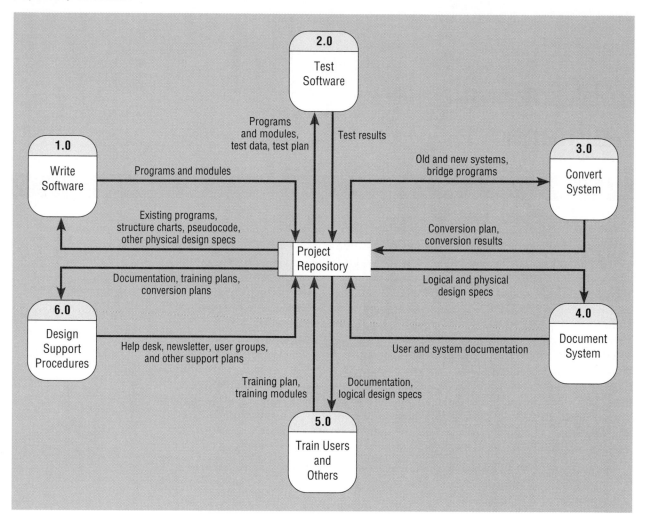

implementation is tightly linked to the next phase—maintenance—which is why we combine these two phases into one section of the book.

As depicted in Figure 2, maintenance includes the following procedures:

- *Responding to requests to change the system*—The backlog of change requests must be prioritized and assigned to maintenance staff and then grouped into batches of work for each new release of the system, a step similar to the project identification and selection phase of the SDLC.

- *Transforming requests into changes*—Assessing if the change can technically be made and, if so, how the change will affect the existing system and determining what work must be done to make the requested changes, a step similar to the project initiation and analysis phases.

- *Designing the changes*—May include activities such as those found in logical and physical design phases.

- *Implementing changes*—Rewriting code, documentation, training plans, and so forth, similar to the work done during the implementation phase.

Figure 2
Steps in maintenance

Maintenance is tightly linked to all phases of the SDLC since it draws upon and adds to information about system requirements, design, and implementation. In fact, maintenance projects are small systems development projects. Maintenance must also keep all documentation, including the CASE repository, up-to-date so that any version of the system can be reconstructed at any time.

We address the variety of work done during system implementation in Chapter 20. Here you will learn about your role in coding a system. Since other courses in your curriculum likely address the skills required in coding, Chapter 20 concentrates on the management of coding, in which you as an analyst will be directly involved. You will learn about testing systems and system components and methods to ensure and measure software quality. As you know from your own programming experience, coding must be tested. Your role as a systems analyst is to develop a plan for testing, which includes developing all the test data required to exercise every part of the system. You start developing the test plan early in the project, usually during analysis, since testing requirements are highly related to system functional requirements. The testing plan you design will usually follow a bottom-up approach, beginning with small modules, followed by extensive testing by the programming group, beta testing with users, and final acceptance testing. A complete history of test data and runs must be kept so that future versions of the system can be compared to demonstrate that discovered problems were fixed and new features will not cause additional problems. Testing ensures the quality of software, by using measures and methods such as structured walkthroughs.

Once built, a system must be installed. For effective installation, existing data must be converted and you must follow a process to "unplug" the existing system and "plug in" the new system. In Chapter 20, we review four popular conversion strategies you can employ and adapt: direct, parallel, single location (pilot), and phased. The comparative advantages and disadvantages of each are discussed so that you can gain insight into the selection of the most appropriate or hybrid strategy for a given system.

Installing a new system involves more than making technical changes to computer systems. Information systems include the people who supply and consume data and information as well as those interested in the organizational units supported by the system. Thus, managing installation involves managing organizational changes as much as it does technical changes. We review several frameworks you can use to anticipate and control human and organizational resistance to change. You will learn about factors such as organizational politics that can affect the successful implementation of a new system.

Chapter 20 contains information on other implementation activities: documenting the system, training, and supporting users. Documentation is extensive for any system. You have already been developing most of the system documentation needed by system maintenance staff by keeping a thorough project workbook or CASE repository. You now need to finalize user documentation: a user's guide, release description, system administrator's guide, and reference manuals. In Chapter 20, you will see a generic outline for a user's guide as well as a wide range of guidelines you can use to develop high-quality user documentation. Remember, documentation is part of the system and it, too, must be tested for completeness, accuracy, and readability.

While documentation is being finalized, user support activities also need to be designed and implemented. First, you must develop a training plan. You may choose to conduct training face-to-face, via computer-based tutorials, or through vendors. New electronic performance support systems are becoming a popular way of delivering on-demand training, and Chapter 20 discusses this and other training methods. Increasingly, training is available from various sources over the Internet or over corporate intranets. Once trained, however, users will still encounter difficulties. So, ongoing support from help desks, newsletters, user groups, on-line bulletin boards, and other mechanisms must be designed, tested, and implemented. You will likely be responsible for designing these support elements, or at least assessing whether such elements exist. You may have to train central information or data center staff on how to handle user questions, how to back up files, and how to recover the system in case of failure. Putting system support operations in place can involve considerable coordination with other system professionals. We conclude Chapter 20 with a brief review of project close-down activities, since the end of implementation means the end of the project.

The end of the project does not mean that work on the system ceases. In fact, the work is only beginning. Today, as much as 80 percent of the life cycle cost of a system occurs after implementation. Because systems can operate for so long and must be constantly updated to correct flaws and changed to work with new technologies and to meet new business conditions and regulations, systems maintenance is a major part of the total systems analysis and design process. In Chapter 21, the last chapter, you will learn about your role in systems maintenance.

There are four kinds of maintenance: corrective, adaptive, perfective, and preventive. You can help control the potentially monumental maintenance cost for a system by making systems maintainable. Various factors affect the maintainability of a system, most of which you can influence, such as the number of defects, the number and skill of users, the quality of documentation, and software structure.

You may also be involved in establishing a maintenance group for a system. You will learn about different organizational structures for maintenance personnel and the reasons for each. You will also learn how to measure maintenance effectiveness, fundamental to controlling the cost and quality of maintenance activities. Configuration management and deciding how to handle changes are at the heart of managing maintenance. You will learn how a systems librarian keeps track of baseline software modules, checks these out to maintenance staff as required, and then how the librarian rebuilds systems. CASE can play a major role in managing documentation, structuring poorly designed system components, and regenerating system modules to implement changes.

Chapter 21 concludes with a discussion of a hypothetical maintenance situation with the Purchasing Fulfillment System at Pine Valley Furniture. In this discussion you will see how a maintenance programmer/analyst applies maintenance procedures to deal with a crisis situation.

20

System Implementation

After studying this chapter, you should be able to:

■ Describe the process of coding, testing, and converting an organizational information system and outline the deliverables and outcomes of the process.

■ Prepare a test plan for an information system.

■ Apply four installation strategies: direct, parallel, single location, and phased installation.

■ List the deliverables for documenting the system and for training and supporting users.

■ Distinguish between system and user documentation and determine which types of documentation are necessary for a given information system.

■ Compare the many modes available for organizational information system training, including self-training and electronic performance support systems.

■ Discuss the issues of providing support for end users.

■ Explain why systems implementation sometimes fails.

■ Compare the factor and political models of the implementation process.

INTRODUCTION

After maintenance, the implementation phase of the systems development life cycle is the most expensive and time-consuming phase of the entire life cycle. Implementation is expensive because so many people are involved in the process; it is time-consuming because of all the work that has to be completed during implementation. Physical design specifications must be turned into working computer code, the code must be tested until most of the errors have been detected and corrected, the system must be installed, user sites must be prepared for the new system, and users must come to rely on the new system rather than the existing one to get their work done.

Implementing a new information system into an organizational context is not a mechanical process. The organizational context has been shaped and re-shaped by the people who work in the organization. The work habits, beliefs, inter-relationships, and personal goals of an organization's members all affect the implementation process. Although factors important to successful implementation have been identified, there are no sure recipes you can follow. During implementation, you must be attuned to key aspects of the organizational context, such as history, politics, and environmental demands—aspects that can contribute to implementation failures if ignored.

Here you will learn about the many activities that the implementation phase comprises. In this chapter, we discuss coding, testing, installation, documentation, user training, support for a system after it is installed, and implementation success. Our intent is not to teach you how to program and test systems—most of you have already learned about writing and testing programs in the courses you took before this one. Rather, this chapter shows you where coding and testing fit in the overall scheme of implementation and stresses the view of implementation as an organizational change process that is not always successful.

In addition, you will learn about providing documentation about the new system for the information systems personnel who will maintain the system and for the system's users. These same users must be trained to use what you have developed and installed in their workplace. Once training has ended and the system has become institutionalized, users will have questions about the system's implementation and how to use it effectively. You must provide a means for users to get answers to these questions and to identify needs for further training.

As a member of the system development team that developed and implemented the new system, your job is winding down now that installation and conversion are complete. Chapter 21 completes the life cycle by focusing on maintenance. The end of implementation also marks the time for you to begin the process of project close-down. You read about project close-down in Chapter 3 when you learned about project management. At the end of this chapter, we will return to the topic of formally ending the systems development project.

After a brief overview of the coding, testing, and installation processes and the deliverables and outcomes from these processes, we will talk about software application testing. The following section presents the four types of installation: direct, parallel, single location, and phased. Afterwards, you will read about the process of documenting systems and training and supporting users as well as the deliverables from these processes. In the next section of the chapter, you will learn about the various types of documentation and numerous methods available for delivering training and support services. Finally, you will read about implementation as an organizational change process, with many organizational and people issues involved in the implementation effort.

SYSTEM IMPLEMENTATION

System implementation is made up of many activities. The six major activities we are concerned with in this chapter are coding, testing, installation, documentation, training, and support (see Figure 20-1). The purpose of these steps is to convert the final physical system specifications into working and reliable software and hardware, document the work that has been done, and provide help for current and future users and caretakers of the system. These steps are often done by other project team members besides analysts, although analysts may do some programming. In any case, analysts are responsible for ensuring that all of these various activities are properly planned and executed. Next, we will briefly discuss these activities in two groups, first coding, testing, and installation, and then, documenting the system and training and supporting users.

Figure 20-1
The systems development life cycle with the implementation phase highlighted

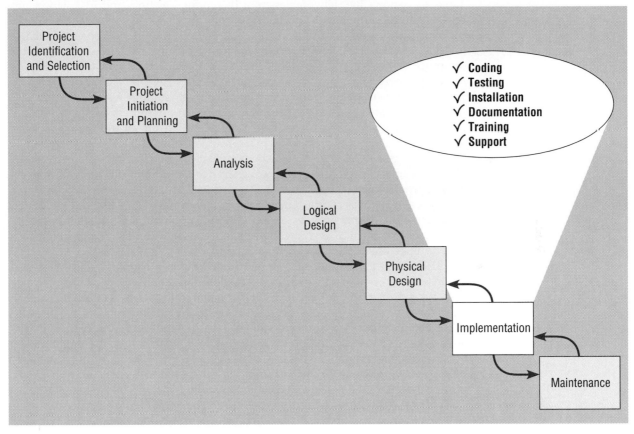

The Process of Coding, Testing, and Installation

Coding, as we mentioned before, is the process whereby the physical design specifications created by the analysis team are turned into working computer code by the programming team. Depending on the size and complexity of the system, coding can be an involved, intensive activity. Once coding has begun, the testing process can begin and proceed in parallel. As each program module is produced, it can be tested individually, then as part of a larger program, and then as part of a larger system. You will learn about the different strategies for testing later in the chapter. We should emphasize that although testing is done during implementation, you must begin planning for testing earlier in the project. Planning involves determining what needs to be tested and collecting test data. This is often done during the analysis phase because testing requirements are related to system requirements.

Installation is the process during which the current system is replaced by the new system. This includes conversion of existing data, software, documentation, and work procedures to those consistent with the new system. Users must give up the old ways of doing their jobs, whether manual or automated, and adjust to accomplishing the same tasks with the new system. Users will sometimes resist these changes and you must help them adjust. However, you cannot control all the dynamics of user-system interaction involved in the installation process.

Deliverables and Outcomes from Coding, Testing, and Installation

Table 20-1 shows the deliverables from the coding, testing, and installation processes. The most obvious outcome is the code itself, but just as important as the code is documentation of the code. Some programming languages, such as COBOL, are said to be largely self-documenting because the language itself spells out much about the program's logic, the labels used for data and variables, and the locations where data are accessed and output. But even COBOL code can be mysterious to maintenance programmers who must maintain the system for years after the original system was written and the original programmers have moved on to other jobs. Therefore, clear, complete documentation for all individual modules and programs is crucial to the system's continued smooth operation. Increasingly, CASE tools are used to maintain the documentation needed by systems professionals. The results of program and system testing are important deliverables from the testing process, as they document the tests as well as the test results. For example, what type of test was conducted? What test data were used? How did the system handle the test? The answers to these questions can provide important information for system maintenance as changes will require retesting and similar testing procedures will be used during the maintenance process.

The next two deliverables, user guides and the user training plan, result from the installation process. User guides provide information on how to use the new system, and the training plan is a strategy for training users so they can quickly learn the new system. The development of the training plan probably began earlier in the project and some training, on the concepts behind the new system, may have already taken place. During the early stages of implementation, the training plans are finalized and training on the use of the system begins. Similarly, the installation plan lays out a strategy for moving from the old system to the new, from the beginning to the end of the process. Installation includes installing the system (hardware and software) at central and user sites. The installation plan answers such questions as when the new system will be installed, which installation strategies will be used, who will be involved, what resources are required, which data will be converted and cleansed, and how long the installation process will take. It is not enough that the system is installed; users must actually use it.

As an analyst, your job is to ensure that all of these deliverables are produced and are done well. You may produce some of the deliverables, such as test data, user guides, and an installation plan; for other deliverables, such as code, you may only supervise or simply monitor their production or accomplishment. The extent of your implementation responsibilities will vary according to the size and standards of the organization you work for, but your ultimate role includes ensuring that all the implementation work leads to a system that meets the specifications developed in earlier project phases. See the box, The Future Programmer, for some insights into the changing role of programming and the nature of systems implementation in systems development.

TABLE 20-1   Deliverables for Coding, Testing, and Installation

1. Coding
   a. Code
   b. Program documentation
2. Testing
   a. Test scenarios (test plan) and test data
   b. Results of program and system testing
3. Installation
   a. User guides
   b. User training plan
   c. Installation and conversion plan
      i. Software and hardware installation schedule
      ii. Data conversion plan
      iii. Site and facility remodeling plan

The Processes of Documenting the System, Training Users, and Supporting Users

Although the process of documentation proceeds throughout the life cycle, it receives formal attention during the implementation phase because the end of implementation largely marks the end of the analysis team's involvement in system development. As the team is getting ready to move on to new projects, you and the other analysts need to prepare documents that reveal all of the important information you have learned about this system during its development and implementation. There are two audiences for this final documentation: (1) the information systems personnel who will maintain the system throughout its productive life and (2) the people who will use the system as part of their daily lives. The analysis team in a large organization can get help in preparing documentation from specialized staff in the information systems department.

Larger organizations also tend to provide training and support to computer users throughout the organization. Some of the training and support is very specific to particular application systems while the rest is general to particular operating systems or off-the-shelf software packages. For example, it is common to find courses on Microsoft Windows™ and WordPerfect™ in organization-wide training facilities. Analysts are mostly uninvolved with general training and support, but they do work with corporate trainers to provide training and support tailored to particular computer applications they have helped develop. Centralized information system training facilities tend to have specialized staff who can help with training and support issues. In smaller organizations that cannot afford to have well-staffed centralized training and support facilities, fellow users are the best source of training and support users have, whether the software is customized or off-the-shelf (Nelson and Cheney, 1987).

> **The Future Programmer**
>
> Where and by whom programming is done continues to change as the nature of programming languages evolves, resulting in improved programming productivity and the opening of programming to less highly skilled personnel. One prediction suggests that future programmers can be grouped into four categories:
> - IS department programmers: the number of people who work in IS are in a clear decline, from nearly 2 million in 1994 to several hundred thousand by 2010; some people believe that these jobs are really being distributed out of the central IS function into business units, possibly under different titles.
> - Software company programmers: These programmers work for consulting and packaged software companies, and the number will likely rise from roughly 600,000 in 1994 to several million by 2010.
> - Embedded software programmers: These programmers produce code that is embedded in other products, like cars, office equipment, and consumer electronics; this group will likely dramatically increase from several million in 1994 to over 10 million by 2010.
> - Occasional programmers: Professionals and technicians (accountants, engineers, managers, and so forth) who program as part of their main duties; this group should rise from roughly 20 million in 1994 to over 100 million by 2010.
>
> One theory is that standard business system components (objects in some terminologies) can be assembled into new systems by less skilled programmers. Thus, the job of what we call today a programmer will be to build these components and to ensure the quality of assembled systems. Although the number of occasional programmers (likely not trained in information systems) is exploding, the need for highly skilled programmers and programming work is far from diminishing.
>
> *Adapted from Bloor, 1994*

Deliverables and Outcomes from Documenting the System, Training Users, and Supporting Users

Table 20-2 shows the deliverables from documenting the system, training users, and supporting users. At the very least, the development team must prepare user documentation. The documentation can be paper-based, but it should also include computer-based modules. For modern information systems, this documentation includes any on-line help designed as part of the system interface. The development team should think through the user training process: Who should be trained? How much training is adequate for each training audience? What do different types of users need to learn during training? The training plan should be supplemented by actual training modules, or at least outlines of such modules, that at a minimum address the three questions stated previously. Finally, the development

TABLE 20-2   Deliverables for Documenting the System, Training, and Supporting Users

1. Documentation
   a. System documentation
   b. User documentation
2. User training plan
   a. Classes
   b. Tutorials
3. User training modules
   a. Training materials
   b. Computer-based training aids
4. User support plan
   a. Help desk
   b. On-line help
   c. Bulletin boards and other
      support mechanisms

team should also deliver a user support plan that addresses such issues as how users will be able to find help once the information system has become integrated into the organization. The development team should consider a multitude of support mechanisms and modes of delivery. Each deliverable is addressed in more detail later in the chapter.

SOFTWARE APPLICATION TESTING

As we mentioned previously, analysts prepare system specifications that are passed on to programmers for coding. Although coding takes considerable effort and skill, the practices and processes of writing code do not belong in this text. However, as software application testing is an activity analysts plan (beginning in the analysis phase) and sometimes supervise, depending on organizational standards, you need to understand the essentials of the testing process.

Testing software begins earlier in the systems development life cycle, even though many of the actual testing activities are carried out during implementation. During analysis, you develop a master test plan. During design, you develop a unit test plan, an integration test plan, and a system test plan. During implementation, these various plans are put into effect and the actual testing is performed.

The purpose of these written test plans is to improve communication among all the people involved in testing the application software. The plan specifies what each person's role will be during testing. The test plans also serve as checklists you can use to determine whether all of the master test plan has been completed. The master test plan is not just a single document but a collection of documents. Each of the component documents represents a complete test plan for one part of the system or for a particular type of test. Presenting a complete master test plan is far beyond the scope of this book. Refer to Mosley's *Handbook of MIS Software Application Testing* for a complete test plan, which comprises a 101-page appendix. To give you an idea of what a master test plan involves, we present an abbreviated table of contents in Table 20-3.

A master test plan is a project within the overall system development project. Since at least some of the system testing will be done by people who have not been involved in the system development so far, the Introduction provides general information about the system and the needs for testing. The Overall Plan and Testing Requirements sections are like a baseline project plan for testing, with a schedule of events, resource requirements, and standards of practice outlined. Procedure Control explains how the testing is to be conducted, including how changes to fix errors will be documented. The fifth and final section explains each specific test necessary to validate that the system performs as expected.

Some organizations have specially trained personnel who supervise and support testing. Testing managers are responsible for developing test plans, establish-

TABLE 20-3   Table of Contents of a Master Test Plan

1. Introduction
   a. Description of system to be tested
   b. Objectives of the test plan
   c. Method of testing
   d. Supporting documents
2. Overall Plan
   a. Milestones, schedule, and locations
   b. Test materials
      1. Test plans
      2. Test cases
      3. Test scenarios
      4. Test log
   c. Criteria for passing tests
3. Testing Requirements
   a. Hardware
   b. Software
   c. Personnel
4. Procedure Control
   a. Test initiation
   b. Test execution
   c. Test failure
   d. Access/change control
   e. Document control
5. Test Specific or Component Specific Test Plans
   a. Objectives
   b. Software description
   c. Method
   d. Milestones, schedule, progression, and locations
   e. Requirements
   f. Criteria for passing tests
   g. Resulting test materials
   h. Execution control
   i. Attachments

Adapted from Mosley, 1993

ing testing standards, integrating testing and development activities in the life cycle, and ensuring that test plans are completed. Testing specialists help develop test plans, create test cases and scenarios, execute the actual tests, and analyze and report test results.

Seven Different Types of Tests

Software application testing is an umbrella term that covers several types of tests. Mosley (1993) organizes the types of tests according to whether they employ static or dynamic techniques and whether the test is automated or manual. Static testing means that the code being tested is not executed. The results of running the code are not an issue for that particular test. Dynamic testing, on the other hand, involves execution of the code. Automated testing means the computer conducts the test while manual means that people do. Using this framework, we can categorize types of tests as shown in Table 20-4.

Let's examine each type of test in turn. **Inspections** are formal group activities where participants manually examine code for occurrences of well-known errors. Syntax, grammar, and some other routine errors can be checked by automated inspection software, so manual inspection checks are used for more subtle errors. Each programming language lends itself to certain types of errors that programmers

Inspections: A testing technique in which participants examine program code for predictable language-specific errors.

TABLE 20-4   A Categorization of Test Types

	Manual	Automated
Static	Inspections	Syntax checking
Dynamic	Walkthroughs	Unit test
	Desk checking	Integration test
		System test

Adapted from Mosley, 1993

make when coding, and these common errors are well-known and documented (for common coding errors in COBOL, see Litecky and Davis, 1976). Code inspection participants compare the code they are examining to a checklist of well-known errors for that particular language. Exactly what the code does is not investigated in an inspection. It has been estimated that code inspections have been used by organizations to detect from 60 to 90 percent of all software defects as well as to provide programmers with feedback that enables them to avoid making the same types of errors in future work (Fagan, 1986). The inspection process can also be used for such things as design specifications.

Unlike inspections, what the code does is an important question in a *walkthrough*. Using structured walkthroughs is a very effective method of detecting errors in code. As you saw in Chapter 6, structured walkthroughs can be used to review many systems development deliverables, including logical and physical design specifications as well as code. Whereas specification walkthroughs tend to be formal reviews, code walkthroughs tend to be informal. Informality tends to make programmers less apprehensive about walkthroughs and helps increase their frequency. According to Yourdon (1989), code walkthroughs should be done frequently when the pieces of work reviewed are relatively small and before the work is formally tested. If walkthroughs are not held until the entire program is tested, the programmer will have already spent too much time looking for errors that the programming team could have found much more quickly. The programmer's time will have been wasted, and the other members of the team may become frustrated because they will not find as many errors as they would have if the walkthrough had been conducted earlier. Further, the longer a program goes without being subjected to a walkthrough, the more defensive the programmer becomes when the code is reviewed. Although each organization that uses walkthroughs conducts them differently, there is a basic structure that you can follow that works well (see Figure 20-2).

It should be stressed that the purpose of a walkthrough is to detect errors, not to correct them. It is the programmer's job to correct the errors uncovered in a walkthrough. Sometimes it can be difficult for the reviewers to refrain from suggesting ways to fix the problems they find in the code, but increased experience with the process can help change a reviewer's behavior.

What the code does is also important in **desk checking**, an informal process where the programmer or someone else who understands the logic of the program works through the code with a paper and pencil. The programmer executes each

Desk checking: A testing technique in which the program code is sequentially executed manually by the reviewer.

Figure 20-2
Steps in a typical walkthrough (Adapted from Yourdon, 1989)

GUIDELINES FOR CONDUCTING A CODE WALKTHROUGH
1. Have the review meeting chaired by the project manager or chief programmer, who is also responsible for scheduling the meeting, reserving a room, setting the agenda, inviting participants, and so on.
2. The programmer presents his or her work to the reviewers. Discussion should be general during the presentation.
3. Following the general discussion, the programmer walks through the code in detail, focusing on the logic of the code rather than on specific test cases.
4. Reviewers ask to walk through specific test cases.
5. The chair resolves disagreements if the review team cannot reach agreement among themselves and assigns duties, usually to the programmer, for making specific changes.
6. A second walkthrough is then scheduled if needed.

instruction, using test cases that may or may not be written down. In one sense, the reviewer acts as the computer, mentally checking each step and its results for the entire set of computer instructions.

Among the list of automated testing techniques in Table 20-4, there is only one technique that is also static, syntax checking. Syntax checking is typically done by a compiler. Errors in syntax are uncovered but the code is not executed. For the other three automated techniques, the code is executed.

The first such technique is **unit testing**, sometimes called module testing. In unit testing, each module is tested alone in an attempt to discover any errors that may exist in the module's code. But since modules coexist and work with other modules in programs and systems, they must be tested together in larger groups. Combining modules and testing them is called **integration testing**. Integration testing is gradual. First you test the coordinating module (the root module in a structure chart tree) and only one of its subordinate modules. After the first test, you add one or two other subordinate modules from the same level. Once the program has been tested with the coordinating module and all of its immediately subordinate modules, you add modules from the next level and then test the program. You continue this procedure until the entire program has been tested as a unit. **System testing** is a similar process, but instead of integrating modules into programs for testing, you integrate programs into systems. System testing follows the same incremental logic that integration testing does. Under both integration and system testing, not only do individual modules and programs get tested many times, so do the interfaces between modules and programs.

Current practice calls for a top-down approach to writing and testing modules. Under a top-down approach, the coordinating module is written first. Then the modules at the next level in the structure chart are written, followed by the modules at the next level, and so on, until all of the modules in the system are done. Each module is tested as it is written. Since top-level modules contain many calls to subordinate modules, you may wonder how they can be tested if the lower level modules haven't been written yet. The answer is **stub testing**. Stubs are two or three lines of code written by a programmer to stand in for the missing modules. During testing, the coordinating module calls the stub instead of the subordinate module. The stub accepts control and then returns it to the coordinating module.

Figure 20-3 illustrates stub and integration system testing. Stub testing is depicted as the innermost oval. Here the Get module (where data are input and read) is being written and tested, but as none of its subordinate modules have been written yet, each one is represented by a stub. In the stub testing illustrated by Figure 20-3, Get is tested with only one stub in place, for its left-most subordinate module. You would of course write stubs for all of the Get module's subordinate modules, just as you would for the Make (where new information is calculated) and Put (where information is output) modules. Once all of the subordinate modules are written and tested, you would conduct an integration test of Get and its subordinate modules, as represented by the second oval. As stated previously, the focus of an integration test is on the inter-relationships among modules. You would also conduct integration tests of Make and its subordinate modules, of Put and its subordinates, and of System and its subordinates, Get, Make, and Put. Eventually your integration testing would include all of the modules in the large oval that encompasses the entire program.

System testing is more than simply expanded integration testing where you are testing the interfaces between programs in a system rather than testing the interfaces between modules in a program. System testing is also intended to demonstrate whether a system meets its objectives. This is not the same as testing a system

Unit testing: Each module is tested alone in an attempt to discover any errors in its code.

Integration testing: The process of bringing together all of the modules that a program comprises for testing purposes. Modules are typically integrated in a top-down, incremental fashion.

System testing: The bringing together of all the programs that a system comprises for testing purposes. Programs are typically integrated in a top-down, incremental fashion.

Stub testing: A technique used in testing modules, especially where modules are written and tested in a top-down fashion, where a few lines of code are used to substitute for subordinate modules.

Figure 20-3
Comparing stub and integration testing

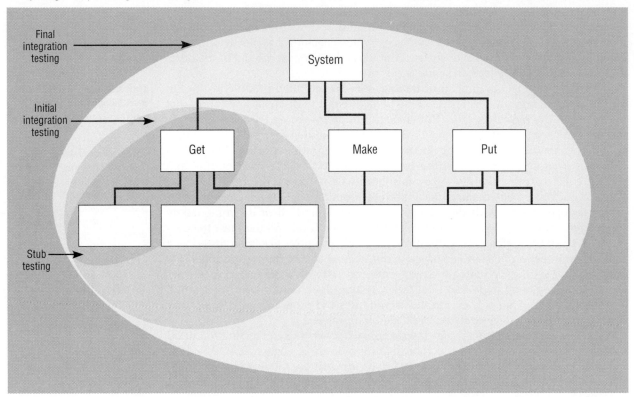

to determine whether it meets requirements—that is the focus of acceptance testing, which will be discussed later. To verify that a system meets its objectives, system testing involves using nonlive test data in a nonlive testing environment. *Nonlive* means the data and situation are artificial, developed specifically for testing purposes, although both data and environment are similar to what users would encounter in everyday system use. The system test is typically conducted by information systems personnel led by the project team leader, although it can also be conducted by users under MIS guidance. The scenarios that form the basis for system tests are prepared as part of the master test plan.

The Testing Process

Up to this point, we have talked about the master test plan and seven different types of tests for software applications. We haven't said very much about the process of testing itself. There are two important things to remember about testing information systems:

1. The purpose of testing is confirming that the system satisfies requirements.

2. Testing must be planned.

These two points have several implications for the testing process, regardless of the type of test being conducted. First, testing is not haphazard. You must pay attention to many different aspects of a system, such as response time, response to boundary data, response to no input, response to heavy volumes of input, and so on. You must test anything (within resource constraints) that could go wrong or be wrong about a system. At a minimum, you should test the most frequently used parts of the system and as many other paths through the system as time permits. Planning gives analysts and programmers an opportunity to think through all the potential problem areas, list these areas, and develop ways to test for problems. As indicated previously, one part of the master test plan is creating a set of test cases, each of which must be carefully documented (see Figure 20-4 for an outline of a test case description).

A test case is a specific scenario of transactions, queries, or navigation paths that represent a typical, critical, or abnormal use of the system. A test case should be repeatable, so that it can be rerun as new versions of the software are tested. This is important for all code, whether written in-house, developed by a contractor, or purchased. Test cases need to determine that new software works with other existing software with which it must share data. Even though analysts often do not do

Pine Valley Furniture Company
Test Case Description

Test Case Number:
Date:
Test Case Description:

Program Name:
Testing State:
Test Case Prepared By:

Test Administrator:

Description of Test Data:

Expected Results:

Actual Results:

Figure 20-4
Test case description form
(Adapted from Mosley, 1993)

the testing, systems analysts, because of their intimate knowledge of applications, often make up or find test data. The people who create the test cases should not be the same people as those who coded and tested the system. In addition to a description of each test case, there must also be a description of the test results, with an emphasis on how the actual results differed from the expected results (see Figure 20-5). This description will indicate why the results were different and what, if anything, should be done to change the software. This description will then suggest the need for retesting, possibly introducing new tests necessary to discover the source of the differences.

One important reason to keep such a thorough description of test cases and results is so that testing can be repeated for each revision of an application. Although new versions of a system may necessitate new test data to validate new features of the application, previous test data usually can and should be reused. Results from use of the test data with prior versions are compared to new versions to show that changes have not introduced new errors and that the behavior of the system, in-

Figure 20-5
Test case results form
(Adapted from Mosley, 1993)

Pine Valley Furniture Company
Test Case Results

Test Case Number:
Date:

Program Name:
Module Under Test:

Explanation of difference between actual and expected output:

Suggestions for next steps:

cluding response time, is no worse. A second implication for the testing process is that test cases must include illegal and out-of-range data. The system should be able to handle any possibility, no matter how unlikely; the only way to find out is to test.

If the results of a test case do not compare favorably to what was expected, the error causing the problem must be found and fixed. Programmers use a variety of debugging tools to help locate and fix errors. A sophisticated debugging tool called a *symbolic debugger* allows the program to be run on-line, even one instruction at a time if the programmer desires, and allows the programmer to observe how different areas of data are affected as the instructions are executed. This cycle of finding problems, fixing errors, and rerunning test cases continues until no additional problems are found. There are specific testing methods that have been developed for generating test cases and guiding the test process (Mosley, 1993). See the box, Automating Testing, for an overview of tools to assist you in testing software.

> **Automating Testing**
>
> Software testing tools provide the following functions, which improve the quality of testing:
> - Record or build scripts of data entry, menu selections and mouse clicks, and input data, which can be replayed in exact sequence for each test run
> - Compare the results of one test run with those from prior test cases to identify errors or to highlight the results of new features
> - Supported unattended script playing to simulate high-volume or stress situations. Such tools can reduce the time for software testing by almost 80 percent.

Acceptance Testing by Users

Once the system tests have been satisfactorily completed, the system is ready for **acceptance testing**, which is testing the system in the environment where it will eventually be used. Acceptance refers to the fact that users typically sign off on the system and "accept" it once they are satisfied with it. As we said previously, the purpose of acceptance testing is for users to determine whether the system meets their requirements. The extent of acceptance testing will vary with the organization and with the system in question. The most complete acceptance testing will include **alpha testing**, where simulated but typical data are used for system testing; **beta testing**, in which live data are used in the users' real working environment; and a system audit conducted by the organization's internal auditors or by members of the quality assurance group.

During alpha testing, the entire system is implemented in a test environment to discover whether or not the system is overtly destructive to itself or to the rest of the environment. The types of tests performed during alpha testing include the following:

- Recovery testing—forces the software (or environment) to fail in order to verify that recovery is properly performed.

- Security testing—verifies that protection mechanisms built into the system will protect it from improper penetration.

- Stress testing—tries to break the system (for example, what happens when a record is written to the database with incomplete information or what happens under extreme on-line transaction loads or with a large number of concurrent users).

- Performance testing—determines how the system performs on the range of possible environments in which it may be used (for example, different hardware configurations, networks, operating systems, and so on); often the goal is to have the system perform with similar response time and other performance measures in each environment.

Acceptance testing:
The process whereby actual users test a completed information system, the end result of which is the users' acceptance of it.

Alpha testing:
User testing of a completed information system using simulated data.

Beta testing:
User testing of a completed information system using real data in the real user environment.

Bugs in the Baggage

Testing a complex software system can be long and frustrating. A case in point was the software to control 4,000 baggage cars at the Denver International Airport. Errors in the software put the airport's opening on hold for months, costing taxpayers $500,000 a day and turning airport bonds into junk status. The airport was supposed to have opened in March 1994, but it did not open until February 1995 because of problems with the baggage-handling system. The system routinely damaged luggage and routed bags to the wrong flights. Various causes of the delay were identified, including last minute design change requests from airport officials and mechanical problems. The bottom-line lesson is that system designers must build in plenty of test and debugging time when scaling up proven technology into a much more complicated environment.

United Airlines, the major carrier at Denver International Airport, took over as systems integrator in October 1994. At the same time, the City of Denver commissioned a traditional conveyor-belt baggage-handling system in the airport for an additional $50 million. When the airport opened in 1995 (and as of this writing), only United used the automated baggage system, and then only to ferry bags to its flights. The system was not able to ferry bags from the planes back to the airport. All the other carriers used the traditional conveyor system. The City of Denver tried to recover $80 million of the system's $193 million cost from BAE Automated Systems Inc., the system's vendor. In 1996, BAE sued United for $17.5 million and the city for $4.1 million in withheld fees. United countersued. In September 1997, all sides settled, and no details were released.

Sources include Bozman, 1994; Lieb, 1997; and Scheier, 1994.

Installation:
The organizational process of changing over from the current information system to a new one.

Direct installation:
Changing over from the old information system to a new one by turning off the old system when the new one is turned on.

Parallel installation:
Running the old information system and the new one at the same time until management decides the old system can be turned off.

In beta testing, a subset of the intended users run the system in their own environments using their own data. The intent of the beta test is to determine whether the software, documentation, technical support, and training activities work as intended. In essence, beta testing can be viewed as a rehearsal of the installation phase. Problems uncovered in alpha and beta testing in any of these areas must be corrected before users can accept the system. There are many stories systems analysts can tell about long delays in final user acceptance due to system bugs (see the box, Bugs in the Baggage, for one famous incident).

INSTALLATION

The process of moving from the current information system to the new one is called **installation**. All employees who use a system, whether they were consulted during the development process or not, must give up their reliance on the current system and begin to rely on the new system. Four different approaches to installation have emerged over the years: direct, parallel, single location, and phased (Figure 20-6). The approach an organization decides to use will depend on the scope and complexity of the change associated with the new system and the organization's risk aversion.

Direct Installation

The direct or abrupt approach to installation (also called "cold-turkey") is as sudden as the name indicates: the old system is turned off and the new system is turned on (Figure 20-6a). Under **direct installation**, users are at the mercy of the new system. Any errors resulting from the new system will have a direct impact on the users and how they do their jobs and, in some cases—depending on the centrality of the system to the organization—on how the organization performs its business. If the new system fails, considerable delay may occur until the old system can again be made operational and business transactions reentered to make the database up-to-date. For these reasons, direct installation can be very risky. Further, direct installation requires a complete installation of the whole system. For a large system, this may mean a long time until the new system can be installed, thus delaying system benefits or even missing the opportunities that motivated the system request. On the other hand, it is the least expensive installation method and it creates considerable interest in making the installation a success. Sometimes, a direct installation is the only possible strategy if there is no way for the current and new systems to coexist, which they must do in some way in each of the other installation approaches.

Parallel Installation

Parallel installation is as riskless as direct installation is risky. Under parallel installation, the old system continues to run alongside the new system until users and

Figure 20-6
Comparison of installation strategies

(a) Direct installation

(b) Parallel installation

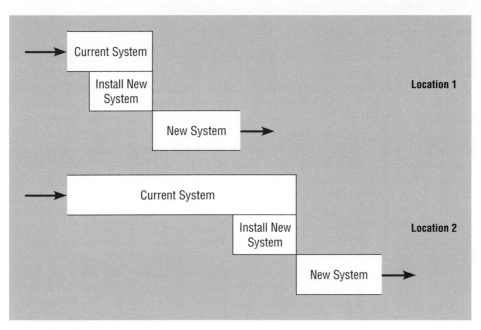

(c) Single location installation (with direct installation at each location)

(d) Phased installation

management are satisfied that the new system is effectively performing its duties and the old system can be turned off (Figure 20-6b). All of the work done by the old system is concurrently performed by the new system. Outputs are compared (to the greatest extent possible) to help determine whether the new system is performing as well as the old. Errors discovered in the new system do not cost the organization much, if anything, as errors can be isolated and the business can be supported with the old system. Since all work is essentially done twice, a parallel installation can be very expensive; running two systems implies employing (and paying) two staffs to not only operate both systems but also to maintain them. A parallel approach can also be confusing to users since they must deal with both systems. As with direct installation, there can be a considerable delay until the new system is completely ready for installation. A parallel approach may not be feasible, especially if the users of the system (such as customers) cannot tolerate redundant effort or the size of the system (number of users or extent of features) is large.

Single Location Installation

Single location installation: Trying out a new information system at one site and using the experience to decide if and how the new system should be deployed throughout the organization.

Single location installation, also known as location and pilot installation, is a middle-of-the-road approach compared to direct and parallel installation. Rather than convert all of the organization at once, single location installation involves changing from the current to the new system in only one place or in a series of separate sites over time (Figure 20-6c depicts this approach for a simple situation of two locations). The single location may be a branch office, a single factory, or one department, and the actual approach used for installation in that location may be any of the other approaches. The key advantage to single location installation is that it limits potential damage and potential cost by limiting the effects to a single site. Once management has determined that installation has been successful in one location, the new system may be deployed in the rest of the organization, possibly continuing with installation in one location at a time. Success at the pilot site can be used to convince reluctant personnel in other sites that the system can be worthwhile for them as well. Problems with the system (the actual software as well as documentation, training, and support) can be resolved before deployment to other sites. Even though the single location approach may be simpler for users, it still places a large burden on IS staff to support two versions of the system. On the other hand, because problems are isolated at one site at a time, IS staff can devote all its efforts to the success at the pilot site. Also, if different locations require sharing of data, extra programs will need to be written to synchronize the current and new systems; although this will happen transparently to users, it is extra work for IS staff. As with each of the other approaches (except phased installation), the whole system is installed; however, some parts of the organization will not get the benefits of the new system until the pilot installation has been completely tested.

Phased Installation

Phased installation: Changing from the old information system to the new one incrementally, starting with one or a few functional components and then gradually extending the installation to cover the whole new system.

Phased installation, also called staged installation, is an incremental approach. Under phased installation, the new system is brought on-line in functional components; different parts of the old and new systems are used in cooperation until the whole new system is installed (Figure 20-6d shows the phase-in of the first two modules of a new system). Phased installation, like single location installation, is an attempt to limit the organization's exposure to risk, whether in terms of cost or disruption of the business. By converting gradually, the organization's risk is spread out over time and place. Also, a phased installation allows for some benefits from the new system before the whole system is ready. For example, new data-capture methods can be used before all reporting modules are ready. For a phased installation, the new and replaced systems must be able to coexist and probably share data. Thus, bridge programs connecting old and new databases and programs often must be built. Sometimes, the new and old systems are so incompatible (built using totally different structures) that pieces of the old system cannot be incrementally replaced, so this strategy is not feasible. A phased installation is akin to bringing out a sequence of releases of the system. Thus, a phased approach requires careful version control, repeated conversions at each phase, and a long period of change, which may be frustrating and confusing to users. On the other hand, each phase of change is smaller and more manageable for all involved.

Planning Installation

Each installation strategy involves converting not only software but also data and (potentially) hardware, documentation, work methods, job descriptions, offices and other facilities, training materials, business forms, and other aspects of the system. For example, it is necessary to recall or replace all the current system documentation and business forms, which suggests that the IS department must keep track of who has these items so that they can be notified and receive replacement items. In practice you will rarely choose a single strategy to the exclusion of all others; most installations will rely on a combination of two or more approaches. For example, if you choose a single location strategy, you have to decide how installation will proceed there and at subsequent sites. Will it be direct, parallel, or phased?

Of special interest in the installation process is the conversion of data. Since existing systems usually contain data required by the new system, current data must be made error-free, unloaded from current files, combined with new data, and loaded into new files. Data may need to be reformatted to be consistent with more advanced data types supported by newer technology used to build the new system. New data fields may have to be entered in large quantities so that every record copied from the current system has all the new fields populated. Manual tasks, such as taking a physical inventory, may need to be done in order to validate data before they are transferred to the new files. The total data conversion process can be tedious. Furthermore, this process may require that current systems be shut off while the data are extracted so that updates to old data, which would contaminate the extract process, cannot occur.

Any decision that requires the current system to be shut down, in whole or in part, before the replacement system is in place must be done with care. Typically, off hours are used for installations that require a lapse in system support. Whether a lapse in service is required or not, the installation schedule should be announced to users well in advance to let them plan their work schedules around outages in service and periods when their system support might be erratic. Successful installation steps should also be announced, and special procedures put in place so that users can easily inform you of problems they encounter during installation periods. You should also plan for emergency staff to be available in case of system failure so that business operations can be recovered and made operational as quickly as possible. Another consideration is the business cycle of the organization. Most organizations face heavy workloads at particular times of year and relatively light loads at other times. A well-known example is the retail industry, where the busiest time of year is the fall, right before the year's major gift-giving holidays. You wouldn't want to schedule installation of a new point-of-sale system to begin December 1 for a department store. Make sure you understand the cyclical nature of the business you are working with before you schedule installation.

Planning for installation may begin as early as the analysis of the organization supported by the system. Some installation activities, such as buying new hardware, remodeling facilities, validating data to be transferred to the new system, and collecting new data to be loaded into the new system, must be done before the software installation can occur. Often the project team leader is responsible for anticipating all installation tasks and assigns responsibility for each to different analysts.

Each installation process involves getting workers to change the way they work. As such, installation should be looked at not as simply installing a new computer system, but as an organizational change process. More than just a computer system is involved—you are also changing how people do their jobs and how the organization operates.

DOCUMENTING THE SYSTEM

In one sense, every information systems development project is unique and will generate its own unique documentation. In another sense, though, system development projects are probably more alike than they are different. Each project shares a similar systems development life cycle, which dictates that certain activities be undertaken and each of those activities be documented. Bell and Evans (1989) illustrate how a generic systems development life cycle maps onto a generic list of when specific systems development documentation elements are finalized (Table 20-5). As you compare the generic life cycle in Table 20-5 to the life cycle presented in this book, you will see that there are differences, but the general structure of both life cycles is the same, as both include the basic phases of analysis, design, implementation, and project planning. Specific documentation will vary depending on the life cycle you are following, and the format and content of the documentation may be mandated by the organization you work for. However, a basic outline of documentation can be adapted for specific needs, as shown in Table 20-5. Note that this table indicates when documentation is typically finalized; you should start developing documentation elements early, as the information needed is captured.

TABLE 20-5 SDLC and Generic Documentation Corresponding to Each Phase

Generic life cycle phase	Generic document
Requirements specification	System requirements specification
	Resource requirements specification
Project control structuring	Management plan
	Engineering change proposal
System development	
Architectural design	Architecture design document
Prototype design	Prototype design document
Detailed design & implementation	Detailed design document
Test specification	Test specifications
Test implementation	Test reports
System delivery	User's guide
	Release description
	System administrator's guide
	Reference guide
	Acceptance sign-off

Adapted from Bell and Evans, 1989

We can simplify the situation even more by dividing documentation into two basic types, **system documentation** and **user documentation**. System documentation records detailed information about a system's design specifications, its internal workings, and its functionality. In Table 20-5, all of the documentation listed (except for System delivery) would qualify as system documentation. System documentation can be further divided into internal and external documentation (Martin and McClure, 1985). **Internal documentation** is part of the program source code or is generated at compile time. **External documentation** includes the outcome of all of the structured diagramming techniques you have studied in this book, such as data flow and entity-relationship diagrams. Although not part of the code itself, external documentation can provide useful information to the primary users of system documentation—maintenance programmers. For example, structure charts and Nassi-Shneiderman charts together provide a good overview of a system's larger structure and the details of its inner workings. Recall that Nassi-Shneiderman charts are themselves used to model specifications for writing code. In the past, external documentation was typically discarded after implementation, primarily because it was considered too costly to keep up-to-date, but today's CASE environment makes it possible to maintain and update external documentation as long as desired.

While system documentation is intended primarily for maintenance programmers (see Chapter 21), user documentation is intended primarily for users. An organization may have definitive standards on system documentation, often consistent with CASE tools and the system development process. These standards may include the outline for the project dictionary and specific pieces of documentation within it. Standards for user documentation are not as explicit.

System documentation:
Detailed information about a system's design specifications, its internal workings, and its functionality.

User documentation:
Written or other visual information about an application system, how it works, and how to use it.

Internal documentation:
System documentation that is part of the program source code or is generated at compile time.

External documentation:
System documentation that includes the outcome of structured diagramming techniques such as data flow and entity-relationship diagrams.

User Documentation

User documentation consists of written or other visual information about an application system, how it works, and how to use it. An excerpt of on-line user documentation for Microsoft Access appears in Figure 20-7. Notice how the documentation has hot links to the meaning of important terms. The documentation lists the steps necessary to actually perform the task the user inquired about. The "notes" section that follows explains specific restrictions and constraints that will affect what the user is attempting. You should also notice how some words in the documentation are underlined with dotted lines and that icons are used to represent Access buttons. This notation signifies that these particular words and buttons are hypertext links to related material elsewhere in the documentation. Hypertext techniques, rare in on-line PC documentation five years ago, are now the rule rather than the exception.

Figure 20-7 represents the content of a reference guide, just one type of user documentation (there is also a quick reference guide). Other types of user documentation include a user's guide, release description, system administrator's guide, and acceptance sign-off (Table 20-5). The reference guide consists of an exhaustive list of the system's functions and commands, usually in alphabetical order. Most on-line reference guides allow you to search by topic area or by typing in the first few letters of your keyword. Reference guides are very good for very specific information (as in Figure 20-7) but not as good for the broader picture of how you perform all the steps required for a given task. The quick reference guide provides essential information about operating a system in a short, concise format. Where computer resources are shared and many users perform similar tasks on the same machines (as with airline reservation or mail order catalog clerks), quick reference guides are often printed on index cards or as small books and mounted on or near the computer terminal. An outline for a generic user's guide (from Bell and Evans,

Figure 20-7
Example of on-line user documentation (from Microsoft Access™)

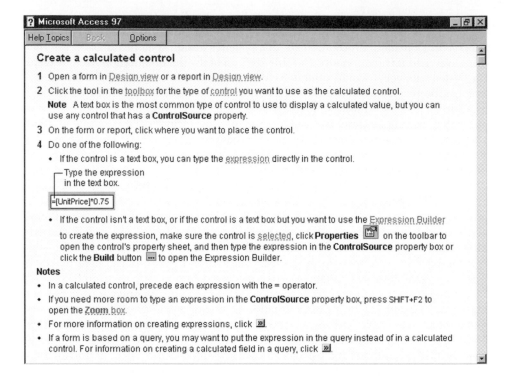

1989) is shown in Table 20-6. The purpose of such a guide is to provide information on how users can use computer systems to perform specific tasks. The information in a user's guide is typically ordered by how often tasks are performed and how complex they are.

In Table 20-6, sections with an "n" and a title in square brackets mean that there would likely be many such sections, each for a different topic. For example, for an accounting application, sections 4 and beyond might address topics such as entering a transaction in the ledger, closing the month, and printing reports. The items in parentheses are optional, included as necessary. An index becomes more important the larger the user's guide. Although a generic user's guide outline is helpful in providing an overview for you of what a user's guide might contain, we have included outlines of user guides from several popular PC software packages in Figure 20-8. Notice how different they are.

TABLE 20-6 Outline of a Generic User's Guide	
Preface	3.3 Save
1. Introduction	3.4 Error recovery
1.1 Configurations	3.n [Basic procedure name]
1.2 Function flow	n. [Task name]
2. User interface	Appendix A—Error Messages
2.1 Display screens	([Appendix])
2.2 Command types	Glossary
3. Getting started	Terms
3.1 Login	Acronyms
3.2 Logout	(Index)

Adapted from Bell and Evans, 1989

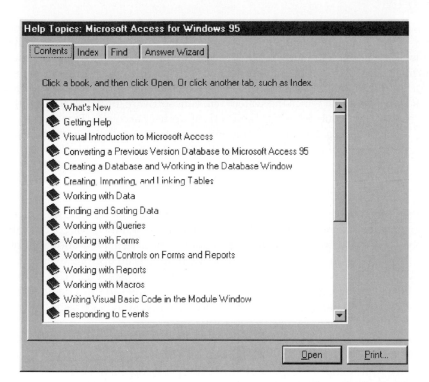

Figure 20-8
Outlines of user's guides
from various popular PC
software packages

(a) Microsoft Access™

(b) WordPerfect™

A release description contains information about a new system release, including a list of complete documentation for the new release, features and enhancements, known problems and how they have been dealt with in the new release, and information about installation. A system administrator's guide is intended primarily for those who will install and administer a new system and contains information about the network on which the system will run, software interfaces for peripherals such as printers, troubleshooting, and setting up user accounts. Finally, the acceptance sign-off allows users to test for proper system installation and then signify their acceptance of the new system with their signatures.

Preparing User Documentation

User documentation, regardless of its content or intended audience, was once provided almost exclusively in big, bulky paper manuals, and it was out of date almost as soon as it was printed. Most documentation is now delivered on-line in hypertext format. Regardless of format, user documentation is an upfront investment that should pay off in reduced training and consultation costs later (Torkzadeh and Doll, 1993). As a future analyst, you need to consider the source of documentation, its quality, and whether its focus is on the information system's functionality or on the tasks the system can be used to perform.

The traditional source of user documentation has been the organization's information systems department. Even though information systems departments have always provided some degree of user documentation, for much of the history of data processing the primary focus of documentation was the system. In a traditional information systems environment, the user interacted with an analyst and computer operations staff for all of his or her computing needs (Figure 20-9). The analyst acted as intermediary between the user and all computing resources. Any reports or other output that went to the user were generated by the operations staff, based on a regular reporting schedule. Since users were consumers and providers

Figure 20-9
Traditional information system environment and its focus on system documentation (Adapted from Torkzadeh and Doll, 1993)

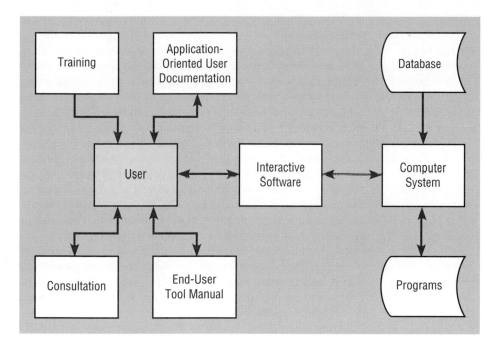

Figure 20-10
End user information system
environment and its focus on
user documentation
(Adapted from Torkzadeh
and Doll, 1993)

of data and information, most documentation developed during a traditional information systems development project was system documentation for the analysts and programmers who had to know how the system worked. Although some user documentation was generated, most documentation was intended to assist maintenance programmers who tended to the system for years after the analysis team had finished its work.

In today's end-user information systems environment, users interact directly with many computing resources, users have many options or querying capabilities from which to choose when using a system, and users are able to develop many local applications themselves (Figure 20-10). Analysts often serve as consultants for these local end-user applications. For end-user applications, the nature and purpose of documentation has changed from documentation intended for the maintenance programmer to documentation for the end user. Application-oriented documentation, whose purpose is to increase user understanding and utilization of the organization's computing resources, has also come to be important. While some of this user-oriented documentation continues to be supplied by the information systems department, much of it now originates with vendors and with users themselves.

TRAINING AND SUPPORTING USERS

Training and **support** are two aspects of an organization's **computing infrastructure** (Kling and Iacono, 1989). Computing infrastructure is made up of all the resources and practices required to help people adequately use computer systems to do their primary work (Kling and Scacchi, 1982; Gasser, 1986). It is analogous to the infrastructure of water mains, electric power lines, streets, and bridges that form the foundation for providing essential services in a city. Henderson and Treacy (1986) identify infrastructure as one of four fundamental issues IS managers must address. They suggest that training and support are most important in the early stages of

Support: Providing ongoing educational and problem-solving assistance to information system users. For in-house developed systems, support materials and jobs will have to be prepared or designed as part of the implementation process.

Computing infrastructure: All the resources and practices required to help people adequately use computer systems to do their primary work.

end-user computing growth and less so later on. Rockart and Short (1989) cite the "development and implementation of a general, and eventually 'seamless,' information technology infrastructure" as a major demand on information technology. They list the creation of an effective information technology infrastructure as one of the five key issues for senior organizational managers in the 1990s. Thus, training and support are critical for the success of an information system. As the person whom the user holds responsible for the new system, you and other analysts on the project team must ensure that high-quality training and support are available.

Although training and support can be talked about as if they are two separate things, in organizational practice the distinction between the two is not all that clear, as the two sometimes overlap. After all, both deal with learning about computing. It is clear that support mechanisms are also a good way to provide training, especially for intermittent users of a system (Eason, 1988). Intermittent or occasional system users are not interested in, nor would they profit from, typical user training methods. Intermittent users must be provided with "point of need support," specific answers to specific questions at the time the answers are needed. A variety of mechanisms, such as the system interface itself and on-line help facilities, can be designed to provide both training and support at the same time.

The value of support is often underestimated. Few organizations invest heavily in support staff, which can lead to users solving problems for themselves or somehow working around them (Gasser, 1986). Adequate user support may be essential for successful information system development, however. One study found that user satisfaction with support provided by the information systems department was the factor most closely related to overall satisfaction with user development of computer-based applications (Rivard and Huff, 1988).

Training Information System Users

Computer use requires skills, and training people to use computer applications can be expensive for organizations (Kling and Iacono, 1989). Training of all types is a major activity in American corporations (they spent $48 billion on training in 1993), but information systems training is often neglected. Many organizations tend to underinvest in computing skills training. It is true that some organizations institutionalize high levels of information system training, but many others offer no systematic training at all.

Some argue that information systems departments are similar to hospitals: both are high-technology environments, both are staffed by well-educated professionals, both are capital-intensive, and both have less than adequate "bedside manners" (Schrage, 1993). In this scenario, users, like patients, are seen as problems to be solved rather than as people. One response to this issue might be to spread more evenly the cost of computer training. Even though users come from all parts of the organization, the information systems department is often stuck paying for most of the computer training itself. Attitudes in information systems towards users and the availability of high-quality training might change if other organizational departments begin to pay their share of the computer training bill.

Others argue that it is difficult to demonstrate any direct benefits from training once the training is complete, since managers are more likely to continually upgrade hardware and software (de Jager, 1994). Progress from upgrading is easy to measure—just look at all the empty cartons— but upgrading may not result in the increases in productivity you would expect. Training users to be effective with the systems they have now may be a more cost-effective way to increase productivity: "If the goal is maximum productivity at the lowest cost, then a day of training usually delivers more productivity per dollar than costly hardware and software up-grades" (de Jager, 1994, p. 86). Though not always taken seriously in practice, the value and cost-effectiveness of information systems training should not be under-estimated.

The type of necessary training will vary by type of system and expertise of users. The list of potential topics from which you must determine if training will be useful include the following:

- Use of the system (e.g., how to enter a class registration request)

- General computer concepts (e.g., computer files and how to copy them)

- Information system concepts (e.g., batch processing)

- Organizational concepts (e.g., FIFO inventory accounting)

- System management (e.g., how to request changes to a system)

- System installation (e.g., how to reconcile current and new systems during phased installation)

As you can see from this partial list, there are potentially many topics that go be-yond simply how to use the new system. It may be necessary for you to develop training for users in other areas so that users will be ready, conceptually and psy-chologically, to use the new system. Some training, like concept training, should begin early in the project since this training can assist in the "unfreezing" element of the organizational change process.

Each element of training can be delivered in a variety of ways. Table 20-7 lists the most common training methods used by information system departments a few years ago. Despite the importance and value of training, most of the methods listed in Table 20-7 are under-utilized in many organizations. Users primarily rely on just one of these delivery modes: more often than not, users turn to the resident expert and to fellow users for training, as shown in how often people use each mode listed in Table 20-7 (see Figure 20-11). One study reported that 89.4 percent of end users consulted their colleagues about how to use microcomputers, but only 48 percent consulted central information systems staff (Lee, 1986). Users are more likely to turn to local experts for help than to the organization's technical support staff because the local expert understands both the users' primary work and the computer systems they use (Eason, 1988). Given their dependence on fel-low users for training, it should not be surprising that end users describe their most common mode of computer training as "self-training" (Nelson and Cheney, 1987). Self-training has been found to be associated with particular sets of user

TABLE 20-7 Seven Common Methods for Computer Training in 1987

1. Tutorial—one person taught at a time
2. Course—several people taught at a time
3. Computer-aided instruction
4. Interactive training manuals—combination of tutorials and computer-aided instruction
5. Resident expert
6. Software help components
7. External sources, such as vendors

Adapted from Nelson and Cheney, 1987

Figure 20-11
Frequency of use of
computer training methods
(Nelson & Cheney, 1987)

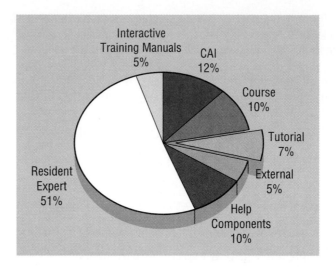

skills: using application development software, using packaged application software, data communication, using hardware, using operating systems, and graphics skills. The last four sets of skills are also highly associated with company-provided training. There appear to be areas of training best accomplished by centralized, company-provided training on the one hand and by self-training on the other.

One conclusion from the experience with user training methods is that an effective strategy for training on a new system is to first train a few key users and then organize training programs and support mechanisms which involve these users to provide further training, both formal and on demand. Often, training is most effective if you customize it to particular user groups, and the lead trainers from these groups are in the best position to do this.

While individualized training is expensive and time-consuming, technological advances and decreasing costs have made this type of training more feasible. Similarly, the number of training modes used by information systems departments today has increased dramatically beyond what is listed in Table 20-7. Training modes now include videos, interactive television for remote training, multimedia training, on-line tutorials, and **electronic performance support systems (EPSS)**. These may be delivered via videotapes, CD-ROMS, company intranets, and the Internet.

Electronic performance support system (EPSS):
Component of a software package or application in which training and educational information is embedded. An EPSS can take several forms, including a tutorial, an expert system shell, and hypertext jumps to reference material.

Electronic performance support systems are on-line help systems that go beyond simply providing help—they embed training directly into a software package (Cole et al., 1997). An EPSS may take on one or more forms: they can be an on-line tutorial, provide hypertext-based access to context-sensitive reference material, or consist of an expert system shell that acts as a coach. The main idea behind the development of an EPSS is that the user never has to leave the application to get the benefits of training. Users learn a new system or unfamiliar features at their own pace and on their own machines, without having to lose work time to remote group training sessions. Furthermore, this learning is on-demand when the user is most motivated to learn, since the user has a task to do. EPSS is sometimes referred to as "just-in-time knowledge." One example of an EPSS with which you may be familiar is Microsoft's Office Assistant™. Office Assistants (Figure 20-12) are animated characters that come up on top of such applications as Access™ and Word™. You ask questions and the Office Assistants return answers that provide educational information, such as graphics, examples, and procedures, as well as hypertext nodes for jumping to related help topics. Microsoft's Office Assistants communicate with the application you are running to see where you are, so you can determine, by

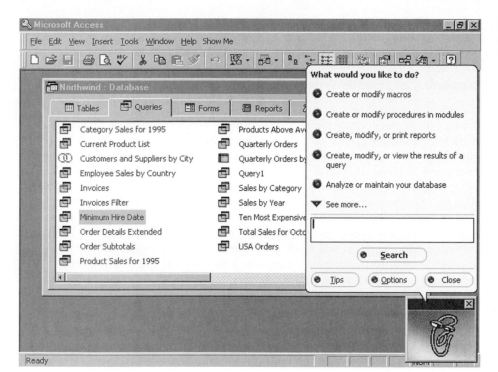

Figure 20-12
A Microsoft Office
Assistant™ note

reading the context-sensitive information, if what you want to do is possible from your present location. Some EPSS environments actually walk the user step-by-step through the task, coaching the user on what to do or allowing the user to get additional on-line assistance at any point.

Training for information systems is increasingly being made available both over company intranets and over the Internet. International Data Corporation projects that the on-line training industry will grow to a $28 billion business by the year 2001 (Dillon, 1997). Individual companies may prepare the training and make it available with the help of vendors who convert the content to work on the Internet. This is the case with Coopers & Lybrand's Tax News Network, which is available to 2000 subscribers as well as 3000 company staffers. Coopers & Lybrand features a two-hour training course on new tax legislation on its password-protected site. Alternatively, an organization may prepare its own training content using course authoring software. An example of this approach is Stanford University's Education Program for Gifted Youth, which Stanford provides over the Internet from its own servers. Still a third alternative is to access training provided by third party vendors. An example of this service is provided by CBT Systems, which offers 279 courses over the Internet. CBT Systems specializes in training on information technology products from multiple vendors, including Microsoft, Oracle, Novell, Powersoft, and SAP. Accessing training over the Internet has the potential to save companies thousands of dollars each year in training costs, especially when it comes to information technology training. Instead of having to send personnel off-site for weeks and pay their travel expenses, companies can gain access to Internet training for lower cost and personnel can get the training at their desks.

As both training and support for computing are increasingly able to be delivered on-line in modules, with some embedded in software packages and applications (as is the case for EPSS), the already blurred distinction between them blurs even more. Some of the issues most particular to computer user support are examined in the next section.

Supporting Information System Users

Historically, computing support for users has been provided in one of a few forms: paper, on-line versions of paper-based support, vendors, or by other people who work for the same organization. As we stated earlier, support, whatever its form, has often been inadequate for users' needs. Yet users consider support to be extremely important. A 1993 J. D. Power and Associates survey found user support to be the number one criterion contributing to user satisfaction with personal computing, cited by 26 percent of respondents as the most important factor (Schurr, 1993).

As organizations moved away from mainframe-based computing to increased reliance on personal computers in the 1980s, the need for support among users also increased. More support was made available on-line, but organizations also began to provide institutionalized user support in the form of information centers and help desks. An **information center** comprises a group of people who can answer questions and assist users with a wide range of computing needs, including the use of particular information systems. Information center staff might do the following:

- Install new hardware or software

- Consult with users writing programs in fourth-generation languages

- Extract data from organizational databases onto personal computers

- Set up user accounts

- Answer basic on-demand questions

- Provide a demonstration site for viewing hardware and software

- Work with users to submit system change requests

When you expect an organizational information center to help support a new system, you will likely want to train the information center staff as soon as possible on the system. Information center staff will need additional training periodically as new system features are introduced, new phases of a system are installed, or system problems and workarounds are identified. Even if new training is not required, information center staff should be aware of system changes, since such changes may result in an increase in demand for information center services.

Personnel in an information center or help desk (we will discuss help desks in a later section in this chapter) were typically drawn from the ranks of information systems workers or knowledgeable users in functional area departments. There was rarely any type of formal training for people to learn how to work in the support area and, in general, this remains true today. As organizations move to client/server architectures, their needs for support have increased even more than during the introduction of PCs, and organizations find themselves in the position of having to rely more than ever on vendor support (From, 1993). This increased need for support comes in part from the lack of standards governing client/server products and the resulting need to make equipment and software from different vendors compatible. Vendors are able to provide the necessary support, but as they have shifted their offerings from primarily expensive mainframe packages to inexpensive off-the-shelf software, they find they can no longer bear the cost of providing the support for free. Most vendors now charge for support, and many have instituted 900 numbers or sell customers unlimited support for a given monthly or annual charge.

Information center: An organizational unit whose mission is to support users in exploiting information technology.

Automating Support In an attempt to cut the costs of providing support and to catch up with the demand for additional support services, vendors have automated much of their support offerings. Common methods for automating support include on-line support forums, bulletin board systems, on-demand fax, and voice-response systems (Schneider, 1993). On-line support forums provide users access to information on new releases, bugs, and tips for more effective usage. Forums are offered on on-line services such as America OnLine,™ over the Internet, and over company intranets. On-demand fax allows users to order support information through an 800 number and receive that information instantly over their fax machines. Finally, voice-response systems allow users to navigate option menus that lead to prerecorded messages about usage, problems, and workarounds. Organizations have established similar support mechanisms for systems developed or purchased by the organization. Internal e-mail, group support systems, and office automation can be used to support such capabilities within an organization.

Other organizations can follow the lead of vendors in automating some of their support offerings in similar ways. Some software vendors work with large accounts and corporations to set up or enhance their own support offerings. The cost to the corporation can go from $5,000 to as much as $20,000. Offerings include access to knowledge bases about a vendor's products, electronic support services, single point of contact, and priority access to vendor support personnel (Schneider, 1993). Product knowledge bases include all of the technical and support information about vendor products and provide additional information for on-site personnel to use in solving problems. Some vendors allow users to access some of the same information that is available in on-line forums through bulletin boards which the vendors set up and maintain themselves and on Internet sites. Many vendors now supply complete user and technical documentation on CD-ROM, including periodic updates, so that a user organization can provide this library of documentation, bug reports, workaround notices, and notes on undocumented features on-line to all internal users. Electronic support services include all of the vendor support services discussed earlier, but tailored specifically for the corporation. The single point of contact is a system engineer who is often based on site and serves as a liaison between the corporation and the vendor. Finally, priority access means that corporate workers can always get help via telephone or e-mail from a person at the vendor company, usually within a prespecified response time of four hours or less.

Such vendor-enhanced support is especially appropriate in organizations where a wide variety of a particular vendor's products is in use, or where most in-house application development either utilizes vendor products as components of the larger system or where the vendor's products are themselves used as the basis for applications. An example of the former would be the case where an organization has set up a client/server architecture based on a particular vendor's SQL server and application programmer interfaces (APIs). Which applications are developed in-house to run under the client/server architecture depends heavily on the server and APIs, and direct vendor support dealing with problems in these components would be very helpful to the enterprise information systems staff. An example of the second would include order entry and inventory control application systems developed using Microsoft's Access™ or Excel™. In this case, the system developers and users, who are sometimes the same people for such package-based applications, can benefit considerably from directly questioning vendor representatives about their products.

Providing Support Through a Help Desk Whether assisted by vendors or going it alone, the center of support activities for a specific information system in many organizations is the help desk. A **help desk** is an information systems department function, staffed by IS personnel, possibly part of the information center unit. The

Help desk: A single point of contact for all user inquiries and problems about a particular information system or for all users in a particular department.

help desk is the first place users should call when they need assistance with an information system. The help desk staff either deals with the users' questions or refers the users to the most appropriate person.

For many years, a help desk was the dumping ground for people IS managers did not know what else to do with. Turnover rates were high because the position was sometimes little more than a complaints department, the pay was low, and burnout rates were high. In today's information systems-dependent enterprises, however, this situation has changed. Help desks are gaining new respect as management comes to appreciate the special combination of technical skills and people skills needed to make good help desk staffers. In fact, a recent survey reveals that the top two valued skills for help desk personnel are related to communication and customer service (Crowley, 1993).

Help desk personnel (as well as the personnel in the more general information center) need to be good at communicating with users, by listening to their problems and intelligently communicating potential solutions. These personnel also need to understand the technology they are helping users with. It is crucial, however, that help desk personnel know when new systems and releases are being implemented and when users are being trained for new systems. Help desk personnel themselves should be well-trained on new systems. One sure recipe for disaster is to train users on new systems but not train the help desk personnel these same users will turn to for their support needs.

Support Issues for the Analyst to Consider

Support is more than just answering user questions about how to use a system to perform a particular task or about the system's functionality. Support also consists of such tasks as providing for recovery and backup, disaster recovery, and PC maintenance; writing newsletters and offering other types of proactive information sharing; and setting up user groups. It is the responsibility of analysts for a new system to be sure that all forms of support are in place before the system is installed.

For medium to large organizations with active information system functions, many of these issues are dealt with centrally. For example, users may be provided with backup software by the central information systems unit and a schedule for routine backup. Policies may also be in place for initiating recovery procedures in case of system failure. Similarly, disaster recovery plans are almost always established by the central IS unit. Information systems personnel in medium to large organizations are also routinely responsible for PC maintenance, as the PCs belong to the enterprise. There may also be IS unit specialists in charge of composing and transmitting newsletters, or overseeing automated bulletin boards and organizing user groups.

When all of these (and more) services are provided by central IS, you must follow the proper procedures to include any new system and its users in the lists of those to whom support is provided. You must design training for the support staff on the new system, and you must make sure that system documentation will be available to it. You must make the support staff aware of the installation schedule. And you must keep these people informed as the system evolves. Similarly, any new hardware and off-the-shelf software has to be registered with the central IS authorities.

When there is no official IS support function to provide support services, you must come up with a creative plan to provide as many services as possible. You may have to write backup and recovery procedures and schedules, and the users' departments may have to purchase and be responsible for the maintenance of their hardware. In some cases, software and hardware maintenance may have to be outsourced to vendors or other capable professionals. In such situations, user interaction and information dissemination may have to be more informal than formal: informal user groups may meet over lunch or over a coffee pot rather than in officially formed and sanctioned forums.

ORGANIZATIONAL ISSUES IN SYSTEMS IMPLEMENTATION

Despite the best efforts of the systems development team to design and build a quality system and to manage the change process in the organization, the implementation effort sometimes fails. Sometimes employees will not use the new system that has been developed for them or, if they do use the system, their level of satisfaction with it is very low. Why do systems implementation efforts fail? This question has been the subject of information systems research for the past 25 years. In this section, we will try to provide some answers, first by looking at what conventional wisdom says are important factors related to implementation success, then by investigating factor-based models and political models of systems implementation.

Why Implementation Sometimes Fails

The conventional wisdom that has emerged over the years is that there are at least two conditions necessary for a successful implementation effort: management support of the system under development and the involvement of users in the development process (Ginzberg, 1981b). Conventional wisdom holds that if both of these conditions are met, you should have a successful implementation. Yet, despite the support and active participation of management and users, information systems implementation sometimes fails (see the box, System Implementation Failures, for examples).

Management support and user involvement are important to implementation success, but they may be overrated compared to other factors that are also important. Research has shown that the link between user involvement and implementation success is sometimes weak (Ives and Olson, 1984). User involvement can help reduce the risk of failure when the system is complex, but user participation in the development process only makes failure more likely when there are financial and time constraints in the development process (Tait and Vessey, 1988). Information systems implementation failures are too common, and the implementation process is too complicated, for the conventional wisdom to be completely correct. The search for better explanations for implementation success and failure has led to two alternative approaches: factor models and political models.

Factor Models of Implementation Success

Several research studies have found other factors that are important to a successful implementation process. Ginzberg (1981b) found three additional important factors: commitment to the project, commitment to change, and extent of project definition and planning. Commitment to the project involves managing the system development project so that the problem being solved is well understood and the system being developed to deal with the problem actually solves it. Commitment to change involves being willing to change behaviors, procedures, and other aspects of the organization. The extent of project definition and planning is a measure of how well planned the project is. The more extensive the planning effort,

System Implementation Failures

In 1985, the New Jersey Motor Vehicles Division implemented a new vehicle registration system. The new system had been developed by a major accounting firm in Applied Data Research's Ideal, a 4GL. Although appropriate for management information systems or decision support systems, 4GLs are not well-suited for high-volume transaction processing systems. As might have been predicted, the vehicle registration system was a disaster. Using the system entailed as much as a 5-minute response time, instead of the 2-second time the Division requested. System use resulted in a large number of incorrect vehicle registrations: over one million drivers in New Jersey had problems with their car registrations. The critical parts of the system had to be reprogrammed in COBOL at a cost of over two million dollars (which the accounting firm paid for) (Zwass, 1992).

Another state system has had an even more colorful history. In 1988, the Department of Health and Rehabilitative Services (HRS) began work on the development of the Florida On-Line Recipient Integrated Data Access system, or FLORIDA for short. The purpose of FLORIDA was to provide a single point of eligibility testing for the welfare services administered by the state, including food stamps, Aid to Families with Dependent Children (AFDC), and Medicaid. Access to FLORIDA would be possible from state welfare offices throughout the state, but FLORIDA and all of its files would reside in Tallahassee, the state capital. In 1989, EDS Federal Corporation won the bid for primary contractor for FLORIDA. One of the contract's stipulations was that the system be developed and implemented within 29 months.

FLORIDA was handed over to the state in June 1992. By the time the system came on-line, it had changed in at least two key aspects from the original design. First, the system was now running on a single mainframe system instead of three. Second, whereas the original design had called for eligibility rulings to be generated overnight, the final system allowed instant, on-line eligibility determinations.

From the time it was first handed over to the state, FLORIDA was a disaster. Response time often approached eight minutes. System crashes, lasting as long as eight hours, were common. Adding to the problems was the fact that, from July 1990 to July 1993, Florida's food stamps, AFDC, and

Medicaid enrollments doubled, from 800,000 to 1.6 million people. FLORIDA was pushed to the limits of its capacity. IBM was commissioned to bring in a new, powerful mainframe system for FLORIDA to run on. As of September 1993, over $173 million had been spent on FLORIDA's development and implementation, almost double the original estimate, and the system was still not complete. Consultants estimated the system had only two more years left to operate, given FLORIDA's then current capacity and projections for the state's welfare enrollments.

The human and financial toll from FLORIDA has easily surpassed those that resulted from New Jersey's vehicle registration system. FLORIDA's use resulted in at least $263 million in welfare over- and underpayments. In 1992, EDS sued HRS for $46 million in payments EDS says it never received. Throughout 1992 and 1993, several key information systems personnel in HRS were fired or forced to resign. In the spring of 1993, the Governor demoted the secretary of HRS and sent the lieutenant governor to HRS to manage the FLORIDA disaster. In August, 1993, a grand jury indicted the former project leader and former deputy secretary of HRS for information systems, for filing false status reports and for falsifying payment reports. In the spring of 1994, all charges were dropped against the former deputy secretary of HRS. The FLORIDA system's former project manager went to trial in May, 1994, and was convicted of two misdemeanor counts of making false statements. The judge in the case overthrew the verdict in June of that year.

In January 1995, the state announced that FLORIDA had been considerably improved, with the error rate for issuing benefits cut to only 12.5%. Yet in October of the same year, the state sued EDS for $60 million for improper business practices in its development of FLORIDA. The state also wanted to ban EDS from ever doing business again in Florida. Two months later, a judge threw out the state's suit. In March 1996, EDS won its 1992 suit against the state. In May of that year, the State of Florida agreed to pay EDS $42.8 million in back payments.

(Compiled from 1993–1996 stories in the Tallahassee Democrat and Information Week.)

the less likely is implementation failure. In other research, Ginzberg (1981a) uncovered another important factor related to implementation success: user expectations. The more realistic a user's early expectations about a new system and its capabilities, the more likely it is that the user will be satisfied with the new system and actually use it.

Although there are many ways to determine if an implementation has been successful, the two most common and trusted are the extent to which the system is used and the user's satisfaction with the system (Lucas, 1997). Lucas, who has extensively studied information systems implementation, identified six factors that influence the extent to which a system is used (1997):

1. *User's personal stake.* How important the domain of the system is for the user; in other words, how relevant the system is to the work the user performs. The

user's personal stake in the system is itself influenced by the level of support management provides for implementation, and by the urgency to the user of the problem addressed by the system. The higher the level of management support and the more urgent the problem, the higher the user's personal stake in the system.

2. *System characteristics*. Includes such aspects of the system's design as ease of use, reliability, and relevance to the task the system supports.

3. *User demographics*. Characteristics of the user, such as age and degree of computer experience.

4. *Organization support*. These are the same issues of support you read about earlier in the chapter. The better the system support infrastructure, the more likely an individual will be to use the system.

5. *Performance*. What individuals can do with a system to support their work will have an impact on extent of system use. The more users can do with a system and the more creative ways they can develop to benefit from the system the more they will use it. The relationship between performance and use goes both ways. The higher the levels of performance, the more use. The more use, the greater the performance.

6. *Satisfaction*. Use and satisfaction also represent a two-way relationship. The more satisfied the users are with the system, the more they will use it. The more they use it, the more satisfied they will be.

The factors identified by Lucas and the relationships they have to each other are shown in the model in Figure 20-13. In the model, it's easier to see the relationships among the various factors, such as how management support and

Figure 20-13
Lucas's model of implementation success, 1997 (Adapted with the permission of the McGraw-Hill Companies. All rights reserved.)

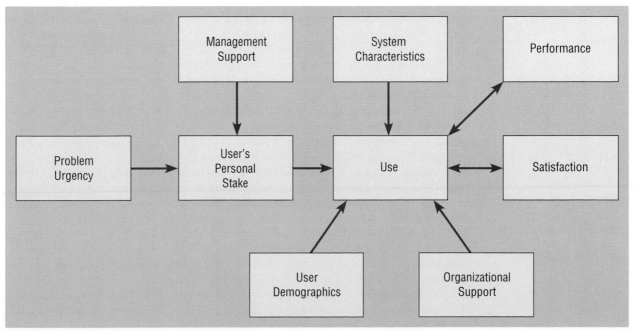

problem urgency affect the user's personal stake in the system. Notice also that the arrows that show the relationships between use and performance and satisfaction have two heads, illustrating the two-way relationships use has with these factors.

It should be clear that, as an analyst and as someone responsible for the successful implementation of an information system, there are some factors you have more control over than others. For example, you will have considerable influence over the system's characteristics, and you may have some influence over the levels of support that will be provided for users of the system. You have no direct control over a user's demographics, personal stake in the system, management support, or the urgency of the problem to the user. This doesn't mean you can ignore factors you can't change. On the contrary, you need to understand these factors very well, because you will have to balance them with the factors you *can* change in your system design and in your implementation strategy. You may not be able to change a user's demographics or personal stake in a system, but you can help design the system and your implementation strategy with these factors in mind.

Political Implementation Models

Factor models of the implementation process have helped analysts better understand implementation and why it may or may not be successful. Certainly, taking the different factors into account and realizing how they work together to influence implementation is important. But just as the conventional wisdom about implementation could not explain the whole story, neither can factor models hope to completely explain the implementation process. Political models have been proposed as another perspective to help you understand how a systems development project can succeed. We will use two examples from the implementation literature in MIS to illustrate the usefulness of political models.

Political models assume that individuals who work in an organization have their own self-interested goals, which they pursue in addition to the goals of their departments and the goals of their organizations. Political models also recognize that power is not distributed evenly in organizations. Some workers have more power than others. People may act to increase their own power relative to that of their coworkers and, at other times, people will act to prevent coworkers with more power (such as bosses) from using that power or from gaining more.

Markus (1981) tells the story of a division of an organization where implementation appears to have succeeded. Workers in two manufacturing plants, called Athens and Capital City, were using the new work-in-progress (WIP) system, which made it possible for management to use a planning and forecasting system based in part on the output of the WIP system. Workers from both plants had been involved in the systems development process, especially workers from the Capital City plant. When workers at Athens resisted using the new WIP system, extensive management pressure seemed to force people at Athens to give in and begin using the new system. It appeared that the conventional wisdom about systems development had prevailed: workers had participated in development, and management had been forcefully supportive. Implementation was a success.

Markus presents a political interpretation of the story that provides another explanation of events (see Figure 20-14). She begins by examining the history and power relationships within the division and the two plants. Although Athens was the plant that resisted using the new WIP system, they actually had superior information systems support at the beginning of the WIP system development process.

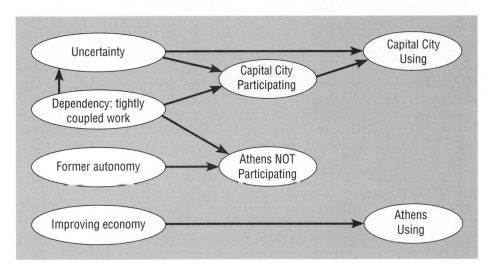

Figure 20-14
Illustrating the political
explanation of system
success at Athens and
Capital City

Athens had once been a separate company and, until the division head decided new WIP and new planning systems were needed, Athens had been allowed a large amount of autonomy in how it operated. Further, the work performed at the two plants was tightly coupled. The Athens plant manufactured airplane parts, which were then refined and finished at Capital City. Athens' manufacturing process was unpredictable and unreliable and resulted in a high scrap rate. Capital City never knew where Athens was in the manufacturing process for any particular part, and this uncertainty complicated Capital City's efforts to complete its work and finish parts in time for promised delivery dates.

According to Markus, when the opportunity arose to develop a system that would lessen the dependency of Capital City on Athens, people at Capital City were anxious to participate in the system's development. With a new WIP system containing data on Athens' production process, data which Capital City could access, the Capital City plant could greatly reduce the uncertainty associated with its own work. Understandably, the people at Athens were not so enthusiastic, and resisted participating in the development process and using the new system. After the WIP system was completed and installed in both plants, the people at Athens continued to use their old WIP system, much to the chagrin of division management and Capital City. Division management applied a great deal of pressure, until finally Athens began to use the system. Markus states, however, that the people at Athens began using the new system not because of management pressure but because the economy began to improve, and managing the work at Athens became too difficult without the new system.

One lesson to be learned from Markus's case study is that factor-based analyses can only go so far in explaining successful implementation in organizations. History and power relationships are also important considerations. Sometimes political interpretations provide better explanations for the implementation process and why events took the course they did.

Once an information system has been successfully implemented, the importance of documentation grows. A successfully implemented system becomes part of the daily work lives of an organization's employees. Many of those employees will use the system, but others will maintain it and keep it running. Documentation is important for both groups of people and is the topic for the next section of the chapter.

PROJECT CLOSE-DOWN

In Chapter 3 you learned about the various phases of project management, from project initiation to closing down the project. If you are the project manager and you have successfully guided your project through all of the phases of the systems development life cycle presented so far in this book, you are now ready to close down your project. Although the maintenance phase is just about to begin, the development project itself is over. As you will see in the next chapter, maintenance can be thought of as a series of smaller development projects, each with its own series of project management phases.

As you recall from Chapter 3, your first task in closing down the project involves many different activities, from dealing with project personnel to planning a celebration of the project's ending. You will likely have to evaluate your team members, reassign most to other projects, and perhaps terminate others. As project manager, you will also have to notify all of the affected parties that the development project is ending and that you are now switching to maintenance mode.

Your second task is to conduct post-project reviews with both your management and your customers. In some organizations, these post-project reviews will follow formal procedures and may involve internal or EDP (electronic data processing) auditors. The point of a project review is to critique the project, its methods, its deliverables, and its management. You can learn many lessons to improve future projects from a thorough post-project review.

The third major task in project close-down is closing out the customer contract. Any contract that has been in effect between you and your customers during the project (or as the basis for the project) must be completed, typically through the consent of all contractually involved parties. This may involve a formal "signing-off" by the clients that your work is complete and acceptable. The maintenance phase will typically be covered under new contractual agreements. If your customer is outside of your organization, you will also likely negotiate a separate support agreement.

As an analyst member of the development team, your job on this particular project ends during project close-down. You will likely be reassigned to another project dealing with some other organizational problem. Maintenance on your new system will begin and continue without you. To complete our consideration of the systems development life cycle, however, we will cover the maintenance phase and its component tasks in Chapter 21.

SUMMARY

This chapter presented an overview of the various aspects of the systems implementation process. In the chapter, you studied seven different types of testing: (1) code inspections, where code is examined for well-known errors; (2) walkthroughs, where a group manually examines what the code is supposed to do; (3) desk checking, where an individual mentally executes the computer instructions; (4) syntax checking, typically done by a compiler; (5) unit or module testing; (6) integration testing, where modules are combined and tested together until the entire program has been tested as a whole; and (7) system testing, where programs are combined to be tested as a system and where the system's meeting of its objectives is examined. You also learned about acceptance testing, where users test the system for its ability to meet their requirements, using live data in a live environment.

You read about four types of installation: (1) direct, where the old system is shut off just as the new one is turned on; (2) parallel, where both old and new systems are run together until it is clear the new system is ready to be used exclusively;

(3) single location, where one site is selected to test the new system; and (4) phased, where the system is installed bit by bit.

You learned about four types of documentation: system documentation, which describes in detail the design of a system and its specifications; internal documentation, that part of system documentation which is included in the code itself or emerges at compile time; external documentation, that part of system documentation which includes the output of diagramming techniques such as data flow and entity-relationship diagramming; and user documentation, which describes a system and how to use it for the system's users.

Training and support are both part of an organization's computing infrastructure. A computing infrastructure is analogous to a city's infrastructure of streets, water mains, and electrical lines. The computing infrastructure allows an organization's computer users to continue to operate, just as a city's infrastructure allows the city to continue to operate. In many organizations, the computing infrastructure and the people charged with providing and maintaining it are underfunded.

Computer training has typically been provided in classes and tutorials. While there is some evidence lectures have their place in teaching people about computing and information systems, the current emphasis in training is on automated delivery methods, such as on-line reference facilities, multimedia training, and electronic performance support systems. The latter embed training in applications themselves in an attempt to make training a seamless part of using an application for daily operations. The emphasis in support is also on providing on-line delivery, including on-line support forums and bulletin board systems. As organizations move toward client/server architectures, they rely more on vendors for support. Vendors provide many on-line support services, and they work with customers to bring many aspects of on-line support in-house. An information center provides general support to all users, and a help desk provides aid to users in a particular department or for a particular system.

You saw how information systems researchers have been trying to explain what constitutes a successful implementation, using conventional wisdom, factor models, and political models. If there is a single main point in this chapter, it is that implementation is a complicated process, from managing programmer teams to the politics that influence what happens to a system after it has been successfully implemented to planning and implementing useful training and support mechanism. Analysts have many factors to identify and manage for a successful systems implementation. Successful implementation rarely happens by accident or occurs in a totally predictable manner. The first step in a successful implementation effort may be realizing just that fact.

KEY TERMS

Acceptance testing	External documentation	Phased installation
Alpha testing	Help desk	Single location installation
Beta testing	Information center	Stub testing
Computing infrastructure	Inspections	System documentation
Desk checking	Installation	System testing
Direct installation	Integration testing	Support
Electronic performance	Internal documentation	Unit testing
support system (EPSS)	Parallel installation	User documentation

REVIEW QUESTIONS

1. Define each of the following terms:
   a. walkthrough
   b. stub testing
   c. computing infrastructure
   d. electronic performance support system (EPSS)
   e. external documentation

2. What are the deliverables from coding, testing, and installation?

3. Explain the testing process for code.

4. What are structured walkthroughs for code? What is their purpose? How are they conducted? How are they different from code inspections?

5. What are the four approaches to installation? Which is the most expensive? Which is the most risky? How does an organization decide which approach to use?

6. What is the conventional wisdom about implementation success?

7. List and define the factors that are important to successful implementation efforts.

8. Explain Lucas's model of implementation success.

9. How would you characterize political models of the implementation process? What can political models do that factor models don't?

10. What is the difference between system documentation and user documentation?

11. What were the common methods of computer training in 1987? What training methods have been added since then?

12. What is self-training?

13. What proof do you have that individual differences matter in computer training?

14. Why are corporations relying so heavily on vendor support as they move to client/server architectures?

15. Describe the delivery methods many vendors employ for providing support.

16. Describe the various roles typically found in a help desk function.

PROBLEMS AND EXERCISES

1. Match the following terms to the appropriate definitions.

   _____ acceptance testing

   _____ direct installation

   _____ parallel installation

   _____ system testing

   a. bringing together all of the programs that a system comprises for testing purposes. Programs are typically integrated in a top-down, incremental fashion

   b. process whereby actual users test a completed information system, the end result of which is the users' acceptance of the system

   c. bringing together all of the modules that a program comprises for testing purposes

   d. changing over from the old system to a new one by turning off the old system as the new one is turned on

_____ integration testing

e. running the old system and the new one at the same time until the old system can be turned off

_____ system documentation

f. detailed information about a system's design specifications, its internal workings, and its functionality

_____ user documentation

g. system documentation that includes the outcome of such structured diagramming techniques as data flow and entity-relationship diagrams

_____ internal documentation

h. written or other visual information about an application system, how it works, and how to use it

_____ external documentation

i. system documentation that is part of the program source code or is generated at compile time

2. Prepare a testing strategy or plan for Pine Valley Furniture's Purchasing Fulfillment System (see Chapter 18 for details).

3. Which installation strategy would you recommend for PVF's Purchasing Fulfillment System? Which would you recommend for Hoosier Burger's Inventory Control System? If you recommended different approaches, please explain why. How is PVF's case different from Hoosier Burger's?

4. Develop a table that compares the four installation strategies, showing the pros and cons of each. Try to make a direct comparison when a pro of one is a con of another.

5. One of the difficult aspects of using the single location approach to installation is choosing an appropriate location. What factors should be considered in picking a pilot site?

6. You have been a user of many information systems including, possibly, a class registration system at your school, a bank account system, a word processing system, and an airline reservation system. Pick a system you have used and assume you were involved in the beta testing of that system. What would be the criteria you would apply to judge whether this system was ready for general distribution?

7. Why is it important to keep a history of test cases and the results of those test cases even after a system has been revised several times?

8. How much documentation is enough?

9. What is the purpose of electronic performance support systems? How would you design one to support a word processing package? A database package?

10. Discuss the role of a centralized training and support facility in a modern organization. Given advances in technology and the prevalence of self-training and consulting among computing end users, how can such a centralized facility continue to justify its existence?

11. Is it good or bad for corporations to rely on vendors for computing support? List arguments both for and against reliance on vendors as part of your answer.

12. Suppose you were responsible for establishing a training program for users of Hoosier Burger's inventory control system (described in previous chapters). Which forms of training would you use? Why?

13. Suppose you were responsible for establishing a help desk for users of Hoosier Burger's inventory control system (described in previous chapters). Which support system elements would you create to help users be effective? Why?

14. Your university or school probably has some form of microcomputer center or help desk for students. What functions does this center perform? How do these functions compare to those outlined in this chapter?

15. Suppose you were responsible for organizing the user documentation for Hoosier Burger's inventory control system (described in previous chapters). Write an outline that shows the documentation you would suggest be created, and generate the table of contents or outline for each element of this documentation.

FIELD EXERCISES

1. Interview someone you know or have access to who works for a medium to large organization. Ask for details on a specific instance of organizational change: What changed? How did it happen? Was it well planned or ad hoc? How were people in the organization affected? How easy was it for employees to move from the old situation to the new one?

2. Reexamine the data you collected in the interview in Field Exercise 1. This time, analyze the data from a political perspective. How well does the political model explain how the organization dealt with change? Explain why the political model does or does not fit.

3. Ask a systems analyst you know or have access to about implementation. Ask what the analyst believes is necessary for a successful implementation. Try to determine whether the analyst believes in factor models or political models of implementation.

4. Prepare a research report on successful and unsuccessful information system implementations. After you have found information on two or three examples of both successful and unsuccessful system implementations, try to find similarities and differences among the examples of each type of implementation. Do you detect any patterns? Can you add to either the factor or political models you read about in the chapter?

5. Talk with people you know who use computers in their work. Ask them to get copies of the user documentation they rely on for the systems they use at work. Analyze the documentation. Would you consider it good or bad? Support your answer. Whether good or bad, how might you improve it?

6. Volunteer to work for a shift at a help desk at your school's computer center. Keep a journal of your experiences. What kind of users did you have to deal with? What kinds of questions did you get? Do you think help desk work is easy or hard? What skills are needed by someone in this position?

7. Let's say your professor has asked you to help him or her train a new secretary on how to prepare class notes for electronic distribution to class members. Your professor uses word processing software and an e-mail package to prepare and distribute the notes. Assume the secretary knows nothing about either package. Prepare a user task guide that shows the secretary how to complete this task.

REFERENCES

Bell, P., and C. Evans. 1989. *Mastering Documentation*. New York, NY: John Wiley & Sons.

Bloor, R. 1994. "The Disappearing Programmer." *DBMS* 7(9) (Aug.): 14–16.

Bozman, J.S. 1994. "United to Simplify Denver's Troubled Baggage Project." *ComputerWorld*, 10(10).

Brooks, F. P. 1995. *The Mythical Man-Month*. Anniversary Edition. Reading, MA: Addison-Wesley.

Cole, K., O. Fischer, and P. Saltzman. 1997. "Just-in-Time Knowledge Delivery." *Communications of the ACM* 40(7): 49-53.

Crowley, A. 1993. "The Help Desk Gains Respect." *PC Week* 10 (November 15): 138.

de Jager, P. 1994. "Are We Just Plain Lazy?" *Computerworld* 28 (February 21): 85.

Dillon, N. 1997. "Internet-based Training Passes Audit." *Computerworld* (November 3): 47-48.

Eason, K. 1988. *Information Technology and Organisational Change*. London: Taylor & Francis.

Fagan, M. E. 1986. "Advances in Software Inspections." *IEEE Transactions on Software Engineering* SE-12(7) (July): 744–51.

From, E. 1993. "Shouldering the Burden of Support." *PC Week* 10 (November 15): 122, 144.

Gasser, L. 1986. "The Integration of Computing and Routine Work." *ACM Transactions on Office Information Systems* 4 (July): 205–25.

Ginzberg, M. J. 1981a. "Early Diagnosis of MIS Implementation Failure: Promising Results and Unanswered Questions." *Management Science* 27(4): 459-78.

Ginzberg, M. J. 1981b. "Key Recurrent Issues in the MIS Implementation Process." *MIS Quarterly* 5(2) (June): 47–59.

Henderson, J. C., and M. E. Treacy. 1986. "Managing End-User Computing for Competitive Advantage." *Sloan Management Review* (Winter): 3–14.

Ives, B. and M. H. Olson. 1984. "User Involvement and MIS Success: A Review of Research." *Management Science* 30(5): 586–603.

Jones, C. 1986. Programming Productivity. New York, NY: McGraw-Hill.

Kling, R., and S. Iacono. 1989. "Desktop Computerization and the Organization of Work." In *Computers in the Human Context*, edited by T. Forester. Cambridge, MA: The MIT Press: 335–56.

Kling, R., and W. Scacchi. 1982. "The Web of Computing: Computer Technology as Social Organization." *Advances in Computers* 21: 1–90.

Lee, D. M. S. 1986. "Usage Pattern and Sources of Assistance for Personal Computer Users." *MIS Quarterly*, 10 (December): 313–25.

Leib, J. 1997. "Baggage Suit Quietly Settled." *The Denver Post Online*, Sept. 11.

Litecky, C. R., and G. B. Davis. 1976. "A Study of Errors, Error Proneness, and Error Diagnosis in COBOL." *Communications of the ACM* 19(1): 33–37.

Lucas, H. C. 1997. *Information Technology for Management*. New York, NY: McGraw-Hill.

Martin, J., and C. McClure. 1985. *Structured Techniques for Computing*. Englewood Cliffs, NJ: Prentice-Hall.

Markus, M. L. 1981. "Implementation Politics: Top Management Support and User Involvement." *Systems/Objectives/Solutions* 1(4): 203–15.

Mosley, D. J. 1993. *The Handbook of MIS Application Software Testing*. Englewood Cliffs, NJ: Yourdon Press.

Nelson, R. R., and P. H. Cheney. 1987. "Training End Users: An Exploratory Study." *MIS Quarterly* 11 (December): 547–59.

Rivard, S., and S. L. Huff. 1988. "Factors of Success for End-User Computing." *Communications of the ACM* 31 (May): 552–61.

Rockart, J. F., and J. E. Short. 1989. "IT in the 1990s: Managing Organizational Interdependence." *Sloan Management Review* (Winter): 7–17.

Russell, D. L. 1994. "Just Say NO to Documentation." *Computerworld* 28 (January 17): 35.

Schneider, J. 1993. "Shouldering the Burden of Support." *PC Week* 10 (November 15): 123, 129.

Schrage, M. 1993. "Unsupported Technology: A Prescription for Failure." *Computerworld* 27 (May 10): 31.

Schurr, A. 1993. "Support is No. 1." *PC Week* 10 (November 15): 126.

Tait, P. and I. Vessey. 1988. "The Effect of User Involvement on System Success: A Contingency Approach." *MIS Quarterly* 12(1) (March): 91–108.

Torkzadeh, G., and W. J. Doll. 1993. "The Place and Value of Documentation in End-User Computing." *Information & Management* 24 (3): 147–58.

Yourdon, E. 1989. *Managing the Structured Techniques*. 4th ed. Englewood Cliffs, NJ: Prentice-Hall.

Zwass, V. 1992. *Management Information Systems.* Des Moines, IA: William C. Brown.

Maintaining Information Systems

After studying this chapter, you should be able to:

■ Explain and contrast four types of maintenance.

■ Describe several factors that influence the cost of maintaining an information system and apply these factors to the design of maintainable systems.

■ Describe maintenance management issues including alternative organizational structures, quality measurement, processes for handling change requests, and configuration management.

■ Explain the role of CASE when maintaining information systems.

INTRODUCTION

> As the twentieth century draws to a close, software development and maintenance operations have become major corporate cost centers. In addition, the magnitude and replacement value of software portfolios have become significant tax liabilities. Finally, the on-rushing "Year 2000" problem brings on a set of new and exceptionally large software costs that will have a major financial impact on corporations and government agencies. (Capers Jones, 1997)

In this final chapter, we discuss systems maintenance, the largest systems development expenditure for many organizations. In fact, more programmers today work on maintenance activities than work on new development. Your first job after graduation may very well be as a maintenance programmer/analyst. This disproportionate distribution of maintenance programmers is interesting since software does not wear out in a physical manner as do buildings and machines.

There is no single reason why software is maintained; however, most reasons relate to a desire to evolve system functionality in order to overcome internal processing errors or to better support changing business needs. Thus, maintaining a system is a fact of life for most systems. This means that maintenance can begin soon after the system is installed. As with the initial design of a system, maintenance activities are not limited only to software changes but include changes to hardware and business procedures. A question many people have about maintenance relates to how long organizations should maintain a system. Five years? Ten years? Longer? There is no simple answer to this question, but it is most often an issue of economics. In other words, at what point does it make financial sense to discontinue evolving an older system and build or purchase a new one? The focus of a great deal of upper IS management attention is devoted to assessing the trade-offs between maintenance and new development. In this chapter, we will provide you with a better understanding of the maintenance process and describe the types of issues that must be considered when maintaining systems.

In this chapter, we also briefly describe the systems maintenance process and the deliverables and outcomes from this process. This is followed by a detailed discussion contrasting the types of maintenance, an overview of critical management issues, and a description of the role of CASE and automated development tools in the maintenance process. Finally, we describe the process of resolving a maintenance request at Pine Valley Furniture.

MAINTAINING INFORMATION SYSTEMS

Once an information system is installed, the system is essentially in the maintenance phase of the SDLC. When a system is in the maintenance phase, some person within the systems development group is responsible for collecting maintenance requests from system users and other interested parties, like system auditors, data center and network management staff, and data analysts. Once collected, each request is analyzed to better understand how it will alter the system and what business benefits and necessities will result from such a change. If the change request is approved, a system change is designed and then implemented. As with the initial development of the system, implemented changes are formally reviewed and tested before installation into operational systems.

The Process of Maintaining Information Systems

Throughout this book, we have drawn the systems development life cycle as the waterfall model where one phase leads to the next with overlap and feedback loops. As shown in Figure 21-1, the maintenance phase is the last phase of the SDLC. Yet, a life cycle, by definition, is circular in that the last activity leads back to the first. This means that the process of maintaining an information system is the process of returning to the beginning of the SDLC (see Figure 21-2) and repeating development steps until the change is implemented.

As shown in Figure 21-1, four major activities occur within maintenance:

1. Obtaining Maintenance Requests
2. Transforming Requests into Changes
3. Designing Changes
4. Implementing Changes

Obtaining maintenance requests requires that a formal process be established whereby users can submit system change requests. Earlier in the book, we presented a user request document called a Systems Service Request (SSR), which is shown in Figure 21-3. Most companies have some sort of document like an SSR to request new development, to report problems, or to request new system features with an existing system. When developing the procedures for obtaining maintenance requests, organizations must also specify an individual within the organiza-

Figure 21-1
Systems development life cycle with maintenance phase highlighted

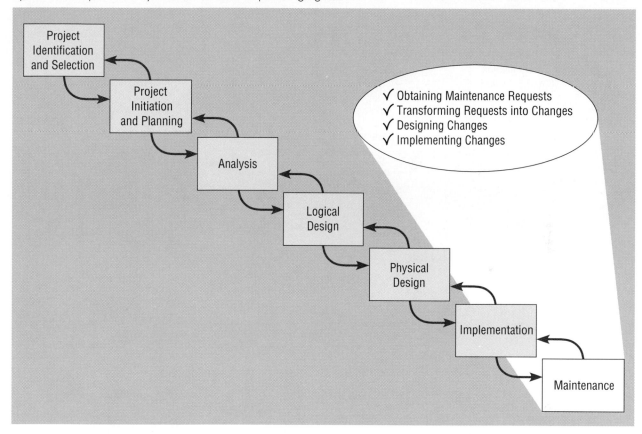

tion to collect these requests and manage their dispersal to maintenance personnel. The process of collecting and dispersing maintenance requests is described in much greater detail later in the chapter.

Once a request is received, analysis must be conducted to gain an understanding of the scope of the request. It must be determined how the request will affect the current system and the duration of such a project. As with the initial development of a system, the size of a maintenance request can be analyzed for risk and feasibility (see Chapter 6). Next, a change request can be transformed into a formal design change which can then be fed into the maintenance implementation phase. Thus, many similarities exist between the SDLC and the activities within the maintenance process. Figure 21-4 equates SDLC phases to the maintenance activities described previously. The figure shows that the first phase of the SDLC—project identification and selection—is analogous to the maintenance process of obtaining a maintenance request (step 1). SDLC phases project initiation and planning and analysis are analogous to the maintenance process of transforming requests into a specific system change (step 2). The logical and physical design phases of the SDLC, of course, equate to the designing changes process (step 3). Finally, the SDLC phase implementation equates to step 4, implementing changes. This similarity between the maintenance process and the SDLC is no accident. The concepts and techniques used to initially develop a system are also used to maintain it.

Figure 21-2
Maintenance phase makes the systems development process a life cycle

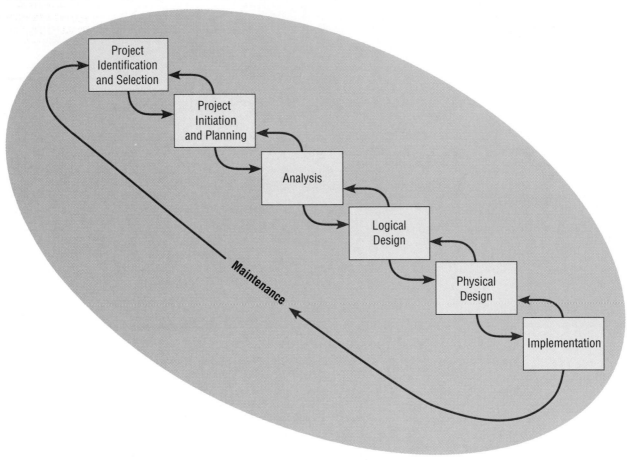

Deliverables and Outcomes

Since the maintenance phase of the SDLC is basically a subset of the activities of the entire development process, the deliverables and outcomes from the process are the development of a new version of the software and new versions of all design documents developed or modified during the maintenance process. This means that all documents created or modified during the maintenance effort, including the system itself, represent the deliverables and outcomes of the process. Those programs and documents that did not change may also be part of the new system. Since most organizations archive prior versions of systems, all prior programs and documents must be kept to ensure the proper versioning of the system. This enables prior versions of the system to be recreated if needed. A more detailed discussion of configuration management and change control is presented later in the chapter.

Because of the similarities between the steps, deliverables, and outcomes of new development and maintenance, you may be wondering how to distinguish between these two processes. One difference is that maintenance reuses most existing system modules in producing the new system version. Other distinctions are that we develop a new system when there is a change in the hardware or software platform or when fundamental assumptions and properties of the data, logic, or process models change.

Figure 21-3
Systems Service Request for Purchasing Fulfillment System (Pine Valley Furniture)

Pine Valley Furniture
System Service Request

REQUESTED BY   Juanita Lopez   DATE   November 1, 1998

DEPARTMENT   Purchasing, Manufacturing Support

LOCATION   Headquarters, 1-322

CONTACT   Tel: 4-3267   FAX: 4-3270   e-mail: jlopez

TYPE OF REQUEST   URGENCY

[X] New System   [   ] Immediate – Operations are impaired or
                                                           opportunity lost

[   ] System Enhancement   [   ] Problems exist, but can be worked around
[   ] System Error Correction   [X] Business losses can be tolerated until new
                                                           system installed

PROBLEM STATEMENT

Sales growth at PVF has caused greater volume of work for the manufacturing support unit within
Purchasing. Further, more concentration on customer service has reduced manufacturing lead times,
which puts more pressure on purchasing activities. In addition, cost-cutting measures force Purchasing
to be more agressive in negotiating terms with vendors, improving delivery times, and lowering our
investments in inventory. The current modest systems support for manufacturing purchasing is not
responsive to these new business conditions. Data are not available, information cannot be summarized,
supplier orders cannot be adequately tracked, and commodity buying is not well supported. PVF is
spending too much on raw materials and not being responsive to manufacturing needs.

SERVICE REQUEST

I request a thorough analysis of our current operations with the intent to design and build a completely
new information system. This system should handle all purchasing transactions, support display and
reporting of critical purchasing data, and assist purchasing agents in commodity buying.

IS LIAISON   Chris Martin (Tel: 4-6204   FAX: 4-6200   e-mail: cmartin)

SPONSOR   Sal Divario, Director, Purchasing

----------------------- TO BE COMPLETED BY SYSTEMS PRIORITY BOARD -----------------------

[   ] Request approved   Assigned to _____
                                          Start date _____
[   ] Recommend revision
[   ] Suggest user development
[   ] Reject for reason _____
                                          _____
                                          _____

Figure 21-4
Maintenance activities in relation to the SDLC

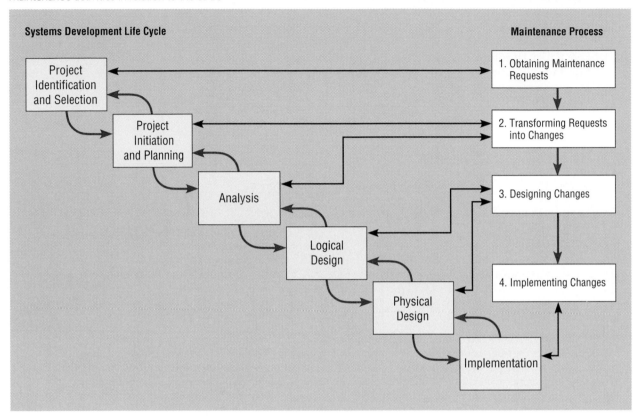

CONDUCTING SYSTEMS MAINTENANCE

A significant portion of the expenditures for information systems within organizations does not go to the development of new systems but to the maintenance of existing systems. We will describe various types of maintenance, factors influencing the complexity and cost of maintenance, alternatives for managing maintenance, and the role of CASE during maintenance. Given that maintenance activities consume the majority of information systems-related expenditures, gaining an understanding of these topics will yield numerous benefits to your career as an information systems professional.

Types of Maintenance

Maintenance: Changes made to a system to fix or enhance its functionality.

Corrective maintenance: Changes made to a system to repair flaws in its design, coding, or implementation.

There are several types of **maintenance** that you can perform on an information system (see Table 21-1). By maintenance, we mean the fixing or enhancing of an information system. **Corrective maintenance** refers to changes made to repair defects in the design, coding, or implementation of the system. For example, if you had recently purchased a new home, corrective maintenance would involve repairs made to things that had never worked as designed, such as a faulty electrical outlet or misaligned door. Most corrective maintenance problems surface soon after installation. When corrective maintenance problems surface, they are typically urgent and need to be resolved to curtail possible interruptions in normal business activities. Of all types of maintenance, corrective accounts for as much as 75 percent of all

TABLE 21-1	Types of Maintenance
Type	**Description**
Corrective	Repair design and programming errors
Adaptive	Modify system to environmental changes
Perfective	Evolve system to solve new problems or take advantage of new opportunities
Preventive	Safeguard system from future problems

maintenance activity (Andrews and Leventhal, 1993). This is unfortunate because corrective maintenance adds little or no value to the organization; it simply focuses on removing defects from an existing system without adding new functionality (see Figure 21-5).

Adaptive maintenance involves making changes to an information system to evolve its functionality to changing business needs or to migrate it to a different operating environment. Within a home, adaptive maintenance might be adding storm windows to improve the cooling performance of an air conditioner. Adaptive maintenance is usually less urgent than corrective maintenance because business and technical changes typically occur over some period of time. Contrary to corrective maintenance, adaptive maintenance is generally a small part of an organization's maintenance effort but does add value to the organization.

Perfective maintenance involves making enhancements to improve processing performance, interface usability, or to add desired, but not necessarily required, system features ("bells and whistles"). In our home example, perfective maintenance would be adding a new room. Many system professionals feel that perfective maintenance is not really maintenance but new development.

Preventive maintenance involves changes made to a system to reduce the chance of future system failure. An example of preventive maintenance might be to increase the number of records that a system can process far beyond what is currently needed or to generalize how a system sends report information to a printer so that the system can easily adapt to changes in printer technology. In our home example, preventive maintenance could be painting the exterior to better protect the home from severe weather conditions. As with adaptive maintenance, both perfective and preventive maintenance are typically a much lower priority than corrective maintenance. Over the life of a system, corrective maintenance is most likely to occur after initial system installation or after major system changes. This

Adaptive maintenance:
Changes made to a system to evolve its functionality to changing business needs or technologies.

Perfective maintenance:
Changes made to a system to add new features or to improve performance.

Preventive maintenance:
Changes made to a system to avoid possible future problems.

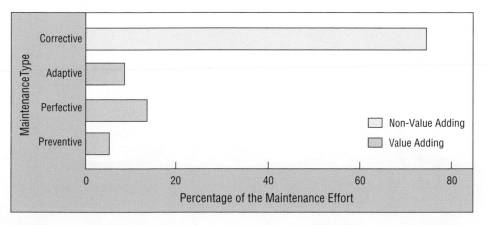

Figure 21-5
Types of maintenance (Adapted from Andrews and Leventhal, 1993)

means that adaptive, perfective, and preventive maintenance activities can lead to corrective maintenance activities if not carefully designed and implemented.

The Cost of Maintenance

Information systems maintenance costs are a significant expenditure. For some organizations, as much as 80 percent of their information systems budget is allocated to maintenance activities (Pressman, 1992). Additionally, the proportion of systems expenditures has been rising due to the fact that many organizations have accumulated more and more older systems that require more and more maintenance. For example, Figure 21-6 shows that in the 1970s, most of an organization's information systems' expenditures were allocated to new development rather than to maintenance. However, over the years, this mix has changed so that the majority of expenditures are now earmarked for maintenance. This means that you must understand the factors influencing the **maintainability** of systems. Maintainability is the ease with which software can be understood, corrected, adapted, and enhanced. Systems with low maintainability result in uncontrollable maintenance expenses.

Numerous factors influence the maintainability of a system. These factors, or cost elements, will determine the extent to which a system has high or low maintainability. Table 21-2 shows numerous elements that influence the cost of maintenance, many of which you can influence as a systems analyst. Of these factors, three are most significant: number of latent defects, number of customers, and documentation quality.

The number of latent defects refers to the number of unknown errors existing in the system after it is installed. Because corrective maintenance accounts for most maintenance activity, the number of latent defects in a system influences most of the costs associated with maintaining a system. If there are no errors in the system after it is installed, then maintenance costs will be relatively low. If there are a large number of defects in the system when it is installed, maintenance costs will likely be high.

A second factor influencing maintenance costs is the number of customers for a given system. In general, the greater the number of customers, the greater the maintenance costs. For example, if a system has only one customer, problem and change requests will come from only one source. A single customer also makes it much eas-

Maintainability: The ease with which software can be understood, corrected, adapted, and enhanced.

Figure 21-6

New development versus maintenance as a percent of software budget (Adapted from Pressman, 1987)

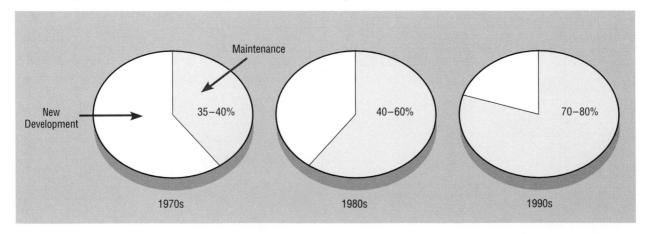

TABLE 21-2 Cost Elements of Maintenance

Element	Description
Defects	Number of unknown defects in a system when it is installed
Customers	Number of different customers that a maintenance group must support
Documentation	Quality of technical system documentation including test cases
Personnel	Number and quality of personnel dedicated to the support and maintenance of a system
Tools	Software development tools, debuggers, hardware, and other resources
Software Structure	Structure and maintainability of the software

Adapted from Jones, 1986

ier for the maintenance group to know how the system is actually being used and the extent to which users are adequately trained. If the system fails, the maintenance group is only notifying, supporting, and retraining a small group of people and updating their programs and documentation. On the other hand, for a system with thousands of users, change requests (possibly contradictory or incompatible) and error reports come from many places, and notification of problems, customer support, and system and documentation updating become a much more significant problem. For example, notifying all customers of a problem is fast and easy when you have a single customer whom you can contact using a telephone, fax, or electronic mail message. Yet, it will be difficult and expensive to quickly and easily contact thousands of users about a catastrophic problem. In sum, the greater the number of customers, the more critical it is that a system have high maintainability.

A third major contributing factor to maintenance costs is the quality of system documentation. Figure 21-7 shows that without quality documentation, maintenance effort can increase exponentially. In conclusion, numerous factors will influence the maintainability and thus the overall costs of system maintenance. System professionals have found that the number of defects in the installed system drive all other

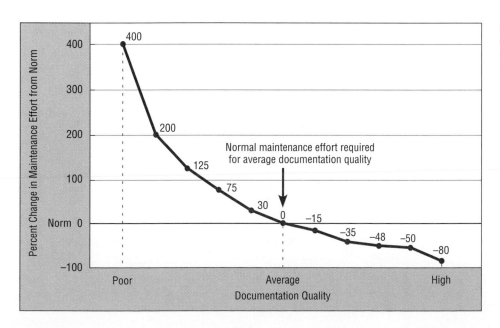

Figure 21-7
Quality documentation eases maintenance (Adapted from Hanna, 1992)

cost factors. This means that it is important that you remove as many errors as possible before installation.

The quality of the maintenance personnel also contributes to the cost of maintenance. In some organizations, the best programmers are assigned to maintenance. Highly skilled programmers are needed because the maintenance programmer is typically not the original programmer and must quickly understand and carefully change the software. Tools, such as those that can automatically produce system documentation where none exists, can also lower maintenance costs. Finally, well-structured programs make it much easier to understand and fix programs.

Managing Maintenance

As maintenance activities consume more and more of the systems development budget, maintenance management has become increasingly important. For example, Table 21-3 shows the worldwide growth of programmers who are working on new development versus maintenance. These data show that the number of people working on maintenance has now surpassed the number working on new development. Maintenance has become the largest segment of programming personnel, and this implies the need for careful management. We will address this concern by discussing several topics related to the effective management of systems maintenance.

Managing Maintenance Personnel   One concern with managing maintenance relates to personnel management. Historically, many organizations had a "maintenance group" that was separate from the "development group." With the increased number of maintenance personnel, the development of formal methodologies and tools, changing organizational forms, end-user computing, and the widespread use of very high-level languages for the development of some systems, organizations have rethought the organization of maintenance and development personnel (Chapin, 1987). In other words, should the maintenance group be separated from the development group? Or, should the same people who build the system also maintain it? A third option is to let the primary end users of the system in the functional units of the business have their own maintenance personnel. The advantages and disadvantages to each of these organizational structures are summarized in Table 21-4.

In addition to the advantages and disadvantages listed in Table 21-4, there are numerous other reasons why organizations should be concerned with how they manage and assign maintenance personnel. One key issue is that many systems

TABLE 21-3   Worldwide Totals of Programmers Working on New Development versus Maintenance

Year	Programmers on New Programs	Programmers on Maintenance
1950	90	10
1960	8,500	1,500
1970	65,000	35,000
1980	1,200,000	800,000
1990	3,000,000	4,000,000
2000	4,000,000	6,000,000

Adapted from Jones, 1986

TABLE 21-4 Advantages and Disadvantages of Different Maintenance Organizational Structures

Type	Advantages	Disadvantages
Separate	Formal transfer of systems between groups improves the system and documentation quality	All things cannot be documented, so the maintenance group may not know critical information about the system
Combined	Maintenance group knows or has access to all assumptions and decisions behind the system's original design	Documentation and testing thoroughness may suffer due to a lack of a formal transfer of responsibility
Functional	Personnel have a vested interest in effectively maintaining the system and have a better understanding of functional requirements	Personnel may have limited job mobility and lack access to adequate human and technical resources

professionals don't want to perform maintenance because they feel that it is more exciting to build something new rather than change an existing system (Martin, Brown, DeHayes, Hoffer, and Perkins, 1999). In other words, maintenance work is often viewed as "cleaning up someone else's mess." Also, organizations have historically provided greater rewards and job opportunities to those performing new development, thus making people shy away from maintenance-type careers. As a result, no matter how an organization chooses to manage its maintenance group— separate, combined, or functional—it is now common to rotate individuals in and out of maintenance activities. This rotation is believed to lessen the negative feelings about maintenance work and to give personnel a greater understanding of the difficulties and relationships between new development and maintenance.

Measuring Maintenance Effectiveness A second management issue is the measurement of maintenance effectiveness. As with the effective management of personnel, the measurement of maintenance activities is fundamental to understanding the quality of the development and maintenance efforts. To measure effectiveness, you must measure these factors:

- Number of failures

- Time between each failure

- Type of failure

Measuring the number and time between failures will provide you with the basis to calculate a widely used measure of system quality. This metric is referred to as the **mean time between failures (MTBF).** As its name implies, the MTBF measure shows the average length of time between the identification of one system failure until the next. Over time, you should expect the MTBF value to rapidly increase after a few months of use (and corrective maintenance) of the system (see Figure 21-8 for an example of the relationship between MTBF and age of a system). If the MTBF does not rapidly increase over time, it will be a signal to management that major problems exist within the system that are not being adequately resolved through the maintenance process.

A more revealing method of measurement is to examine the failures that are occurring. Over time, logging the types of failures will provide a very clear picture of where, when, and how failures occur. For example, knowing that a system repeatedly fails logging new account information to the database when a particular

Mean time between failures (MTBF): A measurement of error occurrences that can be tracked over time to indicate the quality of a system.

Figure 21-8

How the mean time between failures should change over time

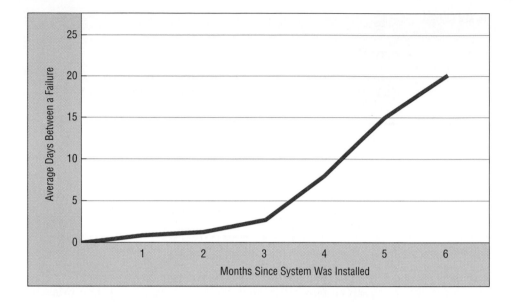

customer is using the system can provide invaluable information to the maintenance personnel. Were the users adequately trained? Is there something unique about this user? Is there something unique about an installation that is causing the failure? What activities were being performed when the system failed?

Tracking the types of failures also provides important management information for future projects. For example, if a higher frequency of errors occurs when a particular development environment is used, such information can help guide personnel assignments, training courses, or the avoidance of a particular package, language, or environment during future development. The primary lesson here is that without measuring and tracking maintenance activities, you cannot gain the knowledge to improve or know how well you are doing relative to the past. To effectively manage and to continuously improve, you must measure and assess performance over time.

Controlling Maintenance Requests   Another maintenance activity is managing maintenance requests. There are various types of maintenance requests—some correct minor or severe defects in the system while others improve or extend system functionality. From a management perspective, a key issue is deciding which requests to perform and which to ignore. Since some requests will be more critical than others, some method of prioritizing requests must be determined.

Figure 21-9 shows a flow chart that suggests one possible method you could apply for dealing with maintenance change requests. First, you must determine the type of request. If, for example, the request is an error—that is, a corrective maintenance request—then the flow chart shows that a question related to the error's severity must be asked. If the error is "very severe," then the request has top priority and is placed at the top of a queue of tasks waiting to be performed on the system. In other words, for an error of high severity, repairs to remove it must be made as soon as possible. If, however, the error is considered "nonsevere," then the change request can be categorized and prioritized based upon its type and relative importance.

If the change request is not an error, then you must determine whether the request is to adapt the system to technology changes and/or business requirements or to enhance the system so that it will provide new business functionality. For adaptation requests, they too will need to be evaluated, categorized, prioritized,

Figure 21-9
Flow chart of how to control maintenance requests (Adapted from Pressman, 1992)

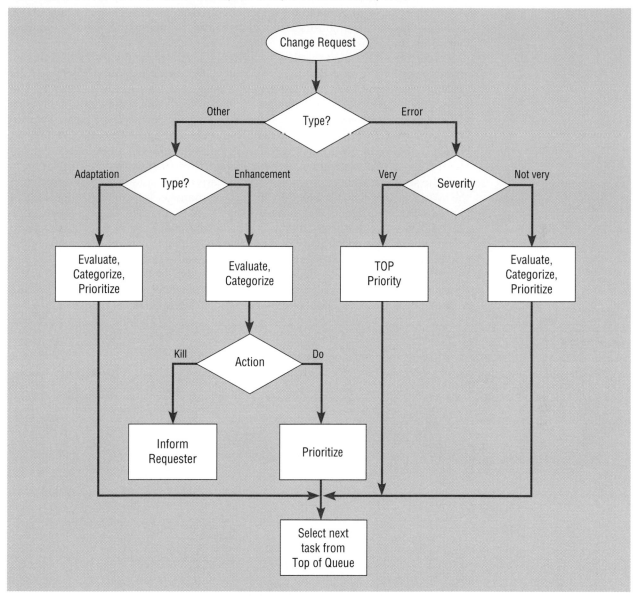

and placed in the queue. For enhancement-type requests, they must first be evaluated to see whether they are aligned with future business and information systems' plans. If not, the request will be rejected and the requester will be informed. If the enhancement appears to be aligned with business and information systems plans, it can then be prioritized and placed into the queue of future tasks. Part of the prioritization process includes estimating the scope and feasibility of the change. Techniques used for assessing the scope and feasibility of entire projects should be used when assessing maintenance requests (see Chapter 6).

The queue of maintenance tasks for a given system is dynamic—growing and shrinking based upon business changes and errors. In fact, some lower-priority change requests may never be accomplished, since only a limited number of changes can be accomplished at a given time. In other words, changes in business needs between the time the request was made and when the task finally rises to the top of the queue may result in the request being deemed unnecessary or no longer important given current business directions. Thus, managing the queue of pending tasks is an important activity.

To better understand the flow of a change request, see Figure 21-10. Initially, an organizational group that uses the system will make a request to change the system. This request flows to the project manager of the system (labeled 1). The project manager evaluates the request in relation to the existing system and pending changes, and forwards the results of this evaluation to the System Priority Board (labeled 2). This evaluation will also include a feasibility analysis that includes estimates of project scope, resource requirements, risks, and other relevant factors. The board evaluates, categorizes, and prioritizes the request in relation to both the strategic and information systems plans of the organization (labeled 3). If the board decides to kill the request, the project manager informs the requester and explains the rationale for the decision (labeled 4). If the request is accepted, it is placed in the queue of pending tasks. The project manager then assigns tasks to maintenance personnel based upon their availability and task priority (labeled 5). On a periodic basis, the project manager prepares a report of all pending tasks in the change request queue. This report is forwarded to the priority board where they reevaluate the requests in light of the current business conditions. This process may result in removing some requests or reprioritizing others.

Figure 21-10
How a maintenance request moves through an organization (Adapted from Pressman, 1987)

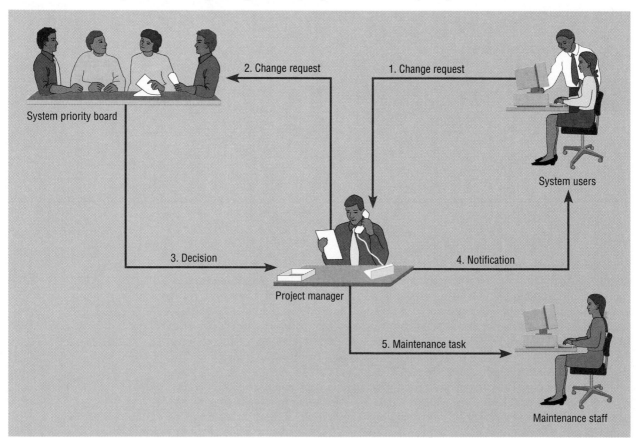

Although each change request goes through an approval process as depicted in Figure 21-10, changes are usually implemented in batches, forming a new release of the software. It is too difficult to manage a lot of small changes. Further, batching changes can reduce maintenance work when several change requests affect the same or highly related modules. Frequent releases of new system versions may also confuse users if the appearance of displays, reports, or data entry screens changes.

Configuration Management A final aspect of managing maintenance is **configuration management,** which is the process of assuring that only authorized changes are made to a system. Once a system has been implemented and installed, the programming code used to construct the system represents the **baseline modules** of the system. The baseline modules are the software modules for the most recent version of a system where each module has passed the organization's quality assurance process and documentation standards. A **system librarian** controls the baseline source code modules. If maintenance personnel are assigned to make changes to a system, they must first check out a copy of the baseline system modules because no one is allowed to directly modify the baseline modules. Only those that have been checked out and have gone through a formal check-in process can reside in the library. Before any code can be checked back in to the librarian, the code must pass the quality control procedures, testing, and documentation standards established by the organization.

When various maintenance personnel working on different maintenance tasks complete each task, the librarian notifies those still working that updates have been made to the baseline modules. This means that all tasks being worked on must now incorporate the latest baseline modules before being approved for check-in. Following a formal process of checking modules out and in, a system librarian helps to assure that only tested and approved modules become part of the baseline system. It is also the responsibility of the librarian to keep copies of all prior versions of all system modules, including the **build routines** needed to construct *any version* of the system that *ever* existed. It may be important to reconstruct old versions of the system if new ones fail, or to support users that cannot run newer versions on their computer system.

Special software systems have been created to manage system configuration and version control activities (see box "Configuration Management Tools"). This software is increasingly necessary as the change control process is complicated in organizations deploying several different networks, operating systems, languages, and database management systems in which there may be many concurrent versions of an application, each for a different platform. One function of this software is to control access to libraried modules. Each time a module is checked out or in, this activity is recorded, after being authorized by the librarian. The software helps the librarian track that all necessary steps have been followed before a new module is released to production, including all integration tests, documentation updates, and approvals.

Configuration management: The process of assuring that only authorized changes are made to a system.

Baseline modules: Software modules that have been tested, documented, and approved to be included in the most recently created version of a system.

System librarian: A person responsible for controlling the checking out and checking in of baseline modules for a system when a system is being developed or maintained.

Build routines: Guidelines that list the instructions to construct an executable system from the baseline source code.

Configuration Management Tools

There are two general kinds of configuration management tools: revision control and source code control. With revision control tools, each system module file is "frozen" (unchangeable) to a specific version level—or "floating"— a programmer may check out, lock, and modify. Only the most recent version of a module is stored; previous versions are reconstructed when needed by applying changes in reverse order. Source code control tools extend the above description to address inter-related files. These tools also help in rebuilding any historic version of a system by recompiling the proper source code modules. They also trace an executable code module back to its source code version.

Role of CASE and Automated Developement Tools in Maintenance

In traditional systems development, much of the time is spent on coding and testing. When software changes are approved, code is first changed and then tested. Once the functionality of the code is assured, the documentation and specification documents are updated to reflect system changes. Over time, the process of keeping all system documentation "current" can be a very boring and time-consuming activity that is often neglected. This neglect makes future maintenance by the same or *different* programmers difficult at best.

A primary objective of using CASE and other automated tools (see Chapter 4) for systems development and maintenance is to radically change the way in which code and documentation are modified and updated. When using an integrated development environment, analysts maintain design documents such as data flow diagrams and screen designs, not source code. In other words, design documents are modified and then code generators automatically create a new version of the system from these updated designs. Also, since the changes are made at the design specification level, most documentation changes such as an updated data flow diagram will have already been completed during the maintenance process itself. Thus, one of the biggest advantages to using CASE, for example, is its benefits during system maintenance.

In addition to using general automated tools for maintenance, two special-purpose tools, reverse engineering and reengineering tools (see Chapter 4), are primarily used to maintain older systems that have incomplete documentation or that were developed prior to CASE use. These tools are often referred to as *design recovery tools* since their primary benefit is to create high-level design documents of a program by reading and analyzing its source code.

Recall that reverse engineering tools are those that can create a representation of a system or program module at a design level of abstraction. For example, reverse engineering tools read program source code as input, perform an analysis, and extract information such as program control structures, data structures, and data flow. Once a program is represented at a design level using both graphical and textual representations, the design can be more effectively restructured to current business needs or programming practices by an analyst. Similarly, reengineering tools extend reverse engineering tools by automatically, or interactively with a systems analyst, altering an existing system in an effort to improve its quality or performance.

We now return to the example from Pine Valley Furniture and the Purchasing Fulfillment System (see Chapter 3 and the *Modern Systems Analysis and Design* web page: http://hepg.awl.com/) to illustrate what may happen to you someday when you are supporting and maintaining systems.

MAINTAINING AN INFORMATION SYSTEM AT PINE VALLEY FURNITURE

Early on a Saturday evening, Juanita Lopez, head of the manufacturing support unit of the Purchasing Department at Pine Valley Furniture (PVF), was developing a new four-week production schedule to prepare purchase orders for numerous material suppliers. She was working on Saturday evening because she was leaving the next day for a long overdue two-week vacation to the Black Hills of South Dakota. Before she could leave, however, she needed to prepare purchase orders for all material requirements for the next four weeks so that orders could be placed during her absence. She was using the Purchasing Fulfillment System to assist her with this activity.

Midway through the process of developing a new production schedule, the system failed and could not be restarted. When she tried to restart the program, an error message was displayed on the terminal:

Data Integrity Error: Corrupt or missing supplier file.

Given that her plane for Rapid City left in less than 12 hours, Juanita had to figure out some way to overcome this catastrophic system error. Her first thought was to walk over to the offices of the information systems development group within the same building. When she did, she found no one there. Her next idea was to contact Chris Ryan, the project manager for the development and maintenance of the system. She placed a call to Chris' home and found that he was at the grocery store but would be home soon. Juanita left a message for Chris to call her ASAP at the office.

Within 30 minutes, Chris returned the call and was on his way into the office to help Juanita. Although it is not a common occurrence, this is not the first time that Chris has gone into the office to assist users when systems have failed during off hours. Chris was looking forward to the day when he could handle all of these problems from home using a home PC and modem; he had been able to do this when all that was required was to scan data files for errors or issue a command to restore a database. Based on Juanita's explanation of the problem and a few quick inquiries from his home PC, Chris decided he had better make the trip to the office where he had all CASE and other tools available.

PVF's system development methodology for performing system maintenance is a formal process in which a user must first write a Systems Service Request (SSR) before maintenance is performed. After it is reviewed by the project manager, it is then forwarded to the Systems Priority Board (see Figure 21-10 for a description of a similar process). For catastrophic problems requiring instant correction so as not to delay normal business operations, the project manager has the discretion to circumvent the normal request process. After arriving on the scene, reviewing the error messages, and learning of Juanita's pending vacation, Chris believed that the failure with the Purchasing Fulfillment System was an instance where he would circumvent the normal maintenance process. His quick investigation suggested a failure in a new version of a system module which had been installed late on Friday afternoon. Chris noticed that the CASE tool records showed that this replacement module had not been tested against a standard test data set related to the type of work Juanita was doing, which made him suspect that this was the source of the problem. After patching the system to make it run, he would have to go back and document and test his changes so that they conformed to the development standards of PVF.

Over the next two hours, Chris used system backups to rebuild the supplier database. He reinstalled a previous version of the system's potentially faulty module (stored in the CASE library) that seemed more reliable, and then he quickly ran a test data set to check that the patches would hold the system together for now. He had to refresh himself on how to mount a tape cartridge on which the backup supplier data had been archived. Juanita was able to complete her task on time to easily make her flight the next morning. She thanked Chris for "going beyond the call of duty." Her appreciation made Chris feel good, but he was still uneasy. When making the "quick-fix" on the system, he did not perform carefully planned testing nor did he confirm what had caused the error. Thus, he knew that the system could fail at any time. He did, however, have a copy of all of Juanita's actions just prior to the system failure. He hoped that through a careful review of those actions he would be able to learn why the system failed. But that would be a job for Monday morning.

SUMMARY

Maintenance is the final phase in the systems development life cycle where systems are changed to rectify internal processing errors or to extend the functionality of the system. Maintenance is where a majority of the financial investment in a system occurs and can span more than 20 years. More and more information systems professionals have devoted their careers to systems maintenance and, as more systems move from initial development into operational use, it is likely that even more professionals will in the future.

It is during maintenance that the SDLC becomes a life cycle since requests to change a system must first be approved, planned, analyzed, designed, and then implemented. In some special cases where business operations are impaired due to an internal system error, quick fixes can be made. This, of course, circumvents the normal maintenance process. After quick fixes are made, maintenance personnel must back up and perform a thorough analysis of the problem to make sure that the correction conforms to normal systems development standards for design, programming, testing, and documentation.

Maintenance requests can be one of four types: corrective, adaptive, perfective, and preventive. Corrective maintenance is used to repair design and programming errors. Adaptive maintenance is used to modify the system to changes in business informational or processing needs, or to migrate the system onto a different technology platform. Perfective maintenance is used to evolve the system so that it can solve new problems or take advantage of new opportunities; in other words, to extend the capabilities of the system beyond those initially intended for the system. Preventive maintenance is used to safeguard the system from future problems.

How a system is designed and implemented can greatly impact the cost of performing maintenance. The number of unknown errors in a system when it is installed is a primary factor in determining the cost of maintenance. Other factors, such as the number of separate customers and the quality of documentation, significantly influence maintenance costs.

Organizations can choose three general methods for managing maintenance personnel. One method is to have a separate maintenance group. A second approach is to have the same people who construct the system also maintain it. A third option is to have maintenance personnel housed within the functional areas of the business that use the system on a day-to-day basis. Each approach has its advantages and disadvantages and no approach is universally best. A second maintenance management issue relates to understanding how to measure the quality of the maintenance effort. Most organizations track the frequency, time, and type of each failure and compare performance over time. Since limited resources preclude organizations from performing all maintenance requests, some formal process for reviewing requests must be established to make sure that only those requests deemed consistent with organizational and information systems plans be performed. A central source, usually a project manager, is used to collect maintenance requests. When requests are submitted, this person forwards each request to a committee charged to assess its merit. Once assessed, the project manager assigns higher-priority activities to maintenance personnel.

Maintenance personnel must be controlled from making unapproved changes to a system. To do this, most organizations assign one member of the maintenance staff, typically a senior programmer or analyst, to serve as system librarian. The librarian controls the checking out and checking in of system modules to assure that appropriate procedures for performing maintenance such as adequate testing and documentation are adhered to.

CASE is actively employed during maintenance. The primary benefit to using CASE is its ability to enable maintenance to be performed on design documents rather than low-level source code. Reverse engineering and re-engineering CASE tools are used to recover design specifications of older systems that were not constructed using CASE or for systems with inadequate design specifications. Once recovered into a design specification, these older systems can then be changed at the design level rather than the source code level, yielding a significant improvement in maintenance personnel productivity.

Business process reengineering is a major source for maintenance requests. BPR is often part of the formal strategic organizational and information systems planning effort where key business processes are redesigned using information technologies to radically improve business performance. Many of the tools and techniques used to design information systems are also used in the BPR process.

KEY TERMS

Adaptive maintenance	Corrective maintenance	Perfective maintenance
Baseline modules	Maintainability	Preventive maintenance
Build routines	Maintenance	System librarian
Configuration	Mean time between	
Management	failures (MTBF)	

REVIEW QUESTIONS

1. Define the following terms:
   a. baseline modules
   b. configuration management
   c. maintainability
   d. mean time between failures
   e. build routines

2. Contrast the following terms:
   a. adaptive maintenance, corrective maintenance, perfective maintenance, preventive maintenance
   b. baseline modules, build routines, system librarian
   c. maintenance, maintainability

3. List the steps in the maintenance process and contrast them with the phases of the systems development life cycle.

4. What are the different types of maintenance and how do they differ?

5. Describe the factors that influence the cost of maintenance. Are any factors more important? Why?

6. Describe three ways for organizing maintenance personnel and contrast the advantages and disadvantages of each approach.

7. What types of measurements must be taken to gain an understanding of the effectiveness of maintenance? Why is tracking mean time between failures an important measurement?

8. What managerial issues can be better understood by measuring maintenance effectiveness?

9. Describe the process for controlling maintenance requests. Should all requests be handled in the same way or are there situations when you should be able to circumvent the process? If so, when and why?

10. What is meant by configuration management? Why do you think organizations have adopted the approach of using a systems librarian?

11. How is CASE used in the maintenance of information systems?

12. What is the difference between reverse engineering and re-engineering CASE tools?

PROBLEMS AND EXERCISES

1. Match the following terms to the appropriate definitions.

   _____ maintenance

   _____ corrective maintenance

   _____ adaptive maintenance

   _____ maintainability

   _____ perfective maintenance
   _____ configuration management

   a. process that assures that only authorized changes are made to the proper software modules
   b. changing a system to take advantage of new opportunities
   c. changing a system in response to environmental changes
   d. repair of design and programming errors
   e. changing or fixing a system
   f. ease with which software can be understood, corrected, adapted, and enhanced

2. Maintenance has been presented as both the final stage of the SDLC (see Figure 21-1) and as a process similar to the SDLC (see Figure 21-4). Why does it make sense to talk about maintenance in both of these ways? Do you see a conflict in looking at maintenance in both ways?

3. In what ways is a request to change an information system handled differently from a request for a new information system?

4. According to Figure 21-5, corrective maintenance is by far the most frequent form of maintenance. What can you do as a systems analyst to reduce this form of maintenance?

5. What other or additional information should be collected on a System Service Request (see Figure 21-3) for a maintenance request?

6. Briefly discuss how a systems analyst can manage each of the six Cost Elements of Maintenance listed in Table 21-2.

7. Suppose you were a system librarian. Using entity-relationship diagramming notation, describe the database you would need to keep track of the information necessary in your job. Consider operational, managerial, and planning aspects of the job.

8. Suppose an information system were developed following a RAD approach (see Chapter 13). How might maintenance be different than if the system had been developed following the traditional life cycle? Why?

9. Software configuration management is similar to configuration management in any engineering environment. For example, the product design engineers for a refrigerator need to coordinate dynamic changes in compressors, power supplies, electronic controls, interior features, and exterior designs as innovations to each occur. How do such product design engineers manage the configuration of their products? What similar practices do systems analysts and librarians have to follow?

FIELD EXERCISES

1. Study an information systems department with which you are familiar or to which you have access. How does this department organize for maintenance? Has this de-

partment adopted one of the three approaches outlined in Table 21-4 or does it use some other approach? Talk with a senior manager in this department to discover how well this maintenance organization structure works.

2. Study an information systems department with which you are familiar or to which you have access. How does this department measure the effectiveness of systems maintenance? What specific metrics are used and how are these metrics used to effect changes in maintenance practices? If there is a history of measurements over several years, how can changes in the measurements be explained?

3. With the help of other students or your instructor, contact a system librarian in an organization. What is this person's job description? What tools does this person use to help him or her in the job? To whom does this person report? What previous jobs did this person hold, and what jobs does this person expect to be promoted into in the near future?

REFERENCES

Andrews. D. C., and N. S. Leventhal. 1993. *Fusion: Integrating IE, CASE, JAD: A Handbook for Reengineering the Systems Organization.* Englewood Cliffs, NJ: Prentice-Hall.

Chapin, N. 1987. "The Job of Software Maintenance." *Proceedings of the Conference on Software Maintenance.* Washington DC: IEEE Computer Society Press: 4–12.

Hanna, M. 1992. "Using documentation as a life-cycle tool." *Software Magazine* (December): 41–46.

Jones, C. 1986. *Programming Productivity.* New York, NY: McGraw-Hill.

Jones, C. 1997. "How to Measure Software Costs." *Application Development Trends* (May): 32–36.

Martin, E. W., C. V. Brown, D. W. DeHayes, J. A. Hoffer, and W. C. Perkins, 1999. *Managing Information Technology: What Managers Need to Know.* 3rd Edition. New York, NY: MacMillan.

Pressman, R. S. 1987. *Software Engineering: A Practitioner's Approach.* New York, NY: McGraw-Hill.

Pressman, R. S. 1992. *Software Engineering: A Practitioner's Approach.* 2d ed. New York, NY: McGraw-Hill.

Glossary of Terms

Note: Chapter or Appendix in which term is defined is listed in parentheses after the definition. Some Glossary entries are defined in articles on the book's website (http://hepg.awl.com/. Use keyword: hoffer.)

Abstract Class   A class that has no direct instances, but whose descendants may have direct instances. (12) *See also* Concrete class.

Abstract operation   Defines the form or protocol of the operation, but not its implementation. (12)

Acceptance testing   The process whereby actual users test a completed information system, the end result of which is the users' acceptance of the system. (20) *See also* System testing.

Access method   An operating system algorithm for storing and locating data in secondary memory. (17) *See also* File organization.

Action stubs   That part of a decision table that lists the actions that result for a given set of conditions. (9)

Activation The time period during which an object performs an operation. (12)

Actor An external entity that interacts with the system (similar to an external entity in data flow diagramming). (12) *See also* Use-case.

Adaptive maintenance   Changes made to a system to evolve its functionality to changing business needs or technologies. (21)

Afferent module   A module of a structure chart related to input to the system. (18) *See also* Efferent module.

Affinity clustering   The process of arranging planning matrix information so that clusters of information with some predetermined level or type of affinity are placed next to each other on a matrix report. (5)

Aggregation A part-of relationship between a component object and an aggregate object. (12) *See also* Composition.

Alias   An alternative name given to an attribute. (16)

Alpha testing   User testing of a completed information system using simulated data. (20) *See also* Beta testing, System testing.

Analysis   The third phase of the SDLC in which the current system is studied and alternative replacement systems are proposed. (1)

Analysis tools   CASE tools that enable automatic checking for incomplete, inconsistent, or incorrect specifications in diagrams, forms, and reports. (4)

Anomalies   Errors or inconsistencies that may result when a user attempts to update a table that contains redundant data. There are three types of anomalies: insertion, deletion, and modification anomalies. (16) *See also* Normalization.

Application independence   The separation of data and the definition of data from the applications that use these data. (1)

Application program interface (API)   Software which allows a specific front-end program development platform to communicate with a particular back-end database engine, even when the front-end and back-end were not built to be compatible. (19)

Application server   A computing server where data analysis functions primarily reside. (19)

Application software   Computer software designed to support organizational functions or processes. (1)

Association A relationship between object classes. (12) *See also* Association role.

Association class An association that has attributes or operations of its own, or that participates in relationships with other classes. (12)

Association role The end of an association which connects it to a class. (12) *See also* Multiplicity.

Associative entity An entity type that associates the instances of one or more entity types and contains attributes that are peculiar to the relationship between those entity instances. Also called a gerund. (10)

Asynchronous message A message in which the sender does not have to wait for the recipient to handle the message. (12) *See also* Sequence diagram, Simple message, Synchronous message.

Attribute A named property or characteristic of an entity that is of interest to the organization. (10) *See also* Multivalued attribute.

Audit trail A list of changes to a data file which allows business transactions to be traced. Both the updating and use of data should be recorded in the audit trail, since the consequences of bad data should be discovered and corrected. (17)

Authorization rules Controls incorporated to restrict access to systems and data and also to restrict the actions that people may take once in the system. (15)

Backward recovery (rollback) An approach to rebuilding a file in which before images of changed records are restored to the file in reverse order until some earlier state is achieved. (17) *See also* Forward recovery (rollforward).

Balancing The conservation of inputs and outputs to a data flow diagram process when that process is decomposed to a lower level. (8)

Baseline modules Software modules that have been tested, documented, and approved to be included in the most recently created version of a system. (21)

Baseline Project Plan A major outcome and deliverable from the project initiation and planning phase which contains the best estimate of a project's scope, benefits, costs, risks, and resource requirements. (6)

Batch processing Information that is collected or generated at some predetermined time interval and can be accessed via hard copy or on-line devices. (14)

Behavior Represents how an object acts and reacts.

Beta testing User testing of a completed information system using real data in the real user environment. (20) *See also* Alpha testing.

Binary relationship A relationship between instances of two entity types. This is the most common type of relationship encountered in data modeling. (10)

Biometric device An instrument that detects personal characteristics such as fingerprints, voice prints, retina prints, or signature dynamics. (15)

Blocking factor The number of physical records per page. (17)

Bottom-up planning A generic information systems planning methodology that identifies and defines IS development projects based upon solving operational business problems or taking advantage of some business opportunities. (5) *See also* Top-down planning, Corporate strategic planning.

Boundary The line that marks the inside and outside of a system and which sets off the system from its environment. (2)

Build routines Guidelines that list the instructions to construct an executable system from the baseline source code. (21)

Business case The justification for an information system, presented in terms of the tangible and intangible economic benefits and costs, and the technical and organizational feasibility of the proposed system. (6)

Business Process Reengineering (BPR) The search for, and implementation of, radical change in business processes to achieve breakthrough improvements in products and services. (7) *See also* Disruptive technologies, key business processes.

Business rules Specifications that preserve the integrity of a conceptual or logical data model. (10)

Calculated field A field which can be derived from other database fields. Also called computed or derived field. (17)

Candidate key An attribute (or combination of attributes) that uniquely identifies each instance of an entity type. (10) *See also* Identifier, Primary key.

Cardinality The number of instances of entity B that can (or must) be associated with each instance of entity A. (10)

CASE *See* Computer-aided software engineering.

Central transform The area of a transform-centered information system where the most important derivation of new information takes place. (18) *See also* Transform analysis.

Class *See also* Object class.

Class diagram Shows the static structure of an object-oriented model: the object classes, their internal structure, and the relationships in which they participate. (12)

Class-scope attribute An attribute of a class that specifies a value common to an entire class, rather than a specific value for an instance. (12)

Client The (front-end) portion of the client/server database system that provides the user interface and data manipulation functions. (19)

Client/server architecture   A LAN-based computing environment in which a central database server or engine performs all database commands sent to it from client workstations, and application programs on each client concentrate on user interface functions. (19)

Closed-ended questions   Questions in interviews and on questionnaires that ask those responding to choose from among a set of prespecified responses. (7) *See also* Open-ended questions.

Closed system   A system that is cut off from its environment and does not interact with it. (2) *See also* Open system.

Code generators   CASE tools that enable the automatic generation of program and database definition code directly from the design documents, diagrams, forms, and reports stored in the repository. (4)

Cohesion   The extent to which a system or a subsystem performs a single function. (2)

Command language interaction   A human-computer interaction method where users enter explicit statements into a system to invoke operations. (15)

Competitive strategy   The method by which an organization attempts to achieve its mission and objectives. (5)

Component   An irreducible part or aggregation of parts that make up a system, also called a subsystem. (2) *See also* Inter-related components.

Component diagram   Shows the software components or modules and their dependencies. (12) *See also* Package.

Composition   A part object that belongs to only one whole object and lives and dies with the whole. (12) *See also* Aggregation.

Computer-aided software engineering (CASE) Software tools that provide automated support for some portion of the systems development process. (4) *See also* Cross life cycle CASE, I-CASE, Lower CASE, Upper CASE.

Computing infrastructure   All the resources and practices required to help people adequately use computer systems to do their primary work. (20) *See also* Support.

Conceptual data model   A detailed model that captures the overall structure of organizational data while being independent of any database management system or other implementation considerations. (10) *See also* Entity-relationship data model, Logical data model.

Concrete class   A class that can have direct instances. (12) *See also* Abstract class.

Concurrency control   A method for preventing loss of data integrity due to interference between users in a multiuser environment. (19)

Condition stubs   That part of a decision table that lists the conditions relevant to the decision. (9)

Configuration management   The process of assuring that only authorized changes are made to a system. (21)

Constraint   A limit to what a system can accomplish. (2)

Constructor operation An operation that creates a new instance of a class. (12) *See also* Abstract operation, Query operation, Update operation.

Context diagram   An overview of an organizational system that shows the system boundary, external entities that interact with the system, and the major information flows between the entities and the system. (8) *See also* Data flow diagram.

Conversion   *See* Installation.

Corporate strategic planning   An ongoing process that defines the mission, objectives, and strategies of an organization. (5)

Corrective maintenance   Changes made to a system to repair flaws in its design, coding, or implementation. (21)

Coupling   The extent to which subsystems depend on each other. (2)

Critical path scheduling   A scheduling technique where the order and duration of a sequence of activities directly affect the completion date of a project. (3)

Cross life cycle CASE   CASE tools designed to support activities that occur *across* multiple phases of the systems development life cycle. (4) *See also* Lower CASE, Upper CASE.

Cross referencing   A feature performed by a data dictionary that enables one description of a data item to be stored and accessed by all individuals so that a single definition for a data item is established and used. (5)

Data   Raw facts about people, objects, and events in an organization. (1)

Data compression technique   Pattern matching and other methods which replace repeating strings of characters with codes of shorter length. (17)

Data couple   A diagrammatic representation of the data exchanged between two modules in a structure chart. (18) *See also* Flag.

Data dictionary   The repository of all data definitions for all organizational applications. (4)

Data flow   Data in motion, moving from one place in a system to another. (1)

Data flow diagram   A picture of the movement of data between external entities and the processes and data stores within a system. (8)

Data-oriented approach   An overall strategy of information systems development that focuses on the ideal organization of data rather than where and how data are used. (1) *See also* Process-oriented approach.

Data store   Data at rest, which may take the form of many different physical representations. (8)

Data type   A detailed coding scheme recognized by system software for representing organizational data. (17)

Database   A shared collection of logically related data designed to meet the information needs of multiple users in an organization. (1)

Database engine   The (back-end) portion of the client/server database system running on the server and providing database processing and shared access functions. (19)

Database management system (DBMS)   Software that is used to create, maintain, and provide controlled access to user databases. (17)

Decision support systems (DSS)   Computer-based systems designed to help organization members make decisions; usually composed of a database, model base, and dialogue system. (Website) *See also* DSS Generators.

Decision table   A matrix representation of the logic of a decision, which specifies the possible conditions for the decision and the resulting actions. (19) *See also* Action stubs, Condition stubs, Rules.

Decision tree   A graphical representation of a decision situation in which decision points (nodes) are connected together by arcs (one for each alternative on a decision) and terminate in ovals (the action which is the result of all of the decisions made on the path that leads to that oval). (9)

Decomposition   *See* Functional decomposition.

Default value   A value a field will assume unless an explicit value is entered for that field. (17)

Degree   The number of entity types that participate in a relationship. (10)

Design strategy   A high-level statement about the approach to developing an information system. It includes statements on the system's functionality, hardware and system software platform, and method for acquisition. (11)

Desk checking   A testing technique in which the program code is sequentially executed manually by the reviewer. (20)

DFD completeness   The extent to which all necessary components of a data flow diagram have been included and fully described. (8)

DFD consistency   The extent to which information contained on one level of a set of nested data flow diagrams is also included on other levels. (8)

Diagramming tools   CASE tools that support the creation of graphical representations of various system elements such as process flow, data relationships, and program structures. (4)

Dialogue   The sequence of interaction between a user and a system. (15)

Dialogue diagramming   A formal method for designing and representing human-computer dialogues using box and line diagrams. (15)

Direct installation   Changing over from the old information system to a new one by turning off the old system when the new one is turned on. (20)

Discount rate   The rate of return used to compute the present value of future cash flows. (6)

Disruptive technologies   Technologies that enable the breaking of long-held business rules that inhibit organizations from making radical business changes. (7) *See also* Business Process Reengineering (BPR).

Distributed database   A single logical database that is spread across computers in multiple locations which are connected by a data communications link. (19) *See also* Location transparency.

Documentation   *See* External documentation, Internal documentation, System documentation, User documentation.

Documentation generators   CASE tools that enable the easy production of both technical and user documentation in standard formats. (4)

Domain   The set of all data types and values that an attribute can assume. (10)

Drop-down menu   A menu positioning method that places the access point of the menu near the top line of the display; when accessed, menus open by dropping down onto the display. (15) *See also* Pop-up menu.

DSS generators   General purpose computer-based tools used to develop specific decision support systems. (Website)

Economic feasibility   A process of identifying the financial benefits and costs associated with a development project. (6)

Efferent module A module of a structure chart related to output from the system. (18) *See also* Afferent module.

Electronic performance support system (EPSS) Component of a software package or application in which training and educational information is embedded. An EPSS can take several forms, including a tutorial, an expert system shell, and hypertext jumps to reference material. (20)

Encapsulation The technique of hiding the internal implementation details of an object from its external view. (12)

Encryption The coding (or scrambling) of data so that they cannot be read by humans. (17)

End users Non-information-system professionals in an organization who specify the business requirements for and use software applications. End users often request new or modified applications, test and approve applications, and may serve on project teams as business experts. (1)

End-user development An approach to systems development in which users who are not computer experts satisfy their own computing needs through the use of high-level software and languages such as electronic spreadsheets and relational database management systems. (1) *See also* Help desk, Support.

Entity instance (instance) A single occurrence of an entity type. (10)

Entity-relationship data model (E-R model) A detailed, logical representation of the entities, associations, and data elements for an organization or business area. (10)

Entity-relationship diagram (E-R diagram) A graphical representation of an E-R model. (10)

Entity type A collection of entities that share common properties or characteristics. (10)

Environment Everything external to a system which interacts with the system. (2)

Event Something that takes place at a certain point in time; a noteworthy occurrence that triggers a state transition. (12)

Exclusive relationships A set of relationships for which an entity instance can participate in only one of the relationships at a time. (Website)

Executive information systems *See* Executive support systems.

Executive support systems Computer-based systems developed to support the information-intensive but limited-time decision making of executives (also referred to as *executive information systems*). (Website)

Expert systems Computer-based systems designed to mimic the performance of human experts. (Website)

External documentation System documentation that includes the outcome of structured diagramming techniques such as data flow and entity-relationship diagrams. (20) *See also* Internal documentation.

External information Information that is collected from or created for individuals and groups external to an organization. (14) *See also* Internal information.

Feasibility *See* Economic feasibility, Legal and contractual feasibility, Operational feasibility, Political feasibility, Schedule feasibility, Technical feasibility.

Field The smallest unit of named application data recognized by system software. (17)

File organization A technique for physically arranging the records of a file on secondary storage devices. (17) *See also* Access method, Hashed file organization, Indexed file organization, Sequential file organization.

File server A device that manages file operations and is shared by each client PC attached to a LAN. (19) *See also* Client/server architecture.

First normal form (1NF) A relation that contains no repeating data. (16) *See also* Normalization.

Flag A diagrammatic representation of a message passed between two modules. (18) *See also* Data couple.

Foreign key An attribute that appears as a nonkey attribute in one relation and as a primary key attribute (or part of a primary key) in another relation. (16)

Form A business document that contains some predefined data and may include some areas where additional data are to be filled in. An instance of a form is typically based on one database record. (14)

Form and report generators CASE tools that support the creation of system forms and reports in order to prototype how systems will "look and feel" to users. (4)

Form interaction A highly intuitive human-computer interaction method whereby data fields are formatted in a manner similar to paper-based forms. (15)

Formal system The official way a system works as described in organizational documentation. (7) *See also* Informal system.

Forward recovery (rollforward) An approach to rebuilding a file in which one starts with an earlier version of the file and either reruns prior transactions or replaces a record with its image after each transaction. (17) *See also* Backward recovery (rollback).

Functional decomposition An iterative process of breaking the description of a system down into finer and finer detail which creates a set of charts in which one process on a given chart is explained in greater detail on another chart. (8)

Functional dependency A particular relationship between two attributes. For any relation R, attribute B is functionally dependent on attribute A if, for every valid instance of A, that value of A uniquely determines the value of B. The functional dependence of B on A is represented as A → B. (16) *See also* Partial functional dependency, Transitive dependency.

Gantt chart A graphical representation of a project that shows each task activity as a horizontal bar whose length is proportional to its time for completion. (3)

Generalization *See* Website.

Hashed file organization The address for each record is determined using a hashing algorithm. (17)

Hashing algorithm A routine that converts a primary key value into a relative record number (or relative file address). (17)

Help desk A single point of contact for all user inquiries and problems about a particular information system or for all users in a particular department. (20) *See also* Computing infrastructure, Information center, Support.

Homonym A single name that is used for two or more different attributes (for example, the term *invoice* to refer to both a customer invoice and a supplier invoice). (16)

Horizontal partitioning Distributing the rows of a table into several separate tables. (19) *See also* Vertical partitioning.

I-CASE An automated systems development environment that provides numerous tools to create diagrams, forms, and reports; provides analysis, reporting, and code generation facilities; and seamlessly shares and integrates data across and between tools. (4)

Icon Graphical pictures that represent specific functions within a system. (15) *See also* Object-based interaction.

Identifier A candidate key that has been selected as the unique, identifying characteristic for an entity type. (10) *See also* Candidate key, Primary key.

Implementation The sixth phase of the SDLC in which the information system is coded, tested, installed, and supported in the organization. (1)

Incremental commitment A strategy in systems analysis and design in which the project is reviewed after each phase and continuation of the project is rejustified in each of these reviews. (5)

Index A table or other data structure used to determine the location of rows in a file that satisfy some condition. (17)

Indexed file organization The records are either stored sequentially or nonsequentially and an index is created that allows software to locate individual records. (17)

Indifferent condition In a decision table, a condition whose value does not affect which actions are taken for two or more rules. (9)

Informal system The way a system actually works. (7) *See also* Formal system.

Information Data that have been processed and presented in a form suitable for human interpretation, often with the purpose of revealing trends or patterns. (1)

Information center An organizational unit whose mission is to support users in exploiting information technology. (20) *See also* Computing infrastructure, Help desk, Support.

Information repository Automated tools to manage and control access to organizational business information and application portfolios as components within a comprehensive repository. (4)

Information systems analysis and design The complex organizational process whereby computer-based information systems are developed and maintained. (1)

Information systems planning (ISP) An orderly means of assessing the information needs of an organization and defining the systems, databases, and technologies that will best satisfy those needs. (5) *See also* Corporate strategic planning, Top-down planning.

Inheritance The property that occurs when entity types or object classes are arranged in a hierarchy and each entity type or object class assumes the attributes and methods of its ancestors; that is, those higher up in the hierarchy. Inheritance allows new but related classes to be derived from existing classes. (1) *See also* Generalization.

Input Whatever a system takes from its environment in order to fulfill its purpose. (2)

Inspections A testing technique in which participants examine program code for predictable language-specific errors. (20)

Installation The organizational process of changing over from the current information system to a new one. (20) *See also* Direct installation, Parallel installation, Phased installation, Single location installation.

Intangible benefit A benefit derived from the creation of an information system that cannot be easily measured in dollars or with certainty. (6) *See also* Tangible benefit.

Intangible cost   A cost associated with an information system that cannot be easily measured in terms of dollars or with certainty. (6) *See also* Tangible cost.

Integrated CASE   *See* I-CASE.

Integration testing   The process of bringing together all of the modules that a program comprises for testing purposes. Modules are typically integrated in a top-down, incremental fashion. (20)

Interface   In systems theory, the point of contact where a system meets its environment or where subsystems meet each other. (2) In human-computer interaction, a method by which users interact with information systems. (15)

Internal documentation   System documentation that is part of the program source code or is generated at compile time. (20) *See also* External documentation.

Internal information   Information that is collected, generated, or consumed within an organization. (14) *See also* External information.

Interrelated components   Dependence of one subsystem on one or more subsystems. (2)

JAD session leader   The trained individual who plans and leads Joint Application Design sessions. (7)

Joint Application Design (JAD)   A structured process in which users, managers, and analysts work together for several days in a series of intensive meetings to specify or review system requirements. (1)

Key business processes   The structured, measured set of activities designed to produce a specific output for a particular customer or market. (7) *See also* Business Process Reengineering (BPR).

Knowledge engineers   Computer professionals whose job it is to elicit knowledge from domain experts in order to develop expert systems. (Website)

Legal and contractual feasibility   The process of assessing potential legal and contractual ramifications due to the construction of a system. (6)

Level-0 diagram   A data flow diagram that represents a system's major processes, data flows, and data stores at a high level of detail. (8)

Level-*n* diagram   A DFD that is the result of *n* nested decompositions of a series of subprocesses from a process on a level-0 diagram. (8)

Local area network (LAN)   The cabling, hardware, and software used to connect workstations, computers, and file servers located in a confined geographical area (typically within one building or campus). (19)

Location transparency   A design goal for a distributed database which says that a user (or user program) requesting data need not know at which site those data are located. (19)

Logical database model   A description of data using a notation that corresponds to an organization of data used by database management systems. (16) *See also* Relational database model.

Logical design   The fourth phase of the SDLC in which all functional features of the system chosen for development in analysis are described independently of any computer platform. (1)

Logical system description   Description of a system that focuses on the system's function and purpose without regard to how the system will be physically implemented. (2)

Lower CASE   CASE tools designed to support the implementation and maintenance phases of the systems development life cycle. (4) *See also* Upper CASE.

Maintainability   The ease with which software can be understood, corrected, adapted, and enhanced. (21)

Maintenance   The final phase of the SDLC in which an information system is systematically repaired and improved; or changes made to a system to fix or enhance its functionality. (1; 21) *See also* Adaptive maintenance, Corrective maintenance, Perfective maintenance, Preventive maintenance.

Management information systems (MIS)   Computer-based systems designed to provide standard reports for managers about transaction data. (Website)

Mean time between failures (MTBF)   A measurement of error occurrences that can be tracked over time to indicate the quality of a system. (21)

Menu interaction   A human-computer interaction method where a list of system options is provided and a specific command is invoked by user selection of a menu option. (15) *See also* Drop-down menu, Pop-up menu.

Method   The implementation of an operation. (12)

Middleware   A combination of hardware, software, and communication technologies that bring together data management, presentation, and analysis into a three-tiered client/server environment. (19)

Mission statement   A statement that makes it clear what business a company is in. (5)

Modularity   Dividing a system up into chunks or modules of a relatively uniform size. (2) *See also* Cohesion, Coupling.

Module   A self-contained component of a system, defined by function. (18)

Multiple classification Shows that an object is an instance of more than one class. (12)

Multiplicity Indicates how many objects participate in a given relationship. (12)

Multivalued attribute An attribute that may take on more than one value for each entity instance. (10)

Natural language interaction A human-computer interaction method where inputs to and outputs from a computer-based application are in a conventional speaking language such as English. (15)

Normal form A state of a relation that can be determined by applying simple rules regarding dependencies to that relation. (16) *See also* Functional dependency.

Normalization The process of converting complex data structures into simple, stable data structures. (16)

Null value A special field value, distinct from 0, blank, or any other value, that indicates that the value for the field is missing or otherwise unknown. (17)

Object An entity that has a well-defined role in the application domain and has state, behavior, and identity. (12; 1) *See also* Object class, Object diagram.

Object-based interaction A human-computer interaction method where symbols are used to represent commands or functions. (15) *See also* Icon.

Object class (class) A set of objects that share a common structure and a common behavior. (12; 1) *See also* Abstract class, Concrete class.

Object diagram A graph of instances that are compatible with a given class diagram. (12)

Object-oriented analysis and design (OOAD) Systems development methodologies and techniques based on objects rather than data or processes. (1)

Objective statements A series of statements that express an organization's qualitative and quantitative goals for reaching a desired future position. (5)

On-line processing The collection and delivery of the most recent available information, typically through an on-line workstation. (14)

One-time cost A cost associated with project start-up and development, or system start-up. (6)

Open-ended questions Questions in interviews and on questionnaires that have no prespecified answers. (7) *See also* Closed-ended questions.

Open system A system that interacts freely with its environment, taking input and returning output. (2) *See also* Closed system.

Operation A function or a service that is provided by all the instances of a class. (12) *See also* Abstract opera-

tion, Constructor operation, Method, Polymorphism, Query operation, Update operation.

Operational feasibility The process of assessing the degree to which a proposed system solves business problems or takes advantage of business opportunities. (6)

Output Whatever a system returns to its environment in order to fulfill its purpose. (2)

Outsourcing The practice of turning over responsibility of some to all of an organization's information systems applications and operations to an outside firm. (11)

Overriding The process of replacing a method inherited from a superclass by a more specific implementation of that method in a subclass. (12)

Package A set of cohesive, tightly coupled classes representing a subsystem. (12) *See also* Component diagram.

Page The amount of data read or written in one secondary memory (disk) input or output operation. For I/O with a magnetic tape, the equivalent term is record block. (17) *See also* Blocking factor.

Parallel installation Running the old information system and the new one at the same time until management decides the old system can be turned off. (20)

Partial functional dependency A dependency in which one or more nonkey attributes are functionally dependent on part, but not all, of the primary key. (16)

Participatory Design (PD) A systems development approach that originated in Northern Europe in which users and the improvement in their work lives are the central focus. (1)

Perfective maintenance Changes made to a system to add new features or to improve performance. (21)

PERT chart A diagram that depicts project activities and their inter-relationships. PERT stands for Program Evaluation Review Technique. (3)

Phased installation Changing from the old information system to the new one incrementally, starting with one or a few functional components and then gradually extending the installation to cover the whole new system. (20)

Physical design The fifth phase of the SDLC in which the logical specifications of the system from logical design are transformed into technology-specific details from which all programming and system construction can be accomplished. (1)

Physical file A named set of contiguous records. (17)

Physical record A group of fields stored in adjacent memory locations and retrieved together as a unit. (17)

Physical system description Description of a system that focuses on how the system will be materially constructed. (2)

Picture (or template) A pattern of codes that restricts the width and possible values for each position of a field. (17)

Pilot installation *See* Single location installation.

Pointer A field of data that can be used to locate a related field or record of data. (17)

Political feasibility The process of evaluating how key stakeholders within the organization view the proposed system. (6)

Polymorphism The same operation may apply to two or more classes in different ways. (12)

Pop-up menu A menu positioning method that places a menu near the current cursor position. (15)

Present value The current value of a future cash flow. (6)

Preventive maintenance Changes made to a system to avoid possible future problems. (21)

Primary key *See* Identifier.

Primitive DFD The lowest level of decomposition for a data flow diagram. (8)

Process The work or actions performed on data so that they are transformed, stored, or distributed. (8)

Process-oriented approach An overall strategy to information systems development that focuses on how and when data are moved through and changed by an information system. (1) *See also* Data-oriented approach.

Processing logic The steps by which data are transformed or moved and a description of the events that trigger these steps. (1)

Project A planned undertaking of related activities to reach an objective that has a beginning and an end. (3)

Project close-down The final phase of the project management process that focuses on bringing a project to an end. (3)

Project execution The third phase of the project management process in which the plans created in the prior phases (project initiation and planning) are put into action. (3)

Project identification and selection The first phase of the SDLC in which an organization's total information system needs are identified, analyzed, prioritized, and arranged. (1)

Project initiation The first phase of the project management process in which activities are performed to assess the size, scope, and complexity of the project and to establish procedures to support later project activities. (3)

Project initiation and planning The second phase of the SDLC in which a potential information systems project is explained and an argument for continuing or not continuing with the project is presented; a detailed plan is also developed for conducting the remaining phases of the SDLC for the proposed system. (1)

Project management A controlled process of initiating, planning, executing, and closing down a project. (3)

Project manager An individual with a diverse set of skills—management, leadership, technical, conflict management, and customer relationship—who is responsible for initiating, planning, executing, and closing down a project. (3)

Project planning The second phase of the project management process which focuses on defining clear, discrete activities and the work needed to complete each activity within a single project. (3)

Project workbook An on-line or hard copy repository for all project correspondence, inputs, outputs, deliverables, procedures, and standards that is used for performing project audits, orientation of new team members, communication with management and customers, scoping future projects, and performing post-project reviews. (3) *See also* Repository.

Prototyping An iterative process of systems development in which requirements are converted to a working system which is continually revised through close work between an analyst and users. (1) *See also* Rapid Application Development (RAD).

Pseudocode A method for representing the instructions in a module with language very similar to computer programming code. (18)

Purpose The overall goal or function of a system. (2)

Query operation An operation that accesses the state of an object but does not alter the state. (12) *See also* Abstract operation, Constructor operation, Update operation.

Rapid Application Development (RAD) Systems development methodology created to radically decrease the time needed to design and implement information systems. RAD relies on extensive user involvement, Joint Application Design sessions, prototyping, integrated CASE tools, and code generators. (13)

Record partitioning The process of splitting logical records into separate physical segments based on affinity of use. (17) *See also* Horizontal partitioning, Vertical partitioning.

Recurring cost A cost resulting from the ongoing evolution and use of a system. (6)

Recursive foreign key A foreign key in a relation that references the primary key values of that same relation. (16)

Reengineering Automated tools that read program source code as input, perform an analysis of the program's data and logic, and then automatically, or interactively with a systems analyst, alter an existing system in an effort to improve its quality or performance. (4) *See also* CASE.

Referential integrity An integrity constraint specifying that the value (or existence) of an attribute in one relation depends on the value (or existence) of an attribute in the same or another relation. (16)

Relation A named, two-dimensional table of data. Each relation consists of a set of named columns and an arbitrary number of unnamed rows. (16)

Relational database model A data model that represents data in the form of tables or relations. (16)

Relationship An association between the instances of one or more entity types that is of interest to the organization. (10) *See also* Instance connection.

Repeating group A set of two or more multivalued attributes that are logically related. (10)

Report A business document that contains only pre-defined data; that is, it is a passive document used solely for reading or viewing. A report typically contains data from many unrelated records or transactions. (14)

Repository A centralized database that contains all diagrams, form and report definitions, data structure, data definitions, process flows and logic, and definitions of other organizational and system components; it provides a set of mechanisms and structures to achieve seamless data-to-tool and data-to-data integration. (4) *See also* I-CASE, Information repository, Project workbook.

Resource Any person, group of people, piece of equipment, or material used in accomplishing an activity. (3)

Reusability The ability to design software modules in a manner so that they can be used again and again in different systems without significant modification. (4)

Reverse engineering Automated tools that read program source code as input and create graphical and textual representations of program design-level information such as program control structures, data structures, logical flow, and data flow. (4) *See also* CASE.

Rules That part of a decision table that specifies which actions are to be followed for a given set of conditions. (9)

Schedule feasibility The process of assessing the degree to which the potential timeframe and completion dates for all major activities within a project meet organizational deadlines and constraints for affecting change. (6)

Scribe The person who makes detailed notes of the happenings at a Joint Application Design session. (7)

Second normal form (2NF) A relation is in second normal form if it is in first normal form and every nonkey attribute is fully functionally dependent on the primary key. Thus no nonkey attribute is functionally dependent on part (but not all) of the primary key. (16) *See also* Functional dependency, Partial functional dependency.

Secondary key One or a combination of fields for which more than one record may have the same combination of values. (17)

Sequence diagram Depicts the interactions among objects during a certain period of time. (12)

Sequential file organization The records in the file are stored in sequence according to a primary key value. (17)

Service *See* Method.

Simple message A message that transfers control from the sender to the recipient without describing the details of the communication. (12) *See also* Asynchronous message, Sequence diagram, Synchronous message.

Single location installation Trying out a new information system at one site and using the experience to decide if and how the new system should be deployed throughout the organization. (20)

Slack time The amount of time that an activity can be delayed without delaying the project. (3)

Smart card A thin plastic card the size of a credit card with an embedded microprocessor and memory. (15)

Source/sink The origin and/or destination of data, sometimes referred to as external entities. (8)

Staged installation *See* Phased installation.

Stakeholder A person who has an interest in an existing or new information system. A stakeholder is someone who is involved in the development of a system, in the use of a system, or someone who has authority over the parts of the organization affected by the system. (1)

State Encompasses an object's properties (attributes and relationships) and the values those properties have. (12) *See also* Behavior.

State diagram   A model of the states of an object and the events that cause the object to change from one state to another. (12)

State transition   Changes in the attributes of an object or in the links an object has with other objects. (12).

Statement of Work (SOW)   Document prepared for the customer during project initiation and planning that describes what the project will deliver and outlines generally at a high level all work required to complete the project. (6)

Structure chart   Hierarchical diagram that shows how an information system is organized. (18)

Structured English   Modified form of the English language used to specify the logic of information system processes. Although there is no single standard, Structured English typically relies on action verbs and noun phrases and contains no adjectives or adverbs. (9)

Stub testing   A technique used in testing modules, especially where modules are written and tested in a top-down fashion, where a few lines of code are used to substitute for subordinate modules. (20)

Support   Providing ongoing educational and problem solving assistance to information system users. For in-house developed systems, support materials and jobs will have to be prepared or designed as part of the implementation process. (20) *See also* Computing infrastructure, Help desk, Information center.

Synchronous message   A type of message in which the caller has to wait for the receiving object to finish executing the called operation before it can resume execution itself. (12) *See also* Asynchronous message, Sequence diagram, Simple message.

Synonyms   Two different names that are used to refer to the same data item (for example, *car* and *automobile*). (16)

System   An inter-related set of components, with an identifiable boundary, working together for some purpose. (2) *See also* Closed system, Open system.

System documentation   Detailed information about a system's design specifications, its internal workings, and its functionality. (20)

System librarian   A person responsible for controlling the checking-out and checking-in of baseline modules for a system when a system is being developed or maintained. (21)

System testing   The bringing together of all the programs that a system comprises for testing purposes. Programs are typically integrated in a top-down, incremental fashion. (20) *See also* Acceptance testing, Alpha testing, Beta testing, Integration testing, Stub testing.

Systems analyst   The organizational role most responsible for the analysis and design of information systems. (1)

Systems development life cycle (SDLC)   The traditional methodology used to develop, maintain, and replace information systems. (1)

Systems development methodology   A standard process followed in an organization to conduct all the steps necessary to analyze, design, implement, and maintain information systems. (1)

Tangible benefit   A benefit derived from the creation of an information system that can be measured in dollars and with certainty. (6) *See also* Intangible benefit.

Tangible cost   A cost associated with an information system that can be measured in terms of dollars and with certainty. (6) *See also* Intangible cost.

Technical feasibility   A process of assessing the development organization's ability to construct a proposed system. (6)

Ternary relationship   A simultaneous relationship among instances of three entity types. (10)

Third normal form (3NF)   A relation is in third normal form if it is in second normal form and no transitive dependencies exist. (16)

Three-tiered client/server   Advanced client/server architectures in which there are three logical and distinct applications—data management, presentation, and analysis—which are combined to create a single information system. (19)

Top-down planning   A generic information systems planning methodology that attempts to gain a broad understanding of the information system needs of the entire organization. (5) *See also* Bottom-up planning.

Transaction analysis   The process of turning data flow diagrams of a transaction-centered system into structure charts. (18) *See also* Transform analysis.

Transaction-centered system   An information system that has as its focus the dispatch of data to their appropriate locations for processing. (18)

Transaction processing systems (TPS)   Computer-based versions of manual organization systems dedicated to handling the organization's transactions; e.g., payroll. (Website)

Transactions   Individual, simple events in the life of an organization that contain data about organizational activity. (Website)

Transform analysis   The process of turning data flow diagrams of a transform-centered system into structure charts. (18) *See also* Transaction analysis.

Transform-centered system An information system that has as its focus the derivation of new information from existing data. (18) *See also* Central transform.

Transitive dependency A functional dependency between two (or more) nonkey attributes in a relation. (16) *See also* Third normal form.

Triggering operation (trigger) An assertion or rule that governs the validity of data manipulation operations such as insert, update, and delete. (10)

Turnaround document Information that is delivered to an external customer as an output that can be returned to provide new information as an input to an information system. (14)

Unary relationship (recursive relationship) A relationship between the instances of one entity type. (10)

Unit testing Method in which each module is tested alone in an attempt to discover any errors in its code. (20)

Update operation An operation that alters the state of an object. (12) *See also* Abstract operation, Constructor operation, Query operation.

Upper CASE CASE tools designed to support information planning and the project identification and selection, project initiation and planning, analysis, and design phases of the systems development life cycle. (4) *See also* Lower CASE.

Usability An overall evaluation of how a system performs in supporting a particular user for a particular task. (14)

Use case A complete sequence of related actions initiated by an actor, it represents a specific way of using the system. (12)

Use-case diagram A diagram that depicts the use cases and actors for a system. (12)

User documentation Written or other visual information about an application system, how it works, and how to use it. (20)

Value chain analysis The process of analyzing an organization's activities to determine where value is added to products and/or services and the cost are incurred for doing so; usually also includes a comparison with the activities, added value, and costs of other organizations for the purpose of making improvements in the organization's operations and performance. (5)

Vertical partitioning Distributing the columns of a table into several separate tables. (19) *See also* Horizontal partitioning.

View A subset of the database that is presented to one or more users. (15)

Walkthrough A peer group review of any product created during the systems development process. Also called structured walkthrough. (6)

Well-structured relation A relation that contains a minimum amount of redundancy and allows users to insert, modify, and delete the rows in a table without errors or inconsistencies. (16) *See also* Normalization.

Work breakdown structure The process of dividing the project into manageable tasks and logically ordering them to ensure a smooth evolution between tasks. (3)

Glossary of Acronyms

Note: Some acronyms are abbreviations for entries in the Glossary of Terms. For these and some other acronym entities, we list in parenthesis the chapter or appendix in which the associated term is defined or introduced. Other acronyms are generally used in the information systems field and are included here for your convenience.

ACM   Association for Computing Machinery (2)

AITP   Association of Information Technology Professionals

API   Application Program Interface (19)

ASM   Association for Systems Management

ATM   Automated Teller Machine

AT&T   American Telephone & Telegraph

BEC   Broadway Entertainment Company (4)

BPP   Baseline Project Plan (6)

BPR   Business Process Reengineering (7)

BSP   Business Systems Planning (5)

CASE   Computer-Aided Software Engineering (4)

CATS   Customer Activity Tracking System (5)

CD   Compact Disk

CDP   Certified Data Processing

CD-ROM   Compact Disk-Read Only Memory

COBOL   COmmon Business Oriented Language

COCOMO   COnstruction COst MOdel

CRT   Cathode Ray Tube

C/S   Client/Server (19)

CUA   Common User Access (15)

DB2   Data Base 2

DBMS   Database Management System (17)

DCR   Design Change Request (20)

DFD   Data Flow Diagram (8)

DPMA   Data Processing Managers Association (2)

DSS   Decision Support System

EDS   Electronic Data Systems

EFT   Electronic Funds Transfer (15)

EIS   Executive Information System

EPSS   Electronic Performance Support System (20)

E-R   Entity-Relationship

ERD   Entity-Relationship Diagram (10)

ES   Expert System

ESS   Executive Support System

ET   Estimated Time (3)

EUC   End-User Computing (20)

FORTRAN   FORmula TRANSlator

GDSS   Group Decision Support System

GSS   Group Support System (7)

GUI   Graphical User Interface

IBM   International Business Machines

I-CASE   Integrated Computer-Aided Software Engineering (4)

IDSS   Integrated Development Support System

IE   Information Engineering

IEF   Information Engineering Facility

I/O   Input/Output

IS   Information System

ISA   Information Systems Architecture

ISAM   Indexed Sequential Access Method

ISP   Information Systems Planning (5)

IT   Information Technology

IU   Indiana University

JAD   Joint Application Design (1)

KLOC   Thousand Lines of Code (20)

LAN   Local Area Network (19)

MIS   Management Information System

M:N   Many-to-Many

MRP   Material Requirements Planning

MTBF   Mean Time Between Failures (21)

MTTR   Mean Time to Repair Defect (20)

NPV   Net Present Value (6)

OA   Office Automation

OO   Object-Oriented

OOAD   Object-Oriented Analysis and Design (1)

PC   Personal Computer

PD   Participatory Design (1)

PERT   Project Evaluation and Review Technique (3)

PIP   Project Initiation and Planning (1)

POS   Point-of-Sale

PTR   Problem Tracking Report (20)

PV   Present Value (6)

PVF   Pine Valley Furniture (1)

RAD   Rapid Application Development (13)

RAM   Random Access Memory

R&D   Research and Development

RFP   Request for Proposal (11)

RFQ   Request for Quote (11)

ROI   Return on Investment (6)

ROM   Read Only Memory

SDLC   Systems Development Life Cycle (1)

SDM   Systems Development Methodology (1)

SNA   System Network Architecture

SOW   Statement of Work (6)

SPTS   Sales Promotion Tracking System

SQL   Structure Query Language

SSR   System Service Request (1)

TPS   Transaction Processing System

TQM   Total Quality Management

TVM   Time Value of Money (6)

UML   Unified Modeling Language

VB   Visual Basic

VBA   Visual Basic for Applications

VSAM   Virtual Sequential Access Method

WIP   Work in Process (20)

1:1   One-to-One

1:*M*   One-to-Many

1NF   First Normal Form (6)

2NF   Second Normal Form (6)

3NF   Third Normal Form (6)

4GL   Fourth-Generation Language

Index

(*Italicized* page number indicates that term is defined on that page.)

Credits

Photos